T0394377

Human Flourishing: The End of Law

Human Flourishing: The End of Law

Essays in Honor of Siegfried Wiessner

Edited by

W. Michael Reisman and Roza Pati

BRILL | NIJHOFF

LEIDEN | BOSTON

The Library of Congress Cataloging-in-Publication Data is available online at https://catalog.loc.gov
LC record available at https://lccn.loc.gov/2023031927

Typeface for the Latin, Greek, and Cyrillic scripts: "Brill". See and download: brill.com/brill-typeface.

ISBN 978-90-04-52482-8 (hardback)
ISBN 978-90-04-52483-5 (e-book)

This book is printed on acid-free paper and produced in a sustainable manner.

Printed by Printforce, the Netherlands

Contents

PART 1
Siegfried Wiessner, The Person

PART 2
Flourishing and Human Dignity: A Theory about Law

PART 5
The Rights of Indigenous Peoples

PART 6
Cultural Heritage Law

PART 10
Law and the Environment

Acknowledgments

The editors are indebted to Lindy Melman of BRILL/ Martinus Nijhoff for her encouragement and patience throughout the production of this *liber amicorum*. At Yale, Cina Santos provided invaluable support.

Tables and Figures

Tables

Figures

Notes on Contributors

Adeno Addis

holds the W. R. Irby Chair and is also the W. Ray Forrester Professor of Public and Constitutional Law at Tulane University School of Law. His current research focuses on two areas: on belonging and displacement (focusing on internal displacement and statelessness) and on optimal constitutional arrangements for fractured societies. In relation to the first area of focus, he has written on *The Dignity of Belonging and the Indignity of Displacement*. In relation to the second area of inquiry, he is co-editing a book entitled *Ethiopia at Constitutional Crossroads: In Search of a Fair and Durable Settlement*.

S. James Anaya

is University Distinguished Professor and the Nicholas Doman Professor of International Law at the University of Colorado Law School (USA), where he teaches and writes in the areas of international human rights and issues concerning indigenous peoples. Professor Anaya served as the United Nations Human Rights Council's Special Rapporteur on the Rights of Indigenous Peoples from 2008 to 2014. In addition to his academic work, Professor Anaya has litigated major indigenous rights and human rights cases in domestic and international tribunals, including the United States Supreme Court and the Inter-American Court of Human Rights.

David A. Armstrong

is President of St. Thomas University, and former President of Thomas More University, Covington, KY. President Armstrong's collaborative, innovative spirit has yielded exciting new ventures and has helped expand the University's regional and national footprint. He has also served as Vice President and General Counsel of Notre Dame College in South Euclid, Ohio. He holds a J.D. degree, Cleveland-Marshall College of Law, and a B.A. in Political Science, Mercyhurst University. He serves on the Stetson University College of Law's Center for Excellence in Higher Education Law and Policy Advisory Council, Board of SACSCOC, and Florida Council 100.

Roy Balleste

is Professor of Law and Law Library Director at Stetson University. He has focused his scholarship on the evolving regulatory challenges of cybersecurity law, cybersecurity in outer space, cyber operations, and cyber conflict. Balleste is a core expert and editorial board member of the Manual on International

Law Applicable to Military Uses of Outer Space (MILAMOS). Balleste holds a J.S.D. and an LL.M. degree in Intercultural Human Rights (St. Thomas University); LL.M. in Air and Space Law (McGill University); M.S. in Cybersecurity (Norwich University); and a J.D. (St. Thomas University).

Mohammad Mahmoud Bayoumi Ibrahim

is Chief Justice at the Egyptian Appellate Court. Dr. Ibrahim obtained an LL.B. in 2000 and an LL.M. in International Law from Ain-Shams University. He also earned an LL.M. and a J.S.D. degree in Intercultural Human Rights from St. Thomas University College of Law. Dr. Ibrahim started off his career as a police officer, then left the Police Force to serve as a Prosecutor at the Office of Egypt's Prosecutor General, and then was promoted to Judge. In the progression of his career, he was deputized in numerous State Bodies and Authorities.

Virgínia Brás Gomes

served as Member of the UN Committee on Economic, Social and Cultural Rights for 14 years, and then as Vice-Chair, Rapporteur, and ultimately Chair of the Committee. She is senior social policy adviser in the Ministry of Employment, Solidarity and Social Security of Portugal. She has served as Distinguished Guest Lecturer in St. Thomas University's LL.M. Program in Intercultural Human Rights. She conducts training on issues of human rights and treaty body reporting in Africa, Asia and Europe, on behalf of the Office of the High Commissioner for Human Rights. She has authored articles in national and international publications.

Gordon Butler

is Professor of Law, St. Thomas University College of Law, Miami, FL. B.E.E., Georgia Institute of Technology; J.D., University of Texas School of Law; LL.M. (Taxation), New York University School of Law; M.B.A. University of Dayton. Professor Butler has taught business law, tax law, and wills and trusts law for more than thirty years, as well as Human Rights and Religion in the Intercultural Human Rights Program since its inception.

Cosmin Corendea

S.J.D. Golden Gate University; LL.M., St. Thomas University, USA. He is Professor and Vice Dean, Jindal School of Environment and Sustainability, India, and teaches Climate Law and Policy, Refugee and Migration Law and International Comparative Law. He is a member of the founding faculty of the LL.M. Programme in Environmental Law, Energy and Climate Change with WWF. He has spent over 15 years in the field of climate change, human mobility, and human rights in the Asia Pacific Region, as a research expert and policy maker, and is credited for developing "international hybrid law," publicized in his seminal book on the subject of *Legal Protection of the Sinking Islands Refugees*.

Lola Cubells Aguilar

is Professor of Constitutional Law at the Universitat Jaume I, Castelló, València, Spain. She holds an International Ph.D. in Human Rights, Peace and Sustainable Development with the Universitat de València. Her expertise is in Indigenous Peoples' Rights, Legal Pluralism and Decolonization. She has been involved in the processes of Indigenous resistance in Chiapas for 20 years.

Ahmed El Demery

holds an LL.M and a J.S.D. in Intercultural Human Rights from St. Thomas University, Miami, and an LL.B. from Cairo University, Egypt. He has published a book on the *Arab Charter on Human Rights: A Voice for Sharia in the Modern World*. He was Visiting Research Student at Oxford University, Faculty of Law. He is Vice President Judge at the Court of Appeals in Egypt, currently seconded to the Department of International and Cultural Cooperation, at the Ministry of Justice in Egypt. He was a legal expert at the Ministry of Justice in Qatar. He also served as Chief Prosecutor at the office of the Prosecutor General of Egypt. He is lecturer at various universities in Egypt.

Jude O. Ezeanokwasa

Ph.D. (Law) & J.C.D. (Canon Law), Lateran University Rome; LL.M. & J.C.L. (Canon Law), Lateran University; B.L. (Barrister at Law), Nigeria; LL.B., Nnamdi Azikiwe University, Awka, Nigeria; B.D.(Divinity), Urban University, Rome; B.A. (Philosophy), Urban University. He serves as Senior Lecturer, Department of International Law and Jurisprudence, and Acting Dean and Head Lecturer on Environmental and Planning Law, at the Faculty of Law, Nnamdi Azikiwe University, Nigeria. He is also a Judge at the Metropolitan Tribunal of the Archdiocese of Miami, Florida, USA and in the Diocesan Tribunal of Catholic Diocese of Awka, as well as a priest of the Catholic Diocese of Awka.

Francesco Francioni

Doctor of Laws, Florence, and LL.M., Harvard, is Professor Emeritus of International Law at the European University Institute, Florence. He is a member of the *Institut de Droit International,* a member of the American Law Institute and of the editorial board of the Italian Yearbook of International Law. He is the co-founder and General Editor, with Ana Vrdoljak, of the Oxford University Press Series "Cultural Heritage Law and Policy" and of the Series "Oxford

Commentaries on International Cultural Heritage Law." He has been judge ad hoc of the Law of the Sea Tribunal and arbitrator at the Permanent Court of Arbitration.

Alfredo Garcia

has over three decades of experience in higher education. He has served as Dean of St. Thomas University College of Law (2007–2010, and 2014–2018) and as Interim Provost of St. Thomas University (2018). He is the first Cuban-born Dean of an ABA-approved law school. He has been a Visiting Professor at American University Washington College of Law and a Visiting Scholar at William and Mary College of Law. He served as prosecutor in Dade County, Florida, and as criminal defense attorney in state and federal courts. He has written extensively in the fields of constitutional criminal procedure, evidence and torts, and he is a contributor to the Oxford Encyclopedia of American Law.

Lauren Gilbert

is Professor of Law at St. Thomas University College of Law, joining the law faculty in 2002. A graduate of Harvard College and Michigan Law School, she was an associate at Arnold & Porter in Washington, D.C. from 1988 to 1991, Fulbright Lecturer in Costa Rica in 1991, researcher for the Inter-American Institute of Human Rights from 1991 to 1992, attorney-investigator for the U.N. Truth Commission for El Salvador from 1992 to 1993, director of the Women and International Law Program at Washington College of Law from 1994 to 1998, and legal services attorney in Miami from 1998 to 2002. She writes on a variety of constitutional topics.

Christian Lee González-Rivera

is an Assistant Professor of Law at St. Thomas University College of Law, in Miami, Florida. His research and writing variously focus on constitutional law, hermeneutics, human trafficking, and international law. He holds a B.A. in Psychology and Philosophy from the University of Puerto Rico (*magna cum laude*) and a J.D. (*magna cum laude*) and LL.M. (*summa cum laude*) in Intercultural Human Rights from St. Thomas University College of Law. He served as senior law clerk for The Honorable Fleur Lobree at Florida's Third District Court of Appeal. He has worked as appellate and trial counsel at the law firm of Butler, Weihmuller, Katz & Craig, LLP.

Craig Hammer

is a Senior Program Manager with the Development Data Group, The World Bank. He specializes in governance reforms open government, and open data initiatives. His work includes strengthening laws, policies, and regulations for improved public service delivery to traditionally marginalized and underserved communities in more than 30 countries in Africa, the Middle East, Latin America, South Asia, and Central Europe. He is a co-author of the *2021 World Development Report: Data for Better Lives*. He is Secretariat Member for the World Bank's Data Governance Body, Member of the Council on Foreign Relations and the Society for the Policy Sciences, as well as a Fellow of the World Academy of Art and Science.

Abadir Ibrahim
is the Associate Director of the Human Rights Program at Harvard Law School. His current research focuses on African approaches to human rights which studies, among other things, the iteration and practice of human rights as impacted by Africa's (post)colonial, religious and traditional heritages. Dr. Ibrahim earned his LL.M. and J.S.D. from the Intercultural Human Rights Program at St. Thomas University College of Law, Miami, where he examined the interaction between democratization and African traditional institutions, labor and professional unions, religious organizations, and other civil society organizations.

Ram S. Jakhu
is Full Professor at the Faculty of Law, McGill University, Montreal, Canada. For four decades, he has been teaching and conducting research in international space law and public international law. He has held various academic positions, including that of the Director of the McGill Institute of Air and Space Law, has served as a Member of the Canadian Human Rights Tribunal, and as a Member of the Advisory Group of Legal Experts on Optional Rules for Arbitration of Disputes Relating to Outer Space of the Permanent Court of Arbitration, at The Hague. He is author of many books, research reports and articles. He is recipient of several academic awards. He holds the degrees of Doctor of Civil Law, LL.M. (McGill) and LL.M., LL.B., B.A. (Panjab).

Kirke Kickingbird
(Kiowa Tribe) has devoted his career to Native American legal issues and has written on them extensively. His stellar service includes positions with the Congressional Relations Office of the Bureau of Indian Affairs; the U.S. Congress American Indian Policy Review Commission; the U.S. State Department Delegation to the International Conference on Discrimination Against Indigenous Populations in the Americas; Institute for the Development of Indian Law in Washington, D.C.; the U.S. Delegation rewriting ILO Indigenous and

Tribal Peoples Convention 1989 (No. 169). He also taught law at Oklahoma City University and has served as Chief Justice of the Supreme Court of the Cheyenne and Arapaho Tribes of Oklahoma.

Michael Kilian

has been a full Professor of Public Law, European Law, and Public International Law as well as Financial and Environmental Law at Martin Luther University of Halle-Wittenberg from 1992 to 2014, having earned his Doctorate in Law (Dr. iur.) and Habilitation at the University of Tübingen. He previously served as Professor of Public Law at the University of Heidelberg. From 1993 to 2000, he also served as a Judge on the Constitutional Court of the German state of Saxony-Anhalt. Since 2015, he has been working of counsel with PHP Law Firm in Leipzig and Dresden.

Eckart Klein

academically originates from the University of Heidelberg and the Max Planck Institute for Comparative Public Law and Public International Law (Dissertation 1973, Habilitation 1980). From 1974 to 1976 he was a law clerk at the German Federal Constitutional Court. He held a professorship for Public Law, Public International and European Law at the Law Faculties of the Universities of Mainz (1981–1994) and Potsdam (1994–2008), where he founded the Human Rights Centre. He was a member of the UN Human Rights Committee (1995–2002) and served between 1998 and 2011 as a Judge *ad hoc* at the European Court of Human Rights in cases against Germany.

Philip Larrey

Ph.D., is a Catholic priest who holds the Chair of Logic and Epistemology at the Pontifical Lateran University in the Vatican, and is Dean of the Philosophy Department. His publications deal with the philosophy of knowledge and critical thinking. He has published several books concerning the effects of the new digital era on society, including *Futuro ignoto* (IF Press) and *Connected World* (Penguin). For years, he has been following the philosophical implications of the rapid development of artificial intelligence and challenges industry leaders to discuss how technology is shaping the fabric of our society. His new book, *Artificial Humanity*, delves into a philosophical discussion of what AI research means for all of humanity.

Lenora Ledwon

is Professor of Law at St. Thomas University College of Law, where she teaches Evidence, Legal Storytelling, and Law and Literature. She holds a J.D. from the University of Michigan and a Ph.D. from the University of Notre Dame. She edited the anthology, *Law and Literature: Text and Theory*, and co-edited *Law and Popular Culture*. She has published articles in Harvard Women's Law Journal; Literature/Film Quarterly; Yale Journal of Women and Law; and Victorian Literature & Culture, as well as chapters for *Harry Potter and Law* and for *Teaching Law and Literature* (Modern Language Association).

Federico Lenzerini

Ph.D., is Professor of International Law and Human Rights at the Department of Political and International Sciences of the University of Siena (Italy). He is Lecturer in the LL.M. Program in Intercultural Human Rights at St. Thomas University College of Law, Miami, and Professor at the Tulane-Siena Summer School on International Law, Cultural Heritage and the Arts. He has been Consultant to UNESCO and Counsel to the Italian Ministry of Foreign Affairs at various international negotiations. He was the Rapporteur of the ILA Committees on the Rights of Indigenous Peoples, and on the Implementation of the Rights of Indigenous Peoples.

Lucas Lixinski

is Professor at the Faculty of Law & Justice, University of New South Wales in Sydney, Australia. He holds a Ph.D. from the European University Institute (Florence, Italy), an LL.M. in Human Rights from Central European University (Budapest, Hungary), and an LL.B. from the Federal University of Rio Grande do Sul (Porto Alegre, Brazil). He writes primarily in the areas of international heritage law and international human rights law. His latest book is *Legalized Identities: Cultural Heritage and the Shaping of Transitional Justice* (Cambridge University Press, 2021).

John Makdisi

is Emeritus Professor of Law and Interim Dean, St. Thomas University College of Law. He has taught and written extensively on American and Islamic law and on issues involving the intersection of law and moral theology. His educational background after receiving his J.D. from Pennsylvania includes an S.J.D. in Islamic Law from Harvard University and a Ph.D. in Moral Theology from Catholic University. He served as dean at three law schools but spent most of his 38+ years of academic life as a professor. Particularly noteworthy is his work on estates and future interests, the Islamic origins of the common law, and St. Thomas Aquinas.

June Mary Makdisi

is Emerita Professor of Law, at St. Thomas University College of Law, an institution she has served for twenty years. She served as law clerk to two Louisiana

State Supreme Court justices. While in law school, she received several awards and served as Editor-in-Chief of the law review. Her primary research focus has been in the field of law and bioethics, topics she has published on extensively. She has also published in the areas of torts, health law, and family law. She is married to John Makdisi, also Professor Emeritus, at STU Law. They have four married children and six grandchildren.

Manuel May Castillo

is an Indigenous scholar originally from the Yucatán Peninsula, Mexico. He holds a Ph.D. in Architectural Heritage from the Polytechnic University of Valencia, Spain. His research focuses on decolonizing heritage, Indigenous archaeology, socio-cultural anthropology, rights and environment. Since 2009, he has worked at several European universities, as assistant professor at the Faculty of Archaeology of Leiden University, The Netherlands, and as a postdoctoral researcher at the Institute of Ancient America of the University of Bonn and at the Institute of Ethnology of Ludwig-Maximilians-Universität München, Germany.

Nishith Mishra

LL.M., Institute of Air and Space Law, Faculty of Law, McGill University. He currently works as a Research Assistant with the Institute and its Center for Research in Air and Space Law. He earned a B.A. LL.B. (Hons.) degree from National Law University Delhi, and certificates from the Indian Law Institute, New Delhi, India. He is winner of multiple awards and scholarships. He has worked as a civil and commercial litigator, and as a private-equity and foreign direct investment lawyer in India. His areas of expertise include international space law and policy, legal regulation of artificial intelligence systems, sustainable development agendas and policies, and the Global Save Soil initiative, and he has published in his areas of interest.

Mariana Monteiro de Matos

is Research Fellow at the Department of Law and Anthropology of the Max Planck Institute for Social Anthropology (Germany). She earned her LL.M. and Doctorate (Dr. iur.) degrees from the University of Göttingen, specializing in international law. Socio-legal studies, constitutional and international law are the main fields of her extensive publication record that includes contributions to Brill Publishers and Oxford University Press. She has delivered lectures in interdisciplinary settings to global audiences. Her research projects have been awarded prestigious grants from several organizations, such as the International Law Association.

Keith Nunes

is a former Fellow of the Woodrow Wilson School of Public Administration and International Affairs of Princeton University, Salzburg Seminar, and University of Chicago Founders' Constitution Seminar, with law degrees from Yale, Leyden, and Cape Town, and diplomas from the Hague Academy of International Law Centre for Research and Study. He edited the Country Handbooks of the *International Contract Manual*, and served as the Director of the Holocaust & Law Institute at Touro Law School and of Kean University's Master's Program in Holocaust & Genocide Studies, and as special assistant to the Touro president. He was a founding Lecturer in the LL.M. Program in Intercultural Human Rights Program of St. Thomas University College of Law.

Jaime Olaiz-González

is Professor of International Law, Constitutional Theory and American Jurisprudence, and Vice Dean for International Programs at Universidad Panamericana School of Law, Mexico City, where he has also served as Dean for the J.D. program. He holds a law degree from Universidad Panamericana, and a J.S.D.'15 and LL.M.'09 from the Yale Law School. He was a Fulbright-García Robles Grantee. He served as Member of the Committee of the United Nations OHCHR for the Diagnosis of the Human Rights' Situation in Mexico City. Professor Olaiz is member of the *Sistema Nacional de Investigadores* (S.N.I.).

Roza Pati

is Professor of Law and Senior Associate Dean for Academic Affairs at St. Thomas University College of Law, Director of the LL.M./J.S.D. Program in Intercultural Human Rights, and Director of the Human Trafficking Academy; Member of the Dicastery for Promoting Integral Human Development and previously Member of the Pontifical Council for Justice and Peace (The Vatican); former Member of Parliament and Cabinet Member, Secretary of State for Youth and Women (Albania). She has been Visiting Professor of Law in India and Romania, and twice Commencement Speaker (Miami and Tirana). She is a globally published author of books, book chapters and articles in multiple languages, and she lectures in academic, governmental and non-governmental institutions. She has earned various academic and service awards. She holds a Dr. iur. (*summa cum laude*, Potsdam, Germany), LL.M. (St. Thomas University), B.A. & LL.B. (Albania).

Fausto Pocar

is Professor Emeritus of International Law at Milan University and Doctor h.c. at Antwerp and Buenos Aires. He is an *ad hoc* judge at the International Court of Justice since 2017, and was a member of UN Human Rights Committee from 1984–2000 (President, 1991–1992), a judge at the International Criminal Tribunal for the Former Yugoslavia from 2000 to 2017 (President, 2005–2008), and an appeals judge at the International Criminal Tribunal for Rwanda from 2000 to 2015. He is a member of the *Institut de Droit International* and Honorary President of the International Institute of Humanitarian Law (President, 2012–2019).

Qerim Qerimi

is a Professor of International Law, International Law of Human Rights, and International Organizations at the University of Prishtina, Kosovo, and a visiting professor and Member of the Law and Development Research Group at the University of Antwerp Faculty of Law. He is a current Member of the Council of Europe's European Commission for Democracy through Law (Venice Commission), and chair of its sub-commission on the protection of national minorities. He serves as Rapporteur for Oxford International Organizations (OXIO). He holds an LL.M. and a J.S.D. degree from St. Thomas University College of Law, Miami, and has pursued postdoctoral research at Harvard Law School on a Fulbright scholarship.

W. Michael Reisman

is Myres S. McDougal Professor Emeritus of Law at the Yale Law School and has been visiting professor in Tokyo, Hong Kong, Berlin, Basel, Paris, Tel Aviv and Geneva. He has been elected to the *Institut de Droit International* and is a Fellow of the World Academy of Art and Science and a Board member of The Foreign Policy Association. He was President of the Arbitration Tribunal of the Bank for International Settlements, President of the Inter-American Commission on Human Rights of the Organization of American States, Honorary President of the American Society of International Law, and Editor-in-Chief of the American Journal of International Law. He has served as arbitrator and counsel in many international cases and was presiding arbitrator in the OSPAR arbitration (Ireland v. UK) and arbitrator in the Eritrea/Ethiopia Boundary Dispute and in the Abyei (Sudan) Boundary Dispute.

Nicholas Rostow

is Member of the New York and District of Columbia bars. He is Senior Partner at Zumpano Patricios & Popok, PLLC, resident in the New York office. He is also a Senior Research Scholar, Yale Law School, and Fellow, Center for Advanced Studies on Terrorism. Other positions held include: Visiting Professor, Cornell Law School, Spring Terms 2022 & 2023; Legal Adviser to the National Security Council, 1987–1993; Staff Director, Senate Select Committee on Intelligence,

1999–2000; and Senior Policy Adviser and General Counsel to the U.S. Permanent Representative to the United Nations, 2001–2005.

Ibrahim Salama

is Chief of the Human Rights Treaties Branch at the Office of the United Nations High Commissioner for Human Rights, where he also leads the Faith for Rights programme. Previously, he headed the UN secretariat for the preparatory process of the 2009 United Nations World Conference Against Racism (Durban Review Conference), was independent expert of the Sub-Commission on the Promotion and Protection of Human Rights, and was elected Chairperson of the Intergovernmental Working Group on the Right to Development.

Jay Sterling Silver

is Professor Emeritus at St. Thomas University College of Law, Miami. His scholarship has appeared in the Vanderbilt, Iowa, Wisconsin, William and Mary, Ohio State, UCLA, Texas A&M, and Rutgers law reviews. His commentary has appeared in *The New York Times*, *The Washington Post*, *The National Law Journal*, *The Guardian*, *CNBC*, *The Christian Science Monitor*, *The Hill*, *The Chronicle of Higher Education*, *The International Herald Tribune*, Madrid's *El Pais*, *The Buenos Aires Herald*, and *The Qatar Tribune*, among others. His writing has been assigned reading in courses at, among others, NYU's Stern School of Business and the law schools at Vanderbilt and American University.

Michael Vastine

has represented individual clients and authored *amicus curiae* briefs in major litigation regarding immigration and crimes and the due process rights of immigrants, representing groups, including the American Immigration Lawyers Association (AILA) and Catholic Legal Services, in cases before the United States Supreme Court, the U.S. Courts of Appeals, the Florida and Connecticut state supreme courts, and the Board of Immigration Appeals, and publishes and presents extensively on these topics. He is a graduate of Oberlin Conservatory of Music, Temple University Graduate School of Music, and Georgetown University Law Center. He is recipient of the AILA (National) Elmer Fried Award for Excellence in Teaching.

Guiguo Wang

is President of the Zhejiang University Academy of International Strategy and Law and University Professor of Law, Guanghua Law School, Zhejiang University, Hangzhou, China; Eason-Weinmann Chair of International and Comparative Law Emeritus, School of Law, Tulane University, New Orleans, USA; J.S.D. (Yale), LL.M. (Columbia). Professor Wang is Chairman of the Hong Kong WTO

Research Institute; Chairman of the National Committee (HK); Titular Member of the International Academy of Comparative Law; and an arbitrator of the China International Economic and Trade Arbitration Commission, the Beijing Arbitration Commission, and the Hong Kong International Arbitration Centre.

Michael Wiener

has been a Visiting Fellow of Kellogg College at the University of Oxford since 2011 and was a Senior Fellow in Residence at the Graduate Institute of International and Development Studies in Geneva (2022). He has been working with the Office of the United Nations High Commissioner for Human Rights since 2006, focusing on the design and implementation of the Rabat Plan of Action as well as the Beirut Declaration and its 18 Commitments on Faith for Rights.

Stephan Wilske

is Partner at Gleiss Lutz, Stuttgart (Germany); FCIArb, admitted to the New York and German bar as well as to various U.S. federal courts, including the U.S. Supreme Court; Maîtrise en droit, Université d'Aix- Marseille III, France; LL.M. (The University of Chicago; Casper Platt Award); Dr. iur. (Tübingen); Lecturer at the Universities of Heidelberg and Jena; Visiting Professor at the National Taiwan University (2010); Senior Committee Member of the Contemporary Asia Arbitration Journal. Since 2011, he has been a member of the American Law Institute (ALI) and, since 2019, a Vice President of the CAAI Court of Arbitration.

Dedication

It gives us enormous pleasure to honor, with this book, our distinguished friend and colleague, Professor Siegfried Wiessner. He has served, since 1985, as Professor of Law, and, since 2001, as Founder and Director of the LL.M. and J.S.D. Programs of St. Thomas University College of Law in Miami, Florida. Siegfried is a brilliant and creative legal scholar, a generous colleague, a gifted teacher and a warm and giving friend. His work addresses real problems and focuses on fashioning alternative policies and legal arrangements that enhance public order and human dignity.

The guiding light of Siegfried's understanding of law has always been that it must serve human beings. The decisions that make up the law at any given time are to be measured by and geared toward the achievement of a public order of human dignity, maximizing access by all to the processes of the shaping and the sharing of all the things people value.

Love impels Siegfried to see the good in every human being he meets, to help lift up those who have fallen, to assist the most vulnerable, the weak and the oppressed, and to insist that the law allow every member of the human race to thrive and to prosper. For many decades now, we have witnessed this passionate dedication in action.

As Siegfried celebrates his seventieth birthday in February 2023, this Festschrift celebrates, in the venerable academic tradition, his many achievements. Each chapter presents an homage to the significant impact Siegfried has had on scholarship and practice in areas as diverse as theory about law, human rights, the rights of indigenous peoples, the rule of law, constitutional law, the rights of migrants, international investment law and arbitration, space law, the use of force, and many more – all integrated by the policy-oriented framework of the New Haven School. This book is entitled "Human Flourishing: The End of Law," for Siegfried sees the purpose of law as allowing human beings to achieve their full potential, both material and spiritual, moving toward a public order in which the common interest will be clarified and implemented peacefully.

We hope that Siegfried will be gratified by this outpouring of affection by colleagues, students and friends, and that readers will be inspired by these essays to take up their challenge and continue Siegfried's work toward the achievement of a world order of human dignity.

The Editors

Siegfried Wiessner: Publications

Books

GENERAL THEORY OF INTERNATIONAL LAW, Volume 1 of AMERICAN CLASSICS OF INTERNATIONAL LAW (Editor, BRILL - Martinus Nijhoff Publishers, 2017), 534 pp.

HANDBOOK ON HUMAN TRAFFICKING, PUBLIC HEALTH AND THE LAW. A SPRING SCHOOL FROM THE NEW HAVEN PERSPECTIVE (Editor, with Wilhelm Kirch and Roza Pati, Georg Thieme Verlag, Stuttgart, New York, 2014), 145 pp.

LOOKING TO THE FUTURE: ESSAYS ON INTERNATIONAL LAW IN HONOR OF W. MICHAEL REISMAN (Editor, with Mahnoush Arsanjani, Jacob Katz Cogan & Robert D. Sloane, BRILL - Martinus Nijhoff Publishers, 2011), 1100 pp.

INTERNATIONAL LAW IN CONTEMPORARY PERSPECTIVE (Casebook, Foundation Press, 2004), with W. Michael Reisman, Mahnoush Arsanjani and Gayl Westerman, 1584 pp.

UNITED STATES AGENCY FOR INTERNATIONAL DEVELOPMENT, M/OP/ENI/DGSR, EVALUATION OF THE RULE OF LAW PROGRAM IN CENTRAL AND EASTERN EUROPE AND THE NEW INDEPENDENT STATES: THE AMERICAN BAR ASSOCIATION/CENTRAL AND EAST EUROPEAN LAW INITIATIVE (ABA/CEELI) - FINAL REPORT, Jan. 28, 1999, with Richard N. Blue, Silvy Chernev and Robyn L. Goodkind, 39 pp., with appendices

DIE FUNKTION DER STAATSANGEHÖRIGKEIT [The Function of Nationality] (Tübingen University Press, 1989), 414 pp.

LAGER UND MENSCHLICHE WÜRDE [Camps and Human Dignity] (Editor, with Claudius Hennig, AS-Verlag , Tübingen 1982), 117 pp.

Book Chapters

Indigenous Peoples: The Battle over Definition, in REFLECTIONS ON INTERNATIONAL LAW. STUDIES IN HONOUR OF LINDY MELMAN 4-40 (Tim McCormack ed., BRILL - Martinus Nijhoff Publishers, 2023)

The Role of the ILA *in the Restatement and Evolution of International and National Law Relating to Indigenous Peoples, in* INTERNATIONAL ACTORS AND THE FORMATION OF LAWS 89-112 (Katja Karjalainen, Iina Tornberg & Aleksi Pursiainen eds., Springer 2022) with Timo Koivurova and Federico Lenzerini

IN HONOUR OF DETLEV VAGTS 174–197 (Pieter H. F. Bekker, Rudolf Dolzer & Michael Waibel eds., Cambridge University Press 2010)

The United Nations Declaration on the Rights of Indigenous Peoples: Selected Issues, in THE DIVERSITY OF INTERNATIONAL LAW. ESSAYS IN HONOUR OF PROFESSOR KALLIOPI K. KOUFA 343–361 (Aristotle Constantinides & Nikos Zaikos eds., Martinus Nijhoff Publishers 2009)

Demographic Change and the Protection of Minorities, in GLOBALER DEMO-GRAPHISCHER WANDEL UND SCHUTZ DER MENSCHENRECHTE 155-185 (Eckart Klein ed., Berliner Wissenschafts-Verlag 2005)

Ethnic Groups, in ENCYCLOPEDIA OF GENOCIDE AND CRIMES AGAINST HUMANI-TY 304-306 (Dinah Shelton ed., Macmillan Reference USA 2005)

Legitimacy and Accountability of NGOs: A Policy-Oriented Perspective, in FROM GOVERNMENT TO GOVERNANCE - 2003 HAGUE JOINT CONFERENCE ON CON-TEMPORARY ISSUES OF INTERNATIONAL LAW 95–101 (W.P. Heere ed., T.M.C. Asser Press 2004)

Policy-Oriented Jurisprudence and Human Rights Abuses in Internal Conflict: Toward a World Public Order of Human Dignity, in THE METHODS OF IN-TERNATIONAL LAW 47–77 (Anne-Marie Slaughter & Steven R. Ratner eds., 2004), with Andrew R. Willard (No. 36, ASIL Studies in Transnational Legal Policy)

Rights and Status of Indigenous Peoples: A Global Comparative and Internation-al Legal Perspective, reprinted in INTERNATIONAL LAW AND INDIGENOUS PEO-PLES 257–328 (S. James Anaya ed., 2003)

Exploring the Edge: The Personal Reach of a Transnational Agreement to Arbitrate, in "IN EINEM VEREINTEN EUROPA DEM FRIEDEN DER WELT ZU DIENEN..." LIBER AMICORUM THOMAS OPPERMANN (Claus Dieter Classen et al. eds., Duncker & Humblot, Berlin 453–473 (2001)

Professor Myres S. McDougal: A Tender Farewell, in MYRES SMITH MCDOUGAL: APPRECIATIONS OF AN EXTRAORDINARY MAN 119-121 (Yale Law School, 1999)

Faces of Vulnerability: Protecting Individuals in Organic and Non-Organ-ic Groups, in THE LIVING LAW OF NATIONS. ESSAYS IN MEMORY OF ATLE GRAHL-MADSEN 217–226 (Gudmundur Alfredsson & Peter Macalister-Smith eds., N. P. Engel 1996)

Law and Minimum World Public Order, with Myres S. McDougal, *in* MYRES S. MCDOUGAL & FLORENTINO P. FELICIANO, THE INTERNATIONAL LAW OF WAR XIX–LXXXII (New Haven Press 1994)

Human Activities in Outer Space: A Framework for Decision-Making, in SPACE LAW: VIEWS OF THE FUTURE 7–20 (Int'l Inst. of Air and Space Law, State Uni-versity of Leyden ed., 1988), *reprinted in* THE SPIRIT OF AMERICAN LAW 514-521 (George S. Grossman ed., 2000)

Die "Vorläufige Wohnheimordnung": Anmerkungen zum Statut des Sammellagers Tübingen, in LAGER UND MENSCHLICHE WÜRDE, LAGER UND MENSCHLICHE WÜRDE 77–102 (AS-Verlag Tübingen 1982)

Articles

Welcome Address, The Death Penalty: A Violation of Human Dignity?, 2022 IHRLR Symposium, 17 INTERCULTURAL HUMAN RIGHTS LAW REVIEW 7–10 (2022)

The ILC at Its 70th Anniversary: Its Role in International Law and Its Impact on U.S. Jurisprudence, 13 FIU LAW REVIEW 1151-1174 (2019), with Christian Lee González, available at https://ecollections.law.fiu.edu/lawreview/vol13/iss6/14/

The Rule of Law: Prolegomena, ZEITSCHRIFT FÜR DEUTSCHES UND AMERIKANISCHES RECHT [German-American Law Review] 82-84 (June 2018), available at https://papers.ssrn.com/sol3/papers.cfm?abstract_id=3293042

Democratizing International Arbitration? Mass Claims Proceedings in Abaclat v. Argentina, 1 JOURNAL OF INTERNATIONAL AND COMPARATIVE LAW 55–83 (2014), available at http://papers.ssrn.com/sol3/papers.cfm?abstract_id=2471271

The Powers of the President, 1 LINCOLN MEMORIAL UNIVERSITY LAW REVIEW 103–130 (2013), available at http://digitalcommons.lmunet.edu/lmulrev/vol1/iss1/13/

The St. Thomas Law Review: Its Ratio Essendi, 25 ST. THOMAS LAW REVIEW 271–273 (2013)

Re-Enchanting the World: Indigenous Peoples' Rights as Essential Parts of a Holistic Human Rights Regime, 15 UCLA JOURNAL OF INTERNATIONAL LAW AND FOREIGN AFFAIRS 239–288 (2010 [2012]), available at http://heinonline.org/HOL/LandingPage?handle=hein.journals/jilfa15&div=10&id=&page=

The Cultural Rights of Indigenous Peoples: Achievements and Continuing Challenges, 22 EUROPEAN JOURNAL OF INTERNATIONAL Law 121–140 (2011), available at http://ejil.org/pdfs/22/1/2128.pdf

Indigenous Sovereignty, Culture, and International Human Rights Law, 110 SOUTH ATLANTIC QUARTERLY 403–427 (2011, with Lorie M. Graham)

The New Haven School of Jurisprudence: A Universal Toolkit for Understanding and Shaping the Law, 18 ASIA PACIFIC LAW REVIEW 45–61 (2010), available at http://papers.ssrn.com/sol3/papers.cfm?abstract_id=2011130

Law as a Means to a Public Order of Human Dignity: The Jurisprudence of Michael Reisman, 34 YALE JOURNAL OF INTERNATIONAL LAW 525–532 (2009), available at https://openyls.law.yale.edu/handle/20.500.13051/6584

The Cuban Embargo and Human Rights: Introductory Remarks, 4 INTERCULTUR-
AL HUMAN RIGHTS LAW REVIEW 5–7 (2009)

*Indigenous Sovereignty: A Reassessment in Light of the UN Declaration on the
Rights of Indigenous Peoples,* 41, VANDERBILT JOURNAL OF TRANSNATIONAL
LAW 1141-1176 (2008), available at https://scholarship.law.vanderbilt.edu
/vjtl/vol41/iss4/4

The New Haven School: A Brief Introduction, 32 YALE JOURNAL OF INTERNATION-
AL LAW 575–582 (2007), with W. Michael Reisman and Andrew R. Willard,
available at https://openyls.law.yale.edu/handle/20.500.13051/6550, and
translated into Spanish as *La New Haven School: Una breve introducción, in*
5 (No. 9) REVISTA TRIBUNA INTERNACIONAL 11–18 (Chile, 2016), available at
https://tribunainternacional.uchile.cl/index.php/RTI/article/view/41956

*The UN Declaration on the Rights of Indigenous Peoples: Towards Re-Empower-
ment,* THIRD WORLD RESURGENCE, Issue No. 206, at 15–17 (October 2007),
with S. James Anaya; *reprinted in* UN DECLARATION ON THE RIGHTS OF IN-
DIGENOUS PEOPLES 45–52 (Tebtebba Foundation 2007), also published,
as *Re-Empowerment of Indigenous Peoples,* at 3(2) ASIAN HUMAN RIGHTS
DEFENDER 44–46 (July-December 2007)

The Articles on State Responsibility and Contemporary International Law, 34
THESAURUS ACROASIUM 247–276 (2006)

The Movement toward Federalism in Italy: A Policy-Oriented Perspective, 15 ST.
THOMAS LAW REVIEW 301–319 (2002)

Policy-Oriented Jurisprudence, 44 GERMAN YEARBOOK OF INTERNATIONAL LAW
96–112 (2001), with Andrew R. Willard

Indigenous Peoples, 10 YEARBOOK OF INTERNATIONAL ENVIRONMENTAL LAW
193-216 (2000); 11 YEARBOOK OF INTERNATIONAL ENVIRONMENTAL LAW 155–
163 (2001); 12 YEARBOOK OF INTERNATIONAL ENVIRONMENTAL LAW 198–208
(2002); 13 YEARBOOK OF INTERNATIONAL ENVIRONMENTAL LAW 249–257
(2004)

Defending Indigenous Peoples' Heritage: An Introduction, 14 ST. THOMAS LAW
REVIEW 271–274 (2001)

Joining Control to Authority: The Hardened "Indigenous Norm," 25 YALE JOURNAL
OF INTERNATIONAL LAW 301–305 (2000)

*The 2000 Revision of the United Nations Draft Principles and Guidelines on the
Protection of the Heritage of Indigenous People,* 13 ST. THOMAS LAW REVIEW
383-390 (2000), with Marie Battiste

*Rights and Status of Indigenous Peoples: A Global Comparative and International
Legal Perspective,* 12 HARVARD HUMAN RIGHTS JOURNAL 57–128 (1999), available
at https://harvardhrj.com/wp-content/uploads/sites/14/2020/06/12_Wiessner
_Rights-and-Status-of-Indigenous-Peoples.pdf

Policy-Oriented Jurisprudence and Human Rights Abuses in Internal Conflict: Toward a World Public Order of Human Dignity, 93 AMERICAN JOURNAL OF INTERNATIONAL LAW 316–334 (1999), with Andrew R. Willard, available at https://www.jstor.org/stable/2997992

¡Esa India! *LatCrit Theory and the Place of Indigenous Peoples within Latina/o Communities,* 53 UNIVERSITY OF MIAMI LAW REVIEW 831-854 (1999), available at https://repository.law.miami.edu/umlr/vol53/iss4/12/, *partially reprinted in* RICHARD DELGADO, LETICIA M. SAUCEDO, MARC-TIZOC GONZÁLEZ, JEAN ANN STEFANCIC, JUAN F. PEREA, LATINOS AND THE LAW: CASES AND MATERIALS 194–195 (West Academic Publishing, 2d ed. 2021)

Professor Myres S. McDougal: A Tender Farewell, 11 ST. THOMAS LAW REVIEW 203-206 (1999)

Marathon Oil Co. v. Ruhrgas AG: Amicus Curiae Brief by Professors of International Arbitration, 9 WORLD ARBITRATION AND MEDIATION REPORT 137–143 (1998)

International Law in the 21st Century: Decisionmaking in Institutionalized and Non-Institutionalized Settings, 26 THESAURUS ACROASIUM 129-153 (1997)

The Proposed American Declaration on the Rights of Indigenous Peoples, 6 INTERNATIONAL JOURNAL OF CULTURAL PROPERTY 356–375 (1997)

American Indian Treaties and Modern International Law, 7 ST. THOMAS LAW REVIEW 567-602 (1995), available at https://heinonline.org/HOL/LandingPage?handle=hein.journals/stlr7&div=40&id=&page=, also published in SOVEREIGNTY SYMPOSIUM VIII (1995)

La Violencia y el Derecho en el Nuevo Orden Mundial, 3 REVISTA DE DERECHO. UNIVERSIDAD CATÓLICA DE LA SSMA. CONCEPCIÓN [Chile] 71–84 (1994)

Federalism: An Architecture for Freedom, 1 NEW EUROPE LAW REVIEW 129–142 (1993)

Law and Peace in a Changing World, 22 CUMBERLAND LAW REVIEW 681–710 (1992), with Myres S. McDougal

Blessed Be the Ties that Bind: The Nexus between Nationality and Territory, 56 MISSISSIPPI LAW JOURNAL 447–533 (1988)

The Public Order of the Geostationary Orbit: Blueprints for the Future, 9 YALE JOURNAL OF WORLD PUBLIC ORDER 217–274 (1983[1985]), available at https://openyls.law.yale.edu/handle/20.500.13051/6814

Die Schiedsfähigkeit internationaler Antitrust-Streitigkeiten, 10 RECHT DER INTERNATIONALEN WIRTSCHAFT 757-765 (1985), with Dieter G. Lange

Barriers to Telecom Trade: A Caveat, 2 TELEMATICS No. 1, 1–10 (1985)

Communications in the Earth-Space Arena: Translating Equity into Hertz and Degrees from the Greenwich Meridian, 52 ITU TELECOMMUNICATION JOURNAL 304–309 (1985)

Vom "verwalteten Grundrecht" zum "verwalteten Menschen"? in POLITISCHES
ASYL UND EINWANDERUNG 92–112 (Ulrich O. Sievering ed., 1984)
Das völkerrechtliche Regime der geostationären Umlaufbahn, 32 AUSTRIAN
JOURNAL OF PUBLIC AND INTERNATIONAL LAW 209–239 (1982), with Rüdiger
Jung
*Die rechtliche Problematik der Sammellager für Asylbewerber in Baden-Würt-
temberg,* 3 INFORMATIONSBRIEF AUSLÄNDERRECHT 261–270 (1981)
Asylverweigerung ohne Anerkennungsverfahren, 7 EUROPÄISCHE GRUNDRECHTE-
ZEITSCHRIFT 473–479 (1980)
Nevil Johnson: Die Institutionen im Studium der Politik [transl. Nevil Johnson,
The Place of Institutions in the Study of Politics], 16 DER STAAT 1-19 (1977)

Lectures and Panel Contributions

Reading the Constitution, Constitution Day Lecture, St. Thomas University,
September 22, 2022
Comments, *Working Session,* ILA *Committee on the Implementation of the
Rights of Indigenous Peoples,* December 5, 2020, 79th ILA Biennial Meeting,
Kyoto, Japan
*Final Report and Remarks, Working Session, International Law Association Com-
mittee on the Rights of Indigenous Peoples,* ILA REPORT OF THE 75TH CONFER-
ENCE HELD IN SOFIA 503–553 (London 2012)
*Interim Report and Remarks, Working Session, International Law Association
Committee on the Rights of Indigenous Peoples,* ILA REPORT OF THE 74TH
CONFERENCE HELD IN THE HAGUE 15-19, 2010 834–923 (London 2010)
The Kurdish Issue and Beyond: Territorial Communities Rivaling the State, 98
PROCEEDINGS OF THE AMERICAN SOCIETY OF INTERNATIONAL LAW 107-108
(2004)
Intellectual Property and Indigenous Peoples: An Overview, 95 PROCEEDINGS OF
THE AMERICAN SOCIETY OF INTERNATIONAL LAW 151-153 (2001)
The Project of Reconfiguration: How Can International Law Be Reconstituted?,
94 PROCEEDINGS OF THE AMERICAN SOCIETY OF INTERNATIONAL LAW 73–74,
79–81 (2000)
Remarks, Panel on *Communities in Transition: Autonomy, Self-Governance and
Independence,* 87 PROCEEDINGS OF THE AMERICAN SOCIETY OF INTERNA-
TIONAL LAW 264–265 (1993)
Developments in the International Law of Telecommunications, 83 PROCEEDINGS
OF THE AMERICAN SOCIETY OF INTERNATIONAL LAW 400–403 (1990)
The Art of the Possible: A Review of Space-WARC 1985-1988, PROCEEDINGS OF THE
32ND COLLOQUIUM ON THE LAW OF OUTER SPACE 266–269 (1990)

Remarks, Panel on *Treaty Law and Outer Space: The Role of the United Nations,* 80 PROCEEDINGS OF THE AMERICAN SOCIETY OF INTERNATIONAL LAW 385 (1988)

Access to a Res Publica Internationalis: The Case of the Geostationary Orbit, PROCEEDINGS OF THE 29TH COLLOQUIUM ON THE LAW OF OUTER SPACE 147–153 (1987)

Book Reviews

Alexandra Xanthaki, Indigenous Rights and United Nations Standards, 103 AMERICAN JOURNAL OF INTERNATIONAL LAW 188–193 (2009)

The Reasons Requirement in International Investment Arbitration. Critical Case Studies (Guillermo Aguilar Alvarez & W. Michael Reisman eds.), 4 (2) GLOBAL ARBITRATION REVIEW 38–39 (2009)

Sandra Voos, Die Schule von New Haven, 96 AMERICAN JOURNAL OF INTERNATIONAL LAW 498–501 (2002)

Gerard-René de Groot, Staatsangehörigkeit im Wandel, 85 AMERICAN JOURNAL OF INTERNATIONAL LAW 422–424 (1991)

Stephen Gorove, The Teaching of Space Law Around the World, 15 JOURNAL OF SPACE LAW 72–75 (1987)

Internet Lecture

The Rights and Status of Indigenous Peoples, United Nations Audiovisual Library of International Law, Lecture Series, at https://legal.un.org/avl/ls /Wiessner_HR.html

Internet Publications

Justice Breyer's Legacy: A Preliminary Assessment, ATTORNEY AT LAW MAGAZINE, February 2, 2022, https://attorneyatlawmagazine.com/justice-breyers-legacy-a-preliminary-assessment

New Haven and the Design of Laws under Therapeutic Jurisprudence, Panel on Legislative Scholarship, Design, Advocacy, and Outcomes, 36th International Congress on Law and Mental Health, Rome, Italy, July 24, 2019, available at https://www.intltj.com/resources/

The Maya Communities in Belize, Interim Report, International Law Association Committee on the Rights of Indigenous Peoples, 77th ILA Biennial

Meeting, Johannesburg, South Africa, August 7–11, 2016 (Member, with Federico Lenzerini)

Final Report and ILA Resolution No. 5/2012, International Law Association Committee on the Rights of Indigenous Peoples, 75th ILA Biennial Meeting, Sofia, Bulgaria, August 26–30, 2012, https://www.ila-hq.org/en_GB/documents/conference-re port-sofia-2012-10 and https://www.ila-hq.org/en_GB/documents/conference -resolution-english-sofia-2012-4 (Chair, with Members)

Remarks, Open Session, International Law Association Committee on the Rights of Indigenous Peoples, ILA Report of the 75th Conference held in Sofia, Bulgaria, August 28, 2012

Interim Report, International Law Association Committee on the Rights of Indigenous Peoples, 74th ILA Biennial Meeting, The Hague, August 2010, at https://www.ila-hq.org/en_GB/documents/conference-report-the-hague-2010-13 (Chair, with Members)

ILA Committee Chair Report, *Rights of Indigenous Peoples,* 87 ABILA NEWS-LETTER 10–11 (September 2010), at http://ila-americanbranch.org/newsletters/201009_ABILA_ NEWSLETTER.pdf

Introductory Note, General Assembly Resolution 61/295 of 13 September 2007 (United Nations Declaration on the Rights of Indigenous Peoples), United Nations Audiovisual Library of International Law, Historical Archives, at https://legal.un.org/avl/pdf/ha/ga_61-295/ga_61-295_s.pdf

ILA Committee Chair Report, *Rights of Indigenous Peoples,* 82 ABILA Newsletter, 7–8 (January 2009), at http://ila-americanbranch.org/newsletters/ABILANews2009-01.pdf

Council Comment: The U.S. Supreme Court's Decision in Medellín v. Texas, ASIL Newsletter, April/June 2008, at 14, at http://www.asil.org/pdfs/asil-news080606.pdf

The UN Declaration on the Rights of Indigenous Peoples: Towards Reempowerment, JURIST Forum, Oct. 3, 2007, at https://www.jurist.org/commentary/2007/10/un-declaration-on-rights-of-indigenous-2/, with S. James Anaya

Council Comment: The International Court of Justice's Decision in Bosnia and Herzegovina v. Serbia and Montenegro, ASIL Newsletter, Spring 2007, at 9, at http://www.asil.org/pdfs/asilnews070625.pdf

A New United Nations Subsidiary Organ: The Permanent Forum on Indigenous Issues, ASIL Insight No. 67, Apr. 2001, at http://www.asil.org/insigh67.cfm, with John Carey

Non-State Actors and Their Impact on International Human Rights Law, AALS Workshop on Human Rights, Oct. 26–28, 2000, at http://www.aals.org/prof dev/humanrights/weissner.html

PART 1

Siegfried Wiessner, The Person

∴

CHAPTER 1

Siegfried Wiessner: A Life in the Pursuit of Human Flourishing for All

W. Michael Reisman and Roza Pati

I

Siegfried Wiessner's scholarship addresses urgent social issues, both domestic and international, with a view to developing solutions that contribute to a public order of human dignity.[1] In analogy to physicians, he sees lawyers as "doctors of the social order."[2] In the tradition of the New Haven School of Jurisprudence, he conceives law as a dynamic process of both authoritative and controlling decision.[3] Thanks to its exhaustive interdisciplinary research, analytical depth and rigorous craftsmanship, judicious appraisal of past and projected future decisions, and thoughtful and innovative proposals, his scholarship has had a profound influence.

His analyses of existing law in his teaching and scholarship are precise, but Siegfried does not worship at the altar of positivism's idol of the golden calf of unalterable rules and institutions. To the contrary, he exposes the fallacies

---

1   Siegfried Wiessner, *The New Haven School of Jurisprudence: A Universal Toolkit for Understanding and Shaping the Law*, 18 Asia Pacific Law Review 45, 51–53 (2010); Siegfried Wiessner & Andrew R. Willard, *Policy-Oriented Jurisprudence and Human Rights Abuses in Internal Conflict: Toward a World Public Order of Human Dignity*, 93 American Journal of International Law 316–334 (1999), also published in The Methods of International Law 47 (Anne-Marie Slaughter & Steven R. Ratner eds., 2004); Siegfried Wiessner, *Law as a Means to a Public Order of Human Dignity: The Jurisprudence of Michael Reisman*, 34 Yale Journal of International Law 525, 530–532 (2009), available at https://openyls.law.yale.edu /handle/20.500.13051/6584.

2   Siegfried Wiessner, *Doctors of the Social Order: Introduction to New Haven Methodology, in* Handbook on Human Trafficking, Public Health and the Law 8 (Wilhelm Kirch, Siegfried Wiessner & Roza Pati eds., Georg Thieme Verlag, Stuttgart, New York, 2014).

3   Siegfried Wiessner, *Michael Reisman, Human Dignity, and the Law, in* Looking to the Future: Essays on International Law in Honor of W. Michael Reisman 21, 26–29 (Martinus Nijhoff Publishers, 2011). *See also* Myres S. McDougal & Siegfried Wiessner, *Law and Minimum World Public Order, in* The International Law of War XIX–LXXXII (Myres S. McDougal & Florentino P. Feliciano, eds., New Haven Press 1994).

and sterilizing effect of extreme positivism and then shows how much can be accomplished once liberated from it.

> The jurisprudence of positivism provides the counter-image to this empirical, dynamic conception of law. Its common focus on "existing" rules, emanating solely from entities deemed equally "sovereign," does not properly reflect the reality of how law is made, applied and changed. Positivism remains fixated on the past, trying to reap from words laid down, irrespective of the context in which they were written, the solution to a problem that arises today or tomorrow in very different circumstances. Without identifying the conditioning factors of the past decisions they rely on – such as the personality, political inclinations, gender and cultural background of the decision makers, as well as the mood of the times, and other societal factors – positivists try hard, in an ultimately futile quest for "certainty" of law, to predict future decisions. But, as they do not take into account changing and changed contexts (e.g., different legislators, judges, shifts in public opinion), their predictions are unlikely to be precise; they may even be inaccurate. Moreover, positivists gain no help from their theory when asked what the law "should" be. Indeed, their theory eschews any creative or prescriptive function.[4]

The contrast between positivism and the jurisprudence he espouses becomes clear in his assessment of the jurisprudence of retiring Supreme Court Justice Breyer. He writes:

> In any event, the respect for the rule of law, as cardinal value and positively ordained, has its limits, according to Breyer: the continuing authority of, and ultimately obedience to, Supreme Court decisions depends on three factors: sanctions for violations, incentives to encourage compliance, and the public's perception that the law is just. This broad term echoes Justice Brandeis' conviction, "if we desire respect for the law, we must first make the law respectable." While correct in principle, it remains tough to designate concretely the contours of injustice that would constitute the outer limits to the reign of positive law, be they the outrages to human dignity of the Nuremberg kind or lesser standards.[5]

---

4   Siegfried Wiessner & Andrew R. Willard, *supra* note 1, at 320.
5   Siegfried Wiessner, *Justice Breyer's Legacy: A Preliminary Assessment,* Attorney at Law Magazine, Feb. 2, 2022, https://attorneyatlawmagazine.com/justice-breyers-legacy-a-preliminary -assessment.

Tough though it would be, Siegfried exposes again and again the *contours of injustice* with precision. A master of analyzing complex and intricate arrangements, he exposes the very different value consequences of these two schools of jurisprudence.

Siegfried is respected around the world as an authoritative scholar of human rights law, especially the plight of indigenous peoples, as well as an ardent advocate for the oppressed. In all these endeavors, Siegfried's base of power is his scholarship, as briefly depicted below.

Siegfried has published widely in the fields of Constitutional Law, International Law, Jurisprudence, The Rule of Law, Space Law, International Arbitration, the Law of Armed Conflict, and International Indigenous Law. His motive for writing has been to enlist the law for those who most urgently need it, the underprivileged, the poor, and the marginalized.

II

Siegfried's ancestors, traditional farmers in Gerhardshofen, a Franconian village in the south of Germany, trace their lineage to 1705. His father, the mayor of the community during Siegfried's youth, was far-sighted and brought industry to the village in the 1960s. It was expected that Siegfried, his only son, would follow in the family tradition. But Siegfried was interested in a wider world and early turned to the Academy. He finished high school in 1972 and then studied law at the Universities of Erlangen, Geneva, and Tübingen. In Tübingen, he became a jurist, passing the first and second bar exams of the State of Baden-Württemberg. In 1977, Professor Hans von Mangoldt, professor of constitutional and international law, and son of Professor Hermann von Mangoldt, Chair of the Parliamentary Council which drafted the Basic Law, the post-WWII Constitution of 1949 of the Federal Republic of Germany, invited him to join his team as a research and teaching associate.

Siegfried's maiden article already showed characteristics that were developed in his later work. He introduced the idea of a necessary procedural dimension to the right to asylum, a right inserted, uniquely among states internationally, in the German Basic Law. While a government decree of 1977 mandated border police and domestic foreigners' offices to disregard an application for asylum that was in their view "evidently abusive," Siegfried's novel argument was that the subjective right to asylum had a procedural dimension that required substantively competent agencies to review these applications.[6]

---

6 Siegfried Wiessner, *Asylverweigerung ohne Anerkennungsverfahren* [Denial of Asylum without Procedure of Recognition], Europäische Grundrechte-Zeitschrift 1980, 473.

The Federal Constitutional Court agreed with this argument and went on to declare the decree unconstitutional.[7] The impact of his idea on the reality of German refugee law was momentous.

Thereafter, he undertook his doctoral thesis, under the direction of Professor von Mangoldt. Siegfried questioned the conventional notion that nationality is a *nudum ius*, a concept devoid of any legal consequences beyond the effects any individual state chose to attach to it. In a global comparative study of the great legal families, he found that common to virtually all legal systems across the world, there are several distinctive legal consequences to the function of nationality transnationally.[8]

In 1979, Siegfried met Keith Nunes, a young South African. It was a life-changing experience. That year, Keith made a number of fiery interventions at the Academy of International Law in The Hague that had the effect of liberating Siegfried from the straitjacket of positivism, and, in an "intellectual rebirth,"[9] introducing him to the New Haven School of Jurisprudence.

In 1982, Siegfried joined Keith, who was already at Yale, and started his life in New Haven in the LL.M. Program at the Yale Law School. He worked closely with one of us, his thesis supervisor, Michael Reisman, and enjoyed this year, which he has often called the best of his intellectual life. He also had many meetings with Professor Myres Smith McDougal. When "Mac" became ill and was unable to travel, he asked Siegfried to deliver the Cordell Hull Centennial Lecture on Law and Peace at Cumberland School of Law in Birmingham, Alabama, in 1991 for him.[10] They also co-authored the introductory update to McDougal's magisterial treatment of the law of war, originally published with Florentino Feliciano in 1961 under the title of *Law and Minimum World Public Order*.[11] Siegfried and Professor McDougal also worked together on several international arbitration cases.

Siegfried applied the New Haven approach rigorously in his article on issues relating to the scarcity of orbital positions and frequencies in the

---

7   BVerfGE 56, 216 (German Federal Constitutional Court Decision of February 25, 1981).

8   Siegfried Wiessner, Die Funktion der Staatsangehörigkeit [The Function of Nationality] (Dr. iur. Dissertation, Tübingen University Press, 1989); *cf.* Siegfried Wiessner, *Blessed Be the Ties that Bind: The Nexus between Nationality and Territory*, 56 Mississippi Law Journal 447 (1988).

9   Siegfried Wiessner, *Professor Myres S. McDougal: A Tender Farewell*, 11 St. Thomas Law Review 203 (1999).

10   Myres S. McDougal & Siegfried Wiessner, *Law and Peace in a Changing World*, 22 Cumberland Law Review 681 (1992).

11   Myres S. McDougal & Siegfried Wiessner, *Law and Minimum World Public Order, in* Myres S. McDougal & Florentino P. Feliciano, The International Law of War xix–lxxxii (New Haven Press 1994).

geostationary satellite orbit.[12] His creative solutions for the equitable sharing of this resource were published, in a shortened version, in the official journal of the International Telecommunication Union.[13] The contrast with an earlier article on the same subject, written with a student using the positivist mode,[14] is striking.[15] Siegfried's article sparked an invitation to join the International Institute of Space Law, which Siegfried accepted. It led to fruitful cooperation[16] and thoughtful predictions in the field.[17]

Siegfried, as a strong proponent of policy-oriented jurisprudence, guided many students to publications using the approach. He also frequently commented on the content and application of the New Haven School. Together with his friend and colleague in the field of political science, Andrew R. Willard,[18] he represented the approach in the 1999 American Society of International Law symposium on international legal theory.[19] The symposium covered the response by proponents of various theories about law to the problem of serious human rights abuses in internal conflict. A Yale symposium yielded a brief theoretical introduction to the New Haven School along with Michael Reisman and Andrew R. Willard.[20] Siegfried added to policy-oriented jurisprudence,

---

12 Siegfried Wiessner, *The Public Order of the Geostationary Orbit: Blueprints for the Future*, 9 Yale Journal of World Public Order 217 (1983[1985]).

13 Siegfried Wiessner, *Communications in the Earth-Space Arena: Translating Equity into Hertz and Degrees from the Greenwich Meridian*, 52 ITU Telecommunication Journal 304 (1985).

14 Siegfried Wiessner & Rüdiger Jung, *Das völkerrechtliche Regime der geostationären Umlaufbahn*, 32 Austrian Journal of Public and International Law 209 (1982).

15 As documented in Siegfried Wiessner, *The New Haven School of Jurisprudence: A Universal Toolkit for Understanding and Shaping the Law, supra* note 1, at 59–61.

16 For presentations at the Institute's annual meetings, see Siegfried Wiessner, *Access to a Res Publica Internationalis: The Case of the Geostationary Orbit*, Proc. 29th Coll. on the Law of Outer Space 147 (1987); and Siegfried Wiessner, *The Art of the Possible: A Review of Space-WARC 1985–1988*, Proc. 32nd Coll. on the Law of Outer Space 266 (1990).

17 Siegfried Wiessner, *Human Activities in Outer Space: A Framework for Decision-Making*, in Space Law: Views of the Future 7 (Int'l Inst. of Air and Space Law, State University of Leyden ed., 1988), reprinted in The Spirit of American Law 514 (George S. Grossman ed., 2000).

18 Siegfried Wiessner & Andrew R. Willard, *Policy-Oriented Jurisprudence and Human Rights Abuses in Internal Conflict: Toward a World Public Order of Human Dignity, supra* note 1.

19 Organized by Steven Ratner and Anne-Marie Slaughter. *Cf.* Steven R. Ratner & Anne-Marie Slaughter, *Appraising the Methods of International Law: A Prospectus for Readers*, 93 American Journal of International Law 291 (1999).

20 W. Michael Reisman, Siegfried Wiessner & Andrew R. Willard, *The New Haven School: A Brief Introduction*, 32 Yale Journal of International Law 575 (2007), and translated into Spanish as *La New Haven School: Una breve introducción, in* 5 (No. 9) Revista Tribuna Internacional 11 (Chile, 2016). *See also* Siegfried Wiessner & Andrew R. Willard, *Policy-Oriented*

inter alia, the designation of a lawyer dedicated to applying the New Haven School's methodology as a "doctor of the social order," diagnosing the social ill using all relevant knowledge and crafting a remedial program specifically designed for the problem.[21] New Haven lawyers focus on the goal of working to find a solution to a societal problem, rather than confining themselves to an analysis, critical or affirmative, of the status quo. Siegfried concluded, "The guiding light for not only the evaluation of past and future decisions, but for effective solutions is the concept of an order of human dignity which allows for the flourishing of all human beings – no minorities left out in the cold – through maximization of access by all to all the processes of shaping and sharing things that human beings value."[22]

Siegfried has communicated to students and colleagues around the world the utility of the New Haven approach, in his lecturing and participation in conferences to organizing workshops abroad, from guiding seminar papers to supervising doctoral dissertations in the field. The BRILL Nijhoff series "Studies in Intercultural Human Rights" under his leadership, has incorporated several excellent theses using New Haven as their guidance.[23]

Michael Reisman, affectionately called "the Dean" of the New Haven School,[24] has been Siegfried's mentor and close friend for many years. With Mahnoush Arsanjani and Gayl Westerman, they published, in 2004, a casebook in the New Haven mold, entitled *International Law in Contemporary Perspective*.[25] With Mahnoush Arsanjani, Jacob Katz Cogan and Robert Sloane,

---

Jurisprudence, 44 German Yearbook of International Law 96 (2001), and Siegfried Wiessner, *The New Haven School of Jurisprudence, supra* note 1.

21   "[T]he ideal role of a lawyer is that of a 'doctor of the social order': just as a medical doctor depends on a thorough diagnosis of a patient's discomfort or disease to prescribe proper treatment, the social doctor, i.e. the lawyer, depends on a comprehensive interdisciplinary study of a problem to prescribe the proper remedies in the form of legal decisions. The non-lawyer experts, in particular, using the methodology germane to their discipline, need to bring to bear their full expertise. Finding the best solutions to societal problems needs thus the combination of law, science and policy: understanding the problem and the past legal decisions with a view to shaping future decisions best designed to approximate an order of human dignity." Siegfried Wiessner, *Doctors of the Social Order, supra* note 2, at 8–9; Siegfried Wiessner, *International Law in the 21st Century: Decisionmaking in Institutionalized and Non-Institutionalized Settings,* 26 Thesaurus Acroasium 129 (1997).

22   *Doctors of the Social Order, supra* note 2, at 15.

23   The most recent being Volume 11: Gabriela Curras DeBellis, Eradicating Human Trafficking: Culture, Law and Policy (2022), supervised by Professor Roza Pati.

24   *Cf.* Harold Hongju Koh, *Michael Reisman, Dean of the New Haven School of International Law,* 34 Yale Journal of International Law 501 (2009).

25   Michael Reisman, Mahnoush Arsanjani, Siegfried Wiessner & Gayl Westerman, International Law in Contemporary Perspective (Foundation Press, 2004).

Siegfried edited, in 2011, a Festschrift in honor of Michael Reisman under the title of *Looking to the Future*, which included his contribution on "Michael Reisman, Human Dignity and the Law."[26] Special mention must be made of Siegfried's brilliant historical and comparative introduction to the first volume of a series of American Classics of International Law, entitled *General Theory of International Law*.[27] This introduction and selection as well as critique of pertinent texts demonstrated a depth of knowledge and discernment about specifically American aspects of theory, as seen by a person socialized outside the American system. It does for American international legal theory what Count Alexis de Tocqueville did for American society.[28]

Siegfried has worked with Michael Reisman on a substantial number of cases in the field of international investment arbitration, particularly in the ICSID system. Prior to his entry into teaching, he practiced international commercial arbitration with the Washington, D.C. law firm of Wilmer, Cutler & Pickering. There, he was of counsel in the successful amicus curiae brief for the International Chamber of Commerce,[29] twice cited by the U.S. Supreme Court regarding the international arbitrability of U.S. antitrust claims in the case of *Mitsubishi Motors Corporation v. Soler Chrysler-Plymouth, Inc.*[30] He also worked with a team of distinguished international arbitration experts in drafting an amicus curiae brief before the U.S. Court of Appeals for the Fifth Circuit in the case of *Marathon Oil Co. et al. v. Ruhrgas AG*.[31] His concern for a broad sharing of benefits manifested itself again in his analysis of and support for the democratization of international arbitration via the admission of mass

---

26   Siegfried Wiessner, *Michael Reisman, Human Dignity, and the Law, in* Looking to the Future, *supra* note 3, at 21. An earlier version of this tribute appeared under the title of *Law as a Means to a Public Order of Human Dignity: The Jurisprudence of Michael Reisman* at 34 Yale Journal of International Law, *supra* note 1.

27   General Theory of International Law, Volume 1, American Classics of International Law 1-78 (Siegfried Wiessner ed., BRILL - Martinus Nijhoff Publishers, 2017).

28   W. Michael Reisman, *Preface to Inaugural Volume*, General Theory of International Law, at xiii.

29   Siegfried Wiessner, Of Counsel, Brief for Int'l Chamber of Commerce as Amicus Curiae, U.S. Supreme Court, Mitsubishi Motors Corporation v. Soler Chrysler-Plymouth, Inc., Nos. 83-1569, 83-1733, December 17, 1984, with Dieter Lange and Sigvard Jarvin.

30   Mitsubishi Motors Corp. v. Soler Chrysler-Plymouth, Inc., 473 U.S. 614 (1985). For a detailed analysis of this decision, see Dieter G. Lange & Siegfried Wiessner, *Die Schiedsfähigkeit internationaler Antitrust-Streitigkeiten,* 10 Recht der internationalen Wirtschaft 757 (1985).

31   Siegfried Wiessner, Of Counsel, Brief for Law Professors Concerned with International Arbitration as Amici Curiae, U.S. Court of Appeals for the Fifth Circuit, Marathon Oil Co. et al. v. Ruhrgas AG, No. 96-20361, February 4, 1998; *Marathon Oil Co. v. Ruhrgas AG: Amicus Curiae Brief by Professors of International Arbitration,* 9 World Arbitration and Mediation Report 137 (1998).

arbitration claims,[32] while his technical proficiency highlighted the various options for extending the scope *ratione personae* of a transnational agreement to arbitrate.[33]

III

While Siegfried has continued to work in all of these areas, his passion has been the law regarding and affecting indigenous peoples, where he is a leading authority. He has developed good relations and is on a first-name basis with many leaders of what have been called the "First Nations." In 1993 and 1994, he gave lectures on the legal status and the empowerment of indigenous peoples to the Sovereignty Symposium in Tulsa, Oklahoma, organized by the Oklahoma Supreme Court and also attended by leaders and rank-and-file of Native American nations and tribes. There he met Susan Ferrell, a beautiful and fearless advocate of the underprivileged and a HUD attorney advisor in charge of Indian housing. She became his Muse, introducing him to the indigenous peoples of Oklahoma, to intertribal dances and drew him to his deep appreciation of their culture. Together with Kirke Kickingbird, a friend and Kiowa leader, they devised and executed the plan for a Tribal Sovereignty Symposium in Miami, more international in nature than its Oklahoma counterpart. Since its inception, it has brought indigenous issues, indigenous leaders and scholars in the field to St. Thomas University.[34] The first such Conference took place on December 1 and 2, 1994 under the title "Tribal Sovereignty: Back to the Future?"

---

32   Siegfried Wiessner, *Democratizing International Arbitration? Mass Claims Proceedings in Abaclat v. Argentina*, 1 Journal of International and Comparative Law 55 (2014).

33   Siegfried Wiessner, *Exploring the Edge: The Personal Reach of a Transnational Agreement to Arbitrate*, *in* "In einem vereinten Europa dem Frieden der Welt zu dienen..." Liber Amicorum Thomas Oppermann 453 (2001).

34   Kirke Kickingbird, *In memoriam Susan J. Ferrell*, 7 St. Thomas Law Review iv (1995). Other Native American leaders include Lawrence Hart, the Peace Chief of the Cheyenne, Ross Swimmer, Principal Chief of the Cherokee Nation, Keller George, the President of the United South and Eastern Tribes, Comanche Leader LaDonna Harris, Onondaga Chief Oren Lyons, representatives of the Navajo and Hopi nations, as well as the leaders of the local Seminole and Miccosukee Tribes, the Osage and Choctaw nations, and many others, including Don Jacinto Tzab, Mayan Wisdom-Keeper from the Yucatán peninsula.

      Erica Daes, inspirational Chairperson of the UN Working Group on Indigenous Peoples, also participated in the meetings and contributed to their success. *Cf.* Erica-Irene A. Daes, *The Indispensable Function of the Sacred*, 13 St. Thomas Law Review 29 (2000). In 2000, at her invitation, Siegfried served as Facilitator for the Drafting Commission of the United Nations Seminar on Draft Principles and Guidelines on the Protection of Indigenous Cultural Heritage, Feb. 28 - March 1, 2000, Geneva, UN Doc. E/CN.4/Sub.2/2000/26 (19 June 2000). *Cf.* Siegfried Wiessner & Marie Battiste, *The 2000 Revision of the United*

To Siegfried's deep and indelible sorrow,[35] Susan was killed shortly thereafter in the Oklahoma City terrorist bombing of April 19, 1995.[36] She was honored later at St. Thomas University with the establishment of the Susan J. Ferrell Intercultural Human Rights Moot Court Competition.[37]

The contributions to eight tribal sovereignty conferences were published in the *St. Thomas Law Review*[38] and, later, in the *Intercultural Human Rights Law Review*.[39] These publications gave the *St. Thomas Law Review* the distinction of having published the third-highest number of articles published from 1985 to 2015 in the field of federal Indian law.[40]

At the first conference on tribal sovereignty, Siegfried presented his fundamental reassessment of treaties of the U.S. government with Indian nations, seeing them as agreements of an international law character rather than domestic contracts. This reconception, based on the history of their creation, the role of the Senate in their approval and the *Western Sahara* opinion of the International Court of Justice, has had important consequences for their validity, interpretation and termination.[41] Thereafter, Siegfried, impressed by the resurgence worldwide of indigenous communities since the 1960s, started his work on the place of indigenous peoples in the legal systems of countries in which they reside. This global survey resulted in his article in 1999 in the *Harvard Human Rights Journal*, demonstrating customary international law rights of indigenous peoples to their traditional lands, resources, cultural heritage, and wide-ranging autonomy.[42] This article, republished on the Internet, ranked #14 in citations among 3,334 articles published in the field of federal

---

       Nations Draft Principles and Guidelines on the Protection of the Heritage of Indigenous People, 13 St. Thomas Law Review 383 (2000).

35   JSW [Siegfried Wiessner], Poem, 7 St. Thomas Law Review ii (1995).

36   She left us her vision for culturally appropriate housing in Native American communities: Susan J. Ferrell, *Indian Housing: The Fourth Decade*, 7 St. Thomas Law Review 445 (1994).

37   St. Thomas University's Susan J. Ferrell Intercultural Human Rights Moot Court Competition, https://www.stu.edu/law/human-rights/moot-court-competition/biography/.

38   Founded in 1987 under Siegfried's leadership. *Cf.* Siegfried Wiessner, *The St. Thomas Law Review: Its Ratio Essendi*, 25 St. Thomas Law Review 271 (2013).

39   Founded in 2005 by both Siegfried and Professor Roza Pati. *Cf.* Siegfried Wiessner, *Dedication*, 1 Intercultural Human Rights Law Review 1 (2006).

40   Grant Christensen & Melissa L. Tatum, *Reading Indian Law: Evaluating Thirty Years of Indian Law Scholarship*, 54 Tulsa Law Review 81, 110 (2018).

41   Siegfried Wiessner, *American Indian Treaties and Modern International Law*, 7 St. Thomas Law Review 567 (1995).

42   Siegfried Wiessner, *Rights and Status of Indigenous Peoples: A Global Comparative and International Legal Perspective*, 12 Harvard Human Rights Journal 57–128 (1999), https://harvardhrj.com/wp-content/uploads/sites/14/2020/06/12_Wiessner_Rights-and-Status-of-Indigenous-Peoples.pdf. *See also* Siegfried Wiessner, *Joining Control to Authority: The Hardened "Indigenous Norm,"* 25 Yale Journal of International Law 301 (2000).

Indian law from 1985 to 2015.[43] Siegfried continued his publications in the field, focusing, inter alia, on the sovereignty of indigenous peoples,[44] their definition,[45] and on the cultural roots of their rights,[46] and, in particular, their rights to land,[47] and has expounded his views at conferences around the world. His lecture on "The Rights and Status of Indigenous Peoples" is a permanent part of the Audiovisual Library of the United Nations.[48] Locally, he helped preserve an indigenous sacred site, the Miami Circle.[49]

---

43   Christensen & Tatum, *supra* note 40, at 98.

44   Siegfried Wiessner, *Indigenous Sovereignty: A Reassessment in Light of the UN Declaration on the Rights of Indigenous Peoples,* 41 Vanderbilt Journal of Transnational Law 1141 (2008), https://scholarship.law.vanderbilt.edu/vjtl/vol41/iss4/4/; Lorie M. Graham & Siegfried Wiessner, *Indigenous Sovereignty, Culture, and International Human Rights Law,* 110 South Atlantic Quarterly 403 (2011).

45   Siegfried Wiessner, *Indigenous Peoples: The Battle over Definition, in* Reflections on International Law. Studies in Honour of Lindy Melman 4–40 (Tim McCormack ed., BRILL – Martinus Nijhoff Publishers, 2023); Siegfried Wiessner, *The United Nations Declaration on the Rights of Indigenous Peoples: Selected Issues, in* The Diversity of International Law. Essays in Honour of Professor Kalliopi K. Koufa 343 (Aristotle Constantinides & Nikos Zaikos eds., Martinus Nijhoff Publishers 2009).

46   Siegfried Wiessner, *The Cultural Rights of Indigenous Peoples: Achievements and Continuing Challenges,* 22 European Journal of International Law 121 (2011), http://ejil.org /pdfs/22/1/2128.pdf. *See also* Siegfried Wiessner, *Culture and the Rights of Indigenous Peoples,* in The Cultural Dimension of Human Rights. Collected Courses of the Academy of European Law 117 (Ana Filipa Vrdoljak ed., Oxford University Press, 2013); Siegfried Wiessner, *The Cultural Dimension of the Rights of Indigenous Peoples, in* International Law for Common Goods: Normative Perspectives on Human Rights, Culture and Nature. Essays in Honor of Francesco Francioni 175 (Hart Publishing, Oxford UK, 2014); and Dalee Sambo Dorough & Siegfried Wiessner, *Indigenous Peoples and Cultural Heritage, in* The Oxford Handbook on International Cultural Heritage Law 407 (Francesco Francioni & Ana Filipa Vrdoljak eds., Oxford University Press, 2020).

47   Siegfried Wiessner, *Indigenous Self-Determination, Culture and Land: A Reassessment in Light of the 2007 UN Declaration on the Rights of Indigenous Peoples,* in Indigenous Rights in the Age of the UN Declaration, ch. 1, at 31 (Elvira Pulitano ed., Cambridge University Press 2012).

48   Siegfried Wiessner, *The Rights and Status of Indigenous Peoples,* United Nations Audiovisual Library of International Law, Lecture Series, February 9, 2009, at https://legal.un.org /avl/ls/Wiessner_HR.html.

49   Rev. Msgr. Franklyn M. Casale, *Sacred Sites and Modern Lives: The Miami Circle and Beyond,* St. Thomas Law Review 3, 4 (2000); Pamela G. Levinson, *Will the Circle be Unbroken – The Miami Circle Discovery and Its Significance for Urban Evolution and Protection of Indigenous Culture,* id. at 283, 307–308; Robert S. Carr & John Ricisak, *The Miami Circle: Beneath the Modern City,* id. at 225 (2000); T.L. Riggs, *The Discovery and Investigation of the Miami Circle,* id. at 229; Bobby C. Billie, *The Miami Circle and Beyond,* id. at 113; Geeta Sacred Song, *Forces of Light: The Spiritual Battle for the Miami Circle,* id. at 221.

Siegfried was elected chairperson of the International Law Association's Committee on the Rights of Indigenous Peoples at its 2008 Rio de Janeiro biennial meeting. Drawing on the work of 30 experts from all over the world, the Committee drafted ILA Resolution No. 5/2012, which found customary and conventional international law rights of indigenous peoples to their self-determination, local and internal autonomy, cultural heritage, and their traditional land, territories and resources.[50] This resolution was uncontested and had the support of the Plenary Assembly of the ILA's Biennial Meeting in Sofia, Bulgaria on August 30, 2012,[51] evidencing international law in the field.[52]

Siegfried has done indispensable work on group rights, in general, particularly those of vulnerable minorities, since

> groups of meaning to individuals are essential extensions of self, necessary parts of a person's identity. Culture, in particular, is a group phenomenon; it cannot be developed by the solipsistic effort of an individual human being. ... In order to respond holistically to human needs and

---

50   ILA Resolution No. 5/2012 on the Rights of Indigenous Peoples, Committee on the Rights of Indigenous Peoples, 75th ILA Biennial Meeting, Sofia, Bulgaria, August 30, 2012, https://www.ila-hq.org/en_GB/documents/conference-resolution-english-sofia-2012-4.

51   For details of its genesis and meaning, see Siegfried Wiessner, *The State and Indigenous Peoples: The Historic Significance of ILA Resolution No. 5/2012, in* Der Staat im Recht. Festschrift für Eckart Klein zum 70. Geburtstag 1357 (M. Breuer et al. eds., Duncker & Humblot, Berlin, 2013). *See also* Timo Koivurova, Federico Lenzerini & Siegfried Wiessner, *The Role of the ILA in the Restatement and Evolution of International and National Law Relating to Indigenous Peoples, in* International Actors and the Formation of Laws 89 (Katja Karjalainen, Iina Tornberg & Aleksi Pursiainen eds., Springer 2022), https://library.oapen.org/viewer/web/ viewer.html?file=/bitstream/ handle/ 20.500. 12657/57316/978-3-030-98351-2.pdf?sequence=1&isAllowed=y.

52   According to the American Law Institute's 1987 Restatement on Foreign Relations Law, the ILA's resolutions enjoy authority as subsidiary means for the determination of rules of international law under Article 38(1)(d) of the Statute of the ICJ on equal footing with the resolutions of the International Law Commission (ILC) and the Institut de Droit International. Restatement (Third) of the Foreign Relations Law of the United States, § 103 reporters' notes 1 (Am. Law Inst. 1987). The ILC has accorded its own proceedings the same authoritative status as the proceedings of the ILA in the context of the identification of customary international law. ILC, Memorandum by the Secretariat, Identification of Customary International Law: Ways and Means for Making the Evidence of Customary International Law More Readily Available, U.N. Doc. A/CN.4/710, ¶¶ 72–73 (Jan. 12, 2018); ILC, Rep. on the Work of Its Sixty-Eighth Session, U.N. Doc. A/71/10, at ¶ 63, commentary to Conclusion 14, ¶ 5 (2016). As to the impact of the ILC, see Siegfried Wiessner & Christian Lee González, *The ILC at Its 70th Anniversary: Its Role in International Law and Its Impact on U.S. Jurisprudence*, 13 FIU Law Review 1151–1174 (2019), https://ecollections.law.fiu.edu/ lawreview/ vol13/iss6/14/.

aspirations, we need to endeavor to protect both individuals and the groups relevant to them. Vulnerability of individuals created the need for individual human rights; the vulnerability of groups—particularly of cultures – creates the need for *their* protection.[53]

Analytically, he started with his work on essential aspects of vulnerability, advancing a crucial distinction between organic and non-organic groups, based on their differential claims of communal self-realization or non-discrimination.[54] He also explored the problématique of unquestioned adherence to ethnic identity,[55] the impact of demographic change,[56] and the legitimacy and accountability of NGOs,[57] focusing, normatively, on the need for comprehensive, holistic solutions.[58]

IV

In the domestic arena, Siegfried amplified and broadened his teaching and research in the field of Constitutional Law. He has written articles on federalism, significantly labelled "an architecture for freedom,"[59] on the powers of the President,[60] on the status of Washington, D.C.,[61] as well as an op-ed on a

---

53   Wiessner, *Indigenous Peoples – The Battle over Definition, supra* note 45.

54   Siegfried Wiessner, *Faces of Vulnerability: Protecting Individuals in Organic and Non-Organic Groups, in* The Living Law of Nations 217 (Gudmundur Alfredsson & Peter Macalister-Smith eds., 1996).

55   *Ethnic Groups, in* Encyclopedia of Genocide and Crimes against Humanity 304–306 (Dinah Shelton ed., Macmillan Reference USA 2005).

56   *Demographic Change and the Protection of Minorities, in* Globaler demographischer Wandel und Schutz der Menschenrechte 155–185 (Eckart Klein ed., Berliner Wissenschafts-Verlag 2005).

57   *Legitimacy and Accountability of NGOs: A Policy-Oriented Perspective, in* From Government to Governance – 2003 Hague Joint Conference on Contemporary Issues of International Law 95 (W.P. Heere ed., T.M.C. Asser Press 2004).

58   *Cf.* Siegfried Wiessner, *Re-Enchanting the World: Indigenous Peoples' Rights as Essential Parts of a Holistic Human Rights Regime*, 15 UCLA Journal of International Law and Foreign Affairs 239 (2010 [2012]), http://heinonline.org/HOL/Landing Page?handle=hein .journals/jilfa15&div=10&id=&page=.

59   Siegfried Wiessner, *Federalism: An Architecture for Freedom*, 1 New Europe Law Review 129–142 (1993).

60   Siegfried Wiessner, *The Powers of the President*, 1 Lincoln Memorial University Law Review 103–130 (2013), http://digitalcommons.lmunet.edu/lmulrev/vol1/iss1/13/.

61   Siegfried Wiessner, *Founding myths, international law and voting rights in the District of Columbia, in* Making Transnational Law Work in the Global Economy: Essays in Honour of

retiring Supreme Court Justice.[62] He helped the construction of democracy in Eastern Europe after the collapse of Communism in the 1990s by serving as an instructor on human rights in a 1992 ABA/CEELI workshop in Lodz, Poland, by assessing draft minorities laws in Romania and a draft press law in Latvia in 1994, and by evaluating, in 1998, the entire ABA Rule of Law Program in Central and Eastern Europe and the New Independent States as a member of a team commissioned by USAID.[63] Comprehensively, he dissected the concept of the rule of law in light of the goal of a public order of human dignity.[64]

St. Thomas University in Miami Gardens, Florida has been Siegfried's academic home since he started teaching at its law school in 1985. In 1990, he became the first Professor of Law tenured through the ranks, and he has taught a number of courses surrounding the broad areas of jurisprudence, international law, and constitutional law ever since.

On Constitution Day 2022, Siegfried delivered a lecture on "Reading the Constitution," which recommended the filling of open concepts of this foundational document of the United States with the values of the New Haven School, which includes the goal of the flourishing of all, including minorities, on the basis of their individual choice of their preferred values.[65] He asked, in essence, what this values-based order could yield, in more granular form, for the interpretation of the Constitution of the United States. He answered: "This interpretation ought to be based on a principled and rational approach and reflect the common interest."[66] This interest ought to be identified with

the concept of an order of human dignity as defined by Myres McDougal and Harold Lasswell. This order would maximize access by all to the processes

---

Detlev Vagts 174–197 (Pieter H. F. Bekker, Rudolf Dolzer & Michael Waibel eds., Cambridge University Press, 2010).

62   Siegfried Wiessner, *Justice Breyer's Legacy: A Preliminary Assessment,* Attorney at Law Magazine, Feb. 2, 2022, https://attorneyatlawmagazine.com/justice-breyers-legacy-a -preliminary-assessment.

63   United States Agency for International Development, M/OP/ENI/DGSR, Evaluation of the Rule of Law Program in Central and Eastern Europe and the New Independent States: The American Bar Association/Central and East European Law Initiative (ABA/CEELI) – Final Report, Jan. 28, 1999, by Richard N. Blue, Silvy Chernev, Robyn L. Goodkind & Siegfried Wiessner, 39 pp., with appendices, *available at* http://pdf.usaid. gov/pdf_docs/pdabro70.pdf.

64   Siegfried Wiessner, *The Rule of Law: Prolegomena,* Zeitschrift für deutsches und amerikanisches Recht [German-American Law Review] 82 (June 2018), https://papers.ssrn.com /sol3/papers. cfm?abstract_id=3293042.

65   Siegfried Wiessner, *Reading the Constitution,* Constitution Day Address, St. Thomas University College of Law (September 22, 2022).

66   *Id.*

of shaping and sharing all things humans empirically value: power, wealth, affection, well-being, enlightenment, skills, respect, and rectitude. After all, the law should serve human beings, not the other way around. The content of open concepts should be filled using this approach, as the goal of law should be the thriving and flourishing of human beings endowed with intrinsic dignity. It should be empowering, not limiting. Principled and rational, this guiding light would transcend decision-making from the gut, based on personal idiosyncracies or rank partisan motivations.

This end of human flourishing also undergirds the LL.M. Program in Intercultural Human Rights, which Siegfried started in 2001 at the suggestion of then Dean John Makdisi, and has continued to develop since 2002, in partnership and with the critical support of the other one of us, Co-Director Professor Roza Pati. The program has graduated some 500 students from over 90 countries, who have often gone on to assume responsible leadership positions in their home states. In 2005, Siegfried and Roza Pati expanded this graduate program with a capstone degree program for the J.S.D. in Intercultural Human Rights, and the *Intercultural Human Rights Law Review*. Human flourishing is part and parcel of Catholic social teaching, deeply embedded in the mission of St. Thomas University and its College of Law.

Nothing makes Siegfried happier than teaching. Students have always been at the center of Siegfried's attention and concern. Aristotle is quoted to have said: "*Educating the mind without educating the heart is no education at all.*" Few teachers can claim the existence of this dual dimension in their work. Siegfried indisputably can. He recommends to his students to give others they encounter the benefit of the doubt, that they are good, that they are well-intentioned.

As a wise protector of good intellectual traditions, Siegfried teaches them to be precise in their analysis, apply sagacity and impartiality while still being vigilant and firm. And to never lose their moral compass. He accompanies them in this journey – always present to resuscitate the hope of any lost or perplexed soul, for "what can life be without hope," as he often states. This love of teaching and of students is probably best evidenced in students' words. Any teacher would be highly pleased to read what students write to and about Siegfried. One of them recently commented online: "Professor Wiessner is a rarity amongst law professors at St. Thomas University. He creates an open forum, allowing for all opinions to be heard while covering the required material. Doing so respectfully and honestly to foster personal and academic growth." Others focus on his brilliance, his care for his students, his "perfect style," and his concise focus on cases, tying together law, theory and history.

Siegfried is keen to make students participate in classroom discussions, briefing cases, identifying rules and underlying policies in Socratic fashion. He encourages them to challenge decisions and opinions of others, as well as to formulate and defend their own opinions on controversial issues. He encourages critical analysis of the black letter law, coherence of argument, and articulation and application of value and policy preferences. This goal of students' mastery of critical review not only deepens their understanding of the holdings of black letter law, as needed for their bar examinations. Most importantly, it also prepares them for a life in the legal profession, which, particularly in the rather open-ended and value-laden field of constitutional law, cannot avoid critical scrutiny, controversial argument, and the development of alternative decisions. Teaching his students to evaluate past decisions and recommendations of future ones in light of logical standards of coherence, experience, and preferred ideas of moral and social order, he brings out the best in them. It was therefore no surprise that, in 2013, Lawyers to the Rescue proclaimed him the Law Professor of the Year.[67]

V

Benjamin Franklin once commented: "I never considered a difference of opinion in politics, in religion, in philosophy, as cause for withdrawing from a friend." Siegfried's life, as teacher, scholar and colleague, daily exhibits his affinity with Franklin. Siegfried is a friend to all he crosses path with. This collection of essays is proof of the diverse friendships that have shaped his life, as much he has shaped theirs. The appreciation of his peers is not only demonstrated by his selection to chair the ILA Committee on the Rights of Indigenous Peoples; he also was chosen to serve as Fernand Braudel Senior Fellow at the European University Institute in Florence, Italy (2009), as member of the Executive Council of The American Society of International Law (2007–2010), and in many other appointments.

But his friends are not only scholars. Being polyglot, he relishes talking with the rank-and-file, diving into new cultures and speaking with everyday people in their own language. All of those who know him recall the warm wisdom of his fluent Spanish, English or French, sometimes seasoned with a slight German accent, and his incessant inclination to seek the betterment of a public order that allows for the shaping and sharing, the production and the distribution of all human values: power, wealth, affection, well-being, enlightenment, skills,

---

67   Lawyers to the Rescue, https://en.everybodywiki.com/Lawyers_to_the_Rescue.

respect, and rectitude. He is there with the people, groups, communities, helping them articulate what base and scope values they have, and at their side,
when such values are threatened, analytical in his written work, or speaking
out at various fora, whether at the UN or at the legislative, executive, or judicial
institutions of various countries.

For Siegfried, the world is one big human family and, on that basis, he
embraces life whether it is in Alaska or Antarctica, in Venezuela's Amazonas or
Johannesburg, in the Gobi Desert in Mongolia or in Tanzania's Arusha, in Athens
or Rome, Serbia or Kosovo, in Israel's Beersheba or Ecuador's Quito, on Bondi
Beach in Australia or Georgia's Tbilisi, in Moscow or Ukraine, Florence or Cairo, to
name only a few of the places in which Siegfried has studied, taught, lectured and
counseled. Everywhere he goes, he follows one star: the guiding light of an order
of human dignity. In his visit to Mongolia in 2015, for example, he rendered advice
and drafted comments on the new Mongolian Criminal Procedure Code from
the perspective of German, comparative and international human rights law at the
invitation of The Honorable Erdenebat Ganbat, The Deputy General Prosecutor
of Mongolia, meeting with representatives of the Mongolian legislature, judiciary,
prosecutor's offices and law enforcement personnel. Just a year later, in Germany,
he engaged faculty and students at the Friedrich Alexander University Erlangen-
Nürnberg, Faculty of Law, on the issue of differences and commonalities in teaching law in the United States and Germany. Then, he moved over to Israel, at the
Ben Gurion University of the Negev, Department of Geography and the University
of Haifa Law School to participate in the workshop on The Legal Geography of
Indigenous Communities: The Bedouins in Comparative Perspective.

VI

As is clear from this abbreviated intellectual portrait, Siegfried is a prolific
writer and a much sought-after academic speaker on a wide range of topics
and in various lands.[68] His scholarship sparkles with erudition and engages

---

68   *See, for instance*, Comments, *Working Session, ILA Committee on the Implementation of the
      Rights of Indigenous Peoples*, December 5, 2020, 79 ILA Biennial Meeting, Kyoto, Japan;
      *Final Report and Remarks, Working Session, International Law Association Committee on
      the Rights of Indigenous Peoples*, ILA Report of the 75th Conference held in Sofia 503–553
      (London 2012); *Interim Report and Remarks, Working Session, International Law Associ-
      ation Committee on the Rights of Indigenous Peoples*, ILA Report of the 74th Conference
      held in The Hague 15–19, 2010 834–923 (London 2010); *The Kurdish Issue and Beyond: Ter-
      ritorial Communities Rivaling the State*, 98 Proceedings of The American Society of Inter-
      national Law 107–108 (2004); *Intellectual Property and Indigenous Peoples: An Overview*,
      95 Proceedings of The American Society of International Law 151–153 (2001); *The Project*

the reader in a readily understood and elegant style. He is a free spirit, but also adapts to the situation. He knows how to be subtle and when to be bold, when to be agile and when to be tranquil. His wisdom is captivating, extending to everyone in his path: students, colleagues, communities, institutions, public or private. His gentle warmth and inner strength singularly distinguish him, and never goes unnoticed by the active interlocutor or the passive audience.

Siegfried's exceptional dedication to the inclusion of all has been a hallmark of his teaching and research efforts at the law school since its inception. For him, all students – and all faculty – have to be treated equally and accorded respect in light of their inherent dignity, because they are made in the image and likeness of God. He likes to note that he traces his devotion to diversity to Susan Ferrell. "Celebrate Diversity!" This message was written on a sticker that Susan Ferrell gave him to proudly display on his office door. In 2001, long before it became a household concept, Siegfried delved deeply into its meaning by asking: "What does this message, often repeated, mean? What should it mean? Is it the celebration of difference as such, the love of the farthest, rather than the nearest? Mindless escapism from the bounds of one's genetic or cultural confines?" And he answers:

> In many ways today, the diversity argument is meant to give strength to the demands and to validate the dreams of groups that perceive themselves to be situated in a status of minority in a given community, lacking in power, wealth and respect by others – all things humans value. They perceive themselves to be sitting at the bottom of the well.
>
> These underrepresented groups demand equal respect for themselves. Often, these groups then define themselves as the entity in the center of reflection, of their universe of concern. Largely because of their marginalization by others, they sometimes tend to band together, stress their features perceived to be unique to them, act as a reliable voting bloc to enhance their comparative power in a balloting society, and then may strive to "take over" in whatever community they have found strength through internal cohesion. To put it differently, if the "takeover" attempt is successful, other groups may be put in the previously disadvantaged position, and the diversity argument is often suspended, at least temporarily.

---

of Reconfiguration: How Can International Law Be Reconstituted?, 94 Proceedings of The American Society of International Law 73–74, 79–81 (2000); Remarks, Panel on *Communities in Transition: Autonomy, Self-Governance and Independence*, 87 Proceedings of The American Society of International Law 264–265 (1993); *Developments in the International Law of Telecommunications*, 83 Proceedings of The American Society of International Law 400–403 (1990); etc.

Isn't there a better way? Is man really man's wolf? Should he/she be? One alternative to the quest for dominance as a group is the institution-alization of respect for minorities, by recognizing their various languages and heritages, their customs and decisionmaking structures, their tradi-tional resources and their use by various distinguishable "organic groups" – to protect the identity and claims of the most vulnerable. The teaching of languages and recognition of autonomy for indigenous people, the quintessential organic group, is just one example of this approach guided by the goal to maintain, to let shine the various bright colors, the beau-tiful individual strands of the fabric of the common cultural heritage of humankind. This approach may be called a "multicultural" one. Just to maintain respect for the previously marginalized group, this approach is an essential starting-point.

It cannot be the final answer, though. Ultimately, we are all part of one race – the human race. All beings with a human face share very similar dreams. As fathers or mothers, we all want our kids to live a better life than we had – whether they live in Manhattan, in Kinshasa, or on an island in the South Seas. Human needs and wants are surprisingly simi-lar. And they can be measured and responded to, as exemplified by the United Nations Development Programme's yearly Human Development Report and Index.

As part of the human race, and in recognition of our fundamental sameness, we need therefore not only celebrate the various groupings we are in, we need to transcend the dangers of group exclusivism and sep-aratism that can culminate, for example, in the killing fields of Hitler's Germany, Rwanda, Phnom Penh and Srebrenica. As important as it is to recognize the claims of others, a worthy celebration of diversity should do even more. Just as any celebration and the joy it arouses comes from a communal activity, the reaching out to others, the recognition of the fact that shared sorrows are only half the sorrows, and shared joy is double the joy, any proper community goal, I submit, should include the inter-action with, the dialogue with the other – be it an individual or a group. This other need not be the one farthest away; it could and should be, first and foremost, our neighbor. A true celebration of humanity must include this "intercultural" aspect: the listening to others, the respect for their innermost concerns, and the quest for a solution that enhances access by all to all the values humans desire. ...

No man is an island. Neither is a group, no matter how closely we identify with it. Thus, ultimately, we need to reach out to each other, "practice random acts of kindness and senseless acts of beauty" – the other bumper sticker that Susan had on her car before her life was taken by the Oklahoma City killer, the "sovereign citizen" so antagonistic to the philosophy of love she stood for. Diversity is thus a goal to be celebrated not in standing apart, but in joining hands and struggling to establish an order free of discrimination and subordination – an order that helps up those who have fallen and an order that gives everybody a fighting chance to build the life of their dreams.[69]

Conclusion

As we celebrate this seventieth birthday of our dear friend and colleague, we know that there is so much left for him to do, to impact the world he lives in. And, for all those who cross his path there is so much more yet to learn from Siegfried – the good teacher who always brings to life the powers and the talents that lie within every human being. His scholarship continues to be of the *bel canto* genre: one that keeps you engaged because you also hear the musicality of the passion that law has the ability to carry. At seventy, his tempo is faster, he presses forward and does not hold back. He ornaments every idea and you always feel the new, the fresh, even in the theme you read before from him. He is anything but businesslike. His motto that we have heard so often remains: "I dance through life" – and even when he pirouettes, he comes right back in sync: crisp, clear, warm, never dry. There is no doubt that Siegfried will continue to be a rainbow in anyone's cloud.[70]

---

69   Siegfried Wiessner, *Celebrate Diversity! – But How?*, St. Thomas Lawyer (2001).
70   Dr. Maya Angelou, *Be a Rainbow in Someone Else's Cloud*, https://www.youtube.com /watch?v=onYXFletWH4.

CHAPTER 2

A Modern-Day Alexis de Tocqueville in our Midst: Siegfried Wiessner, a Foreign-Born Champion of American Democracy and Human Flourishing

David A. Armstrong [*]

As Yale law professor Michael Reisman has remarked, "much as another European, Alexis de Tocqueville," Siegfried Wiessner "was able to see democracy in America with unique penetration and depth."[1] This intriguing cross-century comparison deserves further analysis.

Both scholars, coming from outside the U.S. later in life, could hold a mirror to American political and social realities from their various perches or observational standpoints, and they have demonstrated an abiding friendship and allegiance to the guiding lights of the American Revolution. While there are significant differences, there are surprising similarities in the perception and evaluation of the unique American experiment.

Count Alexis de Tocqueville (1805–1859), born in France as a member of the landed aristocracy and later political scientist, philosopher, historian and post-revolutionary politician,[2] got to know America on only a short trip of nine months in 1831.[3] His resulting book on *Democracy in America*,[4] published in two volumes in 1835 and 1840, however, has arguably been one of the two most important texts on American political life, surpassed only by the Federalist Papers.

It was conceived as a social and political science analysis of how this new, globally irresistible force of the "great democratic revolution" works, in its

---

[*] J.D., President, St. Thomas University.

1   Michael Reisman, *Preface to Inaugural Volume, American Classics in International Law, in* General Theory of International Law xiii (Siegfried Wiessner ed., 2017).

2   *Cf.* Seymour Drescher, *Alexis de Tocqueville*, Encyclopedia Britannica, 27 Sep. 2022, https://www.britannica. com/biography/Alexis-de-Tocqueville (accessed 18 January 2023). *See also* André Jardin, Tocqueville: A Biography (1988).

3   For an account of his travels in America with his friend, Gustave de Beaumont, see Alexis de Tocqueville and Gustave de Beaumont in America. Their Friendship and Their Travels (Olivier Zunz ed., 2011).

4   Alexis de Tocqueville, Democracy in America, Vols. 1 & 2 ([1835 & 1840] trans. by Arthur Goldhammer, 2004).

birthplace and homeland.[5] While France, even after the Revolution of 1789, still had to deal with remaining aspects of its aristocratic past, kept partially alive by the various Napoleonic regimes, America and its political system was the place to look for forecasting the future of the world. Tocqueville saw in America the "image of democracy itself, its inclinations, character, prejudices, and passions."[6]

He was particularly impressed by how deep a hold the concepts of egalitarian democracy had taken in America. Equality of conditions[7] was the antithesis to social and economic life in Old Europe. While France was still governed by remnants of the *Ancien Régime* (feudal conditions of land ownership, nobility, but with rising roles of the business class, the power of the Church, the legal profession and other elites),[8] in his view America had overcome all class distinctions and enjoyed an unprecedented level of equal dignity as well as political and civil liberty. The common man never deferred to elites. This sense of equality shaped laws and policies of this new entity on the world stage. It unleashed the great intellectual and creative talents of humans, irrespective of the strictures of birth, offering an "arsenal open to all from which the weak and poor daily drew arms"[9] – an early statement of the American Dream. And this at a time when, paradoxically, the French Revolution had proceeded under the banner-cry of *liberté, égalité,* and *fraternité,*[10] while America still had slaves and no guarantee of equal protection of the laws.

Tocqueville himself was opposed to the institution of slavery.[11] He did not live to see the Emancipation Proclamation of 1863; still, his wish ultimately became a reality.

At the time of Tocqueville's visit, President Andrew Jackson had instituted his policy of removal of American Indians from the Eastern seaboard, resulting in the cataclysm of the Trail of Tears.[12] While Tocqueville criticized the

---

5   *Id.*, Introduction, at 3.

6   *Id.* at 15.

7   *Id.* at 3.

8   *Cf.* Richard Herr, Tocqueville and the Old Regime (1962).

9   Democracy in America, *supra* note 4, at 5.

10   This national motto of France, coined in the French Revolution, was officially adopted in the Constitution of 1848 as a "principle" of the Republic. France Diplomacy, *Liberty, Equality, Fraternity,* https://www.diplomatie.gouv.fr/en/coming-to-france/france-facts /symbols-of-the-republic/article/liberty-equality-fraternity.

11   Democracy in America, *supra* note 4, at 392–419. His travel companion, Gustave de Beaumont, was more explicit regarding this issue, as expressed in his book Marie or, Slavery in the United States (1835).

12   For details, see Grant Foreman, Indian Removal: The Emigration of the Five Civilized Tribes of Indians (1953); Angie Debo, And Still the Waters Run (1972). For further account

treatment of Native Americans, he saw them doomed to extinction based on their unwillingness to assimilate.[13]

In the economic arena, Tocqueville pointed out that, contrary to Europe, the dominant ethic in the United States was that of hard work and making money; existing inequality was seen as motivation for the poor to gain wealth.[14]

Tocqueville realized that religion is another key feature of American culture: "It was religion that gave birth to the Anglo-American societies. This must always be borne in mind. Hence religion in the United States is inextricably intertwined with all the national habits and all the feelings to which the fatherland gives rise."[15] In addition, "Christianity has ... retained a powerful hold on the American mind, and ... it reigns not simply as a philosophy that one adopts upon examination but as a religion in which one believes without discussion."[16] This is of particular relevance today, as Jefferson's dictum of the wall of separation between church and state is often misinterpreted as separation of religion from society. In fact, in his famous 1802 letter to the Danbury Baptists, Thomas Jefferson had explained that, "I shall see with sincere satisfaction the progress of those sentiments which tend to restore to man all his natural rights, convinced he has no natural right in opposition to his social duties." Such natural rights include the freedom of religion.[17]

The one criticism leveled in Tocqueville's book, much discussed and often rejected in America, is the specter of the "tyranny of the majority."[18] Tocqueville argues that when a majority within American democracy comes to a consensus on a subject, individuals may not want to depart from it for fear of social death. "You are free not to think as I do. You may keep your life, your property, and everything else. But from this day forth you shall be as a stranger among us. You will retain your civic privileges, but they will be of no use to you. For if you seek the votes of your fellow citizens, they will withhold them, and if you seek only their esteem, they will feign to refuse even that. When you approach your fellow creatures, they will shun you as one who is impure. ... Go in peace! I will not take your life, the life I leave you with is worse than death."[19] A majority

---

          of the treatment of Native Americans in the mid-19th century, see Dee Brown, Bury My
          Heart at Wounded Knee (1970).

13   Democracy in America, *supra* note 4, at 371–391, 392 ("The Indians will die, as they lived, in isolation.").

14   *Cf.* Richard Swedberg, Tocqueville's Political Economy (2007).

15   Democracy in America, *supra* note 4, at 486.

16   *Id.*

17   Joshua Charles, Liberty's Secrets 122–123 (2015).

18   Democracy in America, *supra* note 4, at 288.

19   *Id.* at 294.

can "crush a minority without even hearing its screams." From there comes his most controversial statement, "I know of no country where there is in general less independence of mind and true freedom of discussion than in America,"[20] concluding, "freedom of spirit does not exist in America."[21]

His observational standpoint is clear: "I have a passionate love for liberty, law and respect for rights. I am neither of the revolutionary party nor of the conservative. Liberty is my foremost passion."[22]

Professor Siegfried Wiessner also came from another country to the U.S., albeit about 150 years later than Count de Tocqueville. He was born and raised in Germany, on a farm and in a lineage that goes back to his ancestral village of Gerhardshofen, with a first mentioning of his family in the church books of 1705. He holds a law degree as well as a Dr. iur. from the University of Tübingen, and an LL.M. from the Yale Law School. Attracted by the New Haven School of Jurisprudence, he has come and stayed in the United States, now for 40 years, first in the LL.M. Program at Yale, later in practice at the law firm of Wilmer, Cutler & Pickering in Washington, DC, and, since August 1, 1985, as a professor of law at St. Thomas University College of Law. Professor Wiessner has, inter alia, researched, written about, and taught Constitutional Law at the College of Law for more than 30 years. It helped to have researched and taught German constitutional law at the University of Tübingen Faculty of Law prior to coming to America as a research associate to the son of the "father" of the 1949 post-WWII German Constitution, Professor Dr. Hans v. Mangoldt.

Admiring the genius of the American Constitution's division of powers and guarantees of rights, Professor Wiessner has published on key issues in the field. He has written a comparative, policy-oriented article on *Federalism: An Architecture for Freedom*.[23] He has also published a Lincoln symposium lecture on *The Powers of the President*,[24] and assessed the legacy of departing U.S. Supreme Court Justice Stephen Breyer.[25] Most recently, he suggested the filling of open concepts in the Constitution with the idea of a public order of human

---

20   *Id.* at 293.

21   *Id.* at 295.

22   For an analysis of his idea of liberty, see, e.g., Irving M. Zeitlin, Liberty, Equality, and Revolution in Alexis de Tocqueville (1971).

23   Siegfried Wiessner, *Federalism: An Architecture for Freedom,* 1 New Europe Law Review 129 (1993).

24   Siegfried Wiessner, *The Powers of the President,* 1 Lincoln Memorial University Law Review 103 (2013), http://digitalcommons.lmunet.edu/lmulrev/vol1/iss1/13/.

25   Siegfried Wiessner, *Justice Breyer's Legacy: A Preliminary Assessment,* Attorney at Law Magazine, February 2, 2022, https://attorneyatlawmagazine.com/justice-breyers-legacy-a -preliminary-assessment.

dignity, i.e. maximizing access by all to the processes of shaping and sharing all values human beings desire. In other words, the law should enable and promote human flourishing.[26]

Significantly, in his course on Constitutional Law, the first class deals with the question: *What Makes America America?* A constitution, and the reality under it, can only be fully understood by investigation into the values and the culture undergirding it. That requires a Tocqueville-type analysis, aided by the perspective of a fair outside observer.

Contrary to Tocqueville, however, Professor Wiessner would see the Constitution, its structural provisions and the Bill of Rights, in particular the First Amendment, as a significant bulwark against the tyranny of the majority. The Federalist Papers help identify the realistic assumptions about human nature that motivate the constitutional constructions, leading to the separation of powers both on the horizontal as well as the vertical plane, both combined functioning as architectures for freedom. After all, as the Founding Fathers argued: "Ambition must be made to counteract ambition."[27]

The courts also have been used successfully to defend the rights of unpopular minorities; animus against them has not been seen as a legitimate governmental interest.[28] In fact, as Professor Wiessner emphasizes, elections of representatives are not sufficient to constitute a truly free democratic society. Through structural arrangements as well as guarantees of specific rights, the goal of such a society, in the political sphere, must be to arrive at a *realistic chance of the minority of today to become the majority of tomorrow*.[29] Thus the need, in a free democratic system, to provide for freedom of speech, freedom of

---

26   Siegfried Wiessner, *Reading the Constitution*, Constitution Day Lecture, September 22, 2022.

27   Federalist Papers, No. 51, also stating, "If men were angels, no government would be necessary. If angels were to govern men, neither external nor internal controls on government would be necessary." Interestingly, when Tocqueville talks about the "several governments of each State, which the majority controls at its pleasure," he actually cites, approvingly, Federalist Paper No. 51. Democracy in America, *supra* note 4, ch. xv: Unlimited Power of Majority and Its Consequences—Part II.

28   For the first development of the animus doctrine, see U.S. Dep't of Agric. v. Moreno, 413 U.S. 528 (1973), illegitimizing "a bare ... desire to harm a politically unpopular group." *Id.* at 534. *See also* Masterpiece Cakeshop, Ltd. v. Colorado Civil Rights Commission, 38 S. Ct. 1719, 1729–1732 (2018). For an interesting analysis and critique, see Leslie Kendrick & Micah Schwartzman, *The Etiquette of Animus*, 132 Harvard Law Review 133 (12018), but see also Andrew T. Hayashi, *The Law and Economics of Animus*, 89 University of Chicago Law Review 581 (2022).

29   Siegfried Wiessner, *The Rule of Law: Prolegomena*, Zeitschrift für deutsches und amerikanisches Recht [German-American Law Review] 82, 83 (June 2018).

assembly, and freedom of association, including the freedom to found political parties, the existence of vibrant media reflecting the diversity of opinions, free access to the ballot as well as to running as a candidate, and the ensuring of peaceful transitions of power.

He shares the collective statement by the U.S. courts that "[t]he American democratic system is not always based upon simple majority rule. There are certain principles that are so important to the nation that the majority has agreed not to interfere in these areas," including "freedom of religion, speech, equal treatment, and due process of law."[30] Agreeing with their assessment that the "[r]ule of law is a principle under which all persons, institutions, and entities are accountable to laws that are [p]ublicly promulgated, [e]qually enforced, [i]ndependently adjudicated, [a]nd consistent with international human rights principles,"[31] Professor Wiessner's cross-cultural and historical survey of this concept is illuminating and forward-looking.[32]

On the international level, Professor Wiessner has contributed to the development of safeguards for vulnerable communities,[33] in particular, as Chair of the International Law Association's Committee on the Rights of Indigenous Peoples, in finding rights of indigenous peoples to their traditional lands and resources, their cultural heritage, and autonomy under customary international law under ILA Resolution No. 5/2012.[34] Obviously, history has disproved Tocqueville's assumption of the doomed existence of American Indians. They have not vanished from the Earth; they have survived and often even flourished.[35]

---

30   United States Courts, *Overview – Rule of Law*, https://www.uscourts.gov/educational
      -resources/educational-activities/overview-rule-law.

31   *Id.*

32   Wiessner, *Rule of Law, supra* note 29.

33   *Faces of Vulnerability: Protecting Individuals in Organic and Non-Organic Groups, in* The
      Living Law of Nations 217–226 (Gudmundur Alfredsson & Peter Macalister-Smith eds.,
      1996).

34   Final Report, International Law Association Committee on the Rights of Indigenous Peo-
      ples, 75th ILA Biennial Meeting, Sofia, Bulgaria, August 26–30, 2012, https://www.ila-hq
      .org/en_GB/documents/conference-report-sofia-2012-10; ILA Resolution No. 5/2012 on the
      Rights of Indigenous Peoples, August 30, 2012, https://www.ila-hq.org/en_GB/documents
      /conference-resolution-english-sofia-2012-4. For details of its genesis and contents, see
      Siegfried Wiessner, *The State and Indigenous Peoples: The Historic Significance of ILA Res-
      olution No. 5/2012, in* Der Staat im Recht. Festschrift für Eckart Klein zum 70. Geburtstag
      1357–1368 (M. Breuer et al. eds., 2013).

35   Siegfried Wiessner, *Rights and Status of Indigenous Peoples: A Global Comparative and
      International Legal Perspective,* 12 Harvard Human Rights Journal 57, 58 (1999), https://
      harvardhrj.com/wp-content/uploads/sites/14/2020/06/12_Wiessner_Rights-and-Status
      -of-Indigenous-Peoples.pdf.

Rigorously independent, he conducts his class in broad academic freedom. He creates an open forum, allowing for all opinions to be heard and discussed, vigorously debated in Socratic dialogue. I was greatly honored to be invited in two consecutive years to Professor Wiessner's First Amendment Law class to present guest lectures discussing some of the key cases on my favorite topic, the First Amendment freedom regarding symbolic expression, such as burning a draft card or the American flag. I was gleaning first-hand the profound impact of Professor Wiessner's teaching from my interaction with his students, who were perfectly prepared and deeply engaged in the interactive discussion of these controversial subjects.

Independence and mutual respect also characterizes and lies at the foundation of the LL.M. program in Intercultural Human Rights he founded in 2001, and which has now graduated close to 500 students from over 90 countries of the world, attracted largely by its eminent professors and guest lecturers from the United Nations, top scholarly institutions, governmental entities, and non-governmental organizations.[36] The term "intercultural" is its mission, and the first assignment in his class on The International Bill of Rights is devoted to Catholic social teaching, followed by other approaches to rights. As President of this university, I have the duty and pleasure to travel around the country giving lectures, addressing mostly educational audiences. Significantly, I often meet alumni and others from a broad network of academics who come up to me and talk about the LL.M./J.S.D. program, its academic prestige, the impact it has had in their life, its contribution to society, and what lasting impression it has left on them. I attribute this reputation of the program to its leadership.

The Tocqueville analogy is particularly apt regarding Professor Wiessner's selection and introduction of what constitutes "American Classics of International Law" in the field of "General Theory of International Law." As Professor Reisman indicated, similar to Tocqueville, "Siegfried Wiessner, a foreign and American-trained scholar in the United States, brings unique insights and appraisals of America's contribution to theories of and about international law. ... His selection of materials for this volume is judicious and his introductory essay, which is an intellectual *tour de force*, provides a rich historical context within which American theories from the foundation of the Republic to the present are analyzed and related, where relevant, to contemporaneous philosophical and political movements as well as to theories generated abroad. All are trenchantly appraised."[37]

---

36   For details of the program and its distinguished faculty, see St. Thomas University, LL.M. in Intercultural Human Rights, https://www.stu.edu/law/human-rights/llm/.

37   Reisman, *supra* note 1.

In this essay, Professor Wiessner concludes:

1. The United States of America is a unique player in the field of international relations and international law, in its perception of self and in the eyes of others. A clarification of its standpoint in light of its history and its present political, economic, cultural and social circumstances is thus helpful in highlighting the scholarly views of the world that arise or have arisen in its midst.

2. Key historical parameters have shaped American consciousness and, in turn, its scholars' approach to international law: European settlers' conquest of the country's territory from its indigenous inhabitants, the push westward in pursuit of a manifest destiny ordained by providence, the geographic location with no formidable neighboring enemies and two long coastlines in the east and west, as well as the belief in the justness of cause of secession based on the quest for democratic self-rule and Lockean natural rights to liberty and property. These factors have kindled and sustained the pervasive claim of American exceptionalism, and a sense of mission to bring to the world the blessings of freedom, democracy and human rights. They fomented the quest for sea power and power over land as enunciated in the Monroe Doctrine, only just revoked. Coupled with a focus on business and trade, already observed by de Tocqueville, they may have fueled America's rise to a political and economic superpower, the indispensable player in today's world arena. On the other hand, the legacy of slavery and the fraught process of overcoming its vestiges of racial discrimination still impact policy and law.[38]

3. I conclude this survey of American contributions to general theories of international law with a caveat: Ideas know no borders. What seems to clearly hail from one person or place, may actually have a quite different progenitor or place of origin, and that "distinctive" progenitor may have drawn inspiration from a stock of ideas distant in time and space. In Newton's memorable phrase, we stand on the shoulders of others, giants or otherwise. National claims to originality may pale in a world of modern communications technology in which instant access to and interpenetration of ideas is ever more evident.

American theory about international law is, in many respects, a kaleidoscope of ideas with which it has enriched the world. With increasing planetary communication and social and economic exchange, intercultural dialogue will promote a discussion of global values that will

---

38   General Theory of International Law, *Introduction*, at 72 (Siegfried Wiessner ed., 2017).

hopefully bring us closer to an order that respects and fosters human dignity around the world.[39]

This statement leads us back to what attracted Professor Wiessner to the United States in the first place: its openness to a theory about law that is about solving societal problems with a view toward establishing an order of human dignity. Policy-oriented jurisprudence, also called the New Haven School, as defined by its founders Yale Professors Myres S. McDougal, Harold D. Lasswell and W. Michael Reisman, delimits a societal problem using information from all sources of knowledge, describes conflicting claims, looks at past trends in decision and their conditioning factors, predicts future decisions, appraises those decisions, invents alternatives, and recommends solutions in the common interest.[40] Wiessner has called lawyer practitioners of this approach "doctors of the social order,"[41] as they painstakingly diagnose a societal problem before they prescribe proper treatment. The goal of this jurisprudence is to evaluate existing law and develop new solutions, if needed, using the yardstick of an order of human dignity, defined as maximizing access by all to the processes of sharing and sharing things humans value, without leaving minorities out in the cold. This access via the law defines its end: human flourishing and thriving in a productive community.

---

39   *Id.* at 78.
40   W. Michael Reisman, Siegfried Wiessner & Andrew R. Willard, *The New Haven School: A Brief Introduction*, 32 Yale Journal of International Law 575 (2007).
41   Siegfried Wiessner, *Doctors of the Social Order: Introduction to New Haven Methodology*, in Handbook on Human Trafficking, Public Health and the Law 8 (Wilhelm Kirch, Siegfried Wiessner & Roza Pati eds., 2014).

CHAPTER 3

Susan, Siegfried, Oklahoma, and the Rights of Indigenous Peoples

Kirke Kickingbird[*]

The Sovereignty Symposium is an annual inter-tribal conference sponsored by the Oklahoma Supreme Court. The Sovereignty Symposium was established in 1988 to provide a forum in which ideas concerning common legal issues could be exchanged in a scholarly, non-adversarial environment. The Supreme Court espouses no view on any of the issues, and the positions taken by the participants are not endorsed by the Supreme Court.

I participated in the first Sovereignty Symposium that was held in June of 1988 at the Skirvin Hotel in Oklahoma City, Oklahoma. It began with an historical review of sovereignty. Once the context was in place, other topics included economic interaction between the tribe, state and federal governments, potential conflicts of law and resolution of conflicts, cross-deputization of police personnel among those governments to enhance personnel resources and public safety, tribal law and policy development, the Indian Child Welfare Act and an ethics and an independent judiciary panel led by the Oklahoma Attorney General. Participants included Oklahoma judges, law professors, tribal, state and federal officials, attorneys and members of the public and members of Indian tribes.

In 1993, at Sovereignty Symposium VI, the agenda included a panel on the International Year for the World's Indigenous People. One of the panelists was Professor Siegfried Wiessner of St. Thomas University School of Law. Professor Wiessner returned as a panelist on international issues the next year. I had the opportunity and good fortune to meet Siegfried because of his participation on these panels.

The Oklahoma Sovereignty Symposium became the inspiration for the development of a similar conference on indigenous rights at St. Thomas University School of Law that was first held in December of 1994.

---

[*] Of Counsel, Hobbs, Straus, Dean & Walker, LLP, Oklahoma City, OK, Member of the Kiowa Tribe and Kiowa Gourd Clan. Chief Justice of the Supreme Court of the Cheyenne and Arapaho Tribes of Oklahoma and Chairman of the Oklahoma Indian Affairs Commission (1992–1995); Director, Native American Legal Resource Center, Oklahoma City University School of Law (1988–2000).

The article that follows on Susan Ferrell tells you more about the development of the St. Thomas conference. I chose this previously published article because I thought it also provided insight about Siegfried. I expect that the other articles in this volume will have a focus on Siegfried's academic achievements and intellectual gifts. They also may focus on his efforts to turn the law to practical assistance of indigenous people.

The tragedy that engulfed Susan was the bombing of the Oklahoma federal building. It was carried out by domestic terrorists on April 19, 1995. Two anti-government extremists, Timothy McVeigh and Terry Nichols, set off the truck loaded with explosives at 9:02 a.m. and killed 168 men, women and children.

While the focus of the article is Susan, I believe it also presents a personal side of Siegfried that is as important as his intellectual side. It tells you why we admire and respect Siegfried as a friend and colleague.

In Memoriam Susan J. Ferrell[1]

On December 1 and 2, 1994, St. Thomas University held an academic symposium in honor of the First Americans and Indigenous Peoples Around the World. Those conference days, reflected in this symposium issue, were a source of particular pride for Professor Siegfried Wiessner, St. Thomas University School of Law, Susan Ferrell, Legal Advisor at the Department of Housing and Urban Development, Oklahoma City, and me because the three of us had put the final architecture for the conference into place four months earlier at a restaurant in Oklahoma City.

The meeting at the "Painted Desert" in August of 1994 was the first time I had really talked with Susan. We had exchanged pleasantries as we stood with various groups at various Indian law conferences over the years. The last one we attended had been the annual Sovereignty Symposium sponsored by the Oklahoma Supreme Court on June 6–9, 1994.

They did not see me when I entered the restaurant. Susan's golden hair made quite a contrast with Siegfried's coal black mane. I heard a word or two as I approached their table – coins for the gypsy children, castanets, flamenco. I would learn later that dance was one of the greatest joys in Susan's life.

Susan turned to greet me with, "Hello, professor!" At first I thought she was making fun of the pedantic antics of law professors but the ensuing conversation was open and relaxed. When Susan excused herself to make a phone call

---

1   Kirke Kickingbird, *In Memoriam Susan J. Ferrell*, 7 St. Thomas L. Rev. iv (1994–1995).

Siegfried obviously detected my discomfort because he explained to me that Susan's admiration for the academic world and intellectual pursuits was genuine and sincere. Her greeting to me including use of the title, "professor," was a genuine expression of respect. When I learned I was faced with sincerity rather than sarcasm, I let my guard down. When Susan returned to the table, I began to learn about her from what she said about herself and what Siegfried said about her.

Susan had grown up in Chandler, Oklahoma but had been born in Oklahoma City. In fact, she was born at St. Anthony's which was a couple of miles south of our restaurant and just west of her office at HUD. After graduation from the University of Tulsa Law School in 1982, Susan entered private practice for three years. Because helping others was close to her heart, she had accepted a position as an attorney with the U.S. Department of Housing and Urban Development. At HUD, she had become involved with Indian law because of the number of Indian Housing Authority offices in Oklahoma and because she liked to learn about other cultures. Given her profound curiosity, her sense of spirituality, and her love of dance, Susan and the Indians were a perfect match.

As lunch concluded, we returned to business. Siegfried and Susan shaped topic areas and suggested panelists while I verbally edited their suggestions and Siegfried and I scribbled notes of our mutual conclusions on a paper napkin. The most amazing part of the process was that later Susan and Siegfried could take our longhand notes and decipher them.

As Susan and Siegfried drove away that August day I read the bumper stickers on her car. One of them said, "Practice Random Acts of Kindness & Senseless Acts of Beauty," and the other said, "Celebrate Diversity."

As the weeks passed, Susan would convey messages between Siegfried and me. As the conference approached, Susan called more often to confirm whether or not I had gotten certain messages from Siegfried. In the month before the conference, Siegfried and I were talking every other day and making joint calls to invite speakers and tribes to participate. Even with my occasional assistance, Siegfried carried the burden of responsibilities for the conference.

A source of even greater pride came for the three of us when the conference was as successful as we had hoped it would be. As a specialist in American Indian law I want to see strong programs in this field at law schools around the country. Siegfried with his interests in constitutional, international and comparative law and Susan with her background in Indian law and housing complemented me in areas in which I needed assistance with subject matter expertise. We were a good team.

After the December conference Siegfried and I plunged into law school priorities with the start of the second semester in January of 1995 and Susan returned to her work priorities at HUD. We all welcomed the spring break in March. Well, Siegfried and I did. Susan had to put up with our merriment while she worked.

She was delighted at our good fortune and planned a party around the college holidays for the weekend Siegfried had come from Miami.

My wife, Lynn, and I spent a delightful evening with Susan, Siegfried and her friends at her home.

We concluded the evening at Gopuram, an East Indian restaurant in Windsor Hills. Susan loved all kinds of dance. She had taken ballet and tap lessons as a child, and moved on to jazz. Her latest interest was Middle Eastern dancing. She had performed with a dance troupe called "Jewels of the Nile" at the Gopuram. Nancy, Sharon, Celeste, Soraya, and the other "Jewels" were fast friends.

Susan guided us through the menu advising all of us at the table which were meat dishes and which were not for she was a vegetarian. We could see her tender heart could not bear to hurt any creature.

On the next evening, March 25, the Oklahoma City University American Indian Students held their annual pow-wow. I had invited Susan to come dance at the pow-wow. When Susan and Siegfried spotted us in the crowd on Saturday night they joined us. Susan was equipped with a beautiful shawl. She had come prepared to dance and did. The last time Lynn and I saw her she was making the turn on the close side of the drum and passed in front of the drummers and singers with the fringe of her shawl swaying with the rhythms of the dance.

My last class was on April 19, 1995. The spring term ended on the 21st. I knew the summer was going to be very busy. I had three conferences scheduled and two special projects, one of which was for the Governor's Commission on Indian Affairs in Florida. Soon Susan, Siegfried and I would have to design the framework and architecture for the 1995 conference in Florida. We had no idea that it would be architecture that would tear us all apart.

My final class for the semester was scheduled for noon. It was almost nine o'clock and I called my staff at the law school to tell them I would be running late. I made a mental note to get my academic regalia together for the installation ceremony that evening of Dr. Rennard Strickland as our new dean at the law school.

I had just hung up the phone when the sonic boom hit. The windows rattled like they were going to break. Some jet jockey from Tinker Air Field or Vance Air Force Base in Enid was showing off. Or so I thought.

I live twelve miles north of downtown. Oklahoma City's airport is four miles south of downtown. I stepped out onto my back porch, which faces south to listen for the jet. I didn't hear anything. That seemed unusual. I looked at the time. It was five minutes after nine. It was getting late.

I raced south for a mile before remembering that I had left my academic regalia in my haste. I slowed the car to the speed limit and turned on the radio. It announced that there had been an explosion at the Federal Building. The news media was speculating about a leak in a natural gas line. I pulled into my garage, walked through the kitchen and turned on the television in the family room.

The radio had announced that the Federal Building had exploded and said the offices of two federal judges were in the building. Our former dean, Robert Henry, who had been Oklahoma Attorney General, had recently assumed his duties on the 10th Circuit Court of Appeals. I couldn't remember whether all the renovations were completed in the federal courthouse. If they had been completed, all the federal judges had moved back to the court house. If they hadn't, Robert Henry might be in the middle of this crisis.

I called the office and said I would be arriving soon. When I arrived, one student had called to ask if I had seen the television news and asked if we were having class. A gas line explosion was hardly a reason to cancel class.

The radio was reporting shattered windows in downtown office buildings. I became worried about another colleague who officed downtown. Arvo Mikkanen is associate director of our Indian law clinic. He was now an assistant U.S. attorney. The U.S. attorney's office did not answer. I called his home in Norman, he was there. His office had been closed and personnel sent home since the explosion might have weakened water and gas lines in the downtown area. He was awestruck by what he was seeing on television. He said after the explosion he had approached the building from the south until stopped by police lines. He said the building had not looked unusual except for broken glass and smoke.

Looking from the north he said the building looked terrible. There was conjecture by the news media about whether the explosion had been caused by a gas line leak or a bomb. I looked at the time. I had to go to class.

I emerged from the seminar in an encouraged mood. The presentations were solid and the papers were good.

I returned to the office. The radio was announcing casualties were being taken to nearby St. Anthony's hospital and other hospitals in the metropolitan area.

There was a phone call from Siegfried. It was obvious from his anguished voice that he was trying to remain calm. He had just seen the picture of the blown-up building on the television screen, and recognized it from his earlier visits. He hadn't been able to reach Susan nor her parents by phone. "Susan's office is in the building! A window office in the corner of the eighth floor ... Is her area affected? ... Any idea where she is?" It finally sank into my consciousness. Susan's office was in the damaged building. I tried to remember the image from the television screen down the hall. Siegfried's words trailed off and halted. I told him I didn't know anything but would try to find out and call him back.

Everywhere I inquired, I could find only chaos. Every time I found a television set and looked at the building, the bite of the bomb seemed bigger. Even the eighth floor where Susan's office was located had not escaped damage from the blast. We would learn later that parts of the building had collapsed from ground to roof. Except for the outside wall, Susan's office was no more. At 10:30 p.m., the rescue squads were still pulling survivors from the debris as I turned off the television set. I could watch no longer. I called Siegfried and told him that I had no news yet about Susan. I went to bed feeling guilty about the lack of news.

By 8:15 a.m. Thursday, I was at Susan's house. Her car was gone. There was no answer at the door. There was a light on behind the venetian blinds. I couldn't tell if she had come and gone. It would be like Susan to bandage her cuts and scrapes and join a bucket brigade moving debris.

A car stopped out front. The woman driving asked if Susan was home. I said no and she explained that all the neighbors were concerned about her. The neighbor across the street stepped to the curb. We stared at each other a moment. Our daughters had played on the same softball team. We discovered neither of us had any news. It was the same with another neighbor down the street. I left a card at the door asking anybody who knew Susan's whereabouts to call me.

I began to make calls and, through survivors or friends of survivors, ultimately tracked Susan within fifteen minutes of nine. She had calendared a meeting on the ninth floor at nine o'clock. No information was really reliable at this point. Various reports alternated between bad and good.

I briefed my wife, Lynn, on what I knew, and when I was unavailable, Siegfried called her. We couldn't be very encouraging because we didn't know anything and what we did know didn't seem reliable. Siegfried arrived that Thursday night. He had enough adrenaline pumping through his veins to power a Mack truck.

Waiting at Susan's house was like living in hell for Siegfried. He had nothing to do but think. The thoughts flickered across his face as clearly as if they were pictures. If he only could get to the scene and dig through the rubble, he could find Susan alive. He talked to her brother-in-law, Albert Ashwood, who coordinated all of the State agencies involved in the search and rescue effort at the Federal Building.

Unfortunately for Siegfried, the rescue workers were specialists from all over the nation; all others were excluded from getting near the site of destruction. So Siegfried spent the night collecting and dispensing disaster supplies gathered by the Red Cross.

Susan's women friends in the "Jewels of the Nile" had taken over her cats, kitchen and phone on Thursday afternoon. They coordinated information, messages and inquiries and fed the cats—Slim, Zelda, and Momma Tsigane. Everyone we knew was calling the various hospitals to check on Susan.

Those who waited talked about Susan. She kept an open door for stray animals and an open heart for people in distress. In these endeavors, she used all the tools at her disposal. Sometimes she used compassion, sometimes she employed a friendly ear, sometimes she engaged people in occupational therapy in her abundant garden, and sometimes she used her skills as a lawyer to be a defender and champion. Her efforts were appreciated and she was respected and loved.

The vigil at Susan's house had started Thursday afternoon and lasted only forty-eight hours. For Susan's family and friends and all those others caught in the Oklahoma City tragedy, it seemed a lifetime.

On Saturday afternoon we finally found Susan. The federal building has a rectangular shape with the long side of the building running on an east-west axis. The explosive charge on April 19 tore out the supporting pillars which were on the north side of the building directly under her office. As the architecture disintegrated, it tore Susan away from us and broke our hearts. Siegfried had pointed out Susan always did what we did not yet dare to do. This time she had flown away on the wings of angels. Her body died less than a mile from where she was born.

The men and women gathered at her house stood alone and in groups of two or three. It was now after sundown. The hearts and minds assembled were obscured in a darkness almost as profound as that which had engulfed Susan. Some cried softly, some cried with anguished voices and others were racked with silent, uncontrollable sobs.

After an hour Lynn and my daughter, Lauren, came and gathered Siegfried and me. We found a church open nearby, entered the sanctuary, and stood in silent prayer.

Then we, the friends of Susan, went to her parents, Don and Sally and her sister, Cindy, to comfort and console them in their sorrow and their grief. It was Don and Sally who comforted and consoled us in our sorrow and our grief for the parents were as generous as the two daughters.

The Memorial Service for Susan Jane Ferrell was moved from the First Presbyterian Church to the old Chandler High School Auditorium, where Susan had graduated. It was not large enough either. There were 800 people seated or standing in the high school itself and another 400 outside. The music at her' service included Presbyterian hymns, an American Indian flute player using a traditional flute and gospel hymns from the African American Central Baptist Church Inspirational Choir.

The background and number of people at the service conveys just how extraordinary this 37-year-old woman was. Judge Paul Vassar, an old family friend, spoke at her services. He pointed out that Susan distinguished herself in everything she did. With this, no one can disagree. She distinguished herself especially in being our beloved friend.

Susan finished her article before Easter. It appears in this volume and is just one of the fine marks she left as her legacy.[2]

∙∙
∙

Volume 7 of the *St. Thomas Law Review* was dedicated to Susan. Siegfried expressed his feelings, raw as they were, in this poem:[3]

Most beautiful person on Earth. Muse, beloved companion. Friend of all living things adoring nature, Native American culture, life. The widest of arms, the openest of hearts. Lady. Seeing beauty everywhere. Lifting up stray animals, nursing bruised humans, giving them courage and freedom to live, to have joy. Taittinger's. Above all: movement. Full of grace, *con brio*, saying "yes" . . . Pirouetting through life. Putting on the colors of dream, shaking the castanets, doing the flamenco, moving the body softly in Middle Eastern dance. Sneaking up on you quietly when you least expect it. Unconditional support. Aeneas and Aphrodite in one.

Wednesday afternoon, April 19, 1995: The tv's transreal image of the Federal Building. Ripped open, the massive structure, concrete and dark, blown up, the inside laid bare like the entrails of a slaughtered animal. Hell on Earth.

Where is Susan?

Her office, 8th floor, North Side, the room utmost to the left. Gone — in its place, a gaping hole. Only the outside wall remains, shy and lonely, but somewhat defiant. The collection of rocks, the Seminole nameplate, the desk, the angel behind it — gone as if it never existed. Blasted away, the charred remains "pancaked," merged into the rubble of death with children, baby toys, human beings conceived of and sustained by love now frozen in a final moment imposed by a heart cold as stone.

A heart who made himself the judge of who's to live and who's to die. No confrontation; no chance to escape; instant immolation, asphyxiation, or slow flickering off of the candle of life under a mountain of steel and rock; the final crushing. Dante's Inferno.

Mourning. Let the tears flow, the ache cry out. Lament.

Incredulity. Why this? Why Susan?

Spirituality. Chants of yesterday and tomorrow. Gripping. Can't hurt a living thing. Foster and potter: a luscious garden. Overcrowded with flowers. Lion's teeth in the lawn — welcome and respected.

Travel lightly. Give your money to the gypsy boy. You can't take it with you. Don't hurt.

Self-willed judge of life and death: You can't take her away. Susan is here, among us. Her spirit, amazing grace, is in communion with all of us she touched. She will pray for you from above.

See you soon, dearest.

JSW

ii

FIGURE 3.1   Siegfried, Poem for Susan

---

2   Susan J. Ferrell, *Indian Housing: The Fourth Decade*, 7 St. Thomas L. Rev. 445 (1994–1995).

3   JSW, 7 St. Thomas L. Rev. ii (1994–1995).

It was Susan, the exceptional, forever-young woman, whose short presence on earth etched herself not only into Siegfried's heart, but also instilled in him his love for the cause of indigenous peoples. In her memory, together with Professor Roza Pati, he established the Susan J. Ferrell Intercultural Human Rights Moot Court Competition. As judge, I gladly participated in this event. For eleven years, this competition became an Olympics of human rights, a universal intellectual student hub for law students from all over the world – Ethiopia, Hong Kong, India, the United Arab Emirates, Italy, Cayman Islands, and from all over the United States. Each year, the competition revolved around a simulated court proceeding, in which teams representing both sides of the argument prepared written pleadings, with respect to a fictional problem of international human rights law and policy, and presented their arguments in an oral argument before the International Court of Justice. This moot court competition has been key to making the new generation of international lawyers effective advocates in the field. Many of them have already moved to the top of the line in international law, which is ever more relevant to legal practice in an ever more globalizing world. Mostly focusing on issues of indigenous peoples' rights and human trafficking law – the main areas of expertise of its founders –, the competition brought human rights to the fore, a needed specialty in that field that he instilled in the younger generation the dedication to a calling that strives to make possible for all, through the law, a life of fulfillment and human dignity. He rejoiced at seeing law students from every corner of the planet display an excellent knowledge of international law and human rights law, and had tremendous fun at watching these global young citizens and future legal professionals compete fervently to win the beautiful eagle design trophy, bearing Susan's name.

Siegfried's exceptional dedication to the inclusion of all has been a hallmark of his teaching and research efforts at the law school since its inception. For him, all students – and all faculty – have to be treated equally and accorded respect in light of their inherent dignity, because they are made in the image and likeness of God. Siegfried likes to note that he traces his devotion to diversity to Susan Ferrell. "Celebrate Diversity!" This message was written on a sticker that Susan Ferrell gave him to proudly put on his office door. This love for all unites both Siegfried and Susan.

PART 2

Flourishing and Human Dignity: A Theory about Law

∵

CHAPTER 4

The Dignity of Belonging

*Adeno Addis**

1   Introduction

It is a great pleasure to be a part of this celebration of a great scholar whom it has also been my good fortune to call a friend. I have known Professor Siegfried Wiessner since 1982 when we first met at the Yale Law School as graduate students. Over the many years since then I have greatly benefited not only from his instructive scholarship but from his generous friendship as well.

Wiessner's scholarship has a wide reach—from the rights and status of indigenous peoples to the protection of ethnic and other minorities, from the rights of asylum seekers to the nature and function of nationality, from federalism to jurisprudence and the rule of law, and even to activities in outer space. But there is one principle or value that organizes and animates his scholarship: the notion of human dignity. Indeed, human dignity could be said to be central to his whole scholarly enterprise as it is to the jurisprudential school of which he is a prominent member and contributor, the New Haven School of Jurisprudence (New Haven).

What I shall do in this essay is to explore the nature of that fundamental and yet elusive concept of human dignity and to do so in the context of the right to belong, to be more specific in the context of statelessness and the indignity of being a "nowhere" person.

Both the notion of dignity and the right to belong to a community have been central to Wiessner's scholarship. How do we link the two and how does the notion of dignity help us to understand the nature and importance of the right to belong to one or another community?

In one of his articles, Wiessner observes (as he has done in much of his work in one or another form) that New Haven is guided by one "overriding concept," "a global order of human dignity."[1] In another of his articles, he argues that one

---

* W. R. Irby Chair and W. Ray Forrester Professor of Public and Constitutional Law, Tulane University School of Law.

1   Siegfried Wiessner, *Law as a Public Order of Human Dignity: The Jurisprudence of Michael Reisman*, 34 Yale J. Int'l L. 525, 528 (2009). *See also* W. Michael Reisman, Siegfried Wiessner, & Andrew R. Willard, *The New Haven School: A Brief Introduction*, 32 Yale J. Int'l L. 575

manifestation of human dignity is the right to belong to a community. Writing about the rights of indigenous peoples, he observes that the idea of dignifying humans must include the right and the opportunity to belong to a community. One of "[t]he mission[s] of the law," Wiessner writes, is to respond to "the *need* for belonging to groups, entities larger than self."[2] In this sense, dignity is not just about the status and rights of a freestanding individual (if there is such a thing), but it is also about connections and relationships. Indeed, in large measure to be human is to commune or create with others—"shaping and sharing" values, as those writing in the tradition of New Haven would put it.[3]

The community to which one belongs might be a social group or a political community. It might be a small or large community. It might be thick or thin.[4] Whatever the nature of the community, it is within such a community that individuals present themselves and, in the process, create the social and political world in which they live which in turn defines central dimensions of who they are.

2   The Ambiguity of Dignity

What exactly does dignity entail and how does it illuminate the nature and structure of the right to belong? The idea of human dignity, found in almost all legal and political cultures, now plays a very significant role in political and legal discourse.[5]

(2007); Siegfried Wiessner, *The New Haven School of Jurisprudence: A Universal Toolkit for Understanding and Shaping the Law*, 18 Asia Pacific L. Rev. 45 (2010).

2   Siegfried Wiessner, *Re-Enchanting the World: Indigenous Peoples' Rights as Essential Parts of Holistic Human Rights Regimes,* 15 UCLA J. Int'l L. & Foreign Aff. 239 (2010)("The mission of the law should be to answer responsibly to the totality of human aspirations in the crucible between individual self-realization and the need for belonging to groups, entities larger than self.").

3   *See id.* ("Human beings are not atomistic individuals, they are existentially dependent on others to survive and flourish.").

4   For the exploration of the nature of thick and thin communities and the ethical and moral implications for the sorts of arguments about justice, social criticism and nationalist politics, see Michael Walzer, Thick and Thin: Moral Argument at Home and Abroad (1994).

5   *See* Adeno Addis, *Dignity, Integrity and the Concept of a Person*, 13 ICL J. 323 (2019); Adeno Addis, *The Role of Human Dignity in a World of Plural Values and Ethical Commitments*, 31 Neth. Q. Hum. Rts. 403 (2013); Adeno Addis, *Justice Kennedy on Dignity*, 60 Hous. L. Rev. (forthcoming, 2022–23); Adeno Addis, *Human Dignity in Comparative Constitutional Context: In Search of an Overlapping Consensus*, 2 J. Int'l & Comp. L. Rev. 1(2015). But, of course, since its founding by Myres McDougal and Harold Lasswell, New Haven has always put dignity at the center of the scholarly enterprise.

The constitutions of many countries explicitly refer to human dignity or its variations.[6] The concept occupies a prominent place in several national constitutions such as that of Germany, Peru and South Africa[7] and international human rights documents (such as the UDHR and ICCPR8). Some constitutional and conventional laws in fact claim that the pursuit of dignity is (or should be) the central organizing principle of every government.[9] Yet, it is not always clear what this seemingly central concept means or entails. Distinguished scholars across various fields of learning disagree as to what it means to dignify persons or to subject them to indignity. Dignity is one of those terms that most people agree is valuable, even fundamental, but often do not agree on what it precisely means or entails.[10] At times, it is invoked to yield opposite and contradictory outcomes.[11] The concept's popularity often seems to be inversely related to its clarity.

On one point there seems to be an agreement. Dignity is meant to protect personhood itself, dimensions of what it means to be human. Human dignity is the respect we show to people in virtue of their humanity, what the philosopher Stephen Darwall refers to as one of the "moral requirements [to recognize] that are placed on one by the existence of other persons."[12] This "recognition respect," as opposed to what Darwall calls "appraisal respect,"[13] is not earned. It simply is granted by virtue of the fact that the recipient of such

---

6   See Addis, *Human Dignity in Comparative Constitutional Context, supra* note 5, at 8.

7   German Basic Law (1949), art. 1; Peru Const. (2009), art. 1; South Africa Const. (2012), art. 1.

8   See the preambles of those two documents. UDHR, G.A. Res. 217 (III) A, U.N. Doc. A/810 at 71 (1948); ICCPR, G.A. Res. 2200 (XXI) A, U.N. Doc. A/6316 at 52 (1966).

9   The Greek Constitution, for example, provides that "[r]espect for and protection of human dignity constitutes the primary obligation of the State." Greece Const. (2008), art. 2(1).

10   Christopher McCrudden is right in his observation that "[e]veryone could agree that human dignity was central, but not why or how." Christopher McCrudden, *Human Dignity and Judicial Interpretation of Human Rights*, 19 Eur. J. Int'l L. 655, 678 (2008).

11   Assisted suicide, euthanasia, gay rights and abortion are examples where dignity is invoked to yield contradictory results or outcomes. It is marshalled in favor and against autonomy. See the debate in the dwarf tossing case. Manuel Wackenheim v. France, Communication No. 854/1999, U.N. Doc. CCPR/C/75/D854/1999 (2002). And it is invoked in the protection and the ending of life.

12   Stephen L. Darwall, *Two Kinds of Respect*, 88 Ethics 36, 38, 45 (1977).

13   Appraisal respect is the respect we show people in virtue of their achievements or character. It is a respect that is the result of our positive assessment of them as individuals. Darwall, *Two Kinds of Respect, supra* note 12, at 44. Appraisal respect might also accompany individuals in virtue of positions they occupy, their institutional position—e.g., ambassador.

recognition is a human being. It is for this reason that some call human dignity an existential value.[14]

But what are the constituent parts of personhood the interference with which or the attack on which would lead to indignity? That is, what are the minimum, threshold, conditions that must exist to lead us to conclude that the integrity of the person as a person has been protected or diminished (the person is dehumanized or humiliated)? Numerous approaches to the understanding of the nature and scope of dignity vie for recognition and acceptance, each claiming to provide the most robust or complete understanding of what it means to dignify people or conversely to subject them to indignities.

Some think of dignity as a simple label for the collection of rights (values) that people aspire to have, may in fact have, or are entitled to have. This is what can be referred to as the labelling theory of dignity.[15] The theory views dignity simply as a label we use for all of the rights or values that we believe people should have in whatever way (empirically[16] or normatively[17]) the list is developed. Here dignity does not seem to have an independent evaluative or generative power. It does not assist in how or why those specific rights are derived.

To some extent the position of New Haven resembles the labelling theory.[18] Dignity is used as a short-hand description of eight values that people are said to aspire to have. To be sure, I do not believe that New Haven treats the list of eight values as exhaustive, but nonetheless the list indicates that the enterprise is empirical and that the concept of dignity does not have an independent role

---

14   George Kateb, Human Dignity 10 (2011).

15   *See* Adeno Addis, *The Role of Human Dignity in a World of Plural Values, supra* note 5, at 415–419.

16   The New Haven School uses dignity as a label for a list of eight "base" and "scope" values that it claims are empirically ascertained as values that humans have or want to pursue. *See* W. Michael Reisman, Siegfried Wiessner & Andrew Willard, *The New Haven School: A Brief Introduction* 32 Yale J. Int'l L. 575, 576 (2007). To some extent, much of the theorizing in international human rights can be understood in this vein.

17   The views of religious institutions such as the Catholic Church start with the premise that humans are created in the image of God, and they manifest the majesty of that Creator. Quite often, however, it is not clear as to what values, capacities, or interests have to be respected for the human being to remain a manifestation of the majesty of the Creator. But *see, e.g.,* Pontifical Council for Justice and Peace, Compendium of the Social Doctrine of the Church (2004), *available at* https://www.vatican.va/roman_curia/pontifical_councils /justpeace/documents/rc_pc_justpeace_doc_20060526_compendio-dott-soc_en.html. In a world of plural values and ethical commitments, a religious-based theory of dignity will still have difficulty attracting adherents across cultures and systems.

18   Harold Lasswell & Myres McDougal, Jurisprudence for a Free Society: Studies in Law, Science and Policy (1992); Harold D. Lasswell & Abraham Kaplan, Power and Society: A Framework for Political Inquiry (1950).

in the derivation of those values. Dignity here appears to be a label attached to the collection of those empirically ascertained values or claims.

Others view dignity as a concept that acknowledges the existence of, and protects, what is considered to be a central capacity of humanness. An example of such an approach claims that what makes humans different from other animals is their capacity to reason. Treating individuals as if they did not possess that capacity (or undermining the display and exercise of that capacity) is demeaning personhood itself. The "one central capacity" approach to dignity has an incomplete view of what it means to be human to the extent that humanness is viewed as a function of one capacity (however central that capacity may appear to be). Humanness is an amalgam of capacities and needs.

Related to the "one capacity" approach is what can be referred to as the "one condition" approach. An example of such an approach is the claim that humans are dignified to the extent that their autonomy, the one condition that leads to self-determination in its robust sense, is guaranteed.[19] But, of course, autonomy is only one side of the coin. Connecting with others is part of how we develop our humanness as well. Indeed, to be human is both to connect and to separate at the same time.

Still others make a claim (normative or empirical?) that all humans have the same rank and that rank is an elevated one (elevated from other beings).[20] Those who think of dignity as a rank view it as signaling two things: all human beings have an elevated rank (compared to other creatures) and in virtue of that are entitled to certain respects and treatments. And that elevated rank is equally possessed by every human being. Dignity as rank, which appears to be similar to the one capacity approach, however, does not tell us what the nature or source of the rank is and what the principles and values are that define it. The approach does not give a full account or defense of the "equality" or the "elevation" dimension of the claim.[21]

There are other approaches or theories of dignity which do not reduce dignity to one capacity or one condition or one right, but they need not detain us here. As I noted earlier, however different the various approaches are they

---

19   J.S. Mill, On Liberty [1859] (David Bromwich & George Kateb eds., 2008); Immanuel Kant, Practical Philosophy (ed. and trans. Mary J. Gregor (Cambridge University Press, Cambridge 1998). *See also* Eduardo Mendieta, *The Legal Orthopedia of Human Dignity: Thinking Through Axel Honneth*, 40 Phil. & Social Criticism 799, 804–806 (2014).

20   Jeremy Waldron, Dignity, Rank, and Rights (2012).

21   The religious view of dignity (at least that inspired by the three major religions— Christianity, Judaism, and Islam) can be said to be a kind of dignity-as-rank theory. People have dignity because they were created by God (Allah) in his image, greater than others of God's creatures.

are united on the basics. Dignity is about personhood itself. It is meant to vindicate the conditions and circumstances that would make possible the concept of a person. Under this account, indignity is the effacement of personhood. The effacement is described in various ways—humiliation, debasement, dehumanization, etc.—but it is all about the diminishment of what it means to be human. Indignity is about the attack on the threshold conditions for personhood itself. We often realize the scope of dignity through its opposite—the manifestation of indignity. Hannah Arendt astutely observed this phenomenon in relation to the rights to belong, a topic we shall explore in some detail later. As she put it: "[w]e became aware of the existence of a right to have rights ... and a right to belong to some kind of organized community, only when millions of people emerged who had lost and could not regain these rights because of the new global political situation."[22]

For our purpose here, I shall make the claim (defended elsewhere) that a careful and detailed examination of the uses of dignity in the legal, political and philosophical domains shows that the idea of human dignity is invoked in the context of affirming and defending personhood. Protecting the integrity of the person, in its various dimensions—the physical (embodied beings[23]), psychological, and social dimensions of being human—is the purpose of appropriating the concept of dignity.

First, the physical dimension. Whatever else the self may be, it is its body. And being a body is "what makes the self vulnerable to assault and violative deprivation of the other."[24] The body is vulnerable to and is a site of subjugation. When we speak of indignities, physical depredation or violation is what we often have in mind, for "bodily autonomy and bodily integrity [are] immediate ingredients in the human being."[25] Torture is, of course, the most obvious example of depredation of the embodied self.

It is not just interference into the embodied self that would lead to indignity. The withdrawal or denial of the existential minimums for that entity to exist as a human being is another way in which the embodied self can be undermined or diminished. The embodied self has needs to survive, what Giorgio Agamben calls "bare life."[26] It is on this account that the German Constitutional Court and the International Covenant on Economic, Social and Cultural Rights (IESCR) Committee in their own different ways invoke dignity as a way of

---

22   Hannah Arendt, The Origins of Totalitarianism 294 (1951).

23   This is somehow akin to what Hannah Arendt calls natality. See Hannah Arendt, The Human Condition 177(1958). Natality is the basic condition of human life.

24   J.M. Bernstein, Torture and Dignity: An Essay on Moral Injury 13 (2015).

25   Id. at 259.

26   See Giorgio Agamben, Homo Sacer: Sovereign Power and Bare Life (Daniel Heller-Roazen trans. 1998).

explaining the necessity of providing existential minimums.[27] The German Court explicitly ties this existential minimum to dignity. The notion of an "existential minimum" indicates that dignity at bottom is an existential value.

A person, however, is not just a physical and a psychological being. We are not human merely because of bare life,[28] but also because we are social beings with constitutive commitments, such as how and whom to love; whom and how to worship; and with whom to commune and create. These relationships too make us who we are as human beings no less than the physical body we carry or our psychic disposition. To paraphrase Hannah Arendt, humans do not just appear, they *present* themselves.[29] We are not born human. We become human through these interactions, relationships, and commitments. On this account, statelessness, the subject of this essay, resembles "bare" life.[30] In fact, it is bare life which, at times, leads to the demise of the embodied self itself.

An infringement on those aspects of our being is and has been held to be an attack on the dignity of the person. The general point is that dignity is about

---

27 *See* the German Asylum seekers case cited in Addis, *Dignity, Integrity and the Concept of a Person, supra* note 5, at 350. *See also* Robert Alexy, A Theory of Constitutional Rights 290 (2004) ("[T]here cannot be any doubt that the Federal Constitutional Court presupposes the existence of a constitutional right to an existential minimum.") *See also* ICESCR General Comments 3, 4, and 12, *cited in* Addis, *Dignity, Integrity and the Concept of a Person, supra* note 5, at 346–351).

28 Bare life is equivalent to what Arendt calls "the abstract nakedness of being human." Arendt, Totalitarianism, *supra* note 22, at 295.

29 *See* Hannah Arendt, The Life of the Mind 21 (1978) ("In addition to the urge toward self-display by which living things fit themselves into a world of appearances, men also present themselves in deed and word and thus indicate how they wish to appear, what in their opinion is fit to be seen and what is not. ... Up to a point we can choose to how to appear to others, and the appearance is by no means the outward manifestation of an inner disposition; if it were, we probably would all act and speak alike."). *See also* Hannah Arendt, The Human Condition, *supra* note 23, at 176 ("A life without speech and without action ... is literally dead to the world; it has ceased to be a human life because it is no longer lived among men.") *See also* Jürgen Habermas, *The Concept of Human Dignity and the Realistic Utopia of Human Rights,* 41 Metaphilosophy 464, 474 (2010). ("As a modern legal concept, human dignity is associated with the status that citizens assume in the self-created political order.") Habermas too views dignity in political terms where individuals as citizens create and recreate themselves in the context of membership in political communities both as originators and addressees of the law. Arendt's and Habermas' view of human dignity can be characterized as the political ontology of human dignity. Each understood dignity in terms of stance rather than status and stature.

30 *See* Arendt, Totalitarianism, *cited in* John Douglas Macready, Hannah Arendt and the Fragility of Human Dignity 102 (2018) ("The figure of *the stateless human* constituted bare psychological existence for Arendt—mere existence, outside of all political relations.") (emphasis in original).

the protection of personhood itself, from the most basic (the body) to the most reflective (social commitments and membership in political communities) aspects of our being. When a person is forced either legally, administratively, or culturally to abandon or deny (cover) those commitments, the person's self-understanding is shattered or at least disoriented. She suffers humiliation. Humiliation is "the extension of cruelty from the physical to the psychological [and social] realms of suffering."[31] Jürgen Habermas is right when he observes that "human dignity emerges from the plethora of what it means to be humiliated and be deeply hurt."[32]

We are dependent on social others for the recognition of the borders of our personhood, but we are also vulnerable to the violation of those borders by the same social others. The notion of dignity is meant to foster recognition and minimize vulnerability.

3   Statelessness and the Dignity of Belonging

3.1   *Introduction*
If dignity attaches to personhood in its entirety, then dignity might be essential for our understanding and defense of belonging to a national political community and the right to a "home" and the security and protection that it brings. To be human is also to belong to and to participate in an organized society. If torture, genocide, war crimes are paradigmatic examples of an attack on the physical and psychological dimensions of the person, statelessness is its social equivalent. Indeed, statelessness is a condition that opens a person to physical and psychological vulnerability and humiliation as well. Statelessness subjects individuals to "infinite danger," as Michael Walzer would say.[33]

What I shall do in the following pages is inquire into the dignity of belonging to a national political community and the indignity and infinite danger to which statelessness subjects persons.

---

31   Avishai Margalit, The Decent Society 85 (1996).
32   Jürgen Habermas, *The Concept of Human Dignity, supra* note 29, at 468. Habermas seems to argue that the notion of dignity enables us to explain and understand current human rights and to generate more rights. "The features of human dignity specified and actualized in this way can then lead both to a more complete exhaustion of existing civil rights and to the discovery and construction of new ones." *Id.* at 468.
33   Michael Walzer, Spheres of Justice: A Defense of Pluralism and Equality 32 (1983).

3.2   *The Nature and Seriousness of Statelessness*

A stateless person is legally defined as "a person who is not considered as a national by any State under the operation of its law."[34] Nationality is a legal bond between a state and the individuals within its jurisdiction.[35] A stateless person belongs "nowhere,"[36] and, as a consequence, becomes "a virtual non-person," as the UNHCR put it.[37] This description is similar to an observation that Arendt, made a long time ago. Arendt observed that only "the loss of a polity ... expels [a person] from humanity."[38]

Etymologically, statelessness as a human condition affirms or announces the presence (centrality) of the state in its absence. Statelessness describes the paradox inherent in the phenomenon. Everyone is required to submit himself/ herself to the coercive power of a state and yet some individuals have nowhere to belong. Even more significantly, they have no right to belong anywhere. As Michael Walzer argued long ago, the primary social good that we distribute to one another is the social good of membership in some human community, such as membership in a national community.[39] The distribution of membership in a national community (via nationality) is a primary social good of immense importance, for the possession of that social good is the basis for accessing other goods, whether those goods are material or social.[40]

---

34   *See* Convention relating to the Status of Stateless Persons (adopted Sept. 28, 1954, entered into force June 6, 1975) 189 UNTS 117, at art. 1.

35   Nottebohm Case (Liech. v. Guat.), Judgment, 1955 I.C.J. 4 (1955). In this famous case, the Court held that "nationality is a legal bond having as its basis a social fact of attachment a genuine connection of existence, interests and sentiments together with the existence of reciprocal rights and duties." *Id.* at 23.

36   One stateless individual described her status this way: "I feel like nobody who belongs to nowhere. Like I don't exist." *Nowhere People*, http://www.nowherepeople.org/main. The stateless have been described in various other ways. One judicial decision referred to them as "international pariahs." M/V Saiga (No. 2) Case (Saint Vincent and the Grenadines v. Guinea), 1 July 1999, International Tribunal of the Law of the Sea, at para. 63 and 83–84. The UNHCR itself has characterized the stateless as "virtual non-persons." UNHCR, *The Problem of Statelessness Has Become a Live Issue Again*, 112 Protecting Refugees Magazine (1998). At another point in this article, the organization has referred to the stateless as "outcasts from the global political system of states."

37   UNHCR, *The Problem of Statelessness, supra* note 36.

38   Arendt, The Origins of Totalitarianism, *supra* note 22, at 294–95 (1951). Although Arendt exaggerates a bit, the general point is correct. In a world made up of states, it is through membership in national political communities that a person can present herself and co-create the world in which she lives.

39   Walzer, Spheres of Justice, *supra* note 33, at 31 ("The primary good that we distribute to one another is membership in some human community.").

40   Walzer and many others justify the authority of a state to have the exclusive power to admit or exclude as the expression of the "deepest meaning of self-determination"

The United Nations High Commissioner for Refugees (UNHCR) whose mandate now includes stateless persons,[41] estimates that there are about 3.9 million stateless persons spread throughout the world.[42] A mere four or so years ago, even the UNHCR had put the number at around 12 million.[43] The Institute of Statelessness and Inclusion believes that that figure is even higher.[44] Even that number is, however, likely to be a significant undercount if one were to take into account the facts that there are *de facto* stateless people whose nationality is in constant dispute or who are unable to establish their nationality. And there are many persons who are at risk of being rendered stateless at any moment which do not figure in the reported numbers.[45]

It is also the case that governments do not report regularly and accurately the number of stateless persons within their jurisdictions. This is so, either because of a capacity problem or because of lack of good will or incentive. That, too, leads to serious undercounting of the stateless population.[46]

----

without which "there could not be *communities of character*" (emphasis in original). Walzer, Spheres of Justice, *supra* note 33, at 62. Walzer's communities of character are composed of "members *with* memories not only of their own but also of their common life." *See* Walzer, Thick and Thin: Moral Argument at Home and Abroad, *supra* note 4, at 8. As Walzer put it in *Spheres of Justice*, "[o]n the one hand, everyone must have a place to live, and a place where a reasonably secure life is possible. On the other hand, this is not a right that can be enforced against particular host states." *Id.* at 50.

41   In 1996, the UN General Assembly placed the stateless within the UNHCR mandate.

42   Neha Jain, *Manufacturing Statelessness*, 116 Am. J. Int'l L. 237, 249 (2022) ("[T]he UNHCR's statistical count of 3.9 million stateless individuals around the world is likely to be a vast underestimate.").

43   *See* UN News, '*12 million' stateless people globally, warns UNHCR chief in call to States for decisive action*, 12 November 2018, https://news.un.org/en/story/2018/11/1025561. Perhaps UNHCR's recent campaign on eliminating statelessness has led to such drastic decline, but I am very skeptical of such a big drop.

44   Institute on Statelessness and Inclusion, *The World's Stateless 2020: Deprivation of Nationality* (March 2020).

45   The Inter-American Court of Human Rights in its decision responding to the Constitutional Court of the Dominican Republic nullifying Dominican nationality for more than 130,000 persons of Haitian descent extended protection under international law to persons who faced a "risk of statelessness" even though they might not be stateless *de jure* at the particular time. Case of Expelled Dominicans and Haitians v. Dominican Republic, Preliminary Objections, Merits, Reparations and Costs, Judgement, Inter-Am. Ct. H.R. (ser. C) No. 282, ¶ 298. The Inter-American Court put the burden on the Dominican Republic that individuals of Haitian descent did not face a "risk of statelessness."

46   Guy S. Goodwin-Gill made similar observation back in 1994. He wrote: "[n]o one knows how many stateless people there are in the world." *See* GS Goodwin-Gill, *The Rights of Refugees and Stateless Persons, in* Human Rights Perspective and Challenge (in 1990 and Beyond) 378 (KP Saksena ed., 1994). That observation rings true even today.

In this essay, I mean to use statelessness in its broader sense to include those who are de facto stateless with no "effective nationality."[47] Functioning citizenship is what is at stake in any discussion of statelessness.[48] That is, it is not just the right to nationality (having one's own country), but the right to effective nationality (belonging) that is in question. Statelessness is not just a narrow technical legal problem, but a problem of membership in the substantive sense—the lack of full and equal membership and the absence of full integration. The moral claim of social membership (social bonding) is the basis for the legal claim of citizenship. To some extent, the notion of "effective nationality" is assumed in the very definition of statelessness in the very first convention on statelessness, Convention on the Status of Statelessness (Status of Statelessness Convention).[49]

Statelessness is a worldwide problem. No region is immune from it. From West Africa (Côte d'Ivoire) to Southeast Asia (Myanmar[50]), from the Middle East (Kuwait[51]) to the Baltics, from Central America (Dominican Republic) to

---

47 For various examples of how de jure citizenship does not necessarily mean the end of functional statelessness, see Caia Vlieks, Ernst Hirsch Ballin, María José Recalde Vela, *Solving Statelessness: Interpreting the Right to Nationality*, 35 Neth. Q. Hum. Rts. 158 (2017). After listing various examples, the authors then note, "[t]hese examples illustrate that purely legal solutions may reduce numbers, but may have little to no impact on the number of unprotected persons." *Id.* at 160. Laura van Waas defines "ineffective nationality" as a circumstance or condition where a person is "not enjoy[ing] the rights of citizenship enjoyed by other non-criminal citizens of the same state." Laura van Waas, Nationality Matters: Statelessness Under International Law 24 (2008). In relation to African countries, Bronwen Manby notes that, in practice, individual Africans far more often face the practical impossibility of obtaining official documentation than an explicit legal denial of nationality. UNHCR: Citizenship and Statelessness in the Horn of Africa 34 (UNHCR, 2021), https://www.refworld.org/docid/61c97bea4.html. "Universal birth registration has long been an international objective. Yet, with the exception of Djibouti, birth registration rates in the Horn of Africa are amongst the lowest in the world." *Id.*

48 *See* Lindsey N. Kingston, *Statelessness as a Lack of Functioning Citizenship*, 19 Tilburg L. Rev. 127 (2014).

49 Article 1 defines statelessness as one who is not "considered as a national by any State *under the operation of its law*." (emphasis added). The phrase "under the operation of its law" seems to signal that it is not just a lack of de jure status that makes one stateless but also the rendering of the individual through the operation of the law as de facto stateless.

50 Almost a million, mostly Muslim, Rohingya were denied nationality by the ruling junta which is predominantly Buddhist. Many were displaced across Myanmar itself and across the border to Bangladesh and other locations.

51 Zahra Al Barazi & Jason Tucker, *Challenging the Disunity of Statelessness in the Middle East and North Africa*, in Understanding Statelessness 87 (Tendayi Bloom, Katherine Tonkiss & Phillip Cole eds. 2017). The Bidoon in Kuwait are examples of people who live in the shadow of statelessness.

South Asia (Nepal) many live with the knowledge that they are considered not to belong or are in constant fear of being left with nowhere to belong and with no protection that comes only with belonging.[52] Although statelessness is a global problem, Africa and the Asia Pacific regions have the majority of the stateless population.[53]

The causes of statelessness are varied,[54] but the consequences of statelessness are the same. Stateless people live on the margin of society with no access to the rights and privileges that citizenship or nationality provides, with constant fear of expulsion or worse, no access to education and health services, with vulnerability to human trafficking by unscrupulous traffickers, and the like. To be stateless is to lack the basic protections that membership (nationality) provides, to be subject to a "condition of infinite danger."[55] Statelessness

---

52   Even the United States is not immune from the phenomenon of statelessness. There are
      no reliable figures for the number of the stateless population in the country. What is
      undeniable, however, is that there is a sizable group that is at risk of statelessness.

53   *See* Christoph Sperfeldt, *Legal Identity and Statelessness in Southeast Asia, East-West Center* (No. 147, Jan. 2021) ("Around 40 percent of the identified stateless population live in
      the Asia Pacific region, with the majority of them residing in the countries of Southeast
      Asia.") As the article mentions, even though a high percentage of the stateless population is found in Asia, Asian countries have a poor record of signing and ratifying the two
      statelessness conventions, especially Southeast Asian states where a significant stateless
      population resides.

54   They include ethnic and racial conflicts (identity-based conflicts) and hostilities, gender-based discrimination, poor systems of registration, inheritance of statelessness, state
      collapse and state successions, etc. One must not forget the long shadow and impact
      of colonialism, which divided communities between colonial territories and at times
      even transported one group of people from one colonial possession to another part of
      the world (another colonial possession) as laborers, on the statelessness problem. Two
      emerging causes that might be contributors to statelessness, if they are not attended to
      quickly, are climate change (such as the disappearance of islands) that displaces people
      from their homes and international surrogacy, which might be the cause of child statelessness. International surrogacy is unregulated at the international level. Given the fact
      that nationality and citizenship laws vary from State to State, international surrogacy is
      likely to lead to some children being rendered stateless unless there is an international
      regulatory standard. *See* Sanoj Rajan, *International Surrogacy Arrangements and Statelessness, available at* http://children.worldsstateless.org/3/safeguarding-against-childhood
      -statelessness/international-surrogacy-arrangements-and-statelessness.html.

55   Walzer, Spheres of Justice, *supra* note 33, at 32.

has had more impact on certain already vulnerable groups: women and children,[56] nomadic and travelling groups, and indigenous inhabitants.[57]

3.3 Why Worry about Statelessness?

Even though there are claims (generally correct) that the trend in the last few years has been a decline in the stateless population worldwide, there are, as I noted earlier, still too many who live in the shadow and vulnerable to all sorts of threats and exploitative behavior.

At any rate, it is not only the fact that statelessness is currently a serious problem that demands our attention, but also current global political developments that require that we pay close attention to the phenomenon. The emergence of populist nationalism across the globe will increasingly put the issue of who belongs and who does not (and cannot) at the center of political discourse or conversations.[58] There are legitimate fears that hyper-nationalism will lead to forced displacement of a large number of people leading to *de jure* statelessness and an even larger number of people will be rendered *de facto* stateless.[59] Some have argued that just as in the inter-war period (and WWII) statelessness in an era of global populist nationalism might be utilized to consolidate or build "a people." Matthew Gibney argues that one of the reasons for the persistence of statelessness is that "exclusion from membership is often congruent with

---

56   Because of widespread gender-based discrimination in the acquisition of citizenship, women and children are especially vulnerable to statelessness. *See* GiHA Brochure Stateless Women and Girls_060521.pdf. *See also* UNHCR, Report of the Regional Workshop on Statelessness and the Rights of Women and Children, 18–19 November 2011 Manila, Philippines, 50f674c42.pdf (refworld.org).

57   William Conklin, Statelessness: The Enigma of an International Community 96–135 (2014). Nomads or marine mobile populations (refer to as "sea nomads") are particularly vulnerable to statelessness. State-based nationality laws that are premised on a system of fixed territorial links can't accommodate these mobile lifestyles. *See* Greg Acciaioli, Helen Brunt & Julian Clifton, *Foreigners Everywhere, Nationals Nowhere: Exclusion, Irregularity and Invisibility of Stateless Bajau Laut in Eastern Sabah, Malaysia*, 15 J. Immigration & Refugee Stud. 232 (2017).

58   *See* Lars-Erik Cederman, *Blood for Soil: The Fatal Temptations of Ethnic Politics*, Foreign Aff., March/April, 2019, at 61 "[E]thnic nationalism is back with a vengeance. ... [and it is] giving militants more room to attack those who do not belong to the dominant ethnic group"); Nicole Winfield & Derek Gatopoulos, *Pope Warns of Populist Threats Across Europe* (Associated Press story), The Times-Picayune, December 5, 2021, at 7A.

59   The *de jure* stateless have no legal protection or right to participate in the political community in which they find themselves (or any other community) while the *de facto* stateless are unable to access the rights and protections provided by functioning citizenship.

national process of 'people building.'"[60] That is, "[t]he creation of a collective identity is achieved by contrasting the included community with the excluded ones ... and, in so doing, formulating the distinctive character of the national community."[61] Those considered the alien other are often marginalized minority groups. Of course, we know from history that the hostility towards the "Other" that statelessness manifests can lead to an even graver solution such as genocide.[62] Currently, there are examples where states have been accused of having engaged in genocidal acts in relation to their residents that they had rendered stateless. The Myanmar government stands accused before the International Court of Justice[63] and the International Criminal Court[64] of having committed genocide against the Rohingyas.

---

60 Matthew Gibney, *Statelessness and Citizenship in Ethical and Political Perspective, in* Nationality and Statelessness under International Law 55 (Alice Edwards & Laura van Waas eds., 2014).

61 *Id. See also* Neha Jain, *Manufacturing Statelessness*, 116 Am. J. Int'l L. 237 (2022).

62 *See* Adeno Addis, *Genocide and Belonging: Processes of Imagining Communities*, 38 U. Pa. J. Int'l L. 1041 (2017). *See also* Arendt, The Origin of Totalitarianism, *supra* note 22, at 293 ("[A] condition of complete rightlessness was created before the right to live was challenged.") Arendt was of course referring to the Nazi regime's denationalization of its Jewish citizens before it extinguished the lives of many of those citizens. Denationalization (denaturalization) could take mass or individual form. An example of the former is the denationalization of Jews in Germany, the case of Haitians in the Dominican Republic, and the ongoing case of the Rohingya. Of course, there are many examples of individual denaturalization across the globe for various reason and with differing consequences. One prominent example currently is the denaturalization policies of some western countries in the context of the "War on Terror." Craig Forcese, *A Tale of Two Citizenships: Citizenship Revocation for 'Traitors and Terrorists'*, 39 Queen's L. J. 551 (2014); Cassandra Burke Robertson & Irina D. Manta, *(Un)Civil Denaturalization*, 94 N.Y.U. L. Rev. 402 (2019); N R Motaung, *Revocation of Citizenship in the Face of Terrorism*, 50 Comp. & Int'l L. J. S. Afr. 214 (2017). *See also* Matthew J. Gibney, *Denaturalization, in* The Oxford Handbook of Citizenship (Ayelet Shachar ed., 2017). *See also* Audrey Macklin, *Kick-off Contribution, in* The Return of Banishment: Do the New Denaturalization Policies Weaken Citizenship (Audrey Macklin & Rainer Bauböck eds., 2015). Macklin makes the important point that since the "exercise of virtually all rights depends on territorial presence within the state, and only citizens have an unqualified right to enter and remain," to be stripped of the right to enter means that "one is effectively deprived of all other rights that depend (de jure or de facto} on territorial presence." *Id.* at 2. Arendt's "right to have rights" aphorism seem to apply perfectly.

63 Application of the Convention on the Prevention and Punishment of the Crime of Genocide (The Gambia v. Myanmar) ICJ, July 23, 2020); Application of the Convention on the Prevention and Punishment of the Crime of Genocide (The Gambia v. Myanmar) ICJ, July 22, 2022 (Judgment on the preliminary objections).

64 Press Release, *ICC judges authorise opening of an investigation into the situation in Bangladesh/Myanmar*, Nov. 14, 2019, https://www.icc-cpi.int/news/icc-judges-authorise-opening-investigation-situation-bangladesh/myanmar.

We should be concerned about statelessness for another reason. Several nations, mainly developing countries, are highly unstable. State collapse is a real possibility in relation to some of those nations. If that were to occur, it would lead to a large number of displaced people as we saw happened when the former Soviet Union and Yugoslavia broke up into many states. Following the collapse of those two countries, many people found that they were not considered to belong to the new country in which they might have lived their entire lives and even for generations. State collapse, state fragmentation, and the process of state succession which have in the past been sources of large populations of stateless people[65] are distinct possibilities in relation to a number of fractured and unstable states.

4   Statelessness and the Dignity of Belonging

Hannah Arendt, who was herself a stateless person for 18 years (1933–1951) after fleeing her homeland to escape the existential threat from the Nazis,[66] famously observed that a stateless person is not simply expelled from one country, but from all countries. Indeed, "the loss of polity itself expels him from humanity."[67] On this account, the lack of membership in a political community has the consequence of seriously undermining the very personhood or humanity of the excluded. The excluded has been reduced to "bare life."[68]

We become fully human in the process of belonging and interacting and creating with others.[69] We constitute who we are significantly through our words and actions where those words and actions matter to others.[70] In an international order of states, that will occur in significant part if, and when, we are recognized as members of a national political community. On this account, legal personhood becomes a condition for the recognition of the person as

---

65   *See* Ineta Ziemele, *State Succession and Issues of Nationality and Statelessness, in* Nationality and Statelessness under International Law 217–246 (Alice Edwards & Laura van Waas eds., 2014).

66   Arendt fled Nazi Germany at the age of 27 and was stateless until she became a naturalized American citizen in 1951.

67   Arendt, The Origins of Totalitarianism, *supra* note 22, at 295.

68   Giorgio Agamben, Homo Sacer: Sovereign Power and Bare Life (Heller-Roazen, trans. 1998), *see, especially,* at 4–6.

69   *See* Bernard-Henri Lévy, *We Are Not Born Human: Our Humanity is a Process That Begins with Nature,* N.Y. Times, Aug. 22, 2018.

70   *See* Arendt, The Human Condition, *supra* note 23, at 176 ("A life without speech and without action … is literally dead to the world; it has ceased to be a human life because it is no longer lived among men.").

an entity with moral standing, the recognition of personhood itself. Perhaps it is in this sense that Hersch Lauterpacht, one of the most celebrated international legal scholars of the twentieth century and one who thought and wrote about statelessness, referred to nationality as an "essential attribute of human personality."[71] Statelessness, according to Arendt and Lauterpacht, is, therefore, nothing short of an attack on an important aspect of being human, the quest to belong and to enjoy all the benefits and protections that such affiliation brings.

Statelessness is both a wrong and a harm. It is a harm because statelessness exposes people to radical insecurity, to infinite danger. The stateless are highly vulnerable to the arbitrary exercise of private and public power. It is also a wrong in that an international order of states that expects that everyone be subjected to a state's coercive power cannot be legitimate when it regularly produces people who are deemed to belong "nowhere," surplus people.

On several occasions, the United States Supreme Court has made comments that similarly indicate the centrality of citizenship/nationality. In *Klapprott v. United States*, Justice Rutledge described citizenship as "a right no less precious than life or liberty."[72] Writing for the majority, Chief Justice Warren made a similar point in *Trop v. Dulles* characterizing denationalization as one of the worst fates to befall a person, a "total destruction of the individual's status in organized society" and "a form of punishment more primitive than torture."[73] It is more primitive and more consequential to the extent that it strips a person of the very basis for access to other rights. Chief Justice Warren in fact adopts Hannah Arendt's phrase and characterizes citizenship as "the right to

---

71   Hersch Lauterpacht, An International Bill of the Rights of Man 7 (1945). Mira Siegelberg, in her fine book quotes one stateless person's view of nationality. The person was born in Brussels but raised in France. She was married to a person with a Polish passport. The individual exerted great effort to acquire French citizenship, but to no avail. Exasperated, she wrote a letter to the then UN Secretary General, Dag Hammarskjöld, in 1960 pleading that he help her gain French citizenship and put an end to her stateless condition. In the letter, she wrote: "I don't want to die apatride." Then she asked, "[w]hat is it to be human if not to have the right to a nationality." Mira L. Siegelberg, Statelessness. A Modern History 193 (2020).

72   Klapprott v. United States, 336 U.S. 601, 616–617 (1949) (Justice Rutledge, with whom Justice Murphy agrees, concurring in the result.) ("To take away a man's citizenship deprives him of a right no less precious than life or liberty, indeed of one which today comprehends those rights and almost all other rights.").

73   Trop v. Dulles, 356 U.S. 86, 101 (1958). Denaturalization as a punishment is "a total destruction of the individual's status in organized society. It is a form of punishment more primitive than torture, for it destroys for the individual the political existence that was centuries in the development. The punishment strips the citizen of his status in the national and international community. ... In short, the expatriate has lost the right to have rights."

have rights."[74] That is, citizenship or nationality gives access to all other rights (material or social) that are threshold conditions for the existence of the person, including the basic dimension of personhood—the safety and protection of the embodied self. Even "bare life" is contingent on the right to have rights.

Being a legal person in a particular jurisdiction is *necessary* for a person to be recognized as the bearer of rights and privileges—including the right to life, the right to be free from torture, the right to existential minimum, and the right to form stable human relationships. The United States Supreme Court made this very point in *United States v. Wong Kim Ark* when it held that a "man without a country is not recognized by law."[75] It is to capture the fact that the right to have rights (membership in a political community) is the condition to realize all other rights including even those rights denominated as inalienable rights that Arendt made the brilliant observation that the extermination camps of the Nazis exposed that "the world found nothing sacred in the abstract nakedness of being human."[76] A human being was systematically stripped of "qualities [such as nationality] which make it possible for other people to treat him as a fellow-man."[77]

To appropriate a phrase Orlando Patterson used to describe slavery, in an international order of states statelessness is a form of "social death."[78] Indeed, the first formal judicial pronouncement of statelessness in the United States was made in relation to enslaved people. In *Dred Scott v. Sandford*, the United States Supreme Court declared that Blacks, free or enslaved, could not be (and were never meant to be) citizens of the United States.[79] Chief Justice Taney wrote: "In the opinion of the Court, the legislation and histories of the times,

---

74   Trop v. Dulles, at 102.

75   United States v. Wong Kim Ark, 169 U.S. 649 (1898).

76   Arendt, Totalitarianism, *supra* note 22, at 295. Those who perished were still humans with inalienable rights, but without a political community to provide those to them, they merely had the quality of an abstract and naked human. If the Rights of Man had meant anything, it was this very moment that should have triggered it is the point Arendt is making. As she noted elsewhere, a person who is not a member of a political community has a bare life that does not compel others to treat him as a person. *See also id.* at 294 ("Not the loss of specific rights, then but the loss of a community willing and able to guarantee any rights whatsoever, has been the calamity which has befallen ever-increasing numbers of people.")

77   Arendt, Totalitarianism, *supra* note 22, at 296.

78   *See* Orlando Patterson, Slavery and Social Death: A Comparative Study (1982). *See also* Orlando Patterson, Freedom: Freedom in the Making of Western Culture 9–10 (1991) ("The slave is always an excommunicated person. He, most often she, does not belong in the legitimate social or moral community; he has no independent social existence; he exists only through, and for, the master; he is, in other words, natally alienated.")

79   Dred Scott v. Sandford, 60 U.S. 393 (1857).

and the language used in the Declaration of Independence, show, that *neither the class of persons who had been imported as slaves, nor their descendants, whether they had become free or not, were then acknowledged as part of the people*, nor intended to be included in the general words used in that memorable instrument."[80]

In an international political order where almost every inch of the globe is carved into states with mutually exclusive jurisdictions, one's very security and perhaps even life itself is dependent on being claimed by at least one state as a legitimate member, statelessness is the ultimate attack on personhood itself. To be a person is to be recognized that one's words and actions matter to others. For that to occur in a political community, however, one has to be recognized as a legal entity. The stateless live in a legal black hole and consequently as political and even social nonentities.

There are two ways in which statelessness is an attack on personhood itself – on the dignity of the person. First, to the extent that the person is not legally recognized as a member of the political community, the immunities and privileges that are meant to protect the boundaries of the person (either internationally or domestically and physically or otherwise) are unavailable or not fully available.[81] The other, and just as important a loss, is the loss of the idea of home.[82] It is not just about the importance of location and stability. It is also about community and connections. It is about being part of a community of character where relationships are developed and social roots sunk. It is, to quote Arendt, "a place in the world which makes opinions significant and actions effective."[83] Put in another way, the first step to total domination is to kill the juridical person in man. This is precisely what statelessness does.[84] History testifies that complete rightlessness is quite frequently followed by the challenge to the right to life itself. For the stateless during the mid-twentieth century, "the earth had become a death trap."[85]

---

80   *Id.* at 407 (emphasis added).

81   Arendt, Totalitarianism, *supra* note 22, at 291 ("The second loss which the rightless suffered was the loss of government protection.").

82   ("The first loss which the rightless suffered was the loss of their homes, and this means the loss of the entire social structure into which they were born ["social bonding."] and in which they established for themselves a distinct place in the world.") *Id.* at 290.

83   Arendt, Totalitarianism, *supra* note 22, at 293.

84   *Id.* at 296. ("It seems to me that a man who is nothing but a man has lost the very qualities which make it possible for other people to treat him as a fellow-man.") At another point, Arendt refers to that condition as "the abstract nakedness of being human." Id. at 295.

85   Hadji Bakara, *Death Ship Earth: On Mira L. Siegelberg's "Statelessness,"* Los Angeles Review of Books (May 7, 2021), *available at* https://www.lareviewofbooks.org/article/death-ship -earth-on-mira-l-siegelbergs-statelessness/.

5   Guaranteeing and Protecting the Dignity to Belong

Since it is the international order of states, viewed as the will of the aggregate of sovereign states with mutually exclusive jurisdictions, that leads to the phenomenon of statelessness, one could argue that the duty to ensure the dignity of belonging is properly imposed on that international order that produces "surplus people."

How precisely could that duty be discharged? Matthew Gibney mentions in passing that one way might be for the international community simply to apportion existing stateless people among constituent states, in whatever way that apportionment might be done.[86] However, as Gibney himself notes, stateless people live in a particular place and among particular communities where they have sunk roots and have developed relationships. The only thing is that that factual circumstance is not legally recognized or vindicated. Many of these people are properly viewed as "unrecognized citizens" of the particular state. Distributing them across the globe as abstract and unattached beings is neither just nor a long-term solution.[87] Therefore, ultimately the most feasible and just way to impose a duty consistent with the protection of the dignity of the stateless is to do so on individual states in a way that recognizes the specific circumstances of the stateless. The issue then becomes the criteria by which a duty is imposed on a state or states.

To the extent that many stateless people are (and have been) in fact members of national communities (many for generations), the most just way is to put the duty on the particular states to recognize the "unrecognized" members of its community. These individuals have a stake in the future of the particular societies in which they reside (albeit unrecognized). Theorists such as Rainer Bauböck have argued that a morally defensible account of citizenship should give space to all those who have a stake in the future of the particular society. The legalization of those who have been part of the "unrecognized" members of the community is a morally required duty which would justly resolve the stateless problem.[88]

---

86   *See* Gibney, Statelessness and Citizenship, *supra* note 60, at 57–58. The principle of allocation could be a set number to every country or proportionate to the size of the country or to the capacity of the country, or according to another principle of justice, etc.

87   *Id.* at 58 ("The stateless are not, in practice simply deracinated, homeless people, wandering the globe in search of any state that will have them. They are typically, though not exclusively, people settled in particular societies.").

88   *See* Rainer Bauböck, Stakeholder Citizenship: An Idea Whose Time Has Come (2008). For Bauböck, stakeholding is about the idea that one is dependent on that political community for the protection of one's right and how that community develops will have an

The notion of a stakeholder—factual membership – is not very different from the idea of a genuine link that the famous *Nottebohm* case (Liechtenstein v. Guatemala) introduced in the mid-1950s. In that case, the International Court of Justice opined that nationality (citizenship) is "a legal bond having as its basis a social fact of attachment."[89] The bond is constituted from a socio-cultural relationship between or among natural persons. The notion of a legal bond (nationality) as a social bond is nested inside the very discourse about international law and about the international "community of character." As the Court saw it, Nottebohm's habitual residence (factual membership) in Guatemala was an important piece of "evidence of a deeper complex of social relationships experienced there."[90] There are many other indicia of deep complex social relationship—friendship and family, personal and collective memories, place of business, etc. Put simply, one's personhood is developed within the structure and in the context in which one finds oneself. So, the notion of stakeholding and the idea of genuine link that *Nottebohm* seems to suggest accompany the legal bond of nationality are preceded by and assume social relationships. Under this reading, the principles of *jus soli*[91] and *jus sanguinis*[92] are assumed to be indicia of social bonds and stakeholding.

To link this to international law, the international community defined by the human rights regimes (both customary and conventional) takes individuals and their social ties as a starting point. The social relationship amongst natural persons as shared through experience of time and place is the point of departure for affirming the dignity of the person. To respect and protect the dignity of the person is not simply to protect the embodied self from physical attack or to require existential minimum for the individual, but to affirm the commitments, relationships (life-plans) that define the individual. It is to remove the condition (statelessness and internal displacement[93]) that subject the individual to "infinite danger," including the danger to the very life of the person.

---

impact on one's own future. Gibney reinforces this point when he claims: "The question of a right to membership is not decided by the existence of some other state that may formally claim one as a member but is dependent primarily on one's relationship to the state in which one is actually making one's life." Gibney, Statelessness and Citizenship, *supra* note 60, at 60.

89   Liechtenstein v. Guatemala (second phase), (1955) ICJ Rep. 4, 23.
90   Conklin, Statelessness, *supra* note 57, at 189.
91   Citizenship acquired through birth on the territory of the particular country.
92   Citizenship acquired through descent.
93   Internal displacement on the basis of a socially salient factor (such as ethnicity and religion) is also about belonging, who is properly a member of this or that community.

Both the two statelessness conventions and the various international and regional human rights documents seem to affirm this. Several of these provide for citizenship on *jus soli* grounds. Thus, the Convention on the Reduction of Statelessness (Reduction of Statelessness) imposes an obligation on signatory states to grant nationality to children born in their territories in the absence of a right to any other nationality.[94] The American Convention on Human Rights provides for a similar obligation.[95] The European Convention on Nationality also provides that "[e]ach State Party *shall provide* in its internal law for its nationality to be acquired by children born on its territory who do not acquire at birth another nationality."[96]

Although international human rights documents do not explicitly require birthright citizenship for those who would otherwise be stateless, some of them clearly imply it. Thus, the International Covenant on Civil and Political Rights recognizes that "[e]very child has the right to acquire a nationality."[97] Although the article does not impose a duty on the country of birth to provide a nationality in the event that the child will be stateless otherwise, a reasonable implication is that such obligation is imposed. If every child has a right to a nationality and there is no other state to which the child can be said to properly belong, then the default principle seems to be that the appropriate social bond for the child is to the community in which he or she is born.[98] After all, that is the only place to which the child is attached in any reasonable sense. In a very interesting general comment on Article 12 of the ICCPR, General Comment 27, the Human Rights Committee reinforces the proposition that nationality is generally a vindication of a social tie. The Committee read the provision that "[n]o one shall be arbitrarily deprived of the right to enter his own country" as including anyone, citizen or not, who has a "special

---

94   *See* art. 1(1).

95   American Convention on Human Rights (adopted Nov. 22, 1969, entered into force July 18, 1978), 1144 UNTS 144, at art. 20. After declaring that "every person has the right to a nationality," the Convention imposes the duty on "the state in whose territory [the person] was born." But the duty of the state exists only if the person "does not have the right to any other nationality."

96   European Convention on Nationality (adopted Nov. 6, 1997, entered into force March 1, 2000), ETS 166, art. 6(2): (emphasis added).

97   International Covenant on Civil and Political Rights (adopted Dec. 16, 1966, entered into force Mar. 23 1976), 999 UNTS 171, art. 24(3).

98   The Human Rights Committee in General Comment 17, which deals with Article 24, declares that "States are required [by Article 24(3)] to adopt every appropriate measure, both internally and in cooperation with other States, to ensure that every child has a nationality." CCPR General Comment No 17: Rights of the Child (Art. 24), Geneva, 7 April 1988, para. 8.

tie."[99] According to the Committee, this would include stateless persons who have been long-term (habitual) residents of the country. The Committee has reaffirmed this view in the various cases that came before it through the individual petition procedure.[100]

Of course, the requirement that the child be entitled to birthright citizenship in the absence of an alternative nationality will be effective only to the extent that the country of birth has a proper birth registration record. Otherwise, the status of the child will be in constant dispute as is the case now in relation to many people in many parts of the world, especially children from minority groups.[101] ICCPR provides that States are required to register every child immediately after birth.[102] The Convention on the Rights of the Child has a similar provision.[103] Birth registration is an important step towards the acquisition of other forms of legal identity, most crucially nationality.[104] The lack of birth registration is a serious problem in many developing countries, especially in Sub-Saharan Africa.[105] International organizations, both intergovernmental and nongovernmental, must double their efforts to support developing countries to develop systems for child birth registration.

The assumption of a social bond as an important element in the acquisition of membership through nationality is expressed in relation to gender as well.

---

99   UN Human Rights Committee, General Comment No. 27: Freedom of Movement (Article 12), U.N. Doc. CCPR/C/21/Rev.1/Add9, Nov. 1, 1999, para. 20.

100   *See* Human Rights Committee, 'Views: Communication no 1557/2007', U.N. Doc. CCPR/C/102/D/1557/2007, Sep. 1, 2011 (Nystrom v. Australia), *cited in* Michelle Foster & Hélène Lambert, *Statelessness as a Human Rights Issue: A Concept Whose Time Has Come,* 28 Int'l J. Refugee L. 564, 575 (2016). *See also* Steward v. Canada, UN Human Rights Committee, U.N. Doc. CCPR/C/58/D/538/1993(1996).

101   About seventy-five percent of the known stateless population worldwide is said to belong to minorities. *See* U.N. General Assembly, Report of the Special Rapporteur on Minority Issues—*Statelessness: A Minority Issue,* July 20, 2018, U.N. Doc. A/73/205, at 6, para. 21. The Rohingya in Myanmar are a good example of a minority with a statelessness problem.

102   *See* ICCPR Art. 24(2).

103   Convention on the Rights of the Child (adopted Nov. 20, 1989, entered into force Dept. 2 1990) 1577 UNTS 3, art. 7(1). ("The child shall be registered immediately after birth and shall have the right from birth to a name, the right to acquire to a nationality ...").

104   *See* Bronwen Manby, Struggles for Citizenship in Africa 115 (2009) ("Birth registration is usually fundamental to the realization of all other citizenship rights: lack of birth certificates can prevent [presumptive] citizens from registering to vote, putting their children in school or entering them for public exams, accessing healthcare, or obtaining identity cards, passports, or other important documents.").

105   Only 45% of children under the age of five are registered. *See* UNICEF, Birth Registration (June, 2020), *available at* https://data.unicef.org/topic/child-protection/birth-registration/. In the context of Europe, statelessness is a particular problem for the Roma, notably in the post-Yugoslavia states. *See* Katia Binachini, Protecting Stateless Persons (2018).

Thus, human rights treaties make it clear that no woman should be forced to sever her social bond on the account that she is married to a foreigner or that the husband has changed his nationality. The Convention on the Elimination of All Forms of Discrimination Against Women provides under Article 9 that "neither marriage to an alien nor change of nationality by the husband during marriage shall automatically change the nationality of the wife, render her stateless or force upon her the nationality of the husband."[106]

The prohibitions on gender-based discriminations in relation to the acquisition or loss of nationality signal not only that a social bond shall not be severed on the arbitrary ground of gender, but that the distribution of the social good of membership has to be consistent with the international system of human rights that recognizes the "inherent dignity" of everyone. The Convention on the Elimination of All Forms of Racial Discrimination reinforces the equal dignity of all members of the human family and prohibits any distinction on the basis of race for granting or withdrawing nationality.[107]

Gender- and race-based distinctions for purposes of nationality are attacks on the dignity of the person in two ways. First, such discrimination is in itself an attack on the person's human dignity to the extent that he or she is not regarded as having equal moral worth with members of other social groups. Second, such discrimination is an attack on the dignity of the individuals to the extent that the right to belong—the right to have rights—which gives access to all other rights and goods, social and material, essential to flourishing as human beings, are denied them.

The United Nations Human Rights Council has declared that the right to nationality is a fundamental right (a matter of dignity).[108] What makes it a fundamental right is the fact that, in a world constituted by states with mutually

---

106   Convention on the Elimination of All Forms of Discrimination Against Women (adopted Dec. 18, 1979, entered into force Sept. 3, 1981) 1249 UNTS 13, art. 9(1). Article 9(2) also provides that women shall pass on their citizenship to their children on the same basis as men. There are countries that only allow fathers to confer nationality on their children. Brunei is a good example.

107   International Convention on the Elimination of All Forms of Racial Discrimination (adopted Mar. 7, 1966, entered into force Jan. 4, 1969) 660 UNTS 195, art. 1(3). *See also* Convention on the Rights of Persons with Disability (adopted Dec. 13, 2006, entered into force May 3, 2008) 2515 UNTS, art. 18(1)(a).

108   *See* UNHRC Resolutions on Human Rights and Arbitrary Deprivation of Nationality: Resolution 7/10, U.N. Doc A/HRC/RES/7/10, Mar. 27, 2008; Resolution 10/13, U.N. Doc. A/HRC/RES/10/13, Mar. 26, 2009; Resolution 13/2, U.N. Doc. A/HRC/RES/13/2, Mar. 24, 2010; Resolution 20/5, U.N. Doc. A/HRC/RES/20/5, July 16, 2012. *See also* UNHRC, Human Rights and Arbitrary Deprivation of Nationality: Report of the Secretary-General, U.N. Doc. A/HRC/25/28, Dec. 19, 2013.

exclusive jurisdictions it is the means by which a person is recognized as belonging to a national political community. Human rights, even those said to be inalienable, are realizable through the infrastructures of the state. To be stateless, therefore, is to lack access to that infrastructure.

The UN Secretary-General in his report to the Human Rights Council has also opined that the prohibition of arbitrary deprivation of nationality has become a principle of customary international law.[109] The notion of "arbitrary deprivation" applies not only to the arbitrary withdrawal of nationality, but to the arbitrary denials of acquisition of nationality as well. What makes a process arbitrary is not merely non-compliance with the applicable domestic law and procedure,[110] but also inconsistency with applicable conventional and customary international human rights norms and regimes.[111] The notion of "arbitrary deprivation" should, therefore, be understood as a process that fails to acknowledge the special tie or social bond that the individual has with the state and co-members of the community that the rank of nationality is meant to vindicate.

The importance of "special tie" in terms of a right to membership (even if short of a right to citizenship) is affirmed in various human rights documents including the Convention Relating to the Status of Stateless Persons. Article 27, for example, provides that a stateless person has the right to an identity document from his/her state of habitual residence.[112] And under Article 28, the stateless are entitled to travel documents that enable them to leave and return.[113]

However, the notion of special tie or social bond that gives a right to membership also entitles one to abandon that membership when that bond does not seem to work for the particular individual. Indeed, international human rights law acknowledges and enshrines this right. Thus, Article 15(2) of the UDHR declares without any qualification that no one shall be "denied the right

---

109   UNHCR, Human Rights and Arbitrary Deprivation of Nationality: Report of the Secretary General, UN Doc. A/HRC/13/34, Dec. 14 2009, paras. 19–22.

110   See Jorunn Brandvolle, *Deprivation of Nationality: Limitations on Rendering Persons Stateless under International Law, in* Nationality and Statelessness, *supra* note 60, at 194–216. ("Any decision to deprive a person of his or her nationality must also follow certain procedural and substantive standards to avoid being arbitrary. Among the procedural standards to be followed are the right to have the reasoned decision issued in writing, open to administrative or judicial review and subject to an effective remedy." *Id.* at 197).

111   Obvious grounds of arbitrariness in this regard are decisions based on race, color, national or ethnic origin, and descent. *See also* Reduction of Statelessness Convention, art. 9.

112   Status of Stateless Persons, art. 27.

113   Status of Stateless Persons, art. 28.

to change his nationality."[114] This right is linked to other human rights such as the right of persons to leave their country.[115]

6   Conclusion

The world is a common place where human beings are both joined and separated. That process of separation and joining manifests in, and reconciles, our two claims about human rights: their universality and specificity at the same time. The notion of the "inalienability" of rights captures the universality of rights at a general and abstract level. It affirms the equality of humans (in their embodied self, their needs for bare life, and their need and desire to present and constitute themselves). This is the commonality that the notion of inalienability and universality are meant to capture.

However, humans are not abstract beings. They live in a specific place at a specific time within a specific culture. Hence, the universality of rights will have to be vindicated in the particular person with a particular history living in a particular time and space. The "human" of which we talk and for whom we care has a specificity that defines him or her.[116]

In an international order of states with mutually exclusive jurisdictions, it is the right to nationality that makes it possible for people to present themselves both in words and in action as specific individuals with constitutive commitments. In the process of belonging and interaction with others, an individual creates a specific person in a place and at a time. It is in this irreplaceable particularity that a human being has worth or value. Humanity does not have dignity, human beings do.[117] To quote Judith Butler, "the human as a social

---

114   Article 15(2) UDHR.

115   *See* Article 13(2) UDHR: "Everyone has a right to leave any country." *See also* ICCPR, art. 12(2).

116   Macready, Hannah Arendt and the Fragility of Human Dignity *supra* note 30 at 56. "The common world makes stance possible." *Id.* "The world gathers us as human beings (stature) and yet separates us as individuals (status)." *Id.* Arendt was keen to emphasize that the notion of human dignity as an intrinsic, universal principle leaves out an important dimension of dignity—its particularity. That particularity is based on the fact of "human plurality." Arendt reconciles the universal and particular dimensions of dignity with her emphasis that to the extent that humanity exists it is because specific human beings living in specific circumstances exist.

117   *See* Arendt, The Human Condition, *supra* note 23, at 8 ("Plurality is the condition of human actions because we are all the same, that is, human, in such a way that nobody is ever the same as anyone else who ever lived, lives and will live.") And, at another point

being" requires "a place and a community in order to be free."[118] Perhaps this is also what John Douglas Macready meant when he notes that for Arendt "[h]uman beings had dignity only insofar as there was a common space that they could enter as equals and exhibit their unique human talents."[119]

If human dignity is to be guaranteed in a world where every inch of the globe is carved into mutually exclusive territorial jurisdictions, the international community needs to ensure that, as a legal matter, there are no surplus people, no "nowhere people." An international order that requires that everyone submit himself/herself to the coercive power of a state and yet continues to produce "surplus" people cannot be legitimate.

The primary social good that we distribute to one another is the social good of membership in some human community.[120] Membership in a national community (via nationality) is a primary social good of immense importance. It is the means for accessing all other goods, material or social.[121] On this account, statelessness is an attack on the very conditions that ensure the integrity, the dignity, of the person. If the international community of states, which expects every individual to submit herself to the coercive of power of a state, is to honor and defend the dignity of individuals, it must ensure that every individual has access to the most basic right, the right of membership – *the right to have rights.*

---

in the book, Arendt makes the same point with an oft quoted observation that "men, not Man, live on the earth and inhabit the world." *Id.* at 7.

118   Judith Butler, Parting Ways: Jewishness and the Critique of Zionism 147 (2013).

119   Macready, Hannah Arendt and the Fragility of Human Dignity, *supra* note 30, at 55. *See* Arendt, Totalitarianism, *supra* note 22, at 288 ("From the beginning the paradox involved in the declaration of inalienable human rights was that it reckoned with an 'abstract' human being who seemed to exist nowhere.").

120   Walzer, Spheres of Justice, *supra* note 33, at 31 ("The primary good that we distribute to one another is membership in some human community.").

121   The notion of nationality as a primary social good is explained above. *See* text accompanying notes 39 and 40.

CHAPTER 5

Human Dignity in International Law from a Chinese Traditional Cultural Perspective

*Guiguo Wang**

1 Introduction

Human dignity is written into the UN Charter and many other international treaties and has hence been recognized as an obligation of states under international law. Like most international law prescriptions, human dignity is rooted in the national laws of states and can be traced back to the ancient times of human history. As such, it must be a shared value of the whole humankind. This chapter will examine the environment and processes in which it came into being, grew into maturity and is recognized as an international law obligation. It argues that the New Haven School of Jurisprudence has made significant contributions to the realization of human dignity. The Chinese civilization is one of the main civilizations in the world. The question is whether human dignity is also recognized in the Chinese civilization as an inherent value and entitlement of humans. China is a contracting party to the UN Charter and most of the international treaties that recognize human dignity as an international law obligation. The Chinese traditional culture plays an important part in contemporary Chinese foreign policy, national decision makings (including law making) and the life of the Chinese masses. Therefore, where the Chinese traditional culture supports or recognizes human dignity as a shared value, it is likely that it will be enforced, as an international obligation, within China and that China will likely, through its foreign policies and otherwise, help realize human dignity in the world. This chapter will further examine the main schools of Chinese traditional culture to determine if human dignity was appreciated in ancient China, and, if yes, whether the ways and means of its recognition differed from those of Western countries. It argues that human dignity was

* President of the Zhejiang University Academy of International Strategy and Law and University Professor of Law, Guanghua Law School, Zhejiang University, Hangzhou, China; Eason-Weinmann Chair of International and Comparative Law, Emeritus, School of Law, Tulane University, New Orleans, USA; J.S.D. (Yale), LL.M. (Columbia); email: gwang29@tulane.edu.

much emphasized in Chinese traditional culture, though their ways and means for achieving human dignity differed from those of Western cultures. It further argues that Chinese traditional culture and Western cultures can complement and supplement one another for the realization of human dignity for human-kind, thereby contributing to world peace.

I am writing this piece to celebrate the seventieth birthday of Professor Siegfried Wiessner, Professor of Law and Director of the LL.M./J.S.D. Program in Intercultural Human Rights at St. Thomas University, College of Law, Florida, USA. Time flies! Professor Siegfried and I were classmates at Yale Law School under the supervision of our mentor Professor W. Michael Reisman in the early 1980s. It's like yesterday. I remember vividly the discussions and debates among ourselves and with Professor Reisman in class. Even at that time, Siegfried struck me as a deep thinker with sophisticated philosophical ana-lytical skills – a rare, but essential quality for scholarship. Ever since, Professor Wiessner has devoted himself to the study of human dignity and human rights issues as a leading exponent of the New Haven School of Jurisprudence. He has helped introduce the New Haven School of Jurisprudence to Asian countries. I recall that at Professor Reisman's seventieth birthday, we decided to hold a conference on the New Haven School of Jurisprudence at City University of Hong Kong the following year. Professor Reisman, Siegfried and a number of students of Professor Reisman in Asia, the United States and Europe partic-ipated in the conference. It was so successful that it eventually became an annual event with the sponsorship of the Yale Law School and other partners and extended from Hong Kong to the Mainland of China. Last year, we held the 12th International Conference on New Haven School of Jurisprudence and International Law at Zhejiang University sponsored by Yale Law School, Zhejiang University Guanghua Law School, and Tulane University School of Law. At each conference, participants benefitted greatly from Siegfried and other members of the New Haven School of Jurisprudence.

In the circumstance, I thought it would be appropriate to write a piece on human dignity. The concept of human dignity is deeply rooted in all human societies. Chinese culture and tradition for over five thousand years reflect, though in different form, the value of human dignity. This article will first review the basic features of human dignity and its relation to other human rights. Then it will examine the contributions made by the New Haven School of Jurisprudence in promoting human dignity. The New Haven School posits as its goal a public order of human dignity; in the third section, this article will examine the teachings of Chinese traditional culture in relation to human dig-nity and compare them with those of the New Haven School of Jurisprudence. Section four, the conclusion, will argue that human dignity is a shared value of all cultures and that though different communities may appreciate human dignity differently, this diversity of culture will not diminish the force of human dignity as an international obligation. It also argues that as an international obligation and shared value by all humans, the essential features of human dignity must remain unchanged and observed in all cultures.

2   Human Dignity as an International Obligation

Human dignity is contained in the Preamble of the Charter of the United Nations, which states that "we the peoples of the United Nations" are "determined" "to reaffirm faith in fundamental human rights, in the dignity and worth of the human person, in the equal rights of men and women and of nations large and small."[1] It was then included in Article 1 of the Universal Declaration of Human Rights (hereinafter "UDHR"), stating that "All human beings are born free and equal in dignity and rights. They are endowed with reason and conscience and should act towards one another in a spirit of brotherhood."[2] As human dignity is so important and inherent in every human being, even those deprived of liberty must be treated with dignity. On this, Article 10 of the International Covenant on Civil and Political Rights ("ICCPR")[3] provides that "[a]ll persons deprived of their liberty shall be treated with humanity and with respect for the inherent dignity of the human person." A similar expression can be found in the International Covenant on Economic, Social and Cultural Rights ("ICESCR"),[4] in Article 13(1), where the parties agreed that "education shall be directed to the full development of the human personality and the sense of its dignity." It is hence evident that human dignity is well documented in international treaties as a widely recognized principle of international law.

As human dignity is also rooted in national culture, tradition and law there are bound to be diverse understandings of it. Some may consider it as "an antecedent, a consequence, a value, a principle, an experience, and both a contingent and non-contingent exhibition" which can be assessed from

---

1   Charter of the United Nations, *available at* https://www.un.org/en/about-us/un-charter (visited on 9 July 2022).

2   Universal Declaration of Human Rights, *available at* https://www.un.org/en/about-us /universal-declaration-of-human-rights (visited on 9 July 2022).

3   The International Covenant on Civil and Political Rights, *available at* https://treaties.un.org /doc/treaties/ 1976/03/19760323%2006-17%20am/ch_iv_04.pdf (visited on 9 July 2022).

4   The International Covenant on Economic, Social and Cultural Rights, *available at* https:// treaties.un.org/doc/ treaties/1976/01/19760103%2009-57%20pm/ch_iv_03.pdf (visited on 9 July 2022).

"philosophical, legal, pragmatic, psychological, behavioral, and cultural per-spectives."[5] When doing the examination, the question of what human dignity is and what contents it includes is a prerequisite. In assessing human dignity, many Western commentators rely on Kant's kingdom of ends theory:

> In the kingdom of ends everything has a price or a dignity. What has a price can be replaced by something else as its equivalent; what ... is raised above all price and therefore admits of no equivalent has a dignity. ... Morality is the condition under which alone a rational being can be an end in itself, since only through this is it possible to be a law-giving member in the kingdom of ends. Hence morality, and humanity insofar as it is capable of morality, is that which alone has dignity.[6]

Based on Kant's theory, human dignity is considered the basis for other human rights since "it is by virtue of our status as beings with dignity that we possess and should be accorded what we denominate as basic human rights."[7] At the same time, humans must also assume obligations toward each other. For that, it is argued "what we recognize as our obligations we recognize as ours in the sense that we do not merely adhere or conform to them, but own or commit to them as expressions of who and what we are."[8]

Human dignity is viewed as concerning the whole life of humans starting from one's birth, to development, to death. A commentator comparing human flourishing with non-human flourishing, concludes that "human flourishing is much more individualized – that is, diverse and multi-faceted. Human flourishing is not confined primarily to matters of physical development and reproduction, but embraces intentionality, experience, and culture. Whereas one person may flourish in an academic environment, another will flourish when her athletic capacities and interests are able to develop, and a third will flourish when musical talents are encouraged."[9]

In any event, it is often argued that human dignity "is the kind of thing that one can have faith in. It does not need to account for itself by pointing beyond itself to a feature of human nature, reason, or the divine. It is not derivative

---

5   David J. Mattson & Susan G. Clark, *Human Dignity in Concept and Practice*, 44 Policy Sciences 303–319, at 305 (2011).

6   Immanuel Kant, Groundwork of the Metaphysic of Morals 42 (Mary Gregor trans., Cambridge University Press 1998), quoted from John Kleinig & Nicholas G. Evans, *Human Flourishing, Human Dignity, and Human Rights*, 32 L. & Philosophy 539–564, at 553 (September 2013).

7   Kleinig & Evans, *Human Flourishing*, *supra* note 6, at 559–560.

8   *Id.* at 562.

9   *Id.* at 542.

of these features, nor is it cultivated or produced. It is, rather, what defines humans as part of the human family."[10] Human dignity is also considered as the source of political values such as freedom, justice, and peace, the violation of which would lead to outrage and disunity of the society concerned.[11] This raises the question whether human dignity is part of human rights and if not, what its relationship with human rights is. On this issue, some commentators argue that, at least in the Western tradition, human dignity and human rights are two different things, and as such human dignity "justifies the bestowing of rights. ... Simply by being human we are all intrinsically special, thus, we deserve rights, that is, entitlements."[12] Such rights are inalienable or unconditional claims or even conditional, but still strong claims.[13] As rights are demanded in most cases by individuals from their governments, the right holders do not owe any obligation toward other members of the society.

Based on the above, these Western scholars aver that human dignity is inherent in every human being and is the grounding for other rights. As such, it is different from other enumerated human rights, though they are related. Two Chinese scholars, however, consider human dignity as part of human rights. After reviewing and consequently, disagreeing with a number of theories of Western scholars, they argue that, as part of human rights, a violation of human dignity may cause two kinds of harm, namely, "an insulting action and an insulting state. An insulting action causes damage to the victim's self or individuality, positioning him/her in the horrible state of being lorded over, wherein he/she has neither the ability to protect himself/herself nor hope of external assistance. ... An insulting state can be defined as the state in which the complete loss of control of self is sparked by absolute poverty, family tragedy, the tortures of illness, mental breakdown, etc."[14] In their view, where human dignity is considered a right or part of human rights, "it takes as prerequisite the human inviolability and spiritual vulnerability, which apply to everyone, instead of the ability to choose rationally, which has far lesser coverage."[15] So far, this theory does not have as much support as the theory of dichotomy between human dignity and human rights.

---

10   Gaymon Bennet, Technicians of Human Dignity: Bodies, Souls, and the Making of Intrinsic Worth (Just Ideas) 142 (Fordham University Press, 2015).

11   *Ibid.*

12   Mattson & Clark, *supra* note 5, at 306.

13   *Ibid.*

14   Gan Shaoping & Zhang Lin, *Human Dignity as a Right*, 4 Frontiers of Philosophy in China 370–384, at 380–381 (2009).

15   *Id.* at 381.

No matter what view one may hold, it is evident that everyone considers human dignity as an important matter to humankind. In this circumstance, to ascertain the common ground and shared understanding of the term would be beneficial. For that, some scholars argue that "[a]ppeals that simply rouse emotions can motivate and bring attention to issues, but such appeals may not provide enough orientation for people to negotiate widely supported and effective policies. ... We assume that the global prospects for achieving a commonwealth of human dignity would be enhanced by a concept of dignity that allowed for broad participation and contextual sensitivity in application, yet was specific enough, transcending local contexts, to allow for a productive global conversation."[16] Professor Schachter long ago proposed a list of 12 items as contents of human dignity. It could be divided into two categories, "one relates to conduct and ideas that directly offend or denigrate the worth and dignity of individuals; the second, to conduct and ideas that are implicitly incompatible with the basic ideas of the inherent dignity and worth of human persons."[17] Despite the fact that there cannot be a clear line between Schachter's two categories, what is noteworthy is that Schachter's list of human dignity items is not confined to official acts and statements but also includes nonofficial actions, inactions and expressions. For Schachter, in order to have human dignity recognized and implemented, some concrete meaning must be given to it, because otherwise "we cannot easily reject a specious use of the concept, nor can we without understanding its meaning draw specific implications for relevant conduct."[18]

It is submitted that human dignity is an international obligation as it is found in the UN Charter and other conventions. As such, the meaning of human dignity, its scope and application should be determined in accordance with customary international law – the Vienna Convention on the Law of Treaties, in particular its Articles 31 and 32. Accordingly, where the words "human rights" and "human dignity" appear in the same article of the same treaty, they cannot be treated as meaning the same thing. In other words, human dignity and human rights cannot and should not be interpreted as carrying the same meaning. This having been said, it does not mean that human dignity and human rights are totally alienated or separated from each other. To the contrary, they are interrelated and mutually dependent on each other. For instance, without human rights, human dignity may become an empty concept; and without human dignity, human rights may lose their basis. It is also

---

16   Mattson & Clark, *supra* note 5, at 305.

17   Oscar Schachter, *Human Dignity as a Normative Concept*, 77 Am. J. Int'l L. 848, at 852 (1983).

18   *Id.* at 849.

submitted that human dignity is recognized as an important or essential value in most, if not all, national societies out of the need and development of inter-dependence among humans – the issue to be further examined later.

3   The New Haven School's Contributions

The public order of human dignity is the theme of the New Haven School of Jurisprudence. To realize this goal, the New Haven School has developed "a systematic jurisprudence"[19] by advocating the examination of the actual pro-cesses of decision-making rather than just its formal procedures.[20] This is extremely important because decisions and fundamental policies in almost every community are not made exclusively in the formal settings established by laws and prescriptions. They are more often than not made "in a series of informal meetings taking place in country clubs, business lunches, periodic meetings of merchant associations and so on," whilst the body authorized under the law "really does no more than validate or promulgate the decisions and policies clarified elsewhere."[21]

An important contribution of the New Haven School towards human dig-nity is, based on the Universal Declaration of Human Rights (UDHR), its clarifi-cation of the essential values, aspirations inherent in all human beings, which include well-being, affection, respect, power, wealth, enlightenment, skill and rectitude.[22] This list is not regarded as exhaustive but "as a partial indicator of the full complexity of a social equilibrium that would function in harmony with the requirements of human dignity."[23] The purpose of clarifying the val-ues is to spell out the goals and future directions of human dignity so that decision makers will keep them in mind when making decisions.

For the New Haven School, "the clarification of goal is addressed to anyone who is interested in reducing or eliminating self-contradictory impacts on the social process. We take for granted in some cases that the effect of considering goal values will be to dissolve an apparent consensus, and to bring into view

---

19   1 Harold D. Lasswell & Myres S. McDougal, Jurisprudence for a Free Society 167, 728 (New Haven Press, 1992).

20   W. Michael Reisman, The Quest for World Order and Human Dignity in the Twenty-First Century: Constitutive Process and Individual Commitment General Course on Public International Law, Hague Academy of International Law 101–188 (Martinus Nijhoff, 2012).

21   W. Michael Reisman, Jurisprudence: Understanding and Shaping Law – Cases, Readings, Commentary 4 (New Haven Press, 1987).

22   Lasswell & McDougal, *supra* note 19, at 738.

23   *Id.* at 739.

many previously unsuspected differences."[24] Also, the values reflected in the form of human dignity are shared values. As the founders of the New Haven School stated, the "sharing" carries to two sets of meaning, i.e., distributive and formative. "The distributive reference is to participation in the control of value outcomes, described according to the degree of equality or inequality. The formative meaning suggests that the amount of a given value available for sharing may be augmented. In general, we are in favor of higher levels of outcome since we are concerned about the size of the cake as well as the proportional size of the slices."[25] That means that New Haven School does not only concern itself about achieving a higher degree of human dignity for humankind as a whole but also about ensuring each person his/her own share of such values.

For the realization of the values embodied in human dignity, it involves a process of decision-making through which values are shaped. According to Professor Michael Reisman, every decision-making process is a matter of communication:

> All communication involves the mediation of subjectivities or messages. What is distinctive about prescriptive or lawmaking communications is that rather than transmitting a single message, they carry simultaneously *three* co-ordinate communication flows in a fashion akin to the coaxial cables of telephonic communications: the policy content, the authority signal, and the control intention. Unless each of these flows is present and effectively mediated to the relevant audience, a prescription does not result. Equally important, even if the three components are initially communicated, *they must continue to be communicated* for the prescription, as such, to endure; if one or more of the components should cease to be communicated, the prescription undergoes a type of desuetude and is terminated.[26] (*italics in original*)

To ensure effective shaping and sharing of the values of human dignity, attention must be paid to the three communication flows identified by Reisman. It can be said that the value shaping and sharing, just like lawmaking and law enforcement, are two parts of the same decision. In this decision-making process, one must keep in mind the role that the authority and control elements play as well as the differences between the myth system and the operational

---

24   *Ibid.*
25   *Id.* at 740.
26   Reisman, The Quest for World Order, *supra* note 20, at 124.

code.[27] At the same time, the New Haven School considers that there are seven components in each decision-making, namely, intelligence, promotion, prescription, invocation, application, termination and appraisal, and it advocates their application in decision-making processes.[28]

The importance of clarification by the New Haven School of the values embodied in human dignity can hardly be exaggerated. It was the first time that these values were identified and clarified as components of human dignity, which enables imbuing it with concrete meaning. These values of course do not carry the same weight for every person, and not every person is able to possess all of them at a given time. Also, the enjoyment of some values may depend on the realization of others. For instance, power is more important in most cases in determining the outcomes of other values, which makes the disposition of power an important issue. According to the New Haven School, the human community shares the above-mentioned values which are both distributive and formative.[29] The distributive category of values concerns the participation in determining the valued outcomes and hence is about the disposition of power – an equal or unequal disposition of power, as in the real world, the power of a given participant may differ from another, and the degree of control one may exercise varies. The formative values available for sharing may be augmented and the New Haven School is "in favor of higher levels of outcome" since it is "concerned about the size of the cake as well as the proportional size of the slices."[30] Some commentators argue that amongst these eight values, "affection, respect, rectitude, and power have been called deference values, that is, values with particular relevance to social relations or the creation of social space within which people can realize their dignity. People seek and share these values through cultural as well as institutional arrangements, in ways that are shaped by their expectations, desires, and perceived needs."[31] In the view of some commentators, according to the New Haven School, "a commonwealth of human dignity is achieved when: (1) as many people as possible

---

27 W. Michael Reisman, *International Law Making: A Process of Communication, in* Myth System and Operational Code: Selected Essays of W. Michael Reisman 140–171, and 75–96 (Guiguo Wang ed., Law Press, Beijing, China, 2019).

28 Reisman, The Quest for World Order, *supra* note 20, at 150. Among the components, intelligence refers to "the gathering, processing, and dissemination of information relevant to making social choices", whilst invocation is "the provisional characterization of a certain action as inconsistent with a prescription or law that has been established, accompanied by the demand that an appropriate community institution act." *Ibid.*

29 Lasswell & McDougal, *supra* note 19, at 740.

30 *Ibid.*

31 Mattson & Clark, *supra* note 5, at 310.

are involved in deciding what the community ought to produce in terms of both welfare and deference values, (2) the community is successful in producing these outcomes, and (3) the people of that community share broadly in the benefits. This was their formula for achieving dignity, not the dignity itself."[32]

The New Haven School's approach to human dignity has gained support as people "find a value-based frame to be useful in understanding the subjective experience of dignity, to crafting policies to foster a commonwealth of human dignity, and to evaluating policies and practices both before and after they have been implemented. ... Values and value dynamics provide a fundamental framework for talking about the experience of dignity, because they encompass convergent forces arising from the common human experience (e.g., existential concerns) as well as divergent forces arising from different contexts."[33] As with other theories, whether legal or otherwise, the formation, evolution and application of the New Haven School are inescapably affected by the development and trends of the world. Working immediately after the Second World War, the founders of the New Haven School had experienced the suffering of that war and discerned that unless human dignity was given proper attention and could be realized, the development of the world would suffer difficulties.

In the early years of the New Haven School, the world was dominated by the Cold War. Yet its founders, with their keen and sagacious perception, pointed out that "the whole of humankind does today constitute a community, in the sense of interdetermination and interdependence," and believed that the New Haven School must extend "its focus of inquiry to include this largest community, embracing the whole earth-space arena."[34] In their view, "this largest earth-space community process operates through many different lesser communities – from local, through regional and national, to global."[35] Interdependence among nations and other participants of international decision-making or globalization is therefore the basis of the formulations of the New Haven School.

Despite the ups and downs, globalization is still the main trend of the world today, in which the process of interdependence among nations, international organizations, non-governmental organizations, other entities and individuals can hardly be exaggerated. Matters that could be effectively dealt with by sovereign States themselves in the past can no longer be handled without the assistance of other countries and international organizations. At the same

---

32   *Id.* at 310–311.
33   *Id.* at 315.
34   Lasswell & McDougal, *supra* note 19, at 188.
35   *Ibid.*

time, some matters that used to be international in nature must be managed at the national level; in other words, their success depends on the national governments' actions and inactions, legal or political, toward their own lesser communities and private persons. In short, almost every aspect of human life, including birth, aging, sickness and death is a "public good" and must be handled from a world perspective. In pursuing the ultimate goal of human dignity, the New Haven School advocates examination of the social processes of local communities and of the world community in the sense of interdetermination and interdependence. This is a faithful reflection of the reality of this highly globalized world.

4 Chinese Traditional Culture and Human Dignity

Chinese culture is one of the most comprehensive and profound cultures in the world. Chinese traditional culture still has strong impacts on the official decision-making and the life of the Chinese community today. With a history of five thousand years and more, it is extremely difficult, if not impossible, to define what the Chinese traditional culture is or to precisely identify those writings that could be considered to be essential parts of it, let alone to examine in detail their substance. In consequence, those teachings of Chinese traditional culture discussed herein are only the tip of an iceberg. This article will discuss some of the central teachings of Daoism, Confucianism and the New Neo-Confucianism. Daoism and Confucianism have had strong influence throughout Chinese history. In modern-day China, decision-making by government, enterprises and individuals, as well as the behavior of individuals, still bear the marks of the teachings of these philosophies.[36] The New Neo-Confucianism, developed by the late Professor Feng Youlan, is one of the most influential philosophical theories in modern China. Its main contribution is the creation of a comprehensive philosophical theory embracing Daoism, Confucianism and Neo-Confucianism.[37] But Chinese traditional culture is not

---

36   For instance, it was concluded that more than 600 quotations of Chinese traditional culture were made by Xi Jinping between 2013 and 2018 relating to subjects ranging from treatment of people, governance, ethics, foreign policies to rule of law. For details, see Xi Jinping Applies Classics (Xi Jinping Yongdian, Yang Lixin ed., People's Daily Press, 2015), Vol. 1 and Vol. 2 (2018). Also, there is a website for Chinese officials which contains all the references made by Xi Jinping. For details, see https://www.12371.cn/special/blqs/dssj /36xjpyd/ (visited on 11 July 2022).

37   The theory of New Neo-Confucianism is reflected in the following writings by Professor Feng Youlan: A New Treatise on Neo-Confucianism (Xin Li Xue) (Changsha Commercial

confined to the teachings mentioned above. For instance, Buddhism, which is not discussed herein, has influenced Chinese society. The teachings of Daoism, which may be studied as theology, are examined in this article as a philosophical theory.

As discussed earlier, human dignity is inherent in everyone and is therefore an inalienable entitlement of every person, notwithstanding that its contents have been evolving through the history. As such, is human dignity reconcilable with Chinese traditional culture? If yes, to what extent and in what aspects, may Chinese traditional culture reflect the essential components of human dignity? This section will examine these issues by reference to the value-based analysis of the New Haven School.

4.1   *The Dao and Virtue*

According to the teachings of Daoism,[38] everything must follow its *Dao* (way or course) for its coming into being, its maturation and its death. The *Dao* is "something undefined and complete, coming into existence before the Heaven and Earth. How still it was and formless, standing alone, and undergoing no change, reaching everywhere and in no danger (of being exhausted)! It may be regarded as the Mother of all things."[39] The father of Daoism, Lao Zi said: "I do not know its name, and I give it the designation of the *Dao*. Making an effort (further) to give it a name I call it The Great." Neo-Confucianism and the New Neo-Confucianism describe the *Dao* as *Li* (rational principle or law), and in accordance with their views, everything must be in compliance with its own *Li* or it may not be able to exist, develop or reach its perfection.

As the *Dao* is governed by and reflects nature, "[a]ll things stream from the *Dao* and are nourished by *Virtue*. They receive their forms according to the nature of each and are completed according to the circumstances of their

---

Press, 1939); A New Treatise on Practical Affairs (Xin Shi Lun) (Shanghai Commercial Press, 1940); A New Treatise on the Way of Life (Xin Shi Xun) (Shanghai Kaiming Press, 1940); A New Treatise on the Nature of Man (Xin Yuan Ren) (Chongqing Commercial Press, 1943); A New Treatise on Chinese Philosophy (Xin Yuan Dao) (Chongqing Commercial Press, 1945); and A New Treatise on the Methodology of Metaphysics (Xin Zhi Yan) (Shanghai Commercial Press, 1946). All these six books were included in the Classics of Contemporary Chinese Academic Research (Zhong Guo Xian Dai Xue Shu Jing Dian, Liu Mengxi ed., Hebei Education Press 1996).

38   Daoism was created by Lao Zi. Scholars in the Song and Ming Dynasties formulated their theory of Neo-Confucianism based on the teachings of Confucianism, Daoism and Buddhism and further developed the theory of Confucianism. One of the features of Neo-Confucianism is to replace *Dao* with *Li*, something which is shared by the New Neo-Confucianism.

39   Lao Zi, Dao De Jing, ch. 25.

condition. Therefore, all things without exception honor the *Dao*, and exalt *Virtue*. This honoring of the *Dao* and exalting *Virtue* are not the result of any ordination, but because they are what it is."[40] The New Neo-Confucianism adopts a similar attitude: "All things in the world can be comprehended by means of the *Li*. If a thing exists, there must be a *Li* to it. ... Events and things are the actual instances of their *Li*. Since the *Li* is always what it is, it makes no difference whether or not humans know that the *Li* is there, nor whether or not there is an actual instance in existence."[41] "*Li*" in the New Neo-Confucianism carries the same meaning as "*Dao*" of Daoism. In addition to following the *Li*, things may exist or come into being only when the relevant conditions (*Shi*) exist. *Shi* refers to the necessary conditions under which a thing happens and develops. In other words, the emergence and development of a thing must be in accordance with the relevant *Li*. At the same time, there must be necessary and objective conditions (*Shi*) or *Virtue* to enable the thing to emerge and develop. *Virtue* or *Shi* is the necessary condition for a thing to begin and end. For instance, to make an automobile requires, in addition to discovery of the way (scientific theory) for making automobiles, the needed materials, tools and skills – the necessary conditions – which are referred to as *Virtue*. With *Virtue* or conditions evolving, the thing in question will progress or regress. Accordingly, human dignity today must differ from that of ancient China. Yet, Chinese traditional culture can still shine light on the thoughts of the historic Chinese cultural community relating to human dignity.

4.2 *Well-being*

The New Haven School of Jurisprudence considers that well-being of humans includes "the right to 'life, liberty and security of person' and condemnation of 'torture', 'cruel' or 'inhuman' treatment or punishment, as well as the 'right to rest and leisure' and 'social security.'"[42] Chinese traditional culture regards humans as important as the heaven and earth. In the view of Daoism, there are four most important and great things in the universe, namely, the *Dao*, heaven, earth and humans. All these four things must follow certain norms for their existence. In the view of Daoism, the human "takes his law from the Earth; the Earth takes its law from Heaven; Heaven takes its law from the *Dao*; the law of the *Dao* is the nature"[43] or natural law. The New Neo-Confucianism led by the late Professor Feng Youlan argues that "[s]ince we are living in the same world,

---

40   *Id.*, ch. 51.
41   Feng Youlan, A New Treatise on Chinese Philosophy, *supra* note 37, at 795–796.
42   Lasswell & McDougal, *supra* note 19, at 738.
43   Lao Zi, *supra* note 39, ch. 25.

nobody can pursue his own happiness without the influence of others. For the sake of one's own happiness, one must be on good terms with others and help others with the expectation that others will help him. At the same time, for the sake of one's own happiness, one must restrain his desires and suppress any want that may lead to bad results. This is the result of the rational order of the people. But the basis is to maximize the happiness of all people."[44] Thus, the desire for happiness or well-being of humankind is an essential value under Chinese traditional culture.

As humans are important in the universe, they should be treated properly, their well-being must be protected. In order to do so, they must treat others well according to Chinese traditional culture, which states, "One must not have the bad qualities in himself, and then requires that others shall not have such qualities in themselves."[45] Unless humans treat each other mutually well, there will be disasters like in cases where heaven and earth are not treated properly, there would be natural disasters.

4.3 *Respect*

For the New Haven School, respect is a component of human dignity which refers to the precept that "all human beings are born free and equal in dignity and right" and that "everyone is entitled to all rights and freedoms ... without distinction of any kind."[46] One of the essential teachings of Chinese traditional culture is that people must treat each other with respect. Confucius, for instance, once said that "[t]he superior man in the world does not set his mind either for anything or against anything; what is right he will follow."[47] Then what is right? In Chinese traditional culture, there is a rule, which is still followed, that those dead should be given proper respect and should not be ashamed. On this, *Li Ji*,[48] an important component of Chinese traditional culture says that "[w]hen there is a funeral in the neighborhood, do not pound

---

44   Feng Youlan, *Comparison of the Thoughts in the Eighteenth and Nineteenth Century in Europe, in* The Collective Works of San Song Tang 95 (Three Pine Tree House, Feng Youlan ed., Peking University Press, 1984).

45   *The Great Learning, in* The Four Books (James Legge trans., Culture Book Co., 1997, with necessary modifications by this author, hereinafter "*The Great Learning*"), ch. 9, at 25.

46   Lasswell & McDougal, *supra* note 19, at 738.

47   *Confucian Analects, in* The Four Books (James Legge trans., Culture Book Co., 1997, with necessary modifications by this author, hereinafter "*Confucian Analects*"), Book 4, ch. 10.

48   Li Ji is a book that contains an ancient set of norms regulating the behavior of private persons and government officials. In ancient China, these rules were regarded as natural laws with binding force. For a discussion on this issue, see Ju-Ao Mei, *China and the Rule of Law*, 5 Pacific Aff. 863–872, at 868 (1932).

rice with work songs (shanty); when there is a funeral in the village, do not sing songs there."[49] Confucius set an example for people on this: "When the Master was eating by the side of a mourner, he never ate to the full" and "he would not sing on that day but he would be weeping."[50] Why did Confucius act like that and why were people expected to behave the same way? This is because according to Chinese traditional culture people should respect the dignity of others, in particular the dead.

Not only should dead humans be respected, but also they should be treated equally. In ancient times, where a person's family member died, the person was required to mourn the dead person. The time that a person should mourn depended on the dead person's social status. "The one year's mourning was for the great officers, whilst the three years' mourning extended to the Son of Heaven (the Emperor). In the mourning for a father or mother, there was no difference between the noble and the mean."[51] Chinese traditional culture emphasizes respect for the deceased because on the one hand a person is dead and should be allowed to rest in peace and on the other hand, it is also respect for the family and relatives of the deceased. The latter is more important. When a person experiences the pain and grief of losing a loved one and yet his/her neighbors are singing, he/she will feel disrespected and not understood. This will in turn be seen as a violation of the person's dignity and rights.

4.4   Affection

Affection under the New Haven School of Jurisprudence refers to the "right to marry and to found a family" and the "right to a nationality."[52] "Family" has a very special place in Chinese traditional culture, according to which only those whose families are harmonious may be able to serve in a governing position. In this regard, *The Great Learning* taught that "those wishing to govern well their states, they should first manage well their families. Those wishing to manage well their families, they should first cultivate themselves."[53] The theory underpinning this teaching is that "Where the family is a loving family, the whole state becomes a loving state; where the family is courteous, the whole state becomes courteous."[54] Through the process of cultivating individuals and their

---

49   Li Ji, Qu Li Shang, ch. 67.

50   *Confucian Analects, supra* note 47, Book 7, ch. 9.

51   *The Doctrine of the Mean, in* The Four Books (James Legge trans., Culture Book Co., 1997, with necessary modifications by this author, hereinafter *"The Doctrine of the Mean"*), ch. 18.

52   Lasswell & McDougal, *supra* note 19, at 738.

53   *The Great Learning, supra* note 45, ch. 1, at 5.

54   *Id.*, ch. 9, at 24.

families, the entire country would become well governed with love and courtesy. The Book of Poetry says: "They can discharge their duties to their elder brothers. They can discharge their duties to their younger brothers"; with such things going on in the families, "the ruler will discharge his duties to his elder brothers and younger brothers, and then he may teach the people of his state."[55] With examples set by the ruler, his state would be harmonious and peaceful.

Family has always been regarded as the basic unit in the Chinese community. Marriage was not considered a "right", but rather an obligation under Chinese traditional culture. The purpose of getting married is to sustain the continuation of generations. Mencius said, "There are three things which are unfilial, and to have no posterity is the greatest of them."[56] The word "posterity" here refers to male descendants who would carry their family name. In the circumstances, within the basic unit of family, female members could not enjoy equal rights with male members; they should, however, be respected and treated well by their own children. This situation was severely criticized under the influence of modern ideas introduced into the Chinese culture; notwithstanding that, affection remains essential in the Chinese community. It is commonly accepted that where someone does not treat his family members, relatives and friends with affection, that person may not be trusted.

4.5   Power

In ancient China, due to the feudal nature of the community, there could hardly be anything like the "power" element of human dignity articulated by the New Haven School, according to which members of a community are entitled to "take part in the government," "to recognition everywhere as a person before the law," and "to effective remedy by competent national tribunals," the right to "a social and international order."[57] This having been said, it does not mean that a feudal ruler or official would be completely free to do anything he desired. Chinese traditional culture always taught people to become a "superior person" by advocating the principle of reciprocity that "[w]hat you do not like to be done to yourself, do not do to others."[58] It considers the principle of reciprocity as a principle of nature, and that when one exercises the principle of reciprocity, he/her is not far from the *Dao*. Therefore, Daoism's teaching of

---

55   *Id.* at 26.
56   *The Works of Mencius, in* The Four Books (James Legge trans., Culture Book Co., 1997, with necessary modifications by this author), Book IV, Le Low, Part I, ch. 26.
57   Lasswell & McDougal, *supra* note 19, at 738.
58   *The Doctrine of the Mean, supra* note 51, ch. 13.

"[w]ithout acting" does not mean doing nothing. Rather it means that people should behave in accordance with their conscience.

At the same time, Chinese traditional culture emphasizes the role model to be played by those in power and states that "only when the ruler himself is possessed of the good qualities, might he require the good qualities in the people."[59] The Book of Poetry also says, "What rejoiced superior men, parents of the people. They love what the people love; they hate what the people hate."[60] Ancient Chinese metaphorized their governors as parents because according to Chinese traditional culture, those having responsibilities of government are expected to meet the needs of the people. The implication here is that only those officials who could meet the test of loving what the people love and hating what the people hate are good rulers. In assessing "love" or good and "hating" or bad, the principle of justice should be applied. On this matter, a dialogue of the *Confucian Analects* is inspiring: "Tsze-kung asked, 'What do you say of a man who is loved by all the people of his neighborhood?' The Master replied, 'We may not for that accord our approval of him.' 'And what do you say of him who is hated by all the people of his neighborhood?' The Master said, 'We may not for that conclude that he is bad. It is better than either of these cases that the good in the neighborhood love him, and the bad hate him.'"[61] This dialectical analysis of what is good and what is bad by Confucius is instructive. The test of good or bad does not depend on whether everyone considers something as good or bad but depends on whether the thing itself is good or bad by its nature. Then what is the standard or test for determining good and bad?

An example is the teaching of the Book of Poetry, which says that "[t]he admirable, amiable superior men displayed conspicuously their excelling virtue, benefiting their people. The superior men receive what they have from the Heaven, are protected by the Heaven and conduct themselves per the Heaven."[62] In order to be protected by the "heaven," one must have the feeling of commiseration which is regarded as the principle of benevolence, the feeling of shame and dislike, which is regarded as the principle of righteousness, and the feeling of modesty and complaisance, which is regarded as the principle of propriety.[63] Although Chinese traditional culture often refers to "superior man," it considers everyone as equal insofar as one's capacity of becoming a "superior man" is concerned.

---

59   *The Great Learning, supra* note 45, ch. 9, at 25.

60   The Book of Poetry: Xiao Ya – Non Shan You Tai 202 (Situ Bowen ed., Dangdai Shijie Press, 2006).

61   *Confucian Analects, supra* note 47, Book 13, at 311.

62   The Book of Poetry, *supra* note 60, at 334.

63   For reference to these principles, see *The Works of Mencius, supra* note 56, Book 2, Kung-Sun Ch'ow, Part 1, ch. 4.

Once asked a question as to how different he was from others, Mencius replied, "How should I be different from other men! Yao and Shun were just the same as other men."[64] Yao and Shun were ancient emperors before Mencius' time, and they had been loved by their people. Mencius also commented on Shun as to why he had been considered a beloved leader, stating that, "Shun clearly understood the multitude of things and closely observed the relations of humanity. He walked along the path of benevolence and righteousness."[65] On this basis, Mencius concluded that benevolence and propriety distinguished superior men from others, because "[t]he benevolent man loves others. The man of propriety shows respect to others."[66]

Benevolence, propriety, righteousness, reciprocity and love are the most important principles advocated by Chinese traditional culture. Mencius believed that the rulers and ordinary people alike could all observe these principles, as it is in accordance with the principle of nature. In his view, "all things which are the same in kind are like to one another."[67] Then why were humans not an exception to this principle? Mencius argued that "[t]he sage and us are the same in kind." In accordance with Daoism, this would be in compliance with the *Dao* of human dignity. Where individuals are regarded as equals, their right to participation in decision-making should be preserved and protected. In this regard, even though Chinese traditional culture did not use the modern terminology, its teachings do reflect the New Haven's School's theory of power shaping and sharing.

4.6   *Wealth*

In ancient China, land and houses were regarded as valuable properties and for most people those were their only properties, if they were lucky. There was almost no discussion in Chinese traditional culture about the rights of ownership. It does, however, encourage the rulers not to tax the people excessively, as "the accumulation of wealth is the way to scatter the people; and letting it be scattered among them is the way to collect the people."[68] To scatter the people is to drive the people away from supporting the government, because the people did not consider such rulers as having any *virtue*. According to Chinese traditional culture, only those who possess *virtue* could have the support of the people; only those who possess the support of the people could have the

---

64   *Id.*, Book 4, Le Low, Part 2, ch. 32.
65   *Id.*, ch. 19.
66   *Id.*, ch. 28.
67   *Id.*, Book 6, Kaou Tsze, Part 1, ch. 7.
68   *The Great Learning, supra* note 45, ch. 10, at 32.

territory; and only those who possess the territory could have the wealth.[69] Therefore, "the virtuous ruler, by means of his wealth, makes himself more distinguished. The vicious ruler accumulates wealth at the expense of his life."[70] Where the government does not overly tax the people, the people will have more wealth and their standard of living will be improved. This is in a way commensurate with the New Haven School's clarification of wealth as a component of human dignity – "recognition is given to the right to own property and to a 'standard of living adequate for the well-being' of the individual and his family."[71]

4.7   *Enlightenment*

Enlightenment, according to the New Haven School Jurisprudence, is "freedom of opinion and expression" and a right "to seek, receive, and impart information and ideas through any media and regardless of frontiers."[72] Chinese traditional culture does not have the concept of freedom of opinion or expression. It does, however, advocate for the renewal, innovation and dissemination of knowledge. At its beginning, *The Great Learning* states "renovating the people" as its purpose. How could the people be renovated? It is the knowledge and thinking of the people that should be renovated and renewed constantly. The Book of Poetry said, "although Zhou was an ancient state, the ordinance which enlightened it was new."[73] The founder of the Shang Dynasty engraved the following words on his bathtub: "If you can one day renovate yourself, do so from day to day. And let there be daily renovation."[74] The renewal or renovation of knowledge, according to *The Great Learning*, is by extension of knowledge. "Such extension of knowledge lay in the investigation of things."[75] As discussed earlier, Chinese traditional culture focuses on the role model of rulers and superior men. The teachings on renewal of knowledge are hence applicable to all the people. It is submitted that the processes of acquiring and renewing knowledge will help enlighten the community.

4.8   *Skill*

Skill, according to the New Haven School, includes the recognition of the "right to work, to free choice of employment," "to protection against unemployment,"

---

69   *Id.* at 31.
70   *Id.* at 37.
71   Lasswell & McDougal, *supra* note 19, at 738.
72   *Ibid.*
73   *The Great Learning, supra* note 45, ch. 2, at 10.
74   *Ibid.*
75   *Id.*, ch. 1, at 6.

"to education," and "to participate freely in the cultural life of the community, to enjoy the arts and to share in scientific achievement and its benefits."[76] The need of education, in particular, education of the masses, is considered as most important for the community order and harmony. Confucius said, "In teaching there should be no distinction of classes."[77] In ancient China, the wealthy people would invite teachers to teach their children at home. Confucius offered classes himself for the masses and said, "From the man bringing his bundle of dried meat for my teaching upwards, I have never refused instruction to anyone."[78] In those days, teachers made a living by receiving the tuition of students. The above message of Confucius means that he did not care whether or not the payment was adequate and that so long as there were people who wanted to learn and recognized his service (with some dried meat as a token), he would teach them. Following the example set by Confucius, this has become an essential principle of education in China. In addition to formal education, Confucius also emphasized informal learning in life. He said, "When I walk along with two others, they may serve me as my teachers. I will select their good qualities and follow them, their bad qualities and avoid them."[79] Confucius also said, "I have been the whole day without eating, and the whole night without sleeping – occupied with thinking. It was of no use. The better plan is to learn."[80] Confucius is regarded as the god of education. His teachings have far-reaching effects on, including acquisition of skills, all sectors of the Chinese community.

4.9   *Rectitude*

Chinese traditional culture also considers humankind as one of the objects in the universe like the heaven and earth. *Yi Jing*, one of the earliest writings of Chinese traditional culture, says "[t]here are the heaven and earth, then there are all things, There are all things, then there are men and women, there are men and women, then there are husbands and wives, there are husbands and wives, then there are fathers and sons, there are fathers and sons, then there are rulers and ministers, there are rulers and ministers, then there are ups and downs, there are ups and downs, and then there are etiquettes applied."[81] Then

---

76   *Ibid.*

77   *Confucian Analects, supra* note 47, Book 15, Wei Ling Gong, ch. 38, at 357.

78   *Id.,* Book 7, Shu Er, ch. 7, at 202–203.

79   *Id.,* ch. 21, at 209.

80   *Id.,* Book 15, Wei Ling Gong, ch. 30, at 353.

81   Yi Jing, Xu Gua Zhuan, ch. 31, *available at* https://home-nutn-edu-tw.translate.goog
       /xifeng61/@philosophy/iching/le%20ijuann%20Xu%20Gua.htm?_x_tr_sch=http&_x_tr
       _sl=zh-TW&_x_tr_tl=zhCN&_x_tr_hl=zh-CN&_x_tr_pto=sc (visited on 12 July 2022).

what are the etiquettes or norms to be applied to the people and how are they applied? According to Mencius, a prominent figure of Confucianism next to Confucius, the difference between humans and animals is small; the difference is that humans understand and observe benevolence and righteousness. Mencius said, "all men have a mind which cannot bear to see the suffering of others."[82] To illustrate this point, he gave an example that when people suddenly see a child about to fall into a well, they will, without exception, experience a feeling of alarm and distress. "They will feel so," Mencius said, "not as a ground on which they may seek the praise of their neighbors and friends, nor from a dislike to the reputations of having been unmoved by such a thing."[83] They will feel so because they, as humans, have a conscience and feelings toward other humans.

For Confucians, the feeling of commiseration, shame and dislike, modesty and complaisance is "essential to man."[84] These qualities are not only the basis to distinguish humans from animals, but also the requisites to distinguish a superior person from a small person. According to Chinese traditional culture, all humans can become superior persons. When everyone acquires these qualities, human dignity will be realized. This, of course, does not mean that the teachings of Chinese traditional culture think that everyone will become a sage or superior person, though they encourage everyone to be so. Thus, the teachings of Chinese traditional culture are in accord with the New Haven School on rectitude, which considers "freedom of thought, conscience and religion" one's duty "to the community and there is no right to destroy the freedom of others" as components of rectitude.[85]

From the above discussion, it is evident that many teachings of Chinese traditional culture are related to human dignity. These teachings did not, of course, hold the values articulated by the New Haven School as rights of the people. Notwithstanding that, they are helpful in formulating these values for the Chinese community. The fact that China is a signatory of the UDHR and a party to the ICESCR, and has signed the ICCPR should be viewed in the context of Chinese traditional culture as well.

---

82   *The Works of Mencius, supra* note 56, Book 2, Kung-Sun Ch'ow, Part 1, ch. 4.
83   *Ibid.*
84   *Id.,* Book 2, Kung-Sun Ch'ow, Part 1, ch. 4.
85   Lasswell & McDougal, *supra* note 19, at 739.

5   Shared Values, Different Approaches and Diversified Culture

The notion of human dignity is not new and is not confined to Western culture. As people live in different parts of the world, with limited opportunities to interact, the concepts relating to human dignity may differ, but may mean the same thing. It is also amazing that people in ancient times shared some common understanding on humankind, including human dignity. One commentator states that in the ancient Western world "man" was regarded as a small universe or a small world by which "the human race is ennobled by its kinship with the heavenly mind and that of all creatures on earth, only a human shares the mind with the heaven and the stars. ... Accordingly, man has the power to reason, and he also perceives and grows; and by his power of reason alone he has deserved precedence over other animals."[86] This is almost identical to what Mencius said about the difference between men and animals discussed earlier.

Interestingly, ancient Chinese philosophers also related a human to the heaven and earth. They taught people to observe, appraise and analyze everything from a holistic perspective and regard themselves as a component of the cosmos. Wang Yang-Ming,[87] an ancient philosopher once said in *Inquiry on the Great Learning*: "The great man regards Heaven, Earth, and the myriad things as one body. He regards the world as one family and the country as one person. As to those who make a cleavage between objects and distinguish between the self and others, they are small men. That the great man can regard Heaven, Earth, and the myriad things as one body is not because he deliberately wants to do so, but because it is natural to the human nature of his mind that he does so."[88] In other words, not only should people regard themselves as part of the cosmos, but also enshrine benevolence and conscience to others. On this point, Feng Youlan commented that "Yang-Ming said that everyone has 'innate knowledge of good (*liang-zhi*) that one is able to know that it is good or evil when he perceives it'; that is 'what people are able to do without having learned it is an expression of original and good ability. What they know without having to think about it is an expression of original and good knowledge.' What we hold does not need to be the same with Wang Yang-Ming's, but it is not difficult for a person to know what one should do, what ethics one should

---

86   Richard C. Dales, *A Medieval View of Human Dignity*, 38 J. History of Ideas 557, at 559 (Oct. – Dec. 1977).

87   Bryan Van Norden, *Wang Yangming, in* Stanford Encyclopedia of Philosophy (6 September 2019) https://plato.stanford.edu/entries/wang-yangming/ (visited on 7 April 2022).

88   Wang Mingyang, Instructions for Practical Living and Other Neo-Confucian Writings 295–296 (Shou-Jen Wang & Wm. Theodore de Bary eds., Columbia University Press 1963).

observe or what responsibility one should undertake; this is not a problem. To know what one should do and do it continuously without considering gains and losses is compliance or without acting in the Daoism."[89] This passage resembles Kant's theory that "Morality is the condition under which alone a rational being can be an end in itself, since only through this is it possible to be a law-giving member in the kingdom of ends" discussed earlier. The capacity of knowing, without thinking, what is good and what is evil is an essential feature of humans distinctive from other living things like animals and plants.

For Kant, for "the human capacity to make universal law," the "underlying point is that human dignity does not consist primarily in some bare idea of rationality or freedom, however important those may ultimately be to his account. It is the capacity to make universal law, that is, our capacity to bind or obligate ourselves and others."[90] At the same time, "the capacity to make human universal law is constitutive of our human dignity only if those who exercise such capacity also subject themselves to the laws that they make.[91] In a way, this is exactly what Chinese traditional culture advocates – the sage and other peoples should all observe the principle of benevolence, propriety, righteousness, reciprocity and love discussed earlier. Also, the human capacity to make universal law must mean that they are conscious of what the law should be in order to serve the universe well. This again is shared in the teachings of Chinese traditional culture, which emphasizes personal cultivation and rules. According to Confucius, even when sending regards to others, people should demonstrate sincerity, faith and respect – components of human dignity. For instance, where a person "sending complimentary inquiries to a person in another state, he must bow twice when escorting the messenger away."[92] Also, when being asked about how a prince should treat his ministers and vice versa, Confucius replied, "a prince should treat his ministers according to the rules of propriety and the ministers should serve their prince with faithfulness."[93] All these examples affirm that under Chinese traditional culture, individuals were expected and encouraged to be embodied with good human qualities, including to be bound by the rules. From the above, it can be discerned that even though people living in different continents across different eras and times could not have much direct exchanges, they still shared the same values of human dignity which were reflected in their respective cultures.

---

89   Feng Youlan, *Xin Yuan Ren, supra* note 37, at 613.
90   Kleinig & Evans, *supra* note 6, at 553.
91   *Id.* at 554.
92   *Confucian Analects, supra* note 47, Book 10 Heang Tang, ch. 11.
93   *Id.,* Book 3 Pa Yih, ch. 19.

Human dignity as a shared value notwithstanding, writings by Western scholars and Chinese traditional culture apparently adopted different approaches toward it. For the Western part, human dignity is considered the basis for other rights. An extension of this idea is that human dignity is inherent in every person and based on it all other rights arise. As this is the nature of human dignity in Western cultures, Schachter thought that it is "not unrealistic to assume that ideas of this kind will have a role in challenging existing attitudes."[94] And it may also give rise to other rights that do not exist now.[95]

As mentioned earlier, Chinese traditional culture emphasizes educating and cultivating members of their society. The most famous passage is that "[t]hings being investigated, knowledge becomes complete. Their knowledge being complete, their thoughts become sincere. Their thoughts being sincere, their hearts are rectified. Their hearts being rectified, their persons are cultivated. Their persons being cultivated, their families are regulated. Their families being regulated, their states are rightly governed. Their states being rightly governed, the whole world is made tranquil and happy."[96] From this, one can see that under Chinese traditional culture, everyone is expected to be well cultivated and when everyone is well cultivated, one gives due respect to and recognizes the worth of others. This is different from the approach in Western communities, which emphasizes the entitlement of the dignity of every individual and that in view of such, others should respect and recognize such dignity and rights. Yet, even though writings of Western scholars and Chinese traditional culture may approach human dignity from different angles, it does not present any problem, provided human dignity can be realized.

Human dignity has been written into international treaties and other instruments, and hence has the effect of an international law obligation. As such, human dignity must have certain essential features that are universally applicable. Within this general concept, the contents of human dignity may vary slightly from community to community depending on the culture, tradition, legal system, and history thereof. Nor must the measures adopted for the realization of human dignity necessarily be the same. Although it may not be possible to work out a detailed list of components of human dignity, some

---

94   Oscar Schachter, *Human Dignity as a Normative Concept, supra* note 17, at 853.

95   Examples given by Schachter include that "one might suggest that aliens now commonly deprived of rights to take part in civic and political life should as a matter of respect for their worth be given such rights. Other examples might perhaps be inferred from the recognition that vilification and demeaning of group beliefs and aspirations are affronts to dignity and that official behavior involving such vilification or demeaning should be considered as a violation of the rights of the person." *See* Schachter, *ibid.*

96   *The Great Learning, supra* note 45, ch. 1.

common sense will help. Like Mencius once said, "where a man makes shoes without knowing the size of people's feet, yet I know that he will not make them like baskets."[97] This is because all feet of humans are alike and hence their shoes are like one another, though the sizes of the shoes differ. To apply this metaphor to human dignity would mean that as all humans, regardless of their race, nationality, religion, etc., are alike, their inherent entitlement of human dignity must be alike.

Some commentators have stated that compared with other living things, "[h]umans need more – a social engagement that develops their capacities and through which they can learn how to advance themselves. Critical to that environment will be social norms and the acquisition of virtues."[98] It is true that without social norms and acquisition of virtues, humans cannot effectively govern their community. This is also the reason why Confucianism advocates cultivation of humans with virtues and the propriety of rules. At the same time, such social norms and rules must reflect the nature of humans including their development according to Daoism discussed earlier. This again demonstrates that, in diverse cultures, humans share values which evolve together with the development of the world and for the same goals of humanity.

In the end, it is the humans themselves who must take actions to implement the human dignity obligations. In this regard, the New Haven School calls upon the international legal scholars to conduct self-scrutiny "at levels of consciousness so deep that the self is unaware of them" and to serve "the common interests of the most inclusive system of world public order."[99] International legal scholars are also encouraged to invent alternatives for achieving "a better value production and distribution within the requirements of minimum order."[100] Nothing more needs to be added.

In conclusion, human dignity can be traced back to ancient times and is recognized and implemented as an international obligation. In this highly globalized world, cross-border exchanges continue to expand at all levels, but

---

97   *The Works of Mencius*, *supra* note 56, Book 6, Kaou Tsze, Part 1, ch. 7.

98   Kleinig & Evans, *supra* note 6, at 557–8.

99   W. Michael Reisman & Tomo B. Takadi, *How Shall We Fashion International Legal Goals and Criteria for Appraisal in a World of Many Civilizations and Cultures? Review of Onuma Yasuaki's International Law in a Transcivilizational World*, 9 Asian J. Int'l L. 177, 184 (2019).

100   *Ibid.* "As for those negotiating on behalf of a state, though their professional role may require them to champion the interests of their clients, we would suggest that even they would do well to leave their respective civilizations at the door and to focus their efforts, instead, on crafting arrangements that promise the achievement of common interests in terms of value production and sharing," the New Haven School of Jurisprudence counsels. *Ibid.*

this does not mean that the differences among various cultures have disappeared or are disappearing. The world is still diversified in cultures and legal systems. Such diversified sub-cultures and sub-systems make up the world. Nonetheless, the social processes of each sub-culture and sub-system or community are unavoidably affected by the functioning of the social processes of other communities, i.e., they interpenetrate and interact. As the contemporary world is now becoming an integrated whole, the New Haven School's inquiry, which focuses on the social processes of both the community of all humankind and those of smaller communities, is in compliance with the contemporary world trend and therefore meets the needs of humankind.[101] Chinese traditional culture which still has very strong impact on today's official and social decision-makings is rich in teachings relating to human dignity, though their approaches may differ from the writings of Western scholars. In this circumstance, human dignity has become a shared value of the whole world. The recognition and implementation of the international obligation on human dignity will help meet the needs of humanity.

Acknowledgements

The author would like to express his gratitude to Professor W. Michael Reisman for his valuable comments and suggestions.

---

101   Lasswell & McDougal, *supra* note 19, at 188.

CHAPTER 6

Philosophical Implications of Human Flourishing

*Philip Larrey**

1   Introduction: The Concept of Human Flourishing

The notion of human flourishing is quickly becoming an international instrument to measure the true "wealth" of a country, aside from Gross National Product.[1] Human flourishing, or complete human well-being, might be understood as living in "a state in which all aspects of a person's life are good."[2] From a generic point of view, many studies suggest that meaning and purpose in life, mental and physical health, happiness and satisfaction with life, close social relationships, and character and virtue are core constituents of flourishing, and that financial and material stability contributes to sustaining flourishing over time.[3]

For millennia, the notion can be found in various philosophical systems, but only recently has it come to appear in psychological, sociological and even economic studies used to evaluate what constitutes human self-realization and happiness. The first systematic approach to the issue of what constitutes "the good life" is found in the ancient Greek philosopher, Aristotle, with his *Nicomachean Ethics.*[4]

This chapter will consist of the concept of human flourishing, exactly what is human flourishing, and how can we evaluate and measure human flourishing. The five themes to be developed are, first, happiness and personal satisfaction, one of the key elements to human flourishing. Second are the five

---

* Dean, Philosophy Department and Chair of Logic and Epistemology, Pontifical Lateran University, The Vatican; Chairman, Advisory Board, Humanity 2.0.

1 *See* Tyler J. VanderWeele, *On the promotion of human flourishing*, July 13, 2017, 114(31) Proceedings of the National Academy of Sciences 8148–8156, available at https://doi .org/10.1073/pnas.1702996114. *See also* J. Höltge, R. G. Cowden, Matthew T. Lee, A. O. Bechara, S. Joynt, S. Kamble, V. V. Khalanskyi, L. Shtanko, N. M. T. Kurniati, S. Tymchenko, V. L. Voytenko, E. McNeely & T. J. VanderWeele, *A systems perspective on human flourishing: Exploring cross-country similarities and differences of a multisystemic flourishing network*, J. Positive Psychology (2022), available at https://www.tandfonline.com/doi/pdf/10.1080/17439760.202 2.2093784?needAccess=true.

2 *See* VanderWeele, 2017, at 8149.

3 *Id.*

4 Other works by Aristotle or attributed to him that also analyze the issue are *Magna Moralia* and *Eudemian Ethics.*

broad domains of human life. Third, pathways to human flourishing. Fourth, common misconceptions regarding human flourishing. And finally, fifth, Humanity 2.0's goals and how that deals with the subject of human flourishing.

2   Happiness

Although it is difficult to identify with precision, it is safe to say that human flourishing deals with helping people attain self-realization, allowing human beings to fulfill their potential as human beings. This is primarily a philosophical point of view, but, as we will see in the course of these reflections, it becomes very practical also. There is an adage in the English language which says that somebody is clicking on all four cylinders. "I'm clicking on all four cylinders," which means things are working out very well, I am achieving the goals that I set out to achieve, I am using my full capacity in order to do what I want to do.

Human flourishing is relevant in all fields, but today we are going to discuss primarily human flourishing in the workplace, and as a result in society. Human flourishing is an idea that we can actually take to society and ask ourselves, "What can society do, or what can society support (and I mean the institutions of society) in order to enhance human flourishing?" "A state of complete physical and mental social well-being" is how the World Health Organization identified health broadly and, implicitly, human flourishing in the preamble to its Constitution of 1948.[5] This has been something that we have been able to build upon, this concept of health in a state of complete physical and mental and social well-being.

Dr. Laurie Santos is a professor at Yale University who has begun a course called "The Science of Well-Being." This course is now offered free on the website *Cousera*,[6] or at least parts of it are, and there have been more than three million people who have participated in the course so far. It is the most popular class at Yale University. Although Laurie Santos' field of study is psychology, the course which she offers is quite philosophical also. The extreme popularity of this course indicates to us how important the notion of human flourishing is to people. People want to know how to be happy. It sounds obvious, yet it is not obvious. When we talk about the science of well-being, Dr. Santos is using the idea of science in a somewhat broad way. She is not talking about

---

5   1948 Constitution of the World Health Organization, Preamble Principle No. 1: "Health is a state of complete physical, mental and social well-being and not merely the absence of disease or infirmity." http://www.who.int/ governance/eb/who_constitution_en.pdf.

6   Laurie Santos, *The Science of Well-Being*, https://www.coursera.org/learn/the-science-of -well-being.

the "scientific method," as we see in Galileo and what we would consider as strict science today. But she is talking about the fundamental presuppositions of how to be happy, of well-being.

I would certainly suggest enrolling in the class and you will learn a lot of things from her and the material that she suggests. Many of the texts are taken from classical philosophers of Western civilization. One of the things that she does state is the following: in order to be happy, you need to sacrifice and to renounce something. We would not ordinarily consider happiness, or the road to happiness, passing through sacrifice or renouncement. Yet, she does make this point and it is an extremely valid one. If one does not sacrifice something, happiness is not achievable. The point can be confusing, once someone reflects: "Wait, I want to be happy, I don't want to sacrifice." Yet, in reality, one cannot achieve happiness without self-sacrifice and without renouncing.

Let us take an example. Two teams compete for the NBA finals, and one of them wins (last year it was the Golden State Warriors from San Francisco[7]). When you see the final second of the final game, when you see the winner take that trophy, you realize the sacrifice that these men have made for at least one entire year (probably more). In terms of the NBA finals, it happens once a year. The sacrifice and effort put in during one year to win an NBA title is what makes it so important. And that is what makes people happy, especially the men (perhaps some of the most physically and mentally elite of the human race) who win the title. They break down in tears. Why? Because of what it means and because of what went into winning. Achieving human happiness and well-being passes necessarily through the gauntlet of sacrifice and renouncement. Nothing great is achieved without it.

We can look at human flourishing also from within the family, or within a household. We have a home, a family, an extended family. We can look at the importance of one's children's opportunities, and then we have other things which come after that. In terms of the concept of human flourishing, many studies suggest that it begins with the family. Human flourishing starts with the family, yet it does not stop there. We also are approaching this theme through the lens of Western civilization. In Africa, human flourishing will mean something quite different. Although the family is important in Africa, the tribe is more so, because the tribe is the key to success and survival. In Asia, it would mean something quite different. Amartya Sen, for example, the famous professor of economics and philosophy at Harvard University, has written extensively on the issue of "Asian values" and the importance of those values in the

---

7   The Golden State Warriors won the NBA Championship of 2022, *cf.* https://www.nba.com /warriors/championship/ 2022.

global economy. Human flourishing in the Far East or in the Middle East is going to look different in many ways than it does in the West.

The texts that we are using here highlight human flourishing from the Western tradition.

The areas in which we can consider the importance of human flourishing are transportation, public services, health care, ecological environment, safety and security, access to places of worship, shopping, a just salary, free time and vacation, access to psychological assistance. These are the issues that surface when we talk about human flourishing. For example, a good friend of mine lives in Amsterdam, and he pays 65% of his wealth in taxes. Now, that seems like a very large amount to pay in taxes and yet he says, "Oh, I pay it willingly because I know that I get great services as a result." For example, the Dutch enjoy free healthcare, they go to concerts and museums free of charge; they have free public transportation. There are many services that the Netherlands offer in exchange for very high taxes. Most Americans would never pay that amount of taxes, and yet this is all part of human flourishing.

When we ask ourselves, "Are you safe and secure?," because if people are not safe and secure they will not be able to flourish. "Do you have access to psychological assistance?," because flourishing is not only physical, but also psychological. Another issue is free time and vacation: it is very important that we have some but not too much free time. Again, Aristotle would say that the key is in the mean, that virtue is in the middle. We cannot have too little, and neither can we have too much. If we have 50 weeks of vacation in a 52-week year, that is too much; yet, one day of vacation in a 52-week year is too little.

Resilience often goes hand-in-hand with human flourishing. Resilience is now a very common word in our vocabulary, and it is also translated into other languages. In Italian, for example, *"resilienza"* is a way of saying that people overcome hardships, or are steadfast in achieving goals, or eliminating obstacles. Resilience is a very rich word that we use often in society.

Finally, one of the aspects of human flourishing is to strengthen institutions that allow a society to thrive. One of the conditions of human flourishing is to require societal institutions to help individuals and groups to thrive through those institutions which are conducive to flourishing. Such efforts should also be supported by governments. What would that look like? This is exactly what many institutions are trying to achieve. For example, the Templeton Foundation supports many efforts around this theme.[8] Also, we see the Human Flourishing

---

8 Templeton World Charity Foundation, *Innovations for Human Flourishing*, https://www .templetonworldcharity. org/humanflourishing.

program at Harvard University.[9] There is the Jubilee Center at the University of Birmingham,[10] and of course the non-profit foundation Humanity 2.0.[11] There are many others as well. These efforts are attempting to incorporate a paradigm shift in order to move away from the goal of simply making money to enhancing human flourishing on a global basis.

If the future is going to be bright and resourceful, it must entail the shifting of attention to human flourishing.

2.1 Happiness or Personal Satisfaction

The key to human flourishing is happiness or personal satisfaction. This goes back to Aristotle, who wrote a book called the *Nicomachean Ethics*, over 2,500 years ago in which he tried to identify from a philosophical point of view, what happiness was all about. We can talk about measurement of eudaimonia or happiness, which comes in to English from the Greek which speaks about personal satisfaction or happiness. Aristotle said the goal of life is to be happy. This is also where Laurie Santos from Yale is coming from. She actually uses Aristotle. Throughout the history of Western civilization we can appreciate similar ideas in Immanuel Kant, the great modern German philosopher; we can see it in John Stuart Mill; Jeremy Bentham, and up to the 20th century. Philosophers who are writing about human happiness.

The key to happiness in Aristotle are the *virtues*. Virtues used to be taught in school. Yet, today it would probably be politically incorrect, but we can actually study what it means to be happy. There are incredible riches of the past, starting from the ancient Greeks, going up to today, passing through Thomas Aquinas, the medieval philosopher, which would help us achieve us happiness. It is not simply intellectual: Aristotle says happiness is not achieved only by thinking or contemplating (although he does rank that as a very high means of achieving happiness). It is something that has to be existential, has to be lived. This is the definition of Aristotle: "Happiness is attained by action in accordance with virtue." And what are the primary virtues for Aristotle which have carried over also to the Medieval period as well as the Modern period? Prudence, or practical wisdom, is the first. Justice is the second. The third is fortitude or courage, and I would suggest the word we would use today is resilience. And fourth, temperance, or moderation.

---

9   Harvard University, *The Human Flourishing Program at Harvard's Institute for Quantitative Social Science*, https://hfh.fas.harvard.edu/.

10 University of Birmingham, *The Jubilee Centre for Character and Virtues*, https://www.birmingham.ac.uk/research/activity/education/jubilee-centre/index.aspx.

11 Humanity 2.0, *We are a Human Flourishing Accelerator*, https://humanity2-0.org/.

1. *Prudence* or *practical wisdom* is the way in which the general or universal norms are applied in individual situations. Aristotle says that happiness is not achieved only by following universal norms. For example, "Do not kill innocent people," or "Do not steal." Often these norms can be dovetailed with the Ten Commandments, or at the least the last seven. These are universal norms of conduct which all societies accept as right. People may steal what is not theirs, but society can never allow that to be considered as morally correct, or as ethically justifiable. Prudence is the key of applying the general norm to a specific instance. I know what the general norm is, for example, "Do not lie." Lying is bad, it is ethically unacceptable. But in this situation is lying justifiable? We can use the example of the person who is approached by the Gestapo, and they are harboring a Jewish family. The Gestapo askes, "Is there a Jewish family in your home?" The person says "No, there is not," because they are protecting the lives of the Jewish people. Prudence is the application of the general norm. Blind application of the general norm is not adequate in this specific instance. Another famous example is used by the famous French writer, Victor Hugo in his book, *Les Misérables*. Jean Val Jean steals a loaf of bread to feed his family. Stealing is wrong, one should not steal, it is not ethically acceptable. However, in this situation it is morally justifiable because the lives of my family depend on that loaf of bread.

2. The second virtue is *justice*. Of course, Plato asks in *The Republic*, what is justice? It is a very complex issue, but it is fundamental. People need to achieve justice in order to flourish in their lives. Justice is not simply the positive law, which we see in a court of law. In the United States, we have received the Anglo-Saxon way of administering justice. Plato says justice is something greater, it is actually one of the ideas that reside in the soul. Justice is something above positive law, but usually does not contradict it. Sometimes it will contradict positive law, when laws are unjust. Plato speaks a lot on this subject, as does Sophocles. Human beings need justice in order to flourish, justice in an objective sense. Justice can be understood subjectively: what I feel is just for me or for my family; or it can be understood in an objective sense, and that is usually what happens in a court of law, because that is the best forum that as a society we have to find and support justice. The pursuit of justice is one of the main virtues that people must undertake in order to flourish.

3. *Fortitude* or *courage*. Aristotle uses the example of the soldier: a soldier must have courage in order to face death in battle. That is why soldiers need to develop the virtue of courage. A soldier that does not go in to battle when it is necessary, lacks courage or lacks fortitude. Aristotle also states that a soldier has to be cautious, otherwise he will die unnecessarily,

as rushing into a situation that is not going to help. Such is the art of war. Somebody who is courageous, is a good soldier; somebody who does not discern the situation, often ends up dead.

4. *Temperance* or *moderation*. This is one of the most important virtues for Aristotle: "Everything in moderation," because if one exceeds (for example, in pleasure), one may end up destroying it: one can go too far. Temperance can be seen for example in someone who enjoys alcohol, and drinks too much, and therefore ends up feeling terrible. Temperance allows one to achieve the level that is necessary for one's human flourishing. Again, virtue is in the mean: not too little, and not too much. This is one of the most important rules or ways of understanding human flourishing.

3   **Five Broad Domains of Human Life**

These five domains of human life are the ways in which we can and measure human flourishing.

1. Happiness and life satisfaction, which is what we covered briefly in point number one. This is an area that we have identified to be needed in order to achieve flourishing. One's life has to mean something; one's life has to have satisfaction.
2. Health, both mental and physical.
3. Meaning and purpose.
4. Character and virtue.
5. Close social relationships.

The program of human flourishing at Harvard University identifies these five broad domains in order to describe human flourishing. These also will be used in conjunction with ways to promote human flourishing. The first one was already dealt with earlier.

Health, mental and physical, is obviously a crucial dimension of our lives. If one is mentally miserable or physically miserable, it is going to be difficult to achieve human flourishing. Meaning and purpose – if one's life does not have a meaning or a purpose, it is very difficult to flourish. This is one of the reasons why some countries are allowing physician-assisted suicide. Euthanasia for people who are over the age of 18 is something which is quite controversial. Governments are debating the issue all over the globe. In the United States, some states allow physician assisted suicide, while others do not. It is not a federal mandate, but it is up to each state. In Europe, some countries have legalized euthanasia, which means that a person can approach a physician and ask for assisted suicide. The primary reason why people choose to commit suicide with a doctor's help is usually because of a lack of meaning and purpose to their lives. This is a very delicate question, and it is brought up as a way to exemplify of what we understand as having meaning and purpose.

Here is an example in less dramatic form of the importance of *meaning and purpose* in life. Larry Page, cofounder of Google (Alphabet), in 2014 gave an interview with Sergey Brin to Vinod Khosla, in which he was asked about the concept of meaning and purpose in people's lives. The context of the question was around the issue of robots and artificial intelligence taking over people's jobs. We are going to see more of this, although it is going to happen more slowly than some predict. This snippet highlights what we understand as meaning and purpose in people's lives and how that is necessary to achieve flourishing.

"Let us think about the things that you need to make yourself happy – housing, security, opportunities for your kids – anthropologists have been identifying these things. It's not that hard for us to provide those things. The amount of resources we need to do that, the amount of work that actually needs to go into that is pretty small. I'm guessing less than 1 percent at the moment. So the idea that everyone needs to work frantically to meet people's needs is just not true. I do think there's a problem that we don't recognize that. I think there's also a social problem that a lot of people aren't happy if they don't have anything to do. So we need to give people things to do. We need to feel like we're needed, wanted and have something productive to do. But I think the mix with that and the industries we actually need and so on are – there's not a good correspondence. Until we figure that out, we're not going to have a good outcome."[12]

This is why a basic universal income is not that popular of an idea. There have been several countries that have conducted a referendum to their populace on whether or not the government should institute a universal basic income, and they have said no. Switzerland was the first who decided against it.[13] Other countries are actually doing this, in a type of welfare program (like in the U.S.). If you do not have a job, the government will give you a basic income, but you are probably not going to feel fulfilled; you probably are not going to have a high level of meaning and purpose in your life. Often, that comes through one's job, by working. Of course, this is not always the case: all of us know people would prefer to have a basic income and then do amazing things without having to punch a time card, or going to the office from nine to five. However, in the majority of cases, people discover meaning and purpose in their lives by having something to do, and getting paid for it. We can exaggerate

---

12   See *Fireside chat with Google Co-founders Larry Page and Sergey Brin*, https://www .khoslaventures.com/fireside-chat-with-google-co-founders-larry-page-and-sergey-brin.

13   BBC News, *Switzerland's voters reject basic income plan*, 5 June 2016, https://www.bbc .com/news/world-europe-36454060.

and say that money is the only goal that I have, so I am going to simply make money in life. Or, the opposite, "I do not need any money at all, and I can go out in the wilderness and fend for myself." These are both extremes, and they both actually happen: there are people who subscribe to those views, but perhaps not the general population.

The fourth broad domain: *character* and *virtue*. Often, we tend to miss the importance of character and virtue. These can be taught, usually in the family, but also in school. Character and virtue are necessary for human beings to flourish. The Jubilee Center at the University of Birmingham is a clear example.[14] They have many resources and abundant materials that demonstrate the importance of teaching character and virtue as a society and how to do that.

Close social relationships are very important. On the island of Sardinia, there is a village where most of the people live to be over one hundred years old. Many people in Japan also live to be over one hundred. Sociologists and anthropologists flock to these places and ask what is the key to such longevity: is it diet, not smoking, etc.? Most all affirm that the key to longevity is social interaction. People need to interact with other people, and close social relationships are necessary in order for human beings to flourish. Society should help people to thrive in social relationships, and therefore impediments towards creating close social relationships are going to be impediments to human flourishing. This is one of the fundamental goals of the Humanity 2.0 Foundation – to identify obstacles to human flourishing and support projects which overcome those obstacles.

In these five broad domains of human life: happiness and life satisfaction, health, both mental and physical; meaning and purpose; character and virtue; close social relationships; it is vital that they be sustainable. These domains must be stable. We cannot doubt that tomorrow I am going to have an environment more or less the same that I have today. There has to be continuity. These have to be continuous, they cannot be interrupted because the human being will lose trust in those broad domains.

4   Pathways to Human Flourishing

Having identified the five domains of human flourishing, in this next point we have to identify the pathways for that human flourishing. We can see on a graph, if we put the five domains on one side, we put the four pathways to

---

14   *See supra* note 10 ("The Jubilee Centre for Character and Virtues is a pioneering inter-disciplinary research centre focussing on character, virtues and values in the interest of human flourishing").

human flourishing on the other side, we see how they interact. There are many ways in which these categories interact. What are the four pathways?

4.1   Family, Work, Education, and Religious Community

The pathways to human flourishing are the family; your work or your job; the education that one has; and religious community. And again, the issue is not being approached from a religious perspective but rather from a philosophical perspective and therefore religious community is something that we see happens and it is not something that simply religious people can do.

The *family* is still a wide spread institution in Western society, although fewer people are actually getting married. Yet, it is still the majority of people who want to marry and begin a family. Some choose not to; obviously, but the percentage is quite high (over 80%).[15] We see that in families that are stable and loving, there is a higher life satisfaction and there is a greater affective happiness. This sounds obvious, but in a complex society this cannot be taken for granted. If there is an abusive family, this does not work; if there is divorce in the family, we see lower levels of satisfaction and effective happiness. By and large, the key to human flourishing in a family is to have a sound affective relationship among people in the family.

Work: most people are employed. A minority is *not* employed, however flourishing societies require the vast majority of people to have a job. Therefore, work is going to be a pathway to that flourishing and this will come up in the section concerning common misconceptions about flourishing and jobs.

Education: high levels of education correspond to higher satisfaction and happiness. There are some very educated people who are miserable, obviously, but in general, the empirical data primarily using Harvard's program for Human Flourishing tell us that higher levels of education correspond to higher satisfaction and higher happiness. This is not necessarily the case for money. The idea that the more money you have, the happier you are is often not true. Sometimes just the opposite actually happens. This is something that people who set out to make money realize often quickly, that happiness is not proportional to one's income. It can be, but it also may fail to be. And there are many poor people who are very happy, and there are many rich people who are miserable. In terms of actual pathways to human flourishing, strictly identifying

---

15   *See* Tyler VanderWeele, *On the Promotion of Human Flourishing*, in Proc. of the Natl Acad Sci U.S.A (13 July 2017): "Moreover, although marriage rates have been declining, marriage continues to be a very common phenomena with ~80% of Americans aged 25 and older, at some point in time, having been married (42) and thereby having formed a family structure beyond their family of origin." https://europepmc.org/article/pmc/5547610.

monetary value is not one of them. It is actually a subset of that of work, but it is not necessarily one of the pathways itself.

Religious community: 84% of the world population reports a religious affiliation, of some sort.[16] This is a very large number. And in the U.S., it has been even higher. It is true that atheism is on the rise. A most recent Pew Report stated that religious affiliations are going down, with respect to 30 years ago, and the numbers of declared atheists is going up.[17] However, we still have the vast majority in the West organizing themselves in some sort of religious affiliation. There are many, not just the three monotheistic religions (Judaism, Christianity and Islam) but there are almost an infinite amount of religious affiliations that people subscribe to.

The reason this is one of the important pathways to human flourishing is because of the increase of four aspects for people involved in religious communities. One, prayer; two, forgiveness; three, gratitude; and four, trust. These four characteristics thrive in people who adhere to some sort of religious affiliation. These are considered important for human flourishing. Therefore, a religious community is going to help you thrive. A sound religious community.

Along with the five domains of human life, we have the four pathways to human flourishing and they interact with each other in order to achieve levels of flourishing which actually can be empirically verified and also measured.

4.2   *Common Misconceptions and How to Overcome Them*
This section deals with common misconceptions of what human flourishing entails and common misconceptions of the importance of flourishing.

1.   *"The poor do not flourish."* This is a misconception. This is a perception which is actually not the case, it is not verified in reality. "The poor are miserable and do not flourish." This could be something which is woven into the fabric of American society, for example, from the Founding Fathers. Not necessarily, but it is a false conception that we should overcome. Examining suicide rates will give us an indication of people being miserable. The opposite of flourishing is people being miserable and which in its most dramatic form leads to suicide. Of 183 countries identified,

---

16   Pew Research Center, *The Global Religious Landscape*, December 28, 2012, at 9, https://assets.pewresearch.org/wp-content/uploads/sites/11/2014/01/global-religion-full.pdf ("there are 5.8 billion religiously affiliated adults and children around the globe, representing 84% of the 2010 world population of 6.9 billion.").

17   Pew Research Center, *Modeling the Future of Religion in America*, September 13, 2022, https://www.pewresearch.org/religion/2022/09/13/how-u-s-religious-composition-has-changed-in-recent-decades/ ("As recently as the early 1990s, about 90% of U.S. adults identified as Christians. But today, about two-thirds of adults are Christians," and now 29% of Americans state that they have "no religion.").

the United States rank 31 in terms of suicide rates.[18] One being the country with most suicides which is Lesotho, and 183 being the country with almost no suicide at all.[19] The U.S. ranks 31, which is quite high, and the country number 32 is Burkina Faso, which is a country in Africa.[20] The Ukraine is ranked 19th, and South Korea, which is very affluent country ranks 12th.[21] Eleventh out of 183 countries, one of the wealthiest countries, Belgium,[22] tells us that it's not necessarily the case that the poor are miserable and do not flourish.

My own experience has been in Ghana, which is a Western African country and Mexico. I have spent time in both of these countries and among poor people, and I can affirm that poor people in these countries (there are also rich people), they are not miserable, and in fact some of them are quite happy despite not having money. I was fortunate enough to be a part of a foundation which provides free medical health to poor people in Ghana, away from the large cities like Accra, or Cape Coast (there are facilities in major cities). Outside the large cities, people often fend for themselves without adequate health care it is difficult not be miserable. Assuming basic health care and assuming basic sustenance to life, I have found that poor people in general are quite happy. Again, this is not necessarily true; however, I think it is a misconception to base happiness only on economic prosperity.

2.   *"Greater attention to flourishing means a decrease in profits."* This is a common misconception with regard to human flourishing in the workplace. Greater attention to flourishing equals decreased profits. "In my company, if I give too much attention to human flourishing, and if I put my employees at the center, I am going to end up making less money and being less productive." This is not true. Let me offer some examples.

Rick Ridgeway is the VP of public engagement at Patagonia. Patagonia is an outdoor clothing store which employs about 1,500 people. It is one of the companies that enjoys an increasingly high level of human flourishing among its employees. Primarily, they put the employee in the center of the company. Rick gave an interview at the Humanity 2.0 Forum

---

18   See *List of Countries by Suicide Rate* https://en.wikipedia.org/wiki/List_of_countries_by _suicide_rate.

19   *Id.*

20   *Id.*

21   *Id.*

22   *Id.*

in 2019[23] in which he stated exactly the philosophy of the company that makes people want to work there. The company is doing very well. It is not true that the greater attention to human flourishing is going to diminish your returns. It is actually going to make your company thrive even more. Doing good and doing well go hand in hand. A company which endorses ethical values, which supports human flourishing is actually going to be a company which does better than the others. If we look at a list of ethical companies or companies that place human flourishing as one of their priorities, of the principal priorities, we find some "small" companies like Cisco,[24] 3M,[25] Accenture (170,000 employees),[26] IBM,[27] and the list goes on.[28] There are many websites which rank companies according to their ethical code of behavior, or how well their employees flourish, and it is an impressive list. Practically speaking, we can see that this is a misconception, because in fact helping people to thrive in the workplace is going to make your company more productive.

From a philosophical point of view, we should not place human flourishing at the center in order to make more money, because this would go back to making money as the key. Just the opposite: we are doing this as part of human dignity, it is part of the way in which we can help people achieve a greater self-realization, and this is the goal. However, you don't have to sacrifice return on your investment in order to do so. Let me offer three quick negative examples of companies that did not put human flourishing as a priority and did not behave in an ethical way.

---

23   Rick Ridgeway, VP of Public Engagement for Patagonia | Humanity 2.0 – Vatican City, May 2019, video at https://humanity2-0.org/2019-forum/ and https://www.youtube.com/watch?v=bJhJ_2tyuzM.

24   CISCO, *Human Rights in the Supply Chain*, https://www.cisco.com/c/m/en_us/about/csr/esg-hub/supply-chain/human-rights.html.

25   3M *Human Rights Policy*, https://multimedia.3m.com/mws/media/1029705O/human-rights-policy.pdf.

26   Gaston Carrión, *The secret of growth? Reimagining employee experience*, Accenture Business Functions Blog, July 13, 2021, https://www.accenture.com/us-en/blogs/business-functions-blog/the-secret-of-growth-reimagining-employee-experience.

27   Elizabeth Perry & Cait Dowling, *Leading by doing: How IBM is helping employees shift from languishing to thriving*, BetterUp, May 14, 2021, https://www.betterup.com/blog/how-ibm-is-helping-employees-move-from-languishing-to-thriving.

28   Paul Shrivastava & Laszlo Zsolnai, *Wellbeing-oriented organizations: Connecting human flourishing with ecological regeneration*, 31(2) Business Ethics, the Environment & Responsibility 386–397 (April 2022), available at https://online library.wiley.com/doi/full/10.1111/beer.12421.

First, Boeing. The 737 Max is a new model of airplane produced by Boeing in order to compete with Airbus and their new model A320 Neo. It is a midsize plane, it is very fuel efficient and it is quite new, but still considered part of the 737 line which has been around for over 25 years. There were two 737 Max planes that crashed in recent times: one in Indonesia and one in Ethiopia, sold by Boeing. They subsequently grounded all of the planes worldwide. The FAA began the groundings, and then it spread to all over the world. The FAA has now allowed the 737 Max continue flying, but only after a series of changes and greater pilot instruction.[29] Although it is said, "Safety first", the way in which the 737 Max was approved shows that safety was not the first priority. The plane was unsafe, two of them crashed: the crashes were not due to pilot error, but rather the way in which the automatic adjustment system was set up – the software was faulty when operating on erroneous data. We now know that the plane is safe. It took two crashes and hundreds of people dying in order to make it safe. Boeing lost 26 billion dollars in its market cap. It is clear in the end that human flourishing was not the priority.

Second, Volkswagen. vw almost went bankrupt because they cheated on the way diesel emissions were measured in their new cars. They were caught, and there are lawsuits which are still in progress in the United States worth approximately 9 billion dollars. The government of Germany bailed out vw because it was a company "too big to fail" which may actually be true.[30] Lying on your diesel emissions, cheating on the apparatus which measures those emissions is unethical. It is simply wrong. The corruption of the company went to the highest level. This is not placing human flourishing as a priority, not placing ethical behavior as one's priority. The company is facing tremendous amount of problems. The more ethical you are, the better you're going to achieve your goals.

Third, Wells Fargo. Wells Fargo has survived as a bank, but they were caught creating over 3 million fake accounts. The CEO of the company resigned, and the CFO became the CEO, and after 2½ years he resigned also.[31] This was a very serious problem at Wells Fargo. It is unethical to

29   *Boeing 737 Max Flies Again, but Crash Victims' Kin Say Risks Remain*, N.Y. Times, June 27, 2022.

30   *Volkswagen Just Avoided Collapse Because It's 'Too Big To Fail'*, July 8, 2016, https://carbuzz .com/news/volkswagen -just-avoided-collapse-because-it-s-too-big-to-fail.

31   Jennifer Liberto, *Wells Fargo CEO Quits In Wake Of Consumer Financial Scandals*, March 28, 2019, https://www.npr. org/2019/03/28/707738077/wells-fargo-ceo-quits-in-wake-of -consumer-financial-scandals#:~:text=Press,Wells%20Fargo%20CEO%20Timothy%20 Sloan%20Quits%20In%20Wake%20Of%20Multiple,a%20new%20CEO%20is%20 selected.

create false accounts and the reason why the employees were creating false account is because they were given a commission by the bank for each new account. People were inventing accounts which is unethical. You can't do that. What about the conscience of the people doing that? Failing to place ethics or human flourishing as a priority is going to be detrimental to your company, and not the opposite. Obviously, there are companies which thrive by cheating and stealing, and lying. But that's certainly not usually the case, and is certainly not going to be the case in the long term.

3. *"Gross Domestic Product is everything."* This is a misconception. The economic value of a country is not the same as measuring the well-being of a country. The kingdom of Bhutan has put forward the idea of a "Gross National Happiness" index.[32] The small Himalayan country actually has been doing this for many years and other countries are imitating that. For example, the Organization for Economic Cooperation and Development now collects data on life, satisfaction, meaning and purpose.[33] In just classifying a country in terms of its GDP is not the best way of understanding the well-being of the people of that country. The OECD is now understanding that, and using other factors (for example, life satisfaction, meaning and purpose). Not only. We can look at Victoria, British Columbia;[34] Thailand has launched a Gross National Happiness Center.[35] Columbia University has come out with the World Happiness Report, and is edited by John Helliwell, Richard Layer and Jeffrey Sachs.[36] Every year they come out with that report, and, of course, this is one of the most technical ways in which we see human flourishing measured and identified around the world, primarily in the United States. We know that Finland ranks as the most satisfying country: every year people are asked if they are satisfied with their life? Finland is consistently ranked number one.[37] There must be a reason.

---

32   Oxford Poverty and Human Development Initiative, *Bhutan's Gross National Happiness Index*, https://ophi.org.uk/policy/gross-national-happiness-index/#:~:text=The%20phrase %20'gross%20national%20happiness,approach%20towards%20notions%20of%20 progress.

33   OECD Better Life Index, *Life Satisfaction*, https://www.oecdbetterlifeindex.org/topics /life-satisfaction/.

34   Nina Grossman, *Happiness rates high in Greater Victoria: Vital Signs report*, Victoria News, Oct.1,2019,https://www.vicnews.com/news/happiness-rates-high-in-greater-victoria-vital -signs-report/.

35   *Gross National Happiness Centre Thailand*, https://gnhcentrethailand.com/.

36   World Happiness Report 2022, https://worldhappiness.report/ed/2022/.

37   *Id.*,ch.2,https://worldhappiness.report/ed/2022/happiness-benevolence-and-trust-during -covid-19-and-beyond/#ranking-of-happiness-2019-2021.

4. *"People treated well will abuse privileges."* This is a misconception, and is not true. People usually respond to privileges by trusting. It can be the case that people take advantage, that people who are treated well do not correspond by treating others well. This is the Golden Rule: "Treat others as you would have them treat you." However, I would suggest that we should bank on people appreciating being treated well, and corresponding in a like fashion. Here is an example: a Caffé bar here in Italy wanted to start a social experiment. So they approached a person who came in to the Caffè and paid for his espresso (or a cappuccino). It costs a Euro or a Euro and a half. The person serving the coffee says, "Why don't you give me two Euros to pay for the next person's coffee?" The experiment consisted in seeing how far the chain would continue. The next person who comes says, "Can I have an espresso?" And the waiter says, "By the way, the gentleman who just left already paid for your coffee." "Oh, thank you." They wanted to see when the chain ended. Who was going to be first to say, "I am not going to pay for the next person's coffee?" You find that your coffee has been paid for, it is free. The vast majority of people offered to pay for the next person's coffee. The chain reached to over one hundred people. The vast majority of people offered to pay for the next person's coffee. It is not true that people do not care about the next person. Human nature is flawed, people are evil, or selfish. But it is not the majority. From a philosophical point of view, if we sustain the belief that people in general are good-natured, society will flourish.

It is interesting to see these restaurants which offer "All you can eat" for $19.99. You go in to the restaurant, where there is a buffet. What if an entire NFL team goes in there and they all pay $19.99 for all you can eat and they end up eating the place out? They eat everything there. But that's not common. Most people don't eat more than they want. That is why these things work: the owner is not afraid that he is going to end up with no food. Why not? Because most people understand that they have a lunch or dinner, and they eat to a certain extent, and when they are full, they do not eat anymore. You might get the odd person who goes in and eats everything they have. But it is not common. Most people are moderate: they'll pay $19.00, and they will have a salad and a steak. People do not tend to hoard.

5. *"People take advantage of weakness."* This is a misconception, which consists of the idea that people will take advantage of weakness of the system. Again, this cannot be universalized, there are people who will take advantage of weaknesses in the system. People tend to achieve their goals if they are allowed to. If they flourish, they will not take advantage of weaknesses of the system. Here is an example: years ago, MIT built a

new nine-story library, which is beautiful with excellent resources. The head of the library organized a meeting with the staff of the library and asked what type of security system should they use to prevent books being stolen or lost. They required a full-proof security system. In the end, they decided to use the honor system: they knew that their students would be able to break any system they would come up with. After all, these are MIT students! All they need is a reason to break a security system: they would thrive on that. Finding that there is no security system, that it is based on good will, they followed through. The people in charge ended up just leaving it open, and lost very few books. The librarians have statistically seen less and less books being taken from the library. When people are trusted, more often than not, they will trust. It is not always the case, but the alternative is to establish a business context similar to a police state (where people are not flourishing in their jobs).

6. *"People don't care whether their company thrives or not."* This is a misconception, which is not generally true. If people perceive that they have a stake in the company, if they have partial ownership, they will work harder. This is what is called Marcora Law in Italy,[38] named after a politician of the Christian Democrat party after World War II, which established a way of transitioning from a company which is going bankrupt to a worker-recovered enterprise. These are known as WRES, businesses in which the employees become partial owners. This has proven successful many times. A company which is controlled by shareholders, and failing, can be turned around by giving the employees direct responsibility. This also happened in Argentina in 2001, when the country was in a terrible economic crisis and could not sustain their national currency. Many companies followed the example of the Marcora Law and the country came out of the recession.[39] This makes perfect sense, because it instills a greater responsibility on behalf of the people that are working. People will spend more time doing their jobs, they will work longer hours, they will thrive and achieve greater results because they feel it is theirs, and their responsibility and so they are accountable. People do care about their companies, and seeing them thrive.

---

38   Hadfield, M., News, C., Bird, J., Voinea, A., & Grant, A., *The Marcora Law: An effective tool of active employment policy*, Co-operative News, September 22, 2015, https://www.thenews.coop/98000/sector/retail/marcora-law-effective-tool-active-employment-policy/.

39   Kristina Hille, *The empresas recuperadas in Argentina. A way out of the crisis*, *in* International Labor Organization, African responses to the crisis through the social economy. Working document for the International Conference on the Social Economy, Geneva (2009), at 3–14.

7.   *"If people are not watched and disciplined, they will not produce."* Such a misconception goes against human flourishing, but it is simply not true. It is a common misconception. Look at Google, for example. It is a unique company, but it does not require the employees to punch time cards: they have to complete projects. Many engineers are able to meet their goals and then fly to Nepal and ski. Some software programmers work day and night, drinking coffee and Red Bull, and then they spend their time doing other things. The mentality is the key: Google does not demand their employees spend a certain amount of time at their desk, but rather they must complete certain tasks. We can look also at what has happened during the pandemic, with the notion of smart working. People had to start working at home, without being watched nor disciplined, and their productivity has actually increased, in many sectors of society. Not in all sectors, but in many (for example in services it is difficult to have smart working). During "lock down," many companies were forced to have their employees work from home. So much so, many people do not want to go back to the office. In some fields, like education, people want to go back to activities in person instead of using distance learning.

In conclusion, this chapter has attempted to present some of the philosophical implications of human flourishing. The rich concept of human flourishing (or human thriving) is quickly becoming a popular way of identifying that which constitutes the true wealth of a nation, of a social group, or business endeavor. As an appendix to these notions, the reader will see a White Paper which was commissioned by the non-profit organization Humanity 2.0, which will offer a much more detailed account of the notion of human flourishing as understood by the Foundation. Humanity 2.0 has called it "Project Vision," because it provides the intellectual foundation and content behind the Foundation as well as outlining its main goal: to identify obstacles to human flourishing and support those projects which overcome such obstacles. Such is an ambitious goal, but an appropriate one in order to usher in, precisely, the future of humanity, Humanity 2.0.

Appendix: White Paper

Project Vision 2019

What constitutes human flourishing—and its main impediments—for individuals and communities? How should we rank such impediments, and by what standards? A multidimensional, interdisciplinary study.

Ezra Sullivan, op (Project Vision Director: Angelicum)
With thanks to: James Arthur (Birmingham University, UK), Jeffrey Bishop (St. Louis University/Cambridge University), Federico Genoese-Zerbi (Rome), Johannes Moravitz (Austrian Parliament), Craig Steven Titus (Institute for Psychological Science), Candace Vogler (Chicago University)

The Present Opportunity

We live in an era of unprecedented technological development, availability of material resources, and access to information. The opportunities are great, but the dangers are many. And the answers can be confusing. In the era of the encyclopedia, human knowledge was organized alphabetically; in the age of Google and Wikipedia, knowledge is hyperlinked and exists in a web of connections.

Search results are thick with (purported) facts, but thin on integrative insight.

For a deeper approach, we can take inspiration from an ancient story noticed by the professed atheist Peter Singer in his book, *The Most Good You Can Do* (2015). Singer recounts a narrative in which a rich young man came to Jesus of Nazareth and asked, "What good deed must I do, to have eternal life?" (Mt 19:16). In response, Jesus says, "If you would be perfect, go, sell what you possess and give to the poor, and you will have treasure in heaven; and come, follow me" (Mt 19:21).

According to Singer, this is a call for everyone to reconsider their use of material goods—even if we aren't going to give up *everything*, we can nevertheless learn the ways of more effective altruism.

Here we may note that technology puts many of us in the position of the young man: technology offers new "riches" both in terms of material wealth, but also power, opportunities, and questions.

Often in the corners of our conversations there creeps a concern: if technology, material resources, and access to information offer almost unimaginable power over nature, will Lord Acton's concern prove true—and our ultimate power will corrupt us ultimately? On the other hand, many are wondering how technology, resources, and information should be put to best use for the future.

How should we help others? What are some of the greatest obstacles to such help?

This situation calls for a study that can help make sense of the information that confronts us, especially to see whether there are verifiably accurate ways to describe and rank markers of human flourishing and impediments thereto. These are the central issues considered in this 2019 Project Vision Report.

Without minimizing the great desires of any individual, this study is for those who are not seeking perfection. As Singer implies, those who are seeking perfection would not do bad in heeding Jesus's words: "sell what you possess and give to the poor; and come follow me." But ours is not a religious investigation whatsoever. Nor is our research utopianism. We have not created an idealized narrative and in order to fit humanity into that narrative. Our Report is reality-based, as opposed to wish-based, and supported by the best studies wherever available. In this way, we aim to provide compelling answers to questions regarding what constitutes human flourishing—and its main impediments—for individuals and communities. So that we can do the most good possible, our multidimensional, interdisciplinary study also ranks such impediments, thereby giving us indications as to where the solutions may lie in particular projects.

Definitions and Orientations

Human flourishing and its obstacles, appropriately ranked, are among the greatest concerns that humanity faces. The reasons for focusing on these concerns are manifold.

First, we focused on **human** flourishing. Humans exist within a complex global ecosystem that we share with billions of other plants and animals, all of which have their unique properties and natures that organize their nutrition, growth, reproduction, and homeostasis throughout particular life-spans. Without falling prey to negative forms of "speciesism," living things manifest different innate properties common to their species and perform characteristic activities that promote their own welfare. Advanced technologies show the power of humanity to destroy ourselves and everything else with us. It is consequently of utmost importance to consider how we can flourish in harmony with each other and the world as a whole, for as the human race goes, there goes the planet.

Second, we studied the flourishing of humans. There are many benefits to this analogy.

a.   Flourishing is a biological model: apple trees flourish in one way, humans in another. Seeing ourselves as part of the environment emphasizes that, as embodied creatures, we (should) engage with the material world organically, to respect individual natures and nature as a whole.

b.   Flourishing is a model that integrates different levels of human powers, each of which themselves are composed of various factors integrated over time (VanderWeele 2017). One can speak of flourishing in terms of physical health; emotional flourishing; ethical flourishing as manifested in moral conduct; and spiritual flourishing in relation to the highest religious concerns.

c.   The flourishing model scales to different group sizes. Just as one can speak about the flourishing of a single tree, a forest, or the planet, different scales of flourishing exist for humans: for individuals, families, communities, states, and international bodies.

d.   The flourishing model helps organize, integrate, and evaluate various goals. A model of flourishing can help integrate various sub-goals as they are related to a more overarching goal: an apple orchard flourishes when individual trees bear fruit, which is helped by adequate growth, nutrition absorption, photosynthesis, etc. Likewise, a model of human flndividual can help clarify primary and secondary goals for human life. Those goals establish relations among contributors to flourishing on different levels and scales. In this way, flourishing is a model that can evaluate, organize, and integrate mere lists, including the UN's 17 Sustainable Development Goals (UN 2015). Despite the vast research poured into the SDGs, they suffer from a lack of common integration and organization: they are simply listed in numerical order or are depicted as elements in a cycle. Where should we start first: with Goal 9: "Decent Work"? Goal 15: "Life on Land"? More importantly: what counts as "development" in the first place?

e.   Flourishing involves objective measures, unlike studies of well-being which are almost exclusively subjective (Deiner, 2009). Agronomists can objectively measure what factors contribute to an apple tree's flourishing (e.g., amount of sunlight, water, nutrients), and what are signs of its flourishing (e.g., size of apples, density of branch growth). Likewise, our model seeks to identify and rank contributors to human flourishing, as well as objective signs of human flourishing. These will help us accurately identify and rank obstacles to our flourishing.

f.   Flourishing also includes subjective measures. Subjectively, a person may experience flourishing at one level and not at another: for example, a person with chronic illness may flourish ethically despite the lack of full physical flourishing. Comparing objective and subjective concerns helps us make sense of complex data such as quantifiable health measures and qualitative self-reporting. This helps integrate other findings and give more precision to them, e.g., results from a "happiness index" (Helliwell et al. 2017, 2018).

Third, this study considered **obstacles** to human flourishing. We include in our consideration of obstacles both material conditions, such as poverty and lack of access to clean water, and also formal conditions such as political corruption and minimal education.

Fourth, this study evaluated different systems for **ranking** markers of flourishing and its obstacles. We argue that the order involved in ranking can take into account both objective and subjective considerations, without undermining legitimate pluralistic values.

Human Flourishing: Previous Contributions

The Greek thinker Aristotle may be credited with laying the foundations for an understanding of flourishing. With his biological research and philosophical logic, he argued that happiness is something in accord with human excellence, which results in activity that is analogous to the fruit produced by a healthy plant organism. Human excellence has at least five characteristics: it is accompanied by pleasure (NE I.8, 1099a21), is achieved through action (NE I.8, 1099a21), is impossible without friendship (NE VIII.1, 1155a5), has significant content understood by the mind (NE X.7, 1177a26), and seems to need some sort of prosperity or success (NE I.8, 1198a32–33, 1199b6; I.10, 1100b7–10).

Much more recently, the developing branch of "positive" psychology, especially as pioneered by Martin Seligman, has employed the concept of flourishing to describe human excellence. Here is a comparison with Aristotle's five characteristics (Seligman 2012, 16–29).

Seligman	Aristotle
positive emotion	pleasure
engagement	activity
relationships	friendship
meaning	contemplation/use of the mind
achievement	prosperity or success

Because flourishing of the whole person includes flourishing of the body, it makes sense that Seligman's position is supported by biological studies of human health: participants who practiced his version of resiliency had fewer symptoms of physical illness and fewer doctor visits (Seligman 2011, 82–3). One of the most complete empirical reviews indicates that "dispositional optimism" predicts variations in physical flourishing: greater optimism is associated with better health even when various risk factors and psychosocial factors are accounted for (Rasmussen et al, 2009).

Likewise, a number of studies show that stress and depression jeopardize immune functioning, whereas social support, intentional relaxation, and trusting relationships can strengthen it (Peterson 2006, 231). Perhaps more significantly, positive affect in most cases improves problem solving, decision making, and makes thinking more flexible, creative, thorough, and efficient (Isen 2002). In other words, the flourishing of the emotions is intertwined with a flourishing of the brain's neural networks, which removes impediments to the mind's flourishing. This in turn has positive behavioral effects. For these reasons, when Seligman was tasked with defining a biological understanding of health, he found it necessary to include behavioral and even moral elements. He said that "health," which seems to be a necessary element of flourishing, includes biological assets (e.g., the hormone oxytocin, longer DNA telomeres), subjective assets (e.g., optimism, vitality), and functional assets (good marriage, rich friendships, engaging work) (Seligman 2012, 209).

Helpful as Seligman's account of human flourishing may be, by itself it does not capture the essence of human flourishing. Considered in isolation, it is broad enough to coincide with great evil. For instance, if Stalin reported predominantly positive emotions, was fully "engaged" in life, had significant supportive relationships, felt meaning and purpose in his life, and could revel in personal achievements, then—according to this understanding—his totalitarian and murderous life was a great example of human flourishing. To avoid this misunderstanding of human flourishing, Seligman and other thinkers have also discussed what they call "character strengths" or "virtues."

Drawing upon up-to-date data, Tyler VanderWeele's meta-study of empirical research has shown that there are at least nine pathways of human flourishing: certainly including mental and physical health, but also encompassing happiness and life satisfaction, meaning and purpose, character and virtue, and close social relationships (VanderWeele 2017). This may be seen in his diagram:

VanderWeele notes that any adequate account of human flourishing must therefore consider multiple outcomes simultaneously to get a view of the whole. It also ought to look, not just as specific disease or problem prevention,

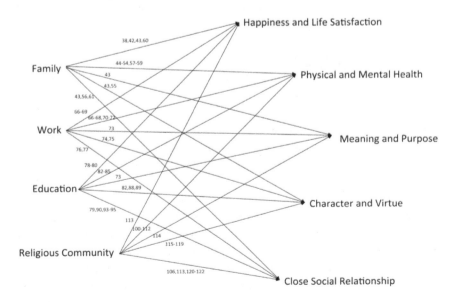

but even more consider broad flourishing outcomes. He notes that his account lacks a causal model to explain the relation among these various elements. We may also observe that among the nine "pathways" there are some missing lateral connections, which raises questions such as: how does work relate to education in terms of flourishing? How does meaning and purpose relate to character?

Here we may take a cue from the American psychologist Abraham Maslow. In his seminal article, "A Theory of Human Motivation," he famously described what became known as the "hierarchy of needs" (Maslow 1943). Because the needs are considered as objectively arranged in a series, it may be portrayed as a pyramid.

Without diminishing the value of this model, a number of questions may arise. For instance, it omits to discuss directly intellectual needs, such as the human hunger for truth. As Augustine once said, we know that everyone loves the truth because even if he does not tell the truth to others, everyone hates to be lied to. Similarly, although Maslow discusses achieving one's full potential, he does not explicitly discuss one's need for moral excellence and positive

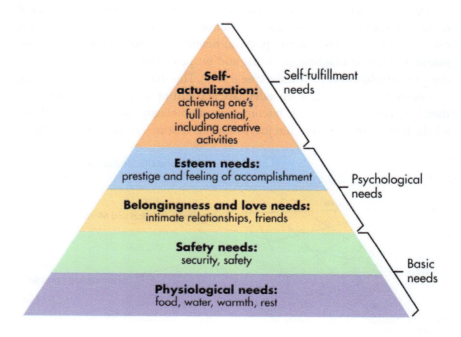

character formation, as evidenced by the universal desire for people to justify their actions as good in some way. However, Maslow does not recognize these needs; and only implicitly includes them under another category—perhaps "self-actualization." With respect to the target subject, Maslow's hierarchy seems to be entirely ego-centric. It does not consider that some goals can be other-centric, or at least focused on a common good that can be shared by individuals commonly. Hence, missing from this analysis are concerns such as entertainment, schools, politics, and civil society.

The Human Flourishing Framework

The philosopher and theologian, Thomas Aquinas, helps to develop some of the insights of other models previously discussed, and to fill in gaps in their thinking. Aquinas addresses the issue of flourishing in a unique way that adds conceptual richness to the analogy. He argues that flourishing is an image derived from nature that helps elucidate the character of human excellence (ST I, q. 37, a. 2). Just as a flower is a sign of hoped-for fruit, so the works of virtue are the hope of ultimate happiness (*Super Gal.*, c. 5, l. 6). Similarly, people flourish in life through their habituation to goodness through good action. Human excellence is the same as virtue: the flourishing of the individual insofar as the acts of virtue are directed towards one's greatest good. Even more, the acts of virtue lead to the full fruition of the human according to different criteria: individual and communal scales; level of value significance; and according to various goals that can be arranged according to a rational order.

Individual and Communal In the highest human flourishing, good habits exist together and mutually support each. Human excellence, seen in virtue, provides balance to a person, shaping his interior life such that no good inclination is in excess but instead is in harmony with human nature, which is composed of a variety of organically united parts (Cessario 2001, 38).

Level Just as a healthy tree will continue to thrive in different seasons, so when one's virtue extends to one's entire life, the virtues will continue to exist and adapt to every new situation.

Goal and Order The human is a complex organism, with various parts: when the parts operate together according to their own goals, and for the good of the whole, they are well-ordered and contribute to the overall flourishing of the person. Health, as a form of physical flourishing, provides an analogy for flourishing in general. A person is healthy when his individual organs operate according to their proper goal in harmony with each other and as contributing to the good of the person as a whole. For example, one goal of blood is to transfer oxygen to the entire body; when this goal is reached, blood achieves its goal and contributes to the good of the body as a whole. The more persons are ordered to their highest good, and are in harmony with the flourishing of their community, the more they flourish individually. And it is this order that Aquinas when he speaks about the "order of charity": how we are hierarchize various things that call for our good will (ST II-II, qq. 25–26).

In addition to Aquinas, an analysis of the Pontifical Council for Justice and Peace (PCJP), an office within the Vatican, offers insights about certain goods that are "basic" for all human beings on the physiological level, as well as the communal levels, with implications for individual needs as well as domains of common goods (PCJP 2005).

With these elements in mind, we propose the following **Human Flourishing Framework.**

Flourishing level	Need type	Individual Good		Common Good/Domain	
Spiritual	Spiritual needs, ultimate meaning	Connecting with ultimate end and meaning		Religion	
Communal	Family need	Doing good for one's family		Family life	
	Community and friendship need	Belonging, doing good for one's society, one's friends	Recognition, esteem	Network of free associations, groups, relationships: "civil society"	Public honor, praise
	Need for organized state	Organizing society, laws		Politics	
Individual	Intellectual-volitional needs	Character formation: becoming a better person Education: knowing		Schools; communications and media	
	Psychological-emotional needs	Feeling good; positive affect Psychological health		Psychological health associations	
	Making and doing needs (including creative activities)	Tools and work Toys and play	Instruments and art	Commerce, technology, Entertainment industries	Common art projects: museums, symphonies, etc.
	Physiological needs	Security, safety where one lives Physiological food, water, warmth,		World peace Healthcare and ecology: natural rest resources equitably shared, reasonably preserved and developed	

Explanation

Flourishing level indicates the locus of flourishing: on an individual level, the communal level, and the spiritual level. Looking at the lowest level of the HFF, we notice that humans may share physiological flourishing along with all living creatures; they may share emotional flourishing with higher animals more capable of emotional experience and expression, including such mammals as dolphins and apes. The higher levels of flourishing, especially intellectual, communal, and spiritual are particular to human beings or expressed among human beings in a qualitatively different way than the rest of the animal kingdom. For this reason, the HFF places those levels of flourishing above levels that are more general and undifferentiated among animal species.

Need type is a development of Maslow (1943) as well as Aquinas (1947), which ultimately is derived from needs found in human nature regardless of time period, culture, or situation.

Individual good provides incomplete examples of goods possessed by individuals that correspond to specific needs. For example, the physiological need of an individual includes food, water, warmth, and rest. Another example: on the communal level, the individual needs community and friendship; one sign of flourishing in this area is recognition and esteem from others.

Common good, domain indicates the kind of good for a group that corresponds to a given kind of need. These are goods possessed by groups together. For example, the physiological need of a group includes healthcare and ecology, which in turn include natural resources equitably shared. Again: on the communal level, a group flourishes when there exists a network of free associations, groups, relationships: "civil society."

Indicators of Individual Flourishing

Following Maslow's insight in his "Hierarchy of Needs" (1943), the Human Flourishing Framework (HFF) is organized according to a hierarchy of needs/values/ends. The lowest are at the bottom of the framework: a base-standard of flourishing in them is necessary in order for a person to mature and flourish in the higher levels. For example, if a person does not have his physiological needs met, such as security and safety, then he or she will find it difficult if not impossible to flourish in a stable way with respect to needs of making and doing—it will be difficult to play, to work, and so on, aside from exceptional circumstances. Likewise, if a person does not flourish in work, then it is likely that he or she will not have their psychological-emotional needs met:

and therefore will not flourish with positive affect. This sort of analysis can be performed for every "flourishing level."

Accordingly, one can extrapolate indicators of flourishing on individual, communal, and spiritual levels. Here we provide indicators only for the individual level.

Indicators of Individual Flourishing

Flourishing type	Indicators	Suppliers	
Intellectual character flourishing	Has a well-formed character Has an adequate education	Schools; communications and media	
Psychological emotional flourishing	Has sound positive affect and psychological health	Psychological health associations	
Experiential flourishing	Has access to necessary tools and adequate work	Commerce, technology,	Common art projects:
	Has access to adequate toys and play	Entertainment industries	museums, symphonies, etc.
	Affirms one's body in a healthy way	Sports, exercise, being in nature	
Physiological flourishing	Lives in safety	Local peace-keeping forces	
	Has access to adequate food, water,	Healthcare services warmth, rest	

It is important to note that the hierarchy of needs could mask that the HFF is a *dynamic system*, such that various goods and agents interact with each other in incredibly complex and often unpredictable ways. In other words, the causality of one level to another is occasionally linear, but more often involves cycles and feedback loops that exist in interdependence. For example, although it is true that some basic physiological flourishing is required for emotional flourishing and intellectual flourishing (indicating a bottom-up causal system), it is likewise true that when a person flourishes intellectually he or she often has a better chance at access to goods that assist physiological flourishing—because he or she can more creatively devise ways to find food, shelter, etc. This indicates that a top-down causal relationship is also at play.

There are also horizontal causal relationships: a person that has access adequate healthcare will also for that reason have better access to food, water, etc.; and a person who has access to technology (a common good) also has more access to tools necessary for work and therefore contributive to experiential flourishing.

There are also diagonal bi-directional causal relationships. This is illustrated by the red arrow below, which indicates that there is a relationship between psychological health and access to healthcare services. From the bottom-up causal direction, easier access to healthcare predicts a better chance at psychological health for an individual predisposed to mental illness—because he or she can receive the help they need. From a top-down causal direction, a person who has more psychological health is more likely to seek out and utilize healthcare opportunities, and to contribute helping others access the same.

Psychological-emotional flourishing	Has sound positive affect and psychological health	Psychological health associations	
Experiential flourishing	Has access to necessary tools and adequate work	Commerce, technology,	Common art projects:
	Has access to adequate toys and play	Entertainment industries	museums, symphonies, etc.
	Affirms one's body in a healthy way	Sports, exercise, being in nature	
Physiological flourishing	Lives in safety	Local peace-keeping forces	
	Has access to adequate food, water, warmth, rest	Healthcare services	

It seems unlikely that all levels, indicators, and suppliers have bi-directional diagonal causal relationships. For example, on a prima facie level, although a person with access to adequate physiological needs (e.g., food and shelter) would seem more likely to seek out entertainment (indicating a diagonal bottom-up causal direction), there is no obvious reason to think that better access to entertainment affects one's access to food, water, etc. (indicating that there is not a top-down causal direction). Given the asymmetry in causal relationships, more studies need to be done to examine where the lines of influence truly exist.

Obstacles to Flourishing

In order to foster human flourishing, we need to consider obstacles and risks that may arise. We distinguish between the two in the following way.

Obstacles are present harms that run contrary to flourishing. For example, ongoing warfare is an obstacle to the safety of individuals in a war zone, as well as the community as a whole—and therefore blocks full physiological flourishing.

Risks to flourishing are future contingents that can slow or prevent flourishing. For example, the lack of food presents a risk to physiological flourishing, and long-term deprivation of nourishment raises the probability from "low risk" to "high risk" or even "certainty" of lack-of-flourishing on account of death. Again, disease presents both an obstacle as well as a risk: it constitutes a present harm to health, and if the disease is chronic and grave, then it risks future impossibility of future flourishing at least on the physiological level.

To narrow the focus of our research, we did not look at global and often unpredictable catastrophic risks, such as effects of tsunamis, earthquakes, solar flares, volcano eruptions, asteroid impacts, etc. (Bostrom 2011). Certainly, work can be done to prevent the worst damage from such harms, but those risks do not constitute present obstacles to flourishing. We argue that flourishing studies ought to identify, evaluate, and rank conditions that currently exist, or will likely exist in the near future, which will significantly slow or prevent block human flourishing.

The Human Flourishing Framework allows researchers to identify obstacles to flourishing in a more nuanced way than ever before. Because it considers different levels of flourishing, it more clearly highlights different kinds of obstacles. Some obstacles concern material conditions for flourishing on the physiological level, such as poverty and lack of access to clean water. Other obstacles concern formal conditions for flourishing on the experiential, psychological, and character levels, such as political corruption and inadequate education.

Ranking Obstacles to Flourishing

Often studies of human happiness, well-being, and flourishing avoid ranking the different factors in comparison with each other, and instead either focus on single factors (e.g., GDP, self-reported satisfaction), or provide a network of different pathways without an explanation of their interaction or an evaluation of their relative importance (VanderWeele, 2017). In contrast, William Macaskill in his explanation for how to like an "effective altruist," astutely notes that not all endeavors to benefit others are equally worthy of one's investment of time and resources (Macaskill 2015). To rank possible altruistic endeavors, he asks questions such as the following:

- **Scale:** How many people benefit, and how much?
- **Opportunity cost:** Is this the most effective thing *you* can do?
- **Market saturation:** Is this area neglected?
- **Tractability:** What are the chances of success, and how good would success be?

With these in mind, one could create a framework for assessing and ranking potential altruistic interventions, as in the following (adapted from Macaskill 2015, 242).

	Scale	Market Saturation	Tractability
Extreme poverty	•••	••	•••
Climate change	••	•••	••
Education	•••	••	••••

Although data should back up the way one measures the rank each potential intervention may have in the different measuring columns, there will be a significant amount of value judgment involved in each measurement, especially depending on the level of specificity considered. For example, change in local education might register very low on the "scale" column (perhaps only one unit dot), but change in nation-wide educational policies can have a huge impact on an entire generation.

Likewise, market saturation for local education may be fairly small—few companies are competing for the direct attention of teachers—but comparatively large nationwide, in which a number of education-related companies are clamoring for government funding.

The question about opportunity cost is more of a personal consideration. It focuses on the abilities of the agent in question, whether a particular individual or a group. It asks: in light of what *you* are capable of doing, with your unique capacities, resources, time availability, etc., will this intervention be more effective than another? Of course, not every individual or group possesses the same mix of these elements. Therefore, what is "most effective" can differ greatly for philanthropic group A possessing a 2 Million funding source but very tech-savvy team members in comparison with philanthropic group B possessing 20 million in funding but with almost no advanced technical resources.

In addition to Macaskill's elements for measurement, our analysis goes a step further and helps rank the possible endeavors by suggesting two additional questions to be asked:
– **Importance:** What interventions are most important in themselves?
– **Causal impact:** What interventions will affect the greatest change?

The issue of importance is addressed in the Human Flourishing Framework, as noted above, in light of the "order of charity" proffered by Aquinas. In his ethical work, he provides a robust analysis that weighs how to assess on an objective level where one should focus his good will (ST II-II, q. 26).

Accordingly, the higher the need and good is on the HFF, the more important it may considered within an objective perspective. That is, all things being equal, we consider one good more objectively important than another insofar as it more clearly contributes or forms a part of flourishing for human beings with respect to their highest capacities. In contrast, some good may be more subjectively important for a given individual or group as a consequence of their circumstances: although a good education may be more important in itself—as tapping into human powers of knowledge and creativity—a nation suffering from starvation urgently needs intervention with food, and if there is a trade-off in the short term educational materials should give way to nourishment.

The issue of causal impact involves identifying foundational causal structures underlying the factors of flourishing, especially as they exist within complex systems (Pearl, 2009). Thus, for instance, education may be considered a "cause of causes," since people who are educated in some realm are enabled to be impactful agents. If a population suffering from drought are educated in efficient water usage, they can then cause a diminishment of water wastage, which in turn causes the negative effects of the drought to diminish. This illustrates a linear top-down causality. An illustration of a virtuous cycle of causality could extend the example further and note that if efficient water usage is taught to a population, the result (diminishing negative effects of drought) may in turn cause a greater number of people to seek out that education, thus impacting the drought even further.

Areas for Future Growth

The goal of Project Vision 2019 was to bring together experts in different fields in order to discuss the nature of human flourishing as well as its obstacles. We worked to synthesize research derived from such varied sources as business, empirical psychology, philosophy, governmental impact studies, and theology, in order to maximize the depth and breadth of our study. This enabled us to recognize points of convergence and to incorporate these insights into our study. The result is a unique, flexible, and robust Human Flourishing Framework. We believe that it presents the best framework yet developed for mapping out the different kinds of flourishing in relation to each other. It thereby also provides a framework for identifying indicators of human flourishing, as well as obstacles of human flourishing—and for comparing and ranking them all.

Our work is just a beginning, a first step to what we hope will be a Human Flourishing Framework that is examined by other experts, tested in the field, and refined where necessary. In that light, we see four areas for future growth with respect to the HFF.

- *External evaluation.* The HFF needs a feedback mechanism: peer review and evaluation of our claims, in order to consider other lists of needs, rankings of objective goods, and so on.
- *Wider dataset.* Wider variety of scholars, who can consider more data points, from a greater variety of viewpoints and expertise, especially regarding the scale, market saturation, and tractability of obstacles of flourishing.
- *Causal analysis and modeling.* We need to consider dynamic models to integrate findings of causal impacts, recognizing elements such as feedback loops, multi-factor causes, long-term versus short-term impact, and the difference between necessary and sufficient causality (Pearl 2009, 2019).
- *Scale expansion.* This research gave an example only of indicators of individual flourishing, but a clearer one would look at flourishing on different scales: families, micro-communities (e.g., neighborhoods), and macro-communities (e.g., civil states).

The result of these four areas of further growth for Project Vision and the HFF is that we will be better able to rank obstacles to flourishing, and to offer metrics for evaluating the effectiveness of different initiatives for overcoming obstacles to human flourishing. In that way, all who use the HFF will be better able to help all people, both individuals and communities, to better flourish and reach their full capacities.

References

Aquinas, Thomas. *Summa Theologica*. Translated by Fathers of the English Dominican Province. New York: Benziger, 1947.

Aquinas, Thomas. *Commentary on St. Paul's Epistle to the Galatians*. Translated by Fabian R. Larcher. Albany, NY: Magi Books., 1966.

Bostrom, Nick, and Milan M. Cirkovic. *Global Catastrophic Risks*. Oxford, UK: OUP, 2011.

Cessario, Romanus. *Introduction to Moral Theology*, rev. ed. Washington, DC: Catholic University of America Press, 2001.

Deiner, Ed, et al (2009). "Defining Well-Being," in *Well-Being for Public Policy*, ed. Deiner et al. Oxford, UK: OUP.

Helliwell, John, Richard Layard, and Jeffrey Sachs (2016, 2017, 2018, 2019). *World Happiness Report*. Manhattan, New York: United Nations Sustainable Development Solutions Network. http://worldhappiness.report/.

Isen, Alice M. "A Role for Neuropsychology in Understanding the Facilitating Influence of Positive Affect on Social Behavior and Cognitive Processes," in *Handbook of Positive Psychology*. Ed. CR Snyder and Shane J. Lope. Oxford, UK: Oxford University Press, 2002, 528–40.

Macaskill, William. *Doing Good Better: Effective Altruism and A Radical New Way to Make a Difference*. London: Guardian Books, 2015.

Maslow, Abraham. "A Theory of Human Motivation." *Psychological Review*, 1943, Vol. 50, no. 4, 370–96.

Pearl, Judea. *Causality: Models, Reasoning, and Inference*. Cambridge, UK: Cambridge University Press, 2009.

Pearl, Judea. *The Book of Why: The New Science of Cause and Effect*. Penguin, 2019.

Peterson, Christopher. *A Primer in Positive Psychology*. New York: Oxford University Press, 2006. Pontifical Council for Justice and Peace, *Compendium of Social Doctrine*. Vatican, 2005.

Rasmussen, Heather N. Michael F. Scheier, and Joel B. Greenhouse. "Optimism and Physical Health: A Meta-Analytic Review." *Annals of Behavioral Medicine* 37, no. 3 (May 2009): 239–56.

Seligman, Martin E. P. *Flourish: A Visionary New Understanding of Happiness and Well-Being*. New York: Atria Books, 2012.

Singer, Peter. *The Most Good You Can Do: How Effective Altruism Is Changing Ideas About Living Ethically*. Yale University Press, 2015.

United Nations General Assembly, Resolution 70/1, "Transforming our world: the 2030 Agenda for Sustainable Development. 25 September 2015. https://www.un.org/ga/search/view_doc.asp?symbol=A/RES/70/1&Lang=E VanderWeele, Tyler J (2017). "On the Promotion of Human Flourishing." *PNAS*, vol. 114, no. 31.

CHAPTER 7

Fraternity in the Law as a Means of Human Flourishing

John Makdisi*

May this essay on fraternity honor my very good friend and colleague, Siegfried Wiessner. He has devoted his life to the encouragement of fraternity throughout the world. His steadfast devotion to this noble goal, coupled with his compassion, integrity, powerful intellect, and strong work ethic, has inspired me and so many others on our own moral and intellectual journeys. Contrary to most *Festschrift*s which are offered upon retirement or death, this one is offered as a milestone along the way of a brilliant career. May God bless your continuing good work, Siegfried, in the many years ahead.

∴

The Declaration of Independence boldly declares that "the Laws of Nature and of Nature's God entitle" a people to a government that secures the self-evident truths "that all men are created equal, that they are endowed by their Creator with certain unalienable rights, that among these are Life, Liberty and the pursuit of Happiness."[1] Government exists to protect life, to ensure liberty and equality, and to enable the pursuit of happiness. Yet today liberty for some has become a banner under which the values of equality, life, and the pursuit of happiness have waned. Equality fails as the ever-widening gap between rich and poor leaves the poor in substandard conditions. Life becomes trivial as our culture of death advocates abortion, euthanasia, and the derogation from marriage as the source of family life. The pursuit of happiness is lost in the

---

* John Makdisi, J.D., S.J.D., Ph.D., is Interim Dean and Emeritus Professor of Law at St. Thomas University College of Law. He has written extensively on Islamic law and American property law among other subjects and now writes in the area of the intersection of law and theology. Dean Makdisi served as Professor of Law at St. Thomas from 1999–2019 and, as Dean from 1999–2003, he helped facilitate the founding of the Intercultural Human Rights Program by Dr. Siegfried Wiessner.
1 The Declaration of Independence, paras. 1–2 (U.S. 1776).

excessive pursuit of possessions, pleasure and power.[2] These failures find their source in the misconceived notion that liberty is a freedom of indifference rather than a freedom for excellence.[3]

This essay examines the misconceived notion of liberty as a freedom of indifference and suggests how we might change it to a freedom for excellence by a greater incorporation of fraternity into our law. Fraternity is love that exceeds a mere desire for the common good. It seeks the good of others as brothers and sisters who share their lives in interdependence and cooperation as they pursue the common good. To reach this level of love is not easy. It involves the conversion of one's natural inclination for self into a natural inclination for the other person, and this can only be done by falling in love:

> Love is patient, love is kind. It is not jealous, [love] is not pompous, it is not inflated, it is not rude, it does not seek its own interests, it is not quick-tempered, it does not brood over injury, it does not rejoice over wrongdoing but rejoices with the truth. It bears all things, believes all things, hopes all things, endures all things.[4]

Love identifies with the other person as with oneself in a unity that in law we call fraternity. It is the excellence that we seek in our pursuit of happiness. It is the perfection of our lives that makes us fully human. It is what makes us truly free.

1   The Claim of Liberty as a Freedom of Indifference

Before examining how we may achieve fraternity as an excellence that makes us free and how we may incorporate fraternity more deeply in the law, it is important to understand the destructive effects of the freedom of indifference more thoroughly. Freedom of indifference has no direction other than to live one's life only for oneself. Living life only for self leads to a denigration of the principles of the Declaration of Independence because it conflicts with the true meaning

---

2 John the Evangelist describes these three temptations as "the lust of the eyes," "the lust of the flesh," and the "pride of life." 1 Jn 2:16. They correspond to the seven deadly vices or sins: greed and sloth seek and despise possessions respectively; lust and gluttony seek pleasure; and wrath, envy and pride seek independence from God and others.

3 The meaning of the terms *freedom of indifference* and *freedom for excellence* are thoroughly defined and explored in Servais Pinckaers, The Sources of Christian Ethics (M. Noble, trans. from 3rd ed. 1995) (1985, 1990, 1993).

4 1 Cor. 13:4–7.

of equality, life, and the pursuit of happiness. The glorification of self sees these ideals as necessary only to enhance one's own welfare, not the welfare of others. It is a Hobbesian attitude that promotes the idea that the welfare of others is a necessary evil to ensure one's own welfare because, without these ideals, one has less freedom to do what one wants.[5] Therefore, the laws that preserve equality, life and the pursuit of happiness become tools to achieve one's own ends. Each person seeks to minimize the effect of these laws on oneself while claiming their full benefit as a right against others. There is no such thing as morality apart from law. The restraint of law exists only to maximize one's ability to do as one pleases with no other direction than that it pleases. This ability is a freedom of indifference. The restraint of law according to this mode of thinking is to ensure the greatest possible freedom of indifference.

The misconceived notion of liberty as a freedom of indifference finds expression in the infamous words of Justice Anthony Kennedy that "at the heart of liberty is the right to define one's own concept of existence, of meaning, of the universe, and of the mystery of human life."[6] Autonomy is projected as the epitome of happiness. Existence, meaning, the universe, and human life are formless clay which each person has the ability to form for oneself in whatever way one wants. Slogans evolve to proclaim that being is nothingness, truth is perception, the world is an illusion, and babies in the womb are not persons. If one but accepts the political correctness of this vision, all will be well with the world.

But all is not well with the world. When John seeks love in Aldous Huxley's pleasure-seeking *Brave New World*, his life ends in despair and suicide.[7] When the animals seek sustenance from the wealth-seeking pigs in George Orwell's *Animal Farm*, their lives end in slavery.[8] When Winston seeks freedom from the power-seeking mind control of Big Brother in George Orwell's *1984*, he ends up succumbing to that control.[9]

The government in each of these stories quells the natural longing of its members for happiness as a function of truth and goodness. It caters to appetites for possessions, pleasure and power to create a world centered on self. The result is death and slavery, both physical and mental. The problem in these societies stems from the willingness of people to allow their government

---

5   *See* Thomas Hobbes, Leviathan or the Matter, Forme, & Power of a Common-Wealth Ecclesiastical and Civill (1651).
6   Planned Parenthood of Se. Pa. v. Casey, 505 U.S. 833, 851 (1992).
7   Aldous Huxley, Brave New World (1932).
8   George Orwell, Animal Farm (1946).
9   George Orwell, 1984 (1949).

to cater to their appetites, dull their senses, and stymie their exercise of will towards the good. When government finally controls them through law, the only morality becomes the obligation under law to follow the pure will of the legislator. Law, as a morality of obligation, serves the purposes of power rather than the true happiness of the common good and ironically limits even the freedom of indifference sought by its citizens.[10]

2   The Claim of Liberty as a Freedom for Excellence

Fraternity is an excellence that frees us from the prison of our desires and enables us to enjoy happiness through the love of other. We can achieve this excellence only through self-understanding, sacrifice and commitment. Self-understanding begins with an understanding that truth and goodness are features of our world that exist apart from our own creation. Our minds incline naturally to know the truth and our wills incline naturally to live in society.[11] The family as the grassroots unit of society shows us that love is the bond that keeps us together and gives us happiness as we live in society. We can choose through a freedom of indifference to reject this truth, but we only lose the one way in which we are free to be happy.

Another truth that we soon learn about ourselves is that our appetites are not always ordered towards the excellence of love. They tend to incline us toward possessions, pleasure and power in ways that promote love of self and detract from the love of other. It requires work and self-sacrifice to re-order our appetites so that they serve our love of other. One does this work by developing habits (virtues) that form a second nature for each of our appetites so that the attractions of possessions, pleasure and power are no longer desired exclusively for the good of ourselves but for the good of the whole of society. A person's appetites are the concupiscible appetite (inclination for pleasure and against pain), the irascible appetite (inclination for fight or flight from danger), and the rational appetite or will (inclination to do good). The chief habits (known as the cardinal virtues) for each of these appetites are temperance, fortitude, and justice respectively. When one has developed these virtues as second natures, love of other comes naturally.

---

10   *See* Pinckaers, *Sources, supra* note 3, at 74 (summary of the different aspects of freedom of indifference).

11   2 Thomas Aquinas, Summa Theologica, pt. I-II, Q. 94, art. 2, at 1009 (Fathers of the English Dominican Province trans. Benziger Bros., Inc. 1947) (hereinafter cited as ST I-II.94.2).

Even after we develop these virtues, however, our work is never finished. Distractions, temptations and other vagaries of life can eat away at one's virtues and cause them to fail if one is not vigilant. In addition to self-sacrifice in the formation of virtue, one must also commit to keeping these virtues throughout one's life. Only then will society live in a stable environment of fraternity enjoying the freedom of excellence that is love.

3   The Nature of Fraternity

Fraternity is love that seeks the good of others as brothers and sisters. There is no greater model for this type of love than Jesus Christ who gave himself for the good of all, especially for the poor, the sick, the needy, and the sinner. He taught that we are our brother's keeper:

> For you were called for freedom, brothers. But do not use this freedom as an opportunity for the flesh; rather, serve one another through love. For the whole law is fulfilled in one statement, namely, "You shall love your neighbor as yourself." But if you go on biting and devouring one another, beware that you are not consumed by one another.[12]

To love one's neighbor as oneself through compassion and service to one's neighbor is the essence of fraternity.

This teaching is no more beautifully illustrated than in the parable of the Good Samaritan. Jesus related the following story when asked "who is my neighbor?"

> A man fell victim to robbers as he went down from Jerusalem to Jericho. They stripped and beat him and went off leaving him half-dead. A priest happened to be going down that road, but when he saw him, he passed by on the opposite side. Likewise a Levite came to the place, and when he saw him, he passed by on the opposite side. But a Samaritan traveler who came upon him was moved with compassion at the sight. He approached the victim, poured oil and wine over his wounds and bandaged them. Then he lifted him up on his own animal, took him to an inn and cared for him. The next day he took out two silver coins and gave them to the innkeeper with the instruction, "Take care of him. If you spend more than

---

12   Gal. 5:13–15.

what I have given you, I shall repay you on my way back." Which of these three, in your opinion, was neighbor to the robbers' victim?[13]

The listener answered Jesus' question by saying "the one who treated him with mercy." Jesus then said "go and do likewise."

In this parable Jesus points out that it does not matter who the actors are. We are all our brother's keeper. He makes the point all the more poignantly by showing that it was not the priest or the Levite who turned away but rather the Samaritan on whom the Jewish community looked down, who was the real brother. As Pope Francis points out, the parable "speaks to us of an essential and often forgotten aspect of our common humanity: we were created for a fulfilment that can only be found in love."[14] It calls us all to give up our indifference to suffering and "emerge from our comfortable isolation" to "identify with the vulnerability of others" and "act instead as neighbours, lifting up and rehabilitating the fallen for the sake of the common good."[15] Only then do we find the true meaning of dignity.

Jesus provides a practical plan to engage in a life of fraternity. In his Sermon on the Mount[16] he offers directives for a person to be blessed (happy) and summarizes them in the Beatitudes.[17] Such a person is one who loves God and neighbor. We begin by dispossessing ourselves of the distractions that feed our appetites for possessiveness, pleasure, and pride and that cause us to turn away from others who are suffering. By learning poverty of spirit, sharing the suffering of others, and removing our arrogance, we prepare our hearts not only to give others their just due and more but to do it with yearning and compassion.[18] When we do this for our neighbor, we do it for God.[19]

---

13   Luke 10:30–36.

14   Pope Francis, Encyclical Letter, *On Fraternity and Social Friendship* 35 (Oct. 3, 2020).

15   *Id.*

16   Mt. 5–7.

17   Mt. 5:3–12.

18   The first five Beatitudes in Mt. 5:3–7. We also realize a purity of heart that allows us to approach sin and heal it, and we become peacemakers as we allow God's peace to penetrate to our very being. These are the sixth and seventh Beatitudes in Mt. 5:8–9. This essay focuses only on the first five beatitudes.

19   Christ calls those blessed who gave food to the hungry, drink to the thirsty, welcome to the stranger, clothes to the naked, care to the sick, and visitation to the prisoner, and he says "whatever you did for one of these least brothers of mine, you did for me." Mt. 25:34–40.

4 Fraternity in the Law

Law cannot command the love that Jesus calls us to live through the Beatitudes. It involves an individual choice to redirect our focus away from self towards the good of the other person. The laws of our nation cannot command this sacrifice. It is an internal affair. Perhaps this is why we do not see fraternity among the values promoted at the beginning of the Declaration of Independence. Nevertheless, the signers of the Declaration recognized that something more was needed if these values were to be maintained, and they did incorporate fraternity in the document by a pledge.

In the last sentence of the Declaration they stated that "for the support of this declaration, with a firm reliance on the protection of Divine Providence, we mutually pledge to each other our lives, our fortunes and our sacred honor."[20] What they recognized was that the key to the success of their endeavor was in their pulling together in fraternity. These words are a personal commitment made by the signers on behalf of the people of the United States to share what they hold most valuable in mutual cooperation in order that their project might work. They are a pledge to live together as one people under God, sharing what is most dear to ensure life, liberty and justice for all. We repeat this pledge each time we pledge allegiance to the flag of the United States of America, which declares us to be "one nation under God, indivisible, with liberty and justice for all."[21]

Fraternity in the Declaration of Independence refers to the people of the United States having the quality of brothers and sisters as they come together to form and maintain their new government. It is a commitment that identifies who we are as a people; it gives us strength in unity; and it promotes human flourishing. This quality involves mutual cooperation based not only on justice but on such love for the common good that one is willing, even desirous, to sacrifice one's fortune, one's honor, and one's very life to assure it. The mutual cooperation described here cannot be commanded, and even if it were, obedience would not be enough. It only works as a commitment in love.

5 Fraternity Encouraged by Law

Even though law cannot command the love that Jesus calls us to live through the Beatitudes, law can encourage it. It does so by adopting policies that work

---

20 Declaration of Independence, *supra* note 1, at para. 32.
21 The Pledge of Allegiance (U.S. 1954).

towards the common good of all, with particular emphasis on the needs of the poor, the suffering and the disadvantaged at the peripheries of our society. In the midst of a growing number of voices clamoring for freedom of indifference, it is important to renew our efforts to incorporate fraternity in the law through these policies—to reject the idea that liberty is merely autonomy and to redouble our efforts to become our brother's keeper.

One note of caution. While law can mandate certain practices to encourage fraternity, it must be careful not to overburden people with laws that are too oppressive. There are limitations on how much one can promote virtue by law. Aquinas maintains that human laws should not forbid all vices but only the more grievous so that people, most of whom are imperfect in virtue, are able to abstain from them because they are not overly burdensome.[22] "The purpose of human law is to lead men to virtue, not suddenly, but gradually."[23] This is done not only to protect victims but also to train perpetrators who "by being habituated in this way [compulsion], might be brought to do willingly what hitherto they did from fear."[24]

With this caution in mind, let us proceed to examine examples of some areas where the law could promote fraternity to better advantage. Since the path to the love that embodies fraternity is through the Beatitudes, these examples will be organized under the first five Beatitudes.

5.1 Blessed are the Poor in Spirit: The Doctrine of Necessity

The vice of possessiveness is an abuse of the concupiscible appetite by greed. The possessive person sees property as part of one's own domain to which no one else has a right. The emphasis is on ownership, not stewardship. In the first Beatitude Christ calls us back from this vice when he says, "Blessed are the poor in spirit."[25] By developing the virtue of temperance one divests oneself of this greed, and develops a second nature for one's concupiscible appetite, making it easier to open one's heart to the needs of others. Law can encourage this virtue by changing the notion that ownership is absolute to one that favors stewardship.

One change in this direction might occur in the doctrine of necessity. The doctrine permits a person seriously in need to use the property of another to prevent harm to one's own person or property. The classic case is *Vincent v.*

---

22 ST I-II.95.1.
23 ST I-II.96.2.ad2.
24 ST I-II.95.1
25 Mt. 5:3.

Lake Erie Transportation Co.[26] in which a captain in a huge storm secured his ship to a dock without the permission of the owner, thus saving his ship but damaging the dock. By permitting the captain to use the property of another in this case, the court encouraged fraternity but then required the ship owner to pay the damages caused to the dock. This made the use of the owner's property a type of loan that had to be repaid.

The court might have used a more fraternal approach by qualifying the use of the dock as a right of the captain arising from his serious need as long as the dock owner was not also in serious need of the dock. The captain's right of use during the period of serious need would give him not only the use but also freedom from liability for any reasonable damages that flowed from the use. With this more fraternal approach, which recalls the just deed of the Good Samaritan, the captain would not have been responsible for the damages to the dock in *Vincent*.

Aquinas maintains that "all things are common property in a case of extreme necessity," and, if the one in need cannot find anyone to help him, he may take another's goods to help himself unless it would put the other in extreme need.[27] The property then belongs to the one in extreme need by reason of that need.[28] The implication is that there is no compensation required in return. Aquinas justifies this doctrine by natural law based on the universal destination of goods.[29] God has given his creation to all, and we all generally

---

26   Vincent v. Lake Erie Transportation Co., 124 N.W. 221 (Minn. 1910).

27   ST II-II.32.7.ad3. It is a duty to help a person in need. Aquinas says that "to keep back what is due to another, inflicts the same kind of injury as taking a thing unjustly." ST II-II.66.3.ad2. On the other hand, "it is altogether wrong to give alms out of what is necessary to us [absolutely]; for instance, if a man found himself in the presence of a case of urgency, and had merely sufficient to support himself and his children, or others under his charge, he would be throwing away his life and that of others if he were to give away in alms, what was then necessary to him."

28   "It is not theft, properly speaking, to take secretly and use another's property in a case of extreme need: because that which he takes for the support of his life becomes his own property by reason of that need." ST II-II.66.7.ad2.

29   "Things which are of human right cannot derogate from natural right or Divine right. Now according to the natural order established by Divine Providence, inferior things are ordained for the purpose of succoring man's needs by their means. Wherefore the division and appropriation of things which are based on human law, do not preclude the fact that man's needs have to be remedied by means of these very things. Hence whatever certain people have in superabundance is due, by natural law, to the purpose of succoring the poor. ... Since, however, there are many who are in need, while it is impossible for all to be succored by means of the same thing, each one is entrusted with the stewardship of his own things, so that out of them he may come to the aid of those who are in need. Nevertheless, if the need be so manifest and urgent, that it is evident that the present need

should treat our ownership of property as stewards, holding it for the good of all.[30] This approach replaces the notion of autonomous ownership with fraternal stewardship.

Of course, law cannot mandate the complete spectrum of virtue. Even though one has a moral duty of stewardship in a case of need, it would be imprudent to require this duty as a matter of law for need that is less serious. Aquinas agrees and states that he does not believe a person is required under penalty of law to aid those whose need is not "so manifest and urgent," even though this does not diminish his moral duty to make a prudent choice to help the less needy.[31] We are all our brother's keeper. The difference between the case of extreme need and the case of lesser need is that the moral obligation does not become a legal obligation in the latter case. Nevertheless, by encouraging a fraternal approach in the extreme case, the law encourages people to use that same approach on their own in the lesser case.

Even if the law were to continue the old regime allowing the use of another's property in the case of extreme necessity on the condition of paying for the damages done, it might nevertheless extend this doctrine to cases with a lesser, albeit significant need. In *Jacque v. Steenberg Homes*[32] the Court protected the property right of a landowner against the use of the landowner's property by one who otherwise would have undergone significant economic loss. The court did not apply the doctrine of necessity but considered the use a trespass. There were no damages, so the court awarded nominal damages to recognize the trespass. However, it then proceeded to award $100,000 in punitive damages. If this award was to confirm the right of the landowner to exclude others

---

must be remedied by whatever means be at hand (for instance when a person is in some imminent danger, and there is no other possible remedy), then it is lawful for a man to succor his own need by means of another's property, by taking it either openly or secretly: nor is this properly speaking theft or robbery." ST II-II.66.7. The principle of the universal destination of goods, which maintains that God intended his creation for all mankind, is found in Genesis 1:28–29.

30   This dominion over external things is natural because we are able to use them for our own profit by our reason and will as they were made for us. ST II-II.66.1. However, we possess them not as our own but as common, so that we are ready to communicate them to others in their need. ST II-II.66.2. Aquinas gives as an example that "a rich man does not act unlawfully if he anticipates someone in taking possession of something which at first was common property, and gives others a share: but he sins if he excludes others indiscriminately from using it." ST II-II.66.2.ad2. The Catholic Catechism quotes St. John Chrysostom and St. Gregory the Great as both affirming that the goods we possess belong to the poor and to give to them is a demand of justice, not charity. Catechism of the Catholic Church, para. 2446, at 587–88 (1994).

31   ST II-II.66.7.

32   Jacque v. Steenberg Homes, Inc., 563 N.W.2d 154 (Wis. 1997).

from his property without regard to their need, the Court missed an opportunity to encourage fraternity. It emphasized the right to exclude as absolute. If, instead, it had recognized the right of the "trespasser" to use the landowner's property as a form of private eminent domain, paying damages but not penalized for the use, it would have supported the idea of mutual cooperation and stewardship in times of need.[33]

The mutual cooperation and stewardship suggested in the *Jacque* case is a form of private eminent domain. In the area of public eminent domain, the government has the power to take private property and convert it to public use under the takings clause of the Fifth Amendment of the Constitution[34] as long as it provides just compensation. There is no constitutional provision that allows for private eminent domain, yet there are several instances where the law allows a private individual to use the property of another—some without payment for the use. Examples include historic preservation laws, environmental laws, the public trust doctrine, access to vital services, nuisance, recovery of property, and deviations from a highway.[35] They have not all been widely adopted due to the resistance of owners who claim the right of absolute ownership. To promote fraternity, these laws themselves might profitably be adopted in jurisdictions that still do not have them.

The concept of property ownership as stewardship applies to more than tangible property. In the area of business, an employer who hires employees for wages that are the mainstay of their lives has a moral duty to pay a living wage to these employees in order that they have the basic necessities of life.[36] Pope Leo XIII in his encyclical on capital and labor states that for an employer "to exercise pressure upon the indigent and the destitute for the sake of gain, and to gather one's profit out of the need of another, is condemned by all laws, human and divine."[37] What this means is that "the wages of the worker must not merely be sufficient for the necessities of life, but should enable the worker to 'possess' a certain modest fortune; that 'bad management, want of enterprise, or out of date methods is not a just reason for reducing the workingmen's wages'; that the right of the worker to a living wage comes before the employer's right to enlarge his plant or the employer's right to advertise to increase his

---

33   For a more detailed analysis of the interpretation of this case, see John Makdisi, *Uncaring Justice: Why* Jacque v. Steenberg Homes *Was Wrongly Decided*, 51 J. Cath. Leg. Stud. 111 (2012).

34   U.S. Const. art. v.

35   For a summary of each of these, see Makdisi, *Uncaring Justice, supra* note 33, at 119–27.

36   These include food, shelter, utilities, transportation, child care, and health care.

37   *Rerum Novarum*: Encyclical of Pope Leo XIII on Capital and Labor, 20 (May 15, 1891).

sales."[38] An employer becomes a steward of his or her business to the extent that he or she recognizes the right of an employee to a living wage through a sharing of profits. The law might encourage fraternity by converting this moral duty into a legal duty by requiring all employers to pay a living wage.

5.2   *Blessed Are They Who Mourn: the Duty to Rescue*

The vice of indifference is an abuse of the irascible appetite by inordinate fear. The indifferent person sees the suffering and afflictions of others as something that would upset the equilibrium of one's life. Therefore, the person chooses to avoid the situation rather than caring for the suffering person. In the second Beatitude Christ calls us back from this vice when he says, "Blessed are those who mourn."[39] Blessed are those who face the suffering of others and allow it to penetrate to the depth of their souls, challenging them in their grief to respond in love.[40] By facing the suffering of others with the virtue of courage one divests oneself of inordinate fear and develops a second nature for one's irascible appetite, making it easier to face the reality of suffering with compassion. Law might encourage this virtue by changing the prevalent notion that permits indifference to the plight of others to one that requires responsibility at least for those needing rescue from a situation of danger.

In contrast to many European countries,[41] only five states in the United States have enforceable duty-to-rescue statutes.[42] In those states that have no duty to rescue, a person can stand by without making any attempt to save the life of another. This happened in 2017 when five Florida teens taunted and filmed a drowning man calling for help without making any attempt to rescue him even after he went under water and did not resurface.[43] They were not held responsible for his death because, despite their callous disregard of

---

38   Fulton J. Sheen, Liberty Equality and Fraternity, Kindle Edition, 71.

39   Mt. 5:4.

40   Servais Pinckaers, The Pursuit of Happiness – God's Way: Living the Beatitudes 82–84 (M. Noble, trans. 1998). God uses suffering to touch hearts of stone and turn them into human hearts. As Pinckaers says, "we see the roadway of affliction, humiliation and patience which Christ once followed, opening up before us." *Id.* at 84.

41   Jay Silver, *The Duty to Rescue: A Reexamination and Proposal*, 26 Wm. & Mary L. Rev. 423, 434–35 (1985).

42   "Hawaii, Minnesota, and Rhode Island have statutes explicitly requiring witnesses to an emergency to notify emergency services, while Vermont, and Wisconsin have statutes implicitly requiring witnesses to do so." Mark H. Okumori, *Germany's Duty-to-Rescue Law Should be Adopted in Every State*, 28 Sw. J. Int'l L. 258, 259 (2022) (footnotes omitted).

43   *Id.* at 258–59, citing Faith Karimi, *Teens Who Laughed and Recorded a Drowning Man in His Final Moments Won 't Face Charges*, CNN, https://edition.cnn.com/2018/06/26/us /florida-teens-no-charges-drowning-man (June 26, 2018, 10:27 PM).

human life, the State Attorney explained that there was "no law that requires a person to provide emergency assistance."[44] This behavior is a serious affront to human dignity which calls us to be our brother's keeper, and it makes a strong case for duty-to-rescue laws. Mutual cooperation in the face of danger to human life is even more important than cooperation in the face of danger to property addressed by the doctrine of necessity.

Christ lauded the traveler in the Parable of the Good Samaritan who took the time to care for the victim of a robbery and beating. The Samaritan was a true model of fraternal friendship. Aquinas confirms the moral of this parable when he states that there is a moral duty to rescue a person who cannot be helped otherwise. Even in the case of an enemy, one must rescue him if he be in danger of death.[45] This duty does not extend to the situation where a rescue would put oneself in danger, although such a supererogatory act would be highly meritorious.[46] Also, if the person needing rescue can be helped otherwise, or by someone who is closer to him or in a better position to help him, the potential rescuer is not bound to help him, although it would be praiseworthy to do so.[47] Still, if a person is in danger of death and there is no one to help except oneself, the law would promote fraternity by requiring one to rescue the person in danger.

5.3 Blessed are the Meek: The Rehabilitation of Felons

The vice of vengeance is an abuse of the will by anger. Anger is "a desire for vengeance, ... aroused chiefly when a man deems himself unjustly injured."[48] When retribution is the infliction of punishment for some good, such as to restrain the wrongdoer from causing further harm or to reform the wrongdoer, retribution is good as a type of justice. But when retribution is the infliction of punishment against the other's evil, the pleasure one takes in this act belongs

---

44   *Id.*

45   If the nature of the excommunicated and the enemies of the common weal "be in urgent need of succor lest it fail, we are bound to help them: for instance, if they be in danger of death through hunger or thirst, or suffer some like distress, unless this be according to the order of justice." ST II-II.31.2.ad3.

46   "Charity does not necessarily require a man to imperil his own body for his neighbor's welfare, except in a case where he is under obligation to do so; and if a man of his own accord offer himself for that purpose, this belongs to the perfection of charity." ST II-II.26.5.ad3.

47   ST II-II.71.1. Aquinas adds: "Therefore an advocate is not always bound to defend the suits of the poor, but only when the aforesaid circumstances concur, else he would have to put aside all other business, and occupy himself entirely in defending the suits of poor people. The same applies to a physician with regard to attendance on the sick."

48   ST II-II.65.2.ad1, citing Aristotle, Rhetoric ii.

to hatred, and retribution is the vice of vengeance as a type of injustice.[49] In the third Beatitude Christ calls us back from this vice when he says, "Blessed are the meek."[50] By developing the virtue of meekness, one divests oneself of the anger that comes from one's desire to change sorrow into the personal pleasure of vengeance and develops a second nature for one's will that finds its happiness in the peaceful possession of oneself through mercy and forgiveness. Such meekness creates the bonds of fraternity that form a true community.[51] Law might encourage this virtue by encouraging models of compassion, forgiveness and mercy as in the treatment of felons in the two examples below.

First example: Before a felon is imprisoned, a victim who has developed the virtue of meekness may wish to forgive his or her perpetrator for the crime committed and may ask for leniency in the sentencing process. As long as the punishment imposed is sufficient to accomplish the interests of the state,[52] the allowance of leniency in punishment beyond the state's interests would encourage fraternity among others in society. Not only would this act of mercy and forgiveness most likely leave a significant impression on the felon himself,[53] but others would think twice about their attitude towards those who have done them wrong. At present, however, many courts exclude testimony by victims asking for leniency.[54] They have not taken sufficient account of the deep human need for fraternity that exists at the core of forgiveness.

Christ modeled this type of forgiveness when he asked his Father to forgive those who mercilessly crucified him[55] and when he forgave the repentant thief on the cross.[56] He showed tremendous strength of character in his meekness. Through suffering, injustice and the anguish of sin he poured out his soul in his Passion. And he calls us to forgive others as he himself forgave and as he called

---

49   ST II-II.108.1.

50   Mt. 5:5. The supreme example of meekness is Jesus Christ "Who, though he was in the form of God, did not regard equality with God something to be grasped. Rather, he emptied himself, taking the form of a slave, coming in human likeness; and found human in appearance, he humbled himself, becoming obedient to death, even death on a cross." Phil. 2:6–8. Christ shows us what it means to be truly human.

51   Pinckaers, Pursuit of Happiness, *supra* note 40, at 72.

52   *I.e.*, deterrence, incapacitation, rehabilitation and education.

53   "While one cannot be certain, it is at least possible that apologetic, forgiven offenders are more likely to take their lessons to heart and less likely to recidivate. Empirical evidence of restorative-justice outcomes certainly suggests that participating offenders are more likely to apologize and be forgiven and less likely to recidivate." Stephanos Bibas, *Forgiveness in Criminal Procedure*, 4 Ohio St. J. Crim. L. 329, 337 (2007).

54   *Id.*

55   Luke 23:34.

56   Luke 23: 42–43.

Peter to forgive.[57] Meekness involves the strength of soul to refuse to succumb to the violence of anger but rather to conquer it with love.

Second example: While felons serve their time before their return to society, the law might promote fraternity by working to remove the stigma of prison through effective rehabilitation. Michelle Alexander describes this stigma in powerful terms:

> Criminals, it turns out, are the one social group in America we have permission to hate. In "colorblind" America, criminals are the new whipping boys. They are entitled to no respect and little moral concern. ... Once released, they find that a heavy and cruel hand has been laid upon them. ... [They] will also be told little or nothing about the parallel universe [they are] about to enter; one that promises a form of punishment that is often more difficult to bear than prison time: a lifetime of shame, contempt, scorn, and exclusion. In this hidden world, discrimination is perfectly legal ... "In this brave new world, punishment for the original offense is no longer enough; one's debt to society is never paid."[58]

This passage resonated deeply with a felon who made a successful return to society but was still marked and excluded as a former felon. When Angel Sanchez got out of prison, he went to law school and graduated in the top 5% of his class, making it onto law review and earning a federal judicial internship. Yet, when it came to getting a job, he found that the concern of the employers with whom he interviewed "was not whether I could be trusted, but whether they could trust the system to give me a chance to practice."[59]

Unless there is real reform of our prison system so that it provides meaningful rehabilitation, a felon will always be marked by the stigma of prison. Sanchez remarked that no level of hard work or amount of academic success could shield him from this stigma and he would never see finality in the payment of his debt to society.[60] Until society decides to devote significant resources to making prisons true centers of rehabilitation, it will never realize the fraternity that necessarily undergirds the principle of liberty for felons. Everyone, including felons who have paid their debt to society, should have

---

57   Christ admonished Peter to forgive one who offended him "'not seven times but seventy-seven times.'" Mt. 18:22. This means that "one should always forgive [sins committed against oneself] and spare our brother when he repents." ST II-II.11.4.ad2.

58   Michelle Alexander, The New Jim Crow 141–42 (2010) (footnotes omitted), as quoted in Angel Sanchez, *In Spite of Prison*, 132 Harv. L. Rev. 1650, 1680 (2019).

59   Sanchez, *In Spite of Prison*, supra note 58, at 1683.

60   *Id.*

an equal chance to pursue happiness as a freedom for excellence. Only when we are meek enough to forgive with true compassion those who have harmed our society will meaningful rehabilitation take place. Only then will the principles of equality, liberty, and the pursuit of happiness in the Declaration of Independence make sense.

The fraternity that can be achieved through meekness in the case of prison reform is modeled by the father in the Parable of the Prodigal Son.[61] After being dishonored by his youngest son who took his inheritance and spent it on wild living, the father did not reject him but waited patiently for his return. When the son finally came to his senses and returned to his father, the father rejoiced and welcomed him back as his son into his house. The forgiveness of the father, full of love without a trace of anger, shows us how to welcome the felon back into society. When a felon is paying his dues to society through his incarceration, the law might encourage fraternity through reform of the prison system to provide meaningful rehabilitation.

5.4   *Blessed are They Who Hunger and Thirst for Righteousness and Blessed are the Merciful: The Promotion of Life*

The fourth and fifth Beatitudes concerning justice and mercy respectively differ from the first three in at least two respects. They do not speak directly to developing virtues that develop second natures for our appetites. They also go together as necessary complements to each other. The justice called righteousness in the fourth Beatitude has its source in God and "must proceed from the heart of man in the form of love."[62] Mercy in the fifth Beatitude favors justice in the heart and "considers the person, always capable of returning to justice with the help of God's grace, and continues to love him in spite of the wrongs he does."[63] The two are inseparable. As Aquinas remarks, "mercy without justice is the mother of dissolution; justice without mercy is cruelty."[64]

The just and merciful person is a person of action. When we begin to detach from the distractions of our appetites as people who are poor in spirit, who mourn, and who are meek, we begin to open our eyes to God's creation in all its beauty and wonder and the place God has given us within it. As the psalmist says:

---

61   Luke 15:11–32.

62   Pinckaers, *Pursuit of Happiness, supra* note 40, at 99.

63   *Id.* at 119.

64   *Super Matthaeum*, Cap. v, L.2.

When I see your heavens, the work of your fingers,
   the moon and stars that you set in place—
What is man that you are mindful of him,
   and a son of man that you care for him?
Yet you have made him little less than a god,
   crowned him with glory and honor.[65]

In light of God's gifts to us, we cannot help but yearn to do God's will as a deer yearns for running streams.[66] It is a natural response to seek to return God's love through action.

Where do we find God in order to return His love? We find Him in the hungry, the thirsty, the stranger, the naked, the sick, and the prisoner.[67] Christ calls us to reach out to these to give them the life, which they, made in the image of God, deserve through our love and care. We have already seen that justice is the virtue of giving people their due. Blessed are the meek who have this sense of justice. But Christ asks for more. He asks us to live this virtue through our actions. Thus, in the fourth Beatitude Christ says, "Blessed are those who hunger and thirst for righteousness,"[68] and in the fifth Beatitude, "Blessed are the merciful."[69] Blessed are they who strive to bring justice to this world with a ready, willing and compassionate heart. The effect of this striving is to create right relationships in which people live more authentically in fraternity.

Taking just one of these categories, the stranger, how might we encourage this fraternity in the law? There are two types of "stranger" in today's society whom we have failed—the unwanted unborn and the immigrant. Despite the recent opinion of *Dobbs*[70] which removed the issue of abortion from the Constitution, there are still many states that promote abortion of the unborn baby in the womb—a stranger to those who avert their eyes from one of the most profound mysteries of this world, the growth of a new human person within the womb. There is also a strong reaction against the immigrant—a stranger to those who forget that we are an immigrant nation and that the person who seeks to immigrate into our country often fits within the categories of those Christ calls us to cherish—the hungry, the thirsty, the stranger, the naked, the sick, and the prisoner. Liberty is a freedom for excellence founded

---

65   Psalm 8:4–6.
66   Psalm 42:1.
67   Mt. 25:34–40.
68   Mt. 5:6.
69   Mt. 5:7.
70   Dobbs v. Jackson Women's Health Organization, 597 U.S. __, 142 S.Ct. 2228.

on fraternity which seeks the good of others as brothers and sisters who share their lives in interdependence and cooperation as they pursue the common good. Law might encourage this fraternity by recognizing and remediating the disfavored status of unborn babies, and by removing barriers to immigration, both of which are motivated by a self-oriented concern to maintain possessions, pleasures and power.

In the case of unborn babies, an example where the law might promote fraternity is in the provision of greater support for families who have difficulty supporting their children. The support in the Family and Medical Leave Act[71] might be changed from unpaid leave to paid leave to give a parent a better chance to bond with a newborn or to care for a child with a serious health condition. In the case of immigration, an example where the law might promote fraternity is in greater respect for the asylum laws. Asylum is an international human right which has been incorporated into U.S. law by the Refugee Act of 1980. In early cases[72] the Supreme Court interpreted the Act to accord with the 1951 United Nations Convention Relating to the Status of Refugees, directing this country's resources to relief of the dire needs of these refugees. In so doing the Court complied with the duty of the state to promote the human rights of every person in its territory and under its jurisdiction and thus promoted fraternity through mercy. Yet, in 1993, in *Sale v. Haitian Centers Council, Inc.*,[73] the Court backpedaled on the effort to protect refugees and returned fleeing Haitians at sea to Haiti without asylum hearings.

∵

Among the principles of life, liberty, equality, and fraternity in the pursuit of happiness, fraternity receives the least emphasis in the Declaration of Independence. This is not because it is the least important. On the contrary, fraternity is essential to realize the other principles because it is the ultimate goal of our lives. Fraternity is love, the epitome of human flourishing. Without love as our goal, liberty becomes a freedom of indifference, equality exists only to promote self, and our lives fail in the pursuit of happiness which can only be achieved in love. Even those who profess not to believe in God recognize human flourishing based on love as the ultimate goal of mankind. The reason fraternity receives the least emphasis is because it cannot be mandated. Nevertheless, the law can and should encourage fraternity through policies

---

71   29 USC 2612(a)(1).

72   *E.g.*, INS v. Cardoza-Fonseca, 480 U.S. 421 (1987).

73   Sale v. Haitian Centers Council, Inc., 509 U.S. 155 (1993).

that motivate us to reach beyond ourselves to unite with our brothers and sisters in a true spirit of other-directedness. Therefore, let us pay particular attention to the concluding words of the Declaration of Independence that "for the support of this declaration, with a firm reliance on the protection of Divine Providence, we mutually pledge to each other our lives, our fortunes and our sacred honor." These words are a pledge to live together as one people under God, sharing what is most dear to ensure life, liberty and justice for all.

CHAPTER 8

Individual and Communal Flourishing through Faith for Rights

*Ibrahim Salama and Michael Wiener**

Abstract

This article considers the cultural and religious factors impacting on human rights, beyond freedom of religion or belief in its narrow boundaries. With migration, conflicts, globalization and communication technologies, diversity has become the main feature and challenge of modern societies. How can human rights tools offer better management of related risks and negative impact on everyone's fundamental freedoms? This article submits that individuals and communities from diverse cultural and religious backgrounds can flourish when the triangle of art, faith and rights is optimized in a conceptually coherent and practically implementable "Faith for Rights" approach.

1   Introduction

Despite its omnipresence in the *travaux préparatoires* of the constituent United Nations human rights texts – from the 1945 UN Charter itself to human rights treaties and declarations such as the 1948 Universal Declaration of Human Rights – the relationship between religion and human rights has never really reached full clarity. In the human rights texts adopted by the United Nations, it was rather confined to the narrower, and often controversial, boundaries of freedom of religion or belief as such.[1] Meanwhile, however, the social interaction and the political manipulation of religious actors and factors continued to develop at the communal level, following their own socio-cultural dynamics.

---

*   Ibrahim Salama, Chief of Human Rights Treaties Branch at the Office of the United Nations High Commissioner for Human Rights, Geneva, Switzerland; and Michael Wiener, Senior Fellow in Residence at the Graduate Institute of International and Development Studies, Geneva, Switzerland. The views expressed in this article are those of the authors and do not necessarily reflect the views of the United Nations.
1   Heiner Bielefeldt, Nazila Ghanea & Michael Wiener, Freedom of Religion or Belief: An International Law Commentary 21–24 (2016).

Observation of, and engagement with, religious actors and factors on human rights issues are important tasks that continue receiving inadequate attention. These tasks are neither well defined, nor systematically fulfilled in a coherent manner in human rights circles. Nevertheless, there have always been more mutual influences between faith and rights than what meets the eye at a first glance on multilateralism.[2] On one side, advocacy efforts of liberal and secular non-governmental organizations on religious issues have been predominantly defensive, denouncing the abuse of religion as a cover-up for human rights violations. On the other side, religious-based organizations sounded mostly conservative, controversial and patriarchal. Both parties did not seem willing for a genuine debate but rather had occasional encounters, for example during side events at the intergovernmental UN Human Rights Council in Geneva. These – allegedly irreconcilable – patterns aggravated the disconnect and mistrust on both sides of the religious and human rights communities in various national and international contexts. Paradoxically, the resulting tensions became ultimately positive, in the sense that they highlighted the underlying problems in a manner that calls for a more thoughtful consideration of rights-based solutions, including through the international human rights mechanisms. A significant example of constructive tensions that led to positive changes is the handling of the controversial resolutions on combating "defamation of religions" (1999–2010),[3] and how the debate has shifted since 2011 to addressing incitement to religious hatred, on the legal basis of article 20 of the International Covenant on Civil and Political Rights, the Rabat Plan of Action,[4] the Beirut Declaration on "Faith for Rights,"[5] general comments of UN treaty bodies,[6] and reports of the Special Rapporteur on freedom of religion of belief.[7] The United Nations human rights expert-based mechanisms have progressively contributed to

---

2   Ibrahim Salama & Michael Wiener, Reconciling Religion and Human Rights: Faith in Multilateralism 252 (2022).

3   Heiner Bielefeldt & Michael Wiener, Religious Freedom Under Scrutiny 60–63 (2020).

4   Rabat Plan of Action on the prohibition of advocacy of national, racial or religious hatred that constitutes incitement to discrimination, hostility or violence (2012), UN Doc. A/HRC/22/17/Add.4, appendix.

5   Beirut Declaration and its 18 Commitments on "Faith for Rights," UN Doc. A/HRC/40/58, annexes I and II.

6   Human Rights Committee, *General Comment No. 34 on Freedoms of Opinion and Expression* (2011), UN Doc. CCPR/C/GC/34; Committee on the Elimination of Racial Discrimination, *General Recommendation No. 35 on Combating Racist Hate Speech* (2013), UN Doc. CERD/C/GC/35.

7   Heiner Bielefeldt, *Report of the Special Rapporteur on freedom of religion or belief* (2015), UN Doc. A/HRC/31/18; Ahmed Shaheed, *Report of the Special Rapporteur on freedom of religion or belief* (2019), UN Doc. A/HRC/40/58.

clarifying human rights norms in this area, identifying the proper demarcation lines between freedom of religion or belief and their abuses in a manner that violates other human rights. One of the main challenges for multilateralism is optimizing all civil, cultural, economic, political and social rights as well as the right to development on truly equal footing. Missing such a balance aggravates both the perceived and real double-standards that aggravate the politicization of human rights.

For decades, the mainstream human rights movement seems to have opted for one of two "easy choices" in dealing with religion: either ignore it altogether or merely denounce its use as justification to violate human rights. Engagement with religious actors was either a non-option or a public relations act. This dynamic has predominantly been putting more external pressure than stimulating critical thinking from within the religious sphere on various human rights issues of common interest. Yet mere advocacy does not necessarily soften dogmas in the religious sphere and could even exacerbate them.

Despite sporadic – albeit useful – attempts to clarify some of its aspects, there has always been a need for a more global and coherent framework on the interaction between religion and human rights. There is a growing demand from the grassroots to progressively enlarge the engagement between faith-based actors, human rights experts and government officials. At the global level, the research-based and expert-led process leading to the development of the above-mentioned Rabat Plan of Action in 2012, Beirut Declaration in 2017 and the #Faith4Rights toolkit in 2020 could be considered a sea change in the pursuit of reconciling religion and rights; they "may help in joining the dots between parallel disciplines and competing actors, widening their common ground and optimizing their mutually enriching diversity."[8]

This article will first explore the conceptual premises of the "Faith for Rights" framework (chapter 2); then outline a rights-based and multicultural approach to managing diversity through Art for Faith for Rights (chapter 3); and lastly share some lessons from peer-to-peer learning as a methodology for implementing the "Faith for Rights" framework (chapter 4).

2   The Conceptual Premises of the "Faith for Rights" Framework

Let justice roll down as waters, and righteousness as a mighty stream.
(Amos 5:24)

---

8   Ibrahim Salama & Michael Wiener, Reconciling Religion and Human Rights: Faith in Multilateralism, *supra* note 2, at 259.

The metaphor in this biblical quote stands at the outset of the message of the conference in Wuppertal on "Strengthening Christian Commitment to Human Dignity and Human Rights," adopted on 12 April 2022. The conference message starts with the title "Hearing the cries," highlighting the story of the gruesome killing – during the same week of the Wuppertal conference – of "Mbodazwe Elvis Nyathi, a 43-year-old Zimbabwean and father of four children, [who] was burnt alive in Diepsloot township in South Africa by a mob protesting crime and poor policing of immigration laws. Elvis is just one of the many cases of mob killings in the black townships, the vestiges of apartheid South Africa."[9] This approach of looking at developments at the grassroots and listening to the victims illustrates what faith can add to the rights-based approaches in promoting social harmony at a much deeper level of human conscience. On the one hand, legal approaches ensure rights by external imposition and imposed enforcement. On the other hand, commitment emanating from faith unleashes individual and communal flourishing more naturally and profoundly. Joyful and enriching coexistence, not just tolerance of others, is the added value of the "Faith for Rights" approach.

For various reasons, including the pushback against both religion and human rights, faith actors increasingly realize the importance of human rights narrative and instruments, while many human rights actors start recognizing the role of religious or belief communities and their leaders in defending human rights. Overcoming doctrinal secularism and dogmatic theologies is by no means an easy task.

The Beirut Declaration and its 18 Commitments on "Faith for Rights" lay down the conceptual premises of this long overdue reconciliation between two disciplines that pursue their trajectories like ships passing in the night, when they should be recognizing and enhancing each other for achieving their shared goal of equal human dignity. The "Faith for Rights" framework builds on international meetings, expert seminars and regional workshops organized by the Office of the United Nations High Commissioner for Human Rights (OHCHR) between 2008 and 2017 in Geneva, Vienna, Nairobi, Bangkok, Santiago de Chile, Rabat, Geneva, Amman, Manama, Tunis, Nicosia, Beirut and Amman. Faith-based and civil society actors working in the field of human

---

9   World Council of Council/Commission of the Churches on International Affairs (WCC/CCIA), United Evangelical Mission (UEM) & Evangelical Church in Germany (EKD), *Strengthening Christian Commitment to Human Dignity and Human Rights – Conference Message* (12 April 2022), *in* Strengthening Christian Perspectives on Human Dignity and Human Rights: Perspectives from an International Consultative Process, 11 (Peter Prove, Jochen Motte, Sabine Dressler and Andar Parlindungan eds., 2022).

rights adopted the Beirut Declaration on 29 March 2017, which stresses at the outset the following vision of a mutually beneficial missing alliance, notwithstanding from different angles: "Faith and rights should be mutually reinforcing spheres. Individual and communal expression of religions or beliefs thrive and flourish in environments where human rights, based on the equal worth of all individuals, are protected."[10]

This vision was echoed by many faith communities in their subsequent reflection and human rights initiatives. The Wuppertal conference message of 12 April 2022 affirmed "the enduring relevance of the Bible as a dynamic resource for churches in the ecumenical movement in its ongoing advocacy for the respect for human rights and the upholding of human dignity."[11] This ownership transforms faith-based actors into human rights defenders who appreciate "the evolution of international human rights protection also through the more specific human rights conventions" and who explicitly urge churches to "engage with the differences in perspective and approach within the ecumenical movement in order to work towards common conclusions and recommendations for churches to reclaim the language of human rights, and to advocate for human rights and rule of law as an integral part of churches' life and witness."[12]

The authors of the Beirut Declaration affirmed in 2017 that their religious or belief convictions are "a source for the protection of the whole spectrum of inalienable human entitlements – from the preservation of the gift of life, the freedoms of thought, conscience, religion, belief, opinion and expression to the freedoms from want and fear, including from violence in all its forms."[13]

---

10   Beirut Declaration, *supra* note 5, at 1.

11   WCC/CCIA, UEM & EKD, *Strengthening Christian Commitment to Human Dignity and Human Rights, Conference Message* (2022), *supra* note 9, at 2.

12   *Id.* at 3.

13   Beirut Declaration, *supra* note 5, at 2, providing the following examples of religious or belief texts to this effect:

⇒"Whoever preserves one life, is considered by Scripture as if one has preserved the whole world." (Talmud, Sanhedrin, 37,a). ⇒"Someone who saves a person's life is equal to someone who saves the life of all." (Qu'ran 5:32) ⇒"You shall love the Lord your God with all your heart, all your soul, all your strength, and with your entire mind; and your neighbour as yourself." (Luke 10:27) ⇒ "Let them worship the Lord of this House who saved them from hunger and saved them from fear." (Sourat Quraish, verses 3,4) ⇒ "A single person was created in the world, to teach that if anyone causes a single person to perish, he has destroyed the entire world; and if anyone saves a single soul, he has saved the entire world." (Mishna Sanhedrin 4:5) ⇒"Let us stand together, make statements collectively and may our thoughts be one." (Rigveda 10:191:2) ⇒ "Just as I protect myself from unpleasant things however small, in the same way I should act towards others with a compassionate and caring mind." (Shantideva, A Guide to the Bodhisattva's Way of Life)

The Beirut Declaration adds that "[r]eligious, ethical and philosophical texts preceded international law in upholding the oneness of humankind, the sacredness of the right to life and the corresponding individual and collective duties that are grounded in the hearts of believers."[14]

History is regrettably full of opposite testimonies and negative examples in real life because – like many other noble values such as patriotism, morality, identity or rights – religions too can also be manipulated for political purpose, exploitation, hegemony, violence or oppression. Mindful of the history of manipulation of religions, faith actors "pledge to disseminate the common human values that unite [them and] undertake to combat any form of exploitation of such differences to advocate violence, discrimination and religious hatred."[15]

The Beirut Declaration identifies the most profound link between religion and human rights, which is the fact that "freedom of religion or belief does not exist without the freedom of thought and conscience which precede all freedoms for they are linked to human essence and his/her rights of choice and to freedom of religion or belief."[16]

Introspectiveness and action-orientation are two shifts in the Beirut Declaration, as opposed to preceding general interreligious statements of compassion and tolerance. The faith-based actors in Beirut identified also gaps in leadership and collective action with the following compelling words: "We hereby solemnly launch together from Beirut the most noble of all struggles, peaceful but powerful, against our own egos, self-interest and artificial divides. Only when we as religious actors assume our respective roles, articulate a shared vision of our responsibilities and transcend preaching to action, only then we will credibly promote mutual acceptance and fraternity among people of different religions or beliefs and empower them to defeat negative impulses of hatred, viciousness, manipulation, greed, cruelty and related forms of inhumanity. All religious or belief communities need a resolved leadership that unequivocally dresses that path by acting for equal dignity of everyone, driven by our shared humanity and respect for the absolute freedom of conscience of every human being. We pledge to spare no effort in filling that joint leadership gap by protecting freedom and diversity through 'faith for rights' activities."[17]

⇒ "Let us put our minds together to see what life we can make for our children." (Chief Sitting Bull, Lakota).

14   *Id.* at 3.
15   *Id.* at 4.
16   *Id.* at 5.
17   *Id.* at 6.

Beyond institutions and leaders of religious or belief communities, the Beirut Declaration emphasizes the individual level of responsibilities it articulates. This explains why the list of its drafters and supporters only indicates their names, ordered alphabetically by their first names, without giving any institutional affiliation and religious or academic titles.[18] This horizontal approach avoids the perception of any hierarchies – each supporter counts equally by virtue of his or her support. Indeed, the "Faith for Rights" framework, composed of the Beirut Declaration and its corresponding 18 commitments, "reaches out to persons belonging to religions and beliefs in all regions of the world, with a view to enhancing cohesive, peaceful and respectful societies on the basis of a common action-oriented platform agreed by all concerned and open to all actors that share its objectives."[19] The Beirut Declaration also charts a vision for global engagement and action based on equality and non-discrimination: "Our main tool and asset is reaching out to hundreds of millions of believers in a preventive structured manner to convey our shared convictions enshrined in this [Faith for Rights] declaration. [...] We will also encourage all believers to assume their individual responsibilities in the defence of their deeply held values of justice, equality and responsibility towards the needy and disadvantaged, regardless of their religion or belief."[20]

The result-oriented nature of the "Faith for Rights" framework emanates from its wide outreach and focus on grassroots-level coalitions. "Building on the present declaration, we also intend to practice what we preach through establishing a multi-level coalition, open for all independent religious actors and faith-based organisations who genuinely demonstrate acceptance of and commitment to the present [Faith for Rights] declaration by implementing projects on the ground in areas that contribute to achieving its purpose. We will also be charting a roadmap for concrete actions in specific areas, to be reviewed regularly by our global coalition of Faith for Rights."[21]

Most importantly, the "Faith for Rights" framework reflects the broad definition of religion or belief in international human law by equally addressing theistic, non-theistic, atheistic or any other believers. The Beirut Declaration also builds on lessons learned from past experiences by pledging to adhere to the following five key conceptual and methodological principles:

---

18   Office of the High Commissioner for Human Rights, *The Beirut Declaration and its 18 Commitments on Faith for Rights: Report and Outlook*, 94–95 (15th ed. 2022), *available online at* https://www.ohchr.org/sites/default/files/Documents/Press/Faith4 Rights.pdf.

19   Beirut Declaration, *supra* note 5, at 7.

20   *Id.* at 11.

21   *Id.* at 9.

a.   Transcending traditional inter-faith dialogues into concrete action-oriented Faith for Rights (F4R) projects at the local level. While dialogue is important, it is not an end in itself. Good intentions are of limited value without corresponding action. [...]

b.   Avoiding theological and doctrinal divides in order to act on areas of shared inter-faith and interfaith vision as defined in the present F4R declaration. This declaration is not conceived to be a tool for dialogue among religions but rather a joint platform for common action in defence of human dignity for all. [...]

c.   Introspectiveness is a virtue we cherish. We will all speak up and act first and foremost on our own weaknesses and challenges within our respective communities. [...]

d.   Speaking with one voice, particularly against any advocacy of hatred that amounts to inciting violence, discrimination or any other violation of the equal dignity that all human beings enjoy regardless of their religion, belief, gender, political or other opinion, national or social origin, or any other status. Denouncing incitement to hatred, injustices, discrimination on religious grounds or any form of religious intolerance is not enough. We have a duty to redress hate speech by remedial compassion and solidarity that heals hearts and societies alike. Our words of redress should transcend religious or belief boundaries. [...]

e.   We are resolved to act in a fully independent manner, abiding only by our conscience, while seeking partnerships with religious and secular authorities, relevant governmental bodies and non-State actors [...].[22]

The Beirut Declaration also re-establishes the inherent link between freedom of religion or belief and freedom of expression as follows: "Speech is fundamental to individual and communal flourishing. It constitutes one of the most crucial mediums for good and evil sides of humanity."[23] This powerful quote highlights that freedom of religion or belief cannot be exercised without freedom of expression. It is practically as simple as that. However, political manipulation managed to juxtapose these two pillars of human rights protection, and this culminated into more than a decade-long controversy within the multilateral context around the notion of "defamation of religions." At the national level, anti-blasphemy laws still hamper in many countries both freedoms, despite the unequivocal call in the Rabat Plan of Action and 18 Commitments to repeal such laws since they have a stifling impact on the enjoyment of

---

22   *Id.* at 10.
23   *Id.* at 20.

freedom of thought, conscience, religion or belief as well as on healthy dialogue and debate about religious issues.[24]

Of course, there can be tensions among various human rights. The resolution of such tensions can be achieved on a case-by-case basis, unless there is a gap of standards. This was the case with respect to finding the demarcation between freedom of expression, as guaranteed by article 19 of the International Covenant on Civil and Political Rights (ICCPR), and advocacy of hatred that constitutes incitement to discrimination, hostility or violence which is prohibited by article 20 of the Covenant. This "standards gap" for distinguishing free speech from hate speech was ultimately filled by the "Faith for Rights" framework and the Rabat threshold test it contains.[25] The latter has been used for example by the national authorities for audio-visual communication in Côte d'Ivoire, Morocco and Tunisia, as well as by UN field presences, Special Rapporteurs, the UN Human Rights Committee, the European Court of Human Rights and Meta's Oversight Board.[26] Such broad usage of these soft law instruments at the national, regional and global levels is remarkable for the short timeframe since the Rabat and Beirut standards were adopted in 2012 and 2017, respectively.

The Beirut Declaration also establishes an interesting analogy with human rights obligations of non-State actors if they exercise significant or effective control over territory and population in times of conflict, by noting that there was "a similar legal and ethical justification in case of religious leaders who exercise a heightened degree of influence over the hearts and minds of their followers at all times."[27] This analogy for treating non-State actors as duty-bearers under international human rights law is based on the general recommendation on women in conflict prevention, conflict and post-conflict situations, adopted in 2013 by the Committee on the Elimination of Discrimination against Women,[28] and the Special Rapporteur's 2014 report on preventing violence committed in

---

24   Rabat Plan of Action, *supra* note 4, at 25; 18 Commitments on "Faith for Rights," *supra* note 5, at XI.

25   18 Commitments on "Faith for Rights," *supra* note 5, at VII-XII; Rabat Plan of Action, *supra* note 4, at 29.

26   Ibrahim Salama & Michael Wiener, *"Faith for Rights": Linking the Dots between Faith-based Actors, Academia, Human Rights Mechanisms and Multilateral Institutions, in* Multilateralism, Human Rights and Diplomacy: A Global Perspective, 361, 366 (David Fernández Puyana ed., 2021).

27   Beirut Declaration, *supra* note 5, at 19.

28   Committee on the Elimination of Discrimination against Women, *General recommendation No. 30 on women in conflict prevention, conflict and post-conflict situations* (2013), UN Doc. CEDAW/C/GC/30, at 16.

the name of religion.[29] This again shows how the findings of UN treaty bodies and special procedures are considered useful and get incorporated into soft law standards.

Far beyond addressing only the negative aspect of combatting the wrong – in this case incitement to discrimination, hostility or violence – the Beirut Declaration capitalizes on the competitive edge of faith as complementary to rights by developing the promising operational notion of remedial speech as a human rights responsibility of faith-based actors. Inspired by, but transcending the opening paragraph of the Constitution of UNESCO,[30] the authors of the Beirut Declaration stated that "[w]ar starts in the minds and is cultivated by a reasoning fuelled by often hidden advocacy of hatred" and that "[s]peech is one of the most strategic areas of the responsibilities we commit to assume and support each other for their implementation through this [Faith for Rights] declaration on the basis of the thresholds articulated by the Rabat Plan of Action."[31] Applying several elements of the Rabat threshold test to religious leaders, the Beirut Declaration adds that "[d]ue to the speaker's position, context, content and extent of sermons, such statements by religious leaders may be likely to meet the threshold of incitement to hatred. Prohibiting such incitement is not enough. Remedial advocacy to reconciliation is equally a duty, including for religious leaders, particularly when hatred is advocated in the name of religions or beliefs."[32]

Previous soft law instruments already alluded that the human rights responsibilities of non-state actors extend to faith-based institutions and individuals.[33] However, the articulation of these responsibilities had not been specific

---

29   Heiner Bielefeldt, *Report of the Special Rapporteur on freedom of religion or belief* (2014), UN Doc. A/HRC/28/66, at 54–55.

30   "The Governments of the States Parties to this Constitution on behalf of their peoples declare: That since wars begin in the minds of men, it is in the minds of men that the defences of peace must be constructed [...]," *Constitution of the United Nations Educational, Scientific and Cultural Organization*, adopted in London on 16 November 1945 and amended by the General Conference at its 2nd, 3rd, 4th, 5th, 6th, 7th, 8th, 9th, 10th, 12th, 15th, 17th, 19th, 20th, 21st, 24th, 25th, 26th, 27th, 28th, 29th, 31st and 40th sessions, *available online at* https://www.unesco.org/en/legal-affairs/constitution.

31   Beirut Declaration, *supra* note 5, at 20.

32   *Id.* at 22.

33   *Id.* at 19, which quotes article 2 (1) of the 1981 UN Declaration on the Elimination of all Forms of Intolerance and of Discrimination Based on Religion of Belief (UN Doc. A/RES/36/55), according to which "no one shall be subject to discrimination by any State, institution, group of persons or person on the grounds of religion or belief." *See also* Heiner Bielefeldt & Michael Wiener, *Introductory Note to the Declaration on the Elimination of All Forms of Intolerance and Discrimination Based on Religion or Belief, in* Audiovisual Library

enough in practical terms that clearly define who owes what to whom in the faith sphere. The Beirut Declaration identifies clearly what is missing: "Both religious precepts and existing international legal frameworks attribute responsibilities to religious actors. Empowering religious actors requires actions in areas such as legislation, institutional reforms, supportive public policies and training adapted to the needs of local religious actors who often are one of the main sources of education and social change in their respective areas of action. International conventions and covenants have defined key legal terms such as genocide, refugee, religious discrimination and freedom of religion or belief. All these concepts have corresponding resonance in different religions and beliefs. In addition, numerous declarations and resolutions provide elements of religious actors' roles and responsibilities that we embrace and consolidate in this [Faith for Rights] declaration."[34]

Accepting such human rights responsibilities of faith-based actors is not in fact initiating new responsibilities as much as it simply connects the dots between both faith and human rights disciplines. The Beirut Declaration emphasizes this forgotten objective convergence in clear terms: "We fully embrace the universally recognised values as articulated in international human rights instruments as common standards of our shared humanity. We ground our commitments in this [Faith for Rights] declaration first and foremost in our conviction that religions and beliefs share common core values of respect for human dignity, justice and fairness. We also ground these commitments in our acceptance of the fact that '[e]veryone has duties to the community in which alone the free and full development of his personality is possible.'"[35] The latter quote from article 29 (1) of the Universal Declaration of Human Rights referring to the "free and full development" is an indicator of individual and communal flourishing.

Faith-based actors have a role to play in this respect, based on their human rights responsibilities that include economic, social and cultural rights as well as the right to development. In this context, a network of partners co-organized in 2021–2022 a series of monthly online peer-to-peer learning events on freedom of religion or belief and the Sustainable Development Goals.[36] Over 100 parliamentarians, civil society actors and faith leaders ultimately called in

      of International Law 1, 3 (UN Office of Legal Affairs 2021), *available online at* https://legal
      .un.org/avl/pdf/ha/ga_36-55/ga_36-55_e.pdf.

34   *Id.* at 15.

35   *Id.* at 14.

36   The series of six high-level dialogues was co-organized by the Freedom of Religion or
    Belief Leadership Network (FoRBLN), International Panel of Parliamentarians for Free-
    dom of Religion or Belief (IPPFoRB), Religions for Peace (RfP), African Parliamentarians
    for Human Rights (AfriPAHR), the "Faith for Rights" Initiative, and the Danish Institute for

their "Leaving No One Behind Statement" on the international community to integrate the experiences of individuals and communities facing inequalities because of their religion or belief within the wider sustainable development agenda.[37] They also recognized that their responses will determine how fast any blind spots in pursuing the Sustainable Development Goals are overcome and the challenges shaping people's and the planet's future are resolved.

3   A Rights-Based and Multicultural Approach to Managing Diversity through Art for Faith for Rights

Having conceptualised the foundations and scope of human rights responsibilities of faith-based actors through the Beirut Declaration, the "Faith for Rights" framework moves to the next level of articulating these responsibilities in the 18 Commitments, which were also adopted on 29 March 2017 in Beirut.

These 18 Commitments on "Faith for Rights" constitute an emerging soft law that clarifies the very concrete, albeit often ignored question, of who owes what to whom? Yet, the 18 Commitments remain a living document as they deal with tensions and complementarities between faith and rights that vary in scope and nature in different times and regions. This unique nature of the "Faith for Rights" framework emanates from the fact that there is not one standard solution that necessarily fits always to issues in the grey zone of tensions among rights or between rights and religion. Hence it is vital to learn from success stories and valuable mistakes, which we will touch upon in the next section about the peer-to-peer learning methodology of the #Faith4Rights toolkit.

It is often hard to keep the debate on the place of religion in societies objective because of a combination of ideological perceptions, mixed with cultural bias, political manipulation and resulting populism as well as the predominantly securitized approaches to any tensions resulting from diversity, including in preventing violent extremism and combatting terrorism. The complexity of managing diversity lies in the nexus of cultural relativism, doctrinal secularism and political populism, all of which claim to defend a certain notion of national identity and public interest. Religion is a powerful horizontal factor, caught at the crossfire of this hazy triangle, hub of dangerously divisive and

---

Human Rights (DIHR), *see* https://www.ippforb.com/newsroom/2021/25/o6leave-no-one
-behind-realising-freedom-of-religion-or-belief-and-the-sustainable-development-goals.

37   International Panel of Parliamentarians for Freedom of Religion or Belief, *Global Commitment to Ensure 'No One is Left Behind' on the Basis of their Religion or Belief* (2022), *available online at* https://www.ippforb.com/newsroom/2022/29/o6global-commitment-to-ensure
-no-one-is-left-behind-on-the-basis-of-their-religion-or-belief.

exploitable confusions, resulting from the unfinished business of reconciling law, culture and religion. The common thread between all tensions related to managing diversity is ignorance, hence the strategic priority of education in all its forms and levels. The problem with education is that it takes time as a long-term solution. Cultural shifts have no fast track. Meanwhile, the lack of governance – or bad management – of diversity in modern societies complicates matters further by deepening social tensions in a manner that obfuscates long-term solutions based on education.

A human rights-based approach to religion is therefore a needed track, parallel to education, but faster and complementary in terms of results. Such an approach, advanced by the "Faith for Rights" framework, while it recognizes the centrality of freedom of religion or belief, still transcends it to the links between freedom of religion or belief and the whole spectrum of the indivisible, interdependent and interrelated human rights. Clarifying these links would provide better protection against the manipulation of fear by populists in the name of national identity and misusing cultural or religious particularities to justify cultural relativism against the universality of human rights.

The "Faith for Rights" framework articulates the human rights responsibilities of faith-based actors in specific soft law standards mode, based on the jurisprudence of relevant UN human rights mechanisms. Beyond its standard-setting function, the framework also enjoys an operational tool of peer-to-peer learning methodology through the #Faith4Rights toolkit with its rights-based vision for the management of religious, cultural and ethnic diversity. Such a vision draws lessons from the limits of a simplistic approach to human rights universality, i.e. one that measures success by mere ratification of international human rights treaties or the number of recommendations accepted by a State during its Universal Periodic Review in Geneva. The multicultural rights-based vision for management of diversity also aspires to learn from the counterproductive doctrinal secularism which assumes that if religious manifestations were banned from the public sphere, then all tensions would miraculously disappear.

Human rights are not only about law, but they are also embedded in all human cultures, including various branches of art. Facilitators of peer-to-peer learning events are encouraged to use artistic expressions for their discussions and each module of the #Faith4Rights toolkit includes examples such as photos, videos, music, improvisation, dance, street art, social media, cartoons and calligraphies.[38]

---

38   Office of the High Commissioner for Human Rights, *#Faith4Rights toolkit*, 8 (2d ed. 2022), *available online at* https://www.ohchr.org/sites/default/files/Documents/Press/faith 4rights-toolkit.pdf.

When art, faith and rights overlap, they stimulate innovation which can generate powerful drives for change in societies. Both faith and rights need artistic expression to unleash their potential by touching the hearts and minds of people. Hence, art is no mere adjunct to faith and rights, but can embody their quintessence, and unpacking the dynamics through which art stretches the boundaries of both faith and rights to the deepest inner circle of human consciousness in a manner that enhances their impact on real life situations of both individuals and communities.

Music and human rights stand in an intimate relationship. The melodies and rhythms that comprise a piano sonata or song, in essence, may encode messages and appeal to moral resistance, for example against the Nazis and against totalitarianism in general.[39] In addition, music may "serve as an inspiring instrument of post-conflict reconciliation," for example through the Fes Festival of Sacred Music, a faith-based initiative founded in 1994 as a tool for rapprochement between people of different cultural and religious origins.[40] As Julian Fifer notes, "[t]he balance sought among human rights principles can be viewed as analogous to the dynamic equilibrium a musician must maintain, moment to moment, in ensemble performance."[41] Compositional equilibria, moreover, follow trajectories that resemble the articulating checks and balances among rights and responsibilities, and this is as true of other forms of art as it is of music.

Every artistic expression is an inspiring claim that sets an agenda for change in its own encoded manner, written in the spiritual vocabulary of artists that reaches hearts in variable ways depending on the recipients. Inspiration is a mystical process. Artistic expressions may stimulate multiple emotions that can liberate recipients from mechanical conformity, from manipulation in the name of religion, and from oppression under the banner of putatively transcendent values, including patriotism. Confronted with artistic expression – in

---

39   Michael Wiener, *Decoding Viktor Ullmann's Last Piano Sonata through Legal Methodology,* *in* The Routledge Companion on Music and Human Rights 416, 434 (Julian Fifer, Angela Impey, Peter G. Kirchschläger, Manfred Nowak & George Ulrich eds., 2022). *See also* Hannelore Brenner, The Girls of Room 28: Friendship, Hope, and Survival in Theresienstadt 77–78 (2009), as well as the song "Ma'agal" which is based on texts written by the girls of room 28, *available online at* https://www.youtube.com/watch?v=DQVtaZG_2cU.

40   Ibrahim Salama, *voice: Ibrahim Salama (Egypt), in* The Routledge Companion on Music and Human Rights 286, 287 (Julian Fifer, Angela Impey, Peter G. Kirchschläger, Manfred Nowak & George Ulrich eds., 2022).

41   Julian Fifer, *Why Music and Human Rights?, in* The Routledge Companion on Music and Human Rights 28, 37 (Julian Fifer, Angela Impey, Peter G. Kirchschläger, Manfred Nowak & George Ulrich eds., 2022).

sharp contrast to unrecognized propaganda – the viewers or hearers feel free to digest, interpret, and conclude for themselves. Therefore, art transmits what legal texts alone can hardly convey. Art emanates from a deep source that links the heart, mind and soul, speaking in turn to all of these. Many people *fear* law, but they all *feel* art. As such, the power of art and its transformative potential with respect to people's attitudes is almost unlimited. Emotions are the strongest of human drives. Hence, it is not just a useful exercise but an important goal to deepen our understanding of how art, especially when associated with faith, interacts with human rights. This is particularly crucial at our present worldwide juncture, when human rights face an existential crisis, including the failure to tolerate diversity and dissent, let alone to celebrate these qualities in a manner that is crucial to achieving vibrant societies in which no group or individual is left behind.

Two common features characterize the mutually enriching dynamics within the triangle of Faith, Rights and Art: their universality and their liberating power. Art, however, enjoys a unique status, in that individuals may hold conflicting views regarding theology, or disagree as to what rights entail, but it is rare that beauty and creativity fail to receive their admiration. This fact substantiates a strategic conclusion: for Faith to stand up for Rights, it needs to rely on the universal language of beauty and creativity that Art provides.

There is ample evidence of the healing and unifying power of art, both in inspiring personal engagement and in achieving inclusive, harmonious societies. Indeed, as UNESCO flagged, "[i]ndividuals are not born interculturally competent, they become competent through education and life experiences. The implication, then, is the critical importance of offering sufficient quality, formal and non-formal learning opportunities for everyone to acquire the intercultural competences required for successful living in the modern complexity of our heterogeneous world."[42] There are few better learning opportunities for intercultural competences than those presented by engagement with the arts. For this and many other reasons, there is also no wonder that artistic expression remains lively and influential in our time. Art has no expiry date. Its spiritual expressions across time and across faith traditions feed continuously into an endless ocean of mystical beauty and creativity. Confronted with such immensity, one can merely glimpse at and seek to appreciate the artistic expressions.

The second horizontal nexus relating Art to Faith to Rights, over and above their universality, is their inextricable association with freedom of expression.

---

42   United Nations Educational, Scientific and Cultural Organization, Intercultural Competences: Conceptual and Operational Framework 38–39 (2013).

None of the three disciplines can survive without freedom of expression. It provides the oxygen that stimulates ideas and allows creative growth in all three disciplines. Performing music, dance or poetry, and producing visual art are manifestations of free expression. Owing to its association with creative imagination, art is often perceived as subversive, a constructive subversion with the flavor of the supreme value of freedom. Numerous examples of censorship by States or attacks by non-State actors, including religious leaders, against compositions deemed "dangerous" or "blasphemous" occur throughout the world.[43] Freedom of expression occupies the same pivotal position within the human rights field itself. All other rights rely on freedom of expression both to defend those rights and to ensure developing their standards.

A third angle of shared DNA between the three disciplines is that human rights – like art and faith – are not static. All three are living disciplines that face pressures, require maintenance, and flourish with progressive development. Even the sky is not the limit for human creativity and adaptation in response to evolving challenges and changing circumstances. Both the legislative and judicial functions, through which States articulate and implement norms, equally require freedom of expression as a fundamental prerequisite. Otherwise, human rights are violated within the structure of oppressive domestic laws.

Undue restrictions on freedom of expression have an equally deleterious effect in the religious sphere. In the presence of such restrictions, compounded with violent extremism and its "unholy alliance" with political populism, religions are increasingly perceived as a threat to fundamental freedoms, with Salman Rushdie calling religion "a mediaeval form of unreason."[44] Grounding critical thinking at the heart of the religious sphere is therefore a strategic leap forward in order to bridge the unfortunate and unnecessary divide between religion and human rights. In the eyes of many, religion is a matter of inviolable dogma, whereas freedom is the very essence of spirituality that employs art to soften dogmas. Art can therefore provide the unspoken language clarifying the grey zone of intersectionality between the seemingly unreconcilable competing disciplines.

According to the former UN High Commissioner for Human Rights, Zeid Ra'ad Al Hussein, however, the "Faith for Rights" framework "provides space for a long-overdue cross-disciplinary reflection on the deep, and mutually

---

43   Freemuse, The State of Artistic Freedom 2021 (2021).

44   English PEN, *Salman Rushdie condemns attacks on Charlie Hebdo* (2015), *available online at* https://www.englishpen.org/posts/campaigns/salman-rushdie-condemns-attack-on-charlie-hebdo/.

enriching, connections between religions and human rights."[45] The rationale underlying this initiative resides in the understanding that failure to reflect on their legitimate possibilities for positive interaction does a disservice to faith, rights and art. Indeed, as High Commissioner Michelle Bachelet stressed, "[r]eligious leaders play a crucial role in either defending human rights, peace and security – or, unfortunately, in undermining them. Supporting the positive contributions of faith-based actors is crucial, as is preventing the exploitation of religious faith as a tool in conflicts, or as interpreted to deny people's rights."[46]

The multiplying effect of freedom of expression on art, faith and rights explains the fact that five of the 18 Commitments on "Faith for Rights" are dedicated to various complementary aspects of freedom of expression, in different but interrelated contexts which we will outline briefly.

Commitment XI addresses freedom of expression in the religious sphere through an interesting multi-pronged approach. It articulates the commitment "not to oppress critical voices and views on matters of religion or belief, however wrong or offensive they may be perceived, in the name of the 'sanctity' of the subject matter and we urge States that still have anti-blasphemy or anti-apostasy laws to repeal them."[47] This statement zeroes in effectively on a nexus of perceived incompatibility between freedom of expression in the religious sphere: the notion of "sanctity." Indeed, the very name of that which is "sacred" inspires in some believers a fear of reflection. Reflection – that is, *doubt* – could be perceived as the negation of belief. This sentiment, which one may well consider a legitimate concern for individual believers, is also what makes religion such a powerful tool for manipulation. Commitment X therefore adds to the mix a "pledge not to give credence to exclusionary interpretations claiming religious grounds in a manner that would instrumentalize religions, beliefs or their followers to incite hatred and violence, for example for electoral purposes or political gains."[48]

In the same vein, Commitment III asserts, "[a]s religions are necessarily subject to human interpretations, we commit to promote constructive engagement on the understanding of religious texts. Consequently, critical thinking and debate on religious matters should not only be tolerated but

---

45   Zeid Ra'ad Al Hussein, *OHCHR expert meeting on "Faith for Rights"* (2017), *available online at* https://www.ohchr.org/en/statements/2017/03/ohchr-expert-meeting-faith-rights?LangID =E&NewsID=21451.

46   Michelle Bachelet, *Global Summit on Religion, Peace and Security* (2019), *available online at* https://www.ohchr.org/en/statements/2019/04/global-summit-religion-peace -and-security?LangID=E&NewsID=24531.

47   18 Commitments on "Faith for Rights," *supra* note 5, at XI.

48   *Id.* at X.

rather encouraged as a requirement for enlightened religious interpretations in a globalized world composed of increasingly multi-cultural and multi-religious societies that are constantly facing evolving challenges."[49] Conscious of the strategic role of education in promoting and protecting human rights, Commitment XII also includes a pledge to review educational programs as follows:

> We commit to further refine the curriculums, teaching materials and textbooks wherever some religious interpretations, or the way they are presented, may give rise to the perception of condoning violence or discrimination. In this context, we pledge to promote respect for pluralism and diversity in the field of religion or belief as well as the right not to receive religious instruction that is inconsistent with one's conviction. We also commit to defend the academic freedom and freedom of expression, in line with Article 19 of the International Covenant on Civil and Political Rights, within the religious discourse in order to promote that religious thinking is capable of confronting new challenges as well as facilitating free and creative thinking. We commit to support efforts in the area of religious reforms in educational and institutional areas.[50]

It is interesting to note that this passage from Commitment XII is supported by the words of twentieth century philosopher Sir A. J. Ayer, the second President of the British Humanist Association, who stated that "the only possible basis for a sound morality is mutual tolerance and respect."[51] Similarly, in connection with Commitment I, the authors of the "Faith for Rights" framework included the following quote from the former head of the Bahá'í Faith from 1892 to 1921, Abdu'l-Bahá: "When freedom of conscience, liberty of thought and right of speech prevail – that is to say, when every man according to his own idealization may give expression to his beliefs – development and growth are inevitable."[52]

The Beirut Declaration also notes that freedoms of thought, conscience, religion, belief and expression are fundamental to individual and communal flourishing, by stressing that "[p]ositive speech is also the healing tool of reconciliation and peacebuilding in the hearts and minds."[53] The special focus on

---

49   *Id.* at III.

50   *Id.* at XII.

51   Alfred Jules Ayer, The Humanist Outlook 10 (1968).

52   'Abdu'l-Bahá, The Promulgation of Universal Peace 197 (2d ed. 1982).

53   Beirut Declaration, *supra* note 5, at 20.

freedom of expression within the "Faith for Rights" framework enhances the potential of artistic expression to become an inspiring ally of both "faith in fundamental human rights"[54] and "faith for rights." The challenge is to enhance the triangle of art, faith and rights in practice, and how to learn lessons from the grassroots.

4   Lessons from Peer-to-Peer Learning as a Methodology for Implementing the "Faith for Rights" Framework

At the first intergovernmental symposium on "Faith for Rights" in Rabat in December 2017, former High Commissioner Zeid Ra'ad Al Hussein stated that "[a]fter the successful shift from dialogue to standards we now hope to move to implementing and supporting concrete 'Faith for Rights' projects by various stakeholders, notably at the grassroots level. Since human rights are by definition a multi-stakeholder vision of society, the 'Faith for Rights' framework is a good example of States, State religious authorities, faith-based and civil society organizations, national human rights institutions and individuals joining forces."[55] This interaction is precisely where artistic expression can carve out a new and much needed space in the human rights world through its newly designed "Faith for Rights" landscape. Art can be the beating heart as well as the gate of beauty and inspiration that finally reconciles religion and rights after decades of – at best – mistrust. Implementing the "Faith for Rights" framework opens a wide horizon in this vein. The 18 peer-to-peer learning modules in the #Faith4Rights toolkit, which correspond to the 18 commitments, dedicate a large space to art as a vehicle for knowledge sharing and joint interfaith action. This opens the new triangular avenue of Art for Faith for Rights[56] in an interdisciplinary manner. After all, human rights norms are not the exclusive concern of lawyers and judges but rather of every individual. Conveying these norms artistically can shift compliance from top-down through coercion to bottom-up with conviction and, thus, from fear to love.

---

54   "Faith in fundamental human rights" is reaffirmed both in the second preambular paragraph of the UN Charter (https://www.un.org/en/about-us/un-charter/preamble) and in the fifth preambular paragraph of the Universal Declaration of Human Rights (https://www.un.org/en/about-us/universal-declaration-of-human-rights).

55   Zeid Ra'ad Al Hussein, *Rabat+5 Symposium on the follow-up to the Rabat Plan of Action* (2017), *available online at* https://www.ohchr.org/en/statements/2017/12/rabat5-symposium-follow-rabat-plan-action-rabat-6-7-december-2017.

56   Ibrahim Salama, *VOICE* (2022), *supra* note 40, at 288.

Indeed, a number of artistic expressions have accompanied the development of the "Faith for Rights" framework from the outset. An Arabic calligraphic exposition was held in the context of the first Walk of Faith for Rights, and these paintings encapsulating the 18 commitments were included in an Arabic compilation of the founding texts of the "Faith for Rights" framework.[57] This constitutes one of the first attempts to employ art as part of a rights-based approach to religion under the auspices of the United Nations. Furthermore, during the first expert meeting in Collonges in December 2018, poetry and music were introduced into the discussion by several participants. A spontaneous collective singing of a religious text took place as a team-building exercise. A participant wrote a poem reflecting on some of the 18 commitments and performed it together with a soprano and pianist. The performance seemed to harmonize perfectly with the surroundings, although nothing was prepared in advance. Subsequently, in May 2019, at the Festival of Religious Freedom at the Adventist campus, several young students from the Orchestre Symphonique du Salève read the 18 Commitments, of which they had articulated summaries, along with a musical performance accompanying their recitation.[58]

Other forms of artistic expression have been used to powerfully convey "Faith for Rights" messages. The Argentinian photographer and visual artist Gaby Herbstein, for example, is leading a multidisciplinary artistic project entitled "Believe to See" that spreads the voice of spiritual leaders of different beliefs, philosophies and cultures from around the world. Herbstein notes that her project is "about 'unity in diversity,' where people will realize that all those teachers, elders and spiritual leaders are saying in different languages and with different tools the same thing. They help us to remember that everything is already within us."[59]

Another project inspired by "Faith for Rights" was implemented by the Portuguese urban artist Vhils, who created impressive murals in the capital of Sierra Leone. As the artist explains on his Instagram page (reproduced in the #Faith4Rights toolkit), Freetown is "a truly remarkable and inspiring place, where I was invited to create a mural that celebrated the country's inter- and intra-religious tolerance. This special project culminated in the depiction of two local children, Paul and Alfreda, who belong to the same family – the boy being a Christian and the girl a Muslim. A country where it is common to have

---

57   https://untrainingcentre.ohchr.org/ar-ae/Documents/Publications/Faith_for_Rights.pdf, at 86–103.

58   *#Faith4Rights toolkit* (2022), *supra* note 38, at 19.

59   *Id.* at 84.

members of the same family belonging to different religions can teach us a lot about tolerance."[60]

Short films are yet another medium of conveying messages, for example to highlight minority rights. The #Faith4Rights toolkit refers to some award-winning short films, including the story of a pianist living amidst war and the tale of a poor child who sneaks into a classroom desperate to be educated; these two films were showcased at the 3By3 Film Festival in Baghdad and during a six-month tour through 17 of Iraq's 19 provinces.[61]

Furthermore, the non-governmental organization Freemuse and OHCHR organized a series of four webinars in 2021. During the first webinar on "Human Rights, Art and Protest," Rabbi Rachel Rosenbluth stressed that the purpose of religion and creation was "for us to be co-creators and transforming and healing the world."[62] The second webinar on "Speaking Truth to Power: Religious or Belief Minority Artists, Voice and Protest" discussed cases where artists have been threatened by anti-blasphemy laws and other forces limiting civic space.[63] The last two webinars focussed on visual artists from a diversity of visual artistic mediums as well as on music inspired by the 18 Commitments, using the hashtag #Music4Faith4Rights.[64] Furthermore, the 2022 international art contest aims at supporting minority artists' work on statelessness and at increasing the visibility of their artwork, while raising awareness on the human rights of stateless individuals and groups belonging to minorities.[65]

Another online conversation on promoting sustainable peace included former OHCHR Minority Fellow Mostafa Betaree, who showed how his civil society organization uses music and dance in engaging with refugees in the Netherlands.[66] In this context, the United States Institute of Peace and OHCHR also conceptualized together with Nazila Ghanea, UN Special Rapporteur on freedom of religion or belief, an online micro-course on "Religion, Human Rights, and Peacebuilding: A 'Faith for Rights' Approach."

The above are all inspiring attempts of linking art, faith and rights. It is important to support and widen the scope of faith-based artistic expressions as a concrete tool for combating intolerance, racism and xenophobia

---

60   *Id.* at 17.

61   *Id.* at 40 and 67.

62   *Id.* at 36.

63   *Id.* at 61.

64   *Id.* at 42.

65   OHCHR, *International Art Contest: Recognizing Minority Artists Working on Statelessness Themes* (2022), *available online at* https://www.ohchr.org/en/minorities/minority-artists -voice-and-dissidence.

66   *#Faith4Rights toolkit* (2022), *supra* note 38, at 86.

in increasingly multi-cultural societies across the globe. Multi-cultural and multi-religious artistic performances are fast tracks to bridging divides and promoting cohesive societies. This can reduce the temptation for political populism that incites to racial and religious hatred under the cloak of patriotism.

On a different – yet related – note, art can also liberate faith from manipulation and reverse fundamentalist trends, especially among youth. There is no wonder that many violent religiously fundamentalist movements consider many forms of artistic expression as sinful and even prohibit music. The singing and dancing rituals in Sufi traditions are a case in point, as even these have been the subject of attacks by mainstream conservative religious groups in the Muslim world. Art provides a natural joyful dose of beauty and of critical thinking that youth in particular appreciate. These features are often missing from religious discourse.

When artistic expression is engaged regarding faith matters, it can be particularly effective in countering religious manipulation because artistic performances empower audiences to exercise their own judgment. Artists communicate various visions and messages to their audience, but each audience member remains the ultimate arbiter of what she or he takes away from the performance. Art, when viewed in this way and combined with a focus on human rights, is indeed a genuine form of critical thinking coupled with an aspiration for change. It provokes, defies, reshapes and traces new horizons. By definition, art and freedom of expression are inseparable from each other.

Human rights law protects artistic expression through numerous hard law norms and soft law standards. Artistic expression is part of religious traditions, as art has served faith since the earliest times. Faith is also essential: the right to freedom of religion or belief can be a support of all other human rights. Through the "Faith for Rights" framework, the faith actors "commit to leverage the spiritual and moral weight of religions and beliefs with the aim of strengthening the protection of universal human rights."[67] The Beirut Declaration even starts with a quote from Rumi, who stated more than seven centuries ago that "[t]here are as many paths to God as there are souls on Earth."[68]

The "Faith for Rights" framework provides both a holistic conceptualization of the interaction between faith and human rights and a methodology for reengineering the dynamics between divine and secular – sometimes opposed – doctrines. Their history of mutual rejection needs to concede for a more open, mature and humble approach of mutual peer-to-peer learning. Human rights are a human product. The same applies to the interpretation of religions

---

67   18 Commitments on "Faith for Rights," *supra* note 5, at xvi.
68   Beirut Declaration, *supra* note 5, preamble.

or beliefs. Reciprocal illiteracy between the religious and rights spheres is an obvious obstacle to their reconciliation, whereas knowledge creates understanding. Peer-to-peer learning is the way forward. The social demand in increasingly multi-cultural societies pushes into this direction. This is why an interdisciplinary approach to developing this methodology of mutual enrichment and flourishing in joyful diversity is of the essence.

Over the past two years, "Faith for Rights" peer-to-peer learning events included diverse participants with practical experiences, for example in safe-guarding religious sites, protecting religious or belief minorities, promoting gender equality, preventing atrocity crimes, countering hate speech and promoting interfaith dialogue. They presented good practices and lessons learnt, identified specific action needed, discussed challenges and opportunities, exploring options for follow-up and further collaboration. In these exchanges it proved vital to capture the conclusions and recommendations in peer-to-peer learning snapshots.[69] At the 2021 High-level Political Forum on Sustainable Development, High Commissioner Michelle Bachelet picked up several of these snapshot recommendations, including that the United Nations could facilitate "safe spaces" in which religious actors and others can engage on issues of faith and human rights, based on the normative human rights framework, soft-law standards and peer-to-peer learning methodology.[70] The High Commissioner also stressed that this implied "listening to each other, sharing experiences what works and what doesn't, and responding jointly to needs at the grassroots level."[71]

Peer-to-peer learning is also founded on a seemingly simple quality which is rather difficult to practice, that is the capacity to genuinely listen to others. One of the simplest exercises of peer-to-peer learning that cultivates this power of listening is asking the participants at the outset of a peer-to-peer learning event to indicate the number and order of identities that define them personally. The self-definitional results always show an amazing diversity of

---

69   OHCHR, *The Beirut Declaration and its 18 Commitments on Faith for Rights: Report and Outlook* (2022), *supra* note 18, at 70 and 93.

70   United Nations Alliance of Civilizations, UN Office on Genocide Prevention and the Responsibility to Protect & OHCHR, *Global Pledge for Action by Religious Actors and Faith-Based Organizations to Address the COVID-19 Pandemic in Collaboration with the United Nations: Peer-to-peer Learning Snapshots and Recommendations* (2021), *available online at* https://www.ohchr.org/sites/default/files/Documents/Issues/Religion/GlobalPledgeRec ommendations.pdf.

71   Michelle Bachelet, *High-level Political Forum on Sustainable Development* (2021), *available online at* https://www.ohchr.org/en/2021/07/side-event-global-pledge-action-religious -actors-and-faith-based-organizations-address?LangID=E&NewsID=27279.

multiple identities that differently shape our perceptions of the same realities. This creates for any group an instant curiosity to listen to each other's different perspectives.

Human rights are not only conceived to protect dignity and equality among individuals, communities and peoples. They are also meant to cherish and unleash, not merely accept and tolerate, human diversity in all its richness. The notion of diversity is not sufficiently common in the mainstream human rights discourse, probably because it may be associated with cultural relativism. For the same reason, in a typically dogmatic manner, the words "religion" and "culture" were tainted at the outset because of the way the 1993 Vienna Declaration and Programme of Action juxtaposes universality and relativism, without fully capturing the deep sense of either of them. The second part of paragraph 5 states that "[w]hile the significance of national and regional particularities and various historical, cultural and religious backgrounds must be borne in mind, it is the duty of States, regardless of their political, economic and cultural systems, to promote and protect all human rights and fundamental freedoms."[72] This formulation suggests that "cultural and religious backgrounds" are more of a potential threat to, rather than a precious asset for, humanity. This background may also partly explain the relative neglect of collective rights in general, and cultural rights in particular.

Human rights, particularly freedom of religion or belief as well as minority rights and cultural rights, are not yet optimally employed to preserve and enhance our human diversity, while they are the most intuitive and natural catalyst that cuts across civilizations, values and identities. The reason may be rooted in the first part of the same paragraph 5 with respect to the relationship between different human rights. It is important to be honest enough to admit that the following pledge – or even "mantra" – of the Vienna Declaration and Programme of Action does not exactly reflect realities on the ground: "All human rights are universal, indivisible and interdependent and interrelated. The international community must treat human rights globally in a fair and equal manner, on the same footing, and with the same emphasis."[73] In practice, however, the politics of human rights are dictated by the relative weights of their respective constituencies, hence the fact that some rights are "more equal" than others.

With a view to countering any ideological impasse, political manipulation and cultural hegemony (either real or perceived), we "should 'secularize

---

72   World Conference on Human Rights, *Vienna Declaration and Programme of Action* (1993), UN Doc. A/CONF.157/23, chapter I, at 5.

73   *Id.*

secularism' (Etienne Balibar) in order not to transform it into a religion, ideology or culture."[74] The international community should heed the pledge from Vienna in 1993 and put equal emphasis on the "orphaned" rights, namely freedom of religion or belief, cultural rights and minority rights, in both their individual and collective dimensions.[75] Interestingly enough, these "orphaned" rights are actually among the richest in terms of protecting diversity, however, they can hardly flourish if doctrinal secularism and mono-culturalism prevail. One of the main sources of these two phenomena is the notion of "tolerance" as it contains three anti-human rights connotations: it presumes that the mainstream is more valuable than the peripheries, it builds on self-proclaimed superiority of values, and it implies a judgmental attitude towards whoever is different in religious or cultural terms – such individuals and communities could at best aspire to be "tolerated."

Yet, it is not enough for the majority in a society to merely "tolerate" members of religious or belief minorities, because their human rights must be fully respected and protected.[76] In this context, the #Faith4Rights toolkit highlights the following objectives of peer-to-peer learning events:

– Participants reach a conviction that religious and cultural diversity is a strength, of which they are custodians. This precious diversity needs to be managed with full respect, not mere tolerance.[77]
– Participants transcend mere tolerance to full respect of the free choice by individuals of their own beliefs, whether theistic, non-theistic, atheistic or other.[78]

Promoting a global vision to all human rights based on their indivisibility and mutual enhancement, while respecting equal emphasis among them, is the tough way forward. Far easier said than done! In practice, such a global vision goes squarely against the political dynamics of unequally dedicated funding and selective international advocacy for specific freedoms, rather than for all human rights. This explains why it is hard to promote such global vision and

---

74   Olivier Roy (Principal Investigator), *Rethinking the Place of Religion in European Secularized Societies: The Need for More Open Societies – Conclusions of the Research Project ReligioWest, in* The (re)construction and formatting of religions in the West through courts, social practices, public discourse and transnational institutions 9 (European University Institute Robert Schuman Centre for Advanced Studies, 2016).

75   Ibrahim Salama & Michael Wiener, Reconciling Religion and Human Rights: Faith in Multilateralism, *supra* note 2, at 16.

76   *Id.* at 146.

77   *#Faith4Rights toolkit* (2022), *supra* note 38, at 12.

78   *Id.* at 19.

why the mantra of paragraph 5 of the Vienna Declaration and Programme of Action remains elusive until deeper clarity is reached on the unfinished business of deeper grounding of human rights universality.

Freedom of religion or belief, minority rights and cultural rights are increasingly both under strain and subject to manipulation. Pushback in these areas in an era of increasingly multicultural societies fuels populism, violent extremism and xenophobia. The current dynamics of interaction between relevant actors is hardly conducive to synergies. Hopes for changing dynamics would remain wishful thinking until a deeper reflection has matured and adapted tools of managing diversity are sharpened through practice. Indeed, the controversies haunting the intersection between culture, religion and law constitute an unfinished business of the human rights movement and doctrine. These controversies reflect a combination of ideological divides and political manipulations. The resulting vicious circle creates multi-facetted impediments to individual and communal flourishing, particularly as they favour populist narratives that discriminate against minorities and migrants in particular, i.e. those who differ from the mainstream. Socio-cultural divides are therefore deepening in many modern societies as well as the grounds for discrimination and hate speech, especially through communication technologies. The resulting socio-cultural tensions and political conflicts explain the pushback we witness against human rights in numerous national and multilateral fora.

However, this vicious circle of misperceptions can be reversed. Controversies around identity hide the blessing of diversity as a permanent and renewable source of human flourishing that enhances genuine universality of all human rights.

Transforming diversity from a problem into a solution has several requirements. The first is to admit that if cultural and religious relativism threaten human rights universality, so does dogmatism in its name. Untangling this self-fulfilling prophecy of ideological dichotomy necessitates more peer-to-peer learning instead of persistent advocacy in a deaf-dialogue mode. In this sense, peer-to-peer learning is not just a methodology. Its deeper roots are grounded in the fact that social questions do not have single answers and that the same good answers are not always those best suited in all times and places.

The most conducive way to enhance human rights universality is to widen and strengthen its historical foundations in different cultures, civilizations and identities that actually define humans at the very personal level, identifying also the conditions where they can or cannot blossom.

This permanent work-in-progress requires adapted and innovative approaches to managing religious and cultural diversity. The "Faith for Rights" framework and its peer-to-peer learning toolkit are among the creative instruments that can help advancing in this direction. Individuals and communities from diverse cultural and religious backgrounds can flourish when the triangle of art, faith and rights is optimized in a conceptually coherent and practically implementable "Faith for Rights" approach.

CHAPTER 9

Neither "Genteel Hoax" Nor "Slot Machine": Constitutional Interpretation in Policy-Oriented Jurisprudence

*Christian Lee González-Rivera**

With whatever doubt, with whatever difficulties a case may be attended, [the Supreme Court] must decide it. ... It has no more right to decline the exercise of a jurisdiction, which is given, than to usurp that, which is not given. The one, or the other would be treason to the constitution.[1]

[Y]ears ago ... Mr. Justice Holmes reaffirmed ancient wisdom in suggesting that the "secret root[s]" from which legal theories draw "all the juices of life" are "considerations of what is expedient for the community concerned," "moral and political theories," "institutions of public policy," "even ... prejudices."[2]

∴

1 Introduction

We've long sought truth in interpretation. And, for just as long, we've been ambivalent about our success. American debate about constitutional interpretation has given rise to an attendant culture. One deeply influenced, if not overdetermined, by partisan and other politics. Increasingly, judges, academics, and even

---

* Assistant Professor of Law, St. Thomas University College of Law, Miami, Florida.
1 Joseph Story, Commentaries on the Constitution 3: § 1570 (1833).
2 Myres S. McDougal & Asher Lans, *Treaties and Congressional-Executive or Presidential Agreements: Interchangeable Instruments of National Policy 1*, 54 Yale L. J. 181, 191 (1945).

laypeople have an opinion about interpretive theory.[3] Especially Originalism.[4] Some say we are all originalists now.[5] Others wish it were not true.[6] Yet others say we've only become textualists—whatever the difference is.[7] The exchange of labels borders on a comedy of errors,[8] since we now speak of *Originalisms* in the plural rather than the earlier, monolithic singular.[9]

---

3 Jamal Greene, *Selling Originalism*, 97 Geo. L.J. 657, 696 (2009) ("The public does not seem to understand the Court or its business with nearly the sophistication of legal professionals and academics, but it is nonetheless willing to offer an opinion on constitutional methodology."); Ozan O. Varol, *The Origins and Limits of Originalism: A Comparative Study*, 44 Vand. L. Rev. 1239, 1242 (2021) ("[N]early half of Americans favor originalism. It is astonishing that nearly half of Americans support a technical legal methodology for interpreting the Constitution."). Of course, the fact is less astonishing if one remembers that, especially in its infancy, Originalism was used for political mobilization. *See, e.g.,* Robert Post & Reva Siegel, *Originalism As a Political Practice: The Right's Living Constitution*, 75 Fordham L. Rev. 545, 548 (2006) ("Although Americans have traditionally incorporated assertions about constitutional text and history into both liberal and conservative arguments, it is almost unknown for a general theory of constitutional interpretation to itself become a site for popular mobilization."). According to Post and Siegel, "[s]ince the 1980s, originalism has primarily served as an ideology that inspires political mobilization and engagement." *Id.* at 554.

4 Throughout this article, I consider "Originalism" to be that theory of constitutional interpretation that deems constitutional meaning as sufficiently fixed when the text was adopted, generally discoverable, and legally binding, and I distinguish between "early" (i.e., founding era), "modern" (i.e., 1960's through the early 1980's (typically called "Old Originalism")), and "contemporary" Originalisms (i.e., since the late 1980's (typically called "New" and "New–New" "Originalism")). I only use these new labels because current nomenclature is too focused on the internal differences within modern Originalism. For a general overview of Originalism, *see* The Challenge of Originalism: Theories of Constitutional Interpretation (Grant Huscroft & Bradley W. Miller eds., 2011); Constitutional Theory: Arguments and Perspectives (Michael J. Gerhardt et al. eds., 2013); Randy Barnett, *An Originalism for Nonoriginalists*, 45 Loy. L. Rev. 611 (1999); Keith Whittington, *Originalism: A Critical Introduction*, 82 Fordham L. Rev. 375 (2013).

5 *See, e.g.,* Elena Kagan, *Clip of Kagan Confirmation Hearing, Day 2, Part 1* (June 29, 2010), *available at* https://www.c-span.org/video/?c4910015/user-clip-originalists.

6 James Fleming, *Are We All Originalists Now? I Hope Not!*, 91 Tex. L. Rev. 1785 (2013).

7 *See, e.g.,* Diarmuid F. O'Scannlain, *"We Are All Textualists Now": The Legacy of Justice Antonin Scalia*, 91 St. John's L. Rev. 303 (2017).

8 As one commentator put it, "[a]s of late, a remarkable array of constitutional theorists have declared themselves originalists of one sort or another, and no one is quite sure why. Or, perhaps more accurately, everyone is sure, but they all disagree with each other." Donald L. Drakeman, *What's the Point of Originalism?*, 37 Harv. J. L. Pub. Pol'y 1123, 1123 (2014).

9 *See, e.g.,* Guha Krishnamurthi, *False Positivism: The Failure of the Newest Originalism*, 46 B.Y.U. L. Rev. 401, 410 n.25 (2020) ("To be sure, originalism itself is not one 'thing'; there are many different originalisms."); James E. Fleming, *The Balkinization of Originalism*, 2012 U. Ill. L. Rev. 669, 671 (2012) ("Given how much ... versions of 'originalism' differ, it would not mean much to claim that we are all originalists now.").

The jury is still out on our success in seeking interpretive truth. Early on, for example, Alexis de Tocqueville stressed that "nothing c[ould] be more obscure ... [for] the common man than legislation based on precedent," noting that "American lawyers resemble somewhat Egyptian priests and are, like them, the sole interpreters of an obscure science."[10] Yet, despite concerns about its "obscurity," de Tocqueville deemed our judicial craft conducive to a free public order.[11] Although our Constitution "can ... vary," he noted, "during its existence it is [still] the fount of all authority."[12] Without a judiciary, it would be "dead letter."[13] John Maxcy Zane, however, writing a few decades after de Tocqueville, insisted that "[t]here [wa]s no more august spectacle than the Supreme Court of the United States when it sits to consider a great constitutional question," since "all the different legal rules of interpretation ... are ... tested .... [and] everything of which the human mind is capable has been used."[14]

"Authority." "Interpretation." "The common man." Concepts long striking a chord in America's legal heart. And for good reason. How can a constitutional provision mean two different things in 1791 and 2023? If its meaning "varies," as de Tocqueville said, how can it authoritatively "bind"? What is interpretation's role in this? For all its bite, the label "obscure science" still managed to pay a half-compliment to our constitutional interpretive practice. At least in the controversial cases, it's always been all art and no science.[15] For over two centuries, perception about our interpretive enterprise has feared two extremes of constitutional "treason," to borrow Story's word: reading either *too little* or *too much* in the Constitution. Describing or prescribing how interpretation can avoid either sums up most constitutional scholarship in the last forty years.

Our need for interpretive truth is fundamental. What if we disagree on loftier questions, like what the purpose of law is, only because we're at odds on

---

10   Alexis de Tocqueville, Democracy in America 312 (Penguin Books ed. 2013).

11   *Id.* at 120–21.

12   *Id.* at 119.

13   *Id.* at 176.

14   John Maxcy Zane, The Story of Law 387 (Liberty Fund ed., 1998).

15   To this day, accusations of "black box" jurisprudence are still hurled at our highest court. *See, e.g.,* Ilya Shapiro, *The Sweet Mystery of Anthony Kennedy, available at* https://www.law. uchicago.edu/recordings/ilya-shapiro-sweet-mystery-anthony-kennedy ("Regardless of how convincing my or anyone's explanation of his jurisprudence might be, if the general perception is that Kennedy decides cases in some inscrutable manner, whether based on policy preferences or some unrecognizable legal theory then he's no better than a black box.").

humbler ones, like what legal language even is or does?[16] *What* and *how* does written law, if ever, *communicate*? *Who* and *how*, if at all, ever *interprets* it? *Whose* interpretation prevails? Most of our questions concern social communication because, objectively, law is one of its chief forms.[17] But they can impact larger, and logically distinct, questions concerning the rule of law, whether broadly defined to encompass human flourishing or narrowly to exclude it. The fact that legal communication encompasses both its *results* (e.g., rules, statutes, constitutions) and the social *processes* producing them (e.g., judicial adjudication, legislation, constitution-making) further complicates things. Our ideas, then, about legal interpretation may not simply *result* from other, grander notions like constitutionalism or political justice: they can, conversely, *cause* some of our commitments to the latter. At the very least, these reinforce or undermine each other. Even as dull a topic as legal interpretation, then, confronts us with a consequential choice.

We all know it. And we're torn about it. Referring to the United States,[18] Siegfried Wiessner notes the "seemingly eternal conflict ... between an interpretation of the Constitution that relies virtually exclusively on its text and original meaning and the other reading which considers it a 'living document.'"[19] The dispute is neither trifling nor academic. Prominent decision makers themselves have spearheaded debate on both sides,[20] in a historically rare episode of the bench steering the lecture halls. Initially, at least. Recently, Wiessner has also warned that "a careful analysis of the problem that impinges upon the rule of law ... is needed to develop a recommendation that promotes

---

16   Ronald Dworkin, *Introduction, in* The Philosophy of Law 1 (Ronald Dworkin ed., 1977) ("Even the debate about the nature of law, which has dominated legal philosophy for some decades, is, at bottom, a debate within the philosophy of language and metaphysics.").

17   *See, e.g.,* John M. Conley & William M. O'Barr, Just Words: Law, Language, and Power 129 (1998) ("Most of the time, law is talk[.]").

18   For opposed views on how parochial our American concern with Originalism is, *see* Jamal Greene, *On the Origins of Originalism,* 88 Tex. L. Rev. 1, 19 (2009) (referring to "the global rejection of American-style originalism" and deeming originalism "an exceedingly unpopular view around the world"); Ozan O. Varol, *supra* note 3, at 1243 (challenging the conventional view and arguing that "originalism has a foreign story").

19   Siegfried Wiessner, *The Powers of the President,* 1 Lincoln Memorial U. L. Rev. 103, 110 (2013).

20   Among them Justice Antonin Scalia and Judge Richard Posner, the latter recently retiring from the bench as "the most-cited legal scholar on record." Jenna Greene, *After Posner retired from 7th Circuit, a grim diagnosis and a brewing battle,* Reuters (Mar. 29, 2022), https://www.reuters.com/legal/litigation/after-posner-retired-7th-circuit-grim-diagnosis -brewing-battle-2022-03-29/.

a public order of human dignity."[21] He recognizes that the interpretation of legal texts is at the heart of such analysis.[22] Emphasizing that Policy-Oriented Jurisprudence[23] "enables one to make [legal] decisions of higher quality," he has continuously invited us to "join th[e] struggle for a world order of human dignity defined in a respectful dialogue of equals."[24] Many of us, interested in more rational interpretive practices, domestically and internationally, have heeded the invitation.[25]

I'd like to ponder exactly what does Policy-Oriented Jurisprudence contribute to contemporary interpretive debate. Scholars have spilled little to no ink on the subject. Contrary to the expected, knee-jerk response, my answer is controversial: some versions of Policy-Oriented Jurisprudence are *squarely compatible* with some versions of contemporary Originalism. If you are committed to either school, odds are my thesis elicits a smile. Especially since Myres S. McDougal, one of New Haven's founders, openly criticized Originalism decades ago. Bear with me. I will also show that Policy-Oriented Jurisprudence asks several questions, and contributes a number of insights, that could and should inform mainstream dialogue. The metaphor framing our current debate as a *false choice* between genteel hoaxes or slot machines, reflected in the title of this piece, comes from McDougal himself, ever the pragmatic, middle-of-the-road trail blazer. Aiming to stir and sharpen debate, I'll be happy to achieve either.

---

21   Siegfried Wiessner, *The Rule of Law: Prolegomena*, Zeitschrift für deutsches und amerikanisches Recht 82, 84 (2018).

22   *Id.*

23   Also called "contextual" and "configurative" jurisprudence, for relevant introductions to the New Haven School's methods, *see* Michael Reisman, Siegfried Wiessner & Andrew Willard, *The New Haven School: A Brief Introduction*, 32 Yale J. Int'l L. 575 (2007); Siegfried Wiessner, *The New Haven School of Jurisprudence: A Universal Toolkit for Understanding and Shaping the Law*, 18 Asia Pacific L. Rev. 45 (2010) [hereafter "Toolkit"]; Frederick Samson, *The Lasswell-McDougal Enterprise: Toward a World Public Order of Human Dignity*, 14 Va. J. Int'l L. 535 (1974); Eisuke Suzuki, *The New Haven School of International Law: An Invitation to a Policy-Oriented Jurisprudence*, 1 Yale Stud. World Pub. Ord. 1 (1974); Michael Schmitt, *New Haven Revisited: Law, Policy and the Pursuit of World Order*, 1 U.S. A.F. Acad. J. Legal Stud. 185 (1990).

24   Wiessner, Toolkit, *supra* note 23, at 53, 61.

25   Siegfried Wiessner is not only my closest academic mentor, now turned colleague, but is a dear and close friend. An example, academic and otherwise, for those of us who know him as much as those who don't. I join in honoring his contributions to jurisprudence across a spectrum of areas. His passion for constitutional and international law, in scholarship no less than in the classroom, is, at once, impressive, inspirational, and even prescient in a world growing ever more connected and concerned about achieving fuller measures of freedom and human dignity.

2   Methodological Caveats

A few words on my focus. In answering the main question, I necessarily address
several narrower others. They include: (1) What is Originalism and how has it
evolved over time?; (2) What theory of legal interpretation did McDougal and
Harold D. Lasswell, the founders of Policy-Oriented Jurisprudence, develop?;
(3) What, if anything, did either say about the cluster of theories comprising
Originalism today?; and (4) How does their interpretive theory compare with
the core and peripheral tenets of contemporary Originalism?

Despite occasionally touching on grander and broader topics, such as "constitutionalism," "constitutional politics," "democracy," "republicanism," or the
"rule of law," my analysis is primarily focused on theories of *interpretation* in
the United States. The difference is critical to avoid confusion. First, I briefly
sketch some salient developments in American Originalism, from its founding to this day. Second, I explain McDougal and Lasswell's interpretive theory.
Third, I analyze the conceptual and practical overlap between New Haven's
interpretive contributions and those of contemporary Originalism. Lastly, I
point out some promising insights articulated by New Haven that could and
should inform current debate.

3   What Fuels Perennial Debate

Our Constitution begs for interpretation. Screams for it, really. And, undeniably, there are *better* and *worse* interpretive answers.[26] One need not be as formidable as Dworkin's Hercules,[27] or believe *all* questions to have right answers,

---

26   Although delving into it exceeds the scope of this paper, I wholeheartedly agree with
      Ronald Dworkin's memorable response to Stanley Fish on the subject:
          People interpret texts and statutes and cases and pictures. The most striking fact about
      this practice is a certain shared conviction. Interpreters for the most part assume that inter-
      preting a text is different from changing it into a new text, that one interpretation may be
      better than another even when this is controversial, that arguments exist for and against
      interpretations, that some of these arguments are stronger, more probative than others,
      that someone who now accepts a particular interpretation of a text may be persuaded
      rather than simply pushed out of it, and so forth. Together these second-order beliefs com-
      pose what we might call a "right-wrong" picture of interpretation, a picture that supposes
      that interpretations may be sound or unsound, better or worse, more or less accurate.
          Ronald Dworkin, *My Reply to Stanley Fish (and Walter Benn Michaels): Please Don't Talk
      About Objectivity Anymore, in* The Politics of Interpretation 289 (W.J.T. Michael ed., 1983).
27   Ronald Dworkin, *Hard Cases*, 88 Harv. L. Rev. 1057, 1083 (1975) ("We might therefore do
      well to consider how a philosophical judge might develop, in appropriate cases, theories

to recognize that, at least most of the time, a legal writer writes to be understood and a reader reads to understand. Especially when the stakes involved are life or limb. Understanding is not a happy accident along our reading journey: it is, hopefully, its destination. Our likelihood of success, and what constitutional methods increase it in the legal context, are at the core of contemporary debate. Disagreement rages, whether one speaks of the Constitution or statutes.[28] Although the Constitution does not prescribe how it is to be interpreted,[29] judicial choice among interpretive methods is *inevitable*. Yet, it is also *desirable*. Revolt against that choice aside, *interpret we must*. Over and over. And that labor, at least in practice, is less reminiscent of Hercules than it is of Sisyphus.

Several factors fuel debate, both internal and external to the social processes of making, interpreting, and enforcing law. Internally, and aside from the *inherent* ambiguity of language, written law is often *deliberately* ambiguous, resulting from political compromise purposefully enacting ambiguous provisions because clarity would have otherwise defeated consensus. For example, international agreement on that catalog of human rights embodied by the historic U.N. Declaration was achieved "provided" that states "[were] not asked why."[30] Our Constitution, no less the result of intense political compromise than the ordinary statute or treaty, contains deliberately unclear language.[31]

---

of what legislative purpose and legal principles require. We shall find that he would construct these theories in the same manner as a philosophical referee would construct the character of a game. I have invented, for this purpose, a lawyer of superhuman skill, learning, patience and acumen, whom I shall call Hercules.").

28   *See, e.g.,* Christopher Serkin & Nelson Tebbe, *Is the Constitution Special?*, 101 Cornell L. Rev. 701 (2016); Kevin Stack, *The Divergence of Statutory and Constitutional Interpretation*, 75 U. Colo. L. Rev. 1 (2004).

29   Of course, even if it did, as a treaty or a contract may do, ascertaining such a provision's meaning and scope will *itself* require interpretation. A curious concession about the inevitability of interpretation is made by Justice Scalia himself, who writes that, "as we see things, 'if you seem to meet an utterance which doesn't have to be interpreted, that is because you have interpreted it already.'" Antonin Scalia & Bryan A. Garner, Reading Law: The Interpretation of Legal Texts 53 (2012).

30   Jacques Maritain, Man and the State 77 (U. of Ch. Press, 1966) ("During one of the meetings ... at which the Rights of Man were being discussed, someone was astonished that certain proponents of violently opposed ideologies had agreed on the draft of a list of rights. Yes, they replied, we agree on these rights provided we are not asked why. With the 'why,' the dispute begins.").

31   Randy Barnett, *The Misconceived Assumption About Constitutional Assumptions*, 103 Nw. U. L. Rev. 615, 633 (2009) ("[T]he Drafters may have deliberately chosen ambiguous language to paper over irreconcilable differences among them. Solum calls this situation 'compromise ambiguity.' It is alleged, for example, that the language of the Necessary and

And not even clear, seemingly unambiguous language is all created equal. Constitutions, including that of the United States, contain different kinds of provisions. Despite perceived clarity, some are hard and fast *rules*, some are broad *standards*, and yet others are loftier, abstract *principles*. This complicates anyone's understanding. And yet, understand we do. And when *we* don't, *courts* still must. At least to decide cases.

Externally, powerful individuals, groups, political institutions, and even cultural movements fan the fires of debate. Academic crossfire over these issues generally takes place under the binary banners of "originalist" and "living" theories of interpretation. A symbiosis of official decision-makers and academics on each side of the divide—often but not always overlapping with wider, political party lines—continuously target judicial adjudication for criticism or praise, depending on how it approximates their preferred interpretive theories. Partly as a result, the composition of the Supreme Court has recently changed and several decisions issued overturning watershed precedent to conform jurisprudence to the majority's peculiar, originalist view of interpretation. Foreseeably, these have elicited originalist, no less than non-originalist, criticism, as well as constitutional cynicism.[32]

At the risk of "enormous[] repetiti[on],"[33] a brief overview of how Originalism developed as a theory and what it stands for today will assist the reader in later appraising how it overlaps, if at all, with New Haven's interpretive commitments. A working definition is, here, necessary. "Originalism" has many meanings. It is a theory of legal interpretation; a social—and political—movement;

      Proper Clause was left deliberately ambiguous to allow both sides of the debate over the scope of federal power to argue later that theirs was the meaning enacted in the Constitution. Finally, it is also possible for the Framers to have deliberately employed ambiguous language to accomplish a nefarious purpose, or at least an unpopular one.").

32   *See, e.g.,* Steven Semeraro, *We Are All Originalists Now ... Or Are We? Bostock's Misperceived Quest to Distinguish Title II's Meaning from the Public's Expectations*, 49 Hofstra L. Rev. 377 (2021); Reva Siegel, *Memory Games: Dobbs's Originalism As Anti-Democratic Living Constitutionalism—and Some Pathways for Resistance*, 101 Tex. L. Rev. (forthcoming 2023), *available at* https://papers.ssrn.com/sol3/papers.cfm?abstract_id=4179622. Despite brewing legal cynicism and overemphasis on the political, and even "hyper-political," aspects of our Judiciary, it is good to be reminded that, although "judges cannot avoid politics in the broad sense of political theory," "law is not a matter of personal or partisan politics, and a critique of law that does not understand this difference will provide poor understanding and even poorer guidance." Ronald Dworkin, *The Politics of Legal Interpretation, in* The Politics of Interpretation 249 (W.J.T. Michael ed., 1983). Partisan and other politics are only a conditioning factor in any comprehensive analysis of legal change.

33   David Fontana, *Comparative Originalism*, 88 Tex. L. Rev. 189, 189 (2010) ("American constitutional scholarship can sometimes seem enormously repetitive. Even if there are truly new ideas or truly new perspectives, they seem to be answering the same old questions.").

and even a cultural trope.[34] As a theory of interpretation, however, it comprises a family or cluster of theories—almost one for every published author, most of which adhere to two tenets. The first one is that the meaning of constitutional provisions and amendments was sufficiently fixed at the time of their enactment (i.e., the "Fixation Thesis"). The second one is that such original meaning should affect and bind subsequent judicial adjudication (i.e., the "Constraint Principle").[35] I believe a third tenet potentially—but not necessarily—implied by the second is that original meaning is sufficiently discoverable *most of the time* (i.e., the "Discoverability Thesis").[36] This cannot simply be a methodological assumption. Yes, the theory's gist is "highly controversial."[37] But it is also intuitively appealing. So much so that, in one form or another, it's always been a part of our constitutional tradition.

4   Collecting "Spirit" from Words: The Founders' Eclectic Originalism

How did the founders themselves interpret the Constitution? After all, the Constitution was historically, politically, and legally unprecedented, not just

---

34   Jack Balkin, *Framework Originalism and the Living Constitution*, 103 Nw. U. L. Rev. 549, 610 (2009) ("Like many revolutionary movements before it, the conservative movement of the late twentieth century has been predicated on a return to an imagined origin, a restoration of proper principles it claims that later generations have abandoned. There is nothing unusual about this: revolutions often use the tropes of return and restoration to promote what is actually change. The conservative originalism of the past several decades has been an attempt to replace a more liberal constitutionalism with a more conservative one. In many ways, it has succeeded.").

35   Lawrence Solum, *What Is Originalism? The Evolution of Contemporary Originalist Theory*, *in* The Challenge of Originalism: Theories of Constitutional Interpretation 182, 198 (Grant Huscroft & Bradley W. Miller eds., 2011). *See also* Ilan Wurman, A Debt Against the Living: An Introduction to Originalism 11 (2017) (defining Originalism as "the idea that the Constitution should be interpreted as its words were originally understood by the Framers who wrote the Constitution in 1787 and by the public that ratified it between 1787 and 1789," and, "[m]ore broadly still ... the idea that words have an original public meaning at the time they were spoken or written and presented to the world").

36   *See, e.g.,* Keith Whittington, *The New Originalism*, 2 Geo. J. of L. & Pub. Pol'y 599, 599 (2004) ("Originalism regards the *discoverable* meaning of the Constitution at the time of its initial adoption[.]") (emphasis added). Of course, Originalism could still be the preferred interpretive method even if only ten percent of the constitutional text (or ten percent of clauses actually litigated) contained discoverable meaning. Especially if one accepts the interpretation-construction distinction advanced by Whittington and described further below.

37   The Challenge of Originalism: Theories of Constitutional Interpretation 181 (Grant Huscroft & Bradley W. Miller eds., 2011).

for its content, but for its written format.[38] Literature on the subject continues to grow, as does that addressing our unwritten Constitution.[39] Here, however, we're concerned with text. One early constitutional dispute representative of mainstream interpretive approaches at the time involved the legality of a national, federal bank.[40] It is a vignette in two acts. First, the dispute over the first bank during George Washington's presidency. Second, the Supreme Court's decision decades later in *McCulloch v. Maryland*.[41] Justice Marshall "did not write on a clean slate in *McCulloch*," given that the bank was "disputed

---

38   Henry Monaghan, *Stare Decisis and Constitutional Adjudication*, 88 Colum. L. Rev. 723, 769 (1988) ("The American Constitution was a watershed in the evolution of thinking about the meaning of a constitution: it culminated a shift from viewing a constitution as simply a description of the fundamental political arrangements of the society to a conception that the constitution stood behind, or grounded and legitimated, those arrangements-and of course constrained them. In this development, the 'writtenness' of the American Constitution was crucial.").

39   For an overview of the concept, *see* Akhil Reed Amar, America's Unwritten Constitution: The Precedents and Principles We Live By (2012). For criticism of the concept of an "unwritten constitution" in the context of constitutional interpretation, *see* Lawrence Solum, *Originalism and the Unwritten Constitution*, U. Ill. L. Rev. 1935, 1936 (2013) ("Opponents of an unwritten constitution do not dispute the existence of judicial decisions that create or articulate rules of constitutional law. In some senses, we do have an unwritten constitution. In other senses, we do not. Framing the issues in terms of the notion of an 'unwritten constitution' obscures rather than illuminates the questions that are at stake.").

40   For an overview of the political and economic implications of the constitutional dispute, *see, e.g.,* Erick Lomazoff, Reconstructing the National Bank Controversy: Politics and Law in the Early American Republic (2018) (providing a comprehensive and nuanced historical review of the developments leading to the First and Second Banks).

41   17 U.S. 316 (1819). Its representativity is also based on its impact, since "the consensus is that the principles for which *McCulloch* stands lie at the heart of the American constitutional order.["] Mark R. Killenbeck, *It's More Than A Constitution*, 49 St. Louis U. L.J. 749, 752–53 (2005). For a deeper account of its context and impact, *see* Richard E. Elliss, Aggressive Nationalism: McCulloch v. Maryland and the Foundation of Federal Authority in the Young Republic (2007); David Schwartz, The Spirit of the Constitution: John Marshall and the 200-year Odyssey of McCulloch v. Maryland (2019). For recent voices suggestively criticizing its wisdom and import, *see* Sanford Levinson, *The Confusing Language of McCulloch v. Maryland: Did Marshall Really Know What He Was Doing (Or Meant)?*, 72 Ark. L. Rev. 7, 29 (2019) (noting *McCulloch* "bequeathed to us a completely muddled and perhaps incomprehensible notion of 'sovereignty'"); Mark A. Graber, *Overruling McCulloch?*, 72 Ark. L. Rev. 79, 80 (2019) ("[T]he Supreme Court probably would have overruled McCulloch's holding that the federal government was constitutionally authorized to incorporate a national bank if a proper vehicle for doing so had come before the court."); John Yoo, *McCulloch v. Maryland, in* Constitutional Stupidities, Constitutional Tragedies 241 (William N. Eskridge, Jr. & Sanford Levinson eds. 1998) (deeming *McCulloch* a "trag[edy]").

since the early days of the Republic."[42] The debate put on display the kind of textualism practiced by the founders. Although some of today's schism existed back then,[43] the most prevalent outlook was an eclectic[44] variety of textualism *consistent*—although not coextensive—*with* contemporary Originalism. This is no anachronism.

Our first Congress considered whether it could and should chart a national bank in 1791. The question was a hot button primarily because expressly including such power had been proposed and rejected at the convention, just years before, in an attempt to make the Constitution more palatable to states with big cities and financial centers. To many, it felt like a kick in the gut to hear that Congress now debated whether to read the opposite of that political compromise into the Constitution. President Washington asked for the opinions of three key cabinet members: Edmund Randolph, Thomas Jefferson, and Alexander Hamilton. "[T]he arguments [they] advanced should be taken seriously as exemplars," and even a "paradigm," "of constitutional argument" at the time.[45]

Randolph answered the question first. His opinion sought to be the most objective and least political.[46] The Attorney General began his analysis making the "obvious" observation that the Constitution did not "expressly" authorize chartering a bank.[47] So—he reasoned—the only way such power could exist was that it be sufficiently "implied" (whether by the "nature" of federal government, its "involve[ment]" in a specified power, or its "proper[ty] and necess[ity]" in carrying out a specified power).[48] Unlike state constitutions, the federal counterpart expressly provides for enumerated powers only, creating a certain

---

42   Daniel A. Farber, *The Story of McCulloch: Banking on National Power*, 20 Const. Comment. 679, 679 (2004).

43   Eric Slauter, The State As Work of Art: The Cultural Origins of the Constitution 29 (2009) ("[T]he modern interpretive divide between those who see the Constitution as a static document and those who see it as a living organism was present in the revolutionary era.").

44   *See* H. Jefferson Powell, A Community Built on Words 208 (2002) ("Eclecticism in the modalities of argument recognized as constitutional has been standard in American constitutional law since the founding."); Robert G. Natelson, *The Founders' Hermeneutic: The Real Original Understanding of Original Intentions*, 68 Ohio St. L.J. 1239, 1259 (2007) (courts "eclectic" in relying on original intent and legislative history).

45   Powell, *supra* note 44, at 22.

46   Walter Dellinger & Jefferson Powell, *The Constitutionality of the Bank Bill: The Attorney General's First Constitutional Law Opinions*, 44 Duke L.J. 110, 112 (1994) (analyzing and reprinting Randolph's bank opinions).

47   *Id.* at 122.

48   *Id.*

presumption against unenumerated ones.[49] The aim, according to Randolph, was to arrive at "a just interpretation of the [Constitution's] words" "upon any principle of fair construction."[50] And the main issue was not so much whether Congress had the power to chart a bank, but whether it had the power to create any corporations, not only banks.[51]

Randolph made the point, perennially debated since, that there is a "real difference" between interpreting statutes and constitutions.[52] "The one comprises a summary of matter, for the detail of which numberless laws will be necessary; the other is the very detail."[53] Thus, statutes are interpreted somewhat liberally, while constitutions are interpreted "with a closer adherence to the literal meaning."[54] How? Mainly through "appeals to ... common sense and common language."[55] Since no power to chart a bank could be reasonably implied through analogical reasoning from any of the specified powers, Randolph last considered the Necessary and Proper Clause. He observed that "necessary" meant "incidental, or ... the natural means of executing a power," while "proper," "if it has any meaning, does not enlarge the powers of Congress, but rather restricts them."[56] Rather than expressly drawing his conclusion that chartering a corporation or, more specifically, a bank, was neither incidental to nor a natural means of executing any specified power, Randolph concluded with a warning: "[L]et it be propounded as an eternal question to those who build new powers on this clause, whether the latitude of construction which they arrogate will not terminate in an unlimited power in Congress?"[57] He later issued a second opinion clarifying that he did not advocate a strict or literalist interpretation that excluded the existence of implied powers. Instead, he conceded the existence and need for such powers, merely denying that the specific power of chartering a bank was anywhere reasonably implied.[58] And he considered the Necessary and Proper Clause surplusage.

---

49   *Id.* at 122–23.

50   *Id.*

51   *Id.* at 123 ("We say charters of incorporation, without confining the question to the Bank; because the admission of it in that instance is an admission of it in every other, in which Congress may think the use of it equally expedient.").

52   *Id.*

53   *Id.*

54   *Id.*

55   *Id.* at 124.

56   *Id.* at 127.

57   *Id.*

58   *Id.* at 130. Today, of course, precedent and doctrine have developed in such a way that many believe the power to charter a bank is reasonably implied by the Borrowing, Commerce, and Spending Clauses. *See, e.g., id.* at 131 n.53.

Jefferson opined next. Because the Tenth Amendment states that all powers "not delegated to the United States ... are reserved to the States or to the people," he framed the inquiry as whether the power to charter the bank had ever been actually "delegated."[59] And he concluded it had not. Like Randolph, after explaining why such a power was not contained in any of the specified ones, he landed on the Necessary and Proper Clause. Jefferson deemed the chartering of a bank unnecessary because all the specified powers "can ... be carried into execution without [it]."[60] That is, he narrowly defined "necessary" as that without which, logically or factually, something cannot obtain.[61] He contrasted the "necessity" of means under the Clause with their mere "convenience," advocated by defenders of the bill. "[A] little difference in the degree of convenience, cannot constitute the necessity which the constitution makes the ground for assuming any non-enumerated power," since, "[i]f such a latitude of construction be allowed ... [i]t would swallow up all the delegated powers, and reduce the whole to one power."[62] For Jefferson, any other interpretation would turn the Necessary and Proper Clause into the Convenient and Desirable Clause.

Ultimately, since Congress could easily carry out its enumerated powers without such a bank, and given the *status quo* of private banking, Jefferson thought the power did not display the "degree" of "necessity" contemplated by the Clause.[63] His strict constructionism, choosing the narrower of two possible meanings for the word "necessary," stood on the shoulders of "a classic 'parade of horribles' presentation," assuming points not made by the bill's defenders.[64] This was likely motivated by one or several extra-interpretive factors, ranging from his agrarianism and distrust of commerce to anti-federalist influences and concern for states rights.[65]

Hamilton intervened last. Despite framing the significance of the matter as one entailing the success or failure of Washington's administration, and in terms of the consequences of defeating the bill, his main criticism of Randolph and Jefferson's opinions was that their "principles of construction ...

---

59   Thomas Jefferson, *Letter to George Washington, February 15, 1791, Opinion on Bill for Establishing a National Bank* at 2, https://memory.loc.gov/service/mss/mtj/mtj1/013/013_0984 _0990.pdf (last accessed July 1, 2022).

60   *Id.* at 4.

61   *Id.* at 5 ("[M]eans without which the grant of power would be nugatory.").

62   *Id.* at 4–5.

63   *Id.* at 6.

64   Charles Reid, *America's First Great Constitutional Controversy: Alexander Hamilton's Bank of the United States*, 14 U. St. Thomas L.J. 105, 183 (2018).

65   *Id.*

would be fatal to the just and indispens[a]ble authority of the United States."[66] According to Hamilton, they had the issue backwards, since "inherent" in the very "definition" of a "sovereign" government is its "right to employ all the means requisite, and fairly applicable to the attainment of the ends of such power," so far as this is "not precluded by restrictions and exceptions specified in the constitution" "or not immoral, or not contrary to the essential ends of political society."[67] That is, admittedly the Constitution specified and enumerated the powers delegated to the federal government. But once the delegation was made, surely that same federal government now had inherent power and discretion in choosing the means to exercise those specified powers. And, since this was true of government in general, Hamilton thought the burden was on Jefferson and Randolph to prove the United States government was the exception to the rule.[68]

Hamilton thought federalism did not change the equation: both federal and state governments were equally sovereign "with regard to [their] proper objects."[69] His syllogism went as follows: (1) it is incidental to sovereign power to erect corporations; (2) the United States is a sovereign power, as shown by the Supremacy Clause; therefore, (3) the United States has the incidental power to erect corporations in relation to the objects or powers entrusted to it by delegation.[70] The only consequence of the federalism and enumeration doctrines was that, where the delegation of authority was "general," as in state constitutions, a government could create corporations in all cases, whereas, here, where the delegation was confined to certain branches of legislation, the United States could only create corporations "in those cases."[71]

Hamilton also addressed Jefferson and Randolph's specific textual arguments. For example, he agreed it was unquestionably true that the Constitution meant only to delegate enumerated powers. However, he regarded what or how much power had actually been delegated by the text an open "question of fact to be made out by fair reasoning and construction upon the particular provisions of the constitution—taking as guides the general principles and general ends of government."[72] Echoing Randolph, it was the fair construction of specific textual provisions, then, what was primarily at stake. Other principles and

---

66   Alexander Hamilton, *Opinion on the Constitutionality of a National Bank*, *in* Alexander
      Hamilton, Writings 613 (Joanne B. Freeman ed., 2001).
67   *Id.*
68   *Id.* at 614.
69   *Id.*
70   *Id.*
71   *Id.* at 615.
72   *Id.*

policy considerations were ancillary and served as mere guides to the primary interpretive task. Hamilton noted that Randolph and Jefferson did not deny the existence of implied powers, delegated just as effectively as express ones.[73] The power to erect a corporation was such a power, since if it could be implied, it could also be pursued as a means to exercise another power.[74] According to Hamilton, the test is "whether the means to be employed ... has a natural relation to any of the acknowledged objects or lawful ends of the government."[75] He reasoned that a corporation may be created in pursuit of collecting taxes, trade with foreign countries, or commerce between states because it is the province of the sovereign federal government to regulate these and do so "to the best and greatest advantage."[76] Thus, his proposed test was satisfied.

Hamilton deemed Jefferson's narrow definition of "necessary" a "restrictive interpretation of the word" too bound by circumstances and the concept of expediency.[77] He stressed that the right to employ unspecified means to exercise a specified power cannot depend on circumstances displaying any particular degree of "necessity:" "the ... right ... must be uniform and invariable," if it is to mean something.[78] Specifically, Hamilton rejected that the "grammatical ... []or popular sense of the term" required Jefferson's construction.[79] Instead, the common meaning of "necessary" was merely "needful, requisite, incidental, useful, or conducive to."[80] This broader meaning was, according to him, "the true one ... to be understood as used in the constitution."[81] From the meaning and structure of the clause, he argued that "it was the intent of the convention" that such clause be afforded a liberal interpretation in the exercise of powers.[82] Jefferson's understanding of the word, therefore, departed from its "obvious and popular sense."[83] It also generated uncertainty as to what should count as a sufficient "degree" of circumstantial necessity.[84] Instead, Hamilton proposed that the criterion for constitutionality under the clause be the logical relationship between the means and the end at issue, not a factual degree

---

73   *Id.* (adding a third variety: "resulting" powers).
74   *Id.* at 616.
75   *Id.*
76   *Id.*
77   *Id.* at 617.
78   *Id.*
79   *Id.* at 618.
80   *Id.*
81   *Id.*
82   *Id.*
83   *Id.*
84   *Id.*

of necessity or utility.[85] He buttressed the point by arguing that Jefferson's reading defied the interpretive principle that constitutional delegations of power "ought to be construed liberally, in advancement of the public good," which he claimed applied to federal as much as state governments.[86] Against Randolph, and potentially in response to Madison's concerns about reading into the Constitution a power specifically voted down during the convention,[87] Hamilton added that "every particular implied in a general power, can be said to be … granted," and while creating a corporation was voted down as an express, specified power, it could still be reasonably implied by other express powers as a means to carrying them out.[88]

President Washington signed the legislation. Despite invoking principles and policy considerations in their reasoning, all three protagonists of the dispute primarily engaged in the interpretation of the constitutional *text*. Their disagreements "emerged out of a common allegiance to the written Constitution."[89] They all "paid careful attention to the text, and each claimed for his argument the virtue of superior fidelity to it."[90] Each claimed to capture the "best" or "true" "popular" "sense" or meaning of the words, even if extra or pre-interpretive commitments played a secondary role in how to choose among competing meanings or interpretations of constitutional design. The dispute was never about anything other than the Constitution's text: *what* it meant to most people and *how* its application best implemented constitutional purpose and design. What the text meant was to be "fixed" through interpretive "reasoning," not fiat, with common law rules, ordinary language, and the "intent" of the convention in mind. True, Jefferson and Hamilton agreed, contrary to Randolph's opinion, that "the Constitution's specific language is to be read in the light of its overall purpose, a purpose that cannot be stated in purely intra-textual terms, and interpretive cruxes are to be resolved by reference to that purpose."[91] But the critical term here is "purely." Overall, when lost or stuck in a hallway of our Constitution, persuasive intra-textual reasoning often unlocks a door to the outside of its language in our quest for meaning.

This persuasion was true of even the more extreme defenders of the bank, such as Fisher Ames. Despite rhetoric asking Congress to legislate "beyond

---

85   *Id.* at 619.

86   *Id.*

87   J. Randy Beck, *The New Jurisprudence of the Necessary and Proper Clause*, U. Ill. L. Rev. 581, 594–98 (2002) (describing Madison's attacks on Hamilton's position).

88   Hamilton, *supra note 66*, at 626–27.

89   Powell, *supra note 44*, at 23.

90   *Id.*

91   *Id.* at 30.

the letter of the constitution," Ames's was a theory of implied powers based on textual provisions, like Hamilton's. The differences in political theory and interpretive commitments did, however, play some role in the differences of outcome.[92] For example, like Jefferson, Madison originally interpreted the specified powers and Necessary and Proper Clause restrictively *because* of his view of the Constitution as primarily a series of limitations on government: a list of things *not to do* collectively. While Ames, like Hamilton, deemed the Constitution a document primarily creating and empowering government, and only secondarily restricting its choices in exercising powers: that is, a list of things *to do* collectively.[93] Unlike Randolph, Jefferson, and Madison, who thought a presumption should exist construing constitutional provisions more narrowly than statutes, Ames thought that the political fact that a government is the highest kind of *corporation* supported a liberal presumption the other way around: it should enjoy latitude in the means it pursues so long as they regard the very goals its powers are meant to achieve.[94] This is also why both Ames and Hamilton often spoke of the power to chart a bank *in tandem* with the power to address emergencies. Thus, to say that Hamilton or Madison—or Jefferson or Randolph, for that matter—"were not ... committed textualists" misses the point.[95] *They were all of textualist ilk, regardless of commitment level.*

Decades later, the Supreme Court decided the question in *McCulloch*.[96] The facts are simple enough. In 1818, Maryland enacted a statute to tax all banks within its territory not charted by its legislature.[97] "[E]veryone understood the

---

92   As Reid observed of the bank controversy:

> Most significantly, of course, from our perspective, is the emergence of alternative theories of constitutional interpretation. Was the Constitution a restraining text? An empowering text? How should enumerated powers be interpreted? What of implied or constructive powers? How faithful must one be to the text? How literally should the text be read? What was the appropriate role for sources external to the Constitution? What of philosophy? What of the writings of jurists such as Vattel? What was the relationship of the states in contrast to the federal government? None of these questions were definitely answered in 1791. None of them have been definitively answered today.

> Reid, *supra* note 64, at 192. For an overview of the main political theories embedded in our constitutional compromise as reflected in debate at the time, *see* Sanford Levinson, An Argument Open to All: Reading the Federalist Papers in the 21st Century (2015); W. B. Allen & Kevin A. Cloonan, The Federalist papers: A Commentary (2009); Morton White, Philosophy, The Federalist, and the Constitution (1987).

93   Reid, *supra* note 64, at 148–51.

94   *Id.* at 149.

95   *Cf., e.g.,* Slauter, *supra* note 43, at 25.

96   For insightful context into the intervening period, *see, e.g.,* Harold Plous & Gordon E. Baker, *M'Culloch v. Maryland: Right Principle, Wrong Case,* 9 Stan. L. Rev. 710, 712–19 (1957).

97   *McCulloch,* 17 U.S. at 317.

measure's real purpose: to curb the influence of the Baltimore branch of the Second Bank of the United States in Maryland, perhaps even to banish it from the state."[98] When the bank continued issuing unstamped (untaxed) bank notes and declined paying the annual $15,000, Maryland's state treasurer sued to collect on the debt.[99] Maryland won in its courts, which upheld the constitutionality of its tax. The bank then sought review from the United States Supreme Court. For nine days, the nation's finest lawyers argued the case, including Daniel Webster. It took the Court only three days to rule.[100]

Justice Marshall agreed that the power to charter a bank was not enumerated anywhere.[101] Why fight the obvious? No matter. This did not end the inquiry. He began by noting that, unlike questions involving the "great principles of liberty," one such as this one, involving instead the "powers" of government under federalism, should factor in how the federal and state governments have behaved and what exercise of powers they have, in practice, tolerated from each other.[102] After all, the federal government had already chartered a bank during Washington's presidency. Turning to his analysis of whether the bill was "[]reconcilable with the Constitution," Marshall reasoned that the latter was not a compact among states, but one by the American people.[103] He then invoked two general principles. First, that the compact created a federal government of delegated, enumerated powers and "the question respecting the extent of the powers actually granted ... will probably continue to arise, so long as our system shall exist."[104] Second, that "the government of the Union, though limited in its powers, is supreme within its sphere of action."[105]

To Marshall, the latter was not just a "result, necessarily, from [government's] nature," but primarily what the Constitution's "express terms" imply by *both* the Supremacy Clause *and* the oath of "fidelity" to it taken by government officials.[106] He observed that, unlike the Articles of Confederation, the Constitution did not expressly exclude implied or incidental powers.[107] Nothing "requires that everything granted shall be expressly and minutely described," which is why

98   Killenbeck, *supra* note 41, at 753.
99   *McCulloch*, 17 U.S. at 318–19; Plous & Baker, *supra* note 96, at 720; Mark R. Killenbeck, *supra* note 41, at 753.
100   Killenbeck, *supra* note 41, at 754; Plous & Baker, *supra* note 96, at 720.
101   *McCulloch*, 17 U.S. at 406.
102   *Id.* at 401.
103   *Id.* at 403.
104   *Id.* at 405.
105   *Id.*
106   *Id.* at 406.
107   *Id.*

the Tenth Amendment omitted the word "expressly," broadly characterizing constitutional powers instead as "delegated."[108] So, powers impliedly delegated exist and the question of whether a particular one has actually been delegated "depend[s] on a fair construction of the whole instrument."[109] According to Marshall, the founders omitted the word "expressly" in characterizing delegated powers "to avoid [the] embarrassments" caused by such an insertion in the Articles of Confederation, the likely culprit for most of their unworkability.[110] Elaborating the point, *while seeking where the power to charter a bank may be textually anchored*, Marshall memorably explained:

> A constitution, to contain an accurate detail of all the subdivisions of which its great powers will admit, and of all the means by which they may be carried into execution, would partake of the prolixity of a legal code, and could scarcely be embraced by the human mind. It would, probably, never be understood by the public. Its nature, therefore, requires, that only its great outlines should be marked, its important objects designated, and the minor ingredients which compose those objects, be deduced from the nature of the objects themselves. That this idea was entertained by the framers of the American constitution, is not only to be inferred from the nature of the instrument, but from the language. ... It is also, in some degree, warranted, by their having omitted to use any restrictive term which might prevent its receiving a fair and just interpretation. In considering this question, then, we must never forget that it is a *constitution* we are expounding.[111]

To those who insisted that the mere absence of the words "to charter a bank" settled the question of whether the power was delegated in Article I, Marshall responded that they confused enumeration with delegation and, since implied powers existed, the absence of an express, enumerated grant merely shifted the question to whether the power may have still been delegated by implication.[112]

---

108   *Id.*
109   *Id.*
110   *Id.* at 406–7.
111   *Id.* at 407.
112   *See, e.g.*, David Schwartz, *McCulloch v. Maryland and the Incoherence of Enumerationism*, 19 Geo. J. L. & Pub. Pol'y 25, 32 (2021) ("Consider Marshall's subtle movement from 'enumerated' to 'granted' to 'actually granted.' Enumerated and granted powers are not the same, especially given *McCulloch*'s conclusion that implied powers are actually granted."). As Schwartz further explains, "Marshall did not relentlessly pursue his own logic of implied powers in *McCulloch*; far from it, he pushed implied powers into a closet, insofar

Showing the absurdity of the opposite, he explained that you take the legal text you interpret as you find it. The Constitution is not a European legal code, with a thousand pages and a host of details—a project he is skeptical about to begin with. Rather, a constitution is meant to be understood by the public. By design, it is only a "great outline" of the "great powers" it recognizes, the "subdivisions" of those powers, and the "means" by which those powers are exercised. Those powers are "important objects" and are, therefore, "designated" through words. However, the means or "minor ingredients" which compose those powers may not be so designated. Instead, they may be "deduced" from the nature of the designated powers themselves. Absent an express requirement otherwise, this is what the Constitution's "language" and "nature" require: an ordinary, "fair and just interpretation" that makes space for reasonable implications from text.

And so, Marshall's analysis immediately turned to those Article I "great powers" from which chartering a bank may be reasonably inferred. He identified several: the right to tax, borrow money, regulate commerce, and raise and maintain armies.[113] Marshall noted that revenue was to be raised, collected, and spent, partly to support armies, throughout the country and its territories "from the Atlantic to the Pacific."[114] This included the need to "transport" treasure in all directions. A bank facilitates this. So, he rhetorically asked: "Can we adopt that construction (unless the words imperiously require it), which would impute to the framers of [the Constitution], when granting these powers for the public good, the intention of impeding their exercise, by withholding a choice of means?"[115] He implied a negative answer. There is no prohibition against creating corporations "if the existence of such a being is essential, to the beneficial exercise of [granted] powers."[116] The only "fair" question was "how far such means may be employed."[117] Well, he concluded that chartering a bank did not go too far. Corporations, whether created for charity or in the process of founding cities, are everywhere always a means to something else. Since federal powers are inherently sovereign as to their objects, "[n]o sufficient reason is ... perceived, why [the power of creating corporations] may not

---

as he shrank from the full implications of recognizing implied commerce powers," "[y]et, the logic of implied powers in *McCulloch* was clear enough, and on the related concept of federal supremacy and its incompatibility with reserved state powers, *McCulloch* self-evidently came down on the side of federal supremacy." *Id.* at 70.

113   *McCulloch*, 17 U.S. at 407.
114   *Id.* at 408.
115   *Id.*
116   *Id.* at 408–409.
117   *Id.* at 409.

pass as incidental to those powers which are expressly given, if it be a direct mode of executing them."[118]

Aside from this "general reasoning,"[119] showing that the power to choose necessary means—like chartering a bank—was sufficiently implied, Marshall also addressed the express grant of power under the Necessary and Proper Clause. The word "necessary" was "controlling."[120] One meaning, advanced by Maryland, was "indispensable, and without which the power would be nugatory."[121] But Marshall questioned whether this was the "sense" in which the word was "always" used, and found another.[122] The second meaning was "convenient, or useful, or essential to another," such that "[t]o employ the means necessary to an end, is generally understood as employing any means calculated to produce the end, and not as being confined to those single means, without which the end would be entirely unattainable."[123] Marshall preferred the latter meaning. He reasoned that, as used, the word seemed figurative and ambiguous.[124] He urged that, where, as here, a word meant both "something excessive" and something less so, it "should be understood in a more mitigated sense," if the latter is also the ordinary or prevailing "sense" in "common usage."[125] Marshall identified intra-textual evidence for this: elsewhere in Article I, the Constitution prohibits states from laying imposts or duties on imports or exports except for what may be "absolutely necessary for executing its inspection laws."[126] Well, this proved that "the convention understood itself to change materially the meaning of the word 'necessary,' by prefixing the word 'absolutely' ... and, in its construction, the subject, the context, the intention of the person using them, are all to be taken into view."[127] Further evidence was the very word "proper:" if "necessary" narrowly meant absolute, physical or logical necessity, then why further qualify the means as "proper," which implies choice?[128] He memorably concluded:

---

118   *Id.* at 411.
119   *Id.*
120   *Id.* at 413.
121   *Id.*
122   *Id.*
123   *Id.* at 413–14.
124   *Id.* at 414.
125   *Id.*
126   *Id.*
127   *Id.* at 414–15.
128   *Id.* at 419.

We admit, as all must admit, that the powers of the government are limited, and that its limits are not to be transcended. But we think the sound construction of the constitution must allow to the national legislature that discretion, with respect to the means by which the powers it confers are to be carried into execution, which will enable that body to perform the high duties assigned to it, in the manner most beneficial to the people. Let the end be legitimate, let it be within the scope of the constitution, and all means which are appropriate, which are plainly adapted to that end, which are not prohibited, but consist with the letter and spirit of the constitution, are constitutional.[129]

Because the choice of chartering a bank satisfied the announced test, Maryland's law was declared unconstitutional and the chartering of the bank was upheld.[130]

There is certainly more to Marshall's holding. And much stimulating dicta. But the core of the analysis, and the arguments of the parties, revolved over the correct "sense" or "meaning" of the words defining the powers enumerated in Article I, especially the Necessary and Proper Clause. And the correct meaning was that in "common" "usage," reflecting the "intention" of the "convention" at the time. It was also the meaning for which most intra-textual evidence existed,[131] and that best served constitutional purpose and design. Marshall's "text and principle" approach, developed in earlier cases, was an example of early constitutional "textualism" that set him apart from some of his colleagues.[132]

---

129   *Id.* at 421.
130   *Id.* at 437.
131   For an analysis and praise of Marshall's "adroit" intra-textualism, *see* Akhil Reed Amar, *Intratextualism*, 112 Harv. L. Rev. 747, 755 (1999). As Professor Amar notes, while "[c]lause-bound textualism reads the words of the Constitution in order, tracking the sequence of clauses as they appear in the document itself," "[b]y contrast, intratextualism often reads the words of the Constitution in a dramatically different order, placing textually nonadjoining clauses side by side for careful analysis." *Id.* at 788.
132   Sylvia Snowiss, *Text and Principle in John Marshall's Constitutional Law: The Cases of Marbury and McCulloch*, 33 J. Marshall L. Rev. 973, 985–86 (2000). As Snowiss explains, in earlier Contracts Clause cases,

   Marshall fixed the meaning of the clause through textual exposition while his colleagues relied exclusively on extra-textual sources, either natural law principle or common law precedent on the law of contracts. It is important to stress that use of textual exposition to determine constitutional meaning was not itself innovative. The decisive innovation was judicial reliance on an arguable exposition to fix the meaning of the Constitution for the purpose of enforcing it against legislation. This made the judiciary the authoritative expounder of constitutional text, attaching, in the process, the judicial

Sturges, another case decided the same month as *McCulloch*, confirms that its textualism was the rule, not the exception. Elaborating on the interplay between the letter and spirit of a constitution, Marshall explained:

> [A]lthough the spirit of an instrument, especially of a constitution, is to be respected not less than its letter, yet *the spirit is to be collected chiefly from its words.* ... But if, in any case, the *plain meaning* of a provision, not contradicted by any other provision in the same instrument, is to be disregarded, because we believe the framers of that instrument could not intend what they say, it must be one in which the *absurdity* and *injustice* of *applying* the provision to the case, would be so *monstrous*, that all mankind would, without hesitation, unite in rejecting the application.[133]

This metaphor of constitutional interpretation as "gathering" "meaning" from words best captures the approach of early Originalism. And, in *Sturges*, whose vantage point is used in ascertaining meaning? According to Marshall, that of an ordinary, reasonable person.[134] It is the "full and obvious meaning" that is sought before a provision may be applied.[135] Why? Because this is the "fair[est]"

---

responsibility in ordinary law to the Constitution and obscuring the difference in kind between them.

Id. However, I disagree with Snowiss' conclusion that, in *McCulloch*, "[t]extual exposition of the Necessary and Proper Clause, undertaken in reply to that made by those denying the existence of implied powers, was subordinate to inference and deduction from constitutional ends, nature, and structure." *Id.* at 1002. Although I lack space to the develop the argument, Marshall's "general reasoning" about implied powers is anchored in text and, most critically, his pronouncement that the holding would have been the same *even if the Necessary and Proper Clause did not exist* is clearly dicta in the form of a *counterfactual.* Although passionate about reasoning about extra-textual factors, to say that Marshall's textual analysis in *McCulloch* was a subordinate, second order affair, turns the holding's rationale on its head. *See, e.g.,* Powell, *supra* note 44, at 22 (explaining that "[t]he role of political sentiment in the debaters' thinking [regarding the national bank] did not ... render their arguments a sham").

133   *Sturges v. Crownshield*, 17 U.S. 122, 202 (1819) (emphasis added).

134   *See id.* at 205 ("No men would so express such an intention. No men would use terms embracing a whole class of laws, for the purpose of designating a single individual of that class."). *See also* Paul Brest, *The Misconceived Quest for the Original Understanding,* 60 B.U. L. Rev. 204, 206 (1980) (explaining that, in *Sturges*, "[t]he plain meaning of a text is the meaning that it would have for a 'normal speaker of English' under the circumstances in which it is used. Two kinds of circumstances seem relevant: the linguistic and the social contexts. The linguistic context refers to vocabulary and syntax. The social context refers to a shared understanding of the purposes the provision might plausibly serve.").

135   *Sturges*, 17 U.S. at 205.

interpretation.[136] What might prevent that meaning from controlling? Only "monstrously" "absurd" or "unjust" applications of such meaning.

Marshall believed that the meaning that controlled was not only that "compatible" with the words chosen by the drafters, but that which was "apparently manifested" by them. That which did not do unjustified "violence" to their "plain meaning." That which resulted from the application of "those rules of construction, which have been consecrated by the wisdom of ages."[137] Marshall's pet peeve about some of the textualism of his time was not *that* it looked chiefly at text, but that *the way* it did so was often wrong and tendentious, giving words "a more limited sense" than they actually had.[138] *Literalism was the danger, not textualism.* The opposite danger was semantic freewheeling. Don't take my word for it. Take Marshall's:

> The powers of [government] are defined and limited; and that those limits may not be mistaken, or forgotten, the Constitution is written. To what purpose are powers limited, and to what purpose is that limitation committed to writing, if these limits may, at any time, be passed by those intended to be restrained?[139]

Despite contemporary wisdom labeling Marshall "the philosophical grandfather" of non-textualist approaches, "his frequently cited landmark opinions such as McCulloch ... were in fact thoroughly rooted in the text of the Constitution."[140] Indeed, "[t]he textual approach, accepted without question for so long, fell from grace suddenly between the 1930s and the 1960s."[141] True,

---

136   *Id.* For a suggestive discussion about the interplay of fair notice in legal documents and interpretation, *compare* Note, 123 Harv. L. Rev. 542 (2009), *with* Benjamin M. Chen, *Textualism as Fair Notice?*, 97 Wash. L. Rev. 339 (2022).

137   *Sturges*, 17 U.S. at 206.

138   *Id.* Again, I must disagree with attempts to explain away Marshall's textualism, especially in *Sturges*. *See, e.g.,* Farah Peterson, *Expounding the Constitution*, 130 Yale L.J. 2, 65 (2020) ("Marshall's commitment to public-law principles of interpretation is underappreciated in part because of the disproportionate importance now assigned to a quote of his that seems in line with modern textualism. ... All this proves, however, is that Marshall was not immune to the charms of using his states' rights adversaries' own logic to defeat them."). It is Marshall's textualism that is unfairly underappreciated when deemed a mere ruse without explanation. An assertion bordering on revisionism.

139   *Marbury v. Madison*, 5 U.S. (1 Cranch) 137, 176 (1803). *See also Poindexter v. Greenhow*, 114 U.S. 270, 291 (1885).

140   Bradley P. Jacob, *Back to Basics: Constitutional Meaning and "Tradition"*, 39 Tex. Tech L. Rev. 261, 265 (2007).

141   *Id.*

"[t]he Bank controversy is but one example of an approach to constitutional interpretation that was developmental rather than static."[142] Yet, as the debates in Washington's first administration and *McCulloch* illustrate, that developing approach was textualist, if eclectic. And it increasingly aimed at better, fairer, and more correct readings, especially in cases where the choice between narrow and broader meanings made all the difference.[143] Critical to that endeavor was the search for "popular," "common," or "usual" meaning.

In sum, that the founding generation's early[144] practice was not an exact copy of *contemporary* Originalism cannot detract from the fact that it did primarily care about text. And in very nuanced ways, including the elucidation of *public ordinary meaning*. An approach consistent with much of contemporary

---

142 Mark R. Killenbeck, *Madison, M'Culloch, and Matters of Judicial Cognizance: Some Thoughts on the Nature and Scope of Judicial Review*, 55 Ark. L. Rev. 901, 913 (2003).

143 As Justice Scalia has noted in this context:

To be sure, in support of its venerability as a legitimate interpretive theory there is often trotted out John Marshall's statement in McCulloch v. Maryland that "we must never forget it is a constitution we are expounding"—as though the implication of that statement was that our interpretation must change from age to age. But that is a canard. The real implication was quite the opposite: Marshall was saying that the Constitution had to be interpreted generously because the powers conferred upon Congress under it had to be broad enough to serve not only the needs of the federal government originally discerned but also the needs that might arise in the future. If constitutional interpretation could be adjusted as changing circumstances required, a broad initial interpretation would have been unnecessary.

Antonin Scalia, *Originalism: The Lesser Evil*, 57 U. Cin. L. Rev. 849, 852–53 (1989).

144 For argument why the founders themselves did not subscribe Originalism, see the now canonical article by H. Jefferson Powell, *The Original Understanding of Original Intent*, 98 Harv. L. Rev. 885 (1985). However, aside from showing that the founders were not *original* intent Originalists—a minority variant of contemporary Originalism, Powell's essay is not useful for much more, as it is admittedly "not concerned ... with ... what ... early interpreters actually did in construing the Constitution." *Id.* at 886. *See also* Wurman, *supra* note 35, at 17 ("When someone says ... that 'originalism refutes originalism' because the Founders themselves weren't originalist (citing H. Jefferson Powell's article), you can respond that original intentions originalism has been severely challenged but that original public understanding originalism has survived the unrelenting counteroffensive."); William Baude, *Were the Framers Originalists (and Does It Matter)?*, Reason (Oct. 24, 2018) (noting that Powell's article "worked against 'original intent' originalism, but as originalist thought became more careful and rigorous, most originalists came to agree that original meaning was controlling, not original intent. In other words, today's originalists share the position of the framers in Powell's article, so there was no mismatch between originalism and the framers."), https://reason.com/volokh/2018/10/24/were-the-framers-originalists-and-does-i/. For subsequent criticism of Powell's work, *see, e.g.,* Charles A. Lofgren, *The Original Understanding of Original Intent?, in* Interpreting the Constitution: The Debate Over Original Intent 117 (Jack N. Rakove ed., 1990).

Originalism. This non-systematic, eclectic method centering around public meaning we can confidently call early Originalism. Of course, it is different from subsequent Originalisms in many ways.

5 Prelude to Modern Originalism

Modern Originalism, the self-conscious theory about constitutional interpretation that arose in the early 1970's, was preceded and shaped by three other events in America's intellectual life: Thayerianism, Alexander Bickel's work on judicial review, and the Warren and Burger Courts' Revolution. It developed in response to all three, embracing Thayerian deference, struggling to answer Bickel's "counter-majoritarian difficulty," and challenging the Warren and Burger Courts' precedent.

Many say that modern constitutional theory in the United States "began"[145] with James B. Thayer's *The Origin and Scope of the American Doctrine of Constitutional Law*.[146] Published in 1893, its main thesis was that statutes should not be voided unless their unconstitutionality is "so clear that it is not open to rational question."[147] Despite disclaiming novelty in doctrine, he effectively ushered into being the "rational basis test" incorporated by our jurisprudence ever since. Thayer's justifications were, variously, that many constitutional provisions admitted of a wide range of reasonable interpretive outcomes, necessarily allowing for legislative choice; that the legislature has as much responsibility to interpret the constitution as the courts; and that too active a judicial review may lead to interbranch conflict and demoralize the people, who will otherwise pay less and less attention to the choices they make, expecting the courts to intervene if they have truly gone astray.[148] "Although the possibility of different branches reaching different interpretive judgments was long contemplated ... Thayer sought to link departmentalism with the standard of review, thereby making an important contribution in formalizing and theorizing the basis for different standards of review."[149]

---

145   Steven G. Calabresi, *Originalism and James Bradley Thayer*, 113 Nw. U. L. Rev. 1419, 1420 (2019).

146   James B. Thayer, *The Origin and Scope of the American Doctrine of Constitutional Law*, 7 Harv. L. Rev. 129 (1893).

147   *Id.* at 144.

148   *Id.* at 136, 142, 146, 156.

149   Vicki C. Jackson, *Thayer, Holmes, Brandeis: Conceptions of Judicial Review, Factfinding, and Proportionality*, 130 Harv. L. Rev. 2348, 2350 (2017).

Thayer's school of judicial deference to democratic rule and self-restraint died for a variety of reasons[150] but "left a legacy: procedural devices for ducking constitutional issues, the notion of restraint as a pragmatic tiebreaker, and a checklist of considerations that argue for restraint in particular cases."[151] Yes, Thayer rejected mechanical and formalistic textual interpretation. But he also praised *McCulloch*'s eclectic approach.[152] Thayerian deference and restraint in constitutional interpretation was gradually displaced—if it ever laid roots— by "[m]odern constitutional theories—whether Bork's or Scalia's originalism, or ... the living Constitution," since they "are designed to tell judges ... how to decide cases correctly rather than merely sensibly or prudently."[153] Richard Posner has even said that modern constitutional theory is "inherently incompatible with [Thayerian constitutional] restraint."[154]

Yet, initially, "[a]dvocacy of originalism often went hand-in-hand with a strong Thayerian deference, which urged judges to strike down statutes only in the most extreme cases when no reasonable defense of the laws could be offered."[155] So much so that some venture that Originalism "was born of a desire to constrain judges," and that "[j]udicial constraint was its heart and

---

150   See Richard A. Posner, *The Rise and Fall of Judicial Self-Restraint*, 100 Cal. L. Rev. 519, 522 (2012) (listing, as likely causes, that "it rested on false premises about judicial deliberation; it lacked coherence-the Thayerians did not constitute a community of thought; it had no stopping point-once you embraced it, you could not explain why a law would ever be declared unconstitutional; it was vulnerable to the rise of constitutional theories; and it was given its coup de grace by a combination of decisions by the liberal Warren Court and the refusal of the conservative successors to Justices of the Warren Court to accept a ratchet theory of judicial succession, in which liberal Justices depart from precedent in order to expand the constitutional rights favored by liberals and their conservative successors 'conserve' those liberal decisions because of a commitment to stare decisis").

151   *Id.*

152   Jackson, *supra* note 149, at 2350; Thayer, *supra* note 146, at 151–52. See also Posner, *supra* note 150, at 524 ("Skeptics of judicial competence often are strict constructionists, in the sense of hewing close to the semantic surface of statutes. They ... defin[e] their role in a way that enables them to apply the law with confidence ('plain meaning'). That is not the character of the Thayerians either; they were ... loose constructionists. And they were not necessarily modest. Their emphasis was not on the inability of judges to understand difficult cases and devise effective remedies, but on the legislature's superior competence, in the sense either of legitimacy or of ability, or both, to legislate with a free hand.").

153   Posner, *supra* note 150, at 535.

154   *Id.* at 537.

155   Whittington, *supra* note 4, at 393 ("Both the substantive content of the original Constitution and the high information requirements for an originalist judge to reach clear conclusions about constitutional meaning suggested to early originalists that democratic majorities would be empowered to act.").

soul—its raison d'être."[156] Although some originalists today have distanced themselves from Thayerianism,[157] this was not always so. Debate persists about Originalism's compatibility with Thayerian deference.[158] One reason why Thayerianism may have been attractive to modern originalists is that, in its most essential form, "Thayerianism is the view that courts should defer to Congress, but that Congress itself should be constrained by the original meaning of the constitutional text."[159]

Be that as it may, Thayerianism and Originalism overlapped early on in strands of conservative constitutional theory.[160] Originalist pioneer Robert Bork, "whose constitutional conservatism cost him a seat on the Supreme Court bench, defined the limited role of the conservative judge" as "translat[ing] the framer's or the legislator's morality into a rule to govern unforeseen circumstances," "abstain[ing] from giving his own desires free play," and "continuing [to] self-conscious[ly] renounc[e] power."[161] Of course, eventually,

---

156   Thomas Colby, *The Sacrifice of the New Originalism*, 99 Geo. L.J. 713, 714 (2011). For criticism that Originalism works out the opposite of restraint, *see, e.g.,* David Strauss, *Originalism, Conservatism, and Judicial Restraint*, 34 Harv. J. L. & Pub. Pol'y 137, 143 (2011) ("If judicial restraint means abjuring one's own views in favor of the law, then originalist interpretation is, contrary to its claims, an open invitation to be unrestrained.").

157   *See* Steven Calabresi, *supra* note 145 at 1421 ("I doubt that Professor Thayer understood how much harm his writing would do, and I hope that if he had understood it, he would have reconsidered. But it is necessary for us, as constitutional law scholars, to tell the history of Thayerian restraint in an unflattering yet true way if we are to properly assess the value of this approach to constitutional decision-making and to expose its opposition to originalism."); Lawrence Solum, *Originalism Versus Living Constitutionalism: The Conceptual Structure of the Great Debate*, 113 Nw. U. L. Rev. 1243, 1261 (2019) ("[W]e might classify various other views as 'living constitutionalism,' including the Thayerian deference approach[.]").

158   Whittington, *supra* note 4, at 393 ("A commitment to judicial deference is a potential add-on to an originalist theory of constitutional interpretation. As such, it might be independently justified as a value that is unrelated to originalism but is nonetheless worth adopting. There is little consensus among current originalists that a general principle of judicial deference is separately attractive. Indeed, many would regard judicial deference as subversive of the primary commitment of originalism to identify and adhere to the original meaning of the Constitution.").

159   Solum, *supra* note 157, at 1273.

160   Of course, "[c]onservatism in politics embraces a spectrum of ideologies, ranging from libertarians to religious conservatives to national security hawks to business conservatives to neoconservatives." Keith Whittington, *Is Originalism Too Conservative?*, 34 Harv. J. L. & Pub. Pol'y 29, 32–34 (2014) (adding that, "[c]onservatism as an intellectual movement is multifaceted. Because of this diversity, originalism as a method of constitutional interpretation is unlikely to produce results that simultaneously satisfy all conservatives.").

161   Thomas E. Baker, *Constitutional Theory in a Nutshell*, 13 Wm. & Mary Bill Rts. J. 57, 109 (2004) (citing Robert Bork, Tradition and Morality in Constitutional Law 11 (1984)).

Originalism and Thayerianism parted ways and cannot now be identified with each other. Just as liberal or progressive constitutionalism defended judicial deference in opposing the *Lochner* Court, only to eschew it during the New Deal and Warren and Burger Courts, conservative constitutionalism once defended *Lochner*, then decried the activism of the Warren and Burger Courts, only to yet again embrace conservative activism during the Rehnquist Court, seeking to correct prior precedent.[162]

Now, between Thayer's work and the Warren and Burger Courts, "conservatism's wilderness years,"[163] the age-old debate over the political morality of judicial review resurfaced. Writing in 1962, Alexander Bickel warned that judicial review—the judicial power to void the acts of the other two branches if found unconstitutional—was a "deviant" practice in democracies like ours.[164] He argued that, although such power could not be found in the Constitution's text, it could still be "placed" in the Constitution.[165] Arguing that a much better job than Marshall's in *Marbury* was needed in today's world to justify the institution,[166] Bickel noted that "judicial review is a counter-majoritarian force in our system."[167] Despite trying to provide an answer to the dilemma, favoring judicial review, Bickel's attempt backfired, fanning rather than quelling the fire of the debate. Both sides of the political spectrum took exception. So, Robert H. Bork, "one of the most conservative constitutionalists on the right," and Mark Tushnet, "one of the most liberal constitutionalists on the left," both published "manifestos against judicial review."[168] As Professor Baker put it, "[t]hese two prominent heretics, and numerous other scholars and commentators who have joined in the intellectual fray, demonstrate how the dogma of judicial review still remains controversial."[169] The debate among originalists of all

---

162   Nimer Sultany, *The State of Progressive Constitutional Theory: The Paradox of Constitutional Democracy and the Project of Political Justification*, 47 Harv. Civ. Rts. & Civ. Lib. L. Rev. 371, 384 n.59 (2012).

163   Ken I. Kersch, The Alternative Tradition of Conservative Constitutional Theory 27 (2019).

164   Alexander Bickel, The Least Dangerous Branch: The Supreme Court At the Bar of Politics 18 (1962).

165   *Id.* at 1.

166   *Id.* at 2.

167   *Id.* at 16.

168   Baker, *supra* note 161, at 67 ("Bork would allow the Supreme Court to continue to decide constitutional cases, but would amend the Constitution to authorize Congress to overrule an interpretation of the Constitution by a simple majority vote. Tushnet would go further to eliminate judicial review in the courts by a constitutional amendment, leaving the task of constitutional interpretation to Congress and populist politics.").

169   *Id.* at 68.

political persuasions over the proper justification and scope of judicial review continues,[170] including the voices of new Supreme Court Justices.[171]

Ultimately, however, "self-conscious originalism in its modern form largely arose as a response to the liberal constitutional decisions of the Warren and Burger Courts."[172] Critics of the Warren and Burger Courts began to argue that "the only legitimate way" of interpreting the Constitution was the intent of the framers: a largely unprecedented call for "methodological exclusivity" in constitutional adjudication.[173] Few disagree with this historical characterization.[174] "Bork would look on a 'liberal judge' relying on moral reasoning and a 'conservative judge' relying on natural law with equal suspicion because he believes that both those sources allow judges to find things in the Constitution that are not there, at least not in Bork's constitution."[175] From the outset, then, originalist pioneers sought a more objective interpretive method that could avoid the pitfalls of judicial activism of *any* sort—it just so happened that conservative political actors at the time had their own, and different, agenda. The fit between academia and politics was not geometrical.

---

170   Sultany, *supra* note 162, at 376 n.21.

171   *See, e.g.,* Amy Coney Barrett, *Countering the Majoritarian Difficulty* 32 Const'l Commentary 61, 77 (2017) (criticizing Randy Barnett's theory of judicial review and proposed presumption of liberty) ("While [Barnett] is right to insist that courts ought not operate based on a distorted understanding of judicial restraint, he overcompensates in the other direction. There is a risk that a faction can run away with the legislative process, but there is also a risk that a faction will conscript courts into helping them win battles they have already lost, fair and square.").

172   Keith Whittington, *supra* note 4, at 29. As Professor Whittington notes:

Judges and scholars turned to history to explain why they thought that the Supreme Court had not only gotten the constitutional law wrong, but had also acted illegitimately in making its rulings. These kinds of critiques culminated in the Reagan administration, the creation of the Federalist Society, and the mobilization of a conservative legal movement that embraced originalism as a core commitment. As a result, many conservatives embrace originalist arguments, and the public often associates originalism with conservatives.

Id. See also Skylar Croy, *The Problem of Change: Rethinking Critiques of "New Originalism,"* Drake L. Rev. Discourse 101, 105 (2019) ("Old originalism emerged as a reaction to the Warren Court's perceived judicial activism. During Richard Nixon's campaign for President, he promised "to appoint only 'strict constructionists who saw their duty as interpreting law and not making law.' .... At his confirmation hearing, soon-to-be Justice Rehnquist stated that he interpreted the Constitution in accordance with 'the language used by the framers, [and] the historical materials available.'").

173   Post & Siegel, *supra* note 3, at 547.

174   Frank Cross, *Originalism: The Forgotten Years*, 28 Const'l Commentary 37, 37 (2012).

175   Baker, *supra* note 161, at 67.

In sum, the ethos of most modern Originalism—deferential, anti-activist, text and history-focused, skeptical of judicial review—must primarily be understood through its early history. Isolating these influences on the tone, ethos, and even political motivations of Originalism, one can better analyze the merits of its theory, and with less distraction. This is critical, since despite its origins, *as a theory*, Originalism is *not* inherently a politically conservative method.

6   Modern Originalism

Modern Originalism—called "Old" Originalism in the literature[176]—came to prominence with Raoul Berger and Robert Bork,[177] at least self-consciously.[178] In 1971, Bork published *Neutral Principles*, lamenting the "disturbing" fact that constitutional law lacked a "theory."[179] As a result of missing "effective criteria," he explained, "we have come to expect that the nature of the Constitution will change, often quite dramatically, as the personnel of the Supreme Court changes."[180]

Rather than offer a theory himself, he purported to merely show "the necessity for a theory."[181] Concerned with the question "[W]hen is authority legitimate?" in the Supreme Court context, he borrowed Herbert Wechsler's argument that the Court could not be an organ of naked power and, instead, must rely on neutral principles in adjudicating cases.[182] According to Bork, the need for principled, neutral adjudication arises from the "seeming anomaly

---

176   *See* Whittington, *supra* note 36, at 599 (coining the label "old originalism" for that appearing between the 1960's and 1980's); Mitchell Berman & Kevin Toh, *On What Distinguishes New Originalism from Old: A Jurisprudential Take*, 82 Fordham L. Rev. 545, 546 (2013) (elaborating on Whittington's distinction and positing that "old originalism was (chiefly) a theory of adjudication, whereas new originalism is (chiefly) a theory of law"); Colby, *supra* note 156, at 714 (explaining that "Old Originalism's promise" was centered on "judicial constraint"); Walter B. Michaels, *A Defense of Old Originalism*, 31 W. New Eng. L. Rev. 21, 22 (2009) (adopting the distinction and defending "old" Originalism against "new" public meaning Originalism).

177   Whittington, *supra* note 36, at 600; Berman & Toh, *supra* note 176, at 559; Colby, *supra* note 156, at 717.

178   Historical inquiry in reconstructing crypto or proto-originalist thought between the Marshall and Warren Courts would tremendously enrich current debate.

179   Robert H. Bork, *Neutral Principles and Some First Amendment Problems*, 47 Indiana L. J. 1, 1 (1971).

180   *Id.*

181   *Id.*

182   *Id.* at 1–2.

of judicial supremacy in a democratic society,"[183] serving as a solution to the counter-majoritarian difficulty. These principles "must ... be neutral in all three meanings of the word: they must be neutrally derived, defined and applied."[184] And they are needed especially in guiding the Court as to how to choose between equally reasonable meanings to words in the Constitution.[185] Although no mention of "original meaning" or "original intent" is made, the concepts are there. He made several references to what the Constitution or its framers "intended" as controlling the Court's quest for meaning,[186] and spoke of two "proper methods" in deriving constitutional rights, one of which was to take from the document specific values that "text or history show the framers actually ... intended."[187] In seeming Thayerian fashion, he "emphasized the imperatives of ... judicial respect for the democratic process."[188] As he went on to later say:

> [W]e need theory, theory that relates the framers' values to today's world. That is not an impossible task by any means, but it is a good deal more complex than slogans such as "strict construction" or "judicial restraint" might lead you to think. It is necessary to establish the proposition that the framers' intentions with respect to freedoms are the sole legitimate premise from which constitutional analysis may proceed.[189]

---

183   *Id.* at 2.

184   *Id.* at 23.

185   *Id.* at 11. He explained in the Equal Protection context:

   The equal protection clause has two legitimate meanings. It can require formal procedural equality, and, because of its historical origins, it does require that government not discriminate along racial lines. But much more than that cannot properly be read into the clause. The bare concept of equality provides no guide for courts. All law discriminates and thereby creates inequality. The Supreme Court has no principled way of saying which non-racial inequalities are impermissible. What it has done, therefore, is to appeal to simplistic notions of "fairness" or to what it regards as "fundamental" interests in order to demand equality in some cases but not in others, thus choosing values and producing a line of cases as improper and as intellectually empty as Griswold v. Connecticut.
   Id.

186   *Id.* at 14, 17, 22.

187   *Id.* at 17.

188   Ilya Somin, *The Borkean Dilemma: Robert Bork and the Tension Between Originalism and Democracy*, 80 U. Chicago L. Rev. Dialogue 243, 244 (2013).

189   Robert H. Bork, Tradition and Morality in Constitutional Law 10 (1984).

Bork's rallying cry was to lay siege to the seemingly anti-textual methods of contemporary First and Fourth Amendment precedent. Some deem it the "opening move" in the development of Originalism.[190]

In 1977, Raoul Berger answered the call and stormed the gates. In his *Government by Judiciary*, he extensively criticized the Warren and Burger Courts' precedent. He devoted a chapter to justify the preference for the framers' intentions over other baselines in constitutional adjudication. He condemned contemporary "indifference" to "original intentions," which he deemed a "recent development."[191] He defined original intent as "the meaning attached by the Framers to the words they employed."[192] Berger resented the scorn with which other scholars treated his position, including Myres McDougal himself, quoted as labeling his approach "verbal archeology" and "filio-pietism."[193] Berger opposed his view of a "fixed" Constitution to that of a "living" one.[194] He favored reliance on the framers' statements and opposed mere resort to dictionaries, especially contemporary ones, to settle disputes, since this still allowed the Court to change past meaning. For instance, he approvingly quoted Paul Brest's example of a hypothetical constitutional use of the word "bi-weekly."[195] Brest had explained:

> [S]uppose that the Constitution provided that some acts were to be performed "bi-weekly." At the time of the framing of the Constitution, this meant only "once every two weeks"; but modern dictionaries, bowing to pervasive misuse, now report "twice a week" (i.e., semi-weekly) as an acceptable definition. To construe the definition now to mean "semi-weekly" would certainly be a change of meaning (and an improper one at that).[196]

Berger deemed this approach as falling within "the accepted view."[197]

Yet, Berger's ideas were different from Brest's. Berger's included not just original intent, but also the framers' *expected applications* of that meaning,

---

190   Solum, *supra* note 35, at 16.
191   Raoul Berger, Government by Judiciary: The Transformation of the Fourteenth Amendment 402 (2d ed. 1997) (1977).
192   *Id.*
193   *Id.* (citing Myres McDougal and Asher Lans, *Treaties and Congressional-Executive or Presidential Agreements: Interchangeable Instruments of National Policy*, 54 Yale L.J. 181 (1945)).
194   *Id.*
195   *Id.* at 408 n.38.
196   Paul Brest, Processes of Constitutional Decisionmaking: Cases and Materials 146 n.38 (1975).
197   Berger, *supra* note 191, at 408 n.38.

as his comments on the Equal Protection Clause suggest.[198] A strange species of fidelity to text, that according to which, where the clear but broad meaning of an open-ended word conflict with the framers' subjective intent that its meaning be more limited, extrinsic evidence trumped text.[199] To develop the "bi-weekly" example, under Berger's logic, even if linguistic usage of the time did show that the word could bear either of the two competing meanings described above, and the contemporary ordinary reader understood this, Berger would have the more restrictive meaning of the drafter's private intent trump that of the ratifying public.

Unsurprisingly, then, Brest authored one of the two most damaging pieces of scholarship against this incipient Originalism—*The Misconceived Quest for the Original Understanding*.[200] His impassioned case against "Strict Originalism" (i.e., original intent Originalism) inoculated many against it, at least for a time, including the young Randy Barnett—one of Originalism's leading figures today. Brest coined the neologisms "originalism" and "originalist" to facilitate his criticism. He broadly defined Originalism as "the familiar approach to constitutional adjudication that accords binding authority to the text of the Constitution or the intentions of its adopters."[201] However, he focused his attacks on "strict textualism," "[t]he most extreme form[] of originalism," which he identified both with "giv[ing] effect to the intent of [the] framers" and "constru[ing] words ... very narrowly and precisely" (i.e., literalism).[202] He showed how daunting, if not outright impossible, the task of ascertaining the framers' intent would be in practice.[203]

However, Brest recognized that what he labeled "moderate" "originalism" or "textualism"—a position that deems the framers' intent mere evidence, not dispositive, of meaning, and that addresses original meaning at higher levels

---

198   *Id.* at 410 ("[T]he debates of the 39th Congress ... left abundant evidence that, for example, in employing 'equal protection of the laws' they had in mind only a ban on discrimination with respect to a limited category of 'enumerated' rights. Disregard of that intention starkly poses the issue whether the Court may 'interpret' black to mean white, to convert the framers' intention to leave suffrage to the States into a transfer of such control to the Supreme Court.").

199   Raoul Berger, *Originalist Theories of Constitutional Interpretation*, 73 Cornell L. Rev. 350, 352–54 (1988) (criticizing the "read[ing of] general words in disregard of the specific intention[s]"); Jonathan O'Neill, Originalism in American Law and Politics: A Constitutional History 127 (2005).

200   Brest, *supra* note 134, at 204.

201   *Id.* at 204.

202   *Id.* at 204, 206.

203   *Id.* at 214, 216, 219–220, 223.

of generality, including purposes[204]—"is a perfectly sensible strategy of constitutional decision making."[205] He admitted that "much" of American constitutional interpretation was "in [its] favor."[206] Brest even asserted that "[t]
he only difference between moderate originalism and nonoriginalist adjudication is one of attitude toward the text and original understanding:" "[f]
or the moderate originalist, these sources are conclusive when they speak
clearly," while "[f]or the nonoriginalist, they are important but not determinative."[207] Nevertheless, he argued that non-originalism was still preferable to
Originalism partly because non-originalism could better accommodate contemporary precedent, was more practicable, and could better guide the development of precedent in difficult cases.[208]

The second blow to early modern Originalism came from Jefferson Powell.
In *The Original Understanding of Original Intent*,[209] he showed that the founding generation did not subscribe original intent Originalism. Powell argued that
the closest original intent theory subscribed in the early republic was a states
rights-oriented form of structural reasoning, not subjective drafters' intent.[210]
Turning Berger's resort to early English commentators on its head, Powell clarified that the long tradition of judicial ascertainment of legislative "intent" was
limited to the words used by legislatures and not their private thoughts, just as
our contracts law addressed interpretation.[211] Powell's was a sort of reduction
to absurdity echoed ever since: if Originalism is exclusively about the original
intent of the framers, and, as a matter of historical fact, the framers did not
expect future generations to look to their private thoughts on matters of interpretation, then Originalism refutes itself and requires us to subscribe a different
theory in order to honor the framers' own preferences that we not be originalists.

Ultimately, modern Originalism's was a death by a thousand cuts within a
single decade. Berger's unprecedented and sustained analysis of the subject,
like Bork's, fell short of articulating a general theory remotely as sophisticated
as the one now identified with Originalism.[212] And the case against original

---

204   *Id.* at 214, 223.
205   *Id.* at 231.
206   *Id.* at 204–205.
207   *Id.* at 229.
208   *Id.* at 231.
209   Powell, *supra* note 144, at 885.
210   *Id.* at 888, 948.
211   *Id.* at 895.
212   *See, e.g.,* Berman & Toh, *supra* note 176, at 559 ("Raoul Berger, as important an old origi-
       nalist as can be found, is best read as maintaining not only (or even principally) that the
       intentions of the Framers provide a useful or reliable guide for judicial decision making

intent Originalism was persuasive: to divine today the exact intentions of a collective group of drafters is impractical, if not impossible. Their intentions actually seem to have been that we not care for them. Insisting on caring for them raised the moral question of why present generations should be governed by the "dead hand" of the past. Original intent originalists have since become a decreasing minority among Originalism's ranks. But the "dead hand" reservation has continued to haunt subsequent Originalisms.

7   Contemporary Originalism: Antonin Scalia's Relaunching of the
       Theory

Contemporary Originalism—encompassing both "New" and "New New" Originalism[213]—was launched by Justice Antonin Scalia in the late 1980's but reached considerable heights in the 2000's. Learning from the crucible of modern Originalism, Scalia steered the ship into the safer harbor of something resembling Brest's "moderate" Originalism: a conceptual "shift" from original intent to "original public meaning" instead.[214]

As noted by Professor Solum,[215] as early as 1986, Scalia urged originalists to "change the label from the Doctrine of Original Intent to the Doctrine of Original Meaning."[216] Without mentioning Powell, he advanced the latter's criticism and quoted Hamilton and Madison to illustrate that they intended the Constitution to be interpreted through its words' original meaning, not the convention's subjective intent.[217] Notably, Scalia weaponized Powell's

---

in a democracy, but that they constitute what the constitutional law is. But insofar as this is his view, he lacked the theoretical sophistication, or even the instinct, to advance much in the way of argument for it.").

213   Peter J. Smith seems to have first adopted the label. Peter J. Smith, *How Different Are Originalism and Nonoriginalism?*, 62 Hastings L. Rev. 707, 709 (2011). *See also* Gary Lawson, *Reflections of an Empirical Reader (Or: Could Fleming Be Right This Time?)*, 96 B.U. L. Rev. 1457, 1472 (2016).

214   Randy Barnett, *Scalia's Infidelity: A Critique of Faint-hearted Originalism*, 75 U. Cin. L. Rev. 7, 9 (2006) ("Justice Scalia was perhaps the first defender of originalism to shift the theory from its previous focus on the intentions of the framers of the Constitution to the original public meaning of the text at the time of its enactment."); Solum, *supra* note 35, at 190.

215   Solum, *supra* note 35, at 190.

216   Antonin Scalia, *Address Before the Attorney General's Conference on Economic Liberties in Washing D.C. (June 14, 1986)*, in Original Meaning Jurisprudence: A Sourcebook 101 (U.S. Dep't of Justice ed., 1987), https://www.ojp.gov/pdff iles1/Digitization/115083NCJRS.pdf.

217   *Id.* at 104–105 (quoting Hamilton saying that, "whatever may have been the intention of the framers of a constitution, or of a law, that intention is to be sought for in the instrument itself, according to usual & established rules of construction").

argument in favor of a newer form of Originalism. Yes, original intent Originalism was self-defeating, since the historical record shows the founders did not believe their subjective intent served as a baseline. But if you do look at what the founders considered the baseline—something Powell did not do, you'd realize they believed that the original meaning of the words controlled.[218] And so original public meaning Originalism came to stay.

Scalia mounted a pragmatic defense of public meaning Originalism rather than a sophisticated, normative one. In *Originalism: The Lesser Evil*, he reiterated that the Constitution is, in its nature, the same sort of legal text judges often construe in daily practice—an enactment that has a fixed meaning "ascertainable through ... usual devices"—and does not require a special interpretive theory.[219] He explained:

> Properly done, the task requires the consideration of an enormous mass of material—in the case of the Constitution and its Amendments, for example, to mention only one element, the records of the ratifying debates in all the states. Even beyond that, it requires an evaluation of the reliability of that material—many of the reports of the ratifying debates, for example, are thought to be quite unreliable. And further still, it requires immersing oneself in the political and intellectual atmosphere of the time .... [I]n short, a task sometimes better suited to the historian than the lawyer.[220]

He took issue with the express rejection of the binding role of constitutional text made by prominent non-originalists like Paul Brest and Lawrence Tribe.[221] His argument in favor of Originalism was primarily that, for all its defects, it was the lesser evil when compared to non-originalism, since the latter: (1) is inconsistent with the mechanism of judicial review (by conflating the kind of law that the judiciary makes with the kind other branches make); (2) does not

---

218   *Id.* at 104 ("But really the trump card to establish that 'original intent' would more accurately be expressed 'original meaning' is this: Even if you believe in original intent in the literal sense you must end up believing in original meaning, because it is perfectly clear that the original intent was that the Constitution would be interpreted according to its original meaning.").

219   Antonin Scalia, *supra* note 143, at 854.

220   *Id.* at 856–57.

221   *Id.* at 853 ("Those who have not delved into the scholarly writing on constitutional law for several years may be unaware of the explicitness with which many prominent and respected commentators reject the original meaning of the Constitution as an authoritative guide.").

offer a consensus alternative to Originalism that can ensure the same degree of stable and predictable results; and (3) falsely promises to expand rights, despite the fact that it is equally compatible, in both theory and practice, with contracting and abolishing preexisting rights.[222]

Admitting that Originalism was sometimes too strong a medicine, he suggested it be watered down with healthy pours of stare decisis and faintheartedness. An example of the latter was the Cruel and Unusual Punishment Clause. He recognized that it *appeared* to be a provision conveying evolutionary content, but denied that the historical evidence supported that interpretation.[223] Yet, he also admitted that, as so many others, he too would likely not uphold a contemporary law imposing flogging despite historical analysis showing that, at the time the Bill of Rights was enacted, flogging was not deemed cruel or unusual.[224] He shrugged off the difficulty as yet another aspect of Originalism that made it imperfect. And he minimized it by deeming it the kind of case that rarely, if ever, takes place: never is the Originalist judge faced with the dilemma of choosing between giving evolutionary content to a provision in the absence of stare decisis requiring it and giving it such content in the absence of historical evidence supporting its evolution (the result making his heart faint).[225] The real debate in most cases—he thought—was not whether some provision allowed for evolutionary content, but whether historical inquiry sufficiently showed that such content had, in fact, evolved.[226] Except for the sake of argument, he denied the existence of evolutionary content in any constitutional provision. Why? Because "the main danger in judicial interpretation" would then be "that the judges will mistake their own predilections for the law."[227] In hard cases, Scalia would resort to the founding generation's reasonable reader's ideas of how a provision would be applied to specific circumstances.[228]

He continued to reframe the debate through the late 1990's, insisting that "the Great Divide with regard to constitutional interpretation is not that between Framers' intent and objective meaning, but rather that between

---

222   *Id.* at 854–56.
223   *Id.* at 861.
224   *Id.* at 863–64.
225   *Id.*
226   *Id.* at 864.
227   *Id.* at 863–64.
228   Note, *Original Meaning and Its Limits*, 120 Harv. L. Rev. 1279, 1279 (2007) ("[Scalia] demands adherence to the Constitution's original meaning and, moreover, construes the original meaning of value-laden language, such as 'unreasonable' and 'cruel,' by reference to the applications it was commonly thought to have at the time of ratification.").

original meaning (whether derived from Framers' intent or not) and *current* meaning."[229] The public's understanding at the time of the enactment ought to control instead.[230] Scalia's theory resonated with many. But his practice of Originalism on the bench caused both friendly and hostile criticism. For example, Randy Barnett argued that Scalia's theory would only enforce the original meaning of rule-like provisions, not broader, vaguer, or open-ended ones like the Ninth Amendment, which Scalia deemed an empty tautology.[231] Thus, Scalia turned "large portions" of the Constitution "nonjusticiable by judicial fiat"[232]—portions people like Barnett deeply care about. According to Barnett, Scalia was unfaithful to the Constitution's text and, thus, no true originalist, in three ways: (1) by his willingness to ignore and not enforce provisions that fell short of his own rule of law theory; (2) by his willingness to avoid objectionable originalist outcomes by resort to precedent; and (3) by his willingness to abandon an originalist result, absent contrary precedent, that he could not personally stomach.[233] Barnett's has not been the only criticism.[234] Non-originalists hurled worse at Scalia's theory and practice, labeling it "disingenuous" and "mean,"[235] "pessimistic" and "fallacious,"[236] and even "politically" "activist."[237] A major criticism was that he could not reconcile public meaning Originalism

---

229   Antonin Scalia, *Common Law Courts in a Civil Law System: The Role of United States Federal Courts in Interpreting Laws and the Constitution, in* A Matter of Interpretation 38 (1997).

230   *Id.* at 37.

231   Barnett, *supra* note 214, at 11 ("Justice Scalia's approach would seem to justify judicial enforcement of only those passages of the Constitution that are sufficiently rule-like to constitute a determinate command that a judge can simply follow. The more general or abstract provisions of the Constitution are hardly rules that fit this description, so should judges ignore them? It turns out that, with respect to the Ninth Amendment, for example, this is precisely the view later adopted by Justice Scalia himself.").

232   *Id.*

233   *Id.* at 13.

234   *See, e.g.,* Enrique Schaerer, *What the Heller? An Originalist Critique of Justice Scalia's Second Amendment Jurisprudence,* 82 U. Cin. L. Rev. 795, 829 (2018) (Scalia "misapplied the textualist principle of originalism when he held that the right protects only those weapons in common use at some ever-changing 'present' time," since "[i]nstead, the right should extend to weapons that are 'lineal descendants' of weapons in common use at the time the Second or Fourteenth Amendment was adopted"); Michael Ramsey, *Beyond the Text: Justice Scalia's Originalism in Practice,* 92 Notre Dame L. Rev. 1945, 1974 (2017) (noting Scalia's practice "encourages more extratextual structural reasoning than strict textualism would permit").

235   *See, e.g.,* Erwin Chemerinsky, *The Jurisprudence of Justice Scalia: A Critical Appraisal,* 22 U. Hawaii L. Rev. 385, 385 (2000).

236   *See, e.g.,* Ken Levy, *Why the Late Justice Scalia was Wrong: The Fallacies of Constitutional Textualism,* 21 Lewis & Clark L. Rev. 45, 46 (2017).

237   *See* Post & Siegel, *supra* note 3, at 549.

with *Brown v. Board of Education*,[238] a common litmus test long applied by non-originalists to Originalisms.[239]

Although Scalia's brand was conservative and Thayerian,[240] unshackled from original intent, public meaning Originalism took on a life of its own. Libertarian, populist, and even progressive iterations have since developed.[241] And yet, "[m]any originalists in the legal academy today no longer fit neatly into one of these."[242] Some have labeled this growing panoply of Originalisms a conceptual "rebooting."[243]

7.1   *Contemporary Originalism Since Scalia*

Since Scalia's contribution, "many contemporary originalists do not emphasize judicial restraint as the primary justification for originalism" anymore.[244] Instead, they seek correct results, "come hell or high water."[245] Restraint or stare decisis are of secondary value. Potentially illustrative of this new spirit

---

238   *See, e.g.,* Ronald Turner, *A Critique of Justice Antonin Scalia's Originalist Defense of Brown v. Board of Education*, 62 UCLA L. Rev. Disc. 170 (2014).

239   *See, e.g.,* Steven G. Calabresi & Michael W. Perl, *Originalism and Brown v. Board of Education*, Mich. St. L. Rev. 429, 432 (2014) ("With respect to the argument that Brown cannot be explained with an originalist understanding, these scholars have claimed that '[t]he evidence is obvious and [un]ambiguous,' the conclusion is 'inevitable' and 'inescapable,' and '[v]irtually nothing' supports the opposite claim, which is said to be 'fanciful.' Therefore, since many believe that Brown and originalism cannot coexist, originalism itself is said ipso facto not to be a legitimate method of constitutional interpretation.").

240   *See, e.g.,* William Baude, *Originalism as a Constraint on Judges*, 84 U. Ch. L. Rev. 2213, 2213 (2017) ("One important feature of Scalia's particular arguments for originalism was constraint—the idea that originalism was centrally a way, the best way, to constrain judicial decisionmaking, whereas nonoriginalist theories would essentially license judges to make up constitutional law as they went along.").

241   Ilan Wurman, *The Founders' Originalism*, 53 Nat'l Aff. (2014) ("In contemporary legal thinking, there have been broadly speaking three schools of originalism—libertarian, progressive, and conservative."), https://www.nationalaffairs.com/publications/detail /the-founders-originalism.

242   *Id.*

243   Stephen M. Griffin, *Rebooting Originalism*, 2008 U. Ill. L. Rev. 1185 (2008).

244   Jack Balkin, *The New Originalism and the Uses of History*, 82 Fordham L. Rev. 641, 648 n.13 (2013).

245   *See, e.g.,* Ken Levy, *supra* note 236, at 49 ("The Popular Theory that the Constitution should be followed 'come hell or high water' itself breaks down into four principles. First is the 'Rule of Law Principle,' the idea that we are 'a government of laws and not of men,' and therefore that the Constitution should determine what the Court says rather than vice versa. When a case is brought before the Court, we want the Court to deliver the correct decision, the constitutionally mandated solution, the decision that the Constitution leaves it no real choice to deliver, not the solution that the justices subjectively prefer.'").

was the Supreme Court's recent decision on abortion in *Dobbs*[246]—one that easily leapt over historically high stare decisis rails. However, as Lawrence Solum has argued, most, if not all, contemporary Originalisms still share the same two theses about historically fixed meaning that binds judicial interpretation today.[247] Of course, they don't share them in the same way.

Critically, the distinction between interpretation and construction in constitutional adjudication is "one of the most interesting developments" in contemporary Originalism.[248] So, I divide post-Scalia perspectives roughly into three groups: those recognizing a distinction between interpretation and construction; those rejecting it; and those making contributions unrelated to it, whether reviving original intent or amplifying history's role in constitutional adjudication.[249]

Keith E. Whittington describes Originalism as "urg[ing] interpreters to look to the text and what a competent reader of the text at the time would have understood it to mean (which may be informed by the broader historical context, purpose, and structure of the document, as well as common linguistic usages of the period)."[250] Importantly, he has drawn a distinction between interpretation and construction in contemporary debate.[251] According to him, in practice, interpretation is "not all" courts do in adjudicating constitutional cases.[252] Instead, the Constitution is often "supplemented through a process

---

246   *Dobbs v. Jackson's Women Health Organization,* 142 S.Ct. 2228 (2022).

247   Solum *supra* note 35, at 182, 198. *See also* Lawrence Solum, *The Fixation Thesis: The Role of Historical Fact in Original Meaning,* 91 Notre Dame L. Rev. 1 (2015); Lawrence Solum, *The Constraint Principle: Original Meaning and Constitutional Practice* (2019), available at https://papers.ssrn.com/sol3/papers.cfm?abstract_id=2940215.

248   Amy Barrett, *The Interpretation/Construction in Constitutional Law: Annual Meeting of the AALS Section on Constitutional Law,* 27 Const'l Commentary 1, 1 (2010), *available at* https://scholarship.law. umn.edu/cgi/viewcontent.cgi?article=1072&context=concomm.

249   I find this grouping of views, within which different political takes overlap, much more informative of the structure of current debate than one based merely on political affiliations, which would tendentiously overstate or mask theoretical agreements and disagreements among such perspectives.

250   Keith Whittington, *On Pluralism within Originalism, in* The Challenge of Originalism: Theories of Constitutional Interpretation 71–72 (Grant Huscroft & Bradley W. Miller eds. 2011).

251   Keith E. Whittington, Constitutional Construction: Divided Powers and Constitutional Meaning 5 (1999) ("Constructions do not pursue a preexisting if deeply hidden meaning in the founding document; rather, they elucidate the text in the interstices of discoverable, interpretive meaning[.]").

252   Keith E. Whittington, *Constructing a New American Constitution,* 27 Const'l Commentary 119, 119 (2010). The claim is empirically correct and even the Supreme Court has long recognized—if never consciously developed – the distinction. *See, e.g., U.S. v. Keitel,* 211 U.S.

of constitutional construction."[253] The need to supplement is apparent when the Constitution is silent on a question—whether because the question concerns an irremediably vague term, an outright gap, or a broad, abstract principle.[254] Before defining "construction," he notes the "continuum" of actions that political actors can—and often do—take in our legal system: at the one end, taking constitutional forms as a given and making policy decisions under them (filling government seats and governing in noncontroversial ways), and at the other, rejecting and replacing the existing constitutional order (revolution).[255] Somewhere between that spectrum lies creation, a revisionary authority that, in our system at least, is partial rather than total and merely amends the Constitution.[256] Well, construction is closer to creation and "picks up" where interpretation "leaves off:"

> Interpretation attempts to divine the meaning of the text. There will be occasions, however, when the Constitution as written cannot in good faith be said to provide a determinate answer to a given question. This is the realm of construction. The process of interpretation may be able to constrain the available readings of the text and limit the permissible set of political options, but the interpreter may not be able to say that the text demands a specific result. Further judgments, further choices, about how to proceed within those bounds are made through the process of construction. Constitutional meaning is no longer discovered at that point. It is built.[257]

All "within boundaries," that is.[258] Construction has no authority to revise text or discoverable meaning, coming into play only when traditional tools of interpretation are exhausted to no avail.[259] It relies on "external" considerations to achieve determinacy, making "normative appeals" to what the Constitution

---

370, 386 (1908) ("That abstractly there may be a difference between the two terms ... finds support in works of respectable authority."). The distinction is not an originalist invention. Lawrence Solum, *The Interpretation-Construction Distinction*, 27 Const'l Commentary 95, 110 (2010) ("Originalists did not invent the interpretation-construction distinction. It has a long pedigree in legal usage—the distinction appears in contract law, the law of trusts and wills, patent law, and in constitutional law, as well.").

253   Whittington, *supra* note 252, at 119.
254   *Id.* 122–25.
255   *Id.* at 120.
256   *Id.*
257   *Id.* at 120–21.
258   *Id.* at 121.
259   *Id.*

"should be," "melding what is known about the Constitution with what is desired."[260] Thus, unlike interpretations, constructions are "temporary:" they always serve the "interests" or "values" of important political actors.[261]

However, because constructions are "essentially political," Whittington notes that the judiciary's power to engage in them is not on a foot with its power to interpret (or the power of other branches to engage in construction).[262] He believes it is "harder" to justify a court's power to strike down governmental action based solely on a construction than it is to justify it on the basis of interpretation.[263] Now, partly since judicial review on the basis of interpretation is justified and that power, itself, is based solely on construction, there is clearly some room for legitimate construction in judicial review.[264] This encompasses standards of deference, the implementation of both concrete and abstract protections (e.g., *Miranda* rights), and what interpretive methods are preferred.[265] Because of its inability to be all-encompassing, all constitutions—not just our own—are a framework that must be supplemented.[266] This supplementation through construction is a form of "constitutional politics."[267] Responding to concerns, Whittington has insisted that construction takes place within the boundaries of interpretation, to supplement and implement, not contradict the meaning of text, and it cannot be avoided by contrived "default rules."[268] He notes that the distinction is "particularly useful" to Originalism in responding to accusations of rigidity or a failure to realistically explain constitutional change.[269]

Reception of Whittington's contribution has not been uniform. For example, Randy Barnett, Lawrence Solum, and Jack Balkin have all openly embraced and developed it in their own ways. From a libertarian point of view, Barnett

---

260   *Id.*
261   *Id.* at 122.
262   *Id.* at 127
263   *Id.*
264   *Id.*
265   *Id.* at 127–28.
266   *Id.* at 130
267   *Id.* at 136.
268   *Id.* at 131–33.
269   *Id.* at 134 ("Originalism qua originalism may provide an adequate account of how the Constitution ought to be interpreted and how courts ought to exercise the power of judicial review, but it may not describe the complete operation of the constitutional order. Originalists may benefit from recognizing more explicitly that constitutional meaning is sometimes indeterminate and that there are limits as to what answers constitutional interpretation can provide.").

has celebrated the development.[270] As he puts it, "Originalists may disagree about many things, but they should all agree on the meaningfulness of this distinction," since "[w]ithout it, [they] are very likely to talk past each other, or their critics, and to confuse themselves and others."[271] He believes that despite Originalism's "usual" and "general" success in many cases, ambiguity becomes irresolvable where evidence of meaning is lost or nonexistent or the ambiguity was deliberate, and vague terms like "reasonable" or "search" "simply do not contain the information necessary to decide matters of application," even when contextually interpreted.[272] The First Amendment is paradigmatic of our need for construction: "time, place, and manner" and similar doctrines are constructions that are "nowhere in the text, but are nevertheless a good way to put into effect what the text does say."[273]

Barnett observes that "Originalism is not a theory of what to do when original meaning runs out. This is not a bug; it is a feature."[274] He warns that originalists "also need a normative theory for how to construe a constitution when its meaning runs out."[275] As he eloquently put it:

> Originalists will not all agree about how to engage in constitutional construction. Part of this disagreement will stem from their differing normative reasons for favoring originalist interpretation. Originalists who ground their commitment to originalism in notions of popular sovereignty can be expected to favor principles of construction that reflect this normative commitment. Likewise, those who favor originalism as a means to protect the background rights retained by the people will likely favor rules of construction that are rights protective. Unless there is some- thing in the text that favors one construction over the other, it is not originalism that is doing the work when one selects a theory of construction to employ when original meaning runs out, but one's underlying normative commitments.[276]

Coming from a different perspective, Lawrence Solum has brought much needed analytical clarity to the debate. Drawing from Linguistics and the Philosophy of Language, he has contributed several concepts and distinctions

---

270   Randy Barnett, *Interpretation and Construction*, 34 Harv. J.L. & Pub. Pol'y 65, 65 (2011).
271   *Id.* at 66.
272   *Id.* at 68.
273   *Id.* at 69.
274   *Id.*
275   *Id.* at 70.
276   *Id.*

to Originalism. For example, he distinguishes between the text's communicative content (the meaning communicated by a legal text in context) and its legal content (the doctrines of the legal rules associated with the text).[277] Additionally, explaining just what kind of communicative content should matter and control, he argues that it should be the "conventional semantic meaning" of the words that constitutes its public meaning.[278] He then reconfigures the "theses" he deems inherent to Originalism. He redefined the known Fixation Thesis as comprising two different sub-theses: the Fixation Thesis (i.e., the semantic meaning of the text was fixed when adopted) and the Clause Meaning Thesis (i.e., that fixed semantic meaning is the text's public meaning). He then reframed the known Constraint Thesis or Principle as comprising two different ones: the Contribution Thesis (i.e., the semantic meaning "contributes" to the content of the law) and the Fidelity Thesis, which controversially "maintains that because the semantic content of the constitution is the supreme law of the land, we are obligated by it, *unless there is an overriding reason of morality to the contrary.*"[279] He also advocates for the incorporation of the distinction between concepts and conceptions in constitutional reasoning: "some constitutional clauses include words or phrases that refer to concepts, requiring a construction that singles out some conception of that concept in light of some theory of construction."[280]

He has embraced Whittington's interpretation-construction distinction.[281] He defines interpretation as "the process (or activity) that recognizes or discovers the linguistic meaning or semantic content of the legal text," and construction as "the process that gives a text legal effect (either by translating the linguistic meaning into legal doctrine or by applying or implementing the text)."[282] Solum argues that "legal theorists cannot do without the distinction."[283] Naturally, he also distinguishes canons of interpretation from canons of construction: the former are rules of thumb that point us to facts about the way language works and to reliable procedures to ascertain linguistic meaning, while the later guide the process by which linguistic meaning is "translated"

---

277   Lawrence Solum, *Communicative Content and Legal Content*, 89 Notre Dame L. Rev. 479, 479 (2013).

278   Lawrence B. Solum, *Semantic Originalism*, 1, 2 (Ill. Pub. L. & Legal Theory Research Papers Series, Paper No. 07-24, 2008), https://papers.ssrn.com/sol3/papers.cfm?abstract_id=1120244 [https://perma.cc/CGF7-7WK2].

279   *Id.* at 2 (emphasis added).

280   *Id.* at 89.

281   Solum, *supra* note 252, at 95.

282   *Id.* at 96.

283   *Id.*

into legal effect.[284] He defines "underdeterminacy," which necessitates the practice of construction, as "referring to cases and issues with respect to which the communicative content of the constitutional text rules out some outcomes but does not fully determine which outcome is correct."[285] Assessing current debate, he states that its "core ... addresses the normative question: What is the best theory of constitutional interpretation *and construction*?"[286] Of course, he realizes that this turn to construction represents a fundamental shift in contemporary debate and Originalism itself, one that most critics have not yet sufficiently processed:

> Some critics of originalism resist an interlocking series of moves within contemporary originalist theory. These moves include: (1) the move from original intentions to original public meaning; (2) the idea that original public meaning of the constitutional text is not controlled by the application beliefs of the drafters, Framers, or public at the time the text was adopted; (3) the claim that some provisions of the constitutional text are moderately underdeterminate with the consequence that the original meaning does not resolve every constitutional issue or case, creating construction zones; and (4) the claim that the political and ideological implications of originalism are mixed, including some results that would be supported by progressives and liberals.[287]

Jack Balkin and Akhil Amar are the two most notable liberal academics on Originalism's camp. One of Balkin's contributions, later embraced by Whittington himself,[288] has been the distinction between the Constitution as a "framework" and as a "skyscraper."[289] Balkin explains that "two types of originalism" based on these two metaphors "differ in the degree of constitutional construction and implementation that later generations may engage

---

284   *Id.* at 113.
285   Solum, *supra* note 157, at 1246.
286   *Id.* at 1244 (emphasis added).
287   *Id.* at 1268. Solum rightly differentiates between Originalism as an academic theory and any equivalent political trope. *Id.* at 1270 ("Most originalist scholars would reject the view that originalism is a thick ideological concept. Outside the realm of scholarly discourse things may be different. For example, political rhetoric or propaganda might deploy a thick ideological conception of originalism, with conservatives selling "originalism" to their base on the basis that it leads to conservative results, and progressives criticizing originalist judges on the basis of the very same assumption. Again, identifying the domain of discourse is important to a clear understanding of originalism as a concept.").
288   Whittington, *supra* 252, at 130.
289   Balkin, *supra* note 34, at 550.

in."[290] "Skyscraper originalism views the Constitution as more or less a finished product," but "Framework originalism, by contrast, views the Constitution as an initial framework for governance that sets politics in motion and must be filled out over time through constitutional construction."[291] In other words, "skyscraper originalism views amendment as the only method of building the Constitution, while framework originalism sees a major role for constitutional construction and implementation by the political branches as well as by the Judiciary."[292]

Elaborating on the type of semantic originalism that he subscribes at the stage of interpretation, he explains that the term "original meaning" is often confusing because it could refer to: (1) semantic content (i.e., the meaning of words); (2) practical applications (e.g., what something "means" in practice); (3) purposes or functions (e.g., the "meaning" of life); (4) specific intentions (e.g., I did not "mean" to hurt you); and (5) private and public associations from culture.[293] However, as he explains:

> Fidelity to "original meaning" in constitutional interpretation refers only to the first of these types of meaning: the semantic content of the words in the clause. We follow the original meaning of words in order to preserve the Constitution's legal meaning over time, as required by the rule of law. Otherwise, if the dictionary definitions of words changed over time, their legal effect would also change, not because of any conscious act of lawmaking (or even political mobilization), but merely because of changes in language. So, for example, when Article IV says that the United States must protect the states from "domestic violence," we should employ the original meaning, "riots" or "insurrections," not the contemporary meaning, "spousal assaults."
>
> Fidelity to original meaning does not, however, require fidelity to any of the other types of original meaning, although these forms of meaning may be relevant evidence of original semantic content. More to the point, these other kinds of meaning may be very important for purposes of constitutional construction.[294]

---

290   *Id.*
291   *Id.*
292   *Id.*
293   *Id.* at 552.
294   *Id.*

Clearly, Balkin differentiates between interpretation and construction. If Balkin's theory sounds like some non-originalist or Living Constitutionalist theories, that's because it is somewhat similar. Enough for Balkin to give it the second name of "Living Originalism."[295] Balkin represents a strand of Originalism that deems some versions of it "compatible" with some versions of non-originalism or Living Constitutionalism.[296] We call this type of school "compatibilist."

Noting the different types of provision, he argues that "the choice of rules, standards, principles, or silence is not accidental:" "Constitutional drafters use rules because they want to limit discretion; they use standards or principles because they want to channel politics but delegate the details to future generations."[297] When it comes to construction, courts engage in it in different ways, variously to "rationalize" the political constructions of other branches (i.e., the process of providing reasons either to "legitimize" or "police" them), to "cooperate" with the dominant forces in national politics by "disciplining" those who "do not share the dominant coalition's values," to strike down laws out of step with a dominant coalition, and to "take responsibility" for decisions that members of the dominant coalition cannot agree on.[298] Most construction he labels "normal science, working out the consequences of previous commitments and countercommitments and reasoning from previous precedents."[299] It involves "the articulation, elaboration, and application of constitutional principles."[300] These principles and doctrines are "not limited" to those available at the time of adoption, but may include new ones.[301] They do not amount to "amendments" to the Constitution and can be limited, distinguished, or overturned.[302] This approach to interpretation and construction that relies on the difference—by design—between rules, standards, and principles Balkin calls the "method" of "text and principle."[303]

---

295   Jack Balkin, *Nine Perspectives On Living Originalism*, 3 U. Ill. L. Rev. 815 (2012).

296   Balkin, *supra* note 34, at 549 ("Original meaning originalism and living constitutionalism are compatible positions. In fact, they are two sides of the same coin. Although not all versions of these theories are compatible, the most intellectually sound versions of each theory are. Recognizing why they are compatible helps us understand how legitimate constitutional change occurs in the American constitutional system.").

297   *Id.* at 553.

298   *Id.* at 571–74.

299   *Id.* at 577.

300   *Id.* at 579.

301   *Id.*

302   *Id.* at 583.

303   Balkin, *supra* note 295, at 817–18 ("Fidelity to the Constitution requires fidelity to the original meaning of the text, and to the choice of rules, principles, and standards in the text.

Amar, on the other hand, has developed a historically conscious, holistic, and accessible approach to constitutional interpretation, reviving the concept and importance of our unwritten Constitution[304]—a move that impliedly accepts Whittington's interpretation-construction distinction.[305] Amar's many contributions include his careful criticism of Justice Scalia's originalist practice as a "dictionaries" "game"[306] insufficiently grounded in history, especially regarding the Reconstruction Amendments.[307] For example, Amar has argued that, although Justice Scalia's interpretation of the Second Amendment based on the time when it was adopted was wrong, he could and should have interpreted it through the lens of the Fourteenth Amendment's Equal Protection Clause, which undeniably contemplated that African Americans in the South be allowed to own weapons for self-defense the same as their White neighbors.[308] During Reconstruction, the meaning of the Second Amendment had

---

It requires us to be faithful both to the principles that are stated in the text and those that we understand to be presupposed by the text or underlie the text, and it requires us to build out constitutional constructions that best apply the text and its associated rules, standards, and principles to our current circumstances. We might call this approach to constitutional interpretation 'the method of text, rule, standard, and principle;' however, as a convenient shorthand, I call it the method of text and principle. The method of text and principle is both originalist, because it requires fidelity to original meaning, and living constitutionalist, because it gives a prominent role to constitutional construction by later generations.").

304   Akhil Reed Amar, America's Constitution: A Biography xi (2005) (explaining Constitution's "meaning and richness" cannot be comprehended without context of historical background). For a short overview of prior literature on the unwritten constitution, *see* John R. Vile, Constitutional Change in the United States: A Comparative Study of the Role of Constitutional Amendments, Judicial Interpretations, and Legislative and Executive Actions 11 n.27 (1994).

305   Solum, *supra* note 39, at 1979 ("Amar doesn't employ the interpretation-construction distinction, but his terms 'gloss' and 'clarify' are consistent with the distinction between interpretation and construction.").

306   Akhil Reed Amar, *A Conversation on Originalism in the Constitution* (44:24) (Sept. 22, 2020), *available at* https://www.youtube.com/watch?v=oF4LLwAiQuo.

307   Akhil Reed Amar, *Heller, HLR, and Holistic Legal Reasoning*, 122 Harv. L. Rev. 145, 148 (2008) ("By contrast, in Justice Scalia's *Heller* opinion, the textual pea swelled to the size of a boulder that no prior judicial mattress could cover up. The Second Amendment's grain of sand became an entire world inviting a fresh and detailed exploration."). Amar notes that, "for all [his analysis'] problems, Justice Scalia reached the right answer," although the better justification lies partly with the Fourteenth Amendment. *Id.* at 174.

308   Akhil Reed Amar, *The Creation and Reconstruction of the Bill of Rights*, 16 S. Ill. U. L.J. 337, 347–48 (1992) ("They try to tell a story, however, that focuses on the original Second Amendment and on framers like George Mason and Elbridge Gerry. Yet those folks were concerned about federalism in large part, and they were talking about militias. The NRA would be much better off if it instead focused on how the right to keep and bear arms was

changed to clearly include an individual's right to gun ownership and adoption of the Fourteenth Amendment must have contributed to a change or evolution of its meaning. The meaning-conferring or meaning-altering effect of amendments on other provisions, even retroactively, is a topic absolutely underdeveloped in contemporary debate.

Other contributions from leading contemporary originalists have either rejected or ignored the interpretation-construction distinction.[309] For example, John O. McGinnis and Michael B. Rappaport have opposed the distinction because "the constructionists have not supplied evidence that the constitutional enactors contemplated construction," "the Framers' generation does not appear to have known about it," and "the evidence suggests that ambiguity and vagueness were resolved by considering evidence of history, structure, purpose, and intent."[310] Responding to their criticism, for example, Balkin has suggested that it matters little whether the founders knew that they were allowing for or engaging in construction. He argues that, although the semantic meaning of "Equal Protection" has remained the same since 1868, how it is applied has changed. The difference between him and McGinnis and Rappaport is that the latter confuse the founding generation's own constructions for part of the text's original meaning. "They believe that we should treat th[is] term[] in much the same way as 'Letters of Marque and Reprisal.'"[311]

Others have revived original intent as Originalism's baseline for meaning.[312] Of course, original intent cannot meet the challenges posed by the

---

transformed during Reconstruction into a much more libertarian and individual-rights oriented idea that blacks, especially had to have guns to protect their homesteads. Hence, individuals have the right to keep and bear arms.").

309   John O. McGinnis & Michael B. Rappaport, *Original Methods Originalism: A New Theory of Interpretation and the Case Against Construction*, 103 Nw. U. L. Rev. 741 (2009) (rejecting the distinction); Richard Kay, *Construction, Originalist Interpretation and the Complete Constitution*, 19 J. Const. L. 1, 25 (2017) ("But the intended meaning of constitutional provisions is a matter of genuine historical fact for which there will be objective, if not always conclusive, evidence. Constitutional construction, on the other hand, is essentially a process of decision-making that involves evaluation of the relative merits and weight of the broad historical and contemporary principles and values that are thought to underlie our social and political institutions. There simply is no fact of the matter about the correct construction applicable to a particular controversy. Constitutional construction, at its heart, puts its trust in human judgment not in historically fixed rules. This is not to put too fine a point on it-the opposite of constitutionalism.").

310   McGinnis & Rappaport, *supra* note 309, at 752.

311   Balkin, *supra* note 295, at 823.

312   *See, e.g.,* Richard S. Kay, *Original Intention and Public Meaning in Constitutional Interpretation*, 103 Nw. U. L. Rev. 703 (2009) (arguing that in practice there should be little difference between original intent and original public meaning and problematizing the concept of

interpretation-construction distinction.[313] Yet others have instead grappled with the role of precedent in originalist methodology, normative justifications, and even "the common good."[314] Many have also focused on the role of historical inquiry in constitutional adjudication.[315] Ultimately, Originalism has diversified so much that some critics claim there are at least *seventy two* different conceptual theses in contemporary Originalism.[316]

8   Winning the Battle; Losing the War?

Originalism has ostensibly won the battle over interpretation. At least on the Supreme Court.[317] But it hasn't won the war over constitutional adjudication. That's because there's more to adjudication than interpretation: there's also construction. Contemporary Originalism has made a critical concession about the conceptual and practical differences between these two aspects of

---

the hypothetical original reader); Jamal Greene, *The Case for Original Intent*, 80 George Washington l. Rev. 1683, 1705 (2012) ("The price of respectability within the legal academy has been self-alienation from a consistent, two-centuries-old practice of intentionalism. Reliance on the authority of the intentions and expectations of the Framers is an entirely respectable and time-honored form of ethical argument in constitutional law, and it is a practice that most originalists are already engaged in."); Michaels, *supra* note 176, at 22.

313   Barnett, *supra* note 270, at 71 ("Perhaps there is a distinctively 'originalist' theory of construction by which we follow what the founding generation would have done when confronted with problems of applying vague language to particular cases. Unlike ascertaining original semantic meaning, however, ascertaining 'what the framers would have done' is a counterfactual, not a factual or historical inquiry.").

314   *See, e.g.,* Thomas W. Merrill, *Originalism, Stare Decisis, and the Promotion of Judicial Restraint,* 22 Const'l Commentary 271 (2005); Richard J. Dougherty, *Originalism and Precedent: Principles and Practices in the Application of Stare Decisis,* 6 Ave Maria L. Rev. 155 (2007); Steven G. Calabresi, *Text, Precedent, and the Constitution: Some Originalist and Normative Arguments for Overruling Planned Parenthood of Southeastern Pennsylvania v. Casey,* 22 Const'l Commentary 1044 (2005); Lee J. Strang, *An Originalist Theory of Precedent: Originalism, Nonoriginalist Precedent, and the Common Good,* 36 N.M. L. Rev. 419 (2006); Josh Hammer, *Common Good Originalism: Our Tradition and Our Path Forward,* 4 Harv. J. L. & Pub. Pol'y 917 (2021); Lee J. Strang, Originalism's Promise: A Natural Law Account of the American Constitution (2019).

315   Brianne J. Gorod, *Originalism and Historical Practice in Separation-of-Powers Cases,* 66 Syracuse L. Rev. 41 (2016).

316   Mitchell N. Berman, *Originalism Is Bunk,* 84 N.Y.U. L. Rev. 1, 14 (2009).

317   A majority of current Justices have either described themselves as originalist or suggested a commitment to original meaning, forming a historic majority for the first time. At least this is the perception. *See, e.g.,* Kelsey Reichmann, *America Gets First Taste of An Originalist Supreme Court,* Courthouse News Service (July 1, 2022), https://www.courthousenews .com/america-gets-first-taste-of-an-originalist-supreme-court/.

adjudication. Clear provisions, such as the entitlement of each state to two U.S. senators, do not require construction. Yet, others do. Take the Equal Protection Clause. Yes, as Justices Harlan and Black have insisted, "equal" means "equal." But neither meaning alone, nor the history of the text's enactment, can tell us whether all or some affirmative action is constitutionally viable, for example. Creative choice and doctrine *consistent with*—though *not present* in—the text is needed to enforce the original meaning of "equal," whatever that meaning is.

Although most agree that Originalism must now prove itself better than Living Constitutionalism in the construction "zone,"[318] originalists disagree on how. Some originalists refuse to recognize the interpretation-construction distinction altogether. And to no one's surprise. After all, construction sounds more like the business of Living Constitutionalism than that of Meese, Bork, or Scalia. Incidentally, the rise of the distinction lends further support to the theory that Originalism and Living Constitutionalism can be compatible. Of course, this threatens the relevance of contemporary debate, forever binary. Even if "we are all originalists now" on matters of interpretation, the interpretation-construction distinction renders the label meaningless unless a distinctively originalist theory of *construction* can exist to guide the courts.[319] Given how broad and abstract contemporary Originalism has become, an equally compelling question is: "[A]re we all moral readers now?"[320] And the answer is likely: yes. Although in a rather strange, subtler, and more text-conscious way than Rawls' or Dworkin's.

Three sets of questions arise in relation to Originalism's new challenge to explain construction. First, *can* Originalism meaningfully *explain* and *guide* construction?[321] Second, *should* it do either? And third, *do* workable originalist theories of construction exist today? Despite skepticism about the possibility of originalist theories of construction among originalists themselves,[322] some

---

318   Barnett, *supra* note 270, at 72 ("If construction is inevitable because the information contained in the text runs out before we have enough information resolve a case or controversy, then originalists need to debate not only the appropriate approach to constitutional interpretation but also the appropriate approach to construction. Some may wish to avoid this normative discussion, but cases still need to be decided.").

319   Smith, *supra* note 213, at 709 ("If we define originalism inclusively enough, we might say that we evidently are all originalists now.").

320   James Fleming, *supra* note 6, at 1797.

321   *Cf., e.g.,* Laura A. Cisneros, *The Constitutional Interpretation/Construction Distinction: A Useful Fiction*, 27 Const'l Commentary 71, 75 (2010) ("Ultimately, the distinction may only prove useful in trying to figure out what the Court is doing rather than trying to figure out what the Court should do.").

322   Barrett, *supra* note 248, at 8 (noting that "[i]t is unrealistic to expect originalists to provide a uniform answer to any of these [construction] questions").

have taken up the challenge.[323] How do they engage with these three sets of questions? Although that assessment exceeds the scope of my inquiry here, I'll discuss some aspects of current originalist theories of construction below in relation to Myres McDougal's own contributions.

Be that as it may, Originalism's embrace of the interpretation-construction distinction is a game changer. Failing to offer its own theory of construction would imply that either there has never been much difference[324] between Originalism and Living Constitutionalism (each simply guiding a different task of constitutional adjudication) or that Originalism is inferior.[325] The very point of the last forty years of debate is at stake.[326]

---

323   *See, e.g.,* Randy Barnett, *The Letter and the Spirit: A Unified Theory of Originalism,* 107 Geo. L.J. 1 (2018); Lawrence Solum, *Originalist Methodology,* 84 U. Ch. L. Rev. 269 (2017); Jack Balkin, *The Construction of Original Public Meaning,* 31 Const'l Commentary 71 (2016).

324   *Compare* Smith, *supra* note 213, at 709 ("The academic debate about originalism remains vibrant and dynamic, and the theoretical case for originalism is more nuanced now than ever before. So nuanced, in fact, that—at least as described by several prominent originalists—originalism is no longer very different, either in theory or in application, from non-originalism."), *with* Eric J. Segall, *The Concession that Dooms Originalism: A Response to Professor Lawrence Solum,* 88 George Washington L. Rev. Arguendo 33, 47 (2020) (arguing construction zone concept renders Originalism and Living Constitutionalism almost indistinguishable and "we should avoid the distraction of a spent and unnecessary 'great debate' over interpretive theories that are not materially different from each other and instead focus directly on the value judgments themselves, at least in the absence of a new and strongly deferential system of judicial review").

325   Michael L. Smith, *Originalism and the Inseparability of Decision Procedures from Interpretive Standards,* 58 Cal. W. L. Rev. 273, 300 (2022). *See also* Michael Dorf, *Majoritarian Difficulty and Theories of Constitutional Decision Making,* 13 J. Const'l L. 283, 292 n.35 (2010) ("[Originalism] must supplement [its] .... theory of interpretation with some other theory to produce normative guidance for adjudication."). In fact, originalist theories of interpretation embracing the concept of construction must also develop a specific standard for telling thin from thick-enough meaning, a threshold question before construction ensues. Illustrative of such critical disagreement is that between Randy Barnett and Jack Balkin on the Commerce Clause. *Compare* Barnett, *supra* note 323 at 33 (deeming Commerce Clause meaning thick enough), *with* Jack Balkin, *Commerce,* 109 Mich. L. Rev. 1, 15–29 (2010) (deeming thin semantic meaning operative and guiding construction).

326   I surmise that, if there cannot exist a workable, distinctively originalist theory of construction, whether in principle or as a matter of fact, then Originalism's Constraint Thesis is in peril of being either false or irrelevant. If so, I wonder whether the Fixation Thesis can alone do the heavy lifting needed for preferring Originalism over other theories. If not, Originalism would be even less useful than most non-originalisms. One possibility is that Originalism be correct and preferable in cases of interpretation with little or no construction, but still useless in construction instances, in a dynamic not unlike physics, where, if I'm allowed the strained analogy, Relativity theory explains well the dynamics of large bodies while Quantum theory best explains minuscule particles, with no potential theoretical unification between the theories on sight. If so, Originalism's defect is but a

9   Myres McDougal's and Harold Lasswell's Theory of Interpretation

Myres McDougal and Harold Lasswell developed a theory of interpretation in parallel to—though in little conversation with—modern Originalism. And one quite critical of original intent Originalism. Although they did not live to see or engage the rise of contemporary Originalism, they were prescient enough to invoke the equivalent of the interpretation-construction distinction central to today's Originalism, as well as to advance arguments against original intent that preceded Brest's or Powell's. Surprisingly, despite McDougal's harsh criticism of Originalism's "unruly youth,"[327] there is much overlap between his theory of interpretation and that of many contemporary originalists. A chronological analysis of McDougal's and Lasswell's ideas on the subject, spanning from 1945 through 1992, illustrates subtle and overt changes in their theory.

9.1   Enforcing "Great Aims": International Agreements outside the Treaty Clause

McDougal first wrote on constitutional interpretation to defend executive and congressional power to enter international agreements outside of the Treaty Clause.[328] The year was 1945. And the stakes could not have been higher, domestically or internationally. An argument was made by some, including Professor Edwin Borchard—McDougal's colleague at Yale—that neither the President nor Congress had the power to enter agreements with other countries unless, per the Treaty Clause, the President obtained the advice and consent of the Senate's two-thirds.[329] Borchard decried the "new cult which attributes the force of a treaty to an executive agreement."[330] He argued that, in drafting the Treaty Clause, the founders had in mind a distinction made by Swiss jurist Emmerich de Vattel between executory agreements committing to long-term action, described as "treaties," and non-executory, administrative agreements fulfillable by few

---

historical—and maybe transitory—accident. And only compatibilists like Balkin would be persuasive.

327   William Baude, *Is Originalism Our Law?*, 115 Col. L. Rev. 2349, 2352 (2015) (referring to early modern Originalism or Original Intent Originalism as "originalism in its unruly youth," when compared to Contemporary Originalism or Public Meaning Originalism).

328   McDougal & Lans, *supra* note 2 at 181 [hereafter "Policy I"]; Myres S. McDougal & Asher Lans, *Treaties and Congressional-Executive or Presidential Agreements: Interchangeable Instruments of National Policy II*, 54 Yale L.J. 534 (1945) [hereafter "Policy II"]. *See also Made in the USA Foundation v. U.S.*, 242 F.3d 1300, 1303 n.5 (11th Cir. 2001) (referring to McDougal as an "early advocate[] of the congressional-executive agreement as an alternative to the Treaty Clause").

329   Edwin Borchard, *Shall the Executive Agreement Replace the Treaty?*, 53 Yale L.J. 664 (1944).

330   *Id.* at 671.

actions or in the short term, which did not count as treaties under the Clause.[331] Borchard rejected that any prior congressional practice allowing the President to negotiate and enter long-term agreements and obtain a mere majority joint resolution from Congress should imply that the President or Congress had such power.[332] Rather, the Treaty Clause was a "definite check" on the President's foreign affairs power and, since the Constitution neither defines "treaties" nor acknowledges the existence of "executive agreements," history should inform what legally relevant differences exist between them.[333] In a way, the Treaty Clause was a "textual prohibition" of anything incompatible with it.[334]

McDougal rejected the argument. Explaining the obvious national needs involved in the aftermath of the recent war, he noted that the Treaty Clause merely granted the President "a permissive power" to make treaties, with the advice and consent of the Senate, conditioned on a two-thirds vote.[335] Additionally, however, the Constitution elsewhere gave the President and Congress "broad powers" over external affairs, "which are meaningless if they do not include the instrumental powers, first, to authorize the making of intergovernmental agreements and, secondly, to make these agreements the law of the land."[336] A "constitutional practice" of 150 years made clear that "all branches" agreed with this interpretation in "hundreds of instances."[337] Contemporary constitutional law, then, "makes available two parallel and completely interchangeable procedures, wholly applicable to the same subject matters and of identical domestic and international legal consequences, for the consummation of intergovernmental agreements," the Treaty Clause two-thirds vote procedure, and Congressional-Executive agreements "authorized or sanctioned by both houses of Congress."[338] McDougal explained:

> Initial choice of the procedure to be followed for securing validation of any particular intergovernmental agreement lies with the President since it is constitutional practice unquestioned since Washington's day that the President alone has the power to propose or dispose in the actual

---

331 *Id.* at 669–70. *See also id.* at 674 ("If a substantial opinion in the Senate demands submission of an agreement for approval as a treaty, no President should resolve the doubt in his own favor and defy the Senate and the Constitution.").

332 *Id.* at 673–675.

333 *Id.* at 675.

334 Edwin Borchard, *Treaties and Executive Agreements—A Reply*, 54 Yale L. J. 616, 664 (1945).

335 McDougal & Asher, *Policy I, supra* note 2, at 187.

336 *Id.*

337 *Id.*

338 *Id.*

conduct of negotiations with other governments. When a specific agreement is submitted to the Congress for approval or implementation, the Congress may of course question the procedure by which the President seeks validation of the agreement, but if the Congress is to act rationally ... it should shape its action in terms of the policy issues involved in the specific agreement and not in terms of some misleading and unhistorical notion that the treaty-making procedure is the exclusive mode of making important international agreements under our Constitution.[339]

To McDougal, Borchard's opinion amounted to "a resistance that is difficult to understand in view of the historical record and of this nation's traditional preference for democracy."[340] A "restrictive theory" of Congressional and Presidential powers spun "from the one brief and ambiguous" Treaty Clause.[341] Citing Holmes and Thayer, McDougal stressed that, in construing ambiguity in this context by recourse to historical practice, national policy and needs "have a special importance in the field of constitutional law, where theories of jurisprudence are inextricably entwined with 'statecraft, and with the political problems of our great and complex national life.'"[342] Borchard, of course, rejected the relevance of any such factors. To him, the entire construction advanced by McDougal was mere cover for a hostile presidential take-over. And too high a price to pay for world peace.

For McDougal, examination of the reasons that motivated the original adoption of the Treaty Clause supported his argument and, alternatively, even if contemporary Congressional-Executive agreements approved by joint resolution were not "within the original contemplation of the Framers," they were still "a development ... within the best traditions of our history."[343] If, as McDougal suggested, Congress and the President have plenary powers over foreign agreements and the Treaty Clause is permissive, then, Congress should be able to choose whether it will opt for the harder or easier path, depending on impending needs.[344] This is especially true when Congress has power to regulate commerce with foreign nations in conjunction with the Necessary and

---

339   *Id.* at 187–188.
340   *Id.* at 188.
341   *Id.* at 189.
342   *Id.* at 191.
343   *Id.* at 194.
344   McDougal & Asher, *Policy II*, *supra* note 328, at 535 ("Full and free responsiveness to democratic control and to the national interest can be made certain by use of the Congressional-Executive agreement as a functional alternative to the treaty, enabling the President to go to both houses of the Congress for confirmation of any particular agreement, either

Proper Clause.[345] Surveying the constitutional convention's debates, as well as those during ratification, McDougal noted three salient facts: (1) the framers and ratifiers devoted "little time" to the topic of the means to exercise foreign affairs powers; (2) the delegates sought to generally keep foreign affairs powers as far as possible from the states; and (3) the permissive nature of the Treaty Clause, coupled with the grants of plenary foreign affairs powers to the national government, "exemplif[ied] the[] [framers'] general realization that it was desirable to grant future generations ample freedom to devise appropriate instruments by which to govern themselves."[346] McDougal also noted that, in adopting the Treaty Clause, the convention voted down a proposal for exclusive control of treaty-making by the Senate and a proposal for the House to participate in negotiations.[347] Because Madison's proposal of a mere majority vote in the Senate was adopted only to later be rejected, McDougal deemed the historical evidence as unable to settle the matter. "[T]he most significant fact about the motives which are supposed to have impelled the Framers to exclude the House of Representatives from the treaty-making process and to require the Senate to give its consent by a two-thirds majority is that none of them have any validity today; most indeed were outmoded within fifty years after the drafting of the Constitution."[348] McDougal's lengthy review of our practice under and outside the Treaty Clause closed with a call to implement original meaning at a higher level of generality and as a whole, in conjunction with Article 1:

> If we allow ourselves to fail again because of the obstructionist tactics of a small group of willful men, archeologists of the future who dig into the ruins of our civilization will have cause for astonishment that a nation which had throughout its history been so successful in making words serve their appropriate purposes should suddenly have become so hypnotized by a single, absolutist notion of the one word "treaty" that it could not see the full meaning, in both reason and tradition, of the many other relevant words of its fundamental charter.[349]

That is, we should enforce the original "great aim of the Framers" "to make our states one as to all foreign concerns," in light of subsequent practice rather

---

in the first instance, or after it has become apparent that an agreement previously submitted to the Senate will be blocked by a minority obdurate in opposing majority will.").

345   *Id.* at 605–607.
346   *Id.* at 536–37.
347   *Id.* at 537–39.
348   *Id.* at 545.
349   *Id.* at 615.

than a restrictive meaning born from now inexistent concerns.[350] Throughout, McDougal speaks of the framers' and ratifiers' "original desires,"[351] "reasons,"[352] "uses,"[353] and "proposals,"[354] as relevant and supportive of his interpretation.

9.2 *Intended Un-Enumeration, the U.S., and the Genocide Convention*

In 1950, McDougal again wrote in support of ratifying the Genocide Convention, in light of opposition to it by the American Bar Association.[355] Concerns included a parade of horribles that the Convention would deprive states of a great field of criminal jurisprudence only to place it in the hands of the federal government and an international tribunal, which required a constitutional amendment and seemed otherwise incompatible with congressional power to punish offenses against the law of nations.[356] McDougal responded that: (1) the framers intended the Treaty Power not to include enumeration precisely to avoid subsequent restrictive interpretations of it that could preclude Congress from acting when it most needs to;[357] (2) this broad interpretation was part of our subsequent legal precedent, especially in conjunction with the Necessary and Proper Clause;[358] (3) nothing in the Constitution required a treaty to be self-executing;[359] and (4) so long as an international tribunal afforded criminals substantially the same due process as our courts do, neither the Constitution would be violated nor the criminal jurisdiction of states usurped.[360] Note that McDougal's reliance on intended un-enumeration and the Necessary and Proper Clause is reminiscent of the arguments over enumeration in the national bank debates leading to *McCulloch*.

9.3 *Legal Systems and Balanced Opposites*

In 1962, McDougal elaborated on the notion that legal systems, including our own, produce and partly consist of principles that generally come in pairs of

---

350   *Id.* at 545.
351   *Id.* at 551.
352   *Id.* at 546.
353   *Id.* at 551 n.84.
354   *Id.* at 611.
355   Myres McDougal & Richard Arens, *The Genocide Convention and the Constitution,* 3 Vand. L. Rev. 683 (1950).
356   *Id.* at 685.
357   *Id.* at 686.
358   *Id.* at 687–89.
359   *Id.* at 693.
360   *Id.* at 695, 705.

complementary opposites.[361] A community's legal principles play the function of communicating to interested audiences its "authoritative policies:" the "'oughts' about projected distributions of values which are to be sustained by ... coercion."[362] Such policy prescriptions, as embodied in principles, embrace "explicit verbal formulations and tacit expression in uniformities of official behavior."[363] Among explicit formulations is the genre of constitutions.[364] And among uniformities of behavior are the practices of state officials.[365] Some principles, stated at high levels of abstraction, are ambiguous enough to "admit of many differing, alternative applications in particular instances," even though based on "equally valid lines of argument."[366] This, however, often happens where decision makers are confronted with two opposite, *competing* principles. Because most systems contain opposing pairs equally applicable to situations, yet leading to opposite results, McDougal thought this reality posed an "ethical challenge" to decision makers in how to choose and apply the correct principle in specific circumstances.[367]

McDougal offered an example from international law. The goal of minimum order (the prevention of unauthorized violence) is sought by a distinction between impermissible (e.g., acts of aggression) and permissible coercion (e.g., self-defense).[368] The shaping and sharing of values by persuasion rather than coercion is, in turn, promoted by principles which both facilitate agreements (e.g., *pacta sunt servanda*) and authorize their termination (e.g., *rebus sic stantibus*).[369] Here, he adds that, when agreements reveal a contradiction, ambiguity, or incompleteness, "the search for the closest possible approximation to the shared expectations of the parties"—the goal of interpretation—is aided by opposing principles of "effectiveness" (i.e., major purposes are to be secured) and "restrictive interpretation" (i.e., purposes should not be imposed on parties).[370] The same—he says—is true of constitutional law:

---

361   Myres S. McDougal, *The Ethics of Applying Systems of Authority: Balanced Opposites of a Legal System*, *in* The Ethic of Power: The Interplay of Religion, Philosophy, and Politics 221 (Harold Lasswell & Harlan Cleveland eds., 1961) [hereafter "Ethics"]. For an earlier statement of the idea, *see* Myres S. McDougal, *Law as a Process of Decision: A Policy-Oriented Approach to Legal Study*, 1 Natural L. F. 53 (1956).

362   McDougal, *Ethics, supra* note 361, at 221.

363   *Id.*

364   *Id.*

365   *Id.*

366   *Id.* at 222.

367   *Id.* at 223.

368   *Id.*

369   *Id.* at 223–24.

370   *Id.* at 224.

> Grants of competence are often balanced by limitations upon competence: powers over war and peace must be exercised in accordance with a bill of rights. The competence of the center may, in geographic location, be balanced against the competence of the periphery: recall the famous tautology of the Tenth Amendment. ... Similarly, balance in the allocation of competence may be sought by a distribution of authority functions among institutions: "legislative," "executive," and "judicial."[371]

Well, McDougal warned that "all this complementarity and adaptability in legal principle may ... be made to serve rational, as well as irrational, community purposes."[372] Our goal, according to him, should be to rationally serve "the common interest" instead.[373] For McDougal, the principles of effectiveness and restrictiveness in interpretation are an example of "polar common interests," "if values are to be shared and shared by persuasion, the major expectations shared by the parties must be secure; it is, however, coercion to impose upon parties expectations that they never entertained."[374]

McDougal explained that, in communities whose constitutive processes project into the future a wide sharing of values among many participants, "under conditions which cannot be anticipated in detail," complementary principles "framed at many different levels of abstraction" "may quite rationally be employed to express both peoples' more fundamental demands and expectations ... and tentative identifications of the different factual contexts in which different [value] distributions are demanded and expected."[375] The mechanism to pierce through complementarity in any unclear case? Authoritative "appliers" of community prescriptions must make an unavoidable "creative choice" in particular instances, "in measure of varying modesty participating even in the prescribing process."[376] Having courts in mind, he added:

> However much the applier may conscientiously defer to the primary competence of the specialized prescriber—accept as he will the goals of ... clarifying basic constitutional principles in terms of the community expectations actually created by the framers and their successors ... there

---

371   *Id.* at 224–25.
372   *Id.* at 225–26.
373   *Id.* at 226.
374   *Id.*
375   *Id.* at 227.
376   *Id.*

still remains to him, whether he be conscious of it or not, a very broad creative, discretion.[377]

The actual subjectivities of the prescribers, or framers, are not available to the judge. Instead, he or she must rely on inferences based on text that may also involve a deliberate use of abstraction.[378] It is necessary to determine whether the facts are *appropriate* for the application of the invoked policies.[379] One cannot hope to avoid the value choice often involved by transforming application into "automation," whether in the guise of "neutral principles" or anything like it, which McDougal labels "escape fantasies."[380]

And because the choice is not only inevitable but also has effects on values,[381] McDougal challenges decision makers to think about "what value criteria" "should" "guide" this "inescapably creative and responsible judgment."[382] He "assumes" that the decision makers he addresses are part of a community "whose basic constitutive process establishes as an overriding goal the progressively more complete fulfillment of the values of human dignity."[383] Such a decision maker's goal should be "to make his every particular decision ... contribute to progress toward this goal" without inferring from this any "license to impose his own unique, idiosyncratic preferences upon the community."[384] To avoid the latter, McDougal insisted that it was necessary that the decision maker identify with the community he represents and "undertake a disciplined, systematic effort to relate the specific choices he must make to a clarified common interest."[385]

But how? McDougal suggested that the decision maker must "improve his intellectual skills" and, to do so, there is no need to resort to religion or philosophy or any other idiosyncratic beliefs.[386] Rather, McDougal and Lasswell recommend a multi-task method to guide creative policy choices: "goal thinking, trend thinking, scientific thinking, developmental thinking, and alternative thinking."[387] Called, among other things, the "New Haven Method," it

---

377 *Id.*
378 *Id.* at 227–28.
379 *Id.* at 228.
380 *Id.* at 228–29.
381 *Id.* at 229.
382 *Id.* at 230.
383 *Id.* at 230.
384 *Id.*
385 *Id.*
386 *Id.* at 230–31.
387 *Id.* at 231.

consists of a systematic, empirical, and analytical sequence of five tasks that aim to maximize human flourishing, defined as the "reciprocal tolerance and honoring of freedom of choice about participation in the shaping and sharing of all values," such as "well-being, enlightenment, power, skill, affection, respect, rectitude, and wealth."[388]

As applied to the context McDougal was addressing, he described the tasks as follows: (1) goal thinking refers to keeping in mind the primacy of goal values and the principle of contextuality, which requires the relation of every specific choice to all values; (2) trend thinking refers to describing past trends in deciding similar issues; (3) scientific thinking explains the factors that conditioned prior decisions; (4) developmental thinking projects future trends in decision avoiding mere extrapolation; and (5) alternative thinking appraises potential solutions and choices in light of the degree to which they advance the specific values at issue and the overriding value of human dignity.[389]

Notably, McDougal refers to the potential benefit of Lasswell's distinction between principles of content and procedure in addressing choice, in lieu of merely complementary legal principles or canons, to "lessen the ambiguities" faced.[390] He observes that, in the context of interpretation, "confusion" ensues from traditional, complementary principles. And even the need to engage in interpretation is often denied, a principle of "presumptive 'plain and natural ... meaning'" being often invoked as "irrefutable."[391] According to McDougal, community-wide meanings ought not be treated like that. In the "verbal melee" and back and forth between semantic and syntactical principles, "the

---

388 Christian Lee Gonzalez-Rivera, *Law as a Means to Human Flourishing: Law, Morality, and Natural Law in Policy-Oriented Perspective*, 14 Intercultural Hum. Rts. L. Rev. 289, 326 (2019). As I have explained elsewhere:

The values that New Haven attributes to human nature and the attainment of which translates into human flourishing find empirical reference in several sources. First and foremost, they derive from cultural anthropology about human behavior and institutional practices, whether we speak of the goals sought by secluded indigenous communities, or the New York City masses. Second, they are interpreted as the legacy bequeathed to us by all the great democratic movements across civilizations, as well as the culmination of many converging trends of thought, both secular and religious, best expressed today by the international consensus on basic human rights. Although the list of eight values is meant to be comprehensive, it is also meant to be brief, and is subject to revision.

Id. at 328. *See also* Reisman et al., *supra* note 23, at 580 ("Starting from the premise that law should serve human beings, the New Haven School anchors its policy-oriented search for a world public order of human dignity in the universe of human aspirations, which are expressed empirically in its characterization of eight values[.]").

389 McDougal, *Ethics, supra* note 361, at 232.

390 *Id.*

391 *Id.* at 233.

closest approximation to the genuine shared expectations of the parties" is often ignored.[392] What is needed is a new and more rational "balance" in interpretation that includes attention to context. That context should encompass frequencies in claimed meanings, depending on the community, and entail logical and syntactical skills to ascertain the range of plausible actual meanings.[393] He added that "words alone do not make a constitution."[394] However, he recognized that such a method of interpretation had not yet been fully developed.

9.4   A Theory for the Interpretation of Agreements

By 1967, McDougal and Lasswell developed such a theory.[395] Yes, it primarily concerned international agreements and treaties. However, it also applied to other kinds of agreement, including democratic constitutions. A core premise was that "the task of interpretation" is "fundamentally the same for all types of prescriptions" and "system[s] of public order," whether international agreements, "constitutions ... and even ... private agreements."[396] So, differences in interpreting these legal documents are not of kind, but of degree and the goals pursued.

According to McDougal, the history of any prescription shows that it is the outcome of a social process, the culminating event in a sequence of communication.[397] In every controversy, decision makers proceed within the frame of reference provided by the basic prescriptions of all the public order systems to which they are responsible.[398] Every such prescription is a communication in which parties seek through signs (i.e., text) and deeds (e.g., practices, negotiations) to mediate their subjectivities and, in private contracts as well as constitutions, this entails difficulties such as contradictions, ambiguities, and degrees

---

392   *Id.*

393   *Id.* at 234. *See also* Myres S. McDougal, *Some Basic Theoretical Concepts About International Law: A Policy-Oriented Framework of Inquiry*, 4 J. Conflict Resol. 337, 352 (1960) (describing process as "beginning with the ... words ... [then] syntactic analysis [of] ... possible meanings ... [then] semantic analysis [of] ... probable meanings ... [and then] systematic ... assessment of ... the closest possible approximation to actual meanings").

394   McDougal, *Ethics, supra* note 361, at 239.

395   Myres S. McDougal, Harold Lasswell, & James C. Miller, The Interpretation of Agreements and World Order (1967).

396   *Id.* at xi. *See also* John Norton Moore, *Prolegomenon to the Jurisprudence of Myres McDougal and Harold Lasswell*, 54 Va. L. Rev. 662, 683 (1968) (noting the treatise "lends itself with some adaptation to the interpretation of prescriptive communications at all levels of social organization, including constitutions").

397   McDougal et al., *supra* note 395, at xi.

398   *Id.*

of completeness.[399] Decision makers facing these difficulties while tasked with interpreting and enforcing prescriptions have comparable chances for relating their decisions to the basic goal values of preferred public order.[400] At least this is what a "realistic" and "consequential" approach yields: it requires, according to McDougal, a clear working conception of what is involved in processes of communication, a preliminary notion of what is meant by interpretation, and a specification of the role of interpretation in the more comprehensive decision process of "application," in which enforcement is related to and integrated with all other community policies.[401]

McDougal emphasizes that law—the kind embodied by all sorts of texts—is the result of a process of communication. So, methods for interpretation and application must be informed and shaped by contemporary developments in Linguistics, Logic, Communications, and all "empirical research" into social and community linguistic practices.[402] Communication is a process involving communicators (i.e., initiators of messages) and audiences (i.e., recipients of messages) making use of signs (e.g., written and oral).[403] Signs mediate the subjective events of two or more parties.[404] These subjectivities or intentions are those of real, individual human beings authorized to engage in the communicative process.[405] And they are not limited to linguistic ones, but include gestures, pictures, and the like.[406] They are to be interpreted considering the forum in which they are employed, as well as the parties' objectives sought in that forum.[407] Objectives encompass "value demands," the perspectives regarding which are "closely tied to expectations about the way in which the preferred events can be made to take place."[408] Attention must also be paid to often "marginally conscious" or "unconscious" demands and expectations.[409]

Parties also employ strategies of communication, including the processing of what is conveyed.[410] The latter is achieved either through *syntactical* (i.e., understanding the interrelations among statements viewed as "a family

---

399   *Id.*
400   *Id.*
401   *Id.* at xi–xii.
402   *Id.* at xii, 371.
403   *Id.* at xii.
404   *Id.*
405   *Id.* at 15.
406   *Id.*
407   *Id.* at xiii.
408   *Id.*
409   *Id.* at xiv.
410   *Id.*

of meaning" in a closed universe) or *semantic* analyses (i.e., understanding the references of the statements regardless of the location of those references inside or outside the message).[411] Lastly, the outcomes of communication often diverge in degrees of completeness of shared subjectivities, and the scientific observer must aim at the best possible basis of inference in ascertaining them.[412] Because every feature of the communication process may affect an outcome by either *facilitating* shared subjectivities or *interfering* with them, an interpreter must give them due consideration in context.[413] From the outset, McDougal ventures that even this cursory appreciation of the factual complexity of communication suggests that it is a mistake to "trust blindly" the assumption that the presence or absence of meaning is to be "read off in simple fashion from the manifest content of particular words embossed or imprinted," since "[i]nterpretation is a far more realistic and subtle challenge."[414] A jab at contemporary textualism that will become a motif throughout the entire treatise.

McDougal structured his entire theory of interpretation around the conceptual and practical difference between *interpretation* and *application*. For him, the primary aim of "genuine" interpretation is to "discover the shared expectations that the parties to the relevant communication succeeded in creating in each other."[415] In doing so, and since the components of communication take on different roles in different contexts, it is "impossible" to impute, in advance, a valid "unvarying weight" to or "hierarchy" among particular features of that process to prevent or remove ambiguities.[416] McDougal labels it an "obvious travesty" to disregard *actual* meaning on account of arbitrary assumptions of one's own.[417] The "grossest, least defensible" kind of arbitrary formalism is, for him, "to arrogate to one particular set of signs—the text of a document—the role of serving as the exclusive index of the parties' shared expectations."[418] McDougal had in mind contemporary textualism, "a violation to the human dignity to choose freely," since it "does violence" to the policy of directing decision makers to respect the preferences of as many members of the community as possible on as many occasions as possible.[419] At bottom,

---

411   *Id.* at xiv–xv.
412   *Id.* at xv.
413   *Id.*
414   *Id.* at xvi.
415   *Id.*
416   *Id.*
417   *Id.* at xvii.
418   *Id.*
419   *Id.*

thus, bad interpretation "is an act of coercion."[420] And much of it was prevalent in his time.

Literalism stops short at words, "with an ascription of meaning to words
taken as final," whereas the better approach "does not neglect the words," but
does engage in "scrutiny of the whole context."[421] This demands an interpreter
to suspend any act of final choice "until all the evidence is in."[422] The process
is two-pronged: on one hand, arranging the manifest content of the text after
considering contradictions, harmonization, and abstraction, and, on the other,
examining this context in light of any information that helps establish the
actual perspectives of the communicator and its audience.[423] These two tasks
track the difference between principles of content, aiding the analysis of the
message, and of procedure, guiding the reconstruction of the situation behind
the message, which affects an interpreter's appraisal of the significance of the
message.[424]

Yet, interpretation is not the only thing a decision maker engages in when
he or she seeks to apply or enforce a textual prescription or agreement.
Application encompasses "primary" interpretation, but when text and context
are not enough to discern the genuine meaning at issue, applying a prescription
also involves ancillary or "supplemental interpretation."[425] Supplementation is
made to cure omissions, fill in gaps, settle ambiguities, and undo vagueness,
"which obviously come within the objectives sought by the parties and give
rise to unnecessary value deprivations if denied."[426] It additionally performs
two functions that "relate the specific controversy to the total context of public
policy:" *policing* and *integration*.[427] Policing and integration entail the evaluation of the parties' expectations or intent for their compatibility with basic,
constitutional policies, and their rejection if they conflict with the latter.[428]

Some principles of content recommended by McDougal are, first, the
contextual principle, requiring the interpreter to focus on the actual, shared

---

420   *Id.*
421   *Id.* at xviii.
422   *Id.*
423   *Id.*
424   *Id.*
425   *Id.* at 29.
426   *Id.* at xix-xx ("No one acquainted with the complex facts of life ever imagines that a
       sequence of words can be arranged to designate in concrete and minute intimacy the
       entire features of a situation, though they can be at least approximately indicated by rea-
       sonably careful language. Life is too short to trap all the abundance of history; hence we
       must be content with sketches, not thumb prints."). *See also id.* at 41.
427   *Id.*
428   *Id.* at 30.

expectations of the parties in their entire factual context, and not to allow any one factor to dominate until all evidence is in.[429] Second, the principle of involvement, which requires assigning individuals' expectations a weight proportional to their involvement or role in the process of communication culminating in the agreement or prescription.[430] Third, the principle of projecting expectations (traditionally called the principle of effectiveness), which requires interpretation to focus on the parties' major objectives, never beyond what they actually expected.[431] Fourth, the principle of anticipated solutions, which entails consideration of the parties' explicitly considered contingencies not expressly incorporated to the agreement or prescription, such that, if these were omitted merely due to convenience, a presumption in their favor should exist, but if they were excluded for other reasons, a contrary presumption should arise.[432] Fifth, the principle of preferred modes of expression, which suggests that, where practice and text collide, often priority is given to sources pertaining to language.[433] Sixth, the principle of logical relationships, which operates in cases of gaps, contradictions, and ambiguities, and requires that an interpreter choose the logical inferences actually shared by the parties, aided by formal methods of logic.[434] Seventh, the principle of the largest shared audience, which requires that, absent contrary evidence, one must assume that terms are intended to be understood as they are generally understood by the largest audience contemporary to the text at issue within the same community the text was produced.[435] Lastly, the principle of probability of agreement, which looks to practices contemporaneous to the agreement or text to help elucidate ambiguities.[436]

As to principles of procedure, McDougal recommends the same contextual principle noted above, but this time split into different "operations." First, adjusting one's effort to the relative importance of the dispute.[437] Second, identifying the focal text or agreement at issue.[438] Third, the historical operation, which requires considering the text in light of the sequence of events that led

---

429   *Id.* at 50.
430   *Id.*
431   *Id.* at 52–53.
432   *Id.* at 53.
433   *Id.* at 56–57.
434   *Id.* at 57.
435   *Id.* at 59.
436   *Id.* at 60.
437   *Id.* at 66.
438   *Id.* at 67.

to its adoption.[439] Fourth, the lexical operation, which elucidates semantic meaning based on the understanding of the audience at the time of adoption of the text, including language, dialect, special usages, culture, class, and other factors.[440] And, in case of texts adopted in the distant past, McDougal warns that community meanings may have changed, so present usages may not indicate the true "original shared expectations" of the communicator and its audience, and the latter must control.[441] Fifth, the logical operation, which entails reliance on several logical aspects of statements to help elaborate their syntactic and semantic meaning (e.g., implications, conjunctions, inclusive and exclusive disjunctions, etc.).[442] Sixth, the operation of assessing scientific credibility, which demands interpreters to rely on those sources with the highest degree of scientific credibility where evidence on language usage conflicts.[443]

All throughout, McDougal's principles are meant to ascertain the key "factors in the estimation of meaning,"[444] which is the "content" of communication.[445] He variously describes the meaning with which interpretation is concerned, including in the case of textual prescriptions, as the communicator's and audience's "original intent,"[446] "original shared expectations,"[447] "original understanding,"[448] "original agreement,"[449] "genuine shared expectations,"[450] "genuine choice,"[451] "expectations current at the time,"[452] and "understanding ... at the time."[453] To ascertain that original meaning, resort must be had to

---

439   *Id.*
440   *Id.*
441   *Id.* at 67–69.
442   *Id.* at 71–72.
443   *Id.* at 74.
444   *Id.* at 70.
445   *Id.* at 11.
446   *Id.* at 83.
447   *Id.* at 67.
448   *Id.* at 57 (adding that focus is needed on "interpretations that were prevalent among persons of approximately the same characteristics ... at the time," in addressing gaps or ambiguities). *See also id.* at 36.
449   *Id.* at 47.
450   *Id.* at 10.
451   *Id.* at 6.
452   *Id.* at 73.
453   *Id.* at 67.

"original usages,"[454] "contemporary usage,"[455] "ordinary" and "public" "signifi-cations,"[456] and, critically, the "public meanings of words."[457]

McDougal deemed contemporary interpretation theory a pendulum often swinging between two extremes. The first extreme was the "plain" or "natu-ral meaning" textualism springing from Vattel. According to McDougal, he exemplified the position that interpretation is more often than not so easy as to be "almost automatic,"[458] a "simple and mechanical routine,"[459] which McDougal deemed "nihilism"[460] and "primitive."[461] Vattel coined the rule that what requires no interpretation should not be interpreted, since its plain, nat-ural, and ordinary meaning should always control despite evidence of contrary intentions or expectations.[462] For McDougal, this *exclusive* resort to ordinary meaning through the use of hypothetical *contemporary* readers frustrates gen-uine interpretation in the case of agreements because it risks substituting the subjectivities of the community for those of the communicator and its audi-ence.[463] There is always a need for interpretation[464] because language, even where clear, is seldom capable of avoiding uncertainty in application, given new circumstances. Yes, interpreters must determine the prima facie "ordinary meaning" of text, but they must also examine the context.[465] Vattel's was an "overemphasis" on the ordinary meanings of words: generally, it should be the "actual" "sense" intended by *the communicator and its audience* that controls.[466] Differentiating it from ordinary meaning, McDougal also rejected the notion of a "natural" meaning to words as unempirical.[467] Context must always be con-sulted regardless of the apparent simplicity and directness of a word.[468] Failing that, reference must be had to the community's fundamental policies.[469] On the other extreme was the equally nihilistic idea that all interpretation was an

---

454   *Id.* at 72.
455   *Id.* at 71.
456   *Id.* at 69.
457   *Id.* at 97.
458   *Id.* at 7.
459   *Id.* at 11.
460   *Id.* at 12.
461   *Id.* at 218.
462   *Id.* at 7–8.
463   *Id.* at 41 n.7.
464   *Id.* at 79–80
465   *Id.* at 81 n.9–10.
466   *Id.* at 82–83.
467   *Id.* at 88 n.38. *See also id.* at 90–91.
468   *Id.* at 93.
469   *Id.*

arbitrary and impossible task, since words are irremediably ambiguous and historic inquiry is impracticable.[470]

However, McDougal's criticisms of "plain meaning" or strict textualism were mainly directed at the interpretation of private and international agreements, not constitutions, and he did not conflate these with "ordinary meaning."[471] He called for the moderate and appropriate use of *ordinary meaning* presumptions, not their rejection.[472] Public ordinary meaning may be a default and starting point, subject to evidence that it has been or should be displaced.[473] But it follows that, in the case of unilateral[474] forms of communication—which our Constitution is, the principle of the largest possible contemporary audience requires the enforcement of the framers and ratifiers' shared "original intent." And in the context of massive participation, this can only mean public, ordinary meaning. What McDougal sought to avoid, in constitutional interpretation as much as in other contexts, were the extremes of those for whom, "on the one hand, interpretation is as automatic as the workings of a well-designed and operated slot machine, and, on the other, [those for whom] all interpretation is a genteel hoax."[475] What we need are better "truth" seeking principles.[476] Yet, these cannot include a single "super-principle" that substitutes for rational, historically driven inquiry.[477] Principles are important because, in applying general or abstract terms, decision makers engage in two tasks: identifying "subordinate terms" (potential semantic meanings) and choosing among these the one most appropriate to the controversy and the facts.[478] The decision maker is often not wholly bound to any one semantic choice.[479] But choice should not be arbitrary, capricious, or irrational.

---

470 *Id.* at 370–73.

471 *Id.* at 90 (explaining that his concern with blind application of ordinary meaning centered around its effect on free commerce and the dignity of choice and societal experimentation). For the conceptual, practical, and even ideological distinctions between "plain," "literal," and "ordinary" meaning conceptions, *see, e.g.,* Brian G. Soclum, Ordinary Meaning: A Theory of the Most Fundamental Principle of Legal Interpretation 20–26 (2015). McDougal seems to have raised the standard objection, identified by Soclum, that "plainness" is often invoked as a ruse to conceal—or shortcut—reasoning and, regardless, offers a simplistic view of language. *Id.* at 24.

472 McDougal et al., *supra* note 395, at 219 n.333.

473 *Id.* at 220–21.

474 *Id.* at 37.

475 *Id.* at 371.

476 *Id.* at 374.

477 *Id.* at 375.

478 *Id.* at 377.

479 *Id.*

Analogizing the Constitution to international agreements just the year before his 1968 treatise, McDougal summarized how he understood the interplay of ordinary dictionary meanings and true original meanings:

> [T]he provisions of our Constitution, whether taken as a document or a more comprehensive flow of communication, exhibit the same complementarities, ambiguities, and incomplete references as do international agreements or customary international law. For supplementing these inadequacies in communication, and in responsible effort to ascertain genuine contemporary community expectation from the whole past flow of relevant communication, an interpreter is authorized to, and must perforce, have recourse to pre-1787 negotiations, subsequent practice by all branches of the government, statutory interpretations, judicial decisions and opinions, and the vast literature of expressions, formal and informal, about preferred public order. Appropriate principles of constitutional interpretation may of course aid in the canvass and assessment of all these different evidences of community expectation and common interest, but there would appear to be as yet no miracle-working formula or computer which can reduce decision to automatic projection. In the last analysis, the interpreter must himself take responsibility for a creative choice[.][480]

Around the same time, McDougal expressed an identical criticism against the inclusion of the Vattelian notion of plain meaning in the future Vienna Convention on the Law of Treaties.[481] Ultimately unsuccessful, he labeled the draft's recognition of a supremacy of plain meaning over extra-textual factors, labeled mere "supplementary means" of interpretation, a development based on an "obscurantist tautology."[482] He recognized that judges often decided interpretive issues relying on relevant dictionaries, but he observed they also needed to look past ambiguous text to effectuate the *actual common interest of parties*.[483] McDougal emphasized that dictionary meanings are often multiple and competing, requiring factual circumstances and history to settle any

---

480   Myres S. McDougal, *Jurisprudence for a Free Society*, 1 Georgia L. Rev. 1, 18 (1966).

481   Myres S. McDougal, *Statement of Professor Myres S. McDougal, United States Delegation, to Committee of the Whole, April 19, 1968*, 62 Am. J. Int'l L. 1021 (1968) [hereafter "Statement"]. *See also* Myres S. McDougal, *The International Law Commission's Draft Articles upon Interpretation: Textuality Redivivus*, 61 Am. J. Int'l L. 992 (1967) (making identical arguments the preceding year).

482   McDougal, *Statement, supra* note 481, at 1023.

483   *Id.* at 1022.

choice.[484] Text and ordinary dictionary meanings are a starting point, not the end of inquiry.[485] He deemed the "poverty of the textuality approach" illustrated by the numerous circumstances where there are multiple versions of authoritative treaty drafts, for which alone the Vienna Convention allowed inquiry into the parties' actual intent.[486] Notably, he insisted that ample choice among competing semantic meanings in dictionaries unmoored from history and circumstances at the time of drafting ironically gave more unbridled discretion to decision makers.[487] Any genuine interpretation must rationally inquire into the relationship of text and original meaning.[488]

9.5 McDougal's Cardozo Lecture: A Manifesto against Incipient Originalism

In 1979, McDougal delivered the annual lecture in honor of Justice Cardozo before the New York City Bar.[489] Building on his legacy of legal realism, he extolled Cardozo's realization that constitutional adjudication often requires a creative choice.[490] This was especially true of the "great generalities of the Constitution," as Cardozo labeled them.[491] Although Cardozo thought they varied from generation to generation and should be supplemented just like the common law, McDougal thought Cardozo's thoughts required systematization.[492] McDougal declared himself a "visiting anthropologist" in the field of constitutional law, analogizing his experience reviewing the extensive literature on the topic to "that of 'eating hay endlessly.'"[493] So, he offered some observations on the goals of interpretation and the intellectual tasks required for it in that context.[494]

First, he labeled the "most primitive" approach that which looks at the Constitution as the single paper document ratified in 1789 and posits as the goal of interpreting it the "original intent of the founding fathers," focusing exclusively on the words of the document alone for such determination.[495] He

---

484   *Id.* at 1024.
485   *Id.*
486   *Id.* at 1025.
487   *Id.* at 1026.
488   *Id.* at 1027.
489   Myres S. McDougal, *The Application of Constitutive Prescriptions: An Addendum to Justice Cardozo*, 1 Cardozo L. Rev. 135 (1979).
490   *Id.* at 136.
491   *Id.*
492   *Id.* at 136–37.
493   *Id.* at 138 n.9.
494   *Id.* at 138.
495   *Id.* at 139.

deems this "extreme ... fidelity to past intentions and words" chimerical and irrational.[496] Instead, he praised Llewellyn's idea of the Constitution as a living institution.[497] Second, he noted the rise of unworkable theories of principled adjudication, matched by the equal rise in calls for unprincipled decision.[498] Third, he observed that value choices are inevitably made in many constitutional cases, and that what we ought to do is not deny that fact but make clear how to specify and apply such values in concrete circumstances.[499] Fourth, he argued that precedent could only ever be one factor in adjudication.[500] Fifth, a systematic and disciplined method is desirable to guide interpretation and application of constitutional provisions to reduce arbitrariness and increase rationality.[501]

Building on his 1968 treatise on interpretation,[502] McDougal recommended several principles and tasks. Among them, he suggests we include in the application of constitutive prescriptions the following: (1) a conception of the Constitution as a comprehensive, continuing process of communication and collaboration; (2) a differentiation of particular claims in terms of factual categories that facilitate the clarification of policy; (3) the explicit recognition of intellectual tasks required for genuine interpretation no less than supplementation and integration; and (4) the systematic employment of principles of content and procedure.[503] Interestingly, he insisted that a better theory of application was needed not just for courts but all branches.[504] The goal of application is to implement the common interest as reflected in our Constitution.[505] McDougal stressed that constitutional law cannot be deemed a mere cover for naked power, and that is precisely what pessimistic, cynical views that give up on potentially workable theories inevitably lead us to.[506] A "fair" "exposition" of the Constitution is possible.[507]

Responding to Justice Rehnquist, McDougal argued that our Constitution is neither solely the document of 1789, nor "a diffuse mass of contemporary

---

496   *Id.* at 140.
497   *Id.* at 141.
498   *Id.* at 144–146.
499   *Id.* at 148.
500   *Id.* at 149.
501   *Id.* at 150.
502   *Id.* at n.70.
503   *Id.* at 151.
504   *Id.* at 152.
505   *Id.*
506   *Id.* at 153.
507   *Id.*

expectations," but rather a "continuous process of communication ... beginning before 1789 and coming down to date."[508] Neither is the Constitution a "continuing constitutional convention." Rather, it is "the whole community."[509] To McDougal, the broad clauses, including the Treaty Clause, Equal Protection, and Due Process, are "invitations" rather than "specifications" for decision, requiring "elaboration from other sources."[510] He argues that application requires interpretation, supplementation, and integration (or policing).[511] Interpretation entails a genuine effort to "approximate the closest possible approximation to the contemporary expectations, about the requirements of decision, created in the general community as a residue of the whole flow of constitutive communication throughout our history."[512] Supplementation fills in gaps and settles ambiguities by reference to "more general basic community policies about the shaping and sharing of values."[513] Integration involves prioritizing among competing or often conflicting values and expectations.[514] McDougal believes that these three operations are inevitable.[515] No principles or computers may substitute for our choice.[516] In discharging that personal responsibility, McDougal recommends pledging to the public order goal value of "human dignity or a free society," since the same is incorporated by our Constitution with varying degrees of explicitness.[517]

He restated some of his principles of content and procedure to apply them in the constitutional context, noting that they needed "sharper refinement and systematization."[518] Principles of content include that of contextuality, which requires preference for considering alternatives in the larger context of constitutive prescriptions; giving effect to the expectations shared by communicators and communicatees in the process of constitutive prescription in so far as they are compatible with human dignity; supplementing expectations; and integrating them.[519] Among principles of procedure, he suggested, again, contextuality; economy; clarification of focus; observing past trends in

---

508   *Id.* at 154.
509   *Id.* at 155.
510   *Id.* at 157.
511   *Id.* at 158.
512   *Id.* at 159.
513   *Id.*
514   *Id.* at 160.
515   *Id.*
516   *Id.*
517   *Id.* at 163.
518   *Id.* at 164 n.110–111.
519   *Id.* at 164–65.

decision and factors affecting it; observing constraints on future possibilities; and inventing and evaluating solutions by relating all options "to basic general community policies" and choosing that which "will promote the largest net aggregate of common interests."[520] Despite earlier rejections of constitutional review viewed as a continuous convention, McDougal still goes on to label it "a comprehensive and continuing plebiscite."[521] One year later, however, he went on to explain that, although pervasive contemporary emphasis on constitutionalism as a set of preferred prescriptions is inadequate to describe the whole constitutive process, it is still "an eloquent and rational affirmation of the more fundamental policies which have historically underlain such process," aiming at securing basic rights.[522] The tension in McDougal's restatement of his interpretive theory, as applied to constitutional law, between the latter's object (including the expectations of the entire community through multiple generations), on one hand, and more fundamental and non-negotiable basic expectations sought to be protected from transient majorities, on the other, is palpable.

9.6   *Jurisprudence for a Free Society*
In their *magnum opus*—published after Lasswell's death, McDougal and Lasswell offered some thoughts, though less systematic, on constitutional interpretation.[523] This time, the point of view adopted was that of those drafting—and anticipating interpretation of—a constitution.

An "advisor-draftsman" faces, among many other questions, whether to include provisions in a constitution that will probably not be enforced.[524] Including them is often justified if it will mobilize support to obtain ratification of the entire document.[525] However, assuming that ratification will not be an issue, McDougal considers the question still. In such a case, he asks, should the provision be construed as an articulation of objectives to be pursued or as a collection of mandates for strict compliance?[526] He explains the difference between these two approaches and tracks the difference between the American and Latin American models. Under the former, the charter is

---

520   *Id.* at 166–67.

521   *Id.* at 169.

522   Myres S. McDougal, Harold Lasswell, & Lung-Chu Chen, Human Rights and World Public Order 472 (1980).

523   Myres S. McDougal & Harold Lasswell, Jurisprudence for a Free Society: Studies in Law, Science, and Policy (Vol II) (1992).

524   *Id.* at 1156.

525   *Id.*

526   *Id.*

mandatory. Under the latter, it is admonitory.[527] However, a workable adjustment is possible by "leaving out specific and impracticable requirements."[528] As an example, McDougal cites the Constitution's preamble, laying down value goals.[529] In the Eighteenth Century, he explains, preambles were given great weight in interpretation.[530] Ever since, however, the opposite became the case: contemporary wisdom deems them rhetorical language devoid of legal effect.[531] McDougal denies that this "narrow" interpretation can be correct.[532]

Another question is to what extent should drafters bind future generations by trying to exclude certain provisions from amendment powers.[533] In diverse societies inexperienced in popular government, restrictions on amendments are critical to protecting civil liberties and minorities.[534] Including them in a charter "crystallizes" the protections.[535] And "[a]ny effort to violate the original 'compromise' will presumably be resisted, not only in the name of particular interests, but of the allegedly authoritative 'contract' entered into at the start."[536] Society will seek to "preserv[e] the weight of the constitutional document."[537] The argument in favor of procedural safeguards is that transitory majorities will otherwise cause grave harm and safeguards will at least require a "pause" that could ensure full consideration and debate of issues.[538] Special safeguards include bills of rights, minority privileges, and states rights.[539]

This insight on interpretation from the perspective of a constitution's drafter or his or her advisor originally came from Lasswell. Two of his earlier contributions are worth mentioning.

First, he recognized the central importance of our Constitution's writtenness. He identified seven phases in the processes of political and legal decision-making: "intelligence (and planning), recommending, prescribing, invoking, applying, appraising, [and] terminating."[540] "Prescribing" referred to "lay[ing]

---

527   *Id.*
528   *Id.*
529   *Id.*
530   *Id.*
531   *Id.* at 1157.
532   *Id.*
533   *Id.*
534   *Id.*
535   *Id.*
536   *Id.*
537   *Id.*
538   *Id.*
539   *Id.*
540   Harold Lasswell, *The Public Interest: Proposing Principles of Content and Procedure*, 5 Nomos: Am. Soc'y Pol. Legal Phil. 54, 54 (1962).

down constitutional provisions, statutes, and the like."[541] "Application" referred
to the "relatively final activities within the frame provided by prescription ...
includ[ing] the disposal of controversies by judicial and regulative bodies."[542]
To "appraise," in turn, meant "to explore and assess the degree to which official
policies have been realized."[543] "Constitutional policy," then, is what ordinarily
is at stake in constitutional adjudication.[544]

It serves critical political purposes. Chief among them, according to Lasswell,
is the setting up of "defense mechanisms" by those "outside the circle of the nominal government" "against arbitrary exercise of authority without some form of
check—the apparatus of constitutionalism and especially of civil rights."[545] He
stressed that certain facts, such as an "unamendable constitution," may be fatal
to the meaningful enforcement of constitutional policy.[546] Lasswell noted that
"[t]he first ten amendments to the Constitution provide *binding written texts*
which give the courts *a peg on which to justify* their defense of private rights and
civilian supremacy."[547] Notice the interplay between the Constitution's *writtenness* and the degree of *justification* the judiciary can achieve in specific adjudi-
cations. The Bill of Rights is what, according to Lasswell, allows the judiciary to
legitimately preclude the establishment of a "garrison state."[548] American political psychology in the constitutional context, explains Lasswell, is well-known
to have developed in relation to cultural tropes about the writtenness of Holy
Scripture.[549] Writtenness, thus, is part of our political theology.

---

541   *Id.* at 55.
542   *Id.*
543   *Id.*
544   *Id.*
545   Harold D. Lasswell, Study of Power 178 (1950).
546   *Id.*
547   Harold D. Lasswell, National Security & Individual Freedom 45 (1950) (emphasis added).
548   *Id.* at 47.
549   Lasswell, *supra* note 545, at 217 ("Issues were argued in the language of conformity with or
       deviation from a body of premises which were presumed to be embodied in a short writ-
       ten document. These patterns of dialectic were familiar to a culture where Protestantism
       prevailed, and where pulpiteering consisted in arguing questions of private and public
       policy in terms of conformity with or deviation from the written Bible. The polemics of
       slavery were carried on in terms of the Constitution and the Bible; so all-embracing were
       these forms of language that the political vocabulary of the United States was enriched
       by no systematic work of social analysis."). *See also id.* at 42 ("Since our Western European
       culture was so long dominated by the symbolism of Christianity, the rising national and
       proletarian movements, quite without premeditation, look over the Christian patterns.
       A classical instance of this is the famous procession at the first session of the Legislative
       Assembly in France in the autumn of 1791, when twelve elderly patriarchs went in search
       of the Book of the Constitution.").

Be that as it may, in Lasswell's opinion, our adjudicative system showcases "intellectual devices by which judges have sought to legitimize the inconsistencies of courts," as well as contradictions, gaps, or vagueness in constitutional policy.[550] One such ordinary, intellectual device is "the presumption of a natural legal order which is self-consistent and superior to any source of inconsistency which might arise from judicial interpretations."[551] Another, "less far-reaching," is "the presumption of consistent intention on the part of the framers of the fundamental principles of the legal order," which "enables many seeming errors to be righted by the judicial organ."[552] Lasswell deemed incipient original intent Originalism an intellectual device, like so many others, aiming at the "logicalization" of our legal system.[553] Lasswell did not criticize such devices.[554] In fact, in his own scholarship on constitutional interpretation, he, no less than McDougal, engaged in originalist and historical inquiry concerning the founding generation's understanding.[555]

Second, Lasswell's preferred perspective in speaking about constitutional interpretation was that of the constitution drafter. According to him, "on fundamental questions pertaining to the whole, the formal language that designates a gathering as a 'constitutional convention' ... does not charm away the tough, hard facts of difference and confusion over the ends to be sought or the

---

550 Harold D. Lasswell, *The Value Analysis of Legal Discourse*, 9 W. Res. L. Rev. 188, 197 (1958).

551 *Id.*

552 *Id.*

553 *Id.*

554 *Id.* at 198 ("The inference is not that since they are open to eventual frustration efforts at logical consistency are futile. It can be forcefully affirmed that in a body politic whose aspiration is toward freedom, it is particularly important to share enlightenment, and therefore to disclose inconsistencies that occur within the legal system."). However, one of McDougal's associates, Professor Michael Reisman, voiced McDougal's criticism of incipient Originalism in describing Lasswell's own theoretical contributions. *See* Michael Reisman, *In Memoriam: Harold D. Lasswell*, 4 Yale Stud. World Pub. Ord. 154, 157 (1978) (criticizing original intent Originalism's assumption that the Constitution was "a sacred talisman to be revered as holy writ and construed in accord with the assumed intentions of the drafters," and stressing "[t]he futility of this approach" as "obvious to the historian"). It is unclear, however, whether Reisman meant to attribute this criticism to Lasswell himself or personally rejected original public meaning or shared expectations as conceived by McDougal (or contemporary Originalism), when he affirmed that "all constitutions are contemporary." *Id.*

555 *See, e.g.,* Lasswell, *supra* note 547, at 59–61, 65, 69–71 (analyzing constitutional convention debates to understand principle of civilian supremacy and noting that "[t]he concern of the Founding Fathers for the protection of the individual against arbitrary official action is fully reflected in the Bill of Rights").

means to be employed."[556] As he colorfully put it, "[t]here is no drug capable of inducing a trance state in the seasoned politician (or the unseasoned citizen, for that matter), by which he becomes a dispassionate spokesman for the common good."[557] Additionally, "[t]he advisor-draftsman will labor to little avail if the ... constitution he produces ... once adopted, is not complied with."[558] So he or she is primarily guided by the *enforceability* of the final *text*. Lasswell recommends several tools to better realize this goal.

For example, with regard to "knowledge," Lasswell suggests that the advisor must make accurate estimates about future compliance. One question he or she should consider is whether "publication" alone will result in "prompt, universal, and continuing compliance."[559] Notice the presupposition that successful compliance with constitutional prescriptions should be "continuing," not suddenly stop 100 years later due to an interpreting court's change of mind. Lasswell also notes that the advisor must be able to sufficiently clarify the goal values embedded in the text. He acknowledged that

> No lawyer, certainly, could imagine that words like "law," "justice" and "liberty" are used in the same way by all men. Yet in our view every responsible citizen (and a fortiori every lawyer) needs to be clear as to what he is talking about, at least when he is talking candidly to himself, even though he may have to abbreviate and simplify in dealings with others (but not for the purpose of shearing the client for the counselor's private advantage). This is the responsible use of the mind: it begins at home. Part of the act of using the mind is the construction of working definitions of fundamental value categories; and this is a major part of the advisor-draftsman's task.[560]

So, Lasswell recommends "translat[ing] some goals into working definitions which are *not likely to be modified by further experience*; and ... translat[ing] many [others] into provisional definitions subject to *relatively easy modification* in the light of further knowledge and experience."[561] That is, ahead of drafting, and depending on the goal, some goals to be embedded in textual

---

556 George H. Dession & Harold D. Lasswell, *Public Order under Law: The Role of the Advisor-Draftsman in the Formation of Code or Constitution*, 65 Yale L.J. 174, 175 (1955).
557 *Id.*
558 *Id.* at 177.
559 *Id.* at 179.
560 *Id.* at 180.
561 *Id.* (emphasis added).

prescriptions will be defined in a way not to be modified later, while others may allow for some modification.

As to what language to use in drafting a provision for the preliminarily defined goal, Lasswell notes that "[t]here are contradictory views current among both scholars and laymen who attempt to evaluate the importance of words in public affairs."[562] On one extreme, "[w]ords are often dismissed with some contempt as idle winds playing over the surface of the fundamental factors in social and political evolution."[563] On the other extreme, words "are hailed as the quintessential instrument of human life and social growth."[564]

Avoiding both extremes, he insists that "[i]n societies with a mass basis the constitution and statutes reach an audience far beyond the confines of the upper level of judges, civil servants, lawyers and professors," "[t]he constitutional charter ... affords an opportunity to focus, crystallize, and remind the body politic of the overriding goals of society."[565] Lasswell explained:

> When innovations are to be introduced that are likely to be resisted by influential minorities, the phrasing of the document can afford to *err in the direction of explicitness*, for if judges recruited from an earlier regime handle the new laws they will in all likelihood narrow uncongenial requirements by *strict construction*. If the purpose of a document is to assist in maintaining free institutions, and to contribute to their growth, the purpose will be served by *providing unequivocal verbal anchors for freedom*. Uneasiness about the security of private rights was a major factor in bringing about the first ten amendments to the Federal Constitution, making explicit certain fundamental guarantees that might have been considered implicit in the Constitution as a whole. *The uneasiness was justified*; and so was the resulting Bill of Rights. This is one of the ways in which "words engrossed on parchment" may be relied upon, in part at least, to "keep a government in order." Some balance is essential between conventional and novel words, phrases and conceptions.[566]

Notice, among other things, Lasswell's agreement that the defenders of the Bill of Rights were justified in thinking that the original Constitution, *as written*, did not sufficiently or reasonably imply, as a whole, the protections sought by

---

562   *Id.* at 181.
563   *Id.*
564   *Id.*
565   *Id.* at 182.
566   *Id.* at 182–83 (emphasis added).

the proposed amendments. Observe also that Lasswell's concern about strict construction suggests an endorsement of moderate, ordinary textualism and an indictment only of literalist or narrow textualism. Above all, realize how he conceives of the Bill of Rights as providing "unequivocal verbal anchors" for adjudication. These, as well as other provisions he notes, will carry either "conventional" or "novel" meanings. From the point of view of the drafter's advisor, what Lasswell recommends anticipating is how the text will be subsequently understood and enforced. The answer is to anticipate the kind of contemporary public or special meaning of words that contemporary Originalism concerns itself with by default.[567]

10   Overlap between New Haven and Contemporary Originalism

McDougal did not further develop the approach outlined in his Cardozo Lecture.[568] Lasswell had also recently passed away. Despite his commendable criticism of incipient Originalism, some of McDougal's core interpretive commitments substantially overlap with some of the tenets of contemporary Originalism. They are worth noting.

First, McDougal's concept of genuine interpretation, as applied to the Constitution, entails the ascertainment of the text's semantic meaning, which embodies the original expectations of the drafters and ratifiers. That meaning, which is binding and ascertained through historical and linguistic inquiry, is the public, ordinary meaning shared by drafters and ratifiers, absent evidence of special meaning or other usage. The point of interpretation is not just to

---

567   Lasswell's assertion that "[j]urisprudence is not properly a branch of lexicography," *id.* at 187 n.18, as well as similar ones, embodied the sentiment that the rational study of law cannot be focused solely on textual prescriptions, but instead should also pay attention to a society's actual enforcement of such prescriptions. It speaks to the Realism behind Lasswell and McDougal's view of the law, as distinguished from Positivism or Natural Law. It had nothing to do with legal interpretation. To the extent it did, Lasswell's sentiment, like McDougal's, was not an early indictment of the future interpretive practices of contemporary Originalism, but of those of original intent Originalism.

568   And, although certain ambiguity in McDougal's restatement of interpretive principles in that lecture seems deliberate, it is much more likely the product of an attempt to minimize the few apparent similarities between his theory and original intent Originalism, the object of his criticism. It is also likely the result of his recognition that Living Constitutionalism, at the time, was conceptually far superior, even if often condemnable. Uneasy to find a clear place in the middle, McDougal's seeming endorsement of one side of the debate should not mislead the reader acquainted with his prior work on interpretation.

ascertain meaning for its own sake. It is to discern the true meaning of our national "social contract," a document full of compromises, gaps, and ambiguities, drafted and ratified by the community and embodying actual protections and expectations. Evidence to be consulted includes not only community-wide linguistic usage, but the debates, private and public expectations about meaning and future applications, and shared understandings of fundamental public policy goals and purposes behind individual provisions and entire sections. The latter are often reflected in drafting history, early judicial cases, and works of jurisprudence, both preceding and following our founding. Substantially, then, McDougal and Lasswell's theory is quite compatible with contemporary Originalism's Fixed Meaning and Constraint theses.

Second, McDougal and Lasswell also recognized the interpretation-construction distinction, articulated as that between primary interpretation and other aspects of application, such as supplementation and policing or integration. Contemporary originalist theories of construction display much of what McDougal and Lasswell packed into the "application" and "supplementation" of constitutional prescriptions.

For example, despite rejecting the notion that the Constitution is a contract, Barnett describes the role of judicial interpretation as including a duty of good faith in construing its provisions—an analogy from the law of contracts.[569] Good faith interpretation and construction entail that, "[l]acking certainty about how to resolve a given case on the basis of the Constitution's linguistic meaning alone, judges must make a decision on the basis of some reason," to wit, by "formulat[ing] a rule with reference to the function—or functions—that a relevant provision is designed to perform."[570] Barnett stresses that "discovering the functions of the Constitution's various clauses and structural design entails investigation into the context in which they were enacted."[571] He recommends several guidelines for engaging in construction: (1) making a good faith effort to determine the original meaning of text and resolving the dispute, if possible, on that basis; (2) failing this, identifying the original functions or spirit of the provision; and (3) formulating a rule to be followed in the case that is (a) consistent with the text and "(b) designed to implement the original functions of (i) the provision at issue or, failing that, (ii) the structure in which the provision appears or, failing that, (iii) the Constitution as a whole."[572]

---

569   Barnett, *supra* note 323, at 30.
570   *Id.* at 32.
571   *Id.* at 34.
572   *Id.* at 35.

These are in the nature of principles of both content and procedure, reminiscent of McDougal's, which also require a judge's genuine and honest scrutiny of text and context (which includes constitutional function or purpose). They are also consistent with McDougal and Lasswell's recommendation that interpretation morph into supplementation (or construction) only where the text is ambiguous, silent, or vague.[573]

In the same vein as McDougal, Solum has also stressed the communicative process behind the Constitution as "attempting to communicate some content to future readers."[574] And just like McDougal, Solum warns that its "content is not fully determined by semantics and syntax," but instead "is almost always partly a function of the context."[575] Moreover, "constitutional construction is required to fill in the content of provisions that are vague, open textured, or irreducibly ambiguous."[576] This is what McDougal thought triggered supplementation. Among Solum's recommended techniques to be used in construction are: (1) precisification (i.e., making vague provisions more precise via rules that draw lines sorting borderline cases); (2) default rules (i.e., rendering open-textured provisions determinate through general default rules, such as Thayerian deference); and (3) precedent and historical practice (i.e., the use of history and prior decisions to liquidate meaning).[577] These principles, some of content and some of procedure, are also reminiscent of McDougal's, including the creation of presumptions in the course of examining text, context, and the community's linguistic usages.

In turn, Balkin argues that "articulating the original public meaning is not a simple job of reporting what happened at a certain magical moment in time;" rather, "it is a theoretical and selective reconstruction of elements of the past, brought to the present and employed in the present for present-day purposes."[578]

---

573   As McDougal emphatically explained:

It would be pointless to deny that a general consensus can on occasion be achieved as to "plain" meanings – in fact, this happens ... much of the time in human communication. Yet there would appear to be a limit to the usefulness of speculative hunches in areas of disagreement as to the "real" plain or ordinary meanings. A more constructive alternative would be for decision-makers to adopt a more thorough, systematic examination[.]

McDougal et al., *supra* note 395, at 252. *See also* Lasswell, *supra* note 550, at 197 ("If contradictions exist they are expected to be resolved by interpretation *unless they are unescapably inscribed in constitutional charters.*") (emphasis added).

574   Solum, *supra* note 323, at 272.
575   *Id.* at 273.
576   *Id.* at 294.
577   *Id.* at 295.
578   Balkin, *supra* note 323, at 78–79.

Much like McDougal, who deemed original public meaning the result of his-torical inquiry aided by a consideration of major purposes and requiring a solution oriented to contemporary needs, Balkin emphasizes both interpreta-tion and construction as primarily the creative construct of a decision maker. Balkin also proposes to restrict original public meaning to semantic meaning, leaving aside the public's expected applications, for example, which may still be relevant later to construction, and to regard this thin, semantic meaning as the binding component of the text.[579]

According to Balkin, "judges must also build out doctrines and institutions on top of the basic framework of the Constitution's original public meaning."[580] The theory, of course, "is a choice, not a description."[581] Like McDougal, who places the entire burden of interpretation on the shoulders of the decision maker's unavoidable duty to make certain choices, Balkin insists that a judge's choice of what background facts are relevant and why is shaped by his or her personal commitments.[582] As attentive as McDougal to the effects of the original understandings we settle on upon present adjudication, Balkin notes that Originalism "filters ... the past because it is designed to produce a legal meaning that lawyers living today might actually use."[583] He argues that "[i]n the practice of constitutional construction, we employ history not as a com-mand but as a resource," and that "we may be more willing-and better able-to take sides in disagreements among constitutional participants in the past, and to say that some constructions were better than others, and more faithful to the Constitution rightly understood."[584] The idea comports with McDougal, including the intuition that, in applying prescriptions through supplementa-tion or integration, decision makers must consider how prior generations—inside and outside of precedent—have resolved disputes over meaning and engage in an evaluation of their own.

Similarly, Whittington's own work on construction is reminiscent of sev-eral of McDougal's intuitions. The former described it as "a creative task involving normative choices in a realm of constitutional indeterminacies."[585] Critical to the legitimacy of judicial construction is that judges "faithful[ly]"

---

579   *Id.* at 80.
580   *Id.* at 80–81.
581   *Id.* at 81.
582   *Id.* at 82.
583   *Id.* at 83.
584   *Id.* at 93.
585   Whittington, *supra* note 252, at 128.

"maintain constitutional understandings widely shared by other political actors."[586] Notably, Whittington commended recognizing the concept and practice of construction, regardless of label, because it helps external observers understand how our constitutionalism actually works.[587] The reader is now familiar with McDougal's emphasis on realistic approaches to ascertaining and implementing widely shared expectations, as well as on the unavoidable and creative choice that application of constitutional prescriptions imposes on the decision maker.

Lastly, McDougal problematized the use of a reasonable person standard in adjudicating ordinary meaning well before contemporary originalists first became troubled by it. Whether the correct construct should be that of a reasonable reader, lawyer, or other kind of person contemporaneously or hypothetically engaged in the relevant process of communication is an aspect of Originalism that is yet to reflect a considered consensus. There is not only an empirical aspect to this debate, but also a normative one. And much of current debate on the issue downplays overt normative reasoning in this regard.

11　New Haven's Suggestive Insights

The conceptual overlap between New Haven's interpretive theory and much of contemporary Originalism is suggestive. But I'd like to stress two features of New Haven that I believe contemporary Originalism, no less than Living Constitutionalism, could profit from: the turns to international law in trying to systematize and harmonize domestic interpretive principles and to normative reasoning. Part of a tradition that spans from Story to Scalia, McDougal believed that the Constitution required no special theory of interpretation, since it is a species of the same kind of agreement that rears its head every now and then, both domestically and internationally, before courts for adjudication. Naturally, he turned to his area of expertise, international law, an arena with a wealth of jurisprudence on functionally indistinguishable constitutive processes of communication. These turns may be promising for several reasons.

First, the long-standing recognition of the interpretation-construction distinction in international law is obvious.[588] One in the development of which

---

586　*Id.* at 129.
587　*Id.* at 134.
588　*See, e.g.,* Anastasios Gourgourinis, *The Distinction Between Interpretation and Application of Norms in International Adjudication,* 2 J. Int'l Dispute Settlement 31 (2011).

McDougal and Lasswell themselves, of course, played a role.[589] Accordingly, and assuming the truth of the assumption that constitutions are not different in kind from international or other agreements, there is much that the venerable body of international jurisprudence on the interpretation-construction distinction may contribute to our debate, especially by way of guidelines and principles.

Second, the growing literature on the overlap and relationship between principles of constitutional and treaty interpretation, as well as their status as customary international law, should inform our domestic debate.[590] Otherwise, it is destined to remain parochial. This includes studying the reciprocal phenomena of the constitutionalization of international law and the internationalization of constitutional law.[591] If Originalism is not merely an American obsession, but objectively says something true or useful of what constitutions like ours are and do, then international practice with regard to functionally identical instruments may inform the debate. And enough international practice, as we know, may eventually bind. Assuming it true, as our own courts do,[592] that the articles in the Vienna Convention on the Law of Treaties concerning interpretation have attained binding customary international law status, is not the United States bound to employ the Convention's Vattelian textualism in interpreting its own treaties? And yet, Vattelianism is at odds with contemporary Originalism. This would mean that the same supreme law of the land—a treaty on one hand, and our Constitution, on the other—would receive, by necessity, two different kinds of reading.

Third, and relatedly, a systematic treatment of the overlap between principles of constitutional interpretation and general principles of law in the

---

589   *Cf. id.* at 47 n.65.

590   *See, e.g.,* Kristen Walker, *International Law as a Tool of Constitutional Interpretation,* 28 Monash U. L. Rev. 85 (2002); Noam Kolt, *Cosmopolitan Originalism: Revisiting the Role of International Law in Constitutional Interpretation,* 41 Melb. U. L. Rev. 182 (2017); Rex D. Glensy, *Constitutional Interpretation through a Global Lens,* 75 Mo. L. Rev. 1171 (2010); Julian Arato, *Treaty Interpretation and Constitutional Transformation: Informal Change in International Organizations,* 38 Yale J. Int'l L. 289 (2013); S.I. Strong, *Beyond the Self-Execution Analysis: Rationalizing Constitutional, Treaty and Statutory Interpretation in International Commercial Arbitration,* 53 Va. J. Int'l L. 499 (2013); Michael Ramsey, *The Constitution's Text and Customary International Law,* 106 Geo. L.J. 1747 (2018).

591   *See, e.g.,* Yuval Shany, *How Supreme Is the Supreme Law of the Land – Comparative Analysis of the Influence of International Human Rights Treaties upon the Interpretation of Constitutional Texts by Domestic Courts,* 31 Brook. J. Int'l L. 341 (2006); Maurizio Arcari, *Creeping Constitutionalization and Fragmentation of International Law: From Constitutional to Consistent Interpretation,* 33 Polish Y.B. Int'l L. 9 (2013).

592   *See, e.g., Ehrlich v American Airlines,* 360 F 3d 366, 373 n.5 (2d Cir. 2004).

context of constitutional adjudication would necessarily be more informative, factually and normatively, than ordinary comparative work, the focus of which is primarily transnational, not international. Just as with customary international law in the realm of interpretation, general principles of interpretation can bind. At the very least, they can inform.

Lastly, New Haven's outlook on the interpretation-construction distinction is not just passive or descriptive. It seeks to be prescriptive and normative. While Barnett speaks of "function" and Balkin of "purpose," McDougal speaks of "shared expectations" about "great aims" and "fundamental policy goals." Unlike Barnett, Balkin, and other originalists, however, McDougal does not merely relegate ascertainment of function or purpose to historical or factual inquiry. Where meaning is at its thinnest, factual inquiry is of no help, and construction is yet unavoidable, McDougal proposes that the latter be performed only within the bounds of an empirical notion of human flourishing derivable from our own Constitution. He means no philosophical free-for-all. But he does ask us to address, at both a normative and empirical level, the unavoidably creative task involved in such instances of construction.[593]

In this context, the notion of human flourishing or dignity stands for two separate but interrelated concepts. On one hand, it means that public order of freedom that McDougal describes as maximizing everyone's participation in the processes of shaping and sharing the things we all value. An empirical and anthropological concept of the common good.[594] On the other hand, and more narrowly, it means the specifically American arrangement of such order,

---

[593] For an overview of the historical, conceptual, and political role of creative choice in constitutional adjudication, *see* Jeffrey M. Shaman, Constitutional Interpretation: Illusion and Reality 1–25 (2001).

[594] *See, e.g.,* Myres McDougal & Gertrude C. K. Leighton, *The Rights of Man in the World Community: Constitutional Illusions Versus Rational Action,* 59 Yale L.J. 60, 61 (1949) ("It is for values ... that men have always framed constitutions, established governments, and sought the delicate balancing of power and formulation of fundamental principle necessary to preserve human rights against all possible aggressors, governmental or other."); Harold D. Lasswell, *A Brief Discourse about Method in the Current Madness,* 57 Am. Soc'y Int'l L. Proc. 72, 76 (1963) ("Consult the constitutional and statutory documents of practically every nation state and you will find that the will and welfare of the people are the proclaimed source and aim of organized society."). "Human dignity," in McDougal and Lasswell's sense, was the equivalent of the concept of a "free society," and did not stand for a separate, obscure, or inherently abstract notion. *See, e.g.,* Myres S. McDougal, *Harold Dwight Lasswell 1902–1978,* 88 Yale L.J. 675, 678 (1979) (referring to "the basic values of human dignity, *or of a free society*") (emphasis added). The notion corresponded, in large measure, with that of the rule of law. *See* Lasswell, *supra* note 546, at 157 ("The growth of constitutional government, of the *Rechtstaat* in place of the *Machtstaat,* is the expression of the determination to protect the (ruled) community against the abuse of the very

as reflected in the fundamental values *actually embedded* in our Constitution.[595] The overlap between these two meanings is not perfect. In cases of insoluble doubt during construction, McDougal's suggestion is that the best interpretive theory should facilitate and default to approximating our current public order to its ideal. Not our *contemporary* ideal, but the *constitutionally entrenched* ideal. This, of course, entails *some* moral reading of critical clauses and original purposes. Although most contemporary Originalism pays lip service to residual and inevitable moral reasoning, it has yet to develop anything resembling a normative theory in this regard. Some may be skeptical of the *content* of McDougal and Lasswell's solution. But none can disparage its *form*: any promising normative guidance must entail a method rational and empirical enough to make it workable both in our democracy and elsewhere.[596]

Siegfried Wiessner, one of McDougal's associates, recently asked: "What could this values-based order consist of, in more granular form, for the interpretation of the Constitution of the United States?" He answered: "It ought to be based on a principled and rational approach and reflect the common interest."[597] "[A]s reflecting this common interest," he proposes

> the concept of an order of human dignity as defined by ... McDougal and ... Lasswell. This order would maximize access by all to the processes of shaping and sharing all things humans empirically value: power, wealth,

---

function which brings community into being. Progress in this direction has been one of the most signal advances in respect for the dignity of human personality.").

595   *See, e.g.,* Lasswell, *supra* note 540, at 57 ("I do not intend to present an idiosyncratic conception of human dignity. What I have in mind is widely understood since it is the dominant theme of the Declaration of Independence in American tradition and of the recent Charter of Human Rights.").

596   What I find most interesting about New Haven's normative component is that it has been incorporated into its interpretive and adjudicative theories by way of procedural principles and presumptions. We could label this a "procedural" normative approach. So, for example, Barnett has proposed a presumption of liberty. *See* Randy Barnett, Restoring the Lost Constitution: The Presumption of Liberty (2003). Presumptions are the subject of constitutional construction. Others, however, propose the use of ultimate value standards that are not embedded in our Constitution for the construction zone. This we can call a more "substantive" normative approach. I find the latter more problematic. However, whether or not New Haven's interpretive theory would allow for the incorporation of what I call "second-order" expectations of authority, based on international or transnational substantive standards, is a different question yet to be developed. *See* Gonzalez-Rivera, *supra* note 388, at 351–61 (explaining the role and content of second order expectations in New Haven's theory of minimal authority expectations behind law and the rule of law).

597   Siegfried Wiessner, *Reading the Constitution*, Constitution Day Address, St. Thomas University College of Law, Miami, Florida (September 22, 2022) (on file with author).

affection, well-being, enlightenment, skills, respect, and rectitude. After all, the law should serve human beings, not the other way round. The content of open concepts should be filled using this approach, as the goal of law should be the thriving and flourishing of human beings endowed with intrinsic dignity. It should be empowering, not limiting. Principled and rational, this guiding light would transcend decision-making from the gut, based on personal idiosyncrasies or rank partisan motivations.[598]

I agree. Debate over degrees of similarity aside, a successful theory of construction, Originalist or not, must take a form *not unlike* that of McDougal and Lasswell. At least not *in kind*. Devoid of any normative commitments, Originalism is a well bound to run dry. A method that only insufficiently, and arbitrarily, taps into the normative springs over which our Constitution is built. Our charter is not *aimless*.

Originalism should not overcompensate for Living Constitutionalism's unprincipled moral musings by opposing all moral reasoning on principle. *Some* principles must shed light on the darkest places of the construction zone. As an originalist, I concede that it is a challenge not just to further develop construction theory in *originalist* terms, but also to do so by integrating New Haven's normative ideas.[599] Yet, as McDougal and Lasswell noted, the concept of human flourishing and dignity undergird our written and unwritten Constitutions. A fact that Originalism must explain and accommodate.[600]

---

598   *Id.*

599   *See, e.g.,* Neomi Rao, *On the Use and Abuse of Dignity in Constitutional Law*, 14 Columbia L. Rev. 201 (2008) (arguing there are consequential differences between American and European conceptions of human dignity when applied to constitutional reasoning). Of course, we should not refrain to do justice by our Constitution's *own* concept of human dignity, informed by our own history, merely because we fear confusing it with its homologue in foreign traditions. Again, if so, we'd be reading less in the Constitution than what it reasonably says in an attempt not to read more. A false, and tragic, choice.

600   Although express provisions for human dignity are a feature of foreign post-World War II constitutions, the concept is implied in our own Constitution. *See* Vicki Jackson, *Constitutional Dialogue and Human Dignity: States and Transnational Constitutional Discourse*, 65 Montana L. Rev. 15, 16 (2004) ("The U.S. Constitution does not refer specifically to human dignity. Yet there are some cognate concepts in the Constitution's text, such as the ban on cruel and unusual punishments, the protections of the due process clause, and others that have been developed in the U. S. Supreme Court's constitutional jurisprudence."); Lawrence H. Tribe, *Equal Dignity: Speaking Its Name*, 129 Harv. L. Rev. 16, 21 (2015) ("[D]ignity is not some alien import with no place in our constitutional tradition. Just as Germany and South Africa adopted universal human dignity as a loadstar of their legal systems after rejecting devastating racist ideologies, so too the United States adopted the Fourteenth Amendment in the wake of the Civil War for strikingly similar reasons – to

Call this "Originalism with a Human Face," the opposite of "Dictionary-Game," "Crypto Normative," and "Value-Free" Originalisms. Wiessner's invitation is one I hope does not fall on deaf ears.

12   Closing Remarks

There's a lot to Jefferson's concern that we should render the Constitution a "blank" paper through construction.[601] And yet, construct we must. However, most non-Originalisms undo the complex but real distinction between what the law is and what it should be to engage in an amorphous process of interpretation calling for contemporary meaning or an outright abandonment of the Constitution as written. They travel perilously under the banner of "Why Should the Constitution Deserve Our Fidelity?" And they are not being rhetorical—for many reasons, ranging from the practical to the normative. Yet, constitutional interpretation, whether art, science, or neither, cannot be conceived of as entailing a sort of Schrödinger's Dead Cat Paradox: holding meaning forever indeterminate, despite history or precedent, until a case arises that "settles" it in light of *present* wants in a sort of *contemporary observer's effect*. That's worse than blank paper. And thoroughly unempirical.

Contemporary Originalism preserves the distinction between what the law is and what it should be, and is currently embarked on the enterprise of rationally ascertaining, in the most principled and empirical manner possible, how constitutional adjudication ascertains what the law is, occasionally implementing and applying it in ways that ever so slightly push the law along the path it should take, but always consistent with the original meaning and purpose of text, at whatever level of generality either is construed. It is Originalism

---

atone for our nation's own original sin and extend our Constitution's promises to all citizens."); W.A. Parent, *Constitutional Commands of Human Dignity: A Bicentennial Essay in Honor of Mr. Justice William J. Brennan, Jr.* , 5 Can. J. L. & Jurisprudence 237, 240 (1992) ("[T]he value of human dignity enjoys a preeminent place in U.S. constitutional morality."). Some have even labeled it the "Dignity Canon." Noah B. Lindell, *The Dignity Canon*, 27 Cornell J. of L. & Pub. Pol'y 415 (2017). For a historical overview of the idea in American constitutional law, *see* Aharon Barak, Human Dignity: The Constitutional Value and the Constitutional Right 185–208 (2015). For its relationship with human rights and the argument that constitutional interpretation theory must default to their advancement, *see* Vincent J. Samar, *Rethinking Constitutional Interpretation to Affirm Human Rights and Dignity*, 47 Hastings Const. L.Q. 83, 84 (2019) ("Human rights serve as the glue for binding the different interpretations together under a higher-ordered set of values, whether by adoption of amendments or Court interpretations.").

601   Powell, *supra* note 44, at 13.

that, living up to McDougal and Lasswell's advice, looks to what contemporary Political Science, Linguistics, History, and other disciplines have to tell us about the communicative process that law is, has been, and will continue to be. I understand that much of Living Constitutionalism deems Originalisms sheep in sheep's clothing; seemingly modest theories with much to be modest about. The opposite is true. Living Constitutionalism is a proud family of theories. But one with little to be proud about, at least when it calls into question *all* sense of fidelity to the Constitution. Even its defenders acknowledge that it is not a "coherently formulated competitor" against Originalism.[602] Simply put, a *written* constitution one cannot betray—whether by reading too little or too much in it—is no constitution at all.

Constitutional interpretation is neither an obscure science, as decried by de Toqueville, nor Maxcy Zane's romanticized, rational, exhaustive, and unimprovable art. Far from it. Nor should it be identified with the opposite extremes of formalistic, rigid, literalist, or ahistorical textualism, on the one hand, or cynical, relativistic, and unprincipled views, on the other, that text is irremediably elastic and only present policy choices may remedy the defect, unanchored from and unconcerned about the bargains and expectations prior generations succeeded in crystallizing into words. Often at a steep price.

McDougal and Lasswell's theory of constitutional law as centuries-long communicative action and interpretation primarily consisting of ascertaining and implementing the public's original, shared expectations in the manner most consistent with the values embedded in the text is relevant. Today as much as fifty years ago. *Especially* today, given how contemporary Originalism has caught up with many of New Haven's prescient intuitions. Whether a dialogue between them takes place now, an entire generation later, is beside the point. What matters most, however, is the promise in New Haven's expansive view of free societies, which prompts us not only to make sense of new, principled ways of interpreting and applying our Constitution, but also to do so without despairing that our success must forever be parochial. At least in principle, whatever approach succeeds in best interpreting and enforcing our Constitution could and should have much in common with those that do the same across our global community. After all, the search for truth in interpretation is not an American affair. So, aside from having a human face, Originalism can and should be meaningfully cosmopolitan.

---

602   David Strauss, *Common Law Constitutional Interpretation*, 63 U. of Ch. L. Rev. 877, 879 (1996).

PART 3

World Order

∴

CHAPTER 10

Ukraine, "Who Decides," and Minimum World Public Order

*Nicholas Rostow**

> We understand that we don't always want to do the right thing, but what they [the audience] have to ask themselves is, "Am I willing to live with the consequences?"
>
> BILL RUSSELL1

∴

1 Introduction

Russia's second invasion of Ukraine in February 2022, intensifying Russia's war launched in 2014, may have torn up the international legal system. In 1945, the world community came together to restate its most important values and create an international organization through which to advance and defend it and avoid a repetition of the two World Wars that gave birth to that organization. The UN founders wanted a workable institution but not a world government. The system never has been more than imperfect and a work in progress, for it reflects the world's history and social and economic development in diverse political systems. In 1945 and today, no state would have agreed to put its ultimate safety

---

* Member of the New York and District of Columbia bars. Senior Partner at Zumpano, Patricios resident in the New York office, Zumpano Patricios & Popok, PLLC, Senior Research Scholar, Yale Law School, and Fellow, Center for Advanced Studies on Terrorism. Among other positions held: Visiting Professor, Cornell Law School, Spring Terms 2022, 2023. I was Legal Adviser to the National Security Council, 1987–93, Staff Director, Senate Select Committee on Intelligence, 1999–2000, Senior Policy Adviser and General Counsel to the U.S. Permanent Representative to the United Nations, 2001–05. The views expressed are my own and do not necessarily reflect the views of the U.S. government or any other institution with which I have been or am affiliated.

1 Harvey Araton, *A Gravelly Voice Dispensing Wisdom Worth the Wait*, N.Y. Times, Aug. 2, 2022, at B8 cols. 2–3.

solely in the hands of such an organization. Russia's invasion of Ukraine has shown again that the UN machinery is not the only way in which the international community can defend its values and respond to aggression. Such responses provide an essential alternative to anarchy in a nuclear age. They show that the international legal system is not a suicide pact when the international machinery cannot address a fundamental challenge so long as the community response is consistent with those values. That is the theme of this chapter.

All states are subject to the norms of the UN Charter. By its terms, the UN Charter is the supreme law of the world; any inconsistent treaty or behavior is without legal force or effect.[2] International organizations like the United Nations, the European Union, and the African Union, to name three, possess certain powers granted by member states.[3] Within the state system and the international structures states have created, the law-making process of authoritative decision has become increasingly complex. The basic law, the UN Charter, has undergone little change since 1945, but the number of actors with power effectively to influence the definition of the international community and that community's values has increased. Decisionmakers apply the law in any given situation in light of these values. Even the most determined leaders who do not respect the values of human dignity and non-aggression claim the protection of other values, such as sovereign equality and non-interference in internal affairs and the sanctity of international agreements and contracts.

All states thus are caught in a complex web of values. Decisionmakers of whatever stripe, applying or claiming to apply the law, even if only giving it lip service, add to the law in question rather like the way a flowing river constantly adds to sediment on its bottom. "Every judgment has a generative power," wrote Justice Benjamin N. Cardozo 100 years ago about the judicial process.[4] His insight is equally appropriate to states and UN bodies in the international system. Their actions add to the development of the law. In the best of circumstances, they hew to Justice Holmes' admonition about common-law judges that they "must and do legislate, but they do so only interstitially."[5] He might have written "sedimentarily." "Who decides" covers the panoply of actors and actions in a global community. It thus concerns processes in which power of various kinds is exerted and resisted and decisions at different levels, often with widespread effects, are taken. Authoritative decision-making begins but

---

2   UN Charter art. 103.

3   In the case of the European Union, the creators or at least some of them hoped that it would evolve into a new state—the United States of Europe.

4   Benjamin N. Cardozo, The Nature of the Judicial Process 21 (1921).

5   Quoted in *id.* at 69.

does not end with states.[6] Nor does it begin or end with the United Nations and its many parts.

Russia, China, and others argue for new approaches to international relations.[7] They resent a system that does not allow them or any other state a free hand to do whatever they want. At the same time, they are jealous of their national prerogatives, including the right not to suffer interference in their "internal affairs" as they define them.[8] They (and so-called "realists," who always, or at least often, seem to favor appeasement of aggression) operate on the basis of the most-often quoted part of the Melian Dialogue: "the strong do what they have the power to do and the weak accept what they have to accept"[9] as reflecting an appropriate attitude toward international relations. While they may recall that part of Thucydides' Melian Dialogue, they ignore a crucially important piece of wisdom and international law thrown back at the Athenians:

> *Melians*: Then in our view (since you force us to leave justice out of account and to confine ourselves to self-interest)—in our view it is at any rate useful that you should not destroy a principle that is to the general good of all men—namely, that in the case of all who fall into danger there should be such a thing as fair play and just dealing, and that such people should be allowed to use and to profit by arguments that fall short of mathematical accuracy. And this is a principle that affects you as much as anybody, since your own fall would be visited by the most terrible vengeance and would be an example to the world.[10]

This statement of more than 2,000 years ago brings to mind, and reinforces the relevance of, Montesquieu's insights that law reflects the nature of things and that the possibility of justice predated formal law.[11] Comity is an important

---

6   *See generally* Rosalyn Higgins, *International Law in a Changing International System*, 58(1) Camb. L.J. 78 (1999). An appropriate metaphor for the process might be the opening few notes of Beethoven's Ninth Symphony.

7   *See, e.g.*, Marc Bennetts & Richard Spencer, *Putin Flies to Iran to Cement New anti-West Alliance*, The Times [London], July 19, 2022, *available at https://www.thetimes.co.uk/article /putin-flies-to-iran-to-cement-new-anti-west-alliance-dvtn2psms*; Jerome A. Cohen, *Law and Power in China's International Relations*, 52 N.Y.U. J. Int'l L. & Pol. 123 (2019); Chris Buckley & Steben Lee Myers, *Xi Builds Security Fortress for China and Himself*, N.Y. Times, Aug. 7, 2022, at A1 col. 2.

8   *Id.*

9   Thucydides, The Peloponnesian War 402 (Rex Warner trans. 1954).

10   *Id.*

11   Charles de Secondat, Baron de Montesquieu, The Spirit of the Laws 1–4 ([1748] 1900).

idea even great powers need to remember; so is the consequence of operating on the basis of hope rather than reason: Athens was defeated and devastated within a dozen years of the Melian Dialogue.

The present international system, which includes international structures and international law, owes more to wars than to any other single source.[12] Russia's invasion of Ukraine, however it turns out, already has concentrated the collective, international mind on strategic, political, and legal issues with the intensity of the prospect of a hanging[13] and much more than the equally unprovoked Russian invasions of Georgia in 2008 and Ukraine in 2014. The invasion again raises questions about the international system and the nature and future of international law as they developed since World War I and the end of the Cold War.

Any evaluation of the impact of the Ukraine war on the international legal system inescapably must analyze the issue of authoritative decision, in other words, "who decides." It also requires another look at the concept of "minimum world public order": does it represent a realistic conception of, and aspiration for, international politics?

2   A System of States and Authoritative Decision-making in a Complicated World

The world structure is based on states. A state is a political division, consisting of a group of people, territory that may or may not be defined by frontiers recognized as final,[14] with a government sovereign within its territory subject to international law, and with authority to enforce its own laws.[15] Each state's

---

12   I recall reading B.H. Liddell Hart (I no longer remember which of his books—*The Ghost of Napoleon* (1934), perhaps) many, many years ago to the effect that military thinkers and leaders have had a bigger impact on more people than all the philosophers put together because millions of soldiers (and civilians) have died or been wounded or simply had their lives turned upside down as a result of the effects of their ideas and their actions in the field.

13   "Depend upon it, Sir, when a man knows he is to be hanged in a fortnight, it concentrates his mind wonderfully." James Boswell, The Life of Samuel Johnson (1791) 748 (1992).

14   For example, the State of Israel came into existence without recognized, final borders.

15   Montevideo Convention on the Rights and Duties of States, Dec. 26, 1933. *Available at* https://treaties.un.org/pages/showdetails.aspx?objid=0800000280166aef. This Convention set forth the minimum qualifications for statehood as a permanent population, defined territory, government, and capacity to enter into foreign relations. What each of these qualifications may mean in a particular case may be subject to inquiry, appraisal, and, ultimately, authoritative decision. The Convention specifies that a state with a federal

sovereignty or power is bounded only by the existence of other, equally sovereign states and such law as states accept as binding. Each state exercises its sovereign power according to its own constitutional process.

In recent decades, the idea that sovereignty implies responsibility has taken hold of people's imaginations. In 2001, for example, the International Commission on Intervention and State Sovereignty, created by the Canadian government, issued a report called *Responsibility to Protect*.[16] The Commission analyzed sovereignty as defined in international law. It concluded that the very legal character of sovereignty implied a requirement of responsible behavior through respecting the sovereignty and territory of other states, the norm of non-intervention, and the requirement to protect a state's own citizens. The Commission wrote: "First, [responsibility] implies that the state authorities are responsible for the functions of protecting the safety and lives of citizens and promotion of their welfare. Secondly, it suggests that the national political authorities are responsible to the citizens internally and to the international community through the UN. And thirdly, it means that the agents of state are responsible for their actions; that is to say, they are accountable for their acts of commission or omission."[17] In 2005, heads of state and government at the United Nations adopted a resolution seeking to commit themselves to act on the basis of the *Responsibility to Protect*: "Each individual State has the responsibility to protect its populations from genocide, war crimes, ethnic cleansing and crimes against humanity. This responsibility entails the prevention of such crimes, including their incitement, through appropriate and necessary means. We accept that responsibility and will act in accordance with it."[18] Russia's

---

structure constitutes a single unit in international law. A-40: Convention on Rights and Duties of States, Virtual Library of Inter-American Peace Initiatives, VIRTUAL LIBRARY OF INTER-AMERICAN PEACE INITIATIVES, https://www.oas.org/sap/peacefund/Virtual Library/SeventhIntConference/Convention/GeneralInformationOfTheTreaty.pdf (last visited Jul. 27, 2022). https://www.oas.org/sap/peace fund/VirtualLibrary/SeventhInt Conference/Convention/GeneralInformationOfTheTreaty.pdf. Garry Wills noted that, after Lincoln's Gettysburg Address, the United States became a singular instead of a plural noun (it went from "the United States are" to "the United States is." Wills ascribes this change to Lincoln. That conclusion may be true as a matter of doctrine. It also is true to see it as a consequence of the Civil War itself and the victory for national unity. Garry Wills, Lincoln at Gettysburg: The Words that Remade America 145 (1992).

16   International Commission on Intervention and State Sovereignty, The Responsibility to Protect (2001), *available at* https://idl-bnc-idrc.dspacedirect.org/bitstream/handle /10625/18432/IDL-18432.pdf?sequence=6&isAllowed=y.

17   *Id.* at 13.

18   G.A. Res. 60/1, 2005 World Summit Outcome, ¶ 138 (Sept. 16, 2005).

wars with Georgia and Ukraine showed that these words did not resonate in Moscow.

By 2022, events, including the invasion of Ukraine, had sapped confidence in the idea of the responsibility to protect and governments' commitment to it. Among the most important blows were the 2003 invasion of Iraq and the 2011 attacks on Libya. Both events damaged the standing of the United States because the United States seemed to be acting as judge and jury in regard to Iraq and, later, even Libya. Neither the context of September 11, 2001, nor the fact that the 2003 invasion arguably was lawful mitigated the negative impact. The argument for lawfulness rested in the main on the proposition that, as a matter of international law, the invasion merely continued in the post-September 11, 2001, context, military operations since 1991 to enforce the Security Council's requirements with respect to limitations on Iraq's armaments and inspections of suspected sites of weapons of mass destruction. Of course, the 2003 invasion was a more intense use of force than even the sustained bombing campaign against Iraq in 1998.[19]

---

19   For a defense of the lawfulness of the invasion, see, e.g., William H. Taft IV (then Legal Adviser of the U.S. Department of State) & Todd F. Buchwald, *Preemption, Iraq, and International Law*, 97 Am. J. Int'l L. 557 (2003), and Nicholas Rostow, *Determining the Lawfulness of the 2003 Campaign Against Iraq*, 34 Isr. Y.B. Hum. Rts. 15 (2004). For an interesting assessment of Operation Desert Fox, the 1998 U.S.–U.K. bombing campaign against Iraq, see William M. Arkin, *The Difference was in the Details*, Wash. Post (Jan. 17, 1999), https://www.washingtonpost.com/wp-srv/inatl/longterm/iraq/analysis.htm. *See also* Rostow, *supra*, at note 44 (enforcement of no-fly zones required thousands of individual sorties). The UN Legal Counsel in 1992, Carl-August Fleischhauer, a future judge of the International Court of Justice (1994–2003), wrote the UN Secretary-General that the cease-fire at the end of Operation Desert Storm in 1991 and UN Security Council Resolutions 686 (1991), S.C. Res. 686 (Mar. 2, 1991), and 687 (1991), S.C. Res. 687 (Apr. 3, 1991), imposing obligations on Iraq, suspended but did not terminate the authorization to use force set forth in UN Security Council Resolution 678 (1990), S.C. Res. 678 (Nov. 29, 1990). His conclusion was that the UN Security Council had to agree: "Since the authorization to use force against Iraq as contained in paragraph 2 of resolution 678 has not been set aside by the cease-fire or resolutions 686 or 687, a sufficiently serious violation of [Iraq's obligations] [(the text contains a typographical error here: "serious violation of Iraq's violation of its obligations under 787")] under 687 withdraws the basis for the establishment if the cease-fire and can re-open the way into the use of the authorization and renewed use of force. The precondition is, however, that the Security Council is in agreement there is a violation and that the Security Council considers the violation sufficiently serious to destroy the basis of the cease-fire. ... Under no circumstances should this assessment be left to individual Member States. Since the original authorization came from the Council, the return to it should also come from that source, and not be left to the subjective evaluation made by individual Member States and their Governments." Fleischhauer to The Secretary-General [Boutros Boutros-Ghali], Aug. 18, 1992. Fleischhauer expected that the Security Council

With regard to Libya, the North Atlantic Treaty Organization (NATO) joined the United States as target for severe criticism. In 2011, at the behest of the Arab League, the Security Council invoked the responsibility to protect and authorized military action.[20] The operation led to the overthrow and killing of Muammar Qaddafi. Russia is not alone in viewing NATO's military actions and consequences as having exceeded the UN Security Council mandate.[21]

---

would express its view by resolution or presidential statement. His view as to form can be read expansively or narrowly. He seems not to have noted the irony that UN Security Council members vote according to instructions (provided the delegations receive them). The votes therefore reflect exactly that "subjective evaluation" by governments Fleischhauer's memorandum suggests does not result in Security Council action. The Security Council is a political body, not some detached Sanhedrin. Fleischhauer's reasoning was in line with what then-Russian UN Ambassador Sergey Lavrov told the Security Council in 1998. U.N. Secretary General, *Letter from the Secretary-General Addressed to the President of the Security Council*, 4, U.N. Doc. S/PV.3955 (Dec. 16, 1998), quoted in Rostow, *supra*, at 25. Fleischhauer's conclusion was not quite in line with what Secretary General Boutros Boutros Ghali signed off on in 1996, Introduction to the United Nations Blue Book Series volume IX: The United Nations and the Iraq-Kuwait Conflict, 1990–1996 29 (1996). The United States and the United Kingdom argued that Security Council Resolution 1441 (2002), S.C. Res. 1441 (Nov. 8, 2002), provided sufficient authority for the invasion. *See* Taft & Buchwald, *supra*; *The Memorandum of Advice on the Use of Force Against Iraq, provided by the Attorney General's Department and the Department of Foreign Affairs and Trade March 18, 2003*, Sydney Morning Herald (March 19, 2003), https://www.smh.com.au /world/middle-east/the-governments-legal-advice-on-using-force-20030319-gdggf5 .html; Committee of Privy Counsellors, *Report of the Official UK Inquiry into Iraq, Volume V*, (July 6, 2016), https://assets.publishing.service.gov.uk/government/uploads/system /uploads/attachment_data/file/535419/The_Report_of_the_Iraq_Inquiry_-_Volume_V .pdf. The Russians and others, including Secretary General Kofi Annan (Patrick E. Tyler, *Annan Says Iraq War Was 'Illegal,'* N.Y. Times (Sept. 16, 2004), https://www.nytimes. com/2004/09/16/international/annan-says-iraq-war-was-illegal.html, disagreed. It often is assumed that Russia and possibly France would have vetoed a resolution after 1441 explicitly authorizing a use of force against Iraq. None was offered for adoption. *See* the discussions in Rostow, *supra*, at notes 53 (reproducing the advice of France's Ambassador to the United States and former Ambassador to the United Nations not to seek a new resolution) and 59; Jane Stromseth, *Law and Force After Iraq: A Transitional Moment*, 97 Am. J. Int'l L. 628 (2003). In the wake of the terrorist attacks of September 11, 2001, emotions ran high, and careful appraisal of events was difficult. *See* Nicholas Rostow & Harvey Rishikof, *9/11 and After: Legal Issues, Lessons, and Irregular Conflict*, in Richard D. Hooker, Jr., & Joseph Collins, eds., Lessons Encountered: Learning from the Long War 347, 378–81 (2015). *Available at* https://ndupress.ndu.edu/Media/News/News-Article-View/Article/717665 /lessons-encountered-learning-from-the-long-war/.

20   S.C Res. 1973, preamble (Mar. 17, 2011), https://documents-dds-ny.un.org/doc/UNDOC /GEN/N11/268/39/PDF/N1126839.pdf?OpenElement.

21   *See, e.g., Full text of Vladimir Putin's Speech Announcing 'Special Military Operation' in Ukraine*, The Print (Feb. 24, 2022, 5:18 PM) https://theprint.in/world/full-text-of-vladimir -putins-speech-announcing-special-military-operation-in-ukraine/845714/. The UN Security

Russia's invasion of Ukraine restored some of the U.S. and NATO standing lost in Iraq and Libya, at least in comparison to Russia. It seems that every international institution wanted to do something to help Ukraine, even when its formal competence appears to lie elsewhere. The International Court of Justice (ICJ) revealed itself to be a case in point. In 2022, Ukraine brought suit against Russia in the ICJ under the Genocide Convention on the ground that Russia alleged genocide by Ukraine as a reason for using force in Eastern Ukraine. The Genocide Convention provides for ICJ dispute resolution in the event parties, such as Ukraine and Russia, disagree about the interpretation or application of the Convention. The Court noted that it "is mindful of the purposes and principles of the United Nations Charter and *of its own responsibilities in the maintenance of international peace and security as well as in the peaceful settlement of disputes under the Charter and the Statute of the Court.*"[22] Nothing in the UN Charter or the Statute of the International Court of Justice would suggest that the Court's responsibilities go beyond adjudication. In any event, the Court's statement of its responsibilities seems to have reflected a majority view. Judge Bennouna, who disagreed with the legal basis for the Court's holding, voted with the majority "because I felt compelled by this tragic situation, in which terrible suffering is being inflicted on the Ukrainian people."[23] The ICJ is not so restricted in its function as U.S. federal courts under Article III of the U.S. Constitution.[24] Yet, the UN Charter is clear that the Court is "the principal judicial organ of the United Nations" empowered only to decide cases between or among states that have agreed to the Court's jurisdiction and to give advisory

---

Council Resolution on Libya, S/RES/1973 (2011), authorized the use of force ("all necessary measures") "to protect civilians and civilian populated areas under threat of attack in the Libyan Arab Jamahiriya, including Benghazi, while excluding a foreign occupation force of any form on any part of Libyan territory," established a no-fly zone in Libyan airspace "in order to help protect civilians," which states were authorized to enforce using "all necessary measures." The Resolution was the basis for NATO's campaign in Libya. The fact that the Arab League wanted the Resolution made adoption possible.

22 Allegations of Genocide under the Convention on the Prevention and Punishment of the Crime of Genocide (Ukraine v. Russian Federation), Order, 2022 I.C.J., ¶ 18 (Mar. 16) (emphasis added), https://www.icj-cij.org/public/files/case-related/182/182-20220316-ORD-01-00-EN.pdf.

23 Declaration of Judge Bennouna, *supra* note 22, at ¶ 1, https://www.icj-cij.org/public/files/case-related/182/182-20220316-ORD-01-02-EN.pdf.

24 U.S. Const. Art. III, §2 (U.S. judicial power extends to cases and controversies). Kathleen M. Sullivan & Noah Feldman, Constitutional Law 34 (18th ed. 2013) (in 1793, Supreme Court rejected Washington's request for an advisory opinion). U.S. Const. Art. III, Sec. 2 (U.S. judicial power extends to cases and controversies).

opinions "on any legal question" to the General Assembly, the Security Council, or other UN bodies authorized to request them.[25]

Whether or not the Court acted because it thought it has responsibilities with respect to the maintenance of international peace and stability bootstrapping from its undoubted role in the peaceful adjudication of disputes, it held that the Genocide Convention dispute resolution provision applied. Quoting President Putin's speech of February 24, 2022, the Court concluded that Ukraine had made out a *prima facie* case that Russia had justified its military operations against Ukraine on the ground that Ukraine had engaged and was engaging in genocide. Second, the Court found that Ukraine had a right not to be subject to such military operations purportedly grounded in the Genocide Convention. At a stage in proceedings where the sufficiency of the pleadings, not the facts, only was at issue, Ukraine's application met the low legal standard by claiming that its rights under the Genocide Convention "not to be subject to a false claim of genocide" were plausible and at risk.[26] Finally, the majority determined that there was a link between the alleged violation of rights and the remedy sought—provisional measures requiring a suspension of military and paramilitary operations by forces under Russia's control or direction, including in the so-called Donetsk People's Republic and the Lugansk People's Republic, and periodic reporting to the Court on implementation of the order.[27] Despite voting with the majority, Judge Bennouna did not agree that there was a legal basis for the Court's decision. His declaration indicated sympathy with President Putin's view of recent history. Bennouna wrote:

> 7. Following the military intervention of the countries of the North Atlantic Treaty Organization (NATO), from 24 March to 10 June 1999, in the Federal Republic of Yugoslavia (now Serbia), without the authorization of the Security Council, which was aimed at preventing a "serious humanitarian disaster in Kosovo", the matter was debated at the international level. The then Secretary-General of the United Nations, Mr. Kofi Annan, underlined the tension that existed within the international community between the need to prevent massive human rights violations and the limits imposed on humanitarian intervention in the context of respect for State sovereignty (*We the peoples: the role of the United Nations in the twenty-first century*, report of the Secretary-General to the

---

25   U.N. Charter arts. 92, 96; Statute of the International Court of Justice, arts. 36, 65–68.

26   Allegations of Genocide, *supra* note 22, at ¶ 52, https://www.icj-cij.org/public/files /case-related/182/182-20220316-ORD-01-00-EN.pdf.

27   *Id.* at ¶¶ 60, 81–3.

Millennium Assembly of the United Nations, doc. A/54/2000, 27 March 2000, para. 218). This was followed, after long discussions, by the adoption at the 2005 United Nations Summit of the concept of "responsibility to protect", according to which it falls to each State to protect its population from massive human rights violations, in particular genocide, and, if necessary, other States may intervene to this end with the authorization of the Security Council (2005 World Summit Outcome, resolution adopted by the General Assembly on 16 September 2005, doc. A/RES/60/1, paras. 138–139).

8. Sadly, in practice, the concept of responsibility to protect has been diverted from its purpose. When, on 17 March 2011, the Security Council authorized Member States to take action through air strikes to protect civilian populations in Libya (resolution 1973, doc. S/RES/1973 (2011)), NATO forces deviated from their initial mandate, by favouring régime change in that country. This saw the end of the concept of responsibility to protect.[28]

Judge Bennouna's declaration seemed to beg the question about whether power should trump law in regard to Russia's invasion of Ukraine. It also raised again the complex question of the role of international law in international relations.[29]

3   UN Decision-making

The operation of the United Nations forms a context within which to evaluate Russia's invasion of Ukraine because Russia has been able to prevent the United Nations from taking effective action.

"Who decides" within the UN system is answered in the UN Charter with respect to the six principal organs—the General Assembly, the Security Council, the Economic and Social Council, the Trusteeship Council, the Secretariat, and the International Court of Justice. These bodies give the United Nations its internal dynamics. A Brazilian observer and one-time UN official aptly described UN group interactions as constituting a play within a

---

28   Bennouna, *supra* note 22.
29   Still one of the most penetrating analyses is Hersch Lauterpacht, The Function of Law in the International Community (1933).

play.[30] They may affect the behavior of the world beyond the walls of the organization. Not every capital knows what its UN mission is doing at any given moment because not every UN Ambassador receives instructions and reports on the mission's activities, diplomacy, and votes on resolutions.[31]

The UN Charter defines the powers of the principal organs. Since there exists no system of review, judicial or otherwise in the United Nations, each principal organ is able to determine its own powers as the ICJ revealed in the Ukraine-Russia case.[32] The Charter authorizes the Security Council to issue decisions, binding on all States.[33] This empowerment of the Security Council constitutes one significant way in which the UN Charter departed from the League of Nations Covenant with the goal of facilitating collective action. The Covenant required unanimity by the League Council or League Assembly to take action. Every member of the League had a veto in each body. The creators of the United Nations deemed that fact to be a structural flaw that contributed to the failure to prevent World War II. Of course, international organizations

---

30   Hernane Tavares de Sá, The Play Within the Play: The Inside Story of the UN IX (1966) ("I found it very difficult and exacting to write about the UN, that complex and unpredictable institution, which is at one and the same time intimately immersed in world events and yet primly self-contained—truly a 'play with the play.' Pascal, if he had lived in our times, might well have written the definitive book about the United Nations—and perhaps would have concluded that *l'ONU a des raisons que la raison ne connaît pas.*") The case of Liechtenstein is illuminating in this connection. Liechtenstein's Permanent Representative to the United Nations since 2002, Christian Wenaweser, exercises enormous influence because no state fears Liechtenstein and because other Permanent Representatives respect his intelligence and skill. Thus, he often chairs meetings and influences outcomes.

31   I recall a colleague who had been U.S. Ambassador to Zimbabwe telling me that he had gone to see President Mugabe to protest how the Zimbabwe Ambassador to the United Nations voted only to be told that Mugabe had no idea what his UN Ambassador was doing because he had issued no instructions to him. There also have been instances of the buying and selling of votes in the UN Security Council.

32   *See generally* Certain Expenses of the United Nations (Article 17, paragraph 2, of the Charter), Advisory Opinion, 1962 I.C.J. Rep. 49 (July 20), espec. at 168. Other UN entities, such as the World Health Organization (WHO), have their own constitutive documents. The WHO Constitution is instructive in that it provides for state ratification, in effect, of actions taken by the Organization. *Constitution of the World Health Organization*, World Health Organization, https://apps.who.int/gb/bd/pdf_files/BD_49th-en.pdf#page=6 (last visited July 28, 2022). Also instructive is the fact that the ICJ concluded that the WHO lacked competence to seek an advisory opinion on the lawfulness of the threat or use of nuclear weapons. Legality of the Threat or Use of Nuclear Weapons, Advisory Opinion, 1996 I.C.J. Rep. 95 (July 8, 1996) *See also generally* Rosalyn Higgins, Phillippa Webb, Dapo Akande, Sandesh Sivakumaran, & James Sloan, Oppenheim's International Law: United Nations (2017).

33   UN Charter art. 25.

usually are unable to make up for members' lack of will. By its actions, the Security Council has determined what it considers to be proper implementation of this power to decide. The response of the larger UN community of states determines whether the Security Council's judgment is correct.[34]

The Charter's articulation of the Security Council's responsibility with respect to the maintenance of peace and security is worth review. The authorizing language is in part of Article 24: "In order to ensure prompt and effective action by the United Nations, its Members confer on the Security Council primary responsibility for the maintenance of international peace and security, and agree that in carrying out its duties under this responsibility the Security Council acts on their behalf."[35] The Charter is silent with respect to situations in which the Security Council is unable to discharge its "primary responsibility" for whatever reason. It may be that one or more of the Permanent Members—China, France, Russia, the United Kingdom, and the United States—veto a substantive resolution. It may be that nine of the fifteen members do not support action. In such situations, the General Assembly and the Secretariat are not powerless with respect to the maintenance of peace, but they lack the power to require states to act (and, judging by the view of its responsibilities noted above in connection with the Ukraine-Russia case, the International Court of Justice believes it can shoulder some of the burden for maintaining or restoring international peace and security as well).

Within their respective means, the General Assembly and the Secretary-General have initiated actions when the Security Council could or would not do so. Since 1950, the General Assembly has debated issues involving international peace and security and made recommendations when it believes the Security Council is deadlocked or rendered unable to act by the exercise of the veto. The General Assembly at least has been able to express its condemnation of Russia's invasion of Ukraine and suspended Russia from the Human Rights Council.

In 1950, the UN Security Council was able to respond to North Korea's attack on South Korea in 1950 solely because the Soviet Union was boycotting the Council. Would the United States and others have sustained their rush to aid

---

34   For example, some commentators wondered whether Chapter VII of the UN Charter authorized the Security Council to establish international criminal tribunals for the Former Yugoslavia (ICTY) and Rwanda (ICTR). *See, e.g.,* Mia Swart, *Tadic Revisited: Some Critical Comments on the Legacy and the Legitimacy of the ICTY*, 3 Goettingen J. Int'l 985 (2011); Eric Rosand, *The Security Council As "Global Legislator": Ultra Vires or Ultra Innovative*, 28 Fordh. Int'l L. J. 542 (2005); Eric Rosand, *Security Council Resolution 1373, the Counter-Terrorism Committee, and the Fight Against Terrorism*, 97 Am. J. Int'l L. 333 (2003).

35   U.N. Charter art. 24, ¶ 1.

and fight alongside South Korea if the Soviet Union had been present to veto Security Council action when North Korea (with the blessing of the Soviet Union and China) invaded South Korea? In this connection, one should recall that the United States sprang into action before the Security Council acted. The Soviet Union objected to the Republic of China (Taiwan) rather than the People's Republic of China holding China's UN seat. The Council authorized States to assist South Korea and created a UN Command. The Council accepted the U.S. offer to fill the UN Commander position and lead the defense of South Korea. When the Soviet Union returned to the Security Council in August 1950, it vetoed continued Security Council action on North Korea. Then, at the urging of the United States, the General Assembly adopted the Uniting for Peace Resolution, taking upon itself responsibility to make recommendations concerning peace and security with regard to the Korean War.[36] As the UN Commander, the United States entered into bilateral agreements pertaining to financing UN forces engaged in this "enforcement action."[37]

The General Assembly and, much less frequently, the Security Council have invoked the Uniting for Peace Resolution since the Korean War. The General Assembly used it in 1957 to establish a UN Emergency Force (UNEF) in the Sinai to separate Egyptian and Israeli forces as part of the settlement of the 1956 Suez crisis.[38] The UN Secretary General also has taken action in regard to peace and security. Dag Hammarskjold established the UN Force in the Congo (UNOC) and mechanisms for financing it, including by assessment, as contrasted with voluntary, payments from the UN membership.[39] Despite the fact that the ICJ opined that expenditures arising from General Assembly or

---

36   G.A. Res. 377(V) (Nov. 3, 1950), https://www.un.org/en/sc/repertoire/otherdocs /GAres377A(v).pdf. *See also* Michael Ramsden, *Uniting for Peace: The Emergency Special Session on Ukraine*, Harv. Int'l L.J. Online, https://harvardilj.org/2022/04/uniting-for -peace-the-emergency-special-session-on-ukraine/; Keith S. Petersen, *The Uses of the Uniting for Peace Resolution since 1950*, 13/2 Int'l Org. 219 (1959); 2 Rosalyn Higgins, United Nations Peacekeeping, 1946–1967, Documents and Commentary: Asia 153–312 (1970). For revelations from the Soviet archives about the origins of the Korean War, including in particular the roles of Stalin and Mao Zedong, which contradict much of the conventional wisdom that had existed for decades, including about the Chinese intervention, see Robert Gellately, Stalin's Curse: Battling for Communism in War and Cold War 330–42 (2013); John Lewis Gaddis, We Know Now: Rethinking Cold War History 54–84 (1997).

37   Rosalyn Higgins, *United Nations Peace-Keeping: Political and Financial Problems*, 21 The World Today 325 (Aug. 1965). "Enforcement action" refers to enforcement of international peace and security, usually pursuant to a Security Council resolution adopted under Chapter VII of the UN Charter.

38   *Id.*

39   *Id.*

Secretariat actions are expenses of the United Nations to be paid out of the UN budget, the Soviet Union objected and never contributed its share.[40]

Kosovo was an example of the real—some might say cynical—international law in action.[41] While scholars worried the bone of authorization and Russia, which promised to veto Security Council authorization for military action against Serbia, fumed, NATO used force to bring an end to what its members considered to be gross human rights atrocities. They also were defending the post-World War II order in Europe by bringing an end to aggression by Serbia against other independent states that formerly were part of Yugoslavia. NATO claimed to be defending the principles and purposes of the UN Charter when the UN mechanisms were unavailable.[42] Such actions inevitably are controversial because they always look legitimate or more legitimate and more lawful when they occur through the UN machinery. But when the UN structure is unavailable for whatever reason, then states are not powerless, doomed to

---

40   Certain Expenses of the United Nations, *supra* note 32, at 49. Legality of the Threat or Use of Nuclear Weapons, *supra* note 32, at 237, ¶ 17 (July 8, 1996). The effect of ICJ Advisory Opinions, in the words of this ICJ advisory opinion, is subject "to appreciation." Russia and France disagreed with the *Certain Expenses* opinion and have never paid their share of expenses for the 1957–67 United Nations Emergency Force (UNEF) stationed between Israel and Egypt after the 1956 Sinai campaign or the UN operation in the Congo in 1960–64. *See also* Higgins, *supra* note 36, volume 3, *Africa*, at 274–303. The failure to pay what is owed to the United Nations has been a recurring issue. The fact that no Member State has lost its vote in the General Assembly because of a failure to pay pursuant to Article 19 of the UN Charter (loss of General Assembly vote if arrears equals or exceeds amount due in preceding two full years) provides an example of how the law at the end of the policeman's billy club may differ from the law in the statute books.

41   I recall Sergey Lavrov, as Russia's UN Ambassador, saying in Security Council informal consultations that he had heard every international law argument made on every side of every issue.

42   Transcript: *Clinton Addresses Nation on Yugoslavia Strike*, CNN (Mar. 24, 1999), https://edition.cnn.com/ALLPOLITICS/stories/1999/03/25/clinton.transcript/ (goals to prevent wider war and stop and prevent massacres); Celestine Bohlen, *Russia Vows to Block the U.N. from Backing Attack on Serbs*, N.Y. Times (Oct. 7, 1998), https://www.nytimes.com/1998/10/07/world/russia-vows-to-block-the-un-from-backing-attack-on-serbs.html. *See also, e.g.*, Mary Ellen O'Connell, *The UN, NATO, and International Law after Kosovo*, 22 Hum. Rts. Q. 57 (2000); *Editorial Comments: NATO's Kosovo Intervention*, 93 Am. J. Int'l L. 824 *et seq.* (1999) (articles by Louis Henkin, Christine Chinkin, Richard Falk, Ruth Wedgwood, and others); Harold Hongju Koh, *Humanitarian Intervention: Time for Better Law*, 111 Am. J. Int'l L. Unbound 287 (2017); Jure Vidmar, *The Use of Force as a Plea of Necessity*, 111 Am. J. Int'l L. Unbound 302 (2017).

accept their fate at the hands of the strong. They have the authority to rally to defend the UN Charter's values—the community's values—at stake.[43]

The General Assembly's use of the Uniting for Peace mechanism has been almost continuous since 1997. It does so by resuming the 10th Emergency Special Session on the Arab-Israeli conflict whenever the Security Council fails to adopt a resolution on the Israeli-Palestine question, usually as a result of a U.S. veto.[44] The General Assembly convened its 38th plenary meeting of the Tenth Emergency Special Session, for example, in response to the U.S. veto on June 1, 2018, of a resolution condemning Israel's use of force against the Great March of Return that resulted in clashes at the Israel-Gaza border. The United States thought the resolution "grossly one-sided."[45] The 10th Emergency Special Session of the General Assembly typically will adopt a resolution akin to the one vetoed. No additional action usually follows. As states in the Middle East have gravitated toward Israel in response to Iran's behavior, there has been less activity at the UN Security Council on the Middle East than previously occurred although there is a monthly meeting on the subject.[46]

In response to Russia's invasion of Ukraine on February 24, 2022, the Security Council met and tried to act. Russia vetoed a resolution introduced by seven members of the Council with the support of more than 60 other states. By the resolution, the Security Council reaffirmed "its commitment to the sovereignty, independence, unity, and territorial integrity of Ukraine within

---

43   *See* UN Charter art. 1 (UN purposes are to maintain international peace and security, develop friendly relations among nations, achieve international cooperation in solving international economic, social, cultural, or humanitarian problems, and to be a forum for harmonizing international actions in the attainment of these common ends).

44   The 10th Emergency Special Session of the General Assembly meets on the subject of "Illegal Israeli actions in occupied East Jerusalem and the rest of the Occupied Palestinian Territory," U.N. Secretary General, Note by the Secretary-General, UN Doc., A/ES-10/1 (Apr. 22,1997),https://documents-dds-ny.un.org/doc/UNDOC/GEN/N97/108/75/PDF/N9710875 .pdf?Open Element, itself a one-sided description of the situation between Israel and its neighbors, including the Palestine Authority.

45   G.A. PV.8274, at 2 (Jun 1, 2018), https://documents-dds-ny.un.org/doc/UNDOC/PRO/N18 /167 /10/PDF/N1816710.pdf?OpenElement. On the Great March of Return, see, e.g., Médecins Sans Frontières, https://www.msf.org/great-march-return-depth.

46   *See, e.g.,* the record of the Security Council meeting, S.C. PV.9046 (May 26, 2022), https:// documents-dds-ny.un.org/doc/UNDOC/PRO/N22/362/02/PDF/N2236202.pdf?Open Element. In effect, the UN General Assembly invokes the Uniting for Peace procedure to discuss the Israeli-Palestinian situation whenever the Palestinians decide they would like such a discussion and can muster the 9 votes on a resolution to force a U.S. veto. The Security Council then typically carries on its review of the situation involving Israel and the Palestine Authority monthly without regard to the General Assembly's actions.

its internationally recognized borders."[47] The Security Council thus rejected changes to Ukraine's borders accomplished by Russia in 2014 when it annexed Crimea and seized parts of Eastern Ukraine. The Council also "[d]eplore[d] in the strongest terms the Russian Federation's aggression against Ukraine in violation of Article 2, paragraph 4 of the United Nations Charter."[48] Russia's veto set in motion the Uniting for Peace process with the distinctive, because rare, variant that the Security Council "decide[d] to call an emergency special session of the General Assembly."[49] This "decision" constituted a non-substantive, procedural resolution, not subject to a Russian veto.[50] On March 2, 2022, the General Assembly condemned the Russian invasion by a vote of 141–5 with 35 abstentions.[51]

Iraq's invasion of Kuwait in 1990 raised the same issues as Russia's invasions of Ukraine in 2014 and 2022. The political context was different. In 1990, the Cold War was over. The Soviet Union was on the verge of dissolution. Hopes ran high for a birth of democracy in Russia and other former European dictatorships. Therefore, in 1990–91, the Soviet Union collaborated at the UN Security Council in defense of Kuwait.[52] Slightly more than thirty years later, Russia vetoed Security Council action on Ukraine because it decided to act as if it were Saddam Hussein's Iraq, even mimicking Saddam's claim that Kuwait was a province of Iraq by denying Ukraine's existence as a real state.[53] The 2022 invasion of Ukraine so incensed members of the General Assembly that they adopted a resolution deciding to debate the exercise by any Permanent Member or Members of the veto in the Security Council within 10 working

---

47 S.C. Res. 2022/155, (Feb. 25, 2022), https://documents-dds-ny.un.org/doc/UNDOC/GEN /N22/ 271/07/PDF/N2227107.pdf?OpenElement.

48 *Id.*

49 UN Doc. s/RES/2623 (2022), Feb. 27, 2022. *Available at*: https://documents-dds-ny.un.org /doc/UNDOC/GEN/N22/271/32/PDF/N2227132.pdf?OpenElement.

50 *Id.*

51 *UN General Assembly Demands Russian Federation Withdraw All Military Forces from the Territory of Ukraine*, European Union (Feb. 3, 2022), https://www.eeas.europa.eu/eeas/un -general-assembly-demands-russian-federation-withdraw-all-military-forces-territory -ukraine_en.

52 *See* John Norton Moore, Crisis in the Gulf: Enforcing the Rule of Law 189 *et passim* (1992) (quoting Soviet Foreign Minister Eduard Shevardnadze).

53 *Compare id.* at 208–20 (claim that Kuwait was always part of Iraq; invention as a state) *with* Putin speech, *supra* note 21.

days.[54] They also suspended Russia from membership in the Human Rights Council.[55]

The UN Charter sets forth the general values and purposes to be pursued. The system is not rigid. Nor does it create a suicide pact if the Charter decision-makers are unable to concur. Indeed, having survived the failure of collective security embodied by the League of Nations, no one in 1945 would have signed up to a system that placed national security or survival solely in the hands of an international organization or in any other system of collective security.[56] That is one of the functions of Article 51: the reaffirmation of the "inherent" right of self-defense.[57] When Russia invaded Ukraine, both in 2014[58] and in 2022, it engaged in armed attacks. Ukraine possessed an inherent right to use proportionate force in self-defense—that level of force reasonably required to bring to an end the situation making necessary the use of force in self-defense.[59] Ukraine had the right to call for military assistance as it has done, and states have had the inherent right of collective self-defense to provide such assistance. They could even send armies as part of this collective self-defense of Ukraine. International relations have never precluded such decision-making. Nor in fact have they precluded decision-making outside formal structures so long as they pursued lawful goals—lawful in terms of such fundamental statements of community policy as contained in the UN Charter.

---

54   G.A. Res. 76/262 (Apr. 28, 2022) (standing mandate for a General Assembly debate when a veto is cast in the Security Council).

55   The vote was 93–24 with 58 abstentions. *UN General Assembly votes to suspend Russia from the Human Rights Council*, United Nations (Apr. 7, 2022), https://news.un.org/en/story/2022/04/1115782.

56   *See, e.g.,* Martin Wight, Power Politics 184–85 (1986).

57   UN Charter Art. 51: "Nothing in the present Charter shall impair the *inherent* right of individual or collective self-defence if an armed attack occurs against a Member of the United Nations, until the Security Council has taken measures *necessary* to maintain international peace and security. ..." Emphasis added. Typical of the international legal system, the ICJ has one view of the meaning of "armed attack," states have another. *See, e.g.,* John Norton Moore, *Jus Ad Bellum Before the International Court of Justice*, 52 Va. J. Int'l L. 903 (2012) (overview and critique of ICJ jurisprudence on the use of force). *See also* Report of the High-Level Panel on Threats, Challenges and Change, A More Secure World: Our Shared Responsibility (2004), *available at* https://www.un.org/peacebuilding/sites/www.un.org.peacebuilding/files/ documents/hlp_more_secure_world.pdf. The Report misquotes Article 51. *See* Nicholas Rostow, *International Law and the Use of Force: A Plea for Realism*, 34 Yale J. Int'l L. 549, 554 n. 28 and accompanying text (2009) (omission of word "necessary" in quotation of Article 51).

58   *Putin Reveals Secrets of Russia's Crimea Takeover Plot*, BBC (March 9, 2015), https://www.bbc.com/news/world-europe-31796226.

59   *See* note 61, *infra*.

That being said, the question then presents itself, what is to be done about situations such as Ukraine? Ukraine, like Georgia in 2008 and even Iraq-Kuwait in 1990 involves a large power deciding to commit aggression against a smaller power it deems unworthy of existence or against which it has claims it cannot satisfy using lawful processes. In 1990, most states understood that Iraq had challenged and threatened an existential interest, shared by each state. (Even if they did not take that view, they understood that Western states did and that, after the Cold War, the preponderance of effective power of those states made it obviously the politically prudent position to join.)

4   Minimum World Public Order

Every legal system confronts the problem of compliance. The international system is no different in this respect. Among its distinctive features is the highly destructive means available to states and non-state actors. War, which involves the most lethal of instruments, has played an important role in the development of international law and is central to the UN Charter's statement of purpose.[60] As a result, a principal function of international law is the marginalization of the use of force. It does so by minimizing the authorities for a use of force and embracing rules embodying proportionality for the conduct of military operations. As a result, the idea of economy of coercion in pursuit of lawful purposes lies at the core of the law governing the use of force—the *jus ad bellum*—and the law governing conduct of force—the *jus in bello*.[61] Honestly applied, the *jus ad bellum* and the *jus in bello* should achieve both "a low level of violence [and] a low *expectation* of violence."[62]

The very idea of minimum world public order emphasizes the foregoing points and implies the existence of world public order itself. The New Haven School of Jurisprudence, to which Professor Wiessner subscribes, offers the most comprehensive definition:

> those features of the world social process, including both goal values and implementing institutions, which are protected by law. The world social

---

60   *See* note 43, *supra*.

61   Myres S. McDougal, *Law and Minimum World Public Order: Armed Conflict in Larger Context*, 3 UCLA Pac. Basin L.J. 21, 26 (1984). *See also* Myres S. McDougal & Florentino P. Feliciano, Law and Minimum World Public Order, espec. 121–29 (1961).

62   W. Michael Reisman, The Quest for World Order and Human Dignity in the Twenty-First Century: Constitutive Process and Individual Commitment 318 (2d ed. 2022).

process, regarded as embracing all the interactions and interdetermi-
nations of peoples across state lines, observably includes a component
process of effective power, in the sense that decisions with international
effects, of many different geographical ranges and intensities in impact,
are in fact continuously being made and enforced. Many of the decisions comprehended in this world process of effective power, are, further, scarcely less observably affected by perspectives of authority, in the
double sense that they are made by the people established by community expectation as appropriate to make such decisions and that they are
"reasoned" decisions—that is, decisions achieved through procedures
and justified in terms of policy criteria established by community expectation. It is these latter decisions, the decisions both attended by effective
power and made in accordance with community perspectives of authority, which establish and protect certain features of the world social process in public orders of varying degrees of universality, including a world
public order—however minimum or rent with dissension that order may
be—and which are, in turn, strengthened and supported by the public
orders they establish or seek to establish. The primary focus of a policy-oriented, contextual jurisprudence, designed to serve the goals of a
world public order of human dignity, must, accordingly, be upon these
complex world social and power processes and their interrelations, and
especially upon the factors which affect particular decisions within such
processes.[63]

In other words, the New Haven School offers a wide-angle vision of international law that tries to take into account and cover human international interaction at all levels and of all kinds. It seeks the law in authoritative decisions
within these interactions consistent with the value of human dignity, decisions
that exercise effective power in accordance with community perspectives of
authority.

Human dignity constitutes a universal value even though states, much less
communities within states, do not always agree on what it means. World public order thus inevitably includes diverse decisionmakers. They may be persons
such as Barack Obama, Joseph Biden, or Volodymyr Zelensky. They may be like
Josef Stalin and successors of his type whoever they may be. Stalin's "deep
commitment to Leninism, his passion for the Communist ideal, combined
with realism, and a ruthlessness in politics" did not mean that Stalin did not

---

63   Myres S. McDougal & Associates, Studies in World Public Order x (1960).

believe he was pursuing and defending human dignity.[64] The existence of the
Stalins of this world means that minimizing coercion that does not conform to
community expectations as set forth in the UN Charter[65] is the best to which
any international legal system can aspire.

Russia's invasion touches profound strategic and moral issues. Strategically,
Russia has implied and been seen to imply a military threat to the independence of other former parts of the Soviet Union. Among those that fear attack
are states such as Estonia, Latvia, and Lithuania, which, not only are independent, but also members of the Atlantic Alliance and NATO. Other neighboring
states against which Russia has engaged in aggression during the past, such as
Finland, and Sweden, have now applied to join NATO. And another victim of
Russian aggression in the past, Poland, has maintained a high level of military
readiness and support for Ukraine in case Russia follows in Soviet and tsarist
footsteps and seeks to take control of Poland. If it were permissible for a state
to decide to take over another state for whatever reason, no state would be safe.
Russia's invasion of Ukraine raises this issue just as Iraq's invasion of Kuwait
did in 1990.

Russia's possession of a large number of the most powerful nuclear weapons
increases the stakes. In 1968, the United States, the Soviet Union, and the United
Kingdom made the following identical statement at the UN Security Council in
connection with the Council's endorsement of the Nuclear Non-Proliferation
Treaty (NPT). Their statements encouraged states to forego possession of
nuclear weapons and join the NPT.

> The Government of the Soviet Union [the United Kingdom, the United
> States] notes with appreciation the desire expressed by a large number
> of States to subscribe to the Treaty on the Non-Proliferation of Nuclear
> Weapons.
>
> We welcome the willingness of these States to undertake not to receive
> the transfer from any transferor whatsoever of nuclear weapons or other
> nuclear explosive devices or of control over such weapons or explosive
> devices directly, or indirectly; not to manufacture or otherwise acquire
> nuclear weapons or other nuclear explosive devices; and not to seek or
> receive any assistance in the manufacture of nuclear weapons or other

---

64   Gellately, *supra* note 36, at 4.
65   UN Charter art. 1, ¶ 1 ("The Purposes of the United Nations are: 1. To maintain inter-
      national peace and security, and to that end: to take effective collective measures for
      the prevention and removal of threats to the peace, and for the suppression of acts of
      aggression or other breaches of the peace, ...").

nuclear explosive devices.

The Soviet Union [the United Kingdom, the United States] also notes the concern of certain of these States, that, in conjunction with their adherence to the Treaty on the Non-Proliferation of Nuclear Weapons, appropriate measures be undertaken to safeguard their security. Any aggression accompanied by the use of nuclear weapons would endanger the peace and security of all States.

Bearing these considerations in mind, the Soviet Union [the United Kingdom, the United States] declares the following:

Aggression with nuclear weapons or the threat of nuclear weapons against a non-nuclear-weapon State would create a qualitatively new situation in which the nuclear-weapon States which are permanent members of the United Nations Security Council would have to act immediately through the Security Council to take the measures necessary to counter such aggression or remove the threat of aggression in accordance with the United Nations Charter, which calls for taking 'effective collective measures for the prevention and removal of threats to the peace, and for the suppression of acts of aggression or other breaches of the peace.' [UN Charter, Art. 1, para. 1] Therefore, any State which commits aggression accompanied by the use of nuclear weapons or threatens such aggression must be aware that its actions will be countered effectively by measures to be taken in accordance with the United Nations Charter to suppress the aggression or remove the threat of aggression.

The Soviet Union [the United Kingdom, the United States] reaffirms its intention as a permanent member of the United Nations Security Council, to seek immediate Security Council action to provide assistance, in accordance with the Charter, to any non-nuclear weapon State, a party to the Treaty on the Non-Proliferation of Nuclear Weapons, that is a victim of an act of aggression or an object of a threat of aggression in which nuclear weapons are used.

The Soviet Union [the United Kingdom, the United States] reaffirms in particular the inherent right, recognized under Article 51 of the Charter, of individual or collective self-defence if an armed attack, including a nuclear attack, occurs against a Member of the United Nations, until the Security Council has taken the measures necessary to maintain international peace and security.

The Soviet Union's [the United Kingdom's, the United States'] vote for the resolution before us and this statement of the way the Soviet Union [the United Kingdom, the United States] intends to act in accordance with the Charter of the United Nations are based upon the fact that the resolution is supported by other permanent members of the Security

Council who are nuclear-weapon States and are also proposing to sign the Treaty on the Non-Proliferation of Nuclear Weapons, and that these States have made similar statements on the ways in which they intend to act in accordance with the Charter.[66]

Everyone familiar with the United Nations during the Cold War knew that the Soviet Union, the United Kingdom, and the United States, if they acted together, could command an overwhelming majority in the Security Council and that neither France nor China likely would exercise its veto in opposition. Indeed, the resolution endorsing the Soviet, UK, and U.S. statements was adopted without opposition (although five states abstained).[67]

In 1994, Ukraine ceased to be home to nuclear weapons that the Soviet Union had stationed on Ukrainian territory and joined the NPT. Among the documents filed in the UN Treaty Office in connection with Ukraine's accession to the NPT is the "Memorandum on security assurances," signed on December 3, 1994, by the Presidents of Ukraine, the Russian Federation (Yeltsin), and the United States (Clinton) and Prime Minister Major of the United Kingdom.[68] By its terms, the Memorandum took effect on signature. In this document, Russia, the United Kingdom, and the United States

[1.] reaffirm their commitment to Ukraine, in accordance with the principles of the CSCE Final Act [Conference on Security and Cooperation in Europe—Helsinki, 1975], to respect the independence and sovereignty and the existing borders of Ukraine[;] ... [2.] reaffirm their obligation to refrain from the threat or use of force against the territorial integrity or political independence of Ukraine, and that none of their weapons will ever be used against Ukraine except in self-defense or otherwise in accordance with the Charter of the United Nations[;]... [3.] reaffirm their commitment to Ukraine, ..., to refrain from economic coercion designed to subordinate to their own interest the exercise by Ukraine of the rights inherent in its

---

66   S.C. PV.1430, ¶ 16 (June 17, 1968). The identical UK and U.S. statements are at 2–3, https://documents-dds-ny.un.org/doc/UNDOC/GEN/N72/357/01/PDF/N7235701.pdf? Open Element.

67   The French abstained on the resolution (S/RES/255 (1968), June 19, 1968, adopted by 10-0-5 (Algeria, Brazil, France, India, Pakistan) regarding the NPT on the ground that France regarded the threat of nuclear war best addressed by elimination of the weapons. *Id.* at 6. Most of the abstaining states expressed doubt as to the necessity for the guarantees.

68   *See* Memorandum on security assurances in connection with Ukraine's accession to the Treaty on the Non-Proliferation of Nuclear Weapons, U.N. 52241 (Dec. 5, 1994), https://treaties.un.org/Pages/showDetails.aspx?objid=0800000280401fbb. The text is at https://treaties.un.org/doc/Publication/UNTS/Volume%203007/Part/volume-3007-I-52241. pdf.

sovereignty and thus to secure advantages of any kind[;] ... [4.] reaffirm their commitment to seek immediate United Nations Security Council action to provide assistance to Ukraine, as a non-nuclear-weapon state party to the Treaty on the Non-Proliferation of Nuclear Weapons, if Ukraine should become a victim of an act of aggression or an object of a threat of aggression in which nuclear weapons are used[;] ... [5.] reaffirm, in the case of Ukraine, their commitment not to use nuclear weapons against any non-nuclear weapon state party to the Treaty on the Non-Proliferation of Nuclear Weapons, except in the case of an attack on themselves, their territories or dependent territories, their armed forces, or their allies, by such a state in association or alliance with a nuclear weapon state. 6. Ukraine, the Russian Federation, the United Kingdom of Great Britain and Northern Ireland, and the United States of America will consult in the event a situation arises which raises a question concerning these commitments.[69]

Obviously, Russia has ignored this Memorandum and the commitments it contains. It also has ignored the Soviet Union's pledge to the world community made at the Security Council in 1968, essentially reaffirmed at the 1995 NPT Review Conference.[70] A wave of acquisitions of nuclear weapons by presently non-nuclear weapon states parties to the NPT, were it to occur, would be a foreseeable consequence of Russia's invasion and disregard of its commitments. While some political scientists would regard such a growth in the number of nuclear weapons states as stabilizing, governments such as the U.S. government take a more cautious approach. They worry that nuclear proliferation increases the risk of nuclear conflict.[71]

President Putin set forth his view of Russia's stakes in Ukraine in his speech of February 24, 2022.[72] Among his points, the following stand out:

For the United States and its allies, it is a policy of containing Russia, with obvious geopolitical dividends. For our country, it is a matter of life and death, a matter of our historical future as a nation. This is not an exaggeration; this is a fact. It is not only a very real threat to our interests but

---

69   *Id.*

70   Susan J. Koch, *Extended Deterrence and the Future of the Nuclear Nonproliferation Treaty*, Comparative Strategy, Vol. 39, No. 3, April 2020.

71   W. Seth Carus, Nuclear Optimists as Proliferation Pessimists: Why U.S. Policy-Makers Who Love the Bomb Don't Think "More is Better" (2013).

72   Vladimir Putin Speech, *supra* note 21. Also available at *Transcript: Vladimir Putin's Televised Address on Ukraine*, Bloomberg News (Feb. 24, 2022), https://www.bloomberg.com/news/articles/2022-02-24/full-transcript-vladimir-putin-s-televised-address-to-russia-on-ukraine-feb-24.

to the very existence of our state and to its sovereignty. It is the red line which we have spoken about on numerous occasions. They have crossed it. ...

I would now like to say something very important for those who may be tempted to interfere in these developments from the outside. No matter who tries to stand in our way or all the more so create threats for our country and our people, they must know that Russia will respond immediately, and the consequences will be such as you have never seen in your entire history. No matter how the events unfold, we are ready. All the necessary decisions in this regard have been taken. I hope that my words will be heard.[73]

Governments understood that this statement, followed by an order to place Russian nuclear forces on alert, constituted a threat to use nuclear weapons against, particularly, a NATO intervention on behalf of Ukraine. Russia thus has used nuclear weapons to try to shield its aggression against Ukraine from a confrontation with non-Ukrainian armed forces.[74]

President Putin went beyond using nuclear weapons as a shield. He also turned the international law of the UN Charter as well as customary international law on its head. The law of the Charter and customary law insist on the need to be attacked or intercept an attack when no reasonable alternative exists as the basis for a use of force.[75] "Containing" Russia, whatever that might mean in the post-Cold War context—resisting Russian territorial expansion at the expense of neighboring, independent states that also are UN members?—does not come close to meeting the requirements of Article 51 of the UN Charter, however expansively one might interpret the "inherent right of individual or collective self-defence."[76] Putin's Russia is violating the fundamental principles of UN Charter international law.

---

73 *Id.*

74 *See, e.g.,* Bryan Bender, *How the Ukraine War Could Go Nuclear*, Politico, Mar. 24, 2022, *available at* https://www.politico.com/news/2022/03/24/how-ukraine-war-could-go-nuclear -00019899.

75 The scholarly debates on the meaning of Article 51 and its use of the term "armed attack" form a voluminous collection. One place to begin is Yoram Dinstein, War, Aggression and Self-Defence 197–260 (6th ed. 2017). *See also* Moore, *supra* note 57.

76 UN Charter art. 51. *See also* China's response to the visit to Taiwan of Speaker Nancy Pelosi: "Beijing says a visit to Taiwan by the third-ranking U.S. politician, Mrs. Pelosi, violated American agreements to honor a One China Policy and may encourage politicians on the island to seek independence. It says it is within its rights to take action to defend its sovereignty. 'China has been compelled to act in self-defense,' Jing Quang, a minister in China's Embassy in Washington told reporters on Friday, Aug. 5, 2022." Wenxin Fan, Joyu Wang,

What is the minimum world public order reality Russia and its allies[77] now confront? At the strategic level, Russia confronts an Atlantic community more united in fear than has been the case in decades. Successive American politicians and Presidents, including Obama[78] and Trump,[79] railed against rich European countries not contributing adequately to Europe's and the Atlantic community's defense and not meeting defense spending obligations in relation to gross domestic product agreed at NATO meetings. As a result of Russia's invasion, Allied defense spending has increased.[80] Finland and Sweden seek membership in the Atlantic Alliance and NATO, surely an unforeseen consequence (at least, viewed from Moscow) of the Russian invasion. In addition, of course, friends of Ukraine such as the United States have contributed billions of dollars in materiel to Ukraine's armed forces fighting Russia. Governments do not have a monopoly on assistance. Non-government organizations, whether companies, bar associations, or other organizations and networks have provided assistance, including with respect to preserving evidence to support eventual legal claims. This outpouring represents a community response. Russia's veto of UN Security Council action forced governments, citizens, and non-government organizations to try other methods to vindicate the values of the UN Charter. Russia also has sharpened the tensions between democratic and

---

& James T. Areddy, *China Steps Up Action In Anger Over Taiwan*, Wall St. J., Aug. 6–7, 2022, at A1, A8. China, of course, violated its 1984 commitments to the United Kingdom when it asserted control over Hong Kong affairs notwithstanding the Joint Declaration on the question of Hong Kong, Dec. 19, 1984. 1399 U.N.T.S. 2339 (Art. 3: "The Hong Kong Special Administrative Region will be vested with executive, legislative and independent judicial power, including that of final adjudication. The laws currently in force in Hong Kong will remain basically unchanged.").

77 Russia is not without friends as it struggles to finish off Ukraine. Iran, North Korea, China, and others have sided with Moscow to a greater or lesser extent. Others, such as South Africa, which remembers Soviet assistance against minoritarian, apartheid rule, and India, which also may remember earlier alignment with the Soviet Union, at the very least hedge their bets on the outcome.

78 Jeffrey Goldberg, *The Obama Doctrine*, The Atlantic (April 2016), https://www.theatlantic .com/magazine/archive/2016/04/the-obama-doctrine/471525/.

79 *See, e.g.*, Julie Hirschfeld Davis, *Trump Warns NATO Allies to Spend More on Defense, or Else*, N.Y. Times (July 2, 2018), https://www.nytimes.com/2018/07/02/world/europe /trump-nato.html.

80 *Face-off with Russia over Ukraine lifts military spending in 2021, Think Tank Says*, Reuters (Apr. 25, 2022), https://www.reuters.com/world/europe/face-off-with-russia-over-ukraine -lifts-military-spending-2021-think-tank-says-2022-04-25/. *See also* Jack Dutton, *Putin's NATO Backfire? How Finnish, Swedish Forces Compare With Ukraine's*, Newsweek (July 19, 2022), https://www.newsweek.com/putins-nato-backfire-finland-swedens-military-versus -pre-war-ukraine-1706926 (Finland and Sweden military strength).

not-so democratic or outright tyrannical governments that have dominated international politics since the end of the Cold War and certainly since the terrorist attacks of September 11, 2001, and the U.S.-led invasion of Iraq of 2003. At the same time, voices such as Henry Kissinger's urge trying to find a negotiated end to the Ukraine war that would leave Russia with Crimea and Donbass and avoid creating a long-lived, perhaps even permanent Russo-Chinese alliance. Kissinger is worried that the West not paint Putin into a corner from which he cannot escape.[81] One journalist called Kissinger "a pragmatic practitioner of *Realpolitik*."[82] But is Kissinger's an appropriate attitude toward international relations and aggression? There are a substantial number of historical examples where aggressors began with a single target and then moved on to others. It is important to recall in this context that Putin painted Russia into the corner in which it finds itself.

Another important consideration has to do with the consequences of Russia's invasion. On the one hand, it has triggered a coalescing of democracies in defense of core UN Charter principles. On the other hand, powers with nuclear weapons who have expansionist or revanchist goals may see a helpful precedent in Russia's ability to sustain military operations, however disappointing the operations must appear from Moscow's point of view. Will it lead to a new consensus that possession of nuclear weapons is crucially important for national defense for countries not in a formal alliance with a nuclear-weapon state? Some observers believe we have been in that situation, recognized or not, since the atomic age began. Does the response to Russia's invasion mean that even such formal alliances may not be taken at face value? De Gaulle's view as to why France needed its own nuclear weapons was multi-faceted and multilayered. It included doubt about Washington's willingness to risk New York City to defend Paris.[83] Russia's invasion also raises a question about deterrence—could Russia have been deterred if sanctions had been imposed before the invasion or if foreign troops had been stationed in Ukraine for the purpose of deterring invasion?

The strategic and legal stakes of Russia's invasion of Ukraine therefore are high. In addition, of course, the moral stakes leap out as Russian forces continue to engage in the kind of indiscriminate attacks on civilian targets that

---

81   *See, e.g.,* Imran Khalid, *Henry Kissinger's Advice on Ending the War in Ukraine is Pragmatic,* Toronto Star, July 4, 2022, *available at* https://www.thestar.com/opinion /contributors/2022/07/04/henry-kissingers-advice-on-ending-the-war-in-ukraine-is -pragmatic.html.

82   *Id.*

83   Jean Lacouture, De Gaulle: The Ruler, 1945–1970 413–33 (Alan Sheridan trans. 1992).

the laws of war aim to prevent or at least punish if they occur. It is difficult to imagine that Russia will find acceptable a negotiated settlement that includes its accountability for war crimes.

5   Conclusion

Wars matter. The Russian invasion of Ukraine already has had important strategic, moral, and legal consequences. Russia's military operations ignore the most fundamental laws of war by ignoring even the pretense of distinguishing between military and civilian targets. Other Russian actions arguably amount to genocide and pillage—plunder.[84] Russia uses nuclear weapons as a shield granting impunity for aggression and war crimes.

The international legal system has fundamental norms regarding the use of force and other subjects such as human rights enforced or advanced through the actions of governments, inter-governmental organizations, and non-government actors. It is a flexible arrangement, particularly where the existence of states is at stake. In September 1965, Secretary of State Dean Rusk put the point well in discussing the role of the State Department Legal Adviser:

> The test of policy by reference to law goes beyond the technical issues of law or even the broader objective of the rule of law. Law is the custodian of the standard of generalized conduct. Our Legal Adviser is responsible for putting to us the questions: What happens if everyone else acts as we are proposing to do? How are we prepared to act if a similar situation arises elsewhere?
>
> The law liberates by making it possible to predict, with reasonable assurance, what the other fellow is going to do. One of the most exciting and hopeful developments of this postwar period, even though largely unnoticed, is the rapid growth of what Wilfred Jenks has called "the Common Law of Mankind". The gravitational pull of law in policy is and must be a powerful factor in policy decision.[85]

What the invasion of Ukraine has put on the table is the future of that gravitational pull toward minimum world public order. Part of that gravitational pull

---

84   *See, e.g.,* Kristina Hook, *Why Russia's War in Ukraine Is a Genocide,* For. Aff., July 28, 2022, *available at* www.foreign affairs.com/Ukraine/why-russias-war-ukraine-genocide.

85   Dean Rusk, *The Anatomy of Foreign Policy Decisions,* Address to the American Political Science Association, Sept. 7, 1965, U.S. Dep't of State, Bull., vol. LII, No. 1370, at 11 (Sept. 27, 1965).

involves answers to the question we began with, "who decides?" The structure of the international system, a system of independent, sovereign, nominally equal states and international organizations to which the states have delegated certain powers without giving up their independence, means that states decide. Their decisions may take place inside or outside international organizations like the United Nations. The point is that, if the relevant international machinery is blocked and unavailable, for whatever reason, the law does not leave states helpless to defend fundamental values under siege. That is the situation raised by the Russian invasion of Ukraine. The answer is neither *sauve qui peut*—everyone for itself—nor submission. A collective, multi-layered and multi-faceted defense of the fundamental values under attack lawfully may be mounted. We have seen the West engage in such an effort in response to Russia's invasion. That is a far better outcome than acceptance of *force majeure*. In a world of nuclear and other weapons of mass and indiscriminate destruction, where international organizations essentially are powerless, there is no acceptable alternative.

Acknowledgements

I wish to thank James A. Rowe, J.D. Cornell 2022, for valuable research assistance and Victoria Okraszewski, Class of 2023, New York Law School, for helping to put the footnotes in proper form.

CHAPTER 11

International Law after the Pandemic: The Contribution of the 2021 Resolution of the *Institut de Droit International*

*Francesco Francioni**

1   Introduction

It is a great pleasure to participate in this *Festschrift* honoring the academic career of Siegfried Wiessner. I was lucky to be associated with Siegfried in several scholarly projects organized both at the European University Institute (EUI) in Florence and at his own institution in Miami. I am referring to the valuable contribution he gave to the courses of the Academy of European Law and Human Rights of the EUI, at a time when I was its co-director, and to his writings on the rights of indigenous peoples that have enriched the publications of the EUI Academy and the Oxford Series on Cultural Heritage Law and Policy. On my side, the association with Siegfried gave me the privilege of participating and teaching in the Master of Laws program in Intercultural Human Rights at St. Thomas University under his direction, and of contributing to the Saint Thomas University's *Intercultural Human Rights Law Review*. These common endeavors on both sides of the Atlantic were always in the spirit of a virtuous application of diverse methods and styles of European and American legal scholarship and of an enduring faith in the progress and modernization of international law through intercultural dialogue.

The topic I have chosen for this contribution is to be an homage to Siegfried's constant attention to the tension between individual human rights and collective rights of the group, of society, and of the international community as a whole.

---

*   Professor of International Law Emeritus, Law Department, European University Institute, Florence.

2   The COVID-19 Pandemic in International Context

The grim experience of the worldwide pandemic of COVID-19 has made dramatically relevant and timely the theme of health as a global public good. At the
same time, it has shown the limits of mainstream international law scholarship
in fully grasping the far-reaching implications of the pandemic and in facing
the challenge of establishing an effective system of international cooperation
for the protection of public health.[1] There are many reasons for these limits.
First, traditional international law scholarship tends to confine the protection
of public health within the boundaries of State sovereignty and domestic jurisdiction. Each state is the trustee of the public health of its people. Second, the
competent international institution, the World Health Organization (WHO),
established in 1948 as a very specialized organization focused on the provision
of medical care, has faced difficulties in dealing with the repercussions that
the protection of public health has on other international regimes, including
human rights, environmental protection, international economic law, and
international security. This has resulted in the tendency to avoid the adoption
of mandatory rules with a clear preference for instruments of soft law that lack
the binding character to effectively contribute to the solution of disputes and
conflicts arising in this field.

Some progress in the system of international sanitary cooperation was
made toward the end of the last century, when the protection of public health
began to acquire the normative value of a global public good that transcends
the narrow national public interest of each state. The painful experience of
the HIV-AIDS pandemic, the opening of State boundaries to free movement of
goods, people, and services with the adoption of the World Trade Organization
(WTO) in 1994, and the looming threat of environmental degradation, made
abundantly clear that with the economic benefits of globalization came new
risks of cross-border diffusion of new pathogens and of world-wide spread of
infectious diseases. The WHO responded to these new challenges by adopting in 2005 a revised text of the International Health Regulations[2] and by
launching the 2016 Health Emergencies Programme, an initiative prompted

---

1   There are excellent scholarly contributions to the subject, but they maintain the character of
     very specialized studies on the international law regime of public health. *See* Global Health
     Law (Gian Luca Burci ed., Cheltenham-Northampton, 2016). For a broader examination of
     the protection of public health within the wider context of public international law, see La
     tutela della salute nel diritto internazionale ed europeo tra interessi globali e interessi parti-
     colari (Laura Pineschi ed., Napoli, 2017).
2   Adopted in 1969 and updated in 1973 and 1981, the text presently in force since 15 June 2007 is
     published in *International Health Regulations,* 3rd edition, World Health Organization, 2016.

by the unsatisfactory response to the 2014 Ebola epidemic in West Africa and designed to deliver rapid and comprehensive support to countries and people facing or recovering from emergencies caused by infectious diseases outbreaks and other hazards to human health.[3]

The COVID-19 pandemic arrived in the wake of these important WHO initiatives. Its impact and worldwide diffusion have caused a humanitarian crisis that has few precedents in the history of modern international law. The reaction of the scientific community has been swift and effective, with the development of a new generation of vaccines at unprecedented speed. But at a political and legal level the international community has emerged from the pandemic fractured and largely unprepared to prevent and control such a serious infectious disease that has caused deaths estimated to be around 20 million worldwide.

The *Institut de Droit International* (IDI), whose mission is to promote the progress of international law, decided to deal with this topic immediately after the onset of the contagion. On 27 March 2020, it established an ad hoc working group (a "Commission") with the task of elaborating a set of draft articles, which, in the IDI's intention, could contribute to the strengthening of the international protection of persons and peoples from the risk of epidemics and pandemics.[4] The working group[5] completed its work in the first half of 2021, and the set of draft articles became the text of a Resolution adopted by the *Institut* at its 80th session (Beijing), held online from 23 to 29 August 2021.

As anyone could have expected, the topic proved to be quite divisive among the members of the working group and of the *Institut*. Different opinions emerged during the preparatory work about the proper role of the World Health Organization, the need to address the causes of the pandemic, the possible responsibilities in preventing and controlling the spread of contagion, as well as about the unavoidable implications of international economic law of the access and equitable distribution of vaccines. In the following sections,

---

3 WHO, 69th World Health Assembly, 5 May 2016, Doc. A69/30.

4 Normally, the *Institut* establishes working groups during the ordinary biennial sessions of the organization, but, in view of the increasing gravity of the epidemic, on March 20, 2020 the secretary general of the Institute, Marcelo Kohen, sent a letter to the members in which he wrote: [Facing the current situation of pandemic,] I invite all our members to reflect on how our Institute can contribute most efficiently in this regard, including by examining issues that we have not yet addressed or that were addressed in an insufficient manner." This invitation was accepted by the members of the *Institut*, and the ad hoc commission on epidemics and pandemics was established. *See* 81 Annuaire de l'Institut de droit international, 80th Session (en ligne) (Paris, 2021), at 43 ff.

5 The present writer was a member of the working group.

I will comment on this Resolution, trying to highlight its innovative aspects as well as its limits. But before undertaking the examination of the substantive aspects of the IDI's Resolution, it is useful briefly to place the topic of the pandemic within the general theme of health as a global public good.

3   The COVID-19 Pandemic and the Law of Global Public Goods

As in previous epidemics, such as HIV-AIDS, Ebola, and SARS, the COVID-19 pandemic has provided a dramatic opportunity to re-focus on health as a public good of international relevance. But, what is the status of international law with regard to "public goods"? This question has for long attracted the attention of international law scholarship, which has tried to analyze it within the perspective of a possible transformation of international law from a system of rules created and applied in order to coordinate spheres of sovereignty to a system of rules and principles capable of protecting also general interests of the international community and of humanity.[6]

From the point of view of economic analysis, the concept of public goods has been defined according to the two criteria of the "non-rivalry" – everyone can benefit from them without diminishing their utility for others – and the "non-excludability" – no one may be denied access and enjoyment.[7] According to economic analysis, such goods may be produced and maintained also by private subjects. But this is the exception – as in the classical case of the lighthouse providing guidance for navigation. The rule is that these goods, such as security, education, environment, and public health, are produced and protected by public authorities and by public expenditure, also in view of discouraging the frequent phenomenon of "free riding," the opportunistic enjoyment of benefits and utilities produced by others' effort.

In the disciplines of political science and international relations, the concept of public goods has been used as an element capable of legitimizing the

---

6   The literature on the subject is vast. Among the many contributions, see, in particular, the joint symposium of the European Society of International Law and the American Society of International Law held at the European University Institute on the topic "Global Public Goods and the Plurality of Legal Orders," published in *European Journal of International Law*, vol. 23, 2012, at 643–792; International Law for Common Goods (Federico Lenzerini & Ana Vrdoljak eds., Oxford and Portland, 2014); Giorgio Gaja, The Protection of General Interests in the International Community, General Course, Hague Academy of International Law (Leiden/Boston, 2014).

7   For an early conceptualization, see Paul A. Samuelson, The Pure Theory of Public Expenditure 387 ff. (1954).

action of international institutions as trustees of the general interest of the international community. This approach has emerged in particular from the work of the United Nations Development Program (UNDP) in defining a shared basis of interests and values in the formulation of the programs of human development. Since UNDP's work occurs against the background of an international reality characterized by state sovereignty, cultural diversity, and political and legal pluralism, the concept of common goods can be a powerful element in support of the legitimacy of the institutional programs.[8]

In international law, the concept of public goods has been expanded into that of "global public goods," which encompasses those goods and values that are essential and non-renounceable, not only for the states but for the international community as a whole. International security, the conservation of the environment that sustains our life, the outstanding expressions of human culture, and, notably, the public health of persons and of humanity are important components of this concept. However, at the international level the production and maintenance of such goods remains problematic. There is no global authority capable of acting as the arbiter of the international common good and as the legitimate agent for the production of global public goods. Rather, there is a plurality of sovereign states, a diversity of legal and political systems variably coordinated at the horizontal level by consensual undertakings and vertically organized by way of international or supra-national institutions in which states, unavoidably, continue to place the notion of public good in a national horizon. The difficulty for international law of organizing a collective action for the protection of a global public good has dramatically emerged in relation to the existential threat of climate change.[9]

It has emerged also in the case of the still lingering health emergency caused by the COVID-19 pandemic. In the first case, the deficiencies of an effective global governance of the crisis have hindered a timely transition to sources of renewable energy and have left ample room to the free-riding of many states, sometimes with the recurring justification that global warming is the historical responsibility of the industrial states and not of the developing countries. In the second case, in contrast with the effective scientific cooperation that has led to the timely production of safe and effective vaccines, the response at the political and legal level has been dictated by sovereignty and national interests, with the effect of weakening the role of the WHO as the competent

---

8   *See* Providing Global Public Goods. Managing Globalization (Inge Kaul et al., UNEP, New York, 2003).

9   It has been revealed also by the inability of international institutions to prevent and stop the breach of international peace caused by the ongoing aggression of Ukraine by Russia.

international organization to fight COVID-19 and even of delegitimizing it as an institution by announcing in some cases the intention of withdrawing from it in the middle of a global sanitary crisis.[10]

The structural deficiencies of international law in matters of collective action required for the protection of global public goods persist even in the face of some progress, at the theoretical level, of the idea that the international community is able to determine that certain public goods must be protected as general community interests. I am referring to the important and often neglected provision of Article 48 para. 1. b) of the International Law Commission's Draft Articles on State Responsibility, which recognizes the *locus standi* of any state, other than the injured state "... to invoke the responsibility of another state ... if the obligation breached is owed to the international community as a whole."[11] This provision adopts the category of *erga omnes obligations* already recognized by the International Court of Justice in a consistent jurisprudence that goes from the early *dictum* in the 1970 *Barcelona Traction* case[12] to the 2020 provisional measure adopted in the case concerning the *Application of the Genocide Convention (The Gambia v Myanmar)*.[13] But it is in the field of natural resources that we can find an explicit recognition of the idea that certain resources are to be considered common goods of the international community. Obviously, I am referring to the concept of the "common heritage of mankind," proclaimed by Article 136 of the 1982 UN Convention on the Law of the Sea, and to the related concept of "common concern of humankind" enunciated in the 1992 conventions on climate and on biodiversity. The latter

---

10 This has been the case with the United States and the decision of July 6, 2020 of the Trump Administration to walk out of the Organization effective July 6, 2021. This decision was promptly reversed by the Biden Administration by letter of January 20, 2021 notifying the UN Secretary General of the intention to reverse the decision of the prior administration.

11 The adoption of this provision was not free of controversy during the works of the International Law Commission, because of the request made by some states (France, Mexico, Slovakia, the United Kingdom) that the phrase "the international community as a whole" should be replaced by "the international community of States as a whole." *See* James Crawford, The International Law Commission's Articles on State Responsibility. Introduction, Text and Commentaries 39 ff. (Cambridge, 2002).

12 Judgment of 5 February 1970, ICJ Reports 1970, paras. 33 and 34.

13 Application of the Convention on the Prevention and Punishment of the Crime of Genocide (The Gambia v. Myanmar), Order of 23 January 2020, ICJ Reports, 2020, https://www.icj-cij.org/public/files/case-related/178/178-20200123-ORD-01-00-EN.pdf. *See also* Judgment of 22 July 2022 on Preliminary Objections in this case, https://www.icj-cij.org/public/files/case-related/178/178-20220722-JUD-01-00-EN.pdf.

convention has further developed the concept of "fair and equitable sharing of benefits" arising from the exploitation of the planet's biological resources.[14]

It is in this general normative context that we need to place the question of the role of international law in protecting and promoting public health in the face of sanitary emergencies such as the COVID-19 pandemic. With this in mind, we can now turn to the examination of the IDI's contribution to the promotion of international law on the protection of persons and peoples against the risk of epidemics and pandemics.

4   The 2021 Resolution of the Institut de Droit International on Epidemics, Pandemics and International Law

This Resolution was adopted by ample majority in the last week of August 2021 during the virtual Beijing session of the *Institut*. It consists of a text of seventeen articles replicating with minor changes the document elaborated by the 12th Commission under the guidance of the rapporteur Shinya Murase of Japan over a very short period of time, slightly over a year. The impulse to undertake this project had come directly from the Secretary General of the *Institut*, Marcelo Kohen, who in March 2020, when the virus was rapidly expanding worldwide, invited all members of the *Institut* to consider possible modes in which it could contribute to identify the role of international law in relation to the pandemic, including the identification of areas and aspects of the matter not sufficiently regulated by applicable norms. The Japanese member of the *Institut*, Shinya Murase, responded promptly by proposing the creation of a new commission and by submitting a short concept paper on objectives and proposed work methods. In view of the urgency of the situation, the Bureau of the IDI decided on March 29 to create a new commission (Commission 12) with the title "Epidemics and international law." The new Commission had Shinya Murase as rapporteur and consisted of 15 members representative of different geographic regions and legal cultures of the world.[15]

---

14   Nagoya Protocol to the Biodiversity Convention on Access to Genetic Resources and the Fair and Equitable Sharing of Benefits Arising from Their Utilization, Montreal, 2011. For a general comment, see Elisa Morgera, Elsa Tsioumani & Matthias Buck, Unravelling the Nagoya Protocol (Leiden/Boston, 2014).

15   The members of the 12th Commission were: José E. Alvarez, Anthony T. Anghie, Eyal Benvenisti, Francesco Francioni, Claudio Grossman, Vanda E. Lamm, Campbell McLachlan, Theodor Meron, Vaclav Mikulka, Gérard Niyugenko, Fausto Pocar, Antonio Remiro Brotons, Bernardo Sepulveda-Amor, Dire Tladi, and Xue Hanqin.

As with all initiatives of the IDI, this one was meant to proceed progressively step by step through the preparation and discussion of successive drafts proposed by the rapporteur on the basis of inputs and comments by members of the Commission. In the case of Commission 12, however, the work leading to the Resolution on epidemics and pandemics has been characterized, on the one hand, by the sense of urgency and by the extremely narrow time frame available for the completion of the project; and, on the other hand, by the plurality and sometimes sharp divergences of views among the members of the Commission. The main points of divergence have proved to be the type of legal instrument to be adopted (a draft convention, draft articles, a resolution), the role of the WHO, the limits of international cooperation in relation to state sovereignty, the difficult balancing between intellectual property rights (IPRs) and access to medication and vaccines as a component of the general interest of the international community to protect public health. As always, the outcome of the work and the adoption of the Resolution were the result of compromise among the discordant positions of the members of the 12th Commission and of the *Institut*.

– *The type of instrument.* The original idea of the rapporteur was that the work of the Commission should lead to the preparation of a draft convention on epidemics and international law. This option, however, was deemed to be too ambitious and unrealistic by the majority of the members of Commission 12. The choice in the end fell to the traditional legal instrument of the *Institut*, i.e. the Resolution. This instrument has in itself the potential of a mere codification of existing norms and principles of international law and of a progressive development of the law applicable to aspects of the pandemic not yet regulated, or not sufficiently regulated.

– *Purposes.* A good part of the Resolution is dedicated to the enunciation of purposes and principles of international law applicable to epidemics and pandemics. The Preamble opens with the statement that "the protection of persons from epidemics without discrimination of any kind and regardless of the sources and cause of the disease is a common concern of humankind." This entails a duty of solidarity and international cooperation in the prevention and control of epidemics and, at the same time, an obligation to respect the human rights of all persons and, in particular, of those who are in a position of vulnerability during the period of application of national and international sanitary measures, such as minors, migrants, persons with disabilities, and people in situations of extreme poverty. The fifth alinea of the Preamble recognizes the "vital role" of the WHO in the protection of public health and the importance of the International Health Regulations as an instrument for the international coordination of states' response to epidemics and pandemics. Finally, the Preamble highlights the necessity that international health law be interpreted and applied in a manner that is coherent with other relevant rules of international law.

- *General Principles.* Article 4 of the Resolution recognizes, among other norms of international law, the prominent role of general principles on the protection of human rights, primarily, the right to life and the right to the enjoyment of the highest attainable standard of health. These principles constitute limits to the sovereignty of every State. The first paragraph of this article also proclaims the right of access of every person to health services, medicines and vaccines. However, it is a pity that this proclamation risks remaining empty rhetoric when we consider that access to medical care and vaccines necessary to combat epidemics and pandemics inevitably have a cost, which many States are not able to afford. The Resolution tries to compensate this weakness of Article 4 by the formulation in Article 6 of a procedural obligation to cooperate at the international level in the spirit of "mutual solidarity" and of "common and shared responsibilities." The duty to cooperate applies not only to States, but also to relations with international organizations, including regional organizations. The aim is to promote scientific knowledge about the causes of the sanitary emergency, their impact on society, as well as the sharing of burdens and benefits of the efforts to combat the epidemic or pandemic (Article 6, para. 3).

- *Due diligence.* Article 5 of the Resolution requires that every State must exercise "due diligence" in the adoption and implementation of legislative, administrative or judicial measures intended to prevent, control or reduce an epidemic or pandemic. However, this article does not specify whether due diligence is to be gauged in accordance with the effective capacity of the relevant State (*diligentia quam in suis*) or in accordance with international law parameters, notably, the International Health Regulations. The concluding phrase of Article 5, para. 1 speaks in favor of the first solution, since it recognizes that "... States shall have due regard for the measures taken by other States to fulfil their obligations in accordance with international law." Unwittingly, this is an indirect manifestation of deference to each State's autonomy in determining the appropriate level of due diligence in preventing and controlling epidemics and pandemics. The consequence is that the due diligence remains anchored to a national standard, rather than to international standards, such as those embodied in the International Health regulations.

- *Norm interaction.* The experience of the COVID-19 pandemic, as of all epidemics, demonstrates that the application of specific rules for the prevention and control of sanitary emergencies may interfere with the observance of other norms of international law, such as those on the protection of human rights and individual liberties, of the environment, of foreign investments and trade, and even with rules and principles concerning international security. Article 7 of the Resolution takes this possibility into account and prescribes that "rules of international law relating to epidemics and other relevant rules of international law should, to the extent possible, be identified, interpreted, applied and implemented as coherent obligations in line with the principles of harmonization and systemic integration, in order to avoid conflicts between obligations." Leaving aside the unhappy linguistic confusion between rules and obligations, this text follows the current practice of "compatibility clauses" included in many international treaties in order to prevent or minimize the risk of "fragmentation" of international law with the proliferation of different legal regimes potentially conflicting one with another. This provision of the Resolution does not include any criterion of prevalence of one type of norms over another. It only affirms the need to seek a reasonable harmonization between norms applicable to epidemics and pandemics and norms relevant to other sectors of international law. At a practical level, the required harmonization can be achieved by application of the principle of "presumption of conformity," which may assist the interpreter in cases of apparent conflict between applicable norms of international law. Unfortunately, the principle of presumption of conformity is not always helpful to resolve conflicts of norms. This is the case, for example, of the obligation of every State to ensure access to health care and vaccines under article 4, para. 1, which may be incompatible with the rigorous observance of the intellectual property rights – patents and technological processes – referred to in Article 7, para. 1.

– *Procedural obligations.* Next to the substantive obligations examined above, the Resolution provides also for a set of procedural obligations binding upon the States affected by the epidemic and other States. Article 9 lays down the obligation to notify the WHO, other interested States and relevant international organizations of any "unexpected or unusual public health event" and of any public health measure adopted and implemented in response to such event. Paragraph 2 of the same Article places upon the affected State the duty to disclose any relevant information regarding the risk of epidemic, as well as the obligation to guarantee access to information by the public and freedom of information and expression by the media in relation to the outbreak of the epidemic. Article 11 requires States affected by epidemics or pandemics promptly to seek external assistance from the WHO, other States or competent actors whenever the danger posed by the health emergency seems to exceed national response capacity. The effective provision of such external assistance presupposes the adoption of measures by the receiving State that may facilitate access to its territory of persons and equipment. At the same time, the State receiving assistance must adopt appropriate measures to ensure protection of relief personnel and of goods and equipment present in its territory for the purpose of providing external assistance (Article 11, para 3). To the duty to seek external assistance corresponds the duty of "other States, along with the WHO, the United Nations and other potential assisting actors to provide assistance. However, this is not an unconditional obligation: it is contingent upon the conclusion of an agreement between the recipient State and the assisting actors and subject to the limiting clause "as appropriate."

– *Special obligations.* The Resolution recognizes that in the exceptional situation of an epidemic or pandemic it may not be possible to guarantee the full enjoyment of all individual rights and freedoms, as prescribed by international and national law. However, Article 12 prescribes that measures restricting such rights and freedoms must be rationally justified on the basis of scientific evidence and applied in accordance with the principles of necessity, proportionality and non-discrimination. The same Article provides for two special obligations of a humanitarian character. The first concerns the prohibition of expulsion, extradition or otherwise transfer of persons to a State affected by an epidemic if it is established that that State is not in a position to provide the necessary measures to protect the health of the persons to be transferred. The second obligation concerns possible sanctions that may be adopted or applied against a State or States affected by an epidemic. Article 12, para. 4 prescribes that States must abstain from adopting economic sanctions such as to undermine the capacity of the targeted State to cope with an epidemic in its territory. A similar obligation concerns the suspension of sanctions already in force insofar as their continuing application may hinder access to medicines, health care and vaccines necessary to control and reduce the epidemic. Unfortunately, these provisions on sanctions neglect to condemn the practice of economic sanctions adopted as a form of retaliation against unwelcome requests by certain States to provide in a transparent and complete manner information and data on the origin and causes of the COVID-19 pandemic. An emblematic case is that of commercial sanctions adopted by China against Australia as a consequence of the latter State's legitimate request to promote within the framework of the WHO an independent inquiry on the origin and causes of the pandemic in China. This has irritated the Chinese government but is not a valid reason for the unilateral adoption of commercial sanctions at a time of a serious international health emergency.

– *Post-epidemic action*. The Resolution recognizes that an accurate evaluation of the action taken by States, the WHO and other relevant actors in the
course of the pandemic is the best guarantee against the recurrence of such
events. Article 14, para. 2 provides that each State that was most seriously
affected by the pandemic shall establish a commission of experts to conduct
a "post-epidemic review to assess the propriety of its own actions and omissions." Also the WHO is bound to conduct a thorough review of its performance in accordance with its constitution and its procedures. At the same
time, the Resolution contemplates the establishment of an independent
panel of experts to review the conduct of "each key State." However, here
the Resolution adopts very soft language as such panel only "may convene"
and not "shall" convene. Also, the Resolution does not specify what is to be
intended by the expression "each key State." Surely, one must assume that
it includes the State on whose territory the virus originated as well as the
States that have mostly contributed to the spreading of the contagion. In
any event, States are bound to share all relevant information among themselves, with the competent organizations and with their population (Article
14, para. 3).

– *International responsibility*. The question of the international responsibility
for the spreading of the pandemic has inflamed the international debate
on the causes of the virus with accusations to China and the WHO of negligence in preventing and controlling the diffusion of the virus and with many
judicial actions brought before national courts to seek damages for the
devastating economic loss caused by the pandemic.[16] But on this important
issue the IDI Resolution remains quite vague and one could say that it limits
itself to stating the obvious. Article 15 provides in para. 2 that: "A breach
of the obligation under international law of a State to prevent, reduce and
control epidemics or to provide early information on the outbreak of epidemics to other States concerned or affected and to the competent international organizations shall entail the responsibility of that State." This is
a simple statement of principle, which eludes the most critical aspects of
the responsibility for damage caused by the pandemic. What is the correct
method for addressing the question of responsibility? Starting from the precise content of the obligation of due diligence? From the damage caused to
other States? Or to communities? Or single individuals? Or should we rather
look at the issue of responsibility in terms of breach of an obligation owed

---

16   *See*, for example, the class action entered by a group of affected business entities on the
Southern District Court of Florida, Case 1:20-cv-21108-UU Document 11, FLSD Docket
05/04/2020.

to the international community as a whole for the enforcement of which any State could act for the protection of health as a global public good? Further, in the case of legal actions undertaken before national courts, what role would have the rule of jurisdictional immunity of the responding State? Finally, why is the responsibility limited to the case in which a State fails to provide information of the outbreak of a virus to other States and to competent organizations and not also to the population of the same State? This is the most direct victim of the possible negligence or the withholding of information on the part of national authorities. It is a pity that a more in-depth examination of these aspects has not been possible because of the time constraints in the adoption of the Resolution.

5   Conclusions

In deciding to elaborate and adopt a Resolution on epidemics and pandemics, the IDI had the stated objective of restating and progressively developing the international law on the protection of persons and of on early and effective response in case of outbreak of epidemics and pandemics. This objective has been achieved at unprecedented speed under the pressure of the seemingly never-ending expansion of the contagion and of the various forms of national response to control and minimize the devastating effects at a sanitary, economic and social level. The result, in my opinion, is more a work of restatement of general principles than of progressive development of international law. The Resolution contributes to reaffirming the principle of *common concern of humankind* and to extending it from the field of environmental law, where it had originally been conceived, to the field of public health. Closely related to this principle is the value of *international solidarity* and of international cooperation in the fight against epidemics and pandemics and in the fulfilment of the responsibility to protect persons from contagion. The reaffirmation of these principles is of vital importance at a time in which the COVID-19 pandemic offers a bleak balance sheet of millions of deaths and the irrational resurgence of nationalism and distrust in the international institutions and even in the scientific evidence of the seriousness of the disease and of the safety and effectiveness of vaccines. These are major obstacles to international solidarity and to meaningful international cooperation. The Resolution contributes to identifying the main substantive and procedural obligations of the States in the event of epidemics or pandemics, both with regard to the prevention and control of contagion in accordance with the principle of due diligence and with regard to the duty of prompt communication of all relevant information concerning the origin and outbreak of the epidemic in their territory. This obligation is of fundamental importance also in view of the persisting uncertainties on the causes of the pandemic and of some residual reluctance of some States to cooperate in ascertaining the origin of the virus. Also, its relevance must be considered in relation to the obligations to request and to offer help whenever the harm caused by the epidemic is likely to exceed the capacity of effective response by the affected State.

Surely, the Resolution could have offered more innovative insights for a progressive development of a law for long treated as a specialized and some-what secluded field of international law. It could have contributed more to the strengthening of international sanitary institutions and of the respective regulations - notably of the WHO and the IHRs. It could have better clarified the relation of IPRs to the global public good of health and the sensitive issue of international responsibility. We shall see if this Resolution will have a fol-low-up dealing with these complex issues. For now, it represents an important testimony of the value of international law as a common language of governments and peoples for continuing to dialogue on how to best protect, in every part of the world, the common good of public health against the risk of epidemics and pandemics.

CHAPTER 12

Governometrics and Rule of Law Transformations in Low- and Middle-Income Countries

Craig Hammer*

Prologue

It is an honor to reflect on the astonishing contributions made by my friend, collaborator, and colleague, Professor Siegfried Wiessner, throughout his long and remarkable career. I am very pleased to dedicate this piece in his honor, and to briefly touch on a few specifics concerning the crucial importance and impact of just some of Siegfried's myriad accomplishments. I have known of and greatly admired Siegfried and his work since I was a student, and I have had the pleasure of being his friend and colleague for more than 10 years. We are both members of the Society for the Policy Sciences, a multidisciplinary organization committed, in short, to solving problems of all varieties, from across the public and private sectors, encompassing both micro and macro issues. This was the ideal forum in which to first interact with Siegfried.

It was in 2012 that I had first attended one of his dazzling presentations on the intersection of poverty alleviation and policy development, and his remarks on indigenous peoples' rights to their lands, culture, and autonomy was an intellectual feast; his analysis included insights from the social sciences, policy studies, and environmental studies, mixing real-world, community-level examples with micro and macro-level theoretical analysis, and he pointed to legal reforms to be pursued to minimize risks. All this he somehow made simultaneously accessible for non-social scientists, non-lawyers, and non-environmental scientists, and still extremely engaging for his colleagues across all three disciplines. I recall being starstruck: at this time, Siegfried was Chair of the International Law Association's (ILA's) Committee on the Rights of Indigenous Peoples and he was busily marshalling global support and expertise which ultimately enabled the ILA's approval of Resolution No. 5/2012, on the Rights of Indigenous Peoples. This was a monumental undertaking. I believe that his drive stems from his deeply held sense of humanism.

* Senior Program Manager with the Development Data Group at the World Bank.

© CRAIG HAMMER, 2023 | DOI:10.1163/9789004524835_013

Siegfried is an eminently ethical and good-natured person, and his modesty and compassion give him interpersonal currency with people from all walks of life. I have been fortunate enough to witness how Siegfried's commitment to poverty alleviation and collaborative support for at-risk peoples has motivated him to design, launch, and manage large-scale initiatives to help enable these underserved communities to become active agents in their own social and economic development. The breadth of Siegfried's skill, knowledge and dedication amply justify his reputation for excellence. Put simply, Siegfried is an internationally recognized and celebrated scholar, scientist, and educator with exceptional records of achievement and accolades in research and operational work, and I am a better person and practitioner for knowing him.

1   Introduction

The words "governance" and "the rule of law" are terms of art often invoked by economists, lawyers, and policymakers to characterize a myriad of understandings concerning legal-political regimes. Neither seems to have a single, precise definition. Their meanings vary within and among organizations and countries, and the words themselves are often conflated. The dominant paradigm refers to effective governance as an outcome made possible at least in part by effective rule of law. Efforts to support the institutionalization of effective governance often occur "through" rule of law strengthening activities and typically focus on top-down, state-centered approaches which concentrate on law reform and government institutions, particularly judiciaries, to build business-friendly legal systems that, it has been argued, bring about poverty alleviation and social development. This understanding has achieved a level of orthodoxy in the international development community and has been widely endorsed by authoritative commentators because it is thought to encourage growth and reduce corruption.

A range of development practitioners – economists, lawyers, social development specialists and more – have interpreted a correlation between the two variables – effective governance through rule of law strengthening or reforms – and concluded that one has a causal impact on the other; the direction of the causal impact depends on the particular author's analysis. In the multilateral context, successive Generals Counsel to the World Bank, starting with Shihata (World Bank General Counsel between 1983 and 1998) and including Tung (1999–2003) and Danino (2003–2006), have emphasized the importance of effective governance made possible by the rule of law for social and economic development. While they refrained from defining their terms in detail, they each set out the conditions in when, they contend, effective governance through strengthening the rule of law prevails. This, in turn, has resulted in increased World Bank attention to how the institution can promote more effective governance through efforts to strengthen the rule of law in low-and-middle income countries, which in recent years has focused on the institutional setting in which policy is created and executed together with customized support for "enablers" (such as increased attention to political accountability, the quality of bureaucracy, and much more).

The World Bank's country support for effective governance through rule of law strengthening and reforms has grown significantly in size and scope across regions throughout the last two decades. The organization has recruited a large number of dedicated rule of law specialists from around the world – and across legal traditions – and designated them "governance specialists" who are co-located in a single department – the World Bank's "Governance Global Practice" – which currently comprises a team of more than 750 specialists worldwide, from a diverse set of disciplines, deployed across World Bank client countries. These specialists are now managing governance projects collectively comprising billions of dollars' worth of technical assistance, loans, and grant-based support. These specialists are additionally involved in more than 1,200 tasks in other sectors. They produce more than 350 studies per year to respond to specific queries from policy makers from around the world and also provide fiduciary support to the implementation of over 2,600 World Bank projects in every country and sector. A cursory summary of current areas and dimensions of rule of law assistance by the World Bank includes: (i) increasing the effectiveness of justice sector institutions and systems; (ii) enhancing openness and transparency in the public sector and engaging and communicating with citizens in ways that do not only deliver on essential public service values but also increase the effectiveness and efficiency of public policies and programs; and (iii) facilitating streamlined delivery of good governance in sectors and key public goods – such as in health, water, education, energy and extractives. These activities complement and otherwise augment other governance support processes, such as efforts to strengthen government financial management, procurement and performance monitoring systems.

As such, the World Bank has folded rule of law support and reform initiatives into its operational portfolio as a central element of its efforts to promote and enable "good governance" in low- and middle-income countries. The Bank's 2017 *World Development Report* on "Governance and the Law" unpacks key governance principles. This report states that "governance" describes: "the process through which state and nonstate actors interact to design and implement policies within a given set of formal and informal rules that shape and are shaped by power."[1] The report goes on to assert that "governance takes place at different levels, from international bodies, to national state institutions, to local government agencies, to community and business associations. These dimensions often overlap, creating a complex network of actors and interests." Chapter 4 of the report is dedicated to the role of law as underpinning effective governance to drive social and economic development and asserts that "[i]t has long been established that the rule of law—which at its core requires that government officials and citizens be bound by and act consistently with the law—is the very basis of the good governance needed to realize full social and economic potential."[2]

Thus, the World Bank has articulated an institutional position concerning the role and importance of the rule of law as a core driver of good governance, to the extent that the latter is impossible without the former. This position is hardly unique. In recent years, the global development community has generally coalesced on the role and value of governance through the rule of law for social and economic development, so much so that promotion and enablement of good governance through the rule of law in developing countries has been prioritized among the Sustainable Development Goals (SDG s) and has been identified as a cross-cutting priority for support in countries around the world in back-to-back IDA replenishments.[3]

The World Bank's – and the broader international development community's – programmatic support to strengthen the quality of governance through rule of law support in emerging economies continues despite persistent questions about its utility and impact in theory and practice, including by Thomas Carothers in his book, *Promoting the Rule of Law Abroad: The Problem of Knowledge*, in which he famously wrote: "The rapidly growing field of rule-of-law assistance is operating from a disturbingly thin base of knowledge at every level—with respect to the core rationale of the work, the question of where the essence of the rule of law actually resides in different societies, how change in the rule of law occurs, and what the real effects are of changes that are produced." In his subsequent paper, *Rule of Law Temptations*, Carothers

1   World Bank, World Development Report: Governance and the Law 41 (2017), *available at* https://www.worldbank.org/en/publication/wdr2017 [hereinafter World Bank 2017].

2   *Id.* at 83.

3   World Bank, *Building Back Better from the Crisis: Toward a Green, Resilient and Inclusive Future* (Report from the Executive Directors of the International Development Association to the Board of Governors Additions to IDA Resources: Twentieth Replenishment, February 17, 2022), *available at* https://documents1.worldbank.org/curated/en/163861645 554924417 /pdf/IDA20-Building-Back-Better-from-the-Crisis-Toward-a-Green-Resilient-and-Inclusive -Future.pdf.

went further and asserted: "[r]elatively few citizens of countries in the former Soviet Union, South America, sub-Saharan Africa, South Asia, and elsewhere would say that the apparent global consensus on the importance of the rule of law has translated into actual marked improvement of the state of law in their societies." Other similar critiques have been made by Ronald Daniels, Colette Rausch, Michael Trebilcock, and Rachel Kleinfeld.

This disagreement about the utility and impact of the effect of rule of law assistance and linked outcomes in the quality of governance focuses on the intrinsic difficulty of knowing how rule of law works or fails in practice from context to context, which encompasses the myriad political economy factors which collectively comprise and condition the enabling – or disabling – environment for rule of law at all levels in a target community, county, region, state, and/or nation, and at all touch points in between. Put a different way, measuring changes in governance over time and across countries, in a valid and reliable manner, remains a contested issue.

2   Problem Statement

This chapter seeks to add value to the relatively narrow, continuing debate about how to improve efforts to promote and enable good governance through rule of law support by the international development community, with an emphasis on efforts by the World Bank. More specifically, the overarching concern of this chapter is to critically evaluate the different measures or indicators of corruption, which might logically be used to inform policymakers across countries and over time, as well as explore potentially viable complements (and alternatives) to these measures. The intention is to determine whether it is possible to associate changes in efforts to promote and otherwise identify institutional features which may incentivize improvements in governance reforms (or strengthening), which may then inform the operational agendas of international development organizations, such as the World Bank. A more thorough understanding of how organizations like the World Bank implement governance through rule of law assistance to combat corruption – in particular how it assesses the scope of corruption challenges to be overcome and the relative effectiveness of interventions – might bring benefits, challenges, and opportunities into focus. It may also surface more shades of gray in what has been a largely black and white disagreement between practitioners and scholars (and consultants straddling both sides) about how to understand and track corruption, as well as how to design governance interventions to strengthen rule of law and combat corruption across country contexts. Indeed, a better understanding might likewise help to move operational teams in international development organizations and government leaders in countries seeking to improve the quality of national or subnational governance toward the development and promulgation of strategy adjustments, such as in the direction of more context-sensitive governance assistance approaches in low- and middle-income countries.

3   Methodology

The methodology applied in this chapter is the Policy Sciences, a useful blueprint for comprehensive issue analysis with related tools and analytical techniques, as devised by Harold Lasswell and Myres McDougal. The Policy Sciences includes approaches designed to clarify the context in which interventions arise, including models to predict and discern problems, as well as techniques to respond to these problems via processes to promote and protect human dignity, which is the fundamental objective of rule of law transformations.[4] The Policy Sciences also includes approaches to understand the layered complexity of the role of observers, participants, and third-party interveners and the extent to which these actors influence or impact the objects of their observation, participants in observed processes, and/or the intervention in part or as a whole. In short, the Policy Sciences provides a framework to enable "configurative thinking"[5] – a balanced approach to analysis which aims

---

4   *See* Myres S. McDougal et al., Studies in World Public Order 987–992 (1960) ("The values we recommend for postulation as the goal values of human dignity are ... merely the traditional values of humanitarianism and enlightenment bequeathed to us by most of the great religions and secular philosophies prevailing in recent centuries"). *See also* Winston Nagan & Craig Hammer, *Communications Theory and World Public Order: The Anthropomorphic, Jurisprudential Foundations of International Human Rights*, 47 Va. J. Int'l L. 725, 742–772 (2007) ("...the New Haven School developed an applied form of its general theory of jurisprudence ... which overarchingly sought to establish a universally applicable theory of human dignity"); *see generally*, Siegfried Wiessner & Andrew R. Willard, *Policy-Oriented Jurisprudence and Human Rights Abuses in Internal Conflict: Toward a World Public Order of Human Dignity*, 93 Am. J. Int'l L. 319 (1999).

5   *See* Harold D. Lasswell & Myres S. McDougal, Jurisprudence for a Free Society: Studies in Law xxx (1992). Winston Nagan and Judit Otvos describe "configurative thinking" as

     ...the establishment of a creative orientation to inquiry and involvement in an effort to influence beneficent outcomes... this is different from the conventional modes of thinking narrowly in terms of the 'is' and the 'ought' or thinking in terms of the logical syllogism. Configurative ... thinking therefore requires normative discourse to guide inquiry, as well as thinking in terms of causes, consequences, trends, future projections, and the creation of policy alternatives. The epistemology of the policy sciences thus requires the use and

"for the most comprehensive map possible ... [and which] tolerate[s] no rug under which ... [to] sweep alleged externalities,"[6] which even accounts for the self-awareness of actors and their roles in the substance of the analysis.

Specifically, this chapter looks to the five intellectual tasks of the policy-oriented approach to evaluate the different measures or indicators of governance and the rule of law used by the World Bank, which might be used to inform policymakers across countries and over time. Section 1 begins by clarifying my own observational standpoint, and then identifies the apparent goals and claims of the primary actors involved in delivering or receiving support for governance reforms through financing and technical assistance for rule of law support from the World Bank. Section 2 then identifies key trends associated with the concept of governance through rule of law assistance, including the origins and implications of this assistance by (and for) the World Bank, as well as estimations of the role and value of efforts to measure and assess the quality of efforts to strengthen governance through rule of law support. Section 3 unpacks several factors which may condition the achievability of the legitimate goals identified, with an emphasis on clarifying the rigor and effectiveness of the World Bank's current efforts to provide governance through rule of law assistance to low- and middle-income countries, as well as global efforts to assess and monitor it. Section 4 synthesizes a series of projections which emerge from the trends and conditioning factors examined, together with an assessment of the likelihood that these projections may come to pass. Section 5 goes on to identify possible alternative strategies, which might enable the World Bank to maximize benefits and minimize risks in its future efforts to strengthen governance processes and outcomes through rule of law assistance. Section 6 thereafter offers some key lessons learned and concluding recommendations.

---

integration of a multitude of intellectual tasks beyond conventional modes of thought, inquiry, and expression. ... [and] assumes critical tasks of creative orientation to observation and participation, as well as responsibility for the political consequences of policy and social values that come under the label of human dignity.

Winston Nagan & Judit Otvos, *Legal Theory and the Anthropocene Challenge: The Implications of Law, Science, and Policy for Weapons of Mass Destruction and Climate Change: The Expanding and Constraining Boundaries of Legal Space and Time and the Challenge of the Anthropocene,* 12 J. L. & Soc. Challenges 150, 156–157 (2010).

6   *See* Lasswell & McDougal, Jurisprudence for a Free Society, *supra* note 5.

4   Where to Start: Establishing a Standpoint

From its inception as a theory for inquiry, the Policy Sciences framework has been intentionally sensitive to the dynamics and implications of inquiry, incident observation, interaction with a range of stakeholders, and the occurrence of events in particular contexts (from the geographic to the temporal and more). The genius of the Policy Sciences is that it accounts for the subconscious bias of the observer as the starting point for any process of inquiry. While the notion that an observer may unintentionally project his or her beliefs onto an external subject or phenomenon is one that anthropologists have long understood, its application to law (and development) is somewhat less familiar territory.[7] Indeed, in the international development context, this inclusion of a focus on the standpoint of the observer/practitioner *ex ante* has only relatively recently achieved mainstream recognition.[8]

Recognition of standpoint is likewise gathering traction in public law. For example, Laurence Tribe suggested that the processes of observation "shapes both the judges themselves and the materials being judged."[9] To the extent that all participants in social process—including specialists in scientific (legal, social or physical) observation—are in some degree observers, they are also in some degree, participants. Thus, "the results courts announce – the ways they view the legal terrain and what they say about it — will in turn have continuing effects that reshape the nature of what the courts initially undertook to review, even beyond anything they directly order anyone to do or refrain from doing."[10] The same may be said for the role of the mediate interventions of scholarship

---

7   An exception was United States Supreme Court Justice Oliver Wendell Holmes, who rejected formalism for a more nuanced conception of the law; he once stated that "the life of the law has not been logic, it has been experience." *See* Stephen Burton, The Path of the Law and Its Influence: The Legacy of Oliver Wendell Holmes, Jr. 2 (S. Burton ed., 2000). *See generally,* Winston P. Nagan, *Not Just a Descending Trail: Traversing Holmes' Many Paths of the Law,* 49 Fla. L. Rev. 463 (1997).

8   For example, the World Bank's 2015 World Development Report entitled *Mind, Society and Behavior* examined "the idea that paying attention to how humans think (the processes of mind) and how history and context shape thinking (the influence of society) can improve the design and implementation of development policies and interventions that target human choice and action (behavior)". *See id.* at 2, *available at* https://www.worldbank .org/en/publication/wdr2015. The World Bank has since launched the "Mind, Behavior, and Development Unit" (eMBeD) to put the report's conclusions into operational practice in the institution's client countries.

9   *See* Laurence Tribe, *The Curvature of Constitutional Space: What Lawyers Can Learn from Modern Physics,* 103 Harv. L. Rev. 1, 20–23 (1989).

10   *Id.*

or of claimants or indeed of legal activists and others. Tribe noted that modern physical theory stresses the salience of pervasive interaction, that is interdetermination and influence between an observer and the observed phenomenon, and that an appreciation of this insight for the legal and social universe, "acknowledges the interconnectedness of legal events and to recognize, as modern physics has, the interdependence between the process of observing and what is observed ... avoid(s) the parochial fallacy of looking at the legal universe only through the eyes of those in power."[11]

Harold Lasswell recognized the limitations of a Newtonian conception of observation. He wrote:

> [I]t is impossible to abolish uncertainty by the refinement of retrospective observations, by the accumulation of historical detail, by the application of precision methods to elapsed events; the crucial test of adequate analysis is nothing less than the future verification of the insight into the nature of the master configuration against which details are constructed. Each specific interpretation is subject to redefinition as the structural potentialities of the future become actualized in the past and present of participant observers. The analyst moves between the contemplation of detail and of configuration, knowing that the soundness of result is an act of creative orientation rather than of automatic projection. The search for precision in the routines of the past must be constantly chastened and given relevance and direction by reference to the task of self-orientation, which is the goal of analysis.[12]

Michael Reisman similarly recognized that "no standpoint is more authentic than another but the scholar must be sensitive to the variations in perception that attend each perspective."[13] With these insights in mind, acknowledging an appropriate observational standpoint and appertaining normative preferences from which to describe and evaluate the state of Rule of Law Development by a multilateral institution such as the World Bank can be a useful starting point to account for this reality that the observer in physics, as in law, is an integral part of the action.

To this end, I am a Senior Program Manager at the World Bank. My role is both operational (in that I lead or collaborate to support World Bank projects

---

11   *Id.* at 38.

12   Harold D. Lasswell, World Politics and Personal Insecurity 13 (1965).

13   W. Michael Reisman, *The View from the New Haven School of International Law, in* W. Michael Reisman et al., International Law in Contemporary Perspective 3 (Foundation Press 2004).

in client countries) and strategic (in that I am responsible for development strategy within my World Bank unit). I specialize in governance reforms, and in particular in open government, open data, and information integrity initiatives. My work at the World Bank has focused on Bank operations, or projects, focusing on strengthening laws, policies, and regulations focused on access to information, open government data, and data-driven decision-making for improved public service delivery to traditionally marginalized and underserved communities in more than thirty countries in Africa, the Middle East, Latin America, South Asia, and Central Europe. In short, my particular focus is on efforts to support governments' decision-making in low- and middle-income countries to rely on robust evidentiary bases, as well as support countries to create legal and policy environments which enable free public access to data and information for mass public consumption and to inform decision-making by citizens on issues which matter to them.

With respect to my work as a development practitioner, I recognize that social and economic development challenges – from the reality and future threat of pandemics, to persistent fragility or conflict in some countries to significant backsliding in others, to refugee crises, to climate change, to biodiversity losses, to significant gaps in sustainable infrastructure and more – are layered, complex, and largely interconnected. Indeed, the list of global challenges to social, economic, and sustainable development seems to get longer each day. Each successive challenge is a further affirmative justification for the need for robust, flexible and effective multilateral development banks and organizations to bring international partnership, coordination, financing, and expertise to bear on the world's most layered, complex challenges.

Drawing from the distinctive insights of Lasswell and McDougal, an objective of this chapter is to explore the intellectual and theoretical challenges of efforts by The World Bank to devise and achieve uptake of "good governance," with an emphasis on both the theory and practice of rule of law reforms in World Bank client countries. This includes a brief overview of present understandings of how governance reforms occur from context to context, and considerations for how organizations such as the World Bank can strengthen the design and implementation of efforts to support good governance and the rule of law in low-and middle-income countries.

5   Goals

To establish goals for this analysis, definitional clarity is important. To do this, I borrow from a host of authoritative commentators. I turn to Lasswell and

McDougal with particular respect to their views on "decisions" and "policy," as well as the roles and importance of "perspectives"[14] and "operations"[15] of decision-makers in general, but more specifically on the perspectives and operations of development practitioners from the point of view of a disengaged observer. In their view, an observer seeks to observe the perspectives and operations of decision-making. The observer is in the role of inquirer. What the observer seeks to observe are the perspectives of the operators (their identifications,[16] demands,[17] and expectations[18]) and what they actually decide in fact.

Accordingly, this section will briefly clarify and appraise goals and claims of a short list of primary actors involved in delivering or receiving governance and rule of law support from the World Bank. This goal clarification exercise will seek to ground relatively abstract goals and claims so that I may briefly parse motivations had by each group; my intention is to then use these abstract goals and claims as the lens through which my larger analysis may be undertaken, with the objective of identifying recommendations for the global development community, including the World Bank, toward helping enable proximity to the formal, legitimate goals of these key actor groups. Even where a goal analysis yields prescriptive signs and symbols that are normatively ambiguous – such as the range of issues inherent in efforts to promote and enable good governance through rule of law assistance by the World Bank – it is hoped that this analysis may nevertheless be useful because it aims to set out a framework to provide clarity where there was little or none before.

---

14   Harold D. Lasswell & Abraham Kaplan, Power and Society 25 (Yale University Press, 1950). "A *perspective* is a pattern of identifications, demands, and expectations."

15   *Id.* at 10. "An *operation* is the nonsymbol event in an act."

16   *Id.* at 11. "*Identification* is the process by which a symbol user symbolizes his egos a member of some aggregate or group of egos (X identifies with Y's if X symbolizes X as a Y)."

17   *Id.* at 17. "A *demand statement* is one expressing a valuation by the maker of the statement. A *symbol of demand* is one used in the demand statements to refer to the value."

18   *Id.* at 21. "An *expectation statement* is one symbolizing the (past, present, or future) occurrence of a state of affairs without demands or identifications. A *symbol of expectation* is one used in expectation statements to characterize the state of affairs. .... One index of how persons or groups will act is the flow of different kinds of expectation statements, and the currency of symbols employed in them. We can classify expectations, for instance, as 'optimistic' or 'pessimistic' about each constituent of the self ... Expectation symbols like 'progress' become sentimentalized and intertwined with demands for the attainment of a better world."

5.1 Formal Goals among Emerging Economies

It seems an understatement to note that the goals of the World Bank's range of low- and-middle-income client countries are indeed varied. It is possible – thanks to the work of a World Bank unit called the Development Finance Vice Presidency, which plays an intermediation role to align World Bank Group and partner resources to meet client country needs[19] – to identify a small number of top-most priorities among the Bank's country clients. These priorities are enshrined in the World Bank's most recent resource replenishment process called the "IDA replenishment." By way of brief background, the International Development Association ("IDA") *process* is the World Bank's primary funding mechanism for low-income countries and mobilizes support from across World Bank member countries in three-year disbursement cycles.[20] Discussions with members focus on specific commitments by the Bank to focus resources on key country priorities (or "special themes"). At a high level, these special themes are:

– Governance and Institutions;
– Fragility, Conflict and Violence-affected states;
– Climate Change;
– Gender; and
– Jobs & Economic Transformation.[21]

The primacy of the "Governance and Institutions" IDA19 and IDA20 commitments across countries is a telling commentary on the importance of strengthening good governance though supporting rule of law and the institutions which enable for countries' other social and economic development priorities. References to a country's goals of improving governance, rule of law, and governance institutions are likewise borne out in a range of World Bank Country Partnership Frameworks,[22] which each detail the full scope of World Bank support for each individual client country in support of enabling that country

---

19   *See* World Bank, Development Finance Vice Presidency, *available at* https://www
      .worldbank.org/en/about/unit/dfi (last visited July 11, 2022).

20   World Bank support for low-income (or IDA) countries comes from contributions from
      across World Bank member countries. World Bank leadership meets with representatives
      of these member countries to replenish this primary funding for low-income countries
      (called the "IDA process") in 3-year periods. The World Bank is presently on its 20th itera-
      tion of 3-year replenishment, hence the "IDA20" designation.

21   *See* World Bank, IDA19 Replenishment, *available at* https://ida.worldbank.org/replenishments
      /ida19-replenishment; and World Bank, IDA20 Replenishment, *available at* https://ida
      .worldbank.org/en/replenishments/ida20-replenishment (last visited July 11, 2022).

22   *See* World Bank, Country Partnership Frameworks, *available at* https://openknowledge
      .worldbank.org/handle/ 10986/23100 (last visited July 11, 2022).

to achieve its development goals. It is clear that this group's goals are at a minimum motivated by key values such as power, enlightenment, respect, well-being, skill, and rectitude.

5.2   *Informal Goals of Some Public Actors in Emerging Economies*

While the above "formal" goals held by government officials leading low- and-middle income countries – as demonstrated by codified summaries of these goals, on which World Bank loans and technical support projects are based – no doubt represent the authentic objectives of many public officials, the phenomena of poor governance and prevalent corruption in many countries around the world indicate that certain "informal" goals likewise exist among some officials. For the purpose of this analysis, these "informal" goals may be abstracted into a high-level concept: "corruption," that is: the abuse of entrusted power for private gain.[23]

Justice Holmes provides a useful insight with respect to this abstracted goal, which has deeply influenced judicial philosophy; in his groundbreaking *The Path of Law*, he suggested that the most practical way to analyze the efficacy of law is to view it from the point of view of the "bad man."[24] His insight is that while not all human beings are necessarily bad (or men), they are capable of holding good and bad perspectives, and so to view law through the prism of a "bad man's" perspective may inform legal scholars' view of not just of legal problems but of the perspectives of the individuals to be governed by it, including their identity, their demands, as well as their claims and expectations. The same concept may be applied to the examination of the efficacy of efforts to support or strengthen governance through rule of law assistance in developing countries, and those government officials with goals and claimswhich may conflict with these efforts.

Nagan and Manausa likewise share valuable insights into how the "bad man's" perspective must be accounted for in operational efforts by organizations like the World Bank to strengthen good governance through rule of law support and reforms, and to combat corruption:

> The bad man is partly a consumer of the law ... [and] economists ... use the bad man's self-interest as the cornerstone of an economic theory based on self-interest. In this sense, the economic man has only his own interest in mind as a consumer. Behind this insight was Holmes' idea of

---

23   Transparency International, *How do you define corruption?*, *available at* https://www
.transparency.org/what-is-corruption#define (last visited July 11, 2022).
24   Oliver Wendell Holmes, *The Path of the Law*, 10 Harv. L. Rev. 457 (1897).

separating law from morality and values. The only real value of concern to the bad man was his economic self-interest.[25]

The problems to which governance reform efforts respond are in fact conflicts about claims or demands for values which, in general, seem to focus in particular on power and wealth. In other words, the problem of the "bad man" vis-a-vis other actors in this section reflect the difference of what claimants *have* and what they *want*. Good governance through rule of law assistance can likewise be abstracted to describe a specialized form of decision-making which adds predictability to these conflicts; it functions as the enabling environment for authoritative and controlling decision-making in the public order. This will thus employ the "bad man's" goal of self-interest (which precipitates corruption), while recognizing (without exploring) the reality that this phenomenon may take any number of forms and be motivated by more complex rationales than pure self-interest.[26] It is important to note that while this goal objectively lacks legitimacy, it is widespread and must be accounted for in this analysis.

5.3   *Goals of the World Bank*

From the creation of the Bretton Woods institutions in 1944, which sought to rebuild both Europe and the global economic order after the horrors of World War II; to a sharpened focus on poverty reduction and post-colonial reforms for social and economic improvements including through the formation of regional development banks; to the nascent recognition of the role of private enterprise as an enabler of development in the 1950s; to a more particular emphasis on investment and support in high-risk sectors and countries to create jobs and raise standards of living; to the advent of interest-free loans, advice, and grants in the 1960s to boost growth, reduce inequalities, and improve living conditions in the world's poorest countries; to a broader recognition of the need to enable better financial investment across regions after a stock market crash and global oil crisis in the early 1970s; to more and better insurance and guarantees to protect and spur foreign direct investments across developing countries in the 1980s; to nascent efforts to broaden development beyond support for government and the launch of direct work with and support for civil

---

25   Winston Nagan & Samantha Manausa, *Judicial Philosophy for Thoughtful Politicians and Business Leaders* 1 Corp. & Bus. L.J. 1, 2 (January 31, 2020), *available at* http://cablj.org /wp-content/uploads/2020/01/W2020-FINAL-W_Nagan.pdf.

26   For more complex rationales which precipitate bad governance and corrupt actions, see, e.g, M. Moore, *Political Underdevelopment: What Causes Bad Governance?*, 1 Pub. Management Rev. 3, 385–418 (2001), *available at* https://gsdrc.org/document-library/political -underdevelopment-what-causes-bad-governance/.

society, indigenous communities, and nongovernmental organizations in the 1980s and 1990s, in particular to improve the quality of social and economic development, shine a light on corruption and push for good governance, and to give voice to demands for government transparency and accountability; to the exponential changes now possible through technology – the World Bank has played an important part in human development for generations.

There are a range of general views concerning the standpoint and comparative advantage of the World Bank relative to other multilaterals, bilateral organizations, national aid agencies, foundations, and other donor organizations across development disciplines, including with particular respect to supporting governance though rule of law reforms. For the purpose of this analysis, I suggest that the comparative advantages of the World Bank include: (i) a focus on strengthening social and/or economic development outcomes in middle-income countries, (MIC s), low-income countries (LIC s), and/or fragile and conflict-affected states countries (FCS); (ii) the ability to work with a spectrum of stakeholders – including across the public and private sectors – at the country-level, the regional level, the global level, or some combination thereof; (iii) in-depth technical knowledge across key sectors; and (iv) the ability to mobilize and leverage significant financing and technical support to help enable countries achieve their social and economic development objectives.

The World Bank has clearly articulated its primary institutional goals in its 2013 "World Bank Group Strategy."[27] This strategy paper outlines the World Bank Group's two overarching strategic goals (or "twin goals"): "(i) End extreme poverty; reduce the percentage of people living on less than $1.25 a day to 3 percent by 2030;[28] and (ii) Promote shared prosperity: foster income growth of the bottom 40 percent of the population in every country." These twin goals were developed to chiefly inform the programming and selection of the World Bank Group's project operations from 2013 forward.

The World Bank Group is a large and diverse organization with a range of sectoral units called "Global Practices"; among these units, the largest and most engaged in the institution's efforts to strengthen client countries' governance through rule of law assistance is the aptly named "Governance Global

---

27   World Bank, A Stronger, Connected, Solutions World Bank Group (2013), *available at* http://documents.worldbank.org/curated/en/602031468161653927/pdf/816970WPov10 WBoBox0379842BooPUBLICo.pdf (last visited, July 11, 2022).

28   *See* World Bank, Fact Sheet: An Adjustment to Global Poverty Lines, *available at* https:// www.worldbank.org/en/ news/factsheet/2022/05/02/fact-sheet-an-adjustment-to-global -poverty-lines#1 (last visited September 16, 2022) (The global poverty threshold was changed to $2.15 per day in September 2022).

Practice."[29] A primary goal of the World Bank's governance efforts under the Governance Global Practice is to understand variation in overall levels of corruption, to be able to combat it in its various forms.[30] The Bank particularly aims to combat corruption through operational projects and technical support for countries focusing on government functions most susceptible to corruption, including: (i) strengthening government financial management, procurement and performance monitoring systems; (ii) facilitating streamlined delivery of good governance in sectors and key public goods, such as in health, water, education, energy and extractives; (iii) increasing the effectiveness of institutions and systems within and beyond the executive branch; and (iv) enhancing openness and transparency in the public sector and engage and communicate with citizens in ways that do not only deliver on essential public service values but also increase the effectiveness and efficiency of public policies and programs.[31]

The Governance Global Practice is able to mobilize substantial technical staff and resources in the pursuit of its goal. It also focuses its work through a specific set of World Bank lending and advisory products, including: project-based financial and technical support for institutional reforms; advisory services through technical assistance and reimbursable schemes; institutional modules and advice in sector projects; public financial management

---

29   World Bank, Governance Global Practice, *available at* https://www.worldbank.org/en
      /topic/governance (last visited July 11, 2022).

30   The World Bank has set out the following indicative framework for its efforts to combat
      corruption in service of the World Bank's overarching twin goals:
          First, every effort must be made to meet corruption at the gate, putting in place insti-
      tutional systems and incentives to prevent corruption from occurring in the first place.
      This includes mitigating and detecting potential risks, as well as addressing weaknesses
      in the institutions critical to this effort. Second, prevention must be built on the shoul-
      ders of credible deterrence, relying on accountability and enforcement mechanisms suf-
      ficiently strong to send a message to potential wrongdoers of the potential cost of their
      misconduct. Deterrence can take many forms beyond criminal consequences, including
      administrative and civil penalties and the Bank has created a world class sanctions and
      debarment mechanism to tackle corruption in its projects. Finally, it is critical to under-
      stand and influence the evolution of norms and standards that can change incentives,
      strengthen public institutions, and thus move the needle towards positive perceptions of
      government needed for longer-term and sustainable efforts to combat corruption. At the
      same time, the Bank Group is increasingly working to understand and address the power
      asymmetries that enable the misuse of funds and other public goods...
          World Bank, Combatting Corruption, *available at* https://www.worldbank.org/en
      /topic/governance/brief/anti-corruption (last visited, July 11, 2022).

31   World Bank, Governance Global Practice: Strategic Priorities, *available at* https://www
      .worldbank.org/en/topic/ governance/overview#2 (last visited, July 11, 2022).

to service delivery in social sectors; research, knowledge dissemination and capacity-building; and diagnosis, measurement and assessment. Overall, in the context of advancing good governance in countries around the world, the values of most any individual World Bank practitioner may be summarized as enlightenment, respect, well-being, skill, rectitude, and affection.

6   Trends

Armed with a better handle on goals had by the primary groups of actors and concerned institutions with respect to the design and implementation of approaches to strengthen governance in emerging economies through rule of law support, certain trends associated with this implementation can now be brought into focus. This section will begin with a description of past trends in theoretical perspectives about the relationship between effective governance and the rule of law, culminating in current efforts to understand and achieve effective reforms in practice. Past trends directly inform the values underpinning the above (legitimate) goals of key groups of actors in the present context seeking to perform value distribution by constituting good governance through rule of law support in countries around the world. So, further trends associated with how governance through rule of law assistance is presently understood, assessed, and monitored in countries can potentially shed light on what may be working, what is not, and help identify opportunities on which organizations like the World Bank might focus to increase the likelihood that the legitimate goals identified in Section 1 might be achieved.

6.1   *Evolution of the Concept of Governance through Rule of Law Assistance*

Across centuries, scholars, jurists and commentators have examined whether and how effective governance can be wrought from implementation of the rule of law; these conceptions have evolved through the years, but continue to influence the myriad efforts to institute governance through rule assistance of law in low- and middle-income countries.

The rule of law concept has been the subject of significant attention for centuries. The contrast between the rule of men versus the rule of law is found in Plato's *Statesman and Laws* and subsequently in Aristotle's *Politics*, in which effective rule of law is understood to mean obedience to positive law and formal checks and balances on rulers and magistrates. Roman jurists adapted ideas of the Stoics and natural law theorists in their expositions of the civil law. This was eventually compiled into the Justinian Roman law Digest, which for centuries embodied the promise of law as "written reason." Effective rule of law was likewise present in early Islamic law and jurisprudence, which recognized the equal subjection of all classes to the ordinary law of the land.

In his biography of Ulpian, Tony Honore describes the Roman law as emerging from a form of communication, which he says comes close to the common law tradition in which law emerges from a dialogue between advocate and judge.[32] Roman jurists crafted tight civil law rules to make it difficult for the emperor to arbitrarily abuse the rights of the Roman citizens. The Roman law of sale was anchored by the principle of good faith, which comes from Greek philosophy.[33] In effect then, the technical crafting of commercial rules outside the formal authority of governance in fact serves as a rule of law restraint on arbitrary governance. From this we understand that law and governance are limited by reason. Aquinas also tells us that there is a God-given faculty of reason.[34] *Marbury v. Madison* follows Locke,[35] Coke,[36] and Bolingbroke[37] in telling us that reason is the foundation of the rule of law. The rule of law is tied to the supremacy of law and that principle implies some sort of higher principle of natural law. *Marbury* gives us the powerful idea of the supremacy of law and judges as a restraint on the possibility of arbitrary governance.[38]

---

32   Tony Honore, Ulpian: Pioneer of Human Rights 94 (2d ed. 2002) (detailing how Ulpian's empirical method of argument distinguished him from other leading Roman lawyers, since he solved problems using an oral style that embraced trial and error, including through the use of phrases, such as "for instance," "it makes little difference if," "but what if," and "unless perhaps," which Honore compares to the Anglo-American common law, in light of Ulpian's emphasis on the role and importance of precedent).

33   *See, e.g.,* H. F. Jolowicz & Barry Nicholas, A Historical Introduction to the Study of Roman Law 406 (1972); F. Pringsheim, The Greek Law of Sale 333 (Weimar, 1950).

34   Thomas Aquinas, De regimine principum [1265–1267], Book I, Chap 1 (trans. JG Dawson) *in* Aquinas: Selected Political Writings 3 (AP D'Entreves ed., 1948) (explaining that man needs no king but himself under God, and has "the full ordering of his own actions by the light of God-given reason").

35   John Locke, Two Treatises on Government 209 (1821) ("God, who hath given the world to men in common, hath also given them reason to make use of it to the best advantage of life, and convenience").

36   Edward Coke, 1 Institutes of the Laws of England 1 (JH Thomas ed., 1836; reprinted 1986) (arguing that "the common law itself is nothing else... but artificial perfection of reason gotten by long study, observation, and experience, and not of every man's natural reason."

37   Lord Bolingbroke, A Dissertation upon Parties, in 2 The Works of Lord Bolingbroke 88 (Henry G. Bohn, 1844) (Bolingbroke, famously a deist who asserts that the phenomenon of God is provable through reason, likewise asserts that a constitution is an "assemblage of laws, institutions, and customs, derived from certain fixed principles of reason").

38   *Marbury v. Madison,* 5 U.S. 137 (1803) (famously holding that the Supreme Court's jurisdiction extends to the limit of what the Constitution provides; the Court was thus empowered to overturn any law passed by Congress if it was determined to be unconstitutional).

Later, Georg Hegel (1820) viewed the rule of law in terms of a "right" in relation to how a social actor enjoys the freedom of self-determination. Specifically, in Hegel's view, it was the role of the state to provide for the capacity of this social actor to strive for an ethical life (which is understood to be relationships structured by what it means to be a self-determining person who has the capability of recognizing others as persons as well).[39] In this, Hegel was clear that the normative ideal for the state is that of the constitutional state. Hegel argued that this self-determination can only be realized in the complex social context of property rights and relations, contracts, moral commitments, family life, the economy, the legal system, and the polity. In other words, a person is not truly "free" unless he/she is a participant in all of these different aspects of the life of the state.

From these early conceptions, two particular schools of thought have emerged as the dominant competing perspectives concerning governance through the rule of law: formalistic ("thin") versus substantive ("thick") conceptions. Formalistic conceptions hold that governance through the rule of law is essentially a "thin," closed set of norms and policy considerations to be applied to the facts at hand; these norms accordingly constrain – and comprise the basis for all – rule of law interpretations to a formalist. Holmes, famous for his formalism, emphasized that governance through the rule of law simply "is" – and that there is no room for judges to venture into what it "ought" to be.[40] Substantive conceptions hold that governance through the rule of law does not distinguish, as the formalistic conception does, between the rule of law and substantive justice; on the contrary, it requires, as a part of the ideal of law, that the rules in the rule book capture and enforce moral rights.

6.1.1 Toward a Contemporary Conception of the Rule of Law, from a Global Development Perspective

These rule of law understandings gradually moved in the direction of economic development, focusing in particular on the extent to which society and the state value institutions which govern their interaction. While the state had long coupled rights and obligations with land and status, it was during the industrial revolution that modern conceptions of contract began to surface, to

---

The Warren court thereafter cemented the power of judicial review in *Cooper v. Aaron* when it held that *Marbury v. Madison* had "declared the basic principle that the federal judiciary is supreme in its exposition of the law of the Constitution"). *See Cooper v. Aaron*, 358 U.S. 1, 18 (1958).

39 Georg Wilhelm Friedrich Hegel, Elements of the Philosophy of Right [Grundlinien der Philosophie des Rechts] (1820).

40 *See* Oliver Wendell Holmes, *The Path of the Law*, 10 Harv. L. Rev. 457 (1897).

establish rules which provided the power to enter into and enforce exchanges. This explains the significant shift in the rule of law towards legal rights and obligations tied to land, rights and obligations based on contract and exchange. Thus, the civil law supported implicitly by the rule of law empowered the critical change of modernization to liberty and freedom of contract to facilitate and expand global trade.[41] English contract law – which was exported on an industrial scale across the empire – demonstrates this understanding, suggesting that securing human exchanges within and across state lines necessitate ordinary rules of contract, agency partnership and various forms of enterprisory association to stabilize principles and expectations, and ensure enforceability.[42]

Weberian economics systematized this analysis and posited that development generally follows the introduction of a market economy. Max Weber understood that economic development generally follows the introduction of a market economy; he believed that the capitalistic order on which a market economy is predicated depended on the existence of a rational, law-bound state.[43] Weber attempted to construct a sociological framework to guide his research into the possible relationship between the rule of law and capitalism. His framework identified the main analytic dimensions of society (polity, social structure, economy, religion, and law) as well as the concrete structures to which they correspond (specifically, the political, social, economic, religious, and legal structures of given societies). The conceptual basis for this approach harkens back to the latter phases of feudalism, when there emerged on the margins of society the merchant class. This class, able to separate itself

---

41   This is evident in the successive development of ever more comprehensive conventions to stabilize private law orderings, from the Hague-Visby Rules to the United Nations Convention on Contracts for the International Sale of Goods to the Hamburg Rules to the Rotterdam Rules, and more. *See* International Convention for the Unification of Certain Rules of Law Relating to Bills of Lading, Aug. 25, 1924, 120 L.N.T.S. 155 (entered into force June 2, 1931), as amended by Protocol to Amend the International Convention for the Unification of Certain Rules of Law Relating to Bills of Lading, Feb. 23, 1968, 1412 U.N.T.S. 128. *See* United Nations Convention on Contracts for the International Sale of Goods (1980), *available at:* https://www.uncitral.org/pdf/english/texts/sales/cisg/V1056997-CISG -e-book.pdf (last visited Feb 26 2016); United Nations Convention on the Carriage of Goods by Sea, Mar. 31, 1978, 1695 U.N.T.S. 3, 17 I.L.M. 608 (entered into force Nov. 1, 1992); United Nations Convention on Contracts for the International Carriage of Goods Wholly or Partly by Sea, G.A. Res. 63/122, UN Doc A/RES/63/122 (Feb. 2, 2009).

42   *See, e.g.,* the Indian Contract Act (1872), which influenced private law orderings across legal systems within the British Empire. *See* AC Patra, The Indian Contract Act 1872, 834–36 (1966).

43   Max Weber, Economy and Society: An Outline of Interpretive Sociology (1914).

from the limits of feudal order, was essentially using mercantile human capital to establish the idea that the maximal development of human capital required freedom, particularly the freedom of contract. Thus, Henry Maine stated that the movement of a progressive society was from "status to contract"; in the status society, human capital is ascribed and thus subject to suppression and expropriation while in the contract society, it is stipulated.[44]

To the Weberian conception Friedrich Hayek added that a key ingredient of a successful market economy is individual freedom which is determined by the rule of law. He argued that civil society and the state are separate under the rule of law, and civil society is legitimated in its demand for as little interference in its affairs as possible.[45] He also asserted that market economies spontaneously allocate societal resources and create order more efficiently than any human design could achieve.[46] Sophisticated private networks are developed which produce and distribute goods and services throughout the economy, and to protect competition. The state is thus limited in principle, and private law orderings are paramount. These networks emerged not by design but as a result of decentralized economic decisions. Dani Rodrik more recently explained that stabilization, privatization, and liberalization contribute to economic development. Much of the early neoclassical institutional analysis followed Demsetz and the law and economics tradition, which held that private law stabilizes expectations about the value of goods and services and is critical for growth and development. Coke likewise pointed out that common law started out as providing ad hoc responses to injustices, but eventually settled down to become a coherent system of rules, which did not alter from judge to judge, and so rises to the level of "artificial reason," which most proximately reflects perfection through time, study, and consistency.[47]

---

44   *See* Henry Maine, Ancient Law: Its Connection With the Early History of Society and its Relation to Modern Ideas 180–181 (2d ed. 1930).

45   Hayek explains that "a spontaneous order ... [since it] has not been created by an outside agency ... may be very serviceable to the individuals which move within such order. In other words, the myriad interactions between ordinary individuals generates a series of desired by each individual, and thus desirable in the aggregate, in ways that could not have been achieved by centralized processes; this decentralized process of individual freedom thus creates "spontaneous order." *See* Friedrich Hayek, Law, Legislation and Liberty: Rules and Order 39 (1973).

46   *See id.*

47   Edward Coke, 1 Institutes of the Laws of England at §138 (JH Thomas, ed. 1836; reprinted 1986) (asserting that the "artificial reason" of the common law has been refined by – and is thus the *summa ratio* of – the natural reason of successions of "grave and learned men," and thus to Coke, law is the "perfection of reason").

Major discussions about the nature of legal theory and legal culture and their connection to social and economic organization emerge from the modern secular state without a bill of rights – the English theorists monopolize this discussion, A.V. Dicey in particular. Dicey focused on how in a system of parliamentary supremacy can judges find and retain the power to limit arbitrary actions by parliament. Dicey set out three principles which together establish the rule of law: the supremacy of regular law over the influence of arbitrary power; equality before the law; and law refers to the rights of individuals set out in a constitution which are defined and enforced by the courts.[48] Dicey's concerns became far more important with the rise of totalitarian state absolutism in the 20th century.

The mid-20th Century brought the Law and Development movement, spearheaded by the U.S. Agency for International Development and the Ford Foundation. A range of scholars have since suggested that the Law and Development movement generated value for successive generations of development practitioners by exemplifying how *not* to approach rule of law development.[49] David Trubek in particular questioned the underlying theoretical assumptions associated with the Law and Development movement. He found this movement to be ethnocentric because it interpreted development in emerging economies in terms of Western history, and evolutionist because it viewed history as a series of generalized stages that have been – and could be – repeated to certain extents in various countries in anticipation of similar outcomes.[50] He argued that both of these perspectives make it impossible to understand the dynamics of legal life in the developing world. Later, the so-called "Washington Consensus" took a somewhat analogous tack though the establishment of a "standard" reform policy prescription for developing countries by Washington, D.C.-based institutions, including the World Bank, the International Monetary Fund, and the US Treasury Department. There are varying perspectives of the relative quality and utility of rule of law assistance during this thirty-year period.

---

48   A.V. Dicey, Introduction to the study of the law of the Constitution 198–203 (10th ed. 1959).

49   *See, e.g.,* Elliot Burg, *Law and Development: A Review of the Literature and a Critique of "Scholars in Self-Estrangement,"* 25 Am. J. Int'l L. 492–530 (1975); John Henry Merryman, *Comparative Law and Social Change: On the Origins, Style, Decline and Revival of the Law and Development Movement,* 25 Am. J. Int'l L. 457–491 (1975); Lawrence Friedman, *On Legal Development,* 24 Rutgers L.R. 11–64 (1969); and David Trubek & Marc Galanter, *Scholars in Self-Estrangement: Some Reflections on the Crisis in Law and Development Studies in the United States,* 4 Wisc. L. Rev. 1062–1102 (1974).

50   David Trubek, *Toward a Social Theory of Law: An Essay on the Study of Law and Development,* 82(1) Yale L.J. 1–50 (1972) [hereinafter Trubek].

This approach to rule of law assistance has been criticized, or otherwise commented upon from a skeptical or curious point of view, time and again. It has been argued, for example, that the rule of law has unproven impacts on economic development, or that activities promoting the rule of law are based on questionable assumptions. It has been argued with particular force that insufficient attention has been paid to the legal needs of historically marginalized and underserved segments of society. Critics also note that careless rule of law development activities have run the risk of creating a ruling elite in client countries, with the power to manipulate through the law. Harvard law professor and critic of rule of law development activities Morton Horwitz has asserted that the "promoti[on] [of] procedural justice enables the shrewd, the calculating, and the wealthy to manipulate its forms to their own advantage."[51] David Trubek, in focusing on attempts to export instrumental legal thought, has suggested that while rule of law assistance can be appropriate in systems characterized by democratic political pluralism, they might actually strengthen authoritarian regimes, which are able to co-opt the legal system and strengthen their own position.[52]

Douglass North's analysis of institutions – which he defines as "humanly devised constraints that structure political, economic and social interactions"[53] – may help to explain the ostensible irreconcilability of the varying perspectives and experiences with rule of law assistance by a range of practitioners and scholars. While in his early analysis North asserted that institutions always evolve in ways to approximate efficiency, it was only after decades of empirical analysis that he refuted his earlier perspective and concluded that societies only aberrantly possess relatively efficient institutions.[54] In other words, institutions are often inefficient. With this conclusion, North opens the door to the possibility that prevailing institutions can actually be hindrances to growth and development. He also explains that differences in economic performance between countries are often caused by differences in institutions or defects in common institutions as well as by "constraints" on these institutions. North defines "constraints" as formal rules, such as constitutions and laws, plus informal restraints, such as sanctions, taboo, customs, and traditions, which

---

51 Morton Horowitz, *The Rule of Law: An Unqualified Human Good?*, 86 Yale L.J. 561, 566 (1977).
52 *See* Trubek, *supra* note 50.
53 Douglass North, *Institutions*, 5 J. Econ. Persp. 97 (1991) [hereinafter North].
54 *See* Douglass North, *Institutions and the Performance of Economies over Time*, *in* Handbook of New Institutional Economics 21–30 (Ménard, C. & Shirley, M. M. eds., 2005).

collectively contribute to the perpetuation of order and safety within a society or market environment.[55]

6.1.2   Implications for the World Bank

North's insight, when viewed through the lens of the gradual evolution of the conceptual foundations of rule of law assistance by international development organizations like the World Bank, would seem to demonstrate the need for context-sensitivity in efforts to advance rule of law support in recipient countries, combined with more and better knowledge capture and impact analysis processes on how specific laws work in practice from context to context. However, as we will see below in this Section, this has not been the primary approach taken by international organizations in their rule of law assistance programs.

Indeed, for the purposes of international development organizations, the evolution of the rule of concept has generated a lack of uniformity in what counts as the rule of law. It has become increasingly associated with development economics during the last twenty years; it has already achieved near worldwide endorsement by experts and authoritative commentators because it is thought to encourage growth and reduce corruption. Many publications by a variety of experts have interpreted a correlation between the two variables – rule of law and economic development – and concluded that one has a causal impact on the other; the direction of the causal impact depends on the particular author's analysis. Economists and lawyers at the World Bank began to seriously examine the development potential of the rule of law after the decline of the Washington Consensus, and in the aftermath of the Asian financial crisis. Outrage over the kleptocratic conduct of a small number of national leaders who had stolen billions of dollars' worth of public funds and international development aid added fuel to the proverbial fire.[56] Development practitioners around the world were shocked into examining what had gone wrong and why. The result was renewed attention to the institutional setting in which policy was created and executed, which necessitated increased attention to political accountability, the quality of bureaucracy, and the rule of law.

Also, modern legal thought generally identifies the state as the prime instrument of governance. The identification of law with sovereignty still commands great influence in the international system; it is obvious that a theory which defines law in terms of the state will have difficulty in accounting for law outside of the state, which is a complicated space for a multilateral organization

---

55   *See* North, *supra* note 53.

56   World Bank and UNODC, Stolen Assets Recovery Initiative, *available at* https://star
       .worldbank.org/ (last visited July 11, 2022).

seeking to promote and enable governance through rule of law reforms. Moreover, a theory which roots all law in the sovereign state will have difficulty accounting for circumstances where the state is subject to international concepts of obligation.[57] This difficulty was obvious to 19th Century theorists as well as more contemporary figures.[58] Indeed, different generations of political commentators, such as Thomas Erskine Holland and Hersch Lauterpacht individually defined extrinsic obligations as the vanishing point of the rule of law.[59] Their approach mirrored Austin's, that the rule of law is determined by and with the sovereign's consent.

Despite its inadequacies, this statist approach to law sets out an infrastructure of command and control that many political elites find comprehensible and justifiable. Unfortunately, this theory has a legacy of unrestrained state absolutism, which was particularly rampant during the 20th Century (and

---

57 *See* Hans Kelsen, Principles of International Law 1 (2d ed., 1967) (examining positivism as a "pure theory of law," the primacy of which is protected by its contextual removal from external interference). *See also* Hans Kelsen, Pure Theory of Law (1967) (1960) (generally examining positivism as a "pure theory of law"). *See also* Prosper Weil, *Towards Relative Normativity in International Law?* 77 Am. J. Int'l L. 413 (1983); and H.L.A. Hart, *Positivism and the Separation of Law and Morals*, 71 Harv. L. Rev. 593, 606–15 (1958).

58 *See* Robert Bork, *The Limits of "International Law,"* The National Interest (Winter 1989 – 1990), at 3, 4 (criticizing the international community's general lack of response to violations of international law); George Kennan, American Diplomacy 95 (1984) (criticizing international law as being insufficiently grounded in reality because of its "legalistic-moralistic approach" to international disputes); Hans J. Morgenthau, Politics Among Nations: The Struggle For Power And Peace 10, 312 (6th ed., 1985) (critiquing international organizations, such as the United Nations, as ineffective mechanisms which seek to displace continuing efforts by various nations to amass power and stating that "that there can be no more primitive and no weaker system of law enforcement than [international law]"); Michael Glennon, *The New Interventionism: The Search for a Just International Law*, Foreign Aff., May - June 1999, at 2, 4 (remarking on perceived failures of the UN Charter with regard to existing measures designed to counter international genocide). *See generally* Reinhold Niebuhr, *The Illusion of World Government*, 5 Bul. Atom. Sci. 290 (October 1949); The Province of Jurisprudence Determined, *supra* n. 30; Robert Stausz-Hupe, Power and Community (1956); Arnold Wolfers, Discord and Collaboration (1962); Kenneth N. Waltz, Theory of International Politics (1979); Kenneth Waltz, *Reflections on Theory of International Politics: A Response to My Critics, in* Neo-Realism and Its Critics 322 (1986); Jed Rubenfeld, *Unilateralism and Constitutionalism*, 79 N.Y.U. L. Rev. 1971 (2004).

59 *See* Hersch Lauterpacht, *The Problem of the Revision of the Law of War*, Brit. Y.B. Int'l Law 382 ("international law is, in some ways, at the vanishing point of law"). *See* Thomas Erskine Holland, The Elements of Jurisprudence 392 (13th ed. 1924) [hereinafter, The Elements of Jurisprudence] ("[International law is] the vanishing point of jurisprudence"). *See also* Winston Nagan, *Lawyer Roles, Identity, and Professional Responsibility in an Age of Globalism*, 13 Fla. J. Int'l L. 131, 144 (2001) [hereinafter, *Lawyer Roles, Identity, and Professional Responsibility*]. *See also* W.W. Buckland, Some Reflections on Jurisprudence (1945).

increasingly so in the 21st Century). Accordingly, for human rights to be firmly grounded in the current reality of international legal order, it must provide a more coherent account of its conceptual and normative bases, which are comprehensible and amenable to rational application in specific instances.

A critical question for international development organizations is thus precisely what differentiates a democratic rule of law state from a totalitarian state? During the 1990s, certain authoritative commentators arrived at a general answer: the ability to constrain arbitrary abuses of power by recourse to law. As noted earlier, Friedrich Hayek argued that a successful market economy depends on individual freedom, which is determined by the rule of law. Private law orderings are thus supremely important, and private networks which drive economic activity emerge not by design but as a result of decentralized economic decisions. William Swadling, Oxford professor of private law, likewise points out that common law started out as providing ad hoc responses to injustices, which eventually became a coherent system of rules which did not alter from judge to judge. This explains the significant shift in the rule of law towards legal rights and obligations tied to land, rights and obligations based on contract and exchange. Exchange could only work on a set of rules that provided the power to enter into and enforce contracts. The state pinned rights and obligations on land and status. Thus, the civil law supported implicitly by the rule of law empowered the critical change of modernization to liberty and freedom of contract. Tony Matthews echoes this understanding in his *Freedom, State Security and the Rule of Law* by suggesting that securing human exchanges within and across state lines necessitates ordinary rules of contract, agency partnership and various forms of enterprisory association.[60]

World Bank rule of law development practitioners and other authoritative commentators, including governance experts, generally agree that institutions do not exist in a vacuum; substantive rules on the books do not capture the essence of a legal system. Recent research in this area has yielded some insights, including so-called "thick" versus "thin" understandings of the rule of law, which run parallel to the natural law/positivism debate. Other analyses focus on capacity development, or the disparity between emerging economies with common law versus civil law traditions, or more specific analyses of the effect of geography and openness to trade on the rule of law. From an operational perspective, the rule of law is closely related to the promotion of good governance because it raises important questions about how and in what environment rulers rule. This implicates understandings about the effectiveness of

---

60   *See* Anthony S. Matthews, Freedom, State Security and the Rule of Law: Dilemmas of the Apartheid Society (1986).

policies devised and implemented by governments, the extent to which society and the state value institutions which govern their interaction, and how governments are selected, overseen, and replaced. In other words, it necessitates a comprehensive idea of what governance and the rule of law are, and how they promote development. However, achieving such a comprehensive understanding of what counts as good governance and the effective rule of law has not been a straightforward process for the international development community. Even a brief and selective review of the various current theoretical discussions about what count as governance and the rule of law may exemplify the myriad, conflicting views at play.

For example, Acemoglu and Johnson have written extensively on the endogeneity challenge which plagues econometric work on institutions and income (i.e. do good institutions raise incomes, or do high incomes result in investments in institutional quality?). They use historical data on settler mortality as an instrument for current institutional quality, and demonstrate a causal link running from institutions (an "expropriation risk" measure serves as a proxy for institutions) to income. Acemoglu and Johnson's analyses have generated significant follow-up literature which suggests that institutions are a key engine for development, which possibly (or even likely) trump all other development drivers. As a result, previous conceptions of development (such as the "geography-as-destiny" point of view) have been sidelined by the view that geography and natural endowments have an indirect role in co-shaping institutional frameworks due to their impact on the development of incentives and constraints of colonizers and local elites. With *Unbundling Institutions*, Acemoglu and Johnson contribute to institutions literature by demonstrating that the rule of law is a broader concept than merely providing formal or informal protection against government and elite predation or expropriation.[61]

---

61   *See* Daron Acemoglu & Simon Johnson, *Unbundling Institutions*, MIT: 2005, *available at* https://www.google.com/url?sa=t&rct=j&q=&esrc=s&source=web&cd=2&ved=2ahUKE wiHlILau5rpAhXEknIEHZzzBhsQFjABegQIARAB&url=https%3A%2F%2 Feconomics.mit.edu%2Ffiles%2F4467&usg=AOvVaw0z97azXysL_uyfdJtTqPTM.Acemoglu and Johnson seek to overcome overlaps between contracting and property rights institutions, as well as to understand the extent to which they are different. They find that while both sets of institutions relate to opportunistic behavior, the nature of this behavior is different. Specifically, contracting institutions regulate transactions between private parties (for example, a debtor and a creditor) and both parties to these transactions may choose to deviate from the specified contractual terms, which they can because of "failures" in implementation and enforcement. Weak contracting institutions can be costly. However, citizens also have certain recourses available to them (they can change the terms of the contracts, they can adapt the nature of their activities to protect themselves from opportunistic behavior, etc.). By comparison, property rights institutions are closely linked to the

By comparison, Berkowitz, Pistor, and Richard examine the determinants of "legality" (which they define as the effectiveness of institutions that enforce the law, as opposed to the law on the books) and the effect of legality on economic development, using data from 49 countries. Specifically, they test the hypothesis that the way a country got its legal system is a more important determinant of legality than the substance of the law, proxied for by the legal family to which the system belongs.[62] The authors find a large and statistically significant "transplant effect." In other words, countries that developed their own legal systems were able to adapt transplanted law or had a population already familiar with the transplanted legal system score much higher on legality indicators than countries that imported law without adaptation or pre-existing familiarity. Additionally, when this transplant effect is included the "legal family" (English common law, French civil law, German civil law, Scandinavian civil law) turns out not to have a statistically significant effect on legality. They argue that the transplanting process has a strong indirect effect on economic development via its impact on legality, while the impact of particular legal families is weaker and not robust to alternative legality measures.[63]

Other authoritative commentators point to other important components of rule of law reforms, for example: that the efficiency of the judiciary is an important component in rule-of-law reforms.[64] These commentators agree

---

distribution of political power in society because they regulate the relationship between ordinary private citizens and the politicians or elites with access to political power. When property rights institutions fail to constrain those in control of the state, the ensuing problems cannot be circumvented by executing alternative contracts to guard against future expropriation because the state (which has a monopoly on legitimate violence), is the ultimate arbiter of contracts. *See id.*

62   *See* Daniel Berkowitz, Katharina Pistor,& Jean-Francois Richard, Economic Development, Legality, and the Transplant Effect (2001).

63   *See id.* Others agree with this school of thought. *See, e.g.,* Edward M Wise, *The Transplant of Legal Patterns* 38 Am. J. Comp. L. 1–22 (1990); Frank Upham, *Ideology, Experience and the Rule of Law in Developing Societies,* Remarks at New York University Law School (September 05, 2001); Ugo Mattei, *Efficiency in Legal Transplants: An Essay in Comparative Law and Economics* 14 Int'l Rev. L. & Econ. 3–19 (1994); Otto Kahn-Freund, *On Uses and Misuses of Comparative Law* 37(1) Modern L. Rev. 1–27 (1974); Alan Watson, Legal Transplants: An Approach to Comparative Law (2nd ed., Athens: University of Georgia Press, 1974/1993).

64   *See, e.g.,* Maria Dakolias, *A Strategy for Judicial Reform: The Experience in Latin America,* 36 Va. J. Int'l L. 167–231 (1995); Richard Messick, *Judicial Reform and Economic Development: A Survey of the Issues,* 14(1) World Bank Research Observer (1999); Linn Hammergren, *Judicial Training and Justice Reform* (Washington: U.S. Agency for International Development, PN-ACD-021, 1998); Mauro Cappelletti, *"Who Watches the Watchmen?" A*

that to increase accountability and transparency among the judiciary, greater publication of court decisions, courts that are open to the public in certain circumstances, and effective hierarchical judicial review are workable strategies. The independence of the judiciary can be protected where governments provide them with sufficient funding, so they might make their own financial and administrative decisions. It has also been suggested that court performance should be evaluated by an independent auditor on a periodic basis. In short, courts must be available to adjudicate disputes and enforce resolutions. For countries that are further along in the reform process, more complex structural reforms that strengthen court capacity (i.e., training judges), independence, and transparency are needed.

Still other analyses add to existing research which demonstrates a link (or otherwise a strong correlation) between various measures of institutional "quality" (including corruption, property rights, bureaucratic delays, and more) and economic development.[65] For example, it has been argued that an indicator of the strength of the rule of law is by measuring the level of corruption in a country's judiciary.[66] Another approach explains the mistake in the previously held (neoclassical economic) assumption that developing countries could take advantage of technological advances developed elsewhere and higher rates of return on capital: in short, institutions designed to protect property and contract rights across the developing world are in many ways deficient. This conclusion is affirmed by quantitative data which suggest that institutional quality is a powerful determinant of a country's ability to achieve a high relative growth rate and to "catch up" with richer countries.[67] Yet another approach examines democracy and the rule of law using game theory, and unpacks the problem of political officials' respect for the rights of citizens

Comparative Study on Judicial Responsibility, 31(1) Am. J. Comp. L. 1–62 (1983); and Mark Ramseyer, *Judicial Independence, in* The New Palgrave Dictionary of Economics and the Law 383–387 (Newman & Peter eds., 1998).

65   Alberto Chong & Cesar Calderon, *Causality and Feedback between Institutional Measures and Economic Growth*, 12(1) Econ. & Politics 69–81 (2000).

66   *See, e.g.,* Edgardo Buscaglia & Maria Dakolias, *An Analysis of the Causes of Corruption in the Judiciary Law and Policy* 1–15 (World Bank: 1999), *available at* http://documents.worldbank .org/curated/en/322431468744322656/An-analysis-of-the-causes-of-corruption-in-the -judiciary; and Lisa Dickieson & Mark Dietrich, *A Methodology for Measuring Judicial Independence*, ABA/CEELI (September 1999).

67   *See* Philip Keefer & Stephen Knack, *Why Don't Poor Countries Catch Up? A Cross-National Test of an Institutional Explanation*, 35 Econ. Inquiry 590–602 (1997).

in particular,[68] while still another argues that certain cultural characteristics have a beneficial impact on economic growth.[69]

Which of these analyses and related lessons – if any – should inform international organizations' approach to rule of law assistance? Which might be most relevant to international development organizations such as the World Bank? And what theory might best underpin an institutional position on rule of law assistance, to be mainstreamed in the Bank's operational portfolio? One can almost hear A.V. Dicey's cynical note that jurisprudence – or legal theory[70] – "stinks in the nostrils of the [practitioner]."[71] It is not uncommon for operational practitioners across technical disciplines to be impatient with theory; they avoid it because they do not see its importance in paradigmatic terms.[72] Indeed, no less than Richard Posner – himself an architect of the jurisprudence of political economy – has suggested that generally, legal theory is intellectually worthless.[73] To many, however, legal theory is a mode of inquiry and a process by which the nature and quality of public order might be better understood, secured, defended and promoted in the common interest. Theory may indeed be crucial because it generates sustainable institutions and expectations about rights and obligations which are critical to even the most elemental ideas of justice and decency. If the worth of legal theory is gauged by its focus on positive outcomes in human dignity, and if it is expressed with precision, it can indeed be a powerful tool to meaningfully enable human development. It might be used to explore a deeper sociology of human relations, as well as basic moral commitments and understandings. This human aspect of legal theory is particularly important to theorists and practitioners dedicated to exploring the empirical and normative roots of what counts as governance and the role of the rule of law in efforts to enable of better lives and livelihoods among the world's poorest, marginalized, and historically least served people.

---

68 *See* Barry Weingast, *The Political Foundations of Democracy and the Rule of Law*, 91(2) Am. Pol. Sci. Rev 245–263 (1997).

69 *See* Alvaro Montenegro, *Constitutional Design and Economic Performance*, 6 Constitutional Pol. Econ. 161–169 (1995).

70 Rudolph B. Schlesinger, Hans W. Baade, Mirjan R. Damaska & Peter E. Herzog, Comparative Law: Cases, Texts, Materials 40 (5th ed. 1988) (stating that the word "jurisprudence" means "a general theory of law," and is also known as "legal theory").

71 Albert Venn Dicey, *The Study of Jurisprudence*, 5 Law Mag. & Rev. 382 (1880).

72 *See* Alfred Denning, The Family Story 38 (1981) ("Jurisprudence was too abstract a subject for my liking. [It is] [a]ll about ideologies, legal norms, and basic norms, 'ought,' and 'is,' realism and behaviorism, and goodness knows what else").

73 *See, generally*, Richard A. Posner, The Problematics of Moral and Legal Theory (1999).

6.2   *Trends: Approaching Definitional Clarity Concerning the Rule of Law through Efforts to Measure it*

In the context of this analysis, legal theory is thus understood to be a tool to explore a deeper sociology of human interaction, to establish moral commitments, to stabilize expectations, and ultimately to enable forward planning.[74] Each determination of what law is and how it works can better enables participants in the evolving discourse to achieve understandings of how to effectively identify, promote, defend, and sustain fundamental human interests, and for international development practitioners, including at the World Bank, to better operationalize these understandings. Further examination of trends which may condition the achievement of these understandings may thus be useful in the instant analysis.

6.2.1   Toward Understanding What Counts as the Rule of Law to Help Enable Good Governance

At a minimum, the above cursory gloss on the evolving conception of the rule of law across centuries demonstrate a certain harmony across contexts and cultures concerning – at a minimum – the importance of the rule of law. Different conceptions of the rule of law have likewise ranged from "thin" to "thick" conceptions. In the arena of international development, "thin" conceptions have generally given way to "thicker" understandings which transcend the procedural and focus on the substantive, and in particular on normative standards of rights and equity.

The World Bank seems to have unofficially adopted a "thick" conception of the rule of law. To understand how and why, it is necessary to examine the conceptual underpinnings and definition of the rule of law concept advanced by the World Bank through its successive generations of its leadership, operational practitioners, and lawyers. In brief, from the late 1980's forward, World Bank development practitioners began to explicitly identify a correlation between the quality of borrowing countries' rule of law and the relative effectiveness of World Bank development loans (across sectors) in those countries.[75] The timing of this emerging recognition of the role and importance of the rule

---

74   *See, e.g.,* H.L.A. Hart, The Concept of Law 97, 110–11, 151 (1961). For a more comprehensive overview of the evolution of understandings about legal theory, *see* Siegfried Wiessner, *The Rule of Law: Prolegomena,* Zeitschrift für deutsches und amerikanisches Recht [German-American Law Review] 82 (June 2018), *available at* https://papers.ssrn.com /sol3/ papers.cfm?abstract_id=3293042.

75   Frank Upham, *Mythmaking in the Rule of Law Orthodoxy,* Carnegie Endowment for International Peace Working Paper: Rule of Law Series, Democracy and Rule of Law Project, Number 30, 9 (September 2002), *available at* https://carnegie endowment.org/files/wp30 .pdf [hereinafter Upham].

of law for development effectiveness is salient; it emerged during the dissolution of the former Soviet Union and during a time of considerable political
crisis across the African continent.[76] It was recognized in contemporary analyses that the rule of law must become a central aspect of efforts to encourage countries in these regions into market economies. It was a flagship 1989
report entitled, *From Crisis to Sustainable Growth – SubSaharan Africa: A Long-
Term Perspective Study,* which first conflated the rule of law with a concept
called "governance."[77] Then-World Bank president Barber Conable introduced
the idea: "A root cause of weak economic performance in the past has been
the failure of public institutions. Private sector initiative and market mechanisms are important, but they must go hand-in-hand with good governance
– a public service that is efficient, a judicial system that is reliable, and an
administration that is accountable to its public."[78] The authors of the report
then elaborated on the governance concept: "By governance is meant the exercise of political power to manage a nation's affairs[,]"[79] and its core objective:
"Ultimately, better governance requires political renewal. This means a concerted attack on corruption from the highest to the lowest levels."[80] This is the
earliest demonstration by World Bank thought leaders of what would become
a norm-establishing effort to connect the concepts of rule of law, governance,
and anticorruption.

This definitional imprecision culminated in an effort by the then-General
Counsel of the World Bank, Ibrahim Shihata, to articulate a formal position
for the World Bank to engage countries with respect to the quality of their
rule of law – also by conflating the concept with other aspects of effective
and efficient public administration and calling it "governance" – as a legitimate consideration in the awarding of World Bank loans, to not fall foul of the
political interference prohibition in the World Bank's Articles of Agreement.[81]
Specifically, Shihata deliberately distanced the concept of rule of law from

---

76   Alvaro Santos, *The World Bank's Uses of the "Rule of Law" Promise in Economic Develop-
      ment,* in The New Law and Economic Development: A Critical Appraisal 268 (David
      Trubek & Alvaro Santos eds., New York: Cambridge University Press 2006) [hereinafter
      Santos].
77   World Bank, *From Crisis to Sustainable Growth – Sub-Saharan Africa : A Long-Term Per-
      spective Study* (Washington, DC: . 198), *available at* http://documents.worldbank.org
      /curated/en/ 49824146874284638/pdf/multi0page.pdf.
78   *See id.*
79   *See id.* at 6.
80   *See id.* at 60.
81   *See* Upham, *supra* note 75 at 9.

politics by calling it "governance" and defining it as "good order," which he posited as a:

> system, based on abstract rules which are actually applied, and on functioning institutions which ensure the appropriate applications of such rules. This system of rules and institutions is reflected in the concept of the *rule of law*, generally known in different legal systems and often expressed in the familiar phrase of a *'government of laws and not of men.'*[82]

Shihata went on to explain that "governance ... conveys the same meaning as government", essentially: "the manner in which a community is managed and directed, including the making and administration of policy in matters of political control, as well as in such economic issues as may be relevant to the management of the community's resources."[83] He merged the rule of law, governance, and anticorruption concepts by defining governance as a "system based on abstract *rules* which are actually applied and on functioning *institutions* which ensure the appropriate application of such rules".[84] Such a system, Shihata argued, can enable economic development through the right combination of laws, policies, and regulation and restrain the arbitrary exercise of power, which may inhibit the effectiveness of World Bank support. Thus, argued Shihata, governance is an arena for World Bank engagement. He stated:

> Reforms cannot be effective in the absence of a system which translates them into workable rules and makes sure they are complied with. Such a system assumes that: (a) there is a set of rules which are known in advance, (b) such rules are actually in force, (c) mechanisms exist to ensure the proper application of the rules and to allow for departure from them as needed according to established procedures, (d) conflicts in the application of the rules can be resolved through binding decisions of an independent judicial or arbitral body and e) there are known procedures for amending the rules when they no longer serve their purpose.[85]

---

82   Ibrahim F. I. Shihata, *The World Bank and 'Governance' Issues in Its Borrowing Members*, *in* The World Bank in a Changing World, Vol. 1, 85 (Franziska Tschofen & Antonio R. Parra, eds.) (1991) [emphasis added].

83   *See id.*

84   *See id.*

85   *See id.*

Shihata then asserted that the World Bank could – within its mandate and in adherence to the institution's Articles of Agreement – support borrowing countries with technical assistance in the reform or development of laws needed for the effective implementation of economic policies, and that the Bank was further free to condition loan disbursements on the adoption of such legal reforms.[86] Shihata thus succeeded in bringing the rule of law into the competence of the World Bank by taking pains to disassociate it from the domestic jurisdiction of borrowing countries by merging it into the larger governance and anticorruption concepts and then demonstrating that good governance (free of corruption) is foundational for social stability and economic growth, and thus a prerequisite for the effective use of World Bank assistance.[87] This larger concept of governance still dominates within the institution, to the point where the meaning of the phrases "rule of law," "governance", and "anticorruption" are often merged (without a distinction as to where one concept stops and the others begin) or else used interchangeably.[88] This may account in part for Alvaro Santos' conclusion that the World Bank has multiple fragmented and inconsistent conceptions of the rule of law, including as an institutional framework for: good governance; the promotion of substantive rights and regulations; the fight against corruption; and for poverty reduction and efforts to enhance human agency.[89]

This conceptual murkiness has been equal parts criticized for its apparent imprecision[90] and lauded for establishing an authorizing environment to enable the implementation of a broader array of projects than was previously

---

86   *See id.* at 86.

87   *See id.* at 85.

88   The World Bank most recently set out a refreshed version of Shihata's definition of governance in the institution's 2017 World Development Report on the subject. It explains that governance is "the process through which state and nonstate actors interact to design and implement policies within a given set of formal and informal rules that shape and are shaped by power." Useful also to note that this World Development Report defines "power" as the ability of groups and individuals to make others act in the interest of those groups and individuals and to bring about specific outcomes. *See* World Bank 2017, *supra* note 1, at 3.

89   *See* Santos, *supra* note 76.

90   Frank Upham, *Mythmaking in the Rule of Law Orthodoxy, in* Promoting the Rule of Law Abroad: in Search of Knowledge 78 (Thomas Carothers, ed., Washington, DC: Carnegie Endowment for International Peace, 2006) (describing the World Bank's language concerning the governance and the rule of law, Frank Upham asserts that "these statements are platitudes ... they present an exclusive path to development ... these statements are evangelical ...") [hereinafter Upham 2006].

possible.[91] Many World Bank practitioners have generally followed the Shihata approach and eschew explaining what the rule of law *is*, to focus on why it (again without distinction from the concepts of governance and anticorruption) is important for the purposes of social, economic, and sustainable development. For example, the World Bank's 2002 Annual Report asserted:

> The rule of law is essential to equitable economic development and sustainable poverty reduction. Weak legal and judicial systems undermine the fight against poverty on many fronts: they divert investment to markets with more predictable rule-based environments, deprive important sectors of the use of productive assets, and mute the voice of citizens in the decision-making process. Vulnerable individuals, including women and children, are unprotected from violence and other forms of abuse that exacerbate inequalities. Ineffectual enforcement of laws engenders environmental degradation, corruption, money laundering, and other problems that burden people and economies around the world.[92]

---

91   For example, Alvaro Santos writes that:
        [The World Bank's] … conceptions [of the governance/rule of law] are overlapping but there are also tensions and contradictions between them. It seems hard that they could all be advanced simultaneously … I … argue that … [b]y advocating several conceptions at once, it becomes easier to justify the goals of any given project. Criticism to any one of the conceptions can be deflected by alternating between the purposes of the different conceptions at play.
        See Santos, *supra* note 76, at 268. Santos likewise points out that the Bank's rule of law/governance/anticorruption projects have been spearheaded by separate and to some extent competing departments, each operating with separate conceptions and different development objectives. *See id.*

92   *See* World Bank, *2002 Annual Report,* at 77, *available at* https://openknowledge. worldbank.org/handle/10986/13931. *See also, e.g.,* Edouard Al-Dahdah et al, *Rules on Paper, Rules in Practice: Enforcing Laws and Policies in the Middle East and North Africa* 1 (World Bank: 2016) (defining rule of law as: "a theoretical concept social scientists use to describe a political order where laws are *predictable* and applied *equally* to all citizens, regardless of their political or economic influence … [such that] no individual or group stands above the law … [which] 'ties the hands' of even the most powerful citizens, including those charged with making and enforcing these same laws." *See also* World Bank, *Legal and Judicial Reform: Observations, Experiences, and Approach of the Legal Vice Presidency* 1 (Washington DC: World Bank, 2002), *available at* http://documents.worldbank.org /curated/en/639721468028843406/Legal-and-judicial-reform-observations-experiences -and-approach-of-the-Legal-Vice-Presidency (The World Bank has clarified that the rule of law prevails where: "(i) the government itself is bound by the law, (ii) every person in society is treated equally under the law, (iii) the human dignity of each individual is recognized and protected by law, and (iv) justice is accessible to all").

Indeed, in this report the phrases "rule of law" and "governance" could be interchanged without altering the meaning of the assertion. This approach to governance/rule-of-law is not unique to the World Bank; key multilateral organizations and technical NGOs have similarly offered unclear conceptual distinctions in efforts to advance social, economic, and sustainable development objectives.[93]

Multiple international development organizations, ostensibly including the World Bank, have seem to have advanced an instrumentalist view of governance/rule-of-law. Doing so, intentionally or otherwise, has arguably opened the door for these organizations to deploy a wide array of avenues and mechanisms for support and reforms in recipient countries. It has also prompted

---

93   The rule of law concept advanced by the United Nations states that it is:

> A principle of governance, in which all persons, institutions and entities, public and private, including the State itself, are accountable to laws that are publicly promulgated, equally enforced and independently adjudicated, and which are consistent with international human rights norms and standards. It requires, as well, measures to ensure adherence to the principles of supremacy of the law, equality before the law, accountability to the law, fairness in the application of the law, separation of powers, participation in decision-making, legal certainty, avoidance of arbitrariness and procedural and legal transparency.

United Nations, *The Rule of Law and Transitional Justice in Conflict and Post-Conflict Societies*, Report of the Secretary-General (S/2004/616) (2004), *available at* https://www .un.org/en/ga/ search/view_doc.asp?symbol=S/2004/616.
Likewise, the World Justice Project defines the rule of law as reflecting the following four principles:
– Government and its officials and agents as well as individuals and private entities are accountable under the law.
– Laws are clear, publicized, stable, and just; are applied evenly; and protect fundamental rights, including the security of persons and property and certain core human rights.
– The process by which the laws are enacted, administered, and enforced is accessible, fair, and efficient.
– Justice is delivered timely by competent, ethical, and independent representatives and neutrals who are of sufficient number, have adequate resources, and reflect the makeup of the communities they serve.

World Justice Project, *What is the Rule of Law*, *available at* http://worldjusticeproject.org /what-rule-law (last visited: July 11, 2022) (explaining that "these four universal principles are further developed in the following nine factors of the WJP Rule of Law Index, which measures how the rule of law is experienced by ordinary people in 99 countries around the globe").

critics of some of these avenues and mechanisms to decry what has been termed a "rule of law orthodoxy,"[94] which describes:

- A focus on state institutions, particularly judiciaries.
- This institutional focus is largely determined by the legal profession, as represented by a nation's jurists, top legal officials, and attorneys, and by foreign consultants and donor personnel.
- As a result, a tendency to define the legal system's problems and cures narrowly, in terms of courts, prosecutors, contracts, law reform, and other institutions and processes in which lawyers play central roles.
- Where civil society engagement occurs, it usually is as a means to-ward the end of state institutional development: consulting non-governmental organizations (NGOs) on how to reform the (narrowly defined) legal system, and funding them as vehicles for advocating reform.
- A reliance on foreign expertise, initiative, and models, particularly those originating in industrialized societies.[95]

Shihata's conflation of the "rule of law" and "governance" in his reference to "government by laws and not of men" is consistent with the "rule of law orthodoxy," which is inherently suspicious of the "rule of men," which connotes arbitrariness, inconsistency, and corruption. Hence the "rule of law orthodoxy" sets out a series of actionable approaches to strengthen institutions and legal and regulatory environments in the same line of strengthening the quality of "governance" which emerges therefrom.[96] This typically includes:

- constructing and repairing courthouses;
- purchasing furniture, computers, and other equipment and materials;
- drafting new laws and regulations;
- training judges, lawyers, and other legal personnel;
- establishing management and administration systems for judiciaries;
- supporting judicial and other training/management institutes;
- building up bar associations; and
- conducting international exchanges for judges, court administrators, and lawyers.[97]

---

94 *See* Upham 2006, *supra* note 90, at 79.
95 Stephen Golub, *The Rule of Law and the UN Peacebuilding Commission: A Social Development Approach*, 20(1) Cambridge Rev. Int'l Aff. 47–67 (March 2007).
96 *Id.*
97 *Id.*

This orthodoxy has likewise been embraced by a range of development organizations seeking to operationalize governance reforms; the institution-strengthening activities described above are considered to be useful mechanisms because they represent an intuitive connection to the quality of governance.[98] However, these are not outcome-oriented indicators. This is a problem for empirically-driven organizations like the World Bank.

6.2.2 Toward Quantifying Governance: Adopting an Outcomes-Based Approach

In practice, in the World Bank has recognized that efforts such as those ubiquitous initiatives associated with rule of law orthodoxy amount to counting *outputs* instead of *outcomes*. There is little evidence that initiatives such as these are enabling transformational impact in the service of social and economic development outcomes because, in short, the entire enterprise "poses certain special problems for measurement."[99] But for any institution to demonstrate progress in the context of governance through the rule of law, clear evidence and replicable results are key. This brings to mind the famous axiom apocryphally attributed to Lord Kelvin: "If you cannot measure it, you cannot improve it." The ability to measure changes in governance through rule of law reforms over time and across countries, in a valid and reliable manner, has been and remains a contested issue.

Rachel Kleinfeld, in her seminal *Advancing the Rule of Law Abroad: Next Generation Reform*, has emphasized the need for a step-change in how reform is assessed with respect to governance through rule of law activities, advocating an "ends-based" definition and approach rather than one which seeks to replicate "good practice" legal institutions and policies.[100] While it is relatively

---

98   *See, e.g.,* Stephen Golub, *Beyond Rule of Law Orthodoxy: The Legal Empowerment Alternative,* Carnegie Endowment for International Peace Working Paper: Rule of Law Series, Democracy and Rule of Law Project, Number 41, 5–7 (October 2003), *available at* https://carnegieendowment.org/files/wp41.pdf.

99   World Bank, *Legal and Judicial Reform: Observations, Experiences, and Approach of the Legal Vice Presidency* 65 (Washington DC 2002), *available at*: http://documents.worldbank .org/curated/en/639721468028843406/Legal-and-judicial-reform-observations -experiences-and-approach-of-the-Legal-Vice-Presidency. *See also,* World Bank, *Measuring Poverty, available at* https://www.worldbank.org/en/topic/ measuringpoverty (last visited July 11, 2022) ("To better understand whether the world is on track to end extreme poverty, and how individual countries are faring, we must regularly measure progress").

100 Rachel Kleinfeld, Advancing the Rule of Law Abroad: Next Generation Reform 11 (2012) ("from an implementation standpoint, institution-based definitions [of the rule of law] lead too easily to institution-modeling, an approach that fails the basic test of strategy: matching resources to ends").

simple to quantify inputs and outputs of interventions which follow the rule of law orthodoxy (as Stephen Golub[101] amply demonstrates), quantifying outcomes is somewhat more difficult. For the purpose of discerning areas where organizations like the World Bank might strengthen their country support to enable good governance and rule of law, it is important to return to the institution's foremost goal in this context: fighting corruption. As indicated in Section I, a core official goal of the World Bank's Governance Global Practice is to preempt or combat corruption in its various forms. While the organization has used different language in recent decades to describe this (from "anticorruption" to "promoting good governance" to "strengthening financial integrity" and more), the fundamental goals remains the same: minimizing "the abuse of public office for private gain."[102]

Accordingly, another trend is clear: the World Bank as well as a wide range of other technical organizations and academic institutions have generated a spectrum of indicator-based mechanisms designed to help identify systemic institutional vulnerabilities and track and measure progress toward good governance outcomes at national and subnational levels in developing countries by focusing in particular on tracking corrupt acts. Indeed, for the World Bank, quantifying corruption in countries at the national or subnational level has become a central exercise to assess the quality of that country or locality's governance and rule of law system. To better substantiate this trend, this section sets out an overview of mechanisms which seek to measure governance, toward better enabling development practitioners design and implement interventions. These mechanisms may be unpacked into three empirical levels, from more aggregate/macro worldwide benchmarking to more in-depth and country specific benchmarking. This specifically includes: (i) Macro-level: worldwide indicators; (ii) Meso-level: cross country analysis, which provide more in-depth data for a select number of countries; and (iii) Micro-level: in-country diagnostic tools.

6.2.2.1   *Macro Level*

At the macro level, Kaufmann, Kraay and Zoido-Lobatón remind us that "governance indicators reflect the statistical compilation of responses on the quality of governance given by a large number of enterprise, citizen and expert survey respondents in industrial and developing countries, as compiled by a

---

101   Stephen Golub, *A House Without a Foundation, in* Promoting the Rule of Law Abroad: in Search of Knowledge 105 (Thomas Carothers, ed., Washington, DC: Carnegie Endowment for International Peace, 2006).

102   The World Bank, Fact Sheet: Corruption, *available at* https://www.worldbank.org/en /news/factsheet/2020/02/19/ anticorruption-fact-sheet (last visited July 11, 2022).

number of survey institutes, think tanks, non-governmental organizations, and international organizations."[103] The collection, analysis, and construction of indicators of worldwide country data on governance and corruption assesses each country in a comparative context for dimensions of governance through aggregation of many variables to create indicators. Macro-level surveys typically cover a spectrum of topics, such as public perceptions of political stability, of the efficiency/quality of public services, of government respect for the rule of law, of the national business climate, and much more. The most general macro-level governance indicators' methodology enables estimates of country-level governance, from which relative country rankings (across dimensions of governance) can be generated, though countries' relative positions are subject to margins of error, which should be indicated clearly. There are several examples of macro-level measures.

Corruption Perceptions Index. The Transparency International Corruption Perceptions Index[104] (CPI) ranks countries in terms of the degree to which corruption is perceived to exist among public officials and politicians. The aim of this index is to measure the abuse of "entrusted power for private gain."[105] The CPI is a composite index, comprised of total of fifteen surveys from nine independent organizations (where at least three surveys are required for a country to be included in the CPI). The way the composite index is developed is that each individual indicator of corruption is standardized (such that each source has the same weight) and then the average (mean) standardized score is calculated. Thus, the CPI score of a country in any one year is the (standardized) average score of all the sources available for that country.

The CPI survey reflects the perceptions of businesspeople and country analysts, both resident and non-resident. Each country receives a score, which can range from 0 (extremely corrupt) to 10 (no corruption) and individual country scores are developed by aggregating and averaging normalised scores of "corruption related data" emanating from a variety of sources. To reduce variations in scoring, the CPI aims to focus on sources available for a given country within the last three years.[106] The list of relevant indicators and scores from

---

103   Daniel Kaufmann, Aart Kraay & Pablo Zoido, *Governance Matters* (August 1999), *available at* https://elibrary. worldbank.org/doi/abs/10.1596/1813-9450-2196 (last visited July 11, 2022) [hereinafter Kaufmann, Kraay & Zoido].

104   Transparency International, Corruption Perceptions Index, *available at* https://www .transparency.org/en/cpi/2021 (last visited July 11, 2022).

105   Transparency International, 2011 Bribe Payers Index, *available at* https://www.transparency .org/bpi2011 (last visited July 11, 2022).

106   The number of sources used to construct the CPI fluctuate over time, since sources must be current from within the last three years and provide consistent comparative

each source are available on a Transparency International document entitled, *Corruption Perceptions Index 2016: Full Source Description*.[107] The surveys used in compiling the CPI pose questions focusing on the misuse of public power for private gain (see Table 12.1). These survey sources include:

- African Development Bank Governance Ratings 2015
- Bertelsmann Foundation Sustainable Governance Indicators 2016
- Bertelsmann Foundation Transformation Index 2016
- Economist Intelligence Unit Country Risk Ratings 2016
- Freedom House Nations in Transit 2016
- Global Insight Country Risk Ratings 2015
- IMD World Competitiveness Yearbook 2016
- Political and Economic Risk Consultancy Asian Intelligence 2016
- Political Risk Services International Country Risk Guide 2016
- World Bank - Country Policy and Institutional Assessment 2015
- World Economic Forum Executive Opinion Survey (EOS) 2016
- World Justice Project Rule of Law Index 2016
- Varieties of Democracy (VDEM) Project 2016

The CPI accordingly builds public awareness of corruption, and low CPI scores have been used to encourage governments to address the root causes.[108] It is thus a potentially "noisy" but nevertheless valid measure of level of corruption.[109]

The Worldwide Governance Indicators. The Worldwide Governance Indicators (WGIS) are another such macro-level measure of governance, which

---

information, and so comparison over long periods are not advised. It is, however, possible to use the CPI year average over a short period of time as a representative score for a country in a given time period. *See, e.g.,* Torsten Persson & Guido Tabellini, The Economic Effects of Constitutions 55 (2003).

107   https://www.transparency.org/news/feature/corruption_perceptions_index_2016.

108   *See* Daniel Treisman, *What have we learned about the causes of corruption from ten years of cross-national empirical research?* 10 Annu. Rev. Polit. Sci. 211–44 (2007) (noting that the CPI has been found to be highly correlated with measures of actual corruption) [hereinafter Treisman].

109   *See* Staffan Andersson & Paul M. Heywood, *The Politics of Perception: Use and Abuse of Transparency International's Approach to Measuring Corruption,* 5 Political Stud. 746–767, 760 (2009), *available at* https://citeseerx.ist.psu.edu/viewdoc/download?doi=10.1.1. 872.5467&rep=rep1&type=pdf ("even though Transparency International cautions against year-to-year comparisons of CPI rankings, it is evident that these are regularly undertaken both by TI chapters themselves, by other leading commentators and – most significantly – by governments and aid organizations. In spite of the shortcomings in the construction of the index, highlighted above, such detailed attention to countries' ranking both reinforces the dominant approach to combating corruption and also serves to underpin the leading role played by TI in formulating anti-corruption strategies").

TABLE 12.1   Representative Components of the CPI (2000)[110]

Source	Who was surveyed/asked?	Question/Assessment (Bureaucratic/Both/ Political)	Availability of data	Sample size (year)?
Political & Economic Risk Consultancy	Expatriate business executives	"Extent of corruption in a way that detracts from the business environment for Foreign companies"	1998, 1999, 2000 in 12–14 Asian countries	280 (1998) 700 (1999-app) 1027 (2000)
Institute for Management Development	Executives in top- and middle-management; domestic and international companies	"Bribing and corruption exists in the public sphere"	1998, 1999, 2000 In 46–47 countries	2515 (1998) 4314 (1999) 4160 (2000)
The Economist Intelligence Unit	Expert staff assessment	"Assessment of the pervasiveness of Corruption among politicians and civil servants"	2000 in 115 countries	NA (expert assessment)
International Crime Victim Survey	General public	"During 1999, has any government official in your own country, asked you to pay a bribe for his service?"	1999, 2000 in 11 countries	20,000 (1999) 20,000 (2000)
The World Bank & EBRD	Senior business-people	"State capture and frequency of irregular, additional payments to public officials"	1999 in 20 countries	3000 (1999)
Freedom House	US academics and Freedom House Staff	"Levels of corruption"	1998 in 28 countries	NA (expert assessment)

(cont.)

110   Alexander Hamilton & Craig Hammer, *Can We Measure the Power of the Grabbing Hand? A Comparative Analysis of Different Indicators of Corruption* 15 (World Bank Policy Research Working Paper No. 8299, 2018), *available at* https://openknowledge.worldbank .org/handle/10986/29162 [hereinafter Hamilton & Hammer].

TABLE 12.1   Representative components of the CPI (2000) (cont.)

Source	Who was surveyed/asked?	Question/Assessment (Bureaucratic/Both/ Political)	Availability of data	Sample size (year)?
The World Economic Forum (Global Competitiveness Report)	Senior business leaders; domestic and international companies	"Irregular, additional payments connected with import and export permits, business licenses, exchange controls, tax assessments, police protection or loan application"	1998, 1999, 2000 in 53– 59 countries	3167 (1998) 3934 (1999) 4022 (2000)
The World Economic Forum (African Competitiveness Report)	Senior business leaders; domestic and international companies	"How problematic is corruption? Irregular, additional Payments are required and large in amount"	1998, 2000 in 20–26 countries	582 (1998) 1800 (2000)
Political Risk Service	Expert staff assessment	"Assessment of 'corruption in government'"	2000 in 140 countries	NA (expert assessment)

includes a specific focus on rule of law. The WGIS cover more than 200 countries, based on more than 350 variables, obtained from dozens of institutions worldwide.[111] The WGIS capture the following six dimensions of governance: (1) Voice and Accountability: measuring political, civil and human rights; (2) Political instability and violence: measuring the likelihood of violent threats to, or changes in, government, including terrorism; (3) Government effectiveness:" measuring the competence of the bureaucracy and the quality of public service delivery; (4) Regulatory burden: measuring the incidence of market-unfriendly policies; (5) Rule of law: measuring the quality of contract enforcement, the police, and the courts, as well as the likelihood of crime and violence; and (6) Control of corruption: measuring the exercise of public power for private gain, including both petty and grand corruption, and state capture. For all six indicators, the partners which produce the WGIS use the

---

111   Daniel Kaufmann & Aart Kraay, *Worldwide Governance Indicators: Methodology, available at* https://info.world bank.org/governance/wgi/Home/Documents (last visited July 11, 2022) [hereinafter Kaufmann & Kraay].

same approach to develop an interval measure of the governance dimension of substantive interest. This entails standardizing the variables and then using an "Unobserved Components Model" (UCM) to develop each indicator. This process therefore enables the development of the control of corruption and government effectiveness indicators that ranges from –2.5 (most corrupt/least effective) to 2.5 (least corrupt/most effective).[112]

The survey methodology, featuring objective measures of performance, initially has been adopted in a number of enterprise surveys.[113] In general, it is more straightforward to gather enterprise-level objective data because much of this information is collected internally within a firm for accounting purposes. Combined datasets, for example household surveys, surveys of public officials, and business surveys, can permit comparisons of perceptions across individuals, from which useful information can be discerned. The WGIs usefully enable comparative monitoring of governance and allow practitioners to raise general "flags" on country performance. Specifically, they allow researchers to examine performance changes across a large number of countries and compare performance across time (within margins of error). Whether one country ranks higher than another country does not mean much in a statistical, practical, economic or policy-oriented way. This is because the measures are not set up to give a definite ranking of a country for a specific variable. Rather, there are large margins of error; looking at the data one sees vertical lines: these are 90 percent confidence intervals. This means that there is a 90% chance that the true variable of governance is somewhere on the vertical bar which depicts the margin of error. Accordingly, data is classified in three broad categories for each governance indicator: "red" (a country is in a governance crisis in that particular component); "yellow" (a country is vulnerable or at risk of falling into a governance crisis); and "green" (a country has better governance and is not at risk). Due to the annual change in the number of sources over time, making inferences regarding the marginal change in a country's score over a short period of time is not advised.[114] Averaging the score of countries over a few years to get a representative average for the time period is not problematic, due to the fact that sources from adjacent years are used to construct the indicator at any one time.

---

112   *Id.*

113   Lixin Colin Xu, Francesca Recanatini & Scott Wallsten, *Surveying Surveys and Questioning Questions - Learning from World Bank Experience* (World Bank Policy Research Working Paper No. WPS 2307 2000), *available at* http://documents.worldbank.org/curated/en/23474146873953o874/Surveying-surveys-and-questioning-questions-learning-from-World-Bank-experience.

114   *See* Kaufmann & Kraay, *supra* note 111.

Key indicators within the WGI for the purpose of this analysis are *Government Effectiveness* and *Control of Corruption*. Given that they rely on a common methodology, it is possible to summarize the coding and some of the issues associated with each indicator jointly. The WGI uses 30 existing data sources to develop each of these indicators. The sources are selected to include the views of citizens, business owners, academics and experts drawn from the public, private, and NGO sectors from across the globe, and the below standard methodology is used.[115] The two indicators are developing using a sub-component of the data sources, as they are available and applicable by year. The 30 data sources can be divided into: (1) surveys of households and firms (nine sources), (2) commercial intelligence information generators (e.g. the Economist Intelligence Unit, four sources); (3) NGOs (nine sources, including Freedom House) and Public Sector Organizations (such the World Bank).

Control of Corruption Cluster/Governance Dimension. The aim of this measure, like the CPI, is to capture the extent to which public policy-makers abuse their public office for private gain. The aim of the index is thus: "... designed to capture ... [the] extent to which public power is exercised for private gain, including both petty and grand forms of corruption, as well as 'capture' of the state by elites and private interests."[116]

The CC – like the CPI – is primarily comprised of sources focused on measuring political and bureaucratic corruption, some of which overlap with the CPI. Specifically, three out of five of the CC's representative sources focus on general corruption (e.g. "pervasiveness of corruption"); one is focused on bureaucratic corruption ("an assessment of the intrusiveness of the country's bureaucracy") and one is focused on political corruption ("is corruption in government widespread?"). Given that one of the CC's representative sources is focused on corruption by bureaucrats, the CC may skew toward unelected officials more so than the CPI. Like the CPI, the indicator is focused on surveys of experts, though to a lesser extent, and it focuses on both grand political and more petty corruption.

Government Effectiveness (GE) Cluster/Governance Dimension. The scope of the GE is similar to that of the CPI and the CC in that all three aim to capture abuses of public power by policy makers. It is qualitatively different because it measures the extent to which corruption takes place via unit cost increases, rather than a focus on levels of bribes. Hence, while measures comprising the CPI and CC are designed to capture the extent to which public policy makers extract rents, such as extortion and bribery, the GE is designed to capture the

115   *Id.*
116   *Id.*

TABLE 12.2   Representative Components of the CC[117]

Source	Who Was surveyed/asked?	Question/Assessment of (Bureaucratic/Both/Political)	Source Type
Economist Intelligence Unit Risk-wire & Democracy Index	Expert Staff	"Pervasiveness of Corruption"	Commercial Business Information Provider
World Economic Forum Global Competitiveness Report	Survey- Senior business leaders; domestic and international companies	"Public trust in financial honesty of politicians. Diversion of public funds due to corruption is common" "Frequent for firms to make extra payments connected: (1) trade permits, (2) public utilities, (3) tax payments, (4) loan applications, (5) awarding of public contracts, (6) influence laws, policies regulations, decrees, (7) to get favourable judicial decisions."	Non-Government Organization
Gallup World Poll	Survey-general public	"Is corruption in government widespread?"	Commercial Business Information Provider
Institutional Profiles Database	Expert Staff	"Level of petty, large-scale and political corruption"	Government
Global Insight Business Conditions and Risk Indicators	Expert Staff	"An assessment of the intrusiveness of the country's bureaucracy. The amount of red tape likely to countered is assessed, as is the likelihood of encountering corrupt of officials and other groups"	Commercial Business Information Provider

---

117   See Hamilton & Hammer, supra note 109, at 15.

extent to which public policy makers abuse their office by reducing their workloads, enhancing their benefits, and related activities. In short, "Government Effectiveness (GE) – [is designed to capture] perceptions of the quality of public services, the quality of the civil service and the degree of its independence from political pressures, the quality of policy formulation and implementation, and the credibility of the government's commitment to such policies."[118] This focus on bureaucratic corruption is a key value-addition by the GE. Only one of the five representative sources of the GE is not focused on bureaucratic corruption (i.e. "quality of the supply of public goods: education and basic health and the capacity of political authorities to implement reforms" (see Table 12.3).

Given that the GE does focus on political corruption, it is likely to be correlated with measures of political corruption because of the relationship between politicians and bureaucrats. The sources for the Worldwide Governance Indicators are as follows:

Global Corruption Barometer. The Global Corruption Barometer (GCB) provides information on perceptions of corruption by the general public; this is a key distinguishing characteristic since other measures like the CPI focus on the perceptions of elites, such as experts and industry participants. Since 2003, Transparency International has collaborated with Gallup International to develop a questionnaire focusing on different elements of corruption.[119] These questions are part of Gallup's Voice of the People survey.[120] The number of countries the survey covers has varied over time (47–86), and in some countries the authorities have barred politically sensitive questions. The sample survey is national in scope, though it is confined to urban centers in some emerging economies and has historically been conducted via face-to-face or telephone interviews. The sample framework is either random or by quota, depending on the country in question, and sample sizes have generally been large though the final results are weighed by demographic characteristics (age, groups, and sex) to help ensure that the results are as representative of the general population as possible. The summary statistics of a typical GCB are as follows:

The questions in the GCB have evolved over time. Questions of particular interest for respondents were launched in the 2003 survey, and included asks

---

118   Daniel Kaufmann, Aart Kraay & Massimo Mastruzzi, *The Worldwide Governance Indicators: A Summary of Methodology, Data and Analytical Issues* (World Bank Policy Research Working Paper no. 5430, 2010), *available at* https://papers.ssrn.com/sol3/papers.cfm?abstract_id=1682130.

119   Transparency International, *Corruption Perceptions Index; Global Corruption Barometer, available at*https://www.transparency.org/en/gcb (last visited July 11, 2022) [hereinafter Transparency International].

120   *Id.*

TABLE 12.3   Representative Components of the GE[121]

Source	Who was surveyed/asked?	Question/Assessment of (Bureaucratic/Both/Political)	Source type
Economist Intelligence Unit	Expert Staff	"Quality of bureaucracy / institutional effectiveness"	Commercial Business Information Provider
World Economic Forum Global Competitiveness Report	Survey-Senior business leaders; domestic and international companies	"Quality of general infrastructure Quality of public schools Time spent by senior management dealing with government officials"	Non-Government Organization
Gallup World Poll	Survey-general public	Satisfaction with public transportation system Satisfaction with roads and highways Satisfaction with education system	Commercial Business Information Provider
Institutional Profiles Database	Expert Staff	"Quality of the supply of public goods: education and basic health Capacity of political authorities to implement reforms"	Government
Political Risk Services International Country Risk Guide	Expert Staff	"Bureaucratic Quality"	Commercial Business Information Provider
Global Insight Business Conditions and Risk Indicators	Expert Staff	"An assessment of the quality of the country's bureaucracy. The better the bureaucracy, the quicker decisions are made and the more easily foreign investors can go about their business. Policy consistency and forward planning. How confident businesses can be of the continuity of economic policy stance-whether a change of government will entail major policy disruption, and whether the current government has pursued a coherent strategy. This factor also looks at the extent to which policy-making is far-sighted, or conversely aimed at short-term economic advantage."	Commercial Business Information Provider

---

121   *See* Hamilton & Hammer, *supra* note 109, at 17.

TABLE 12.4   Descriptive Statistics of the Global Corruption Barometer (2003)[122]

Number of questions	Number of countries	Questions of interest	Sample size	Demographic data controls
6	47	"Corruption is a significant problem in: political life" (no/yes, slightly/yes significantly)	40,838 (19,488) female (21,390) male	Age, Education attainment. Income level

of respondents whether "corruption had a not/significant/somewhat significant/very significant effect on (1) personal and family life, (2) the business environment, and (3) political life."[123] Results were reported by percentage of respondents, were interval in nature, and presented a range of responses from 0% to 100%. Results over the years have presented significant variation in respondents' perceptions of corruption in different policy domains. For example, of the six questions on the 2003 GCB, one asked respondents: "[Is] Corruption is a significant problem in: political life [Yes or No]?" Given that the GCB questionnaire is put to one type of respondent (i.e. the general public) and in light of questions like this one – i.e. one which turns on levels of awareness or engagement by citizens with respect to the behavior of top government officials, and which does not combine with other indicators of corruption to account for the possible effect of unrepresentative results – raises questions about the efficacy of the extent of the GCB's practical value for governance analyses and suitability to inform operational responses.

Bribe Payers index. Transparency International launched the Bribe Payers index (BPI) 1999. The BPI ranks exporting countries on the degree to which international companies headquartered in these countries are perceived to pay bribes to senior public officials in emerging economies. In short, the BPI focuses on perceptions of the supply-side of bribery.

Global Financial Integrity. Strengthening governance through rule of law assistance is often explicitly tied to the recognition that government financial management, procurement and performance monitoring systems are important, including to facilitate streamlined delivery of good governance in public

---

122   See Hamilton & Hammer, *supra* note 110, at 19.
123   *See* Transparency International, *supra* note 120.

sectors and key public goods, such as in health, water, education, energy and extractives. Analyzing financial flows is thus of paramount importance to assess and improve governance situations in countries. With this in mind, the Global Financial Integrity (GFI)[124] uses sources of data and analytical methodologies used by international institutions and governments to surface information on gaps, such as gaps in balance of payments data and gaps in trade data, since the difference indicates an inflow or outflow that was not recorded, or a re-invoicing of transactions between export from one country and import into another country.[125]

The Institute for Economics and Peace. The Institute for Economics and Peace is a think tank dedicated to developing metrics to analyze peace and seeks to quantify its economic value, including by developing global and national indices, calculating the economic cost of violence, and analyzing country level risk and understanding positive peace.[126] The Institute generated an analysis focusing on the measurement of SDG 16, and set out a range of relevant indicators to relevant to ascertaining the quality of governance and the relative strength of rule of law in countries. Key proposed indicators include:

− Total volume of inward and outward illicit financial flows
− Illicit financial flows as a percentage of GDP
− Total value of inward and outward illicit financial flows (in current USD)
− Adherence/ratification of the International Convention for the Suppression of the Financing of Terrorism and the Convention against Transnational Organized Crime
− Percentage of criminal cases in which the defendant/people does not have legal or other representation in court
− Percentage of defendants in criminal cases who are represented by legal counsel

---

124   Global Financial Integrity, Research and Analysis, *available at* https://gfintegrity.org/reports/ (last visited July 11, 2022).
125   *Id.* Indicators and data sources used include:
  − IMF: Balance of payments data, contributing to the analysis of net errors and omissions; Direction of Trade Statistics (DOTS), enabling analyses of discrepancies in trade between pairs of reporting countries.
  − World Bank: data on debt, contributing to the analysis of broad capital flight.
  − UN COMTRADE: data on bilateral trade in commodity groups.
  − US Dept. of Commerce: data on trade transactions by Harmonized System coding categories.
  − European Statistics: data on trade transactions by Harmonized System coding categories.
126   Institute for Economics and Peace, *available at* https://www.economicsandpeace.org/ (last visited July 11, 2022).

- Conviction rates for indigent defendants provided with legal representation as a proportion of conviction rates for defendants with lawyer of their own choice
- Ratio of conviction rates (violent crimes) for impoverished defendants who are provided with free legal representation vs. conviction rates for defendants with legal representation of their own choosing
- Value of illicit production and trafficking of natural resources, as a total and as a percentage of GDP
- Extractive industries transparency initiative status (compliant, candidate, suspended, or other, EITI)
- Resource Governance Index (Revenue Watch Institute)
- Active participation in (co-operation with) Forest Law Enforcement, Governance and Trade (FLEGT) or equivalent illicit logging control initiative/the Egmont Group of Financial Intelligence Units/the Kimberley process/the UN Programme of Action on SALW/Interpol
- Value of illicit production and trafficking of drugs, as a total and as a percentage of GDP
- Global volume of money laundering
- Drug-related crime per 100,000 population
- Number of investigations and convictions against suspicious financial activity relating to organized crime, money laundering, bribery and corruption, and financing of terrorism
- Number of investigations and convictions against suspicious financial activity relating to bribery and corruption
- Total number of cases analyzed by the body in charge of fighting money laundering and illicit flows in the last 12 months
- Total number of reported cases to the body in charge of fighting money laundering and illicit flows that were addressed by the justice system
- Conviction rate for all corruption cases in the justice system/year
- Proportion of corruption cases that are cleared by the judiciary system within 12 months
- Assets and liabilities of BIS reporting banks in international tax havens by country
- Ratification of UNCAC and up-to-date legal framework against bribery and corruption, which facilitates stolen asset recovery
- World Economic Forum Question: To what extent does organized crime (mafia-oriented racketeering, extortion) impose costs on businesses in your country?
- Percentage of population who paid a bribe to a public official, or were asked for a bribe by these public officials, during the last 12 months

- Existence of mandatory public register that discloses the beneficial owner-ship of trust funds and companies
- Percentage of persons who paid a bribe to a security, police or justice official or were asked a bribe by these public officials, in the past 12 months
- Percentage of persons who had at least one contact with a public official, who paid a bribe to a public official, or were asked for a bribe by these public officials, during the last 12 months
- Proportion of the population admitting having paid bribes in the last 12 months
- Proportion of the population admitting knowing someone who has paid bribes in the last 12 months
- Percent of population that reports paying a bribe when obtaining a public service or when interacting with a public official
- Proportion of [persons/businesses] that did, were asked or were expected to pay a bribe or provide a product or service to a public official
- Reported rates of bribery (individual experience) in basic public services
- Existence of a reporting mechanism through which citizens can report cor-ruption cases
- Percentage of businesses that paid a bribe to a public official, or were asked for a bribe by these public officials, during the last 12 months
- Percentage of businesses that paid a bribe to a public official, or were asked a bribe by these public officials, during the last 12 months
- Percentage of businesses who had at least one contact with a public official, who paid a bribe to a public official, or were asked for a bribe by these public officials, during the last 12 months
- Percentage of firms identifying corruption as a major constraint
- Percentage of public officials who have been hired through formal and stan-dardized procedure
- Asset declaration requirement & wealth made public
- Existence of legislation that requires public officials to declare assets
- Laws in place requiring disclosure of assets by key political and administra-tive leaders
- Existence of a law requiring the disclosure of private donations to political parties (yes/no)
- Share of staff recruited using merit-based practices
- Survey Question: In practice, civil servants are appointed and evaluated according to professional criteria
- Percentage of cases of corruption prosecuted
- Executive (the head of state, the head of government, and cabinet minis-ters) bribery and corrupt exchanges

- Executive embezzlement and theft
- Bribes to the judiciary
- Corrupt activities in the legislature
- Public sector embezzlement and theft; public sector corrupt exchanges
- Rate of compliance with binding resultant judgments of bilateral and multilateral investment treaty disputes
- Number of legally binding bilateral and/or multilateral investment treaties[127]

Gallup World Poll Survey. The Gallup World Poll tracks public perceptions via nationally representative surveys (face-to-face or by telephone) in more than 160 countries, and include indicators relevant to ascertaining public sentiment on the quality of governance and the rule of law, including questions such as: "Do you think the government of your country is doing enough to fight corruption, or not?" and "Do you think the level of corruption in this country is lower, about the same, or higher than it was 5 years ago?"[128]

World Justice Project Rule of Law Index. The World Justice Project Rule of Law (WJPROL) Index focuses collects original data on the rule of law from 128 countries and jurisdictions, based on more than 130,000 household and expert surveys to measure how the rule of law is experienced and perceived by the general public worldwide.[129] The WJPROL Index focuses on grouping forty-four indicators under the following eight "factors":

- Constraints on Government Powers (Factor 1)
- Absence of Corruption (Factor 2)
- Open Government (Factor 3)
- Fundamental Rights (Factor 4)
- Order and Security (Factor 5)
- Regulatory Enforcement (Factor 6)
- Civil Justice (Factor 7)
- Criminal Justice (Factor 8)[130]

---

127   Institute for Economics and Peace, *Measuring Goal 16: Identifying Priority Indicates Based on Key Statistical and Normative Criteria* (September 2014), *available at* https://www .economicsandpeace.org/wp-content/uploads/2015/06/Measuring-Goal-16.pdf.

128   Gallup, Global Research, *available* ahttps://www.gallup.com/analytics/318875/global -research.aspx (last visited July 11, 2022).

129   World Justice Project, Our Approach, *available at* https://worldjusticeproject.org /about-us/overview/our-approach (last visited July 11, 2022).

130   World Justice Project, *World Justice Project Rule of Law Index 2021* 15 (2021), *available at* https://worldjusticeproject. org/sites/default/files/documents/WJP-INDEX-21.pdf.

The Index also references "Informal Justice" as Factor 9, though notes that it is not included in the Index's aggregate scores and rankings.[131] The WJP report goes so far as to identify what the indicators seek to measure[132] and rely on perception data to discern the effectiveness of governance and the rule of law, for example with respect to instances of bribery, improper influence by public or private interests, misappropriation of public funds or other resources, and more across institutions of government, including the executive branch, the judiciary, the military and police, and the legislature.[133]

6.2.2.2   Meso Level

Meso-level data sets out more detail than macro-level data and feature consistent questions across countries over time. It can be useful for "deeper dive" analyses of bribery and illicit financial flows in a country than is possible at the macro level. A meso-level cross-country analysis can enable practitioners to track specific aspects of government performance over time.

Global Competitiveness Report. The Global Competitiveness Report assesses the competitiveness landscape of 138 economies and sets out insight into the drivers of their productivity and prosperity. The Report series remains one of the most comprehensive assessments of national competitiveness. The 2017 edition particularly highlighted that declining openness is threatening growth and prosperity.[134]

Leadership Council of the Sustainable Development Solutions Network. The Leadership Council oversees the work of the Sustainable Development Solutions Network.[135] It comprises eminent experts on sustainable development from academia, business, civil society, and the public sector. The Council produced a report in March 2015, which proposed a series of indicators and a monitoring framework[136] for the SDGs, including for SDG 16, the "Governance Goal." These include:

---

131   *Id.* at 16.

132   *Id.* at 16–19.

133   *Id.*

134   Global Competitiveness Report, *available at* https://reports.weforum.org/global-compet-itiveness-index-2017-2018/ (last visited July 11, 2022).

135   Sustainable Development Solutions Network, Leadership Council, *available at* https://www.unsdsn.org/leadership-council (last visited July 11, 2022).

136   Leadership Council of the Sustainable Development Solutions Network, *Indicators and a Monitoring Framework for the Sustainable Development Goals: Launching a data revolution for the SDGs* (A report by the Leadership Council of the Sustainable Development Solutions Network, March 20, 2015), *available at* https://knowledge4policy.ec.europa.eu /publication/indicators-monitoring-framework-sustainable-development-goals-launching -data-revolution_en.

- Proportion of legal persons and arrangements for which beneficial owner-ship information is publicly available
- Revenues, expenditures, and financing of all central government entities are presented on a gross basis in public budget documentation and autho-rized by the legislature
- Perception of public sector corruption
- Percentage of people and businesses that paid a bribe to a public official, or were asked for a bribe by a public official, during the last 12 months.

Enterprise Surveys. A key example of multi-country enterprise survey instru-ments is the World Bank's Enterprise Surveys.[137] An Enterprise Survey is a firm-level survey of a representative sample of an economy's private sector. The surveys cover a range of business environment topics, including compe-tition and performance measures, but also topics like corruption and bribery. The World Bank has collected this data from face-to-face interviews with top managers and business owners since 2002, from more than 155,000 companies in 148 economies. The Bank's findings and recommendations are designed to help policy makers identify, prioritize and implement reforms of policies and institutions that support efficient private economic activity.

It is important to note that World Bank relies on enterprise surveys as a key source of corruption and bribery indicators. These enterprise survey indica-tors capture the prevalence of different types of bribery in 139 countries, with results based on surveys of more than 127,000 firms. For example, enterprise survey indicators indicatively include:

- Bribery incidence (percent of firms experiencing at least one bribe payment request)
- Bribery depth (% of public transactions where a gift or informal payment was requested)
- Percent of firms expected to give gifts in meetings with tax officials
- Percent of firms expected to give gifts to secure government contract
- Value of gift expected to secure a government contract (% of contract value)
- Percent of firms expected to give gifts to get an operating license
- Percent of firms expected to give gifts to get an import license
- Percent of firms expected to give gifts to get a construction permit
- Percent of firms expected to give gifts to get an electrical connection
- Percent of firms expected to give gifts to get a water connection
- Percent of firms expected to give gifts to public officials "to get things done"
- Percent of firms identifying corruption as a major constraint

---

137   World Bank, Enterprise Surveys, *available at* topics/corruption (last visited July 11, 2022).

– Percent of firms identifying the courts system as a major constraint[138]

As of 2017, the enterprise surveys have indicated that one in four firms in low-income and lower-middle-income countries encounter requests for bribes and informal payments from officials, while one in five are expected to offer gifts to tax officials.[139] Bribery often occurs in transactions necessary for a private firm to conduct business: paying taxes; obtaining an operating license, import license, or construction permit; and obtaining an electrical or water connection. In the economies worst affected, more than half the firms encounter such requests, adding to their costs. The requests also impede the creation and growth of firms.[140]

6.2.2.3   *Micro Level*

Micro-level data are collected via in-depth, governance diagnostic surveys in a single country, for example of public officials, households, and enterprise managers. They allow us to distill key links between governance and the quality of services, growth and the specific characteristics of the public sector. Micro-level analyses can be aimed to identify both weak institutions (in need of reform) and strong institutions (examples of good governance) and can be instructive to unbundled corruption by type administrative, capture of the state, bidding, theft of goods and public resources, purchase of licenses and regulations. Further, they help to assess the costs of each type of corruption on different groups of stakeholders and ultimately help in the development of policy recommendations.

The United Nations Survey of Crime Trends and Operations of Criminal Justice Systems. This is a survey compiled and collected by the Crime Prevention and Criminal Justice Division of the United Nations. The survey launched in 1970 and compiles annual data on incidences of crime in UN member states.[141] The survey focuses on relevant public authorities in each UN member state and solicits the provision of data from each member state's own national statis-

---

138   World Bank Enterprise Surveys, Explore Indicators, *available at* https://www.enterprise-surveys.org/en/enterprise surveys (last visited July 11, 2022).

139   World Bank, 2017 Atlas of Sustainable Development Goals: Data Topics (2017), *available at* https://datatopics.worldbank.org/sdgatlas/archive/2017/SDG-16-peace-justice-and-strong-institutions.html (last visited July 11, 2022).

140   *Id.*

141   United Nations Office on Drugs and Crime, United Nations Survey of Crime Trends and Operations of Criminal Justice Systems, *available at* https://www.unodc.org/unodc/en/data-and-analysis/United-Nations-Surveys-on-Crime-Trends-and-the-Operations-of-Criminal-Justice-Systems.html (last visited July 11, 2022).

tics, concerning incidences of crime. This survey includes a range of indicators of the quality of governance and prevalence of corruption, for example including the number of prosecutions for bribery per 100,000 members of the country's population. The rate of prosecution per 100,000 can, hypothetically, vary from 0 to 100,000 (interval range). To focus on this indicator specifically using results from the survey completed in 2000 for illustrative purposes, there is significant variation in the number of prosecutions for bribery per 100,000 people, while on average there were 3.5 prosecutions for bribery per 100,000 of the population. The standard error is greater than the mean (9.6), the lowest per capita prospection is 0.01 per 100,000 (Pakistan), while the highest rate was in Romania (52.3 per 100,000).[142]

Certain challenges arise with respect to attempting to use bribery data as a measure of corruption. The first is that the word "bribery" lacks definitional clarity: it varies by jurisdiction and definitions have evolved over time, which make cross-country comparisons and comparisons over time difficult or impossible. Second, prosecution for bribery does not necessarily measure levels of overall corruption; some countries might have low levels of prosecution due to the lack of corruption, or due to the limited capacity of the domestic legal system to undertake prosecutions. Conversely, a high prosecution rate might indicate high levels of bribery or else efforts to use prosecution as a deterrent. In short, since use of prosecution may vary significantly across contexts, its relevance as a cross-sectional measure of increased or decreased corruption is questionable.[143]

Evidence on the propensity of diplomats from different countries to break the law (i.e. "Tickets"). There is evidence that social, cultural, and institutional norms which create incentives and shape expectations may indeed condition the propensity for individuals to abuse public office for private gain when the opportunity arises. Fishman and Miguel have explored this phenomenon by examining the conduct of United Nations diplomats in New York – who are immune from prosecution – with respect to the number of parking tickets issued to individual diplomats.[144] From this analysis, they have developed a per capita measure of the abuse of parking violations by UN diplomats.

---

142   United Nations Office on Drugs and Crime, The Seventh United Nations Survey on Crime Trends and the Operations of Criminal Justice Systems (1998 - 2000), *available at* https://www.unodc.org/unodc/en/data-and-analysis/Seventh-United-Nations-Survey-on-Crime-Trends-and-the-Operations-of-Criminal-Justice-Systems.html.

143   Johann Lambsdorff, *Corruption: An Empirical Approach*, 61 Am. J. Econ. & Sociology 829–853 (2004).

144   Raymond Fishman & Edward Miguel, *Cultures of Corruption: Evidence From Diplomatic Parking Tickets*, 115(6) J. Pol. Econ. 1020–1048 (2007).

Specifically, they divide the number of tickets issued to UN diplomats of a certain nationality between 1998 and 2000, by the number of diplomats in that country's UN delegation.

The number of parking tickets per capita (size of the diplomatic delegation) is an interval indicator ranging from 0-249. Fishman and Miguel found significant variation in the number of tickets issued per capita, with the standard error (33.0) larger than the mean (19.7). For many countries, especially high-income (OECD) countries in Northern Europe, the number of parking tickets issued was 0, while as a region, the Middle East had the highest rate of ticketing (Kuwait had the highest rate of all countries: 249.4).[145]

This measure has certain weaknesses; it might only measure a narrow form of corrupt act, and diplomats may not necessarily be representative of a population. However, it also has several strengths: it does correlate strongly with Control of Corruption and CPI subjective survey data on corruption. Also, while diplomats might not be representative of a population, they are more likely to be similar to the senior policymakers who may undertake large scale corruption. Likewise, data is available for a large number of countries (146); it is comparable, and does exist over a time period (1998–2001) for which corruption indices exist. For these reasons, *Tickets* can be used as a robustness check for CC and CPI subjective results.

Country Policy and Institutional Assessment. The World Bank's Country Policy and Institutional Assessment (CPIA) aims to (annually) assess the quality of a country's present policy and institutional framework for enabling poverty reduction, sustainable growth, and the effective use of development assistance.[146] The World Bank rates low-income countries each year using the CPIA to determine the amount of resources a country may receive from the International Development Association (IDA). Specifically, the CPIA rates countries on a low-to-high scale for each of sixteen criteria that are grouped in four clusters: (i) economic management; (ii) structural policies; (iii) policies for social inclusion and equity; and (iv) public sector management and institutions. CPIA criterion #16 focuses on "Transparency, Accountability, and Corruption in the Public Sector."[147] Country scores depend on the degree of country performance in a given year, assessed against the criteria for which

145   *Id.*

146   World Bank, Country Policy and Institutional Assessment, *available at* http://data .worldbank.org/data-catalog/CPIA (last visited July 11, 2022).

147   World Bank, 2005 Country Policy and Institutional Assessment questionnaire, *available at* http://siteresources. worldbank.org/IDA/Resources/CPIA2005Questionnaire.pdf (last visited July 11, 2022).

ratings are assigned by World Bank staff. Scores are then averaged to first identify a per-cluster score, and then to calculate a composite country rating as the
average of all four clusters. Each country rating is based on a range of indicators, as well as experts' observations and research of countries' promulgated
policies and performance.

Afrobarometer. The Afrobarometer is a face-to-face public perception survey
which is conducted in 39 African countries, focusing in particular on democracy, governance, economic conditions, and related issues, which is repeated
every two years.[148] Samples are designed to be a representative cross-section
of voting-age citizens in each country, and have typically been either 1200 or
2400,[149] with governance-related results communicated in a series of report,
including "SDG 16 summary scorecards," which compare Afrobarometer survey findings of citizens' perspectives to official UN efforts to track progress of
Sustainable Development Goal 16.[150]

CEPII Institutional Profiles Database. The Centre d'Etudes Prospectives et
d'Informations Internationales (CEPII) Institutional Profiles Database (IPD)
sets out a measure of countries' institutional characteristics through composite indicators built from perception data.[151] The object of the database is
to enable research on potential relationships between country institutions,
economic growth, and different forms of development.[152] For example, the
2012 edition of the database covered 143 countries and was comprised of 130
indicators, derived from 330 variables which describe a range of institutional

---

148   Afrobarometer, Sampling, *available at* https://www.afrobarometer.org/surveys-and
       -methods/sampling/ (last visited July 11, 2022).

149   *Id.*

150   *See, e.g.*, Afrobarometer, *SDG 16 summary scorecard: Peace, justice and strong institutions
       (Indicator 1: Increase trust in police, judiciary and Parliament)* (July 19, 2022), *available at*
       https://www.afrobarometer.org/publication/sdg-16-summary-scorecard-peace-justice
       -and-strong-institutions-indicator-1-increase-trust-in-police-judiciary-and-parliament/;
       Afrobarometer, *SDG 16 summary scorecard: Peace, justice and strong institutions (Indicator
       2: Reduce perceived corruption in police, judiciary and Parliament)* (July 19, 2022), *available
       at* https://www.afrobarometer.org/ publication/sdg-16-summary-scorecard-peace-justice
       -and-strong-institutions-indicator-2-reduce-perceived-corruption-in-police-judiciary
       -and-parliament/; Afrobarometer, *SDG 16 summary scorecard: Peace, justice and strong insti-
       tutions (Indicator 3: Paid bribe for public services within the past year)* (July 19, 2022), *avail-
       able at* https://www.afrobarometer. org/publication/sdg-16-summary-scorecard-peace
       -justice-and-strong-institutions-indicator-3-paid-bribe-for-public-services-within-the
       -past-year/.

151   Centre d'Etudes Prospectives et d'Informations Internationales (CEPII), Institutional
       Profiles Database, *available at* http://www.cepii.fr/institutions/en/ipd.asp (last visited
       July 11, 2022).

152   *Id.*

characteristics clustered in the following nine areas: (i) political institutions; (ii) security, law and order, control of violence; (iii) functioning of public administrations; (iv) free operation of markets; (v) coordination of stakeholders, strategic vision and innovation; (vi) security of transactions and contracts; (vii) market regulations, social dialogue; (viii) openness; and (ix) social cohesion and social mobility.[153]

FATF compliance ratings. The Financial Action Task Force (FATF) is an inter-governmental body established in 1989 by the Ministers of its Member jurisdictions. The FATF works to set standards and promote implementation of legal, regulatory and operational measures to combat money laundering, the financing of terrorist activities, and other threats to the integrity of the international financial system.[154] The FATF also works to strengthen political will in countries to support legislative and regulatory reforms focused on these priorities, including though the latest iteration in 2012 of the FATF Recommendations.[155] The FATF also monitors member states' progress in undertaking relevant reforms and counter-measures for money laundering and other abuses of the international financial system.

UNCAC National Review Reports and Self-Assessments. The United Nations Convention Against Corruption (UNCAC) Implementation Review Mechanism is within the remit of the United Nations Office on Drugs and Crime (UNODC). It is a peer review process that helps state parties of the UNCAC to monitor implementation of the Convention.[156] Specifically, each state party must nominate up to fifteen governmental experts to undertake a review of their country, using a focused assessment covering six criteria: (i) Guiding principles of the Mechanism; (ii) Transparent, efficient, non-intrusive, inclusive and impartial; (iii) Non-adversarial and non-punitive, without any form of ranking; (iv) Opportunities to share good practices and challenges; (v) Technical, promoting

---

153   Centre d'Etudes Prospectives et d'Informations Internationales (CEPII), Presentation of the Institutional Profiles Database 2012, *available at* http://www.cepii.fr/institutions/doc /ipd_2012_cahiers-2013-03_en.pdf (last visited July 11, 2022).

154   Financial Action Task Force, About, *available at* http://www.fatf-gafi.org/about/ (last visited, July 11, 2022).

155   Financial Action Task Force, *International Standards on Combating Money Laundering and the Financing of Terrorism and Proliferation - the FATF Recommendations* (Paris, 16 February 2012), *available at* http://www.fatf-gafi.org/media/fatf/documents/recommendations/pdfs /FATF%20Recommendations%202012.pdf.

156   United Nations Office on Drugs and Crime, Comprehensive Self-Assessment Checklist on the Implementation of the United Nations Convention Against Corruption, *available at* https://www.unodc.org/unodc/en/corruption/self-assessment.html (last visited July 11, 2022).

constructive collaboration; and (vi) Complements existing international and regional review mechanisms.

6.3   *Toward Global Consensus on Metrics to Track and Assess Governance and the Rule of Law around the World: Sustainable Development Goal 16*

The above indices and indicators were each developed with the objective of broadening our understanding of what counts as effective governance and the rule of law – with an emphasis on identifying and assessing the severity of corruption – by unpacking these concepts into actions that can be counted, monitored, assessed, and counteracted over time and across countries. Each metric offers a unique view of potential entry points and opportunities to combat corruption and to strengthen the building blocks of effective governance and the quality of the rule of law through institutional strengthening, policy reforms, and gap-filling.

However, given this proliferation of metrics, it is worth noting that broad consensus as to what counts as good governance what effective rule of law regimes look like arguably occurred only relatively recently. Efforts by scholars and practitioners to agree on a clearer and measurable definition of what counts as governance and the rule of law have arguably culminated most recently in the definition and adoption of the Sustainable Development Goals (SDGs).

The Sustainable Development Goals (SDGs) are a set of targets relating to future international development, which replaced the Millennium Development Goals when they expired at the end of 2015. The SDGs were first formally discussed at the United Nations Conference on Sustainable Development held in Rio de Janeiro in June 2012 (Rio+20). Then-United Nations Secretary-General Ban Ki-Moon established the UN System Task Team in September 2011 to lead UN preparations for the post-2015 UN development agenda.[157] The SDGs – the set of targets and indicators relating to future international human and sustainable development – thus replaced the Millennium Development Goals at the end of 2015.[158]

---

157   United Nations Development Policy and Analysis Division, Preparing for the Development Agenda Beyond 2015, *available at* http://www.un.org/en/development/desa/policy /untaskteam_undf/ (last visited July 11, 2022).

158   United Nations, The Sustainable Development Agenda, *available at* http://www.un.org /sustainabledevelopment/ development-agenda/ (last visited July 11, 2022) ("On 1 January 2016, the 17 Sustainable Development Goals (SDGs) of the 2030 Agenda for Sustainable Development—adopted by world leaders in September 2015 at an historic UN

The development of the SDGs was a multi-year process in which hundreds of global experts weighed in to create the 17 SDGs, their 169 targets, and their 232 unique indicators.[159] The SDGs were first formally discussed at the United Nations Conference on Sustainable Development held in Rio de Janeiro in June 2012 ("Rio+20").[160] At Rio+20, UN Member States agreed to establish an intergovernmental process to develop a set of "action-oriented, concise and easy to communicate" sustainable development goals (SDGs) to help drive the implementation of sustainable development.[161] The Rio+20 outcome document, *The Future We Want*, also calls for the goals to be coherent with the United Nations development agenda beyond 2015.[162] A 30-member Open Working Group (OWG) of the General Assembly was tasked with preparing a proposal on the SDGs, as well as a concrete list of targets and measurable indicators to ensure that progress against the SDGs can be tracked.[163] This Open Working Group thereafter proposed 17 goals covering a broad range of sustainable development issues.[164] On September 25, 2015, the United Nations General Assembly accepted that the Open Working Group's proposals would become the basis of the post-2015 development agenda. These 17 SDGs officially came into force on January 1, 2016 and the global indicator framework was later adopted by the UN General Assembly on July 6, 2017.

Summit—officially came into force...The SDGs build on the success of the Millennium Development Goals (MDGs) and aim to go further to end all forms of poverty.").

159   United Nations Department of Economic and Social Affairs, Statistics Division, SDG Indicators: Global indicator framework for the Sustainable Development Goals and targets of the 2030 Agenda for Sustainable Development, *available at* https://unstats.un.org/sdgs/indicators/indicators-list/#:~:text=The%20global%20indicator%20framework%20includes,of%20SDG%20indicators%20is%20248 (last visited July 11, 2022).

160   United Nations, United Nations Conference on Sustainable Development, Rio+20, *available at* https://sustainable development.un.org/rio20 (last visited July 11, 2022).

161   United Nations, *The Future We Want* at para. 247, G.A RES/66/288, UN Doc A/RES/66/288 (July 27, 2012), *available at* http://www.un.org/ga/search/view_doc.asp?symbol=A/ RES /66/288&Lang=E (last visited July 11, 2022).

162   *Id.* at para 75.

163   *Id.* at para 248.

164   United Nations, Open Working Group Proposal for Sustainable Development Goals, *available at* https://sustainabledevelopment.un.org/content/documents/1579SDGs%20 Proposal.pdf (last visited July 11, 2022); *Integrated and coordinated implementation of and follow-up to the outcomes of the major United Nations conferences and summits in the economic, social and related fields, Sustainable development: implementation of Agenda 21; the Programme for the Further Implementation of Agenda 21 and the outcomes of the World Summit on Sustainable Development and of the United Nations Conference on Sustainable Development; Follow-up to the outcome of the Millennium Summit*, G.A. RES/68/970, UN Doc A/68/970 (Aug 12 2014), *available at* http://www.un.org/ga/search/view_doc .asp?symbol=A/68/970&Lang=E (last visited July 11, 2022).

SDG 16 is to "Promote peaceful and inclusive societies for sustainable development, provide access to justice for all and build effective, accountable and inclusive institutions at all levels."[165] Often called the "peace and governance" goal, it has 12 targets and progress is measured against 23 indicators (see Table 12.5). Taken together – and given the scope of consultations which generated it and of breadth of international agreement on its promulgation – the SDG 16 text, its targets and indicators may comprise a compelling global consensus as to what the achievement of good governance and effective rule of law entails, in a framework designed to be measured and evaluated over time.

A range of development organizations, including the United Nations and the World Bank, are currently working to measure and monitor progress against SDG 16, with the objective of understanding and assessing countries' governance environments largely through objective metrics.[166] However, the effective measurement of SDG16 is conditioned by a range of realities which have collectively meant that the ability to undertake effective decision-making across governance priorities may be curtailed.

7 Conditioning Factors

The previous section demonstrated the still-fashionable trend of developing measures or indicators of governance. This trend has resulted in a range of macro, meso, and micro level metrics available to development practitioners, government officials, and other actors involved in supporting reforms, to inform them about changes in governance across countries and over time. The previous section also provided an overview of the ostensible culmination of this trend: the clearest indication to date of consensus from experts around the world concerning what counts as governance through rule of law strengthening for the purposes of the Sustainable Development Goals.

At this point, it may be useful to question how these measures, including those comprising SDG 16, are fit-for-purpose and what, if anything, the World Bank might internalize from these metrics for its own operational portfolio in service of its client countries. To answer these questions, this section will

---

165   United Nations, Goal 16: Promote just, peaceful and inclusive societies, *available at* https://www.un.org/sustainabledevelopment/peace-justice/ (last visited July 11, 2022).

166   *See, generally*, OECD-DAC, *Sourcebook on Measuring Peace, Justice and Institutions: Report of the Virtual Network of stakeholders for the development of indicators on peaceful societies, justice and effective institutions for SDG 16* (July 2015), *available at* https://www.oecd.org /officialdocuments/publicdisplaydocumentpdf/?cote=DCD/DAC/GOVNET/RD(2015)2 /RD2&docLanguage=En [hereinafter OECD-DAC].

TABLE 12.5   SDG Targets and Indicators

SDG 16 targets	SDG 16 indicators
16.1 significantly reduce all forms of violence and related death rates everywhere	16.1.1. Number of victims of intentional homicide per 100,000 population, by sex and age
	16.1.2. Conflict-related deaths per 100,000 population, by sex, age and cause
	16.1.3. Proportion of population subjected to physical, psychological or sexual violence in the previous 12 months
	16.1.4. Proportion of population that feel safe walking alone around the area they live
16.2 end abuse, exploitation, trafficking and all forms of violence and torture against children	16.2.1. Proportion of children aged 1–17 years who experienced any physical punishment and/or psychological aggression by caregivers in the past month
	16.2.2. Number of victims of human trafficking per 100,000 population, by sex, age and form of exploitation
	16.2.3. Proportion of young women and men aged 18–29 years who experienced sexual violence by age 18
16.3 promote the rule of law at the national and international levels, and ensure equal access to justice for all	16.3.1. Proportion of victims of violence in the previous 12 months who reported their victimization to competent authorities or other officially recognized conflict resolution mechanisms
	16.3.2. Unsentenced detainees as a proportion of overall prison population
16.4 by 2030 significantly reduce illicit financial and arms flows, strengthen recovery and return of stolen assets, and combat all forms of organized crime	16.4.1. Total value of inward and outward illicit financial flows (in current United States dollars)
	16.4.2. Proportion of seized, found or surrendered arms whose illicit origin or context has been traced or established by a competent authority in line with international instruments
16.5 substantially reduce corruption and bribery in all its forms	16.5.1. Proportion of persons who had at least one contact with a public official and who paid a bribe to a public official, or were asked for a bribe by those public officials, during the previous 12 months
	16.5.2. Proportion of businesses that had at least one contact with a public official and that paid a bribe to a public official, or were asked for a bribe by those public officials during the previous 12 months

(cont.)

TABLE 12.5   SDG Targets and Indicators (*cont.*)

SDG 16 targets	SDG 16 indicators
16.6 develop effective, accountable and transparent institutions at all levels	16.6.1. Primary government expenditures as a proportion of original approved budget, by sector (or by budget codes or similar)
	16.6.2. Proportion of the population satisfied with their last experience of public services
16.7 ensure responsive, inclusive, participatory and representative decision-making at all levels	16.7.1. Proportions of positions (by sex, age, persons with disabilities and population groups) in public institutions (national and local legislatures, public service, and judiciary) compared to national distributions
	16.7.2. Proportion of population who believe decision-making is inclusive and responsive, by sex, age, disability and population group
16.8 broaden and strengthen the participation of developing countries in the institutions of global governance	16.8.1. Proportion of members and voting rights of developing countries in international organizations
16.9 by 2030 provide legal identity for all including birth registration	16.9.1. Proportion of children under 5 years of age whose births have been registered with a civil authority, by age
16.10 ensure public access to information and protect fundamental freedoms, in accordance with national legislation and international agreements	16.10.1. Number of verified cases of killing, kidnapping, enforced disappearance, arbitrary detention and torture of journalists, associated media personnel, trade unionists and human rights advocates in the previous 12 months
	16.10.2. Number of countries that adopt and implement constitutional, statutory and/or policy guarantees for public access to information
16.a strengthen relevant national institutions, including through international cooperation, for building capacities at all levels, in particular in developing countries, for preventing violence and combating terrorism and crime	16.a.1. Existence of independent national human rights institutions in compliance with the Paris Principles
16.b promote and enforce non-discriminatory laws and policies for sustainable development	16.b.1. Proportion of population reporting having personally felt discriminated against or harassed in the previous 12 months on the basis of a ground of discrimination prohibited under international human rights law

critically evaluate the strengths and weaknesses of several of the more robust of these metrics. The aim is to identify indicators which are both valid and reliable and to unpack several conditions which may influence the effectiveness of these measures with respect to the achievement of the legitimate goals of the key actors identified in Section 1 – chiefly focusing on combating corruption – and parse any resultant lessons for the international development community, including the World Bank.

7.1 Subjective versus Objective Metrics for Governance: Is One Better than the other?

A potentially useful entry point is to examine whether one type of indicator is more valid and reliable than another with respect to measuring governance and the quality of the rule of law. Accordingly, the focus of this section is to attempt to account for variation in levels of governance in general (instead of a specific policy domain, such as health, infrastructure, or procurement). To understand how variations of governance are assessed and tracked, attempts to measure governance and the rule of law can be divided into two categories: (1) *objective indicators* which use "real" data to calculate the magnitude of waste and abuse in public administration; and (2) *subjective indicators*, which use survey data (for example, of experts, elites, or the public) to attempt to measure perceptions and/or the lived experience of corruption by different groups.

Objective indicators of corruption are less standardized and less numerous than composite subjective indicators. Three types of objective indicators have generally been developed: (1) input-output analysis of anticipated (versus actual) costs of construction and provision of services; (2) criminal statistics concerning the number of bribery prosecutions; and (3) natural experimental data on the behavior of policymakers.[167]

7.2 Deriving Lessons on the Robustness of Corruption Indicators on the Basis of Trends Examined, to Inform Projections

Hamilton and Hammer (2018) undertook a critical review of authoritative literature concerning the comparative strengths and weaknesses of subjective and objective indicators of corruption with respect to their general validity and reliability, and drew conclusions about which most likely capture variation in overall levels of corruption that is of theoretical interest to development practitioners in the international development community, including the World

---

167   *See* Hamilton & Hammer, *supra* note 110, at 20.

Bank.[168] These conclusions, when combined with other relevant analysis, collectively comprise lessons which might add value to the international development community's governance portfolio development, as well as further efforts to develop global public goods relevant to combatting corruption.

7.2.1 Lesson #1: Using Objective Indicators as a Complementary Robustness Check

The pros and cons of each type of indicator may act as a check on the weaknesses of the other type of indicator. Subjective indicators might enable measurement of broad types of corruption, and where they are valid measures, they will correlate with objective indicators of corruption. Notwithstanding the continuing debate in the literature,[169] there is an emerging consensus both objective and subjective indicators can indeed be valid and can serve as crosschecks for each other. A growing corpus of research suggests that both forms of indicators of corruption often highly correlated with each other, particularly where the standard errors of both are taken into account,[170] and skepticism of subjective indicators is thus misplaced.

7.2.2 Lesson #2: Which Corruption Measure Might Better Capture the Theoretical Interest of World Bank Practitioners, with Respect to Overall Levels of Corruption?

When viewed through the lens of the World Bank's ostensible institutional goal of understanding variation in overall levels of corruption to be able to assess, combat, and track progress in scaling down instances of corruption in low- and middle-income countries, the most valid and reliable measures of corruption are the ones that are most likely to capture those elements of corruption associated with both politicians and the broader public sector. It has been shown that of particular importance to the robustness of corruption measures is the development of composite survey-based indicators of corruption, which try to use multiple survey sources to increase the accuracy of their measures. From this, it is possible to argue that the CPI, CC, the GCB, and the Ticket data are most likely to satisfy these criteria, since these indicators focus on overall corruption. While there are many other subjective indicators

---

168   *See* Hamilton & Hammer, *supra* note 110.
169   For a summary, *see generally* Treisman, *supra* note 108.
170   *See* Daniel Kaufmann, Aart Kraay & Massimo Mastruzzi, *Measuring Corruption: Myths and Realities* (Africa Region Findings and Good Practice Infobriefs no. 273), World Bank, Washington, DC. (2007), *available at* https://open knowledge.worldbank.org/handle /10986/ 9576.

of corruption, focusing on these aggregate indicators may arguably be a more useful for development practitioners since individual indicators may be more prone to deficiencies in representation or measure corruption in a narrower way. While reliance on composite indicators is justified with regard to validity and reliability, it is arguably useful to consider one specific indicator, which might serve as a robustness check on findings of composite indicators.

Comparing the relative value of these indicators is somewhat complex because of the way these indicators are constructed, and how they generate costs and benefits. Narrowly focused indicators are generally less "noisy," given that they point to a particular dimension of corruption. This is the case with the GCB and Ticket data. However, it may be the case that these narrow indicators do not capture the complexity or multi-dimensionality of corruption. Conversely, indices which combine multiple sources might offer more texture in corruption assessments. This may be the case with the CPI and the CC; however, it follows that since they rely on perceptions, they might be more "noisy."

It is possible to argue that composite subjective indicators, such as the CPI and the CC, comprise a useful starting point for an empirical analysis of corruption since they are relatively more comprehensive and might thus capture more elements of corruption than narrowly focused indicators. While both the CPI and CC are based on perceptions, the major subjective indicators are highly correlated with more narrow objective indicators, and with outcomes associated with corruption, which chips away at the argument that objective indicators have a comparative advantage that is "validity-based." Plus, subjective indicators have additional advantages, such as that they focus on overall levels of corruption (as opposed to narrower indicators such as specific instances of corruption in a particular sector). They are also more reliable when it comes to measuring cross-sectional variation in perceived corruption, which opens the door for researchers to undertake cross-sectional regression analyses. With these arguments in favor of the comparative advantage of subjective indicators in mind, objective indicators have significant value and can be used in complementary ways, such as for robustness checks of initial subjective-based results, which can strengthen confidence in the validity and reliability of these initial results.

It is thus important to emphasize how much public perceptions matter to countries' governance arrangements. In the seminal *The Quality of Growth*,[171] Vinod Thomas and co-authors remind us that how people view society can impact their expectations, which can have actual knock-on effects across sectors. For example, public expectation of a currency devaluation can result in

---

171   *See generally* Vinod Thomas et al., The Quality of Growth 2000 [hereinafter Thomas et al.].

an actual devaluation as a result of changes in speculation on future events; firms make investment decisions based on perceptions of how well a country's regulatory system functions; examples abound of the societal and economic effects of public perceptions.[172] Thomas and colleagues continue that for various aspects of governance, subjective survey results matter "at least as much as official data."[173] Composite subjective indicators can help depict the difference between *de jure* and *de facto* state of governance. The existence of anticorruption bodies or institutions, from election monitors to anti-corruption commissions and the any related legal or regulatory regimes, does not shed light on the effectiveness of these institutions or bodies, whereas good quality perception data – like that generated by the cpi and cc – can.

7.2.3   Lesson #3: Toward Mainstreaming Context-Sensitive Approaches
An important lesson emerging from the totality of the above analysis is that in any international development context – planning, policy selection, implementation, and evaluation are intricately intertwined processes; they are complex, integrated or layered parts of a whole which should be considered comprehensively, and not necessarily unpacked into convenient constituent or indicative parts for analysis for evaluation, parsing lessons, replication, and more. William Ascher acknowledges this complexity and emphasizes that important realities are often ignored in analysis of operational development based on, in his view, a delimited view of the features of the development problem.[174] With particular respect to governance through rule of law international assistance, Carothers criticizes efforts to provide "rule of law aid" for failing to sufficiently extend deeply into the legal and cultural context in recipient countries.[175]

Put another way, and by definition, subjective and objective indicators-based analyses of an international development problem can illuminate part of the picture. Where nuance and context are missed, the resulting analysis and operational or policy response might additionally exhibit gaps which could condition the overall effectiveness of part or all of the response. This recognition has enabled leading policy scientists to eschew reductive approaches and assess a range of development problems comprehensively, which has added substantial value to the international development discourse.[176] Deploying the Policy

---

172   *See generally* Walter Lippmann, Public Opinion (1922).

173   Thomas et al., *supra* note 171 at 167.

174   *See* William Ascher, Understanding the Policymaking Process in Developing Countries (Cambridge University Press, 2017).

175   *See* Thomas Carothers, *The Rule of Law Revival*, 72(2) Foreign Aff. 95 (1998).

176   *See* Winston Nagan, Contextual-Configurative Jurisprudence: The Law, Science and Policies of Human Dignity (2013); Charles Norchi & Karuna Chibber, *A Technical Note for*

Sciences also forces the development practitioner to remain conscientiously pragmatic when it comes to assessing actual impact – they must account comprehensively for extremely complicated, context-sensitive processes that require (at a minimum) multiple years of consistent focus and perseverance, flexibility and adaptation, a spectrum of "soft" skills in combination with "hard" (technical) skills and relevant experience, and much more, before something approximating a meaningful impact or outcome may be possible.

This recognition of the primacy of context-sensitivity is a relatively more recent phenomenon within international development organizations' governance support efforts, with particular respect to unpacking the political economy of corruption, bribery, and illicit financial flows in low- and middle-income countries.[177] Jain explains that a corrupt act has three features: (1) discretionary power with respect to rule definition and/or rule application; (2) an expectation of economic rent associated with discretion; and (3) the expected cost of corruption.[178] Thus, the range of what counts as a corrupt act is broad, from a single act of a payment in contravention of established law to

Value-Based Participatory Planning, Monitoring, and Evaluations in Community-Driven Development (World Bank: 2003), *available at* https://pdfs.semanticscholar.org/bca6/fc7b0a5ee1f5452e055c5e6c2d8853fd056f.pdf?_ga=2.179725284.1980954982.1588458147-1047454741.1588458147; Siegfried Wiessner, *International Law in the 21st Century: Decision-Making in Institutionalized and Non-Institutionalized Settings,* 26 Thesaurus Acroasium 129–153 (1997); Susan Clark, The Policy Process: A Practical Guide for Natural Resource Professionals (2002); Michael Reisman, The Quest for World Order and Human Dignity in the Twenty-first Century: Constitutive Process and Individual Commitment (2d ed. 2022); Michael Reisman & Aaron Schreiber, Jurisprudence: Understanding and Shaping Law: Cases, Readings, Commentary (1987); and Ron Brunner & Amanda Lynch, Adaptive Governance: Integrating Science, Policy, and Decision Making (2005).

177 *See generally* Treisman, *supra* note 108; Dele Olowu, *Roots and Remedies of Governmental Corruption in Africa,* 7(3) Corruption & Reform 227–236 (1993); Sahr Kpundeh, *Political Will in Fighting Corruption. Corruption & Integrity Improvement Initiatives in Developing Countries* (Seminar paper, UNDP) 70–87 (October 1997), *available at* http://www.undp-aciac.org/publications/other/undp/fc/corruption97e.pdf ; Michael Johnston, *Fighting systemic corruption: Social foundations for institutional reform* 10(1) Eur. J. Dev. Res. 85–104 (1998); Stephen Riley, *The Political Economy of Anti-Corruption Strategies in Africa,* 10(1) Eur. J. Dev. Res. 129–159 (1998); Timothy Besley & Robin Burgess, *The Political Economy of Government Responsiveness: Theory and Evidence from India,* 117(4) Q. J. Econ.1415–1451 (2002), *available at* https://doi.org/10.1162/003355302320935061; and Margit Tavits, *Causes of Corruption: Testing Competing Hypotheses* (Nuffield College, Working Papers in Politics, No. 2005-W3, 2005), *available at* https://www.nuff.ox.ac.uk/Politics/papers/2005/Tavits%20Nuffield%20WP.pdf.

178 Arvind K. Jain, *Corruption: A Review,* 15(1) J. Econ. Surv. 71–121 (2001).

an endemic malfunction of a political and economic system.[179] Since the scope of corruption can be so varied, the conditions which may enable corrupt acts may vary as well, and the literature on the contributing causes of corruption has shown this, and offers a multiplicity of explanations for this phenomenon. Much of the literature notes that it is difficult or impossible to discern a single specific cause for a corrupt act. Both the different types of corruption and the scope of corruption in countries can have very different causes.

It follows that it is difficult to establish a clear distinction between the causes and costs of corruption from context to context. Corduneanu-Huci, Hamilton and Ferrer note that costs feed into the causes and vice versa. Specifically, they explain that small-scale corruption may be symptomatic of rapid moderniza- tion and – in certain contexts – it may be a natural expression of social capital.[180] They continue that – again, in certain contexts – the side effect of large-scale corruption might include more resources for private investment; increased mar- ket access by the poor and marginalized; and/or a form of "compensation" for low levels of tax revenue.[181] Moreover, they point to North, Wallis, and Weingast, who explain that in some contexts trade-offs exist between a corruption and conflict, essentially that dismantling corrupt patronage relationships may have the unintended effect of destabilizing governance arrangements, which could result in or contribute to conflict.[182] In short, these concepts must be under- stood more comprehensively with considered regard for the context in question before an assessment of the causes and costs of corruption and its relative effect on the quality of governance can be persuasively established. At a minimum, this recognition underscores the importance of complementary, political econ- omy analyses to ascertain the context in which corrupt acts occur to more fully understand each act and their implications for prevailing governance arrange- ments, particularly where efforts to design and implement a counteracting inter- vention are anticipated.

---

179   Jens Chr. Andvig & Odd-Helge Fjeldstad with Inge Amundsen, Tone Sissener & Tina Søreide, *Corruption: A Review of Contemporary Research*, Bergen: Chr. Michelsen Institute (CMI Report R 2001:7) (2001), *available at* https://www.cmi.no/publications/861-corruption -a-review-of-contemporary-research [hereinafter Andvig et al.].

180   Cristina Corduneanu Huci, Issel Masses Ferrer & Alexander Hamilton, Understanding Policy Change: How to Apply Political Economy Concepts in Practice 71 (2012), *available at* http://documents.worldbank.org/curated/en/364691468326141374/Understanding-policy -change-how-to-apply-political-economy-concepts-in-practice [hereinafter Corduneanu Huci et al.) (citing Patrick Chabal & Jean-Pascal Daloz, Africa Works: The Political Instru- mentalization of Disorder 1999).

181   *Id.*

182   *Id.*

8   Projections

A few key projections emerge from careful analysis of the identified trends and conditioning factors, which include both optimistic and pessimistic constructs relative to the desired (legitimate) goals of the key stakeholders identified in Section 1.

8.1   *Projection: The International Development Community Will Continue to Rely Heavily on Objective Indicators-Based Analysis, Which Will Spur More Investment in Gap-Filling for Objective Indicators to Track and Assess Governance and Corruption*

In short, this projection suggest that the international development community will not move to implement Lessons #1 and #2 emerging from the analysis in Section 7 above, despite the increasing recognition that national data and statistical systems are chronically under-financed.[183]

To explore this projection in a bit more detail, it is important to first understand that overall donor financing for data collection and statistical capacity building in developing countries has decreased significantly in the last several years.[184] The effect of this under-investment in statistical systems has been

---

183   In 2017, the World Bank's Independent Evaluation Group published an evaluation of the World Bank's support for client countries' data and statistics entitled, "Data for Development – An Evaluation of World Bank Support for Data and Statistical Capacity". The report presents an extensive description of lessons learned from the World Bank's work in supporting countries to produce, share, and use data—as well as the Bank's own work—to curate, disseminate, and analyze development data. The evaluation recognizes the Bank's global reputation and effectiveness in development data activities as well as its leading role in global data partnerships, but finds that the Bank must intensify efforts to mobilize and deliver long-term funding and technical support in collaboration with countries, to implement a more comprehensive model of statistical capacity. For the full report, see World Bank, Independent Evaluation Group, *Data for Development – An Evaluation of World Bank Support for Data and Statistical Capacity* (2017), *available at* http://ieg .worldbankgroup.org/evaluations/data-for-development.

184   The NGO PARIS21 has found that the total share of Official Development Assistance (ODA) dedicated to data/statistics has stagnated at 0.3% (or approximately USD $600 million) per year, despite record ODA highs in recent years. They calculate that the cost for more comprehensive support for data and statistical systems will be approximately USD $5.6 billion per year between 2019 to 2030 for 75 low and low-middle-income and 69 upper middle-income countries, of which an estimated USD 4.3 billion (77%) of costs would be covered by domestic resources. They continue that, should current levels of ODA remain the same, this will leave a financing gap of USD 1.3 billion (23%) per year for *other* financing, such as external assistance from multilateral and bilaterals, as well other domestic sources. PARIS21 qualifies that these calculations speak to the full implementation of the Cape Town Global Action Plan for Sustainable Development Data, which

significant gaps in high-quality data in low- and middle-income countries around the world. The country-level policy failures, ineffective service delivery, allocative inefficiencies, and the extent to which poor and historically underserved populations have been further marginalized or driven deeper into poverty occasioned by these data gaps cannot be calculated. These gaps in development data also threaten the effectiveness the achievement of most all the SDGs,[185] including and particularly SDG 16, as well as the World Bank's full spectrum of social and economic development initiatives, from human capital investments to governance reforms.

With particular respect to SDG 16 (the "peace and governance goal"), in an effort to support the definition and harmonization of governance indicators (with contributions of leadership and technical input from the World Bank), the United Nations Statistical Commission (UNSC) established a new City Group – the Praia City Group on Governance Statistics – to address issues of conceptualization, methodology and instruments in what it described as the "new domain" of governance statistics.[186] The Praia City Group met for the first time in June 2015 to launch prioritization processes and prepare the Group's first SDG16 roadmap for presentation to ECOSOC. The Group also indicated its intention to develop a handbook on governance statistics for national statistical

---

was informally launched at the first UN World Data Forum on 15 January 2017 in Cape Town South Africa, and adopted by the United Nations Statistical Commission at its 48th Session in March 2017. The Action Plan elaborates the scope of support needed to support national statistical systems, and address gaps in national statistics and statistical coordination to achieve the 2030 Agenda. *See* Andrew Rogerson & Rachael Calleja, *Mobilising Data for the SDGs: How could a Data Acceleration Facility Help, and How Might it Work?* PARIS21 Discussion Paper, No. 15 January 2019, *available at* https://www.google .com/url?sa=t&rct=j&q=&esrc=s&source=web&cd=1&cad=rja&uact=8&ved=2ahUKE wjonNTqhpjpAhVloXIEHbTmBXwQFjAAegQIAxAB&url=https%3A%2F%2Fparis21 .org%2Fsites%2Fdefault%2Ffiles%2F2019-01%2FMobilising%2520Data% 2520for%2520the%2520SDGs%2520%2528DP15%2529_0.pdf&usg=AOvVaw2hy Xeo5COmyKqDCIVyp2x.

185   *See* Johannes Jütting & Ida McDonnell, *Overview: What Will it Take for Data to Enable Development?*, *in* Development Co-operation Report 2017: Data for Development. Paris: OECD (2017) (reporting that as of 2017, nearly two-thirds of the 231 unique SDG indicators had no available data; that 88 of these indicators had no defined methodology and are thus uncollectable; that a further 55 of these indicators have a methodology but data is not yet being collected and reported for them in most countries; all of which means that even countries with sophisticated national statistical offices may have the ability to collect only 40% of all SDG indicators).

186   United Nations Statistical Commission, Report of Cabo Verde on governance, peace and security statistics, E/CN.3/2015/17 (9 December 2014, *available at* http://unstats.un.org /unsd/statcom/doc15/2015-17-CaboVerde.pdf).

offices, to contribute to establishing international standards and methods for the compilation of governance statistics by enlisting relevant expertise from across countries and from the international, academic and non-profit sectors.

Unlike the MDGs, measuring and monitoring progress of SDG 16 is a periodic (aspirationally annual[187]) process, predominantly using "administrative data, surveys (including household and labor force surveys), as well as direct monitoring from organizations."[188] UN Member States have emphasized that the role of the IAEG-SDG's members should include consultation and coordination within their own national statistical system, and should also involve reaching out for contributions by global observers and development institutions. The IAEG-SDGs likewise stressed the important contributions of regional and international agencies, in particular as entities responsible for the compilation of indicators at the global level and for the conceptual and methodological development in their specific areas of work based on their existing mandates and that it will invite them to contribute their expertise during its consultations. It further stressed the important contributions of Major Groups and other stakeholders in the indicator development process, and has committed to ensure multi-stakeholder involvement through continuing consultations, toward ensuring timely and effective tracking of all SDGs.

Based on the analysis in Sections 2 and 3 above, it is clear that efforts to achieve systematic measures of governance in several countries is still a relatively nascent field – indeed, less than two decades ago, the majority of policy advice, action program formulation, and research writings in these subject areas were typically done without rigorous empirical measurement.[189] However, more recent research has sharpened and unbundled some of the notions of governance and corruption, which has permitted a better

---

187   Sustainable Development Solutions Network, *Indicators and a Monitoring Framework for the Sustainable Development Goals: Launching a Data Revolution for the SDGs* (Sustainable Development Solutions Network, New York; 2015, *available at* http://unsdsn.org/wp-content /uploads/2015/05/150612-FINAL-SDSN-Indicator-Report1.pdf).

188   *Id.*

189   *See generally* Treisman, *supra* note 108; Daniel Kaufmann, Francesca Recanatini & Sergiy Biletsky, *Assessing governance: Diagnostic tools and applied methods for capacity building and action learning* (The World Bank, Washington D.C.) (2002), *available at* http://web .worldbank.org/archive/website00818/WEB/PDF/KAUF_REC.PDF [hereinafter Kaufmann, Recanatini & Biletsky]; and Susan Rose-Ackerman, *The Political Economy of Corruption— Causes and Consequences* (Public Policy for the Private Sector Note No. 74, World Bank: April 1996), *available at* https://documents1.worldbank.org/curated/en/231001468 762302694 /pdf/16933-Replacement-file-074ACKER.pdf.

understanding of the causes and consequences of corruption and its effects of governance through objective indicators.[190]

As these approaches to unbundle and measure aspects of governance has evolved in recent years, so, too, have grown vocal arguments to exclusively anchor this measurement in objective indicators rather than subjective or composite subjective indicators or a complementary approach comprising both. These arguments were particularly vocal throughout the establishment of the SDG 16 indicators. For example, powerful members of the IAEG-SDGs and Praia City Group advising the indicator-setting process, such as OECD-DAC and pointed out that "Objective indicators that are specific and measurable are considered to be "objectively verifiable indicators" – they contribute to transparency and accountability as they can be reliably replicated by others and yield the same result ... [whereas] [s]ubjective assessments may introduce reporting biases. Careful design can account for uncertainty around estimates, but cannot necessarily identify the extent of bias."[191] Likewise, the European Statistical Advisory Committee argued forcefully that "In this Goal [SDG 16], subjective indicators are over represented; non-official subjective indicators should be replaced with objective, more easily measurable indicators."[192] As such, it follows that dependency on objective indicators-based analysis of governance and corruption – including efforts to track and assess country progress under SDG16 – is likely.[193]

Nonetheless, as we have seen, the viability of objective indicators-based measures of governance and corruption is contingent on the availability of evidentiary data underpinning each indicator. As the breadth of the problem of chronic under-investment in many statistical systems, particularly in developing and least developed countries and its damaging implications – including significant gaps in governance and anticorruption data – are increasingly well understood, an important projection is that members of the international development and national statistics communities will join forces to correct it.

---

190   *See, e.g.*, Kaufmann, Kraay & Zoido, *supra* note 103.

191   *See, e.g.*, OECD-DAC, *supra* note 164.

192   *See* European Statistical Advisory Committee, *Opinion on a Pre-final Draft EU SDG Indicator Set* (March 22, 2017), at 8, *available at* https://ec.europa.eu/eurostat/documents/735541 / 749923/ESAC+opinion_ESAC+Doc.+2017_22+ESAC+opinion+EU+SDG+indicator+set+ Final+20032017.v1.4.pdf/a5717c79-fbb1-4619-a3aa-fb3f8e1df17a.

193   For an example of the back-and-forth between expert advisors concerning reliance on objective and/or subjective indicators to track SDG 16, *see, e.g.*, Mark Orkin, *An empirical prioritization of key Goal 16 indicators* (Presentation to PRIO/UNDP Expert Meeting on Measuring SDG 16 Targets, Oslo) (February 28–29, 2016).

A possible pessimistic construct is that this collaboration may look (unhelpfully) familiar. In the past, external support for development data funding has often been tied to the monitoring of specific donor-supported investments in other thematic areas, such as health. Funding volumes have been small and often in support of one-off instruments, with little harmonization among different donors and streamlining with national statistical plans.[194]

A slightly more optimistic construct is also possible. Since 2015, multilateral and bilateral development partners and philanthropies have made new global commitments for data and statistics. For example, in 2015 the World Bank, working with a range of developing countries and several international partners, committed to conducting triennial household-level surveys in the 78 poorest nations. The estimated cost of the initiative, of $300 million for every three-year period (2015–2030), is expected to be borne by a mixture of countries' own resources, donor funding and World Bank financing.[195] Also in 2015, several developing countries and development organizations, including the World Bank and the World Health Organization, launched the Global Civil Registration and Vital Statistics Scaling-Up Investment Plan that covers activities in 73 countries over a 10-year period. Its projected total cost is $3.82 billion (excluding India and China), with an estimated funding gap of $1.99 billion, to be closed by a combination of additional domestic and international resources.[196] Further commitments for sectoral data funding have likewise been prioritized under the 20th replenishment of the International Development Association (IDA20).[197] This includes some further financial support for data relevant to tracking and assessing governance and corruption in low- and middle-income countries.

While these initiatives mobilize sizable international and domestic investments, financing gaps remain and must be closed. In addition, many initiatives focus on data funding for specific sectors. Funding mechanisms with a specific

---

194   Bern Network, *Financing more and better data to achieve the SDGs*, 16–17 (2019), *available at* https://paris21.org/sites/default/files/2019-07/BernDraftReport_SoftCopy_FINAL.pdf [hereinafter Bern Network].

195   World Bank, *World Bank's New End-Poverty Tool: Surveys in Poorest Countries* (Press release, October 15, 2015), *available at* https://www.worldbank.org/en/news/press-release /2015/10/15/world-bank-new-end-poverty-tool-surveys-in-poorest-countries (last visited July 11, 2022).

196   World Bank and World Health Organization, *Global civil registration and vital statistics scaling up investment plan 2015–2024* (Washington, D.C.: World Bank, May 2014), *available at* https://www.worldbank.org/en/topic/health/publication/global-civil-registration-vital -statistics-scaling-up-investment.

197   World Bank, *IDA20 Replenishment*, *available at* https://ida.worldbank.org/en/replenishments / ida20-replenishment (last visited October 1, 2022).

sectoral focus can have the advantage of galvanizing donors – including new donors such as philanthropies – around their shared priorities, thus increasing overall funding for data and statistics, as well as leveraging sectoral expertise and becoming hubs for knowledge-sharing.[198]

Renewed efforts to increase and harmonize funding also include strengthened global partnerships and targeted multi-stakeholder cooperation. Such an approach could prioritize the pooling of donor funds and coordination of resource allocation within specific sectors, in this context governance and corruption. Doing so may also help leverage additional concessional and non-concessional resources such as World Bank IDA or International Bank for Reconstruction and Development (IBRD) resources, which can be complemented by increased domestic financing from recipient countries. Such a three-pronged approach – pooling donor resources, leveraging additional resources and increasing domestic financing – could contribute to a step-change in more sustainable financing for data and statistics. The World Bank and several key partners have also spearheaded the launch of an umbrella trust fund for data called the Global Data Facility to scale up this approach across key sectors and a range of low-income and middle-income countries, while ensuring a country-led, flexible, and adaptive approach to strengthen the capacity of national data and statistical systems.[199] This could substantially help to close financing gaps for data which underpin objective indicators of governance and corruption.

It is important to note that all of these efforts, important as they are, are particularly designed to support data systems and data capital which by and large do not include closing gaps in data for objective measures underpinning SDG16.[200] Just as importantly, these efforts do not include a deliberate effort to simultaneously support composite subjective indicators to identify, assess, and track corruption and help discern the quality of governance in client countries more reliably than via objective indicators, as demonstrated by the analysis and lessons learned in Section 3. This seems to be a missed opportunity.

---

198   *See, e.g.,* Bern Network, *supra* at 194.

199   *See* Haishan Fu & Craig Hammer, *Toward a new, collaborative global financing architecture for fragile, low, and middle-income countries' data priorities,* 38(3) Statistical J. IAOS 741–748 (2022).

200   *See* Umar Serajuddin & Marco Scuriatti, *The World Bank's role in SDG monitoring* (January 31, 2019), *available at* https://blogs.worldbank.org/opendata/world-bank-s-role-sdg-monitoring (The World Bank participates in IAEG-SDGs as an observer and is a custodian or co-custodian (with other agencies) for 20 indicators, and is involved in the development and monitoring of an additional 22 indicators. Altogether, the World Bank is formally engaged with the monitoring of 42 of [the more than 230] SDG indicators.).

8.2   *Projection: The IAEG-SDG Will also Continue to Rely on Objective Indicators-Based Analysis for SDG monitoring, but May Grow to Rely on Composite Subjective Indicators to Track SDG 16*

This projection suggests that in light of the above analysis, the IAEG-SDGS may eventually act on Lessons #1 and #2 emerging from Section 3 above. It is important to recall that the IAEG identified objective indicators for SDG 16 which – as noted above – might better serve as complementary to composite subjective indicators to discern the quality of governance and overall levels of corruption in countries for the purposes of the SDGs.

This projection is predicated on the same findings brought to light in the above projection concerning the financing gap for key data for objective indicators identified above. And so, despite the heartening, implicit validation of the importance of governance and rule of law assistance for social and economic development set out in SDG 16, the challenging reality is that in many cases, the IAEG identified objective indicators for SDGs (including SDG 16) for which there are no currently available data sources. Indeed, as of 2021 there are presently only 6 of the 17 SDGs for which more than two-thirds of countries have data to report on progress.[201] This will make demonstrating countries' progress under SDG 16 difficult or impossible, and this projection asserts that the IAEG-SDGs will thus be forced to look elsewhere to track indicators which are relatively consistent with SDG 16 targets, for which data are available.

8.2.1   Conditions Influencing Global Capacity to Track Corruption under SDG 16

As alluded to earlier, statistics and the generation of governance-relevant data are often plagued by under-investment by government in low- and middle-income countries. Data are collected variably by National Statistics Bureaus (NSBs), individual line ministries and other public sector bodies (especially the Ministry of Finance, the Central Bank, and the Ministry of Health), as well as by parastatals, universities and other non-governmental entities. Due to a combination of factors, official statistics are often reported erratically, sometimes altered for non-technical reasons, and not always disseminated in a timely manner or a user-friendly format, and other actions which severely limits the use of such data in decision-making.[202]

---

201   United Nations Department of Economic and Social Affairs, Statistics Division, Sustainable Development Goals Report 2021: Investing in data to save lives and build back better, *available at* https://unstats.un.org/sdgs/report/2021/investing-in-data-to-save-lives-and-build-back-better/ (last visited July 11, 2022).

202   World Bank, World Development Report 2021: Data for Better Lives 59–62 (2021), *available at* https://www. worldbank.org/en/publication/wdr2021.

Efforts across regions to surface government data systematically and to otherwise make what data exists accessible for public analysis have been complicated by the lack of political will, a lack of (or unenforceable) legal and regulatory enabling environment for information freedom, as well as related policies to mandate machine readable standards, to unpack categories of government data, and more. Often – when it exists – governance-related data is dated; several URLs on government-sponsored virtual platforms are broken; and much of the data are in non-machine readable format, such as in pdfs. Moreover, it is often the case that at ministry and state levels there is little or insufficient digital record keeping, and thus an insufficient supply of current (and historical) national and subnational data and statistics for long-term continuing analysis relevant to the governance context. Non-national holdings of relevant governance data (such as by the World Bank, among other organizations) are robust, and have provided a useful stop-gap for statistics capacity development and development of knowledge products, but this is not a sustainable solution.

Even in the case of the Millennium Development Goals (MDGs) – perhaps some of the most widely tracked indicators globally between 2000–2015 – the global development community still lacks timely and reliable data across the 36 indicators.[203] Disaggregation of data by sex, or areas in which conflict is prevalent, remains erratic across country contexts, including and particularly among fragile states and low-income countries. This fact impedes the ability to assess the situation of women and girls and conflict-affected persons effectively; due to either poor quality of data or a lack of data entirely, poor and marginalized communities across regions have in effect been left behind.

8.2.2 Recognition of these Constraining Conditions for Discerning and Tracking Corruption under SDG 16

Concerns about measuring and monitoring progress of the SDGs have already been voiced by a range of authoritative commentators. For example, the International Council for Science (ICSU) and the International Social Science Council (ISSC) released a 2015 analysis of the 169 SDG targets and asserted that only 29% are "well-developed"; that 54% "could be strengthened by being more

---

203   *See* Steve MacFeely, *The 2030 Agenda: An Unprecedented Statistical Challenge* (Friedrich Ebert Stiftung: International Policy Analysis) 5 (November 2018), *available at* https://library.fes.de/pdf-files/iez/14796.pdf (reporting that as of 2015, the target year in which the Millennium Development Goals were meant to be achieved, countries reported on average data for only 68% of the MDG indicators).

specific"; and that 17% "require significant work".[204] In particular, the authors found SDG 16 "overly timid," stating that "the way ... SDG [16] is formulated, narrowly emphasizing justice, accountability and inclusion, is arbitrary and disconnected from research on how governance affects sustainable development." The authors conclude that "SDG 16 ... falls short of what the evidence suggests is needed ... [and] because the SDG 16 elements point a spotlight overwhelmingly on poor countries, whereas the broader set of governance targets require action universally, the choice of targets undermines the overarching ambitions of the goal."[205]

Measuring and monitoring progress against SDG 16 will accordingly be challenging because of limitations associated with the evidence base and the ecosystem of governance statistics across regions. Without clear, evidence-based understandings of the political economy issues surrounding governance data, there is a substantial risk of failing to effectively monitor progress against SDG 16. The additional risk of doing harm exists – for example, where poor quality data may be used to make policy decisions. The lack of capacity and technical knowhow when it comes to governance data means that, without help and support, many of the World Bank's priority countries may find they are unable to measure and track progress against SDG 16. This would amount to a significant missed opportunity in the global fight against corruption and in efforts to promote and enable stronger governance around the world.

8.2.3   The Praia City Group May Eventually Look to Complementary Efforts to More Effectively Monitor SDG 16

While efforts to adequately finance data and statistics could enable more and better efforts to track governance and corruption through indicators, it will not occur in time to make a difference for the tracking of SDG 16. Give the above constraining conditions countries around the world are facing in reporting on their progress under SDG 16, the Praia City Group may eventually look to complementary, non-SDG16 indicators for which data are available to augment SDG indicators for which data are not available. Indeed, the UN specifically

---

204   International Council for Science, *International Social Science Council, Review of Targets for the Sustainable Development Goals: The Science Perspective* (2015), *available at* http://www.icsu.org/publications/reports-and-reviews/review-of-targets-for-the-sustainable-development-goals-the-science-perspective-2015/SDG-Report.pdf).

205   For evidence of governance challenges faced in high-income countries, see, e.g, Alexander Hamilton, *Small Is Beautiful, at Least in High-Income Democracies : The Distribution of Policy-Making Responsibility, Electoral Accountability, and Incentives for Rent Extraction* (World Bank Policy Research Working Paper No. 6305, 2013), *available at* https://openknowledge.worldbank.org/handle/10986/12197 [hereinafter Hamilton].

mandates the Praia City Group the authority to generate complementary indicators to help countries develop context-specific ways of measuring and monitoring progress against SDG 16. Put another way, it is therefore possible that the Praia City Group could augment the objective indicators on which SDG 16 relies with composite subjective indicators, as recommended in lessons #1 and #2 in Section 7 above.

8.3 *Projection: The World Bank Will Increasingly Mainstream Context-Sensitivity in Efforts to Track and Understand Governance and Corruption*

This projection suggests that the World Bank may scale up efforts to implement Lesson #3 emerging from the analysis in Section 7 above. World Bank experts have already developed increasingly sophisticated political economy analyses, an analytical process which deploys tools and techniques which are analogous to the Policy Sciences in its recognition of the importance of contextual drivers and stakeholders for development reforms. Specifically, the World Bank's annual flagship publication, the *World Development Report*, has relatively recently assayed the complexities and realities of developing country-context policy and reform processes in detail,[206] and a several World Bank development practitioners have followed suit with more targeted analyses (see, for example, Figure 12.1 for the political economy model proposed by this group).[207] While objective indicators-based work will no doubt continue, the Bank is producing ever more comprehensive political economy analyses, including in the governance contexts in low- and middle-income countries.[208]

In light of these and related emerging approaches to introducing a political economy model for use by World Bank governance practitioners, it may be useful to set out a further approach (which could, for example, augment that described in Figure 12.1) which better recognizes that the likelihood of

---

206 *See, e.g.,* World Bank, World Development Report 2015: Mind, Society, and Behavior (2015), *available at* https://openknowledge.worldbank.org/handle/10986/20597; World Bank, World Development Report 2004: Making Services Work for Poor People (2004), *available at* https://openknowledge.worldbank.org/handle/10986/5986 ; World Bank, World Development Report 2003: Sustainable Development in a Dynamic World–Transforming Institutions, Growth, and Quality of Life (2003), *available at* https://openknowledge .worldbank. org/handle/10986/5985 ; World Bank, World Development Report 2000/2001: Attacking Poverty (2001), *available at* https://openknowledge.worldbank.org/handle /10986/11856.

207 *See, e.g.,* Verena Fritz, Brian Levy & Rachel Ort, Problem-Driven Political Economy Analysis : The World Bank's Experience (2014), *available at* https://issuu.com/world.bank .publications/ docs/9781464801211.

208 *Id.*

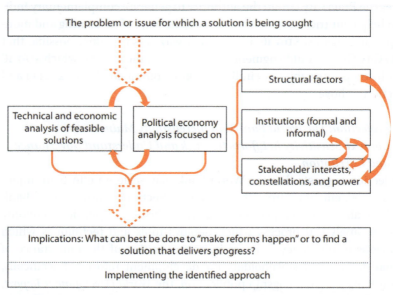

FIGURE 12.1   Layers and Key Aspects of Problem-Driven Political Economy Analysis[209]

achieving good governance outcomes (including combatting corruption) is conditioned by human action and is therefore informed by basic human values. As such, the advanced legal theory of Lasswell and McDougal might help achieve a more integrated and comprehensive understandings of the values that would count in processes to operationalize rule of law development. Specifically, this legal theory has identified and associated eight values with institutional mechanisms specialized to their realization in social practice: power, wealth, enlightenment, respect, well-being, skill, rectitude, and affection.[210] To achieve a better and more nuanced understanding of how these values influence or condition rule of law development, it may be useful to look again to Lasswell and McDougal, who examined the global political process by identifying, unpacking, and mapping a spectrum of social, cultural, economic, psychological, and other fundamental building blocks which underpin of human social structures, behaviors, and actions.[211]

---

209   *Id.* at 5.

210   *See* Myres S. McDougal & Harold D. Lasswell, *The Identification and Appraisal of Diverse Systems of Public Order*, 53 Am. J. Int'l L. 1 (1953), *reprinted in* International Rules: Approaches From International Law And International Relations 113, 126–36 (Robert J. Beck et al. eds., 1996).

211   *See generally* Harold Lasswell, Politics: Who Gets What, When, How (1936); *see also* Harold Lasswell, World Politics Faces Economics (1945); *see also* Harold Lasswell & Abraham

To create a contextual map the New Haven school set out three processes: the "social process," the "power process," and the "constitutive process." The "social process" describes the way in which people promote their values through institutions (small "i," such as family and faith-based communities) and Institutions (capital "I," such as government bodies, corporations, and bilateral/multilateral non-governmental organizations). The "power process" describes the way in which people pursue power through these institutions and Institutions. The "constitutive process" describes the way in which institutions that manage power are developed, essentially as an exercise in stabilizing expectations about how decision-making authority is allocated. These processes cascade, such that the "constitutive process" is an aspect of the "power process," and the "power process" is an aspect of the "social process."[212]

This section thus undertakes a literature review to identify several considerations which may inform the (projected) increased reliance by the World Bank on political economy analysis approaches to more comprehensively understand the phenomena of rule of law, governance, and corruption, using conceptual markers to describe and clarify the interrelations of the social, power, and constitutive processes. By accounting for these social process, power process, and constitutive process considerations, the Bank may thereafter be better equipped to undertake both a detailed analysis of particular dimensions of the focus of inquiry and one which achieves levels of abstraction to generate analytical value beyond that which is possible through purely objective indicators-based analyses. It may thus further enhance the achievability of key actors' legitimate goals in this chapter (as described in Section 1).[213]

8.3.1   Social Process Considerations

Corruption as Normative. The decision to commit a corrupt act might be triggered or otherwise informed by values of greed, personal gain and/or resignation to corruption. People are capable of accommodating illegal acts they deem normative. When politically corrupt transactions become so pervasive in a political system that they become an expected norm in transactions involving government officials, a culture of political corruption may be said to exist.[214]

Kaplan, Power and Society: A Framework of Political Inquiry (1950); *see also* Harold D. Lasswell & Myres S. McDougal, Jurisprudence for a Free Society (1992).

212   *Id.*

213   *See* Myres S. McDougal et al., *The World Community: A Planetary Social Process*, 21 U.C. Davis L. Rev. 807 (1988) (suggesting that to achieve a realistic understanding of world order, a comprehensive map of the global social process is needed).

214   *See, e.g.,* VT LeVine, Political Corruption: The Ghana Case (Stanford, CA: Hoover Institution) (1975).

Such legitimization of values have been regarded elsewhere as contributing to corruption.[215] A discussion of the values which pertain to acts of corruption have likewise been examined through the lens of societal and cultural norms. Some studies find that societies characterized by ethnic divisions are correlated to corruption.[216] Other studies warn that certain forms of relatively recent societal behavior, for example concerning changes in human behavior associated with colonialism, should not be abstracted into cultural representations.[217]

Kinship ties. It is important to emphasize that kinship loyalties do not necessarily lead to corruption. It has been asserted that traditional societies do not encourage or condone corruption.[218] Depending on the context, a gift can be used for positive or negative purposes – is not necessarily a bribe, for it depends on circumstance and intent. This focus on the concept of intent suggests that when kinship loyalties are advanced at the expense of loyalty to the state, this typically results in circumnavigation of official rules to maintain them; it may thus be possible to conclude that corruption can occur as a result of attitudes and patterns of behavior rooted in the socio-cultural fabric of a particular group, akin to a patron-client network, based on customs and connections.[219] Familiar examples of this might include using kinship ties to determine who receives a government job or which organization wins a government contract. This is true for developed and developing countries alike.

Bad Incentives. Corruption undermines the state's ability to carry out its functions in the economy (IMF 2016). When a state fails to perform its functions, the economic costs can be high. But if the costs are so high, it is prudent to ask why people resort to corruption at all. The reasons may lie in a given set of incentives that lead people to commit corrupt acts. The role of the government in the economy also has an impact on levels of public corruption. Mancur Olson advises that changes in institutions can be better understood by

---

215   *See, e.g.,* Jean-François Médard, *Corruption in the Neo-Patrimonial States of Sub-Saharan Africa in* Political Corruption 379–402 (Heidenheimer & Johnson eds., 2002) [hereinafter Médard]; and Syed Hussein Alatas, Corruption: Its Nature, Causes, and Functions 122 (1990) (criticizing the attribution of corrupt acts to external causes, such as the legacy of colonialism or inefficiencies of bureaucratic government functions).

216   *See, e.g.,* Andrei Shleifer & Robert Vishny, *Corruption* (NBER Working Paper No. w4372, May 1993), *available at* SSRN: https://ssrn.com/abstract=227027; and Paolo Mauro, *Corruption and Growth,* 110(3) Q. J. Econ. 681–712 (1995), *available at* https://doi.org/10.2307/2946696.

217   *See* Médard, *supra* note 215.

218   Bertha Osei-Hwedie, *The Political, Economic, and Cultural Bases of Corruption in Africa, in* Corruption and Development in Africa (Hope, K.R., Chikulo, B.C., eds., Palgrave Macmillan, London, 2000).

219   *See id.*

considering the incentives of those in power.[220] Nagan and Manausa identify self-interest as the cornerstone of all analysis under the neoliberal economic model.[221] Campante et al. find a relationship between corruption and political stability, and describe the interplay of two effects: (1) a "horizon effect," where higher levels of state instability lead individual incumbents to embezzle more during a short window of opportunity; and (2) a "demand effect," where the private sector is more willing to bribe stable incumbents.[222] They find integrating reelection incentives into electoral systems (which also includes an eventual term limit) may lower incentives for corruption.

In practice, individuals resort to bribery and theft of public money when the incentives in the systems do not work well. "Incentives" in this instance means some form of encouragement – material or immaterial – to motivate an individual to decide to take a particular action. Incentives typically include bonuses for high quality work or public recognition. Bad incentives might include an overly rigid or burdensome architecture of rules which make achievement of outcomes unnecessarily difficult, such as in the economies ranked at the bottom of the World Bank's *Doing Business Report* in the "ease of doing business" category – in certain countries, it takes months to start a business (for example as of a 2017 analysis, it takes 230 days for a small-to-medium-sized company to formally start operations in Venezuela, as compared to approximately one-half of one day to do the same in New Zealand).[223] When it is overly difficult to start a business, the incentive structure is not working properly. Despite some progress made in the analysis of the interplay between incentives and corruption, Olken and Pande suggest that evidence that directly links performance pay or other incentive schemes with corruption outcomes is largely lacking.[224]

---

220 Mancur Olson, Power and Prosperity: Outgrowing Communist and Capitalist Dictatorships (New York: Basic Books, 2000).

221 Winston Nagan & Samantha Manausa, *Judicial Philosophy for Thoughtful Politicians and Business Leaders*, 1 Corp. & Bus. L.J. 1, 2 (January 31, 2020), *available at* http://cablj.org/wp-content/uploads/2020/01/W2020-FINAL-W_Nagan.pdf ("Thus, modern political economy finds its roots in the jurisprudential idea of the role of the bad man in the definition of law.").

222 Filipe Campante, Davin Chor & Quoc-Anh Do, *Instability and the Incentives for Corruption*, 21(1) Econ. & Politics 42–92 (2009), *available at* https://dash.harvard.edu/bitstream/handle/1/4778510/Campante-InstabilityIncentives.pdf?sequence=1.

223 World Bank, 2017 Doing Business Report: Equal Opportunity for All (2017), *available at* http://www.doing business.org/data/exploretopics/starting-a-business.

224 Benjamin Olken & Rohini Pande, *Corruption in Developing Countries*, 4 Ann. Rev. Econ. 479–509 (September 2012), *available at* https://doi.org/10.1146/annurev-economics-080511-110917 [hereinafter Olken & Pande].

Good incentives have also been identified as crucial for the implementation of lasting governance reforms. For example, Al-Dahdah et al. argue that:

> ... the drafting and implementation of laws and regulations that are compatible with principles of the rule of law depend on the incentives both lawmakers and implementing agencies have. If laws and their enforcement align with the goals of the ruling elites, effective implementation is a far more likely outcome. The incentives elites have to build and support rule-of-law institutions themselves derive from the distribution of power, especially the number and the relative strength of competing political interests in society. A society's power structure is partly a historical given. The point ... is that it is not deterministic. Realigning the *incentive structures* for reform among key actors and organizations can dramatically improve the chances that rule-of-law institutions will take root. Building the capacity of organizations without first changing institutional incentives is likely to lead to perverse outcomes, with the capacity ultimately channeled toward goals the reformers never envisioned.[225]

To this end, over the years the World Bank has inaugurated a range of monetary and non-monetary incentives programs in countries around the world, with varying results.[226]

Low Wages. It has been argued that competitive wages are a necessary condition to avoid corruption. It is not uncommon in many low- and middle-income countries for government officials to have relatively low or uncompetitive salaries. Several cross-country studies have found that higher public wages are associated with lower levels of corruption, though Olken and Pande note that these studies are essentially cross-sectional in nature.[227] Niehaus and Sukhtankar studied the premise that rents from retaining one's job can deter corruption today while preserving tomorrow's opportunities and found an 80% reduction

---

225   Edouard Al-Dahdah, Cristina Corduneanu-Huci, Gael Raballand, Ernest Sergenti & Myriam Ababsa, Rules on Paper, Rules in Practice: Enforcing Laws and Policies in the Middle East and North Africa (Washington, DC: World Bank) (2016), *available at* https://openknowledge.worldbank.org/handle/10986/24715.

226   *See, e.g.,* Sebastian James, *Incentives and Investments: Evidence and Policy Implications* (Investment Climate Advisory Services, World Bank Group, June 2009), *available at*: https://openknowledge.worldbank.org/handle/10986/27875; and Sebastian James, *Tax and non-tax incentives and investment: Evidence and Policy Implications,* (Investment Climate Advisory Services, World Bank Group, June 2014).

227   *See* Olken & Pande, *supra* note 224.

in daily theft by officials in the period after a wage increase.[228] It may seem intuitive that if a public official earns insufficient income, taking bribes may be viewed as a way to augment one's income and sustain one's livelihood, however more analysis of any possible balance between necessity and greed must be better understood to generate any potential insights into what size salary a public official must earn to become less corruptible from context to context. It is important to note that Van Rijckeghem and Weder studied this balance and found that while higher pay for public servants may indeed reduce corruption, the benefits may be smaller than the added costs.[229] Their research further demonstrates that civil service wages are highly correlated with measures of rule of law and the quality of bureaucracy may also have additional indirect effects on levels of corruption among public officials.[230] What is clear, however, is that higher or more competitive wages will not eradicate high-level or "grand" corruption. This is the form of corruption which is most damaging to governance and development: the theft of state funds by elites.[231] Corruption at this level is evidently not necessarily influenced or exacerbated by official pay scales. Raising salaries alone is thus not a singular solution; doing so must be accompanied by further, substantial reforms.

Post-colonial considerations. The decades during and following de-colonization across regions has left a fraught political legacy for contemporary leaders. Various post-independence leaders assumed power in contexts characterized by centralized control, and with institutions to match. Writing on post-colonial states of Pakistan and Bangladesh, Hamza Alavi adds that the colonial state featured a powerful bureaucratic-military apparatus and mechanisms of government which enabled subordination of the national classes.[232] He explains that the post-colonial society inherits the overdeveloped apparatus of state and its institutionalized practices, through which the operations of indigenous social classes are regulated and controlled.[233]

---

228   Paul Niehaus & Sandip Sukhtankar, *Corruption Dynamics: The Golden Goose Effect*, 5(4) Am. Econ. J.: Econ. Pol'y 230–69 (2013).

229   Caroline Van Rijckeghem & Beatrice Weder, *Corruption and the Rate of Temptation: Do Low Wages in the Civil Service Cause Corruption?* (IMF Working Paper no. WP/97/73, 1997), *available at* https://www.imf.org/en/Publications/ WP/Issues/2016/12/30/Corruption -and-the-Rate-of-Temptation-Do-Low-Wages-in-the-Civil-Service-Cause-Corruption -2246.

230   *Id.*

231   World Bank, Helping Countries Combat Corruption: The Role of the World Bank, *available at* http://www1.worldbank. org/publicsector/anticorrupt/corruptn/cor02.htm (last visited July 11, 2022).

232   Hamza Alavi, The State in Post-Colonial Societies: Pakistan and Bangladesh (1973).

233   *Id.*

Chazan et al. also explain that many post-independence leaders effectively inherited a structure of control but lacked a power base from which they could effectively establish priorities and pursue policies.[234] Post-independent governments accordingly had to deal with the issue of power consolidation in a political environment in which their own legitimacy was delicate and in which expectations from the populace were high. Several leaders chose to further concentrate power at the center. Maxon posits that the "authoritarian structure and statist tendencies" of the postcolonial state in East Africa is the inevitable consequence of the politico-administrative policies pursued during the colonial period.[235] Oyugi and Ochieng explain the characteristics of centralized power in such post-colonial contexts: centralized governance; law and order-focused administration; and authoritarianism in political life.[236]

Post-colonial states often became the primary employer and provider of services. In an overly-expansive state, the public is typically forced to maneuver a large and often complex bureaucracy for any transaction. Hope illustrates the bureaucratic hoops through which post-colonial citizens must jump, such as "getting a driver's license, telephone service, subsidized credit, tax administration decisions, government contracts for goods and/or services, or permits to sell crops."[237] This resulted in widespread corruption, since bribes were extracted for transactions to be completed. Corrupt acts then become self-reinforcing since public officials retain control over the instruments regulating socio-economic benefits, and private parties remain willing to make illegal payments to secure those benefits.[238]

Persson and Tabellini contend that an electoral system, legacy or otherwise, may affect levels of corruption and overall effectiveness of a governance regime; they illustrate this contention by setting out examples of how a country's constitution can influence incidences of corruption among public officials.[239] Specifically, they explain that electoral rules may encourage or

---

234 *See generally*, Naomi Chazan et al., Politics and Society in Contemporary Africa (1999).

235 Robert Maxon, East Africa: An Introductory History 175 (1994).

236 *See generally*, Walter Oyugi & Jimmy Ochieng, *East Africa: Regional Politics and Dynamics*, in Oxford Encyclopedia of African Politics (N. Cheeseman ed., 2020).

237 Kempe Ronald Hope, *Corruption and Development in Africa*, *in* Corruption and Development in Africa: Lessons from Country Case Studies 20 (K. Hope & B. Chikulo eds., 2000).

238 Jacqueline Coolidge & Susan Rose-Ackerman, *High-Level Rent Seeking and Corruption in African Regimes: Theory and Cases* (World Bank Policy Research Working Paper, 2013), *available at* https://doi.org/10.1596/1813-9450-1780.

239 Torsten Persson & Guido Tabellini, *Political Institutions and Policy Outcomes: What are the Stylized Facts?* (CESifo Working Paper Series No. 459, April 2001), *available at* SSRN: https://ssrn.com/abstract=270935.

discourage corrupt acts. Examples cited include constitutional provisions permitting election of politicians from party lists rather than individually, which may create a free-rider problem because it lessens individual accountability and may thus increase incidences of corruption. They continue that small electoral districts with higher barriers to entry may also increase corruption by reducing the choices available to voters and thus incentivizing corrupt acts.[240] Accordingly, Persson, Tabellini, and Trebbi conclude that a plurality electoral system, in which the candidate who polls more votes than any other candidate is elected, should result in a lower incidence of corruption than a proportional representation electoral system because the former permits the direct accountability of elected officials to the electorate and the latter does not.[241] Kunicova and Rose-Ackerman argue that proportional representation electoral systems offer greater opportunities to party leaders to commit corrupt acts than plurality electoral systems for the same reason.[242] Hamilton adds that the distribution of policymaking responsibilities between electorally accountable decision-makers and their electorally unaccountable public policy-making counterparts may determine the level of rents extracted in a high-income democracy context.[243]

8.3.2 Power Process Considerations

Government institutions. Any effort to mainstream context-sensitive analyses into multilateral efforts to understand the quality of governance and how to combat corruption in a particular location and time must acknowledge that there are a range of forces shaping the power process at work which result in poor governance and corruption. Corruption is one of the manifestations of institutional weaknesses in a governance system, in short: if institutions are weak, corruption can follow. Hernando de Soto finds that government institutions in developing countries can be so dysfunctional that they effectively push populations into the informal sector of the economy, which can both promote corruption generally and even help to institutionalize corruption in the bureaucratic institutions of the state.[244] Johnson, Kaufmann, and Schleifer find that instances of "bad equilibrium," where the interplay of politics and economic and institutional incentives influence the growth of the unofficial

---

240   *Id.*

241   Torsten Persson, Guido Tabellini & Francesco Trebbi, *Electoral Rules and Corruption*, 1(4) J. Eur. Econ. Ass'n 958–989 (2003), *available at* https://doi.org/10.1162/154247603322493203.

242   Jana Kunicova & Susan Rose-Ackerman, *Electoral Rules and Constitutional Structures as Constraints on Corruption*, 35(4) Brit J. Pol. Sci. 573–606 (2005).

243   *See* Hamilton, *supra* note 205.

244   *See generally*, Hernando de Soto, The Mystery of Capital (2000).

economy, which in turn affects economic performance, reflect institutional weakness.[245] Weak institutional capacity undermines a government's ability to implement and enforce policies, which opens the door to corrupt acts. Other opportunities for corrupt acts stem from institutional characteristics, such as extensive regulations, discretion of public officials, and the lack of accountability.

Bureaucracy. Tanzi finds that factors which contribute to corruption directly can include the quality of bureaucracy, the level of public sector wages, the strength of penalty systems, institutional control, and the quality of leadership.[246] The relative strength of each of these factors directly conditions the effectiveness of the rule of law in a country. Weak (or nonexistent) rule of law and unpredictability of public administration create opportunities for corruption. Lack of rule of law protections can results in capture of the formal bureaucracy by the state, which may use bureaucratic functions for personal gain, occasionally including state instruments for law and order. Kaufmann and Wei find that where government regulations are vague or lax, and where public officials are willing to abuse their power, corruption breeds inefficiency.[247] Egregious examples abound where the lack of rule of law contributed to corruption, such as in the Congo where former President Mobutu Seso Seko had diverted more than US$5 billion into foreign accounts, businesses and real estate holdings; in Indonesia, where Mohamed Suharto embezzled between USD $15–35 billion; and in the Philippines where Ferdinand Marcos stole an estimated USD $5–10 billion in public funds.[248]

Involvement of the state in the economy. Levels of corruption are higher in countries with higher degrees of state ownership in the economy, excessive business

245   Simon Johnson, Daniel Kaufmann & Andrei Shleifer, *The Unofficial Economy in Transition* 159–239 (2 Brookings Papers on Economic Activity, 1997), *available at* https://www .brookings.edu/wpcontent/uploads/1997/06/1997b_bpea_johnson_kauf mann_shleifer _goldman_weitzman.pdf.

246   Vito Tanzi, *Corruption Around the World: Causes, Consequences, Scope and Cures* (IMF Working Paper no 63, 1998), *available at* https://www.imf.org/en/Publications /WP/Issues/2016/12/30/Corruption-Around-the-World-Causes-Consequences-Scope-and -Cures-2583.

247   Daniel Kaufmann and Shang-Jin Wei, *Does 'Grease Money' Speed Up the Wheels of Commerce?* (IMF Working Paper no. 64, 2000), *available at* https://www.imf.org/external /pubs/ft/wp/2000/wp0064.pdf.

248   UNODC and World Bank, *Stolen Asset Recovery (StAR) Initiative: Challenges, Opportunities, and Action Plan* 11 (2007), *available at* https://www.unodc.org/documents/corruption /StAR-Sept07-full.pdf.

regulation and taxes, arbitrary application of regulations, and trade restrictions.[249] This is the case even in stable high income democracies. Monopolized economies also typically exhibit higher levels of corruption. State power, coupled with insider information, creates opportunities for public officials to promote their own interests, or those of their allies.[250] Ades and Tella find that corruption is higher in countries with economies dominated by a small number of firms or where domestic firms are sheltered from foreign competition by high tariffs.[251] Tanzi and Davoodi find that corruption motivates government leaders to increase public spending.[252] Rose-Ackerman argues that bribes are paid for two reasons: to obtain government benefits and to avoid costs. Specifically, she finds that when governments sell goods or services at below-market prices, firms will often pay off officials for access to state supplies.[253] She also finds higher incidences of corruption when government officials have amassed valuable information which individuals and firms may be willing to pay for – such as bidding specifications for forthcoming lucrative government procurement – and shows that firms and individuals will pay to avoid costs of delay.[254]

Discretion. Corruption in the bureaucracy occurs when the rewards and penalties for certain services are under an official's control, the public official has the discretion in the allocation of resources, and the accountability of officials for decisions and actions taken is lacking.[255] Some government branches are more susceptible for corruption, especially places where public officials have discretion, can operate autonomously, where people are very dependent on

---

249   OECD, *State-Owned Enterprises and Corruption: What Are the Risks and What Can Be Done?*
         20–22 (2018), *available at* https://www.oecd-ilibrary.org/governance/state-owned-enterprises
         -and-corruption_9789264303058-en.

250   World Bank Institute and Global Organization of Parliamentarians Against Corruption,
         Controlling Corruption: A Parliamentarian's Handbook 24 (2005), *available at* https://
         parlcent.org/wp-content/uploads/2020/07/Controlling_Corruption_Handbook_EN.pdf
         ("Corruption is more likely to proliferate in countries where governments create monop-
         olistic economic settings ... [and s]tate power, coupled with insider information, creates
         opportunities for public officials to promote their own interests or those of their allies")
         [hereinafter WBI and GOPAC].

251   Alberto Ades & Rafael Di Tella, *The Causes and Consequences of Corruption: A Review of
         Recent Empirical Contributions, in* Liberalization and the New Corruption (B. Harris-White
         & G. White, eds.), 27(2) IDS Bulletin 6–11 (1996), *available at* https://bulletin.ids
         .ac.uk/index.php/idsbo/article/view/1503/PDF.

252   Vito Tanzi & Hamid Davoodi, *Corruption, Public Investment, and Growth* (IMF Working
         Paper no 139, 1997), *available at* https://www.imf.org/external/pubs/ft/wp/wp97139.pdf.

253   Susan Rose-Ackerman, Corruption and Government: Causes, Consequences and Reform
         51–53 (Cambridge: Cambridge University Press, 1999).

254   *See id.*

255   *See* Andvig et al. *supra* note 179.

the services rendered. An example of government unit particularly vulnerable to corrupt acts is the customs agency, which characterized by a range of opportunities for graft.[256] This is because customs officials clear goods and are tasked with ensuring that the necessary requirements for products entering the country are met and that required taxes are paid. When officials have a level of discretion, they are thus in a position to accelerate, delay, or halt clearing processes, instances of bribery increase. This is only one example of the challenges faced by bureaucracies around the world; the very existence of bureaucratic discretion can create opportunities for individuals to abuse privileges associated with administrative office.

Professionalism and independence of the public service. Rauch and Evans examined processes to recruit and promote civil servants across developing countries and found higher levels of corruption in countries where recruitment and promotions are based less on merit than other factors.[257] Weak levels of professionalism in a bureaucracy can also lead to corruption. When there is a weak separation between civil service and the party politic, policies designed by the civil service can be captured. In extreme cases, government officers may not have an incentive to perform their official duties since they receive relatively little formal income and receive substantial income through soliciting bribes.[258]

Institutionalization of transparency and accountability. Lack of transparency and accountability based on the rule of law and democratic values of public officials coupled with distortion in policy priorities, is a significant cause of corruption. In some countries, politicians and bureaucrats control access to valuable benefits and can impose costs on private citizens. Public officials may be tempted to leverage their positions for private gain by soliciting bribes, and private individuals may likewise be willing to pay bribes to get what they want from government.[259]

---

256 *See, e.g.*, Gerard McLinden, *Integrity in Customs, in* Customs Modernization Handbook (De Wulf & Sokol eds., 2005).

257 James Rauch & Peter Evans, *Bureaucratic Structure and Bureaucratic Performance in Less Developed Countries*, 75 J. Pub. Econ. 49–71 (2000), *available at* https://citeseerx.ist.psu .edu/viewdoc/download?doi=10.1.1.203.288&rep= rep1&type=pdf.

258 *See generally* Jeremy Foltz & Kweku Opoku-Agyemang, *Do Higher Salaries Lower Petty Corruption? A Policy Experiment on West Africa's Highways* (Working Paper, University of Wisconsin-Madison and University of California, Berkeley, 2015), *available at* https:// cega.berkeley.edu/assets/miscellaneous_files/118_-_Opoku-Agyemang_Ghana_Police _Corruption_paper_revised_v3.pdf.

259 World Bank, World Development Report 1997: The State in a Changing World 103 (1997), *available at* https://openknowledge.worldbank.org/handle/10986/5980.

The importance of transparency and accountability in general is increasingly well understood as foils to corrupt acts. Islam finds that countries with better information flows have better quality governance.[260] Kaufmann and Bellver find that transparency is associated with reduced corruption and relatively more effective government agencies than countries with less transparency.[261] Countries with higher level of budget transparency tend to achieve positive development outcomes than countries with lower levels of transparency.[262] Benito and Bastida find evidence of both a positive relationship between political turnout and transparency, and a positive relationship between national government fiscal balance and budget transparency.[263] Bernoth and Wolff find that fiscal transparency reduces risk premiums while creative accounting increases the spread.[264] Glennerster and Shin find that when countries become more transparent, they experience notable declines in borrowing costs.[265] Hameed analyzes indices of fiscal transparency based on IMF fiscal Reports on Standards and Codes (ROSCs) and – while he emphasizes that the underlying data is partial in nature and is careful not to make a causal claim—finds that after controlling for other socioeconomic variables, countries that are more transparent tend to have better credit ratings, better fiscal discipline, and less corruption.[266] Hameed subsequently analyzes the

---

260   Roumeen Islam, *Do More Transparent Governments Govern Better?* (World Bank Policy Research Working Paper no. 3077, 2003), *available at* https://openknowledge.worldbank.org/handle/10986/18169.

261   Daniel Kaufmann & Ana Bellver, *Transparenting Transparency: Initial Empirics and Policy Applications* (Draft Policy Research Paper, 2005), *available at* http://web.worldbank.org/archive/website00818/WEB/PDF/TRANSP-5.PDF.

262   OECD, Best Practices for Budget Transparency (2002), *available at* https://www.oecd.org/gov/budgeting/best-practices-budget-transparency.htm (last visited July 11, 2022).

263   Bernardino Benito & Francisco Bastida, *Budget Transparency, Fiscal Performance, and Political Turnout: An International Approach*, 69(3) Pub. Admin. Rev. 403–417 (2009), *available at* https://onlinelibrary.wiley.com/doi/full/10.1111/j.1540-6210.2009.01988.x.

264   Kerstin Bernoth & Guntram Wolff, *Fool the Markets? Creative Accounting, Fiscal Transparency and Sovereign Risk Premia* (Bundesbank Series 1 Discussion Paper No. 2006), *available at* http://dx.doi.org/10.2139/ssrn.2785245).

265   Rachel Glennerster & Yongseok Shin, *Does Transparency Pay?* (55(1) IMF Staff Papers, 2008), *available at* https://www.imf.org/external/pubs/ft/staffp/2008/01/pdf/glennerster.pdf.

266   Farhan Hameed, *Fiscal Transparency and Economic Outcomes* (IMF Working Paper No. 05/225, 2005), *available at* https://www.imf.org/external/pubs/ft/wp/2005/wp05225.pdf.

2008 Open Budget Survey results[267] and finds that more transparent countries tend to have higher credit ratings.[268]

The body of literature on budget accountability and participatory processes as aspects of good governance continues to grow.[269] Efforts to improve budget accountability are predicated on the assumption that improving budget transparency is not only an important goal in itself, but that it would achieve better development outcomes for people, or human development (in other words, lack of transparency creates opportunities for public officials to abuse their office for private gain). The relationship between fiscal transparency and improved fiscal outcomes, although well recognized, is not an automatic one. Some countries make improvements in fiscal transparency, but experience limited improvement in financial governance. In this respect, the difference between nominal and effective transparency is often emphasized, as well as the need for clear "proactive" transparency policies that ensure that the right information is released at the right time and in the right way to ensure that external stakeholders to the executive, like parliaments and citizens, can play an accountability role.[270]

8.3.3   Constitutive Process Considerations

Elite capture. Elite capture can occur in a variety of ways, such as the domination by elites of natural resources, patronage, political cronyism – in some instances, government dominates all aspects of the economy. In short, elite capture creates a climate for systematic exploitation of the state by public officials.[271] In certain contexts, the ruling party controls the legislature and influences decisions and the recommendations of various parliamentary committees.[272] Systems of government that have traditionally been dominated by

---

267   *See* International Budget Partnership, Open Budget Survey 2008, *available at* https://
       internationalbudget.org/ publications/open-budget-survey-2008/ (last visited July 11, 2022).

268   Farhan Hameed, *Budget Transparency and Financial Markets* (IBP Working Paper No. 1, 2011),
       available at https://internationalbudget.org/wp-content/uploads/IBP-Working-Paper-1
       -Budget-Transparency-and-Financial-Markets.pdf.

269   *See generally* World Bank 2017, *supra* note 1.

270   *See, e.g.,* Mary McNeil & Takawira Mumvuma, *Demanding Good Governance: A Stocktaking of Social Accountability Initiatives by Civil Society in Anglophone Africa* (World Bank Institute, 2006); and Dennis Arroyo & Karen Sirker, *Stocktaking of Social Accountability Initiatives in the Asia and Pacific Region* (World Bank Institute, 2005).

271   Sahr Kpundeh, *Corruption and Corruption Control in Africa* (working paper prepared for a workshop organized by the Gulbenkian Foundation on "Democracy and Development in Africa" in Lisbon, Portugal, June, 2000), *available at* https://citeseerx.ist.psu.edu/viewdoc /download? doi=10.1.1.595.4791&rep=rep1&type=pdf.

272   *See id.*

the executive or the military typically have a weak or nonexistent civil society. Governance arrangements without effective accountability mechanisms, such as transparent institutions, checks and balances, and robust third-party monitoring are particularly vulnerable to abuses of power.[273]

Hellmann, Jones, and Kaufmann examine elite capture in the transitional economies and distinguish two types of monopolization of private sector policies.[274] They first define state capture as the capacity of firms to shape and affect the formation of basic rules of the game (i.e. laws, regulations, and decrees) through private payments to public officials and politicians. They next define the use of influence as the capacity to do the same without recourse to such payments.[275] They further explain that that while firms that use influence are usually incumbents with influence inherited from the past (with reasonably secure property rights and both formal and informal ties with the state). These firms use state capture as a strategy to compete against existing influential firms by trying to purchase benefits from the state including protection for their own property and contract rights.[276]

Enforcement. One explanation of why corruption occurs has to do with enforcement of the law. If there are many rules and no capacity to enforce, the enforcement of rules becomes random. Enforcement might thus be exercised based on "extralegal" factors, such as the ability to pay a bribe. Examples abound, such as in the contexts of traffic enforcement,[277] trade restrictions,[278]

---

273 John Ackerman, *Social Accountability in the Public Sector: A Conceptual Discussion* (World Bank Social Development Paper 82, March 2005), *available at* https://www.worldbank .org/content/dam/Worldbank/Event/MNA/yemen_cso/english/Yemen_CSO_Conf _Social-Accountability-in-the-Public-Sector_ENG.pdf.

274 Joel S. Hellman, Geraint Jones & Daniel Kaufmann, *Seize the State, Seize the Day: An Empirical Analysis of State Capture and Corruption in Transition Economies* (paper prepared for the ABCDE 2000 Conference, Washington, D.C.: April 18–20, 2000), *available at* https:// www.researchgate.net/profile/Daniel-Kaufmann-11/publication/228724476_Seize _the_State_Seize_the_Day_An_Empirical_Analysis_of_State_Capture_and_Corruption _in_Transition_Economies/links/564bf05808ae4ae893b81303/Seize-the-State-Seize-the -Day-An-Empirical-Analysis-of-State-Capture-and-Corruption-in-Transition-Economies .pdf.

275 *Id.*

276 *Id.*

277 Gorkem Celik & Serdar Sayan, *To Give In or Not To Give In To Bribery? Setting the Optimal Fines for Violations of Rules when the Enforcers are Likely to Ask for Bribes* (Working Paper, Bilkent University and Ohio State University, August 3, 2005), *available at* https://citeseerx .ist.psu.edu/viewdoc/download?doi=10.1.1.584.1228&rep=rep1&type=pdf.

278 Sami Bensassi, Joachim Jarreau, *Price discrimination in bribe payments: Evidence from informal cross-border trade in West Africa*, 122 World Development 462–480 (2019), *available at* https://doi.org/10.1016/j.worlddev.2019.05.023.

subsidies[279] and tax evasion.[280] Enforcement policies are widely used, including in places where clear governance problems persist, and so these policies may offer greater opportunities for corruption to emerge and become entrenched.[281]

8.3.4   Bringing this Projection to Fruition

Bratton and van de Walle describe governance as the "interactive process by which state and social actors reciprocally probe for a consensus on the rules of the political game."[282] Hence, the ambition of the above exercise is to better position the World Bank to undertake contextual mapping of these "rules of the political game" with respect to the quality of governance and the rule of law, and the prevalence of corruption in a particular context within the Bank's client countries. As we have seen, aspects, or "ingredients," of this reciprocal relationship include political freedom, civil liberties and freedom of the press, security, confidence in the economy and social, economic and political stability, and more – can be countervailing forces to government overreach. Looking at many low- and middle-income countries it is clear that several, most, or in certain cases, all of these ingredients are not present. The very institutions that should be enabling or delivering these ingredients are often the ones often preventing them from occurring.

Of course, the above considerations are just the beginning. To truly create a contextual map of the range of complex and dynamic factors which influence or condition the quality of governance and the prevalence of corruption within low-and-middle-income countries, key steps would necessarily include a methodology such as that of the Policy Sciences: identifying operative participants in the world social and power processes; clarifying their perspectives, demands, and expectations; determining their bases of power; clarifying the contexts in which they operate; unpacking how they develop strategies to achieve specific outcomes; understanding what action is taken to implement

---

279   Fabian Teichmann, Marie-Christin Falker, Bruno Sergi, *Gaming Environmental Governance? Bribery, Abuse of Subsidies, and Corruption in European Union Programs* (Energy Research and Social Science, 66(10141) (2020), *available at* https://doi.org/10.1016/j.erss.2020.101481.

280   Meghana Ayyagari, Asli Demirgüç-Kunt & Vojislav Maksimovic, *Are Innovating Firms Victims or Perpetrators? Tax Evasion, Bribe Payments, and the Role of External Finance in Developing Countries* (World Bank Policy Research Working Paper No. 5389, 2010), *available at* https://elibrary.worldbank.org/doi/abs/10.1596/1813-9450-5389.

281   *See* WBI and GOPAC, *supra* note 251.

282   Michael Bratton & Nicholas van de Walle, *Toward Governance in Africa: Popular Demands and State Responses*, *in* Governance and Politics in Africa 27–55 (G. Hydén & M. Bratton eds., 1992).

these strategies; ascertaining whether the desired outcomes are achieved; and finally determining the effects of the action.

The literature review in this Section clearly demonstrates that power in society is expressed in terms of decision-making. This decision-making has created and sustains an enabling environment for poor governance and contraventions of rule of law, and results in corrupt acts across country contexts. These corrupt acts undermine opportunities for a range of other social and economic development outcomes, from increased domestic resource mobilization through tax efficiency to gender equality and social/ethnic inclusion to water and sanitation service provision to climate change mitigation efforts and more.

To help bring this projection into effective fruition, the World Bank could consider scaling up implementation of the work of one of its expert consultants, Charles Norchi, who piloted the institution's first Value-Based Participatory Planning, Monitoring, and Evaluation (VBPP) project in service of a Community-Driven Development initiative in Afghanistan in 2003.[283] In inaugurating the World Bank's first operational case study using a value-based methodology, Norchi undertook a comprehensive contextual mapping approach to enable community design, development, and participation in implementing a grassroots development project based on their own community values, based on the explicit recognition, identification, and clarification of these values. In so doing, Norchi found significant convergence in perspectives among community participants in a variety of contexts.[284]

Such a contextual mapping exercise could help enable World Bank practitioners to map the values underpinning the quality of governance or prevalence of corruption in a particular context in terms of the problems generated and the values challenges which these problems present. For example, by examining the power value and its institutional process of interaction, the Bank practitioner could eschew a purely *de jure* analysis and isolate a series of markers which point to *de facto* governance problems arising from social interaction. The identification of these problems could in turn enable clarification of the value aspect which each problem implicates, which could then inform the development of a theory to anticipate each value aspect and improve the likelihood of solving or circumventing these problems. A comprehensive map of these value aspects might identify problems related to:

---

283 Charles Norchi & Karuna Chibber, *A Techical Note for Value-Based Participatory Planning, Monitoring, and Evaluations in Community-Driven Development* (World Bank: 2003), *available at* https://pdfs.semanticscholar.org/bca6/fc7b0a5ee1f5452e055c5e6c2d8853fd056f .pdf?_ga=2.179725284.1980954982.1588458147-1047454741.1588458147.

284 *See id.*

- Institutional practices ("participants, perspectives, situations, base values, strategies, [and] outcomes") of the range of decision-makers in global social process relevant to sustainable development;[285]
- Arenas of social interaction (spatial, temporal, institutional, or characterized by crisis);[286]
- Power accessible to and used by decision-makers[287] (and how it is "continually ... renewed, recreated, defended, and modified ... [and] continually resisted, limited, altered, [and]] challenged by pressures")[288]; and
- Coercive or persuasive modalities (as "an inducement ... [or] constraint" to ensure effective prescription, application, and enforcement, including the threat or use of military force, economic pressure, diplomatic engagement, and propaganda).[289]

Mapping the values inherent in each problem category could surface valuable insights on what enhances or retards the likelihood of efforts to strengthen governance and combat corruption from context to context. This is because the creation and distribution of effective power is an important outcome of the global social process.

As the World Bank increasingly deploys political economy analyses in its governance agenda, it signals a new paradigm of development support for low- and middle-income countries around the world. Adding tools and processes explicitly designed to support value clarification as part of broader contextual mapping efforts could further help enable the institution to transcend disciplinary boundaries and adapt project design and implementation approaches to resolve challenges which identify conflicting claims, priorities and interests for which concerted efforts at reconciliation are necessary, and respond with interrelated and interdependent implementation of development solutions. It could likewise help enable the institution to improve its focus on how effective

---

285   Lasswell & McDougal, Jurisprudence for a Free Society, *supra* note 5, at 324.

286   *See id.* at 614.

287   *See id.* at 113, citing Timasheff, An Introduction to the Sociology of Law 17, 303 (1939) ("constitutional order ... exists as long as it is recognized by the active power center" which is "generally complex and highly structuralized" from which may come "a hierarchy of legal rules").

288   *See* Raymond Williams, Marxism And Literature 112 (1977) (suggesting that power is an outcome of the social process).

289   Lasswell & McDougal, Jurisprudence for a Free Society, *supra* note 5, at 415, 1457. *See also* Stephen D. Krasner, *Structural Causes and Regime Consequences: Regimes as Intervening Variables, in* International Regimes 1, 2 (S. Krasner ed., 1983); Harold Lasswell, Propaganda Technique in the World War (1927); Harold Lasswell, *The Theory of Political Propaganda*, 21 Am. Pol. Sci. Rev. 627 (1927); and Harold Lasswell, *The Function of the Propagandist*, 38 Int'l J. Ethics 258 (1928).

and controlling decisions are made in particular contexts and put into effect in
the public interest of all social participants. Unpacking this public and private
decision-making could thus be a necessary first step toward understanding the
creation and the distribution of the values which underpin the policy process
of the conventional paradigm, to strengthen the institution's theory of change
in its governance portfolio.

9   Conclusions, Lessons Learned, and Recommendations

"Governance" has emerged in the last twenty years as a specialized field and practitioners involved in its discourse tend to be scholar-specialists. The discourse
within this universe of specialists has made the study of governance and the role
of rule of law reforms a challenging and serious matter. Frequently, the practical
issues which emerge for the governance practitioner in low- and middle-income
countries deal with fundamentals of social organization which challenge them
to more deeply understand the moral and value foundations upon which the
infrastructure of a society is established. There is, at the same time, something
of a tension here. Those who are governance practitioners may be impatient
about the relevance of theory to their day-to-day work. In this sense, they may
be functioning in a world that is somewhat distinct from the actual discourse
and influence of theoretical specialists. As a consequence, there is a tendency
to conclude that theory is too far removed from practice to be of direct value to
their work. Thus, there is a serious specialists' discourse about governance, and,
from a practical point of view, the possibility of a disconnect in terms of how
the insights of theory define the role of the governance practitioner, which are
in turn redefined by practical experiences. The World Bank is in a rarified position to close this gap between theory and practice with respect to governance
through rule of law reforms by reflecting on key lessons learned and contemplating a new (or at least complementary) model for operational engagement.

Lessons can be discerned from the above analysis, together with complementary literature reviews on anticorruption measures focusing on governance institutions and non-government anticorruption and accountability actors; as well as
a series of case studies examining the role and impact of Social Accountability
initiatives focusing on anti-corruption Third-Party Monitoring activities around
the world and a summary of evidentiary studies of the effectiveness and impact of
selected anticorruption initiatives. While several of these measures and analyses
help to raise awareness of corrupt practices, a key lesson emerging from this chapter is that most measurements described above are somewhat lacking. Several
do not provide much in-depth information about the forms, prevalence and

problems of corruption in different countries. They are useful as initial assessment tools but if we would like to investigate the core causes of corruption and governance assessment in a country we need to have more specialized tools to do so.

More accurate measurement tools have since been developed which enable researchers to target different aspects of governance. Advances in the field demonstrate that well-designed indicators can help researchers identify the institutional triggers of mis-governance and its effects. By discerning specific vulnerabilities in institutions, practitioners can focus anticorruption efforts for greater effect. At the same time, it is also clear that further developments in measurement are possible with the use of comprehensive methodologies, which incorporate several conventional methods and are purportedly designed for a specific type of analysis. With this in mind, a few recommendations seem to come into focus.

9.1 *Toward New Insights in Understanding, Tracking, and Measuring Governance, the Rule of Law, and Efforts to Counter Corruption*

Kaufmann, Recanatini and Biletsky pose the key question: how can such a rich and complex phenomenon as governance be measured consistently and across countries?[290] Munck and Verkuilen set out a design framework for mechanisms to analyze the quality of democracy, including at the conceptual level, considerations for measurement, and for the aggregation of data.[291] They emphasize the importance of conceptual clarity, attribute identification, and an analysis of how these attributes relate to each other and whether they might be aggregated after measurement. According to Kaufmann, Recanatini and Biletsky, this framework can be successfully implemented when developing empirical tools to assess the quality of governance and consists of the following steps: (1) Clearly define the concept to be measured, being deliberate about avoiding too broad or too narrow definitions; (2) Identify the significant features of the governance variables to be measured; (3) Undertake the measurement using multiple, unbiased indicators which could contribute to a single conceptual attribute and which can be crosschecked using multiple sources to enhance quality assurance; and (4) Aggregate, or compile, the data from across sources to create an index, ideally without losing much key data in the process.[292]

---

290   *See* Kaufmann, Recanatini & Biletsky, *supra* note 189.
291   Gerardo Munck & Jay Verkuilen, *Conceptualizing and Measuring Democracy: Evaluating Alternative Indices*, 35(1) Comp. Pol. Stud. 5–34, *available at* https://doi.org/10.1177/001041400203500101.
292   *See* Kaufmann, Recanatini & Biletsky, *supra* note 189.

McGee and Gaventa remind us that "how to measure" must be at the center of any commentary on the effectiveness of efforts to stem corruption and enable improved governance.[293] They assessed the effectiveness of a range of anticorruption programmatic work and focused on five sectors which are historically prone to corruption: (1) service delivery; (2) budget processes; (3) freedom of information; (4) natural resource governance; and (5) aid transparency. Their analysis yielded several findings, foremost of which was that the evidence of impact was uneven at best given the amount of attention and donor funding flowing into anticorruption efforts. They found that those studies with longer time horizons were unsurprisingly more robust, particularly with regard to service delivery and budget transparency, but that even in longstanding research areas more analysis was needed to discern the effectiveness of anticorruption efforts. They further found that in newer areas, such as relatively recent initiatives on natural resource transparency and aid transparency, there is likewise unsurprisingly less of a knowledge base from which to draw general conclusions about impact and effectiveness.[294] They subsequently argue in that in light of the relatively uncertain evidence of impact of anticorruption accountability and transparency programming, a need exists to re-think what "impact" actually means with respect to governance and anticorruption efforts.[295] They suggest a stronger focus on corruption triggers conditioned by power and politics, revising the larger theory of change concerning the potential relationship between transparency, accountability and corruption, and adapting efforts to monitor and evaluate corruption to account for practical insights which may emerge.[296]

With this in mind, it might be useful to set out several steps which could enable the effective measurement of governance, with an emphasis on tracking and combatting corruption.

Step 1: Unbundle and clearly define the concepts of governance and the rule of law. As mentioned earlier, the concepts of "governance" and "rule of law" have long been the subject of definitional imprecision, and have variously covered the quality of decision-making or policy-making processes; the processes

---

293   Rosemary McGee &John Gaventa, *Synthesis Report – Review of Impact and Effectiveness of Transparency and Accountability Initiatives* (Institute of Development Studies, working paper prepared for the Transparency and Accountability Initiative Workshop on October 14–15, 2010), *available at* https://www.ids.ac.uk/download.php?file=files/dmfile/IETASynthesisReportMcGeeGaventaFinal28Oct2010.pdf.

294   *Id.*

295   Rosemary McGee & John Gaventa, *Shifting Power? Assessing the Impact of Transparency and Accountability Initiatives* 1–39 (IDS Working Paper, Issue 383, November 2011), *available at* https://onlinelibrary.wiley.com/doi/ epdf/10.1111/j.2040-0209.2011.00383_2.x.

296   *Id.*

by which governments are selected or succeeded; the quality or efficiency of the implementation of selected government functions, such as public service delivery, and more. Articulation – and adherence – to singular and consistent definitions of both concepts, which are acknowledged and adopted across governometric instruments would add key value to efforts to strengthen these phenomena, as well as to better track and counteract disablers of good governance and the effectiveness of the rule of law, such as widespread corruption.

   Step 2: Explicitly identify key aspects of good governance practices and what counts as the effective rule of law. This is linked to, and build upon, Step 1 above, since only by defining both concepts can they be disaggregated into their respective constituent aspects which might be cross-applicable across contexts. For example, when one considers how a government is constituted (aspect 1), specific measures may include the level of input citizens have had the selection or election of government leaders; whether and to whom these leaders are accountable for their decisions and actions; whether and how redress mechanisms are in place; and whether and how successive governments are constituted. The relative fragility or stability of the government can also be measured, as can whether citizens believe that the government selection process is legitimate. Likewise, when one considers the responsiveness and effectiveness of policy-making to citizens' needs (aspect 2), specific measures may likewise include public perceptions about the quality of service delivery; the extent to which businesses, including SMEs, experience burdens by administrative processes or regulation; the extent to which transparency mechanisms are in place to provide clear and timely data and information on policy implementation and related quality assurance processes. When one considers whether citizens approve of government decisions and actions and the extent to which government is honoring its social contract with the people it governs (aspect 3), specific measures may again include public perceptions and approval ratings for particular government policies or actions; and perceptions about the prevalence of corruption at the national or subnational level. These are only indicative aspects, but each identified aspect would ideally comprise a set of measures based on good quality and timely data from traditional[297] or new[298] sources, which can be analyzed separately or collectively to provide an indication about the quality of national or sub-national governance in a country.

---

297   *See, e.g.,* World Bank, The World Development Indicators, *available at* https://datatopics .worldbank.org/world-development-indicators/ (last visited July 11, 2022).

298   *See, e.g.,* World Bank, *Big data in action for government: big data innovation in public services, policy, and engagement* (2017), *available at* https://documents.worldbank.org/en /publication/documents-reports/documentdetail/176511491287380986/big-data-in -action-for-government-big-data-innovation-in-public-services-policy-and-engagement.

Step 3: Deploy a considered range of measurement tools and good quality data sources. To quantify and help explain the quality of governance and the rule of law in a particular context, a range of tools and data sources should be used. This includes traditional survey methods (which exhibit the standard best practice features, including a statistically representative sample), which can gather respondent input across their perceptions and experiences, and which can likewise focus on objective measures. Survey tools include household surveys; public opinion polls; enterprise surveys; surveys of public officials; surveys of subject matter experts; and more. Other sources of data can likewise be useful as complements to assess the quality of governance and the rule of law where available, such as administrative data, and relatively newer sources of data obtained, for example, from mobile devices, sensors, satellites, and other third-party or big data sources.

Step 4: Aggregate. Aggregation refers to the process of summarizing information which contained in multiple variables and highly correlated in one (i.e. the factor) which is selected as the most authoritative to describe the relationships among them. The aggregation method is always the same (i.e. factor analysis or unobservable components); the difference is the level, or aggregate information by country to enable cross-country comparisons, or aggregate information by institutions to enable cross- institutional comparisons. The most effective aggregation is undertaken without losing much information in the process, and so researchers should be deliberate when selecting the level of aggregation for their analysis.

Step 5: Consider context. As mentioned earlier, governance can not only be viewed as formal institutions, rules and regulations; it is also comprised of informal rules, norms, and third-party actors which can individually or collectively affect governance outcomes. Corduneanu-Huci, Hamilton and Ferrer explain that the political-economic environment that accounts for the various complex interactions which collectively comprise governance – including root problems, why they persist, and how they can be changed – must be understood in order to effectively navigate a policy landscape.[299] Measuring these interactions is complicated, as Ian Bremmer has pointed out "Politics, after all, is influenced by human behavior and the sudden confluence of events, for which no direct calibrations exist."[300] An effective political economy analysis accordingly deploys a range of proxy variables to quantify the quality of governance.

---

299   *See* Corduneanu Huci et al., *supra* note 180, at 71 (citing Patrick Chabal & Jean-Pascal Daloz, Africa Works: The Political Instrumentalization of Disorder (1999)).

300   Ian Bremmer, *Managing Risk in an Unstable World*, Harv. Bus. Rev. (June 2005), *available at* https://hbr.org/2005/06/managing-risk-in-an-unstable-world.

9.2   *The Policy Sciences May Help Enable Multilateral Organizations,*
        Including the World Bank, to Inaugurate a New Global Paradigm of
        Support for Good Governance

With the above steps in mind, and particularly in light of step 5, multilateral organizations could benefit from more consistent use of analytical frameworks like the Policy Sciences to enable more and better support for governance and rule of law in low- and middle-income countries. In devising the Policy Sciences framework, Lasswell and McDougal created a new paradigm for inquiry about governance and the rule of law, and both conditions for and approaches to the effective institution of related reforms. The Policy Sciences likewise offers a range of pragmatic insights about the socio-cultural, political implications, and policy consequences of generating and communicating knowledge in societies in which that knowledge is a base of power and authority, and a vital part of social, political and cultural development. The framework particularly emphasizes the role and importance of human decision-making. A range of scholars and practitioners – including and particularly in the governance and rule of law development space – have only relatively recently begun to understand the need for comprehensive understandings of layered, interconnected, and complex web of human relationships and values, and their combined impact on decision processes in context, as necessary preconditions before an effective reform process could even be conceptually possible; in other words, many are now arriving at conclusions and recommendations which Lasswell and McDougal comprehensively articulated more than six decades ago.

As suggested above, to create a contextual map of the quality of governance, the effectiveness of the rule of law, and the prevalence of corruption in a country context, the first priority is to identify operative participants in the world social and power processes, then clarify their perspectives, demands, and expectations, determine their bases of power, clarify the contexts in which they operate, unpack how they develop strategies to achieve specific outcomes, understand what action is taken to implement these strategies, ascertain whether the desired outcomes are achieved, and determine the effects of the action. Mapping the values inherent in each problem category could likewise surface valuable insights on what enhances or inhibits the likelihood of achieving sustainable development. Put another way, the necessary elements of a new paradigm of governance and rule of law support could include approaches which are: (i) context-sensitive; (ii) problem-oriented; (iii) multi-method; and (iv) interdisciplinary, with a focus on the dynamics of global interdependence and global inter-determination.[301]

---

301   Winston Nagan, Craig Hammer & Maxat Akhmetkaliyeva, *Toward a New Theory of Sustainable Development: Drawing on Insights from Developments in Modern Legal Theory* 45–57, 3 Cadmus 2 (May 2017).

To illustrate, a contextual mapping exercise which focuses on governance and the implicit values which condition the likelihood of localized or widespread laws that align with social norms, could create a stronger basis for better understanding the appropriate theory and prospects of what counts as good governance in the common global interest, and how to customize approaches to local context more effectively. By way of a simple example, it may be useful to look to the work of Richard Posner, who views economics as a matter concerned with wealth and wealth generation. In short, he has asserted that wealth is a justifiable economic objective, and has set out a model of economic social process based on wealth acquisition. His model postulates that legal rules and political institutions in general should efficiently maximize the benefit-to-cost ratio and thus increase the wealth of society in the aggregate, where efficiency is indicated by the total amount of individual "willingnesses to pay," which Posner uses as shorthand to describe an individual's value judgment of whether it is worth moving – or worth resisting a move – from one social state to another.[302] In this model, wealth is both a desired goal and a base of power from which to acquire more wealth. The problem with this model is that it limits the focus of the economic inquirer, since it excludes other values associated with basic human needs and claims, which are fundamental to human and social capital and are thus important to a sustainable political economy for the future.

With this in mind, advanced legal theory has generated a series of intellectual tasks to underpin a new paradigmatic approach to measure and support governance and rule of law transformations; these tasks include:

- Identification and description of good governance and rule of law policy perspectives (i.e. normative aspects of how to support and enable good governance);
- Identification and descriptions of good governance and rule of law policy in actual operation (the 'operational code which supports good governance and enables effective rule of law);
- Emphasis on decision-making and qualities of authority and control relevant to good governance and rule of law in the global social process;
- Emphasis on authoritative decision from global to local arenas relating to good governance and rule of law at different levels of social organization;
- Focus on society and the human agents who enable and constrain the exercise of good governance and the effectiveness of rule of law, and related social consequences (explicit identification of the human capital resources); and

---

302   Richard Posner, Economic Analysis of Law 4 (1972).

– Focus on public and private policy interventions implicating human capital
  in good governance and rule of law with local to global impacts and results.
In short, legal theory provides robust guidance for the development of a
more comprehensive and effective development paradigm to support and
enable good governance and the effective rule of law, which has largely been
absent from conventional economic theory. By setting out a series of tools and
approaches to enable clarification of the value institutional foundations of
economic order vital to good governance and the effective rule of law, cataloguing and analysis of legally relevant events, and understanding of the anatomy
of decision-making through contextual mapping, legal theory further clarifies
a spectrum of options – and related strategies for or against – economic and
policy interventions from persuasion to coercion, cutting across diplomacy,
propaganda, economic incentives or pressure, and the threat or use of force.

The central contributions that modern legal theory can bring to a more realistic and responsible theory for inquiry about the political economy of good
governance and effective rule of law in essence focus on the role of the individual observer, who carries the weight of their creativity, invention, experience,
enterprise, social and human capital, and more into his or her role as observer;
on the standpoint of this observer, such that a contextual inquiry is undertaken from as comprehensive a vantage point as possible to maximize the likelihood of objective observation, or else acknowledges and aims to account for
the various forces acting on the observer which might affect the process of
observation and thus condition or influence any insights discerned; and on
the overarching importance of policy-centered intervention, such that this
observer is prepared to provide policy guidance through interventions which
aim to solve the problems discerned to advance the common interest.

The creation and distribution of effective power is an important outcome
of the global social process. Power in society is expressed in terms of decision-making. Decision-making by operational actors in the conventional
paradigm has created and sustains the enabling environment for corruption,
poor governance, ineffective rule of law, and the drift toward plutocracy in the
global community. A new paradigm of governance and rule of law support
should focus on how effective and controlling decisions are made and put into
effect in the public interest of all social participants. Unpacking this public and
private decision-making is a necessary first step toward understanding the creation and the distribution of the values which underpin the policy process of
the conventional paradigm, and the enabling conditions of good governance
and effective rule of law.

Key lessons have emerged from legal philosophy throughout history and
from operational experience through practice by multilaterals like the World

Bank, toward the development of a new paradigm in which support for good governance and the effective rule of law can transcend narrow disciplinary boundaries, emphasize open access to new knowledge, facilitate the availability of new tools for human productivity, embrace the primacy of interrelated and interdependent implementation of governance solutions and eschew partial or sectoral approaches, surface, implement, and celebrate global solutions and coordinated actions by the international community, and recognize that approaches to resolve challenges are subject to conflicting claims, priorities and interests, for which concerted efforts at reconciliation are necessary.

PART 4

Human Rights

..

CHAPTER 13

Ensuring Compliance with and Execution of Human Rights Commitments

*Eckart Klein**

1 Introduction: The Copernican Turn of International Law

The topic opens a vast field and goes to the basics of international law. Human rights are today an essential part of public international law. As long as only States, international organizations, and some special entities for historical reasons – like the Holy See – figured as subjects of international law, rights of individuals could not become a matter for international regulation. Only indirectly favourable effects for individuals could follow from the existence of objective international rules based on customary international law or general principles of law or could be created by the conclusion of treaties providing for respective protective State obligations. The manifestation of human rights in international law was dependent on the recognition of individuals as holders of rights on the international plane, and, consequently, as subjects of international law.

As of today, a multitude of human rights have been acknowledged on the universal and regional level. These acknowledged rights entitle the individuals to claim them in their own right, without being mediated by their State.[1] The appearance of the individuals and their rights on the international scene has changed public international law as a whole and has led to far-reaching consequences. They were essentially summarized by the dictum of the International Criminal Tribunal for the Former Yugoslavia (ICTY) in the *Tadić*

---

* Dr. iur.utr. habil. (1980 Heidelberg), 1969–1981 Research Fellow at the Max Planck Institute for Comparative Public Law and Public International Law Heidelberg, 1974–76 Law clerk with the President of the German Federal Constitutional Court in Karlsruhe, Professor of Public Law, Public International and European Law (University of Mainz 1981–94, University of Potsdam 1994–2008), Founder and Director of the Human Rights Centre of the University of Potsdam 1994–2009, judge at the Higher Administrative Court of the Land Rhenania Palatinat 1984–95 and Land Brandenburg 1995–2001, judge at the Constitutional Court of the Land Bremen 1995–2011, member of the UN Human Rights Committee 1995–2002, ad hoc judge at the European Court of Human Rights in Strasbourg between 1998 and 2011.

1 This statement does not mean that the procedural way to claim the rights is always open; see *infra* 3.2.

Case: "A State-sovereignty-oriented approach has been gradually supplanted by a human-being-oriented approach", moving human rights to the centre of international law.[2] The move to a human-being-oriented approach was well justified. In earlier times, public international law was only concerned with the relations among States as expressed by rules governing their behaviour in times of peace and war. Both, peace and war, were equally accepted as legal ways of realizing the States' interests.[3] In open contrast to this position, the Preamble of the UN Charter (1945) clearly indicates the connection between human rights and peace: it spells out that the peoples of the UN are determined "to save succeeding generations from the scourge of war" and "to reaffirm faith in fundamental human rights."

The Preamble of the Universal Declaration of Human Rights (1948) underlines this idea stating that, "the recognition of the inherent dignity and of equal and inalienable rights of all members of the human family is the foundation of freedom, justice and peace in the world." Since human rights form an indispensable basis of peace and, conversely, peace alone can assure the full enjoyment of human rights, (aggressive) wars can no longer be considered a legally acknowledged state of affairs. The prohibition of waging war is thus no longer merely an idea that should remove unhappy and finally destructive conduct from the States themselves; the more important pillar now is the realization that human rights are severely endangered, and mostly directly violated by warfare. The idea of human rights necessarily leads to the perception that the State exists to serve human beings and not the other way around.[4] Here the Copernican turn of international law becomes understandable. Just as any interference with human rights needs to be justified, going to war has to be justified too – and there are not many possibilities for that. If, therefore, human rights have acquired a central place from which public international law must be conceived, compliance with human rights commitments must be a permanent concern of very high priority for all subjects of international law.[5]

---

2 ICTY, *Prosecutor v. Tadić, Decision on the Defense Motion for Interlocutory Appeal on Jurisdiction*, Case No. IT-94-1-A (Appeal), 2.10.1995, para. 97.

3 Carl von Clausewitz, Vom Kriege 34 (Frankfurt a.M., Berlin, Wien 1981, originally 1832). See for the development to the prohibition of military force Christian Tomuschat, *Enforcement of International Law. From the Authority of Hard Law to the Impact of Flexible Methods*, 79 Zeitschrift für ausländisches öffentiches Recht und Völkerrecht (ZaöRV) 579, 587–597 (2019).

4 *Cf.* Art. 1 First Draft of the Basic Law (Entwurf von Herrenchiemsee) of 1948, in 1 Jahrbuch des öffentlichen Rechts 48 (Gerhard Leibholz & Hermann von Mangoldt eds., Tübingen 1951).

5 At this point, one may recognize a certain convergence of general interest and individual interest, but by no means their identity. Limitations of the individual rights for the sake of the common good, but also curtailment of the general interest in favour of the right of the

Consequently, the ways and means that are available to ensure compliance are not just technical niceties, but cornerstones of the international law edifice (2. and 3.). The same is true for the devices available to enforce legal behaviour after the appeal to the law has been ignored (4.). A conclusion will round out this contribution (5.).

The following thoughts about these issues are, hopefully, not an unworthy gift for my good friend and colleague Siegfried Wiessner. He has dedicated his academic and much of his private life to supporting human rights in theory and practice, generally and very concretely for members of minorities and indigenous peoples.[6] His selflessness was always inspiring. The establishment of the LL.M./ J.S.D. Program in Intercultural Human Rights at his home University, St. Thomas, in Miami has enabled hundreds of students from all over the world to gain insights into the importance of human rights and manifold problems which their protection repeatedly presents. I am grateful to Siegfried that since the beginning of that project I have been able to participate in this endeavour over the years.

2   Human Rights and Ensuring Compliance: Definitions

Human rights are subjective legal entitlements of individuals or groups of human beings and, by the same token, objective legal obligations for the States and all public authorities.[7] These obligations are, on the international level, binding on States just by their existence. Their binding force is not dependent on their incorporation into domestic law. As legal obligations, they need a valid

---

individual may result from this never permanently fixed relationship; *see* Eckart Klein, *On Limits and Restrictions of Human Rights. A Systematic Attempt, in* Strengthening Human Rights Protections in Geneva, Israel, the West Bank and Beyond (Joseph E. David, Yaël Ronen, Yuval Shany & J.H.H. Weiler eds., Cambridge 2021).

6   Siegfried Wiessner's great contribution to the Final ILA Report on the Rights of Indigenous Peoples (Sofia 2012) as Chair of the pertinent ILA Committee must be particularly mentioned; see further from the rich work of Siegfried Wiessner, *The Cultural Rights of Indigenous Peoples: Achievements and Continuing Challenges*, 22 Eur. J. Int'l L. 121–140 (2011); id., *The State and Indigenous Peoples: The Historic Significance of ILA Resolution No. 5/2012, in* Der Staat im Recht. Festschrift für Eckart Klein 1357–1368 (Marten Breuer et al. eds., Berlin 2013).

7   This does not mean that only States are obligated; also international organizations can be bearers of obligations; *cf.* Frédéric Mégret & Florian Hoffmann, *The UN as a Human Rights Violator? Some Reflections on the United Nations Changing Human Rights Responsibilities*, 25 Hum. Rts. Q. 314, 314–42 (2003). For the much discussed issue of the importance of human rights for corporations, see only Denise Wallace, Human Rights and Business. A Policy-Oriented Perspective (Leiden Boston 2014).

legal ground. Most human rights today are treaty-based, obligating all States that have ratified the treaty, not having withdrawn from it and not having declared admissible reservations. Another legal basis may be presented by customary international law or general principles of law. Soft law as such will not suffice, but one must always examine whether a specific provision has grown into a legal norm or should be taken into consideration in the interpretation process. Similarly, mere moral norms cannot form the basis of a legally relevant decision.[8] It is quite another issue as to how far legal rules may depart from any morality without losing the claim of validity.[9]

The legal expectation regarding norm compliance is directed at the complete fulfilment of the obligations concerned. This means that non-compliance is equated with a breach of a legal obligation; not merely representing a technical problem in the dynamic process of fulfilment.[10] In order to determine a breach one has to take account of the scope and content of the obligations; including the limits and possible restrictions of the rights which have to be respected, protected, and ensured by States.[11] Likewise, admissible derogations from the existing legal commitments must be considered.[12] All these steps require careful interpretation to be achieved on the basis of the Vienna Convention on the Law of Treaties of 1969 (VCLT), whose relevant articles are recognized by the International Court of Justice (ICJ) as reflecting customary international law.[13]

Compliance with human rights commitments primarily means a conduct of the States that fully realizes their obligations, and, therefore, avoids any violations of human rights guarantees.[14] Beside this preventive purpose, ensuring compliance also includes cessation, non-repetition and reparation if a human

---

8   Eckart Klein, *The Importance and Challenges of Values-Based Legal Orders*, 10 Intercultural Hum. Rts. L. Rev. 1, 8 (2015).

9   *See* Georg Jellinek, Die sozialethische Bedeutung von Recht, Unrecht und Strafe 45 and 47: „Recht als ethisches Minimum" (2nd ed. Berlin 1908); critically Gustav Radbruch, Rechtsphilosophie 138 (5th ed. Stuttgart 1956).

10   *See* to this definition Dinah Shelton, *Introduction, in* Commitment and Compliance. The Role of Non-Binding Norms in the International Legal System 5 (Dinah Shelton ed., Oxford 2000); different Martti Koskenniemi, The Gentle Civilizer of Nations. The Rise and Fall of International Law 1870–1960, 496 n. 295 (Cambridge 2002).

11   Beth A. Simmons, Mobilizing for Human Rights 27 *et seq.* (Cambridge 2009).

12   E.g., Art. 4 ICCPR, Art. 15 ECHR.

13   Bosnia and Herzegovina v. Serbia and Montenegro, 2007 ICJ Reports para.160 (Judgment of 26 February).

14   It is doubtful whether the term "may be necessary to give effect to the rights" (Art. 2, para. 2, ICCPR) asks for more than to avoid any violation or rather demands optimization.

right has been violated.[15] In a broader sense, ensuring compliance as it is understood here, also entails the possibility of execution of legal findings of violations declared by competent international entities or bodies.[16]

3   Ways and Means of Ensuring Commitments

3.1   *Self-Responsibility of States*

Regarding the compliance with human rights obligations foremost the approach of the States themselves to their accepted duties is decisive. Too many States do not take these duties seriously, having adopted them just for reasons of propaganda instead of well-intentioned concern for their citizens.[17] It certainly helps the State organs to apply their international obligations if they have been introduced into domestic law, because the organs, of course, are more familiar with their own internal law than international law. The interpretation of the norms by national organs can differ from international bodies' understanding. The difficult question of who has the final word can hardly be evaded. At any rate, the honest preparedness of States to honour their obligations is the best condition for a particularly effective protection of human rights. If the States act in this spirit there is a good chance that human rights violations can be avoided from the outset, or, if not, can at least be repaired according to the remedies provided for by the national or international system. The good will of the State organs can be supported by NGOs as far as they are able and willing to have a sharp look at the human rights situation in the country. It is always a clear indication of a failing interest of the State when the work of NGOs is neglected or characterized as directed from outside or even prohibited.

One has to take account of the difficult relationship of States to human rights. States are addressed by human rights norms as the most probable violators, on the one hand, and as guarantors of the rights on the other. In many cases, States do not meet the expectations as protector of these rights. In the

---

15 Arts 27, 30, 31, 34 on Responsibility of States for Internationally Wrongful Acts (ARS), UN Doc. A/RES/56/83, Annex (28 January 2002).

16 Sometimes "enforcement" is strictly distinguished from "compliance." *See* Rainer Grote, Mariela Morales Antoniazzi & Davide Paris, *Compliance in Human Rights Law: Issues, Concept, Methodology, in* Research Handbook on Compliance in International Law 1, 3 (Rainer Grote, Mariela Morales Antoniazzi & Davide Paris eds., Cheltenham, UK, Northampton, USA 2021).

17 On the various reasons why States ratify human rights treaties, see Stephen D. Krasner, Sovereignty: Organized Hypocrisy 121–123 (Princeton 1999).

course of the growing institutionalisation of international law that started with the League of Nations and accelerated after World War II with the foundation of the UN, international institutions were created endowed with the competence to interpret and apply human rights norms, thus restricting the power of exclusive self-interpretation by the States.[18] Many varied entities of different nature were established. They range from courts and quasi-judicial bodies to political institutions on the global and the regional level. It is not the intention of this contribution to give a detailed description of all these bodies; rather, I shall try to emphasize some characteristic traits of the institutions involved and the instruments they use to perform their duties, and to generally analyse their work.

Usually, international bodies will only get the opportunity to tackle human rights issues, if the claim of a violation has already been made. Human rights issues will be brought to the attention of the institutions just mentioned in two main ways. Either the individuals themselves are enabled to claim a violation of their rights by a certain State (individual complaints), or a State may refer an alleged breach of the human rights obligations by another State to such an international body (inter-State cases).

3.2 *International Courts*

Particularly two aspects point to courts as the institutions best qualified to determine whether human rights violations have occurred: First, the institutionalized independence and impartiality of the members of the courts, and, second, their capacity to hand down final and legally binding decisions. Without these two prerequisites, States would hardly abide by the judgments since the underlying facts of a case will be very often controversial. Actually, all founding treaties or statutes of international courts provide such independence (from other State organs) and impartiality (with respect to the parties to the dispute or interested others) of the judges as well as the binding force of the judgments. Since all the judges of international Courts are elected, their elections are subject to substantial rules. For example, according to the European Convention of Human Rights (ECHR) the judges of the European Court of Human Rights (ECtHR) are elected by the Parliamentary Assembly of the Council of Europe by a majority vote on the basis of criteria including their independence and impartiality from a list containing three nominations

---

18   *Cf.* Hersch Lauterpacht, International Law and Human Rights 79 fn. 15 (London 1950), quoting from one of his earlier lectures in 1943: "The habitation of the rights of man within the exclusive precincts of the sovereign State has proved insecure."

proposed by the State whose judge has to be elected; every State has one judge on the bench.

Nominees have to introduce themselves to a special committee of the Council which then adopts a recommendation for the vote of the Assembly's Plenary. When the elected judges take their seat for the first time, they have to swear or give a solemn declaration that they will act independently and impartially.[19] If a judge is biased in a concrete case and therefore cannot participate in the procedure, the home State of the judge may nominate another person as judge *ad hoc* who also has to fulfil all the criteria to be elected.[20] The Rules of Court also fix certain political, administrative or professional activities that would be incompatible with the performance of the judicial duties.[21] The exclusion of re-election after a period of nine years at the Court prevents pressure on the judges by their States.[22] The possibility that the national judge is inclined to decide in favour of his home State can still not be completely eliminated. But to exclude the national judge from the deliberations of the court just because of this natural affiliation would deprive the court of knowledge of the legal order where the case had evolved.

The judgments of international courts are final; they definitely decide a case and can bring the dispute to rest. Regarding the ECtHR, the judgments of the Grand Chamber become immediately final and binding, those of the Chambers only if they were not appealed to the Grand Chamber or the appeal is not accepted by a committee of the Grand Chamber.[23] In spite of the finality and binding force of judgments, States are not always ready to respect them. This would not only be a (further) violation of the treaty, but also generate another dispute if more than one State had participated in the procedure (inter-State cases). Such inter-State procedures are provided for by all the three regional human rights systems and were not in common use, but their number has recently increased perhaps indicating a better understanding of the States parties' collective responsibility for human rights.[24]

---

19   Art. 22 ECHR, Art. 3 Rules of ECtHR.

20   Art. 29 Rules of ECtHR.

21   Art. 4 Rules of ECtHR.

22   Art. 23 ECHR.

23   Arts. 44 and 46, para. 1, ECHR.

24   Michel de Salvia, *Chronique du contentieux interétatique devant la Cour européenne des droits de l'homme,* 33 Revue trimestrielle des droits de l'homme 295–304 (2022). From 1956 to 2021, only 28 inter-State cases came before the Court.

Up to now, there is no special human rights court on the global level.[25] This does not mean that other international courts on this plane do not contribute to the protection of human rights. E.g., the International Court of Justice (ICJ) may in an inter-State affair assess the claim of a State that another State has violated the human rights of its citizens[26] or, by an advisory opinion, express a similar view.[27] While in the first case the judgment of the Court would be legally binding on the parties,[28] an advisory opinion lacks this effect,[29] but because of the high reputation of the ICJ it is still a very authoritative voice in the international legal discussion, that should not be undervalued. On the regional basis, advisory opinions can also play an important role, but only at the request of Member States or the Organisation. Thus the African Court on Peoples' and Human Rights (ACtHR) and the Inter-American Court of Human Rights (IACtHR) are competent to provide advisory opinions in human rights matters.[30] A prominent recent example is the Opinion of the IACtHR of 9 November 2020, at the request of Colombia regarding the consequences of the separation of Venezuela from the inter-American system, and from the OAS for the future protection of human rights in this country.[31] Also the International Criminal Court (ICC) has a human rights-protective function. Though its jurisdiction is restricted to crimes of genocide and against humanity, war crimes and the crime of aggression, human rights will always be affected by those crimes, and obtain at least indirect protection if the crimes are brought to justice before the ICC.[32]

---

25   The proposal to set up an International Court of Human Rights was made by Australia during the discussion of the UN Commission on Human Rights on the drafting of a Covenant on Human Rights in June 1949; see Lauterpacht, International Law, *supra* note 18, at 278–279, 308.

26   LaGrand (Germany v. United States of America), ICJ Reports 2001, 466, paras. 77 and 89 (Judgment of 27 June 2001); Application of the International Convention on the Elimination of All Forms of Racial Discrimination (Georgia v. Russian Federation), Preliminary Objections, ICJ Reports 2011, 70 (Judgment of 1 April 2011).

27   Legal Consequences of the Construction of a Wall in the Occupied Palestinian Territory, ICJ Reports 2004, 136 (Advisory Opinion of 9 July 2004).

28   The same is true for orders of the Court on interim measures, *infra* note 85.

29   Art. 94, para.1, UN Charter, Arts 59 and 60 Statute of ICJ; Art. 96 UN Charter, Art. 65 Statute ICJ.

30   Art. 4 Protocol to the African Charter; Art. 64 American Convention on Human Rights (ACHR). However, the ECtHR is excluded from giving advisory opinions in matters where it is competent to decide on cases regarding alleged violations of the human rights enshrined in the ECHR, Art. 47 para. 2 ECHR.

31   IACtHR, Advisory Opinion OC-26/20 of 9 November 2020, 41 Hum. Rts. L.J. 29–67 (2021).

32   For the legal relationship between humanitarian law (IHRL) and human rights law, see Christian Tomuschat, Human Rights. Between Idealism and Realism 337–338 (Oxford 3rd ed. 2014).

As holders of rights, individuals should be enabled to claim and defend them. However, to draw this consequence was another important step in the evolution of human rights law and, because of the general mediation of individuals by their States, by no means obvious. This is why still today individuals do not regularly have immediate access to international human rights courts. Rather, this track has to be opened by the consent of the States establishing a court and its procedural law. While the ECHR and the African (Banjul) Charter on Human and Peoples' Rights (ACHPR) have now provided for such a procedure, no such opportunity exists under the American Convention on Human Rights (ACHR) and the Rules of Procedure of the Inter-American Court of Human Rights (IACtHR). Four steps of the evolution are discernible. At a first step, the individuals may lodge petitions, not to a human rights court, but to a commission that is competent to assess the case and find a violation, but not to decide the case with binding force.[33] At a second step, a court has been established and the commission may submit the case to the court, if the State concerned has accepted the jurisdiction of the court.[34] At a third step, individuals may institute cases directly before the court, but only if the State involved has declared its acceptance to receive cases of this kind.[35] Finally, at a fourth step, individuals have direct access to the human rights court, without dependence on an intermediate procedure before a commission or a special consent of the States parties to the human rights treaty. Rather, the compulsory jurisdiction of the court is automatically acknowledged by becoming a State party.[36] Of course, the procedural conditions of admissibility of the complaints or petitions must always be met, inter alia the requirement of the exhaustion of domestic remedies. Further, the regional courts and, in the case of the inter-American system, the Commission shall always be open to reach a friendly or amicable settlement in a case pending before them.[37]

---

33   So until Protocol to the African Charter on Human and Peoples' Rights on the Establishment of an African Court on Human and Peoples' Rights of 1998, operational since 2009; *see* Art. 56–59 African Charter on Peoples' and Human Rights (African Charter).

34   This was the case according to the ECHR at the beginning of the system in 1950. This is still the situation under the Inter-American system, where the IACtHR can only be approached by the States parties and the Commission, Art. 61 ACHR.

35   Arts 5, para. 3, and 34. para. 6 Protocol to the African Charter. Of the 31 States having ratified the Protocol only nine allowed the Court to decide on individual complaints, and four States have withdrawn their permission until the end of 2021; *see* Martin Faix & Ayyoub Jamali, *Is the African Court on Human and Peoples' Rights in an Existential Crisis?*, 40 Netherlands Q. Hum. Rts. 56, 63–64 (2022).

36   Art. 34 ECHR, since 1998. Consequently, the European Commission of Human Rights has been abolished at the same time.

37   Art. 9 Protocol to the African Charter; Art. 39 ECHR; Art. 48, para. 1 lit. f ACHR.

3.3   Quasi-Judicial Bodies

In practise, quasi-judicial bodies play a more important role on the universal plane than courts, indicating the clearly recognizable caution of States regarding legally binding judgments. Most international human rights treaties have established committees in order to monitor the compliance of the States parties; the only exception is the Convention on the Prevention and Punishment of the Crime of Genocide whose early adoption, on 9 December 1948, one day before the Universal Declaration of Human Rights, shows the sovereignty-based reserve of the States to admit a permanent control of their conduct.[38] From the creation of the International Convention on the Elimination of Racial Discrimination (1961), and the two International Covenants on Civil and Political Rights (1966), and Economic, Social and Cultural Rights (1966) to the International Convention for the Protection of All Persons from Enforced Disappearance (2006), a Committee was established for monitoring tasks.[39]

The numbers of the Committee members range from 10 to 23.[40] They are elected by secret ballot from a list of persons nominated by the States parties at a meeting of these States for a period of 4 years. While the former conventions allow indefinite re-election if the person has again been nominated by a State party, the more recent conventions provide only for one re-election.[41] This change represents a prudent strengthening of the independence of the members. The Committee members are serving in their personal capacity independently and impartially. As the rules of procedure of the various committees organise the performance of their work quite similar to that of courts, one must actually speak of quasi-judicial bodies having in mind that the committees cannot hand down legally binding judgments.

Common to all these committees is their task to receive periodic reports on the enjoyment of the human rights guaranteed in the respective treaty, to discuss the situation, welcoming or criticising the developments, and, finally,

---

38   The provision on the competence of the ICJ for the interpretation and fulfilment of this Convention in cases of disputes between the Contracting parties (Art. IX) was a courageous step, but reservations to this provision are possible; see Reservations to the Convention on the Prevention and Punishment of the Crime of Genocide, Advisory Opinion, 1951 ICJ Reports 15–69 (28 May 1951).

39   Also the above mentioned Commissions working within the regional human rights systems should be counted for quasi-judicial bodies though they are performing their task in close connection with a court.

40   10: Committees on Torture and Enforced Disappearance; 23: CEDAW. Four committees, among them the committees of the two Covenants count 18 members. Migrant workers: 14.

41   Art. 34 para. 7 Convention of the Rights of Persons with Disabilities (2006) and Art. 26 para. 4 International Convention for the Protection of All Persons from Enforced Disappearance (2006).

to adopt concluding observations containing recommendations, which are either, delivered to the State concerned and published in a report sent to the UN General Assembly, and/or to the Economic and Social Council. A follow-up mechanism attempts to ensure that the recommendations are seriously taken into account. The discussion of the next report will usually take up the deficiencies that had been noticed before and not yet repaired.[42]

A second task, which is not common to all committees from their creation, is to receive and consider communications from individuals claiming to be victims of a violation of any right set forth in the relevant Convention by a State party. This procedure, seen from the point of view of earlier perceptions of international law, is quite revolutionary; because it submits the behaviour of a State in relation to individuals, including their own nationals, to international control, it is up to the States parties to accept this competence of the committees by a special act, as the adoption of a protocol to the convention or a declaration under an article of the relevant convention.[43] The committee, beside a possible decision of inadmissibility, can adopt a view finding a violation of the rights or not. In case of a violation, the committee will ask the State concerned for cessation of the violation, for non-repetition and for an effective remedy. Though the views, different from judgments, do not entail a legal obligation for the State, this must not be equated with legal meaninglessness. Rather the State has to take the views seriously and to examine whether it will comply, or not, with its requests, and give understandable reasons for that.[44] The committees have established follow-up mechanisms to put pressure on the State for compliance. The highest numbers of individual communications are received by the UN Human Rights Committee and the Committees of CERD and CAT.[45]

---

42   For the discussion of the States reports see David Kretzmer & Eckart Klein, *The Human Rights Committee: Monitoring States Parties Reports*, in 45 Israel Y.B. on Hum. Rts. 133, 140 *et seq.* (2015).

43   E.g., Optional Protocol: ICCPR; ICESCR; CEDAW; CRC; CRPD (since 2007). Declarations: CERD, CAT, CED, CMW.

44   Tomuschat, Human Rights, *supra* note 32 at 266–268; UN Human Rights Committee (UNHRCtee), General Comment (GC) No. 33/2008 para. 13, UN Doc. CCPR/C/GC/33 (2008).

45   The UNHRCtee alone has issued 1,812 views (finding in 1,342 views violations) since 1977 when it started its work; *see* https://www.ungeneva.org/en/news-media/meeting-summary /2022/03/human-rights-committee-adopts-annual-report. The report was adopted on 24 March 2022. For the procedure of the UNHRCtee, see more closely Anja Seibert-Fohr & Christine Weniger, *Compliance Monitoring Under the International Covenant on Civil and Political Rights*, *in* Research Handbook on Compliance, *supra* note 16, at 425, 428 *et seq.*

There is a third instrument provided for by most conventions that can be used by the committees to protect human rights. Seven of the nine universal conventions provide for a procedure by which one State party can complain against another State party about violations of human rights,[46] but again such inter-state communications are not applicable without a special act of acceptance by a declaration, under a specific article of the convention or by a protocol.[47] While in the past no State had made any use of this protective instrument, in 2018 three inter-State communications were brought before the Committee on the Elimination of Racial Discrimination. The complaints of *Qatar v. Kingdom of Saudi-Arabia and United Arab Emirates* have been suspended, on the request of Qatar in 2021; the case of *State of Palestine v. Israel* is still pending.

Finally, speaking of the instruments at the committees' disposal, one should also mention the general comments (or recommendations) which have been emancipated from a part of the State reporting procedure to an autonomous monitoring instrument.[48] Based on the previous practice of the committees, the general comments (GC) include comments for the States regarding the content of their reports, commentaries to specific articles of the conventions, remarks to more general issues as denunciation or reservations and legal yardsticks for all those (branches of government, individuals, NGOs, national human rights institutions) who are willing to observe the human rights situation in a given country and are interested in the realization of the human rights guarantees according to the interpretation of the committees. The committees themselves frequently cite their own general comments in their views, and also general comments of other committees. This practice integrates the general comments in its monitoring work, and helps to form a coherent interpretation and application of the rights protected by the conventions.[49] It remains to be said that in this case the committees' emanations have no legally binding force but should be assessed as "authoritative interpretations" of the rights and the corresponding state obligations.[50]

---

46   Not CEDAW and CRPD.

47   E.g., Arts. 11–13 CERD; 41–43 ICCPR; Art. 21 CAT; Art. 32 CED; Art. 10 OP ICESCR; Art. 12 OP CAT.

48   *See, e.g.,* Art. 40 para. 4 ICCPR; Eckart Klein & David Kretzmer, *The UN Human Rights Committee: The General Comments – The Evolution of an Autonomous Monitoring Instrument,* in 58 German Y.B. Int'l L. 189–229 (2015).

49   Klein & Kretzmer, *ibid.* 226–227.

50   Helen Keller & Leena Grover, *General Comments of the Human Rights Committee and their Legitimacy, in* UN Human Rights Treaty Bodies: Law and Legitimacy 116, 187 (Helen Keller & Geir Ulfstein eds., Cambridge 2012).

Regional independent expert bodies occupied with human rights protection are very numerous and cannot be dealt with here in detail. Just to give two examples from Europe in the field of minority protection: The European Charter for Regional or Minority Languages of 1992 and the Framework Convention for the Protection of National Minorities of 1995 have established monitoring mechanisms to protect the relevant rights. The core of the mechanisms is a reporting procedure. The reports of the States parties to the treaties on the performance of their obligations are directed to the Committee of Ministers of the Council of Europe, which is supported by an Advisory Committee (Framework Convention), and a Committee of Experts (European Charter). Both independent bodies consider the periodic reports, and send their opinion (Convention), or evaluation report (Charter), back to the Committee of Ministers which usually adopts them including their recommendations. The monitoring process of the Committee of Experts (European Charter) is particularly interesting, because in preparing the report it widely uses written and oral information from the civil society, highly enriched by on-the-spot visits. However, in neither case has an individual complaint procedure been established.[51] Of course, one should also mention, beyond Europe, the important African Commission on Human and Peoples' Rights and the Inter-American Commission on Human Rights.[52]

3.4   *Political Bodies*

Numerous political bodies can be found on the global level, in particular in the UN system, being involved in the protection of human rights. Probably the most prominent actor in this field today is the UN Human Rights Council (HRC), a subsidiary body of the UN General Assembly, created in 2006, whose 47 State representatives are elected by the General Assembly for a three year term.[53] The HRC closely cooperates with the Office of the UN High Commissioner for Human Rights (UNHCHR). The Council's main task is to perform the Universal Periodic Review (UPR). According to this procedure, all 193 UN Member States, during a four-and-a-half year period, and again during the subsequent periods,

---

51   Stefan Oeter, *Conventions on the Protection of National Minorities, in* The Council of Europe. Its Law and Policies 542, 557 *et seq.* (Stefanie Schmahl & Marten Breuer eds., Oxford 2017); Rainer Hofmann, *Die Rahmenkonvention des Europarates zum Schutz nationaler Minderheiten,* 5 Menschenrechtsmagazin 63–73 (2000).

52   *See* Arts. 30–62 African (Banjul) Charter on Human and Peoples' Rights of 1981 (African Charter), OAU Doc. CAB/LEG/67/3 rev. 5; Arts 34–51 Inter-American Convention on Human Rights (American Convention) of 1969, OAS, Official Records OEA/Ser. K/XVI/I:I., Doc. 65, Rev. 1.

53   UN Doc. A/RES/60/251.

have to present a report on the human rights situation in the country taking as yardstick the Universal Declaration of Human Rights. The State reports are supplemented by documents of the Office of the UNHCHR based on the findings of the relevant UN human rights bodies as the treaty bodies, and of NGOs. The examination of the report takes 3.5 hours, giving the State under review the opportunity to present its own picture of the human rights situation in the country, followed by a general discussion about the situation including the suggestions of recommendations. A group of three States (troika) prepares the outcome document – containing the results of the debate including the recommendations made – and the voluntary commitments accepted by the State under review. Before the adoption of the report by the Council's plenary, there is another opportunity to point to critical issues. The State concerned is expected to inform the Council during the next two years about the steps undertaken to fulfil the accepted recommendations.[54]

Apart from the UPR, the HRC is also occupied with a complaint procedure, more or less taken over from its predecessor institution, the Human Rights Commission established by ECOSOC. Here individuals, groups and NGOs may turn to the Council, alleging consistent patterns of gross, and reliably attested, violations of human rights and fundamental freedoms everywhere in the world. Two working groups deal with the complaint. If investigations are necessary, and appear to be justified a report is brought to the attention of the Council which confidentially examines the complaint. The Council may discontinue the consideration, or keep it under review, by appointing an expert to examine the situation and reporting back to the Council, or even to discontinue the confidential consideration of the matter and transfer it to public consideration. However, on the whole the procedure is generally characterized by strict confidentiality, and this trait, apart from the fact that Council members are not independent experts, but representatives of their States subject to instructions, clearly distinguishes the Council's procedure from that of the treaty bodies.[55]

The UN General Assembly itself, by its albeit not legally binding resolutions, is able to influence States as to their behaviour in human rights matters; examples are the rights of women, child soldiers, or, more generally,

---

54   Miloon Kothari, *From Commission to the Council: Evolution of UN Charter Bodies, in* The
      Oxford Handbook of International Human Rights Law 587, 601–608 (Dinah Shelton ed.,
      Oxford 2013); Christian Tomuschat, *Universal Periodic Review: A New System of International Law With Specific Ground Rules?, in* From Bilateralism to Community Interest.
      Essays in Honour of Judge Bruno Simma 609–628 (Ulrich Fastenrath et al. eds., Oxford
      2011).

55   Tomuschat, Human Rights, *supra* note 32, at 193.

the administration of justice.[56] Probably the main contribution of the UN Security Council is that it has, by acknowledging serious human rights violations as a "threat to the peace" or a "breach to the peace" (Art. 39 UN Charter), enabled itself to make use of its enforcement powers,[57] beyond its power just to propose or recommend the respect of human rights. However, both institutions are mainly governed by the political interests of their members, and this, of course, deeply impacts their human rights activities. Less influenced by political interests, though still visible, is the work of the UN Specialized Agencies as far as their task in the human rights field is concerned.[58] Examples include the activities of the International Labour Organization (ILO), and the World Health Organization (WHO).

3.5 Conclusion of this Section

In view of the great number of bodies engaged on the international scene for human rights monitoring, and the variety of tools at their disposal, the foregoing survey is evidently not comprehensive. However, what I wanted to show is the multitude, and mixture, of the bodies, and their instruments, tackling human rights monitoring from a legal and a more political point of view. This combination presents an added value. All these mechanisms together enhance the accountability of States because their (alleged) human rights violations do not pass unnoticed and require answers before an international forum.[59] Still both approaches—legal and political – should take account of the sensitivity of human rights issues which rightly or wrongly (very wrongly according to my mind) is a fact for many States shielding behind the sovereignty argument, and maintaining that international control illegally intervenes in the area of their domestic jurisdiction. This does not mean that the legal bodies should not apply the law, or political bodies should merely keep in mind the political interests of the States involved. But prudence should always govern the decisions, and the possible results should not be overwhelmed by the relevant

---

56   E.g., UN Doc. A/RES/66/130 (women and political participation), A/RES/69/149 (trafficking in women and girls); A/RES/51/77 (child soldiers). Also, the role of ECOSOC would have deserved to be stressed.

57   Art. 40–42 UN Charter. This development started with the assessment of Apartheid as "a potential threat to peace and security," UN Doc. S/RES/282 (1970), followed up by many resolutions becoming more and more determined, e.g., S/RES/733 (1992) concerning Somalia.

58   Eckart Klein, *United Nations, Specialized Agencies, in* Max Planck Encyclopedia of Public International Law (MPEPIL) Vol. X 489 MN 80 (Rüdiger Wolfrum ed., Oxford 2012).

59   Bruno Simma & Andreas L. Paulus, *The Responsibility of Individuals for Human Rights Abuses in Internal Conflicts*, 93 Am. J. Int'l L. 302, 313 (1999).

bodies.[60] However, despite all efforts to come to a fair solution in human rights disputes, again-and-again, one is confronted with the unwillingness of States to accept the judgments and recommendations of the monitoring bodies, be it for reasons of a specific or even principled resistance.[61] The argument is often supported by reference to national constitutional law prohibiting the internal application of international law, and decisions based thereon, if the said international emanations are colliding with the constitution and the competent national court has so held. Thus, the question becomes inevitable: What about the chances to enforce the international decisions and to overcome the States' resistance under those circumstances?

4   Enforcement of Judgments and other Decisions

4.1   *Preliminary Remarks*

Seen from the perspective of law, non-compliance with the obligations is – at least after the legal clarification of the issue has taken place – a completely destructive attitude, because it is the purpose of law to be respected. But it would be unrealistic to close one's eyes to the possibility that legal rules can be, and actually are, breached. One has not to follow Hans Morgenthau's opinion that only (forcible) sanctions create the reality of norms,[62] but any national or international legislator is well advised to see to this case and take the necessary precautions. Certainly, in reality violations of law can be sanctioned. In national law, the law can and will be executed, if needed even by physical force. The monopoly of power lies with the State.[63] In international law, however, States confront each other as sovereign equals, and have to respect the core obligation to obey the prohibition of threat or use of military force in their international relations (Art. 2, para. 4, UN Charter). Thus the question arises: for which constellations of human rights violations are military sanctions available?

---

60   *Quidquid id est prudenter agas et respice finem.*
61   See the various contributions in Principled Resistance to ECtHR Judgments – A New Paradigm? (Marten Breuer ed., Berlin 2019).
62   Hans Morgenthau, La réalité des normes, en particulier des normes du droit international 242 (Paris 1934).
63   Eckart Klein, *Staatliches Gewaltmonopol, in* Verfassungstheorie 635–656 (Otto Depenheuer & Christoph Grabenwarter eds., Tübingen 2010).

4.2   *Military Sanctions*

The only (more or less) clear case for military sanctions in our human rights context is provided by Art. 94, para.2 UN Charter. It regards the failure of a party to a case decided by the ICJ to perform the relevant judgment. It is well possible that States bring their disputes on human rights questions before the ICJ.[64] The other party may apply to the UN Security Council "which may, if it deems necessary, make recommendations or decide upon measures to be taken to give effect to the judgment."[65] The operative part of the judgment is the reference point of the content of the legal obligation.[66] The other party as well as the Security Council have discretion whether they wish to make use of their possible ways of acting. The Council can restrict itself to recommenda-tory remarks or decide on measures in the sense of Art. 41 and 42 UN Charter, which may include military measures (Art. 42). It is disputed whether such measures can be decided upon at any rate, or only if the general conditions for measures in the sense of Art. 39 UN Charter ("existence of any threat to the peace, breach of the peace, or act of aggression"), apply.

Personally, I am in favour of the first opinion because if the prerequisites of Art. 39 are given, the Security Council could anyway make use of the measures according to Art. 41 and 42, without being required to have recourse to a special legal foundation (Art. 94 UN Charter).[67] If the Security Council takes action on the basis of Art. 94, para. 2 UN Charter, the voting rules of Art. 27 UN Charter must be observed; therefore, an attempt to adopt decisions on measures, but probably also mere recommendations addressed at a permanent member of the Council, would fail because of its veto power. The same is true for a military humanitarian intervention ordered, or recommended by the Security Council (Art. 39 UN Charter). At this time, we can only state that there is an important lack of executory possibilities to the disadvantage of human rights protection.

Unilateral military humanitarian interventions – not expressly legitimized by the Security Council[68] – are for general reasons (Art. 2 para. 4 UN Charter)

---

64   E.g., the case of Georgia v. Russia, ICJ Reports 2011, *supra* note 26, at 70.

65   Art. 94, para. 2 UN Charter covers only judgments, not advisory opinions or orders of interim protection by the Court notwithstanding their binding force; *see* LaGrand, ICJ Reports 2001, *supra* note 26, at para. 108.

66   Polish Postal Service in Danzig, PCIL Rep. Ser. B No. 11, 6, 29–30 (16 May 1925).

67   Otherwise, Art. 94 (2) would only contain a procedural rule regarding to the applicant ("other party"). On the different opinions, see Karin Oellers-Frahm, *in* The Charter of the United Nations. A Commentary, Art. 94 MN 23 (Bruno Simma, Daniel-Erasmus Khan, Georg Nolte & Andreas Paulus eds., 2nd edition, Oxford 2012).

68   In case of a clear prohibition or condemnation by the Council, the intervention would be doubtlessly illegal.

seriously disputed.[69] However, they should not be completely excluded from the range of possibilities to enforce respect for human rights. Human rights and peace belong together, they are conditioning each other, and this creates a serious dilemma, if force is used in order to protect human rights. The legal values of peace and human rights have the same weight, and that is why there is no principled priority among them. For this reason, the concrete circumstances have to be assessed in any case and the consequences of each action carefully weighed. It is only the result of this balancing that will decide on the international legality of the intervention.

4.3   *Other Enforcement Measures of Binding International Decisions*

Binding international decisions can be issued by judicial, quasi-judicial and political bodies. The most prominent example of the latter is presented by the Security Council's ordering under Art. 39 UN Charter of an immediate cessation of serious human rights violations in a given country.[70] While the Council could decide measures under Art. 42 UN Charter, it could also order measures not involving the use of armed force, to give effect to its decisions according to Art. 41 UN Charter. Here again, the Security Council is not obliged either to decide a measure, or a certain measure, but it has full discretion. Whatever the Council will decide or not, the result will depend on its appraisal of the political situation.

With the exception of the judgments of the ICJ, judgments, or other decisions, or orders of international courts cannot be executed by military force.[71] This is even true concerning orders for provisional measures of the ICJ itself; because these orders are not judgments.[72] Still the Security Council could be engaged on the basis of Arts. 35 and 36 UN Charter, or *proprio motu*, under the conditions of Art. 39 UN Charter.[73]

---

69   *See* Vaughan Lowe & Antonios Tzanakopoulos, *Humanitarian Intervention, in* MPEPIL Vol. V MN 47–49 (Rüdiger Wolfrum ed., Oxford 2012).

70   E.g., Syria: UN Doc. S/RES/2401(2018); Yemen: S/RES/ 2216 (2015).

71   Again: If the non-execution of such a decision, etc. causes a situation under Art. 39 UN Charter, the Security Council could tackle the issue under this provision.

72   *See supra* note 65. Judgments are "final decisions," Karin Oellers-Frahm, in The Statute of the International Court of Justice. A Commentary, Art. 41 MN 103 (Andreas Zimmermann et al., 2nd ed. 2012). The latest example is presented by the case Allegations of Genocide under the Convention on the Prevention and Punishment of the Crime of Genocide, Application for Provisional Measures (Ukraine v. Russian Federation), para. 86 (ICJ, Order of 16 March 2022).

73   On the enforcement of the judgments of the ICC, see Arts. 103–111 Rome Statute, particularly as to the role of the "State of enforcement" and the supervision of the enforcement of sentences and conditions of imprisonment by the ICC.

The judgments of the regional human rights courts have their own specific enforcement mechanisms. Art. 46 paras. 2–5 ECHR contains the relevant rules for the judgments of the ECtHR. According to this provision, the final judgments are transmitted to the Committee of Ministers (CM); which shall supervise their execution. The CM is a main organ of the Council of Europe (CoE); composed of the Foreign Ministers of all members of this organization or their deputies – and deals with the supervision issues in special human rights meetings – it is supported by the Department for the Execution of Judgments of the ECtHR.[74] This means that the execution of all judgments is supervised; if no problems arise, the procedure will be closed by a final resolution of the CM. The CM may ask the ECtHR for clarification, if it considers that a problem of interpretation is impeding the execution (interpretation procedure). If the CM considers that a State party to the case refuses to abide by the judgment, it may adopt a decision, by a two-thirds majority vote of all representatives entitled to sit on the CM, and refer the question to the Court whether the State has failed to fulfil its obligations, not without having before formally noticed the State concerned (infringement procedure).[75] If the Court does not find a violation, the CM will close its examination of the case. If the Court, however, finds a violation, the case is sent back to the CM "for consideration of the measures to be taken" (Art. 46 para. 5 ECHR).

The further steps of the procedure are not determined. By drafting Art. 46 para. 5 ECHR the Member States found that, the finally adopted procedure would suffice to put enough pressure on States hesitating or refusing to comply with the judgments. This assessment is rather doubtful. The CM is by nature, a clearly political body. Some States have shown that in cases where important political interests are at stake, they are not willing to accept the judgment.[76] Some States even have built up a legal shield against the performance of their obligations by empowering their constitutional courts to check whether the ECtHR judgment corresponds with their constitutional rules.[77]

---

74   On the whole procedure, see Supervision of the Execution of Judgments and Decisions of the European Court of Human Rights, 15th Annual Report of the Committee of Ministers 2021; Julie-Enni Zastrow, Die Rolle des Ministerkomitees bei der Umsetzung der Urteile des Europäischen Gerichtshofs 111- 142 (Berlin 2018).

75   For more details, see Raffaela Kunz, *Securing the Survival of the System: The Legal and Institutional Architecture to Supervise Compliance with the ECtHR's Judgments*, in Research Handbook on Compliance, *supra* note 16, at 16, 26–27, 35–36.

76   Simon Palmer, *The Committee of Ministers*, in The Council of Europe, *supra* note 51, at 137, 149–150 MN 6.52.

77   *See* as to the case of Russia, Vladislav Starzhenetskiy, *The Execution of ECtHR Judgements and the 'Right to Object' of the Russian Constitutional Court*, in Principled Resistance to ECtHR Judgments – A New Paradigm?, 245, 259–269 (Marten Breuer ed., Berlin 2019).

Theoretically, the CM could make use of Art. 8 in conjunction with Art. 3 Statute of the CoE, and suspend the member from its rights of representation, or request it to withdraw from the Organization, and even determine the date of the cessation of its membership. But this sharp sword is hardly a suitable instrument for the stubborn failure to comply with a certain judgment. Thus, only very serious or permanent fundamental violations of the obligations will in practice lead to the use of this instrument.[78] The general experience that the enforcement of rules on the international level is merely weakly developed is certainly true for the field of human rights.

Art. 29 of the Protocol to the African Charter on Human and Peoples' Rights on the Establishment of an African Court on Human and Peoples' Rights of 1998[79] provides that the judgments of this Court shall be notified to the parties to the case and transferred to the AU members and the African Commission on Human and Peoples' Rights. Art. 30

Protocol reads: "The States parties to the present Protocol undertake to comply with the judgment in any case to which they are parties within the time stipulated by the Court and to guarantee its execution." The only means provided by the Protocol to put pressure on the non-complying State is the annual report of the Court to the AU Assembly – the highest organ of the AU and composed of the heads of State and government – which "shall specify, in particular, the cases in which a State has not complied with the Court's judgment" (Art. 31 Protocol). But, nothing is said about the measures at the Assembly's disposal. Thus, the pressure is reduced to a naming and shaming method.

A new Protocol on the Statute of the African Court of Justice and Human Rights of 2008 – whose main purpose is the merger of the African Court on Human and Peoples' Rights and the Court of Justice of the African Union – tries to enhance the pressure. While the naming of States not complying with the judgment in the annual activity report of the Court is still present (Art. 57), Art. 46 Protocol 2008 is tightening up the possible reactions to non-compliance. It has provided that, the Court refers the matter (the individual case) directly to the Assembly, and not only via a list contained in its report. The Assembly "shall decide upon measures to be taken to give effect to that judgment" and "may impose sanctions by virtue of paragraph 2 of Article 23 of the Constitutive Act [of the AU]." This provision indicates sanctions "such as

---

78   Now the CM has excluded Russia from the CoE, CM/Res (2022)2 (16 March 2022).

79   The Protocol entered into force in 2004. *See* in more detail Frans Viljoen, *Forging a Credible African System of Human Rights Protection by Overcoming State Resistance and Individual Weakness: Compliance at a Crossroads, in* Research Handbook on Compliance, *supra* note 16, at 365 *et seq.*

the denial of transport and communications links with other Member States, and other means of a political and economic nature to be determined by the Assembly." As these means are not exclusive ("such as"), the price for not abiding by the judgment could really become very high. However, apart from the fact that the Protocol has not yet entered into force, it is not very probable that the Assembly which decides by consensus or, if necessary, by a two-thirds majority of the AU Member States, would make extensive use of its competences. Again, we have a result which does not secure the execution of the judgments.[80]

Individuals and groups of individuals do not have access to the Inter-American Court of Human Rights, but they are enabled to direct their petitions to the Inter-American Commission on Human Rights; which may bring the case before the Court (Arts. 44 to 51 American Convention on Human Rights) after having dealt with the matter itself, and not securing a friendly solution between the person and the State concerned. The Court's judgment is final and not subject to appeal (Art. 67 American Convention), and will be notified to the parties to the case and transmitted to States Parties of the Convention (Art. 69 Convention). According to Art. 68, the "States Parties to the Convention undertake to comply with the judgement in any case to which they are parties."[81] Further, by the same Article, it is ordered that the part of a judgment "that stipulates compensatory damages may be executed in the country concerned in accordance with domestic procedure governing the execution of judgments against the state." Regarding the compliance with its judgments, the Court has developed its own procedure of supervision by reacting to submissions of petitioners or the Commission, calling for hearings, or issuing binding instructions as to the fulfilment of reparations orders.[82] If States are still not willing to comply, Art. 30 of the Statute of the Inter-American Court of Human Rights

---

80 Frans Viljoen, International Human Rights Law in Africa 472–473 (Oxford 2007) remarks that the protection of human rights finally depends on the will of the States and their domestic legal system. In a later contribution, Viljoen sounds a bit more optimistic, Frans Viljoen, *supra* note 79, at 386: "Still in its infancy, ... the Court's insistence on naming non-implementing states, provide promising building blocks for an improved implementation management system and practice." Faix & Jamali, *supra* note 35, at 64 come to the result that "the Court cannot be perceived as a legitimate and effective judicial human rights body in Africa."

81 Thomas M. Antkowiak & Alejandra Gonza, The American Convention on Human Rights. Essential Rights 308 (Oxford 2017), stress Art. 68 (1) ACHR as "the cornerstone of the Inter-American System's enforcement authority."

82 Antkowiak & Gonza, *id.* at 310; Rene Urueña, *Compliance as Transformation: The Inter-American System of Human Rights and its Impact(s)*, in Research Handbook on Compliance, *supra* note 16, at 225, 231–237.

provides that the Court in its annual report to the OAS General Assembly (Art. 65 Convention), "shall indicate those cases in which a State has failed to comply with the Court's ruling." In the report, the Court requests the Assembly to "urge" compliance by the State. The Assembly, by the Permanent Council, has to consider the report, but there are no rules concerning the measures it may take.[83] Here again, it is a political body that is ultimately deciding.[84]

Not only judgments are legally binding, but also other international decisions by courts or quasi-judicial entities may have this legal effect. Decisions on interim or provisional measures are a good example. The UN Human Rights Committee has been the forerunner in this respect. In 2000, it has held that its orders on interim measures issued in the individual communication procedure had to be obeyed though its final views on such cases lack this binding force. It was reasoned that by consenting to the communication procedure the States must not undermine it by obstructing the Committee's efforts to find a correct decision.[85] Shortly after this decision, the ICJ changed its previous jurisprudence and attributed provisional measures legally mandatory character, too.[86] The ECtHR also followed.[87] If the orders on provisional measures are not complied with, no particular procedure is in place. The relevant body can only take up this failure by the final decision on the case, and the enforcement of this decision, be it a judgment or another emanation, will be determined by the rules already discussed above.

4.4   *Enforcement of Non-Binding International Decisions*
The views of the monitoring bodies – with regard to individual communications – are not legally binding as far as the statement of violation is concerned, but they obligate the State to react to the recommendation by explaining in good faith, why it is not willing to accept the statement. In the follow-up procedure which the UN Human Rights Committee, taking it as an example, has developed, the State concerned is asked through diplomatic channels to comply with the views, the result is described in the Committee's annual report to

---

83   Arts 54 lit. f and 91 lit. f Charter OAS.
84   James L. Cavallaro & Stephanie Erin Brewer, *Revaluating Regional Human Rights Litigation in the Twenty-First Century: The Case of the Inter-American Court,* 102 Am. J. Int'l L. 768, 783–784 (2008) stress the insufficient support of the OAS for the Court. A more positive view of the system is taken by Ureña, *supra* note 82, at 237 *et seq.*
85   HRCtee, Piandiong, Morallos and Bulan vs. The Philippines, Communication No. 869/1999, Views of 19 October 2000.
86   LaGrand, ICJ Reports 2001, 466, *supra* note 26, at paras 98–116.
87   ECtHR, Mamatkulow and Askarov v. Turkey, No. 46827 et al., MN 102, 125 and 128 (Judgment of the Grand Chamber, 4 February 2005).

the UN General Assembly, and the State is pressed again for a positive reply in the next round of monitoring its report according to Art. 40 ICCPR.[88]

4.5   *Measures taken on the Basis of the Law of State Responsibility*

Non-compliance of a State with a legally binding international decision constitutes a breach of an international obligation; and is therefore, an internationally wrongful act.[89] Such an act entails the obligations to cease it, to guarantee non-repetition, and to make full reparation for the injury caused by it. Of course, these obligations leave the duty of the State concerned to perform the obligation breached unaffected.[90] To apply the law of State responsibility, if a State refuses to abide by binding decisions under a particular human rights treaty might be doubtful, because the treaty could have established a self-contained legal regime. The question is whether, human rights treaties form a subsystem of a system (public international law) to which it belongs; and whether, this subsystem has obtained a *lex specialis* design that would not tolerate a fall-back on the general rules.[91] But do human rights treaties contain, by their rules for implementation and enforcement of the human rights commitments, such special rules that exclude resort to the general rules?[92] This is certainly an issue of interpretation. There are good reasons to understand the human rights treaties as special rules as far as they establish a particular procedure for the examination of any alleged violation of the accepted obligations, and for the enforcement of the binding outcomes.[93] But, to assume that a recourse to instruments of enforcement outside the treaty would be inadmissible – if all possibilities of the treaty are exhausted – would hardly be reasonable, because

---

88   For more details of the follow-up procedure, see Anja Seibert-Fohr & Christine Weniger, *supra* note 45, at 436–441.

89   Arts. 1 and 2 of the Articles on Responsibility of States for internationally wrongful acts (ARS), UN Doc.A/RES/56/83 (12 December 2001), Annex. Most of the articles are viewed as codification of customary international law, *cf.* Gabcikovo-Nagymaros (Hungary v. Slovakia), ICJ Reports 1997, 7 paras 50 *et seq.* (Judgment of 25 September 1997); Application of the Convention on the Prevention and Punishment of the Crime of Genocide (Bosnia and Herzegovina v. Serbia and Montenegro), ICJ Reports 2007, 43, paras 385 and 398 (Judgment of 26 February 2007).

90   Arts. 28–31 ARS.

91   Eckart Klein, *Self-Contained Regime,* in MPEPILVol. IX 97 MN 1–3 (Rüdiger Wolfrum ed., Oxford 2012).

92   *See* Art. 55 ARS.; *cf. also* Art. 55 ECHR.

93   This would also include the initiating of an inter-State procedure according to the rules of the respective human rights treaty.

otherwise the purpose of the treaty could not be attained.[94] Thus, the application of the rules of State responsibility is possible, if the special procedures of the human rights treaties fail to create redress for the victim.

The home State of the violated person may invoke the responsibility of another State, if the obligation breached is owed to the home State. The Permanent Court of International Justice (PCIJ) has held in the context of diplomatic protection, that the violation of one of its nationals, in his or her rights, is injuring the State itself empowering it to claim protection.[95] This idea fits also the protection of nationals by their home State, allowing it to use the instruments given by the law on the responsibility of States.

The home State could take countermeasures (or reprisals) against the State whose human rights violation had been affirmed, of course only under the conditions relating to the legal resort to those measures, which must not affect the prohibition of the use of force, the obligations of fundamental human rights, or of a humanitarian character, or obligations under peremptory norms of general international law.[96] By taking countermeasures the State can put unilateral pressure upon the other State to bring it back to lawful behavior (for example, by suspending its own obligations created by treaties or based on customary law *vis-à-vis* the violator) but only as long as the other State does not fulfil its legal obligations.[97] If a State has committed a serious breach of an obligation arising under a peremptory norm of general international law, then all States are called upon to cooperate to bring to an end such serious breaches through lawful means, and not to recognize as lawful a situation created by this breach.[98]

Although the instruments made available by the law of State responsibility are not weak and can really make a difference, their use is not without risks. The responsible State will often deny its own responsibility – as it had probably done before – by refusing to comply with the judgment or other binding

---

94   *See* Eckart Klein, *Self-contained Regime, supra* note 91, at MN 14; Malgosia Fitzmaurice, *Interpretation of Human Rights Treaties, in* The Oxford Handbook of International Human Rights Law 739, 741 (Dinah Shelton ed., Oxford 2013): "No such regime is ever completely separated from general law." Further Bruno Simma & Dirk Pulkowski, *Of Planets and the Universe: Self-contained Regimes in International Law* 17 Eur. J. Int'l L. 483–529 (2006). See also Tomuschat, *supra* note 3, at 627–628.

95   Mavrommatis Palestine Concessions, PCIJ, Series A No. 2 (Judgment of 8 August 1924).

96   Arts 49–52 ARS; *see* regarding the problem Wilfried Fiedler, *Gegenmaßnahmen, in* 37 Berichte der Deutschen Gesellschaft für Völkerrecht 9, 25–26 (Heidelberg 1998); Eckart Klein, *Gegenmaßnahmen, id.* at 39, 55–57.

97   *See* Art 53 ARS.

98   Arts. 40 and 41 ARS. A serious breach is defined as involving "a gross or systematic failure by the responsible State to fulfil the obligation."

decision, and argue that the taken countermeasures are themselves illegal justifying it to take (counter-)countermeasures by itself, possibly leading to a spiral of measures, which under normal conditions would all be illegal. More or less necessarily, a new dispute will arise that has to be resolved by peaceful means. This brings the issue back to resolution through political and diplomatic channels, or by judicial decisions. And the game may start anew.

5   Conclusions

The result of this scrutiny is rather disillusioning. It is difficult not to agree with Dzehtsiarou's statement: "International human rights instruments are hardly ever effective when there is no will and desire coming from the states to engage and to comply."[99] Actually, in many cases human rights guarantees cannot prevent their violations, and likewise the procedures to clarify the alleged violations and to repair the material, or immaterial damage done by an effective remedy; and lastly, if needed, the existing enforcement mechanisms are not respected. Such disrespect seems to grow even in regions where, for decades, a basically functioning human rights system had been founded on a rather sophisticated protective mechanism.

Despite all this, that only quite exceptionally armed force can be used to enforce legally binding international decisions should not be deplored, because, war principally contradicts the perception of the international order set up after World War II. To conduct war for self-defence or the possibility to use armed force in order to execute binding decisions of the UN Security Council, or judgments of the ICJ were (and are) merely resigned concessions to the evidently unalterable fact that, sometimes only military power can terminate serious violations of international law. In view of the risk combined with military actions, it is always open to the discretion of the competent body or State to take this step. States usually invoke their sovereignty when they oppose international binding decisions, and their enforcement. However, in many cases, this invocation will not justify the infringement of the relevant legal norms; because, the State has made use of its sovereignty by voluntarily accepting the legal obligation, whether it is of a material, or procedural nature. But again, this argument is blunted if the State insists on its position and does not bow to the legal devices. Then the question arises: what can be done for the law to be respected?

---

99   Kanstantsin Dzehtsiarou, *Can Human Rights Law Live Up to Its Promises?*, Eur. Hum. Rts. L. Rev. 1 (2022).

For the reasons just mentioned, it has been suggested that, "the whole concept of sovereignty needs to be reconsidered."[100] As this would hit the State itself as the holder of sovereignty, one would have to ask whether the international order would, hereby, not become dangerously affected. The States are not only subjects, but also in spite of their deficiencies, not replaceable pillars for the whole edifice of public international law and particularly important for the protection of human rights – as absurd this might sound in view of their frequent violations of these rights.[101] But, the human rights situation in failed, or failing, States confirms this statement.

As to sovereignty, one has to remind its critics that in the international law of our days, the legal meaning of this term has already been decisively reduced by the prohibition of the threat, and use of armed force. The problem we are confronted with is not the lack of norms, or the need to give a new meaning to terms of international law, but only to bring States to compliance with their commitments, even if they do not want to.

Of course, the problem has been seen and discussed for a long time, and a solution proposed was to refer the problem to the empire of politics. The sole rational way to accommodate the divergent national interests showing up in non-compliance with legal rules (including human rights norms) would be the forging of political compromises which could, by definition, not reflect the valid legal norms, but had to find their own way.[102] This way would probably be determined by the most powerful States, and the solutions found would swiftly take effect as elements of an order set up by these States. Even if a World State could be established on the ground of a general agreement of all States, the probability of the emergence of a hegemon would be very strong. It is true that divergent interests could be eliminated in such a world order, but the necessary degree of pressure on and suppression of the peoples and individuals would be completely contrary to the idea of human beings as autonomous – self-responsible – persons. The area of liberty and freedom of the individual would essentially shrink; because otherwise, the existing very different moods, traditions and interests could not be reduced to a common denominator and evolving conflicts could not be resolved. No, this is not an acceptable alternative.

---

100   Dzehtsiarou, *id.* at 5. Louis Henkin, in a private discussion with the author, called sovereignty the "s-word".

101   Regarding the dilemma of States, see *supra* 3.1.

102   *Cf.* on this Hans Morgenthau, *Emergent Problems of United States Foreign Policy, in* The Relevance of Law. Essays in Honor of Leo Gross 47, 55 (Karl W. Deutsch & Stanley Hoffmann eds., Cambridge, 1968); Koskenniemi, The Gentle Civilizer, *supra* note 10, at 480–482.

There is no international order that is adequate to the self-determination of peoples and the autonomy of human beings, if it is not essentially based on law informed by the value of the free personality. Only such law can assure the equality of States, and of individuals, and protect against arbitrariness. All the violators, and violations of international law, and human rights notwithstanding, there is no other more promising way than to have trust in such a law and, if necessary, to insist that it be complied with, and to open as many as possible ways for accountability of human rights violators. One should not underestimate the power and the educative force of law, which may often take a long time. We all know that setbacks are possible and even very probable. The whole evolutionary process is marked by progress and retrogression. But we likewise know that ideas such as peace and human dignity, once thought, do not perish, rather they always aspire to be realized. Actually, they have been realized, if not perfectly (there is still so much room for evolution), but at least to an important degree by existing international law. The pure lust for power exercised by dictators and their States can only for a while threaten the order they are combating. These are certainly highly dangerous moments, but defending the order, and adhering to the prescribed legal avenues to reach legal solutions, is not only possible but necessary to keep its promises. The best way to defend the law against its violators is to maintain it. The widely shared condemnation of Putin's war against the Ukraine will finally demonstrate the strength of the law and not its failure.

CHAPTER 14

Islamic Law-Ethics and the Struggle against Slavery and Human Trafficking

*Abadir M. Ibrahim**

1   Introduction

It costs more for a girl with blue eyes.[1]

These were the words of ISIS fighters chatting eagerly about an impending date slotted for the slave market where enslaved women would be walked on a runway for fighters to bid on, purchase, and keep for sexual and labor exploitation. The words, images and reporting coming out of ISIS territory, were utterly shocking especially to Muslims from whose broader faith community these fighters come. If it were not for the high-profile incidents such as the aggressively visible reintroduction of slavery by ISIS, the sale of human beings at an auction in Libya, or the kidnapping and forced marriage of the Chibok girls in Nigeria, most Muslims would have rarely thought about slavery – let alone as something that is explicitly promoted as mandated by their faith. When they did think about slavery, it would have mostly been as a relic of history.

The predisposition of most Muslims on slavery was recently summarized by Havva Guney-Ruebenacker at the annual meeting of the American Society of Comparative Law when she described it through the thoughts evoked by a movie, *The Message*, and a television miniseries, *Roots*.[2] Both productions tell stories of suffering endured by two African slaves with whom it is hard not to empathize. Unlike Kunta Kinte and other characters in *Roots*, the African/Ethiopian slave Bilal in the Muslim origination story is freed and would become one of the central figures of early Islam known for his origination of the format for the call for prayer (*adhan*) and as a governor of Medina.[3] The commonly held belief is one that combines a strong revulsion towards slavery, and in this case to racism, and

---

* Associate Director, Human Rights Program at Harvard Law School.

1   Paul Wood, *Islamic State: Yazidi Women tell of Sex-Slavery Trauma*, BBC News (22 Dec. 2014).

2   *An Islamic Version of The Dred Scott Problem: Has Slavery Always Been an Evil in Islamic Law or have Juristic Sentiments Evolved?* 2021 Annual Meeting, Am. Soc'y Comp. L. (22 Oct. 2021).

3   Bernard K. Freamon, *Straight, No Chaser: Slavery, Abolition, and Modern Islamic Thought, in* Indian Ocean Slavery in the Age of Abolition 62 (Robert Harms ed., 2013) (also making reference to how the Bilal story is a central theme about how Muslims think about slavery).

a feeling of contentment with how Islam brought about "the end of slavery and the beginning of universal abolition as we know it"[4] is indeed an apt description.

The upbeat view about the role of Islam in bringing about the end of slavery is, of course, not one that is shared only by contemporary Muslims raised in front of TV screens. It is a view that is widely expressed by most Islamic scholars including most Islamists. A prominent example is Abul A'la Mawdudi (d. 1979) who was a leading conservative intellectual and a founding figure in South Asian political Islam. Writing at a time when the revival of slavery was not on the horizon, Mawdudi weaves together an abolitionist narrative that combines a strong sense of revulsion against slavery, which he exemplifies with the transatlantic slave trade, and praise of the abolitionist impetus of Islam. Calling the enslavement of free-born human beings a "primitive practice" that is "clearly and categorically forbidden," he concludes that the result of Islam's policy of encouraging the freeing of slaves "was that by the time the period of the Rightly-Guided Caliphs was reached, all the old slaves of Arabia were liberated."[5] Mawdudi even boasts that "the problem of the slaves of Arabia was solved" with the advent of Islam, "in a short period of thirty or forty years."[6]

How one gets from this apparently shared feeling of revulsion towards slavery amongst Muslims to an attempt to reinstitute slave markets by other contemporaneous Muslims is at the crux of this study. One has to note at the outset that neither the emergence of slavery and human trafficking,[7] nor the initiatives to end them, can be ascribed to Islam as a religion as such.[8] Like in most places, slavery, and in today's world human trafficking, are commonplace in Muslim-majority regions with a great deal of overlap in the types of

---

4   Guney-Ruebenacker, *supra* note 2.

5   Abul A'la Mawdudi, Human Rights in Islam 6–8 (Trans. Ahmed Said Khan 1976); note also that he goes not to treat the issue of subsequent slavery as a sort of necessary evil wherein it was allowed to keep prisoners of war as slaves as the only alternative to that is to execute them or keep them in Siberia-like concentration and labor camps, *ibid.*

6   *Ibid.*

7   Note that this chapter adopts its definitions of slavery and human trafficking from international treaty law. Accordingly, "slavery" is used to signify a situation in which legal ownership is exercised over a person while human trafficking signifies overlapping sets of practices without formal ownership. Compare, *e.g.*, Art. 1 of the Slavery Convention of 1926, 60 L.N.T.S. 253 and Art. 3 of the UN TIP Protocol, U.N. Doc. A/55/49 (Vol. I) (2001).

8   The social, economic and other structural determinants of slavery and human trafficking are quite varied and are not unique to any religious tradition. ECOSOC, Sub-Comm'n on Promotion & Prot. of Human Rights, Report of the Working Group on Contemporary Forms of Slavery on its Thirtieth Session, 36(17)(c), U.N. Doc. E/CN.4/Sub.2/2005/34 (July 7, 2005); *also see* Janie Chuang, *Beyond a Snapshot: Preventing Human Trafficking in the Global Economy*, 13 Ind. J. Global Legal Stud. 137 (2006).

exploitation, practices of recruitment and transfer, and government responses to curb them.[9] Though there will be unique manifestations that emanate from the Islamicate cultural and religious settings, parts of which are discussed in this chapter, slavery and human trafficking are human phenomena.

This, however, does not mean that Islam does not have a role to play in the fight against, or the exacerbation of, slavery and human trafficking. Being a belief system that informs the values of close to two billion human beings, about a quarter of the world's population, Islam should be expected to have an impact on how slavery and human trafficking are perpetrated and fought. The potential contribution of Islamic discourses to combatting slavery and trafficking is enormous and should not be overlooked. Muslims and Islamic scholars, as believers, members of communities, scholars, leaders, and victims should also be concerned about slavery and human trafficking as these phenomena are guaranteed to be in their communities. Slavery and human trafficking raise challenges that are relevant to Islam as a religious system, as these phenomena are intricately connected with questions of ethics, ways of living a good life, and a good afterlife.[10]

This chapter examines the potential role of Islamic law and ethics in the fight against slavery and human trafficking by approaching the matter by adopting the methodologies of policy-oriented jurisprudence originally developed by Harold Lasswell and Myres McDougal.[11] Expanding the understanding of policy-oriented jurisprudence of law as an ongoing social process of authoritative and controlling decision to include a discussion of Islamic ethics, the chapter first outlines the different classical and contemporary Islamic positions on slavery and their evolution into contemporary discussions of human trafficking. After highlighting some challenges posed by the lack of a broad-based and deep-rooted consensus on the topic of slavery, the chapter then proceeds to identifying the controlling factors that have affected past trends in decision that support or oppose Islamic abolitionism. While the chapter does not delve into a projection of future trends, it proposes some strategic interventions in support of a public order of human dignity.

---

9   Generally, Giuseppe Calandruccio, *A Review of Recent Research on Human Trafficking in the Middle East*, 43 Int'l Migr. 267, 269, 276–77, 278–285 (2005); Mohamed Y. Mattar, *Trafficking in Persons, Especially Women and Children, in Countries of the Middle East: The Scope of the Problem and the Appropriate Legislative Responses*, 26 Fordham Int'l L.J. 721, *passim* (2003).

10 For a discussion of the role of religion in combatting human trafficking see Roza Pati, *Marshalling the Forces of Good: Religion and the Fight against Human Trafficking*, 9 Intercultural Hum. Rts. L. Rev. 1 (2014).

11 Harold D. Lasswell & Myres S. McDougal, Jurisprudence for a Free Society: Studies in Law, Science and Policy (1992). For a brief exposition of the method, see Siegfried Wiessner & Andrew R. Willard, *Policy Oriented Jurisprudence and Human Rights Abuses in Internal Conflict: Toward a World Public Order of Human Dignity*, 93 Am. J. Int'l L. 316 (1999).

2 Key Islamic Ethico-Legal Concepts (and an Introduction to their Indeterminacy)

Typically, the topic of Islam in relation to slavery and/or human trafficking is discussed from the point of view of Islamic law. While this contribution does not depart too far from that approach, it also treats the same discussion as an ethical one. A facet of Islam that is particularly important in this connection is that its legal and ethical systems overlap to a great extent. A discussion among family members or friends about whether it is ethical to treat a household employee a certain way will, almost inevitably, weave in and out of legal reasoning. It will, for example, include discussions about whether a certain way of acting is allowed (*halal*), discouraged (*makruh*), or forbidden (*haram*). Such a conversation could draw from the Quran and from stories from the Prophet's or his companions' lives and can easily pull in the local Imam or a learned person if it is considered a particularly important subject. While the discussion will almost certainly contain appeals to non-legal notions such as appeals to empathy or indifference, the discussion can on occasion advance, or devolve depending on how one sees it, into convoluted arguments about the precedent of different schools of thought on the subject.

These conversations would fall under legal discourse to the extent that they involve the interpretation of legal texts and judicial precedents, debates about whether these texts or precedents contain communications of policy or are backed by control intent, whether actors making legal pronouncements have the authority to do so, and whether such pronouncements are made in accordance with acceptable criteria and procedures. Although debates that inform the ethical decisions of Muslims overlap with and stand on one or more Islamic legal traditions, the discussion is both a legal and ethical one, or may also be only one of those, depending on the context of the conversation. The same legal reasoning may be applied in the context of a court, or a discussion among friends, with the former situation leading to a fine or imprisonment, and the later to moral censure. Thus, since neither law nor ethics can fully capture the types of discourses in this chapter, "ethico-legal," "law-ethics," or "law and ethics" are used to denote this mostly but not always overlapping discourse. Even where "ethics" or "law" are used separately, the two are generally used interchangeably unless specifically indicated otherwise.[12]

---

12   The insight about the overlap between Islamic law and ethics is not new. However, most of the literature focuses solely on legal discourse and remains within legal literature even where the discussion is a non-legal one. *See, e.g.,* Khaled Abou El Fadl, *Qur'anic Ethics and Islamic Law*, 1 J. Islamic Ethics 7 (2017); also see the introduction and the contributions of

At the base of Islamic ethico-legal discourse sits its single most important source text, the Quran, which is considered to be the word of God. Even though the Quran is cited quite often in ethical and legal discussions, its meaning is rarely straightforward. According to Islamic theological history, the Quran was revealed to Mohamed through installments over a period of 23 years.[13] This creates layers of revelation which shift in tone and substantive pronouncements over time and context. As a result, one cannot simply pick up the Quran and purport to understand what its ethical and legal implications are without a process of contextualization that makes up the stuff of Quranic exegesis and the "science" of abrogation.[14] This makes the interpretation of the Quran dependent mostly on the second primary source of Islamic law-ethics – the Hadith.

The Hadith contain the stories, sayings, actions, and omissions of the Prophet Mohamed and are referred to as the prophetic traditions (or the *Sunnah*) which are meant to be imitated or used as a source of inspiration by believers. While the Quran was systematically compiled within decades of the prophet's death, the systematic compilation of the Hadith did not start for about a century in a process that would become more stable two to three centuries after the Prophet's death.[15] The sheer volume of the Hadith material, the length of time over which it was compiled, the wider geography of its compilation, the diversity of its sources and compilers, and the political and social upheavals during its compilation, lead to a situation where the authenticity and content of the Hadith material is often extremely controversial among Islamic jurists and scholars. Thus, although the theory of Islamic legal interpretation is meant to operate with the Quran and Hadith as its primary sources and move on to other sources where the two do not provide definitive answers, what you have in reality is a large volume of primary source texts whose content is uncertain and whose interpretive outcomes are highly indeterminate.

Abdulaziz Sachedina, Ebrahim Moosa, and Carl Ernst in Islamic Law and Ethics (David R. Vishanoff ed., 2020).

13   Hamid Naseem Rafiabadi, *Revelation of the Quran*, in World Religions and Islam: A Critical Study 235 (Hamid Naseem Rafiabadi ed., 2003).

14   "Abrogation" is usually used to denote situations in which a Quranic declaration is overruled or amended by a later revelation. In most contexts, the abrogated verses can be found in the Quran although there are also verses that were "forgotten" or excluded from what would later be compiled as a book. *See* John Burton, *The Exegesis of Q. 2: 106 and the Islamic Theories of "naskh: mā nansakh min āya aw nansahāna'ti bi khairin minhā aw mithlihā"*, 48 Bull. Sch. Orient. & Afr. Stud. 452 (1985).

15   Chibli Mallat, *From Islamic to Middle Eastern Law a Restatement of the Field (Part I)* 51 Am. J. Comp. L. 699, 719–7 (2003); Abū Ruqayyah Farasat Latif, *The Qur'aniyūn of The Twentieth Century*, Submitted in Partial fulfilment of the MA Degree Loughborough University (Sept. 2006).

The level of indeterminacy of the meaning of the primary text material is, however, reduced by the fact that interpretation is usually undertaken within interpretive communities that are made up of jurists and scholars. What lies between the source texts and legal and ethical conclusions is a body of Islamic law and jurisprudence that limits possible interpretive outcomes of legal rulings (*fiqh*), for example, on whether something is *halal*, and therefore morally acceptable or, *haram* or *makruh*, and therefore also morally objectionable. Most Islamic schools of law deploy methodologies of interpretation, developed through a field of Islamic jurisprudence, which are considered to be the secondary sources of Islamic law next to the Quran and Sunnah. The most important ones include reasoning/wisdom (*'aql*), derivation of rules through analogical reasoning (*qiyas*), individual or independent juristic reasoning (*ijtihad*) and what can be defined as scholarly, and in the early post-prophetic period community-wide consensus (*ijmā*).

Another notion that developed after the schools of law took concrete shape is what could be described as the binding precedent within specific schools which is followed or "imitated" (*taqlid*) by students of each school.[16] In situations where a school or a sub-set of a school determines that a precedent has been set, graduates of that school are precluded from exercising independent judgement (*ijtihad*) on that topic in deciding legal cases or issuing declarations (*fatwas*) on specific topics, cases, or questions.[17] The notion that *ijtihad* is no longer available on matters on which there is *taqlid* is usually referred to as the closure of the gates of *ijtihad*.[18]

While surviving Islamic schools of law agree on this overall framework, and therefore providing for the basis of the determinacy of outcomes, it is also important not to overstate the determinacy of the outcomes of decision, especially when one is engaged in a comparative approach that crosses school lines or when one looks at decisions across different periods of time. There are always going to be technical debates on the meaning and scope of any one method of reasoning, on the hierarchies of methodologies, and the resulting jurisprudential interpretations.[19] Thus, the different Islamic legal positions available today

---

16   *See, generally,* Mohammad Hashim Kamali, *Methodological Issues in Islamic Jurisprudence,* 11 Arab L. Q. 3 (1996); *also* Bernard Weiss, *Interpretation in Islamic Law: The Theory of Ijtihād,* 26 Am. J. Comp. L. 199 (1978); Nabil Shehaby, *'Illa and Qiyās in Early Islamic Legal Theory,* 102 J. Am. Oriental Soc'y 27, 28 (1982); Wael B. Hallaq, *On the Authoritativeness of Sunni Consensus,* 18 Int'l J. Middle East Stud. 427, 427 (1986).

17   Anver M Emon, *Shari'a and the Modern State, in* Islamic Law and International Human Rights Law 61–62 (Anver M. Emon, Mark S. Ellis & Benjamin Glahn eds., 2012).

18   *See, e.g.,* Weiss, *supra* note 16, at 208–209.

19   *See, e.g., generally,* Hallaq, *supra* note 16, *passim*; Mohammad Omar Farooq, Toward Our Reformation: From Legalism to Value-oriented Islamic Law and Jurisprudence,

are diverse and have not remained static in the centuries they took to take form and this process is still ongoing.[20] As we will see later, the ability of the traditional schools to enforce their precedent through internal discipline has been greatly disrupted by the emergence of reformist scholarship.

A final category of law that is relevant to this study is what we will call here secular law understood within the Islamic ethico-legal point of view. Whereas the determination of law and its application is considered to be the reserve of Islamic law and therefore Islamic jurists, there is a reserve power left to rulers who can legislate on topics that are not within the jurisdiction of the jurist class. This category of legislative power, which in many contemporary societies can either be exercised by monarchs or by secular political legislative bodies, is considered to be the lowest rung in the hierarchy of law and can only cover matters that are not already covered by a pre-existing corpus of Islamic law sources. This category of law (*qānūn*), also referred to as governance in accordance with Sharia (*siyasa shar'iyya*), is exercised by monarchs or other secular legislative bodies as a sort of administrative law and is considered to be valid under Islamic law in so far as it does not contradict *fiqh* that is validly derived by jurists.[21] While the influence of the government over Islamic law outcomes can take the form of the ability to determine which school or movement is recognized, favored, disfavored or persecuted, this reserve authority has also expanded over the centuries especially following the establishment of the modern state.[22]

3   Conflicting Claims and Past Trends in Decision

Granting some generalization, we will divide the approaches to this topic into traditionalist and reformist viewpoints.[23] It is, it should be noted, difficult to begin a discussion of Islamic law-ethics without a deluge of disclaimers as

---

esp. chapters 3–5 (2012). Ahmed Hassan, *The Classical Definition of Ijma': The Nature of Consensus*, 14 Islamic Stud. 261 (1975).

20   Abdullahi Ahmed An-Na'im, Toward an Islamic Reformation: Civil Liberties, Human Rights, and International Law 18 (1990); Muhammad Asad, This Law of Ours and Other Essays (1987); Wael B. Hallaq, *Considerations on the Function and Character of Sunnī Legal Theory*, 104 J. Am. Oriental Soc'y 679, 681 (1984).

21   Emon, *supra* note 17, at 52; Kristen Stilt, Islamic Law in Action: Authority, Discretion, and Everyday Experiences in Mamluk Egypt 26–32 (2012).

22   Boğaç A. Ergene, *Qanun and Sharia*, *in* The Ashgate Research Companion to Islamic Law (Rudolph Peters & Peri Bearman eds. 2014).

23   *See, e.g.,* Khaled M. Abou El Fadl, The Great Theft: Wrestling Islam from the Extremists 26–44, 155–59 (2007).

to both contemporary and historical positions on any issue which can, to borrow from Lena Salaymeh, be contingent, multivariant, and shaped by multiple legal-theological hermeneutic communities, in addition to social or political factors that determine the way decisions evolve and change.[24] The first disclaimer that needs to be made for the purposes of this chapter is that the traditionalist and reformist categories are themselves diverse. They are not only connected by sets of intermediate positions that create a continuum, but the fact that any specific scholar or school we cite holds one position on a topic does not necessarily mean that she or he will hold a traditionalist or reformist line on other topics.

The second, possibly the most important, disclaimer is that almost all the positions have an important commonality in relation to the Islamic tradition. In addition to an overlapping body of source texts and methodologies, an important commonality includes their reverence for and idealization of an imagined and historical Islamic tradition. To the extent that both the traditionalist and reformist positions show reverence to or even romanticize the past, they could all be called traditionalist.[25] Their difference lies not in relation to the past in general, but rather to parts of the past they identify with. What are identified as traditionalist identify with the schools of law that existed immediately before the advent of colonialism and which survive to date. Reformists, on the other hand, typically identify with traditions and schools that fall outside of these schools. Thus, the traditionalist and reformist labels are meant here to distinguish the two positions from a contemporary vantage point by taking modernity as the starting point for the distinction.

An additional overlap between the traditionalist and reformist viewpoints is that both have to deal with the vagaries of contemporary social issues and challenges. Granting that reformist positions are going to be relatively more responsive to contemporary issues, the difference is one of degree and not absolute as traditionalist schools do have adaptability built into them. The contemporary issue that is especially relevant to this study is the need of Islamic scholars to respond to the need for, and the ubiquity of, human rights in contemporary political and ethical discourse. Although both positions generally maintain a positive posture towards human rights the differences in their foundational assumptions and methodologies begin to manifest when dealing

---

24   Lena Salaymeh, The Beginnings of Islamic Law: Late Antique Islamicate Legal Traditions 5 (2016).

25   Another option that could have been adopted is that of orthodoxy. That would, however, not have solved the challenge being alluded to here and the traditionalist-reformist dichotomy is also helpful in the way it describes the positions held on slavery.

with conflicting norms between traditional *fiqh* positions and human rights standards. In the section that follows we will briefly address the attitudes of the traditionalist and reformist viewpoints on human rights in general before continuing to slavery and human trafficking.

3.1   Hesitant Abolitionism: The Traditionalist Baseline

At the base of the classical-traditionalist position on slavery lies a qualified reception of human rights which supports the notion of human rights but is willing to accept specific human rights norms only in so far as they do not conflict with their respective traditional *fiqh* positions. The traditionalist position rests on a voluminous discourse and apologia literature that contends that the modern notion of human rights only give recognition to what has been preached and practiced in Islam for centuries. The preface to the Universal Islamic Declaration of Human Rights (1981) states that, "Islam gave to mankind an ideal code of human rights fourteen centuries ago."[26] The Cairo Declaration on Human Rights in Islam (1990), a document adopted by the Organization of the Islamic Conference (OIC),[27] states that "fundamental rights and freedoms according to Islam are an integral part of the Islamic religion ... contained in the Revealed Books of Allah" implying that human rights in Islam are as old as the Quran itself.[28] An apt rendition of this position is provided by Ayatollah Ali Khamenei, the current supreme leader of Iran, when he stated:

> We Muslims, of course, know it very well that if the Western world and the Western civilization have paid attention to this matter in the recent centuries, Islam has dealt with it from all the various aspects many centuries back. ... [it is obvious] that the verses of the Quran and the traditions handed down from the Prophet (SA) and the Imams of his Household (AS), each one of them emphasizes the fundamental rights of man something which has caught the attention of men in recent years. ... I would say, that today it is big responsibility on the shoulders of the Islamic society to make this reality known to the world.[29]

---

26   Universal Islamic Declaration of Human Rights, Paris (19 September 1981).

27   The organization has now been renamed the Organization of the Islamic Cooperation, which retains the OIC acronym.

28   Preamble of the Cairo Declaration on Human Rights in Islam, Aug. 5, 1990, U.N. GAOR, World Conf. on Hum. Rts., 4th Sess., Agenda Item 5, U.N. Doc. A/CONF.157/PC/62/Add.18 (1993).

29   Ayatollah Khamenei, *Human Rights in Islam*, Delivered on the occasion of the 5th Islamic Thought Conference 29–31st January, 1987 (trans. 1989 by Sayid Khadim Husayn Naqavi), http://www.iranchamber.com/history/ akhamenei/works/human_right_islam.pdf. For a

Although the conclusion that historic Islamic law-ethics is compatible with modern human rights ideals is not problematic on its own, challenges arise when this notion is applied at the practical and normative levels. This challenge is especially poignant when traditional Islamic normative standards clash with modern human rights norms. The interest of most traditionalist scholars in dealing with human rights is to defend conservative beliefs from any moral and normative paradigm that challenges pre-existing norms or the scholar's place of moral authority. Therefore, rather than reinterpreting religious text to revise traditional *fiqh* positions in a way that is protective of human rights, they tend to reinterpret human rights by accepting only those rights that fit their pre-existing normative positions. Both the Universal Islamic Declaration of Human Rights and the Cairo Declaration on Human Rights in Islam are good examples of this as they give little room for doubt as to the inviolability of traditional *fiqh* positions rather than that of human rights. The two documents diverge even on basic notions such as human equality by accepting supremacist and patriarchal notions inherited from Islam's imperialist phase where Muslim adult males are granted a privileged existence while women and non-Muslims are granted significantly subservient social and legal positions.[30]

The traditionalist position on slavery or human trafficking parallels the approach to human rights. At its core are two conflicting claims that emanate from positions taken by classical and premodern jurists who allowed slavery to thrive but who also tried to regulate it with differing levels of interest either to protect slave owners' rights or those of slaves. This is, for the most part, not surprising because the authors of the classical *fiqh* positions lived in slave-owning societies which had a continuity with all the practices described in all the religious texts on which they relied. For early and premodern Muslims, similar to the Islamic scholars and great prophets in the holy books, raiding for slaves, raping women and children from vanquished societies, making slaves do laborious work including fighting wars and all the other things that one

broader, but similar statement by Prince Abdullah bin Abdul Aziz bin Abdul Rahman, see Joseph A. Kechichia, Succession in Saudi Arabia 2–3 (2001). For a discussion of similar conclusions by others, see Ebrahim Moosa, *The Dilemma of Islamic Rights Schemes*, 15 J. L. & Relig. 185, 195–196 (2000–2001).

30   Ebrahim Moosa, *The Dilemma of Islamic Rights Schemes*, 15 J. L. & Relig. 185, 196–200 (2001); Zehra F. Kabasakal Arat, *Forging a Global Culture of Human Rights: Origins and Prospects of the International Bill of Rights*, 28 Hum. Rts. Q. 416, 432–33 (2006); N. K. Singh, Social Justice And Human Rights In Islam 34–37 (1998); Ann Elizabeth Mayer, *Universal Versus Islamic Human Rights: A Clash of Cultures or a Clash with a Construct?*, 15 Mich. J. Int'l L. 307, 329–332 (1994); Ann E. Mayer, Islam and Human Rights: Tradition and Politics 90–91, 121–122 (2013).

might associate with slavery, were a reality of life. That was simply what normalcy looked like and Islam was no exception in its accession to the norm.

This did not, however, mean that early and premodern Muslims were not moved by an aversion towards exploitation and abuse or were unaware of the ethical dilemmas surrounding slavery. Many classical scholars, even while allowing slavery on legal-technical grounds, recognized slavery to be the worst possible affront to human dignity describing it as a form of humiliation, degradation and even as a form of death.[31] As a result of this awareness, these scholars obviously did not wish slavery upon themselves or their families, and they also put restrictions on the acquisition of new slaves including by claiming *ijmā* on these restrictions. Examples include the prohibition of *de novo* enslavement of free Muslims, the re-enslavement of freed slaves, the sale of the mothers of a slave-owner's child, or the speculative sale of an unborn fetus of a slave.[32]

Early Islamic law and ethics also set some minimum standards of treatment of slaves and encouraged maximalist standards. Minimum standards, for example, included the prohibition of physically assaulting slaves and the abolition of slave prostitution.[33] Examples of maximalist standards included the encouragement of slave owners to treat their slaves as members of the family, for instance, by feeding and clothing them the same as members of one's family.[34] This notion of kindness and comity is captured by the Quran itself which implores believers to "Be good to your parents, to relatives, to orphans, to the needy, to neighbors near and far, to travelers in need, and to your slaves."[35]

---

31   Havva G. Guney-Ruebenacker, *An Islamic Legal Realist Critique of the Traditional Theory of Slavery, Marriage and Divorce in Islamic Law*, J.S.D. Dissertation, Harvard Law School (2011).

32   Younus Y. Mirza, *Remembering the Umm al-Walad: Ibn Kathir's Treatise on the Sale of the Concubine, in* Concubines and Courtesans: Women and Slavery in Islamic History 297 (Matthew S. Gordon & Kathryn A. Hain eds., 2017). *See also* Myada Omar El-Sawi, *Beyond the "Tiers" of Human Trafficking Victims: Islamic Law's Ability to Push the Muslim World to the Top of the United States Trafficking Tier Placements and into Compliance with International Law*, 39 Ga. J. Int'l & Comp. L. 391, 401 (2011); Ghislaine Lydon, *Islamic Legal Culture and Slave-Ownership Contests in Nineteenth-Century Sahara*, 40 Int'l J. Afr. Hist. Stud. 391, 421–422 (2007).

33   Usually citing Quran 4:25, 24:32–33 and 33:5. *See generally also* Elizabeth Urban, Conquered Populations in Early Islam Non-Arabs: Slaves and the Sons of Slave Mothers 24–37 (2020).

34   Mohamed Y. Mattar, Combating Trafficking in Persons in Accordance with the Principles of Islamic Law 20 (2012).

35   Quran 4:36.

Another area in which one sees an attempt to minimize ills of slavery is in the encouragement of manumission. The Quran makes the freeing of slaves one of the deeds loved by God and a sure way to enter heaven: *"Righteousness is not that you turn your faces toward the east or the west, true righteousness in ...* [*those who*] *free slaves ...*"[36] *"Zakah expenditures",* declares another verse, "[*should go towards*] *the freeing of Slaves.*"[37] The Quran tells Muslims that if they killed a fellow believer, whether in war or in peace time, they should free a slave irrespective of whether they owed the aggrieved any compensation or apology.[38] The Quran also prescribed the freeing of slaves for the atonement of sins such as the breaking a promise or canceling a divorce after proclaiming it.[39]

An instructive anecdote that weaves these abolitionist notions is found in the story of Zayd ibn Harithah, the first male convert to Islam, who was adopted by the Prophet Mohammad as a son. What makes this story compelling is that Zaid, who was abducted and sold into slavery as a child, chose to live as a slave with Mohammad even though his family found him after years of searching and offered to ransom him. He was freed and adopted by Mohamed after he declined the opportunity to reunite with his family and tribe.[40] This story is seen as an embodiment of the Prophet's Sunnah which wraps together the encouragement of manumission and notions of the humane treatment of slaves that blurs the lines between slavery, and therefore ownership, and familiality. Invocations encouraging the humane treatment of, and the freeing of, slaves are so prevalent in the primary texts, that most Islamic scholars agree that the common thread that connects them is an urge to encourage the freeing of slaves.

An abolitionist impetus in Islam has also led to proto-abolitionist initiatives that included attempts to expand limitations on the enslavement of Muslims or limit the valid ways through which non-Muslim slaves can be acquired. Jonathan Brown traces attempts to expand limitations on enslavement to Abu Muhammad Juwayni an Ash'ari Islamic scholar from the 1000s.[41] There is some indication of an Islamic scholarly endeavor by a Timbuktu-based scholar Ahmad Baba who critiqued and embarked upon a mission to mitigate the harms of the racialized slave raiding business in West Africa in the early late 1500s or early 1600s.[42] Rudolph T. Ware traces Islamic abolitionism

---

36   Quran 2:177; see also 47:4; 90:12–-13.

37   Quran 9:60.

38   Quran 9:42.

39   Quran 5:89; 58:3.

40   David S. Powers, Zayd 21–24 (2014).

41   Jonathan A.C. Brown, Slavery and Islam 98 (2019).

42   Timothy Cleaveland, *Ahmad Baba al-Timbukti and his Islamic Critique of Racial Slavery in the Maghrib,* 20 J. North Afr. Stud. (2015).

to an African Muslim anti-slavery movement that was started around 1770 by an Islamic teacher called Sulaymaan Baal.[43] This movement would eventually succeed in the abolition of and the disruption of the transatlantic slave trade in parts of Senegambia in the 1780s under the leadership of ʿAbdul-Qadir Kan.[44] Ware goes on to show how subsequent West African scholars, including the famous Sufi scholar and pioneer of non-violence Amadu Bamba, had visceral reactions to the enslavement of the "Walking Qur'an" – African children so named for their recitation of the Quran from memory.[45]

The abolitionist impetus would, however, reach a high point only after the abolition of slavery in Europe and subsequent diffusion of abolitionism globally including through pressures created by colonial policies. While there had been earlier initiatives of partial restrictions under the Ottoman Emperor Abdulmejid I,[46] the first complete abolition of slavery and the closure of slave markets under the rubric of Islamic law came in 1846 as a royal decree of Ahmad Bey of Tunisia, who was himself the son of an enslaved woman.[47] The Islamic narrative of the emancipation movement was expressed in a 1854 Ottoman law which announced "[m]an is the most noble of creatures God has formed, in making him free; selling people as animals, or articles of furniture, is contrary to the will of the Sovereign Creator."[48]

Influenced in part by reformist movements discussed in the next section, the following century saw a wave of public opinion turning against legal slavery and a cascade of similar bans against slavery in other Muslim polities.[49] Legally sanctioned slavery would not come to an end in the Muslim world until recently, with Qatar (1952) Saudi Arabia (1962) and Mauritania (1981) being the last three countries to ban the practice. Although the process of legally banning slavery was spearheaded by the governments of Muslim-majority states, it is worth noting that traditionalist scholars were at the forefront of resisting abolitionism starting in the mid-1800s. Since the traditionalist scholars

---

43   Rudolph T. Ware III, The Walking Qur'an 110–111, 119–124 (2014).
44   Id. at 125–133; Molefi Kete Asante, The History of Africa: The Quest for Eternal Harmony (2014).
45   Id. Ch. 3.
46   See Bernard Lewis, Race and Slavery in the Middle East: An Historical Enquiry (Oxford University Press 1990).
47   Bernard K. Freamon, Possessed by The Right Hand: The Problem of Slavery in Islamic Law and Muslim Cultures 365 (Brill 2019).
48   Bernard K. Freamon, Slavery, Freedom, and the Doctrine of Consensus in Islamic Jurisprudence, 11 Harv. Hum. Rts. J. 1, 58 (1998), citing Murray Gordon, Slavery in The Arab World 47 (1989).
49   See Willian Gervase Clarence-Smith, Islam and the Abolition of Slavery 221 (Oxford University Press 2006).

believed that the right to legislate, albeit through the interpretation of "God's law," belonged to them, they saw the abolition of slavery as prohibiting something that God has explicitly allowed in the Quran.[50] In places like the Hijaz (modern-day Western Saudi Arabia) where slavery was common, the resistance to the abolition of black slavery energized the scholastic class to ally with slave traders and call for revolts against abolitionist authorities labeling them as heretics and even polytheists who can be killed and, ironically whose children can be taken as slaves.[51]

While slavery is abolished throughout the Muslim world today, there are two important caveats, both caused by the traditionalist resistance against abolitionism, that need addressing. First, although one no longer sees an active resistance from traditionalist scholars, their underlying discomfort with the abolition of slavery or at least an unwillingness to condemn slavery never went away. With the drying up of trade routes with the abolition of slavery globally and the banning of slave markets in Muslim polities, most traditionalists simply acquiesced to the new status quo. The most typical argument with which they justified their acquiesce was a procedural one – the only valid way to acquire slaves is through a duly declared jihad, there is no duly declared jihad today or there cannot be one because only a duly constituted Caliphate (an institution that does not exist today) can declare one, therefore making the issue of slavery redundant.[52]

Second, since the normative pronouncements in classical schools of Islamic law (*fiqh*) did not ban slavery, and since traditionalist scholars did not support abolition, the abolition of slavery was achieved through reserve power left to rulers (*qānūn* or *siyasa*). In other words, the traditionalist understanding of the prohibition of slavery does not have a basis in the form of an *ijmā* or *taqlid*, and is, therefore, neither forbidden (*haram*), nor discouraged (*makruh*).[53] Based on the regulatory powers of the state comparable to traffic, customs, or tax regulations, the use of non-divine state law once again provided a compromise where

---

50   Based on, among other things, the Quran's statements such as "O believers! Do not forbid the good things which Allah has made lawful for you" (5:87) and "O Prophet, why do you forbid what Allah has made lawful for you?" (66:1).

51   Guney-Ruebenacker, *supra* note 31, at 29–32; Freamon, *supra* note 48, at 60; William Ochsenwald, *Muslim-European Conflict in the Hijaz: The Slave Controversy, 1840– 1895*, 16 Middle E. Stud. 115, 119–21 (1980).

52   *See, e,g.,* William Gervase Clarence-Smith, *Islamic Abolitionism in the Western Indian Ocean from c. 1800, in* Robert Harms ed., *supra* note 3, at 81. For similar conclusions of Shia scholars in Iran during the abolition period see Seyed Masoud Noori and Zhra Azhar, *Shīʿī Ideas of Slavery: A Study of Iran in the Qājar Era Before and After the Constitutional Revolution*, 3 J. Islamic L. 57 (2022).

53   A notable but rare exception to this is the Universal Islamic Declaration of Human Rights which declares "slavery and forced labor are abhorred" at Par. G (iii).

slavery would be banned in practice without active support or opposition from traditional scholars.

The fact that the traditionalist view on abolition is a rather technical one and one that is based on subsidiary legislation has a number of adverse ethical and legal implications. Slavery not being forbidden (*haram*) or discouraged (*makruh*), and abolition being based on a trivial technicality, the violation of this prohibition is not going to be seen as a significant moral failing. Legislation aimed at combatting human trafficking, which would also be based on *qānūn* or *siyasa*, would also face similar challenges. From a purely technical Islamic law point of view, although considered to be binding under Islamic law, the prohibition of slavery through a regulatory-administrative feat can be as easily annulled through the ruler's discretion. This makes the abolition of slavery temporary, or a form of suspension,[54] which is less secure than the prohibitions against smoking or backbiting both of which are *haram*.

3.2   *Reformists: Moving from Slavery to Human Trafficking*
To fully grasp the place of reformist movements and their contributions to the fight against slavery and human trafficking, it is important to point out what Arnold Yasin Mol calls a hermeneutic of continuity.[55] Despite reaching conclusions that diverge from traditionalists their starting point is also the classical Islamic tradition. Most reformist scholars, emerge from or harken back to a rationalist tradition within Islam which leans heavily on a purposive approach to Islamic jurisprudence and puts different concepts of justice, individual rights, and public interests, rather than traditional *fiqh* or *taqlid* outcomes, at the center of its reasoning.[56] In order to overcome traditional *taqlid* positions reformists also generally hold that *taqlid* never really closed the gate of ijtihad or that the gate is now reopened.[57] Another important characteristic of reformist positions is that, although embroiling themselves in theological and jurisprudential debates that sometimes date back a millennium and a half,

---

54   *See, e.g.,* Guney-Ruebenacker, *supra* note 31, at 34–38. *Also see* Clarence-Smith, *supra* note 52, at 81–82.

55   Arnold Yasin Mol, *Islamic Human Rights Discourse and Hermeneutics of Continuity*, 3 J. Islamic Ethics 180 (2019).

56   *Id.* at 191–196. Adis Duderija, *A Case Study of Patriarchy and Slavery: The Hermeneutical Importance of Qurʾānic Assumptions in the Development of a Values-Based and Purposive Oriented Qurʾān-sunna Hermeneutic*, 11 J. Women Middle E. & Islamic World 58 (2013).

57   Ali Khan, *The Reopening of the Islamic Code: The Second Era of Ijtihad*, 1 Univ. St. Thomas L. J. 341 (2003); *also see* Wael B. Hallaq, *Was the Gate of Ijtihad Closed?* 16 Int'l J. Middle East Stud. 3 (1984) (arguing the gates of ijtihad were never closed).

contemporary issues and contexts are an important vantage point even when approaching classical traditions.

It is this later vantage point that would allow reformist scholars to interpret the Quran, Islamic history, theology, law and ethics in ways that defied over a century of orthodoxy in a process that began in the middle of the eighteenth century in the Indian subcontinent and in the late nineteenth century in the Middle East.[58] One finds the abolitionist discourse on slavery pick up pace in the nineteenth century paralleling a rise in reformist discourse.[59] Some argued that the Quran had always mandated immediate abolition but for the non-implementation of this mandate by generations of Muslims who went against the precedent of the Prophet Mohammad who is reported to have freed all his slaves.[60] Others contended that the Quranic impetus was abolitionist, although, since full abolition could not be achieved in slave-based economies, the Quran aimed for gradual abolition, which has now been achieved.[61] Since a wide range of reformist scholars supports the abolitionist position, including prominent progressive Islamist scholars,[62] it will not be easy to summarize or categorize these positions. What unites these positions is that they revisit the source texts from an abolitionist point of view to conclude that, rather than merely minimizing the ways in which slaves are acquired, espousing some standards of treatment, and encouraging manumission, Islam had actually always intended to set all slaves free – just like the Prophet Mohammad did. Islamic abolitionists thus take the abolitionist impetus of the source texts to their logical conclusion declaring slavery to be a moral wrong that has no place in contemporary society.

Moving beyond slavery, the equal emphasis on continuing the classical tradition and the subject position of contemporary inheritors of the tradition allowed reformists, to move from the abolition of slavery to more elaborate

---

58   Abdullah Saeed, Interpreting the Qur'ān: Towards a Contemporary Approach 10–12, 20–21 (2006); Daniel W. Brown, Rethinking Tradition in Modern Islamic Thought 22 (1996) (also citing mid-18th century reformists not only from the Indian Sub-continent but also from Yemen); David Johnston, *A Turn in the Epistemology and Hermeneutics of Twentieth Century Uṣūl al-Fiqh*, 11 Islamic L. & Soc'y 233, 254–280 (2004).

59   *See, e.g.*, Mansoor Moaddel, *Conditions for Ideological Production: The Origins of Islamic Modernism in India, Egypt, and Iran*, 30 Theory & Soc'y 669 (2001).

60   For the most extensive defense and explanation of this position see Guney-Ruebenacker, *supra* note 31, *passim.*

61   *See, e.g.*, Amina Wadud, Qur'an and Woman: Rereading the Sacred Text from a Woman's Perspective 82, 101 (1999). For a survey of these and especially the reformist positions see Clarence-Smith, *supra* note 52, at *passim*; Brown, *supra* note 41, at 230–232, 243–248.

62   For a discussion on Abul A'la Mawdudi, see the introduction of this chapter and on Ayatollah Murtaza Mutahhari and Sayyid Qutb, see Bernard K. Freamon, *ISIS, Boko Haram, and the Human Right to Freedom from Slavery Under Islamic Law*, 39 Fordham Int'l L. J. 245, 284–290 (2015).

approaches to the challenges posed by human rights violations. Placing Islamic principles and concepts such as human dignity, human equality, human brotherhood, justice, natural law, natural rights and the universality of human nature at the center of their theology and jurisprudence allowed contemporary scholars to come up with rather progressive Islamic constructs of human rights.[63] It is within this interpretive community that one finds a willingness to connect the dots between abolitionism and human trafficking. The mantle of bridging the intellectual discourse on abolitionism and contemporary human trafficking was taken up by Mohamed Mattar, a contemporaneous scholar of human trafficking law.[64]

Mattar relies on a notion of gradual abolition which he derives in a two-step way. He begins by restating and reemphasizing a variant of Islamic abolitionism which combines the abolitionist impetus of early Islam with the notion of "gradual social change", or what Abdullahi Ahmed An-Na'im describes as the "evolutionary approach",[65] wherein entrenched social ills, such as intoxication or usury, are prohibited over time because too radical a change would be impractical. Like many other abolitionists, Mattar brings into contestation parts of the Quran and Hadith that traditionalist and classical hermeneuts deemphasize or interpret away to justify slavery.[66] Building on wider pre-existing discourse of gradual social reform especially common amongst abolitionist[67] and other[68] reformist Islamic circles, Mattar extends the prohibition of slavery to human trafficking which he notes is the modern iteration of slavery.

The second and a more expansive argument that Mattar espouses is based on a compilation of *sui generis* prohibitions which he builds into a broader

---

63   For a summary of these positions, see Abadir M. Ibrahim, *A Not-So-Radical Approach to an Islamic Understanding of Human Rights* 96 J. Relig. 346, 347–357 (2016); *also see* Anver M. Emon, *Natural Law and Natural Rights in Islamic Law*, 20 J. L. & Rel. 351 (2004).

64   Mattar, *supra* note 34, at 18–20.

65   Abdullahi Ahmed An-Na'im, Toward an Islamic Reformation: Civil Liberties, Human Rights, and International Law 175 (1990).

66   For example, these include a Quranic verse that requires the emancipation of a slave who requests it, or a Hadith that says that Allah does not accept the prayer of someone who enslaves a free person, which make it quite a compelling starting point for Islamic abolitionism. *Id.* at 19.

67   *See, e.g.,* Freamon, *supra* note 47, 122–23; David L. Neal & Ashraful Hasan, *Distinctions Between Muslims and Dhimmis: The Human Rights of Non-Muslims Under Islamic Law*, *in* Human Rights Dilemmas in Contemporary Times: Issues and Answers 9, 10 (Ashraful Hasan ed., 1998). Chouki El Hamel, Black Morocco: A History of Slavery, Race, and Islam 17–50 (2014).

68   *See, e.g.,* Mohammed Moussa, Politics of the Islamic Tradition: The thought of Muhammad al-Ghazali 98, 100–108, 115–16 (2016) (combining it with the notions of reform (*islah*), and renewal (*tajdid*) especially in the context of politics and democratization).

notion of the prohibition of exploitation. In addition to listing Islamic prohibitions of misappropriation of another's property, gambling, bribery, monopolistic, practices and the prohibition of labor and sexual exploitation, which he builds into an Islamic notion of the prohibition of exploitation, he also alludes to how such practices are connected to contemporary human trafficking to make a case for the connection between these Islamic prohibitions and human trafficking. Closely following the types of exploitation contained in the definition of human trafficking in international law, he argues that there is an abundance of Islamic norms that prohibit exploitation and therefore human trafficking.[69]

Although not as specialized or as extensive, one finds contemporary Islamic ethical and legal discourse that parallels Mattar's arguments in relation to human trafficking in the Muslim world. The human rights abuses connected with the Kafala system of migration and employment that emanates from Islamic law has, for example, generated religiously grounded condemnation from Muslim and Islamic scholars.[70] The condemnation includes a ripple of *fatwas* coming from conservative religious establishments in the Gulf region.[71] Probably the most notable example of such arguments is contained in the fatwa of Yusuf Al-Qaradawi, one of the most prominent contemporary Islamic scholars, who called for the abolition of some of the Kafala systems in the Gulf because of the exploitation and abuse they have resulted in.[72]

3.3   *Challenges to the Abolitionist Consensus*
In order to fully capture the conflicting claims on slavery and human trafficking it is helpful but not sufficient to see the discursive field in binary terms – as divided between supporters of slavery and abolitionists or between

---

69   Mattar, *supra* note 34, at 21–28.

70   *See e.g.*, El-Sawi, *supra* note 32, at 403–406; Mohammad A. Auwal, *Ending the Exploitation of Migrant Workers in the Gulf*, 34 Fletcher F. World Aff. 87, 105 (2010).

71   Calandruccio, *supra* note 9, at 282; Mattar, *supra* note 9, at 758; Ray Jureidini & Said Fares Hassan, *The Islamic Principle of Kafala as Applied to Migrant Workers: Traditional Continuity and Reform*, *in* Migration and Islamic Ethics: Issues of Residence, Naturalisation and Citizenship 92 (Ray Jureidini & Said Fares Hassan eds., 2020); BBC News, *Saudi Cleric Preaches Workers' Rights* (3 Sept. 2002).

72   Mohamed Y. Mattar, *Human Rights Legislation in the Arab World: The Case of Human Trafficking*, 33 Mich. J. Int'l L. 101, 129–130 (2011) (quoting Qaradawi's fatwa). The UN Special Rapporteurs on slavery, on migrants and on human trafficking have recently reached the same conclusion regarding Saudi Arabia calling for the abolition of the kafala system, AL SAU 7/2021.

traditionalists and reformists. One has to take into account that if there is a traditionalist-reformist consensus on the abolition of slavery, this consensus is rather superficial. To exemplify this point, it may be instructive to revisit the shared sentiment of Guney-Ruebenacker and Mawdudi's concurrence on the loathsomeness of slavery. One would assume that Guney-Ruebenacker, a radical abolitionist and a critical feminist,[73] would agree with Mawdudi when he writes:

> Islam has clearly and categorically forbidden the primitive practice of capturing a free man, to make him a slave or to sell him into slavery. On this point the clear and unequivocal words of the Prophet (S) are as follows: "There are three categories of people against whom I shall myself be a plaintiff on the Day of Judgement. Of these three, one is he who enslaves a free man, then sells him and eats this money."[74]

The concurrence between the two cannot however be farther than the reality. One could walk away from a reading of Mawdudi with an impression that he is arguing that the value system of Islam has unquestionable disdain towards slavery. A closer inspection of his broader body of work will, however, reveal that he is not an abolitionist at all. To the contrary, although he effectively summons the abolitionist impetus of Islam and rails against transatlantic slavery, he is opposed to slavery only when it is not of the Islamic variety. He would have no qualms reinstating this variety of slavery had a truly Islamic political system existed.[75] The superficiality of the consensus creates a false sense of the irrevocability of the abolition of slavery thus masking two important continuities – the continuity in the patterns of slavery and human trafficking in some Muslim-majority countries in ways that trace pre-modern practices and the continuity of resistance against abolitionism amongst traditionalist and some reformist scholars.

One sees a continuity of this anti-abolitionist posture in countries like Mauritania where black slavery and human trafficking are still being justified

---

73   Her work is partially described in the text accompanying *supra* & *infra* notes 60, 92–93.

74   Mawdudi, *supra* note 5, at 19.

75   His publication on human rights in Islam only implies this and does not make pro-slavery statements probably for polemical reasons. However, his position on slavery, equality between men and women, and slavery under a truly Islamic system comes out more clearly in Abul A'la Mawdudi, Purdah and the Status of Woman in Islam 17, 81, 96–99, 139 (trans. Al-Ash'ari 1972).

in Islamic ethical and juristic terms,[76] where runaway slaves are prosecuted by courts, and anti-slavery activists are persecuted as heretics with the active traditionalist participation and leadership.[77] In Sudan, where the famous abolitionist and reformist scholar Mahmud Muhammad Taha was executed for heresy,[78] Islamic law and ethics constituted a centerpiece for the justification and encouragement of slave raids during the civil war, resulting in countless civilians of "African/Black" descent being forced into sexual slavery or household labor.[79] In many Western and Northern African countries one sees this continuity mostly in the form of human trafficking which parallels pre-abolition social and economic relations but can also take a form that is very similar to formalized slavery in contexts where traditionalist Islamic norms (and other customary practices) are recognized by the legal system and enforced by the judiciary.[80] Even in Egypt, which has been cited often for its early success in abolishing slavery, judges still seems to be willing to convict individuals who criticize slavery under the country's apostasy laws.[81]

Unfortunately, there has also been a steady stream of traditionalist scholars who have sought to go beyond merely rejecting the formation of consensus on Islamic abolitionism by supporting the formal reinstitution of slavery. In Saudi Arabia, despite the *fatwas* discussed earlier on human trafficking mentioned

---

76   The connection between slavery and religions leaders is so acute that anti-slavery activists mockingly call slavery a "sacred institution." *See* Zekeria Ould Ahmed Salem, *The Politics of the Haratin Social Movement in Mauritania, 1978–2014, in* Social Currents in North Africa (Osama Abi-Mershed ed., 2018).

77   Brahim El Guabli, *Biram Ould Abeid and Slavery in Mauritania*, Reset Dialogues on Civilizations (31 May 2012); Humanists International, *Cases of Concern: Mohammed Ould Shaikh Ould Mkhaitir* (27 Jan. 2022); *also see* Benjamin N. Lawrance & Ruby P Andrew, *A "Neo-Abolitionist Trend" in Sub-Saharan Africa? Regional Anti-Trafficking Patterns and a Preliminary Legislative Taxonomy*, 9 Seattle J. for Soc. Just. 599, 605–616 (2011) (for a summary of the history of slavery and trafficking in Mauritania); Irwin Cotler & Judith Abitan, *Mauritania abolished slavery in 1991, so why is it criminalizing slavery opponents?*, National Post (4 Sept. 2018); John D. Sutter, *Attorney: Charges against Liberated Mauritanian Slave Dropped*, CNN (23 Oct. 2014).

78   *See* Mayer, *supra* note 30, at 183–183.

79   Sarah L. Dygert, *Eradicating Sudanese Slavery: The Sudanese Government and the abuse of Islam*, 3 Regent J. Int'l L. 143, 144, 156–57 (2005); Nhial Bol, *Sudan-Human Rights: Children Still being Sold into Slavery*, Inter Press Service (24 July 1997).

80   *See* Helen Duffy, *Hadijatou Mani Koroua v Niger: Slavery Unveiled by the ECOWAS Court*, 9 Hum. Rts. L. Rev. 151 (2009); Benedetta Rossi, *African Post-Slavery: A History of the Future*, 48 Int'l J. Afr. Hist. Stud. 303 (2015).

81   Guney-Ruebenacker, *supra* note 31, at 40–41; Paul Marshall & Nina Shea, Silenced: How Apostasy and Blasphemy Codes are Choking Freedom Worldwide 77 (2011); *see also generally* El Hamel, *supra* note 67, Ch. 7–8.

above there have also been fatwas in support of slavery.[82] For instance, one of the most prominent scholars in the country, Saleh Al-Fawzan, has been advocating for the re-legalization of slavery and accusing critics of heresy.[83] In Egypt, one of the debates that took place in the Constituent Assembly which drafted the 2012 Islamist Constitution ended with the exclusion of an unequivocal statement prohibiting slavery and human trafficking from the 2012 Constitution.[84] In western academia one finds in the work of Jonathan Brown, a prominent Islamic studies academic based in Georgetown University, the most systematic attempt to undermine the Islamic abolitionist consensus and, more broadly, in the defense of traditionalist positions.[85]

While Muslims in a state of contentment and complacency received a rude awakening by recent images coming out Nigeria and Libya, which can be seen as symptomatic of this continuity, the most serious attempt to reinstate slavery came from a rather new modernist Islamist movement – the so-called Islamic State of Iraq and Syria (ISIS).[86] The fact that human trafficking surfaced following the breakdown of economic and legal order is neither surprising nor interesting for an inquiry about slavery or human trafficking. What makes these phenomena interesting to this study is how readily the ethical system

---

82   Fundamental Human Dignity and the Mathematics of Slavery (Jun. 2006), *available at* https://papers.ssrn.com/sol3/papers.cfm?abstract_id=2131265.

83   Abou El Fadl, *supra* note 23, at 255–256.

84   Salafi members of the Constituent Assembly who opposed the inclusion of the prohibition of slavery did not get everything they wanted as they also espoused the reduction of the legal marriageable age to six and they did allow some references to human trafficking which they thought did not contradict their understanding of Islamic law. Moushira Khattab, *Women's Rights Under Egypt's Constitutional Disarray*, 15 Viewpoints: Woodrow Wilson Center for Int'l Scholars (17 Jan. 2013). *Also see* Abadir M. Ibrahim, *Post-Revolutionary Islamism and the Future of Democracy and Human Rights in Egypt*, 30 Am. J. Islamic Soc. Sci. 19, 24–31, 34 (2013) (arguing that the resulting 2012 Constitution was "an Islamist document with democratic hallmarks or vice versa" and that it remained vague as to whether it was moving away from many democratic and human rights ideals and minimum standards which were to be determined through sub-constitutional practices).

85   Brown, *supra* note 41, at 1–9 and *passim* (Brown, among other things, recycles a lengthy catalogue of critical and deconstructive arguments against both Islamic and non-Islamic abolitionism, however, suspending all critical faculties when he comes to the traditionalist position on slavery which he sets out to defend because not doing so "would be to condemn the Quran, the Prophet Muhammad and God's law as morally compromised." *Id.* at 312). For a range of reactions to Brown's first public presentation of his work, see Valerie Strauss, *Georgetown professor under fire for lecture about slavery and Islam*, Wash. Post (17 Feb. 2017).

86   Wood, *supra* note 1; Freamon, *supra* note at 62, *passim*; Nima Elbagir et al., *People for sale: Where lives are auctioned for $400*, CNN (15 Nov. 2017); Paul, *Islamic State: Yazidi Women tell of Sex-Slavery Trauma*, BBC News (22 Dec. 2014).

of Islam was retrofitted in justifying a proto-state complete with a legal and administrative system that enforces, and in fact strongly encourages, a system of slavery. ISIS may be a hyper-modern reformist movement[87] and it may be denounced by most traditionalist and reformist scholars.[88] However, its position on slavery is not ethically that different from that of traditionalists. In so far as the traditionalist version of abolition is contingent upon the survival or the acceptance of the authority of the state and not the inherent worth of slavery, the traditionalist position will continue to reinforce modes of thinking that constitute the baseline for the reinstitution of slavery.

The most important outcome of the superficiality of the abolitionist consensus, and the inability to see the continuities between premodern and contemporary slavery and human trafficking, is that it has led to contemporary complacency among Muslims who assume that slavery is a thing of the past. This creates an atmosphere in which the reinstatement of legal slavery is much easier than one would expect in situations where the authority of modern states falters or where actors that challenge the legitimacy of the abolition of slavery take state power. Short of these worst-case scenarios, with the inability of scholars to find consensus on viewing slavery to be sinful or morally problematic, Muslim communities will have difficulties in finding common ground in order to fight human trafficking.

This can be exemplified by looking at the need to protect victims of human trafficking from being revictimized and retraumatized by state authorities through prosecution or administrative measures such as deportation. While countries with Islamic legal systems face the challenge of protecting victims as well as most other states,[89] countries with Islamic legal systems or those which have a stronger traditionalist influence are also going to face additional challenges that are connected with traditional *fiqh*. In addition to the fact that traditional Islamic legal rules are going to be inadequate in dealing with the

---

87   Generally, on its connections with modernity and modern movements, see Hassan, *The Sectarianism of the Islamic State: Ideological Roots and Political Context*, Carnegie Endowment for International Peace (2016); Thorsten Botz-Bornstein, The Political Aesthetics of ISIS and Italian Futurism (2018). More broadly on the modernist credentials of Islamist movements see Roxanne L. Euben, Enemy in the Mirror: Islamic Fundamentalism and the Limits of Modern Rationalism (1999).

88   *See, e.g.,* Mohamed al Yacoubi, *Muslims Against ISIS Part 1: Clerics & Scholars*, Wilson Center (2014); Open Letter to Dr. Ibrahim Awwad Al-Badri, alias 'Abu Bakr Al-Baghdadi', to the Fighters and Followers of the Self-Declared 'Islamic State' (19 Sept. 2014) (hereinafter "Open Letter to Baghdadi"); AFP, Sunni cleric says Iraq caliphate violates Sharia (5 Jul. 2014) (reporting on Yusef al-Qaradawi's condemnation of ISIS and its declaration of a caliphate).

89   *See, e.g.,* United States Department of State, Trafficking in Persons Report (2021).

multifaceted sides of human trafficking in general,[90] traditional *fiqh* rules would make it almost impossible for victims of trafficking for sexual exploitation to report perpetrators as they can face severe punishment for adultery. In addition, if victims are rescued, they would be automatically exposed to layers of social, emotional and even physical trauma connected with their prosecution under traditional Islamic law.[91]

4   Controlling Factors

Some of the determining factors that that will influence whether Islamic law-ethics will support slavery or abolition are hermeneutical. Thus, the substance of the source texts such as the Quran and hadith, the relationship of classical and contemporary hermeneutic communities to these texts, and the methodologies they apply will inform the conclusions they reach on slavery. These differences, however, do not explain why these interpretive communities act in in certain ways. As we have seen in previous sections, the range of Islamic positions on slavery is quite wide, and no one of these positions is uniquely more Islamic than the others in as far as they are all rooted in a hermeneutic tradition that entertains a great deal of indeterminacy of interpretive outcomes. It is, therefore, important to interrogate predispositional and environmental conditioning factors causing some, and not other, Islamic hermeneutic communities to fail to join the abolitionist social and juristic consensus.

Havva Guney-Ruebenacker, in exploring classical positions on slavery, finds early jurists to have been preoccupied by a desire to build a knowledge structure and an ethical system that justified and entrenched existing power relations between slaves and the "master class" to which jurists belonged, aspired to belong, or were dependent upon.[92] Reviewing the literature on the mid-nineteenth century when the Muslim World began abolishing slavery, Bernard Freamon joins Guney-Ruebenacker, in identifying a number of controlling factors that played a role in facilitating or hampering abolitionist

---

90   Mattar, *supra* note 9, at 734–745 (2003).
91   Liz Kelly, *"You Can Find Anything You Want": A Critical Reflection on Research on Trafficking in Persons within and into Europe*, 43 Int'l Migr. 235, 256 (2005); Sarah Zimmerman, *Mending the Protection and Prosecution Divide: Looking at Saudi Arabia Human Trafficking Flaws and Possibilities*, 15 Wash. U. Global Stud. L. Rev. 536 (2016); Human Rights Now, Women's Rights Report: Discrimination in the Punishment of Women (Jul. 2018).
92   Guney-Ruebenacker, *supra* note 31, at 45–57.

initiatives.[93] In addition to varying degrees of pressure from colonial powers, these factors include the prevalence of slavery in the economy, public support for abolitionism, development of reformist Islamic scholarship, and the level of support or opposition to abolition from traditional Islamic scholars. In places like Tunisia, Sudan, Egypt and the Indian sub-continent, there had already been public support for abolition and the religious establishment was also not opposed to it. In the Hijaz and the Eastern African coast, however, abolitionism faced fierce resistance both from the economic and religious establishment.

These studies are especially instructive for contemporary contexts in which Islamic scholars and judges are operating in societies in which slavery and human trafficking are prevalent in the economy. A judge or government official in Mauritania will have strong and personal incentives to resist abolitionism and to directly or indirectly support the persecution of anti-slavery activists through blasphemy and apostasy laws. Where the conditioning factors that incentivized the classical scholars to build pro slave-owner hegemonic discourses are still applicable, a meaningful conversation about why contemporary traditionalist scholars support slavery or human trafficking would have to address those conditioning factors. Rather than focusing merely on building logically tidier or more convincing hermeneutical abolitionist arguments, which frankly already exist, one would have to ask more fundamental questions about the root causes of slavery and human trafficking. The promotion of abolitionist hermeneutical constructs may be important in challenging the ability of the beneficiaries of slavery or human trafficking to justify exploitative relations and entrench their socio-economic positions, but more will be needed to change social and economic structures as well. Coming back to the Mauritanian example, where a large proportion of the population is enslaved along racial lines,[94] one cannot expect to bring slavery to an end, let alone address long-term post-slavery challenges such as casteism, racism and human trafficking, without first changing the economic, social and political structures that underlay slavery.

This approach does not, however, fully explain why traditionalists in societies that have abolished slavery over a century and a half ago, and therefore

---

93   *Id.* at *passim*; Freamon, *supra* note 47, *passim*; and Freamon, *supra* note 48, *passim*.

94   Since the country does not provide statistical data on the subject, estimates can vary widely from two to up to twenty percent. *See* Sebastian Bouknight & Timothy Hucks, *Slavery Hidden in Plain Sight in Mauritania*, Inside Arabia (30 Jan. 2019); John D. Sutter, *Slavery's Last Stronghold*, CNN (Mar. 2012); Global Slavery Index, Regional Analysis: Africa https://www.globalslaveryindex.org/2018/findings/regional-analysis/africa/ (2018).

having no direct or indirect material interests in slavery, should resist abolitionism. Part of the initial resistance to abolitionism, especially in the early period
of abolition during European imperialism, may be explained both by direct
economic interests and a resistance to colonial impositions which would have
been especially offensive to scholars who themselves were at the helm of an
imperialist belief system. Since these traditionalist institutions have survived
the shocks of modernity and the challenge of reformist movements and continue today,[95] one can hypothesize that these institutions simply carried over
the hegemonic social and economic attitudes from pre-modern slave-owning
days.

One can imagine that traditionalist institutions may increasingly move
from their hesitant toleration of abolitionism towards supporting more stable forms of abolitionism within the confines of traditionalist hermeneutic
structures suggested in the next section. One of the challenges that Islamic
discourses continue to face is that the pre-modern schools were confronted by
colonialism, postcolonialism, and modernity in quick succession which threw
a deluge of ethical and legal challenges with which these schools, or Islamic
discourses in general, have not been able to keep up. Thus, one can be optimistic about the willingness of these schools to slowly change positions that
were held in premodern times. However, given the perseverance of hegemonic
discourses in general and given the continuity of pre-modern socio-economic
exploitative relations in some parts of the Muslim world, one should also
expect traditionalist resistance to abolitionism to persist.

Finally, there is the role of the modern postcolonial states, especially those
in Muslim-majority parts of the world, and the role of human rights advocacy
in shaping their role. Modern states have played a central part in the abolition of slavery and continue to do so with regard to human trafficking. The
recent resurgence of slavery and human trafficking in connection with ISIS or
Boko Haram is also directly related to dysfunction and collapse of these states
caused by foreign invasion or internal weakness. It goes without saying, therefore, that support for state stability, and advocacy aimed at states, is going to
have a direct positive effect on the fight against slavery and human trafficking.
Modern states can, of course, be problematic where they lack legitimacy or rely
on human rights abuse to maintain power. In these situations, although they
may maintain abolitionist policies and ensure abolitionist structures, they can
also either cause resentment that leads to support for anti-abolitionist Islamic

---

95   *See, e.g.,* Muhammad Qasim Zaman, The Ulama in Contemporary Islam: Custodians of
      Change (2010); Ahmet T. Kuru, *The Ulema-State Alliance: A Barrier to Democracy and
      Development in the Muslim World,* Tony Blair Institute for Global Change (2021).

movements or can also align with such actors in their bid to maintain power. It is, therefore, important to conceive of ways of building as wide a pan-Islamic consensus on abolitionism as possible, one that includes traditionalists and reformists. Some strategies for doing so, applicable both with and outside of the support of states, are explored in the next section.

5   Strategies for a Public Order of Human Dignity

Many strategies for supporting the abolition of slavery and the advocacy against human trafficking jump out from the previous sections. One can, for example, pick up from the discussion on the role of structural determinants of slavery and human trafficking to discuss how these structural changes can be introduced. One can similarly discuss how the role of modern states and state law can be enhanced. One can also approach the topic from the point of view of how foreign policies of global powers can be leveraged for instance through the utilization of the Trafficking in Persons (TIP) Report.

Rather than revisiting all the determining factors and the large number of possible strategies, the remainder of the chapter stays within what Abdullahi Ahmed An-Na'im describes as an "internal cultural discourse."[96] It explores strategies that can support abolitionism within the Islamic law-ethics discursive space. The strategies recommended assume that traditionalist schools are going to persist and that there is sufficient flexibility in their hermeneutic tools that allow them to take more abolitionist positions.

5.1   *Expanding and Deepening the Abolitionist Consensus*
It may be true that a consensus has arisen over the last century in Muslim circles including among Muslim scholars that considers the debate on the complete abolition of slavery to have been resolved on the side of abolition. However, it is only among Muslim publics and reformist scholars that this consensus is abolitionist in the sense that it sees slavery to be an unacceptable way to treat other human beings. Abolitionist Muslims and Muslims who seek to fight against human trafficking must realize that the abolitionist consensus does not have deep roots in traditionalist circles. Since traditionalist teachings continue to have a role in the education of a significantly large number of Mosque leaders, jurists, and Islamic court judges, and have a significant presence in the

---

96   See *generally,* but esp. at 2–29, Abdullahi Ahmed An-Na'im ed., Human Rights in Cross-Cultural Perspectives (University of Pennsylvania Press 1995).

spiritual lives and the religious education of millions of Muslims around the world. Thus, one of the things that scholars, activists and concerned Muslims can do is work on the entrenchment of the abolitionist consensus among traditional hermeneutic circles.

While most reformist scholars simply assume that there is a juristic consensus on the abolition of slavery,[97] Bernard Freamon has taken a more proactive approach towards expanding and entrenching abolitionism by calling for a more explicit declaration of an *ijmā*-level consensus.[98] In addition to producing a sizable list of academic work on the topic, Freamon has launched a project to place the prohibition of slavery on more solid grounds. The project invites Islamic scholars to *"consider whether there is or should be an ijmā', declaring that slavery and slave trading are now illegal under the aegis of Islamic law and those practices should be considered to be abolished."*[99] If successful, especially among traditional scholars, a project focusing on expanding an Islamic scholarly consensus that genuinely hopes to combat slavery ought to be able to establish the strongest type of precedent which will be extremely difficult to reverse and make it easier to engage Islamic scholars and courts as allies against slavery and human trafficking. A scholastic consensus can also allow non-Islamic institutions that occasionally overlap with Islamic ones, such as courts in legally plural jurisdictions and international human rights bodies, to deploy this consensus against those who wish to defend slavery and slavery-like practices by deploying Islamic law.

Although how effectively an *ijmā* against slavery can be built from an advocacy or strategy point of view is not explored in this study, it will be noted that Muslims who are opposed to slavery and their allies need to make sure that they and their communities are not inadvertently supporting the opponents of Islamic abolitionism. One of the more immediate things that Muslims and Muslim abolitionists ought to consider is seeking ways to diminish the demand for pro-slavery Imams and Quran teachers. Decreasing the demand for pro-slavery Imams and teachers, for example by ensuring that slavery is put on the criteria for the selection of Imams or the selection of where one sends their child to Quran school, should loop an anti-slavery feedback to traditional schools. More importantly, such steps should at least ensure that abolitionists

---

97   *See, e.g.,* Mattar, *supra* note 34, at 18–20; El Fadl, *supra* note 23, at 255.; Parveen Shaukat, Human Rights in Islam 71 (1995); William Gervase Clarence-Smith, *supra* note 49, at 197; Open Letter to Baghdadi, *supra* note 88, at Sec. 12.

98   *See* Freamon, *supra* note 47; Freamon, *supra* note 48; Freamon, *supra* note at 62.

99   *See* "Statement of the Problem," on https://ijma-on-slavery.org/.

can shield their own children and communities from pro-slavery religious teachings, while avoiding personally funding anti-abolitionist enterprises.

Typically, an "internal cultural discourse" in the Islamic discursive space is occupied by Muslims. This space can, however, involve non-Muslims where it overlaps with other discourses. When this happens especially in human rights and constitutional law circles, it is important for "outsiders" to this discourse not to support the pro-slavery and other traditionalist positions by falling into an essentialist trap that portrays these positions as the only possible interpretation of Islam. The portrayal and reinforcement of traditionalist positions as representative of the entirety of Islam is unfortunately visibly present in the academic literature that attempts to briefly capture the essence of Islam, for example, in the context of comparing different "civilizations."[100] The issue of slavery in Islam has reached international tribunals such as the African Commission on Human and Peoples' Rights and the Community Court of Justice of the Economic Community of West African States, both of which have for the most part avoided the position of Islamic law on slavery.[101] The European Court of Human Rights, on the contrary, has fallen into the essentialist trap and came out more explicitly on the side of traditionalism when it decided "Sharia" is both "stable and invariable" and "faithfully reflects the dogmas and divine rules laid down by religion."[102]

The African Commission, which has generally chosen to avoid making pronouncements on Islamic law and jurisprudence,[103] made a brief foray into

---

100   The most obvious example of this is Huntington who falls in this trap in attempting to capture the essence of different "civilizations." *See* Samuel P. Huntington, The Third Wave: Democratization in the Late Twentieth Century 300–314 (1991). One can also see the same trend in the human rights field where Donnelly argues that an Islamic concept of human rights is non-existent and, at any rate, not desirable based on a very small sample among Muslim authors. *See* Jack Donnelly, *Human Rights and Human Dignity: An Analytic Critique of Non-Western Conceptions of Human Rights*, 76 Am. Pol. Sci. Rev. 303, 306–307 (1982).

101   *Bah Ould Rabah v. Mauritania*, Afr. Comm'n, Comm. No. 197/97 (2004); *Hadijatou Mani Koraou v. Niger*, Community Ct. Just. of the ECOWAS, ECW/CCJ/JUD/06/08 (2008).

102   *Refah Partisi et al. v. Turkey*, Eur. Court Hum. Rts., App. Nos. 41340/98, 41342/98, 41343/98 and 41344/98, Par. 123 (2003). These statements are repeated almost verbatim in *Gündüz v. Turkey*, Eur. Court Hum. Rts., App. No. 35071/97 (2003).

103   *Curtis Francis Doebbler v. Sudan*, Afr. Comm'n, Comm. No. 236/2000, *par.* 41 (2003) (in this case the Commission held Sudan to be in violation of the African Charter on Human and Peoples' Rights for its laws on corporal punishment, it explicitly avoids the topic noting that "it was not invited to interpret Islamic *Shari'a* Law"). Another case in which due process rights in Islamic Courts was brought to the African Commission although it was not decided on admissibility because the complainant inexplicably withdrew the case. *Safia Yakubu Husaini and et al. v. Nigeria*, Afr. Comm'n, Comm. No. 269/2003 (2005). The

Islamic law in *Amnesty International et al. v. Sudan* where it conflated the freedom of religion of Muslims, with the Sudanese government's application of "Sharia" and its persecution of religious minorities.[104] Reformist scholars would have vehemently opposed this characterization as they often have to emphasize the distinction between "Sharia," a broad and generic reference to *a priori* guiding principles of divine inspiration, and *"fiqh,"* which is a temporal and a purely human endeavor to translate the divine inspiration into specific substantive rules through the different interpretive methods described in the first section of the chapter.[105] Although this is not a distinction that traditionalists necessarily reject, those who seek to implement traditional *fiqh* in contemporary societies, including the government of Sudan that was in power at the relevant time, usually conflate the two under "Sharia" to raise the profile of *fiqh* positions they espouse and to simultaneously deny the interpretive flexibility they would have to concede if they cast their positions as *fiqh* or the opinion of mere mortals. In fact, many of the forms of persecution that the Sudanese government was engaged in, such as attempts at forced conversion or the prohibitions against the building of Churches, the harassment of clergy, and the denial of access to food aid to minorities, are unlikely to stand the test of "legal prescription"[106] even under classical and traditionalist *fiqh* positions.[107]

International Criminal Court has, in the *Al-Hassan* and *Al Mahdi* cases, been confronted with similar issues although not in connection with slavery. While the ICC did not address this matter in *Al Mahdi* because it was pleaded, *Al-Hassan* had not been decided at the time of writing.

104   Afr. Comm'n, Comm. Nos. 48/90-50/91-52/91-89/93, *par.* 19, 72–73 (1999) [hereinafter *"Amnesty International et al. v. Sudan"*] (specifically holding that "Shari'a is the national law," and that "[t]here is no controversy as to Shari'a being based upon the interpretation of the Muslim religion").

105   An-Na'im, *supra* note 20, 19–20; Khaled Abou El Fadl, *The Human Rights Commitment in Modern Islam, in* Human Rights and Responsibilities in the World Religions, (Joseph Runzo, Nancy M. Martin & Arvind Sharma eds., 2002); Amina Wadud, *Shari'ah Is Not the Law*, Religion Dispatches Magazine (2011); Zainah Anwar, *Introduction: Why Equality and Justice Now, in* Wanted: Equality and Justice in the Muslim Family 15 (Zainah Anwar ed., 2009).

106   The African Commission considers a right to have been violated unless it is shown that a limitation is, among other things, "prescribed by [a] law" that is "duly enacted." *See Amnesty International et al. v. Sudan,* Par. 58–59; *Constitutional Rights Project and another v. Nigeria,* Comm. No. 102/93 Afr. Comm'n (ACHPR, 1998) at Par. 42; *Purohit and another v. Gambia,* Comm. No. 241/2001 Afr. Comm'n (ACHPR, 2003) para. 64.

107   Although one can make the case that Islamic imperialism has, in practice, led to situations of forced or partially coerced conversions that are sanctioned by the state, forced conversions and most forms of explicit persecution of religions minorities have always been against established *fiqh* from a strictly doctrinal point of view. *See* Michael Bonner, Jihad in Islamic History 87–91 (2008).

In addition to domestic judiciaries and human rights bodies in legally plural jurisdictions, international human rights institutions, human rights NGOs, and litigators ought to tread more carefully in this regard as such a monolithization of Muslims in the traditionalist mold privileges those engaged in interpreting Islam as opposed to human rights, while undermining the efforts of progressive Muslim scholars, human rights activists, and feminists who are already being persecuted by the former.[108] Human rights actors ought to collaborate with progressive Muslims and Muslim groups to ensure that they approach Islam in a more nuanced manner. Until that happens, it is best to take a "do no harm" approach or, to borrow a leading Islamic legal maxim, "it is more advantageous to prevent the occurrence of harm."[109] This may mean finding human rights violations by states purporting to utilize Islamic law without having to go into what constitutes Islamic law and what does not.

5.2   *Holistic Approaches to Moving beyond Slavery*

In a previous section it was noted that reformist Muslim scholars have been developing Islamic ethico-legal approaches to addressing human trafficking. Granting that the need to promote abolitionism cannot be underestimated, these anti-trafficking approaches and the development of additional technical-legal arguments ought to be promoted. However, these arguments are also excessively technical, in part, because they stand on two highly technical fields, that of Islamic law-ethics in addition to domestic or international human trafficking laws. This makes them inaccessible to most but a small subset that is familiar with both fields. In addition, there is also a need to develop intermediary discourses that contextualize and place these technical arguments in broader Islamic social, cultural, and religious contexts.

---

108   *See* Ann Elizabeth Mayer, *Universal Versus Islamic Human Rights: A Clash of Cultures or a Clash with a Construct?* 15 Mich. J. Int'l L. 307, 384–402 (1994) (warning against essentializing Muslims and outlining the activism of and persecution against progressives); Abdullahi Ahmed An-Na'im, *The Islamic Law of Apostasy and its Modern Applicability: A Case from the Sudan*, 16 Religion 197, 197–198, 204–210 (1986) (describing the persecution of progressive Muslims in Sudan); Heiner Bielefeldt, *Muslim Voices in the Human Rights Debate*, 17 Hum. Rts. Q. 587, 602–615 (1995) (generally classifying Muslim views on human rights 'conservative', 'liberal', and 'pragmatic'); also Charles Kurzman, *Liberal Islam, Prospects and Challenges*, 3 Middle East Rev. Int'l Aff. 11, 11–13 (1999) (categorizing Shi'a Muslim views into "liberal Shari`a", "silent Shari`a" and "interpreted Shari`a").

109   Luqman Zakariyah, Legal Maxims in Islamic Criminal Law: Theory and Applications 162 (2015).

A comparatively more successful example for how a holistic approach may be provided by the feminist movement within Islam. Similar to the discourse on slavery, reformist women's rights discourse has been taking place over the last hundred plus years with concomitant hermeneutic approaches, legal reform initiatives, and a range of successes and failures that stretch from traditionalist resistance to reformist attempts to push the limits all the way to the radical groups that seek to impose imagined versions of a glorious past. However, what sets women's rights movements apart is that they have, at least in the last four decades, transformed into proper religious and social movements that seek to address power and patriarchy in Islam and Muslim societies more broadly.

What can be described as Islamic feminist discourse spans from the intricate exegetical works[110] to a tremendously diverse academic literature, social media advocacy and polemics, and even works of art.[111] Islamic feminist fields of action, some of which are conducted through formally organized groupings,[112] range from advocacy for the reform of Islamic law and especially family law,[113] to building alliances, creating inclusive spaces within their religious communities and protesting discriminatory religious institutions and spaces,[114] to creating nonprofits that provide for women's and other social needs,[115] and establishing women-friendly and women-led mosques.[116] Granted that it may

---

110   For the exegetical work, see, e.g., Wadud, *supra* note 61, *passim*; Asma Barlas, Believing Women in Islam: Unreading Patriarchal Interpretations of the Qur'an 186–187 (Karachi: Sama, 2004); Aziza Al-Hibri, *A Story of Islamic Herstory: Or How did We ever get into this Mess?*, 5 Women's Stud. Int'l Forum 207–219 (1982).

111   *See, e.g.,* Valerie J. Hoffman-Ladd, *Polemics on the Modesty and Segregation of Women in Contemporary Egypt*, Int'l J. Mid. E. Stud. 23 (1987); Wen-Chin Ouyang, F*eminist Discourse Between Art and Ideology: Four Novels by Nawāl Al-Sa'dāwī*, 30 Al-'Arabiyya 95 (1997); Rachel Epp Buller, *Un/Veiled: Feminist Art from the Arab/Muslim Diaspora*, 24 Al-Raida 116 (2007).

112   The most notable social organizations include Women Living Under Muslim Laws (WLUML), Sisters in Islam, Global Movement for Equality and Justice in the Muslim Family (Musawah). *See* Eva F. Nisa, *Women and Islamic Movements*, *in* Handbook of Islamic Sects and Movements (Muhammad Afzal Upal & Carole M. Cusack eds., 2021).

113   Kristin Stilt, Salma Waheedi & Swathi Gandhavadi Griffin, *The Ambitions of Muslim Family Law Reform*, 41 Harv. J. L. & Gender 301 (2018); Andra Nahal Behrouz, *Women's Rebellion: Towards a New Understanding of Domestic Violence in Islamic Law*, 5 UCLA J. Islamic & Near E. L. 153 (2006).

114   For example, the UnMosqued and Feminist Islamic Troublemakers of North America (FITNA) are good examples of activist communities that fall within this category.

115   For example Adis Duderija, The Imperatives of Progressive Islam 148 (2017).

116   For what has come to be known as the "Wadud Prayer" where progressive Muslims and rights advocates held a congregation in which women called for and led Muslim prayer,

take another couple of decades to fully understand whether or how successful the Islamic feminist movement will be, there are tentative lessons that Muslim abolitionists can learn from this movement. This movement is also a natural ally to abolitionism because of the overlaps between the concerns of feminists and abolitionists.

One of the tentative lessons that Muslim abolitionists can learn from Islamic feminists is the placement of abolitionist discourse within a larger progressive discourse, not on standalone issues such as slavery or human trafficking, but in the development of Islamic discourses on and alliances around equality and exploitation. These two values are deeply rooted in the source texts of Islam and Islamic scholars and pre-modern jurists had developed anti-exploitative discourses that ranged from slavery to usury, monopoly, underpayment for labor, the mistreatment of laborers and so on.[117] Similar to the discourse on human trafficking, the implications of Islamic law-ethics on labor and capitalism is a niche subject that is accessible only to scholars who are able to traverse a number of fields including religion and other political and economic issues, ideology, and political economy.[118] Despite being relevant to millions of Muslims, this discourse is probably too esoteric and inaccessible to have been picked up by either labor or Islamic movements.[119]

---

see Laury Silvers & Ahmed Elewa, 'I Am One of the People': A Survey and Analysis of Legal Arguments on Woman-Led Prayer in Islam, 26 J. L. & Relig. 141 (2011); apparently Muslims in China have also followed a similar path underlining that while the text allows such an interpretation it is the interpreter who chooses not to take it there, see Louisa Lim, Chinese Muslims forge isolated path, BBC News (15 Sept. 2004) http://news.bbc.co.uk/2/hi/asia-pacific/3656180.stm.

117 Mattar, supra note 34, at 21–28. For a discussion of pre-modern discourses that were supported exploitative relations and opposed them, see Maya Shatzmiller, Labor in the Medieval Islamic World 375–380 (1994).

118 See, e.g., Khalil Ur Rehman, The Concept of Labor in Islam (2010); Bayu Taufiq Possumah, Abdul Ghafar Ismail & Shahida Shahimi, Bringing Work Back in Islamic Ethics, 112 J. Bus. Ethics 257 (2013); Adnan A. Zulfiqar, Religious Sanctification of Labor Law: Islamic Labor Principles and Model Provisions, 9 U. Pa. J. Lab. & Emp. L. 421 (2007); Radwa S. Elsaman, Corporate Social Responsibility in Islamic Law: Labor and Employment, 18 New Eng. J. Int'l & Comp. L. 97 (2012).

119 Probably as a result of this, neither of the Islamist parties that won elections in Tunisia and Egypt were able to capture the support of labor either at a policy or discursive levels. See Gilbert Achcar (trans. G. M. Goshgarian), The People Want: A Radical Exploration of the Arab Uprising 235–46 (2013); Jamie Allinson, Class Forces, Transition and the Arab Uprisings: A Comparison of Tunisia, Egypt and Syria, 22 Democratization 294 (2015).

6   Conclusion

Most post-emancipation societies fight an uphill battle to overcome the legacies of slavery which linger for generations following emancipation. In the United States, putting aside multifaceted challenges that pervade systems of education, housing, healthcare, and state violence, the legacies of slavery are palpably visible in human trafficking statistics.[120] In addition to newer trends in human trafficking, one can expect what Kevin Bales describes as "vestiges of old slavery"[121] to persist in post-emancipation societies including those with large Muslim populations and majorities.[122] Having explored the potentialities of legal and ethical discourses of Islam on slavery, one could be forgiven for coming out with a pessimistic disposition. Despite the apparent consensus on the abolition of slavery among Muslim populations and reformist scholars, the consensus is rather thin.

With traditionalist scholars only superficially disapproving of slavery and being unable to portray slavery as sinful or immoral, it is going to be difficult to enlist them in combatting the vestiges of old slavery and contemporary human trafficking. This situation is probably going to be frustrating, and sometimes dangerous, for Muslims who are engaged in combatting human trafficking. The challenges they will face can range from difficulties in finding allies in their local imams, to religious leader who will vehemently oppose them, or even put them in jail or have them executed for apostasy or blasphemy. On the positive side, all countries with Islamic legal systems and Muslim majority populations have formally abolished slavery, are parties to international treaties prohibiting human trafficking, and have national legislation prohibiting human trafficking.[123] While this gives actors combatting slavery and human trafficking some respite, there is still a long way to go in terms of bringing

---

120   Cheryl Nelson-Butler, *The Racial Roots of Human Trafficking*, 62 UCLA L. Rev. 1481–83, 1496–1502 (2015) (noting that African Americans are significantly more vulnerable, constituting about 40% of sex trafficking victims despite constituting about 13% of the population, and are also more likely to be prosecuted than protected by the justice system).

121   Kevin Bales, Disposable People: New Slavery in the Global Economy 6–7 (2012) (*also see id.* at 80–120 on Mauritania).

122   For an instructive summary and collection on race and racism in North Africa and the Middle East, see the collection of articles in Vol. 10 of Lateral: J. Cultural Stud. Ass'n, *passim* (2021); Laura Menin, *Being 'black' in North Africa and the Middle East*, Open Democracy (12 Feb. 2018).

123   Mattar, *supra* note 9, at *passim*; also see United Nations, Treaty Series, Vol. 2237, Doc. A/55/383, 319 (showing that every UN member state except Congo and Uganda is a party to the UN TIP Protocol).

the full force of the Islamic value system behind the fight against slavery and human trafficking.

Acknowledgments

I would like to thank Gerald L. Neuman and María Cecilia Ercole for comments that helped inform and improve this work, and Roza Pati for the many conversations that led me to the topic of Islam and human trafficking.

CHAPTER 15

From Non-Discrimination to Substantive Equality: The On-Going Struggle

*Virgínia Brás Gomes**

1   Introduction

> Where, after all, do universal human rights begin? In small places, close
> to home – so close and so small that they cannot be seen on any maps
> of the world. Yet they are the world of the individual person; the neigh-
> bourhood he lives in; the school or college he attends; the factory, farm
> or office where he works. Such are the places where every man, woman
> and child seeks equal justice, equal opportunity, equal dignity without
> discrimination. Unless these rights have meaning there, they have little
> meaning anywhere. Without concerned citizen action to uphold them
> close to home, we shall look in vain for progress in the larger world.
>
> ELEANOR ROOSEVELT

Non-discrimination and equality have long been part and parcel of our aspirations, our legal and institutional frameworks, policies, and programs. In spite
of some progress, in certain countries more than in others, in combatting traditional forms of discrimination, as times evolve, the nature of discrimination
is becoming more interwoven with contemporary trends. It has acquired forms
that are more complex, which lie at the heart of unrest and potential conflict,
and therefore are more difficult to overcome.

The assessment reflected in this article stems from my work as a member of the UN Committee on Economic, Social, and Cultural Rights (CESCR)
that enabled me to understand how deeply discrimination contributes to the
non-realization of human rights, particularly for the most disadvantaged and
marginalized individuals and groups, and how sound and adequately implemented public policies can combat inequalities at all levels.

---

* Chair, United Nations Committee on Economic, Social and Cultural Rights, 2018.

2   Non-Discrimination in Human Rights Treaties

The twin principles of equality and non-discrimination are the bedrock of the international human rights framework. A frequently used definition of discrimination is set out in Article 1(1) of the International Convention on the Elimination of All Forms of Racial Discrimination as "any distinction, exclusion, restriction or preference based on race, colour, descent, or national or ethnic origin which has the purpose or effect of nullifying or impairing the recognition, enjoyment or exercise, on an equal footing, of human rights and fundamental freedoms in the political, economic, social, cultural or any other field of public life."[1]

The Universal Declaration of Human Rights (UDHR) sets forth a broad list of grounds for discrimination – "race, colour, sex, language, religion, political or other opinion, national or social origin, property, birth or other status."[2] This list, that is also included in the two International Covenants, that on Civil and Political Rights (ICCPR)[3] and that on Economic, Social and Cultural Rights (ICESCR),[4] does not attempt to be exhaustive since it includes the reference to "other status" to leave open the possibility for the inclusion of other grounds for discrimination that may eventually become necessary.

Later human rights treaties took on board new grounds for discrimination, or identified particular groups as being victims of discrimination, or even provided guidance on how to overcome problems caused by discrimination. For example, Article 2 of the Convention on the Rights of the Child includes ethnic origin and disability,[5] while Article 1 of the International Convention for the Protection of the Rights of all Migrant Workers and Members of their Families[6] refers to age for the first time as a ground for discrimination. In turn, Article 6 of the Convention on the Protection of Persons with Disabilities expresses the recognition by States parties that "women and girls with disabilities are subject to multiple discrimination," while Article 5(3) states that "in order to promote

---

1 International Convention on the Elimination of All Forms of Racial Discrimination (CERD), art. 1(1).

2 Universal Declaration of Human Rights, 10 December 1948, U.N.G.A. Res. 217 A), art. 2(1).

3 International Covenant on Civil and Political Rights (ICCPR), 16 December 1966, U.N.G.A. Res. 2200A (XXI), art. 2(1).

4 International Covenant on Economic, Social and Cultural Rights (ICESCR), 16 December 1966, U.N.G.A. Res. 2200A (XXI), art. 2(1).

5 Convention on the Rights of the Child (CRC), 20 November 1989, U.N.G.A. Res. 44/25, art. 2(1).

6 International Convention on the Protection of the Rights of All Migrant Workers and Members of Their Families, 18 December 1990, U.N.G.A. Res. 45/158, art. 1(1). It also refers to "economic position" and "marital status."

equality and eliminate discrimination, States Parties shall take all appropriate measures to ensure that reasonable accommodation is provided."[7]

While all the grounds indicated in the core human rights treaties remain valid, evolving societal norms and individual behaviors reflected in diverse ways of living have given rise to new grounds, which have led the UN treaty bodies in charge of interpreting their respective treaties to reflect these additional grounds in their guidance to States parties regarding the implementation of the rights listed therein. For example, in its General Comment (GC) 20, on non-discrimination in economic, social and cultural rights, the Committee on Economic, Social and Cultural Rights (CESCR) added sexual orientation and gender identity to the list of grounds for discrimination.[8] In the same GC, the CESCR took advantage of the "other status" clause in Article 2(2) of the ICESCR, and recognized that poverty and discrimination are mutually reinforcing, adding economic, and social situations as a ground for discrimination.[9]

3   Discrimination at Home

The ratification of the core international human rights instruments requires that States parties must immediately eliminate formal, or *de jure,* discrimination established by law, by amending such discriminatory legislation, and adopt measures for the elimination of *de facto* discrimination or discrimination in practice as soon as possible.

How have States translated the comprehensive international legal framework into national legislation and regulations? More importantly, how far have they made it real in policy formulation and implementation?

Very seldom have they taken the option to enact comprehensive anti-discrimination legislation that would provide the overarching legal architecture for a coherent non-discriminatory environment and integrated policies to

---

7   13 December 2006, U.N.G.A. Res. A/RES/61/106, arts. 5(3) and 6.

8   CESCR, General Comment No. 20, Non-discrimination in economic, social and cultural rights (art. 2, para. 2, of the International Covenant on Economic, Social and Cultural Rights), 2 July 2009, U.N. Doc. E/C.12/GC/20, para. 32.

9   *Id.* para. 35. The nature and manifestations of discrimination are different depending on the context, and they evolve over time. A flexible approach to the ground of "other status" is thus needed in order to capture other forms of differential treatment that cannot be reasonably and objectively justified and are of a comparable nature to the expressly recognized grounds in article 2, paragraph 2 of the ICESCR. These additional grounds are commonly recognized when they reflect the experience of social groups that are vulnerable and have suffered and continue to suffer marginalization (*id.,* para. 27).

combat the root causes of discrimination. There are, in a number of countries, ample regulations against discrimination in the field of education, work and employment, and social security, with legal avenues for complaints and redress, yet the absence of a framework law that tackles the problem across the board allows for huge implementation gaps.

For example, according to Article 14 of the European Convention for the Protection of Human Rights and Fundamental Freedoms, "the enjoyment of the rights and freedoms set forth in this Convention shall be secured without discrimination on any ground such as sex, race, colour, language, religion, political or other opinion, national or social origin, association with a national minority, property, birth or other status."[10]

However, the two anti-discrimination European Union Directives in place – the Racial Equality Directive 2000/43/EC,[11] implementing the principle of equal treatment between persons irrespective of racial or ethnic origin, and Council Directive 2000/78/EC,[12] establishing a general framework for equal treatment in employment and occupation – do not follow the overall non-discrimination blanket provision of Article 14 of the European Convention.

These Directives have been transposed to the national legislative frameworks of the EU Member States, reproducing the existing loopholes by mostly covering unequal treatment on grounds of race and gender, and for employment and occupation issues.

The draft horizontal EU anti-discrimination Directive, also known as the Equal Treatment Directive, that would expand protection throughout the European Union against discrimination on the grounds of age, disability, religion or belief, and sexual orientation, to the areas of social protection, healthcare, education, housing and access to goods and services, has been under discussion since 2008.[13]

At present, these four grounds are only covered in employment and vocational training. The grounds of sex and ethnic, or racial, origin are, by contrast, protected across a much broader range of social areas.

---

10   European Convention for the Protection of Human Rights and Fundamental Freedoms, 4 November 1950, European Treaty Series – No. 5, art. 14.

11   European Union, Council Directive 2000/43/EC of 29 June 2000 implementing the principle of equal treatment between persons irrespective of racial or ethnic origin, https:// eur-lex.europa.eu/legal-content/EN/TXT/?uri= celex%3A32000L0043.

12   European Union, Council Directive 2000/78/EC of 27 November 2000 establishing a general framework for equal treatment in employment and occupation, https://eur-lex .europa.eu/legal-content/EN/TXT/?uri =celex%3A32000L0078.

13   See Equinet, *Time to adopt the Equal Treatment Directive*, 25 June 2018, https://equineteurope .org/time-to-adopt-the-equal-treatment-directive.

Despite overwhelming support from the European Commission, a vast majority of EU member states, and the European Parliament, the Equal Treatment Directive remains in a position of deep freeze since it requires unanimous agreement from all the Member States.

The non-adoption of the Directive has several practical consequences. It reinforces the notion that some forms of discrimination are more acceptable than others and is deeply unfair to those groups who would benefit the most from the added protection the directive would provide. Besides calling into question the EU's commitment to its founding values of respect for human dignity, freedom, democracy, equality, the rule of law, and respect for human rights, as stipulated in Article 2 of the Treaty of the European Union, it also limits the ability of the EU to provide redress to discrimination victims and bring perpetrators to account.

The African Charter on Human and Peoples' Rights of 1981 recognizes a wide range of civil, political, economic, social, and cultural rights of individual human beings, including a provision on freedom from discrimination on any grounds in the enjoyment of the rights and freedoms guaranteed in the Charter,[14] that closely follows the formulation of Article 2 of the UDHR.

In turn, the African Court on Human and Peoples' Rights has adjudicated a number of cases related to individual and group discrimination.[15]

In general terms, national implementation of the Concluding Observations of UN treaty bodies to African States Parties has neither been consistent nor effective. For example, during its last session, the CESCR, in its dialogue with the Democratic Republic of Congo, noted with concern the absence of a comprehensive anti-discrimination law as well the lack of effective measures to combat *de facto* discrimination in the effective enjoyment of economic, social, and cultural rights experienced by indigenous peoples, in particular the Batwa, internally displaced persons, and persons with disabilities.[16] The Committee also raised the issue of discrimination on grounds of sexual orientation and gender identity since the State's Criminal Code is often used to

---

14   African Charter on Human and Peoples' Rights of 1981, art. 2: "Every individual shall be entitled to the enjoyment of the rights and freedoms recognized and guaranteed in the present Charter without distinction of any kind such as race, ethnic group, colour, sex, language, religion, political or any other opinion, national and social origin, fortune, birth or any status."

15   *See, e.g., The matter of African Commission on Human and Peoples' Rights v. Republic of Kenya,* Application No. 006/2021 Judgement (Reparations), 32 June 2022, pertaining to the Ogiek Indigenous People.

16   CESCR Concluding Observations (2021) on the sixth periodic report of the Democratic Republic of Congo, (E/C.12/COD/CO/6), paras. 26 and 27.

criminalize same-sex marriages, recommending that the State party combat discrimination and stigmatization faced by lesbian, gay, bisexual, transgender, and intersex persons by conducting awareness raising campaigns and ensuring that the Criminal Code is not used to criminalize relations between persons of the same sex.[17] The Committee also expressed its concern at the persistent gender stereotypes that perpetuate gender inequality, particularly in the areas of labor market access, equal pay and conditions of work, and participation in public and political life.[18]

In the Americas, the American Convention on Human Rights[19] and the Additional Protocol to the American Convention on Human Rights in the Area of Economic, Social, and Cultural Rights (Protocol of San Salvador)[20] guarantee the exercise of rights without discrimination of any kind for reasons related to race, color, sex, language, religion, political or other opinions, national or social origin, economic status, birth, or any other social condition. The Inter-American Commission on Human Rights, in charge of promoting the observance and protection of human rights in the Americas, furthers its mandate through inter alia, receiving, analyzing, and investigating individual petitions regarding alleged human rights violations committed either by a Member State of the Organisation of American States (OAS) that has ratified the American Convention or by one that has not done so, as well as observing the general situation of human rights in the Member States.[21] Some of its more recent thematic reports raise these issues and provide guidance on combatting discrimination based on gender and race.[22]

In turn, recently, the Inter-American Court of Human Rights found *Intersectional Discrimination, Labor Violations of Rights of Workers in Fireworks Factory Explosion* in Brazil. In its decision, it requires the state to actively protect groups at higher risk, especially women and children, from the danger of

---

17   *Id.*, paras. 28 and 29.

18   *Id.*, para. 30.

19   American Convention on Human Rights, 22 November 1969, art.1: Obligation to respect rights.

20   *Id.* art.3: Obligation of non-discrimination.

21   Charter of the OAS, 1948, art. 6.

22   Economic, Social, Cultural and Environmental Rights of Persons of African Descent, https://www.oas.org/en/iachr/reports/pdfs/DESCA-Afro-en.pdf; Report on Trans and Gender-Diverse Persons and Their Economic, Social, Cultural, and Environmental Rights, http://www.oas.org/en/iachr/ reports/pdfs/TransDESCA-en.pdf (oas.org); *IACHR: States and Society Must Protect Girls and Adolescents from All Forms of Violence*, October 11, 2022, https://www.oas.org/en/IACHR/jsForm/?File=/en/iachr/ media_center/PReleases /2022/226.asp.

unsafe, unsanitary, and particularly dangerous working conditions by enforcing and supervising the implementation of protective regulations.[23]

Despite some progress in repealing direct discrimination in laws and policies, indirect discrimination has turned out to be more complex, especially when legal provisions appear to be neutral but, in effect, lead to discrimination when implemented. Of particular concern are intersectional discrimination and culturally ingrained discrimination. The former is derived from the cumulative and compounded effects of discrimination on several grounds while the latter (culturally ingrained discrimination) is the most difficult to tackle, because it results from the explicit or implicit imposition of dominant societal values on those who do not share them. The most important gaps in antidiscrimination practice lie in the lack of recognition by States of intersectional or compounded discrimination and the particularly negative and long-lasting effects it has on women and persons belonging to vulnerable groups. There is also a lack of recognition of systemic discrimination based on deeply rooted societal prejudices. Governments are reluctant to recognize such discrimination because it amounts to a failure of the measures they have taken to combat discrimination without really addressing its root causes. One only needs to look at discrimination against the poor, or minority groups such as the Dalits, the Roma people, or indigenous communities, to know this is true.

4   Recurrent Patterns of *De Facto* Discrimination against Certain Groups

Discrimination and conflict have never been so close and yet so far apart. So close, because all States have recognized the undeniable links between them and yet so far apart, because this recognition has not been matched by the political will and the closing of non-discrimination policy implementation gaps. Discrimination against the Dalits[24] and the Roma provide good examples of these contradictory trends, the lack of political will, and the inability to combat deep-rooted societal patterns, and misconceptions.

---

23   *Empregados da Fábrica de Fogos de Santo Antônio de Jesus e seus Familiares vs. Brasil*, 15 July 2021, https://www.escr-net.org/caselaw/2021/empregados-da-fabrica-fogos-santo-antonio-jesus-e-seus-familiares-vs-brasil.

24   According to the International Dalit Solidarity Network, there are an estimated 260 million Dalits worldwide. The Dalit live in South Asia (India, Nepal, Bangladesh, Pakistan, and Sri Lanka) and in communities who migrated from South Asia across the globe.

Over 2,000 years old, the caste system is perhaps the oldest surviving social hierarchy in the world. The dialogue with the national delegations and NGO representatives of some of the States with Dalit communities have provided human rights treaty bodies with the opportunity for extensive discussions on the difficulties of changing ingrained societal discrimination patterns legitimized by tradition and cultural practices.

In the Indian legal system, discrimination of Scheduled Castes (SC's) and Scheduled Tribes (ST's) is prohibited. This stems from Article 17 of the Indian Constitution that abolishes untouchability, which is greatly due to the efforts of Dr. B. R. Ambedkar, himself a Dalit, one of the leaders of the Indian independence movement, and considered chief architect of the Indian Constitution. In his writings and speeches, he consistently used the designation "Depressed Classes" to refer to the Dalit communities. In his words, "[p]olitical democracy cannot last unless there lies at the base of it social democracy. What does social democracy mean? It means a way of life which recognizes liberty, equality and fraternity as the principles of life."[25]

A host of other legal prohibitions are in place, most notably the 1989 Scheduled Castes and Scheduled Tribes (Prevention of Atrocities) Act to prevent discrimination and crimes against Dalits and Adivasis,[26] and to provide relief and rehabilitation for victims of the extensive listing of offences under the Act that covers violations of civil, cultural, economic, political, and social rights.

Affirmative action has been implemented in India by way of a reservation policy that though subject to contestation by some sectors of society and even challenged in court, enables members of the lower castes to access public education and employment on a priority basis. However, qualitative representation is still short of the prescribed quota. Regardless of legal safeguards,

---

25   https://www.brainyquote.com/quotes/b_r_ambedkar_753200.
26   With respect to the legal terminology in India, the National Commission for Scheduled Castes and Scheduled Tribes has held the term "Scheduled Castes" to be the proper constitutional usage for the castes identified as Dalits. A Dalit is hence a person who belongs to one of the castes identified as Scheduled Caste.
      "Adivasis" literally mean "indigenous people" or "original inhabitants," though the term "Scheduled Tribes" is not coterminous with the term "Adivasis." Scheduled Tribes is an administrative term used for purposes of "administering" certain specific constitutional privileges, protection and benefits for specific sections of peoples considered historically disadvantaged and "backward."

atrocities against members of the SC's account for 89% of the crimes against SC's and ST's combined.[27]

Even though the National Commission for Scheduled Castes and Scheduled Tribes has extensive powers of investigation and inquiry in this area and can fix responsibility and recommend action, its recommendations are not binding. Much more needs to be done by the Commission to strengthen the judicial protection for Dalits to ensure the effective implementation of anti-discrimination public policies and programmes, and create a better structured platform for dialogue with civil society organizations working on Dalit issues. Perhaps, most importantly, it needs to review and step up its efforts to identify social practices that promote discrimination in order to help change deeply rooted societal prejudices.

The National Campaign on Dalit Human Rights, that works with victims of violence to advocate for justice and compensation from the government, while providing economic and psychological services for families, has continuously raised issues related to the marginalization, stigma, and violence suffered by the Dalit communities, such as pervasive sexual violence, trafficking and harmful cultural practices targeting women and girls as well as hate speech, and on-line discrimination and abuse.[28]

The Committee on the Elimination of all Forms of Discrimination against Women notes the State party's efforts to enact a legal framework to prevent and respond to violence against women, including women from the marginalized castes and communities, and the establishment, in 2013, of the Justice Verma Committee on Amendments to Criminal Law to review existing normative gaps. However, it remains concerned over the escalation of caste-based violence, including rape against women and girls, and the downplaying by key State officials of the grave criminal nature of sexual violence against women and girls, as well as the poor implementation of the Scheduled Castes and the Scheduled Tribes (Prevention of Atrocities) Act, and the impunity of perpetrators of serious crimes against women.[29]

In its dialogue with India, another treaty body, the CESCR, had also voiced its concerns at the obstacles faced by victims in seeking access to justice, including the high costs of litigation, the long delays in court proceedings,

---

27   *See* https://www.insightsonindia.com/social-justice/issues-related-to-sc-st/national -commission-for-scheduled-castes/.

28   *See* Beena Pallical in OHCHR, *The Dalit: Born into a life of discrimination and stigma,* 19 April 2021, https://www.ohchr.org/en/stories/2021/04/dalit-born-life-discrimination-and -stigma.

29   CEDAW Concluding Observations (2014) CEDAW/C/IND/CO/4–5, paras. 10(c)(d).

and the non-implementation of court decisions by government authorities. Of particular concern was the low rate of prosecution of crimes against persons belonging to scheduled castes and scheduled tribes, which is tied to a serious obstacle in the victims' access to justice, stemming from discriminatory attitudes and prejudices in the enforcement of the law.[30]

A blanket recommendation addressed to the State party was to strengthen the enforcement of existing legal prohibitions of discrimination and, consider enacting comprehensive administrative, civil and/or criminal anti-discrimination legislation guaranteeing the right to equal treatment and protection against discrimination.[31]

In 2019, in its *Concluding Observations on India*, the Committee on the Rights of Persons with Disabilities (CRPD) regretted the absence of measures to combat multiple and intersecting discrimination against inter alia persons with disabilities in scheduled castes and scheduled tribes, including Dalits and Adivasi.[32]

More recently, in the context of the Universal Periodic Review, a number of recommendations on the non-discrimination normative framework and practices were made and supported by India.[33] Only time will tell if such support will lead to proactive efforts and the accountability of the public duty bearers in the future.

Nepal is another case study that illustrates the disappointing implementation of non-discrimination provisions, even when and where there have been political, institutional, and legislative changes in the right direction.

The Interim Constitution of Nepal adopted in December 2006, already prohibited caste-based discrimination recognizing that economic, social, and cultural discrimination of Dalits and other minorities was one of the legitimating factors of the People's War. It is true that the earlier 1990 Constitution already prohibited such discrimination. But it is equally true that it also contained a

---

30   CESCR, Concluding Observations (2008), U.N. Soc. E/C.12/IND/CO/5, paras. 13 and 14.

31   *Id.*, para. 52.

32   CRPD/C/IND/CO/1: Concluding Observations on the initial report of India (Advance Unedited Version), 29 October 2019, https://www.ohchr.org/en/documents/concluding -observations/crpdcindco1-concluding-observations-initial-report-india-advance.

33   Report of Working Group: India, Universal Periodic Review, Third Cycle (2017–2020), U.N. Doc. A/HRC/36/10. Recommendations. Continue the fight against discrimination, exclusion, dehumanization, stigmatization and violence suffered by scheduled castes (Peru) (161.81); Take urgent measures to repeal the norms that discriminate against castes, and investigate and sanction the perpetrators of acts of discrimination and violence against them, in particular against the Dalits (Argentina) (161.82); Take the necessary measures to ensure effective implementation of the Scheduled Castes and Scheduled Tribes Act, notably through the training of State officials (France) (161.83).

number of exemptions. For example, in religious contexts, which rendered the constitutional provision almost ineffective.

The new Constitution, adopted at the end of a wide consultative process in 2015, enshrined non-discrimination and equality clauses that provide legislative protection against discrimination on several grounds.[34] In fact, a joint reading of both clauses brings us close to a comprehensive anti-discrimination law that all human rights monitoring bodies have been calling for as the best tool to combat intersectional and systemic discrimination. However, as noted by the CEDAW Committee, there is still further need for the definition of discrimination against women, encompassing elements of direct and indirect discrimination, as well as multiple and intersecting forms of discrimination in the public and private spheres, that would guarantee effective remedies for victims, as well as the repeal of previous discriminatory laws, and provisions in the Civil Code that restrict women's rights to citizenship, access to employment abroad, and marital property upon divorce.[35]

In the same vein, the CERD Committee questioned the definition and criminalization of racial discrimination, insofar as the Caste-based Discrimination and Untouchability (Offence and Punishment) Act of 2011 does not prohibit discrimination based on color, or national or ethnic origin, and does not expressly prohibit both direct and indirect forms of discrimination.

---

34   Constitution of Nepal, art. 24: Right against untouchability and discrimination (…) (1) No person shall be treated with any kind of untouchability or discrimination in any private or public place on grounds of caste, ethnicity, origin, community, occupation, or physical condition (…) (5). All forms of untouchability or discrimination contrary to this provision shall be punishable by law as a serious social crime, and the victim of such an act shall have the right to compensation as provided for by law.

     Id. art.18: Right to equality (1) All citizens shall be equal before law. No person shall be denied the equal protection of law. (2) There shall be no discrimination in the application of general laws on the grounds of origin, religion, race, caste, tribe, sex, physical conditions, disability, health condition, matrimonial status, pregnancy, economic condition, language or geographical region, or ideology or any other such grounds. (3) The state shall not discriminate among citizens on grounds of origin, religion, race, caste, tribe, sex, economic condition, language or geographical region, ideology and such other matters. Provided that nothing shall be deemed to bar the making of special provisions by law for the protection, empowerment or advancement of the women lagging behind socially and culturally, Dalits, Adibasi, Madhesi, Tharus, Muslims, oppressed class, backward communities, minorities, marginalized groups, peasants, laborers, youths, children, senior citizens, sexual minorities, persons with disability, pregnant, incapacitated and the helpless persons, and of the citizens who belong to backward regions and financially deprived citizens including the Khas Arya.

35   CEDAW, Concluding Observations on the sixth periodic report of Nepal, 14 November 2018, U.N. Doc. CEDAW/C/NPL/CO/6, paras. 8(a)(b). 2018.

Consequently, the State party was urged to ensure that its domestic legislation defines and criminalizes all forms of racial discrimination specified in Article 1 of the Convention on the Elimination of all Forms of Racial Discrimination, including discrimination on the basis of color, and national or ethnic origin, and prohibits both direct and indirect racial discrimination in all fields of public life.

The CERD Committee also remained concerned by reports of the persistence of caste-based segregation. In an extensive recommendation that covers a number of structural constraints, the State party was required to monitor, investigate, prosecute and sanction incidents of violence linked to inter-caste marriage and caste-based segregation. In addition to offering protection and remedies for victims, there was a mandate to conduct country-wide public awareness and education campaigns designed to eliminate the notion of racial or caste-based hierarchies, end social segregation practices, and prevent inter-caste violence. This helped to ensure that educational curricula and textbooks condemn caste-based discrimination and untouchability, contain positive representations of the culture and contributions of all castes, and omit derogatory or otherwise discriminatory language against any caste. Furthermore, in order to combat caste-based occupational specialization, that obstructs socioeconomic mobility and assigns members of certain castes to degrading and/or exploitative occupations, the CERD Committee recommended that the State party implement measures to guarantee and promote occupational mobility for marginalized castes, including through hiring incentives, vocational training, community-based awareness, and empowerment programs.[36]

The root of the caste-based discrimination in Nepal is likely due to social inclusion policies and the national Three Year Plans for development, which are ambiguous as they fail to adequately address the issue of diversity and intersectionality within Nepali society. Moreover, they continue to identify exclusion as a developmental issue, and poverty alleviation as the solution rather than exclusion as a consequence of discriminatory policies that should be changed and practices that must be abolished. The hesitation to use the term Dalit, which is often replaced by 33 euphemisms such as "oppressed," "depressed," "backward," "deprived," and "disadvantaged," shows the unwillingness to

---

36   CERD, Concluding Observations on the combined seventeenth to twenty-third periodic reports of Nepal, 29 May 2018, U.N. Doc. CERD/C/NPL/CO/17–23, paras. 7, 8, 13, 14, 31 and 32.

recognize caste discrimination as a part of the problem formulation and to combat structural caste discrimination.[37]

Article 21 of the EU Charter of Fundamental Rights prohibits any discrimination because of ethnic or social origin or membership of a national minority. Since 2000, EU law (Racial Equality Directive, 2000/43/EC) has promoted equal treatment and prohibited direct and indirect discrimination. However, Roma individuals and communities[38] continue to face widespread discrimination, segregation, and institutional and societal non-acceptance and non-recognition of their specific characteristics and ways of living.[39]

The Decade for Roma Inclusion (2005–2015)[40] represented an action framework for governments to promote, with the effective participation of the Roma people themselves, strategies programmes action plans and affirmative action, and to closely monitor progress in accelerating social inclusion and improving the economic and social status of the Roma people across the region. In spite of some progress, the political commitment to break the cycle of poverty and exclusion, and close the gap in welfare and impoverished living conditions between the Roma and the non-Roma people has not materialized. Roma communities still face widespread discrimination by private and public employers and national, regional and local authorities responsible for social benefits and social services.

---

37 Aastha Kc, *Caste-Based Discrimination in Contemporary Nepal: A problematisation of Nepal's national policies that address discrimination based on caste*, Spring 2020, https://www.diva-portal.org/smash/ get/diva2:1482580/FULLTEXT01.pdf.

38 According to Amnesty International, there is no official or reliable count of Romani populations worldwide. In Europe, there are between 10 and 12 million Roma. Most of them around two thirds – live in Central and Eastern European countries, where they make up between 5 and 10 per cent of the population. There are also sizeable Romani minorities in Western Europe, especially in Italy (around 150,000 Roma and Travellers), Spain (600,000–800,000), France and the UK (up to 300,000 in each country). *The Roma in Europe: 11 things you always wanted to know.* There are an estimated one million Roma in the United States and 800,000 in Brazil, most of whose ancestors emigrated in the 19th century from Eastern Europe. *Romani people – Wikipedia.*

39 Widely known as *Gypsies* (or *Gipsies*), which is considered a pejorative term by Romani people due to its connotations of illegality and irregularity as well as its historical use as a racial slur. Cognates of the word exist in many other languages (e.g. *tzigane* in French; *gitano*, in Spanish; *zingaro*, in Italian; *Cigano*, in Portuguese; *Tigan*, in Romanian; and *Zigeuner*, in German). At the first World Romani Congress in 1971, its attendees unanimously voted to reject the use of all exonyms for the Romani people, including *Gypsy*, due to their aforementioned negative and stereotypical connotations.

40 Adopted by eight countries in Central and Southeast Europe (Bulgaria, Croatia, the Czech Republic, Hungary, Macedonia, Romania, Serbia and Montenegro, and Slovakia) and supported by the international community.

A great majority of Roma families are frequently denied access to social housing, leading them to live in slum settlements, without access to running water, adequate sewerage and, with no security of tenure. Notwithstanding the fact that their life expectancy remains considerably lower than that of the non-Roma population, they are discriminated against in their access to health care services. There are still many States that have a persistent pattern of segregating Roma children in separate schools, for example, placing Roma children in special remedial schools for children with mental disabilities, or in separate substandard "catch-up" classes within schools. Discriminatory ethnic profiling by police officers undermines trust in public authorities and there continue to be a lack of disaggregated data on complaints received by the police, inspectorates, and judicial bodies in the context of the implementation of the Racial Equality Directive.

Roma communities were also deeply impacted by the COVID-19 social and health crisis, that reflects the vulnerability of many Roma communities that have not only experienced a higher risk of contagion, but have also been more affected by the confinement measures that left many Roma families unemployed and without other means of subsistence. Moreover, during the pandemic, Roma have been subjected to discrimination, antigypsyism[41] attitudes, and violations of their fundamental rights.[42]

A cursory search for the opinion of treaty bodies on discrimination against the Roma yielded an excellent example of concerns and recommendations in this field, as expressed by the CESCR, after its dialogue with the national delegation from the Czech Republic earlier this year.

While acknowledging the Strategy for Roma Equality, Inclusion and Participation 2021–2030, and initiatives such as the national Roma platform, the Committee reiterated its concerns about the stigmatization, poverty, and widespread discrimination experienced by the Roma in the areas of health, education, housing, and employment, recommending that the State party intensify its efforts to address the socioeconomic disparities and discrimination faced by Roma persons in accessing health care, education, adequate housing, employment, and public services, paying particular attention to Roma women and children; proactively address negative prejudices and stereotypes against Roma, including through awareness-raising campaigns, and

---

41   The term "antigypsyism" is used by the Council of Europe to characterize this form of discrimination. *Cf.* https://www.coe.int/en/web/roma-and-travellers/antigypsyism -/-discrimination.

42   EURoma, FRA Report on Fundamental Rights in Europe 2021, https://www.euromanet .eu/news/fra-report-on-fundamental-rights-in-europe-2021/.

provide information to Roma about their rights; undertake steps to address mistrust among the Roma of public institutions, including by involving Roma representatives in the formulation, monitoring, and evaluation of policies that concern their rights; and improve its data collection system with a view to producing reliable data disaggregated on the basis of prohibited grounds of discrimination.[43] More specifically, the Committee recommended that the State party intensify its efforts to support employment for Roma,[44] implement a national policy and strategy with a time-bound action plan to accelerate progress towards deinstitutionalization, in support of community-based and family-based options, giving particular attention to children with disabilities, Roma children, and very young children, in order to reduce the high number of institutionalized children.[45] The Committee was also concerned that inflation would depress the value of the subsistence minimum that did not include the cost of housing and was constantly decreasing with a negative impact on people who rely on social benefits that are calculated on the basis of this indicator, especially Roma. Among its recommendations are the development and effective implementation of a human-rights based national strategy on housing, the adoption of a housing law, and the increase availability of adequate and affordable housing, particularly by expanding the supply of social housing and housing subsidies.[46]

Among other concerns expressed by the Committee are the forced sterilization of Roma women[47] and the insufficient level of inclusive education for Roma and migrant children as well as the insufficient coverage of Roma children by preschool education. It is recommended that the State party intensify its efforts to ensure that Roma children have access to high quality mainstream education, including preschool education and take targeted measures to improve enrolment and completion rates among Roma children, in particular Roma girls, at the various levels of education.[48]

It is also worth noting that in accordance with the procedure on follow-up to concluding observations adopted by the Committee, the State party requested to provide, within 24 months of the adoption of the concluding observations, information on the implementation of the recommendations contained in

---

43   CESCR, Concluding Observations on the third periodic report of Czechia (E/C.12/CZE/
      CO/3), https://www.ecoi.net/en/document/2070826.html, paras. 14 and 15.
44   *Id.*, para. 21(b).
45   *Id.*, para. 31(b).
46   *Id.*, paras. 34 and 37.
47   *Id.*, paras. 40 and 41.
48   *Id.*, paras. 48 and 49.

paragraphs 31(b) (children in institutions) and 37(a) (adequate housing) that focus on the Roma.

5   Moving towards Substantive Equality, the Obligations of States to Fulfill Economic, Social, and Cultural Rights

The lack of constitutional recognition of economic, social, and cultural rights (ESCR) in a number of countries deeply impacts the political relevance of these rights and the corresponding obligations to realize them. States that do not have these rights in their constitutions hold the view that there is no provision in the ICESCR that requires them to incorporate the Covenant or to accord to it a specific status in the domestic legal order, and that other methods of implementation of the ICESCR, through appropriate legislation and administrative measures, ensure the fulfilment of their obligations. Formally, this may be correct, but in reality, the lack of constitutional recognition weakens the status and the scope of these rights. However, Covenant rights cannot be applied directly by domestic courts, which restricts access to effective legal remedies in case of violations. The incorporation of the Covenant would also help States to adopt a National Human Rights Action Plan enabling them to operate more strategically to ensure their human rights efforts are better coordinated and human rights progress on the ground is more effectively monitored.

It may be true that constitutional rights primarily set aspirational goals, but it is certainly true that rights that are in a Constitution, or in a Bill of Rights, are much more likely to be the further object of framework laws to guarantee universal and implementation with built-in accountability mechanisms. A case in point is countries that were under fiscal adjustment programs during the Austerity period. One of the first measures to be taken during this time was to drastically cut social spending which corresponded with a negative impact on the enjoyment of a number of rights. But countries that had constitutionalized some or all of the ESCR had some safeguards in place that protected rights holders from even more long-lasting consequences.

When ESCR are not given the relevance they deserve in domestic law and policy, but rather remain to be realized by fragmented programs and ad-hoc support measures that do not comply with a human rights-based approach, there are obvious consequences in the allocation of resources guaranteed by the national budget, which can be scarce and subject to negotiation between line ministries at times with conflicting priorities.

On the other hand, generally speaking, progressive realization of ESCR seems to have come to some kind of a standstill across the board. Again, constitutional recognition of ESCR is a permanent reminder to States of their overarching political and social contract with all those living under their jurisdiction.

Another frequent argument for non-incorporation is that the direct applicability of the Covenant rights is incompatible with the doctrine of the supremacy of the parliament. In other words, if these rights were to become the basis for judicial decisions, judges would be entitled to enter the realm of politics, which is reserved for the parliament.

Fortunately, against the artificial division of human rights into first class rights that ensure the freedoms and second-class rights that are mostly aspirational, various landmark judgments of regional and national courts regarding violations of ESCR have proved that the separation of powers among the different branches of government and their independence can be fully retained and that they are, in fact, mutually reinforcing.

In any case, and irrespective of the constitutional framework, to ensure that substantive equality goes beyond formal equality before the law, and has a real transformative effect on people's lives, States must have core obligations towards the progressive realization of rights.

The core obligations of States are to address, as a matter of absolute priority, the needs of target groups traditionally subject to discrimination, such as ethnic and national minorities and indigenous and tribal communities. For them, the legal framework is often incomplete and the implementation gaps always considerable due to the limited access to justice which is often complicated, delayed, and generally too expensive.

For those countries that have ratified the ICESCR,[49] there is an immediate obligation to ensure the satisfaction of, at the very least, minimum essential levels[50] for each of the Covenant rights for these target groups with time-bound measurable benchmarks that set the targets to be achieved, as well as the economic and social measures to achieve them.

The strengthening of the concept of core obligations has been perhaps one of the most important contributions the Committee on Economic, Social and Cultural Rights has made, from considerations on the nature and content of such obligations in General Comment No. 3 on the domestic application of the Covenant, to spelling out the core obligations in later General Comments on substantive rights.[51] The Committee is often questioned as to why it includes a national plan of action in the core obligations. The answer is that it is a

---

49   171 States parties.
50   CESCR General Comment No. 3 (1990) on the nature of States parties obligations.
51   *See* General Comments Nos. 12, 13, 14, 15, 17, 18, 19, 21, 22, 23 and 25.

procedural core obligation of the utmost importance, because it requires that the human rights principles of participation of rights holders and accountability of duty bearers be interwoven with the material content of the right.

Article 2(1) of the Covenant[52] obliges each State party to take the necessary steps "to the maximum of its available resources," which means that overall national priorities should ensure that resource allocation is in conformity with the States party's obligations under the Covenant.[53]

States must take deliberate, concrete and targeted steps to progressively realize the rights using domestic resources as well as international cooperation and assistance. Not all obligations are tied to resources or are to be achieved in the long term. For example, States parties have an immediate obligation to "guarantee that the rights enunciated in the Covenant will be exercised without discrimination of any kind." This obligation frequently requires the immediate adoption and implementation of appropriate legislation but does not necessarily call for significant resource allocations. The obligation to fulfill rights, on the other hand, often requires positive budgetary measures, and criteria need to be developed in order to assess whether such measures are sufficient, adequate, and reasonable.

Lack of resources can certainly affect the full enjoyment of economic, social, and cultural rights, but Article 2.1 of the Covenant obliges each State party to take the necessary steps "to the maximum of its available resources". In order for a State party to be able to attribute its failure to meet at least its minimum core obligations to a lack of available resources it must demonstrate that every effort has been made to use all resources that are at its disposition in an effort to satisfy, as a matter of priority, those minimum obligations. Without such obligations, the Covenant would be deprived of all meaningful content. In sum, where several policy options are available, States should adopt the option that least restricts Covenant rights and all steps should take into account the precarious situation of individuals and families living in deprivation, with the utmost priority to be given to grave situations.

Obviously, States cannot allocate resources they do not have. But they can certainly generate resources to promote public policies for the enjoyment of

---

52   ICESCR art. 2(1): "Each State Party to the present Covenant undertakes to take steps, individually and through international assistance and cooperation, especially economic and technical, to the maximum of its available resources, with a view to achieving progressively the full realisation of the rights recognized in the present Covenant by all appropriate means, including particularly the adoption of legislative measures."

53   CESCR Statement on an evaluation of the obligation to take steps to the "maximum of available resources" under an optional protocol to the Covenant, 10 May 2007, https://www2.ohchr.org/english/bodies/cescr/docs/statements/Obligationtotakesteps-2007.pdf.

economic, social, and cultural rights, therefore supporting social transfers to mitigate inequalities that grow in times of austerity and fiscal adjustment programs, most recently as a consequence of the COVID-19 pandemic. But they need the political will to do so. As the CESCR has indicated, it is incumbent on States exiting bail-out programs to move towards increasing their revenues in a transparent and participatory manner, to restore the pre-crisis levels of public services and social benefits, including by reviewing their tax regimes. It is also incumbent for States to ensure that effective protection of their rights is enhanced in line with expected post-pandemic economic recovery.

To comply with their obligation to protect, States are also required to take measures to prevent third parties from interfering with the enjoyment of the rights, an obligation that is becoming increasingly relevant.

In the context of public policy norms and regulations, there is general agreement that States are required to set the enabling normative framework and to regulate, bearing in mind their obligation to guarantee fulfillment of economic, social, and cultural rights without discrimination. This means that laws, policies and regulations must ensure that non-State actors act in conformity. Furthermore, given the advancement of economic globalization, the human rights of individuals, groups and peoples are increasingly affected by, and dependent on, the extraterritorial acts and omissions of States. When the decision making power of nation-states is weak, either due to the failure of governments or an overall unfavorable economic and development environment, transnational corporations have several options to carry out their activities at national and extra territorial levels. The co-relation of power between States and the private sector is rather unbalanced. Perhaps the ongoing discussion in the Human Rights Council on a new binding treaty on business and human rights in light of an evolving understanding of international solidarity at all levels will provide the opportunity to craft sound solutions to match the size of the challenge. It would also be wise for States to push beyond simply adopting National Action Plans, and rather implement the UN Guiding Principles on Business and Human Rights,[54] which is, of course, a positive development in and of itself.

Compliance by States with their human rights obligations must also enable an on-going assessment that allows for corrections if the impact of the measures is not as expected. This can only be achieved through the meaningful participation of the affected groups in the process. Two recurrent dimensions of the struggle of any discriminated community are the lack of representation

---

54   *See* OHCHR, *UN Guiding Principles on Business and Human Rights,* https://www.ohchr
        .org/sites/default/ files/documents/publications/guidingprinciplesbusinesshr_en.pdf.

of members of such communities in decision making bodies and the multiple tiers of discrimination faced by women, who suffer the most and are at the lower levels of society, impoverished and invisible citizens. Therefore, participation, in particular women's participation, is indeed an essential tool to advancing non-discrimination and substantive equality. Participation of rights holders calls for accountability on the part of duty bearers using any mechanisms they consider appropriate, provided they are accessible, transparent and effective.

The principle of equality and non-discrimination requires States to disaggregate data by income, age, gender, geographic region, race, ethnicity, education, wealth quintile, and other distinctions as locally relevant. Disaggregated data over a medium time frame will assist in identifying patterns of discrimination against specific groups as well as disparities in, and barriers to, access to health care, social protection, housing, food, education, water, and sanitation, thereby contributing to an inclusive rights implementation framework that leaves no one behind. As part of its work on lists of illustrative indicators on civil and political rights, as well as economic, social, and cultural rights, the Office of the High Commissioner for Human Rights (OHCHR) has developed a list of structural, process, and outcome indicators to monitor the realization of several human rights.[55]

Table 14 on the right to non-discrimination, identifies four characteristic attributes of the right: equality before the law and protection of person, direct or indirect discrimination by public or private actors nullifying or impairing access to an adequate standard of living, health and education, and equality of livelihood opportunities, as well as special measures for participation, including in decision-making.

Disaggregated indicators need to be comparable over time, as well as understood and recognized by all the stakeholders. In many States such indicators are still not available, although examples of indicators and benchmarks established at the grass roots level by the affected groups have proved to be

---

55   *See* OHCHR, Human Rights Indicators A Guide to Measurement and Implementation, https://www.ohchr.org/sites/default/files/Documents/Publications/Human_rights_indicators_en.pdf, at 88–101 on the rights to liberty and security of person; adequate food; enjoyment of the highest standard of physical and mental health; not to be subjected to torture, or to cruel, inhuman or degrading treatment or punishment; participate in public affairs; education; adequate housing; work; social security; freedom of opinion and expression; fair trial; violence against women; non-discrimination; life.

  See also The OPERA Framework—Center for Economic and Social Rights, https://www.cesr.org/opera-framework/ (Outcomes, Policy Efforts, Resources and Assessment) to analyse various dimensions of the obligation to fulfil economic and social rights.

relevant to their impact assessment which opened windows of opportunity for a bottom-up process that is useful to the other levels of planning and assessment. This is indeed what meaningful participation can bring to policy formulation.

Meaningful participation of rights holders and accountability of duty bearers are increasingly relevant for the full enjoyment of all human rights. In fact, they are two sides of the same coin. All rights holders, particularly the most disadvantaged, should be guaranteed a means to participate in decisions that affect the enjoyment of their rights. At the collective level, civil society organizations constituted by citizens who organize themselves formally and informally around common interests of a particular sector or the whole of society (for example, grass-roots organizations, welfare associations, advocacy networks or social movements) should also participate in policy making, implementation and evaluation. It is all about building a culture of human rights and the capacity needed to bring in the rights-based approach through meaningful participation that largely moves beyond token consultation. It is also about building up hope by providing affected groups with the practical tools to monitor the various stages of the rights implementation process.

6   The Long Quest for Substantive Equality between Men and Women: A Case in Point

In spite of ample legislation on non-discrimination and equality, in tandem with the implementation of temporary special measures that aim at reducing and/or eliminating the causes and circumstances that give rise or contribute to situations of *de facto* discrimination, women continued to be denied right to education, training, work, social security, health, land, and other livelihood resources. The following three basic assumptions frame this discussion.

First, women represent approximately half of the world's population, but have been given very unequal roles to play. Despite some progress in certain regions of the world, flagrant imbalances persist, and the negative effects of such imbalances infringe upon the enjoyment of women's rights. Moreover, on the level of national development, women bear the cost of high economic and social achievements.

The second assumption is that girls and women are often in a disadvantaged position compared to men, whether it is accessing education, participation in the labor market, or in relation to poverty in general, due to their unequal access to resources, goods, and services. Women continue to face enormous difficulties in accessing land and other livelihood resources, which propels the cycle of poverty due to unpaid work that is not recognized as a contribution to economic growth. Unpaid workers who contribute to a family business, or are account workers, have no safety net to protect them against income loss.

The third assumption is that women, more often than men, continue to be out of the labor market and that the great majority of so-called "working" women are more likely to be employed in informal, precarious, low-paying jobs, with little to no access to social insurance benefits such as pension schemes, paid maternity leave, or unemployment insurance. Additionally, even if women are in the labor market, they often experience lower labor force participation rates, higher levels of part-time and temporary work, and informal employment (especially informal self-employment). They face persistent gender pay gaps and a disproportionately higher share of unpaid care work, which national social protection strategies often fail to recognize, consequently leaving them without social security benefits such as a maternity leave, pensions or health care.

All of these outcomes are associated with persistent patterns of inequality, discrimination and structural disadvantage.

Public policies to fulfil women's rights may have eliminated formal discrimination to some extent but there is much to be done in adopting measures for the elimination of *de facto* discrimination. For example, the intersectional discrimination to which women workers are subject leads to accumulated disadvantages in their professional and personal lives. Progress on the three key interrelated indicators for gender equality in the labor market is far from satisfactory. The glass ceiling limits women's access to top decision-making posts in both public services and private sector companies. The gender pay gap and the sticky floor perpetuates vertical and horizontal job segregation. All these obstacles impede women's substantive equality.

Change will be difficult if States continue to take piecemeal measures to deal with a problem that is systemic. General measures to address negative stereotypes that perpetuate gender inequality in the labor market, such as a comprehensive system of protection to combat gender discrimination that includes equal pay for equal work or work of equal value, should be topped by specific work-related measures. For example, to protect the safety and health of pregnant workers, day-care services should be set up in the workplace, to facilitate flexible working arrangements, and allow for diversified vocational training and retraining programs.

The provision of equal pay for equal work, or work of equal value, is covered by international human rights law, proclaimed in the ILO Constitution and enshrined in national constitutions as the framework for labor legislation. The formulation in Article 7(a)(ii) of the ICESCR, which refers to fair wages and equal remuneration for work of equal value without distinction of any kind, guarantees conditions of work not inferior to those enjoyed by men, with equal pay for equal work, has been interpreted by the CESCR as remuneration for workers that should be equal even when their work is different but nonetheless of the same value when assessed by objective criteria. This requires an on-going evaluation of whether the work is of equal value, and whether the remuneration received is equal across a broad selection of functions. In order to assess the value of work, it is important to include skills, responsibilities and efforts required by the worker as well as working conditions. Remuneration set through collective agreements should seek equality for work of equal value.[56]

The violation of the right to equal pay for equal work or work of equal value is one of the documented reasons for the gender pay gap that, together with labor market segregation and unequal opportunities for promotions and career advancement, continue to affect women negatively at all stages of their careers.

Another area that requires particular attention from public authorities is social protection. In work-related social security schemes where contributions represent an integral component of the remuneration and benefits are a proportion thereof, States need to take continuous steps "to eliminate the factors that prevent women from making equal contributions to such schemes, (for example, intermittent participation in the workforce on account of family responsibilities and unequal wage outcomes) or ensure that schemes take account of such factors in the design of benefit formulas (for example by considering child rearing periods or periods to take care of adult dependents in relation to pension entitlements)".[57]

In the past, social security rights for women were often derived from male rights holders with negative consequences, such as creating dependency on the direct rights holder and discouraging women from joining the labour market, since women were entitled to social protection through their husbands. One of the positive outcomes of the entry of women into the labor market is that they are acquiring more individual work-related social rights and are thus no longer dependent on their husbands or partners as male breadwinners. But the reverse side of this coin is the need for a vast range of measures to reconcile professional, family, and personal life. For example, parents need to have clearly defined rights of securing a place for their children in childcare services to qualify for individual and non-transferable entitlements to paid paternity

---

56   See CESCR General Comment No. 23 (2016), on the right to just and favourable conditions of work, paras. 11–17.

57   See CESCR General Comment No. 19, on the right to social security, para. 32.

and parental leaves, and to have the contributions during these leave periods credited as work periods and not as periods of incapacity to work. These are all very important issues for the individualization of rights for women and men.

Gender-based discrimination in employment throughout their lives has a cumulative impact in old age, forcing older women to live on disproportionately lower incomes and pensions, or even no pension, compared with men. In fact, more women than men fall below the poverty line, and the depth of poverty is greater for extremely poor women. Overall, in spite of the extension of tax-financed universal pensions in many parts of the world, women who rely exclusively on such pensions often struggle with low benefit levels and where tax-financed pensions are means-tested at the household level, many older women still do not benefit from this source of income because of either narrow eligibility criteria or stigmatization.

Gender-responsive social protection requires the mainstreaming of gender equality into public policies in order to tackle the impact of discrimination, in particular intersectional discrimination on working and non-working women.

Unpaid work, including care work, further restricts girls and women from enjoying all their rights, since they become invisible in policy planning, implementation and evaluation as individual rights holders. Their so-called "societal" obligations linked to child rearing, care for older and dependent members of the family and, more generally, their responsibility towards the well-being of their families and communities, normally push their own rights totally out of the picture.

One of the frequently used arguments to justify the unequal caring burden is that women may choose to stay at home for emotional reasons, forgetting that what is at stake is not their choice. However, the fact that child care facilities as well as facilities to care for dependent adults are not considered a priority in national economic and social policies leaves women with no other choice except to stay at home. It is true that countries with a faster changing gender balance have more women participating in the labor market. As a result, activities that were traditionally provided free of charge such as, informal care, now have to be provided by the State and/or the private non-profit or for-profit sectors. This is particularly true for what is considered the production of family well-being, which was almost exclusively entrusted to women, the so–called "l'Etat Providence caché," the hidden welfare State. Yet, even in these countries, public services including care facilities are unevenly distributed between urban and rural areas, and often not physically or economically accessible.

From a socio-economic perspective, social services are an important component of the infrastructure required for the smooth functioning of the economy through the full integration of women in the labor market.For this social integration to be part of the harmonious development of children, and the care of older or dependent persons, access to, and use of, social services require that they comply with criteria of accessibility (physical, economic, and of information in user-friendly and in minority languages); availability (in remote areas and traditionally deprived neighbourhoods); adequacy or adaptability (to different cultural contexts, norms, and traditions); and quality in service delivery (design, implementation, and evaluation with full participation of users).

Access to quality social services is crucial for the acquisition of individual work-related rights for women. Lone parents and/or low-income persons and families are especially dependent on affordable, or, if need be, subsidized social services in order to work and escape from benefit dependency. The absence or insufficiency of adequate, accessible, and affordable social services will likely reinforce old divisions of social welfare and give rise to new ones.

In the last several decades, the crumbling of the welfare state has particularly impacted the provision of public social services. The state is no longer the sole provider of social services, but rather the enabler of an overall favorable environment for social development and social inclusion with increased responsibility for ensuring equitable delivery of, and access to, quality social services through an effective legal and fiscal framework and an accountable public sector.

Issues of both subsidiarity and complementarity of social services have come very much to the foreground due to the changes in the role of the public sector. It is assumed that these services can, in most cases, be delivered most effectively and efficiently by entities closest to local communities that are therefore more aware of their needs. It is also part of present public policy formulation and practice to consider decentralisation, privatisation, public/private partnerships, as well as the introduction of competitive market-based structures as complementary and alternative approaches to the delivery of social services that often restricts the access of low-income individuals and families. In sum, irrespective of the provider and the modality, it is the responsibility of the State to guarantee non-discrimination and equal access for all, especially those that are most vulnerable and disadvantaged.

The economic impact of the COVID crisis hit women particularly hard and exacerbated pre-existing gender inequalities such as the gender pay gap and gross imbalances in the distribution of unpaid care and domestic work, which is also likely to lead to women giving up participating in labor market beyond the pandemic. Several studies have shown that the involvement of men in household work has increased compared to pre-COVID times, but the burden on women is still disproportionate. Recovery efforts need to build on measures taken to combat the pandemic and integrate them into general policy frameworks in the labor and social security systems.

7 Justiciability of Economic, Social and Cultural Rights as an Essential Tool to Combat Discrimination

Human rights are about individuals and lived injustices that require redress and reparation. The provision of remedies is therefore of fundamental value. Though the existence of an accessible, independent, and impartial judicial review system remains a requirement necessary to secure the observance of the rule of law principles by all stakeholders, the right to an effective remedy need not be interpreted as always requiring a judicial remedy. Administrative, financial, educational and social remedies will, in many cases, be adequate, and those living within the jurisdiction of a State have a legitimate expectation, based on the principle of good faith, that all administrative authorities will comply with human rights obligations in their decision-making. In addition to non-discrimination and substantive equality policy failures, the obstacles faced by victims in access to justice, including the burdens of high costs of litigation, drawn-out court proceedings and the non-implementation of court decisions by government authorities, certainly all lead to violations of their rights. Of particular concern is the low rate of prosecution of crimes against persons belonging to discriminated groups and the fact that discriminatory attitudes and prejudices in the enforcement of the law, especially by the police, are serious obstacles in the victims' access to justice.

Various national and regional courts have adjudicated individual complaints in which the non-enjoyment of economic, social, and cultural rights is underpinned by discrimination and inequality.[58]

---

58 In the recent case of *Mahlangu and Another v Minister of Labor and Others*, in November 2021,the South African Constitutional Court decided that the exclusion of domestic workers employed in private homes from making claims to the Compensation for Occupational Injury and Illness Act (COIDA), in cases of illness, injury, disablement or death at work, violates their rights to social security, equality and dignity, and it made this finding retroactively applicable from 1994, the date the South African constitution was enacted. *See next page* In so doing, the court articulated a theory of intersectional discrimination and moved forward its own, jurisprudence on indirect discrimination, infusing the right to social security, dignity and retrospective application with an intersectional analysis. It also reframed the narrative on domestic workers. https://www.solidaritycenter.org /health-and-safety-south-african-domestic workers-no-longer-invisible/.

In the context of international judicial remedies, victims of potential violations of the right to social security can claim remedies under the Optional Protocol to the ICESCR.[59]

The case of *Trujillo Calera v. Ecuador*[60] is another example of the effects of indirect discrimination on women. After assessing the admissibility and merits of the complaint, the CESCR found that Ecuador had violated her right to social security by denying her a retirement pension. The views of the CESCR were that the victim suffered discriminatory treatment on the basis of her gender due to the conditions of her affiliation with the voluntary contribution pension system and that her situation was exacerbated by the fact that Ecuador did not have a comprehensive non-contributory old-age pension scheme. The State was asked to grant the complainant the benefits she was entitled to as part of her right to a pension, other social security benefits, enabling her to have an adequate and dignified standard of living, as well as to adopt legislative and administrative measures to ensure, to the maximum of its available resources, that similar situations did not occur in the future.

8   Conclusion

The drafters of the UDHR and of the two Covenants were wise and forward-looking to have included the "other status" clause in these instruments. In fact, not only are the original grounds for discrimination still there, but new grounds are now having an impact on peoples' daily lives. It is true that non-discrimination provisions have not been consistently implemented or enforced, certainly not with the political will and institutional capacity that

---

59   Entry into force in 2013, with 26 ratifications so far. The OP enables victims, who have exhausted domestic remedies, to claim their economic, social and cultural rights at the international level. It also enables the CESCR, in charge of its enforcement, not only to provide reparation, compensation or rehabilitation in case of individual complaints but also to require States to ensure guarantees of non-repetition through general policy measures. One of the most interesting features of the OP is its provision on a standard of review that has to take into account the reasonableness of steps taken by the State party. This means that the Committee, in order to determine the violation of any right, has to consider the reasonableness of measures taken by the State in conformity with Article 2(1) of the Covenant, on the use of maximum available resources, while keeping in mind the possibility of States to adopt a variety of measures to implement Covenant rights.

60   CESCR, Trujillo Calera vs Ecuador, 26 March 2018, U.N. Doc. E/C.12/63/D/10/2015, https://www.escr-net.org/caselaw/2018/marcia-cecilia-trujillo-calero-v-ecuador-cescr-communication-102015-un-doc.

a problem of this magnitude deserves. If we consider the number of affected persons and families, the nature and extent of human rights violations they face and the depth of economic, social, and cultural exclusion in which they live, however, some progress has been achieved that has made a difference to some individuals and groups, but it is far from sufficient.

What is more important is the general consensus that inequality and inequalities are not simply the result of historic discrimination, cultural bias, or individual choices. They are driven directly by the decisions governments make, or fail to make, to address legal and structural barriers and to advance and realize comprehensive equality that goes beyond formal and protective equality. Indeed, just as laws that reinforce structural inequalities can have wide-ranging harms, undoing this inequality in the law can have—and has had—wide-ranging benefits.

In addition to the obligations States committed to when they ratified human rights treaties, they also committed to the achievement of the UN Sustainable Development Goals. The underlying call in the 2030 Agenda for no one to be left behind can strengthen the non-discrimination and equality framework. We will have to wait to find out whether this is really how States are planning to put it into practice, or whether it risks remaining an unrealized intent of purpose.

The concept of equality shapes definitions of citizenship. If we think that some people deserve more rights than others, then citizenship takes different forms for different groups.[61] What we need, more than ever, is substantive equality that underpins transformative laws, policies and, above all, results on the ground for all those individuals and groups that still feel discriminated, frustrated and disenfranchised.

Against the persistent and wide-ranging challenges derived from territorial and ethnic strife, conflicts, insecurity, scarcity of resources, poverty, and the many on-going crises – food, economic, financial, global warming, and unparalleled global refugee and migration movements – the rights to non-discrimination and equality reaffirm the intrinsic dignity and inalienable worth of every individual. What really matters is to keep in mind that in this changing world, States have to cover traditional risks, as well as face new ones, in an active and preventative manner, within a context of scarce resources, with clear goals and strategies for integrated economic and social policies. Central to these goals and strategies is the principle of "equality of rights,

---

61　Michael Bellesiles, in *Weaponizing Citizenship*. Academia Letters, March 2021. https://www.academia.edu/45602360/Weaponizing_Citizenship, at 6.

conditions, and opportunities, which refer broadly to ways in which people are able to participate fully in society as citizens, to exercise their entitlement to resources, and their ability to contribute to the well-being of themselves, their families and their communities.

It is indeed a huge endeavor, but also one from which no one is exempted.

CHAPTER 16

Asylum from the Perspectives of International and Islamic Law: A Comparative Analysis

Mohammad Bayoumi[*]

1   Introduction

The increasing incidence of armed conflict, persecution, and violence on a worldwide scale makes this study very important. At least 82.4 million people were forced to leave their homes by the end of 2019.[1] There are about 26 million refugees who have fled their homelands because of war, persecution, or other devastation.[2] These figures are unprecedented in human history.[3]

The inclusion of Islamic law considerations raises the significance of this study. Over the past decade, the vast majority of refugees around the world have come from Muslim-majority or mostly Muslim countries.[4] The largest numbers of refugees worldwide have been hosted by Turkey, Bangladesh, Jordan, and Pakistan.[5] Specifically, Turkey has hosted the highest refugee population in the world, with the majority of these individuals escaping the violence in neighboring Syria.[6] Since the beginning of the Syrian crisis in 2011, 6.31 million individuals have fled the country. About a third of the world's refugees live in these areas.[7] Thus, Islam is the most widely prevalent religion among both refugees and host nations, and its laws, beliefs, and teachings have a direct influence on the protection of refugees that governments and the international community may afford to refugees.[8]

---

[*]   J.S.D., Chief Justice, Egyptian Appellate Courts.
1   *Figures at a Glance*, UN High Commissioner for Refugees (UNHCR), https://www.unhcr.org /figures-at-a-glance.html (last visited July 25, 2022).
2   *Id.*
3   Nehaluddin Ahmad, *A Study of Evolution and Practices of Asylum and Rights of Refugees in Islamic Traditions and International Law*, 22 Rutgers J. L. & Religion 518, 519 (2021–22).
4   Speech of Antonio Guterres, *in* The Right to Asylum between Islamic Shari'ah and International Refugee Law: A Comparative Study 307 (2009).
5   2018 Global Trends Report, UN High Commissioner for Refugees (UNHCR).
6   *Id.*
7   *Id.*
8   Ahmad, *supra* note 3, at 519–20.

This study is of the utmost importance due to the severity of the problems and challenges that a large number of forced migrants and asylum seekers are currently facing. It compares Islamic law with international asylum standards and evaluates the strengths and weaknesses of each system in order to determine whether or not refugees' rights are genuinely protected, and whether or not they confront a variety of severe obstacles that must be redressed.

The study will begin with an explanation of asylum under international law, followed by a discussion from an Islamic standpoint. In addition, the paper will end with a conclusion drawing parallels and differences between the two systems.

2   Asylum under International Law

This section will define asylum, describe the three facets of the right to asylum, and explain what it means to be a refugee. The paper will then zero in on the key themes surrounding asylum, the concept of persecution, and the principle of non-refoulement. The paper will also address the topic of asylum restrictions.

2.1   *The Meaning of "Asylum"*

The Latin term "asylum" is the equivalent of the Greek word "asylon," which means liberty from seizure.[9] Asylum has always been seen as a haven of refuge where one may be free from the grasp of a pursuer. Scholars agree that the tradition of asylum dates back to the dawn of time, with the first safe havens built in religious structures.[10]

Despite its long existence and widespread use, the term "asylum" lacks a universally acknowledged definition.[11] In spite of this fact, when discussions shifted from the definition of "asylum" as a concept to its definition as a right, scholars were able to specify important elements of that right.[12]

The right to asylum has been characterized as including the following concrete "manifestations of state conduct"[13]; "to admit a person to its territory"; to allow the person to remain there; "to refrain from expelling the person"; "to

---

9   Atle Grahl-Madsen, The Status of Refugees in International Law 3 (1972).

10   S. Prakash Sinha, Asylum and International Law 5 (1971); Roman Boed, *The State of the Right to Asylum in International Law*, 5 Duke J. Comp. & Int'l L. 1 (1994).

11   Atle Grahl-Madsen, Territorial Asylum 50 (1980).

12   Boed, *supra* note 10, at 3.

13   *Id.*

refrain from extraditing the person"; and "to refrain from prosecuting, punishing, or otherwise restricting the person's liberty."[14]

International law recognizes three aspects of the asylum right: the right of states to grant asylum; the right of individuals to seek asylum; and the right of individuals to obtain or be granted asylum. Each of these rights will be clarified as follows:

2.2 *The States' Right to Grant Asylum*

In international law, the right of a state to provide asylum is well-established. It derived from the principle that all sovereign states are presumed to have exclusive sovereignty over their territory and, by extension, over their inhabitants.[15] This universally accepted principle implies that every sovereign state has the authority to grant or deny asylum to those within its borders.[16] Thus, in international law, the right to asylum has traditionally been seen as a state's right rather than an individual's.[17]

Everyone appears to have the right to enjoy asylum under customary international law. This right is stated in Article 14 of the first international human rights document, the Universal Declaration of Human Rights (UDHR), stipulating that "everyone has the right to seek and to enjoy in other countries asylum from persecution."[18] The right to enjoy asylum was also repeated in similar or almost identical language in a number of other international and regional human rights documents.[19] However, the phrase "the right to enjoy asylum" appears to avoid placing a weight on states to provide asylum.[20] It is challenging to define the meaning of the right to enjoy asylum. It would have been more explicit and effective to use terminology like "the right to asylum" or "the right to obtain asylum" when establishing asylum under international law.[21]

---

14   *Id.*
15   Felice Morgenstern, *The Right of Asylum*, 1949 Brit. Y.B. Int'l L. 327, 327.
16   *Id.* at 327.
17   *Id.* at 335.
18   G.A. Res. 217 (III) A art. 14(1), Universal Declaration of Human Rights (Dec. 10, 1948) [hereinafter UDHR].
19   Declaration on Territorial Asylum, at preamble, G.A. Res. 2312, U.N. GAOR, 22d Sess., Supp. No. 16, at 81, U.N. Doc. A/6912 (1967); Asian-African Legal Consultative Organization [AALCO] Bangkok Principles on the Status and Treatment of Refugees, at art. 2(1) (Dec. 31, 1966), https://perma.cc/LL2A-3VRT [hereinafter Bangkok Principles] ("Everyone without any distinction of any kind, is entitled to the right to seek and to enjoy in other countries asylum from persecution.").
20   Timothy E. Lynch, *Refugees, Refoulment, and Freedom of Movement: Asylum Seeker's Right to Admission and Territorial Asylum*, 36 Geo. Immigr. L.J. 73, 88 (2021).
21   *Id.* at 89.

This, however, is not the intention of Article 14, as it avoids using the terms "to seek and be granted" asylum, as discussed below.

Article 1(1) of the Declaration on Territorial Asylum states that "asylum granted by a State, in the exercise of its sovereignty, to persons entitled to invoke Article 14 of the Universal Declaration of Human Rights... shall be respected by all other States."[22] Likewise, Article 1(3) of this Declaration enables the state of refuge to examine the reasons for granting asylum.[23]

In addition, Article 2(1) of the OAU Convention Governing the Specific Aspects of Refugee Problems in Africa states that member states "shall use their best endeavors consistent with their respective legislations to receive refugees."[24] Similarly, Article 1 of the Convention on Territorial Asylum, which was adopted by the Organization of American States in 1954, states that "every State has the right, in the exercise of its sovereignty, to admit into its territory such persons as it deems advisable, without, through the exercise of this right, giving rise to complaint by any other State."[25] Likewise, Article 2 (2) of the Bangkok Principles, states that "[a] State has the sovereign right to grant or refuse asylum in its territory to a refugee."[26] Furthermore, Article 2 of the Declaration on Territorial Asylum, adopted in 1977 by the Committee of Ministers of the Council of Europe, affirms the authority of governments to provide asylum.[27] In addition to these regional agreements, a large number of states also have local procedures for determining asylum claims.[28]

2.3 Individuals' Right to Seek Asylum

An individual's right to seek asylum is the second aspect of the asylum right. A person has the fundamental right to leave his country of residence in search of refuge. Since no nation-state can legitimately claim ownership over its citizens or permanent residents, it is a basic human right for anybody to flee their home country in search of protection.[29]

The right to seek asylum is enshrined in numerous international and regional human rights instruments, which appear to be established in

---

22   Declaration on Territorial Asylum, *supra* note 19, art. 1(1).

23   *Id.* art. 1(3).

24   OAU Convention Governing the Specific Aspects of Refugee Problems in Africa, Sept. 10, 1969, art. II(1), 1001 U.N.T.S. 45, 48.

25   Convention on Territorial Asylum, Mar. 28, 1954, OEA/Ser.X/1, art. 1.

26   Bangkok Principles, *supra* note 19, at art. 2(2).

27   Declaration on Territorial Asylum, Nov. 18, 1977, art. 2.

28   Boed, *supra* note 10, at 3.

29   Grahl-Madsen, *supra* note 9.

customary international law.[30] Article 13(2) of the UDHR states that "everyone has the right to leave any country, including his own,"[31] whereas Article 14 (1) of the Declaration stipulates that everyone has the right to "seek... asylum from persecution".[32] In addition, Article 12 (2) of the ICCPR states that "[e]veryone shall be free to leave any country, including his own."[33]

In addition, a large number of regional human rights conventions and declarations ensure an individuals' right to seek asylum. Article 12 (3) of the African Charter on Human and Peoples' Rights,[34] Article 22 (7) of the American Convention on Human Rights,[35] and Article 28 of the Arab Charter on Human Rights stipulate the right to seek asylum in a foreign nation to avoid persecution.[36] In addition, concerning the non-binding documents, Article 27 of the American Declaration of the Rights and Duties of Man,[37] Article 12 of the Cairo Declaration on Human Rights in Islam,[38] and Article 2(1) of the Bangkok Principles on the Status and Treatment of Refugees[39] specify this right explicitly.

2.4 Individuals' Right to be Granted Asylum?

The right of an individual to be granted asylum is the third component of the asylum right. However, international law has not yet adopted a uniform

---

30   Lynch, *supra* note 20, at 87.

31   UDHR, *supra* note 18, art 13(2).

32   *Id.* art. 14(1).

33   International Covenant on Civil & Political Rights art. 12 (2), *opened for signature* Mar. 23, 1976, 999 U.N.T.S. 171 (entered into force Dec. 16, 1966) [hereinafter ICCPR].

34   Org. of African Unity, African Charter on Human and Peoples' Rights art. 12.3 (Jun. 27, 1981) ("Every individual shall have the right, when persecuted, to seek and obtain asylum in other countries in accordance with the laws of those countries and international conventions.").

35   Organization of American States, American Convention on Human Rights art. 22.7, Nov. 22, 1969, O.A.S.T.S. No. 36, 1144 U.N.T.S. 123 ("Every person has the right to seek and be granted asylum in a foreign territory, in accordance with the legislation of the state and international conventions, in the event he is being pursued for political offenses or related common crimes.").

36   League of Arab States, Arab Charter on Human Rights art. 28 (May 23, 2004) ("Everyone shall have the right to seek political asylum in other countries in order to escape persecution.").

37   Organization of American States, American Declaration of the Rights and Duties of Man, May 2, 1948, at art. XXVII ("Every person has the right, in case of pursuit not resulting from ordinary crimes, to seek and receive asylum in foreign territory, in accordance with the laws of each country and with international agreements.").

38   Organization of Islamic Cooperation, Cairo Declaration on Human Rights in Islam, art. 12 (Aug. 5, 1990) ("Every man ... is entitled to seek asylum in another country").

39   Bangkok Principles, *supra* note 19, at art. 2(1).

standard of protection for this right.[40] It is clear from the many treaties and conventions, which address issues of human rights, asylum, and refugees at the international and regional levels, that no one has a legal entitlement to be granted asylum protection under current international law.[41]

Article 14 (1) of the UDHR guarantees the right "to seek and to enjoy in other countries asylum from persecution."[42] Scholars in the field of human rights agree that this provision only grants the individual the right to seek refuge, not the right to receive it.[43] They challenge the wording of Article 14 (1) for granting an individual the right to seek refuge without specifying who is accountable for upholding that right.[44] Consequently, the Declaration did not add anything new to the existing international legal framework.[45]

In addition, the ICCPR has no provisions regarding asylum. As a result, states are not required to provide asylum under its provisions.[46] Equally absent from the International Covenant on Economic, Social, and Cultural Rights is any mention of the right to asylum.[47] Even the 1951 Convention[48] Relating to the Status of Refugees and the 1967 Protocol on the Status of Refugees,[49] the two primary international instruments for protecting refugees, do not guarantee the right to obtain asylum. In addition, the European Convention on Human

---

40   Boed, *supra* note 10, at 8.

41   *Id.* at 8–9.

42   UDHR, *supra* note 18, art. 14(1), at 4.

43   Stephen B. Young, *Between Sovereigns: A Reexamination of the Refugee's Status, in* Transnational Legal Problems of Refugees 339, 347 (Michigan Yearbook of International Legal Studies ed., 1982); Boed, *supra* note 10, at 9.

44   *Id.*

45   Similarly, the Vienna Declaration and Program of Action did not extend the conventional concept of the right to asylum. Article 23 of the Vienna Declaration just reiterates the principles of Article 14(1) of the UDHR stipulating that "everyone, without distinction of any kind, is entitled to the right to seek and to enjoy in other countries asylum from persecution." The Vienna Declaration and Programme of Action, June 25, 1993, *in* United Nations, World Conference on Human Rights 36 (1993).

46   Alfred De Zayas, *Human Rights and Refugees, in* Migration and Migration Policy 25, 26 (International Organization for Migration ed., 1992).

47   Sinha, *supra* note 10, at 90.

48   Convention Relating to the Status of Refugees, July 28, 1951, 19 U.S.T. 6259, 189 U.N.T.S. 150 [hereinafter 1951 Refugee Convention].

49   Protocol Relating to the Status of Refugees, Jan. 31, 1967, 19 U.S.T. 6223, 606 U.N.T.S. 267 [hereinafter Refugee Protocol].

Rights is silent on the topic of asylum.[50] No mention of asylum is made in that convention.[51]

While regional instruments in Africa and the Americas recognize the right to asylum, they do so with a high regard for state sovereignty, making them of limited practical use to asylum-seekers. Article 2(1) of the African Refugee Convention requires states to accept refugees in accordance with their laws.[52] Similarly, Article 27 of the American Declaration of the Rights and Duties of Man stipulates that "[e]very person has the right, in case of pursuit not resulting from ordinary crimes, to seek and receive asylum in foreign territory, in accordance with the laws of each country and with international agreements."[53] In addition, Article 22(7) of the American Convention on Human Rights states that "every person has the right to seek and be granted asylum in a foreign territory, in accordance with the legislation of the state and international conventions."[54] Individuals' right to be granted asylum remains within the scope of state authority under each of these treaties. Accordingly, no one has a guaranteed right under international law to obtain or be granted asylum. This issue lies within the discretionary power of each individual state.

2.5   The Meaning of "Refugee"

Under international law, the terms "refugee" and "migrant" are not interchangeable.[55] Migrants, unlike refugees, choose to relocate not because they face immediate persecution or death, but to better their lives by seeking jobs, or in some circumstances for purposes of a better education, family reunification, or other reasons.[56] In contrast to refugees, migrants face no barrier to return to their home countries. If they want to return, they will continue to be protected by their government.[57]

---

50   European Convention on Human Rights, Nov. 4, 1950, 213 U.N.T.S. 221.

51   Terje Einarsen, *The European Convention on Human Rights and the Notion of an Implied Right to de facto Asylum*, 2 Int'l J. Refugee L. 361, 362 (1990).

52   OAU Convention Governing the Specific Aspects of Refugee Problems in Africa, art. II(1), Sept. 10, 1969, 1001 U.N.T.S. 45 [hereinafter African Refugee Convention].

53   The American Declaration of the Rights and Duties of Man, May 2, 1948, art. 27, O.A.S Off. Rec. OEA/Ser.L/V/II.23/Doc. 21/Rev.6.

54   American Convention on Human Rights, *supra* note 35.

55   UN High Commissioner for Refugees (UNHCR), *'Refugees' and 'Migrants'* – (UNHCR) https://www.unhcr.org/news/latest/2016/3/56e95c676/refugees-migrants-frequently -asked-questions-faqs.html (last visited July 28, 2022).

56   UNHCR, *What Is a Refugee? Definition and Meaning*, https://www.unhcr.org/asylum -and-migration.html (last visited July 25, 2022).

57   *Id.*

Similarly, under international law, a refugee differs from an internally displaced person. A refugee is a person who crosses international borders to seek safety, protection, or asylum in another country. Although an internally displaced person may have the same goals as a refugee, he/she remains on the territory of his/her state, and is thus subject to its laws.[58]

In accordance with international law, treaties, customary law, obligatory norms, and other international legal instruments are all utilized for the protection of refugees' rights. However, the only international documents directly applicable to refugees are the 1951 Convention,[59] and its 1967 Protocol.[60]

The 1951 Refugee Convention and its 1967 Protocol are the cornerstone of the worldwide refugee protection framework. The vast majority of states have ratified them.[61] The Convention describes the situation of refugees as frequently "perilous and intolerable" because they cross national borders in search of safety in neighboring countries and thus become internationally recognized as "refugees" with access to aid from the UN High Commissioner for Refugees (UNHCR), other states, and other relevant organizations.[62] The 1951 Convention was formed specifically for the purpose of protecting and recognizing refugees, who are in urgent need of protection due to the possibility of persecution in their home country.[63]

Article 1(A)(2) of the 1951 Convention defines a refugee as a person who has fled his or her homeland "owing to a well-founded fear of being persecuted for reasons of race, religion, nationality, membership of a particular social group or political opinion, is outside the country of his/her nationality, and is unable to, or owing to such fear, is unwilling to avail himself/herself of the protection of that country."[64]

This definition lays forth the criteria that an individual must meet in order to be classified as a refugee:

– *First*: physical presence outside of one's home country.

---

58   UNHCR, *What Is a Refugee?*, https://www.unrefugees.org/refugee-facts/what-is-a-refugee (last visited July 25, 2022).

59   1951 Refugee Convention, *supra* note 48.

60   Refugee Protocol, *supra* note 49.

61   Maja Janmyr, *The 1951 Refugee Convention and Non-Signatory States: Charting a Research Agenda*, 33 Int'l J. Refugee L. 188, 188–89 (2021).

62   Ahmad, *supra* note 3, at 523.

63   Sharifah Nazneen Agha, *The Ethics of Asylum in Early Muslim Society*, Refugee Survey Q. 30, 31 (2008).

64   1951 Refugee Convention, *supra* note 48, at art. 1(A)(2).

- *Second*: a well-founded fear of persecution (the Convention does not define the word "persecution," but it is thought to include all serious infringements and abuses of human rights).
- *Third*: the inability to enjoy the protection of one's own country against anticipated persecution.[65]

When these conditions are met, an individual is deemed a refugee. In other words, an individual does not become a refugee if his or her request for protection is granted. Recognizing someone as a refugee is an affirmative action; it serves to certify the refugee status.[66]

Three regional instruments define the term "refugee." The first is the African Refugee Convention,[67] which regulates the specific aspects of refugee problems in Africa. The remaining two instruments are non-binding regional declarations: the Cartagena Declaration on Refugees[68] of the Organization of American States (OAS) and the Bangkok Principles.[69]

The concept of "refugee" as defined by the 1951 Refugee Convention is reflected in all three of these documents, but its scope is enlarged to include persons who have fled their home countries for reasons not specified in the 1951 Convention.[70]

- *The African Refugee Convention* defines a refugee as a person who is forced to leave his country of origin or nationality because of "external aggression, occupation, foreign domination, or events seriously disrupting public order in either part or the whole of his country of origin or nationality."[71]
- *The Cartagena Declaration*'s definition of "refugee" encompasses people "who have fled their country because their lives, safety or freedom have been threatened by generalized violence, foreign aggression, internal conflicts, massive human rights violations or other circumstances which have seriously disturbed public order."[72]

---

65   *Id.*
66   Frances Nicholson & Judith Kumin, *Refugee Protection: A Guide to International Refugee Law,* UNHCR, at 17 (2017).
67   African Refugee Convention, *supra* note 52.
68   Organization of American States, Cartagena Declaration on Refugees, *Colloquium on the International Protection of Refugees in Central America, Mexico and Panama,* Nov. 22, 1984, OAS/Ser. L/V/11.66, doc. 10, rev. 1, at 190–93, https://perma.cc/U7AA-GG39 [hereinafter Cartagena Declaration].
69   Bangkok Principles, *supra* note 19.
70   Lynch, *supra* note 20, at 82.
71   African Refugee Convention, *supra* note 52, at art. 1(2).
72   Cartagena Declaration, *supra* note 68, at part III, P 3.

– *The Bangkok Principles* define "refugee" broadly to include those protected by the African Refugee Convention, as well as people escaping persecution based on their ethnicity or gender, and any refugee's legal dependents.[73]

2.6 The Meaning of "Persecution"

It should be clear by now that the term "persecution" is the key identifier of a refugee under international law. It is the main factor that separates refugees from non-refugees. However, the 1951 Convention and its 1967 Protocol do not include a clear definition of the term "persecution."[74] Each state has considerable discretion in deciding who is a "refugee" based on the extent to which they have suffered alleged harm at the hands of the asylum seeker's home country. While some countries interpret this term exceedingly leniently, others do not.[75] Undoubtedly, not every instance of harm merits a claim of persecution.[76] If persecution is interpreted widely, a substantial portion of the global population would be eligible for refugee status. Accordingly, harm may only qualify as persecution if it reaches a specific level of severity.[77]

Since international refugee law does not define "persecution," the study should look for a definition in other sources of international law.

The *Universal Declaration of Human Rights (UDHR)*[78] is relevant in defining "persecution" since it includes provisions protecting fundamental human

---

73   Bangkok Principles, *supra* note 19, at art. 1.
74   Lynch, *supra* note 20, at 79.
75   *Id.*
76   Selimi v. Ashcroft, 360 F.3d 736, 740–41 (7th Cir. 2004).
77   Scott Rempell, *Defining Persecution*, 2013 Utah L. Rev. 283, 310 (2013).
78   UDHR, *supra* note 18. The UDHR is possibly the most important decision of the United Nations General Assembly. On December 10, 1948, the United Nations General Assembly adopted the UDHR as a non-binding resolution outlining the fundamental human rights to which all people are entitled. Nicholas R. Bednar, *Asylum's Interpretative Impasse: Interpreting "Persecution" and "Particular Social Group" Using International Human Rights Law*, 26 Minn. J. Int'l L. 145, 174 (2017). The UDHR has been the most important international instrument for the protection of fundamental human rights since its adoption. This declaration inspired the development of a number of human rights instruments, including the ICCPR and the International Covenant on Economic, Social, and Cultural Rights (ICESCR). *Id.* at 175. Numerous scholars believe that the UDHR has largely been elevated to binding customary international law because of its prominence and the frequency with which it has been cited and applied in international and domestic laws. *Id.* at 175.

    Concerning refugee rights, the preamble of the 1951 Convention makes specific reference to the UDHR. 1951 Refugee Convention, *supra* note 48, at preamble. In addition, as stated in Article 14 of the UDHR, individuals have the right to seek and enjoy refuge from persecution in another country. UDHR, *supra* note 18, art. 14.

rights. Article 3 ensures the right to "life, liberty, and security of person."[79] Article 4 prohibits slavery and servitude.[80] Article 5 protects the right to be free from torture or "cruel, inhuman or degrading treatment or punishment".[81] Article 13 guarantees the freedom to leave any country, including one's own.[82] Article 16 guarantees not just the freedom to marry, but also the right to consent to marriage, which is crucial for domestic violence claims.[83]

All of these clauses, along with others, may be cited in asylum applications to support the argument that violations of fundamental human rights may constitute persecution.[84]

The International Covenant on Civil and Political Rights (ICCPR)[85] contains a number of significant clauses that may contribute to the interpretation of the term "persecution." Article 6 protects the right to life.[86] Article 7 protects the right to be free from torture or humiliating treatment.[87] Article 8 prohibits slavery.[88] Article 9 prohibits arbitrary arrests or detention.[89] Article 18 protects the right to freedom of thought, conscience, and religion.[90]

Furthermore, article 23 of the ICCPR requires potential spouses to give informed permission, and therefore it might be relevant to domestic violence and gender-based claims.[91] Consequently, it could be argued that forced marriages constitute a form of persecution.[92] In addition, Article 23(4) stipulates that states parties should take all appropriate measures to maintain equality of rights and duties between spouses.[93] On the basis of this paragraph, domestic

---

The UDHR has been quoted and relied upon more frequently than the vast majority, if not all, other international instruments. Bednar, *supra* note 78, at 174–75. Several domestic courts, including U.S. courts, have frequently cited the UDHR in numerous asylum cases. Tai-Heng Cheng, *The Universal Declaration of Human Rights at Sixty: Is It Still Right for the United States?*, 41 Cornell Int'l L.J. 251, 272 (2008); Zheng v. Gonzales, 192 Fed. App'x 733 (10th Cir. 2006).

79   UDHR, *supra* note 18, art. 3.
80   *Id.* at art. 4.
81   *Id.* at art. 5.
82   *Id.* at art.13.
83   *Id.* at art.16.
84   Bednar, *supra* note 78, at 176.
85   ICCPR, *supra* note 33.
86   *Id.* at art. 6.
87   *Id.* at art. 7.
88   *Id.* at art. 8.
89   *Id.* at art. 9.
90   *Id.* at art.18.
91   *Id.* at art.23(3).
92   Bednar, *supra* note 78, at 174.
93   ICCPR, *supra* note 33, at art. 23(4).

violence might be considered persecution, particularly when the government is reluctant to interfere or adopt legislation criminalizing domestic violence.[94]

The Convention on the Elimination of All Forms of Discrimination Against Women (CEDAW)[95] provides broad protection to women, and the interpretations of its articles by the CEDAW Committee are crucial for gender-based asylum petitions.[96] General Recommendations No. 32 and No. 14 of the CEDAW Committee give the most pertinent and substantial support for asylum petitions based on domestic violence.[97]

General Recommendation No. 32 expressly addresses gender-based asylum claims.[98] The CEDAW Committee specifically explains that one of the objectives of this general recommendation is to assist countries in addressing gender discrimination in order to protect the rights of women seeking asylum.[99] In paragraph 15 of the recommendation, the Committee listed the following as examples of "gender-related forms of persecution": "[T]he threat of female genital mutilation, forced/early marriage, threat of violence and/or so-called 'honour crimes,' trafficking in women, acid attacks, rape and other forms of sexual assault, serious forms of domestic violence, the imposition of the death penalty or other physical punishments existing in discriminatory justice systems, forced sterilization, political or religious persecution for holding feminist or other views and the persecutory consequences of failing to conform to gender-prescribed social norms and mores, or for claiming their rights under the Convention."[100] For the purposes of the 1951 Convention, this paragraph could be used to show that these types of gender-based domestic violence

---

94 Bednar, *supra* note 78, at 174.

95 Convention on the Elimination of All Forms of Discrimination Against Women, Dec. 18, 1979, 1249 U.N.T.S. 13 (entered into force Sept. 3, 1981) [hereinafter CEDAW]. CEDAW is the foremost international treaty addressing violations of human rights based on gender. Article 1 defines discrimination against women broadly as any "distinction, exclusion, or restriction" based on sex that impairs or nullifies women's "recognition, enjoyment, or exercise", regardless of marital status, of human rights and basic freedoms in the political, civil, economic, social, cultural, or any other field. *Id.* art. 1.

96 Comm. on the Elimination of Discrimination Against Women, General Recommendation No. 12: Violence Against Women, U.N. Doc. A/44/38 (1989).

97 Bednar, *supra* note 78, at 168.

98 Comm. on the Elimination of Discrimination Against Women, General Recommendation No. 32: On the Gender-Related Dimensions of Refugee Status, Asylum, Nationality, and Stateless Women, U.N. Doc. CEDAW/C/GC/32, https://documents-dds-ny.un.org/doc/UNDOC/GEN/N14/627/90/PDF/N1462790.pdf? OpenElement.

99 *Id.* at para. 4.

100 *Id.* at para. 15.

constitute forms of persecution and are, therefore, valid and accepted reasons for asylum.[101]

The CEDAW Committee's General Recommendation No. 14 regarding female genital mutilation (FGM) is particularly pertinent and significant.[102] Despite the fact that this recommendation does not explicitly state that FGM is a form of persecution, a number of domestic courts have cited it to support this position.[103] For example, in *Abay v. Ashcroft*, a U.S. domestic court applied this recommendation to conclude that FGM is a serious violation of the rights of women and female children, and therefore constitutes persecution.[104]

The Convention on the Rights of the Child (CRC)[105] recognizes that children are distinct from their parents and are entitled to their own rights and safeguards.[106] Regarding the definition of "persecution" as it pertains to children, the CRC may be helpful to the development of arguments on this issue. For example, Article 36 requires states parties to protect the child against any type of "exploitation prejudicial to any aspects of the child's welfare."[107] Under Article 37, children are protected against torture and humiliating treatment.[108] In addition, states parties are required under Article 38 to prohibit children under the age of 15 from directly participating in hostilities or the armed forces.[109]

The United Nations High Commissioner for Refugees (UNHCR) is the institution tasked with monitoring, overseeing, and providing international protection to refugees across the world.[110] States members to the 1951 Convention are required "to cooperate with the [UNHCR], or any other agency of the United

---

101 Bednar, *supra* note 78, at 169.
102 Comm. on the Elimination of Discrimination Against Women, General Recommendation No. 14: Female Circumcision, U.N. Doc. A/45/38 and Corrigendum (1990), http://www .refworld.org/docid/453882 a30.html.
103 Abankwah v. INS, 185 F.3d 18, 23 (2d Cir. 1999).
104 Abay v. Ashcroft, 368 F.3d 634, 638 (6th Cir. 2004).
105 Convention on the Rights of the Child, Nov. 20, 1989, 1577 U.N.T.S. 3 [hereinafter CRC]. The CRC acknowledges and protects extensively the fundamental rights of children. It is considered the most broadly approved treaty in history. UNICEF and the CRC, *Convention on the Rights of the Child, A World of Difference: 25 CRC Achievements*, UNICEF.
106 CRC, *supra* note 105, art. 12.
107 *Id.* art. 36.
108 *Id.* art. 37.
109 *Id.* art. 38.
110 Bednar, *supra* note 78, at 162–3. UNHCR defines international protection that should be granted to a refugee as "all actions aimed at ensuring equal access to and enjoyment of the rights of refugees and asylum-seekers, whether women, men, girls and boys, in accordance with the relevant bodies of law, including international refugee law, international humanitarian law, and international human rights law". Organization of the Islamic Conference (OIC) Ministerial Conference on the Problems of Refugees in the Muslim

Nations which may succeed it, in the exercise of its functions, and shall in particular facilitate its duty of supervising the application of the provisions of this Convention."[111]

The UNHCR provides two different types of materials that explain the provisions of the 1951 Convention and might be helpful in defining the term "persecution": a handbook and guidelines.[112] However, UNHCR publications are only persuasive, and their interpretations do not bind member states.[113]

Concerning gender-based asylum petitions, the UNHCR's Guidelines on International Protection: Gender-Related Persecution might be referenced.[114] These guidelines are important in situations involving domestic violence, rape, sexual assault, and other forms of gender-based persecution.[115]

On the other hand, the UNHCR has issued Guidelines on International Protection: Child Asylum Claims. In these guidelines, the UNHCR supports a child-sensitive interpretation of the refugee definition in accordance with the CRC.[116] According to the UNHCR, the CRC requires adjudicators to prioritize the best interests of the child in all child-related decisions.[117] These guidelines may assist in creating arguments for asylum claims involving child trafficking and labor, underage recruitment, female genital mutilation, domestic violence, and other child-specific types of persecution. In other words, these guidelines may be relevant for arguing that any of these actions constitute persecution.[118]

2.7   *The Principle of Non-Refoulement*

The most significant and crucial principle of international refugee law is the principle of *non-refoulement*.[119] According to this principle, a refugee must not

---

World: Working Document No. 1: Enhancing Refugee and IDP Protection in the Muslim World' 27–29 November 2006 (*UNHCR*) 2.

111   1951 Convention *supra* note 48, at art. 35.

112   Bednar, *supra* note 78, at 163.

113   INS v. Cardoza-Fonseca, 480 U.S. 421, 439 n.22 (1987).

114   UNHCR, *Guidelines on International Protection: Gender-Related Persecution*, U.N. Doc. HCR/GIP/02/01, (May 7, 2002).

115   Bednar, *supra* note 78, at 165.

116   UNHCR, *Guidelines on International Protection: Child Asylum Claims*, at 4, U.N. Doc. HCR/GIP/09/08, (Dec. 22, 2009).

117   *Id.*

118   Bednar, *supra* note 78, at 166.

119   Concerning the right to freedom of movement, Article 12 of the ICCPR stipulates that everyone legally present on the territory of a state has the right to freedom of movement and to choose his or her place of residence. ICCPR, *supra* note 33, at art. 12. However, Article 12 (3) of the Covenant permits states to restrict internal freedom of movement and freedom of residence when necessary to protect public order, national security, public health or morals, or the rights and freedoms of others. *Id.* at art. 12(3). Regarding

be returned to a country where they suffer grave risks to their life or freedom. This principle is accepted as customary international law.[120]

The 1951 Convention states that "[n]o Contracting State shall expel or return (*"refouler"*) a refugee in any manner whatsoever to the frontiers of territories where his life or freedom would be threatened on account of his race, religion, nationality, membership of a particular social group or political opinion."[121] However, under the Convention, a refugee who poses a threat to the community of the nation in which he is located or who has been convicted of a very serious crime by a final judgment is not eligible to claim refugee status under this provision.[122]

The following are some considerations of the principle of non-refoulment as stipulated in the 1951 Convention:

- *First*: the principle of non-refoulement applies only to refugees as defined by the 1951 convention.[123]
- *Second*: this principle applies to all refugees, documented or not. It is not limited to refugees who have been granted permission to reside in a foreign host nation.[124]
- *Third*: this principle is connected to threats of persecution based on a refugee's "race, religion, nationality, membership of a particular social group or

---

international refugee law, Article 26 of the 1951 Convention stipulates that states must provide refugees with the right to choose their place of abode and to travel freely inside the state. 1951 Convention, *supra* note 48, art. 26. In addition, Article 28 of the Convention requires States Parties to provide refugees with travel documents allowing them to leave the country unless compelling public order or national security considerations require otherwise. *Id.* art. 28.

   Concerning the right to family life, according to Article 23 of the ICCPR, the family is the natural and essential group unit of society, deserving of protection from both society and the state. ICCPR, *supra* note 33, at art. 23. Several nations grant dependent relatives protection in relation to this right. Therefore, if a person is given asylum, his or her dependent relatives will also enjoy protection. Nevertheless, the concept of a dependent relative differs according to each state's cultural concept of family. Ahmad, *supra* note 3, at 543. The "spouse, civil partner, unmarried or same-sex partner, or minor child accompanying [the applicant]" is considered a dependent in the United Kingdom. However, in Kenya, "any dependent grandparent, parent, grandchild, or ward living in the same household as the refugee" is considered a dependent relative. *Id.*

120   *Id.*
121   1951 Refugee Convention, *supra* note 48, at art. 33(1).
122   *Id.* art. 33(2).
123   Lynch, *supra* note 20, at 97.
124   *Id.*

political opinion". Other threats, such as natural disasters and widespread civil violence, are unrelated to the principle.[125]

– *Fourth*: the 1951 Convention provides an exception to this principle for refugees who endanger the host country's security.[126]
– *Fifth*: the 1951 Convention lacks a provision prohibiting states from rejecting asylum seekers at their borders, even if they are fleeing persecution in a nearby country.[127]

The African Refugee Convention states that "[n]o person shall be subjected by a Member State to measures such as rejection at the frontier, return or expulsion, which would compel him to return to or remain in a territory where his life, physical integrity or liberty would be threatened for the reasons [which qualify a person as a refugee under this convention]."[128]

This provision, in contrast to the 1951 Convention, indicates that the principle of non-refoulement extends to all individuals, not only refugees.[129] This demonstrates that refugee status is not required to enjoy the right of non-refoulement under this regional convention. In addition, persons who seek asylum at the border of a state party are protected by the non-refoulement principle if being turned away would force them to remain in their country of persecution.[130] Therefore, such individuals cannot be denied entry if the border is with a government persecuting them or threatening to deport them to a persecuting country.[131]

In order to guarantee that they do not violate the non-refoulement principle, states parties are obligated to admit asylum-seekers who request refuge at their borders.[132] It could be argued that every asylum applicant at the border must be permitted because, otherwise, a state would be unable to determine whether the rejection of a person would violate the Convention's prohibition of non-refoulement.[133] To further guarantee that such a violation does not occur, states must conduct a thorough assessment of the individual's position. The initial stage of such an assessment is "admitting the asylum seeker" so that the assessment may commence.[134]

---

125   *Id.*
126   1951 Refugee Convention, *supra* note 48, at art. 33(2).
127   Lynch, *supra* note 20, at 97.
128   African Refugee Convention, *supra* note 52, at art. 11.3.
129   Lynch, *supra* note 20, at 107.
130   *Id.*
131   *Id.*
132   *Id.*
133   *Id.*
134   *Id.*

Other human rights treaties include the principle of non-refoulement, such as the Convention Against Torture (CAT),[135] the International Convention for the Protection of All Persons from Enforced Disappearance (ICPPED),[136] the American Convention on Human Rights (ACHR),[137] and the Inter-American Convention to Prevent and Punish Torture (IACPPT).[138]

In addition, many courts and human rights bodies have interpreted several provisions of other international and regional treaties to include non-refoulement prohibitions, such as the International Covenant on Civil and Political Rights (ICCPR),[139] the Convention on the Elimination on All Forms of Discrimination against Women,[140] the Convention on the Rights of the Child,[141] the Convention on the Rights of Persons with Disabilities(CRPD),[142] the International Convention on the Elimination of All Forms of Racial Discrimination (CERD),[143] and the European Convention for Human Rights (ECHR).[144]

Customary international law protects the principle of non-refoulement as well. This fact has been supported by numerous courts, international

---

135   Convention against Torture and Other Cruel, Inhuman or Degrading Treatment or Punishment, art. 3.1, Dec. 10, 1984, 1465 U.N.T.S. 85.

136   International Convention for the Protection of All Persons from Enforced Disappearance, art. 16, para. 1, Dec. 20, 2006, 2716 U.N.T.S. 3.

137   American Convention on Human Rights, *supra* note 35.

138   Inter-American Convention to Prevent and Punish Torture, art. 13, para. 4, Dec. 9, 1985, O.A.S.T.S. No. 67.

139   In General Comment No. 31, the Human Rights Committee (HRC) stipulates that "the Article 2 [of the ICCPR] obligation requiring that States Parties respect and ensure the Covenant rights for all persons in their territory and all persons under their control entails an obligation not to extradite, deport, expel or otherwise remove a person from their territory, where there are substantial grounds for believing that there is a real risk of irreparable harm." Para. 12, U.N. Doc. CCPR/C/21/Rev.1/Add.13 (Mar. 29, 2004).

140   Committee on the Elimination of Discrimination against Women [CEDAW Committee], General Recommendation No. 32 on Gender-Related Dimensions of Refugee Status, Asylum, Nationality and Statelessness of Women, PARAS. 17–23, U.N. Doc. CEDAW/C/GC/32 (Nov. 14, 2014).

141   Committee on the Rights of the Child [CRC Committee], General Comment No. 6 (2005): Treatment of Unaccompanied and Separated Children Outside Their Country of Origin, para. 27, U.N. Doc. CRC/GC/2005/6 (Sept. 1, 2005).

142   Committee on the Rights of Persons with Disabilities, Decision Adopted by the Committee Under Article 2 of the Optional Protocol, Concerning Communication No. 28/2015, O.O.J. v Sweden, para. 10.3, U.N. Doc. CRPD/C/18/D/28/2015 (Aug. 18, 2017).

143   Committee on the Elimination of Racial Discrimination, General Recommendation XXX on discrimination against non-citizens, para. 27 (Oct. 1, 2002).

144   Article 3 of the European Convention on Human Rights has been interpreted by the European Court of Human Rights as prohibiting member states from extraditing a person to a country where there is a real risk of being subjected to torture or inhuman treatment. Soering v. United Kingdom, App. No. 14038/88, Eur. Ct. HR, para. 111 (July 7, 1989).

institutions and, international law scholars.[145] Customary international law bans refoulement for anyone who would be eligible for protection under the 1951 Convention, the Refugee Protocol, or the Convention against Torture, according to the vast majority of experts in the field.[146] However, the traditional non-refoulement principle's applicability may extend further.[147] Human rights discourse has had a strong influence on the non-refoulement principle and other established rules of international refugee law throughout the past four decades.[148] It is therefore no longer universally accepted that states may return refugees to persecution on the basis of extradition demands or national security concerns.[149]

2.8 *Restrictions on Asylum*

Article 1(F) of the 1951 Convention relates to a person who is unqualified for international protection and is thus excluded from the Convention's applicability. With respect to such a person, there must be "serious reasons for considering" that:

a. he has committed a crime against peace, a war crime, or a crime against humanity, as defined in the international instruments drawn up to make provision in respect of such crimes;

b. he has committed a serious non-political crime outside the country of refuge prior to his admission to that country as a refugee;

c. he has been guilty of acts contrary to the purposes and principles of the United Nations.[150]

Evidently, the purpose of these restrictions is to prevent criminals and human rights violators from acquiring refugee status and fleeing prosecution.

In addition, it should be noted that the 1951 Convention clearly excludes certain groups from its protection. Article 1(D) stipulates that the Convention is not applicable to people "who are at present receiving from organs or agencies

---

145 Hirsi Jamaa v. Italy, App. No. 27765/09, Eur. Ct. H.R., P 23 (Feb. 23, 2012); U.N. Doc. E/AC.32/SR.21, paras. 6–15; *ICRC*, 2018, 99 Int'l Rev. Red Cross 345, 346 (2017); International Law Association, *Resolution 6/2002 on Refugee Procedures* (*Declaration on International Minimum Standards for Refugee Procedures*) (Apr. 6, 2002).

146 Cathryn Costello & Michelle Foster, *Non-refoulement as Custom and Jus Cogens? Putting the Prohibition to the Test*, 46 Neth. YB Int'l L. 273, 300 (2015); Evan J. Criddle & Evan Fox-Decent, *The Future of Fiduciary Law Symposium: The Authority of International Refugee Law*, 62 Wm. & Mary L. Rev. 1067, 1082–83 (2021).

147 *Id.*

148 Alice Edwards, *Human Rights, Refugees, and the Right "to Enjoy" Asylum*, 17 Int'l J. Refugee L. 293, 294–96 (2005).

149 Costello & Foster, *supra* note 146, at 1083.

150 1951 Refugee Convention, *supra* note 48, at art. 1(F).

of the United Nations other than the United Nations High Commissioner for Refugees protection or assistance."[151] As a result, the Convention eliminates from its protection more than 3 million Palestinians, who are supported by the United Nations Relief and Works Agency for Palestine Refugees in the Near East (UNRWA).[152]

3   Asylum under Islamic Law

This section examines the Islamic Sharia's position on the right to asylum, starting with the Qur'an and moving on to the well-known Sunnah narrations. In addition, this section will explicate the concept of non-refoulment in Islam and identify the restrictions on asylum.

3.1   *The Meaning of Asylum*

The Arabic word "aman," which may be translated into English as "asylum," "protection," or "safety," is the foundation of refugee protection in Islamic law.[153] The word "aman" is used in numerous contexts that are important in Islamic law. For purposes of this study, "aman" is best described as the act of providing safety and security to those who have fled their native country due to threats to their safety or freedom.[154]

On the other hand, a refugee is defined more broadly in Islam than in international refugee law.[155] Unlike international refugee law, Islamic law affords the same protection to refugees, internally displaced persons, forced migrants, and stateless individuals.[156]

Asylum is an integral part of Islamic law. The Qur'an and Sunnah, the most fundamental Islamic sources of law, discuss asylum and refugees in explicit and comprehensive detail.

3.2   *Asylum in the Qur'an*

This study will explain the Qur'anic protection framework for the right to asylum in the following points:

---

151   *Id.* art 1(d).

152   Ahmad, *supra* note 3, at 536.

153   *Id.* at 525.

154   *Id.*

155   Fausto Aarya De Santis, *Refugee Protection under Islamic Law*, Peace and Conflict Monitor (2015), http://www.monitor.upeace.org/printer.cfm?id_article =1081 (last visited July 23, 2022).

156   *Id.*

– The Qur'an guarantees the right to seek asylum. In addition, it encourages individuals who are persecuted in their own country to seek asylum in a new nation. In this respect, the Qur'an states: "As for those who emigrated in the cause of Allah after being persecuted, We will surely bless them with a good home in this world. But the reward of the Hereafter is far better, if only they knew."[157] In addition, the Qur'an says: "Indeed, those whom the angels take [in death] while wronging themselves – [the angels] will say, "In what [condition] were you?" They will say, "We were oppressed in the land." The angels will say, "Was not the earth of Allah spacious [enough] for you to emigrate therein [...] except the men, women, and children who were indeed too feeble to be able to seek the means of escape and did not know where to go.... maybe Allah shall pardon these, for Allah is All-Pardoning, All-Forgiving."[158]

– The Qur'an guarantees the right to be granted asylum. It obligates the country where asylum is sought to grant it. In addition, the Qur'an provides crucial guidelines for the proper reception and treatment of asylum seekers.[159] The Qur'an says: "But those who before them, had homes (in Medina) and had adopted the Faith, – Show their affection to such as came to them for refuge, and entertain no desire in their hearts for things given to the (latter), but give them preference over themselves, even though poverty was their (own lot) and those saved from the covetousness of their own souls, – They are the ones that achieve prosperity."[160]

– The Qur'an explicitly protects the right to be granted asylum for non-Muslims. The Qur'an states: "And if anyone of the disbelievers seeks your protection, then grant him protection so that he may hear the word of Allah, and then escort him to where he will be secure."[161] In other words, the Qur'an does not compel non-Muslim asylum seekers to embrace Islam, but rather respects their right to choose their own religion or belief. The Qur'an says: "Let there be no compulsion in religion, truth stands out clear from error."[162]

---

157   *Surah An-Nahl*, verse 41.
158   *Surah An-Nisa*, verses 97–9.
159   Ahmad, *supra* note 3, at 534.
160   *Surah Al-Hashr*, verse 9. In other verses, the Qur'an provides guidance on how to treat refugees and migrants. It encourages citizens of the country of refuge to help refugees and praises those who do so. The Qur'an says: "Allah has already forgiven the Prophet and the Muhajireen and the Ansar who followed him in the hour of difficulty after the hearts of a party of them had almost inclined [to doubt], and then He forgave them. Indeed, He was to them Kind and Merciful." *Surah At-Taubah*, verse 117.
161   *Surah At-Taubah*, verse 6.
162   *Surah al-Baqarah*, verse 256.

- The Qur'an promotes the principle of equality for asylum seekers. In other words, asylum seekers should have the same rights as citizens of the host country. The Qur'an states: "O mankind, indeed We have created you from male and female and made you peoples and tribes that you may know one another. Indeed, the most noble of you in the sight of Allah is the most righteous of you. Indeed, Allah is Knowing and Acquainted."[163]
- The Qur'an grants special protection to vulnerable refugees, including women and children.[164] The rationale behind this protection is that the most vulnerable members of the refugee community deserve special protection.[165]

Accordingly, the Qur'an offers a comprehensive and distinctive refugee protection framework. It ensures the right to seek and obtain asylum, with a particular emphasis on non-Muslim asylum seekers. In addition, it provides significant guidelines for the care and reception of asylum seekers. Furthermore, it promotes the principle of equality for asylum seekers and affords protection to particularly vulnerable refugees, including women and children.

3.3 Asylum in the Sunnah

There are two main incidents in the Sunnah that formed early Islam and were closely connected to asylum:

The first incident took place in 615 A.D., when the Prophet Mohammad (PBUH) urged his followers to flee persecution in Mecca and go to Abyssinia (present-day Ethiopia), where they were welcomed and granted asylum by the King (Negus) of Abyssinia.[166] This incident occurred at the Prophet's request, but he did not personally take part in it. This incident is also regarded as one

---

163 *Surah* al-Hujurat, verse 13. The Qur'an also states: "And of His signs is the creation of the heavens and the earth and the diversity of your languages and your colors. Indeed, in that are signs for those of knowledge." *Surah Ar-Rum,* verse 22.

164 Ahmad, *supra* note 3, at 527. Many verses in the Qur'an stipulate special protection for women and children. For example, the Qur'an states: "And give to the orphans their properties and do not substitute the defective [of your own] for the good [of theirs]. And do not consume their properties into your own. Indeed, that is ever a great sin." *Surah An-Nisa,* verse 2. The Qur'an also states: "And let those [executors and guardians] fear [injustice] as if they [themselves] had left weak offspring behind and feared for them. So let them fear Allah and speak words of appropriate justice". *Surah An-Nisa,* verse 9. In addition, the Qur'an says: "And do not approach the property of an orphan, except in the way that is best, until he reaches maturity. And fulfill [every] commitment. Indeed, the commitment is ever [that about which one will be] questioned." *Surah Al-Isra,* verse 34.

165 Ahmad, *supra* note 3, at 527. It should be obvious that the Qur'an requires equality, justice, and fairness among all mankind. The Qur'an states: "Indeed, Allah orders justice and good conduct and giving to relatives and forbids immorality and bad conduct and oppression. He admonishes you that perhaps you will be reminded." *Surah An-Nahl,* verse 90.

166 Ahmad, *supra* note 3, at 531–32.

of the earliest interactions between Muslims and Christians, during which Muslims received support and protection from a non-Muslim ruler.[167]

Upon hearing of their departure, the ruling Quraysh tribe of Mecca moved quickly to demand the extradition of a group they falsely claimed to be "rebels or fugitives from justice."[168] Nevertheless, after careful consideration, the king granted Muslims asylum, telling them, "Go your ways, for ye are safe in my land. Not for mountains of gold would I harm a single man of you."[169] The King represented what we now refer to as the role of the "host state" that provides refuge for asylum seekers and protects people seeking its protection.[170] The king's favorable treatment of asylum-seekers became a key point of reference for Muslim-Christian relations in the future.[171] This event exemplifies the contemporary principle of non-refoulement.[172]

It is essential to note that three key asylum principles may be inferred from this incident:[173]

– Asylum is likely sought due to fears of persecution.
– The purpose of asylum is to protect refugees.
– It is unlawful to extradite a refugee who could be persecuted in the requesting country.[174]

The second incident took place when the Prophet Mohammad left Mecca because of the Quraysh's animosity and sought refuge in Medina, where he was welcomed by the hosts.[175] This event serves as the center around which refugee protection in Islamic law revolves.[176]

As soon as the Prophet arrived in Medina, a city with a diverse cultural and religious population, he laid the foundation of a peaceful and integrated community.[177] Through an important document he developed, the Medina Charter,

---

167   *Id.*

168   *Id.*

169   Adil Salahi, Muhammad: Man and Prophet 124 (Leicestershire, The Islamic Foundation, 2002).

170   Agha, *supra* note 63, at 30.

171   Ahmad, *supra* note 3, at 532.

172   *Id.*

173   Ahmed Abou-El-Wafa, The Right to Asylum between Islamic Shari'ah and International Refugee Law: A Comparative Study 106 (2009).

174   Ahmad, *supra* note 3, at 532.

175   *Id.* at 530.

176   Kirsten Zaat, *The Protection of Forced Migrants in Islamic Law*, (2007) UNHCR New Issues in Refugee Research, Research Paper No. 146. 15.

177   Muhammad Husain Haykal, The Life of Muhammad 102 (Ismail Raji al-Faruqi, Kuala Lumpur, Malaysia, Islamic Book Trust, 2002).

the Prophet created justice and equality for all segments of society.[178] The
Medina Charter expanded on ensuring friendly relations between the refugees
and the host community by granting civil and political rights to the Meccan
refugees within a mutually accepted legal framework.[179]

Indeed, the Sunnah is a significant and exceptional source of asylum in
Islam because the Prophet himself sought refuge and encouraged his early followers to do the same. In addition, the Sunnah indicates the friendly and outstanding relationship between Muslims and non-Muslims, because Muslims
got assistance and protection from a Christian ruler. The Medina Charter is
a historic and exceptional document that provided mutual support between
refugees and people of the host nation and enabled refugees to obtain civil,
political, and many other rights. This charter might serve as a model for our
modern approach to refugee protection.

3.4   The Principle of Non-Refoulement

The principle of non-refoulment is protected in Islam. A Muslim nation cannot
compel a refugee to return to his home country, where he may face persecution. There are several arguments that could be made to support this position,
including:

- *First*: it is evident that sending a refugee to a country where he or she may
  be persecuted or tortured breaches the Islamic concept of "aman," or "protection," as the study previously indicated.[180]
- *Second*: Islam prohibits committing treason by returning a refugee to a
  country where his life may be in danger or his fundamental rights will be
  violated.[181]

In this regard, it should be highlighted that the behavior of the Abyssinian
king, with whom early Muslims sought refuge, is a perfect example of non-
refoulment. When delegates of the Quraysh arrived and requested that
asylum-seekers be returned to their home country, Makkah, the king replied:
"Nay, by God, they shall not be betrayed – a people that have sought my protection and made my country their abode and chosen me above all others!
I will not give them up, until I have summoned them and questioned them
concerning what these men say of them. If it be as they have said, then will I

---

178   Ahmad, *supra* note 3, at 530–31.
179   *Id.* at 531.
180   *Id.* at 544.
181   Abou-El-Wafa, *supra* note 173, at 55.

deliver them unto them, that they may restore them to their own people. But if not, then I will be their good protector, so long as they seek my protection."[182]

In Islam, the principle of non-refoulement is absolute. A refugee cannot be sent back to a country where his life or freedom might be in danger.[183] It was even argued that Islam was the first to create the non-refoulment principle and the non-extradition rule of refugees who committed political crimes.[184]

3.5   Restrictions on Asylum

Similar to international law, Islam allows a host country to deny refuge to a non-political criminal who has committed a crime in his or her own country and is seeking asylum as a method to escape punishment.[185]

However, the asylum-seeker should not be sent to a country where he or she may face persecution. The country that denies asylum must not breach the principle of non-refoulment; the asylum applicant must be permitted to seek protection elsewhere.[186]

4   Conclusion

After illustrating the asylum protection framework under international refugee and Islamic law, it is possible to briefly conclude with the following points:

- International refugee law protects the right to seek asylum. However, this right may be ineffective and useless if states do not accept asylum requests. International law does not obligate states to grant asylum; every sovereign state has the authority to grant or deny asylum. Thus, no one has a guaranteed right to obtain or be granted asylum under international law.
- *In contrast*, under Islamic law, a country is required, not entitled, to grant asylum. Individuals' right to obtain or be granted asylum is fully guaranteed by Islamic law.
- International refugee law protection is based on refugees' fears of persecution based on "race, religion, nationality, membership in a particular social group or political opinion." However, this protection does not apply if the victim is subjected to other threats, such as natural disasters and extensive civil violence.

---

182   *Id.* at 109.
183   *Id.* at 53.
184   *Id.*
185   Ahmad, *supra* note 3, at 546–47.
186   Abou-El-Wafa, *supra* note 173, at 55.

- *In contrast*, Islamic law applies widely to all reasons for seeking asylum. In other words, unlike international refugee law, Islam has no specific requirements for granting asylum.
- International refugee law recognizes the concept of "fears of persecution" as the key criterion for determining who is a refugee but does not define this concept. As a result, states have wide discretion in assessing the degree of alleged harm inflicted on asylum seekers and determining who qualifies as a refugee.
- *In contrast*, this controversy does not exist in Islamic law. Concerns about persecution and other motives for seeking asylum are regarded equally. Under Islamic law, the country has an obligation to accept and welcome all asylum seekers.
- International refugee law's principle of "non-refoulement" is only applicable to threats of persecution based on "race, religion, nationality, membership in a particular social group, or political opinion," but other risks, including natural disasters and widespread civil violence, are irrelevant to this precept. In addition, international refugee law provides an exception to the non-refoulement principle for refugees who endanger the host country's security. Furthermore, this principle does not apply to asylum seekers at the borders of the country in which they request asylum, even if they are fleeing persecution in a neighboring country.

The author argues that these exceptions may amount to serious and flagrant violations of several fundamental human rights, including the right to life, the right to liberty and security of person, and other basic rights.

- *In contrast*, Islam avoids this issue. The right to non-refoulement is absolute under Islamic law; a refugee must not be forced to return to his home country, where he may be persecuted.
- International refugee law does not provide special protection for vulnerable groups, such as women and children. However, other instruments of international law could be used to provide this protection.
- *In contrast*, Islamic law explicitly protects vulnerable populations, including women and children.
- International refugee law excludes from protection more than three million Palestinians, who are supported by the United Nations Relief and Works Agency for Palestine Refugees in the Near East (UNRWA).

The author sees that Islamic law provides protection to refugees within an outstanding and comprehensive framework. Islamic law ensures the right to seek and be granted asylum, provides significant guidelines for the care and reception of asylum seekers, enables refugees to have many rights, protects the principle of equality between asylum seekers and citizens of the host states, affords special protection for vulnerable refugees, and most importantly regards refugees' right to non-refoulement as absolute.

The author argues that the interesting asylum legal system under Islamic law is vastly superior and preferable to international law, which has the following weaknesses and flaws:

- International refugee law does not guarantee an individual's right to receive or be granted asylum.
- International refugee law allows exceptions to the non-refoulement principle.
- International refugee law does not protect people suffering from a variety of threats, such as natural disasters and severe civil violence.
- International refugee law protects refugees solely on the basis of the imprecise and undefined concept of persecution.
- International refugee law provides no special protection to vulnerable groups, including women and children.

Accordingly, the author concludes that international refugee framework requires a substantial amount of revision and modification in order to provide better protection for refugees and assist in resolving and overcoming a number of obstacles, challenges, and problems that refugees currently face. The international community should enhance the international refugee system and provide refugees with broader and more comprehensive protection. Improving the international refugee system and strengthening and expanding refugee protection should be a top priority for the international community as it faces the challenges of often forced migration long not seen in world history.

CHAPTER 17

The Dilemma of Forgiveness: The Personal in the Holocaust

*Keith D. Nunes**

In der Hoffnung, der Weg der Menschheit führt von der Bestialität
zur Humanität

Siegfried Wiessner, May 10, 1982, Dedication to the Author in LAGER UND
MENSCHLICHE WÜRDE (Claudius Hennig & Siegfried Wiessner eds., 1982)

∵

Prologue

The Nazis tried their damndest to trump the question "Can injustice be framed
into law?"[1] "[A] corrupt throne ... that brings on misery by its decrees?"[2] They
used the powerful instruments and strategies of the state to carry the weight
of their nefarious policies of law and order. The mission of the Nazis was not
only to disenfranchise but also to dehumanize a certain minority of the citizens of the Weimar Republic, characterizing them as an inferior race, both
Jews and Roma-Sinti (so-called Gypsies with exogamous marriages), with the
ultimate aim to wipe these citizens from the face of the earth because they
were *Untermenschen*: The category they created of subhumans, the inferior
people, included: Jews, Roma and Sinti, and Slavs (i.e., Poles, Serbs, Ukrainians,
and Russians).[3]

---

* A former Fellow of the Woodrow Wilson School of Public Administration and International
Affairs of Princeton University, Salzburg Seminar, and University of Chicago Founders'
Constitution Seminar, with law degrees from Yale, Leyden, and Cape Town, and diplomas
from the Hague Academy of International Law Centre for Research and Study.
1 Psalm 94, Authorized Daily Prayer Book, Chief Rabbi Lord Jonathan Sacks, OBM 151 (2007).
2 *Ibid.*; The Koren Tehillim, tr. Rabbi Eli Cashdan 480 (2017).
3 Timothy Snyder observes that an account of mass atrocities in Europe really extends to
the context between 1933 and 1945 to encompass "bloodlands" shared between Berlin and

The genesis of this national degradation of law was the rule of law of the Weimar Republic that had been declared amidst defeat, national humiliation, revolution, chaos and disorder. The Weimar constitution itself was flawed, giving rise to Nazi rule. Article 48 gave the president authority to suspend the Reichstag and rule by decree without parliamentary support. Weimar's proportional representation encouraged the growth of an unstable coalition government and gave cranks and extremists a voice in the Reichstag. Many of the multiple parties opposed democracy, notably, the parties agitating for a Marxist revolution, the Communist Party and Independent Social Democrats. On the extreme right nationalist and ultra-right-wing groups sought to replace the republic with a military dictatorship.

Hitler and the Nazi Party threatened Weimar's democracy, which, from 1924 to 1929, seemed secure with an economy that showed encouraging signs of recovery, a period when reparations were not causing Franco-German antagonism. The Party's rise was based on its use of racial doctrines that had deep roots in many German states and in the extreme racial nationalism and antisemitism of Martin Luther. German antisemites were influenced by Luther and Johann Gottlieb Fichte in Germany, Arthur de Gobineau, Louis-Ferdinand Céline and Robert Barsillach in France, and Houston Chamberlain in England.[4] For them, race predicted the rise and fall of nation-states. The antisemitism of the 1890s fed into the complicated angst of the extreme political right, with its national socialism after the First World War period, and fringe lobby groups (the extreme nationalist pan-German League, the National Germanic League

---

Moscow. The German death factories stand alongside the Soviet murder sites and must be added to the Soviet killing sites to encompass 14 million civilians and prisoners of war who were killed in these bloodlands from central Poland to western Russia, as he identifies the sites. Timothy Snyder, Bloodlands—Europe Between Hitler and Stalin (2010). *See* on the history in the Prologue, Saul Friedländer, Nazi Germany and the Jews: The Years of Persecution, 1933–39 (1998) and Nazi Germany and the Jews: the Years of Destruction, 1939–45 (2008); Michael Burleigh, The Third Reich: A New History (2001); Richard J. Evans' "Third Reich Trilogy": The Coming of the Third Reich (2005), The Third Reich in Power (2006),The Third Reich at War (2009); Michael Marrus, The Holocaust in History (1987); Alan Bullock, Hitler. A Study in Tyranny (1962); Ian Kershaw, Hitler (1991); Alan Bullock, Hitler and Stalin: Parallel Lives (1991); William Sheridan Allen, The Nazi Seizure of Power: The Experience of a Single German Town, 1930–1935 (1965); Heinz Höhne, Die Machtergreifung (1983); Martin Gilbert, The Holocaust. The Human Tragedy (1985); Martin Gilbert, Kristallnacht. Prelude to Destruction (2006).

4   Houston Stewart Chamberlain was the son-in-law of Richard Wagner whose ferocious antisemitism looked back to a mythical Germany that was pre-Christian with the myths of flaxen-blond-haired heroes and heroines of his operas.

of Clerks, and the Agrarian League). Propaganda exaggerated the degree of influence of the Jews on the elite, professions, and especially the banks and stock market. Jews were portrayed as not only "alien" to the German race, but as wielding too much power and influence in Germany inimical to Aryan "cultural superiority." The Nazis built up the concept of racial superiority to become the central component of Nazism.

The *Burgfrieden* (truce) between political right and left in Germany included the Jews until Germany began to lose World War I when anti-Jewish prejudice revived—despite the 12,000 German Jews who gave their lives for the "Fatherland." Right-wing circles propagated the *Dolchstosslegende*—the stab in the back myth to the effect that Jews had betrayed Germany by fomenting revolution when the German army was actually winning the war, and that the Jews profited financially from the First World War. For right-wing German nationalists, the Bolshevik Revolution of 1917 in Russia was a sinister link between Jews and communism. Walter Rathenau, a future foreign minister of postwar Weimar Republic, was made responsible as a Jew for the German revolution of 1918. All this despite the fact that, although Trotsky and Zinoviev were Jewish, the Bolshevik Revolution was neither Jewish-led, nor was the German Revolution in 1918.

De-mobbed German soldiers rejected the democracy of the Weimar Republic as corrupt and ineffectual, drawn to the political right's racism and identification of Jews as malignant to their nationalist views of "their" body politic. Conflating Jews and communists as allies, the nationalists wanted to see them neutralized to overcome the shame and their defeat of 1918. Hitler's Vienna of 1908 and 1913 was one of endemic antisemitism under the mayor Karl Lueger, who, with the propagandist August von Schönerer, stirred up the ferocity of Austrian hatred and resentment of Jews and led to Hitler's hysterical welcome on his "triumphal" return to Vienna in 1938.

When imprisoned in the comfort of Landsberg prison for 5 years for high treason against the Weimar Republic, of which he served but 13 months in 1924, because of the Munich beer hall putsch of November 1923, Hitler started to write *Mein Kampf* (My Struggle). This turgid manifesto is markedly different from the *Letter from Birmingham Jail*, the open letter written on April 16, 1963, by Dr. Martin Luther King Jr., where he says, "Injustice anywhere is a threat to justice everywhere." Hitler radically pushed for ferocious antisemitism and a racial state. Dr. King's overriding goal, in sharp contrast, was civil and political rights for all Americans, most inclusively, in view of their legal and social exclusion, black Americans.

1   The Sunflower[5] and Simon Wiesenthal

Simon Wiesenthal was a prisoner in the forced labor camp of Janowska where *Sonderkommando* 1005 used a machine to grind the bones of victims after their bodies were burned in the camp.[6]

As an inmate at Janowska *lager*, Simon Wiesenthal was sent on a forced labor detail to Lemberg, his student town, to clear medical waste from the Reserve Hospital set up for wounded German soldiers. Here at his rebranded technical school, Wiesenthal is approached by a nurse who risks asking him if he is a Jew, although his identification seemed apparent to him from his clothing and, perhaps, his features. The nurse leads Wiesenthal to a patient in what was the principal's office. The man in the hospital bed is totally bandaged— only his mouth, nose, and ears are free of bandages. Could he be a Jew? An OJP, i.e. with one Jewish parent? At his bedside, the soldier tells him that he is on his deathbed.

The soldier, Karl, tortured by his experiences in "the field," wants to speak to a Jew. Wiesenthal shows his civility by picking up a letter from his mother, brought by the nurse, that slipped from the soldier's hand. He reflects that he will not receive any letter because his mother was cruelly dragged to her death from the Ghetto. Karl relates that he joined the SS as a volunteer over his parent's vehement objections, disabusing Wiesenthal's idea that he could be a Jew. Karl holds Wiesenthal's hand and confesses to heinous crimes on the battlefield. Wiesenthal thinks that despite the heinousness of his crimes, he will be rewarded with a sunflower on his military grave as he saw marking the graves of Nazi soldiers en route to the reserve hospital. Wiesenthal thinks: "For me there would be no sunflower. I would be buried in a mass grave, where corpses would be piled on top of me. No sunflower would ever bring light into my darkness, and no butterflies would dance above my dreadful tomb."[7] For him, the sunflower heads seemed to be mirrors absorbing the sun's rays into the ground and that a periscope enabled the butterflies from flower to flower to send messages to the dead from grave to grave.[8] He drops Karl's hand.

Karl's family background speaks to human values. His father was a committed social democrat and a factory manager. His mother brought him up

---

5   Reliance is on Simon Wiesenthal, The Sunflower—On the Possibilities and Limits of Forgiveness (1998).
6   United States Holocaust Memorial Museum, Holocaust Encyclopedia, https://encyclopedia .ushmm.org/content/ en/photo/bone-crushing-machine-in-janowska.
7   *Supra* note 5, at 14–15.
8   *Id.* at 14.

as a Catholic. After he joined the Hitler Youth, his parents no longer spoke to him about politics since they feared he would shop them to the Nazis. Volunteering for the SS caused him vehement criticism from his father. Karl held Wiesenthal's hand tighter as he tried to release it on hearing that joining the SS was for Karl part of something exciting and grand.

Richard Evans explains the underlying motive for the zeal Karl had to join the SS: "Nazi propaganda was most effective in the younger generation of Germans, who after all had had few chances to form their own firm values and beliefs before the regime began, and who were subjected to massively intensive and unremitting indoctrination from the schools, from the Hitler Youth, and from the mass media orchestrated by Goebbels. It was overwhelmingly young people, for example, who joined in the antisemitic violence of the *Kristallnacht* and shouted insults at Victor Klemperer in the streets."[9]

As Wiesenthal wonders why he is at the bedside of this bandaged soldier, why a Catholic priest is not called to hear his confession, he "as a matter of course" waves away a bluebottle for which Karl thanks him. He wants to leave, their backgrounds share nothing, and he thinks of his own dying unremembered by a Sunflower. Wiesenthal's deep humanity, however, keeps him at Karl's bedside whom he sees as helpless as himself.

Karl tells Wiesenthal harrowing crime upon crime. In a Ukrainian village they had "inhumanly" shot at Russians hiding in a farmhouse which Karl describes as "mak[ing] history."[10] Towards Dnepropetrovsk in a large square they drove almost 200 Jews into a nearby house including "many children who stared at us with anxious eyes. A few were quietly crying. There were infants in their mothers' arms, but hardly any young men; mostly women and graybeards."[11] A truck-full of Jews was also jammed into the house. The Jews had been forced to carry cans of gasoline into the upper floors of the house. The doors were locked, and a machine gun guarded the exit. Karl obeyed the command to remove the safety pins from their hand grenades and throw them through the house's windows. The building was engulfed in flames. Karl saw a man on the second floor holding a small child in his arms. His clothes were burning. The woman at his side seemed to be the child's mother. The man covered the child's eyes with his free hand and jumped into the street followed by

---

9   Richard J. Evans, *Coercion and Consent in Nazi Germany, Raleigh Lecture on History*, The British Academy, 151 British Academy Proc. 53,73 (2006), https://www.thebritishacademy .ac.uk/publishing/review/10/coercion-and-consent-nazi-germany/. *See* Victor Klemperer, I Shall Bear Witness: The Diaries of Victor Klemperer, 1933–41 (tr. Martin Chalmers 1998).

10   Sunflower, *supra* note 5, at 38.

11   *Id.* at 40.

the woman. Burning bodies fell from the other windows and ... they shot at them. "[T]hat one family I shall never forget—least of all the child."[12] He cries in remembrance of the eyes of the child. Their platoon leader dismisses the haunted screams, sleepless nights, his companions not being able to look each other in the face—since Jews are not human beings.

Wiesenthal is reminded of the last Jewish child from the Ghetto, Eli, a pet name for Eliyahu—Elijah the prophet—for whom at Passover Seder the customary fifth cup of wine is set aside and the door opened at the end of the Seder with a prayer for him to come in and drink the wine. "He doesn't drink more than a tear!"[13] is the response he gets from his grandmother on why the cup remained full. For them as children, Eliyahu was their protector. By staying home, Eli the ghetto boy survived the Nazi raid taking the children from their fake kindergarten to the gas chambers. Karl's horrific story of the baby, in his father's hands leaping to their death, reminds Wiesenthal of Eli—the last Jewish child he saw. And, he names the boy Eli.[14]

The last Jewish baby born in Vienna under Hitler, Dr Fritz Ruben Bittmann, is my friend. His parents were "submarines," i.e. living in the underground in the second district of Vienna. They received food packets, to keep them alive and share with other Jews hidden in the underground, from Turkey, from where they were shipped by a close relative under the auspices of the Apostolic Delegate to Turkey and Greece, who used his office for the benefit of the Jewish Underground namely Angelo Giuseppe Roncalli, subsequently Pope John XXIII.[15]

Karl's brutality flows, as Richard Evans says, from Nazi indoctrination and inculcation of violence in young Germans: "It is only by recognizing that large numbers of Germans had become willing administrators of coercion and repression, and that millions of younger Germans had been heavily influenced by Nazi indoctrination, that we can explain the extraordinarily savage behaviour of the forces that invaded Poland in 1939."[16] "Toughness, hardness, brutality, the use of force, the virtues of violence, had been inculcated into a whole generation of young Germans from 1933 onwards."[17]

---

12   *Id.* at 43.
13   *Id.* at 44.
14   *Id.* at 63.
15   *See* Biography of Pope John Paul XXIII at https://www.vatican.va/content/john-xxiii/en /biography/documents/hf_j-xxiii_bio_16071997_biography.html.
16   Evans, supra note 9, at 78.
17   *Id.* at 79.

Karl does not discuss the theft and looting of Jewish[18] and Polish property, the Nazis assumed to be freely available to them, along with their brutal beatings and murder, massacring Jews, and sending men off as slave laborers to Germany along with ethnic cleansing and population transfers.

In Crimea towards Russian-held Taganrog, with intense artillery fire over weeks and many military cemeteries and sunflowers, Karl cried "My G-d," "My G-d," and where, in climbing out of the trench, he was hit by an exploding shell. "In that moment I saw the burning family, the father with the child and behind them the mother—and they came to meet me. 'No, I cannot shoot at them a second time.' The thought flashed through my mind …. And then a shell exploded by my side. I lost consciousness … It was a miracle that I was still alive—even now I am as good as dead … So I lie here waiting for death. The pains in my body are terrible, but worse still is my conscience … I cannot die … without coming clean … In the last hours of my life you are with me. I do not know who you are. I only know that you are a Jew and that is enough … In the long nights while I have been waiting for death, time and time again I have longed to talk about it to a Jew and beg forgiveness from him. Only I didn't know whether there were any Jews left … I know that what I am asking is almost too much for you, but without your answer I cannot die in peace."[19]

Karl begs Wiesenthal to forgive him for his crimes. He cannot die in peace without receiving forgiveness. Wiesenthal's sympathy evaporated with each terrible crime. Yet, he cannot tear himself away from Karl's bedside. He feels there is a "warm undertone in [Karl's] voice as he spoke about the Jews."[20] Indeed, he has experienced good things from their Jewish family physician whose medical treatment his mother trusted exclusively.[21] Otherwise, he was acquainted with a few other Jews whom they gave food to when they were cleaning their army quarters in Poland, and he left food on the table. But then they were plied with the Nazi disinformation that the Jews were to blame for all Germany's troubles: war, unemployment, poverty, and hunger in Germany.

In particular ways this experience with the nurse, who "keeps cavey" in order for Karl to speak with Wiesenthal, is formative for him. When I met with Simon Wiesenthal in Vienna, shortly after 9/11, Wiesenthal informed me that his work as a Nazi hunter had nothing to do with the erroneous interpretation of an eye

---

18   "[A]lmost universal" according to Richard Evans, id., citing his The Third Reich at War (2008), ch.1.

19   Sunflower, *supra* note 5, at 50–54.

20   *Id.* at 40.

21   *Id.*

for an eye,[22] whereby the perpetrator is required to be punished equal in kind to the offense. Authoritative Jewish decision-making have always interpreted this statement of the Torah as a matter of compensation. Measure for measure.

When Karl tells Wiesenthal that he was born in Stuttgart and was only 21 years old and really too young to die, Wiesenthal thinks that for the Nazis Jewish children were never too young to die—policies carried out by Eichmann and Hoess. When Karl intuited Wiesenthal's thought, he asked whether, without paying attention to his circumstances of his behavior in the war, he really is too young to die.

Wiesenthal told me that people would come to him, to pressure him, and complain that he should not prosecute old or crippled or injured Nazis. Instead, they should be dealt with in a compassionate and a humanitarian way because of their age or infirmity. Wiesenthal's policy was not a policy of vengeance. His policy was to focus on seeking justice for the victims of the Holocaust.

Simon Wiesenthal leaves Karl without heeding his dying request for forgiveness of his crimes. The next day, the nurse approaches him again and takes him not to Karl's room but to a storage room. Here she tells Wiesenthal that Karl passed away in the night. She offers him Karl's belongings since Karl wanted him to have them. Instead of accepting Karl's bequest, Wiesenthal asked the nurse to let Karl's mother have his bundle of belongings.

Simon Wiesenthal is profoundly affected by his experience with Karl. Back in the stable of the concentration camp where he sleeps with 150 other men, he eventually tries to discuss Karl's plea with his little group: Josek who is pious and sensitive and his two other friends Arthur and Adam. Arthur's reply is "one less,"[23] and Adam, a lawyer and writer, cynically says that he would like the murderer to die ten times a day.[24] Josek worries that Wiesenthal might forgive Karl since he cannot forgive crimes done against other people.

Wiesenthal asks Josek to consider his view that Karl was sincere in wanting forgiveness, with true repentance,[25] and in anguish[26] over his conduct. Josek responds that severe physical and mental suffering is part and parcel of the soldier's punishment for his crimes. Wiesenthal thinks Karl was looking to him as a representative of his victims. Arthur intervenes that, if Wiesenthal had forgiven Karl out of superhuman kindness, he would not have forgiven himself. The irony is that Arthur says Wiesenthal should have called for a priest

---

22   Lev. 24:19–21. *Cf.* Simon Wiesenthal, Justice, Not Vengeance: Recollections (1990).
23   Sunflower, *supra* note 5, at 64.
24   *Id.*
25   *Id.* at 53.
26   *Id.* at 42.

to hear Karl's confession and give him absolution from his crimes. Wiesenthal questions the relativity of each religion on ethics absent general laws of guilt and penitence.

Wiesenthal's friends die in the camp: Arthur in his arms from typhus, Adam from execution for a sprained ankle, and Josek shot for a high fever. Over the next years of the war, time and again, through all his suffering, Simon thought of Karl and wondered if he should have forgiven him.

Uppermost in Simon Wiesenthal's mind is his encounter with Karl: "[O]ught I to have forgiven him? ... Was my silence at the bedside of the dying Nazi right or wrong? This is a profound moral question ... The crux of the matter is, of course, the question of forgiveness. Forgetting is something that time alone takes care of, but forgiveness is an act of volition ..."[27]

"Forgiveness," Nelson Mandela in the movie says, "liberates the soul, it removes fear. That's why it's such a powerful weapon."[28] Mandela used this perspective to constructive effect, as the movie portrays, to get black and white and politically opposite South Africans to cooperate to forge the new South Africa, but forgiveness is a complicated if not also a subtle matter. There is the complex question of how can we forgive the unforgivable? Are the acts Wiesenthal witnesses at the bedside of Karl "unforgivable"? Jacques Derrida thinks so and says, "[Y]es, there is the unforgivable. Is this not, in truth, the only thing to forgive? One cannot, or should not, forgive: there is only forgiveness, if there is any, where there is the unforgivable."[29] Simon Eder disagrees on the basis of "Jewish tradition which treads the narrow tightrope between both justice on the one hand and mercy on the other ..." He emphasizes Wiesenthal's experience in *The Sunflower* as a case in point where it is not in Wiesenthal's remit to usurp the divine prerogative to forgive.[30] Namely, the thirteen attributes of divine compassion written in the Torah "forgiving iniquity, rebellion and sin, and absolving the [guilty who repent]." Simon Eder is referring to the most profound and hidden aspect of G-d's attribute of mercy, mysteriously present and providing forgiveness for sins of commission that are otherwise unforgivable.

Bolek, a new inmate for Wiesenthal in his last camp Mauthausen, a young Catholic Pole priest candidate, agrees: "One thing is certain: you can

---

27   *Id.* at 97–98.

28   The Mandela post-Apartheid biographical sports drama, 2009, directed by Clint Eastwood. Mandela suffered 18 of his 27 years in incarceration on Robben Island off Cape Town.

29   Jacques Derrida, Cosmopolitanism and Forgiveness 36 (2001), *cited by* Simon Eder, *Is Forgiveness Even Possible?*, Jewish Quest, https://jewishquest.org/writing/is-forgiveness-even-possible/.

30   Eder, *id.*

only forgive a wrong that has been done to yourself,"[31] But, then, he ripostes, Wiesenthal should have forgiven Karl because he had no one else to turn to and those he had wronged were dead. Bolek finds fault with Wiesenthal who should have forgiven Karl since he was a dying man repenting for his sins. But ... even Bolek wavers from his initial position at the end.[32]

Josek had previously pointed out something important though: In the World to Come the dead would ask him who gave him the authority to forgive their murderer.[33] There is here the case of the oppressed black South African woman who courageously testified at the Truth and Reconciliation Commission established in 1995 to heal the country. She sided succinctly with Josek. Her family had endured the severest of deprivations. Her husband had been tortured by the police, and then they killed him summarily. She was emphatic: "A commission or a government cannot forgive. Only I, eventually, could do it. And I am not ready to forgive."[34] This victim of apartheid, amongst so many others, is saying something crucial: I am not ready to forgive the unforgivable because forgiveness is premature. This is not a matter of political forgiveness to transcend apartheid and our hatreds for a future of co-operation in the new South Africa. "[O]nly the sufferer is qualified to make the decision."[35]

Simon Wiesenthal was barely alive when Mauthausen was liberated by the 11th Armored Division of the Third U.S. Army on May 5, 1945. But he continued to think about, and question, his decision of silence to refuse to express forgiveness to the soldier Karl and he subsequently asked a long list of Jewish and non-Jewish thinkers to consider his decision.[36] Each struggles with the dilemma, clarifiable by the constructive jurisprudence of Myres McDougal,[37] and comes to different conclusions of when to forgive and when to seek justice. Judaism eschews radical forgiveness that calls upon adherents of one's faith to forgive the most egregious and heinous of crimes. Judaism believes in a forgiving G-d and promotes forgiveness as an essential human virtue. It does

---

31   Sunflower, *supra* note 5, at 81.

32   *Id.* at 83.

33   *Id.* at 66–67.

34   Cited by Derrida, *supra* note 47, at 43.

35   Sunflower, *supra* note 5, at 98.

36   *Id.*, Book Two: The Symposium, at 99–274, for the fifty-three varied responses and experiences.

37   *See and Cf.* W. Michael Reisman & Aaron Schreiber, Understanding and Shaping Law: Cases, Readings, Commentary (1987); Myres S. McDougal et al., Studies in World Public Order (1960); Harold D Lasswell & Myres S McDougal, Jurisprudence for a Free Society (1992); W. Michael Reisman, *Myres S. McDougal: Architect of a Jurisprudence for a Free Society*, 66 Miss. L.J. 15 (1996–1997).

believe that there are crimes that cannot be forgiven and for which punishment is justified.

C.S. Lewis expresses surprise that the psalmists believe in G-d's judgment: "Judgement [sic] is apparently an occasion of universal rejoicing. People ask for it: 'Judge me, O Lord my G-d, according to thy righteousness'" (Psalm 35:24).[38]

There is, as Simon Eder writes, "ambiguity that lies surrounding questions of forgiveness – namely what is being asked of when one seeks forgiveness? Who is being asked? Something or someone?"[39] Permanent forgiveness? Assistance in the process of repentance? Regaining G-d's favor? Capacity to be happy again? In short, the Teshuvah—the asking for forgiveness from G-d is a return process to the status ante quo which calls for more than a vicar who is domestically authorized to dispense absolution. As David in Psalm 51 illustrates, the repentance dialogue continues with G-d long after grant of the initial forgiveness.[40]

To conclude, Is there a measure of forgiveness when Wiesenthal recalls the address of Karl's mother on the bundle the nurse said Karl wanted him to have when, four years after his momentous meeting with Karl, reminded by a sunflower, he shows his humanity en route to Munich by visiting Karl's mother, Frau Maria S.[41] in Stuttgart, an infirm widow living in the rubble of her former home? Was Wiesenthal being asked for unconditional forgiveness in the sense of something found in the confession box? More particularly, is there forgiveness without forgetting, when Wiesenthal keeps silent about her son's culpability and direct participation in crimes against humanity and mass murder? He does not disabuse her about her view that her son was a "good boy"? Karl's father has died implacable against his son's Nazi activities.

Simon Wiesenthal in a quiet, tender manner writes: "I looked at the old lady who was clearly kindhearted, a good mother and a good wife. Without doubt, she must often have shown sympathy for the oppressed, but the happiness of her own family was of paramount importance to her. There were millions of such families anxious only for peace and quiet in their own little nests. These were the mounting blocks by which the criminals climbed to power and kept it."[42] The human drive to keep one's head down and to look after one's own to be safe and secure leads to untenable compromises for humanity, and, in the

---

38   C.S. Lewis, *Judgement in the Psalms – Mere CS Lewis*, http://merecslewis.blogspot
       .com/2011/04/judgement-in-psalms.html.

39   Eder, supra note 29.

40   By G-d through Nathan II Sam. 12.

41   Sunflower, *supra* note 5, at 86.

42   *Id.* at 91.

instant case of Nazi Germany, gave rise to the unique and virulent "elimina-tionist antisemitism" in German identity as Daniel Goldhagen observed.[43]

Antisemitism was not a particularly German doctrine. It is a pervasive European-wide phenomenon. In Russia between 1880 and the outbreak of the First World pogroms (anti-Jewish atrocities) were the order of the day encour-aged by the Tsar.

In the most cultivated territorial community, France, a Jewish army officer Alfred Dreyfus, from Alsace, was accused of spying for Germany and dismissed from the army in 1894 and sent to the penal colony of Devil's Island in French Guyana. His case divided France.

Simon Wiesenthal remarks: "I asked myself if it was only the Nazis who had persecuted us. Was it not just as wicked for people to look on quietly and with-out protest at human beings enduring such shocking humiliation? But in their eyes were we human beings at all?"[44]

Forgiveness, which Karl was seeking, Tzvi Hersh Weinreb[45] reminds one, "is an act of G-d for which there are no intermediaries. Only G-d can forgive but undoing not only sin but the consequences of sin." Is that not the crux of the matter Simon Wiesenthal was seized of?

Haunted by his experience with Karl, and his mindful flashbacks to the young six-year-old boy in the ghetto, Eli, Wiesenthal asks plaintively: "There are many kinds of silence. Indeed it can be more eloquent than words, and it can be interpreted in many ways. Was my silence at the bedside of the dying Nazi right or wrong?" Or, one may add, when visiting his mother? "Well, I kept silent when a young Nazi, on his deathbed begged me to be his confessor. And later, when I met his mother, I again kept silent rather than shatter her illusions about her dead son's inherent goodness. And how many bystanders kept silent as they watched Jewish men, women, and children being led to the slaughter-houses of Europe?"[46] Silence does have an emotional, even spiritual dimen-sion. Consider: "Three things are fitting for us—upright kneeling, motionless dancing, and silent screaming."[47] "... We can kneel even when we are upright; and we can stand erect and yet be humble and reverent. Dancing ... can ... be

---

43   Daniel Goldhagen, Hitler's Willing Executioners: Ordinary Germans and the Holocaust (1996).

44   Sunflower, *supra* note 5, at 57.

45   Tzvi Hersh Weinreb, *in* The Koren Tehillim 676 (tr. Elli Cashdan with introduction and commentary by Weinreb, 2017).

46   Sunflower, *supra* note 5, at 97. Wiesenthal questions his decision of silence not to for-give Karl so deeply that he approaches a long list of non-Jewish and Jewish thinkers who respond in their own way in The Sunflower.

47   Rabbi Menahem Mendel of Premislan, Siddur Hadash 349 (2000).

an inner mood. ... We can, indeed, cry out silently."[48] It seems that Wiesenthal has been "crying out silently" ever since. ... Did the world, did responsible decision-makers hear his cry ... at least to bring the Nazis to justice? The record on Nazi prosecutions is uneven. Yes, there is Nuremberg, Jerusalem, trials in Germany and even Austria, Australia, and the quirky way the U.S. deals with the issue (via removals of citizenship and deportation of exposed Nazis). There is the Holocaust settlement, art restorations, but have we done enough? Could we additionally have used South Africa's model of reconciliation in some cases? What about the business involvement in the Holocaust? Was there not a promise to deal with corporations after the settlements with Germany, France, Switzerland?

There is a different inclusive approach. Rather than relativizing values as set by different faith communities, we can give due recognition to the claims people make everywhere in their communities to what they really want—claims that are distillable in terms of the human values of respect, wealth, enlightenment, power, skills, rectitude (moral and ethical guides), well-being, and affection. For Karl, there are questions of culpability, and its degrees, intent or negligence, causation, mitigating factors, and repentance—all issues that relate to these values which are a democratic asset for a community to adjust individual claims with those of the public interest, i.e., to distill common values and the inclusive interest of the community in a continuum of degrees of shared participation in the social process.[49] Forgiveness along with repentance would fall outside the functions of the criminal justice process. As far as a truth and reconciliation process, the woman in South Africa, whose name I wish I knew, is surely right in relation to forgiveness when she says forgiveness must come from within the victim.

Simon Wiesenthal stood for the liberal process of justice to keep and to promote a public order of human dignity. He insisted that the Nazis should be charged with their crimes against humanity or released. He would have no truck with vigilantism or extra-judicial activities. He stood squarely against collective guilt and acts of wreaking vengeance[50] upon his tormentors. Just as the 21 defendants were indicted at Nuremberg, Nazi perpetrators had a right to defend themselves through pro bono defense counsel in open court and have the case proved against them. For him the trials were also a matter of didactic legality, as Lawrence Douglas names it.[51] He wanted an historical

---

48   *Id.*
49   McDougal, Studies in World Public Order, *supra* note 37, at 157.
50   Like King David in Psalm 142, for instance.
51   Lawrence Douglas, The Memory of Judgment 3 (2001).

tutelage to educate the public, politically and in human values, and to shape collective memory for future law and policy. "To succeed as a didactic spectacle in a democracy, a trial must be justly conducted insofar as one of the principal pedagogic aims of such a proceeding must be to make visible and public the sober authority of the rule of law."[52]

But Wiesenthal actually is deeply compassionate, instanced by his considered treatment of Karl and the compassionate visit to his mother and keeping the truth of her son's Nazi conduct from her, and, when he comes to the heavenly court, he wants to be accounted for what he did for the six million. This is encapsulated in the story of his Sabbath evening dinner in the Manhattan home of a Mauthausen co-prisoner when his host, who became a prosperous jewelry manufacturer, asked him this question:

"Simon, if you had gone back to building houses, you'd be a millionaire. Why didn't you?" "You're a religious man," replied Wiesenthal. "You believe in G-d and life after death. I also believe. When we come to the other world and meet the millions of Jews who died in the camps and they ask us, 'What have you done?', there will be many answers. You will say, 'I became a jeweler.' Another will say, 'I have smuggled coffee and American cigarettes.' Another will say, 'I built houses.' But I will say, 'I did not forget you.'"[53]

Wiesenthal and the black South African woman at the Truth and Reconciliation Commission share something positive. They have in common a sense of ingrained justice. Justice ingrained into the spirit and conscience. They do something which many did not do in the Holocaust; they use it. "There is room for forgiveness. But it is achieved only after justice has been done."[54] Both of them spoke, not blinded by malice toward their perpetrators, for public justice. Proceeding with wisdom premised on policy and law not passion. They want what is right and just in the sense Myres McDougal sees law as existentially grounded authoritative decisions determinative of effective human behavior.[55] Simon Wiesenthal and the woman before the South African Truth

---

52   *Id.*

53   Clyde A Farnsworth, *A Sleuth with 6 Million Clients*, N. Y. Times Magazine, February 2, 1964, *cited by* Mary Cate Kelleher, *The Life of Simon Wiesenthal as Told by the New York Times*, https://digitalcommons. salve.edu/pell_theses/6/; and Biography, Museum of Tolerance, https://www.museumoftolerance.com/about-us/about-simon-wiesenthal / biography.html.

54   Tzvi Hersh Weinreb, *supra* note 45, at 402.

55   *See supra* note 37.

and Reconciliation Commission demand what Jonathan Sacks calls "[j]ustice, the application of law."[56]

2   Post Script

My visit with Simon Wiesenthal also broached his motivation for not taking a position against Kurt Waldheim and for becoming a Nazi hunter.

Waldheim in the 1986 Austrian presidential election had autobiographically dissembled about his service in Greece and Yugoslavia as an intelligence officer in the Wehrmacht of Nazi Germany during World War II. Claims were made that he had engaged in war crimes. Wiesenthal insisted that he would take a stand against Waldheim on unequivocal evidence that he had actually engaged in war crimes. Where was evidence that there was blood on his hands? Criticized for his stand, perhaps costing him a share in the Nobel Peace Prize,[57] Wiesenthal was vindicated by the highly regarded, domestically and internationally, Social Democrat president of Austria Federal President Heinz Fischer, whose wife is Jewish, who, at Waldheim's funeral, said he was "a great Austrian" and that he had been wrongfully accused of committing war crimes. Heinz Fischer praised Waldheim for his unstinting efforts to solve international crises and contributions to world peace.

As a Nazi hunter, Simon Wiesenthal contributed to the intelligence on the whereabouts of Adolf Eichmann in Argentina in 1953, where he was abducted in 1960 and tried in Jerusalem.[58] He had an intelligence network running through the Survivors of the Holocaust around the globe. His motivation for his work as Nazi hunter was this: "Justice, justice you shall pursue" as the Torah insists.[59] The repetition of justice emphasizes the importance of action being addressed to both the goal and the process of achieving it. It was not just his leitmotiv, but his seriously committed goal, singleness of purpose. There is just as assuredly another dimension to Simon Wiesenthal. In *The Sunflower*, Simon and Arthur are skeptical of Josek's deep faith. He, for instance, asks Josek: why if we are all created equally in G-d's image, some are victims and some are murderers?

---

56   Jonathan Sacks, The Authorized Daily Prayer Book of the United Hebrew Congregations of the Commonwealth 148 (4th ed. 2007); The Koren Siddur, *supra* note 2, at 186.

57   Encyclopedia Britannica, https://www.britannica.com/biography/Simon-Wiesenthal#ref1117425.

58   *See* Keith D. Nunes, *Justice for the Holocaust—Eichmann's Jerusalem Trial*, 28 Cal. Int'l L.J. 29 (2020).

59   "Justice, justice you shall pursue, that you may thrive and occupy the land that Adonai your G-d is giving you." Deuteronomy16:20.

He is concerned about how relative religion is so that each religion leads to different views on guilt and repentance with no universal moral and ethical guide. He thought the law of death "logical, certain, and irrefutable" and the universal law for the basis of judgment, i.e. authoritative decision. Something he experienced existentially in the camps. "Why," Simon Wiesenthal asked, "is there no general law of guilt and expiation? Has every religion its own ethics, its own answers?"[60]

Acknowledgments

My high regard for Siegfried's human values (respect, enlightenment, well-being, rectitude, wealth, power, skills, affection) and activities since we were students at the Hague Academy of International Law and our subsequent meetings at the Universities of Tübingen and Yale obliges this essay in his honor. I would like to thank Bruce Afran for his edits, former Chief Rabbi of Austria Arie Folger and David Newton of Princeton for their thoughtful comments, and Rabbi Dov Elkins of Jerusalem and Andrew Newton of London for their gracious readings.

---

60   Sunflower, *supra* note 5, at 67.

CHAPTER 18

The Sermon on the Mount: Going the Extra Mile and Flourishing

*Gordon T. Butler**

Behold, the days come, saith the Lord God,
that I will send a famine in the land,
not a famine of bread, nor a thirst for water,
but of hearing the words of the Lord.

AMOS 8:11

∴

1 Introduction

It is an honor to contribute to the Festschrift for Professor Siegfried Wiessner, a colleague and friend for over thirty years. Professor Wiessner was the Associate Dean at the Law School during the Academic Year 1990–1991. In the spring of 1991, I was invited to St. Thomas for an interview and was given an employment offer. Being an efficient Associate Dean always seeking to fill teaching needs, Professor Wiessner asked if I was willing to teach Wills & Trusts, and I agreed. Four professors were hired that year. The early years of the Law School were years of considerable strife and uncertainty with regard to the tenure process. Of the four professors hired during Professor Wiessner's year as Associate Dean, I was the only one tenured. At the time I was hired, I knew very little about academic life, having practiced law for nearly twenty years. That I succeeded

---

* Professor of Law, St. Thomas University College of Law, Miami, FL. B.E.E. Georgia Institute of Technology; J.D. University of Texas School of Law; LL.M. (Taxation) New York University School of Law; M.B.A. University of Dayton. Professor Butler has taught Human Rights and Religion in the Intercultural Human Rights Program since the program's inception.

in being tenured was in many ways the result of Professor Wiessner's guidance and support during the tenure-track process.[1]

Professor Wiessner is well known for his support of the scholarship of young professors, and I was no exception. He reviewed and made valuable suggestions to my first law and religion article. In fact, he proposed the title, *Cometh the Revolution: The Case for Overruling McCollum v. Board of Education.*[2] On later articles on tax and on religion, he was tireless in his support and guidance. When he inaugurated the Intercultural Human Rights Program, Professor Wiessner extended me the opportunity to co-teach the course on Human Rights and Religion with a Priest, a Rabbi, and an Imam. This opportunity proved to be a rich experience, and I now teach the entire course. Over the years, Professor Wiessner and I discussed religion, and he invariably would refer to the Sermon on the Mount. The discussion would always end up in a debate over Jesus' reference to the Old Testament command "an eye for an eye and a tooth for a tooth"[3] and its continuing application in today's world. Earlier this year, Professor Wiessner and I were in a Bible study that decided to study the Sermon on the Mount.[4] I led the study and was surprised at how little I had known about this wonderful sermon. I learned a great deal and I trust Professor Wiessner did as well. His probing questions spurred much discussion from the members of the study.

Professor Wiessner's observations suggested to me that this Festschrift would provide an opportunity to explore Jesus' teaching on the Old Testament command of "an eye for an eye and a tooth for a tooth" which was being distorted by the religious leaders of that time (*i.e.,* the "scribes and Pharisees").[5] Jesus' discussion of "an eye for an eye" is in the context of six examples demonstrating the proper understanding of the Old Testament law.[6] The fifth

---

1 Many others on the faculty both current and past also owe a debt of gratitude to Professor Wiessner for his support during the tenure process.

2 Gordon T. Butler, *Cometh the Revolution: The Case for Overruling McCollum v. Board of Education,* 99 Dick. L. Rev. 843 (1995).

3 *Matthew* 5:38. References to the Bible are to the King James Version throughout this article.

4 The Sermon on the Mount is found in the Bible in the Book of Matthew chapters 5, 6, and 7.

5 *See Matthew* 5, 6, & 7. Rabbi Alexandra Wright, *The Sermon on the Mount: a Jewish View,* 70 The Blackfriars, April 1989 at 182, 183 (stating that "Modern Judaism-orthodox and liberal-is rooted in the Pharisaic tradition" and that it was formed around the synagogue as a place of worship that existed before the destruction of the Temple in 70 A.D.). "... only Judaism of the Pharisees survived antiquity. .... Hence, all the vicissitudes that have marked Jewish-Christian relations are rooted in antagonism which had its beginnings in the hostility marring the relationship between Jesus and the Pharisees." *Id.* at 184, citing Ellis Rivkin, A Hidden Revolution: The Pharisee's Search for the Kingdom Within 72 (1978).

6 *Matthew* 5.

example is "an eye for an eye" and the sixth example is the command to "love your neighbor."[7] These two examples have been seen as a comparison between the harsh rules of the Old Testament versus the soft, tender, loving message of the New Testament. This dichotomy has led some to view the God of the Old Testament as a totally different God than the God of the New Testament.[8] It is my hope that this paper will demonstrate that the same God is at work, following the same rules in both testaments. Indeed, the two examples stand independently and are both fully applicable today when rightly understood. This article will deal with the fifth example. To do so, the Sermon on the Mount must be seen in its overall context. Near the end of the Sermon Jesus advises his disciples to enter into the narrow gate that leads to life. This author believes that once you go through the gate the Sermon shows you the path upon which you will travel, and on that path you will find life in a way that is truly human flourishing.

2   Background for the Sermon on the Mount

The sermon begins with Jesus going onto a mountain.[9] When He was set, His disciples came to Him and He began to teach them by setting forth the qualities that must be present in those who would enter the kingdom of heaven.[10] By the time He finished the sermon, multitudes had gathered and were astonished at his teaching because he was teaching as one having authority and not as the scribes taught.[11] In fact, much of the sermon undermines the teaching of the scribes as being distorted and superficial.[12]

To understand the Sermon on the Mount, it is necessary to put the sermon in perspective. In an insightful article our colleague, Dean John Makdisi, identified two pillars necessary for such an understanding: the need to be poor in spirit and the need of the Holy Spirit.[13] First, the sermon begins with and is built on the Beatitudes (Latin for "Blessings") in which Jesus identifies specific

---

7   *Matthew* 5:38–48.
8   Jonathan T. Pennington, The Sermon on the Mount and Human Flourishing: A Theological Commentary 195 (2017).
9   *Matthew* 5:1.
10   *Matthew* 5:1–11.
11   *Matthew* 7:28–29.
12   *See Matthew* 5, 6, & 7.
13   John Makdisi, *A Christian Response to Laws that Require Immoral Acts, in* 19 Nova et Vetera 1147–79 (English Edition 2021).

characteristics that will be true of His followers.[14] Each Beatitude carries a specific promise appropriate to the characteristic. All Christians to a greater or lesser degree show the presence and growth of all of these characteristics in their lives.[15] The Beatitudes are found in The Gospel of St. Matthew 5:3–12:

> Blessed are the poor in spirit: for theirs is the kingdom of heaven.
> Blessed are they that mourn: for they shall be comforted.
> Blessed are the meek: for they shall inherit the earth.
> Blessed are they which do hunger and thirst after righteousness: for they shall be filled.
> Blessed are the merciful: for they shall obtain mercy.
> Blessed are the pure in heart: for they shall see God.
> Blessed are the peacemakers: for they shall be called the children of God.
> Blessed are they which are persecuted for righteousness' sake: for theirs is the kingdom of heaven.
> Blessed are ye, when men shall revile you, and persecute you, and shall say all manner of evil against you falsely, for my sake.
> Rejoice, and be exceeding glad: for great is your reward in heaven: for so persecuted they the prophets which were before you.

Dean Makdisi identifies "poor in spirit" as the foundation stone of the sermon.[16] To define "poor in spirit," we first recognize that it does not mean being poor in a material sense. The sermon in Luke's Gospel (sometimes referred to as the Sermon on the Plain because of Luke's description) states, "Blessed are ye poor: for yours is the kingdom of God."[17] Some have argued that Luke is correct and that Matthew spiritualized the sermon. As a result, they see Jesus making a social or sociological judgment regarding the poor and hungry and promising food and riches in the kingdom of God.[18] This interpretation is not likely since Jesus resisted the temptation to turn stones into bread during his temptation

---

14   *Matthew* 5:1–11. Lloyd-Jones identifies lessons to be learned from the Beatitudes: "*all Christians are to be like this*"; Lloyd-Jones *infra* note 85 at 33; "*all Christians are meant to manifest all of these characteristics,*" *id.* at 34; "*none of these descriptions refers to what we may call a natural tendency,*" *id.* at 35; "These descriptions … indicate clearly … *the essential, utter difference between the Christian and the non-Christian,*" *id.* at 36; and "*The truth is that the Christian and the non-Christian belong to two entirely different realms,*" *id.* at 39.

15   *Matthew* 5:3–12. *See* John Stott, The Message of the Sermon on the Mount 31 (1978) [hereinafter, "Stott, The Sermon on the Mount"].

16   Makdisi, *supra* note 13, at 1150.

17   *Luke* 6:17, 20.

18   Stott, The Sermon on the Mount, *supra* note 15, at 31.

and refused the people's request when they wanted to make him king following the feeding of the 5,000 in the wilderness.[19] Most importantly and unambiguously, Jesus later stated to the Roman governor, Pontius Pilate, that "My kingdom is not of this world."[20]

The concept of "blessing" is often misunderstood as simply being "happy." Happiness is a subjective condition whereas Jesus is making an objective judgment about the state of these people. Essentially, "He is declaring not what they may feel like ('happy'), but what God thinks of them and what on that account they are: they are blessed."[21] The characteristics in the Beatitudes are the responsibilities of the citizens of the kingdom of heaven and the corresponding blessings are the privileges of citizens of the kingdom.[22] George Eldon Ladd has summarized the kingdom of God nicely:

> The Kingdom of God is basically the rule of God. It is God's reign, the divine sovereignty in action. God's reign, however, is manifested in several realms, and the Gospels speak of entering the Kingdom of God both today and tomorrow. God's reign manifests itself both in the future and in the present and thereby creates both a future realm and a present realm in which men may experience the blessings of His reign.[23]

The blessings have a present and future enjoyment, notwithstanding only the first and eighth Beatitudes state the blessing in terms of present enjoyment ("for theirs *is* the kingdom of heaven") while the other six are stated in future terms (*e.g.*, "for they *shall be* comforted").[24]

---

19   *Matthew* 14:13–21; *Mark* 6:32–44; *Luke* 9:10b-17; *John* 6:1–15. The feeding of the 5,000 is the only miracle that appears in all four gospels. This is because it shows Jesus as God who was able to feed them in the wilderness. Following the feeding in John, the gospel goes into Jesus' discourse on the bread of life that came down from the Father, concluding: "it is the spirit that quickeneth; the flesh profiteth nothing: the words that I speak are spirit, and they are life." *John* 6:26–59 & 6:63.

20   *John* 6:15 & 18:36.

21   Stott, The Sermon on the Mount, *supra* note 15, at 33.

22   *Id.*

23   George Eldon Ladd, The Gospel of the Kingdom. Scriptural Studies in the Kingdom of God 24 (1959).

24   *Matthew* 5:3–12 (emphasis added in quotations). Another view is that the Sermon is Jesus' attempt to bring in the kingdom of God but, when the people rejected his teachings, he decided to go to the cross as an alternative leaving the promises of the Sermon to be fulfilled in a future "kingdom age." This view is known as the dispensational view and was popularized by J. N. Darby in his 1909 Scofield Reference Bible. Stott, The Sermon on the Mount, *supra* note 15, at 35–36.

3   The First Pillar: Blessed are the Poor in Spirit

Looking now at the first Beatitude blessing the "poor in spirit."[25] We often look at someone as being poor in spirit who, because of life's situations, is downcast and has reached a condition of hopelessness. This might lead someone to recognize that he is powerless to change his condition and reach out to God for help. Just as likely, however, he might turn away from God and curse God as Job's wife suggested.[26] Being "humble" is another way of looking at being poor in spirit. Certainly, if we compare ourselves to others we might think of ourselves as being "better than others" but it is just as likely we would conclude that others are superior to ourselves in talent, good looks, personality, popularity, material wealth, intelligence and a myriad of other qualities. This may lower our view of ourselves and others may call us humble. Looking at a dictionary definition, we see humble defined as "having a low opinion of oneself and one's abilities" or "lowly, modest, unpretentious."[27] But this is not being poor in spirit. In fact, the scripture tells us, "For we dare not make ourselves of the number, or compare ourselves with some that commend themselves: but they measuring themselves by themselves, and comparing themselves among themselves, are not wise."[28]

Humility that is of the nature of poor in spirit is that which we find in comparing our righteousness with the righteousness and majesty of God. It is in this encounter that we see not only our wretchedness but also how deserving we are of eternal punishment. Jonathan Edwards summed it up in his commentary, *Charity and Its Fruits*, as follows:

> Humility may be defined to be a habit of mind and heart corresponding to our comparative unworthiness and vileness before God, or a sense of our own comparative meanness in his sight with the disposition to a behavior answerable thereto. ....[29]

---

25   *Matthew* 5:3.

26   *Job* 2:9. The literal Hebrew would translate as "Bless God and die" but the King James Version reflects the editorial; position that the words were sarcastic and really mean to curse God and die. Job lived c 2000 BC about the time of Abraham. He was a wealthy businessman who God allowed to lose all his property, his children died tragically, and his health failed. It was at this point that his wife said to him, "Doest thou still retain thine integrity? curse God, and die." *Id.* God eventually restored Job's health, family, and wealth. *See* Steven J. Lawson, Holman Old Testament Commentary: *Job* 4, 7–8 (2004).

27   Chambers, 21st Century Dictionary 655 (1996).

28   *2 Corinthians* 10:12.

29   Jonathan Edwards, Charity and its Fruits 130 (photo. reprint 1978) (1852).

Once we understand our meanness before God then we can recognize our meanness before our fellow men. Edwards continues:

> For man is not only a mean creature in comparison with God, but he is very mean compared with multitudes of creatures of a superior rank in the universe; and most men are mean in comparison with many of their fellow-men. And when a sense of this comparative meanness arises from a just sense of our meanness as God sees it, then it is of the nature of true humility. He that has a right sense and estimate of himself in comparison with God, will be likely to have his eyes opened to see himself aright in all respects. Seeing truly how he stands with respect to the first and highest of all beings, will tend greatly to help him to a just apprehension of the place he stands in among creatures. ...[30]

A few scriptural examples of the experience will demonstrate the point. These will be taken from the Old Testament because, rightly understood, the Old and New Testaments should be read as a single document.[31] The first example is Abraham's reaction when he learned that God would refrain from destroying Sodom if He found 50 righteous people in the city.[32] When Abraham realized he was speaking with God and was about to negotiate a lower threshold for saving the city, Abraham cried, "Behold now, I have taken upon me to speak unto the Lord, which am but dust and ashes."[33]

---

30   *Id.* at 130. An interesting note is the anti-levelling element described by Edwards:

> Humility will further tend *to prevent a levelling behavior.* Some persons are always ready to level those above them down to themselves, while they are never willing to level those below them up to their own positions. But he that is under the influence of humility will avoid both these extremes. On the one hand, he will be willing that all should rise just so far and as their diligence and worth of character entitle them to; and on the other hand, he will be willing that his superiors should be known and acknowledged in their place, and have rendered to them all the honours that are their due. He will not desire that all should stand on the same level, for he knows it is best that there should be gradations in society; that some should be above other and should be honoured and submitted to as such.

> *Id.* at 142–143 (citing *Romans* 13:7 and *Titus* 3:1) (emphasis added).

31   Peters, *infra* note 73, sets forth "Proposition 16. This kingdom cannot be properly comprehended without acknowledging an intimate and internal connection existing between the Old and New Testaments."

32   *Genesis* 18:22–26. Abraham lived circa 2166–1991 BC. Bible dates are estimates at best and subject to much controversy. The dates set out in this article are traditional dates taken from Rose Publishing, LLC, *Bible Time Line* (2001).

33   *Genesis* 18:27.

Another example is Isaiah's response to seeing God when he was called to take a message to the people of Israel.[34] Isaiah recounts:

> In the year that king Ŭzzĭăh died I saw also the Lord sitting upon a throne, high and lifted up, and his train filled the temple. Above it stood the seraphims: each one had six wings: with twain he covered his face, and with twain he covered his feet, and with twain he did fly. And one cried unto another, and said, Holy, holy, holy, is the Lord of hosts: the whole earth is full of his glory. And the posts of the door moved at the voice of him that cried, and the house filled with smoke. Then said I, Woe is me: for I am undone; because I am a man of unclean lips, and I dwell in the midst of a people of unclean lips; for mine eyes have seen the King, the Lord of hosts. Then flew one of the seraphims unto me, having a live coal in his hand, which he had taken with the tongs from off the altar: and he laid it upon my mouth: and said, Lo, this hath touched thy lips; and thine iniquity is taken away, and thy sin purged. Also I heard the voice of the Lord, saying, Whom shall I send, and who will go for us? Then said I, Here am I; send me.[35]

Isaiah recognized the true state of his nature when compared to God's, but also the state of those around him and his only response was, "Woe is me."[36] This is the response that renders one poor in spirit. King David experienced God's continuing call to be poor in spirit when Nathan the Prophet confronted him for his adulterous relationship with Bathsheba and the murdering of her husband.[37] David acknowledged his sin to God saying, "For I acknowledge my transgressions: and my sin is ever before me. Against thee, thee only have I sinned, and done this evil in thy sight: that thou mightiest be justified when thou speakest and be clear when thou judgest."[38] David goes on to recognize God's desire:

> For thou desirest not sacrifice: else would I give it: thou delightest not in burnt offering. The sacrifices of God are a broken spirit: a broken and a contrite heart, O God, thou wilt not despise.[39]

---

34   *Isaiah* 6:1–8. Isaiah lived circa 760–673 BC.
35   *Id.*
36   *Isaiah* 6:5.
37   *Psalm* 51. David lived circa 1011–971 BC.
38   *Psalm* 51:3–4.
39   *Psalm* 51:16–17.

Perhaps the most dramatic example of the humbling of an Old Testament prophet in an encounter with God was the encounter of the prophet Elijah.[40] Elijah had just experienced the most spectacular display of God's power on Mount Carmel. There he challenged 450 prophets of Baal to see who could cause fire to come from heaven to burn the altar. After hours of calling on their gods to no avail, the prophets of Baal gave up. Elijah then stepped up and called down fire from heaven and all the people fell down on their faces and shouted, "The Lord He is the God."[41] Elijah then had the 450 prophets of Baal slaughtered. If that were not enough, Elijah then called on the Lord to send rain after three years of draught. The rains came and Elijah raced King Ahab's chariot back to Jĕźreel on foot in the downpour where Queen Jezebel threatened Elijah's life the very next day. Elijah fled to the wilderness dejected even though he had just performed great miracles in the sight of all Israel.

After fleeing into the wilderness for forty days and being fed by angels, Elijah came to a cave where God approached him and asked what Elijah was doing there. Elijah said that he had done these great deeds for the Lord but that he was the only prophet left and they were trying to kill him. The Lord then told Elijah to go stand by the cave and suddenly a mighty windstorm passed by, and then an earth quake, and then a fire. But God was not in the wind, the earthquake, or the fire, and:

> ... after the fire a still small voice. And it was so, when Elijah heard it, that he wrapped his face in his mantle, and went out, and stood in the entering in of the cave. And behold, there came a voice unto him, and said, What doest thou here, Elijah?[42]

Elijah then repeats the same answer he gave when the Lord asked the question the first time, but now the situation was different. Elijah had been humbled and he understood God's majesty and power. And God gave Elijah instructions on things to do and then addressed Elijah's lament that he was the only prophet left in Israel:

---

40   *See 1 Kings* 18–19. Elijah lived circa 870–845 BC. The events of Elijah described in the following paragraphs of this article are found in the Bible in the book of *1 Kings* chapters 18 and 19.

41   *1 Kings* 18:30–39.

42   *1 Kings* 19:12–13.

Yet I have left me seven thousand in Israel all the knees which have not bowed unto Baal, and every mouth which has not kissed him.[43]

An early twentieth century theologian summarized the lessons to be learned from this event in Elijah's life as follows:

We close then with a word of warning and one of encouragement. We must not identify our cause with God's cause; our method with God's methods; or our hopes with God's purposes. The word of encouragement: God's cause is never in danger; and what He has begun in the soul or in the world, He will complete unto the end.[44]

Many Christians rejoiced when the United States Supreme Court overturned its decisions *Roe v. Wade*, 410 U.S. 113 (1973), and *Planned Parenthood of Southeastern Pennsylvania v. Casey*, 505 U.S. 833 (1992), and sent the abortion issue back to the states. This was something that they had been seeking for nearly fifty years. Many had given up hope that, even if inclined to overrule those cases, the justices may not have the courage to do so in the face of public outrage. Then, on June 24, 2022, the seemingly impossible occurred and the cases were overruled.[45]

The poor in spirit know that the will of God will be done in earth as it is in heaven. They pray for it daily.[46]

4   The Second Pillar: The Office and Work of the Holy Spirit

We now come to the second pillar of the Sermon on the Mount, which is the necessity of the active work of the Holy Spirit in carrying out the commands of the Sermon.[47] A superficial reading of the Sermon will convince anyone in their natural state of the impossibility of carrying out the commands.

---

43   *1 Kings* 19-18.

44   Benjamin B. Warfield, Faith & Life 13 (Banner of Truth Trust ed. 1974) (1916).

45   *Dobbs v. Jackson Women's Health Org.*, 142 S.Ct. 2228 (2022). *Dobbs* overturned the 1973 and 1992 decisions proclaiming and upholding the Constitutional right to an abortion.

46   *Matthew* 6:10.

47   Makdisi, *supra* note 13, at 1150, 1151, 1155, 1165, 1166, and 1178. For example, Makdisi, in speaking of the ability to hunger and thirst after righteousness states:
       This yearning is the hunger and thirst for righteousness that makes one blessed. We cannot hope to develop this yearning on our own. It is an act of love moved by the Holy Spirit and penetrating much deeper in our souls than a mere desire to be good. We need to be open and say yes to Christ's call.

For example, humility is not something that man in his natural state is able to attain. In his autobiography, Benjamin Franklin set out to methodically incorporate and practice a set of common virtues into his life.[48] He listed 12 such virtues but added humility as a thirteenth virtue at the suggestion of a colleague.[49] Franklin's list included: temperance, silence, order, resolution, frugality, industry, sincerity, justice, moderation, cleanliness, tranquility, chastity, and humility.[50] Humility proved difficult for Franklin because the more he became humble the more he became proud of that fact.[51] He states:

> In reality, there is, perhaps, no one of our natural passions so hard to subdue as *pride*. Disguise it, struggle with it, beat it down, stifle it, mortify it as much as one pleases, it is still alive, and will every now and then peep out and show itself; you will see it, perhaps, often in this history; for, even if I could conceive that I had completely overcome it, I should probably be proud of my humility.[52]

The blessing promised to the poor in spirit is the kingdom of heaven.[53] In John 3:3, Jesus says to the Pharisee Nicodemus, "verily, verily, I say unto thee, Except a man be born again (or born *from above*), he cannot see the kingdom of God." This makes abundantly clear that the poor in spirit are those that have undergone a great spiritual change before they could even qualify for the blessing of the first Beatitude.[54] Jesus continued stating the reason this great spiritual change was necessary, "That which is born of the flesh is flesh; and that which is born of the Spirit is spirit."[55] Jesus was amazed that Nicodemus, a master of Israel, did not understand these things.[56]

---

48   Benjamin Franklin, Franklin's Autobiography, at Part IX (1916), *available at* https://www .gutenberg.org/ files/20203/20203-h/20203-h.htm.

49   *Id.*

50   *Id.*

51   *Id.*

52   *Id.* (emphasis added).

53   *Matthew* 5:3.

54   James Buchanan, The Office and Work of the Holy Spirit 3–21 (photo. reprint 1966) (1843). Buchanan describes in detail the work of the Holy Spirit in the conversion of the Philippian Goaler, The Dying Malefactor, Paul, The Ethiopian Treasurer, Cornelius, Lydia, Timothy, the Conversions at Pentecost, and in Revivals. *Id.* at 131–236.

55   *John* 3:6.

56   *John* 3:6, 10. W. M. Ramsay describes the impact of the divine on man as follows:
      When the Divine power manifests itself to man, he knows it, and it becomes to him a possession forever, to rule in him or to destroy him: there is no middle way. When it has revealed itself to others, we recognize the truth by its effect on them; but we cannot

Christians are Trinitarians in that they believe that God exists in the form of three equal persons which are designated the Father, the Son, and the Holy Spirit. Augustine so emphasized the unity as to teach the full equality of the "persons":

> And there is so great an equality in that Trinity, that not only the Father is not greater than the Son, as regards divinity, but neither are the Father and the Son together greater than the Holy Spirit; nor is each individual person, whichever it be of the three, less than the Trinity itself.[57]

The office and work of the Holy Spirit is the least taught element in the doctrine of the trinity, yet it is critical to an understanding of what is meant that the Sermon on the Mount is addressed primarily to Christians. I say primarily because the Sermon will show non-Christians their inability to please God (this was also the evangelical purpose of the ten commandments[58]) and send them to Jesus for justification. Understand, the Sermon on the Mount is not the Gospel. Justification is the result of Jesus' death, burial, and resurrection, as payment for the sins of His people and is imputed to them for righteousness. In the same way

---

understand in what way the Divine truth has revealed itself to them nor can they explain the process to us.

W. M. Ramsay, The Education of Christ: Hillside Reveries 17 (photo. reprint 1979) (1902).

In traveling through the Central Anatolian plateau, Ramsay began to sense the impact of geography on his thinking in a way resembling a religious conversion. *See id.* Indeed, he was thinking of how Paul must have reacted to the plateau as he traveled extensively through it on his missionary journeys. In trying to explain the impact, Ramsay found a perfect analogy in the fascinating account in a western novel of the experience of cowboys on the western prairies of America who are profoundly and noticeably changed after spending time on the vast plains. *Id.* at 6–15.

57   *See generally* St. Augustine, *On the Holy Trinity, in* Nicene and Post-Nicene Fathers: First Series, Volume III St. Augustine: On the Holy Trinity, Doctrinal Treatise, Moral Treatises 115 (Philip Schaff ed., photo. reprint 1998) (1887). Recognizing the difficulty of understanding the Trinity Augustine advises that "we must supplicate, with most devout piety, that He will open our understanding" and that his readers to preserve this rule "that what has not yet been made clear to our intellect, be nevertheless not loosened from the firmness of our faith." *Id.*

58   John Stott summarizes the impact of the law on the non-believer as follows:

Not until the law has bruised and smitten us will we admit our need of the gospel to bind up our wounds. Not until the law has arrested and imprisoned us will we pine for Christ to set us free. Not until the law has condemned and killed us will we call upon Christ for justification and life. Not until the law has driven us to despair of ourselves will we ever believe in Jesus. Not until the law has humbled us even to hell will we turn to the gospel to raise us to heaven.

Stott, The Sermon on the Mount, *supra* note 15, at 93.

Abraham was justified by the imputation of righteousness.[59] Once justified, the Sermon becomes a guide showing the Christian how to live and please God and their need daily to rely on the work of the Holy Spirit in their lives.[60]

It is important to understand the nature of man in order to understand the need for the rebirth announced by Jesus to Nicodemus. When God created man, He breathed the breath of life into man's nostrils and he became a living soul.[61] In breathing the breath of life into man, God imparted not only physical life but spiritual life in the form of the Holy Spirit.[62] Later, man disobeyed God's command not to eat of the tree of the knowledge of good and evil and our first parents received the penalty for disobedience, which was that "in the day that thou eatest thereof thou shalt surely die."[63] When God executed the penalty for man's disobedience, man became subject to physical death. He also died spiritually in that the Holy Spirit was removed from man and man became flesh, as we see in Jesus teachings to Nicodemus where he said, "That which is born of flesh is flesh and that which is born of the Spirit is spirit."[64] Jesus here acknowledges what is often called original sin. The Apostle Paul would be very clear in his recognition of man's total inability to apprehend spiritual matters when he said:

---

59 *Genesis* 15:6 (providing, "And he (Abraham) believed in the Lord; and he counted it to him for righteousness."). The study of "salvation" is called soteriology. The Apostle Paul gave a clear statement of the Gospel as: "For I delivered unto you first of all that which I also received, how that Christ died for our sins according to the scriptures; And that he was buried, and that he rose again the third day according to the scriptures; And that he was seen of Cephas, then of the twelve: ..." 1 *Corinthians* 15:3–5.

60 John R. Stott, The Message of Galatians 36 (1968) (originally published under the title Only One Way).

61 *Genesis* 2:7.

62 George Smeaton, The Doctrine of the Holy Spirit 10–17 (photo. reprint 1974) (1889). Smeaton states:

That he not only bore a likeness to God's perfections in his mental, moral, and religious constitution, but that he placed in a peculiarly close relation to all the persons of the Trinity,--nay, in a conscious personal relation to all the divine Persons--is clearly intimated in the words: "Let us make man in our image, after our likeness." [*Genesis* 1²⁶].

Id. at 11. He further concludes: "The arguments against the view that Adam had the Spirit are wholly destitute of Biblical ground, and have no validity or weight." *Id.* at 15.

63 *Genesis* 2:17.

64 *John* 3:6; *see also* Smeaton, *supra* note 62, at 17 (pointing out also that not only was the Spirit lost but man became captive to Satan (Ephesians 2:2) and the image of God was replaced by the corruption of man's nature (John 3:6)).

But the natural man receiveth not the things of the Spirit of God: for they are foolishness unto him: neither can he know them because they are spiritually discerned.[65]

Scriptures make clear that this necessary rebirth is the work of God as we see in Colossians 1:12–14 where Paul states:

Giving thanks unto the Father, which hath made us meet to be partakers of the inheritance of the saints in light: who had delivered us [i.e., "rescued us"] from the power of darkness, and hath translated us into the kingdom of his dear son: in whom we have redemption through his blood, even the forgiveness of sins.[66]

Once translated into the kingdom, the Holy Spirit continues His work by cleansing us and causing us to walk in ways pleasing to God as described in the Sermon on the Mount.[67] This process is called sanctification and will not be completed in this lifetime, although Jesus called on us to be perfect.[68] Paul is particularly graphic in his denunciation of the Galatians in trying to make themselves perfect through human (fleshly) efforts:

O foolish Galatians, who hast bewitched you, that ye should not obey the truth, before whose eyes Jesus Christ hath been evidently set forth,

---

65   *1 Corinthians* 2:14.

66   *See* Stott, The Message of Galatians, *supra* note 60, at 36. Stott translates the word deliver in Galatians 1:4 as "rescue." *Id.* It would seem appropriate to do the same in Colossians 1:13. Nicholas Byfield says the word translated "delivered:" "doth not signify only to let out, or lead out, or buy out; but it noteth forcibly to snatch out. Man is not gotten so easily out of Satan's hands; nor will the world and flesh let him go without force, or without blows." Nicholas Byfield, On Colossians 102 (photo. reprint 2007) (1869); *see also* Ethelbert W. Bullinger, A Critical Lexicon and Concordance to the English and Greek New Testament 214 (photo. reprint 8th ed. 1957) (1877).

67   Jesus' death, burial, and resurrection is the blood sacrifice sealing the new covenant as set forth in well-known passages such as Jeremiah 31:31–34 in which God says, "I will put my law in their inward parts, and write it in their hearts, and will be their God, and they shall be my people," and *Ezekiel* 36:25–29 where God promises that "A new heart also will I give you, and a new spirit will I put within you: and I will take away the stony heart out of your flesh, and I will give you a heart of flesh. And I will put my spirit within you and cause you to walk in my statutes, and ye shall keep my judgments, and do them." For a further explanation of the new covenant, see Paul's discussion in Hebrews chapters 8 through 10. *See generally* Louis F. DeBoer, The Divine Covenants 118–41 (2000). Unfortunately, emphasis on the covenants has waned in the modern church.

68   *Matthew* 5:48.

crucified among you? This only would I learn of you, Received ye the Spirit by the works of the law, or by the hearing of faith? Are ye so foolish? Having begun in the Spirit, are you now made perfect by the flesh?[69]

Having been translated into God's kingdom,[70] the new Christian can now read and understand the Sermon on the Mount. Having been brought to see God as Abraham, David, Elijah, and Isaiah did before him, he can now understand the meaning of the other Beatitudes: to mourn, to be meek, to hunger and thirst after righteousness, to be merciful, to be pure in heart, to be a peacemaker, and to rejoice when being persecuted for righteousness sake. You will

---

69   *Galatians* 3:1.
70   Translation into the kingdom of God is here presented as exclusively God's work because of man's inability to even perceive spiritual matters, let alone make a "decision" for Christ as generally presented in evangelical circles. This doctrine is greatly debated around the question of predestination that is not discussed here. However, advocates asserting the necessity of man's acceptance (i.e., his decision through the exercise of his will) before being born from above need to reconcile man's inability with God's sovereignty. In other words, a spiritually dead person cannot make a decision that requires spiritual perception. The traditional explanation is that God has provided a special grace called "prevenient grace," which is grace preceding the grace of salvation which gives man the ability to make a decision for Christ. The concept is well stated in Chapter V of The Canons and Dogmatic Decrees of the Council of Trent A.D. 1563 as follows:
    The Synod further declares that, in adults, the beginning of the said Justification is to be derived from the prevenient grace of God through Jesus Christ, that is to say, from his vocation, whereby, without any merits existing on their parts, they are called; that so they, who by sins were alienated from God, may be disposed through his quickening and assisting grace, to convert themselves to their own justification, by freely assenting to and co-operating with that said grace: in such sort that, while God touches the heart of man by the illumination of the Holy Ghost, neither is man himself utterly inactive while he receives that inspiration, forasmuch as he is also able to reject it; yet is he not able by his own free will, without the grace of God, to move himself unto justice in his sight. Whence, when it is said in the sacred writings: *Turn ye to me, and I will turn to you* [*Zechariah*. 1:3], we are admonished of our liberty; and when we answer: *Convert us, O Lord, to thee, and we shall be converted* [*Lamentations* 5:21], we confess that we are prevented (anticipated) by the grace of God.
    The Creeds of Christendom: Volume I, The Greek and Latin Creeds 92 (Philip Schaff ed., photo. reprint 1983) (1931). A. W. Tozer states:
    Christian theology teaches the doctrine of prevenient grace, which briefly stated means this, that before a man can seek God, God must first have sought the man. Before a sinful man can think a right thought of God, there must have been a work of enlightenment done within him; imperfect it may be, but a true work nonetheless, and the secret cause of all desiring and seeking and praying which may follow.
    A. W. Tozer, The Pursuit of God 11 (1948), *available at* https://www.gutenberg.org /files/25141/25141-h/25141-h.htm.

have followed Jesus' command to deny yourself and take up your cross and will follow him.[71] The same is stated by Paul: "Therefore if any man be in Christ, he is a new creature: old things have passed away; behold, all things are become new."[72] Life in the kingdom of God[73] is now the central objective of your life.

5   The Core of Jesus' Teaching

We now understand that the Sermon on the Mount is a sermon to the faithful who have been born of the spirit and are seeking God's righteousness. We also understand that the Beatitudes are a summary of character traits in and maturing in the faithful. Jesus now begins detailing the life the faithful should expect. He first refers to their mission as the "salt of the earth" and "light of the world."[74] He then addresses the question as to the continuing importance of the "law and the prophets."[75] This question arises because some might think that there is no longer a need for the Old Testament law and prophets. In fact, some may think the Beatitudes replace the ten commandments. Jesus responds:

> Think not that I am come to destroy the law, or the prophets: I am not come to destroy but to fulfill. For verily I say unto you, Till heaven and earth pass, one jot or one tittle shall in no wise pass from the law, till all be fulfilled. Whosoever therefore shall break one of these least commandments, and shall teach men so, he shall be called least in the kingdom of heaven: but whosoever shall do and teach them, the same shall be called

---

71   *Matthew* 16:24; *Mark* 8:34; *Luke* 9:23.

72   *2 Corinthians* 5:17.

73   The kingdom of God is another neglected area of Christian doctrine. George N. H. Peters, The Theocratic Kingdom of our Lord Jesus, the Christ, (photo. reprint 1988) (1884). In his comprehensive and exhaustively annotated, three-volume treatise on the kingdom of God, Peters states:

The Scriptures cannot be rightly comprehended without a due knowledge of this kingdom. It is a fact, attested to by the multitude of works, and constantly presented in all phases of Biblical literature, that the doctrine respecting the kingdom has materially affected the judgments of men concerning the canonical authority, the credibility, inspiration, and the meaning of the writings contained in the Bible. If in error here, it will inevitably manifest itself, *e.g.*, in exegesis and criticism. ...

Id at 29. Peters supports his thought as to the importance of the Kingdom of God by noting that it is "a subject which embraces a larger proportion of Revelation than all other subjects combined" and "was the leading subject of the preaching of John the Baptist, Christ, the disciples and apostles," among other things. *Id.* at 30.

74   *Matthew* 5:13, 14.

75   *Matthew* 5:17.

great in the kingdom of heaven. For I say unto you, That except your righteousness shall exceed the righteousness of the scribes and Pharisees, ye shall in no case enter into the kingdom of heaven.[76]

Our initial thought is that, if no one has ever been able to keep the law perfectly, how can Christians think they will be able to do so. The simple answer is that, in the new covenant, Jesus' mission inaugurates a new era with an expanded role for the Holy Spirit who writes the law on believers' hearts and causes them to walk in them.[77] The result is that believers will cry out like David, "O how love I thy law! It is my meditation all the day."[78] Or as Paul says, "Abba Father."[79] These are the words of those persons "which are born, not of blood, nor of the will of the flesh, nor of the will of man, but of God."[80]

Jesus has a greater purpose in bringing up the law and telling his followers that their righteousness must exceed that of the scribes and the Pharisees.[81] He will spend the remaining 28 verses of Matthew chapter 5, from verses 21 to 48, to provide six examples of how the scribes and Pharisees have distorted the law. These six examples begin with "Ye have heard it said ..." and address the false teachings on murder, adultery, divorce, oaths, an eye for an eye (taking revenge), and loving your neighbor.[82] Jesus then explains the correct view of each example beginning with the words, "But I say to you ..." and focuses on a correct teaching.[83] Jesus is asserting, on his own authority, that he is not seeking to contradict Moses but correcting the corruption of Moses as instilled in the

---

76   *Matthew* 5:17–20.

77   *Jeremiah* 31:31–34; *Ezekiel* 36:25–29; *see also* DeBoer, *supra* note 67, at 118–41.

78   *Psalm* 119:97.

79   *Romans* 8:15; *Galatians* 4:6.

80   *John* 1:13.

81   Wright *supra* note 5, at 185, citing Rivkin, Hidden Revolution, *supra* note 5, at 87 (asserting that the Pharisee's standard is the standard for Christians because the Pharisees showed undeviating loyalty to every jot and tittle of the law and were the models for the legally normative). Wright does not acknowledge that the standard for the Christian is an inner standard rather than the outward formality of the Pharisees. However, Wright notes that Jews are uneasy with Jesus' sense of personal authority in asserting His positions whereas the Pharisees are always careful to use Biblical authority to support their positions. Wright *supra* note 5, at 188–89. Christians would agree that Jesus speaks on his own authority since he is God incarnate and indeed He and the New Testament writers place Him in the Center of the Gospel. *See* Machen's Notes on Galatians 37–42 (John H. Skilton ed., 1977). Skilton collects articles by J. Gresham Machen appearing in *Christianity Today* from 1931–1933 and adds additional material of Machen's to complete the study of Galatians.

82   *Matthew* 5:27–48.

83   *Id.*

inherited traditions going back centuries. Jesus is replacing these corruptions of the law "with his own accurate and authoritative interpretation of God's law."[84]

6   Ye Have Heard that it Hath been Said, "An Eye for Eye, and Tooth for Tooth ..."

Jesus begins to correct six areas in which the scribes and Pharisees had distorted the law and the prophets. In each example, Jesus focuses on the state of one's heart as opposed to focusing solely on the physical act.[85] It is with the fifth example, "an eye for an eye," and the sixth example, "love your neighbor" that some commentators see the high point of the Sermon on the Mount.[86] People have suggested that an eye for "an eye and a tooth for a tooth" is symbolic of the Old Testament and that "love your neighbor" is of the New Testament approach to private relationships and public actions. Indeed, the first fruit of the Holy Spirit is love.[87] However, it is self-evident that the demand for justice and revenge are powerful human instincts which are as powerful today as they were four thousand years ago. Is Jesus overthrowing the principle of "an eye for and eye" and replacing it with a principle of not resisting evil?

The language of Jesus' fifth example is as follows:

> Ye have heard that it hath been said, An eye for an eye, and a tooth for a tooth: But I say unto you, That ye resist not evil: but whosoever shall smite thee on thy right cheek, turn to him the other also. And if any man will sue thee at the law, and take away thy coat, let him have thy cloak also. And whosoever shall compel thee to go a mile, go with him twain. Give to him that asketh thee, and from him that would borrow of thee turn not thou away.[88]

Jesus begins with the Old Testament phrase: "An eye for an eye, and a tooth for a tooth." He immediately addresses the error of the scribes and Pharisees by pointing to the true response when someone seeks to injure you: "that ye resist not evil." In other words, you are not to take revenge or to retaliate. To

---

84   Stott, The Sermon on the Mount, *supra* note 15, at 215.
85   *See generally* 1 D. Martyn Lloyd-Jones, Studies in the Sermon on the Mount 180–320 (combined volume, 1977).
86   Stott, The Sermon on the Mount, *supra* note 15, at 103.
87   *Galatians* 5:22.
88   *Matthew* 5:38–42.

understand the meaning of his admonition He provides four short illustrations (referred to as "cameos"[89]) on how properly to address the command. Jesus is wanting his followers to approach the command differently than do the scribes and Pharisees, the religious leaders and the role models for keeping the law. Keep in mind that Jesus is not proposing to destroy the law and the prophets but to fulfill it.

The command of "an eye for an eye and a tooth for a tooth," is a direct quote out of the Mosaic Law.[90] From the context, it is a direct instruction to judges[91] known as the *lex talionis*:

> ... the principle of an exact retribution, whose purpose was both to lay the foundation of justice, specifying the punishment which a wrongdoer deserved, and to limit the compensation of his victim to an exact equivalent and no more. It thus had a double effect of defining justice and restraining revenge. It also prohibited the taking of the law into one's own hands by the ghastly vengeance of the family feud.[92]

For example, the punishment for being a false witness was that, after the judges have made "diligent inquisition," to do to the witness what he sought to do against his brother.[93] The punishment would put the evil out of the community:

> And those which remain shall hear, and fear, and shall henceforth commit no more any such evil among you. And thine eye shall not pity; but life shall go for life, and eye for eye, tooth for tooth, hand for hand, foot for foot.[94]

This rule of justice was part of Moses' civil law, which was instituted to govern the people as a Hebrew nation and was distinct from the moral law. It is likely that by the time of Jesus the literal retaliation had been replaced by an award for money damages. Even under Moses' law, if a man caused injury to his servant's eye or tooth, the penalty was to free the servant rather than take the

---

89 Stott, The Sermon on the Mount, *supra* note 15, at 105–06 where he states" The four mini-illustrations which follow all apply the principle of Christian non-retaliation..... They are vivid little cameos drawn from different life-situations."

90 *See Exodus* 21:24; *Leviticus* 24:20; *Deuteronomy* 19:21.

91 *See, e.g., Deuteronomy* 19:16–21.

92 Stott, The Sermon on the Mount, *supra* note 15, at 104.

93 *Deuteronomy* 19:18–19.

94 *Deuteronomy* 19:20–21.

eye or tooth of the man.[95] One commentator pointed out the purpose of the Mosaic legislation as follows:

> The main intent of the Mosaic legislation was to control excesses. In this case in particular, it was to control anger and violence and the desire for revenge.[96] ... The object, therefore, of this Mosaic legislation was to control and reduce this utterly chaotic condition to a certain amount of order. ... God, the Author of salvation, the Author of the way whereby mankind can be delivered from the bondage and the tyranny of sin, has also ordained that there shall be a check upon sin. The God of grace is also the God of law, and this is one of the illustrations of the law.[97]

It is generally agreed among commentators that the Old Testament teaching of "an eye for an eye" was legislation directed toward the judges of Israel and not at individuals as noted by the following commentator:

> But perhaps the most important thing is that this enactment was not given to the individual, but rather to the judges who were responsible for law and order amongst the individuals. The system of judges was set up amongst the children of Israel, and when disputes and matters arose the people had to take them to these responsible authorities for judgment. It was the judges who were to see to it that it was an eye for an eye and a tooth for a tooth and no more... Its main object was to introduce this element of justice and of righteousness into a chaotic condition and to take from man the tendency to take the law into his own hands and to do anything he likes.[98]

The scribes and Pharisees ignored the fact that the teaching was for judges only but they recognized it as an individual right to be insisted upon.[99] They were taking a negative injunction and making it positive and then teaching

---

95   *Exodus* 21:26–27.

96   Lloyd-Jones, *supra* note 85, at 271.

97   *Id.* at 271–72.

98   *Id.* at 272; *see also* James Morrison, A Practical Commentary on the Gospel According to St. Matthew 81 (photo. reprint 1981) (1884).

99   Lloyd-Jones, *supra* note 85, at 273. Martin Luther said,

> As now in previous passages he rebuked and rejected their teaching and false interpretations, he here also takes up the passage, that stands recorded in the law of Moses, for those to whom was committed government authority, and who were to punish with the sword that they should and had to take eye for eye and tooth for tooth; in such a way, that

others to do so. The Pharisees regarded it "as a matter of right and duty to have an 'eye for an eye, and a tooth for a tooth.' To them it was something to be insisted upon rather than something which should be restrained."[100] One commentator explained it thus:

> The error of the rabbinical teachers lay in not explaining to the people that the principle of *eye for eye* was intended, not to encourage and foster a fiery spirit of revenge, but to discourage and repress a fiery spirit of revenge. They did not explain, moreover, that it was a principle which was, as Michaelis remarks (*Mosaisches Recht,* §242), eminently fitted to promote the security of the poor, and to set as a check on the passion of masters and other superiors. Pecuniary punishments as he observes, are not very formidable to men of opulence. "But" adds he, "when the greatest and richest man in the realm knows that if he puts out the eye of the peasant the latter has a right to insist that his eye be put out in return; that a sentence will actually be pronounced if the matter comes before a court; and the said punishment inflicted, without the least respect to his rank, or his noble eye being considered as one whit better than the peasant's, and that he has no possible way of saving it, but by humbling himself before the other, as deeply as may be necessary to work upon his compassion and make him relent, besides paying him as much money as he deems a satisfactory compensation for his loss; everyone will be convinced that the nobleman will bethink himself before he put out any one's eye. The rabbinical teachers, overlooking the benevolent side of the statute, seem to have adduced it for the purpose of inculcating what would amount to a haughtily malevolent spirit.[101]

Jesus was addressing the distortion of the command by the scribes and Pharisees, who taught the principle could be taken from the courts into the personal realm thereby allowing people to take personal revenge. This violated Leviticus 19:18 that provided, "Thou shalt not avenge, nor bear any grudge against the children of thy people, but thou shalt love thy neighbor as thyself: I am the Lord." These religious leaders had found a way to use a

---

they sinned just as heavily if they failed to use the commanded sword and punishment, as did the other who seized the sword and took revenge themselves, without command.

Luther *infra* note 121, at 125.

100   *Id.* at 273.

101   Morrison, *supra* note 98, at 81.

principle of justice as an excuse to do the very thing the principle was designed to prevent.[102]

Thus, Jesus is not seeking to undermine the principle of justice. The Bible speaks of judgment throughout, both in this life and the next. Jesus refers to the final judgment in the Sermon on the Mount in which He will be the judge.[103] What He is doing is rejecting the application of the principle to our personal relations. Jesus recognizes that the principle addressed in "an eye for an eye" is "revenge" and restores a correct understanding by focusing on the individuals' attitude toward his fellow man when he is wronged by his fellow man. Jesus gives us four cameos that demonstrate a loving response to personal insult. To repeat: Jesus said, "But I say unto you, That ye resist not evil:"

1.   But whosoever shall smite thee on the right cheek, turn to him the other also.
2.   And if any man will sue thee at the law, and take away thy coat, let him have thy cloak also, and
3.   Whosoever shall compel thee to go a mile, go with him twain,
4.   Give to him that asketh thee and from him that would borrow of thee turn not thou away.[104]

Before addressing what Jesus means when he says, "resist not evil," and the cameos illustrating that principle, we will look at how they have been used as a rule of social policy. There have been times when "resist not evil" has been taken quite literally and applied it to social affairs. Others have seen in the sermon commands to incorporate it into social teaching. We now briefly address those efforts.

7   The Sermon on the Mount as Public Policy

One person who carried "resist not evil" to an extreme was the nineteenth century novelist, Leo Tolstoy. In his book, *What I Believe*, Tolstoy described how, as he read and re-read the Sermon on the Mount, it came to him suddenly that Jesus' command not to resist evil required a complete prohibition of physical violence.[105] He concluded that if everyone followed this precept that the

---

102   Stott, The Sermon on the Mount, *supra* note 15, at 104–05 (citing John W. Wenham, Christ and the Bible 35 (1972)).
103   *Matthew* 7:1–6, 21–23.
104   *Matthew* 5:39–42.
105   For example, Tolstoy stated: "The first point that struck me, when I understood the commandment, 'Do not resist evil,' in its true meaning, was that human courts were not only contrary to this commandment, but in direct opposition to the whole doctrine of Christ,

kingdom of God would indeed have come.[106] Another individual influenced by the Sermon on the Mount and by Tolstoy's interpretation of it was Gandhi, who sought to implement his non-violence ethic into India.[107] Being inspired by Gandhi, Martin Luther King pursued a non-violent protest for equal rights for minorities in the United States with great success.[108] He faced evil men and persecution but he did not seek revenge and relied on the redemptive power of love.[109]

There have been churches and denominations, often referred to as "peace churches," which would attach Jesus' teaching in the Sermon on the Mount to "the rules for magistrates and police in their public capacity."[110] The author of one of the books cited herein was raised in such a denomination that grew out of the German pietistic tradition of the early eighteenth century.[111]

A recent article argues that differing views of President Donald Trump held by evangelical Christians can be traced back to differing views of the Sermon on the Mount held by advocates of the Social Gospel movement and the Fundamentalist movement of the late nineteenth and early twentieth centuries.[112] Heirs of the Fundamentalist movement, which the author equates with the "religious right," assert that the Sermon on the Mount has application to individual believers and to churches.[113] Heirs of the Social Gospel movement, which the author refers to as Neo-Bryanites, acknowledge the Sermon has application primarily to individuals and churches but assert that it has implications for secular justice.[114]

The Neo-Bryanites are not as strident as their forebears who advocated that Jesus' admonition to love our neighbors as ourselves should serve as the

---

and that therefore He must certainly have forbidden them. Leo Tolstoy, What I Believe, ch. 3 (1886), https://en.wikisource.org/wiki/What_I_Believe_(Tolstoy_,_Popoff)/Chapter_3 (last visited August 16, 2022).

106   Stott, The Sermon on the Mount, *supra* note 16, at 108–09 (providing a fuller description of the efforts of Leo Tolstoy); *see also* Lloyd-Jones, *supra* note 85, at 274–75.

107   *See* Stott, The Sermon on the Mount, *supra* note 15, at 109–10 (providing a fuller description of the efforts of Gandhi).

108   *Id.* at 113–14 (providing a fuller description of the efforts of Martin Luther King).

109   *See id.* Stott acknowledged that King understood Jesus' teaching better than either Tolstoy or Gandhi. *Id.* King was defending the principle of equality before the law and not himself from personal insult. *See id.*

110   Robert D. Culver, Civil Government: A Biblical View, at footnote 207 (2000 First Canadian ed.) (1974).

111   *Id.* (listing a number of scholarly works on the nonresistance movement); *see also, e.g.,* War, Peace, and Non-resistance (Guy F. Herschberger ed.,1959).

112   David Skeet, *Divided by the Sermon on the Mount*, 47 Pepp. L. Rev. 495 (2020).

113   *Id.* at 495.

114   *Id.* at 517.

guiding principle for all of American life, not just as a command for individual Christians,[115] and that the Kingdom of God called for by Jesus in the Sermon on the Mount could be achieved in American society.[116] What seems clear to the author is that both groups acknowledge the Bible teaches action against poverty and injustice but the two sides have different views about how best to achieve those actions: i.e., through governmental or private initiatives.[117]

Earlier in the Sermon on the Mount Jesus commanded His followers to be the salt of the earth and the light of the world and would later advise them not to worry about food, drink, or clothing but to seek first His kingdom and His righteousness.[118] Following these commands will always impact the society around them. Indeed, the blessing of the Beatitude to rejoice when you are persecuted for righteousness sake for yours is the kingdom of heaven.[119] Dean Makdisi's article on the Sermon on the Mount addresses how people living out the Beatitudes might react when they encounter problems that were the subject of recent litigation.[120]

Martin Luther witnessed confusion in the Sermon on the Mount in his day where some would undermine Jesus' teaching as too impractical and others would push it to the point of saying you should have nothing of your own or should not act as a judge or ruler.[121] Luther saw the Sermon as applying to Christians alone in contrast to the carnal notions of Christ's disciples, who still clung to the idea that Jesus had come to establish an earthly kingdom in which they would rule as lords.[122] Luther also recognized that the focus was on the heart and that, if you were called upon to protect yourself or your family or to

---

115   *Id.* at 502.
116   *Id.* at 501. In footnote 136, Skeet refers to the late nineteenth century optimism that the world was getting better. This he attributes to the postmillennial eschatology holding that the world would be perfected prior to Jesus' return for the 1,000 year reign. The goals of the Neo-Bryanites and other modern groups asserting the application of the Sermon on the Mount to social issues as less ambitious than their predecessors. *Id.* This may be accounted for by two world wars in the twentieth century that blunted enthusiasm for the view that the world was being perfected.
117   *Id.* at 500. Perhaps those advocating governmental solutions should ponder Jesus' refusal to be made king by the people after they experienced the feeding of the 5,000. *John* 6:15.
118   *Matthew* 5:13–16 and *Matthew* 6:31–34, respectively.
119   *Matthew* 5:10.
120   *See* Makdisi, *supra* note 13; Skeet, *supra* note 112 (illustrating Christians as salt and light); *see also* Steven D. Smith, *One Step Enough*, 47 Pepp. L. Rev. 549 (2020) (describing ways in which Christians address difficult choices in the academy).
121   Martin Luther, Commentary on the Sermon on the Mount vii–ix (photo. reprint 2017) (1892).
122   *Id.* at 126.

administer justice as a civil servant, you do so without any hatred or spirit of vengeance in your heart.[123]

Again, the Sermon on the Mount is addressed to believers who have been born from above. As one commentator put it:

> For the world, and for a nation, and for non-Christians the law still applies, and it is the law which says 'an eye for an eye, and a tooth for a tooth.' These people are still under that justice which restrains and holds man back, preserving law and order and controlling excesses. In other words, that is why a Christian must believe in law and order, and why he must never be negligent of his duties as a citizen of a State. He knows that 'the powers that be are ordained of God,' that lawlessness must be controlled, and vice and crime kept within bounds—'an eye for an eye, and a tooth for a tooth,' justice and equity. In other words the New Testament teaches that, until a man comes under grace, he must be kept under the law. It is at this point that all this modern muddle and confusion has entered in. People who are not Christian talk vaguely about Christ's teaching concerning life, and interpret it as meaning that you must not punish a child when it does wrong, that there must be no law and order, and that we must first love everybody and make them nice. And now we are seeing the results! But this is heresy. It is 'an eye for an eye, and a tooth for a tooth' until the spirit of Christ enters into us. Then, something higher is expected of us, but not until then. The law exposes evil and keeps it within bounds and it is God Himself who ordained this, and all 'the powers that be' that are to enforce it.
>
> This is our first principle. This has nothing to do with nations or so-called Christian pacifism, Christian socialism and things like that. They cannot be based on this teaching; indeed they are a denial of it. That was the whole tragedy of Tolstoy, and alas, poor man, he himself became a tragedy at the end when he faced the utter uselessness of it all. That was quite inevitable from the beginning as he would have seen had he truly understood the teaching.[124]

---

123   *Id.* at 130.
124   Lloyd-Jones, *supra* note 85, at 276–77.

8   A Note on the Christian View of Government

Efforts to incorporate the command not to resist evil as an element of civil government leads to results undermining the entire purpose of government. As repeatedly asserted herein, the Sermon on the Mount is given to individuals, and not to all individuals, but solely to Christians.[125] It is impossible for anyone else to conform to the standards and, indeed, it appears as foolishness to them. The New Testament does however address civil government, so it is helpful to consider a few passages.

In the book of Genesis, God organized life around three divinely ordained institutions that continue to this day.[126] The first was the *Family*. It was established in Genesis 2, prior to the fall of man into sin, and is in a covenant between man and woman in which they are to be fruitful and multiply. The second is *Civil Government*. It is established in Genesis 9 by means of the covenant with Noah. Civil government was established to restrain the evil tendencies of man to injure other men. Thus, man is given the power of the sword to enforce its laws. The third is the *Church*. It is established in Genesis chapters 15 and 17 in the covenant with Abraham and has authority to receive and teach God's word, administer the sacraments, and enforce discipline.[127] A thriving and growing society requires all three institutions to be strong and independent. Such a society would possess an "ordered liberty."[128] In fact, religion and law must interact for either to perform its duties appropriately.[129] However, here we will discuss only civil government.

---

125   Culver, *supra* note 110, at 205 (emphasizing the point: "The law in question was given for guidance to civil judges in execution of public law, not to individuals for adjustments of private grievances.").

126   Paul Woolley, Family, State, and Church: God's Institutions (1965).

127   Wayne Grudem, Systematic Theology: An Introduction to Biblical Doctrine 864–67 (1994). Grudem identifies Lutheran and Reformation definitions that both include the concepts of correct preaching of the Word of God and the correct administration of the sacraments as the elements of the true church. *Id.* The administration of the sacraments would involve an element of church discipline although Grudem does not address discipline.

128   The concept of "ordered liberty" is used in the recent case, *Dobbs v. Jackson Women's Health Organization*, 597 U.S. ____ (2022), to define the standard for guaranteeing rights that are not mentioned in the United States Constitution. The standard is that such rights must be "deeply rooted in the Nation's history and tradition" and "implicit in the concept of ordered liberty." *Id.* slip op. at 12.

129   Harold Berman, The Interaction of Law and Religion 11 (1974) (stating, "Despite the tensions between them, one cannot flourish without the other. Law without (what I call) religion degenerates into a mechanical legalism. Religion without (what I call) law loses its social effectiveness."). Berman identifies four characteristics common to religion and law:

Government always has a religious foundation because it must always operate with some authority.[130] The Bible's approach to government is no exception. Following the creation and fall of man into sin, the population of the world grew. Unfortunately, man in his fallen state was unable to follow a righteous life. When God viewed his fallen state, He "saw that the wickedness of man was great in the earth and that every imagination of the thoughts of his heart was only evil continually."[131] God determined to destroy the world by a flood, but Noah found grace in the eyes of the Lord and God directed Noah to build an ark, which would save Noah, his wife, children and their spouses, and pairs of animals. After the flood waters subsided, God declared that he would not again destroy the world by water. At that point, God established the Noahic Covenant authorizing the use of the sword by man against his brother stating:

> And surely your blood of your lives will I require; at the hand of every beast will I require it, and at the hand of man; at the hand of every man's brother will I require the life of man. Whoso sheddeth man's blood, by man shall his blood be shed: for in the image of God made he man.[132]

Luther is credited with tying this text to the establishment of coercive human government. Luther states:

> Here, however, God shares his power with man and grants him power over life and death among men, provided that the person is guilty of shedding blood ... him God makes liable not only to his own judgment but also to the human sword.[133]

The principle ways in which law channels and communicates transrational values are fourfold: first, through *ritual*, that is, ceremonial procedures which symbolize the objectivity of law; second, through *tradition*, that is, language and practices handed down from the past which symbolize the ongoingness of law; third, through *authority*, that is, the reliance upon written or spoken sources of law which are considered to be decisive in themselves and which symbolize the binding power of law; and fourth, through *universality*, that is, the claim to embody universally valid concepts or insights which symbolize the law's connection with an all – embracing truth. These four elements ... are present in all legal systems, just as they are present in all religions.

Id. at 31. "Religion to be true must be constantly growing. It cannot become stagnant without falsifying itself. The nation which does not increase in its power Divine purpose, and fails to produce a succession of listeners to and interpreters of the Divine voice, has become dead to the Divine message." Ramsay, *supra* note 56, at 27.

130 Culver, *supra* note 110, at 52.

131 *Genesis* 6:5.

132 *Genesis* 9:5–6.

133 Culver, *supra* note 110, at 72–73 (citing Luther's Works, at II. vi-xiv (Jaroslav Pelikan & Daniel E. Poellat eds., 1960)).

Luther continues:

> Therefore we must take careful note of this passage, in which God estab-
> lished government to render judgment not only about matters involving
> life but also matters less important than life. Thus a government should
> punish the disobedience of children, theft, adultery and perjury ... This
> text is outstanding ... for here God establishes government and gives it
> the sword to hold wantonness in check, lest violence and other sins pro-
> ceed without limit.[134]

The state is created "both to punish the wrongdoer (i.e. to 'resist one who is
evil' to the point of making him bear the penalty of his evil) and to reward
those who do good."[135]

Jesus' teaching on civil government comes from the well-known story of the
payment of the poll tax.[136] The Pharisees were attempting to entangle Jesus in
a conflict between the civil authorities and His God. Jesus responded, "Render
therefore unto Caesar the things which are Caesar's; and unto God the things
that are God's."[137]

> Tell us therefore, What thinkest thou? Is it lawful to give tribute unto
> Caesar, or not? But Jesus perceived their wickedness, and said, Why tempt
> ye me, ye hypocrites? Shew me the tribute money. And they brought unto
> him a penny. And he saith unto them, Whose is this image and super-
> scription? They say unto him, Caesar's. Then saith he unto them, Render
> therefore unto Caesar the things which are Caesar's; and unto God the
> things that are God's.[138]

Jesus recognizes clearly the dual loyalty between what is owed God and what
is our duty as citizens. Luther developed his two kingdom teaching from this
story.[139] He distinguished between what we do in the secular world and what

---

134   *Id.*
135   Stott, The Sermon on the Mount, *supra* note 15, at 110–11 (citing *Romans* 13:1–10).
136   *Matthew* 22:17–21.
137   *Matthew* 22:21. Jesus' answer has been described as "One of the wisest, deepest, and yet
      simplest maxims ever uttered in human language. It gleams in its own light. With what
      instant effect must it have shown in upon the minds of His questioners, dispelling into
      nonentity the little cloud of fog which they had joined hand in hand to distil over the trap
      which they had laid. Morrison *supra* note 98, at 411.
138   *Matthew* 22:17–21.
139   Stott, The Sermon on the Mount, *supra* note 15, at 112.

we do in the heavenly world.[140] In the secular world, we have the office of magistrate or judge and we resist evil, but in the spiritual kingdom we do not resist evil. We return evil with good.[141] A Christian lives simultaneously in two kingdoms: the kingdom of God and the kingdom of the earth. How the two kingdom theory has developed historically, its impact in society, and the controversy surrounding Luther's treatment of the subject are beyond the scope of this article but various sources are available.[142] Nevertheless, even though we are living in the Kingdom of God now, we still live in this natural world and have duties and responsibilities here. As stated by J. Gresham Machen,

> The Christian does indeed live still in this world. It is a travesty on this Pauline doctrine when it is held to mean that when he escapes, inwardly, from the present evil world by the redeeming work of Christ the Christian can calmly leave the world to its fate. On the contrary, Christian men, even after they have been redeemed, are left in this world, and in this world they have an important duty to perform.[143]

Alfred Endersheim's evaluation of Jesus' words here is well done:

> Christ's kingdom is not of this world; a true Theocracy is not inconsistent with submission to the secular power in things that are really its own; politics and religion neither include, nor yet exclude, each other; they are, side by side, in different domains. The State is Divinely sanctioned, and religion is Divinely sanctioned—and both are equally the ordinance of God. On this principle did Apostolic authority regulate the relations between Church and State, even when the latter was heathen the question about the limits of either province has been hotly discussed by sectarians on either side, who have claimed the saying of Christ in support of one or the opposite extreme which they advocated. And yet, to the simple searcher after duty, it seems not so difficult to see the distinction, if

---

140   *Id.*

141   Stott, The Sermon on the Mount, *supra* note 15, at 112–13; *see also* Luther, *supra* note 121, at 124–34.

142   *See* John Witte, Jr., The Blessings of Liberty: Human Rights and Religious Freedom in the Western Legal Tradition 81–89 (2022); Jürgen Moltmann, On Human Dignity: Political Theology and Ethics 61–77 (1984).

143   Machen's Notes, *supra* note 81, at 32.

only we succeed in purging ourselves of logical refinements and strained inferences.[144]

A further quote recognizing the limitations on the civil magistrate and the broad authority of God is the following:

> Thus Jesus' whole position toward the State is clearly circumscribed, precisely in the duality it entails throughout. On the one hand, the State is nothing final. On the other hand, it has the right to demand what is necessary to its existence—but no more. Every totalitarian claim of the state is thereby disallowed. And the double imperative logically follows: on the one hand, do not let the Zealots draw you into a purely political martial action against the existence of the Roman State; on the other, do not give the Sate what belongs to God! In the background we hear the challenge; if ever the state demands what belongs to God, if ever it hinders you in the proclamation of the kingdom of God, then resist it. The whole leitmotiv [i.e., a recurrent theme] of the complex New Testament attitude toward the State is formulated by Jesus here in this saying.[145]

The government officials are ministers of God granted the power of the sword to restrain evil and reward good.[146] As Paul explains in Romans 13:4:

> For he is the minister of God for good. But if thou do that which is evil, be afraid for he beareth not the sword in vain: for he is the minister of God, a revenger to execute wrath upon him that doeth evil.

Romans 13 is not a formula supporting tyrants. Under appropriate circumstances, tyrants can be resisted. Indeed, Christians may have a duty to resist tyranny.[147] Paul goes on to make clear that the proper sphere of government

---

144   Alfred Edersheim, The Life and Times of Jesus the Messiah 2:386 (1907) (cited and quoted in Culver, *supra* note 110, at 203).

145   Oscar Cullmann, The State in the New Testament 33 (1956) (cited and quoted in Culver, *supra* note 111, at 204, and citing *Matthew* 22:21 and *Mark* 12:13).

146   *Romans* 13:1–10.

147   Stephanus Junius Brutus, Vindiciae, Contra Tyrannos xxvi, 45 (George Garnet ed., 1994) (1579). The book addresses four questions regarding the power of the people and the princes. Question number 2 was "Whether it be lawful to resist a prince who is breaking the law of God and devastating God's church: by whom, how, and to what extent." *Id.* at 35. When the prince ruins religion, he ought to be resisted. Magistrates have control over the prince. Private men ought to offer a passive resistance until magistrates call them to

is limited to the areas covered by the second table of the ten-commandments: the commandments against murder, adultery, stealing, lying, and coveting. In that the family is a God-ordained institution, the authority of the government is limited to violations in the family of the other commandments the government is charged with enforcing. Commandments of the first table, having no other God, not making images, not taking the Lord's name in vain, and remembering the Sabbath day, are not included in Paul's list of those commandments subject to government enforcement.

In the Massachusetts Bay Colony, Roger Williams asserted numerous claims against the legitimacy of acts and the constitution of the colonial government. An early claim of Williams was that "civil magistrates had no authority to punish Sabbath-breakers, 'as it was a breach of the first table.'"[148] As one author recounts:

> The Cambridge Platform, adopted by the leaders of Massachusetts churches in 1648 as a statement of belief, declared that 'it is the duty of the magistrate, to take care of matters of religion and to improve his civil authority for the observing of the duties commanded in the first, as well as for observing of duties commanded in the second table.' Williams, however, maintained that civil government in Massachusetts had authority only to enforce the commands of the second table—which contained the law of nature, the law moral and civil—and had no legitimate power to enforce the obligations of the first.[149]

Limiting government to the second table of the commandments comes directly from Romans chapter 13. The prohibitions of the second table have counter parts in most all civil codes and have received a great deal of approval in most civilizations. One author, who sees the second table as a minor limitation on

---

arms. *Id.* at 45–48. *See* Constitutionalism and Resistance in the Sixteenth Century: Three Treatises by Hotman, Beza, and Mornay 149–151 (Julian H. Franklin ed., 1969). Franklin provides abridged editions of three landmark works in the history of political thought clearly marking the transition from medieval to modern constitutional ideas. *Id.* at 11. *See also* Witte, *supra* note 142, at 100–04 (discussing the duty to resist tyrannical governments). Witte notes that Johannes Althusius (1557–1638) listed "the right to carry arms" among the natural liberties of man. *Id.* at 99.

148 Timothy L. Hall, Separating Church and State: Roger Williams and Religious Liberty 33 (1998) (citations omitted). Williams also asserted that "the king's patent was an insufficient basis for claiming title to lands in the New World. No one, Williams declared, could assert legitimate title unless he had 'compounded with the natives.'" *Id.*

149 *Id.* at 37 (citations omitted).

life considering all the freedom that remains, argues they are the basis of a happy life:

> In regard to the Second Table of the Law its prohibition of violence in the sixth commandment is a blessing and not a penalty. We all live more happily if the threat of violence in our lives is reduced to a minimum, and life would be better still if all violence could be eliminated. Similarly, it may be momentarily pleasant to possess the neighbor's wife, but a coldly calculating mind will eventually end up with the conclusion that the game is not worth the candle; eventually, there can be only disorganization and unhappiness; figure it out for yourself, if you have a brain. And similarly, there is no abiding happiness in theft or in fraud or in falsehood. The only happy and prosperous societies are those in which lives are safe (sixth commandment), possession of mate is safe (seventh commandment), possession of property is safe (eighth commandment), truthfulness is observed (ninth commandment), and contentment prevails (tenth commandment).[150]

With this limitation, you are free to live your life as you see fit. The same author suggests that this is the freedom you have to love yourself and at the same time love your neighbor as yourself:

> ... loving yourself consists in that freedom which permits you to set your own individual values on all aspects of life and permits you to pursue those values freely (except there be no exploitation of the neighbor). And when you love your neighbor as yourself you leave him equally free to set his own values and select his own choices and live his own life (but he may not exploit you and others).[151]

The Christian is a citizen of the world as well as a citizen of the kingdom of God. As a citizen of the world, the Christian may have responsibilities as a government employee as a vocation or possibly as a member of the military in time of war. It is at this point that it is important to recognize the legitimate

---

150 Frederick Nymeyer, *Understanding and Misunderstanding The Hebrew-Christian Law of Love, in* 1 First Principles in Morality and Economics 60 (1955).

151 *Id.* at 61. Nymeyer's concept of "ordered liberty" is more restrictive than the United States Supreme Court's concept as set forth in *Planned Parenthood of Southeastern Pennsylvania v. Casey*, 505 U.S. 833 (1992), which formulated the concept as: "At the heart of liberty is the right to define one's own concept of existence, of meaning, of the universe, and of the mystery of human life." *Id.* at 851.

area of governmental activity such that a Christian has the responsibility to carry out the administration of justice in an appropriate manner. The nature of modern warfare poses a particular challenge for Christians called upon to serve in the military, but this question goes beyond what Jesus was teaching in the Sermon on the Mount.[152] Paul summarized the balance called for by Jesus when he said in Romans 12:17–21:

> Recompense to no man evil for evil. Provide things honest in the sight of all men. If it be possible, as much as lieth in you, live peaceably with all men. Dearly beloved, avenge not yourselves, but rather give place unto wrath: for it is written, Vengeance is mine; I will repay, saith the Lord. Therefore if thine enemy hunger, feed him; if he thirst, give him drink: for in so doing thou shalt heap coals of fire on his head. Be not overcome of evil, but overcome evil with good.

The "Biblical distinction between response to evil in the area of private conduct and in the area of public duty of civil magistrates"[153] was well known to those listening to Jesus preach the Sermon on the Mount.[154] In the last quoted statement by Paul, he quoted from Deuteronomy 32:35 ["Vengeance is mine"] and Proverbs 25:21–22 ["if thine enemy hunger"].[155]

The form of government is another issue that can require study. Democracy, aristocracy, and monarchy among others are all possibilities.[156] Tocqueville suggested that:

> Every religion has an affinity with some political opinion.
> Allow the human spirit to follow its bent and it will impose a uniform rule on both political society and the divine city. It will seek, if I may put it this way, to harmonize earth with Heaven.[157]

---

152 *See* Stott, The Sermon on the Mount, *supra* note 15, at 111–14 (discussing the application of Jesus' teaching to war and Martin Luther's two kingdom theory, which has been used to justify Christians participating in governmental actions without any responsibility, to question the morality of those actions).

153 Culver, *supra* note 110, at 207.

154 *Id.* at 206.

155 *Romans* 12:19–20.

156 All three forms can be traced back to Aristotle and the Greeks. Calvin thought all three forms could be good and useful but that each can also be corrupted. For a general discussion of this topic, see R. M. Kingdom, *Calvinus Regulator: the 1543 'Constitution' of the City-State of Geneva, in* Calvinis Servus Christi 225, 228–31 (Wilhelm H. Neuse ed., 1986)

157 1 Alexis de Tocqueville, Democracy in America 332 (Arthur Goldhammer trans., 2004) (1835, 1840).

Christian religious organizations include the prelacy model in which decision making comes from the hierarchical structure. The Roman Catholic Church is an example of a hierarchical church which employs the principle of subsidiarity to push decisions down to the lowest practical level.[158] A second model is the presbytery model, in which individual churches unite and send representatives to presbyteries which hold judicial authority over the churches.[159] Presbyteries then send representatives to a synod which asserts judicial power over the presbyteries. Finally, the synods send representatives to a general assembly which makes the final decision on matters that cannot be resolved at the lower levels. This type of structure is seen in the United States where we have city, county, state, and national governments. The third model is the independency model in which decisions are all made by independent local churches from which there is no possibility of appeal.[160]

As noted above God's three institutions must be strong and independent for society to prosper. Today in societies in the West, religion and the family have a diminishing influence on society and the Word of God is rarely heard in civil discourse.[161] Government has grown and now determines the moral

---

158   Thomas Witherow, The Apostolic Church, Which Is It? 59–62 (photo reprint 1967) (1879). Witherow describes the various forms of church government and tests each by the standards of scripture. The Roman Catholic Church also has the principle of subsidiarity in which decisions are to be made at the lowest organizational level if possible.

159   Id. at 66–71.

160   Id. at 62–66.

161   Martin Luther, in his final sermon, lamented the neglect of the Word of God:

   In times past, we would have run to the ends of the world if we had known of a place where we could have heard God speak. But now ... Father and mother and children sing and speak of [Him]. The preacher speaks of [him] in the parish church—you ought to lift up your hands and rejoice that we have been given the honor of hearing God speaking to us through his Word. "Oh," people say, "what is that? After all, there is preaching every day, often many times every day, so that we soon grow weary of it. What do we get out of it?"

   https://dennistheeremite.blogspot.com/2017/10/reformation-martin-luthers-last -sermon.html (last visited August 20, 2022). Excerpt from Martin Luther's last sermon preached on February 15, 1546, three days before his death. The text was Matthew 11:25–30. Similarly, in 1847 a Bible commentator observed the way in which Church members of his day differed little from non-Christians:

   .... Christianity occupies their heads; but heathenism their hearts. They pretend to have faith; but, as for "the faith that overcomes the world," they know nothing about it. Their whole life, instead of being occupied in a progressive transformation of the soul after the Divine image, is one continued state of conformity to the world; and instead of regarding "the fellowship of the world" as a decisive proof of their "enmity against God," they affect it, they seek it, and they glory in it.

   Charles Simeon: Expository Outlines on the Whole Bible, Vol. 17 Galatians, Ephesians, 3 (1874), cited in Rousas John Rushdoony, Romans & Galatians 317 (1997).

standards for society and how wealth will be used and distributed. Tocqueville has observed that, as religion loses its influence, the society degenerates and loses its ability to grow and prosper:

> This is especially true of men who live in free countries.
>
> When a people's religion is destroyed, doubt takes hold of the highest regions of the intellect and half paralyzes all the others. Individuals become accustomed to making do with confused and fluctuating notions about the matters of greatest interest to themselves and their fellow men. They defend their opinions badly or give them up altogether, and because they despair of resolving on their own the greatest problems with which human destiny confronts them, they cravenly cease to think about such things at all.
>
> Such state inevitably enervates the soul; it weakens the springs of the will and prepares citizens for servitude.
>
> Not only will citizens then allow their liberty to be taken from them; in many cases they surrender it voluntarily.[162]

William Ramsay came to a similar conclusion from his travels in Anatolia. He writes:

> Religion to be true must be constantly growing. It cannot become stagnant without falsifying itself. The nation which does not increase in its power of interpreting the Divine purpose, and fails to produce a succession of listeners to and interpreters of the Divine voice, has become dead to the Divine message. In that country, where a true national character has never been allowed scope to develop, the history of religion has been one of degradation and of increase in the polytheistic spirit, which constitutes an infallible index of growing insensibility to the Divine nature. You learn there more clearly than in any other country that religion cannot be real and permanent except through the continuous revelation of the Divine nature to man.[163]

As a final thought on religion and the state, Roger Williams saw that, whenever the state sought to enforce a religion, tragic results were inevitable. The reasons for William's book, *The Bloudy Tenent*, include:

---

162   Tocqueville, *supra* note 157, at 502–03.

163   Ramsay, *supra* note 56, at 27–28.

First, that the blood of so many hundred thousand souls of Protestants and papists, spilled in the wars of present and former ages for their respective consciences, is not required nor accepted by Jesus Christ the Prince of Peace. ....

Eighthly, God requires no uniformity of religion to be enacted and enforced in any civil state; which enforced uniformity, sooner or later, is the greatest occasion of civil war, ravishing of conscience, persecution of Christ Jesus in his servants, and of the hypocrisy and destruction of millions of souls.[164]

These concepts of keeping government out of religion and allowing religion to flourish are reflected in the First Amendment to the United States Constitution. They are also reflected in James Madison's *Memorial and Remonstrance against Religious Assessments*, in which Madison enumerated 15 specific reasons government has no authority to interfere with or use public money to support religious activities.[165] Roger Williams' 1644 book lays out Christian arguments for religious liberty in which people of all religions can live together on the basis of Biblical teaching and not merely as a practical solution.[166]

9   Jesus Explains "Resist not Evil"

"Resist not evil" has been controversial and led people to embrace extreme approaches to non-resistance. Perhaps our translation is giving the wrong impression since elsewhere in the Bible we are told to resist evil.[167] Essentially, it is a direction not to avenge oneself when we are wronged. Others translate the prohibition as "But I tell you not to resist an evil person"[168] or "do not retaliate or seek revenge by evil means."[169]

If we look to Jesus' conduct as He was accused, brought before the council, and before the Roman governor, we see Him falsely accused, ridiculed, spat

---

164   Roger Williams, The Bloudy Tenent of Persecution, for Cause of Conscience 3 (reprint 2001) (1644). Religious liberty allows all religions to flourish in society. Toleration allows only the major religions to prosper. Intolerance only allows the dominant religion to prosper.

165   James Madison, *Memorial and Remonstrance Against Religious Assessment* (1785), *available at* https://founders.archives.gov/documents/Madison/01-08-02-0163.

166   Williams, *supra* note 164.

167   *Ephesians* 6:13; *1 Peter* 5:8–9; *James* 4:7.

168   *See, e.g., Matthew* 5:39 (New King James).

169   Pennington, *supra* note 8, at 194 n.56.

upon, struck with the palms of hands, whipped, and forced to wear a crown of thorns without resisting.[170] Indeed, when one of His disciples sought to resist Jesus' arrest and drew a sword; Jesus rebuked him saying:

> Thinkest thou that I cannot now pray to my Father, and he shall presently give me more than twelve legions of angels? But how then shall the scriptures be fulfilled, that thus it must be.[171]

Jesus followed His teachings to the letter. Jesus was an example of meekness in His response to His enemies. According to the nineteenth century English preacher, C. H. Spurgeon, we "are to be as the anvil when bad men are the hammers."[172]

Jesus is not calling everyone to suffer and die as an alternative to resisting an evil person. While some Christians may be called upon to give up their lives rather than deny the faith, Jesus is not addressing that situation. In other situations, we see Jesus resisting the money changers in the temple and questioning the acts of the High Priest when He is struck.[173] On one occasion Paul the Apostle resisted Peter the Apostle to his face when Peter withdrew from eating with gentiles to avoid being accused by the Judaizers.[174] On another occasion Paul used his Roman citizenship to challenge his Roman captors when they proposed to examine him by scourging. When Paul was asked by the governor whether he would go to Jerusalem to stand trial on charges by his Jewish accusers,[175] he refused and stood on his right to stand at Caesar's judgment seat in Rome.[176] Christians also should resist when called upon to do evil or to participate in the world's evil.

Jesus is giving general directions to the individual encountering demands in his everyday life where the first reaction of the natural man is to resist and defend one's self against the evil doer. The four cameos illustrate the principle of non-retaliation when someone seeks to injure you. That is, when you are slapped, sued for your coat, compelled to assist someone and go a mile, and when someone asks for money.[177] Jesus' well-known advice is to turn the

---

170   *See Matthew 26 & 27.*
171   *Matthew 26:53–54.*
172   Stott, The Sermon on the Mount, *supra* note 15, at 107.
173   *Matthew 21:12–13; John 18:19–23.*
174   *Galatians 2:11–14.*
175   *Acts 25:9–12.*
176   *Id.*
177   *Matthew 5:39–42.*

other cheek, give them your cloak, go an extra mile, and give the money.[178] This advice goes against our natural response, which is to resist and retaliate.

D. Martyn Lloyd-Jones has given us a couple of principles of interpretation that should be kept in mind. First, the Sermon on the Mount is not a code of ethics or set of rules covering our conduct in detail.[179] It is a matter of emphasizing the spirit of the law. Second, we do not apply the precepts mechanically.[180] It is the spirit not the letter that is important. Third, if our interpretation appears ridiculous or puts us in a ridiculous position, it is incorrect.[181] Fourth, if our interpretation makes the teaching look impossible, it is incorrect.[182] If our interpretation contradicts the plain meaning of other scripture, it is incorrect.[183]

We have already shown that the Sermon is not addressed to governmental policy. It is addressed to individual Christians. These are the people described in the Beatitudes. The teaching is impossible for anyone who lacks these qualities. How then could it possibly be made into public policy? Here, we deal only with the Christian's reaction to things done to him individually.

John Stott, seeing the only limit to the Christian's generosity is the limit love itself imposes, states as follows:

> Further, however conscientious we may be in our determination not to sidestep the implications of Jesus' teaching, we still cannot take the four little cameos with wooden, unimaginative literalism. This is partly because they are given not as detailed regulations but as illustrations of a principle and partly because they must be seen to uphold the principle they are intended to illustrate. That principle is love, the selfless love of a person who when injured, refuses to satisfy himself by taking revenge but studies instead the highest welfare of the other person and of society, and determines his reactions accordingly. He will certainly never hit back, returning evil for evil, for he has been entirely freed from personal animosity. Instead, he seeks to return good for evil. So he is willing to give to the uttermost—his body, his clothing, his service, his money—in so far as these gifts are required by love.[184]

---

178   *Id.*
179   Lloyd-Jones, *supra* note 85, at 273.
180   *Id.* at 274.
181   *Id.*
182   *Id.*
183   *Id.*
184   Stott, The Sermon on the Mount, *supra* note 15, at 107 (citing C. H. Spurgeon, The Gospel and the Kingdom 30 (1893)).

It is easy to conclude that Jesus is not seeking to encourage the world to take advantage of Christians expecting them to be drained of their assets.[185] D. Martyn Lloyd-Jones sees the key to the command in the fourth cameo namely, "Give to him that asketh thee, and from him that would borrow of thee turn not thou away."[186] At first glance, this seems inconsistent with the thrust of the other cameos. But Lloyd-Jones sees Jesus' concern is with your image of self. He sees the issue as first dealing with the reflex of self-defense that arises instinctively when some wrong is done to me. Then comes the attitude toward your possessions. We see that it is self all the time and not just when I am threatened with some injury. The defense arises even when someone would merely borrow. We're protecting "self."

Jesus is not just talking about outward material responses. This is what the scribes and Pharisees do. Jesus is "concerned with the condition of the heart, with the inner attitude of mind."[187] As Lloyd-Jones puts it:

> 'No,' says Christ in effect, 'it is a matter of the spirit, it is a matter of your whole attitude, especially your attitude towards yourself; and I would have you see that if you are to be truly My disciples you must become dead to yourself.' He is saying, if you like: 'if any man would be My disciple, let him deny himself (and all his rights to himself and all the rights of self), and take up his cross, and follow Me.'[188]

These cameos are illustrations as to how you might examine your own heart and attitude. They are not detailed examples of how to react to every situation in mechanical response. Looking at the first cameo again, "But I say unto you, That ye resist not evil: but whosoever shall smite thee on thy right cheek,

---

185   The early church in Jerusalem began on a principle of having all goods in common while recognizing that committing your goods was strictly a voluntary decision. *See Acts* 4:34–5:11 & 24:17. Whatever the benefit of this early experiment, it was not too long before the leaders of the Jerusalem church asked Paul to remember the poor. Paul did, and the churches Paul established in Galatia were joyfully making collections to support the poor in the Jerusalem church as was prophesized. *Acts* 11:27–30. Paul's trip to Jerusalem at that time was to bring famine relief to Jerusalem. *Acts* 12:25. It is uncertain if this famine relief visit is the same visit described in *Galatians* 2:1–10. Paul also brought alms and offerings to Jerusalem on his final visit. *Acts* 24:17.

186   *Matthew* 5:42.

187   George Eldon Ladd, *supra* note 23, at 88. Jesus has said, ""For out of the heart proceed evil thoughts, murders, adulteries, fornications, thefts, false witnesses, blasphemies: These are the things which defile a man:" *Matthew* 15:18–19a.

188   Lloyd-Jones, *supra* note 85, at 279 (citing *Matthew* 16:24).

turn to him the other also."[189] The first cameo is a case of physical abuse and addresses the insulting nature of the abuse that we are to tolerate. If we are being physically assaulted, we defend our person. We would also expect law enforcement to carry out its duty to prosecute the individual. Jesus is calling us to look at our hearts. Lloyd-Jones identified the core problem in these cameos is our natural effort to protect ourselves. That is, from the insult.

Thus, when we have been smitten on the right cheek by a person having evil motives, we naturally want to use our best efforts not only to resist but to retaliate. This comes out of a motive and desire for revenge. A bit of self-examination quickly reveals to us that we are doing exactly what Jesus prohibits. If we are truly being motivated by the Beatitudes, we will know that our hearts are in the wrong place when we seek revenge. We are to be peacemakers. We should instantly put that motive aside and turn the other cheek. In other words, we should seek by whatever means available to defuse the situation and end the conflict. We do this to the point of taking more-than-reasonable efforts. And if we must use force to resist, we use the method most likely to cause the least injury. Those seeing our efforts will see our good will and praise God. We might say that the guidance Jesus is giving is resist not him who is evil by improper motivations nor by improper means.[190]

The restriction against private revenge permeates the Old Testament. One example is the story of a wealthy shepherd near Carmel named Nabal.[191] He was churlish and evil in his doings. David encountered Nabal's servants in the field and sent them away unharmed. Later, David sent emissaries to Nabal requesting supplies and Nabal refused, thereby insulting David. Being angry, David armed 600 men to take revenge on Nabal. Nabal's wife, Abigail, prepared food and supplies for David and intercepted him on the way. David stated his intention: "he hath requited me evil for good. So and more also do God unto the enemies of David, if I leave of all that pertain to him by the morning light

---

189   *Matthew* 5:39.

190   Frederick Nymeyer, *Scriptural Corrections of Popular Errors Concerning Law Requiring Brotherly Love*, *in* 1 First Principles in Morality and Economics 85, 95 (1955). In a later article, Nymeyer quoted Talleyrand in a letter to Napoleon after the latter had achieved a triumph in words similar to our view of this cameo on resisting evil:

    Sire, three centuries of civilization have bequeathed to Europe a law of nations for which, in the words of a famous writer, human nature will never be grateful enough. This law is founded on the principle that nations should in time of peace do each other the most good, and in time of war the least possible harm.

    Frederick Nymeyer, *The Quest for Ramparts for Liberty*, *in* 1 First Principles in Morality and Economics 284, 293 (1955).

191   *1 Samuel* 25.

any that pisseth against the wall."[192] Abigail humbled herself before David and pleaded with David, recognizing that at times David had fought the battles of the Lord in his civil capacity but that shedding Nabal's blood was causeless. David accepted the advice stating: "And blessed be thy advice, and blessed be thou, which hast kept me this day from coming to shed blood, and from aveng-ing myself with mine own hand."[193] Here David demonstrates the Beatitude of meekness and his refusing to repay evil with evil.

Another example of David's willingness to set his self-interest aside is when he had the opportunity to kill King Saul who was pursuing him to kill him.[194] King Saul had gone into a cave for rest and it was the same cave in which David was hiding. David had the opportunity to take revenge but instead merely cut a piece from Saul's clothing and later showed the piece to Saul to demonstrate his goodwill to the king. In taking this action David said he would not lift a hand against God's anointed king.[195] Another example is when Abraham was lead-ing his large family and flocks through an area later to be the nation of Israel.[196] Abraham and his nephew Lot had large flocks that needed feeding and con-flict arose between the two families. Abraham being senior was in charge and called Lot to him and asked Lot to choose between the two parts of the land. Lot chose the most desirable part and Abraham accepted what was left rather than insisting on his rights as senior. Both of these are examples of meekness. Moses' action in bearing the burdens and complaints of the Israelites in the wilderness earned him the title as the meekest man in the land.[197]

The second cameo is "and if any man will sue thee at the law, and take away thy coat, let him have thy cloak also."[198] Under Jewish law, it was not lawful to sue for the outer garment, only the inner garment.[199] Jesus is again looking to the inner man who is always thinking about defending their rights whatever

---

192   *1 Samuel* 25:21–22.

193   *1 Samuel* 25:33; *see also* Culver, *supra* note 110, at 206–07 (discussing the distinction between private conduct addressed in the Sermon on the Mount and actions by the civil magistrate which are not).

194   *1 Samuel* 24.

195   *Id.* After David showed Saul the piece of Saul's skirt that he cut off to prove his goodwill to Saul, David said:

    The Lord judge between me and thee, and the Lord avenge me of thee: but mine hand shall not be upon thee. As saith the proverb of the ancients, Wickedness proceedeth from the wicked: but mine hand shall not be upon thee.

    1 Samuel 24:12–13.

196   *Genesis* 13:1–12.

197   *Numbers* 12:3.

198   *Matthew* 5:40.

199   Lloyd-Jones, *supra* note 85, at 283.

the cost. In the defense of personal rights, you are effectively insisting on recognition of your personal dignity. There are examples in scripture where, when struck by the palm of an officer's hand who said, "Answerest thou the high priest so? Jesus answered him, if I have spoken evil, bear witness of the evil: but if well, why smithest thou me?," Jesus protests the action of the officer.[200] On another occasion, Paul and Silas were imprisoned in Philippi with their feet bound in stocks. When the magistrates realized they had imprisoned them wrongfully, he sent word to release them quietly from the prison. But Paul said, "they have beaten us openly uncondemned, being Romans, and have cast us into prison; and now do they thrust us out privily? nay verily; but let them come themselves and fetch us out."[201] Neither of these examples involve personal rights. Both are rebuking the officer for breaking the law and Paul is insisting that the dignity and honor of the law be upheld. Give him your cloak also is an effort to defuse a personal conflict and involves the natural man's demand that his personal rights be vindicated.[202] To this Jesus says, "give him your cloak also."

The third cameo is "And whosoever shall compel thee to go a mile, go with him twain."[203] Jesus is referring to the custom that allowed the government to commandeer a man to carry baggage for a particular distance and then commandeer another to continue on to the final destination.[204] This illustrates natural man's resistance to the government and others imposing obligations on people. The natural reaction is to resent the action. While Jesus wants us to submit outwardly He also tells us to do so inwardly and willingly. Indeed we must be ready to go beyond what is demanded. The Apostle Peter tells us,

> Submit your selves to every ordinance of man for the Lord's sake: whether it be to the king, as supreme; Or unto governors, as unto them that are sent by him for the punishment of evildoers, and for the praise of them that do well. For so is the will of God, that with well doing ye may put to silence the ignorance of foolish men.[205]

The apostle Paul provides another admonition to give willingly stating:

---

200 *John* 18:22–23.
201 *Acts* 16:35–38.
202 Lloyd-Jones, *supra* note 85, at 284–85.
203 *Matthew* 5:41.
204 Lloyd-Jones, *supra* note 85, at 286.
205 *1 Peter* 2:13–15. Peter also admonishes, "servant, be subject to your masters with all fear; not only to the good and gentle, but also to the forward." *1 Peter* 2:18.

But this I say, He which soweth sparingly shall reap also sparingly; and he which soweth bountifully shall reap also bountifully. Every man according as he purposeth in his heart, so let him give, not grudgingly, or of necessity: for God loveth a cheerful giver.[206]

There are limits as to the authority of government when the government commands what is against God's law.[207] The command here does not prohibit working for change in government but requires that you do so lawfully. But we should never allow our resentment against the imposition by government or other authority over us such as employers to interfere with our duties and attitudes as Christians.[208]

The final cameo is "give to him that asketh thee, and from him that would borrow of thee turn not thou away."[209] Perhaps this is the most difficult for many people who hold their money and other possessions as their own and no one has a right to infringe on their ownership. Jesus is not saying to give to professional beggars or frauds or those who would obviously misuse any funds given. He is admonishing us not to close our hearts to those with genuine needs. Again, it is a matter of the condition of the heart and how we are to be different from the natural man whose reaction to any request is to hold tight to that which is his. The Apostle John states it well:

But whoso hath this world's good, and seeth his brother have need, and shutteth up his bowels of compassion from, him, how dwelleth the love of God in him? My little children, let us not love in word, neither in tongue; but in deed and truth.[210]

The responses called for by Jesus in these four cameos are things not found naturally in mankind. The Sermon on the Mount is only for those that have been born again and are now seeing the attitudes of the Beatitudes developing in their lives. Our attitudes toward personal insults, being sued, legislation, and charity are different than that of the world. The difference is a matter of what

---

206   2 *Corinthians* 9:6–7.
207   When the authorities ordered Peter not to teach in the name of Jesus, Peter replied: "We ought to obey God rather than man." *Acts* 5:27–29.
208   Lloyd-Jones, *supra* note 85, at 286–88.
209   *Matthew* 5:42.
210   *1* John 3:17–18; Lloyd-Jones, *supra* note 85, at 288–89.

we are rather than what we do.[211] What we do is reflective of what we are.[212] Lloyd-Jones highlights this point about denying the self:

> The whole trouble in life, as we have seen, is ultimately this concern about self, and what our Lord is inculcating here is that it is something of which we must rid ourselves entirely. We must rid ourselves of this constant tendency to be watching the interests of self, to be always on the look-out for insults or attacks or injuries, always in this defensive attitude. That is the kind of thing He has in mind. All that must disappear, and that of course means that we must cease to be sensitive about self. This morbid sensitiveness, this whole condition in which self is 'on edge' and so delicately and sensitively poised and balanced that the slightest disturbance can upset its equilibrium, must be got rid of. The condition which our Lord is here describing is one in which a man simply cannot be hurt. Perhaps that is the most radical form in which one can put that statement.[213]

Lloyd-Jones then illustrates the principle from the life of George Müller, a well-known nineteenth century evangelist and founder of the Ashley Down Orphanage in Bristol, England.[214] Müller stated,

> There was a day when I died, utterly died, died to George Müller and his opinions, preferences, tastes and will; died to the world, its approval or censure; died to the approval or blame of even my brethren and friends; and since then I have studied only to show myself approved unto God.[215]

We have already demonstrated that you must be born again before these standards can become real to you. You must say with Paul the Apostle, "I am crucified with Christ: nevertheless I live; yet not I, but Christ liveth in me; and the life which I now live in the flesh I live by the faith of the Son of God who loved me, and gave himself for me."[216]

---

211   George Eldon Ladd, *supra* note 23, at 83.
212   Lloyd-Jones, *supra* note 85, at 290.
213   *Id.* at 291.
214   *Id.*
215   *Id.* at 291–92.
216   *Galatians* 2:20; Lloyd-Jones, *supra* note 85, at 293.

10 Conclusion

We now see the demands being made on Christians. It is only left for us to examine ourselves and determine how we are doing on our road to life. Concern over self is the cause of our unhappiness and we must put it aside. Holiness is the removal from the self-centered life. We have the ultimate example in Jesus Christ, who left His throne in heaven and made Himself in the likeness of man so that He could suffer and die for the sins of man so man could be set free from the dominion of sin. The final directions in the Sermon on the Mount are to seek Christ's kingdom and righteousness and to seek to enter in by the narrow gate which few find.[217]

The Beatitudes are qualities of character existing and growing in every Christian. To be poor in spirit is more than just being unhappy with life and looking for Jesus to change everything. It is a recognition that, in the face of a holy and omnipotent God, neither you nor any of the things you have done have anything of value to this God. In this condition, you readily deny yourself any right to make demands on God or anyone else. You know that sin has corrupted you so that you are worthy only of eternal punishment. Furthermore, you look around you and realize that everyone is in the same condition. This situation causes you to mourn and to hunger and thirst after righteousness and, because you are in such need of mercy, you readily extend it to others. Realizing you are unclean, you seek to cleanse and purify your heart and avoid strife and anger with those around you. You seek to make peace wherever possible. In this state of despair, you realize that the only thing worthy of your attention and effort is to seek to glorify God who alone is worthy. Unfortunately, you become very unpopular with those around you who prefer not to think about such things. They want to suppress all such uncomfortable ideas and to suppress you and persecute you because you remind them of what they lost somewhere in the distant past. At this point, the blessing associated with each Beatitude becomes real to the believer. The promise of both the first and eighth Beatitude is the kingdom of heaven, which you are now seeking along with His righteousness above all things.[218] Jesus's command to "be ye perfect" becomes music to your ears. These are the people who shall inherit the earth. They now love God with all of their heart, soul, and mind and to keep their heart with all diligence, for out of it come the issues of life.[219]

---

217 *Matthew* 7:7–27.
218 *Matthew* 5:3, 10 and 6:33.
219 *Matthew* 22:37 and *Proverbs.* 4:23, respectively.

Jesus ends the Sermon on the Mount with words of encouragement and words of caution.[220] His words of encouragement are that, if you hear His words and do them, you are like a wise man who built his house upon a rock and, when the rains and winds and floods came, the house did not fall. But, if you fail to hear His words and do them, you are like a foolish man who built his house upon sand and, when the rains and winds and floods came, the house fell and great was its fall.[221]

Jesus gives the instruction to enter by the strait gate because wide is the gate and broad is the way that leads to destruction and many go in. In other words, it is easy to go along with the crowd and ignore Jesus' teaching. But the believer is to enter in by the strait gate because narrow is the way that leads to life and few there be that find it.[222] This is another way that Jesus is telling us not to worry about what we will eat or drink or wear but to seek first His kingdom and His righteousness and all these things will be added to you.[223] The emphasis is again to keep your priorities in order.

Jesus' final instruction confirms what we already know. Those who are called of Christ are called to be radically different from the world. By answering the call and striving to enter that strait gate that leads to life you are on the path to true human flourishing. We live in a time when there is little recognition of the Word of God in society. Hence, the initial quote from Amos 8:11. This article dealt with only a very few verses but purging all thought of revenge from our hearts is a small step into that strait gate that leads to human flourishing or. as Jesus would later say, "I am come that they might have life, and have it more abundantly."[224]

11   Dedication

Two verses bring this article to a conclusion. In 2021, Professor Wiessner experienced the profound loss of his mother. His mother had been a wonderful testimony to the love of Christ ever since she experienced the preaching of Billy Graham in the late 1950s. The verse that commemorated her life was 1 John 4:16:

---

220   *Matthew* 7:24–27.
221   *Id.*
222   *Matthew* 7:13–14.
223   *Matthew* 6:31–34.
224   *John* 10:10.

And we have known and believed the love that God hath to us. God is love; and he that dwelleth in love dwelleth in God, and God in him.

Professor Wiessner found comfort in his sorrow from Psalm 4:8:

I will both lay me down in peace, and sleep: for thou, Lord, only makest me dwell in safety.

It is the prayer of this author that all who read this article will live a life worthy of 1 John 4:16 and find the comfort in sorrow that Professor Wiessner found in Psalm 4:8.

CHAPTER 19

Native | Emigrant: The Curious Immigration Case of Forcibly Displaced Native Americans and Examination of the Rights of the Wampanoag Tribal Descendants in Bermuda

*Michael Vastine**

Contributing to a book honoring my friend Siegfried Wiessner, when asked, was more than an easy "yes," it is a privilege. However, as an interloper in the field, *e.g.*, writing on an issue relating to indigenous persons' rights, in a text which will inevitably be read by Siegfried and some of his distinguished friends and colleagues, is admittedly a bit reckless. Further reckless is hazarding an attempt to quantify a legal issue, describe an injustice, and pose a conundrum that belongs to a culture, without perpetuating the imperialist and colonial impulses that gave rise to it. In this regard I raise a question hopefully worth exploring further, although any "answer" should and must incorporate deeper and more culture-centric and culturally-informed perspectives than the present space allows.

My usual legal practice dwells on minutiae, the legal distinctions that often make the difference between an immigrant being deportable for a criminal conviction, or not. Minute as these arguments may appear to be, they are of tremendous, often vital importance to my clients and me, giving life to humanity's grand, macro-level principles every day.

---

* Michael Vastine joined the faculty of St. Thomas University College of Law in 2004, where he is Professor of Law and Director of Clinical Programs. Michael has both represented individual clients and authored amicus curiae briefs in major litigation regarding immigration and crimes and the due process rights of immigrants, representing groups including American Immigration Lawyers Association (AILA) and Catholic Legal Services in cases before the United States Supreme Court, the U.S. Courts of Appeals, the Florida and Connecticut state supreme courts, and the Board of Immigration Appeals. Michael also publishes on these topics and has made hundreds of presentations at conferences of the immigration bar. He is a graduate of Oberlin Conservatory of Music, Temple University Graduate School of Music, and Georgetown University Law Center. In 2013, Michael received the AILA (National) Elmer Fried Award for Excellence in Teaching.

© MICHAEL VASTINE, 2023 | DOI:10.1163/9789004524835_020

A beauty of my field of immigrant defense is that beyond the technical legal theory, every case comes with an origin story, as every client is on their distinct arc of international migration, one that both fits archetypal norms and takes uniquely personal twists. Every case is interesting, even compelling, just as the client behind the case is the product of their own fascinating experiences. The following essay attempts to illustrate a situation rooted both in my world and in Siegfried's: How could descendants of indigenous Native Americans, ripped from their ancestral homeland by slavery, have no claim to their native soil? Unlike my typical "law reform" objective-driven writing, I don't ultimately have a solution, but in fleshing out a riddle, I hope to pique the reader's curiosity about a paradox of modern civilization, the product of arbitrary circumstances informed by colonial errors and overlooked atrocities, one that might have— consistent with the themes of the tome in which this piece is but a chapter - a different and more equitable resolution in a world beyond the "end of law."

1   The Client

Picture the painted concrete block walls and the spartan industrial furniture of the attorney-client visitation room at the Krome Service Processing Center, a forced home to about 800 deportable immigrants. Krome, a converted cold war military base located at Miami-Dade County's western development boundary – immediately beyond Krome's perimeter, the Everglades – a "deten- tion center" that feels like a "jail" in every aspect but its name. The room's only décor is a panic button, to summon staff in the infinitesimal chance that a client meeting goes awry.

I am there to see a client from Bermuda, my second ever, and also the second that has found his way to detention based on a criminal conviction involving cannabis.

My first client had been of African-Bermudian origin, and had split his child- hood between Bermuda's capital, Hamilton, and London, and possessed a sort of British-centric view of being from Bermuda. In his case, we had eventually challenged whether he was deportable at all, based on a peculiarity in Bermuda's criminal law: Bermuda included in its definition of "cannabis" all parts of the cannabis plant (aside from sativa stalk fibers processed into hemp textiles),[1]

---

1   *See* Bermuda Misuse of Drugs Act 1972 : 159(1):
   "Cannabis" (except in the expression "cannabis resin") means any plant or part thereof within the botanically designated genus Cannabis, but does not include any fiber produced from the stalk of the plant.

while the U.S. (federal) Controlled Substances Act, 21 U.S.C. § 802, excluded the euphorically useless parts of the plant, such as the roots and the entire stalks.[2] This overbreadth in the Bermuda definition meant a conviction didn't "categorically," i.e., necessarily, match the federal standard. Florida's criminal code was written the same way, and it became my life's quest to exploit the distinction as a way of fighting against the deportability of immigrants convicted of Florida drug offenses.[3]

Thus, I find myself in the concrete block interview room, knowing not much about the new client I was expecting to see. I knew only: 1) Bermuda, and 2) cannabis conviction. I am buoyed by the potential promise in the legal theories of the case. Internally, I rehearse the theory – of mismatched drug definitions – and clever ways of explaining the then-novel defense to a non-lawyer, one who might not have much hope.

The guard's keys clatter from the prisoner-side access door to the room. In comes L–, polite, medium complexion, in nice Nike sneakers below the red jumpsuit assigned to detainees whose crimes the Immigration and Customs Enforcement (ICE) officers had classified – correctly, or not – as serious "aggravated felonies."[4] After some pleasantries, I summarize why I want to study his conviction records and what I would be looking for.

He departs to his barrack and returns shortly with his criminal papers. I see that he was convicted in *United States federal* court – bad news – for growing cannabis. It won't be possible to argue that the federal definition of cannabis didn't apply in his case. It is a federal conviction, invoking that very definition.

---

2   The federal substance is enumerated at 21 U.S.C. § 802 as follows:

(16) The term "marihuana" means all parts of the plant Cannabis sativa L., whether growing or not; the seeds thereof; the resin extracted from any part of such plant; and every compound, manufacture, salt, derivative, mixture, or preparation of such plant, its seeds or resin. Such term does not include the mature stalks of such plant, fiber produced from such stalks, oil or cake made from the seeds of such plant, any other compound, manufacture, salt, derivative, mixture, or preparation of such mature stalks (except the resin extracted therefrom), fiber, oil, or cake, or the sterilized seed of such plant which is incapable of germination (emphasis added to highlight distinctions).

3   Ultimately, a colleague won a case presenting this theory at the United States Court of Appeals for the Eleventh Circuit, which provides federal review of immigration court decisions that originate within the state of Florida. *See Said v. United States AG,* 28 F.4th 1328 (11th Cir. 2022) (reversing a published decision of the Board of Immigration Appeals addressing the same issue, *Matter of Navarro Guadarrama,* 27 I&N Dec. 560 (BIA 2019)). As a result of *Said,* Florida "cannabis" convictions now cannot be found to trigger immigration consequences.

4   The long list of qualifying types of offenses is found at 8 U.S.C. § 1101(a)(43) and ranges in weight from extremely serious (murder, rape, and arms trafficking) to not (theft offenses with suspended sentences, recidivist simple drug possession).

Curses. I don't look so clever, anymore. This case may be impossible. Instead of strategizing, I prepare him for that reality.

As often happens in my client meetings, eventually our conversation drifts far afield. He's happy for the company and I'm always interested in building rapport and learning a bit about my clients – I'll learn something about the world and inevitably get a tip for a good local restaurant to seek out, later: "the best place for -----," from a client's culture.

He is worried that if he loses his case, he will almost certainly be deported straight from the detention center, taken from the jail to the airport and flown to Bermuda accompanied by a marshal or DHS officer. In this case, he will be unable to wrap up his life in the U.S. and manage his property. His affairs will be a disaster. He will inevitably lose the full value of his possessions, including vehicles, by liquidating them in his absence.

He is also worried about his extended family. For some reason, while talking about families, he recounts recently taking some ancestry/DNA tests with his family members to confirm that their ancestors were Native American.

[Cue the sound of shrieking brakes.]

Native American? The journey begins.

2   The Basics: Bermuda

Bermuda. 20 square miles of land mass (*one-sixtieth* the size of Rhode Island, the smallest U.S. state) across some 180 islands and islets, including seven main islands, located 650 miles east of North Carolina.

Bermuda. Encountered in 1505 by Spanish explorers. Colonized in 1609 after a hurricane-induced misadventure forced the landing of an English ship (or ships) intending to resupply the Virginia Company's settlement at Jamestown, Europe's first permanent foothold in the Western Hemisphere. News of the shipwreck contributes to the scene-setting in a play being scripted at the time by William Shakespeare, *The Tempest.*

Bermuda. Racially integrated by the slave trade, as early as 1616. Slavery abolished August 1, 1834, 30 years after Haiti accomplished the same via revolution, and 30 years before the U.S. accomplished emancipation via civil war.

Bermuda. Tourism. Pink sands. Mopeds. Actor Michael Douglas a citizen (via his mother). Complicated rules for foreigners' land ownership, which recently became more relaxed.

Bermuda. Gross Domestic Product (GDP) of $110, 859.50, sixty percent higher than that of the United States.[5] GDP bested only by Liechtenstein, Luxemburg, and Monaco. Major industries: insurance and financial services.[6]

Bermuda. Population 65,000. 52% identify as Black. Recent genetic demographic study revealed 1% to be Native American.[7]

3   The Basics: Native American Assistance of New England Colonizers; Retribution

Every American schoolchild is indoctrinated in our national origin stories, with primacy awarded to the historic legends of Columbus, Jamestown/John Smith/ Pocahontas, and Plymouth Colony/Mayflower/Pilgrims. The basics of the latter, of course, involved members of the reform-minded "puritan" Protestant movement within the Church of England (thereby, by definition, an outsider group finding itself in conflict with both the Crown and the larger Church of England), eventually setting forth to establish a colony in New England with the Massachusetts Bay Company. Notably, the Pilgrims did not "discover" the area, even from a Euro-centric perspective. The region was perhaps visited by Italian explorer John Cabot (*i.e.*, Giovanni Cabotto, who sailed under an

---

5   *GDP per capita (current US$) – Bermuda*, World Bank (2022), https://data.worldbank.org /indicator/NY.GDP. PCAP.CD?locations=BM&most_recent_value_desc=false.

6   *Bermuda – Economic Indicators*, Moody's Analytics, https://www.economy.com/bermuda /indicators.

7   Discussed more, *infra*, the relative isolation of St. David's Island, Bermuda, combined with its historic population of known former Native American slaves, invited a genealogical study, completed in 2009. The scientists involved concluded that "[i]n light of genealogical and oral historical data from the St. David's [Island Committee], the low frequency of Native American [...] lineages may reflect the influence of genetic drift, the demographic impact of European colonization, and historical admixture with persons of non-native backgrounds, which began with the settlement of the islands. By comparing the genetic data with genealogical and historical information, we are able to reconstruct the complex history of this Bermudian community, which is unique among New World populations." Jill B. Gaieski, Amanda C. Owings, Miguel G. Vilar, Matthew C. Dulik, David F. Gaieski, Rachel M. Gittelman, John Lindo, Lydia Gau, Theodore G. Schurr & Genographic Consortium*Genetic ancestry and indigenous heritage in a Native American descendant community in Bermuda*, 146 Am. J. Physical Anthropology 392–405 (2011), *available at* https://pubmed.ncbi.nlm.nih .gov/21994016/.
    The phenomenon of "genetic drift" tends to erase minority genetic types over generations, thus explaining the apparent dissonance between the known genealogy of Native American Bermudians and the relatively low outcomes in the modern genetic study.

English flag) over a century prior, and was minimally surveyed by John Smith, of Jamestown fame, and dubbed "New England" by Smith no later than 1616.

Nonetheless, after landing on the eastern tip of Cape Cod and eventually disembarking 25 miles west across Cape Cod Bay at Plymouth on the eve of the winter of 1620, nearly half of the Pilgrim settlers died in their first year in North America. Those who survived famously celebrated with a feast of "thanksgiving" the following autumn, the genesis of the modern national holiday celebrated the fourth Thursday in November across the United States.

The colony was further notable for its political documents. Being as weather-related navigational challenges forced the group to settle well outside the northern confines of the Virginia Colony, the group was briefly located in a geopolitical anomaly: literally, a land beyond law. Like Voltaire's view on the almighty,[8] and proving the human need for declarative collective governing principles as a bulwark against anarchy,[9] the overwhelming majority of the adult men on board agreed upon a foundational document of communal principles, to impose order. Later, this charter came to be known as the Mayflower Compact,[10] nicknamed after their famous transatlantic sailing ship, within which these signatories enumerated their commitment to collective governance.

Of course, the intrepid European settlers were not the first custodians of New England. Native Americans had populated the region for 9,000–12,000 years,[11] so at the time the Pilgrims arrived, the Europeans encountered a patchwork of Native American nations, collectively comprising a complex regional civilization, but each with its own complex political realities. As is increasingly acknowledged, the Pilgrims directly encroached upon the land of the Wampanoag tribe, which controlled much of southeastern Massachusetts

---

8   *The Three Imposters* (1769) ("If God did not exist, it would be necessary to invent Him" (*"Si Dieu n'existait pas, il faudrait l'inventer"*)).

9   Rivka Galchen, *Why Do We Obey Rules?*, The New Yorker (July 6, 2022) (reviewing "'Rules: A Short History of What We Live By,' by the science historian Lorraine Daston, and examin[ing] why rules exist, why we follow them, and how their history can express, in part, the history of humanity itself.").

10   Initially known as *Agreement Between the Settlers at New Plymouth: 1620* and establishing that the signatories would "enact, constitute, and frame, such just and equal Laws, Ordinances, Acts, Constitutions, and Officers, from time to time, as shall be thought most meet and convenient for the general Good of the Colony." *See e.g.*, Mayflower Compact: 1620, *compiled by* The Avalon Project, Yale Law School, https://avalon.law.yale.edu/17th_century/mayflower.asp.

11   *See* National Park Service, *New England Archeological Time Periods*, https://www.nps.gov/articles/000/archeological-time-periods.htm.

(along with the islands of modern-day Nantucket and Martha's Vineyard[12]) and had its own reasons for strategic rapprochement with the newcomers, who happened to settle into a former Wampanoag village recently decimated, if not eradicated, by disease, with the pestilence likely also traceable to prior European contact.[13]

Both legend and the historical record establish that the Pilgrims managed, nearly immediately, to establish a method for coexisting with the Wampanoag. The Wampanoag political leader, or *sachem*, Massasoit, elected to assist the English, being as his alternative was conflict with both the Europeans *and* a neighboring federation.[14] Massasoit took the path of (immediate) least resistance, certainly not suspecting the long-term path of assured self-destruction he set in motion, via his help of the colonizers.

In his interactions, Massasoit was likely assisted by the interpretation skills of Tisquantum (aka, the "Squanto" known throughout popular history),[15] if not a small number of other Native Americans who had learned English to varying degrees *in England* during years abroad after being taken captive by earlier explorers.[16] The point being, even as early as the Pilgrims' landing, there was *already* a complicated interplay in culture, identity, and power dynamics, as the "butterfly effect"[17] of the earliest European contact with the Native population began to manifest in earnest. It is perhaps jarring to consider that even the Pilgrims' own interactions were informed by their place in a continuum that preceded their arrival, but that is the historical reality.

---

12   Martha's Vineyard is known to the federally recognized Aquinnah Wampanoag tribe as *Noepe*, upon which the tribe holds nearly 500 acres of land. *See The Creation of Noepe*, The Wampanoag Tribe of Gay Head Acquinnah, https://wampanoagtribe-nsn.gov/ancientways.

13   *See* Charles C. Mann, *Native Intelligence,* Smithsonian Magazine (December 2005), https://www.smithsonian mag.com/history/native-intelligence-109314481/.

14   *See id.*

15   *See, e.g.,* G. Brockell, *The life and mysterious death of Squanto, whose remains may now lie under a Cape Cod golf course,* Wash. Post (November 25, 2021), https://www.washingtonpost .com/history/2021/11/25/squanto-death-murder-golf-course/.

16   *See, e.g., The Story of Squanto,* Mayflower 400, https://www.mayflower400uk.org /education/ native-america/2020/june/the-story-of-squanto/; *Squanto,* Encyclopedia Britannica, https://www.britannica.com/ biography/Squanto.

17   In popular culture, the expression, with its origins in Dr. Edward Lorenz's question "does the flap of a butterfly's wings in Brazil cause a tornado in Texas?" refers to the outsize impact of minute disturbances of norms, but Lorenz actually referred to the inevitability of the operation of any complex system toward a predictable cumulative outcome. *See* Jamie Verdon, *Understanding the Butterfly Effect,* The American Scientist (2013), https:// www.americanscientist.org/article/understanding-the-butterfly-effect.
      Here, the author thinks the popular *and* intended use of the phase are equally *apropos*.

With the benefit of hindsight, any realistic twenty-first century reader can surmise the outcome of inevitable territorial jealousy between the Pilgrims and their initially tolerant Native American neighbors, particularly when the land in question included the Wampanoag-controlled real estate that comprises Nantucket and Martha's Vineyard.[18] The pastoral image of the first Thanksgiving and the mythologized solidarity between the settlers and the colonized, gave way to negotiated land deals extending the holdings of the ever-increasing number of Europeans, and eventually to mortal conflict.

In the Spring of 1621, the Wampanoag and the Puritans signed the first treaty between Native and European groups, a peace that would largely endure for 50 years, and – as an initial matter – ensure a safe growing season for the Puritans in that first Summer of their colony, leading to the sustenance for the aforementioned "Thanksgiving" and the subsequent winter. A simple agreement against mutual aggression and for mutual aid,[19] the Wampanoag treaty was recently commemorated as the reverse side of the U.S. Dollar coins (aka Sacajawea golden dollars), in 2011.[20] This vital relationship is not obviously not totally forgotten.

---

18   Frances Karttunen, *How many Wampanoags were on Nantucket when the first English settlers arrived in 1659?*, Nantucket Historical Association. https://nha.org/research /nantucket-history/history-topics/how-many-indians-were-on-nantucket-when-the -first-english-settlers-arrived-in-1659/ (noting that population estimates for the mid-1600s range from 1,500 to 2,000 Wampanoag, broken into different groups, each with their own *sachem* leader).

19   Worth reprinting in full, the treaty established:
  1.   That neither he [Massasoit] nor any of his should injure or do hurt to any of our people.
  2.   And if any of his did hurt to any of ours, he should send the offender, that we might punish him.
  3.   That if any of our tools were taken away when our people were at work, he should cause them to be restored, and if ours did any harm to any of his, we would do the like to them.
  4.   If any did unjustly war against him, we would aid him; if any did war against us, he should aid us.
  5.   He should send to his neighbor confederates, to certify them of this, that they might not wrong us, but might be likewise comprised in the conditions of peace.
  6.   That when their men came to us, they should leave their bows and arrows behind them, as we should do our peace when we came.
  7.   Lastly, that doing thus, King James would esteem of him as his friend and ally.
  Nathan Dorn, *The Treaty That Saved Plymouth Colony* (blog), Library of Congress (March 22, 2017), https://blogs.loc.gov/law/2017/03/the-treaty-that-made-thanksgiving/.

20   In 2011, the U.S. Mint issued Native American Silver Dollars commemorating the treaty. *See* http://www.usmint.gov/mint_programs/nativeamerican/?action=2011NADesign.

However, by 1670, the Wampanoag were governed by Sachem (chief) Metacom (aka Metacomet, otherwise known as King Philip), a son of Massasoit.[21] Facing persistent land encroachment, the reality that the English were not fulfilling (at minimum) the first four prongs of 1621 treaty, and untenable pressure from the English to unilaterally disarm, Metacom led the Wampanoag and their allies in armed conflict that was ultimately triggered by alleged or actual assassinations on each side.[22] The ensuing war lasted from 1675 to 1676, ending with the capture of Metacom's wife and son, and the execution of Metacom in 1676.[23] Commonly referred to as King Philip's War, historians regard the conflict as likely the country's most bloody, per capita, with perhaps forty percent of the Wampanoag decimated, their numbers reduced to figure estimated as low as 400.[24] The majority of the surviving Wampanoag were captured and sold into slavery, to settle wartime debts incurred by the prevailing English colonists.

---

21   *See, e.g., King Philip's War and its impact on America,* Mayflower 400, https://www
      .mayflower400uk.org/education/native-america/2020/july/the-story-of-king-philips
      -war/.

22   *See The Story of Squanto,* Mayflower 400, https://www.mayflower400uk.org/education
      /native-america/2020/june/the-story-of-squanto/; *see also* Carol Berkin et al., Making
      America Volume 1: To 1877: A History of the United States 72–73 (2014).
      In 1636, the Pequot (the larger Indian Nation within New England) War had begun,
      with the Indians under attack from both the Massachusetts and Connecticut armies and
      their Indian allies, the Narragansetts and the Mohicans ... The brutal war did not end until
      all the Pequot men had been killed and the women and children sold into slavery.
      For almost three decades, an uneasy peace existed between new England colonists
      and Indians. But the struggle of the land continued. When war broke out again, it was two
      longtime allies – the Plymouth colonists and the Wampanoags who took up arms against
      each other. By 1675, the friendship between these two groups had been eroded by Pilgrim
      demands for Indian lands. Chief Metacomet, known to the English as King Philip, made
      the difficult decision to resist. ... With the help of Iroquois troops sent by the governor of
      New York, the colonists finally defeated the Wampanoags. Metacomet was murdered, and
      his head was impaled on a stick.
      Indian objections to colonial expansion in New England had been silenced. Several
      tribes had been wiped out entirely in the war, or their few survivors sold into slavery in
      the Caribbean.

23   *See id.; see also* Sarah Pruitt, *Why the Wampanoag Signed a Peace Treaty with the Mayflower
      Pilgrims,* history.com, https://www.history.com/news/wampanoag-pilgrim-peace-treaty
      -thanksgiving.

24   Jessie Little Doe Baird, *A Brief Timeline of Wampanoag History,* https://mashpeewampa-
      noagtribe-nsn.gov/timeline.

Many of the captives, perhaps including Metacom's own surviving family members,[25] were sold to traders who transported these new Wampanoag slaves out of New England, to Bermuda.

4   Beyond Law: Inherent/Perpetual Right of Passage for Indigenous Persons (and the Treaties Recognizing It)

Like conceiving a universe beyond the edge of space,[26] we are so accustomed to an imposed system of order and government, that it is difficult to imagine a world *beyond* law. However, the perfect state of being might reflect a natural and balanced order, based upon logical principles. And those principles may have been held among humans all along, whether noticed or not, prior to codification by the earliest societies.

When the Europeans settled, populated, and ultimately carved up the geography of North America into new political units, the various European powers did not operate in a vacuum; they did so within complicated relationships with allies and enemies, against a backdrop of the historic native civilizations and their collective symbiotic relationships with the natural world. Thus, in the several multilateral and bilateral treaties that formed the 1783 "Peace of Paris" resolving the (American) Revolutionary War, the major national players – the United States, Britain, France, and Spain (and to a significantly lesser extent, the Netherlands) – agreed upon new international territorial boundaries, primarily in North America.

Remarkably, within the Treaty of Paris, the United States and Britain agreed upon recognizing inherent principles that applied to indigenous Native Americans who traditionally occupied lands that straddled the new northern

---

25   Rick Green, *For Early Colonists, Indians Were A Bloody Enemy And The Spoils Of War*, The Hartford Courant, September 29, 2002, reprinted at Battlefields of the Pequot War, http://pequotwar.org/2012/02/did-you-know-after-the-pequot-war-pequot-women-children-were-sold-into-slavery-isle-of-nevis-bermuda-providence-isle/.

26   *See* Cormac O'Raifeartaigh, *Albert Einstein and the origins of modern cosmology*, https://physicstoday.scitation.org/do/10.1063/PT.5.9085/full/ (revisiting and questioning whether a physicist as great as Albert Einstein could have been correct in his seminal 1917 *Cosmological Considerations In The General Theory Of Relativity*, which was premised upon a static, three-dimensional universe, rather than his rejection of this concept in favor of theories accepting an ever-expanding, and therefore infinite one); Paul Sutter, *Is there Anything Beyond the Universe?*, January 25, 2022, https://www.space.com/whats-beyond-universe-edge; Patchen Barss, *What if the Universe has no End*, bbc.com (January 19, 2020), https://www.bbc.com/future/article/20200117-what-if-the-universe-has-no-end.

U.S. border with Canada.[27] The countries recognized that Canadian Indians – those who have no political or tribal ties to the United States,[28] but do possess a 50% Indian blood quotient – possessed an inherent right of passage to the United States, and thus the right to permanently reside there.[29]

Again, this "right of passage" is based on Native peoples' aboriginal right to movement within the greater North American land mass that was formerly not subject to the boundaries of the political footprint of the United States, as drawn by the European colonizers. As it is proclaimed and recorded in a treaty, this inherent right of Native movement lives on to the present, and must be read into – and trumps – U.S. statutes which seemingly might conflict with or limit the "right of passage."[30] This provision enumerating the rights of Native Canadians was subsequently confirmed by the Treaty of 1796, in the "Explanatory Article to the Third Article of the Treaty of November 19, 1794, Respecting the Liberty to Pass and Repass the Borders and to Carry on Trade and Commerce," which reiterated the historic rights and explicitly compacted the understanding that the "right of passage" would continue, unabridgeably, into the future.[31]

---

27   Discussed at some length in *Matter of A-*, 1 I&N Dec. 600, 601, n. 1 (BIA, November 13, 1943), quoting:
      "It is agreed that it shall at all times be free to his Majesty's subjects, and to the citizens of the United States, and also to the Indians dwelling on either side of the said boundary line, freely to pass and repass by land or inland navigation, into the respective territories and countries of the two parties, on the continent of America."

28   Otherwise, they would eventually be legislated to be U.S. citizens, pursuant to the Indian Citizenship Act of 1924.

29   Immigration and Nationality Act § 289, 8 U.S.C. § 1359, reads:
      Nothing in this title shall be construed to affect the right of American Indians born in Canada to pass the borders of the United States, but such right shall extend only to persons who possess at least 50 per centum of blood of the American Indian race.

30   *See, e.g.,* Carlos Manuel Vazquez, *Treaties as Law of the Land: The Supremacy Clause and the Judicial Enforcement of Treaties*, 122 Harv. L. Rev. 599 (2008).

31   The Explanatory Article expounds:
      They the said Commissioners, having communicated to each other their full powers, have in virtue of the same, and conformably to the spirit of the last Article of the said treaty of Amity, Commerce, and Navigation, entered into this explanatory Article, and do by these presents explicitly Agree and declare, That *no stipulations in any treaty subsequently concluded by either of the contracting parties with any other State or Nation, or with any Indian tribe, can be understood to derogate in any manner from the rights of free intercourse and commerce* secured by the aforesaid third Article of the treaty of Amity, commerce and navigation, to the subjects of his Majesty and to the Citizens of the United States and to the Indians dwelling on either side of the boundary-line aforesaid; but that all the said persons shall remain at full liberty freely to pass and repass by land or inland navigation, into the respective territories and countries of the contracting parties, on either side of the said boundary-line, and freely to carry on trade and commerce with

The only land at issue that implicated Indian freedom of movement was the northern U.S. border, a boundary created at the conclusion of the Revolutionary War. Thus, Canadian Indians required and received unique treaty-recognized treatment that would survive into contemporary times as ratified treaty-based rights.[32] Of course, this northern border was further under dispute and was again resolved at the conclusion of the War of 1812 fought, again, between the nascent United States and Great Britain. The war itself could be viewed as a militaristic withdrawal from the Jay Treaty. However, philosophically, the principles contained therein *pre-existed* that treaty, and the rights of Indians acknowledged under the Jay treaty were explicitly reestablished by the Treaty of Ghent, which thus concluded the War of 1812.[33]

Unsurprisingly, our nation's courts have had need to examine this intersection between the treaty-based rights and U.S. immigration law.[34] The premise that a

---

each other, according to the stipulations of the said third Article of the treaty of Amity, Commerce and Navigation. (emphasis added).

Explanatory Article to Article 3 of the Jay Treaty, signed at Philadelphia (May 5, 1796), https://avalon.law.yale.edu/ 18th_century/jayex1.asp

32   *See* Greg Boos & Greg McLawsen, *American Indians Born in Canada and the Right of Free Access to the United States*, Border Policy Research Institute Publication 69 (2013), https:// cedar.wwu.edu/cgi/viewcontent.cgi?article=1068&context=bpri_publications.

33   Treaty of Peace and Amity Between the United States and Great Britain ("Treaty of Ghent"), Art. IX (1814), https://www.archives.gov/milestone-documents/treaty-of-ghent, is dedicated to resolving Native participation in the conflicts, and provides:

The United States of America engage to put an end immediately after the Ratification of the present Treaty to hostilities with all the Tribes or Nations of Indians with whom they may be at war at the time of such Ratification, and forthwith to *restore to such Tribes or Nations respectively all the possessions, rights, and privileges which they may have enjoyed or been entitled to in one thousand eight hundred and eleven previous to such hostilities.* Provided always that such Tribes or Nations shall agree to desist from all hostilities against the United States of America, their Citizens, and Subjects upon the Ratification of the present Treaty being notified to such Tribes or Nations, and shall so desist accordingly. And His Britannic Majesty engages on his part to put an end immediately after the Ratification of the present Treaty to hostilities with all the Tribes or Nations of Indians with whom He may be at war at the time of such Ratification, and forthwith to restore to such Tribes or Nations respectively all the possessions, rights, and privileges, which they may have enjoyed or been entitled to in one thousand eight hundred and eleven previous to such hostilities. Provided always that such Tribes or Nations shall agree to desist from all hostilities against His Britannic Majesty and His Subjects upon the Ratification of the present Treaty being notified to such Tribes or Nations, and shall so desist accordingly (emphasis added).

34   Not limited to the immigration context, treaty-based rights have recurring presence in Native American legal issues. *See, e.g., Herrera v. Wyoming* 587 U.S. ___, 139 S. Ct. 1686 (2019); Jessica Gresko, *High court sides with Crow tribe member in hunting dispute*, APNews (May 20, 2019), https://apnews.com/article/414e8576c64542bdb4461e5414f63618

Native Canadian can enter and live in the United States, entitled to public benefits and some exemptions from international duties and import prohibitions, and without fear of deportation therefrom, has not gone without challenge.[35] Perhaps the most cited modern case from the Board of Immigration Appeals, the appellate body of the Executive Office for Immigration Review (which also includes the nation's immigration trial courts, all within the Department of Justice), is the 1978 case, *Matter of Yellowquill*, which provides a helpfully illustrative factual scenario.[36]

Ms. Yellowquill, a Native Canadian, had a serious problem. She had been convicted in Texas for possessing heroin. Any controlled substance offense makes a non-citizen deportable, so she was apparently subject to deportation from the United States.[37] She pointed out to the BIA that, if deported, she had a treaty-recognized right of passage to reenter the United States. In her view, it was therefore ludicrous, factually, for her to be subject to an ineffective deportation and therefore, legally, she should not be subject to removal at all. She won.

Yellowquill effectively reversed one of the earliest BIA decisions (literally, from volume 1 of the reported appellate immigration cases), *Matter of A-*,[38] involving a registered Canadian member of the Chemainus Band, who was found to be deportable for becoming a "public charge" within five years of entering the United States. His problems were based on medical conditions – collateral manifestations of syphilis – which arguably triggered three bases for removal. Recognizing that "A-" had a "right of passage" and that deportation was a toothless exercise which failed to prevent "A-'s" immediate reentry into

---

(describing case holding, that treaty-based hunting rights held by the Crow tribe which predated Wyoming's statehood, cannot be abrogated by modern Wyoming law).

35   *See generally* Jay Treaty, *supra; see also Border Crossing Rights between the United States and Canada for Aboriginal People*, Pine Tree Legal Assistance (calling into question whether the "United States implement[s] promise of duty-free carriage of 'proper goods'"), https://www.ptla.org/border-crossing-rights-jay-treaty; *see, e.g., Travelling to the United States with Eagle Items: Guidelines for Indigenous People* (July 5, 2017) https://www.canada.ca/en/environment-climate-change/services/convention-international-trade-endangered-species/wild-animal-plant-protection-act/travelling-eagle-items-guidelines-aboriginal.html#_02.

36   16 I&N Dec. 2664 (BIA 1978).

37   *See* 8 U.S.C. § 1227(a)(2)(B):

      Any alien who at any time after admission has been convicted of a violation of (or a conspiracy or attempt to violate) any law or regulation of a state, the United States, or a foreign country relating to a controlled substance (as defined in section 802 of Title 21), other than a single offense involving possession for one's own use of 30 grams or less of marijuana, is deportable.

38   *Matter of A-*, 1 I&N Dec. 600 (BIA November 13, 1943).

the United States, the BIA ordered deportation anyway, in a transparent effort to pass off this burdensome "ward" on another caretaking country, Canada. The BIA was effectively trying to make "A-" miserable enough (by the inconvenience of facing perpetual enforcement if he returned) that he would no longer avail himself of his rights to return to the United States. One could suppose that the BIA reasonably found that "A-" presented poor facts: while he apparently had no family, job, or stable home, he *did* have gonorrhea, syphilis, unpaid medical bills (for treatment of the foregoing) and numerous arrests for alcohol-related offenses.[39] Thus, the BIA made every effort to make "A-" into Canada's problem, consistent with the BIA's view that "only those Indians who are considered undesirable, whether because they are criminals or have certain physical or mental disqualifications, will be ordered deported."[40]

Matter of A- is also informative for its use of the terms of the day, dismissively referring to "A-" as a "ward" of Canada, and thereby invoking the paternalistic tradition of state treatment of natives and their affairs that continues, with controversy, to the present.[41] The BIA also refers to "A-" as having never being "enfranchised," the paternalistic process – via marriage or familial relationship, or professional achievement – in which a tribal member might come to be regarded as a non-Native (*i.e.*, not *dis*enfranchised), full member of Canadian society.[42] Further, the BIA addressed the paternalistic (yet helpful) presumptions to be used when delineating the rights of non-Native Americans, namely

---

39   *Id.* at 604–605.

40   *Id.* at 603.

41   Until 1951, the 1876 Canadian *Indian Act,* which established and defined "Indian" as a legal identity forced many Status Indian men and women to "enfranchise"—give up status rights for citizenship rights. Gaining the franchise, joining the military, obtaining a college degree or becoming a professional automatically resulted in the loss of Indian status. In addition, any Status Indian who resided outside of Canada for five years or longer resigned his or her status). *See e.g. Indian Status*, The Canadian Encyclopedia (May 11, 2020), https://www.thecanadianencyclopedia. ca/en/article/indian-status.

42   Karrmen Crey & Erin Hanson, *Indian Status. What is Indian Status?*, First Nations & Indigenous Studies, University of British Columbia, https://indigenousfoundations.web. arts. ubc.ca/indian_status/ ("Initially, any Indians who obtained a university degree and/or became a professional such as a doctor or lawyer would automatically lose their status. The same process would occur for any Indian who served in the armed forces, or any status Indian woman who married a non-status man. When a woman was enfranchised, as with any enfranchised Indian, she was not provided with compensation or support, nor could she be guaranteed access to her community of origin since her band membership would have been removed as well. Essentially, she lost her Indian rights. Of course, once someone had lost their status, or was enfranchised, they were unable to pass along Indian status (and hence the associated rights) to their children, thus severing ties to their ancestry and community—their Indian ancestry was no longer legally recognized, and in

that ambiguities in treaties or statutes must be construed in favor of the Indian whose rights are affected by that statute.

As discussed above, the contemporary right of passage is recorded in a ratified treaty, but the aboriginal right itself is inherent, running to and from time immemorial. Thus, it predates the Peace of Paris and the 1794 Jay Treaty. As basis for *Yellowquill*, the BIA referenced and accepted an earlier court holding in *Akins v. Saxbe*,[43] which the BIA presented as the best judicial explanation of those rights of Canada-born Indians, in a case discussing those early treaty-based statements.[44] Although *Akins* was not directly an immigration case, it is illustrative to use for further clarification.

Akins is a 1974 federal district court decision from Maine, addressing border crossing and customs issues for a cross-boundary business operated by Penobscot Indians, some of whom lived on each side of the U.S.–Canada border, in a case requiring the court to construe the impact of the 1928 Immigration and Nationality Act (INA) on the free passage right. To figure out what the 1928 Congress would have understood this right to entail, the *Akins* court drew on pre-1928 court precedent that would have informed congressional knowledge, whether actual or constructive, in its passing of the immigration statute.[45] Central in this body of cases was the then-recent 1927 U.S. District Court decision out of Pennsylvania, *U.S. ex rel Diabo v. McCandless*.[46] The year before Congress acted (in passing he INA), *McCandless* had clearly explained the principle that the historic aboriginal right to move "unobstructed" was *recognized*, and not created by, the Jay treaty, in 1794.[47] Therefore, pursuant to this foundational aboriginal right, Canadian-born American Indians are not "aliens," subject to removability.[48]

---

many cases they were further separated from their communities physically, geographically, socially, spiritually, psychologically, and emotionally.").

43   380 F.Supp. 1210 (N.Dist. ME 1974).

44   *See Yellowquill* at 578 ("the Service [...] has stated it considers *Akins* correct").

45   A recurring theme in immigration litigation is discerning – and then applying – the generic meaning of undefined Congressional terms, which can be surmised by determining the prevailing generic understanding of the term at the time of usage by Congress. *See e.g. Esquivel-Quintana v. Sessions*, 137 S. Ct. 1562 (2017) (in a case contemplating the meaning of a term defining criminal deportability, explaining "[t]he everyday understanding of" the term used [...] "should count for a lot here, for the statutes in play do not define the term, and so remit us to regular usage to see what Congress probably meant," and proceeding to canvass the 50 states' criminal codes to determine prevailing norms).

46   18 F.2d 282 (E.Dist. PA 1927).

47   *Akins, supra*, at 1220, n.7.

48   *McCandless*, at 283.

In passing the 1928 INA, Congress was aware (literally or constructively) of *McCandless*, as it is referenced in the legislative history.[49] Congress did not intend to circumvent *McCandless*; rather, Congress' purpose was to recognize and secure the pre-existing right of free passage as it had been guaranteed in the treaty and delineated in *McCandless*, not determined by (or dependent upon) the present validity of the Jay Treaty.[50]

Thus, *Yellowquill, Akins, and McCandless* all reference the intrinsic aboriginal right – free passage - that flows as an inherent part of Indian existence, notwithstanding treaties or codification within statutes. The lesson in these cases is of indigenous supremacy in certain contexts, subject to statutory implementation. More practically speaking, Congress has codified the Canadian program, in which Canadian Indians of "pure enough" native bloodlines, but without ethnic or tribal ties to the United States, may nonetheless exercise fundamental rights to enter and remain in the United States.

Notwithstanding this long-established right, sometimes the United States government makes errors. A fairly recent example involved Fred Macdonald, whose mother was 100% Native Canadian of the native Squamish Nation, based in British Columbia.[51] MacDonald was also a registered member of the Nation. In 2009, the Department of Homeland Security detained MacDonald and initiated removal proceedings against him, based upon his convictions in San Diego, California, for possession of cocaine with intent to sell. Typically, nearly all controlled substance offenses, including MacDonald's, trigger deportability,[52] and all commercial drug offenses are considered "aggravated felonies"[53]

---

49   *See Akins*, at 1220–1221.

50   *See id.*

51   *MacDonald v. United States*, CASE NO. 11-cv-1088 - IEG (BLM) (S.D. Cal. Dec. 23, 2011).

52   *See* 8 U.S.C. § 1227(a)(2)(B)

      Any alien who at any time after admission has been convicted of a violation of (or a conspiracy or attempt to violate) any law or regulation of a state, the United States, or a foreign country relating to a controlled substance (as defined in section 802 of Title 21), *other than a single offense involving possession for one's own use of 30 grams or less of marijuana*, is deportable (emphasis added).

53   8 U.S.C. §§ 1101(a)(43)(B) (the term aggravated felony means [...] illicit trafficking in a controlled substance (as defined in section 802 of Title 21), including a drug trafficking crime (as defined in section 924(c) of Title 18); 1227(a)(2)(A) (Any alien who is convicted of an aggravated felony at any time after admission is deportable; *see, e.g., Lopez v. Gonzales*, 548 U.S. 47 (2006) (distinguishing commercial from non-commercial offenses as triggering "illicit trafficking" deportability, establishing that state offenses that match elements of a federal felony offense also trigger "drug trafficking crime" deportability); *Moncrieffe v. Holder*, 569 U.S. 184 (2013) (reiterating *Lopez'* holding that a state offense must necessarily match a federal felony to trigger "drug trafficking crime" deportability and that, in the case of a conviction under an ambiguous statute, the immigrant enjoys a presumption

that mandate removal by barring discretionary relief.[54] Compounding matters, either of these bases for deportation also triggered mandatory detention while MacDonald fought his case before the immigration court.[55] In a twist that should have been dispositive in MacDonald's proceedings, when DHS attorneys filed records to establish the basis for deportation, its own documentation established MacDonald's immigration status as a lawful permanent resident was premised upon being a "Canadian Born American Indian." Nonetheless, the U.S. government pursued and achieved MacDonald's deportation. Apparently, MacDonald acquiesced, knowing that fighting his case would result in months in detention, if not longer.[56] After eventually reentering the U.S. by reasserting his "right of passage," MacDonald sued the United States government for having detained and deported him, resulting in a year spent outside of the country in violation of his rights. MacDonald ultimately lost his monetary claim, under the stringent parameters for bringing suit against U.S. officials, but nonetheless he was entitled to resume his resident status.

Turning back to the subject of this essay, native *Americans* are obviously not part of this class of privileged Canadians.[57] They possess superior rights in the United States, relative to native Canadians, as they are, of course, U.S. citizens, not interfacing with the domestic immigration system at all. But who exactly

---

that their conviction rested upon the least culpable act criminalized); *Mellouli v. Lynch*, 135 S.Ct. 1980 (2015) (applying *Moncrieffe* to determination of the type of drug involved in a conviction, which must necessarily relate to a federally proscribed substance, enumerated under 21 U.S.C. § 802, to trigger immigration consequences).

54   *See* 8 U.S.C. § 1229b(a)(3) (barring the Attorney General's discretionary power to grant "cancellation of removal" to a deportable permanent resident if they have a conviction for an aggravated felony).

55   *See* 8 U.S.C. § 1226(c) (enumerating offenses, including controlled substance offenses and enumerated "aggravated felonies" that prohibit an immigration judge from considering a non-citizen's release on bond); *Demore v. Kim*, 538 U.S. 510 (2003) (upholding mandatory detention scheme as constitutional).

56   *See MacDonald*, at 3 ("He feared that if he did contest the charges, he would be held in custody for at least another 6 months, or even one to three years. Rather, in order to secure his release as quickly as possible, MacDonald decided not to contest the charges, with the intention to 'challenge the situation from the outside'").

57   For a discussion of complicated questions related to children of slaves and immigrants, touching on the related complex questions of native American citizenship in the nineteenth century, *see* Gabriel J. Chin & Paul Finkelman, *Birthright Citizenship, Slave Trade Legislation, and the Origins of Federal Immigration Regulation*, 54 U.C. Davis L. Rev. 2215 (2021) (discussing in part *Elk v. Wilkins*, 112 U.S. 94 (1884) (holding that an Indian born in the U.S. in tribal relations was not a birthright citizen) and providing examples of related questions including how "Indians not in a tribal relation could be birthright citizens," noting that "determinations of citizenship for Native American were often problematic and idiosyncratic").

is "Native American" is a question of cultural and political rights, subject to definition by each tribe.

5   Mashpee Wampanoag Recognition and Membership

The U.S. government finally granted federal recognition to the Mashpee (MA) Wampanoag tribe, in 2007, in findings "[p]repared in response to a petition submitted to the Associate Deputy Secretary for Federal Acknowledgment that this group does exist as an Indian tribe."[58] The Proposed Finding, approved by Associate Deputy Secretary of the Interior James Cason on March 31, 2006, affirmed key historic events, including the tribe's 1620 contact with Pilgrims (and ensuing epidemiological and political challenges in coexistence, King Philip's War of the early 1670's and resulting population decimation to about 100 survivors, per the report), summarized above.

The report also detailed that, beginning in 1788, official Massachusetts oversight of native land rights assured that native "proprietors" of land could only transfer to other Mashpee Wampanoags, ensuring a line of geographic tribal connection and succession. Finally, in 1870, Massachusetts gave the tribe and other natives state citizenship. For over the next century, until 1974, Mashpee Wampanoag held political control of the municipality of Mashpee, Massachusetts, town council, a feat enabled by the fact that tribal members comprised the majority of the town. However, the Mashpee Wampanoag could claim an even longer period of running continuous government, first through its period of governing the town of Mashpee, and then continued self-government through its tribal council, which continues to the present day.

This continuous governance gained heightened importance and scrutiny in 1975, when the tribe applied for federal recognition, through the Department of Interior. The tribe also launched Land Claim Litigation,[59] in which it lost under narrow construction of the statutory term "tribe" pursuant to Indian

---

58   *See* Department of the Interior, *Proposed Finding on the Mashpee Wampanoag Indian Tribal Council, Inc.* (March 31, 2006), https://www.bia.gov/sites/default/files/dup/assets /as-ia/ofa/petition/015_mashpe_MA/015_pf.pdf , a 186-page government report summarizing 20 years of application materials, including political, cultural and genealogical documentation.

59   *See e.g.* Department of Justice, *History of Land Claims Litigation*, https://www.justice.gov /enrd/history-indian-claims-litigation (summarizing the Department of Justice's role "in defending the United States and/or particular federal agencies against suits brought by Indian tribes or individual Indians. Suits seeking the award of money damages have been filed in the United States Court of Federal Claims (and its predecessor courts) seeking

Non-Intercourse Act(s), which dictate federal approval of sale of Indian lands passed to tribes pursuant to treaties. Unfortunately, under fluctuating historic standards, the Mashpee Wampanoag were not considered a "tribe" in 1790 or in three different assessments between 1869 and 1876, although they were considered as such when assessed in 1834 and 1842. Long story short, following decades of struggle, the tribe finally re-earned federal recognition in 2007.[60]

Membership in the tribe, as in all tribes, is subject to tribal law, which necessarily requires establishing parameters for asserting membership and transmitting the same through family lines.[61] In the case of the Mashpee Wampanoag, an applicant for recognized membership must prove: their "direct lineal descent"; that they have not publicly denounced or disavowed membership in the tribe; physical residence within 20 miles of Mashpee, Massachusetts for the prior 20 years, or similar presence of family members with involvement in community affairs; and a demonstrated community and cultural commitment, both by participation in certain public-facing events and continued contributions to the spiritual, traditional, and social well-being of the tribe.[62]

---

additional compensation for lands ceded to the United States by treaty or agreement; asserting mismanagement of tribal lands and/or natural resources").

60 *See* Mashpee Wampanoag Tribe, https://mashpeewampanoagtribe-nsn.gov ("The Mashpee Wampanoag Tribe, also known as the People of the First Light, has inhabited present day Massachusetts and Eastern Rhode Island for more than 12,000 years. After an arduous process lasting more than three decades, the Mashpee Wampanoag were re-acknowledged as a federally recognized tribe in 2007. In 2015, the federal government declared 150 acres of land in Mashpee and 170 acres of land in Taunton as the Tribe's initial reservation, on which the Tribe can exercise its full tribal sovereignty rights. The Mashpee tribe currently has approximately 2,600 enrolled citizens.").

61 *See Enrollment Department*, Mashpee Wampanoag Tribe, https://mashpeewampanoagtribe-nsn.gov/enrollment:

  The Mashpee Wampanoag Tribe is a living, functioning Tribal entity consisting of blood-related families that have existed on or near the same land since time immemorial. The continued existence of the Tribe has been based on those families living, interacting and surviving together against all odds while sharing a distinct traditional culture.

  To prove yourself a citizen of this Tribe it is expected that you and your family have and will continue to be involved in the social, political and cultural well-being of the Tribe.

  Throughout time there have been a number of changes in our circles of life, complicating our ability to live in or near Mashpee, however, there has been an expectation that some social, political and cultural connection has always been maintained.

62 *See* 2017-ORD-006, Enrollment Ordinance, Section 3 (Definitions), Section 4 (Enrollment Requirements).

  The reader may note that in a parallel context, the General Society of Mayflower Descendants pursues its goal of documenting and confirming living descendants of the original Pilgrams, via genealogically-confirmed history project. *See generally*

The element of "direct lineal descent" requires that the applicant prove, through genealogical records, that their forebears "were registered in the Report to the Governor and Council, concerning the Indians of the Commonwealth, Under the Act of April 16, 1859, written by John Milton Earle and published in 1861 by William White, Printer to the State, in Boston, Massachusetts (the Earle Report)."[63] The Earle Report served as a census and assessment of numerous aspects of Native American life in Massachusetts in 1859 and reported some 370 members of the Mashpee Wampanoag among nearly 1,650 total Native Americans identified.[64] The Report further acknowledged that many Wampanoag were likely lost to the non-Massachusetts diaspora and were therefore uncounted. It further explained that the then-current count inevitably had undergone significant genealogical evolution, via multi-cultural inter-marriage, from the populations that lived locally at the times of colonization.[65] While nearly certainly true, the commentary can hardly be divorced from the condescending and racist tone of the larger document, which ultimately found the Massachusetts native population unworthy of citizenship.[66]

---

https://themayflowersociety.org; *see also* A. Farmer, *Persistence in the Genes: Connecting the Dots to the Mayflower*, New York Times (November 27, 2013) ("The society has actually relaxed its standards, no longer requiring applicants to submit character references from two current members. It still demands an exhaustive trove of primary documents that can include deeds, wills and birth, death and marriage certificates, as well as census data. The society has fairly conclusively mapped out the first five generations of Mayflower descendants, helping to speed the process. But as many as 10 more generations can separate a current applicant from a presumed Mayflower ancestor.").

63   *See Enrollment Ordinance,* at Section 3(c).

64   Note: totals tallied made by the author, via review of the Earle Report census, which itself attributes racial identities of "white," "African," "colored," and "unknown" to several included persons, not included in the author's total of 370.

65   *See* J. Earle, *Report to the Governor and Council, Concerning the Indians of the Commonwealth, Under the Act of April 16, 1859* (1861) ("Earle Report"), at 9–10 ("When it is considered that the intermixture, both with the whites and the blacks, commenced more than two hundred years ago, and than, in the course of ten or twelve generations, there has been an opportunity, from intermarriages among themselves, for the foreign blood early introduced to permeate the whole mass, and when it is considered, that the intermixture has been constantly kept up, from the outside, also, down to the present time, it would be a marvel indeed, if any Indian of the pure native race remained.").

66   *Id.* at 12. Embedded in the text describing the subjects' repugnance and poverty, Earle speculates: "perhaps some Moses may yet arise among these, who will prepare the minds of the people, and lead the way to their social emancipation."

      Modern anthropologists studying one of the three modern Wampanoag tribes, the Seaconke (which is presently recognized at the state, not federal level) describe the genealogical question more artfully. *See* Sergey I. Zhadanov, Matthew C. Dulik, Michael Markley, George W. Jennings, Jill B. Gaieski, George Elias, Theodore G. Schurr & The

6   The Diaspora: Wampanoag in Bermuda

Starting in 1619, the historical record is clear regarding the enslavement of Native Americans, within Bermuda, where they were forced into servitude for purposes of agriculture and Bermuda's primary commerce: international ship-ping and seafaring. Scholars and researchers have combed historic files and observed that Bermuda records note 347 commercial transactions involving the exchange of black and Indian slaves.[67] Determining the exact Native American population at any historic moment is complicated by inconsistencies in demo-graphic acknowledgement. Indians and "mulattoes" were reported individually in deeds, court records, and probate inventories, but island-wide censuses made only white and Negro designations; thus, figures given for Bermuda's black pop-ulation included a variety of interracial and multiethnic offspring.[68]

The 500-acre St. David's Island is historically the primary center of Indian-Bermudians. Descendants of American Indians were relatively isolated on

---

Genographic Project Consortium, *Genetic Heritage and Native Identity of the Seaconke Wampanoag Tribe of Massachusetts*, 142 Am. J. Physical Anthropology 579–589 (August 2010):

> Because of repeated epidemics and conflicts with English colonists, including King Philip's War of 1675–76, and subsequent colonial laws forbidding tribal identification, the Wampanoag population was largely decimated, decreasing in size from as many as 12,000 individuals in the 16th century to less than 400, as recorded in 1677. To investigate the influence of the historical past on its biological ancestry and native cultural identity, we analyzed genetic variation in the Seaconke Wampanoag tribe. Our results indicate that the majority of their mtDNA haplotypes belongs to West Eurasian and African lineages, thus reflecting the extent of their contacts and interactions with people of European and African descent. On the paternal side, Y-chromosome analysis identified a range of Native American, West Eurasian, and African haplogroups in the population, and also surpris-ingly revealed the presence of a paternal lineage that appears at its highest frequencies in New Guinea and Melanesia. Comparison of the genetic data with genealogical and histor-ical information allows us to reconstruct the tribal history of the Seaconke Wampanoag back to at least the early 18th century.

67   Michael J. Jarvis, *Maritime Masters and Seafaring Slaves in Bermuda, 1680–1783*,The William and Mary Quarterly Vol. 59, No. 3, Slaveries in the Atlantic World, at 585–622 (2002).

68   *See id.* Popular anthropology of Bermuda also accounts for the continued presence of the Native American descendants of the early slaves: The population of Bermuda is 62,997 (2000 estimate). Blacks have been in the majority since some point in the late eighteenth century, and now comprise between 60 and 70 percent of Bermudians. The majority of the remaining ethnic components are northern European, mainly British; they are fol-lowed by Portuguese, who are mainly of Azorean origin, and the descendants of a number of Native American tribes.

> *See Bermuda*, Countries and their Cultures, (Forum, Culture of Bermuda) http://www .everyculture.com/A-Bo/Bermuda.html#ixzz2GGaMT1xR.

Saint David's, both during and subsequent to the slavery era, lumped together and labeled with a common "Mohawk" pejorative misnomer by non-Indians. The isolation had both a geographic and social division between "blacks" and whites which began soon after the colony was established, through the slaves imported to serve the needs of the colonists. Descendants of the original white settlers established a system of racial segregation in both government and social life that they perpetuated for over two centuries.[69]

As local historian Jean Foggo Simon (himself lineally a member of the Fox family tree of Wampanoag), discovered in his recent familial research, conducted from the contemporary perspective of a Bermudan:

> Nowhere did I find the word "Mohawk" associated with the St. David's [Parish, Bermuda] Islanders in the documents. I began to investigate further.
>
> Many books had been written over the centuries about the capture of Native Americans from along the coast of Massachusetts and Connecticut. There were lists of Natives being sold and shipped into slavery, some to Bermuda and some to other parts of the world. It was the record about King Philip's War and after his death the Massachusetts authorities had dispatched to Bermuda some 40–50 of their most able-bodied young warriors. That shipment of slaves, some say, also included King Philip's wife and young son.
>
> I then discovered that one of my ancestors was "a native Bermudian of strongly marked Indian features; reputed to be of Indian descent, and probably descending from one of the Pequot captives." He died in 1875 at the age of 84 years. His name was Jacob Minors. Jacob married Ruth Fox, a half Irish/half Native woman.
>
> For decades, the only family names in our St. David's native families were: Minors, Fox, Foggo, Pitcher, Lamb, Burchall and Millett. Descendants of families who arrived to colonize the island and whose names were listed on a 1716 list are still prevalent today: Cox, Higgs, Burchall, Fox, Hayward, Gibbons, Tucker, Watlington, Hall, Dill, Wingood, Packwood, Outerbridge, etc.[70]

Thus, it is common for a Bermudian of Native American descent to be able to trace their genealogy to 1716, if not further.

---

69   *Id.*
70   Jean Foggo Simon, *St. David's Indian Committee, St David's, Bermuda*, http://www.rootsweb .ancestry.com/ ~bmuwgw/stdavidislanders.htm.

In his definitive history of St. David's Island, the Wampanoag-Bermudian police official turned cultural historian St. Clair "Brinky" Tucker records the facts and folklore of the region. Through his work on the Bermuda Human Rights Commission and Heritage Month Committee of Bermuda, he was central to 2002 and 2003 festivals, engaged jointly with the Mashpee Wampanoag tribe and the St. David's Island Reconnection Indian Committee, in which the Massachusetts tribe celebrated with its Bermudian counterparts. With access to various archives and libraries in Bermuda, Tucker has compiled the historic record regarding "Indian slavery, especially as it relates to St. David's Islanders, including how they were treated *en route* [to Bermuda]; what tribes they were members of; the trading port in Bermuda at which they arrived; what work they performed; how they died; how and where they were buried; how they conducted themselves on Emancipation Day and after; interracial marriages [the first of which was recorded in 1622]; education; executions;" and other matters.[71] Tucker accounts for Native American slave populations primarily from the Wampanoag and Pequot tribes, but with additional slaves identified as Narragansett, Mohegan, and Cherokee.

Mr. Tucker documented a Native American population in Bermuda of 400 to 500 by the early 1700's, against a total population of about 6,000. At the time, St. David's population was over 46% Native American.[72] Dwarfed, relatively speaking, by Bermuda's Main Island, St. David's – totaling just 503 acres – was relatively isolated for its first 300 years, until it was finally connected to the mainland by the Severn Bridge in the 1930's.[73]

The reader can easily deduce that this was not even four generations ago.

7   Convergence: the Bermuda Paradox

1616   Slavery begins in Bermuda.
1675   Wampanoag tribe suffers massive defeat in King Philip's War, many
       survivors sold into slavery in Bermuda.
1776   Americans declare independence from Britain.
1834   Slavery ends in Bermuda.

---

71   St. Clair "Brinky" Tucker, St. David's Island, Bermuda, Its People, History, and Culture 1
     (2009).
72   *See id.* at 7.
73   In telling discriminatory urban planning, this hub of minority population was made the
     site of a U.S. military base in the 1940's and now houses Bermuda's L.F. Wade International
     airport on its east end.

1859 Earle Report delineates recognized members of Massachusetts Tribes, only descendants of those listed in this census may be considered part of tribes.

1863 Slavery ends in United States.

1924 Indian Citizenship Act (Snyder Act).

1965 Voting Rights Act.

2007 Federal recognition of Mashpee Wampanoag.

8 Limitations of Tribal Law

As discussed above, Indian governments within the United States are free to devise their own methodology for determining membership in each tribe. This is a hotly contested issue in some tribal communities and for some, the genealogical requirement can trigger an existential crisis.[74] A check on this power is the related power, by the Department of the Interior, to deny tribal recognition to groups that lack the requisite geographic, ethnographic/genealogical and cultural continuity that distinguish the tribes given federal designation.[75] For the Mashpee Wampanoag, population continuity is relatively less of a concern, as tribal membership may pass through either a mother or a natural father.[76] In comparison, the Aquinnah Wampanoag tribe of Martha's Vineyard has a matrilineal system for tribal transmission. Neither has a minimum blood quantum threshold for retaining and transmitting membership.

---

74 *"One of our Elders who addressed our Tribal Council concerning wording in our constitution defining who could be a member and who couldn't. He said, 'When are our grandchildren no longer our grandchildren?' and left."* Warren Petoskey, *Less than blood quantum*, www .nativenewsnetwork.com, April 24, 2012 (referencing a citizenship debate within the Little Bay Bands of Odawa Indians, Harbor Springs, Michigan).

75 *See Proposed Finding on the Mashpee Wampanoag Indian Tribal Council, Inc., supra* note 58:
   The acknowledgment regulations under 25 CFR Part 83 establish the procedures by which non-recognized groups may seek Federal acknowledgment as Indian tribes with government-to-government relationships with the United States. To be entitled to such a political relationship with the United States, the petitioner must submit documentary evidence that the group meets all seven mandatory criteria set forth in section 83.7 of the regulations. Failure to meet anyone of the mandatory criteria will result in a determination the group is not an Indian tribe within the meaning of Federal law. The Office of Federal Acknowledgment (OFA) within the Office of the AS-IA has responsibility for petition review and analysis.

76 *See* 2017-ORD-006, Enrollment Ordinance, Section 3 (Definitions), Section 7 (Determining Paternity to Establish Constitutional Requirement of Direct Lineal Descent) (requiring genetic testing only in circumstances of uncertain paternity).

Indian blood quantum laws are outlying race-based distinctions in American law, which are generally frowned upon. For example, the Iowa Supreme Court recently reviewed state legislation that defined Indians solely by ancestry, with no requirement of tribal membership, under strict scrutiny, and struck a provision in the state's version of the Indian Child Welfare Act as an impermissible racial classification.[77]

In contrast, it bears addressing that the blood quantum restriction on Native Canadians' right of free passage is a rare example of an explicitly racial distinction in legislation, which the federal courts may review to determine whether it violates equal protection principles under a strict scrutiny analysis. The Supreme Court has gravitated toward considering Indian status as a "political," rather than "racial" distinction, which would seem to come into direct conflict with a "blood quantum" requirement in a statute.[78] It bears further noting that U.S. immigration policy has withdrawn from other former racial (and racist) distinctions, including Asian discrimination, and loss of citizenship via marriage to non-citizens.

The Native Canadian free passage distinction based on blood quantum is further anomalous within both immigration and Indian Law. U.S. tribes are free to make their own distinct membership schemes (which may or not have strict blood quantum requirements). Canada itself does not follow a "blood quantum" scheme for determining Indian-ness and, in fact, invoked a broader definition of Indian in its 1982 constitution, relying upon an undefined and general concept of "aboriginal peoples of Canada."[79]

Native American tribes are political entities with extensive powers of self-government. For thousands of years, American Indians and Alaska Natives governed themselves through tribal laws, cultural traditions, religious customs, and kinship systems, such as clans and societies.[80] Through their tribal governments, tribal members generally define conditions of membership, regulate domestic relations of members, prescribe rules of inheritance for reservation property not in trust status, levy taxes, regulate property under tribal jurisdiction, control the conduct of members by tribal ordinances, and administer justice.[81] They also continue to utilize their traditional systems of

---

77   *See In re A.W.*, 741 N.W. 2d 793 (Iowa 2007).

78   *See generally Morton v. Mancari*, 417 U.S. 535 (1974); P. Spruhan, *The Canadian Indian Free Passage Right: The Last Stronghold of Explicit Race Restriction in United States Immigration Law*, 85 N. Dak. L. Rev. 301 (2009).

79   *See* Spruhan, at 327.

80   *See Frequently Asked Questions*, Bureau of Indian Affairs, Dep't of the Interior, http://www.bia.gov/FAQs/index.htm.

81   *See id.*

self-government whenever and wherever possible.[82] Additionally, according to the U.S. Department of Justice, Office of Tribal Justice:

> As a general principle, an Indian is a person who is of some degree Indian blood and is recognized as an Indian by a Tribe and/or the United States. No single federal or tribal criterion establishes a person's identity as an Indian. Government agencies use differing criteria to determine eligibility for programs and services. Tribes also have varying eligibility criteria for membership.
>
> It is important to distinguish between the ethnological term "Indian" and the political/legal term "Indian." The protections and services provided by the United States for tribal members flow not from an individual's status as an American Indian in an ethnological sense, but because the person is a member of a Tribe recognized by the United States and with which the United States has a special trust relationship.[83]

9   Outcomes

It is not this author's privilege to say what the Bermudian Wampanoag descendants "deserve" or what they should want, out of their situation. There is something remarkable about the richness of their modern circumstances, to the extent that the group owns and celebrates their identity and their ancestral past, overcoming time and distance to preserve their culture and their Native American origins. And, of course, there is the fact that they live *in Bermuda*. As Wampanoag-Bermudian historian Brinky Tucker remarked in an interview, "it is a beautiful country, the quality of life is excellent, and the average Bermudian lives comfortably."

In some of the author's email correspondence while working on this article, contacts wondered if the "lawyer" interest in this story might be one of generating some self-interested conflict, perhaps via litigation or profiting from outlining the story. Nothing could be further from the truth. However, plagued by a sense of nagging injustice, I do think there is a bit of potential prescriptive thinking, if the actors wished to engage in self-advocacy. The "what if?" aspect of the story is interesting.

---

82   *See id.*
83   Frequently Asked Questions, Office of Tribal Justice, U.S. Department of Justice, http://www.justice.gov/otj/nafaqs.htm.

Reckonings are difficult, as evidenced by the United States' halting efforts to deal with modern impacts of historic slavery and destruction of Native American culture, which as recently as August 2022 has drawn critical attention by the United Nations, explicitly suggesting that the Unites States consider modern realities through the informed lens of its discriminatory past.[84] Recent political discourse and resulting academic censorship reveals that many within the United States prefer to ignore our history, much less grapple with it and mitigate its modern manifestations, so tangible steps may be unlikely. Nonetheless, I think it is important to acknowledge historic realities. What we subsequently do about those realities is a political question, I suppose. But it is fair and important to ask, "what rights *should* the displaced Wampanoag – and other Native Americans similarly situated – possess"? And whatever that answer is, how should we feel about it?

Mr. Brinky Tucker, the historian, has hopes for an adequate museum in Bermuda, complete with the research library and archival genealogical data dating back centuries, so that at a minimum the history is not lost, but is preserved and elevated. The United States could easily contemplate the same, or at least make a formal federal acknowledgment of the shared history and celebrate it.

On the legal front, though, how is it that a Native American population, sold internationally (primarily) in the 1670's is no longer "native"? What should we make of the historical fact that the Wampanoag survivors of King Phillip's War were sold to Bermuda *a century* before the American Revolution, and *nearly two centuries* before the Massachusetts 1861 Earle Report set the legal parameters of the modern recognized tribe? What about those grandiose acknowledgements of inherent rights of indigenous persons, in the Jay Treaty and the Treaty of Ghent? Should Native American descendants with demonstrable

---

84 United Nations Committee on the Elimination of Racial Discrimination, *Concluding observations on the combined tenth to twelfth reports of the United States of America*, CERD/C/USA/CO/10–12 (August 30, 2022) recommending that the United States:
   a. Adopt all necessary measures to ensure that human rights education, including on the fight against racism and racial discrimination Indigenous Peoples' history, culture and languages, as well as on respect for diversity and the promotion of equal treatment, is part of the curriculum at all school levels;
   b. Take further measures to ensure that the history of colonialism and slavery and their legacies is part of the school curriculum at all levels, including by adopting federal national standards or guidelines in this regard;
   c. Undertake additional efforts to effectively protect teachers and school personnel from harassment, threats, intimidation and violence in this context.

genealogies be afforded, at minimum, a right of passage and protections from removal similar to those discussed in *Yellowquill* and *MacDonald*?

This would seem the time to consider any action, or at least more deeply memorialize the legal situation, as attempted in these pages. Certainly, no freed Bermudian Native American would have brought any claim of "belonging" prior to the U.S.'s emancipation of slaves, or the 1924 Indian Citizenship Act. A disenfranchised person of color would further hardly be likely to make any race-based claim prior to the Civil Rights Act. Separately, a Wampanoag descendant would face specific legal impossibilities prior to the federal recognition of the tribe, which happened a mere fifteen years ago, in 2007. But what about now, if they demanded rights that were not inferior to those of Native Canadians, or, at minimum, claimed rights less arbitrarily denied than by being excluded from an 1861 Massachusetts census?

As an initial matter, if there was to be a legal remedy of injustice, we need not be overwhelmed by "floodgates" concerns that plague a lot of cases involving reopening old cases (and wounds).[85] Classic examples as disparate as the post-*Gideon v. Wainwright* criminal justice environment (in which right to counsel was assured, and tens of thousands of pre-*Gideon* state convictions made in violation of the right to counsel were subject to being revisited) and the Mariel boatlift (120,000–125,000 Cubans arriving in Miami, between May and September, 1980),[86] show that even in the case of seismic social occurrences, legal and social economies simply expand to meet the new realities, without undermining the effective functioning of the prior system.

Further, in contrast to other immigration policies, the scale of any tangible remedy for the Wampanoag-Bermudians would be negligible compared to historic immigration "amnesties," visa programs, and temporary or discretionary programs created to resolve inequities or historic injustices or policy objectives. A few examples illustrate this: despite its overwhelming

---

85   *See, e.g., Chaidez v. United States*, 568 U.S. 342 (2013) (in the immigration context, the Supreme Court declining to apply retroactively the right to effective representation announced in *Padilla v. Kentucky, Padilla v. Kentucky*, 559 U.S. 356 (2010), for immigrant defendants to be informed of the immigration consequences of a criminal proceeding, joining states which used their own retroactivity jurisprudence – and floodgates concerns – to nearly universally conclude the same).

86   David Card, *The Impact of the Mariel Boatlift on the Miami Labor Market*, Industrial & Labor Relations Rev., Vol. 43, No. 2, (Jan. 1990), http://links.jstor.org/sici?sici=0019-7939%28199001%2943%3A2%3C245%3ATIOTMB%3E2.0.CO%3B2-Z (explaining that all levels of the labor market were effectively unimpacted by the influx, countering assumption that domestic unskilled labor, particularly of Black Miamians, must have been negatively impacted by the sudden infusion of Cuban labor).

inadequacies, the nascent U.S. refugee program admitted 27,000 Germans in 1940;[87] in 2021, President Biden set a target of 125,000 refugee admissions for fiscal year 2022,[88] a decision made months prior to the Russian invasion of Ukraine, which resulted in a temporary program to protect an additional 100,000 Ukrainians via "parole," for a two-year period;[89] in 1998, in recognition of decades of discriminatory policies against Haitians,[90] Congress passed the Haitian Refugee and Immigration Fairness Act (HRIFA), triggering over 40,000 applications by 2006;[91] curing similar problems for cases largely originating in Central America, Congress produced the Nicaraguan Adjustment and Central American Relief Act (NACARA), providing resident status to a huge swath of

---

87   *How Many Refugees Came to the United States from 1933–1945?*, Americans and the Holocaust, United States Holocaust Memorial Museum, https://exhibitions.ushmm. org/americans-and-the-holocaust/how-many-refugees-came-to-the-united-states -from-1933–1945.

88   *See Memorandum for the Secretary of State on Presidential Determination on Refugee Admissions for Fiscal Year 2022* (October 8, 2021), https://www.whitehouse.gov/briefing-room /statements-releases/2021/10/08/memorandum-for-the-secretary-of-state-on-presidential -determination-on-refugee-admissions-for-fiscal-year-2022/.

89   *See Uniting for Ukraine*, United States Citizenship and Immigration Services (September 29, 2022), https://www.uscis.gov/ukraine ("As a result of the Russian military's unprovoked full-scale invasion of Ukraine and ongoing aggression, millions of Ukrainians have been forced to flee their homes. The Biden-Harris Administration remains committed to welcoming 100,000 Ukrainians and others fleeing Russia's aggression. To meet this commitment, the Administration intends to utilize the full range of legal pathways to the United States, including new processes such as *Uniting for Ukraine* and existing opportunities such as immigrant and nonimmigrant visas, and refugee resettlement processing."). Notably, as "parolees," Ukrainians with certain qualifying family and professional relationships will be able to apply for lawful permanent resident status, pursuant to Immigration and Nationality Act § 245(a).

90   *See Haitian Refugee and Immigration Fairness Act*, The Immigration and Ethnic History Society.https://immigrationhistory.org/item/haitian-refugee-immigrant-fairness-act/,2019 ("HRIFA acknowledged the legitimacy of the Haitian refugee crisis by allowing some Haitians to regularize their status. Steady influxes of Haitian "boat people" began arriving in December 1972, in flight from the brutal Duvalier dictatorship. Because Duvalier was an anti-communist ally that the United States did not want to offend, the U.S. government categorized the overwhelmingly poor and black migrants as economic migrants and not as refugees, making them ineligible to receive asylum and remain in the United States. To deter future asylum seekers from Haiti, the government placed the Haitians in detention centers, jails, and prisons. Treatment of Haitians contrasted sharply with that meted out to their neighboring Cubans, who as opponents of the communist Castro government receive the greatest consideration to gain admission as refugees.").

91   *See Immigration Benefits: Fifteenth Report Required by the Haitian Refugee Immigration Fairness Act of 1998*, GAO-07-168R (November 9, 2006), https://www.govinfo.gov/content /pkg/GAOREPORTS-GAO-07-168R/html/GAOREPORTS-GAO-07-168R.htm.

the undocumented population, including some 150,000 Nicaraguans, 5,000 Cubans, 200,000 Salvadorans and 50,000 Guatemalans;[92] in order to increase the worldwide availability of visas, Congress created a diversity lottery that awards 50,000 visas annually to applicants from countries underrepresented in recent immigration;[93] and the well-publicized temporary protection from removability awarded to immigrants brought to (and/or remaining in) the U.S. without status since they were children, Deferred Action for Childhood Arrivals (DACA) includes some 741,000 participants.[94] Dwarfing all of these programs, the 1986 Reagan-era Immigration Reform and Control Act contained an amnesty, through which an approximate 2.7 million undocumented persons acquired lawful permanent residence.[95]

In contrast, Bermuda's *total* population is about 65,000.

10   **The Client, Revisited**

Faced with the prospect of lengthy detention by the Department of Homeland Security, L---- and I had a difficult conversation. He was going to be deported.

Despite sharing common ancestors in a family tree that forked in 1676, with his ancestors being sold to Bermuda, and with the remaining 1676 tribe members' lineages, eight to ten generations later, eventually being registered in the 1861 Earle Report, L---- could not possibly be a member of the Mashpee Wampanoag tribe. Regardless of the St. David's Island anomaly – the isolation of a fixed, largely Native American population for 300 years, that was

---

92   *The Nicaraguan Adjustment and Central American Relief Act: Hardship Relief and Long-Term Illegal Aliens*, Congressional Research Service (July 15, 1998), https://www.everycrsreport .com/files/19980715_98-3_08ea932ffbb5b70b21888bb84863bfba90bfba25.pdf.

93   INA 203(c).

94   United States Citizenship and Immigration Services, *Approximate Active DACA Recipients: As of March 31, 2020*, https://www.uscis.gov/sites/default/files/document/data/Approximate %20Active%20DACA%20Receipts%20-%20March%2031%2C%202020.pdf.

95   Nancy Rytina, *IRCA Legalization Effects: Lawful Permanent Residence and Naturaliza-tion through 2001, Office of Policy and Planning Statistics Division*, U.S. Immigration and Naturalization Service, https://www.dhs.gov/sites/default/files/publications/IRCA _Legalization_Effects_2002.pdf:

[T]hree million persons applied for legalization. The applicants represented most legalization eligible aliens given an estimated illegal immigrant population of 3–5 million in 1986 (Hoefer, 1991). The approval rates for temporary and permanent residence were fairly high among both legalization (pre-1982 applicants) and SAW applicants. Nearly 2.7 million persons – nearly nine in ten applicants for temporary residence – were ultimately approved for permanent residence.[...]

By 2001, one-third of IRCA LPRs had naturalized.

perhaps genealogically comparable (or at least somewhat parallel) to the 1861 Massachusetts population – he certainly wasn't descended from an 1861 Earle Report Wampanoag enrollee, and definitely had never lived in the vicinity of Mashpee, Massachusetts.

Had he been a native Canadian, his blood quantum would have been relevant, because if he had been a recognized member of a Canadian tribe with 50% or higher native blood, he might exercise his right of passage to remain in the United States.

Thus, the curious and unsettling irony: a demonstrable claim of being Native American really did not help at all.

Acknowledgments

The author would like to thank Mr. St. Clair "Brinky" Tucker for his writings and generous sharing of his text and thoughts on the history of Native Americans in Bermuda. Further thanks go to the clients and colleagues – and a judge – with whom the shared experience of litigating a case presenting the paradox of deportable Native Americans served to reveal and shape this author's thoughts and curiosity. Finally, this work was helped along by the thoughtful encouragement of participants at an "incubator session" at the 2014 ImmProf conference, and was subsequently generously supported by a research stipend provided by St. Thomas University College of Law.

CHAPTER 20

Protecting Women and Children under Egyptian Family Law: A Journey of Increasing Rights

Ahmed Mohamed El Demery*

First and foremost, thanks to God for everything. Through this article, I express my deep and sincere gratitude to Professor Siegfried Wiessner, who gave me the exceptional opportunity to do my J.S.D. and LL.M. degrees at St. Thomas University. His dynamism, vision, sincerity and motivation have deeply inspired me, and I consider it a great privilege and honor to have worked and studied under his guidance. His gracious hospitality, generosity and humility are unmatched. He picked me up from the airport the first time I arrived to Miami to join the LL.M. program, and he welcomed and accompanied us, students, with kindness and empathy throughout our academic journey. I thank him heartily for sharing his immense knowledge, for the support, sincerity, patience and encouragement to pursue graduate studies not to make money, but rather to be passionate about law, human rights, and make a difference for the good in the world. Professor Wiessner is as much an ideal model of how a professor should be as he is an eminent scholar in the field of international law and jurisprudence. He generously offered his time and his wisdom in guiding me through the doctoral dissertation process, in offering insightful comments, and he brought out the best in me.

1   Introduction

Equality between men and women is one of the fundamental international principles of human rights; it is to be found in all human rights treaties and instruments. For example, it is implied in Article 1 of the Universal Declaration of Human Rights when it states that "All human beings are born free and equal in dignity and rights."[1] The International Covenant on Civil and Political Rights

---

*   Vice President Judge at Egyptian Court of Appeal, currently seconded to the Department of International and Cultural Cooperation at the Ministry of Justice in Egypt.
1   Universal Declaration of Human Rights, G.A. Res. 217A, art. 15, U.N. GAOR, 3d Sess., 1st plen. mtg., U.N. Doc. A/810 (Dec. 10, 1948).

© AHMED MOHAMED EL DEMERY, 2023 | DOI:10.1163/9789004524835_021

expressly states that, "The States Parties to the present Covenant undertake to ensure the equal right of men and women to the enjoyment of all civil and political rights set forth in the present Covenant."[2] The International Covenant on Economic, Social and Cultural Rights sets forth that "The States Parties to the present Covenant undertake to ensure the equal right of men and women to the enjoyment of all economic, social and cultural rights set forth in the present Covenant."[3]

The Arab Charter on Human Rights, which is inspired by Sharia law, provides that:

1. Each State party to the present Charter undertakes to ensure to all individuals subject to its jurisdiction the right to enjoy the rights and freedoms set forth herein, without distinction on grounds of race, colour, sex, language, religious belief, opinion, thought, national or social origin, wealth, birth or physical or mental disability.

2. The States parties to the present Charter shall take the requisite measures to guarantee effective equality in the enjoyment of all the rights and freedoms enshrined in the present Charter in order to ensure protection against all forms of discrimination based on any of the grounds mentioned in the preceding paragraph.

3. Men and women are equal in respect of human dignity, rights and obligations within the framework of the *positive discrimination established in favour of women* by the Islamic Shariah, other divine laws and by applicable laws and legal instruments. Accordingly, each State party pledges to take all the requisite measures to guarantee equal opportunities and effective equality between men and women in the enjoyment of all the rights set out in this Charter.[4] [emphasis added]

This provision of the Arab Charter on Human Rights directly qualifies the idea of "equality between men and women" with the idea of "positive discrimination." The Arab Charter explains that, "All persons are equal before the courts and tribunals. The States parties shall guarantee the independence of the judiciary and protect magistrates against any interference, pressure or threats.

---

2   International Covenant on Civil and Political Rights, Dec. 16, 1966, 999 U.N. T.S. 171, at art. 3.
3   International Covenant on Economic, Social and Cultural Rights, Dec. 16, 1966, 993 U.N.T.S. 3, at art. 3.
4   Arab Charter on Human Rights, (*entered into force* March 15, 2008), at art. 3, https://digitallibrary .un.org/record/551368?ln=en.

They shall also guarantee every person subject to their jurisdiction the right to seek a legal remedy before courts of all levels."[5]

In ancient Egypt, the societal position of a woman was determined by the position of her father, brother, or husband. It did not matter whether she was educated or not as women did not play any significant role in society at that time. Women and children have taken revolutionary steps forward in an effort to strengthen all of their rights in Egypt. The successes achieved would not have been accomplished without the support and ongoing strategy of the Egyptian governments throughout the past decades. For example, the law was amended by raising the age of maturity of a child to be 18 years in compliance with Article 1 of the Convention on the Rights of the Child. The Egyptian Constitution states that "A child is considered to be anyone who has not reached 18 years of age."[6] In addition, the law was amended to raise the minimum age of marriage to 18 years in order to comply with the international standard of the legal minimum age of marriage. The Concluding Observations of the Committee on the Elimination of Discrimination against Women in its report on Egypt state that "The Committee also welcomes the adoption of the new child law (Law No. 126 of 2008), which raises the age of marriage from 16 to 18 years for both males and females and criminalizes female genital mutilation."[7] The Egyptian law was amended to allow Egyptian women to have their full human rights of transferring their nationality to their children. The Egyptian Constitution states that, "Citizenship is a right to anyone born to an Egyptian father or an Egyptian mother."[8] Egypt withdrew its reservation regarding Article 9 of the Convention on the Elimination of All Forms of Discrimination against Women, which states that "States Parties shall grant women equal rights with men with respect to the nationality of their children." The Concluding Observations of the Committee on the Elimination of Discrimination against Women states in its report on Egypt that "The Committee commends the State party for its withdrawal of its reservation to article 9, paragraph 2, of the Convention. The Committee notes that the nationality law has been amended under Law No. 154 of 2004, which grants gender equality regarding the transfer of Egyptian

---

5   *Id.* at art. 12

6   Article 80 of the Egyptian Constitution of 2014 with Amendments through 2019 https://www .constituteproject.org/constitution/Egypt_2019.pdf?lang=en.

7   Concluding Observations of the Committee on the Elimination of Discrimination against Women, CEDAW/C/EGY/CO/7, https://www2.ohchr.org/english/bodies/cedaw/docs/co / CEDAW-C-EGY-CO-7.pdf (last visited Dec. 18, 2022).

8   Article 6 of the Egyptian Constitution.

nationality to the children of a man or a woman who marries a foreigner."[9] On the other hand, in order to protect the bonds of the family, several laws aggravated the punishment if the victims are women and children. This includes Law No. 1 for 2018 on Combating Human Trafficking and Law No. 82 for 2016 on Combating Illegal Migration and the Smuggling of Migrants.

In Egypt, there is more than one law regarding family or personal status matters since the laws differ according to the person's religion. For example, if the spouses are Muslims, then the Egyptian family law for Muslims applies. On the other hand, if the spouses are Coptic Orthodox Christians, then the Egyptian family law for Coptic Orthodox Christians would apply.[10] Therefore, it is necessary to establish the religion of the parties in order to apply the appropriate Egyptian family law.

The diversity of applicable laws is due to the fact that The Egyptian Constitution states, "The principles of the laws of Egyptian Christians and Jews are the main source of laws regulating their personal status, religious affairs, and selection of spiritual leaders."[11]

Egypt has taken great strides toward the protection of general human rights, and specifically women's and children's rights. The Constitution of the Arab Republic of Egypt, which was adopted in 2014, declares that Egypt is an Arab Republic with a democratic system.[12] Article 53 of the Egyptian Constitution states:

> All citizens are equal before the Law. They are equal in rights, freedoms and general duties, without discrimination based on religion, belief, sex, origin, race, color, language, disability, social class, political or geographic affiliation or any other reason. Discrimination and incitement of hatred is a crime punished by Law. The State shall take necessary measures for eliminating all forms of discrimination, and the Law shall regulate creating an independent commission for this purpose.[13]

Egypt also has a very strong independent legislative and judicial system. "The House of Representatives is entrusted with legislative authority and with approving the general policy of the state, the general plan of economic and

---

9   Concluding Observations of the Committee on the Elimination of Discrimination against Women, *supra* note 7.
10 The Family Law of Copts Orthodox, 1938.
11 Article 3 of the Egyptian Constitution.
12 *Id.* at article 1.
13 *Id.* at article 53.

social development and the state budget. ...."[14] The judicial authority in Egypt is exercised through several courts: the Supreme Constitutional Court, the Court of Cassation, the seven courts of appeal in the various Governorates, and the Summary Tribunals in the districts.

The Egyptian Constitution safeguards the protection of women, motherhood, childhood, and combat discrimination against women. Article 11 states:

> The state commits to achieving equality between women and men in all civil, political, economic, social, and cultural rights in accordance with the provisions of this Constitution. The state commits to taking the necessary measures to ensure appropriate representation of women in the houses of parliament, in the manner specified by law. It grants women the right to hold public posts and high management posts in the state, and to appointment in judicial bodies and entities without discrimination. The state commits to the protection of women against all forms of violence, and ensures women empowerment to reconcile the duties of a woman toward her family and her work requirements. The state ensures care and protection and care for motherhood and childhood, and for breadwinning, and elderly women, and women most in need.[15]

At the international level, Egypt has moved in the direction of providing protection for women's and children's rights by ratifying many important human rights and women rights conventions and treaties. For example, Egypt ratified the International Covenant on Civil and Political Rights on January 14, 1982,[16] the International Convention on the Elimination of all Forms of Racial Discrimination on May 1, 1967,[17] the Convention on the Elimination of all Forms of Discrimination Against Women (CEDAW) on September 18, 1981,[18] the Convention on the Rights of the Child on July 6 1990,[19] and the International Covenant on Economic, Social, and Cultural Rights on January 14, 1982.[20]

---

14   *Id.* at article 101.

15   *Id.* at article 11.

16   International Covenant on Civil and Political Rights, *supra* note 2. The ratification dates by Egypt of the various human rights treaties are listed at https://tbinternet.ohchr.org /_layouts/15/TreatyBodyExternal/ Treaty.aspx?CountryID=54&Lang=EN.

17   International Convention on the Elimination of all Forms of Racial Discrimination, Dec. 21, 1965, 660 U.N.T.S. 195.

18   Convention on the Elimination of All Forms of Discrimination against Women, Dec. 18, 1979, 1249 U.N.T.S. 13.

19   Convention on the Rights of the Child, Nov. 20, 1989, 1577 U.N.T.S. 3.

20   International Covenant on Economic, Social and Cultural Rights, *supra* note 3.

Egypt made a general reservation to Article 2 of CEDAW, stating that "Egypt is willing to comply with the content of this article, provided that such compliance does not run counter to the Islamic Sharia."[21]

Egypt also made a reservation to Article 16 of CEDAW by stating that:

> Concerning the equality of men and women in all matters relating to marriage and family relations during the marriage and upon its dissolution, without prejudice to the Islamic sharia provisions whereby women are accorded rights equivalent to those of their spouses so as to ensure a just balance between them. This is out of respect of their sacrosanct nature of the firm religious beliefs which govern marital relations in Egypt and which may not be called in question and in view of the fact that one of the most important bases of these relations is an equivalency of rights and duties so as to ensure complementarity which guarantees true equality between the spouses not a quasi-equality that renders the marriage a burden on the wife. The provisions of the sharia lay down that the husband shall pay bridal money to the wife and maintain her full rights over her property and is not obliged to spend anything on her keep. The sharia therefore restricts the wife's rights to divorce by making it contingent on a judge's ruling, whereas no such restriction is laid down in the case of the husband.[22]

The CEDAW Committee noted that "reservations incompatible with the object and purpose of the convention were not permitted according to its article 28."[23] The Egyptian representative to the Committee stated:

> Under Islamic law, the marriage was entered into by contract, and it was obligatory for the spouses to abide by its terms. The husband had the primary responsibility for all financial expenditures. That provision was even discriminatory against men, as women were allowed to spend their own money freely. Under Islamic law, a woman had the right to divorce her husband at any time if such a stipulation was made in the marriage

---

21   Declarations, reservations, objections and notifications of withdrawal of reservations relating to the Convention on the Elimination of All Forms of Discrimination against Women, CEDAW/SP/2006/2, https://documents-dds-ny.un.org/doc/UNDOC/GEN/N06/309/97/PDF/N0630997.pdf?OpenElement (last visited 4 Dec. 2022).

22   Id.

23   CEDAW Committee, Concluding Observations, Egypt, CEDAW A/39/45 (1984), 34th and 39th Mtgs (Mar. 30 & Apr. 3, 1984), http://www.bayefsky.com/html/egypt_t4_cedaw.php (last visited December 4, 2022).

contract. In addition, a woman could divorce her husband under certain conditions. Some of those conditions were that her husband had married a second wife, he was concealing a first marriage, he did not give his wife any money or that he was in a prison for a period of three years. With regard to the granting of the same rights and responsibilities during marriage and at its dissolution, Egypt had made a reservation on article 16 of the Convention.[24]

The reservation expressed by Egypt does not mean that there is discrimination against women, but rather that, as stated by the Arab Charter on Human Rights, there is positive discrimination and there are more rights in favor of women.[25] "There should be more understanding of the philosophy of Sharia law. There are many shared values between Sharia law and the international human rights standards. The reservations expressed by Arab countries that are based on Sharia law should be examined."[26]

Article 6 of the Cairo Declaration on Human Rights in Islam states "Woman is equal to man in human dignity, and has rights to enjoy as well as dutiesto perform; she has her own civil entity and financial independence, and the right to retain her name and lineage [and] the husband is responsible for the support and welfare of the family."[27]

The Egyptian Constitution states that Islamic law is the main source of law for Muslims. Islam emphasizes the equality between men and women regarding their rights[28] and obligations.[29] The Quran says,

---

24   *Id.*

25   Ahmed El Demery, The Arab Charter of Human Rights: A Voice of Sharia in the Modern World 202 (2015).

26   *Id.*

27   Cairo Declaration on Human Rights in Islam, Aug. 5, 1990, U.N. GAOR, World Conf. on Hum. Rts.,

28   Quran 9:72 ("Allah has promised to the believers – men and women – Gardens under which rivers flow to dwell therein forever, and beautiful mansions in Gardens of Adn (Eden Paradise). But the greatest bliss is the Good Pleasure of Allah. That is the supreme success."). The Quran is the Islamic religious book. Each chapter in the Quran is composed of several verses, which vary in length. When citing the Quran in this book, the number of the chapter precedes the number of the verse. The chapter and the verse are separated by a colon.

29   *Id.* at 6:152: "Say (O Muhammad SAW): 'Come, I will recite what your Lord has prohibited you from: Join not anything in worship with Him; be good and dutiful to your parents; kill not your children because of poverty – We provide sustenance for you and for them; come not near to Al-Fawahish (shameful sins, illegal sexual intercourse, etc.) whether committed openly or secretly, and kill not anyone whom Allah has forbidden, except for a just cause (according to Islamic law). This He has commanded you that you may understand.'

And the believers, men and women, are protecting friends one of another; they enjoin the right and forbid the wrong, and they establish worship and they pay the poor-due, and they obey Allah and His messenger. As for these, Allah will have mercy on them. Lo! Allah is Mighty, Wise.[30]

There is a longstanding legal debate in which Egyptians are asking: is the law for or against women's rights in Egypt? Some may think that women do not have any legal or human rights. Many are also wondering if the law is affected by culture, and goes in the wrong direction by discriminating against women and putting them under bad legal standards. Others are wondering if the culture is affected by law, while there are some in the middle who say that both the culture and the law are affecting each other.

It should be noted that non-Muslims have their own family law. As stated above, the Egyptian Constitution provides that "The canon principles of Egyptian Christians and Jews are the main source of legislation for their personal status laws, religious affairs, and the selection of their spiritual leaders."[31]

This article will focus on the law of family affairs of Muslims and will shine light on some parts of Islamic family law. It is important to draw attention to the fact that human rights are not always absolute; there are limits to them. In other words, every individual can enjoy his right freely on the condition that he or she does not prevent other people from freely enjoying their rights. It has been said that, "your right to swing your arm ends just where the other person's nose begins. One person's right is another person's duty.[32] Sharia law balances between individual rights and duties.[33]

Women's rights are placed in a supreme position in Sharia. In Quran, Jesus said, "And dutiful to my mother, and made me not arrogant, unblest."[34] In Islam, mothers are given more care than fathers. A mother bears the baby and suffers during pregnancy and at the time of delivery of the baby. A Companion

---

'And come not near to the orphan's property, except to improve it, until he (or she) attains the age of full strength; and give full measure and full weight with justice. We burden not any person, but that which he can bear. And whenever you give your word (i.e. judge between men or give evidence, etc.), say the truth even if a near relative is concerned, and fulfill the Covenant of Allah, This He commands you, that you may remember.'"

30   *Id.* at 9:71.

31   Article 3 of the Egyptian Constitution.

32   El Demery, *supra* note 25, at 95 (*citing* Kathryn English & Adam Stapleton, The Human Rights Handbook: A Practical Guide to Monitoring Human Rights 5 (1995)).

33   *Id.* at 96 (*citing* Jason Morgan-Foster, *A New Perspective On The Universality Debate: Reverse Moderate Relativism In The Islamic Context*, 10 ILSA J. Int'l & Comp. L. 35, 59 (2003)).

34   Quran 32:19.

asked the Prophet, "'Who deserves my good treatment most?' 'Your mother,' said the Prophet. 'Who next?' 'Your mother.' 'Who next?' 'Your mother.' 'Who after that?' 'Your father.'" Therefore mothers receive three times the care from their children, which is more than the father deserves.[35] Muslims must be kind to their parents even if the parents do not believe in God or they want their son or daughter to not believe in God. It is said in the Quran: "But if they [both] strive with you to make you join in worship with Me others that of which you have no knowledge, then obey them not; but behave with them in the world kindly, and follow the path of him who turns to Me in repentance and in obedience. Then to Me will be your return, and I shall tell you what you used to do."[36]

There are many commonalities that exist between Sharia law and international law. However, the principle of the "margin of appreciation" can play a very important role as a way of reconciling Sharia Law and international human rights law.

The margin of appreciation is a doctrine the Court uses to interpret certain Convention provisions. It generally refers to the amount of discretion the Court gives national authorities in fulfilling their obligations under the Convention.[37]

> Margin of appreciation is a means by where member states are conferred a privilege to balance between the rights of the individual with the rights of the public at large. When there is a conflict between the security of public with the individual human rights then it is for the state to determine whether it is within the margin of appreciation that they can violate that individual's human rights without being held liable for violation... Nonetheless, the extent of margin of appreciation vary in accordance with the type of right the states authorities are interfering with and each case depended upon the circumstances and merits of the case.[38]

The margin of appreciation has been developed by the European Court of Human Rights in many cases. The first case that mentioned the margin of

---

35 El Demery, *supra* note 25, at 58 (*citing* Dr. I. A. Arshed. *Parents' Rights Relationship in Islam*, http://www.islam101.com/sociology/parchild.htm (last visited Dec. 10, 2022)).

36 Quran 31:15.

37 El Demery, *supra* note 25, at 127 (*citing* Jeffrey A. Brauch, *The Margin of Appreciation and the Jurisprudence of the European Court of Human Rights: Threat to the Rule of Law*, 11 Colum. J. Eur. L. 113, 115 (2004)).

38 *Margin of appreciation*, http://www.ukessays.com/essays/law/margin-of-appreciation .php (last visited Dec. 10, 2022).

appreciation is that of *Handyside v. the United Kingdom.*[39] In this case, the Court states that

> it is not possible to find in the domestic law of the various Contracting States a uniform European conception of morals. The view taken by their respective laws of the requirements of morals varies from time to time and from place to place, especially in our era which is character- ised by a rapid and far-reaching evolution of opinions on the subject. By reason of their direct and continuous contact with the vital forces of their countries, State authorities are in principle in a better position than the international judge to give an opinion on the exact content of these requirements as well as on the "necessity" of a "restriction" or "penalty" intended to meet them.[40]

The principle of the margin of appreciation can allow for co-existence between Sharia and international human rights law. For instance, the meaning of posi- tive discrimination in favor of women according to Sharia law is that husbands are financially responsible to their wives even if the wife is richer than her hus- band. In this example, there is no equality between men and women, as men have to pay to women. Therefore, the doctrine of the margin of appreciation can be used to protect the rights given to women according to Sharia law.[41]

"The constitution expanded the identification of rights and freedoms."[42] A whole chapter, from Article 51 to Article 93, is devoted to human rights, free- doms, and duties. Another whole chapter is devoted to the rule of law.

The Egyptian Constitution references the Universal Declaration of human Rights. Its preamble provides that "[w]e are drafting a Constitution that paves the way to the future for us, and which is in line with the Universal Declaration of Human Rights, which we took part in the drafting of and approved."[43]

The protection of the fundamental freedoms and human rights is guaran- teed in the Egyptian Constitution. The Constitution states that

---

39   El Demery, *supra* note 25, at 127 (*citing* Handyside v. the United Kingdom, (5493/72) [1976] ECHR 5 (7 December 1976)).

40   *Id* at 128.

41   *Id.* at 129

42   Moushira Khattab *Women's Rights Under Egypt's Constitutional Disarray*, https://www .wilsoncenter.org/sites/default/files/media/documents/publication/womens_rights _under_egypts_constitutional_disarray.pdf (last visited Dec. 17, 2022).

43   Preamble of the Egyptian Constitution.

Citizens are equal before the law, possess equal rights and public duties, and may not be discriminated against on the basis of religion, belief, sex, origin, race, color, language, disability, social class, political or geographical affiliation, or for any other reason. Discrimination and incitement to hate are crimes punishable by law. The state shall take all necessary measures to eliminate all forms of discrimination, and the law shall regulate the establishment of an independent commission for this purpose.[44]

The Constitution emphasized the important of equality between men and women. In addition, it gives more care to women and children. As stated above, the Constitution provides that:

The state commits to achieving equality between women and men in all civil, political, economic, social, and cultural rights in accordance with the provisions of this Constitution. The state commits to taking the necessary measures to ensure appropriate representation of women in the houses of parliament, in the manner specified by law. It grants women the right to hold public posts and high management posts in the state, and to appointment in judicial bodies and entities without discrimination. The state commits to the protection of women against all forms of violence, and ensures women empowerment to reconcile the duties of a woman toward her family and her work requirements. The state ensures care and protection and care for motherhood and childhood, and for breadwinning, and elderly women, and women most in need.[45]

Egypt ratified eight core international human rights instruments and a number of regional instruments within the Arab and African human rights systems. A special status was conferred in the Constitution for the first time to international human rights instruments.[46] The Constitution provides that "The state is committed to the agreements, covenants, and international conventions of human rights that were ratified by Egypt. They have the force of law after publication in accordance with the specified circumstances."[47]

---

44   Egyptian Constitution, Article 53.

45   *Id.* at art 11.

46   Supreme Standing Committee for Human Rights, National Human Rights Strategy 2021–2026, https://sschr.gov.eg/media/gapb5bq4/national-human-rights-strategy.pdf (Last visited Dec. 11, 2022).

47   Egyptian Constitution, Article 93.

The Concluding Observations of the Committee on the Elimination of Discrimination against Women on Egypt state that the Egyptian Constitution:

> includes provisions on the commitment of the State party to achieve gender equality in all civil, political, economic, social and cultural rights and to ensure the protection of women against all forms of violence, as well as the affirmation that citizens' core rights and freedoms cannot be suspended or derogated, and that no law that regulates the exercise of rights and freedoms may restrict them in such a way as to undermine their essence.[48]

Egypt adopted a national human rights strategy 2021–2026. The importance of this strategy is that it is the first integrated national human rights strategy in Egypt. It builds on the progress achieved and takes into consideration opportunities and challenges at the national level.[49]

The strategy is based on a vision aiming at advancing all human rights in Egypt through enhancing respect for and protection of all civil, political, economic, social and cultural rights, stipulated for in the Constitution, national laws and international and regional instruments ratified by Egypt. The ultimate goal is to enhance equality and equal opportunities without any discrimination. The strategy is a ambitious national roadmap on human rights and a significant tool for self-development in this field.[50]

2   Past Trends in Authoritative and Controlling Decisions

2.1   *Divorce – "talaq"*

The Concluding Observations of the Committee on the Elimination of Discrimination against Women on Egypt state that "the Committee notes the State party's efforts and commitment to review all discriminatory personal status laws regarding marriage and family relations."[51] On the other hand, "the Committee is concerned about the fact that men have the right to unilaterally

---

48   Concluding Observations on the combined eighth to tenth periodic reports of Egypt, Committee on the Elimination of Discrimination against Women, CEDAW/C/EGY/CO/ 8–10, https://documents-dds-ny.un.org/doc/UNDOC/GEN/N21/356/11/PDF/N2135611.pdf? OpenElement (last visited Dec. 17, 2022).

49   Supreme Standing Committee for Human Rights, *supra* note 46.

50   *Id.*

51   Concluding Observations on the combined eighth to tenth periodic reports of Egypt, *Supra* note 48.

divorce their spouses (*talaq*), including verbally with a one-week period for official registration of the divorce, which leaves many women in precarious situations."[52]

It should be noted that there is a new proposed law for family matters. The committee working on this law is examining the verbal divorce. The President of Egypt is concerned about the verbal divorce, as he requested the competent authorities to amend the law by banning verbal divorce.[53]

According to Egyptian law, women do not have the right to make a unilateral decision to be divorced from their husbands, unless they wrote this condition into their original marriage contract. Any woman can divorce herself, at her own will, if she states in the marriage contract that she has that right. If she did not write in this condition, then she cannot be divorced except in two cases: her husband agrees to divorce her, or she can sue her husband and ask the court to divorce her. The wife can sue her husband for various reasons. For one, she can request the court to divorce her due to the harm she had experienced.[54] Second, she can claim divorce due to an unsolved concrete problem.[55] Third, she can claim divorce without any specific reason, which is called divorce by "*Khula.*"[56]

If a husband divorces his wife or if she won the cases of divorce, except the *Khula,* then she can sue her husband via the *Al-Motta* case.[57] The *Al-Motta* is a kind of remedy granted due to the moral harm endured by the woman as a result of the divorce. There are many laws which have been adopted in Egypt with the goal of supporting women. According to Egyptian Civil Law,

> The effects of marriage, including its effects upon the property of the spouses, are regulated by the law of the country to which the husband belongs at the time of conclusion of the marriage. Repudiation of marriage is governed by the law of the country to which the husband belongs at the time of repudiation, whereas divorce and separation are governed by the law of the country to which the husband belongs at the time of the commencement of the legal proceedings.[58]

---

52   *Id.*
53   Speech of the Egyptian president requesting to prohibit verbal divorce, https://www .youtube.com/ watch?v=UaJgeyuDrbA (Last visited, Dec. 17, 2022).
54   Divorce Law due to harm [harm], Law No. 25 of 1929.
55   Divorce Law due to unsolved concrete problem [problems], Law No. 100 of 1985.
56   Divorce Law due to *Khula*, Law No. 1 of 2000.
57   Motta Law [Motta], Law No. 25 of 1929.
58   Article 13, Egyptian Civil Law, http://hrlibrary.umn.edu/research/Egypt/Civil%20 Law.pdf.

With respect to the financial obligations that result from marriage, the Egyptian Civil Law provides that "[o]bligations as regards payment of alimony to relatives are governed by the (national) law of the person liable for such payment."[59] As explained above, any woman can write a condition into the marriage contract stating that she can divorce her husband at her own will. If she did not write this condition into the contract, she can be divorced by mutual consent with her husband, or sue her husband requesting divorce. On the other hand, the husband has the right to divorce his wife without the need to sue his wife in court. One of the main reasons for giving the husband this right is because of his financial obligation towards his wife before, during, and after the dissolution of marriage.[60] The ability for husband and wife to obtain a divorce by mutual consent, without resorting to the courts, is the fastest and easiest way. On the other hand, there are kinds of divorce that need a reasonable cause submitted to the court. Furthermore, there is *Khula*, which can be done by either mutual agreement of both parties, without going to the court, or by submitting a case to the court. *Khula* cases are the fastest judicial avenues that do not need any reason to be submitted. This article will shed some light on samples of Egyptian laws that concern divorce.

2.1.1   Divorce due to Harm

Before the adoption of the *Khula* law,[61] no woman could be divorced unless a cause stated in the law existed. For example, a woman could ask for a divorce if her husband caused harm to her[62] or due to her husband's absence or being jailed.[63] There is more than one condition and regulation for the family court to fulfill in order to divorce a woman from her husband. If a wife wanted to be divorced due to the "harm" that was caused to her, she had to prove that there was harm caused by her husband. Harm meant any act that was done by the husband to the wife which caused a detriment to her. This harm includes both moral and physical harm. Furthermore, the wife, due to this harm, must show that she could not bear living with her husband anymore.[64] Instances of moral harm differed from case to case, as the court has discretionary authority to

---

59   *Id.* at article 15.

60   El Demery, *supra* note 25, at 226.

61   Law No. 1 of 2000, on family matters.

62   Article 20, Law No. 1 of 2000.

63   Divorce Law due to imprisonment of the husband, Law No. 25 of 1929.

64   Ta'lemat El Naeb El Aam Besha'n Tatbeek Kanoon Mahkamet El Osraa Al Sader bel kanon rakam 10 lesanaat 2004 [The Prosecutor General, The Instructions of The Prosecutor General Regarding the Establishment of The Family Court by The Law No 10 of 2004], at 58.

decide whether there is harm or not depending on the circumstances of each case. An example of moral harm is a husband's attempt to create and develop a false bad reputation of his wife or intentionally treat her in a poor manner.

In order for the wife to win her case, she must provide the court with the necessary witnesses and evidence to prove her claims to the judge. The decision of the judge will depend on all of the materials presented in the case.[65] Before rendering the court's decision, the judge must request from both the husband and the wife an attempt to reconcile and solve their dispute. Additionally, if the spouses have children, then the judge must request from them, more than once, time to reconcile and solve the problem.[66] If the judge failed to ask the spouses to reconcile and solve the dispute, then the case and the final decision of the court would be considered null and void.[67]

According to the "divorce due to harm," women must pay judicial fees, in order to be able to start a case before the court. An amendment to the law is proposed to allow the waiver of judicial fees, as is done in financial responsibility cases. This suggested amendment would allow women, who are not able to bear paying the fees of the court, to still have their case before the court without the need to any judicial fees.

In financial responsibility cases, the law allows women to sue their husband in court without the need to appoint a lawyer on her behalf. The court can appoint a lawyer on behalf of women who cannot bear the expenses of the lawyers. In addition, in financial responsibility cases women are not required by law to pay judicial fees.[68] This law is successfully helping women who would otherwise be unable to pay expenses to lawyers.

The *Khula* law was set forth to enable women to be divorced from their husbands by their own will.[69] The *Khula* law requires from the wife to relieve her husband of any financial obligations towards her, as it is her choice to end the marriage immediately.[70]

Wives can ask for a ruling to be divorced from their husbands, if they informed the court by evidence that their husbands are absent for one year or more without knowing anything about them. Law No. 25 of 1929 states that: "If the husband is absent for a year or more without an acceptable excuse, his wife

65   *Id.* at 59.
66   *Id.*
67   *Id.*
68   Article 3, Law No. 1 of 2000.
69   *Supra* note 62.
70   *Id.*

may ask the judge to divorce her irrevocably if she is harmed due to his absent, even if he has money from which she can spend."[71]

Regarding divorce, the Quran states:

> And when you divorce (your) women (a revocable divorce), and they approach the end of their 'Iddat (-the prescribed period of waiting after divorce) then either retain them in an equitable manner or send them away (- freeing them) in an equitable manner. And do not retain them wrongfully that you may exceed the proper limits (and do them harm and maltreat them). And whosoever does that he has indeed done wrong and injustice to himself. Do not take Allâh's commandments in a light way; and remember Allâh's favour upon you and what He has revealed to you of the Book and the Wisdom, wherewith He exhorts you. And take Allâh as a shield and know that Allâh has perfect knowledge of everything.[72]

2.1.2   The Khula

"'Khula' is meant to be an equitable solution. According to Prophetic precedent, a woman who does not like her husband through no fault of his own has the option of leaving him, so long as she returns the *mahr* [dowry]."[73] The literal meaning of *Khula* is to disown or to repudiate; a woman can repudiate her marriage.[74] The *Khula* law was issued in 2000.[75] The aim of the law is to protect women's rights. According to the *Khula* law, any woman can request from the court to divorce her, without saying any reason, except that she hates living with her husband. In addition, she must waive her financial rights. In other words, she will return back the dowry that he paid to her and she cannot request *Al-Motta*.[76] Women are appreciative of this *Khula* law because it is the easiest, fastest way to be divorced. Many women prefer to solve the family disputes in a quick way that protects the privacy of the family and children. The origin and roots of *Khula* is in the Islamic law, so when applying this law people feel that this is not only a national law, but also a divine law.

---

71   Article 12, Law No. 25, 1929, https://manshurat.org/node/12369 (last visited, Aug. 22, 2022).

72   Quran 2:231.

73   El Demery, *supra* note 25, at 228. (*citing* Azizah Al-Hibri, *Islam, Law, and Custom: Redefining Muslim Women's Rights*, 12 Am. U, J. Int'l L. & Pol'y 1, 24 (1997)).

74   Asghar Ali Engineer, The Rights of Women in Islam 136 1992.

75   *Supra* note 62. Article 20 of Law No. 1 of 2000.

76   *Id.*

The *Khula* law came from the *Quran* and *Hadith*.[77] It is stated in the *Quran* that,

> If you fear that they would not be able to keep the limits ordained by Allah, then there is no sin on either of them if she gives back (the Mahr i.e. dowry or a part of it) for her *Khula* (divorce). These are the limits ordained by Allah, so do not transgress them. And whoever transgresses the limits ordained by Allah, then such are the Zalimoon (wrong-doers, etc.).[78]

The *Khula* law states that the spouses can agree together to be divorced by *Khula*, without needing to go to court. If the husband does not agree, his wife can sue him requesting *Khula*, and gives up her financial rights. In this case, the court must divorce her, after requesting reconciliation between them.[79]

Although the *Khula* law does not have strict long regulations like the divorce by harm, there are some easy requirements that must be fulfilled in the *Khula* law before the judge divorces the spouses. The court itself must do its best to try to solve and reconcile the dispute. Also, the court must appoint two professional arbitrators in family matters; the arbitrators will have only three months to try to solve the dispute. Their mission will only be to try to solve and reconcile the dispute; it is forbidden for the arbitrators to know why the wife is asking to be divorced by the *Khula*. The duty of the arbitrators is to attempt to convince both parties to return back again to live together.[80] The arbitrators

---

77   *Quran* is the Holy Islamic book, the *hadith* is the prophet's wordings. there is a famous *hadith* that the legislative authority used it to guide them in issuing the *Khula* law, this hadith states that El Bokhary narrates after Ben Abbas: "The wife of Thabet Ibn Kayes went to Prophet Mohamed and told him: 'Oh prophet, Thabet is a pious, good-mannered person yet I loathe him and I fear blasphemy.' The Prophet asked her: 'would you return his garden? (Presented as his dowry to her)'. She agreed to do so. The prophet asked her husband to accept the garden and divorce her." We can understand from the prophetic tradition about Thabet's wife though she attests that her spouse enjoys good conduct, is religiously devout and definitely is good company in view of his religious integrity and good manners. She asks for divorce as she loathes him and fears actions that will amount to blasphemy should she pursue life with him. The prophet Mohamed did not rebuke her nor compel her to sustain her matrimonial life. Prophet Mohamed respected her opinion, answered her demand and agreed to grant her a divorce.

78   Quran 2:229.

79   *Supra* note 62.

80   *Supra* note 64, at 57.

then submit a report to the court. However, the opinion of the arbitrators is not binding upon the Court.[81]

The Concluding Observations of the Committee on the Elimination of Discrimination against Women on Egypt state that "women who seek divorce by unilateral termination of their marriage contract (*khula*) under Act No. 1 of 2000 can only obtain such a divorce if they forgo alimony and return their dowry."[82] The Committee recommends that Egypt accelerate the adoption of the amendment to the Personal Status Law to ensure that it guarantees equal grounds and procedures for obtaining a divorce.[83]

Due to the fact that women ask judges to divorce them without mentioning any reason, they should return back to their husbands the bridal money (dowry) that was given to them by their husbands. The wife also must forfeit her right to alimony including the "*Motta*."[84] On the other hand, divorce by *Khula* law, does not affect the financial obligations of the husband towards his children. In addition, *Khula* does not affect the right of the woman to have custody of the children. It should be clear that if a husband divorces his wife; he has no right to return back the alimony and the dowry. In addition, his ex-wife can claim *Al-Motta*.

The wife or her lawyer should clearly say to the judge that she cannot bear living with her husband anymore, and that she fears not being able to keep the limits ordained by Allah (God).[85]

After the *Khula* law was applied, thousands of cases were brought before the courts; many women were attracted to this law because of its simple regulations and the short time the case would take in the court.

Under the *Khula* law, the wife does not need to explain the harm that was caused by her husband to her, even if her husband was very good with her, caring, and generous. If she hates living with him and she fears that she can't keep the limits ordained by Allah, divorce can be obtained. In the *Khula* law, Article 20 states that the decision of the court is final. So, if the court divorced the woman via the *Khula* law, the husband cannot appeal.[86] An example of a *Khula* case occurred when a man submitted a case to the Egyptian Constitutional Court claiming that Article 20 of the *Khula* law is unconstitutional and against Sharia law. He clarified that the *Khula* judgment cannot be appealed. The

---

81   Article 19, Law No.1 of 2000.
82   Concluding Observations on the combined eighth to tenth periodic reports of Egypt, *supra* note 48.
83   *Id.*
84   *Supra* note 62.
85   *Id.*
86   *Id.*

Constitutional Court affirmed the legal and the Islamic Sharia justifications of the law. Regarding the legal justification, the Court said that the law aims to lift the injustice of the wives who suffer from the intransigence of their husbands, when the aversion is strong and the treatment is difficult. The Court added that the law also removes from the husbands any financial burden that may result from the termination of the marital relationship. The wife waives all of her legal financial rights, and returns the dowry that the husband paid to her, which is confirmed in the marriage contract or estimated by the court in the event of a dispute. In addition, she declares that she hates life with her husband, and that there is no way to continue living with him. Furthermore, she declares that she fears that she will not establish the limits of God because of this hatred. If the husband does not agree to the divorce, the court plays its role to attempt reconciliation between the spouses and then appoints two arbitrators to continue the effort. The Court added that there is no obligation on the wife to show reasons that the wife does not want to disclose. If reconciliation was not achieved, and the two arbitrators were unable to do so, the court divorces her after she returns back the dowry.[87]

With respect to Islamic Sharia, the Constitutional Court said that the marriage was originally entered into to continue for a lifetime between the spouses. However, when hatred replaces affection and mercy between spouses, God permits the husband to end the relationship by divorce, using it when needed and within the limits drawn by the wise legislator for him. God also permitted the wife to request to divorce herself by *Khula*, after returning back to her husband what he had paid (dowry).[88]

An Egyptian mother of two children has become the first woman to file for divorce, in January 2000, under the *Khula* law.[89] The wife said in her petition to the family court that she had no particular complaint against her husband but hated living with him.[90] Her husband had previously refused to divorce her. The wife added that she was ready to give up all her financial rights, as required under the legislation, in order to be divorced from her husband. The court decided to divorce her by *Khula* law.[91]

---

87   The Constitutional Court, Case No. 201 for the Judicial Year No. 23, http://hrlibrary.umn.edu/arabic/Egypt-scc-sc/Egypt-scc-201-Y23.html.

88   *Id.*

89   *First Egyptian Woman Files for Divorce*, BBC News (Jan. 29, 2000), http://news.bbc.co.uk/1/hi/world/middle_east/623875.stm.

90   *Id.*

91   *Id.*

2.1.3   The Home of the Divorced Woman who has Child Custody

Any man, who has children from his divorced wife, should prepare a suitable separate home for the children and the woman who has custody over the child.[92] If the home is rented, the husband is legally responsible for paying the rent. If the home is owned by the husband, then the husband has the right not to leave that home if he prepared another suitable home for the woman and the children.[93]

The Judge gives the woman the choice of either living in the same home she was used to live with her husband, or to take the cost of the rent, and then she can choose freely another place to live.[94]

The woman, who requests child custody, should fulfill certain conditions, in order to have the right to stay in the home with the children after the divorce, for example:[95]

1.   At the time of divorce the children should be in the age of child custody (under 15 years old).
2.   The woman should fulfill the conditions of the capability to have custody over the child. For example, she should be mature and not suffering from insanity. She should be capable to raise the children. The woman should not live with the children in a home in which someone else is living with them, who hates the children.
3.   She should live with children in the home of custody.

The father of the children has the right to return back to stay in the home that he prepared for the woman and the children under certain conditions:[96]

1.   If the children are more than 15 years old.
2.   The right of the woman to have the children custody was withdrawn from her due to any reason.
3.   If the woman chooses to take money and not to stay in his home.
4.   If the father of the children prepared for them another suitable home.

2.2   *Financial Responsibility*

It should be clear that, according to Islamic Sharia law, a woman is owed unique special care, whether she is a mother, sister, or wife. For example, wives have separate and independent financial budgets. The husband is responsible to pay each and everything, including the cost of the house, the

---

92   Article 18 bis 3 of Law No. 25 of 1920, amended by Law No. 100 of 1985.
93   *Id.*
94   *Id.*
95   *Supra* note 64, at 77.
96   *Id.* at 78.

electricity bill, the education fees, the medical expenses, the food and the clothes of the wife and the children. In other words, her husband cannot force her to pay anything against her will. She can help him, if she wants, out of her own will, but she is not required by law or Sharia or customs to pay anything.

The following scenario explains the financial obligations and duties imposed on women and men: a father has a son and a daughter. If the son wants to get married, he has to pay dowry for his wife. However, when his sister gets married, she will receive a dowry from her husband. On the other hand, her brother has to buy or rent an apartment to live in with his wife. Also, he has to pay for the expenses of his children and wife such as food, clothes, medicine, medical insurance, etc. However, his sister will not pay for anything because her husband is financially responsible for all the expenses.[97] If the brother divorces his wife, he has to pay her: *Al-Motta*, child's alimony, the nursery fee, the house rent fees until the end of the child custody, etc. On the other hand, if his sister is divorced, her husband will pay her *Al-Motta*, child's alimony, the nursery fee, the custody accommodation rent (rent of the place they are living) until the end of the child custody, etc.

2.2.1   The Financial Responsibility toward the Divorced Woman: *Al-Motta*

The *Al-Motta* law[98] is a very old law. It constitutes a very important protection for women, as it protects them from the arbitrary abuses that can be inflicted upon them by their husbands. Each and every husband is obliged to pay the divorced woman *Al-Motta* if two conditions are fulfilled together, according to article 18 bis of the Law. First, if her husband was the one who initiated the divorce. Second, in the case that she requested the divorce and the abuse or pain was proven in the court.[99] The reason behind imposing the financial responsibility is due to the moral harm that happened to the women because of the divorce. So, this financial responsibility is a kind of remedy for her.[100]

The family law stated that the amount of money that the ex-husband will pay is counted as if he were paying her expenses (food, clothes, etc.) for at least two years. In other words, the total amount of two years worth of the expenses are considered the financial responsibility that the ex-husband owes

---

97   El Demery, *supra* note 25, at 53.
98   Article 18 bis of Law No. 25 of 1920 amended by Law No. 100 of 1985.
99   *Id.; see also supra* note 64, at 79.
100   *Supra* note 64, at 79.

his ex-wife.[101] The judge's decision should be in the light of the ex-husband's income, the circumstances and reasons of the divorce, and the numbers of years the spouses were married.[102]

The *Al-Motta* protects the rights of women because it is considered a kind of compensation and reparation for damage. The judge orders the ex-husband to give her a reasonable amount of money, i.e. at least her total expenses of at least two years.[103] For example, if a woman was married for 10 years and got divorced, the judge can render a decision that the ex-husband must pay 7 years of *Al-Motta*. In addition, women can claim the right to the *Al-Motta* if her husband divorced her by his own will.

An example of the judicial cases of *Al-Motta*: a woman sued her husband to be divorced due to harm. After she was divorced, she sued her ex-husband to pay *Al-Motta*. The ex-husband claimed that the conditions of article 18 bis of the Law are not fulfilled, because the divorce happened with the consent and upon the request of the wife. The Supreme Court of Cassation expanded the interpretation of the meaning of the consent of the wife in article 18 bis. The Court stated that, in the light of Islamic Sharia law, it is not considered consent of the wife to be divorced, if her husband forced her by his harm to ask for the divorce.[104] The Supreme Court of Cassation added that if the wife's recourse to the judge to divorce her from her husband because of his harm to her, she can still claim *Al-Motta*. The Court also added that the existence of this harm was proven by evidence to the court. Therefore, the divorce is not considered as brought about by her consent, but by the harm caused to her.[105]

On the other hand, if the woman asked for the divorce due to *Khula*, she does not have the right to ask for *Al-Motta* because divorce via *Khula* does not need any proof of harm.[106] Divorce due to *Khula* is on condition of the wife's waiving her financial rights. In *Khula* law, it is enough for the woman to claim it without harm being done to her; she just needs to tell the court that living with her husband is unbearable. According to the *Khula* law, the judge does not investigate any harm that happened to the wife, he divorces her because she just wants to be divorced.[107] Therefore, if she is divorced by the *Khula*, then she doesn't have the right to the *Al-Motta*.

---

101   Article 18 bis of Law No. 25 of 1920 amended by Law No. 100 of 1985.

102   *Id.*

103   *Id.*

104   Case Number 6 for the Judicial Year No. 63, (March 10, 1997), https://www.cc.gov.eg /judgment_single?id=111118839&ja=16204 ; *see also supra* note 25, at 79.

105   *Id.*

106   *Supra* note 64.

107   *Id.*

There are many cases which prove that the *Al-Motta* law plays a very important role in protecting and securing women's rights. For example, there were two cases in the Family Court of Cairo. In the first case, the family court decided that the husband must pay his ex-wife five hundred thousand Egyptian Pounds for the *Al-Motta* of his wife. In the second case, the Court decided that the husband should pay his ex-wife four hundred and twenty thousand Egyptian Pounds. In both cases, the two wives gave evidence to the court that there ex-husbands are businessmen. The wives submitted to the court the documents that prove the wealth of their husbands. Also, they explained to the judge that their husbands arbitrarily divorced them without their consent and even without them committing any fault.[108]

In another case, the Family Court in Cairo decided to divorce a woman, who works as a teacher in a school, from her husband. The court decided that her husband must pay one hundred thousand Egyptian pounds as *Al-Motta*. The women said to the court that her husband informed her that he wants to marry another woman. She added that she was beaten by him because she refused this new marriage. After a few days, when she returned home from the hospital, she found her husband with his new wife in her bedroom. The husband confessed to the court that he had beaten his wife.[109]

Therefore, the *Al-Motta* law was placed on the side of the women, so that they are not left helpless and without income after being divorced. It is a kind of compensation and reparation of damages. The *Al-Motta* is paid to the woman even if she is working and her income is higher than her ex-husband's. According to the law, even after *Al-Motta* money is paid, the husband is still obligated to pay a monthly allowance for his children separately.[110]

2.2.2   The Financial Responsibility of the Husband toward his Wife

According to customs, traditions, and religion a man has to pay "*Mahr*" (dowry) to the woman he wants to marry.[111] A marriage dowry is given by the groom

---

108   http://www.elakhbar.org.eg/issues/16810/1100.html.

109   http://www.algomhuria.net.eg/algomhuria/today/accedents/detail08.asp (It should be noted that the woman in this case have the right to sue her husband at the criminal court because he beat her.).

110   The Law of the Financial Responsibility of the Father Toward his Children, Law No. 25 of 1929.

111   Islam states that the relation between the husband and wife should be in good faith and respect from both sides. When any Muslim man wants to marry a woman he has to pay the woman "*Mahr*" (obligatory bridal money toward his wife, dowry). As it was stated in the Quran in Chapter 4 Verse 4, "And give to the women (whom you marry) their *Mahr* (obligatory bridal money given by the husband to his wife at the time of marriage) with a

to the bride for her own personal use. The "*Mahr*" is based on the marriage entered into. The amount of dowry differs from place to place and from family to family depending on the circumstances.

From the first moment the husband marries his wife, he is responsible for paying for all the necessary needs of his wife, even if his wife believes in another religion different from his own.[112] Also, the husband is responsible to pay the expenses of his wife and children when they are sick and ill.[113] In addition, the husband should pay the reasonable expenses of his wife even if she is working and has a higher salary than his salary. In short, he is responsible for paying everything, even if his wife is richer than he is.[114] The financial responsibility of the husband includes his wife's food, clothes, the cost of the rent of the home they are living in, etc.[115]

The husband is legally responsible and legally in debt to pay the amount of money to his wife from the date he stopped paying it. This debt must be paid to the wife. It can be waived only if the wife agreed and stated explicitly that the debt is waived.[116]

The laws and regulations which are rooted in Islamic Sharia law totally secure and protect women rights. It is stated in a *hadith* that the "Messenger of Allah said, 'A dinar [money] you spend in Allah's way, or to free a slave, or as a charity you give to a needy person, or to support your family, the one yielding the greatest reward is that which you spend on your family.'"[117] In another *hadith*, it is stated "Messenger of Allah said, 'Neglecting one's own dependents is a reason enough for a man to commit a sin.'"[118] Another example, which is demonstrated by the story of a woman who came to Prophet Mohammed complaining that her husband was niggard, scarce and did not provide her with enough money for herself and her child. She added that she takes money from him without telling him. The Prophet told her to take all the money that satisfies you and your child, *belma'roof* (in line with what is reasonable).[119]

---

good heart, but if they, of their own good pleasure, remit any part of it to you, take it, and enjoy it without fear of any harm (as Allah has made it lawful)."

112 Article 1 and 16 of Law No. 25 of 1920 amended by Law No. 100 of 1985; *see also supra* note 64, at 65.

113 *Supra* note 64, at 65.

114 *Id.*

115 *Id.*

116 *Id.*

117 Riyad as-Salihin, Hadith 289, https://sunnah.com/riyadussalihin:289.

118 Riyad as-Salihin, Hadith 294, https://sunnah.com/riyadussalihin:294.

119 Sahih al-Bukhari 5364, Book 69, Hadith 14, https://sunnah.com/bukhari:5364.

The financial debts of the husband to his wife and children have priority, and they take precedence over any other debts he owes toward anyone else.[120] Women's rights should be protected and secured, especially because, in some cases, husbands try to not pay a cent to their wives. On the other hand, some wives try to take more money than their husband is able to pay. The court has full discretionary authority to decide how much the husband should pay.[121] The court decides this issue in the light of the husband's financial situation, at the time of examining the case. For example, whether he is poor or rich, even if he is poor, he is still responsible to cover the necessary basic needs of his wife.[122] The court requests from the police investigation office its investigation regarding the husband's salary and income. In addition, the courts also issue an order requesting from his workplace an official document indicating his total salary. In some cases, the husband is working in a different country, outside of Egypt. Egypt signed several bilateral and regional treaties in this regard. The office of International Cooperation at the Ministry of Justice plays an important role in sending Mutual Legal Assistance (MLA) requests of the court to the judicial authorities of the requested country, regardless of whether there exists a pertinent treaty with that country or not. The reason of sending an MLA request is to protect the human rights of the children and their mother. Due to different legal systems, there are some countries that do not reply. Other countries delay in sending the official document indicating the total salary of the husband. This may lead to financial problems and suffering of the mother and her children. There should be international treaties regarding mutual legal assistance requests in family matters. This treaty should establish a time frame and find easier and faster regulations for implementing the court's decision. This proposed treaty should also find ways in deducting the amount of money the court decided from his salary by transferring it to the women and her children.

Due to the potential delay that may occur until the final decision is taken, the judge orders the husband to pay quick temporary financial support to his wife and children until the final decision is rendered. If the judge found that all the conditions are fulfilled, the court should issue a temporary decision. That temporary court decision is to be issued within, at a maximum, two weeks from the day the wife sued her husband. The temporary court decision states that the husband should pay his wife a specific amount of money (as

---

120   *Supra* note 112; Article 77 of Law No. 1 of 2000.
121   *Supra* note 64, at 66.
122   *Id.*

determined by the court), that covers her necessary basic needs, until the court issues its final verdict.[123]

After the final verdict, the husband can deduct the amount of money that he paid to his wife, i.e. the money that he paid after the temporary decision of the court, from the total amount of money he has to pay to his wife after the final decision.[124]

This law is effective, because it gives women financial support. It imposes the responsibility on husbands to pay the needs of their wives. Also, the most important thing in this law is the authority of the judge to issue a quick temporary decision. This quick decision reduces the problems that women suffer due to the potential delay that may occur until the final decision. Also, this law secures women's financial rights and ensures that they are financially supported regardless of their own financial situation and whether they work or not.

This law is derived from Islamic Sharia law. The Quran provides that "Let the man of wealth provide according to his means. As for the one with limited resources, let him provide according to whatever Allah has given him. Allah does not require of any soul beyond what He has given it. After hardship, Allah will bring about ease."[125]

The Kingdom of Saudi Arabia explained the purposes and objectives of Sharia law with respect to the financial obligations of men in its report submitted to CEDAW. It stated that

> a son in relation to daughters and a brother in relation to sisters, the male receives double the share of the female. The reason for this is that a man will provide for his wife and children while his sister, by virtue of the fact that she is not burdened with outlay but will herself be provided for, will invest her share, thus making the outcome, after a short time, equal or even favourable to the woman.[126]

---

123   *Id;* Article 16 of Law No. 25 of 1929, as amended by Law No. 100 of 1985.
124   *Id.*
125   Quran 65:7.
126   El Demery, *supra* note 25, at 228. (*citing* U.N. Committee the Elimination of All Forms of Discrimination against Women, U.N. Committee on the Elimination of Discrimination against Women (CEDAW), Combined Initial and Second Periodic Reports of States Parties, Saudi Arabia, U.N. Doc. CEDAW/C/SAU/2, at 11 (Mar. 29, 2007)).

2.2.3   The Financial Responsibility of the Father toward the Woman who has Custody over their Child

Before writing about child custody, it is important to differentiate between the financial responsibility of the husband towards his children and the financial responsibility of the husband towards the woman who is entitled to a nursery fee. The father is legally responsible to pay alimony of the children.[127] On the other hand, the nursery fee is paid to the woman, whether she is the mother of the children or not; it is not the fee for breastfeeding, and it is not the child's alimony.[128] It is paid to the woman because she takes care of the children.

With respect to child custody, the law protects and respects the rights of women who have custody over the child. Egyptian family law states that fathers shall pay the woman who has the custody of the children a nursery fee, because she is responsible to serve and take care of the children. The fee is owed to the woman from the first day of the custody.[129]

According to the law, women have inherent child custody. The father of the children has the responsibility of paying the nursery fee to the woman, until his children turn fifteen years old. After this age, they are deemed old enough, and they can stay with the father in his home. In another words, children after the age of fifteen have the right to stay with their father.[130] If they decide to continue living with their mother, the mother will not be paid the nursery fee of child custody.[131] In all cases, the father is still responsible of paying the expenses of the child's alimony.

The law states that the father is responsible to pay the expenses of his children (child's alimony), even if they are living with their mother. The law differentiates between daughter and son, by giving more protection to the woman. The father pays for his daughter and covers her expenses until she is married or earns enough to support herself. In addition, the father should cover the expenses of his son until he is fifteen years old and capable to work. The son is considered not capable to work, for example, if he has still not graduated from school and university or if he suffers from a mental disease.[132]

The Supreme Constitutional Court of Egypt rendered many decisions in favor of women that are in compliance with women's rights. An example is a

---

127   *Supra* note 64, at 67; Article 18 bis 2 of Law No. 25 of 1920, as amended by Law No. 100 of 1985.

128   Article 20 of Law No. 25 of 1920, as amended by Law No. 100 of 1985; *see also supra* note 64, at 67.

129   *Id.*

130   *Id.*

131   *Id.*

132   *Id.*

case concerning the financial obligations of the father to pay for guardianship. In 1989, a court decided that a father had to make payments to a mother for her guardianship of their infant child dating back to 1973 and continuing forward until the date at which the mother no longer was the guardian of their child.[133] In this case, the father claimed that subsection 4 of Article 18 of the Personal Status Law was unconstitutional with respect to its stipulation that the father was obliged to pay for guardianship beginning at the date that he stopped doing so. He asserted this violated Article 2 because of the Hanafi religious doctrine.[134] The Hanafi doctrine stated that payment for the upbringing of children was only due from the date of the court's ruling. The Constitutional Court stated that the long existence of one of these rules does not mean that it could not be substituted by a new rule provided that the new rule was in the best interest of the society and not contrary to the main purposes and norms of the Sharia. The Court added that the view of the Hanafi was that the child had been otherwise provided for during this period and therefore no longer required the costs claimed. The court asserted that this view was neither consistent with what actually occurred in practice nor was it in the best interests of the family. Furthermore, the court added that the father was the only person responsible for the costs of guardianship of his child in accordance with the words of the Prophet: "it is a great sin for the person to abandon whom he feeds.[135] The court also clarified that the child's rights do not lapse until full payment has been made. The payment was necessary for both the mother and the child. The court clarified that the Quran states that, "neither shall a mother be made to suffer harm on account of her child, nor a father on account of his child."[136]

The law imposes this obligation upon the husband to support the woman who has child custody until the end of the child custody and the child's alimony. The law is ideal in protecting and safeguarding the rights of women and children. The father of the children has a full obligation to pay all the expenses of his wife and children. The roots of this law are in Islamic law. For instance, the Quran provides general guidance by stating the following general rule:

> "Divorced" mothers will breastfeed their offspring for two whole years, for those who wish to complete the nursing "of their child." The child's father will provide reasonable maintenance and clothing for the mother

---

133   El Demery, *supra* note 25, at 208 (*citing* Case No. 29, Judicial Year 11, 26th Mar. 1994).
134   Hanafi religious doctrine is the official doctrine that is followed in Egypt.
135   El Demery, *supra* note 25, at 209 (*citing* Case No. 29, Judicial Year 11, 26th Mar. 1994).
136   Quran 2:233.

"during that period." No one will be charged with more than they can bear. No mother or father should be made to suffer for their child. The "father's" heirs are under the same obligation. But if both sides decide—after mutual consultation and consent—to wean a child, then there is no blame on them. If you decide to have your children nursed by a wet-nurse, it is permissible as long as you pay fairly. Be mindful of Allah, and know that Allah is All-Seeing of what you do.[137]

2.2.4. The Financial Responsibility of the Father toward the Breastfeeding Woman

Family law states that the father of the children shall pay the woman who is responsible to breastfeed his children, whether this woman is the mother of the children or not.[138] The salary of the woman is for two years from the first day that she breastfeeds the babies.[139]

This law is considerate of the role that women play in society, in terms of appreciation of her breastfeeding the children, and acknowledging that she should be financially rewarded for doing so.

2.3 *Child Custody*

The law has given women superiority regarding child custody. This is derived from Islamic Sharia. The Quran states:

And your Lord has decreed that you worship none but Him. And that you be dutiful to your parents. If one of them or both of them attain old age in your life, say not to them a word of disrespect, nor shout at them but address them in terms of honor.[140]

---

137   Quran 2:233.

138   *Supra* note 64, at 68.

139   *Id.*

140   Quran 17:23 (Islam gives parents the highest position and rank over all people. Due to their important major role, God mentions them after He mentions His name directly.); *see, e.g.,* Quran 31:13–14 ("And (remember) when Luqman said to his son when he was advising him: 'O my son! Join not in worship others with Allah. Verily joining others in worship with Allah is a great Zulm (wrong) indeed. And We have enjoined on man (to be dutiful and good) to his parents. His mother bore him in weakness and hardship upon weakness and hardship, and his weaning is in two years – give thanks to Me and to your parents. Unto Me is the final destination.'"); *see also* Quran 4:36 ("Worship Allah and join none with Him in worship, and do good to parents, kinsfolk, orphans, *Al-Masakin* (the poor), the neighbour who is near of kin, the neighbour who is a stranger, the companion by your side, the wayfarer (you meet), and those (slaves) whom your right hands possess.

In Sharia, mothers are given more care than fathers. Mothers raise children; in addition, they suffer pain during pregnancy and at the time of delivering the baby.[141]

A very famous hadith says:

A man came to the Prophet Muhammad and said, "O Messenger of God! Who among the people is the most worthy of my good companionship?" The Prophet said,

> "Your mother"
> The man said, "Then who?"
> The Prophet said, "Then your mother."
> The man further asked, "Then who?"
> The Prophet said, "Then your mother"
> The man asked again, "Then who?"
> The Prophet said, "Then your father."[142]

Egyptian family law has ensured the right of the mother to have custody of the children until they are fifteen years old.[143] Even after the children become fifteen years old, the father does not have the right to arbitrarily take the children away from the mother. If the father wants his children to live with him and they refused, or his ex-wife refused, then the court will render its decision according to the law. Once the children are fifteen years old, the judge will give the children the choice to either stay with the father or the mother.[144] The judge will give daughters and sons the full choice to either live with their father

---

Verily, Allah does not like such as are proud and boastful."); *see also* Quran 46:15 ("And We have enjoined on man to be dutiful and kind to his parents. His mother bears him with hardship and she brings him forth with hardship, and the bearing of him, and the weaning of him is thirty (30) months, till when he attains full strength and reaches forty years, he says: "My Lord! Grant me the power and ability that I may be grateful for Your Favour which You have bestowed upon me and upon my parents, and that I may do righteous good deeds, such as please You, and make my off-spring good. Truly, I have turned to You in repentance, and truly, I am one of the Muslims (submitting to Your Will)) (Although both parents in Islam have this important position but when comparing between the father and the mother, then the mother will be in a higher position than the position of the man in Islam. Women suffered so much in pregnancy and taking care of the baby and also suffer in raising their child.).

141   El Demery, *supra* note 25, at 58.

142   Riyad as-Salihin, Hadith 316, https://sunnah.com/riyadussalihin:316.

143   Article 20 of Law No. 25 of 1920, amended by both Law No. 100 of 1985 and No. 4 of 2005, *supra* note 128.

144   *Id.*

or continue living with their mother until the daughter is married and the son is twenty-one years old.[145]

Even if the mother of the children is not alive, this does not mean that the children's father will have the right to take them. Priority is given to women in the case of child custody.[146] The priority is given first to the mother of the children. If the mother is dead or incapable of having custody due to any reason, then this right is given to the maternal grandmother of the children, and so on. If all are dead or are incapable to have custody, then this right is given to the paternal grandmother; after that, it is given to the paternal great-grandmother, and so on.[147] After that, this right is given to the sister of the child if she is old enough and capable to take care of the child. Then, this right is given to the sisters of the mother then the sisters of the father, etc.[148] If all these women are dead or not capable for any reason, then the child's custody will be transferred to the men, and priority will first be given to the grandfather.[149]

From all these examples, we can clearly understand how the law has honored and highly respected women. This is due to the fact that God created women with special skills and feelings which help them in raising the children in an ideal way. Due to the importance of child custody and the fact that many cases take a long time in court, the prosecutor general of Egypt gives instructions to all prosecutors of the family office regarding child custody. This instruction states that if a dispute happens regarding child custody, the prosecutor shall not wait until the court renders the final decision. The prosecutor should issue a quick legal order, after investigation and after asking all the parties of the dispute.[150] The legal order shall name the person that has the child custody, until the court issues its final decision.[151] This quick legal order of the public prosecution helps the pending cases regarding child custody in Egyptian Family Courts.

Any woman can sue her ex-husband, claiming her right to have custody over the child. The ex-husband cannot defend himself by saying that his ex-wife agreed to forfeit her right to the child custody. The court decision will be in favor of the woman because as it is the mother's rights and for the best interest of the child. The child custody is not only the right of the mother, but also a

---

145   *Id.*
146   *Id. See also supra* note 64, at 71.
147   *Id.* at 71.
148   *Id.*
149   *Id.*
150   *Supra* note 64, at 54.
151   *Id.*

fundamental right of the children. Therefore, for the best interest of the children, they should be with their mother.

2.4   *The Efficiency and Effectiveness of the Family Court*

2.4.1   The Enforceability of the Family Court Decisions

In order to protect women's and children's rights, the decisions of the court of first instance with respect to financial matters are enforceable, even if they are appealed.[152] For example, the court of first instance rendered a decision stating that father should pay monthly 2000 Egyptian pounds to his wife and children as financial responsibility towards his wife and children. In addition, the court rendered a decision that the man should pay 100 pounds monthly for bedding. The husband must pay this amount of money, even if he submitted an appeal to the appeal court. The enforceability of the decisions of the family courts in financial matters is very important in guaranteeing children and women rights to live an adequate life. The woman can also appeal the decision of the court, requesting the court of appeal to increase the amount of money. Usually women appeal the decision of the court of first instance, by claiming that the amount of money determined by the court of first instance is not enough, compared to the increase in living expenses and the high income and salary of her husband. It should be noted that regardless of whether women appeal the decision of the court of first instance or not, they always have the right to sue and bring a new case after a while requesting from the court to increase the amount of money previously determined by the court of first instance and the court of appeal. For example, women may claim that her living expenses increased and/or his income increased or he worked in a new job with a higher salary or he inherited money from his family. On the other hand, the husband can submit a case requesting to reduce the amount of money decided by the court. For example, he can claim that his income was reduced or he left his job because of a disability. In short, it is a case-by-case decision; the court will examine the circumstances of each case.

2.4.2   The Sanction of Imprisonment

From all that is mentioned above, we can easily conclude that the family court always tries to do a great job in protecting the right of children and women. Egyptian family law precisely aims to protect the rights of children and women. On the other hand, some fathers and husbands try to escape their financial responsibility. The family court is given the legal power to render a

---

152   Article 54, Law No. 1 of 2000.

decision of imprisoning the father or husband who intentionally refuses to pay his financial obligations. This allows the family court to be more efficient and effective.

According to the family law, if certain conditions are fulfilled, the family court has the right to issue a court decision of imprisoning irresponsible men:

1. if there was a final verdict with regard to the financial responsibility of the man;
2. if the man refused to pay the money owed, after the imprisonment case was raised against him;
3. if the court found by evidence that this man is capable of paying all the money that he is responsible to pay; and
4. if the court ordered the man to pay but he refused to pay.[153]

After the fulfillment of all of these conditions, the family court, upon the request of the woman, has the right to issue a court decision of imprisoning the man.[154]

If the man still insists on not paying the money, she can also sue him according to the Criminal Code in the misdemeanor court; in this case, the imprisonment can be ordered for up to one year.[155]

The main goal of the family court is not to imprison men, but pursue the main goal that the family, including husband, wife and children, live again together in good relations. This goal is clear as the law requires the court to request reconciliation between the parties of each case. Even in some articles of the family law, reconciliation is requested at least two times; otherwise the court's final decision will be null and void.

If the husband pays the money, then the decision of the imprisonment will not be applied on him. If he was imprisoned, then he will have his freedom immediately after paying the money due.[156]

The Supreme Court held that, according to Islamic law, only the father is responsible to pay his children's expenses (home, food, clothes, medicine, education fees, etc.). The Court added that he cannot forfeit this obligation, even if he is insolvent, as long as he is able to earn something.[157]

---

153   Law No. 1 of 2000, Article 76 bis, as amended by Law No. 91 of 2000.
154   *Id.*
155   Egyptian Criminal Law, Article 293, https://sherloc.unodc.org/cld/document/egy/1937 /criminal _code_of_egypt_english.html (last visited Sep. 3, 2022).
156   *Id.*
157   The Supreme Court, Case No. 3938 for the Judicial Year 85 (Aug. 18 2020), https://www .cc.gov.eg/judgment_single?id=111646017&ja=285751.

2.4.3   The Insurance System

In some cases, the potential loser tries to use all the legal possible ways to extend the length of the trial, in order not to pay their children. In addition, the potential loser tries to escape from justice by not implementing the court's decision. The delay in paying the money is an injustice. The new proposed family law should focus on the enforcement issue, by finding more effective ways for implementation. Any woman having a family dispute hopes to raise one case that covers all possible disputes. One case means less money being paid to lawyers and also means having a quick court decision instead of waiting for a couple of decisions after bringing several different cases.

Many women and children may suffer until they get the money from the man (husband or father) as the delay in receiving the money may affect their lives totally. For example, in many cases the children need to pay tuition fees of their school on time. Also, the mother or the children may need medical treatment forcing them to go to the hospital immediately without delay. In many real cases, the woman does not work, and even if she is working, her salary cannot cover all the necessary expenses (food, clothes, medical treatment, home rent, etc.).

Often, in most countries in the world, if a person wants to obtain insurance, the beneficiary of the insurance must pay a certain amount of money continuously. In Egypt, however, the legislators proposed an ideal solution for women who face the difficulty of being unable to pay for all expenses, i.e. a national insurance system. With this, the wife will have the benefit of the insurance, but she will not sign any contract for the insurance, and she will not have to pay for it. According to this insurance, "Nasser Social Bank" (a governmental bank) will immediately pay the amount of money that was determined by the judge.[158] The family law gives the woman the right to go to the bank nearest to her home and take the money from that branch.[159] Nasser bank, however, does not pay the amount of money that was determined by the judge for *Al-Motta*.[160]

According to the law, Nasser Bank was given the right to deduct this amount of money from the salary of the husband. This authority was given to the bank regardless of the place the man was working at, e.g., in the public sector, private sector, etc.[161] If the man was not working in Egypt, or if he did not have Egyptian citizenship, the Office of the Prosecutor General and the Office of

---

158   *Supra* note 25, at 210; *see also supra* note 156.
159   *Id.*
160   Ta'lemat El Naeb El Aam, *supra* note 64, at 211.
161   *Id.*

International Cooperation at the Ministry of Justice of Egypt would use all suitable diplomatic ways to get the money back.

The husbands themselves are responsible of financing the family insurance. The family insurance is funded in a very smart way. Every man that wants to marry a woman must pay a certain amount of money before signing the official marriage paper.[162] In addition, every husband must pay a certain amount of money, if he wants to divorce his wife, or if he wants to return her back after the divorce by a new marriage contract.[163] In order to obtain an official birth certificate, every father must pay fees for each baby when he applies for the birth certificate.[164] The new draft of family law will establish an Egyptian Family Support and Care Fund. This fund will play an important than the current existing insurance System. The Egyptian president said that the idea of establishing a fund for the Egyptian family is to provide support for children, as Nasser Social Bank became indebted to the state by about 350 million pounds. According to President Al-Sisi, Nasser Bank is already providing funds for this group of children and mothers. The President added that the Family Support and Care Fund is a safety valve for young children who, due to the separation of their parents, suddenly turned into victims. The divorce incident and the anger of the parents deprived the children of financial care for their needs in life. He added that the state must protect them and pay these risks for them. The human rights of the children and their mother should not be lost when a dispute or divorce occurs. Furthermore, he added that the government and newly married people will contribute to financing the Egyptian Family Support and Care Fund.[165]

2.4.4   Lawyers

Many women suffer when having to pay large amounts of money to lawyers in the court while some women do not have enough money to pay for the lawyers at all. Family law has put an end to these suffering situations, as any person can raise any case of financial responsibility without a lawyer. If the family court finds it necessary, then the court can appoint a lawyer on behalf of the person who raised the case. The financial department will be responsible in paying all the expenses of the lawyer.[166]

---

162   *Id.* at 207.
163   *Id.*
164   *Id.*
165   Egyptian president, Egyptian Family Support and Care Fund, https://www.youtube.com /watch?v=HqIgZzVsQgE.
166   *Id.; see also supra* note 111.

2.4.5   No Fees Required

According to Egyptian family law, no person will pay a cent in raising any of the cases of the financial responsibility at any stage of litigation.[167] In other words, if any woman wants to sue her husband or ex-husband, then she does not have to pay any fees. There are no fees even if she wants to appeal the decision of the first court.[168]

2.4.6   The Reconciliation Office

The family law's priority is to protect the bonds of the family. According to the family law, no person has the right to bring a case before the family court unless this person applies first to the reconciliation office. This office charges no fees and using its services is a precondition to submit a case to the family court, for example, divorce due to harm, divorce due to unsolved concrete problem, *Khula*, financial cases, etc.[169] So, in order not to waste time and to make it easier, if anyone brought a case without having first applied to the dispute reconciliation office, then the court itself can return the case to the dispute reconciliation office.[170]

The reconciliation office is under the authority of the Ministry of Justice. This office contains many specialized legal, sociological and psychological employees. The duty of these professional employees is to try to solve, reconcile, and settle the disputes between a man and a woman as they have the authority to speak with both parties in an effort to solve the problems between them.[171] The reconciliation office does not collect any fees from the parties as their services are free.[172]

In order to not waste the time of either party, according to the family law, the reconciliation office has fifteen days from the day of application, to resolve the dispute. These fifteen days can be extended only to an extra fifteen days, totaling thirty days, if both parties agreed to extend the time limit.[173] If the dispute was solved, then the president of the reconciliation office will give the parties an official certificate of the reconciliation.[174]

---

167   *Id.*
168   *Id.*
169   *Id.* at 44; Articles 5 to 9 of Law No. 10 of 2004.
170   *Supra* note 64, at 178; *see also* Articles 5 to 9 of Law No. 10 of 2004.
171   *Id.* at 44.
172   *Id.*
173   *Id.*
174   *Id.* at 44.

2.4.7   Highly Experienced Judges at the Family Court

According to the family law, each court of first instance shall consist of three judges. At least one of them has to be a senior judge, and his job title is "President at the Court of First Instance."[175] The parties have the right to appeal the judgment at the court of appeal.[176] The court of appeal of family law shall consist of three judges; at least one of them has to be a senior judge, his job title being "President at the Court of Appeal."[177] The main goal is to make sure that there are highly experienced judges at the family court.

Once again, family law tries to protect the rights of women. In addition, the law ensured that highly ranked judges are in family court to ensure good expertise in adjudicating the family disputes. Also, the law states that in all the family courts there should be two specialized professionals, one of them should be sociological and the other should be psychological.[178] Furthermore, one of them at least must be a woman.[179] These two professionals have no authority to decide a case, they only submit a report to the judges on the sociological and the psychological aspects of the case.

3   Prediction of Future Decisions

There are many rights stated in the family law, but the legislators and the Ministry of Justice are keen to adopt a new law to give more effective protection and rights. The government wants to protect the family bonds, especially women and children. The Egyptian President stated several times in public speeches that the percentage of divorce and separation is alarming in Egypt. He recommended that there should be solutions for this important issue. He added that there should be a committee of highly experienced experts and judges to evaluate the current law and submit solutions.[180] In June of 2022, the Minister of Justice issued a ministerial decree establishing a judicial committee

---

175   *Supra* note 64, at 178; Article 2 of Law No. 10 of 2004.
176   *Id.* at 46.
177   *Id.*
178   Article 2 of Law No. 10 of 2004.
179   *Id.*
180   Sada Elbalad, *Editorial Hall – President Abdel Fattah El-Sisi's intervention with the media, Azza Mustafa, in the Editorial Hall Program,* YouTube (May 10, 2020), https://www .youtube.com/watch?v=jRtSDTgHfd8; *see also* DMC, *President El-Sisi: Divorce Rates Reach 44%, An Indication of a Serious Issue in Society,* YouTube (July 28, 2018), https://www .youtube.com/watch?v=HCdfkSDvS-o.

to draft a proposal of a new law on family affairs.[181] The proposed new law will have a balanced vision that guarantees the rights of all family members. In addition, it will take into account the multiple interests of all parties concerned and address family as well as societal concerns in this regard.[182]

This judicial committee has several duties including finding possible solutions to reduce family conflicts, maintaining balanced interests among family members, and applying justice effectively and swiftly. The committee receives proposals and suggestions from all competent authorities.[183] Furthermore, any person can submit their suggestions to the committee. The Minister of Justice said that the final proposal of the law, once it is finished, will be presented for whole of society dialogue.[184] The Committee is expected to finish drafting of the new law in 2023.

On the other hand, the government has already started to gradually begin digitalizing and computerizing the courts. The reason of doing so is to facilitate to the parties of cases and the judges the proceedings of the cases and ensure prompt decisions. It is expected in the next few years that all the courts will be computerized and digitalized.

4   Opinion and Recommendations

With respect to the Committee which is currently working on drafting a new law on family affairs, it is expected that the new law will be a great achievement for the Egyptian family affairs due to the composition of the judicial committee including highly specialized experts in the field of family affairs. The government and all of society are doing their best to find solutions. All judicial regulations regarding the family matters should be revised so as to decrease the amount of time cases take in the court and to further protect and support women. The Committee is receiving thousands of proposals and ideas regarding family affairs from competent authorities, lawyers, and individuals. This clearly shows that society has strong confidence and great expectations regarding the outcome of the Committee's work. There will be one unified

---

181   Minister of Justice Decree No. 3805 of 2022 (June 5, 2022).

182   *Id.; see also* Sada Elbalad, *The Minister of Justice Reveals the Details of Issuing a Ministerial Decision to Form the Competent Committee for the Personal Status Law tomorrow*, YouTube (June 4, 2022), https://www.youtube.com/watch? v=o68SLmYPKLI.

183   ON, A final word – the Minister of Justice Reveals the Details of Forming a Committee to Prepare the Personal Status Law ... and Sends Important Messages, YouTube (June 5, 2022), https://www.youtube.com/watch?v=hKrtKr27Mk4.

184   *Id.*

comprehensive new code of family law, instead of having several laws with several amendments.[185] Having one law make it much easier for parties of the case, lawyers, and judges, to understand and implement. The Chairman of the Committee for the Preparation of the draft Personal Status Law (Family Law) said that the new draft personal status law provides for immediate alimony for the wife or divorced woman, until the case is decided.[186] The new draft Personal Status Law approved the establishment of the Egyptian Family Support and Care Fund. The goal of the Fund is to ensure the implementation of the final judgments issued to determine alimony for the wife, the divorced woman, her children, and to support and care for the Egyptian family. The Minister of Justice said that this fund[187] is important to maintain the stability of the family at the same level they were living in.[188]

The digitalization of the courts and case management including family courts is very important. It will help the parties of the case, especially women and children, access electronically the decisions of the courts and the court's proceedings. The remote trials will make it easier for the parties to attend court hearings online, especially when there is a global pandemic, like COVID-19. In addition, the parties will be able to see information about their case online and upload documents. Furthermore, digitalization and computerizing will enable the court and judges to make database management for all the cases and enable the judges to render finial decisions promptly.

One of the challenges that are facing the family courts is the possibility of the existence of several cases separately for each spouse. In other words, there may be five cases or more for each family separately, the wife or the husband can sue each other separately in several cases. For example, the wife can sue her husband in the following cases: divorce due to harm; *Al-Motta*; children's expenses; children's school fees; child custody; housing wages; expenses for clothes and bedding; maid salary; medical expenses, etc. In my opinion, there should be only one case for each family that includes and covers all of the possible disputes within the family. So, the parties of the case and the judge will review a checklist that includes all relevant claims. Afterwards, the court will render one decision that includes all of the possible claims. This proposal will reduce the huge number of separate cases in front of the courts.

---

185   Details of the draft personal status law, https://www.elaosboa.com/638004/.

186   The Chairman of the Committee for the Preparation of the draft Personal Status Law (Family Law), https://www.cairo24.com/1717032.

187   The Family Welfare Fund solves divorce problems and provides a decent life for divorced women and her children, https://www.vetogate.com/4774837.

188   It protects the children. The Minister of Justice reveals the tasks of the Egyptian Family Support Fund, https://www.youtube.com/watch?v=6vwFDMAkgXU.

The family disputes are not usefully solved in courts by saying which one is right or wrong; the court should render its decision in light of the best interests of the child and the family. There should be profound studies from all competent authorities with expertise to find concrete solutions. These decisions should be taken with a view toward protecting the family bonds and fundamental interests of the children and family.

The National Council for Women will continue to undertake an active role in protecting and enhancing women's human rights, freedoms, empowerment, and non-discrimination.[189] The government will continue its efforts in improving the educational level of women, especially in villages and rural areas, as highly educated women know and claim their human rights. The Concluding Observations of the Committee on the Elimination of Discrimination against Women on Egypt state that "The Committee notes the focus of the National Strategy for the Empowerment of Egyptian Women for 2016–2030 on rural women with concern."[190] Also, the Committee notes with concern "[t]he high rates of illiteracy, including digital illiteracy, and school dropout among girls and women."[191] The Committee recommends that Egypt "[a]dopt and implement legal and policy measures to ensure that rural women effectively have access to education."[192]

The Egyptian Constitution provides that "[u]niversities are committed to teaching human rights, and professional morals and ethics relating to various academic disciplines."[193] The government and nongovernmental organizations are trying to eradicate illiteracy and lower the school dropout rate, especially for girls. All the government and nongovernmental organizations should do their best to encourage women and children to become educated. The Egyptian Constitution states that "[t]he state commits to developing a comprehensive plan to eradicate alphabetical and digital illiteracy for all citizens from all age groups. It commits to developing implementation mechanisms with the participation of civil society institutions according to a specific timeline."[194]

In some cases, men try to escape from implementing the court decision. They refuse to pay the basic needs to their children and wife, although the documents submitted to the court prove that these men are rich. One of the

---

189   Supreme Standing Committee for Human Rights, *supra* note 45.
190   Concluding observations on the combined eighth to tenth periodic reports of Egypt, *supra* note 47.
191   *Id.*
192   *Id.*
193   Egyptian Constitution, Article 24.
194   *Id.* at art. 25.

possible ideas to solve this issue is to prevent these men from requesting any government services unless they meet all their financial responsibilities.

Usually divorced women do not have enough money to pay all the expenses of their children, especially because of the delay in the courts. The government and non-governmental organizations should work together to find possible ways to help the children of the divorced women. This can be done by exempting children of divorced women from paying educational fees in the governmental schools, or finding possible funds or at least reducing the tuition for them.

5 Conclusion

The Egyptian National Human Rights Strategy states:

> Over the past years, Egypt achieved significant national milestones in the field of human rights, at the legislative, executive and institutional levels. However, enhancing the protection of human rights is an ongoing and recurrent process which has accumulative and gradual impact. Any efforts exerted or achievements attained in this field will not lead to perfection; challenges relating to the equal enjoyment of rights and fundamental freedoms by everyone will remain. This implies more efforts to address accumulated challenges and existing shortcomings.[195]

There is no doubt that the family affairs law is issued for the sake of protecting women's rights, the family's stability, and eventually a stable society overall. Women and children in Egypt are currently in a unique position in society, and their rights are protected and granted. For example, the financial cases and the *Khula* Law are great achievements for securing and protecting wives and children. The *Khula* law is ideal as it protects women's rights, and it does not need a proof of harm, the court's decision is final and cannot be appealed.

The law of the financial responsibility of the husband towards his wife is effective, as the law gives women financial support whether they are rich or poor. The father is responsible to cover the expenses of his daughter until she gets married or until she starts working and earns enough money to support herself. In addition, the father is also responsible to cover the expenses of his son until he concludes his undergraduate and graduate education. The

---

195   Supreme Standing Committee for Human Rights, *supra* note 45.

financial debts of the husband towards his children and wife have priority and superiority over any other debts he owes toward other people. Even if the wife is wealthier than her husband, he is still responsible to cover the necessary basic needs of his wife and children. One of main reason that leads the legislator to state that the husband should pay expenses of his wife, even if she is richer than him, is because of cultures, traditions, and the Quran. The Quran states that "men are the protectors and maintainers of women, because Allah has made one of them to excel the other, and because they spend (to support them) from their means."[196] In addition, the Quran provides that "who hoard their wealth and enjoin avarice on others, and hide that which Allah hath bestowed upon them of His bounty. For disbelievers We prepare a shameful doom."[197] So, from this verse we can understand that Islam wants husbands to be generous with their wives. Sharia law emphasizes the importance of individual duties in society, therefore in order for the husband to have rights, a duty to his wife and children must be fulfilled. Unlike Sharia law, the International Covenant on Economic, Social and Cultural Rights only creates general rights and does not focus on individual duties.[198]

In addition to the financial responsibility towards the wife, there is an additional financial responsibility towards the woman who breastfeeds the child, whether she is the mother of the child or not. This law respects the woman, regardless if she is the true mother or not, and gives her the expenses for the two years of nursing. This law protects and secures the right of the mother or the woman who breastfeeds the child. On the other hand, the Al-Motta law also protects the right of women as it provides women with their expenses for, at least, two full years, according to the financial status of the ex-husband.

In the light of what I have clarified in this article, "we can see that the husband holds a lot of responsibility before, during, and after marriage. Because of this, he is given some rights in return."[199] There is positive discrimination in favor of women which is stated in Article 3 (3) of the Arab Charter on Human Rights.[200]

The right of the women relates not only to the financial responsibility, but also to the right to custody over the children. Like the *Khula* law, the root of custody is derived from Islam. The priority is given to women because they are

---

196   Quran 176:34.

197   Quran 176:37.

198   El Demery, *supra* note 25, at 96–97; Jason Morgan-Foster, *A New Perspective on the Universality Debate: Reverse Moderate Relativism in the Islamic Context*, 10 ILSA J. Int'l & Comp. L. 35, 59 (2003).

199   *Id.* at 228.

200   *See supra* note 4.

capable of taking care of children; God created them with special unique skills and feelings that help them in raising their children in an ideal way.

The high percentage of divorce rate in Egypt should be studied and evaluated by all the authorities and the research institutes to know the reasons behind it and find possible ways of solving this issue. The current committee that is working drafting a new law is expected to do a great progress, and to find very good solutions.

Sharia, which is the main source of the constitution on Muslims' family matters, encourages the romantic life of the family together – husband, wife and children.[201] The Quran states that "O my Lord! Grant unto us wives and offspring who will be the comfort of our eyes, and give us (the grace) to lead the righteous."[202] It should be clear that Sharia did not say that the husband will be at a higher level in paradise than his wife, they are equal. The Quran states, "Enter Paradise, you and your wives, in happiness."[203] Also, the Quran states, "They and their wives, in pleasant shade, on thrones reclining."[204]

In conclusion, although there are continuous great achievements in family law matters, still there are several challenges to face. For example, the committee should find solutions regarding implementing the court decisions promptly, especially regarding financial cases of women and children. The national human rights strategy sheds light on the need to create a national mechanism for the immediate enforcement of alimony and custody rulings. It also emphasizes the importance to amend laws with the aim of enhancing women's rights, ensuring the child's best interest, and facilitating women's access to their rights and their children's rights without delay.[205] The family law in general is a great step forward toward protecting the bonds of the families and safeguarding and securing the rights of children and women. The most important thing is to find the reasons of divorce and try to find solutions and reduce its occurrence. No country can have a strong community without strong united families. Children should be raised living with their parents. To achieve this goal, the collaborative work of the government, community, society, the Church and the Mosque is needed in order to find best solutions. The Egyptian President said that there are 9 million children whose parents are divorced. In addition, there are 15 million, children whose parents are separated but not

---

201   El Demery, *supra* note 25, at 118.
202   Quran 25:74.
203   *Id.* at 43:70.
204   *Id.* at 36:56.
205   Supreme Standing Committee for Human Rights, *supra* note 45.

divorced officially. He added that all of society must confront this phenomenon and protect the community.[206]

Acknowledgements

I would like to thank Professor W. Michael Reisman, Myres S. McDougal Professor of International Law at the Yale Law School, and Professor Roza Pati, Executive Director of the LL.M./ J.S.D. Program in Intercultural Human Rights and the Director of the Human Trafficking Academy, for giving me the opportunity to write this article and for providing invaluable guidance throughout this research. I am extremely grateful to my parents for their love, prayers, caring and sacrifices to educate and prepare me for the future. I am most thankful to my wife and my children for their love, understanding, prayers and continuing support to complete this article. I also express my thanks to my sister.

---

206   DMC, *President El-Sisi: Divorce Rates Reach 44%, An Indication of a Serious Issue in Society*, YouTube (July 28, 2018), https://www.youtube.com/watch?v=HCdfkSDvS-0.

PART 5

The Rights of Indigenous Peoples

∵

CHAPTER 21

Indigenous Peoples in the United States: Justice Still Needed

*S. James Anaya**

1   Introduction

Indigenous peoples in the United States occupy a complex and challenging place in the American social and political landscape, one that requires reflection on the country's injustices toward them to contemplate the path forward. With their vastly diverse identities, Native Americans together stand as a beacon of resilience in the face of an often brutal and unforgiving history. Genuine movement is needed to resolve the persisting injustices and inequities they face.

The situations of indigenous peoples in the United States and elsewhere have gained attention internationally, and in 2007 the United Nations adopted a Declaration on the Rights of Indigenous Peoples.[1] The UN has also established mechanisms that work to advance the human rights of indigenous peoples worldwide in accordance with the Declaration, including the mandate of Special Rapporteur on the rights of indigenous peoples, one of the UN Human Rights Council's several independent expert positions established to examine particular areas of human rights concern.[2]

I was privileged to have been appointed the UN Special Rapporteur on rights of indigenous peoples for two consecutive terms, serving from 2008 to 2014. In that capacity I conducted examinations of the human rights situation of indigenous peoples in several countries, including the United States. As part of this work, in May 2012, I held consultations with indigenous peoples, tribes, and nations as well as federal and state government authorities in several

---

* University Distinguished Professor and Nicholas Doman Professor of International Law, University of Colorado Law School.
1 G.A. Res. 61/295, Sept. 13 2007.
2 Other UN mechanisms focused on indigenous peoples' concerns include the seven-member Expert Mechanism on the Rights of Indigenous Peoples, which also reports to the UN Human Rights Council, and the 16-member Permanent Forum on Indigenous Issues, which reports to the UN Economic and Social Council. *See generally* U.N. Office of the High Comm'r, *Indigenous Peoples and the United Nations Human Rights System, Fact Sheet No. 9/Rev.2*, at 11–15 (2013).

parts of the United States, including Arizona, Alaska, Oregon, South Dakota, Washington state, and Washington D.C.

What follows in this chapter is a modified and updated version of the report I concluded as Special Rapporteur addressing the human rights situation of indigenous peoples in the United States. These peoples constitute vibrant communities that have contributed greatly to the life of the country. In the next sections a brief description of the diverse indigenous nations, tribes, and communities in the country is followed by a summary of U.S. laws and policies regarding indigenous peoples. I then examine the disadvantaged conditions of indigenous peoples in the United States and assess the present-day legacies of historical wrongs. Finally, I recommend steps forward, highlighting the significance of the Declaration on the Rights of Indigenous Peoples and its essential role in guiding efforts to generate just solutions. Ultimately, I concluded that the United States must adopt new approaches, in accordance with the Declaration, to advance toward justice for indigenous peoples and address persistent, deep-seated problems related to historical wrongs, failed policies of the past, and continuing systemic barriers to the full realization of their rights.

2   The Indigenous Peoples of the United States

2.1   *The Diverse Indigenous Nations, Tribes, and Communities*
The indigenous peoples of the United States include a vast array of distinct groups that fall under the generally accepted designation of Native Americans, which include American Indians and Alaska Natives; also included are the people indigenous to Hawaii, or Native Hawaiians. These indigenous peoples form tribes or nations – terms used interchangeably herein – and other communities with distinctive cultural and political attributes.

Broadly speaking, Native Americans living in the contiguous United States constitute tribes or nations with diverse cultural and ethnic characteristics that can be grouped geographically. Linguistic families and other cultural markers, however, cross rough geographic categories, and within these categories differences abound. For historical and other reasons, Alaska Natives and Native Hawaiians are considered distinct from Native Americans in the contiguous United States.

The United States presently recognizes and maintains what it refers to as government-to-government relations with approximately 574 American Indian and Alaska Native tribes and villages,[3] around 229 of these being Alaska

---

3   *Federal and State Recognized Tribes*, National Conference of State Legislatures, https://www
    .ncsl.org/legislators-staff/legislators/quad-caucus/list-of-federal-and-state-recognized-tribes
    .aspx (last visited Aug. 15, 2022).

Native groups.[4] For the most part each of these tribes and villages determines its own membership. While having some form of federal recognition, Native Hawaiians do not have a similar status under United States law as that of American Indians and Alaska Native groups. Many other groups in the United States that identify as indigenous peoples have not been federally recognized, although some of these have achieved recognition at the state level.

It is estimated that prior to colonization, the indigenous population within the territory that now constitutes the United States numbered several million and represented diverse cultures and societies speaking hundreds of languages and dialects. After the arrival of Europeans, the indigenous population suffered significant decline due to the effects of disease, war, enslavement, and forced relocations.

According to the most recent U.S. census data, people who identify as Native American represent approximately 2.9 percent of the overall population of the United States, with 9.7 million persons identifying as American Indian or Alaska Native, either alone or in combination with one or more other races.[5] It should be noted that this number significantly exceeds the number of those who are enrolled or registered members of federally recognized indigenous groups. In addition, there are roughly half a million persons that identify entirely or partly as Native Hawaiians.

Characteristically, the federally recognized tribes have reservations or other lands that have been left to or set aside for them and over which they exercise powers of self-government. While the land holdings vary significantly among the tribes, in all cases they pale in comparison to the land areas once under their possession or control. Still, the diminished landholdings provide some physical space and material bases for the tribes to maintain their cultures and political institutions and to develop economically.

While many indigenous persons live on reservations or other Native-controlled land areas, many others live in urban areas beyond the boundaries of indigenous lands. It is quite common, however, for indigenous persons living in urban areas to maintain close ties to the land-based communities of the tribes with which they are affiliated and to develop bonds of community with other indigenous persons in their urban settings.

---

4 *Tribal Nations and the United States: An Introduction*, National Congress of American Indians, https://www.ncai.org/about-tribes#:~:text=There%20are%20574%20federally%20recognized, villages)%20in%20the%20United%20States (last visited Aug. 15, 2022).

5 Nicholas Jones, Rachel Marks, Roberto Ramirez, Merarys S. Ríos-Vargas, *2020 Census Illuminates Racial and Ethnic Composition of the* Country, U.S. Census Bureau (Aug.12, 2021), https://www.census.gov/library/stories/2021/08/improved-race-ethnicity-measures-reveal -united-states-population-much-more-multiracial.html.

Several indigenous peoples live in border areas and face unique challenges, especially tribes living along the United States-Mexico border, where heightened border security measures implemented by the federal government in recent years have increasingly made cross-border contact between members of the same tribes very difficult.

2.2 *The Contributions of Indigenous Peoples to the Broader Society Despite Persistent Stereotypes*

Within the United States, stereotypes persist that tend to render Native Americans relics of the past, perpetuated by the use of Indian names by professional and other high-profile sports teams, caricatures in the popular media, and even mainstream education on history and social studies. Such stereotypes have served in the broader society to obscure understanding of the reality of Native Americans today and to help to keep alive racially discriminatory attitudes.

Beyond the stereotypes, however, one readily sees vibrant indigenous communities, both in reservation and other areas, including urban areas, which have contributed to the building of the country and continue to contribute to the broader society. Of course, their greatest contribution is in the vast expanses of land that they gave up, through treaty cessions and otherwise, without which the United States and its economic base would not exist. Native Americans have also added to the defense and security of the United States and are represented among the ranks of the United States military services at a rate higher than that of any other ethnic group.[6]

Today, indigenous peoples in the United States face multiple disadvantages, which are related to the long history of wrongs and misguided policies that have been inflicted upon them. Nonetheless, American Indians, Alaska Natives, and Native Hawaiians have survived as peoples, striving to develop with their distinct identities intact and to maintain and transmit to future generations their material and cultural heritage. While doing so, they add a cultural depth and grounding that, even while often going unnoticed by the majority society, is an important part of the country's collective heritage. Further, the knowledge that they retain about the country's landscapes and the natural resources on them, along with their ethic of stewardship of the land, are invaluable assets to the country, even if not fully appreciated.

---

6   American Indians and Alaska Natives serve in the Armed Forces at five times the national average and have served with distinction in every major conflict for over 200 years. *See American Indian Veterans Have Highest Record of Military Service*, National Indian Council on Aging, Inc (Nov. 8, 2019), https://www.nicoa.org/american-indian-veterans-have-highest -record-of-military-service/.

Increasingly effective activism by indigenous peoples over the last half century has elevated national awareness about their contributions as well as about their ongoing concerns. Encouraged by the Black Lives Matter and #MeToo movements, young indigenous activists have raised their voices, and stories reflecting their realities are filtering into popular media, including television programs and magazines.[7]

3   United States Law and Policy Regarding Indigenous Peoples

Laws and policies related to indigenous peoples have developed over centuries since the colonial era, and today they comprise a complex array of decisions by the United States Congress, the executive branch of the federal government, and the federal courts, in particular the United States Supreme Court.

3.1   *The Basic Framework*

The Constitution of the United States (1787) makes little reference to indigenous peoples, the principal mention being in its article I, section 8, which provides Congress the power to "regulate commerce with ... with the Indian Tribes." This provision signals that, within the federal structure of the government of the United States, competency over matters relating to indigenous peoples rests at the federal, as opposed to state, level.

Looking beyond the constitutional text to historical practice and the colonial-era law of nations, the United States Supreme Court established, in a series of early 19th century cases, foundational principles about the rights and status of Indian tribes that largely endure today.[8] Supreme Court doctrine recognizes that Indian tribes are inherently sovereign with powers of self-government; indeed, they are "nations" with original rights over their ancestral lands. Within this same body of doctrine, however, the sovereignty and original land rights

---

7   For example, FX television series "Reservations Dogs" (depicting the adventures of a group of indigenous teenagers in Oklahoma who are trying to make their way to California) and Peacock's "Rutherford Falls" (following two friends, one indigenous, navigating colonialism and its legacy on their town and families) are hits on their respective networks; *see also* Charlotte Collins, *Quannah Chasinghorse is the Model of the Moment and We Can't Look Away*, InStyle Magazine (Nov. 18, 2021), https://www.instyle.com/awards-events/fashion-week /quannah-chasinghorse (detailing the rise of a young Han Gwich'in and Sicangu/Oglala Lakota woman to high fashion and her work to raise awareness about indigenous culture and land rights).

8   *See* Johnson v. M'Intosh, 21 U.S. 543 (1823); Cherokee Nation v. Georgia, 30 U.S. 1 (1831); Worcester v. Georgia, 31 U.S. 515 (1832).

of tribes are deemed necessarily diminished and subordinated to the power of the United States. This subordination is considered to be a result of discovery or conquest by the European colonial powers or the successor United States.

The federal power to regulate commerce with the Indian tribes is accordingly enlarged to one that is deemed plenary in nature and that can be used to unilaterally modify or extinguish tribal sovereignty or land rights.[9] This power is also related to and justified by a duty of protection the federal government is deemed to have over Indian tribes, in a so-called trusteeship. In all, tribes are sovereign nations with certain inherent powers of self-government and original rights, but they are rendered, in words penned by the famous Supreme Court Justice John Marshall, "domestic dependent nations," subject to the overriding power of the federal government.[10]

While there are positive characteristics of the rights-affirming strain of this judicial doctrine, the rights-limiting strain of this doctrine is out of step with contemporary human rights values. As demonstrated by a significant body of scholarly work, the use of notions of discovery and conquest to find Indians' rights diminished and subordinated to plenary congressional power is linked to colonial-era attitudes toward indigenous peoples that can only be described as racist.[11] Early Supreme Court decisions themselves reveal perceptions of Indians as backward, conquered peoples, with descriptions of them as savages and an inferior race.[12]

At times, however, the Supreme Court and lower courts have been protective of indigenous peoples' rights by affirming original Indian rights to the extent consistent with operative doctrine, or more often by enforcing treaty terms, legislation, or executive decisions that are themselves protective of indigenous rights.[13]

3.2   The Evolution of Federal Policy and Legislation

Federal legislative and executive action, in the exercise of the broad authority over indigenous affairs affirmed by the Supreme Court, has evolved over time along with shifting policy objectives shaped by historical circumstances and prevailing attitudes of the time. After achieving its independence, the United States

---

9   See Lone Wolf v. Hitchcock, 187 U.S. 553 (1903).
10   Cherokee Nation v. Georgia, 30 U.S. 1 (1831).
11   See, e.g., Walter Echohawk, In the Courts of the Conqueror: The 10 Worst Indian Law Cases Ever Decided (2010); Robert A. Williams, Jr., The American Indian in Western Legal Thought (1990).
12   See, e.g., Tee-Hit-Ton v. United States, 344 U.S. 272 (1955).
13   See, e.g., McGirt v. Oklahoma, 591 U.S. ___ (2020); Peoria Tribe of Indians of Oklahoma v. United States, 390 U. S. 468 (1968); United States v. Mitchell, 463 U.S. 206 (1983) (Mitchell II); Hodel v. Irving, 481 U.S. 704 (1987); Confederated Tribes of the Colville Reservation v. United States, 964 F. 2d 1102 (Fed. Cir. 1992); White Mountain Apache Tribe of Arizona v. United States, 26 Cl. Ct. 446 (1992).

continued the practice that had been established by Great Britain and other colonial powers of treaty-making with Indian tribes. These treaties were means both by which the United States or its colonial precursors acquired land from Indian tribes, as well as means by which the tribes retained rights over lands and resources not ceded. The treaties, moreover, dealt with diverse issues and provided a foundation for the United States' relations with tribes on the basis of their recognition as nations with inherent sovereignty. Although the United States ceased dealing with Indian tribes through treaties in 1871,[14] after having consolidated its control over the territory it had acquired across the continent, many of the historical treaties with tribes continue in force as part of federal law and to define United States-tribal relations. At the same time, numerous flagrant violations of historical treaties constitute some of the principal wrongdoings committed by the United States towards indigenous peoples, which remains a recurring subject of concern for many Native American communities today.

Subsequent to the end of the treaty-making era, United States law and policy was characterized by a series of steps aimed at acculturating indigenous peoples in the ways of the dominant society and diluting or eliminating their sovereignty and collective rights over lands and resources. In the late nineteenth century, a vast government bureaucracy emerged under a United States Commissioner of Indian Affairs to consolidate and manage the system of reservations, pueblos, rancherias, and settlements that were home to the surviving indigenous peoples in the country.

Under the General Allotment Act of 1887,[15] tribal landholdings were broken up into individual plots that could become alienable, which eventually resulted in a substantial further loss of Indian land and a complex system of interspersed Indian and non-Indian titled land that now characterizes tenure within many reservations. The Allotment Act resulted in even greater impoverishment and social upheaval among the tribes, and consequently, after conferring United States citizenship on all Indians in 1924, Congress passed the Indian Reorganization Act of 1934 (IRA)[16] as a major reform measure. The IRA included provisions to secure the Indian land base from further erosion and provided for establishing reservation-based governments akin to local municipalities under the authority of the Secretary of Interior of the federal government, on the basis of model constitutions that were developed by the Secretary. While providing a degree of self-government, the Act was considered a transitional measure to prepare the Indians for, in the words of its chief

---

14   *See* Indian Appropriations Act, 25 U.S.C. §71 (1871).
15   24 Stat. 388 (1987) (also known as the "Dawes Act").
16   25 U.S.C. 461 et seq., 48 Stat 984 (1934), amended through Pub.L. No. 109–221 (2006).

architect, United States Indian Commissioner John Collier, "real assimilation."[17] Many Indian tribes today continue under the IRA regime.

In the 1950s the United States Government attempted to complete its program of assimilation with Congress' adoption of a formal policy of "termination,"[18] which involved steps to end the special status of Indian tribes and convert their lands to private ownership. The termination policy was eventually abandoned, but not before several tribes lost federal recognition and their self-governing status, and saw their landholdings dissipate, with invariably devastating social and economic consequences that are still apparent today.

3.3   *The Contemporary Federal Legislative and Policy Regime*

In the face of past federal programs of assimilation and acculturation, Native Americans continued to make clear their determination, as they still do, to hold on to and recover their own distinctive cultures and institutions of self-government as a basis for their development and place in the world. With this resolve eventually came a change in federal policy, as it moved to reflect, if not entirely accommodate, indigenous peoples' own aspirations. In 1970, the President of the United States advanced this change in a message to Congress, in which he affirmed, "The time has come to break decisively with the past and to create the conditions for a new era in which the Indian future is determined by Indian acts and Indian decisions."[19]

The contemporary thrust of federal policy is marked by several pieces of major legislation, including the Indian Self-Determination and Education Assistance Act of 1975,[20] by which tribes are able to assume the planning and administration of federal programs that are devised for their benefit; the Indian Child Welfare Act of 1978,[21] which favors indigenous custody of indigenous children; the American Indian Religious Freedom Act of 1978,[22] which directs federal officials to consult with tribes about actions that may affect religious practices; the Native American Graves Protection and Repatriation Act of 1990,[23] which directs federal agencies and museums to return indigenous remains and sacred objects to appropriate indigenous groups; and the Native American

---

17   *Hearings on Readjustment of Indian Affairs Before the H. Comm. of Indian Affairs*, 73rd Cong., 2nd sess., 21 (1934).

18   H. Cong. Res. 108, 3d Cong., 1st Sess., 67 Stat. B137 (1953).

19   H.R. Doc. No. 91–363, 91st Cong., 2d Sess. (July 8, 1970).

20   25 U.S.C. §§ 5301 et seq., Pub. L. No. 93–638 (1975).

21   25 U.S.C. §§ 1901 et seq., Pub. L. No. 95–608 (1978).

22   42 U.S.C. § 1996, Pub. L. No. 95–341 (1978).

23   25 U.S.C. §§ 3001 et seq., Pub. L. No. 101–601 (1990).

Languages Act of 1990,[24] which provides support for the use and recovery of indigenous languages through educational programs. A number of other laws provide protections for indigenous religion and culture, and still others address Indian economic and natural resource development, education, and civil rights.

In alignment with the existing federal legislation, there are dozens of executive directives and programs that apply specifically to indigenous peoples that reflect a significant level of dedication on the part of the federal government to address indigenous concerns within the self-determination policy framework. Several agencies throughout the government are dedicated specifically to indigenous affairs, the principal one being the Department of the Interior, which includes the Bureau of Indian Affairs. Under federal law, pursuant to its historical protectorate, or trusteeship, the United States holds in trust the underlying title to the Indian lands within reservations and other lands set aside by statute or treaty for the tribes. The Department is responsible for overseeing some 55 million surface acres and the subsurface mineral resources in some 59 million acres.[25]

There are numerous other indigenous-specific agencies and programs in various parts of the Government. Notably, and especially in recent years, the Government has made an important, increased effort to appoint indigenous individuals to high-level government positions dealing with indigenous affairs, including the position of Assistant Secretary for Indian Affairs, which heads the Bureau of Indian Affairs, and the Secretary of the Interior, which heads the Department of the Interior. Also significantly, the Obama and Biden administrations established senior policy advisor positions in the White House to advise on issues related to indigenous peoples.[26]

4   The Disadvantaged Conditions of Indigenous Peoples: The Present-Day Legacies of Historical Wrongs

United States laws and policies in the last few decades undoubtedly have contributed to halting the erosion of indigenous identities and have weighed in favor of placing indigenous peoples on a path toward greater self-determination,

---

24   25 U.S.C. §§ 2901 et seq., Pub. L. No. 101–477 (1990).

25   Congressional Research Service, U.S. Department of the Interior: An Overview 11 (Jun. 23, 2021), https://sgp.fas.org/crs/misc/R45480.pdf.

26   *See, e.g., PaaWee Rivera, Senior Advisor and Tribal Affairs Director for the White House Office of Intergovernmental Affairs*, The White House Office of Intergovernmental Affairs https://www.whitehouse.gov/iga/meet-the-team/paawee-rivera/ (last visited Aug. 18, 2022).

as well as economic and social health. Nonetheless, the conditions of disadvantage persist with the continuing effects of a long history of wrongs and past misguided policies.

4.1   *Economic and Social Conditions*

Soon after my consultations in the United States as Special Rapporteur, I received a manila envelope stuffed with letters written by students from a class at White River High School in South Dakota – a school where a majority of the students are from the nearby reservation of the Rosebud Sioux Tribe. In a cover letter the class's teacher explained that the students "would like to feel they have a voice as it is so desolate here that it is sometimes hard to remember there is an outside world. Despite all the hardships here, these kids are so incredibly resilient and talented."

The teacher's words were a poignant introduction to the first letter in the stack, which was from a 15-year-old girl who lamented:

> Life here is very hand to mouth. Out here, we don't have the finer things. You get what you get and you don't throw a fit. And I'm going to be honest with you, sometimes I don't eat. I've never told anyone this before, not even my mom, but I don't eat sometimes because I feel bad about making my mom buy food that I know is expensive. And you know what? Life is hard enough for my mom, so I will probably never tell her. My parents have enough to worry about. I do not know what you can do, but try your very best to help us. Please help us. We can do this. Yes we can!

The evident hardship combined with resilience was reflected in the other letters, giving a highly-personalized gloss on the conditions of disadvantage faced by indigenous peoples in the United States. These conditions vary widely among the diverse indigenous tribes, nations, and communities. United States census data and other available statistics, however, show Native Americans do fare much worse along social and economic indicators than any other ethnic group in the country.

For example, Native Americans, especially on reservations, have disproportionately high poverty rates, rising to nearly double the national average.[27]

---

27   Valerie Wilson and Zane Mokhiber, 2016 ACS Shows Stubbornly High Native American Poverty and Different Degrees of Economic Well-Being for Asian Ethnic Groups, Policy Commons (Sept. 15, 2017), https://policycommons.net/artifacts/1407215/2016-acs-shows-stubbornly-high-native-american-poverty-and-different-degrees-of-economic-well-being-for-asian-ethnic-groups/2021476/. *See also* Jull Fleury DeVoe et al., Statistical

Along with poverty, Native Americans disproportionately suffer poor health conditions with low life expectancy and high rates of disease, illness, alcoholism and suicide.[28] The COVID-19 pandemic magnified this health crisis, disproportionately affecting American Indian and Alaska Native populations across the country.[29]

As for education, 88.6 per cent of Native Americans aged 25 or older hold a high school diploma or alternative credential as compared with 91.1 percent of the general population, while 33.1 percent of Native Americans hold a basic university degree as compared to 37.9 percent of the general population.[30] Indigenous peoples also face disproportionate rates of incarceration, and rates of violent crime on Indian reservations exceed those of any other racial group and are double the national average.[31]

The image now often popularized of Native Americans flush with cash from casinos is far from the norm. A number of tribes do have casino operations as part of economic development efforts, taking advantage of special exemptions from ordinary state regulation and taxation that are available to them under federal law. While most tribes do not have casinos, those that do experience lower poverty and unemployment rates among their tribal members.[32] Despite

---

Trends in the Education of American Indians and Alaska Natives: 2008, at 22 (2008), https://nces.ed.gov/pubs2008/2008084_1.pdf.

28 American Indians and Alaska Natives continue to die at higher rates than other Americans in many categories, including from chronic liver disease and cirrhosis, diabetes mellitus, unintentional injuries, assault/homicide, intentional self-harm/suicide, and chronic lower respiratory diseases. *See Indian Health Disparities*, Indian Health Service (Oct. 2019), https://www.ihs.gov/newsroom/factsheets/disparities/.

29 American Indians and Alaska Natives had infection rates over 3.5 times higher than non-Hispanic whites, were over four times more likely to be hospitalized as a result of COVID-19 and had higher rates of mortality at younger ages than non-Hispanic whites. *See Coronavirus (COVID-19)*, Indian Health Service, https://www.ihs.gov/coronavirus / (last updated July 18, 2022).

30 *American Indian and Alaska Native Data Links, Detailed Demographic Profile, 2019: ACS 1-Year Estimates Selected Population*, U.S. Census Bureau (2019), https://data.census.gov /cedsci/table?q=S0201#; *Census Bureau Releases New Education Attainment Data*, U.S. Census Bureau (Feb. 24, 2022), https://www.census.gov/newsroom/press-releases/2022 /educational-attainment.html#:~:text=In%202021%2C%2029.4%25%20of%20men ,women%20and%2046.9%25%20were%20men.

31 Steven W. Perry, American Indians and Crime–A Bureau of Justice Statistics Statistical Profile, 1992–2002, at 4–11, 18–24 (2004), https://bjs.ojp.gov/content/pub/pdf/aic02.pdf.

32 *See* Alan Meister, Casino City's Indian Gaming Industry Report, Newton: Casino City Press 3 (2017).

these economic gains, tribal communities remain well below the national income average.[33]

4.2   Violence against Women

The continuing vulnerabilities of indigenous communities are highlighted by alarmingly high rates of violence against indigenous women, a grave and persistent problem that has been well documented.[34] A United States Department of Justice study published in 2016 estimated that more than four in five American indigenous women (84.3 percent) had experienced violence, and that more than half had experienced sexual violence.[35] A 2013 study by the National Congress of American Indians showed that American Indians and Alaska Natives were 2.5 times as likely to experience violent crimes – and at least two times more likely to experience rape or sexual assault crimes – compared to all other demographic groups.[36]

Estimates are that the vast majority (up to 96 percent) of indigenous female victims of sexual violence experience violence at the hands of non-indigenous perpetrators,[37] many of whom have made their way into indigenous communities but who, until recently, were not subject to indigenous prosecutorial authority because of their non-indigenous status. In response to this systemic impunity, Congress passed key reforms in the Violence Against Women Act to bolster tribes' ability to prosecute these cases. The Violence Against Women Reauthorization Act of 2013 (VAWA 2013) included a historic provision to address the jurisdictional gap by recognizing tribes' inherent authority to exercise "special domestic violence criminal jurisdiction" over both Indians and

---

33   *See* Jonathan B. Taylor and Joseph Kalt, Cabazon, The Indian Gaming Regulatory Act, and the Socioeconomic Consequences of American Indian Governmental Gaming: A Ten Year Review xiii (2005), https://nnigovernance.arizona.edu/sites/default/files/attachments /text/2005_TAYLOR_kalt_HPAIED_databook.pdf.

34   *See, e.g., Report of the Special Rapporteur on Violence Against Women, Causes and Consequences: Mission to the United States of America*, ¶¶ 62 – 66, U.N. Doc. A/HRC/17/26/Add.5 (June 6, 2011) (Rashida Manjoo, Special Rapporteur).

35   André B. Rosay, Violence Against American Indian and Alaska Native Women and Men: 2010 Findings from the National Intimate Partner and Sexual Violence Survey 43 (2016), https://www.ojp.gov/pdffiles1/nij/249736.pdf.

36   National Congress of American Indians, Policy Insights Brief: Statistics on Violence Against Native Women, National Congress of American Indians 2 (2013), https://www .ncai.org/attachments/PolicyPaper_tWAjznFslemhAffZgNGzHUqIWMRPkCDjp FtxeKEUVKjubxfpGYK_Policy%20Insights%20Brief_VAWA_020613.pdf.

37   *See* National Congress of American Indians, Policy Research Update: State of the Data on Violence Against American Indian and Alaska Native Women and Girls 4 (2021), https:// www.ncai.org/policy-research-center/research-data/prc-publications/NCAI_VAWA _Data_Update_2021_FINAL.pdf.

non-Indians who assault Indian spouses, intimate partners, or dating partners, or who violate certain protection orders in Indian Country.[38] In 2022, President Biden signed into law VAWA 2022, which built on this framework and added additional categories of criminal conduct that can be prosecuted against non-Indians in tribal court.[39] While these changes advance tribal capacity to respond to violence against Native women, unfortunately a pattern of violence against women continues.

In order to escape violent situations, many victims are forced to leave their homes and communities, which is particularly troubling in the context of indigenous communities. As one Tlingit woman expressed to me, "when I left, I didn't just leave my family. I left my culture behind ... I ran away from my traditions, from my songs, my dances, and my heritage."

4.3   *Lands, Resources, and Broken Treaties*

The conditions of disadvantage of indigenous peoples undoubtedly are not mere happenstance. Rather, they stem from the well-documented history of the taking of vast expanses of indigenous lands with abundant resources, along with active suppression of indigenous peoples' cultures and political institutions, entrenched patterns of discrimination against them and outright brutality, all of which figured in the history of the settlement of the country and the building of its economy.

Many Indian nations conveyed land to the United States or its colonial predecessors by treaty, but almost invariably under coercion following warfare or threat thereof, and in exchange usually for little more than promises of government assistance and protection that usually proved illusory or worse. In other cases, lands were simply taken by force or fraud. In many instances treaty provisions that guaranteed reserved rights to tribes over lands or resources were broken by the United States under pressure to acquire land for non-indigenous interests. It is a testament to the goodwill of Indian nations that they have uniformly insisted on observance of the treaties, even regarding them as sacred compacts, rather than challenge their terms as inequitable.

---

38   Violence Against Women Reauthorization Act, 2013, 42 U.S.C. 13701. *See also* U.S. Dep't of Justice, Office on Violence Against Women, 2018 Biennial Report to Congress on the Effectiveness of Grant Programs Under the Violence Against Women Act 2 (2018), https://www.justice.gov/ovw/page/file/1292636/download.

39   Indian Civil Rights Act, 25 U.S.C.§§ 1304, as amended by the Violence Against Women Act, 2022. VAWA 2022 expands the crimes over which tribes have inherent criminal jurisdiction over non-Indians and enacts other amendments that enhance tribal authority and due process measures.

In nearly all cases, the loss of land meant the substantial or complete under-mining of indigenous peoples' own economic foundations and means of sub-sistence, as well as cultural loss, given the centrality of land to cultural and related social patterns. Especially devastating instances of such loss involve the forced removal of indigenous peoples from their ancestral territories, as happened for example, with the Choctaw, Cherokee, and other indigenous people who were removed from their homes in the southeastern United States to the Oklahoma territory in a trek through what has been called a "trail of tears," in which many of them perished.

Another emblematic case involves the Black Hills in South Dakota, part of the ancestral territory of the Lakota people that, under the Treaty of Fort Laramie of 1868, was reserved to the Lakota and other tribes known collec-tively as the Great Sioux Nation. Following the discovery of gold in the area, in 1877 Congress passed an act reversing its promise under the treaty and vesting ownership of the Black Hills in the government. The Lakota and other Sioux tribes have refused to accept payment required in accordance with a 1980 Supreme Court decision[40] and continue to demand the return of the Black Hills; this is despite the fact that the people of these tribes are now scattered on several reservations where there are high rates of poverty. Today, the Black Hills are designated national forest and park lands, although they still hold a central place in the history, culture, and worldviews of surrounding tribes and, at the same time, serve as a constant visible reminder of their loss.

In addition to millions of acres of lands lost, often in violation of treaties, a history of inadequately-controlled extractive and other activities within or near indigenous lands, including nuclear weapons testing and uranium min-ing in the western United States, has resulted in widespread environmental harm and has caused serious and continued health problems among Native Americans. More recent activities that are causing or could potentially cause environmental harm to indigenous habitats include increased min-ing activity in the Little Rockies in Montana, just south of the Fort Belknap Indian Reservation;[41] the Big Canyon dam project near cultural sites that are

---

40   In *United States v. Sioux Nation of Indians*, 448 U.S. 371 (1980), the Supreme Court found that the government had breached the Treaty of Fort Laramie such that the tribes were entitled to compensation, but not to return of the land.

41   *See* Stephanie Woodard, *Mining Companies Strike Gold by Destroying Public Lands*, In These Times (June 2, 2022), https://inthesetimes.com/article/native-american-indigenous -peoples-mining-mine-cleanup-environmental-justice-epa-bureau-of-land-management (also discussing the environmental threats to Native people of hardrock mining in Nevada).

important to the Navajo Nation and other tribes;[42] and the Willow oil development project near Nuiqsut, Alaska.[43]

In many places, including in Alaska and the Pacific Northwest in particular, indigenous peoples continue to depend upon hunting and fishing, and the
maintenance of these subsistence activities is essential for both their physical
and their cultural survival, especially in isolated areas. However, indigenous
peoples face ever-greater threats to their subsistence activities due to a growing surge of restrictive state and federal regulatory regimes, environmental
harm, and competing activities often fueled by racism.[44]

4.4   *Sacred Places*

With their loss of land, indigenous peoples have lost, and are still threatened
with losing, control over and access to places of cultural and religious significance. Particular sites and geographic spaces that are sacred to indigenous
peoples can be found throughout the vast expanse of lands that have passed
into government hands. The ability of indigenous peoples to use and access
their sacred places is often curtailed by mining, logging, hydroelectric, and
other development projects, which are carried out under permits issued by
federal or state authorities. In many cases, the very presence of these activities
represents a desecration.

A case that I examined in detail as UN Special Rapporteur involved the San
Francisco Peaks in Northern Arizona – an area sacred to the Navajo, Hopi, and
other indigenous peoples, where under a federal permit the Snowbowl ski resort
proceeded with plans to make artificial snow using recycled sewage effluent.[45]
The affected tribes sought to prevent the permitting of artificial snowmaking

---

42   *See* Haln'e, *Sign A Petition to Save Big Canyon from Destructive Water Project*, Save the Con-
     fluence (July 8, 2022), https://savetheconfluence.com/news/sign-a-petition-to-save-big
     -canyon-from-destructive-water-project/ (critiquing the risks of the Big Canyon dam con-
     struction on the environmental and spiritual health of the local Native communities).

43   *See* Victoria Petersen, *Alaska's Willow Project Promises Huge Amounts of Oil – and Huge
     Environmental Impacts,* High Country News (August 3, 2022), https://www.hcn.org/articles
     /north-energy-industry-alaskas-willow-project-promises-huge-amounts-of-oil-and
     -huge-environmental-impacts (highlighting the local community's concerns over the
     impending oil and gas project in Nuiqsut, Alaska).

44   *See* Elisabeth Sherman, *Indigenous Fishing Rights in the Pacific Northwest Are Being Threat-
     ened*, Matador Network (Oct. 2, 2020), https://matadornetwork.com/read/indigenous
     -fishing-rights-pacific-northwest/ (discussing the complicated and difficult position of
     tribes in the Pacific Northwest to assert and protect their fishing rights).

45   *See Report of the Special Rapporteur on the rights of indigenous peoples,* U.N. Doc. A/
     HRC/18/35.Add.1, Annex X (August 22, 2011) (S. James Anaya, Special Rapporteur);
     Communications Report of Special Procedures, U.N. Doc. A/HRC/19/44 (Feb. 23, 2012).

through communications with the U.S. Department of Agriculture, the U.S. Forest Service, the U.S. Department of Justice, and the Department of the Interior, informing these agencies of the need to protect and maintain the natural environmental qualities that have formed the religious and spiritual relationship between the tribes and the San Francisco Peaks.[46] The tribes also sought redress in the U.S. Courts and international human rights mechanisms, to no lasting avail.

Also illustrative: The federal government approved a wind energy facility in an area where there are sacred places, including burial grounds, of the Viejas Band of Kumeyaay Indians.[47] The Havasupai tribe has seen many of its sacred places contaminated by mining operations and struggles to prevent further such desecration.[48] Today, Apache people face the potential destruction of a place sacred to them in the area known as Oak Flat in Arizona as a result of a large-scale mining project authorized by the U.S. Congress.[49] The desecration of and lack of access to sacred places inflict grave harm on indigenous peoples, for whom these places are important parts of identity, culture, and social fabric.

4.5   *The Removal of Children from Indigenous Environments*
Historically, added to the taking of indigenous lands was the direct assault on indigenous cultural expression that was carried out or facilitated by the federal and state governments. Likely the program of this type with the most devastating consequences, which are still felt today, was the systematic removal of indigenous children from their families to place them in government or church-run

---

46   *See* Inter-Tribal Council of Arizona, *Supporting the Decision of the Ninth Circuit Court of Appeals to Protect the Sacred San Francisco Peaks*, Res. 0709 (April 13, 2007), https:// itcaonline.com/wp-content/uploads/2011/10/LettertoUnitedNationsSpecial   Rapporteur Anaya.pdf.

47   *See Report of the Special Rapporteur on the rights of indigenous peoples: The situation of indigenous peoples in the United States of America*, ¶ 162, U.N. Doc. A/HRC/21/47/Add.1, Appendix II (August 30, 2012) (James Anaya, Special Rapporteur). *See generally* Toby McLeod, CA *Tribe Fights Wind Farm on Sacred Land*, Sacred Land Film Project (May 23, 2012), https://sacredland.org/ca-tribe-fights-wind-farm-on-sacred-land-blog/ (discussing U.S. Department of Interior's approval of Pattern Energy's Ocotillo Wind Energy Facility and its threat to the ancestral graves of the Quechan Tribe).

48   *See* Debra Utacia Krol, *How Legal and Cultural Barriers Keep Indigenous People from Protecting Sacred Spaces Off Tribal Land*, USA Today News, https://www.usatoday.com /in-depth/news/nation/2021/08/17/indigenous-people-legal-barriers-protect-sacred -spaces/ 8152992002/ (last updated Nov. 24, 2021).

49   *See* Dana Hedgpeth, *This Land Is Sacred to the Apache, and They Are Fighting to Save It*, The Washington Post (April 12, 2021) .

boarding schools, with the objective of expunging them of their indigenous identities. Captain Richard Pratt, founder of the Carlisle Indian school, coined the phrase, "kill the Indian in him, save the man,"[50] in instituting the boarding school policy in the 1880s which continued well into the mid-1900s.

Emotional, physical, and sexual abuse within the boarding schools has been well-documented. Typically, upon entering a boarding school, indigenous children had their hair cut, were forced to wear uniforms, and were punished for speaking their languages or practicing their traditions. The compounded effect of generations of indigenous people, including generations still living, having passed through these schools cuts deep in indigenous communities throughout the United States.

On May 11, 2022, the U.S. Secretary of the Interior released a long-awaited first investigative report on the Indian boarding schools.[51] The report identified 408 such schools that operated in the United States between 1819–1969 and over 1,000 other federal and non-federal institutions that may have involved the education of Native children during this time period, many of which received support from religious institutions.[52] Fifty-three Indian boarding schools were identified where students were buried on the premises.[53] The report documented that 19 Indian boarding schools accounted for some 500 child deaths, and as the investigation continues, these numbers are expected to increase.[54]

Additionally, a pattern of placing indigenous children in non-indigenous care under state custody proceedings, with similar effects on indigenous individuals and communities, continued until well into the 1970s. That pattern was blunted by the passage of the Indian Child Welfare Act in 1978,[55] federal legislation that advances a strong presumption of indigenous custody for indigenous children but that continues to face barriers to its implementation. Today, the Indian Child Welfare Act is being challenged as being in violation of the U.S. Constitution's guarantee of equal protection – a cruel irony.[56]

---

50   R.H. Pratt, *The Advantages of Mingling Indians with Whites*, in Proceedings of the National Conference of Charities and Correction, at the 19th Annual Session held in Denver, Col, June 23–29, 1982, (Isabel C. Barrows, ed., 1892).

51   *See* Department of Interior, Federal Indian Boarding School Initiative Investigative Report (2022), https://www.bia.gov/sites/default/files/dup/inline-files/bsi_investigative_report _may_2022_508.pdf.

52   *Id.* at 6.

53   *Id.* at 8.

54   *Id.* at 9; National Indian Child Welfare Association, Child and Family Policy Update (June 2022), https://www.nicwa.org/policy-update/.

55   Pub. L. No. 95–608, 92 Stat. 3069 (1978).

56   Brackeen v. Haaland, 942 F.3d 287 (5th Cir. 2021) *cert granted*, __U.S. __ (No. 21–380) (2022).

4.6   *Open Wounds of Historical Events*

The open wounds left by historical events are plentiful, alive in intergenerational memory if not experience. During my consultations in the U.S. as Special Rapporteur, I heard emotional testimony from a direct descendant of victims of one of the most egregiousatrocities committed against Native Americans – the massacre at Sand Creek in 1864. Hundreds of Cheyenne and Arapaho were attacked by surprise and massacred by close tos 700 armed United States troops acting under direct orders of their superiors. Previously, the tribes had signed a treaty with the United States, under which they willingly gave up their arms and flew a flag of truce at the Sand Creek camp. It was not until 2000 that Congress designated Sand Creek as a national historic site in recognition of the massacre, and in 2007 the site was finally dedicated and formally opened to the public. Still, no action was ever taken against those responsible for the massacre and, despite the promises made in a later treaty of reparations for the descendants of the victims at Sand Creek, none has yet been made.[57]

A more recent incident that continues to spark feelings of injustice among indigenous peoples around the United States is the well-known case of Leonard Peltier, an activist and leader in the American Indian Movement, who was convicted in 1977 following the deaths of two Federal Bureau of Investigation agents during a clash on the Pine Ridge Reservation in South Dakota. After a trial that has been criticized by many as involving numerous due process problems, Mr. Peltier was sentenced to two life sentences for murder and has been denied parole on various occasions. Pleas for presidential consideration of clemency by notable individuals and institutions have not borne fruit. .

4.7   *Self-Government*

In all locations I visited across the United States as Special Rapporteur, indigenous leaders stressed the importance, to the cultural survival and well-being of their peoples, of securing ties to land and natural resources and enhancing self-government capacity. As previously noted, several federal programs are in place to address the concerns of indigenous peoples and to provide them substantial assistance. Indigenous leaders, however, stressed that the solution lies fundamentally in further strengthening indigenous peoples' ability to develop

---

57   In 2013, descendants sued the federal government for reparations. The federal district court dismissed the suit on the ground that the government had not waived its sovereign immunity. The Tenth Circuit Court of Appeals upheld the decision and the Supreme court declined to review the Tenth Circuit decision. *See* Homer Flute et al. v. United States, 808 F.3d 1234 (10th Cir., 2015), *cert. denied*, 580 U.S. 826 (2016).

and implement their own programs for economic development and job creation, education, preservation and development of cultural expressions and knowledge, and public order, including the protection of indigenous women and children. Yet, the U.S. government policy of indigenous self-determination in place for half a century has not prevented problematic restrictions that have been imposed on indigenous peoples' self-government.

As a general matter, the sovereignty of federally recognized Indian tribes, as far as it goes, displaces the authority of the states over so-called Indian country, that is, reservation and other lands where there is a substantial Indian presence. But United States courts have continued to see the inherent sovereignty of tribes, and hence their self-governance authority, as an implicitly diminished sovereignty, and this view has served to limit the powers of tribal regulatory and judicial authorities especially in relation to non-indigenous persons. Additionally, tribal sovereignty may succumb to substantial state sovereignty interests,[58] and the Supreme Court has restrictively interpreted the Indian Reorganization Act to prevent many tribes from extending their sovereignty over recovered or newly acquired lands.[59]

Judicially-established limitations on tribal sovereignty are in addition to those imposed by Congress, especially under acts devised under the earlier eras of assimilation. These include the Major Crimes Act of 1885,[60] which established paramount federal jurisdiction over certain crimes committed in Indian country, whether by an indigenous or non-indigenous person; and Public Law 280 of 1953,[61] which extended state criminal and civil jurisdiction to Indian country in specified states. Especially in light of inadequate state and federal law enforcement on reservations, these jurisdictional limits imposed on indigenous tribes result in situations in which, as one tribal judge lamented in a conversation I had with him, "we can't police and punish people who come into the community and cause harm to that community and its people." As Special Rapporteur, I heard numerous frustrations based on concerns that jurisdictional limitations send the constant message to tribes that their institutions are incompetent and inferior, no matter how capable they have demonstrated themselves to be. Further impeding self-governance capacity are financial constraints.

---

58   *See* Nevada v. Hicks, 533 U.S. 353 (2001).
59   *See* Carcieri v. Salazar, 155 U.S. 379 (2009).
60   18 U.S.C. § 1152.
61   67 Stat. 588–590 (1953).

It is important to note, however, that despite these impediments, many tribal governments and justice systems are gaining strength. The resilient determination of tribes to continue building their governance institutions despite systemic resistance is admirable. During a Special Rapporteur consultation in Oklahoma, the Principal Chief of the Cherokee Nation put it this way: "As the Principal Chief of the largest Indian Tribe in the United States, my vision for our people is one of becoming great."[62]

4.8   *Recognition*

In order for its powers of sovereignty, or self-government, to be recognized and officially functional within the United States legal system, or to be eligible for assistance designated for Indian tribes, an indigenous group must have specific recognition by the federal government. A number of indigenous peoples, for reasons related to the same cluster of historical events that have broadly affected indigenous peoples in the country, lack such federal recognition and hence are especially disadvantaged. Several of these are tribes that were stripped of their federal status as a result of the termination policies of the 1950s.

Numerous unrecognized indigenous groups have been striving to achieve federal recognition for decades, principally through an administrative process provided for this purpose by the Department of the Interior. Concerns regarding the cost and the length of the federal recognition process, and the challenges faced by lack of recognition, were repeatedly brought to my attention when I was Special Rapporteur. Indigenous groups had invested millions of dollars and filed thousands of documents in support of their claims. Figures about the pace of the recognition process yield differing perspectives. Nonetheless, as described to me by one U.S. Senator, "it is not a system that is working under any stretch of the imagination."

---

62   Later, the Cherokee Nation and other tribes in Oklahoma were successful in regaining jurisdiction over substantial territory in that state. In *McGirt v. Oklahoma*, 591 U.S.__ (2020), the U.S. Supreme Court ruled that the U.S. Congress never acted sufficiently to "disestablish" the reservations of the Five Civilized Tribes in Oklahoma when granting its statehood, and thus almost half the state was still considered to be Indian country under the jurisdiction of the tribes. Not long afterwards, in *Oklahoma v. Castro-Huerta*, 597 U.S.__(2022), the Supreme Court held federal and state law enforcement have concurrent jurisdiction to prosecute crimes committed by non-Indians against Indians in Indian country.

4.9   *Alaska*

Indigenous peoples in Alaska have federal recognition within a unique legal regime that developed under a specific set of circumstances. In 1971 Congress enacted the Alaska Native Claims Settlement Act (ANCSA),[63] which extinguished "all claims of aboriginal title," as well as "any aboriginal hunting and fishing rights that may exist," throughout Alaska. In exchange, the act set up a system of native-run corporations with assets provided under the settlement, and Alaska Natives born as of the date of the act were given shares in the corporations.

With its design of replacing rights in land and resources with individual shares in corporations, ANCSA can be seen as being driven by the policy of assimilation that had long been in place and that presumably was coming to an end around the time of the act's adoption. Yet ANCSA continues to define realities for indigenous peoples in Alaska, leaving in its aftermath precarious conditions for indigenous peoples in their ability to maintain the subsistence and cultural patterns that have long sustained them amid abundant fish and wildlife resources, or to craft their own vehicles of self-determination. Subsequent federal legislation has done little to restore Alaska Native hunting and fishing rights; instead, it has left indigenous hunting and fishing subject to the same regulatory regime that applies to non-indigenous activities.[64] And this regulatory regime is a highly complex, difficult one to navigate, in which both the federal government and the state play a part, with the state in effect having a dominant role. The matter of subsistence hunting and fishing remains crucial both for cultural purposes and for food security. However, subsistence activities are subject to a state regulatory regime that allows for, and appears to often favor, competing land and resource uses such as mining and other activities, including hunting and fishing for sport, that may threaten natural environments and food sources.

When I visited Alaska as Special Rapporteur, representatives of Alaska Native tribal governments, villages, corporations, and organizations generally expressed the view that ANCSA was faulty in its inception. There were divergent views, however, about the extent to which the corporations can and are being responsive to the needs and aspirations of Alaska Natives, within the limitations of the corporate model. There are indications that, in many respects, the native-run corporations are functioning to provide important economic and

---

63   3 U.S.C. §§1601 et seq.
64   *See generally* Meghan Sullivan, *Can Indigenous Subsistence Rights Still Be Protected in Alaska?*, Alaska Public Media (Oct. 14, 2021), https://alaskapublic.org/2021/10/14 /subsistence-is-absolutely-critical-to-our-survival-can-indigenous-subsistence-rights -still-be-protected-in-alaska/ (discussing the unstable status of Alaska Native subsistence rights).

other benefits to Alaska Natives. At the same time, there are indications that the economic and cultural transformations accelerated by ANCSA have bred or exacerbated social ills among indigenous communities, manifesting themselves, for example, in high rates of suicide, alcoholism, and violence.

Several Alaska Native advocates hold the view that the problem runs deeper than ANCSA, to the incorporation of Alaska into the United States as a federal state through procedures that allegedly were not in compliance with the right of the indigenous people of Alaska to self-determination.

4.10   *Hawaii*

Also in a uniquely vulnerable situation are the indigenous people of Hawaii, having experienced a particular history of colonial onslaught and resulting economic, social, and cultural upheaval. They benefit from some federal programs available to Native Americans, but they have no recognized powers of self-government under federal law. And they have little by way of effective land-holdings, their lands largely having passed to non-indigenous ownership and control with the aggressive patterns of colonization initiated with the arrival of the British explorer James Cook in 1778. Indigenous Hawaiians have diffuse interests in lands "ceded" to the United States and then passed to the state of Hawaii, under a trust that is specified in the 1959 Statehood Admission Act and now managed by the Office of Hawaiian Affairs.

Remarkably, the United States Congress in 1993 issued an apology "to Native Hawaiians on behalf of the people of the United States for the overthrow of the Kingdom of Hawaii on January 17, 1893 with the participation of agents and citizens of the United States."[65] The apology recognized that the overthrow resulted in the suppression of the "inherent sovereignty of the Native Hawaiian people" and called for "reconciliation" efforts. Despite important steps taken,[66] the call for reconciliation remains largely unfilled, while a growing movement of indigenous Hawaiians challenges the legitimacy and legality of the annexation of Hawaii following the overthrow, as well as the process by which Hawaii moved from its designation as a non-self-governing territory under United Nations supervision to incorporation into the United States as one of its federal states in 1959. In the meantime, indigenous Hawaiians see their sacred places under the domination of others, and they continue to fare worse than

---

65   Pub. L. No. 103–150, 103rd Congress. Joint Res. 19 (1993).

66   In 2022, the President signed into law legislation that would provide millions in funding to advance the specific and often unique cultural, economic, educational, health, and other needs of Native Hawaiians. Consolidated Appropriations Act, Pub. L. No: 117–103 (2022).

any other demographic group in Hawaii in terms of education, health, crime, and employment.[67]

5   More Needs to be Done

5.1   *Welcomed, but Still not Sufficient, Government Initiatives*

The high level of attention to indigenous peoples' concerns represented by numerous acts of Congress and federal executive programs demonstrates some acknowledgment of the historical debt acquired toward the country's first peoples, and it partially fulfills historical treaty commitments. It is evident that the federal government has taken steps in recent years to strengthen programs pertaining to indigenous peoples' rights and interests, including initiatives to develop consultation policies and open spaces of dialogue with tribes on a "government to government" basis; to increase support for the recovery of indigenous languages; to address indigenous health disparities; to settle outstanding claims for mismanagement of indigenous assets held in trust by the federal government; to promote economic opportunity and community development; to ensure the safety of and prevent violence against indigenous women; to clean up environmental pollution caused by historical natural resource extraction; to bolster tribal education; enhance tribal capacity and cooperative arrangements in the area of law and order; and to protect Native American voting rights, among others.[68]

Yet, the adequacy of effective implementation of the highly developed body of law and government programs concerning indigenous peoples is insufficient. While welcoming improved consultation procedures, for example, many indigenous leaders assert that they have yet to see sufficientchange in the decision-making of government agents about matters of crucial concern to their peoples – in particular decisions about lands that are outside of indigenous-controlled areas but that nonetheless affect their access to natural or cultural resources or environmental well-being.

---

67   See Profile: *Native Hawaiian/ Pacific Islanders*, U.S. Department of Health and Human Services, Office of Minority Health, https://minorityhealth.hhs.gov/omh/browse.aspx?lvl =3&lvlid=65 (last visited Sept. 6, 2022).

68   *See generally* The White House Tribal Nations Summit Progress Report, Domestic Policy Council (Nov. 2021), https://www.whitehouse.gov/wp-content/uploads/2021/11/WH-Tribal -Nations-Summit-Progress-Report.pdf; Exec. Order No. 13647, 78 Fed. Reg. 39539 (June 26, 2013), Establishing the White House Council on Native American Affairs, https://www .govinfo.gov/content/pkg/FR-2013-07-01/pdf/2013-15942.pdf.

Additionally, there remains a lack of adequate funding for housing, health, education, environmental remediation, women's health and safety, language, and other programs; a concern echoed by both federal officials and representatives of indigenous peoples. The complicated and confusing bureaucratic procedures, coupled with a faulty understanding and awareness among many federal and state government officials about tribal realities or even about the content of relevant laws and policies themselves, remain significant barriers to the needed institutional changes necessary to adequately support and empower indigenous communities.

It can be observed that the overall thrust of the policy underlying the federal legislation and programs adopted since the latter part of the 20th century – a policy of advancing indigenous self-determination and development with respect for cultural identity – is a shift from prior, historical policy and bends toward the aspirations expressed by indigenous peoples. The problems signaled are that the laws and programs do not go far enough to meet those aspirations and that they are underfunded or inadequately administered. Moreover, they fail to go so far as to ultimately resolve persistent, deep-seated problems.

5.2   *The Need for Determined Action and Justice*

Numerous matters relating to the history of misdealing and harm inflicted on indigenous peoples are still unresolved. Historical wrongs continue to live in intergenerational memory and trauma, and together with current systemic problems, they still inflict harm. Across the United States, indigenous representatives have made abundantly clear that these problems continue to breed disharmony, dislocation, and hardship.

Unless genuine movement is made toward resolving these pending matters, the place of indigenous peoples within the United States will continue to be an unstable, disadvantaged, and inequitable one, and the country's moral standing will continue to suffer. Determined action should take aim at closing the latent wounds and building just and equitable conditions, and at providing needed redress consistent with the United States' human rights obligations.

The government took a step that could be one on a path toward justice, when in 2010 Congress adopted a resolution of apology to the indigenous peoples of the country, following in the spirit of the apology previously issued to Native Hawaiians. Acknowledging widespread wrongdoing, the Apology states: "The United States, acting through Congress … apologizes on behalf of the people of the United States for the many instances of violence, maltreatment and neglect inflicted on Native Peoples by citizens of the United States

[and] expresses its regret."[69] The apology also "urges the President to acknowledge the wrongs of the United States against Indian tribes in the history of the United States in order to bring healing to this land."[70] The full text of the apology bears reading. However, strangely, the apology was buried deep in a defense appropriations act, and apparently few indigenous people, much less the public in general, were made aware of it.

Such an apology should not go unnoticed. Rather, it should be a point of public awakening and mark a path toward justice, a path for concrete steps to address issues whose resolution is essential to defeating disharmony, and a path toward more enlightened framing of relations between indigenous peoples and the United States.

Among the pending issues that should be addressed with firm determination are the severed or frayed connections with culturally significant landscapes and sacred sites, such as those resulting from the taking of the Black Hills or from environmental pollution in countless places; imposed limitations on indigenous self-governance capacity, such as that preventing indigenous authorities from acting with full force to address problems within their communities; the pathologies left by the removal of indigenous children from their communities; and other persistent symbols of subordination, such as the refusal of the United States thus far to make good on its long-standing promise to provide reparations for the Sand Creek massacre. Also to be addressed are the pervasive problems left in the aftermath of Alaska Statehood and the Alaska Native Claims Settlement Act and the still not remedied, yet acknowledged, suppression of indigenous Hawaiian sovereignty.

Noteworthy is the previous significant effort made by the United States to comprehensively resolve the grievances of Indian tribes by its creation in 1946 of the Indian Claims Commission and by extending the Commission's authority widely to include claims based on "fair and honorable dealings," inter alia.[71] Over its life, the Commission determined hundreds of land claims based on treaties or ancestral occupation, but the only remedies provided under the relevant statute were for monetary compensation upon a finding of extinguishment or taking of rights, a product of the assimilationist frame of thinking from the period in which the Commission was created. Limiting remedies to

---

69 Department of Defense Appropriations Act of 2010, H.R. 3326, 111th Cong. §8113(a)(4)5) (2010).

70 *Id.* at §8113(a)(6).

71 Indian Claims Commission Act of 1946, Pub. L. No. 79–726, § 2, 60 Stat. 1049, 1050–56 (1946).

monetary ones left many fundamental issues unresolved or further complicated.[72] Still the establishment of the Commission represents the capacity of the United States to take sweeping action to address evident wrongs on the basis of prevailing policy preferences.

What is now needed is a resolve to take action to address the pending, deep-seated concerns of indigenous peoples, but within current notions of justice and the human rights of indigenous peoples. Exemplifying the kind of action to be taken consistent with contemporary human rights values is the federal legislation returning the sacred Blue Lake to Taos Pueblo in 1970[73] and restoring land to the Timbisha Shoshone Tribe in Death Valley, in 2000.[74] Both land areas were restored from land under federal administration, with no consequence for any individual property interests. Other exemplary actions are the more recent co-management initiative between the Oglala Sioux Tribe and the state of South Dakota to oversee shared natural resources,[75] and the agreement between the federal government and an inter-tribal coalition to co-manage the Bears Ears National Monument in southeastern Utah.[76] Such measures reveal an=important level of understanding of the centrality of land and geographic spaces to the physical and cultural well-being of indigenous peoples, in accordance with standards now prevailing internationally and in principle accepted by the United States.

---

72   For example, the members of the Western Shoshone Nation sought to affirm aboriginal title as a defense to a federal trespass action, but ultimately the U.S. Supreme Court ruled that any efforts to claim extant aboriginal title to the land in question was barred by a Commission's monetary award for the presumed taking of the land. *See* United States v. Dann, 470 U.S. 39 (1985).

73   Pub. L. 91–550, 84 Stat. 1437–39 (1970).

74   Timbisha Shoshone Homeland Act, Pub. L. 106–423, 114 Stat. 1875–1882 (2000).

75   Cooperative Agreement Between the Oglala Sioux Parks and Recreation Authority and the South Dakota Department of Game, Fish and Parks, Apr. 26, 2017, https://sdtribalrelations .sd.gov/docs/SDGFP_OST_Cooperative_Agreement.pdf.

76   Inter-Governmental Cooperative Agreement between the Tribal Nations whose representatives comprise the Bears Ears Commission, the Hopi Tribe, Navajo Nation, Ute Mountain Ute Tribe, Ute Indian Tribe of the Uintah and Ouray Reservation, and the Pueblo of Zuni and the United Stated Department of the Interior, Bureau of Land Management and the United States Department of Agriculture, Forest Service for the Cooperative Management of the Federal Lands and Resources of the Bears Ears National Monument (Jun. 18, 2022), https://www.blm.gov/sites/blm.gov/files/docs/2022-06/BearsEarsNational MonumentInter-GovernmentalAgreement2022.pdf; *see* Maxine Joselow, *Native American Tribes to Co-Manage National Monument For First Time*, Bears Ears Inter-Tribal Coalition, https://www.bearsearscoalition.org/coalition-to-co-manage-bears-ears/(lastupdatedJune 20, 2022).

6 The Significance of the Declaration on the Rights of Indigenous Peoples

The United Nations Declaration on the Rights of Indigenous Peoples[77] stands as an important impetus and guide for measures to address the concerns of indigenous peoples in the United States and to move toward bridging the justice gap. An authoritative instrument with broad support, the Declaration marks a path toward remedying the injustices and inequitable conditions faced by indigenous peoples, calling on determined action to secure their rights, within a model of respect for their self-determination and distinctive cultural identities.

The Declaration represents a global consensus among governments and indigenous peoples worldwide that is joined by the United States as well as by indigenous peoples in the country. It was adopted by the United Nations General Assembly with the affirmative votes of an overwhelming majority of UN Member States amid expressions of celebration by indigenous peoples from around the world. At the urging of indigenous leaders from throughout the country, the United States declared its support for the Declaration on December 16, 2010, reversing its earlier position.

By its very nature as a resolution and not a treaty, the Declaration on the Rights of Indigenous Peoples is not itself a legally binding document. Nonetheless, the Declaration is an extension of the legal commitment assumed by United Nations Member States – including the United States – to promote and respect human rights under the United Nations Charter and multilateral human rights treaties to which the United States is a party, including the International Covenant on Civil and Political Rights, and the International Convention on the Elimination of All Forms of Racial Discrimination.[78] Further, the core principles it represents, which build upon widely-accepted human rights norms, represent customary international law.[79]

---

77   G.A. Res. 61//295, Sept. 13, 2007.
78   *See Report of the Special Rapporteur on the situation of human rights and fundamental freedoms of indigenous people,* ¶¶ 18–43, U.N. Doc. A/HRC/9/9 (August 11, 2008) (S. James Anaya, Special Rapporteur).
79   *See* Int'l Law Ass'n [ILA], Resolution No. 5/2012 on the Rights of Indigenous Peoples, 75th Biennial Meeting of the International Law Association, Sofia, adopted August 30, 2012, *available at* https://www.ila-hq.org/index.php/committees (accessed 21 August 2022), finding, upon detailed analysis by 30 experts from around the globe, that indigenous peoples have rights under customary international law to their traditional lands and resources, their culture, and wide-ranging autonomy. The analysis leading to the conclusions in the resolution is in: Interim Report of the Committee on the Rights of Indigenous

Whatever its precise legal significance, the Declaration embodies a convergence of common understanding about the rights of indigenous peoples, upon a foundation of fundamental human rights, including rights of equality, self-determination, property, and cultural integrity. It is a product of more than two decades of deliberations in which the experiences and aspirations of indigenous peoples worldwide, along with failures and successes of the relevant laws and policies of governments, were closely examined, with a view toward promoting human rights.

With these characteristics, the Declaration is now part of United States domestic and foreign policy, as made clear in the United States' announcement that its endorsement of the instrument:

> ... reflects the U.S. commitment to work with [indigenous] tribes, individuals, and communities to address the many challenges they face. The United States aspires to improve relations with indigenous peoples by looking to the principles embodied in the Declaration in its dealings with federally recognized tribes, while also working, as appropriate, with all indigenous individuals and communities in the United States.[80]
>
> Moreover, the United States is committed to serving as a model in the international community in promoting and protecting the collective rights of indigenous peoples as well as the human rights of all individuals.[81]

As part of United States policy, an extension of its international human rights obligations, and its commitments to indigenous peoples in the United States, the Declaration should now serve as a beacon for executive, legislative, and judicial decision-makers in relation to issues concerning the indigenous peoples of the country. All such decision-making should incorporate awareness and close consideration of the Declaration's terms. Moreover, the Declaration

---

Peoples, ILA (2010), https://www.ila-hq.org/index.php/committees, and Final Report of the Committee on the Rights of Indigenous Peoples, ILA (August 28, 2012), at 31–32, https://www.ila-hq.org/index.php/committees. For further background, see Siegfried Wiessner, *Rights and Status of Indigenous Peoples: A Global Comparative and International Legal Perspective*, 12 Harv. Hum. Rts. J. 57–128 (1999); and *id.*, *The State and Indigenous Peoples: The Historic Significance of ILA Resolution No. 5/2012, in* Der Staat im Recht. Festschrift für Eckart Klein zum 70. Geburtstag 1357–1368 (M. Breuer et al. eds, Duncker & Humblot, Berlin, 2013).

80   U.S. Dep't of State, Announcement of U.S. Support for the United Nations Declaration on the Rights of Indigenous Peoples—Initiatives to Promote the Government-to-Government Relationship & Improve the Lives of Indigenous Peoples 2 (Jan. 12, 2011), https://2009-2017.state.gov/documents/organization/ 154782.pdf.

81   *Id.*

is an instrument that should motivate and guide steps toward still-needed justice for the country's indigenous peoples.

7   Conclusions and Recommendations

Indigenous peoples in the United States – including American Indian, Alaska Native, and Native Hawaiian peoples – constitute vibrant communities that contribute greatly to the life of the country. Yet they face significant challenges related to widespread historical wrongs and misguided government policies that today manifest themselves in various indicators of disadvantage and impediments to the exercise of their individual and collective rights.

Many acts of Congress and federal programs that have been developed over the last few decades – in contrast to earlier exercises of federal power based on misguided policies – in significant measure respond to indigenous peoples' concerns. But more must be done. Despite positive aspects of existing legislation and programs, new measures are needed to provide redress for persistent, deep-seated problems and achieve genuine justice for indigenous peoples.

Measures of healing and redress should include, among others, initiatives to address outstanding claims of treaty violations or non-consensual takings of traditional lands to which indigenous peoples retain cultural or economic attachment, and to restore or secure indigenous peoples' capacities to maintain connections with places and sites of cultural or religious significance, in accordance with the United States international human rights commitments.

Other measures should include efforts to identify and heal particular sources of open wounds. And hence, for example, promised reparations should be provided to the descendants of the Sand Creek massacre, and new or renewed consideration should be given to clemency for Leonard Peltier. Issues of self-governance, environmental degradation, language restoration, and federal recognition, as well as the particular concerns of indigenous peoples in urban settings and border areas, among other matters, should also be addressed. The federal executive and Congress should respond to initiatives promoted by indigenous peoples for new or amended legislation and programs, in accordance with the international human rights commitments of the United States.

The United Nations Declaration on the Rights of Indigenous Peoples is an important impetus and guide for improving upon existing measures to address the concerns of indigenous peoples in the United States and for developing new measures to advance toward justice. The Declaration represents an international standard accepted by the United States, at the urging of indigenous peoples from across the country and is an extension of the United States' historical leadership and commitment to promoting human rights under various sources of international law. With these characteristics, the Declaration is a benchmark for all relevant decision-making by the federal executive, Congress, and the judiciary of the United States.

The federal executive should work closely with indigenous leaders, at all levels of decision-making, to identify and remove any barriers to the effective implementation of existing government programs and directives, and to improve upon them. Appointing indigenous leaders to significant federal positions of is an important means of strengthened federal executive responsiveness to indigenous concerns.

In keeping with the expressed commitment of the United States to the principles of the Declaration on the Rights of Indigenous Peoples and its related international human rights obligations, the President should issue a directive to all executive agencies to adhere to the Declaration in all their decision-making concerning indigenous peoples. Independently of such a presidential directive, given that the Declaration has already been adopted as part of United States policy, all executive agencies that touch upon indigenous affairs should become fully aware of the meaning of the Declaration in relation to their respective spheres of responsibility, and they should ensure that their decisions and consultation procedures are consistent with the Declaration. To this end, there should be a crosscutting executive level campaign to ensure awareness about the content and meaning of the Declaration.

For its part, Congress should act promptly on legislative proposals advocated by indigenous leaders for the protection of their peoples' rights and ensure that any legislation concerning indigenous peoples is adopted in consultation with them. Particular, immediate priority should be placed on legislation advocated by indigenous peoples and proposed by the executive to enhance access to education and protect voting rights, among other legislative priorities.[82]

Congress should hold hearings to educate its members about the Declaration on the Rights of Indigenous Peoples and to consider specific legislative measures that are needed to fully implement the rights affirmed therein. Attention should be paid to aspects of already existing legislation that should be reformed and to new legislation that could advance still needed measures to achieve justice. Further, consideration should also be given to providing judicial remedies for infringements of rights incorporated in the Declaration. Moreover, any legislation adopted by Congress should be in alignment with the human rights standards represented by the Declaration. To this end, Congress

---

82   *See Indian Law Bulletins—U.S. Legislation, 117th Cong., Proposed Legislation,* Native American Rights Fund, https://narf.org/nill/bulletins/legislation/117_uslegislation.html (last visited July 27, 2022).

should consider adopting a resolution affirming the Declaration as the policy of United States and declaring its resolve to exercise its power to advance the principles and goals of the Declaration.

At a minimum, Congress should continuously refrain from exercising any purported power to unilaterally extinguish indigenous peoples' rights, with the understanding that to do so would be morally wrong and against expressed United States domestic and foreign policy, and that it would incur responsibility for the United States under its international human rights obligations.

Finally, the federal judiciary should adjudicate cases involving indigenous rights in a manner consistent with the Declaration. The U.S. judiciary, in particular the United States Supreme Court, has played a significant role in defining the rights and status of indigenous peoples. While affirming indigenous peoples' rights and inherent sovereignty, it has also articulated grounds for limiting those rights on the basis of colonial-era doctrine that is out of step with contemporary human rights values. Consistent with well-established methods of judicial reasoning, the federal courts should discard such colonial-era doctrine in favor of an alternative jurisprudence infused with the contemporary human rights values that have been embraced by the United States, including those values reflected in the United Nations Declaration on the Rights of Indigenous Peoples.

Furthermore, just as the Supreme Court looked to the law of nations of the colonial era to define bedrock principles concerning the rights and status of indigenous peoples, it should now look to contemporary international law, as expressed by the Declaration, for the same purposes. Accordingly, the federal courts should interpret, or reinterpret, relevant doctrine, treaties, and statutes in light of the Declaration, both in regard to the nature of indigenous peoples' rights and the nature of federal power.

If the federal courts were to function in this way, and if the Congress and the federal Executive were similarly to modernize their approaches and take bold steps to address matters of concern to the first peoples of the land, the United States would be a better country. The needed healing and justice would be in motion. And the country would be farther along the path toward a more perfect Union.

Acknowledgments

I would like to acknowledge the important work of Professor Siegfried Wiessner to advance the rights of indigenous peoples in the United States and elsewhere. Many of the ideas set forth here draw inspiration from that work. Additionally, I'm thankful to Alex Kinsella and Maia Campbell who assisted with the research for this chapter.

CHAPTER 22

ILA Resolution No. 5/2012 and the Rights of Indigenous Peoples

*Federico Lenzerini**

1 One Day, in Cidade Maravilhosa

According to a famous saying, in Rio de Janeiro every cop has to make a choice. He either turns dirty, keeps his mouth shut, or goes to war. When in August 2008 I travelled to Rio de Janeiro, with the purpose of attending the 73rd biennial Conference of the International Law Association (ILA), I could not imagine that—metaphorically speaking—I, too, had to prepare to go to "war." Obviously, it would not have been a "war" as dangerous for my personal physical integrity as the struggle that everyday cops have to fight in Rio de Janeiro is for them; certainly, it would not have been a "war" fought with firearms and other weapons of war; rather, it would have been an academic and professional "war," the outcome of which could have some importance for peoples who, for centuries, have been persecuted, marginalized and discriminated and who, in the first years of 2000s, were struggling for their political, social and cultural renascence. I had to prepare to fight a "war" for the rights of Indigenous peoples, in the context of which, fortunately, I would not have been asked to either turn dirty or keep my mouth shut. Even more fortunately, there was another thing that I did not know yet, i.e. that I would have fought that war for human dignity side by side with a great academic ally and, eventually, friend, Professor Siegfried Wiessner.

I was introduced to Professor Wiessner by a member of the ILA Committee on the Rights of Indigenous Peoples (hereinafter: the Committee) in the hall of the InterContinental Hotel, location of the ILA Conference in Rio de Janeiro. The main task of the Committee was to develop a study on the legal

---

* Ph.D., International Law; Professor of International Law and Human Rights, University of Siena, Department of Political and International Sciences of the University of Siena (Italy); Professor at the LL.M. Program in Intercultural Human Rights, St. Thomas University School of Law, Miami (FL), USA; Rapporteur of the International Law Association (ILA) Committee on the Rights of Indigenous Peoples (2008–2012); Rapporteur of the ILA Committee on the Implementation of the Rights of Indigenous Peoples (2014–2020).

significance of the *United Nations Declaration on the Rights of Indigenous Peoples* (UNDRIP), adopted by the UN General Assembly on 13 September 2007.[1] Professor Wiessner had just been formally appointed Chair of the Committee, replacing Professor S. James Anaya, who, on his turn, had been nominated UN Special Rapporteur on the Rights of Indigenous Peoples. He asked me whether I wanted to become a member of the Committee, and I obviously accepted. I had the first working meeting with Professor Wiessner and the other members of the Committee in the afternoon of that same day, outside the InterContinental Hotel, under the sun shining in the Cidade Maravilhosa. I was the newest member of the Committee, and for this reason I was mainly listening to the discussion, trying to learn and observe. I immediately noted that Professor Wiessner was a very dynamic Chair. His views on the rights of Indigenous peoples were innovative, as shaped by the results of a global comparative and international legal study concerning such rights he had published in 1999. [Siegfried Wiessner, *Rights and Status of Indigenous Peoples: A Global Comparative and International Legal Perspective*, 12 Harv. Hum. Rts. J. 57–128 (1999)]. His findings in this respect might not initially have been shared by some of the Committee members, but it was undoubtedly fully in line with my own views on the subject.

2   The Road to ILA Resolution No. 5/2012

Shortly after the Rio Conference, the Committee's first rapporteur, Gregory Marks from Australia, had unfortunately to resign from his role due to health reasons. Professor Wiessner then asked me to become the new rapporteur of the Committee, a proposal which I enthusiastically accepted, although I think that, when I received Professor Wiessner's proposal, I was not fully aware of the responsibilities that that role brought with itself. What happened afterwards has been described by Professor Wiessner himself:

> The new Rapporteur of the Committee, Professor Federico Lenzerini from the University of Siena, coordinated the process, integrating work done at an intersessional workshop at the European University Institute in Florence, Italy, and combined subcommittee reports in a 52-page interim report for the ILA's 74th Biennial Meeting in The Hague. After another intersessional meeting conducted at the University of Anchorage

---

1   U.N. Doc. A/RES/61/295.

in Alaska in August 2011, at the invitation of Inuit Committee member Dalee Sambo Dorough, the final report of the Committee and a resolution for the ILA's 75th Biennial Meeting in Sofia was prepared. The final report supplemented the interim report of 2010.

The package of both the interim and the final report, plus the resolution, were presented for discussion and adoption at the Open Session of the Committee on August 28, 2012. This session was open to all members of the ILA. The session was chaired by Ralph Wilde (University College London) and was well attended. Upon the presentation of the report and resolution by the Chair and Rapporteur, interventions from the floor from among the Committee members present—Dalee Sambo Dorough, Mahulena Hofmann, Willem van Genugten, Rainer Hofmann, Ana Vrdolyak, Christina Binder and Katja Goecke—and comments and questions from non-Committee members of the ILA, all supportive and informative, the Chairman of the Session put the Committee's proposal to a vote. All ILA members voting in that room raised their hands emphatically in favour—save one abstention by a late arrival to the meeting, who did not feel knowledgeable enough about the subject to cast a substantive vote.

After this decision, the ILA Steering Committee put its finishing touches on the resolution, without changing the substance of the Committee's proposal. A question was asked as to why the resolution did not include a definition of the term "Indigenous peoples". The [Committee Chair (Professor Wiessner)] responded that the Committee as a whole, in particular its indigenous members, was unwilling to present a formal definition as this was seen, inter alia, as another attempt at colonization. Still, in the final report, a section had been included to clarify the understanding of the term. Two essential elements of that multi-factorial description of Indigenous peoples were self-identification as such and indigenous peoples' special, often spiritual relationship with their ancestral lands. The Steering Committee was satisfied with this response.

At the closing plenary session of August 30, 2012 in the Aula of the University of Sofia, the Chairman of the ILA Executive Council, The Rt Hon the Lord Mance, Justice of the United Kingdom Supreme Court, and Open Session Chairman Wilde introduced Resolution No. 5/2012. Dr. Wilde stated:

> This resolution represents the culmination of six years of very hard work on this important and cutting-edge topic. Its conclusions and recommendations are based on a wide-ranging and rigorous study

of state practice in this area, as reflected in the Committee's two lengthy reports. The resolution and those reports are clearly destined to play a major role in influencing the understanding and development of international law in this field.

And then he commended the adoption of the Resolution—to the rousing applause of the audience. As with the prior resolutions, Lord Mance, after waiting for objections, which did not come, declared the resolution properly offered, seconded, and passed. The session fittingly ended with a violinist playing Beethoven's "Ode to Joy."[2]

The "war" I referred to in the previous section took place, in particular, during the Open Session of the Committee at ILA's 74th Biennial Meeting in The Hague, in August 2010, under the chairmanship of Professor James Crawford. That Session was the theatrical stage of a very fervent and sometimes vehement academic debate, during which the Chair and the Rapporteur of the Committee—backed by other Committee members, particularly Dalee Sambo Dorough—fought like two visionaries who were aware that the results of that debate would have represented a crucial step in the future developments of international law in the field of Indigenous peoples' rights. Relying on the indisputable evidence offered by pertinent international practice, they eventually defeated the resistance of the more conservative members of the Committee, paving the way for the approval, two years later, of ILA Resolution No. 5/2012 by the ILA Executive Council.

3 A Look at the UNDRIP

As noted *supra*, in section 1, the main task of the Committee was to develop a study on the legal significance of the UNDRIP. ILA Resolution No. 5/2012 represents the synthesis and the *operative completion* of such a study. It is therefore appropriate to provide a brief survey of the UNDRIP and of its most important provisions, in order to describe the main legal background from which the Resolution originated.

The UNDRIP was adopted by the UN General Assembly following twenty-two years of negotiations in which representatives of Indigenous peoples coming

---

2 Siegfried Wiessner, *The State and Indigenous Peoples: The Historic Significance of ILA Resolution No. 5/2012, in* Der Staat im Recht. Festschrift für Eckart Klein zum 70. Geburtstag 1357, 1363–64 (M. Breuer et al. eds., 2013) (footnotes omitted).

from all around the world were fully involved. Its genesis was quite complicated, to the point that, for a long time, it appeared almost impossible to overcome the impasse determined by the conflicting views of State and Indigenous representatives concerning some key provisions included in its text. One of these provisions was represented by the article of the Draft Declaration recognizing the right of Indigenous peoples to self-determination (in the adopted text of the UNDRIP the article in point is Article 3), for the reason that States were scared by the implications traditionally attached to this right under international law, i.e. a right to secession. However, the impasse determined by the presence of this provision was eventually surmounted thanks to the inclusion in the Declaration's text of Article 46, paragraph 1, stating that "[n]othing in this Declaration may be interpreted as implying for any State, people, group or person any right to engage in any activity or to perform any act contrary to the Charter of the United Nations or *construed as authorizing or encouraging any action which would dismember or impair, totally or in part, the territorial integrity or political unity of sovereign and independent States*".[3] Another provision that was the object of controversy during the whole length of the negotiations leading to the adoption of the UNDRIP is its Article 28, which states that

1. Indigenous peoples have the right to redress, by means that can include restitution or, when this is not possible, just, fair and equitable compensation, for the lands, territories and resources which they have traditionally owned or otherwise occupied or used, and which have been confiscated, taken, occupied, used or damaged without their free, prior and informed consent.

2. Unless otherwise freely agreed upon by the peoples concerned, compensation shall take the form of lands, territories and resources equal in quality, size and legal status or of monetary compensation or other appropriate redress.

The presence of this article in the Declaration's text was probably the main reason for the negative vote expressed at the moment of its adoption by Australia, Canada, New Zealand and the United States,[4] particularly concerned by the amount of the lands located in their respective national territories which were potentially to be returned to Indigenous communities in the event of a

---

3 Emphasis added.

4 The UNDRIP was adopted on 13 September 2007 with 144 votes in favour, four votes against (Australia, Canada, New Zealand and the United States) and 11 abstentions (Azerbaijan, Bangladesh, Bhutan, Burundi, Colombia, Georgia, Kenya, Nigeria, Russia, Samoa and Ukraine).

strict and literal application of the provision in point.[5] However, in reality, this provision must be interpreted with a due degree of flexibility, implying that, although the main option provided for by its text is restitution, in many cases the latter may not be objectively practicable or may conflict with fundamental interests of the national community as a whole, which are often protected by international law as well. The drafters of Article 28 must have been fully aware of this, as evidenced by the fact that the provision accepts that, depending on the specific circumstances of each concrete case, restitution may be replaced by "just, fair and equitable compensation." The four countries originally voting against the adoption of the UNDRIP soon became mindful of this, and, between 2009 and 2010, all of them, in addition to Colombia and Samoa, officially endorsed the UNDRIP, thus making support for the Declaration virtually universal.

The operational provisions of the UNDRIP entail two principal general features.[6] First, they proclaim the *inherently* collective nature of Indigenous peoples' rights, in addition to reiterating that members of Indigenous communities are entitled to the full enjoyment of individual human rights and fundamental freedoms—"as recognized in the Charter of the United Nations, the Universal Declaration of Human Rights and international human rights law" (Article 1)—to an identical extent as all other human beings and without "any kind of discrimination ... in particular that based on their indigenous origin or identity" (Article 2).

Secondly, although the text of the UNDRIP never explicitly mentions the expression "Indigenous sovereignty,"[7] it actually defines its attributes. In

---

5   *See* Federico Lenzerini, *Reparations, Restitution, and Redress: Articles 8(2), 11(2), 20(2), and 28, in* The UN Declaration on the Rights of Indigenous Peoples. A Commentary 573, 585 (Jessie Hohmann & Marc Weller eds., 2018).

6   The following description of the contents of the UNDRIP is based on a previous writing of mine; *see* Federico Lenzerini, *Declaration on the Rights of Indigenous Peoples (UNDRIP), in* Elgar Encyclopedia of Human Rights (C. Binder, M. Nowak, J.A. Hofbauer & P. Janig eds., 2021).

7   On Indigenous sovereignty, see Federico Lenzerini, *Sovereignty Revised: International Law and Parallel Sovereignty of Indigenous Peoples*, 42 Texas Int'l L.J. 55 (2006). In that article, I wrote that "indigenous sovereignty entails, at a minimum, the following rights, protected by international law: (a) the right of indigenous peoples to live in, and maintain ownership of, their traditional lands (including natural resources) with no external interference (except in strictly and objectively exceptional cases and/or pursuant to their effective, prior, free and informed consent); (b) the right to maintain their own identity and right to enjoy, manifest, preserve and transmit to future generations their own culture (including political and social systems, traditional customs, medicine, language, and religious beliefs); (c) the right to self-government of their internal affairs according to their own customary law, including the right to use their own traditional judicial procedures (providing that they are consistent

addition to the right to self-determination—conceived by Article 3 as a prerogative allowing Indigenous peoples to "freely determine their political status and freely pursue their economic, social and cultural development"—the
related right to autonomy and self-government is established, with regard to
"matters relating to their internal and local affairs, as well as ways and means
for financing their autonomous functions" (Article 4). Article 5 UNDRIP adds
that "Indigenous peoples have the right to maintain and strengthen their distinct political, legal, economic, social and cultural institutions, while retaining their right to participate fully, if they so choose, in the political, economic,
social and cultural life of the State." The latter right is strictly interrelated with
the one sanctioned by Article 18, according to which "Indigenous peoples have
the right to participate in decision-making in matters which would affect their
rights, through representatives chosen by themselves in accordance with their
own procedures, as well as to maintain and develop their own indigenous
decision-making institutions." Article 20(1) adds that "Indigenous peoples have
the right to maintain and develop their political, economic and social systems
or institutions, to be secure in the enjoyment of their own means of subsistence and development, and to engage freely in all their traditional and other
economic activities," while Article 23 recognizes the right of the peoples concerned to determine and develop priorities and strategies for exercising their
right to development; this right attains political significance in so far as it presupposes a right "to be actively involved in developing and determining health,
housing and other economic and social programmes affecting them and, as far
as possible, to administer such programmes through their own institutions."

Another attribute of Indigenous sovereignty is the right to preserve and
transmit to future generations their own distinctive cultural identity and integrity. The implications of this right are expressed by a number of provisions
included in the UNDRIP. In particular, Article 8 states that "Indigenous peoples and individuals have the right not to be subjected to forced assimilation
or destruction of their culture"; this right entails the following prerogatives:
(a) right to preserve their integrity as distinct peoples, their cultural values and
ethnic identities; (b) right to keep possession of their traditional lands, territories or resources; (c) right not to be subjected to forced population transfer;
(d) right not to be subjected to any form of forced assimilation or integration;
(e) prohibition of any form of propaganda designed to promote or incite racial
or ethnic discrimination directed against them. One further concrete specification subsumed within the right of Indigenous peoples to the preservation

---

with internationally recognized human rights); and d) the right to effective participation, at
all levels of decision-making, in decisions which may affect them" (at 187–88).

and protection of their own distinctive identity and integrity is indicated by Article 11 UNDRIP, which affirms the right of such peoples "to practise and revitalize their cultural traditions and customs," which includes "the right to maintain, protect and develop the past, present and future manifestations of their cultures, such as archaeological and historical sites, artefacts, designs, ceremonies, technologies and visual and performing arts and literature."

This provision is complemented by the subsequent Article 12, establishing the rights of Indigenous communities "to manifest, practise, develop and teach their spiritual and religious traditions, customs and ceremonies ... to maintain, protect, and have access in privacy to their religious and cultural sites ... [as well as] to the use and control of their ceremonial objects; and the right to the repatriation of their human remains." Furthermore, Article 13 provides for the right of Indigenous peoples "to revitalize, use, develop and transmit to future generations their histories, languages, oral traditions, philosophies, writing systems and literatures, and to designate and retain their own names for communities, places and persons," while Article 14 asserts their right "to establish and control their educational systems and institutions providing education in their own languages, in a manner appropriate to their cultural methods of teaching and learning."

Article 16 UNDRIP also protects Indigenous peoples' cultural identity through affirming their right "to establish their own media in their own languages and to have access to all forms of non-indigenous media without discrimination." Article 31 articulates the right of Indigenous communities "to maintain, control, protect and develop their cultural heritage, traditional knowledge and traditional cultural expressions, as well as the manifestations of their sciences, technologies and cultures, including human and genetic resources, seeds, medicines, knowledge of the properties of fauna and flora, oral traditions, literatures, designs, sports and traditional games and visual and performing arts," whilst Article 34 recognizes their right "to promote, develop and maintain their institutional structures and their distinctive customs, spirituality, traditions, procedures, practices and, in the cases where they exist, juridical systems or customs, in accordance with international human rights standards."

Indigenous sovereignty also includes the right of Indigenous peoples "to the lands, territories and resources which [they] have traditionally owned, occupied or otherwise used or acquired," affirmed by Article 26(1) UNDRIP. There is no need to emphasize how crucial this right is for Indigenous peoples. Its nature and significance are famously described in a frequently quoted excerpt from the judgment of the Inter-American Court of Human Rights (IACtHR) in the *Awas Tingni* case:

Among indigenous peoples there is a communitarian tradition regarding a communal form of collective property of the land, in the sense that ownership of the land is not centered on an individual but rather on the group and its community. Indigenous groups, by the fact of their very existence, have the right to live freely in their own territory; the close ties of indigenous people with the land must be recognized and understood as the fundamental basis of their cultures, their spiritual life, their integrity, and their economic survival. For indigenous communities, relations to the land are not merely a matter of possession and production but a material and spiritual element which they must fully enjoy, even to preserve their cultural legacy and transmit it to future generations.[8]

This right is not only especially significant per se, but—embodying a formidable example of the relationship of deep interdependence generally existing between all Indigenous peoples' rights—it is also functional to the safeguarding of the very distinct cultural identity of Indigenous peoples and of their survival and flourishing as different human communities, for which the preservation of the special spiritual relation they have with their ancestral lands is essential.[9] The UNDRIP deals with the right in point in a number of provisions.

Article 25, in particular, emphasizes that "Indigenous peoples have the right to maintain and strengthen their distinctive spiritual relationship with their traditionally owned or otherwise occupied and used lands, territories, waters and coastal seas and other resources and to uphold their responsibilities to future generations in this regard," while Article 26(2) attributes to the peoples concerned "the right to own, use, develop and control the lands, territories and resources that they possess by reason of traditional ownership or other traditional occupation or use, as well as those which they have otherwise acquired"; this presupposes an obligation of States to "give legal recognition and protection to these lands, territories and resources. Such recognition shall be conducted with due respect to the customs, traditions and land tenure systems of the indigenous peoples concerned" (Article 26(3)). In addition, as required by Article 27 UNDRIP, States

---

8   See Case of the Mayagna (Sumo) Awas Tingni Community v. Nicaragua, Series C No. 79, Judgment of 31 August 2001 ((Merits, Reparations and Costs), para. 149. Regarding this case see, among others, Jonathan P. Vuotto, Awas Tingni v. Nicaragua: International Precedent For Indigenous Land Rights?, 22 Boston U. Int'l L.J. 219 (2004); Bryan Neihart, Awas Tingni v. Nicaragua Reconsidered: Grounding Indigenous Peoples' Land Rights in Religious Freedom, 42 Denv. J. Int'l L. & Pol'y 77 (2013).

9   See Siegfried Wiessner, Re-Enchanting the World: Indigenous Peoples' Rights as Essential Parts of a Holistic Human Rights Regime, 15 UCLA J. Int'l & Foreign Aff. 239, 259 (2010).

shall establish and implement, in conjunction with indigenous peoples concerned, a fair, independent, impartial, open and transparent process, giving due recognition to indigenous peoples' laws, traditions, customs and land tenure systems, to recognize and adjudicate the rights of indigenous peoples pertaining to their lands, territories and resources, including those which were traditionally owned or otherwise occupied or used. Indigenous peoples shall have the right to participate in this process.

The protection of the relationship existing between Indigenous peoples and their ancestral lands is completed, in the UNDRIP, by Article 32—providing for the right of such peoples "to determine and develop priorities and strategies for the development or use of their lands or territories and other resources"—by Article 10—establishing that Indigenous peoples "shall not be forcibly removed from their lands or territories" and that no relocation "shall take place without the free, prior and informed consent of the indigenous peoples concerned and after agreement on just and fair compensation and, where possible, with the option of return"—and by Article 28, reproduced *supra*.

Among the other rights recognized by the UNDRIP in favour of Indigenous peoples the following are included: the "right, without discrimination, to the improvement of their economic and social conditions, including, inter alia, in the areas of education, employment, vocational training and retraining, housing, sanitation, health and social security" (Article 21); the "right to their traditional medicines and to maintain their health practices, including the conservation of their vital medicinal plants, animals and minerals ... [as well as] right to access [by Indigenous individuals], without any discrimination, to all social and health services" (Article 24); and the right "to the recognition, observance and enforcement of treaties, agreements and other constructive arrangements concluded with States or their successors and to have States honour and respect such treaties, agreements and other constructive arrangements" (Article 37).

One rule of special importance established by the UNDRIP is the one according to which the free, prior and informed consent (FPIC) of the Indigenous communities concerned must be obtained for legitimately carrying out certain activities in their lands or territories or actions that, in any event, may significantly impair the rights protected by the Declaration. This requirement is established by Article 10 as regards the relocation of Indigenous peoples from their lands or territories; by Article 11(2) with respect to the appropriation of their cultural, intellectual, religious and spiritual property; by Article 19 as a necessary condition for adopting and implementing legislative or administrative measures that may affect them; by Article 28 as regards the confiscation, taking, occupation, use or damage to lands, territories and resources which they have traditionally owned or otherwise occupied or used; by Article 29(2) for the storage or disposal of hazardous materials in the lands or territories of Indigenous peoples; as well as by Article 32(2) "prior to the approval of any project affecting their lands or territories and other resources, particularly in connection with the development, utilization or exploitation of mineral, water or other resources."

Last, but not least, the UNDRIP dedicates extensive space to the right of Indigenous peoples to reparation and redress for the wrong suffered. This right is, in particular, contemplated by Article 8(2) for violations threatening the cultural identity and integrity of Indigenous peoples; by Article 11(2) as regards the "cultural, intellectual, religious and spiritual property taken without their free, prior and informed consent or in violation of their laws, traditions and customs"; by Article 20(2) for the situations when Indigenous peoples are "deprived of their means of subsistence and development"; by Article 28 "for the lands, territories and resources which they have traditionally owned or otherwise occupied or used, and which have been confiscated, taken, occupied, used or damaged without their free, prior and informed consent"; and by Article 32(3) for damages determined by projects "affecting their lands or territories and other resources ... [producing] adverse environmental, economic, social, cultural or spiritual impact."[10]

These provisions are complemented by Article 40, providing for the right of Indigenous peoples "to access to and prompt decision through just and fair procedures for the resolution of conflicts and disputes with States or other parties, as well as to effective remedies for all infringements of their individual and collective rights. Such a decision shall give due consideration to the customs, traditions, rules and legal systems of the indigenous peoples concerned and international human rights."

The adoption of the UNDRIP represented a ground-breaking event in the context of the legal movement for the recognition of the rights of Indigenous peoples and for their legal and cultural renaissance. Since the immediate aftermath of its adoption, the UNDRIP has had a propulsive force in advancing the rights of Indigenous peoples in the context of international human rights law, especially due to the use made of it by international human rights monitoring bodies (including, among others, the IACtHR, the African Commission and Court of Human and Peoples' Rights and the Caribbean Court of Justice), by domestic courts and other State organs, in addition to the fact of being

---

10   More extensively on reparation and redress see Lenzerini, *supra* note 5, *passim.*

explicitly mentioned in the text of important international treaties posterior to it.[11] The most important aspect of this practice is that the relevant bodies agree in considering the UNDRIP as the main instrument defining the standards that *States are obliged to comply with* in the context of Indigenous peoples' rights. A notable, recent, addition in the field of domestic practice is represented by Canadian Bill C-15, *An Act respecting the United Nations Declaration on the Rights of Indigenous Peoples*,[12] which received Royal Assent on 21 June 2021 and incorporated the UNDRIP into national legislation, declaring that "[t]he Government of Canada must, in consultation and cooperation with Indigenous peoples, take all measures necessary to ensure that the laws of Canada are consistent with the Declaration."[13] This and other developments demonstrate that the "UNDRIP has been a milestone of re-empowerment [of Indigenous peoples], from the down of the *Cayuga Indians* Award of 1926 which denied indigenous peoples the status of a 'legal unit of international law' to their membership, on a level of equality with states, on the UN Permanent Forum on Indigenous Issues and beyond."[14]

4   The Significance of ILA Resolution No. 5/2012 on the Rights of Indigenous Peoples and its Place in International Law

Professor Wiessner has explained the significance of ILA Resolution No. 5/2012, writing that "[t]he resolution is historic. Not only does it recognize collective human rights; it also specifies a number of rights that have become part and parcel of customary international law".[15] In a statement of endorsement of the Committee's final report and resolution, the then UN Special Rapporteur on the Rights of Indigenous Peoples, S. James Anaya, wrote that

> [t]he committee's work before you reflects the highest standards of our profession. It is structured thematically around key aspects of indigenous

---

11   For more details see Federico Lenzerini, *Implementation of the UNDRIP around the World: Achievements and Future Perspectives. The Outcome of the Work of the ILA Committee on the Implementation of the Rights of Indigenous Peoples*, 23 Int'l J. Hum. Rts. 51 (2019), at 56–8; *id., supra* note 6, paras. 20–24.

12   *Available at* https://www.parl.ca/LegisInfo/en/bill/43-2/c-15 (accessed 17 June 2023).

13   *See* para. 5.

14   *See* International Law Association, Committee on the Rights of Indigenous Peoples, The Hague Conference (2010), Interim Report, *available at* https://www.ila-hq.org/en_GB /committees/rights-of-indigenous-peoples (accessed 17 June 2023), at 2 (footnotes omitted).

15   *See* Wiessner, *supra* note 2, at 1364 (footnotes omitted).

peoples' rights, including culture and identity, lands and resources, and self-determination and autonomy. It recognizes the goal of protection of cultural diversity, which undergirds the novel phenomenon of communal and collective rights being introduced into international law. Importantly, on the basis of accepted methods of international legal analysis, the report not only expounds upon the content of the various provisions of the UN Declaration on the Rights of Indigenous Peoples, it also engages in a review of pertinent international and state practice to ascertain the international legal status of the various rights formulated in that document. One example is the thoughtful discussion of the principles of consultation and consent in the final report. Given the thorough research undertaken by the committee, the conclusions as formulated in its final report and resolution are highly authoritative.[16]

In writing this statement, the UN Special Rapporteur confirmed his previous recognition of the authority of the conclusions of the Committee—as they would eventually flow into Resolution No. 5/2012—expressed in his position of a member of the ICSID Arbitral Tribunal in the *Grand River Award*. In that award, he stated that

> [i]t may well be ... that there does exist a principle of customary international law requiring governmental authorities to consult indigenous peoples on governmental policies or actions significantly affecting them. One member of the Tribunal has written that there is such a customary rule. Moreover, a recent study by a committee of several international law experts assembled under the auspices of the International Law Association, after an exhaustive survey of relevant state and international practice, found a wide range of customary international law norms concerning indigenous peoples, including "the right to be consulted with respect to any project that may affect them."[17]

The position authoritatively expressed by the UN Special Rapporteur attributes further legitimation to a cutting-edge stance taken by ILA Resolution

---

16   *See* Statement of Endorsement of Committee Final Report and Resolution by S. James Anaya, Annex to the International Law Association's Committee on the Rights of Indigenous Peoples Final Report, Sofia Conference (2012), *available at* https://www.ila-hq.org /en_GB/committees/rights-of-indigenous-peoples (accessed 17 June 2023) 31, at 32.

17   *Grand River Enterprises Six Nations, Ltd., et al. v. United States of America*, Award, 12 January 2011, *available at* https://www.italaw.com/sites/default/files/case-documents/ita0384.pdf (accessed 17 June 2023), para. 210.

No. 5/2012, i.e., exactly, that the most fundamental rights of Indigenous peoples are today protected by rules of customary international law. This aspect was characterized by controversial views within the Committee, and it certainly was the main reason of the fervent debate which developed during its Open Session at ILA's 74th Biennial Meeting in The Hague, as described in the previous section. However, as noted in the Committee's Interim Report,

> the overwhelming voting majority with which the UNDRIP has been approved, the subsequent endorsement of the Declaration by ... the few governments that had voted against it, the unequivocal judicial and para-judicial practice of treaty bodies, as well as the pertinent state practice at both the domestic and international level, unequivocally show that a general *opinio iuris* as well as *consuetudo* exists within the international community according to which certain basic prerogatives that are essential in order to safeguard the identity and basic rights of indigenous peoples are today crystallized in the realm of customary international law.[18]

The main argument used by those opposing the existence of rules of customary international law in the field of Indigenous peoples' rights was based on the fact that the rights sanctioned by those rules are the object of frequent breaches all around the world. However, this argument may be quite easily rebutted through relying on an *ontological* assessment of legal rules in general and customary international law in particular. In fact, violation is inherent in the very existence of a legal rule; in epistemological terms, the simple fact of defining a given behaviour as "violation" or "breach" confirms the existence of the rule that is assumed as being violated. This axiom has been confirmed— with specific regard to international law—by the International Court of Justice (ICJ) in the renowned and very often quoted passage from its *Nicaragua* judgment:

> for a rule to be established as customary, the corresponding practice must [not] be in absolute rigorous conformity with the rule. In order to deduce the existence of customary rules, ... it [is] sufficient that the conduct of States should, in general, be consistent with such rules, and that *instances of State conduct inconsistent with a given rule should generally have been treated as breaches of that rule* ... If a State acts in a way prima facie incompatible with a recognized rule, but defends its conduct

---

18   *See* Committee on the Rights of Indigenous Peoples, *supra* note 14, at 43.

by appealing to exceptions or justifications ..., then whether or not the State's conduct is in fact justifiable on that basis, the significance of that attitude is to confirm rather than to weaken the rule.[19]

In the context of international practice concerning the rights of Indigenous peoples, it is quite unusual that States not applying or not properly implementing them in concrete cases use the argument that such rights would not exist or would not be productive of any State obligations. They rather rely on the presumed existence of particular circumstances which would justify exceptions to or derogations from such rules. And, of course, one cannot assume that arguments of this kind are always legally ungrounded. Actually, in the doctrinal debate, it appears that the discussion concerning the existence of rights of Indigenous peoples under customary international law is centered on a kind of *epistemological misunderstanding*, based on the inaccurate assumption that, once certain customary rules recognizing such rights are considered as existing and in force, they would determine obligations of absolute character that States would not be allowed to disregard, irrespective of the specific circumstances of concrete cases. In reality, instead, the rules under discussion are to be treated like any other provision of customary international law, which can be the object of derogation in the presence, for instance, of a circumstance precluding wrongfulness[20]—or, in any event, in case of material impossibility of performing it—and, most importantly, are subject to *balancing* with conflicting values also sanctioned by provisions of customary international law. Balancing "involves weighing competing rights against each other and analysing the relative strengths of many factors."[21] Although technical methods exist for carrying out this operation—particularly the use of the *lex specialis derogat legi generali* and *lex posterior derogat legi priori* principles—it is evident that "[t]he question of the normative weight to be given to particular rights and obligations at the moment when they appear to clash with other rights and obligations can only be argued on a case-by-case basis."[22] Certainly, the rights

---

19   *Case concerning Military and Paramilitary Activities in and against Nicaragua* (*Nicaragua v. USA*), Judgment of 27 June 1986, *I.C.J. Reports* 1986, at 14, para. 186 (emphasis added).

20   *See* International Law Commission, Articles on 'Responsibility of States for Internationally Wrongful Acts, *available at* https://legal.un.org/ilc/texts/instruments/english/draft _articles/9_6_2001.pdf (accessed 17 June 2023), Articles 20–27.

21   *See Balancing, The Free Dictionary, available at* https://legal-dictionary.thefreedictionary .com/ Balancing (accessed 17 June 2023).

22   *See* Fragmentation of International Law: Difficulties Arising from the Diversification and Expansion of International Law, Report of the Study Group of the International Law

of Indigenous peoples usually have prominent normative weight, to an extent that sometimes they may even reach the point of grazing the peak of *jus cogens*.

Indeed, a denial of Indigenous peoples' rights—including cultural rights— may translate in practice into forms of deep suffering and pain for their members, reaching the threshold of inhuman and degrading treatment, a human rights violation prohibited by a peremptory norm of general international law.[23] However, this is not always the case, and therefore one cannot assume a priori that the rights of Indigenous peoples must always prevail over competing interests; as a consequence, it may be possible that "States are unable, for concrete and justified reasons," to guarantee proper respect and realization of such rights.[24] This may happen, for instance, in the event of conflicts between Indigenous peoples' collective land rights and other competing property rights over the same territories, although two *caveats* are imperative: first, appropriate

---

Commission, finalized by Mr. Martti Koskenniemi, UN Doc. A/CN.4/L.682 and Add.1, 13 April 2006, para. 474.

23   An example of this reality is offered by the case of the N'djuka Maroon village of Moiwana, in Suriname, which, on 29 November 1986, was attacked by members of the national armed forces, who allegedly massacred over 40 men, women and children, and razed the village to the ground. In examining the case, the IACtHR found that the fact that the physical remains of the deceased members of the community had not been returned to it by the government of Suriname gave rise, to the detriment of the surviving members, to a violation of Article 5(1) of the *American Convention of Human Rights* (adopted in 1969, 1144 UNTS 123), establishing the right to humane treatment, in particular that "[e] very person has the right to have his physical, mental, and moral integrity respected." This finding was based on the assumption that 'Moiwana community members ... endured significant emotional, psychological, spiritual and economic hardship—suffering to a such a degree as to result in the State's violation of Article 5(1) of the American Convention" (*Case of the Moiwana Community v. Suriname*, Series C No. 124, Judgment of 15 June 2005 (Preliminary Objections, Merits, Reparations and Costs), para. 103). In fact, "the N'djuka people have specific and complex rituals that must be precisely followed upon the death of a community member. Furthermore, it is extremely important to have possession of the physical remains of the deceased, as the corpse must be treated in a particular manner during the N'djuka death ceremonies and must be placed in the burial ground of the appropriate descent group. Only those who have been deemed unworthy do not receive an honorable burial. If the various death rituals are not performed according to N'djuka tradition, it is considered a profound moral transgression, which will not only anger the spirit of the individual who died, but also may offend other ancestors of the community. ... This leads to a number of 'spiritually-caused illnesses' that become manifest as actual physical maladies and can potentially affect the entire natural lineage. ... The N'djuka understand that such illnesses are not cured on their own, but rather must be resolved through cultural and ceremonial means; if not, the conditions will persist through generations" (*id.*, paras. 98–9).

24   *See* IACtHR, *Case of the Yakye Axa Indigenous Community v. Paraguay*, Series C No. 125, Judgment of 17 June 2005 (Merits, Reparations and Costs), para. 149.

consideration must be paid to the impact that deprivation of their traditional lands may have on the very survival of Indigenous peoples as distinct cultural communities and even for their physical existence, especially for the reason that—consistent with the considerations right above—"[d]isregarding the ancestral right of the members of the indigenous communities to their territories could affect other basic rights, such as the right to cultural identity and to the very survival of the indigenous communities and their members";[25] secondly, when it happens that Indigenous peoples' rights are disregarded or impaired because a competing right is considered as prevailing over them, the Indigenous communities concerned are entitled to compensation for the damages suffered, which "must be guided primarily by the meaning of the land [or, in any event, by the value of the loss undergone] for them".[26]

Having said that, however, it must be reiterated that recognizing the existence of Indigenous peoples' rights under customary international law—as done by ILA Resolution No. 5/2012—does not necessarily mean depriving national governments of any kind of control over the parts of the national territory traditionally belonging to Indigenous communities. At the same time, when balancing Indigenous peoples' rights with other fundamental interests of the national communities, States are bound to use good faith and attribute adequate weight to the concrete consequences that denial or impairment of such rights would produce to the prejudice of the preservation of the cultural identity of the Indigenous peoples concerned, as well as of the individual rights of their members. This means in practice that the rights of Indigenous peoples can only be sacrificed when it is indispensable to protect a fundamental interest of the State or of its national community and no other way exists for achieving such an interest.

Obviously, ILA Resolution No. 5/2012 does not consider all the provisions included in the UNDRIP as corresponding to rules of customary international law. On the contrary, this treatment is only reserved to a very limited part of them, specifying that "[t]he 2007 United Nations Declaration on the Rights of Indigenous Peoples (UNDRIP) as a whole cannot yet be considered as a statement of existing customary international law. However it includes several key provisions which correspond to existing State obligations under customary international law."[27]

---

25   *Id.* para. 147.

26   *Id.* para. 149.

27   *See* para. 2. The text of ILA Resolution No. 5/2012 is available at https://www.ila-hq.org /en_GB/committees/rights-of-indigenous-peoples (accessed 17 June 2023).

First, ILA Resolution No. 5/2012 affirms that "States must comply with the obligation—consistent with customary and applicable conventional international law—to recognise, respect, protect, fulfil and promote the right of indigenous peoples to self-determination, conceived as the right to decide their political status and to determine what their future will be, in compliance with relevant rules of international law and the principles of equality and non-discrimination."[28] This right represents the basis for the effective enjoyment of any other human rights recognized in favour of Indigenous peoples. As declared by the government of Australia at the moment of its official endorsement of the UNDRIP, the right to self-determination entitles "Indigenous peoples to have control over their destiny and to be treated respectfully."[29] It is to be conceived as a right entitling "the peoples concerned ... to exercise an opportune degree of autonomy and self-government within the State in which they live, without providing authorization to carry out acts contrary to the territorial integrity or political unity of States[, consistent with Article 46, para. 1 UNDRIP]. This said, however, indigenous peoples continue to have the same right that all other peoples have to move toward secession in appropriate cases."[30] The last sentence implies that, like any other people, Indigenous peoples are entitled to pursue secession in the cases when it is established by international law, i.e. in situations of colonization, in the event of foreign occupation, and, possibly, when they are "denied meaningful access to government to pursue their political, economic, social and cultural development."[31]

The second right of Indigenous peoples that ILA Resolution No. 5/2012 confirms as being recognized by customary international law (in addition to applicable conventional international law) is the right to autonomy or self-government.[32] The Resolution explains that this right

> translates into a number of prerogatives necessary in order to secure the preservation and transmission to future generations of their cultural identity and distinctiveness. These prerogatives include, *inter alia*, the right to participate in national decision-making with respect to decisions that may affect them, the right to be consulted with respect to any project

---

28 *Id.* para. 4.

29 *See* Statement on the United Nations Declaration on the Rights of Indigenous Peoples, 3 April 2009, *available at* https://parlinfo.aph.gov.au/parlInfo/search/display/display .w3p;query=Id:%22media/pressrel/418T6%22 (accessed 17 June 2023).

30 *See* Committee on the Rights of Indigenous Peoples, *supra* note 14, at 10.

31 *See Re: Secession of Quebec*, [1998] 2 S.C.R. 217, Supreme Court of Canada, 37 I.L.M. 1340, 1373, para. 138.

32 *See* ILA Resolution No. 5/2012, *supra* note 27, para. 5.

that may affect them and the related right that projects significantly impacting their rights and ways of life are not carried out without their prior, free and informed consent, as well as the right to regulate autonomously their internal affairs according to their own customary laws and to establish, maintain and develop their own legal and political institutions.[33]

ILA Resolution No. 5/2012 then attests the existence, under customary international law—and, again, under applicable conventional international law—of a State obligation "to recognise, respect, safeguard, promote and fulfil the rights of indigenous peoples to their traditional lands, territories and resources, which include the right to restitution of the ancestral lands, territories and resources of which they have been deprived in the past."[34] The text makes it clear that "Indigenous peoples' land rights must be secured in order to preserve the spiritual relationship of the community concerned with its ancestral lands, which is an essential prerequisite to allow such a community to retain its cultural identity, practices, customs and institutions."[35]

Last but not least, the obligation of States "under customary and applicable conventional international law—to recognise and fulfil the rights of indigenous peoples to reparation and redress for wrongs they have suffered, including rights relating to lands taken or damaged without their free, prior and informed consent,"[36] is recognized. It is an obligation which presupposes that "[e]ffective mechanisms for redress—established in conjunction with the peoples concerned—must be available and accessible in favour of indigenous peoples. Reparation must be adequate and effective, and, according to the perspective of the indigenous communities concerned, actually capable of repairing the wrongs they have suffered."[37]

In this regard, the fact that "today a general *opinio juris* exists within the international community confirming that States are *required* to provide some form of reparation for the wrongs suffered by Indigenous peoples, especially in the event of deprivation of, or damage to, their traditional lands", is corroborated by the UNDRIP negotiations as well as by the "the massive consistent [international and] domestic practice recently developed in the field."[38] In addition, it is also confirmed by a reasoning of legal logic. In fact, considering

---

33   *Id.*
34   *Id.* para. 7.
35   *Id.*
36   *Id.* para. 10.
37   *Id.*
38   *See* Lenzerini, *supra* note 5, at 596–7 (italics in the original text).

that reparation is essential for guaranteeing the effective enjoyment of human rights, any obligation existing in the field of human rights inherently incorporates the requirement that any breach of the obligation concerned is adequately redressed. It logically follows that any rule protecting human rights which exists under customary international law necessarily presupposes the parallel and indivisible existence of an obligation—*also sanctioned by customary international law*—that adequate reparation is guaranteed in the event of violation of the rule concerned.

This automatically implies that, as regards the rights of Indigenous peoples protected by customary international law, corresponding obligations exist, *also according to customary international law*, binding States to provide effective and adequate reparation in favour of Indigenous peoples for the breaches of the said rights they have suffered.[39]

This right has a minimum requirement, namely that reparation is *adequate* and *effective*, meaning that it must be capable of eliminating, to the maximum extent possible, the effects of the wrong suffered *as they are perceived by the communities concerned* or by their members.[40]

The paragraphs attesting the existence of Indigenous peoples' rights under customary international law do not exhaust the contents of ILA Resolution No. 5/2012. Indeed, the latter clarifies that

> [t]he provisions included in UNDRIP which do not yet correspond to customary international law nevertheless express the aspirations of the world's indigenous peoples, as well as of States, in their move to improve existing standards for the safeguarding of indigenous peoples' human rights. States recognised them in a "declaration" subsumed "within the framework of the obligations established by the Charter of the United Nations to promote and protect human rights on a non-discriminatory basis" and passed with overwhelming support by the United Nations General Assembly. This genesis leads to an expectation of maximum compliance by States and the other relevant actors. The provisions included in UNDRIP represent the parameters of reference for States to define the scope and content of their existing obligations—pursuant to customary and conventional international law—towards indigenous peoples.[41]

---

39   *Id.* at 597.
40   *Id.*
41   ILA Resolution No. 5/2012, *supra* note 27, para. 3.

The spirit and the formulation of this paragraph—particularly the use of the word "yet"—clearly show the dynamic character of the evolution of international law on Indigenous peoples, a process *in fieri* in the context of which the amount of rights recognized by rules of customary international law promises to grow progressively, as they are functional to the fulfilment of the aspiration of Indigenous peoples themselves to give full realization to their cultural identity, distinctiveness, and rights. In fact, in the fourteen paragraphs composing ILA Resolution No. 5/2012 each word was carefully selected and pondered not only with the purpose of reflecting the current status of international law on Indigenous peoples' rights, painted with the colors of Indigenous view of life and cosmology. Setting and describing the existing legal standards in the field was indeed only a part of the task, probably, in the end, not even the most challenging one. It was contextually necessary to pave the way for the establishment of a legal and social background conducive to the further positive evolution of international law in the field, consistent with Indigenous peoples' own needs and life expectations, with the ultimate purpose of allowing them to harmoniously develop and transmit their own cultural identity to future generations. The first paragraphs of the Resolution exactly reflect this awareness, clearly illustrating that the outcomes achieved so far simply represent a starting point, the fuel for a propulsive process of positive legal evolution and "ideological" enlightenment aimed at ensuring that Indigenous peoples may effective enjoy the full measure of (collective and individual) human rights necessary for living their lives consistent with their own wishes and desires. This is particularly clear in paragraph 1 of the Resolution, according to which "Indigenous peoples are holders of collective human rights aimed at ensuring the preservation and transmission to future generations of their cultural identity and distinctiveness. Members of indigenous peoples are entitled to the enjoyment of all internationally recognised human rights—including those specific to their indigenous identity—in a condition of full equality with all other human beings."

The dynamic character of this text rests in the *complementary dichotomy* of the message it conveys. On the one hand, it clarifies that no differences exist between members of Indigenous peoples and other peoples as regards the right to enjoy *all* internationally recognized human rights; this way, the paragraph fixes the results of the evolution of international human rights law for Indigenous peoples. On the other hand—and contextually—it advocates that existing human rights standards must be *collectivized* and moulded so as to achieve the purpose of "ensuring the preservation and transmission to future generations of their cultural identity and distinctiveness." It therefore endorses the process of *evolutive interpretation* of human rights standards developed by international human rights monitoring bodies (particularly the IACtHR), consisting in attributing a collective dimension to individual human rights with the specific purpose of meeting the particular needs and concerns of Indigenous peoples.[42]

Paragraph 3 of ILA Resolution No. 5/2012—previously reproduced[43]—is also particularly meaningful in the part where it affirms that "[t]he provisions included in UNDRIP represent the parameters of reference for States to define the scope and content of their existing obligations—pursuant to customary and conventional international law—towards indigenous peoples". As described in the previous section, this statement actually reflects the contemporary practice prevailing among international human rights monitoring bodies and in many countries, consisting in considering the UNDRIP as the main parameter of reference in defining the contents of State obligations towards Indigenous peoples.

ILA Resolution No. 5/2012 also does not miss the occasion of emphasizing the importance of other Indigenous peoples' rights—in addition to those previously mentioned—irrespective of whether or not they are sanctioned by rules of customary international law. In this regard, the Resolution has indeed followed a rigorous and scrupulous approach, avoiding to declare the existence of rules of customary international law with respect to those rights for which such an assumption was not plainly grounded on a sufficient and verified amount of *diuturnitas* and *opinio juris*. This notwithstanding, for a right in particular it is hard to maintain that it is not protected by a rule of general international law, of binding character for all countries. It is the right to cultural identity and integrity. As regards this right, ILA Resolution No. 5/2012 affirms that

---

42   *See*, among the many relevant academic works, Isabel Madariaga Cuneo, *The Rights of Indigenous Peoples and the Inter-American Human Rights System*, 22 Ariz. J. Int'l & Comp. L. 53 (2005); Gabriella Citroni & Karla I. Quintana Osuna, *Reparations for Indigenous Peoples in the Case Law of the Inter-American Court of Human Rights, in* Reparations for Indigenous Peoples. International and Comparative Perspectives 317 (F. Lenzerini ed., 2008); Jo M. Pasqualucci, *International Indigenous Land Rights: A Critique of the Jurisprudence of the Inter-american Court of Human Rights in Light of the United Nations Declaration on the Rights of Indigenous Peoples*, 27 Wis. Int'l L.J. 51 (2009–2010); Vasiliki Saranti, *International Justice and Protection of Indigenous Peoples—The Case-Law of the Inter-American Court of Human Rights*, 9 US-China L. Rev. 427 (2012); Alejandro Fuentes, *Protection of Indigenous Peoples' Traditional Lands and Exploitation of Natural Resources: The Inter-American Court of Human Rights' Safeguards*, 24 Int'l J. Minority & Group Rts. 229 (2017).

43   *See supra* note 41 and corresponding text.

States are bound to recognise, respect, protect and fulfil indigenous peoples' cultural identity (in all its elements, including cultural heritage) and to cooperate with them in good faith—through all possible means—in order to ensure its preservation and transmission to future generations. Cultural rights are the core of indigenous cosmology, ways of life and identity, and must therefore be safeguarded in a way that is consistent with the perspectives, needs and expectations of the specific indigenous peoples.[44]

This paragraph does not explicitly refer to the existence of an obligation of customary international law providing for a right of Indigenous peoples to have their cultural identity and heritage respected and preserved. However, it is easy to see how—on account of the previously noted strict interdependence existing between all Indigenous peoples' rights—the violation of this right would inevitably translate into a breach of other rights recognized in favor of those peoples by customary international law, particularly the right to self-determination. As noted by the renowned Australian Aboriginal activist Michael Dodson with specific regard to cultural heritage, "[f]or Indigenous peoples, the impact of separating us from our heritage goes directly to the heart that pumps life through our peoples. To expect a people to be able to enjoy their culture without their cultural heritage and their sacred belongings is equivalent to amputating their legs and digging up the ground and asking them to run the marathon."[45] It logically follows that the obligation to respect and protect the right to self-determination and other rights explicitly recognized by customary international law *implies* the existence of a State responsibility to adequately protect and preserve Indigenous peoples' cultural identity and integrity.

Another right the existence of which is explicitly recognized by ILA Resolution No. 5/2012 is the right of Indigenous peoples to establish their own educational institutions and media, as well as to provide education to Indigenous children in their traditional languages and according to their own traditions. The Resolution, in particular, highlights that "States have the obligation not to interfere with the exercise of these rights."[46] The nature

---

44   *See* ILA Resolution No. 5/2012, *supra* note 27, para. 6.
45   See 'Cultural Rights and Educational Responsibilities', Speech by Michael Dodson, Aboriginal and Torres Strait Islander Social Justice Commissioner, The Frank Archibald Memorial Lecture, 5 September 1994, University of New England, *available at* https://humanrights .gov.au/ about/news/speeches/cultural-rights-and-educational-responsibilities-dodson-1994 (accessed 17 June 2023).
46   *See* ILA Resolution No. 5/2012, *supra* note 27, para. 8.

of this obligation, with specific regard to language rights, is clarified in the Committee's Final Report, in which it is stated that

> [a]t the moment ... [the pertinent] legal evolution ... has probably not yet reached the point of leading to the existence of a rule of customary international law dictating a *positive* State obligation to take all possible measures in order to allow indigenous peoples to preserve their languages and transmit them to future generation. At the same time, it is clear, from the history and context of the UNDRIP, that such an obligation actually exists in *negative* terms, in the sense that States are bound not to create any obstacles to the efforts and activities carried out by indigenous peoples in order to preserve their own languages as an element of their cultural identity.[47]

Paragraph 9 of ILA Resolution No. 5/2012 addresses a very controversial issue, i.e. the one concerning Indigenous peoples' treaty rights. On account of such a controversial character, the approach adopted by the Resolution concerning this issue is quite cautious, as it asserts that "States must cooperate in good faith with indigenous peoples in order to give full recognition and execution to treaties and agreements concluded with indigenous peoples in a manner respecting the spirit and intent of the understanding of the indigenous negotiators as well as the living nature of the solemn undertakings made by all parties." While treaties concluded between Indigenous peoples and States in the past should be regarded as equivalent to international treaties—for the reason that they were negotiated and adopted between nations effectively equipped with sovereignty in their respective territories—in contemporary practice they are actually treated as "domestic treaties", State governments retaining the freedom to unilaterally disregard and/or modify them.[48] Although in terms of legal logic this appears to be an ontological irrationality, it nevertheless reflects the state of things emerging from relevant practice; hence, the position taken by ILA Resolution No. 5/2012 on this issue could reasonably not be different.

The final part of the Resolution includes some recommendations addressed to the various actors involved in the context of Indigenous peoples' rights protection. First, States are recommended ("ought to")

---

47   *See* Committee on the Rights of Indigenous Peoples Final Report, Sofia Conference (2012), *supra* note 16, at 15.

48   On this issue see Federico Lenzerini, McGirt v Oklahoma *and the Right of Indigenous Peoples to Have Their Treaties Concluded with States Respected: Is the Glass Half-Full or Half-Empty?*, 21 Hum. Rts. L. Rev. 486 (2021).

to restructure their domestic law with a view to adopting all necessary measures—including constitutional amendments, institutional and legislative reforms, judicial action, administrative rules, special policies, reparations procedures and awareness-raising activities—in order to make the full realization of indigenous peoples' human rights possible within their territories, consistently with the rules and standards established by UNDRIP.[49]

Secondly, Indigenous peoples themselves

are encouraged to cooperate actively and in good faith with States, to facilitate the implementation of States' international obligations related to indigenous peoples' rights, consistently with the rules and standards established by UNDRIP. Indigenous peoples are obligated to respect the fundamental human rights of others and the individual rights of their members, consistently with internationally recognised human rights standards.[50]

Thirdly, the Resolution underlines that the civil society, "in all its components, ought to promote a favourable environment for the affirmation of indigenous peoples' rights, especially by nurturing a positive understanding within society as a whole of the value of indigenous cultures as well as of the positive role which may be played by indigenous peoples to further sustainable life in the world".[51]

Finally, the

competent bodies, specialized agencies and mechanisms of the United Nations system—including the Human Rights Council, the Permanent Forum on Indigenous Issues, the Expert Mechanism on the Rights of Indigenous Peoples and the Special Rapporteur on the Rights of Indigenous Peoples—are encouraged to continue and strengthen their activity, in cooperation with States and indigenous peoples, in order to ensure further protection, promotion and improvement of indigenous peoples' rights throughout the world, consistently with the rules and minimum standards of human rights established by the UNDRIP.[52]

49　　*See* ILA Resolution No. 5/2012, *supra* note 27, para. 11.
50　　*Id.* para. 12.
51　　*Id.* para. 13.
52　　*Id.* para. 14.

5   The End of Law

Professor Wiessner has written that

> Resolution No. 5/2012 transcends the writings of individual scholars, no
> matter how well-researched and persuasive their work is. It has come
> about to help complete the circle of protection for the most vulnerable
> and precious peoples on the face of the Earth. May they avail themselves
> in their peaceful legal fight for survival of this new arm in their quiver,
> and may thus law achieve its noblest end: to make peace through justice,
> ever aiming for a public order in which dignity for all is assured.[53]

ILA Resolution No. 5/2012 aimed at strengthening the international legal
movement which—through rewinding the tape of a long past of prevarication,
abuses and genocide—pursues the purpose of fully reintegrating the human
dignity of Indigenous peoples, engaging in an attempt to give realization of the
noblest end of law, as emphasized by Professor Wiessner himself. It is not by
chance that Professor Wiessner has been at the forefront of the struggle leading to the adoption of the Resolution, because that of helping law to achieve its
noblest end has always been the mission of his academic life.

Writing this chapter has represented, for me, a pleasant journey back to one
of the most important and emotional exercises of my own professional and academic career. As I have made it clear in the previous pages, it was a journey accomplished side by side with Professor Wiessner. I cannot forget all the exchanges of
ideas we had, the many intercontinental calls at any time of the day and the night;
the huge flow of emails on the Miami-Siena axis; the vehement discussions on the
points of disagreement between us (only a very few, in reality); the deep determination in developing our ideas without forgetting even for a single moment that
we had to remain strictly adherent to the objective status of international law in
the field of Indigenous peoples' rights; as well as the celebrations in conference
venues or in convenient bars or restaurants around the world. When I started
writing about the rights of Indigenous peoples—back in 2005—I was profoundly
touched by the bitter remembrance of the massacre of Wounded Knee by Black
Elk, the charismatic leader of the Sioux Oglala, who said that "[at Wounded Knee,
with all the killed women and children], something else died there in the bloody
mud, and was buried in the blizzard. A people's dream died there. It was a beautiful dream."[54] I like to think that ILA Resolution No. 5/2012 actually represents one
of the stones paving the road leading that dream to revivify.

---

53   *See* Wiessner, *supra* note 2, at 1368.
54   John G. Neihardt, Black Elk Speaks 145 (4th Ed. 2014).

CHAPTER 23

K'úilich Ha' – Sacred Water, Autonomy and Self-Determination-Based Normative Systems of the Maya

Manuel May Castillo* and Lola Cubells Aguilar**

The Maya communities of the Yucatán Peninsula, Mexico, face the impact of neoliberal megaprojects and state policies that contravene fundamental principles of their rights as Indigenous Peoples. Legal concessions for the planting of transgenic crops, agro-industry, overexploitation of water, and the *Plan de Reordenamiento Territorial Tren Maya* development project, for example, reveal the lack of harmonization between the principles of international law as recognized in the Mexican Constitution and the Maya normative systems. Such lack of harmonization violates, among others, their rights to Autonomy, Self-Determination and Free, Prior and Informed Consent.

In this chapter, we reflect on the land-territory-spirit connection and the notion of water as territory in accordance with the Maya *cosmovivencia,*[1] as a canvas on which we outline a proposal for harmonizing Maya normative systems, those of the State, and those of international law. The proposal arises from collective reflections with, for and by members of Maya communities taking place in the Chenes region of Hopelchen, Campeche, Mexico in the context of the defense of Sacred Water and their ancestral territories.[2]

---

* Ph.D., Department of Social Sciences – Universidad Carlos III de Madrid (Spain).

** Ph.D., Department of Public Law, Jaume I University, Castellón (Spain).

1 We use this compound term from the Spanish words *Cosmos* and *vivencia* instead of Cosmovision to refer to a particular way of being, living and cohabiting (with) the (living) world rather than just a vision or contemplation.

2 This chapter has been prompted by the recent academic call to embark on a co-theorization of human rights from the bottom up by including diverse ontological ways of understanding and relating to water. Lieselotte Viaene, *Indigenous water ontologies, hydro-development and the human/more-than-human right to water: a call for critical engagement with plurilegal water realities,* 12 Water 1660 (2021).

1   Introduction

In 2019, members of Maya communities in Hopelchen denounced the over-exploitation of aquifers for rice cultivation, a non-native crop in the region, which negatively impacts these communities. On the one hand, artisanal water wells in nearby communities such as San Juan Bautista Sahcabchen are running out of water to supply daily household consumption and, on the other hand, agrochemicals such as glyphosate have entered people's bodies due to the consumption of contaminated water from the wells. Based on this complaint, a work team[3] was created comprised of members of Mayan communities convened the organization *Ka' Kuxtal Much Meyaj A.C.*, lawyers[4] and researchers with diverse profiles in the spirit of building bridges of dialogue between Indigenous norms and the norms of positive law, which will result in respect for their right to Autonomy and Self-Determination during the enforcement of water governance policies in Mexico.

Cultural plurality in Mexico is evident both in the diverse and differentiated practices of the Maya Peoples of southern Mexico and in their shared wisdom. The languages of the Maya family and their forms of relationship with Mother Earth are clear examples of such shared knowledge, the result of fluid interactions from the ancestral past to the present. The ways of naming water *Ha'* are remarkably similar in the diverse Maya languages of Mexico and Guatemala, as are the ways of existing, being and coexisting with water. In the coexistence between the Maya peoples and water, relationships of respect are established based on norms that are often recreated in the ritual sphere. That is to say, in rituals, norms of mutual respect and coexistence with water and nature in general are established. These interdependent relationships occur among spiritual beings and are identifiable in rain ceremonies or rituals at water sources performed throughout the Maya region, from the highlands of Guatemala to the lowlands north of the Yucatán Peninsula.

The synergy produced between Maya rituals and Catholic practices gave birth to one of the most important festivals in the Maya region of southeast

---

3 We are grateful to lawyer Lizy Peralta Mercado. Without her enourmous patience and wisdom the interdisciplinar/intercultural work wouldn't be possible.

4 In our international and multidisciplinary team we are privileged to count on the support of Professor Dr. Siegfried Wiessner, Chair of the International Law Association (ILA) Committee on the Rights of Indigenous Peoples (2008–2012), who contributes, together with Professor Dr. Federico Lenzerini, Rapporteur of this Committee, and Professor Dr. Willem van Genugten, Chair of the ILA Committee on the Implementation of the Rights of Indigenous Peoples (2013–2020) to this collective work by providing international legal advice on the rights of Indigenous Peoples.

Mexico: the Feast of the Holy Cross on May 3. This important ritual was the subject of an ethnographic record by the Tseltal anthropologist Mª Patricia Pérez of the *Pat'otan* (Greetings or hugs from the heart):

> Estas palabras poéticas del corazón y para el corazón de los *Ajawetik*, dioses, están acompañadas de alimentos y bebidas sagradas (caldo de pollo, el cacao, el trago, los cigarros), así como de incienso, velas, música tradicional, bailes y del buen corazón de los hombres y de las mujeres. Sólo así se puede llegar al corazón del *Ajaw*, de la tierra, del agua, del tiempo y del cosmos. Cuando vemos concretizado esto, nuestros corazones regresan alegres a la casa; de ocurrir lo contrario, habrá una pena profunda en el corazón.[5]

This Other way of relating to Mother Earth involves not only practices but also shows the pluriverse ways of living-being-thinking and inhabiting the world. From these wisdoms of the heart or philosophies of life, normative practices of coexistence and defense of the territory are instituted.

The Mayan concepts of water and its related norms presented here come from collective reflections carried out in four participatory workshops in the Mayan region of the Chenes from March 2021 to October 2022. An average of 16 people participated in each of these four workshops, women and men, members of the Mayan communities of the region, including elders, adults and youth. Two non-indigenous women lawyers assisted in understanding the legal principles and norms of water. The analyses presented here are drawn from written reports and participatory observation, and from informal conversations with members of Ka Kuxtal. The working sessions were conducted bilingually, in Yucatec Maya and Spanish, which allowed for a deeper understanding of the concepts of water as expressed in the native language.

2   Land, Territory/Water, Spirit

In the Maya communities of the Chenes, it is said that everything that casts a shadow has a spirit: *Tuláakal ba'alo'ob yaan u oochelo'ob, yaan u Óolo'ob*. From

---

5 "These poetic words spoken from the heart and for the heart of the Ajawetik, gods, are accompanied by sacred foods and drinks (chicken soup, cacao, drinks, cigars), as well as incense, candles, traditional music, dance and the warm-heartedness of men and women. This is the only way to reach the heart of the Ajaw, the earth, the water, the time and the cosmos. When we see this materialized, our hearts return joyfully home; otherwise, there will be a deep sorrow in the heart" (translation by the authors). Mª Patricia Pérez Moreno, O'tan-o'tanil. Stalel tseltaletik yu'un Bachajón, Chiapas, México = Corazón. una forma de ser, estar, hacer, sentir, pensar de los tseltaletik de Bachajón, Chiapas, México 77 (1st ed. 2014).

this perspective, from the vision of the Maya Peoples, there are no lifeless things in the territory because they all have a shadow and a spirit. That is to say, stones, metals, etc. have a spirit, or more precisely, they all have an Óol. Although we translate the concept Óol as spirit, it is a concept that may also be translated as energy or vital force. Often it is used as synonym of *Pixan*: soul or spirit of the deceased.

A definition of territory is practically absent in modern Maya-Spanish dictionaries,[6] which is not at all surprising if we consider that the broad use of this concept is relatively new. In its modern sense, it emerges in the European Middle Ages and it is in the 17th century that it becomes a subject of study in political theory.

This concept is bound up with the politics, governance and control of the geographies occupied by modern nation-states.[7] In Mexico, in particular, the notion of territory comes from the colonial tradition, in turn rooted in the European imperialist expansion that we trace back to the Roman Empire. Territory, according to Elden,[8] is a concept shaped by perpetual practice. In its more contemporary sense, territory is also conceived as a set of practices intertwined with dominion,[9] power, control, legal jurisdiction and political strategy aimed at the governance of a people and a given space.

The absence of a similar concept in Yucatec Maya is an indicator that law on land, territory and resources still lacks an approach to Maya ontologies. Instead, Eurocentric and state-centric notions take precedence in the exercise of governance in Mexico. This deficiency is symptomatic of the asymmetry and unidirectionality established by the Mexican State in its relationship with the Maya peoples when the former legislates over the space and lands ancestrally occupied by the latter. With regard to the Mexican State, land, and therefore territory, are conceived as sources of exploitable resources (land-territory-resource) and related practices are legislated under the same understanding. On a global scale, the same is true of other States.

---

6   Juan Ramón Bastarrachea Manzano, Ermilo Yah Pech & Fidencio Briceño Chel, *Diccionario básico español-maya-español* (1st ed. 1992), https://www.mayas.uady.mx/diccionario/index .html (last visited Oct. 23, 2022); Terrence Kaufman & John Justeson, *A Preliminary Mayan Etymological Dictionary* (2003), http://www.famsi.org/reports/01051/pmed.pdf (last visited Oct. 23, 2022); Javier Abelardo Gómez Navarrete, Diccionario introductorio español-maya, maya-español (Chetumal: Universidad de Quintana Roo, 2009).

7   Stuart Elden, *How Should We Do the History of Territory?*, 1 Territory, Politics, Governance 5 (2013).

8   *Id.*

9   Behind the concept of dominion lays a legal and philosophical framework of domination enshrined in the colonial Doctrine of Discovery. *See* Sarah Augustine, The Land Is Not Empty: Following Jesus in Dismantling the Doctrine of Discovery 14 (Kindle ed. 2021).

How do we understand the territory from the *cosmovivencia* of the Maya peoples?[10] As a result of community-based research, we were able to learn from the Maya communities in Hopelchen that Mother Earth is a being with a spirit. Indeed, when we delved deeper into the territory, through participatory workshops[11] with the indigenous organization in Hopelchen and through concepts in Maya language, we learned that the territory is made up of a set of spiritual beings. From Yucatec Maya, the term *lu'um*: earth, is the ground we walk on but is also meant as a living being and simultaneously as a community of living beings: *"U lu'umil hach tuláakal. Leti' le péepeno'obo', le ch'íich'o'obo', le ba'alche'obo', le k'áaxo', le ke'elo'obo'. Tuláakal ba'ax ku kuxaánobo'jach k lu'umil"*;[12] "Territory is everything. It's the butterflies, birds, animals, jungle, insects. Everything that lives is our territory." The territory is made up of spiritual beings. These beings are the territory itself. The territory and the beings that comprise it have an Óol (spirit) – by the fact of having a shadow – and as a spiritual community they also take part in the ceremonies.[13] For example, during the *Ch'a' Cháak* (rain ceremonies) the spirits of the four directions *Lak'in Ik', Xaman Kan, Chik'in Ik', Nojol Ik', Yúum Cháak* (Lord/ess Rain) and the guardians of the jungle, among others, are invoked. Birds, frogs and toads are also invoked through the reproduction of their songs. Mimicking the singing of frogs and toads is a role normally played by children. During the ritual acts, it is understood that a large community of spiritual beings participates, with whom a communion is established for the invocation of Rain. It is not, therefore, an exclusive conversation between people and Lord/ess Rain, but a conversation open to other beings in the territory, which are also the territory. From the spiritual relations between people and the territory it is possible to establish the *Lu'um-Lu'umil-Óol* (land-territory-spirit) linkage, which contrasts with that of land-territory-resources.

Lu'um is a living being with whom harmonious relations of coexistence must be maintained. It is a spiritual being on whose skin the *milpa* is cultivated. It is through Yucatec Maya expressions that the spiritual essence of Mother Earth can be understood. For example, the *Ts'íik Lu'um*, are "tierras que desorientan,

---

10   *See*, in comparison, the anthropological-legal analysis of the rights to territory and water from the perspective of the Q'eqchi' people in Guatemala. Lieselotte Viaene, La Hidroeléctrica Xalalá en territorios maya q'eqchi' de Guatemala ¿Qué pasará con nuestra tierra y agua sagradas? Un análisis antropológico-jurídico de los derechos humanos amenazados 70–80 (2015).

11   Workshop on water and rights in July 2022 in Hopelchen, Campeche.

12   Taught by Don Gaspar Cauich from the community of *Xka'lot Ak'al*, Hopelchen.

13   *See* the concept Muhel, "spirit" and its connection with "shadow" established by Lieselotte Viaene, Nimla Rahilal. Pueblos indígenas y justicia transicional: reflexiones antropológicas 141 (2019).

que nublan el entendimiento. El remedio es encenderles una vela o veladora."[14] We are confident that the remedy cited above is the *Jeets' Lu'um* ceremony (reassuring the earth) that is widely performed in the communities of the Yucatan Peninsula. It is intended to re-establish harmony with the spiritual guardians of the territory: "Ceremonia mediante la cual se presentan ofrendas a los dueños míticos del monte, antes de empezar a explotar un terreno."[15] A similar expression *Jeets' Óol*: to be calm,[16] expresses a spirit-centered state of mind. It literally means to have a calm or harmonious spirit. After *lu'um, lu'umil* is used as an interpretation of the Western concept of "territory". Nonetheless, from the Maya *cosmovivencia* and the expressions in the native language, the spiritual essence is placed at the center, as discussed above. *Kaab* or *Yóok'ol Kaab* also means land in various Maya languages,[17] although in Hopelchen communities it is more often translated as world.[18] The notion of territory as a spiritual living being is part of the millenary cultural heritage of the Maya peoples. In fact, within Classic period hieroglyphic writing (600–900 C.E.) we recognize symbols for *Kaab;* land, represented with the head of a rodent (Figure 23.1) or *Witz*: mountain, depicted as the head of a divine being.

Aside from its spiritual nature, the territory is a ceremonial space as perceived in contemporary ceremonies in the jungle, such as the *Jeets' lu'um* and from archaeological evidence. In pre-colonial times the territory was often represented as a two-headed serpent. In the mural paintings of San Bartolo in Guatemala, the territory is portrayed as the body of a snake, the mouth of which depicts a cave where a ritual takes place in which a germinating seed is offered.

Territory/Water. Under the same principle that land and territory are living beings, water is conceived as an essential element of their bodies. In Yucatec, this idea is conveyed as follows: "*Le ha'o' jach k'i'ik'el k ki'ichpam na' lu'um*":[19] "Water is the blood of the beautiful Mother Earth." In addition, due to the fact that it casts a shadow, water has an Óol. According to its diverse manifestations, his/her Óol manifests itself in the form of a serpent or in anthropomorphic

---

14 "[L]ands that disorient, that blur our understanding. The remedy is to light a candle" (translation by the authors). Gómez Navarrete, *supra* note 6, at 104.

15 "ceremony through which offerings are presented to the mythical owners of the forest, before beginning to exploit a piece of land" (translation by the authors). Through this definition, we recognize some Mayan norms for harmonious coexistence with the land. Bastarrachea et al., *supra* note 6.

16 Gómez Navarrete, *supra* note 6, at 133.

17 Kaufman & Justeson, *supra* note 6, at 414.

18 Gómez Navarrete, *supra* note 6, at 138.

19 Statement by Doña Leocadia Uitz Chin of the community of *Ixk'ix* and president of the organization *Ka' Kuxtal Much Meyaj A.C.* We are grateful for the translations from Maya to Spanish by Adriana Cauich from *Xkalot Ak'al*, Hopelchen.

FIGURE 23.1
Hieroglyph for Kaab. KAB' (kab') (T758c) > n.
"earth" ... "Represents the head of a rodent with
T526 KAB'AN infixed to the forehead."[21]
DRAWING BY MANUEL MAY

FIGURE 23.2   Serpent motifs next to *Yuum Cháak* representations in *Hochob, Hopelchen,*
Campeche, Mexico
PHOTO MANUEL MAY, 2019

form: the serpent *Tzucan* is the guardian of the cenotes and watering holes[20]
and *Yúum Cháak* is Lord/ess Rain to whom the *Ch'a' Cháak* ceremonies are
consecrated. Much like the depictions for earth and world, the serpent icon is
likewise used to depict the spiritual manifestations of water. Some illustrations
of these energies can be found in pre-colonial codices and temples (Figure
23.2),[21] but more than myths of the past, such spiritual connections remain in
force and are being reformulated by Maya communities in the present.

---

20   https://www.gob.mx/conagua/articulos/tzukan-la-serpiente-protectora-de-cenotes?
      idiom=es.
21   *See* another example in San Bartolo's Mural published at: https://arqueologiamexicana
      .mx/mexico-antiguo/hallazgo-las-excepcionales-pinturas-de-san-bartolo-guatemala.

3   Autonomy and Self-Determination in the Defense of Territory/
       Water

While exercising their right to Autonomy and Self-Determination, the claims
of the Maya communities of Hopelchen encounter numerous obstacles in
the inter-legal[22] translation of water concepts and in the dialogue between
their own normative systems and those of the Mexican State. In international
law, instruments such as ILO Convention No. 169[23] and the United Nations
Declaration on the Rights of Indigenous Peoples (UNDRIP)[24] aim to serve as
a bridge for dialogue between Maya peoples and the State. These instruments
are conceived as a way of condensing into a text the essential rights that must
be guaranteed to the Indigenous Peoples of Abya Yala so that they can continue to exist.

If the Maya peoples are to fully enjoy their collective rights to maintain
their cultural identity, their lands, their ancestral territories and their spiritual
relationships with them, it is essential that their right to Autonomy and Self-
Determination, as established in the UNDRIP, be guaranteed in the first place.
The collective rights of Indigenous Peoples in Mexico focused on Autonomy
and Self-Determination, culture, lands, territories and resources have resonated and found increasing support at the international level. The Committee
on the Rights of Indigenous Peoples of the International Law Association (ILA)
has taken a step forward in "clarifying, elucidating and providing guidance" on
the provisions of the UNDRIP, and recognizes, as adopted in the ILA's authoritative Resolution No. 5/2012 on the Rights of Indigenous Peoples, that:

> Indigenous peoples are holders of collective human rights aimed at
> ensuring the preservation and transmission to future generations of their
> cultural identity and distinctiveness. Members of indigenous peoples are
> entitled to the enjoyment of all internationally recognised human rights
> – including those specific to their indigenous identity – in a condition of
> full equality with all other human beings.[25]

---

22   Boaventura de Sousa Santos' concept of "interlegality" refers to the "complex relationship
      between two rights, state law and local law, using different scales". Boaventura de Sousa San-
      tos, Critica De La Razon Indolente. Contra El Desperdicio De La Experiencia 237, 251 (2003).
23   ILO Convention (No. 169) Concerning Indigenous and Tribal Peoples in Independent
      Countries, *adopted* June 27, 1989, *reprinted in* 28 Int'l Legal Mat. 1382.
24   United Nations Declaration on the Rights of Indigenous Peoples, G.A. Res. 61/295,
      Annex, U.N. Doc. A/RES/61/295 (Sept. 13, 2007), https://www.un.org/development/desa
      /indigenouspeoples/wpcontent/ uploads/sites/19/2018/11/UNDRIP_E_web.pdf.
25   ILA Resolution No. 5/2012, Rights of Indigenous Peoples, Conclusion No. 1, https://
      www.ila-hq.org/en_GB/documents/conference-resolution-english-sofia-2012-4 (last visited

This resolution recognized Indigenous Peoples' right to self-determination[26] as well as autonomy[27] under customary international law.

The ILA Committee on the Rights of Indigenous Peoples was chaired by our honoree, Professor Siegfried Wiessner, succeeding Professor S. James Anaya. Elsewhere, Professor Wiessner stated that the principle of Self-Determination is already outlined in ILO Convention No. 169 and ultimately enshrined in the UNDRIP after a complicated history of negotiation between States and Indigenous Peoples.[28] Throughout, representatives of the various Indigenous Peoples reiterated that the right to Self-Determination should be treated as an umbrella principle under which all other rights of Indigenous Peoples should be considered.[29]

The enjoyment of Self-Determination therefore derives from the respect for the normative systems of the Maya Peoples and their principles of coexistence with the territory, as a spiritual being. The appropriate interpretation of these principles is of utmost importance when designing water management and exploitation policies in Mexico. In inter-legal translation, a culturally

---

Oct. 23, 2022). For the history and legal valence of this resolution, see Siegfried Wiessner, *The State and Indigenous Peoples: The Historic Significance of ILA Resolution No. 5/2012*, *in* Der Staat im Recht. Festschrift für Eckart Klein zum 70. Geburtstag 1357 (Marten Breuer et al. eds., 2013). For a Spanish translation, see *El Estado y los pueblos indígenas: la importancia histórica de la resolución No. 5/2012 de la ILA* (*Asociación de Derecho Internacional*), Ars Iuris (2016) Núm. 51, https://scripta.up.edu.mx/handle/ 20.500.12552/ 4566.

26   ILA Res. No. 5/2012, Conclusion No. 4: "States must comply with the obligation – consistently with customary and applicable conventional international law – to recognise, respect, protect, fulfil and promote the right of indigenous peoples to self-determination, conceived as the right to decide their political status and to determine what their future will be, in compliance with relevant rules of international law and the principles of equality and nondiscrimination."

27   ILA Res. No. 5/2012, Conclusion No. 5: "States must also comply – according to customary and applicable conventional international law – with the obligation to recognise and promote the right of indigenous peoples to autonomy or self-government, which translates into a number of prerogatives necessary in order to secure the preservation and transmission to future generations of their cultural identity and distinctiveness. These prerogatives include, inter alia, the right to participate in national decision-making with respect to decisions that may affect them, the right to be consulted with respect to any Project that may affect them and the related right that projects significantly impacting their rights and ways of life are not carried out without their prior, free and informed consent, as well as the right to regulate autonomously their internal affairs according to their own customary laws and to establish, maintain and develop their own legal and political institutions."

28   Siegfried Wiessner, *Re-Enchanting the World: Indigenous Peoples' Rights as Essential Parts of a Holistic Human Rights Regime*, 15 UCLA J. Int'l L. & Foreign Aff. 239, 248, 249–253 (2012).

29   *Id.* at 250 n. 44.

appropriate interpretation of Territory/Water would bridge the lack of under-standing between the parties, in which different meanings are often understood even when the same terms and a *lingua franca*, namely Spanish, are used. The subject of (culturally appropriate) legal interpretation is still a pending task for States such as Mexico and Guatemala when legislating on Maya territories.

With regard to the Mexican State, land is conceived as an exploitable resource under the land-territory-resources linkage and is legislated as such, differenti-ating between laws on water and those on land. Within such an asymmetrical context, where the Eurocentric/State-centric understanding and relationship with the land predominates, ILO Convention No. 169 and UNDRIP include negotiated principles related to ancestral land rights. Principles that, within the framework of international law, have a significant influence on the relationships between States and Indigenous Peoples around the world. Despite the attempt to translate Indigenous *cosmovivencia* into positive international law, the link between land, territory and resources in international law shows how it contin-ues to be permeated by an understanding that is separate from the spirit-being, and which dismembers the territory into each of these three elements. There are, however, other territorialities that do not respond to the modern capitalist logic that conceives nature as an object separated into land, territory and natu-ral resources. As Arturo Escobar points out: the territorialities-territorializations of the movements are linked to an ontological dimension.[30]

Recognizing the Maya peoples' own way of understanding territory/water requires reinterpreting some of the articles of ILO Convention 169 and UNDRIP from a critical and anticolonial perspective. It is, in the words of Alexander Pinto, an epistemic rupture in the understanding of water conflicts as a com-mon good, as opposed to the water-commodity binary; it claims water-terri-tory as a way of reflecting the inseparability of the two.[31]

Let us first look at ILO Convention 169. On the one hand, we must bear in mind the importance of Article 5, which states that in applying the provisions of the Convention, "social, cultural, religious and spiritual values and practices shall be recognized and protected."[32] Thus, both Articles 14 and 15 should be applied taking into account the social, cultural and spiritual practices of the Maya. In the first case, the right of the Maya people to traditionally occupied lands and territories. It even states that in "appropriate cases" the right of Maya

---

30   Arturo Escobar, Sentipensar con la tierra. Nuevas lecturas sobre desarrollo, territorio y diferencias (2014).

31   Alexander Panez Pinto, *Agua-Territorio en América Latina: Contribuciones a partir del análisis de estudios sobre conflictos hídricos en Chile*, 8 Revista Rupturas 193 (2018).

32   ILO Convention 169, *supra* note 24.

peoples to use lands that they do not occupy but to which they have had access for their traditional and subsistence activities should be protected. Here the notion of territory should be extended to the water bodies that through social, cultural and spiritual practices become sacred places as they remain places of offering and petition. And that, as we have detailed in the previous paragraph, are an inseparable part of the territory. They are one and the same being together with the rainforest and humans themselves: "nuestra fe es la voz del bosque, de la lluvia, es el dios *Cháak*. Traemos la lluvia. Somos lluvia".[33]

On the other hand, Article 15 of the Convention refers, as mentioned above, to natural resources, as distinct from land and territory. It also refers to the right to use, manage and conserve them. Regarding the management of natural resources owned by the State, the international standard provides that the State must carry out consultations to obtain the Consent of the Indigenous Peoples and assess the extent to which they may be harmed. These consultations should be carried out prior to prospecting or exploitation on their lands in the understanding that free, prior, and (well) informed Consent is pursued.

In Hopelchen, agribusiness has spread over thousands of hectares, leading to the loss of approximately 185,000 ha of primary forest between 2001 and 2021.[34] In the territories of the community of San Juan Bautista Sahcabchen alone, multiple well concessions have been granted without prior consultation and in violation of the right to Consent of the Maya people. Even the recognition of the possibility of compensating native peoples for the damage caused is striking. This is something that members of the Maya communities of Hopelchen often reject, pointing out that compensation implies that it is taken for granted that there is and will be damage to the Territory/Water. Their preference is for the laws to function as preventive rather than remedial tools. The principles of the Convention can be interpreted in both ways; as preventive and/or remedial.

Similarly, the right to compensation appears in Article 27 of the UNDRIP, clarifying that compensation shall consist of lands and territories of equal quality and extent. These characteristics ignore the ancestry and the link with the sacred sites, which are not only based on quality and extent, but also on the history of resistance, knowledge and spiritual relationships woven into the territories. The members of the Maya organization point out that their struggle is for the cancellation of all projects that exploit, pollute and destroy the Territory/Water. As we well know, ILO Convention 169 (1989) arose within the framework of neoliberal economic globalization whose doctrines materialized

---

33   "Our faith is the voice of the forest, of the rain, it is the god *Cháak*. We bring rain. We are rain." Remarks by Doña Leocadia Uitz, chair of the Maya indigenous organization at the "Workshop on water and rights" in July 2022, Hopelchen, Campeche.

34   *See* Global Forest Watch data, *available at* https://www.globalforestwatch.org/.

in Mexico with NAFTA (1994). In such a neoliberal context, the Convention was intended to create legal instruments for the protection of the rights of Indigenous Peoples, historically marginalized and discriminated against in the economic and labor policies of the States. Among other things, it was designed to curb extractivism and territorial dispossession, and therefore assumed the need to compensate the peoples for possible damages caused.

Along the same lines, UNDRIP refers to the triad of land, territory and natural resources in Article 26. The most important issue in both international norms is recognition of the traditional possession of territory and natural resources, beyond ownership. The UNDRIP refers the right to lands, territories, resources that they have traditionally owned, occupied "or otherwise used or acquired." How are these principles implemented in the Maya ancestral territory that is being occupied, modified and affected by the *Proyecto de Reordenamiento Territorial Tren Maya* development project or by agribusiness or pig farms? The Maya communities are well aware that their spiritual, economic and cultural practices with the Territory/Water conflict with these projects. Despite the significant milestone represented by international norms on Indigenous rights, an ontological[35] difference still prevails between how native peoples conceive their territorialities and how it is regulated in these international and national norms. On the other hand, a detailed study of state practice and *opinio juris* reflected in ILA Resolution No. 5/2012 came to the conclusion that Indigenous Peoples' land rights under customary international law "must be secured in order to preserve the spiritual relationship of the community concerned with its ancestral lands, which is an essential prerequisite to allow such a community to retain its cultural identity, practices, customs and institutions."[36] In

---

35   Here we pick up the concept of ontology as defined by Arturo Escobar, *supra* note 31, at 95: "... our way of understanding what it means that something or someone exists."

36   ILA Resolution No. 5/2012, *supra* note 26, Conclusion No. 7. As Professor Michael Reisman has stated, "it is the integrity of the inner worlds of [indigenous] peoples—their rectitude systems or their sense of spirituality—that is their distinctive humanity. Without an opportunity to determine, sustain, and develop that integrity, their humanity—and ours—is denied." W. Michael Reisman, *International Law and the Inner Worlds of Others*, 9 St. Thomas L. Rev. 25, 26 (1996). Similarly, Professor Wiessner commented that "[i]t is this sense of spirituality that is overlooked when an indigenous people is conceived of as just another minority community suffering socio-economic oppression." Wiessner, *supra* note 29, at 242 n. 7. Jaime Martínez Luna, a Zapotec anthropologist, made this important point:

The need to survive causes us to view everything from a materialistic perspective. ... But here is where the difference from indigenous thinking springs forth. *Comunalidad* is a way of understanding life as being permeated with spirituality, symbolism, and a greater integration with nature. It is one way of understanding that human beings are not the center, but simply a part of the great natural world. It is here that we can distinguish the enormous difference between Western and indigenous thought.

any event, the fulfilment of Indigenous rights should address the practices of Maya peoples and their own territorialities, which should direct public policies, development and judicial practice. The latter is in charge of reviewing the demands for the defense of normative systems, in this case, Maya law.

There are numerous State laws in which the recognition of the rights of Indigenous Peoples and their ontological relationship with the Territory/Water has not been appropriately integrated, such as, for example, the Mexican National Water Law[37] on the use, protection and administration of water as a resource of the Nation.

4   Maya Law

The *cosmovivencia* of the Maya people with the Territory/Water and its relevance in social, cultural and spiritual practices is reflected in the different norms that make up Maya law as an instrument for the safeguarding and defense of water in the face of neoliberal attacks reconfigured in megaprojects such as the *Tren Maya* development project, agribusiness or pig farms. Oral expressions and daily and ritual practices transmit a spiritual connection between the Maya peoples of the Yucatán Peninsula and the land and territory. Based on the practices, we are able to identify some normative systems of use and coexistence with the Territory/Water that are in force in the Maya communities of Hopelchen.

A normative system is understood as the norms that native peoples create based on their own philosophy of life. This is what Professor Jesús de la Torre has called the law that springs from the people or the right to utter law.[38] Indigenous norms should not be understood only as "customs" practiced ancestrally without any kind of change, but as oral or written norms that peoples establish and reformulate to defend their way of relating to other spiritual beings, to protect and defend them. Therefore, practices that defend water demonstrate, on the one hand, a way of understanding the relationship with Territory/Water that rejects the Eurocentric/State-centric separation of territory-land-natural resources made by international norms. It is true that the

---

Jaime Martínez Luna, *The Fourth Principle, in* New World of Indigenous Resistance 85, 93–94 (Lois Meyer & Benjamín Maldonado Alvarado eds., 2010).

37   Ley de Aguas Nacionales, *available at* https://www.diputados.gob.mx/LeyesBiblio/ref/lan.htm.

38   Jesús Antonio de la Torre Rangel, El Derecho que nace del pueblo (2006).

Inter-American Court of Human Rights has already pointed out in repeated rulings that Article 21 of the American Convention of Human Rights mandates the protection of the special connection between territory and natural resources for Indigenous Peoples.[39]

Equitable distribution and care of water and respect as a spiritual being (*K'íilich Ha'*: Sacred Water) are some of the norms that arise from daily practices and rituals. The ritual of requesting permission to take the *Suhuy Ha'* (pure water) from the cenotes is an example of the Maya communities' compliance with the norm of respect. Even when the norms are not written, the communities ensure that they are duly complied with. Thus, for example, the norm of respectful coexistence with the Territory/Water and its guardian spirits is fulfilled through ritual acts in the *Jeets' Lu'um*. When a collective meal is offered and words of respect are ritually uttered for the wider community of the territory, human and non-human, it formalizes and gives substance to the norm.[40] The purpose of this norm is to maintain or re-establish harmony with the territory as mentioned above. The rules of respect convey a holistic principle of equity that includes all beings. All have a shadow and a spirit and, consequently, are also subjects of Indigenous norms. An illustrative example of such principle of equity can be inferred from the interrogative pronoun in Yucatec Maya *Max*; who, used for both humans and other beings. For example, in the questions *Max a Na'*; Who is your mother?, *Max a Che'*; Who is your tree? and *Max a Uaban*; Who is your plant?, we understand that plants and trees are beings equal to people. In contrast, to refer to things or abstract concepts, the interrogative pronoun *Bax*; what or which is used. E.g. *Bax a dzulbal*; What is your lineage?[41]

---

39   Francisco López Bárcenas, *Agua, propiedad y derechos indígenas*, 2 Argumentos. Estudios críticos de la sociedad 99 (2020).

40   For a connection between acts, ritual utterances, norms and communal morality see the erudite work of Roy A. Rappaport, Ritual and Religion in the Making of Humanity 29–32, 132–134, 152–155 (10th ed. 1999).

41   Ramón Arzápalo Marín, El Ritual de los Bacabes 22–23 (2d ed. 2007). The similarity in the use of interrogative pronouns for people and plants was detected in the translation of a text from the XVI century thanks to the teaching of Selena Uc Pantí from the community of *Xmejía*, Hopelchen and member of *the work team*. Although the forms of pronoun usage have varied up to the present, the principles of equitable respect are still in force, as can be seen when asking permission and thanking medicinal plants for providing their leaves or roots for healing as taught by Doña Marta Madera likewise a member of the work team in Hopelchen.

5   Final Thoughts

The land-territory-resources linkage cannot be taken for granted in the Maya worldview. From the practices of the Indigenous communities in Hopelchen, it is feasible to identify a notion of territory that is comprehensive, indivisible and centered on its spiritual essence. The land-territory-spirit link is evident in the daily practices and rituals of the Maya peoples. From the practices of these communities, including those of territorial advocacy, it is possible to gradually bring to light the norms of use and coexistence with Water/Territory that these communities claim and advocate as fundamental for the dialogue between their own normative systems and those of the Mexican State. In these dialogues, a matter of utmost importance is to seek an appropriate translation of concepts and practices related to the territory of Maya peoples into legal principles related to governance.

Recognizing the progress that has been made at the international level through the approval of norms such as ILO Convention 169 or the UNDRIP and the development of customary international law, the water defense workshops carried out with Maya communities in Hopelchen provide us with water defense practices that are part of what we call the Maya normative system and that should guide the interpretation of international norms. In Mexico, the constitutional reform of Article 1 in 2011 means that international human rights norms are on the same hierarchical level as the Mexican Constitution and should guide the interpretation of the Constitution and other legislation. This means that all legislation and policies that disregard the rights of Indigenous Peoples contained in international norms should be declared null and unconstitutional.

In this sense, the collective right to lands, territories and resources should be interpreted jointly with the right to normative systems that guide the way to defend the possession of the Maya territory, understood as such, the Territory/Water. The ancestral possession of the territory is demonstrated through the different Indigenous norms with which the sacred water is defended, but also through ceremonies or rituals that continue to be performed in cenotes or caves, regardless of not having property titles over the Territory/Water that is being extracted, polluted and over-exploited due to the proliferation of agribusiness in municipalities such as Hopelchen, promoted for decades by the State itself. As López Bárcenas rightly points out, to overcome the civilizational crisis:

> ... no basta con perfeccionar la forma de administrar, gestionar y usar el agua, se requiere cambiar el modelo en que tales actividades se realizan, poniendo en el centro uno que privilegie la existencia de la vida presente

y futura, así como las culturas de las diversas sociedades, entre ellas las de los pueblos indígenas de México.[42]

As customary international law acknowledges the obligation of the State to recognize, respect, protect and promote the rights of Indigenous Peoples to their traditional lands, territories and resources, we advocate that Territory/ Water should be understood as an indivisible whole from the normative practice of the Maya people, since from their *cosmovivencia* there is no such understanding of water as a resource but holistically understood as Territory/ Water-spirit; *lu'umil* or *Yook'ol Kaab*. The Territory/Water is, therefore, a whole that cannot be conceived independently and which the States, through their public policies, must respect. From this perspective, it is easy to understand that territorial reorganization megaprojects or the proliferation of monocultures, which cause deforestation and severe pollution of the Territory/Water, should not only be considered as an environmental crime but also as a violation of various rights of Indigenous Peoples recognized in the international norms that are ratified by the Mexican State and, therefore, legally binding.

The redrafting of legal frameworks in Mexico, where respect for the Autonomy and Self-Determination of the Maya peoples and their conception of Territory/Water-spirit becomes a reality, could certainly detonate a *re-flourishing* and *re-enchantment* of society on both a national and global scale, thus sowing a seed of hope for future generations.

6 Acknowledgments

The authors wish to thank the Maya communities of Hopelchén, in particular to San Juan Bautista Sahcabchen, Ich Ek, Crucero San Luis, and Suctuc as well as to the Maya youth and Elders whose names are mentioned through these chapter. In addition, we wish to acknowledge that part of the results presented here have been made possible thanks to the support of the DAAD P.R.I.M.E. 2017 programme funded by the Federal Ministry of Education and Research of Germany (BMBF) and the European Union (EU) through the Marie Curie/ COFUND Actions of the Seventh Framework Programme of the European Union (FP7/2007-2013), grant agreement REA n° 605728.

---

42 "... [I]t is not enough to improve the way water is administered, managed and used; it is necessary to change the model in which such activities are carried out, placing at the center one that privileges the existence of present and future life, as well as the cultures of diverse societies, including those of Mexico's indigenous peoples." (translation by the authors). Francisco López Bárcenas, *supra* note 40, at 86.

CHAPTER 24

Expert Evidence in Indigenous Land Claims: Legal Framework and Anthropological Features in the *Awas Tingni* Case

*Mariana Monteiro de Matos**

1 Introduction

"Indigenous" is a crucial term in groundbreaking developments in international law. In 1993, the United Nations General Assembly proclaimed the first International Decade of the World's Indigenous Peoples, which spanned from 1995 to 2004 and was extended for another decade, until 2015. Indigenous peoples were progressively recognized, from a "buzzword of the nineties"[1] to global players in international law and policy-making.

Professor Siegfried Wiessner is a pioneer of legal scholarship on the global indigenous peoples' movement. Under his chairmanship, the eminent Committee on the Rights of Indigenous Peoples of the International Law Association concluded its work with a cutting-edge report and, most importantly, the proposal of the subsequently passed International Law Association Resolution No. 5/2012. This document is a standard-setting reference in international law and was crucial for the consolidation—and further development—of the legal framework on the rights of indigenous peoples.[2]

---

* Dr. iur., Göttingen (Germany), 2018; LL.M., Göttingen (Germany), 2013; LL.B., Belém (Brazil), 2011. She is research fellow at the Department of Law and Anthropology of the Max Planck Institute for Social Anthropology (Germany). Socio-legal studies, constitutional law, and international law are the main fields of her extensive publication record, which includes contributions to Brill Publishers and Oxford University Press. Dr. iur. Monteiro de Matos has delivered lectures and workshops in interdisciplinary settings to global audiences. Her research projects have been awarded prestigious grants from several organizations, including the International Law Association. ORCID: https://orcid.org/0000-0002-2439-8872.

1 2 Rodolfo Stavenhagen, Pioneer on Indigenous Rights 107 (2013).

2 Timo Koivurova et al., *The Role of the ILA in the Restatement and Evolution of International and National Law Relating to Indigenous Peoples*, *in* International Actors and the Formation of Laws 89–112 (Katja Karjalainen et al. eds., 2022); Siegfried Wiessner, *El Estado y los Pueblos Indígenas: La Importancia Histórica de la Resolución No. 5/2012 de la ILA* (*Asociación de Derecho Internacional*), 1 Ars Iuris (2018), https://revistas-colaboracion.juridicas.unam.mx/index.php /ars-iuris/article/view/34182 (last visited Jul 5, 2022); Siegfried Wiessner, *The State and*

By the time of the International Law Association's Resolution No. 5/2012, Wiessner was already a leading expert on the rights of indigenous peoples. His interest in this field was intertwined with his unique conception of law, which developed throughout his career as a *Volljurist*. As he elucidated: "The mission of the law should be to answer responsibly to the totality of human aspirations in the crucible between individual self-realization and the need for belonging to groups, entities larger than self."[3]

Wiessner's seminal contribution to the *Harvard Human Rights Journal* contains a powerful legal analysis of international and comparative law concerning indigenous peoples, embedded in the related contextual issues.[4] His *avant-garde* paper had a revolutionary impact on international human rights law— in books and in practice. A remarkable result was the citation of Wiessner's paper by the Inter-American Commission of Human Rights (hereinafter IACHR or Inter-American Commission) to advance a final key argument in a landmark case.[5]

It is thus not a coincidence that this contribution to the volume honoring Siegfried Wiessner focuses on a subject dear to him: the rights of indigenous peoples. Inspired by his scholarship dealing with topical issues of procedure,[6] this chapter examines the role of expert witnessing in indigenous land claims in the Inter-American Human Rights System (IAHRS).

The *Awas Tingni* judgment delivered by the Inter-American Court of Human Rights (hereinafter IACtHR or Inter-American Court) is "the" landmark judgment on indigenous land rights.[7] It represents the first time that an international tribunal upheld the protection of indigenous territory, not to mention that it crafted "communal property" as a central concept under international human rights law. A lesser-known piece of information regarding this case's pioneering role is that it represents the first time that the IACtHR held an

---

Indigenous Peoples: The Historic Significance of ILA Resolution No. 5/2012, in Der Staat im Recht: Festschrift für Eckart Klein zum 70. Geburtstag 1357–1368 (Marten Breuer et al. eds., 2013).

3 Siegfried Wiessner, *Re-Enchanting the World: Indigenous Peoples' Rights as Essential Parts of a Holistic Human Rights Regime*, 15 UCLA J. Int'l L. Foreign Aff. 239–288, 240 (2010).

4 Siegfried Wiessner, *Rights and Status of Indigenous Peoples: A Global Comparative and International Legal Analysis*, 12 Harv. Hum. Rts. J. 57–128 (1999).

5 Inter-American Commission of Human Rights, Mayagna (Sumo) Awas Tingni Community v. Nicaragua, Final Written Arguments, https://www.corteidh.or.cr/docs/casos/mayagna /agficidh.pdf (last visited Jul 5, 2022).

6 *Cf.* Siegfried Wiessner, *Asylverweigerung ohne Anerkennungsverfahren: Zur grundrechtlichen Relevanz sog. mißbräuchlicher Asylanträge*, 7 Europäische Grundrechte-Zeitschrift 473–479 (1980).

7 Inter-American Court of Human Rights, Mayagna (Sumo) Awas Tingni Community v. Nicaragua, Merits, Reparations and Costs, Series C No. 79 (2001).

extensive public hearing to receive additional oral evidence and cross-examine experts.[8] Much has been written about this leading judgment whose influence on the Inter-American case law—and beyond—is substantial.[9]

Legal scholarship has dedicated itself to grasping the sophisticated hermeneutics that Inter-American judges used to interpret the American Convention of Human Rights (hereinafter ACHR) in the *Awas Tingni* case. However, it has barely explored the procedural issues related to the case, such as evidence,[10] that were fundamental for the judicial reasoning, outcome, and reparation orders.[11] In this regard, a critical issue refers to oral evidence and, more specifically, to proof submission by expert witnesses (hereinafter experts). Notably, the *Awas Tingni* judgment is a rare example of the IACtHR's case law on indigenous land rights containing a detailed account of the expert testimonies received, highlighting their unique role in legal fact-finding.

To fill this gap, this chapter addresses how expert evidence was articulated in the *Awas Tingni* case by the parties involved and by the IACtHR. Put differently, it aims to examine the role and impact of oral expert evidence in this case. By analyzing the judgment, the background of the experts involved becomes clear. They had either training in law or sociocultural anthropology (hereinafter anthropology), which explains the substantive amount of anthropological literature available regarding the case.[12]

---

8   Jonas Bens, The Indigenous Paradox: Rights, Sovereignty, and Culture in the Americas 141 (2020).

9   S. James Anaya & Maia S. Campbell, *Gaining Legal Recognition of Indigenous Land Rights: The Story of the Awas Tingni Case in Nicaragua, in* Human Rights Advocacy Stories 117–153 (Deena R. Hurwitz et al. eds., 2009); S. James Anaya & Claudio Grossman, *The Case of Awas Tingni v. Nicaragua: A New Step in the International Law of Indigenous Peoples,* 19 Ariz. J. Int'l. & Comp. L. 1–15 (2002); Claudio Nash Rojas, *Los Derechos Indígenas en el Sistema Interamericano de Derechos Humanos,* 1 Inter-Am. & Eur. Hum. Rts. J. 61–86, 68 (2008); Jo M. Pasqualucci, *The Evolution of International Indigenous Rights in the Inter-American Human Rights System,* 6 Hum. Rights L. Rev. 281–322 (2006); Elizabeth Salmón, Los Pueblos Indígenas en la Jurisprudencia de la Corte Interamericana de Derechos Humanos: Estándares en Torno a su Protección y Promoción 41–42 (2010).

10   An exception is Anaya & Grossman, *supra* note 9, at 5.

11   Inter-American Court of Human Rights, *supra* note 7, Joint Separate Opinion of Judges Cançado Trindade, Pacheco Gomez and A. Abreu Burelli, at 2; *id.,* Concurring Opinion of Judge Sergio García Ramírez, at 4.

12   Bens, *supra* note 8; Edmund T Gordon et al., *Rights, Resources, and the Social Memory of Struggle: Reflections on a Study of Indigenous and Black Community Land Rights on Nicaragua's Atlantic Coast,* 14 HUM. ORGA. 369–381 (2022); Charles R. Hale, *Using and Refusing the Law: Indigenous Struggles and Legal Strategies after Neoliberal Multiculturalism,* 122 Am. Anthropol. 618–631 (2020); Charles R. Hale, *Activist Research v. Cultural Critique: Indigenous Land Rights and the Contradictions of Politically Engaged Anthropology,*

The role of sociocultural anthropologists (hereinafter anthropologists) as experts in a courtroom setting is at the heart of the dialogue between law and anthropology. The challenges that anthropologists face in legal adjudication are widely explored in anthropology under the umbrella terms of "anthropological expertise" and "cultural expertise."[13] Answering this chapter's research question is, therefore, not only a matter of examining legal scholarship concerning human rights law; it also requires an examination of anthropological literature to grasp the notion of expert evidence. Therefore, this chapter offers the reader a comprehensive and interdisciplinary reading on expert evidence.

In terms of structure, this chapter proceeds as follows. After this introduction, the second part elucidates the *Awas Tingni* case, including the facts and outcome, to give the reader a sense of familiarity with indigenous land claims. The third part then frames the role of socio-anthropological expert witnessing in the IAHRS with a focus on this case, and the fourth part examines the influence of anthropology-based oral testimonies on the final judgment. Lastly, final remarks are presented as a conclusion.

2   Awas Tingni Community v. Nicaragua: Context and Ruling

Indigenous land issues follow a pattern. In most cases, indigenous peoples enjoy land possession, which is essential for their survival; however, states do not always recognize associated rights and even authorize concessions in claimed indigenous lands. This section clarifies this pattern in light of the *Awas Tingni* case.[14] Its goal is to familiarize the reader with the critical interests at stake in indigenous land claims by using this case as an example. In this way,

---

21   Cult. Anthropol. 96–120 (2006); Theodore MacDonald, *Internationalizing Community Land Rights*, Centerpiece, 2001, 2–3.

13   Marie-Claire Foblets et al., *Introduction: Mapping the Field of Law and Anthropology*, in The Oxford Handbook of Law and Anthropology 5 (2020); Marie-Claire Foblets, *Prefatory Comments: Anthropological Expertise and Legal Practice: About False Dichotomies, the Difficulties of Handling Objectivity and Unique Opportunities for the Future of a Discipline*, 12 Int. J. L. in Context 231–234 (2016); Anthony Good, *Cultural Evidence in Courts of Law*, 14 J. R. Anthropol. Inst. S47–S60, 48–50 (2008); Livia Holden, Cultural Expertise: An Emerging Concept and Evolving Practices (2020), https://www.mdpi.com/books/pdfview /book/1973 (last visited July 28, 2022); Lawrence Rosen, *The Anthropologist as Expert Witness*, 79 Am. Anthropol. 555–578 (1977).

14   This section is based on the original IACtHR's decision, the IACHR's complaint before the IACtHR, and the summary provided here: Mariana Monteiro de Matos, Indigenous Land Rights in the Inter-American System: Substantive and Procedural Law 42–51 (2021).

the reader will better understand the role of anthropological expertise in these claims.

The Inter-American Commission has dealt for a long time with controversies over indigenous territories in the geographical region that corresponds to Nicaragua. As with other peoples around the globe, indigenous peoples there have struggled, since colonial times for their lands. When the Sandinista movement seized power in 1979, the local situation started to be aggravated to the point that indigenous peoples raised allegations of genocide. The international community witnessed those bloody issues through media coverage by human rights organizations and legal proceedings brought before the International Court of Justice.[15] It was in this context that the *Awas Tingni* case developed.

The Awas Tingni is a Mayagna indigenous community on Nicaragua's Atlantic coast.[16] Mayagna refers to the larger indigenous ethnolinguistic group to which the Awas Tingni and its members belong. The community is organized under a customary leadership structure recognized by domestic laws, and its economy is based on familiar agriculture, hunting, fishing, fruits, and medicinal plant gathering.

The Nicaraguan government had long been granting concessions for the exploitation of natural resources. These concessions affected the Awas Tingni's ancestral territory, although they did not involve the community in any consultation process. In 1995, the Nicaraguan Natural Resources Ministry began negotiating a concession with a company called by its acronym SOLCARSA. One year later, it authorized this concession to extract timber from the Awas Tingni lands, despite the community's protests. The Supreme Court condemned the act and ordered the concession's suspension; nevertheless, the state delayed compliance with this decision. Nicaragua's untimely action resulted in negative environmental footprints on the Awas Tingni territory.

---

15   International Court of Justice, Military and Paramilitary Activities in and against Nicaragua (Nicaragua v. United States of America), Merits, ICJ Reports 14–150 (1986).

16   The current terminology in international law pertaining to indigenous groups *lato sensu* is "indigenous peoples" in accordance with the United Nations Declaration on the Rights of Indigenous Peoples (UNDRIP). However, this chapter uses sometimes the nomenclature of "indigenous communities," since this was the wording of the original complaint before the IAHRS, which was concluded prior to the UNDRIP adoption and, thus, before the current terminology. "Indigenous peoples" and "indigenous communities" have different legal implications in international law. For an overview on this issue, see Ian Brownlie, *The Rights of Peoples in Modern International Law, in* Rights of People: Symposium: Selected Papers 1–16 (James Crawford ed., 1988).

The case went through the regular dual-stage procedure on the Inter-American level. It started before the IACHR, went through a friendly settlement, and landed in San José. The IACHR accused Nicaragua of property rights violations due to the failure to adopt measures securing communal land rights. According to the IACHR, Article 21 of the ACHR, in conjunction with Article 1(1), protected indigenous land tenure. In addition, the IACHR claimed that Nicaragua violated the community's right to be consulted by unilaterally authorizing the exploitation of Awas Tingni communal lands. The IACHR's petition asked for several reparations to the victims, including official recognition of communal land rights.

In response, the historic judgment issued by the IACtHR upheld indigenous land rights. Building on an autonomous interpretation of international human rights law, the IACtHR examined the ACHR in light of the current living conditions of the Awas Tingni community. It attributed a violation to the state due to the failure to delimitate, demarcate, and title the territory belonging to the indigenous community and to issue concessions to third parties. Thus, the IACtHR concluded that the state had violated Article 21 of the ACHR in connection with Articles 1(1) and 2 thereof to the detriment of the Awas Tingni community members. The evidentiary process behind this outcome is the topic of the next section.

3   Evidence-Building in the IAHRS: The Landmark *Awas Tingni* Case

The *Awas Tingni* case is regarded as a leading decision due to the groundbreaking interpretation of property rights developed by the IACtHR. It is evident that the IACtHR had to use sophisticated legal tools to solve the challenge of expanding an individualistically conceived right to protect several persons as a whole group. What is less obvious is the significant leeway that the IACtHR had to extend before beginning such complex hermeneutical activity. In legal practice, one must establish the facts before considering the applicable laws. Simply put, "any lawyer knows that to win a case, good arguments are important, but good evidence is crucial."[17]

In the *Awas Tingni* case, the facts were controversial, since the claimed indigenous territory was neither demarcated nor titled. In addition, indigenous communities of the Nicaraguan Atlantic coast did not have a legal personality, and domestic court decisions concerned only state concessions, not

---

17   Margherita Melillo, *Forms of Evidence, in* Max Planck Encyclopedias of Public International Law 1 (2021), https://opil.ouplaw.com (last visited Jul 28, 2022).

their recognition as a community or their land rights. The state used this legal vacuum strategically to advance its own arguments, as demonstrated in its final allegations: "The Inter-American Commission did not succeed in contradicting the fact that the Awas Tingni community consisted of a reduced number of persons who do not belong to the same ethnicity and, therefore, they have neither a common history nor ancestral possession of the claimed lands." Such a line of argument contesting ethnicity is common in lawsuits concerning indigenous land rights.[18]

In the case under analysis, at issue were the "people" and the "place." These had to be established to avoid undermining the decision's legal value and the IACtHR's authority. The IACtHR needed cutting-edge evidence to produce a solid precedent. Both the IACHR and the Awas Tingni's legal representatives knew it. Indeed, they may have assumed that the case would be decided against the community without expert evidence.[19]

Evidence in the IAHRS is the product of an intricate process. Similar to other regional human rights systems,[20] the IAHRS's basic documents—the ACHR and the IACtHR Statute—provide little guidance on the IACtHR's evidentiary activity. As a result, a general feature of the IACtHR's evidentiary system is that procedural aspects evolve according to the IACtHR's established procedural rules and case law, inspired by international legal adjudication.[21] Another feature worth mentioning is that the IACtHR has an autonomous role *vis-à-vis* the IACHR and domestic courts, since previously established facts do not bind the court.[22]

---

18   Monteiro de Matos, *supra* note 14, at 167/243–245; Marie-Catherine Petersmann, *Contested Indigeneity and Traditionality in Environmental Litigation: The Politics of Expertise in Regional Human Rights Courts*, 21 Hum. Rts. L. Rev. 132–156, 137 (2021). For an example outside the Inter-American system, see Maria Sapignoli, *"Bushmen" in the Law: Evidence and Identity in Botswana's High Court*, 40 PoLAR: Political Leg. Anthropol. Rev. 210–225, 217 (2017).

19   Hale, *supra* note 12, at 621.

20   Melillo, *supra* note 17, at 31–32.

21   Alirio Abreu Burelli, *La Prueba en los Procesos Ante la Corte Interamericana de Derechos Humanos*, *in* Memoria del Seminario: El Sistema Interamericano de Protección de los Derechos Humanos en el Umbral del Siglo XXI 113–125, 114 (2003), http://ru .juridicas.unam.mx:80/xmlui/handle/123456789/28023 (last visited Jul 5, 2022); Héctor Fix-Zamudio, *Orden y Valoración de las Pruebas en la Función Contenciosa de la Corte Interamericana de Derechos Humanos*, *in* Memoria del Seminario: El Sistema Interamericano de Protección de los Derechos Humanos en el Umbral del Siglo XXI 197–215, 198 (2003), http://ru.juridicas.unam.mx:80/xmlui/ handle/123456789/57120 (last visited Jul 28, 2022); Melillo, *supra* note 18, at 31.

22   Álvaro Paúl, *Evidence: Inter-American Court of Human Rights (IACtHR)*, *in* Max Planck Encyclopedias of Public International Law 3 (2018), https://opil.ouplaw.com (last visited Jul 28, 2022).

Based on legal practice, this chapter divided the evidence development process under the IACtHR's contentious jurisdiction into three stages. The first is the submission of written evidence and the request for oral evidence to be produced. If authorized by the Inter-American Court, testimonies are received in the second stage. Finally, in the third stage, the IACtHR evaluates the evidence presented and decides on its admission. These three stages are examined below in light of the *Awas Tingni* case. They demonstrate the articulation of expert evidence in the IAHRS procedure.

3.1   *Backstage: Framing Judicial Expertise*

The IACHR's initial petition submitted a substantive amount of written evidence while also asking the IACtHR to authorize it to produce even more. If authorized, the evidence-building appeared to be not very taxing, since the *Awas Tingni* community had been under the spotlight of multiple research projects for over a decade. In other words, the expert-evidence-making process for this case had started at least ten years before it, thus revealing the IAHRS legal proceedings to be at the tip of the iceberg concerning indigenous territorial claims.

Despite scientific data on the *Awas Tingni* community, producing oral testimonies before the IAHRS was a sophisticated task for the parties, who had to abide by the rules in the IACtHR's case law and those in the 1996 rules of procedure.[23] In this regard, two elements were crucial for the parties: timing and type. Regarding the former, procedural rules differentiated between witnesses and experts (hereinafter declarants) without defining them.[24] The IACtHR's case law provided a general notion of the type of declarants, as it explained that witnesses' testimonies may refer to "facts of which the witnesses had direct knowledge" concerning the relevant case.[25] Conversely, experts could give their opinions about the facts.[26] In practice, as detailed below, the difference

---

23   Inter-American Court of Human Rights, Rules of Procedure, approved by the Court at its XXXIV Regular Session, Sep 9–20, 1996, https://www.corteidh.or.cr/reglamento .cfm?lang=en (last visited Jul 28, 2022).

24   For the sake of this analysis, this chapter borrows from the IACtHR's current rules of procedure (Nov 16–18, 2009, Article 2, no. 10) the word "declarants" as referring to witnesses and expert witnesses. It does not differentiate between witnesses and alleged victims. Please note that the rules of procedure in force at the time of the *Awas Tingni* case did not use the terminology of "declarants."

25   Inter-American Court of Human Rights, Suárez-Rosero v. Ecuador, Merits, Series C No. 35 32 (1997).

26   The current rules of procedure (Article 2, 23) provide a definition of expert witness: "The term 'expert witness' refers to the person whom, possessing particular scientific, artistic, technical, or practical knowledge or experience, informs the Court about issues in contention inasmuch as they relate to his or her special area of knowledge or experience." In

between the two types of declarants was often blurred. However, in any case, the parties had to state the capacity of each declarant selected in the adequate written pleadings.

In the *Awas Tingni* case, classifying a declarant as a witness or expert had two main consequences. Firstly, upon participation in the hearing, and depending on the capacity, the witness or expert had to take a slightly different oath, the violation of which implied domestic sanctions (Articles 47 and 51 of the 1996 rules of procedure). Secondly, witnesses and experts had different amounts of time available for testimony, with a ten-minute advantage for the latter. The party offering a declarant had to cover the expenses for his/her appearance in the courtroom (Article 45 of the 1996 rules of procedure).[27] Notably, Article 50 of the 1996 rules of procedure protected the declarants and their families from state pressure on account of their appearance before the IACtHR.[28]

Regarding timing, the appointment of witnesses and experts in the IAHRS has a specific procedural moment. At the time of the complaint under analysis, the IACHR had to indicate the names of the witnesses and experts in the application or preliminary objections. In contrast, the state had to do so either in reply to the application or preliminary objections, according to Article 43 of the 1996 rules of procedure.[29] Following the procedural dimension of the equality principle,[30] suggestions of witnesses or experts presented by the parties in an untimely manner had to be justified and would be admitted by the IACtHR only in exceptional circumstances, provided the opposing party's right of defense had been exercised.[31]

The reason behind the strict procedural stages for indicating declarants was related to the principle of due process of law that was—and still is—interwoven with the parties' right to raise objections. According to Articles 48

---

addition, according to Articles 35(f) and 36(f), expert witnesses must also submit their *curricula vitae*. See also: Inter-American Court of Human Rights, Cabrera García and Montiel Flores v. Mexico, Preliminary Exceptions, Merits, Reparations and Costs, Series C No. 220 47–48 (2010). For other differences between experts and witnesses, see Mónica Feria-Tinta, *Declarant: Inter-American Court of Human Rights (IACtHR)*, in Max Planck Encyclopedias of Public International Law 7 (2021), https://opil.ouplaw.com (last visited Jul 28, 2022); Álvaro Paúl, *Prueba Testifical y Pericial en la Práctica de la Corte Interamericana de Derechos Humanos*, 25 Ius et Praxis 19–48, 30–34 (2019); Paúl, *supra* note 22, at 28.

27   This rule is similar to Article 60 of the current rules of procedure.
28   This rule is found in Article 53 of the current rules of procedure.
29   Those rules are partially equivalent to Articles 35(1)(f) and 41(1)(c) of the current rules of procedure. For the differences, *see* Paúl, *supra* note 26, at 23–25.
30   Abreu Burelli, *supra* note 21, at 119.
31   This rule is found in Article 57(2) of the current rules of procedure.

and 49 of the 1996 rules of procedure,[32] the IACtHR had to examine eventual objections and to decide. It had the discretion to admit and produce evidence that it deemed relevant (Article 44 of the 1996 rules of procedure), a power that the IACtHR has regularly used.[33] Legal scholarship explains that the IACtHR has progressively adopted a strict approach to the procedural moment for offering evidence.[34]

In the case at hand, the IACHR submitted in its application in 1998 a list of names of witnesses and experts, suggesting the scope of their testimonies, to which Nicaragua did not object. In February 2000, the IACtHR secretariat requested that the IACHR send a final list of witnesses and experts that would be summoned to the hearing scheduled for June 13th, 2000.[35] In response, the IACHR sent a shortlist, reducing the number of previous declarants in the original petition. Nevertheless, the IACtHR postponed the scheduled hearing to November.

In September 2000, the IACtHR's secretariat again requested the IACHR's final list of witnesses and experts.[36] The IACHR submitted the shortlist of names provided in February with a slight difference. It changed the capacity of Dr. Theodore Macdonald, a Harvard anthropologist who had conducted ethnographic research among the Awas Tingni community, from witness to expert without justification. Despite no objections, the IACtHR strictly interpreted the procedural rules and denied this modification. Therefore, Macdonald was kept on the list only as a witness.

The opposite party, Nicaragua, submitted a list of witnesses and experts in a 2000 written submission, to which the IACHR objected as time-barred.[37] The IACtHR ruled that the state submission did not follow the procedural moment established in the 1996 rules of procedure—as explained above. It clarified that Nicaragua had not justified such a delay, contradicting the rules of procedure; thus, the state's request for testimonies was inadmissible. The short lapse

---

32   Those rules are equivalent to Articles 47 and 48 of the current rules of procedure. In that regard, *see* Fix-Zamudio, *supra* note 21, at 204–205.

33   This rule is equivalent to Article 58 of the current rules of procedure. On the active role in obtaining evidence, see *id.* at 205–206; Rüdiger Wolfrum & Mirka Möldner, *International Courts and Tribunals, Evidence, in* Max Planck Encyclopedias of Public International Law 49–56 (2013), https://opil.ouplaw.com (last visited Jul 28, 2022).

34   Feria-Tinta, *supra* note 26, at 19.

35   Inter-American Court of Human Rights, Resolution of the President, Mar 20, 2000.

36   Inter-American Court of Human Rights, Resolution of the President, Sep 14, 2000, at 4.

37   *Id.* at 5.

in naming the declarants put the state in a difficult position to defend itself without oral testimonies.

Voluntarily, following its legal framework and the principle of obtaining the best possible evidence to judge the case,[38] the IACtHR decided to hear one of the witnesses proposed by the state, Mr. Marco Centeno Caffarena, director of the Nicaraguan office for rural titling. It defined a threefold scope for his testimony: proceedings for titling indigenous land rights, criteria for establishing the geographical area to be recognized, and an overview of indigenous land claims.

3.2   *Oral Proceedings: Receiving Expert Testimonies*

The hearing occurred during the XLIX ordinary period of sessions at the seat of the Inter-American Court in San José of Costa Rica. Between November 16th and 18th, 2000, according to Chapters III and IV of the 1996 rules of procedure, the Judges of the Inter-American Court and the involved parties heard, interrogated, and cross-examined witnesses and experts.[39] Following the IACtHR's decision,[40] four experts had to testify in the *Awas Tingni* case. The first and most illustrious was Professor Dr. Rodolfo Stavenhagen.

On the first day, Stavenhagen testified. The German-born Mexican scholar had worked for almost fifty years as an anthropologist and sociologist at the National Indigenist Institute of Mexico.[41] Shortly after the hearing, he officially became the first United Nations Rapporteur on the Human Rights and Fundamental Freedoms of Indigenous Peoples. During his mandate, he appeared in several cases before the IACtHR. In *Awas Tingni*, he testified about indigenous peoples and their connections with their ancestral lands.

On the second day of the hearing, the IACtHR received the remaining three experts. It started with Professor Dr. Charles Hale, an anthropologist based at the University of Texas, who was the director of the Institute of Latin American

---

38   *See, for example,* Inter-American Court of Human Rights, Villagrán Morales et al. v. Guatemala, Merits, Series C No. 63 222 (1999).

39   An audio recording of this hearing is available at: https://soundcloud.com/search? q=Comunidad%20Mayagna%20(Sumo)%20Awas%20Tingni%20Vs.%20Nicaragua (last visited July 22, 2022). For an unofficial transcript of this hearing, see *Arizona Journal of International and Comparative Law* Vol. 19, No. 1: http://arizonajournal.org/ archive/vol-19 -no-1/ (last visited Jul 29, 2022).

40   Inter-American Court of Human Rights, *supra* note 36.

41   Transcripción de la audiencia pública sobre el fondo, celebrada los días 16, 17 y 18 de Noviembre de 2000, en la sede de la Corte, 1 88 (2000).

Studies.[42] His testimony's scope concerned the indigenous peoples of the Nicaraguan Atlantic coast and their land use patterns, which had been the focus of his research for over twenty years.

While the first two experts focused on the anthropological aspects of indigenous peoples, those remaining tackled legal issues associated with indigenous land tenure. After Hale, Mr. Roque Roldán, a prominent Colombian lawyer, provided his expert testimony. He had worked as a consultant for several international institutions and states, including Nicaragua.[43] He addressed indigenous peoples in the Americas and compared the legal framework on the rights of indigenous peoples in other Latin American countries with the Nicaraguan law and legal practice.

The final expert to testify was Mrs. Lottie Cunningham, a Nicaraguan attorney and public notary. Based on her six years of experience as legal counsel to indigenous communities in Nicaragua,[44] she testified about the alleged absence of domestic legal remedies for violations of the rights of indigenous communities.

Notably, the objectives of the testimonies were deeply entangled. They related not only to the facts but also to controversial legal issues. None of the experts had conducted empirical research among the Awas Tingni community. The only person to have done so was Macdonald, who, due to procedural issues explained above, the IACtHR accepted as a witness. The IAHRS evidentiary procedure established that the selected experts did not have to provide a written report before the hearing—a nowadays outdated practice.

Moreover, the IACtHR and the parties had agreed on how to conduct the hearing, which was only defined in more recent rules of procedure.[45] The only rule by the time of *Awas Tingni* was that the IACtHR's president had to conduct the hearing smoothly, according to Articles 40–41 of the 1996 rules. To overcome this absence of regulation, it was established in a meeting before the audience that each of the four rounds of expert testimony would begin with a thirty-minute questioning by the IACHR, assisted by the community's legal representative, Dr. James Anaya, a Professor of International and Constitutional Law. Subsequently, state representatives would have the same amount of time for interrogation. If one party exceeded its time, the other party would receive additional minutes to comply with the principle of equality of arms. Finally,

---

42   *Id.* at 187.

43   *Id.* at 204–205.

44   *Id.* at 219.

45   For instance, *see* Articles 51–52 of the 2009 rules of procedure.

each testimony would be concluded with a round of questions formulated by the judges, who often wanted to clarify issues, even beyond the expert's scope of testimony.[46]

3.3   Post-Hearing: Evaluation and Admission
The third and final stage of the evidentiary process in the IAHRS contentious jurisdiction relates to the evaluation and final decision on the admission of the evidence produced. Parties will only know if and to what extent the evidence presented will be considered in the ruling at this point. Thus, this is when the evidence submitted takes its final shape.

In the *Awas Tingni* case, this stage was reflected under part VI of the judgment. In four concise pages, the IACtHR explained its criteria for evaluating the evidence before admitting the expert evidence "only insofar as it is in accordance with the object of the respective examination."[47]

Following its established case law, the IACtHR evaluated the evidence submitted in light of many principles, among which the "*sana crítica*" played a crucial role. This may be translated as "sound judicial discretion" and reflects how the common law system weighs the evidence.[48] Accordingly, such a principle demands a logical and comprehensive analysis of the evidence presented, for which the object and purpose of the ACHR are to be considered.[49] This principle is beneficial in assessing the role of evidence: "If the reader wishes to know the evidence that supports a particular finding, he or she must read the section of proven facts, where the IACtHR will include in a footnote all the evidence that contributed to its finding, without mentioning the different value that it grants to each means of evidence."[50] The following section scrutinizes the role of expert evidence in the final judgment.

---

46   Transcripción de la audiencia pública sobre el fondo, celebrada los días 16, 17 y 18 de Noviembre de 2000, en la sede de la Corte, *supra* note 41, at 137.

47   Inter-American Court of Human Rights, *supra* note 7, at 100.

48   Paúl, *supra* note 22, at 9.

49   Inter-American Court of Human Rights, *supra* note 7, at 88; Abreu Burelli, *supra* note 21, at 124; Fix-Zamudio, *supra* note 21, at 212–213.

50   Paúl, *supra* note 22, at 10.

4   The Critical Role of Anthropological Expert Evidence in the Awas
         Tingni Case

There is no machine or sociolegal tool to measure the impact of anthropological expert witnessing in legal complaints.[51] Such an impact is not tangible and
sometimes even hidden between the lines. Therefore, an exhaustive analysis
of the impact of anthropological expertise on the *Awas Tingni* case is not feasible from a scholarly perspective. Despite this limitation, a closer examination
is vital.

This section immerses itself in legal and anthropological scholarships to
illustrate the influence of expert witnessing on the main aspects of the present
case. It starts with indicating and assessing direct references to expert evidence
in the official factual background. Then, it elaborates on the anthropological
links between expert evidence, and the cultural identity-based framework that
was the normative basis of the case at hand and that constitutes the river on
which the Inter-American case law on indigenous land rights navigates. Lastly,
it analyzes the influence of expert evidence on the differentiation between
individual and group rights, which the IACtHR grasped in the merits and
post-merits sections of the judgment.

4.1   *Zooming In: Explicit References by the Inter-American Court*
Following legal doctrine and the principle of *sana crítica*, the section's footnotes concerning the proven facts are the first to be examined in assessing the
impact of expert evidence. They contain references to each item of evidence
considered by the IACtHR to establish a given fact. In the case at hand, as
explained in the previous section, the critical issues were "people" and "place."

Footnote fourteen refers to the "people" (the Awas Tingni community).[52]
Here the IACtHR mentioned two official documents, the written expert evidence submitted by the Central American and Caribbean Research Council
and the University of Iowa, and the witness testimony of a member of the
Awas Tingni. Also referring to the community, footnote seventeen used similar
authorities but cited Macdonald's ethnographic study.[53]

To establish the "place" (*i.e.*, the Awas Tingni's claimed land), the IACtHR
referred to oral testimonies by witnesses (footnote eighteen), among other

---

51   Holden, *supra* note 13, at 1.
52   Inter-American Court of Human Rights, *supra* note 7, at 103.
53   *Id.*

sources.[54] These included Macdonald's testimony as well as his ethnographic study. In addition, they cited the research by the University of Iowa. Further footnotes regarding the territory at issue (footnotes nineteen to twenty-one) concerned written evidence—expert and non-expert. The mention of oral expert evidence is only found in footnote nineteen, namely Hale's testimony that relates to the overlapping communal lands.[55]

Given these footnotes, a preliminary analysis may lead to the (wrong) conclusion that expert evidence played a weak role in the case at hand. The IACtHR hardly used it as an explicit reference. Neither Stavenhagen nor Roldán was quoted in establishing the facts. The relatively more frequent reference to Macdonald's work does not contradict this inference, since Macdonald was heard only as a witness despite his qualification as an anthropologist.[56] However, his testimony can be considered neither expert nor witness evidence.[57] This analysis sustains that it had a unique character: witness-expert evidence.

Likewise, the examination of the court transcripts and judgment demonstrates that Macdonald played the role of a *testigo-perito* (literally, a witness-expert).[58] Officially, this figure does not exist in Inter-American procedural law, but it has appeared in its case law.[59] In practice, Macdonald declared not only about his first-hand experiences. He also expressed his knowledge as an anthropologist—something that a regular witness is not allowed to do, as explained in the previous section. During the trial, the state raised some objections against Macdonald for playing this role.[60] His overall performance during the hearing and the resulting oral evidence differed from those of other declarants qualified as experts.

Given the witness-expert character of Macdonald's oral testimony, it is crucial to remember how the IACtHR weighs the evidence. As explained in the previous section, neither IAHRS's basic documents nor the IACtHR's case law supports a strict hierarchy regarding the different types of evidence.[61] In other terms, Macdonald's testimony did not have less weight than expert

---

54   *Id.*

55   *Id.*

56   *See* the previous section for a detailed explanation of it.

57   For an opposite view, *see* Bens, *supra* note 8, at 145.

58   Transcripción de la audiencia pública sobre el fondo, celebrada los días 16, 17 y 18 de Noviembre de 2000, en la sede de la Corte, *supra* note 41, at 55–86.

59   Paúl, *supra* note 26, at 30–36.

60   Transcripción de la audiencia pública sobre el fondo, celebrada los días 16, 17 y 18 de Noviembre de 2000, en la sede de la Corte, *supra* note 41, at 63.

61   Paúl, *supra* note 26, at 36.

testimonies, nor did it play a minor role. This chapter recognizes the singularity and relevance of Macdonald's declarations while remarking that it legally does not constitute anthropological expert evidence.

The reason behind the scant references to oral expert evidence may be that the IACtHR wanted to avoid giving an impression of "artificiality" regarding the factual basis. By relying on the first-hand experience of witnesses through testimonies, some of them by indigenous community members, the IACtHR reinforced the controversial "cultural authenticity," which was employed as a central point to claim land rights. In doing so, it established an international legal precedent regarding accepting indigenous oral traditions as evidence—something still objected to in some jurisdictions—and bolstered the victims' role in legal adjudication.

By the time of the *Awas Tingni* judgment, frequent references to research conducted by outsiders as evidence could have raised political issues. According to the literature, such references could have created an eventual suspicion that an "authentic culture" was being fabricated abroad and endorsed by the IACtHR to modify territorial boundaries or even to interfere in domestic affairs.[62] These issues are especially sensitive in many American countries, including Nicaragua, given their historical experience with foreign intervention in domestic settings, resulting in violations of state sovereignty.

Concisely, controversies regarding "cultural authenticity" underlie the *Awas Tingni* case and expose the role of anthropological expertise therein. The following section elaborates on such debates through an interdisciplinary lens.

4.2 The Cultural Identity–Based Framework: Sketching Culture with Anthropology

The case at hand represents the beginning of the cultural identity–based framework for property rights in the IACtHR's case law.[63] Given the absence of a specific provision in the ACHR regarding collective property, the IACtHR

---

62   Bens, *supra* note 8, at 145.
63   Christopher A. Loperena, *Adjudicating Indigeneity: Anthropological Testimony in the Inter-American Court of Human Rights*, 122 Am. Anthropol. 595, 596 (2020); Mariana Monteiro de Matos, *Cultural Identity and Self-determination as Key Concepts in Concurring Legal Frameworks for the International Protection of the Rights of Indigenous Peoples*, *in* Cultural Heritage and International Law: Objects, Means and Ends of International Protection 273, 273 (Evelyne Lagrange et al. eds., 2018); Mariana Monteiro de Matos, *Das Recht indigener Völker auf natürliche Ressourcen und die entsprechenden Teilnahmerechte: Eine Analyse der VN-Erklärung über die Rechte indigener Völker sowie der Rechtsprechungen des VN-Menschenrechtsausschusses und des Interamerikanischen Gerichtshofes für Menschenrechte*, October 10th, 2013.

developed *de lege ferenda* the right to cultural identity as the quintessence of protecting indigenous land rights. The creation of a new right through legal decision-making received inspiration from many sources, including—but not limited to—anthropological knowledge via written and oral expert evidence. The following passage, which has been widely quoted across the globe, synthesizes this legal framework (emphasis added):

> Indigenous groups, by the fact of their very existence, have the right to live freely in their own territory; *the close ties of indigenous people with the land must be recognized and understood as the fundamental basis of their cultures*, their spiritual life, their integrity, and their economic survival. For indigenous communities, relations to the land are not merely a matter of possession and production but *a material and spiritual element* which they must fully enjoy, even to preserve their cultural legacy and transmit it to future generations.[64]

This chapter notes that such a statement exposes the very notion of culture behind the case at hand, which parallelly illustrates the Inter-American case law's approach regarding indigenous land rights. Notably, this paragraph goes beyond the popular understanding of culture as a synonym for arts or erudition. Rather, it involves both tangible (land) and intangible (spiritual life and integrity) elements. It echoes anthropological scholarship and the testimony of the experts heard by the IACtHR, which grasp culture as a broad term responsible for translating a range of independent activities among human groups (*i.a.*, land use).[65] Indeed, culture embraces several elements, but it is not defined by them.

To clarify, anthropologically speaking, culture is non-consensual. After extensive debate and investigation, anthropology has widely accepted the absence of a universal definition of culture. In the literature, this word can be found to express everything, nothing, or something, such as society or lifestyle. As Clifford explained in the context of a court case involving indigenous claims, "Culture appeared to have no essential features. Neither language, religion, land, economics, nor any other institution or custom was its sine qua non. It seemed to be a contingent mix of elements."[66] Controversies in anthropological

---

64   Inter-American Court of Human Rights, *supra* note 7, at 149.
65   I and II Edward B. Tylor, Primitive Culture: Researches into the Development of Mythology, Philosophy, Religion, Language, Art and Custom 1 (1874).
66   James Clifford, The Predicament of Culture: Twentieth-Century Ethnography, Literature, and Art 323 (1986).

scholarship spin around the polysemic meaning of culture.[67] Still, there is no solution for this issue because such a concept is deeply ingrained in contemporary worldviews and academic disciplines, including law and anthropology.[68] This term constitutes an essential component of human communication.

The entanglements between anthropology and law have been broadly discussed in both fields.[69] Establishing effective communication requires a stretching effort for the subjects involved when these types of knowledge encounter each other. As persons from different disciplines, lawyers and anthropologists have singular ways of expressing ideas, and, therefore, a *de facto* translation process of concepts must occur during technical dialogues. "The nature of cultural translation is an old anthropological problem, but the globalization of human rights discourse raises it in a new guise,"[70] warned the leading anthropologist Sally Engle Merry in view of contemporary challenges regarding law and anthropology.

What is striking in the IACtHR's statement quoted above is the intertwinement between indigenous peoples and lands. This quotation demonstrates a unique understanding of property rights, contrasting with the traditional notions stipulated in legal documents, which draw upon Roman Law. Also notable in this landmark judgment is the mention of "indigenous," given that this concept is absent in Inter-American basic legal documents. By comparison, in many countries belonging to the IAHRS, judges handle cases on indigenous land rights with the full support of specific legislation, complemented by expert evidence on the matter that accurately defines indigenous peoples and their lands. However, the IACtHR's judges had to decide without an indigenous-focused normative basis. In this gap, the role of anthropological expertise flourished.

Instead of defining "indigenous," the IACtHR explained a range of elements around the concept, at risk of criticism for "essentializing" this category and

---

67   For other controversies, see Thomas Hylland Eriksen, What is Anthropology? 26–31 (2004).

68   Roque de Barros Laraia, *Cultura*, *in* Antropologia & Direito: Temas antropológicos para estudos jurídicos 55, 58 (2012).

69   Jonas Bens, *Anthropology and the law: Historicising the epistemological divide*, 12 Int. J. Law in Context 235 (2016); Marie-Claire Foblets et al., *Legal Scholars Engaging with Social Anthropology: Hardships and Gains*, 23 German L.J. 911, 912 (2022); Randy Frances Kandel, *How Lawyers and Anthropologists Think Differently: Six Differences in Assumptions and Outlook between Anthropologists and Attorneys*, 11 NAPA Bulletin 1 (1992).

70   Sally Engle Merry, *Transnational Human Rights and Local Activism: Mapping the Middle*, 108 Am. Anthropol. 38, 40 (2006).

raising paradoxical effects for indigenous peoples and their complaints.[71] This criticism of the IACtHR is found in the literature concerning indigenous land claims as a detrimental effect of the legal treatment of cultural-based practices.[72] Anthropological literature reveals that in the translation process from local issues in indigenous territories to legal settings, indigenous peoples and their legal representatives often need to use the essentialization or cultural-ization of indigenous image as a legal strategy.[73] The main reasons behind such a strategy lie in either the absence of a legal definition concerning indig-enous peoples or the distance between local indigenous practices and the legal requirements of indigeneity, which usually rely on the so-called cultural differentiation.

Likewise, a key requirement regarding indigeneity—besides self-identification—is cultural differentiation from the rest of the society, which is present in the legislation of many countries under the Inter-American system.[74] Indigenous peoples acting as plaintiffs must comply with this requirement to assert their rights; this implies, in practice, the performance of subjective identities in judicial proceedings as culturally differentiated. As a result, in accordance with some authors, cultural subtleties disappear, and popular notions associated with indigenous lifestyles materialize before the courts.[75] By crafting Otherness, indigenous peoples encapsulate their diversity to make it fit into legal terms—an inadequate but essential process to access justice.

In that sense, cultural difference associated with ethnicity or indigene-ity in legal adjudication contrasts with local realities. Indigeneity in legal proceedings can be understood as a reflexive meta-discourse on culture, to borrow the expression from Carneiro da Cunha,[76] in the sense that it articulates the idiosyncrasies of indigenous peoples under a different logic compared to subjective intraethnic accounts. Far from criticizing it as less organic, anthropological theory explains that there are ever-evolving ways of expressing identities that vary across contexts and groups.

By the same token, it is evident that self and external classifications must not always coincide. Ethnic identification corresponds to a classificatory act

---

71   On the paradoxical effects, see Sapignoli, *supra* note 18, at 210.
72   Loperena, *supra* note 63, at 595.
73   Clifford, *supra* note 66, at 10–11; Petersmann, *supra* note 18, at 148–156.
74   João Pacheco de Oliveira Filho, *Os Instrumentos de Bordo: Expectativas e Possibilidades do Trabalho do Antropólogo en Laudos Períciais, in* A perícia antropológica em processos judiciais 121 (1994).
75   Adam Kuper, *The Return of the Native*, 44 Curr. Anthropol. 389–402, 395 (2003).
76   Manuela Carneiro da Cunha, Cultura com Aspas e Outros Ensaios 373 (1st ed. 2009).

performed by a subject within a given situational context.[77] In the *Awas Tingni* case, Macdonald's witness-expert testimony vividly describes the different sides of this classificatory act.[78] Put differently, subjective and objective classifications of indigeneity can be opposed in some cases, as identity cannot be classified in a ranking list.

The culturalization of indigenous land rights results from the sophisticated translation process of indigenous and non-indigenous worldviews that occurs in courtroom settings, for which anthropological expertise is essential. Expert evidence is needed to make "identity tangible, 'legalized' and recognizable in the terms required by state law."[79] In this regard, a broad debate in anthropology has developed over the years—from the neutrality of expert witnessing to the very nature of anthropological knowledge. Rosen points out three related challenges concerning anthropological expertise that, in the case of indigenous land claims, effectively began to emerge in the United States before the Indian Claims Commission.[80] In pragmatic terms, the "essentialization of culture" is a tricky legal strategy,[81] as the *Awas Tingni* case exposed.

During the *Awas Tingni* hearing, the essentialization of indigenous culture raised a race-related controversy. Hale explained that the Awas Tingni legal strategy privileged reified notions of community and indigeneity to the detriment of race and gender inequities within the community.[82] Accordingly, expert evidence combined the ideas of culture and ancestrality. *Mayagna* culture could be traced back to pre-Hispanic times, as expressed in the expert testimonies of Hale and Stavenhagen.

Similar to other indigenous complaints,[83] the state tackled the "cultural authenticity of the community." It argued based on the submission of written proof—a 1995 state census—showing the community's interethnic background: almost forty percent of the Awas Tingni community was composed of *mestizos* and persons with a *Miskito* origin.[84] Accordingly, there was no

---

77   Pacheco de Oliveira Filho, *supra* note 74, at 121.

78   Transcripción de la audiencia pública sobre el fondo, celebrada los días 16, 17 y 18 de Noviembre de 2000, en la sede de la Corte, *supra* note 41, at 64.

79   Sapignoli, *supra* note 18, at 210.

80   Rosen, *supra* note 13, at 567.

81   For a comprehensive examination, see Karen Engle, The Elusive Promise of Indigenous Development: Rights, Culture, Strategy 163–182 (2010).

82   Hale, *supra* note 12, at 114.

83   Loperena, *supra* note 63, at 599–600; Sapignoli, *supra* note 18, at 216.

84   Transcripción de la audiencia pública sobre el fondo, celebrada los días 16, 17 y 18 de Noviembre de 2000, en la sede de la Corte, *supra* note 41, at 290.

collective shared past, and thus, the community could not claim common ancestral occupation of the claimed lands. This line of argumentation simultaneously challenged the key controversial elements in the complaint: "people" and "place." The implicit reference to the notion of cultural identity being grounded in biological features has been the object of considerable discussion in legal anthropological scholarship.[85] Put differently, the state contended the degree of purity of the Awas Tingni community,[86] and in doing so, it shook the core of the pro-Awas Tingni legal arguments.

In response, the IACHR provided a solid counter-argument to the state's allegation regarding Awas Tingni's authenticity. Notably, it replied in its final arguments that international treaties do not require racial purity for recognizing ancestrality or indigenous land rights.[87] Although not explicitly indicating the relevant international treaties, this analysis points out that such a statement aligns with the *ius cogens* principle of non-discrimination. Additionally, it notes that the rhetorical effect before the IACtHR was striking.

The IACtHR agreed with the IACHR's argument regarding the classification of Awas Tingni as an indigenous people without elaborating on the interethnic composition of the group. In more recent judgments, it did so, consolidating the trend that began with the present case and contributing to the expansion of the category of "indigenous" in international human rights law.[88]

Observed through an anthropological looking-glass, the state argument regarding Awas Tingni's cultural authenticity does not have a substantial foundation. This chapter notes that it touched upon the outdated notion of assimilation or acculturation of indigenous peoples through interethnic contacts to push forward the false dichotomy between—rephrasing in contemporary terms—"true or fake indigeneity." However, the main point of contention concerned the continuity of indigenous cultures, without which the notion of ancestrality could not be legally sustained.

Anthropology has consistently demonstrated that continuity in indigenous land claims has a unique meaning due to the fluidity of cultural processes and the complex colonial history behind indigenous trajectories. Groups are not static, and several indigenous peoples are constantly on the move—by their own choice or as a result of the use of force. Many countries around the globe have acknowledged indigenous peoples' historical marginalization through

---

85   For instance, *see* Good, *supra* note 13, at 553; Kuper, *supra* note 75, at 392.
86   Bens, *supra* note 8, at 152.
87   Transcripción de la audiencia pública sobre el fondo, celebrada los días 16, 17 y 18 de Noviembre de 2000, en la sede de la Corte, *supra* note 41, at 295.
88   Monteiro de Matos, *supra* note 14, at 243.

assimilation policies.[89] Several ethnographies have documented these turbulent historical experiences as well.[90] Through those dynamics, indigenous traditions have connected to new environments and reinvented themselves over the years. The leading anthropologist Oliveira Filho gives a comprehensible explanation regarding continuity:

> As sociocultural units, indigenous peoples have a form of existence that should not be described through categories, such as life and death or apex and decline. A specific culture and indigenous people do not die due to a biological cycle. A group can disappear if all its members are killed and its existence is entirely suppressed from local memory, including the destruction of archives and documents. Except for this extreme situation, nothing prevents, as a result of more favorable socio-political conditions, cultural elements from re-emerging, even if modified and in different contexts, updated by people who claim the same identity.[91]

This explanation clarifies the inadequacy of the concept of extinction for describing indigenous cultures or the legal notion of causal nexus, commonly used in civil law countries, to analyze cultural processes. In addition, it implies that establishing the continuity of indigenous cultures in legal proceedings is complex and, *per se,* an interdisciplinary endeavor. In examining indigenous land claims and continuity, the law should build on a non-reductionist approach to cultural identities and processes in line with contemporary anthropological scholarship,[92] as reflected in the quotation above. Expert evidence in judicial adjudication is a fabulous tool for building the bridge between law and other disciplines, such as anthropology.

Framing this non-reductionist approach in the context of the *Awas Tingni* case implies that continuity does not mean a linear, chronological order of events or persons connected to the land dating back to pre-Hispanic times. Instead, in metaphorical terms, continuity is a hypertext forged by unbroken

---

89   Canada, *Statement of apology to former students of Indian Residential Schools,* (2008), https://www.rcaanc-cirnac.gc.ca/eng/1100100015644/1571589171655 (last visited Oct 19, 2022); Relatório da Comissão Nacional da Verdade: Textos temáticos – Volume II, (Comissão Nacional da Verdade ed., 2014).

90   Clifford, *supra* note 67, at 341.

91   João Pacheco de Oliveira Filho, *Perícia Antropológica, in* Antropologia & Direito: Temas antropológicos para estudos jurídicos 125, 133. Free translation by the author from Portuguese.

92   Mark Goodale, Anthropology and Law: A Critical Introduction 152 (2017).

historical chains of coherent, even if contrasting, subjective narratives of the Awas Tingni community in a commonly shared place and time.

4.3   *Indigenous Land Rights: Remarks on Individual and Group Rights*
The influence of anthropological expertise becomes even more evident when scrutinizing the court transcripts and the judgment. The merits section mentioned expert testimony to sustain the absence of domestic proceedings for indigenous land titling,[93] leading to the recognition of the violation of Article 21 of the ACHR. In addition, the collective dimensions of the right to property are an essential development in the decision's rationale. To achieve them, the IACtHR wandered a rocky path softened by expert testimonies.

During the trial, the relationship between individual and group rights, which concerns the bedrock of modern human rights law, came up several times. The judges took turns questioning the witnesses and experts on issues, such as the rights that individual community members have, or if they have desires, aspirations, or interests regarding an individual assignation of the land. In this regard, the dialogue between the expert anthropologist Rodolfo Stavenhagen and Judge García Ramírez is emblematic (emphasis added):

> Judge García Ramírez: Mr. Stavenhagen, you have stated your status as a sociologist and anthropologist, an eminent one by the way, not necessarily a lawyer; but you have explored in depth the rights of indigenous peoples and done so from a human rights perspective. I would like to know your point of view on the human rights of indigenous people. Does the indigenous relationship with the land lead us to configure a special form, a particular modality of human rights? What is the experience of the indigenous community and its members from the point of view of their rights, of their rights concerning the land, and how would you characterize this experience, if I can put it that way, from a human rights perspective, which you have explored so extensively?
>
> Expert Witness Rodolfo Stavenhagen: Your Excellency, you asked me the one-million-dollar question. Indeed, I believe that this is the fundamental problem. Of course, as you pointed out, since they are human rights, they are essentially human and correspond to the human person. *However, in certain conditions, specific circumstances, and given historical contexts, the rights of the human person are guaranteed and can only be fully exercised if communal rights are recognized. These collective rights*

---

93   Inter-American Court of Human Rights, *supra* note 7, at 124.

concern the community to which a person belongs from birth and of which he is a part, giving him the necessary elements to feel fully realized as a human being, which also means being social and cultural. The counterpart of this affirmation is that when the rights of a community are violated, whatever they may be, linguistic, religious, ethnic, cultural, indigenous or not, but which apply, of course, also in the first place to indigenous peoples. When the rights of these communities to continue subsisting as such and to be able to reproduce themselves as the units and identities that they are historically are violated, I am convinced that a fundamental human right or a series of basic human rights are fundamentally violated, namely the right to culture, the right to participate, the right to identity, and even the right to survive, and this is what has been demonstrated by many studies on indigenous peoples and communities in the Latin American region.[94]

Considering the post-merits section, the degree of impact of this dialogue and, more generally, of expert testimony is indisputable. This section contains elaborated explanations by the judges on several points of the decision, commonly designated by the name of opinions, that offer valuable insights into the IACtHR's elements of decision-making. As a general rule, more opinions mean more controversies.

In the *Awas Tingni* case, several opinions were issued: the Joint Separate Opinion of Judges Cançado Trindade, Pacheco Gómez, and Abreu Burelli; the Concurring Opinion of Judge Salgado Pesantes; the Concurring Opinion of Judge García Ramírez; and the Dissenting Opinion of Judge Montiel Argüello. Except for this last one, all opinions touched upon anthropology or mentioned oral anthropological evidence.

Judge García Ramírez's opinion referred explicitly to the above dialogue in explaining the relationship between individual and group rights. In his terms: "It must be recalled that individual subjective rights flow from and are protected by these community rights, which are an essential part of the juridical culture of many indigenous peoples and, by extension, of their members."[95] His opinion contributed substantially to solidifying *Awas Tingni*'s perennial echo in human rights law.

---

94   Transcripción de la audiencia pública sobre el fondo, celebrada los días 16, 17 y 18 de Noviembre de 2000, en la sede de la Corte, *supra* note 42, at 99. Free translation by the author from Spanish.

95   Inter-American Court of Human Rights, *supra* note 7. Concurring Opinion of Judge García Ramírez, at 14.

Finally, it is worth mentioning that the relationship between individual and group rights is hardly explainable due to its complexity. There is even disagreement about the terminology, namely, if "collective rights" should be called "group rights." In the *Awas Tingni* case, the IACtHR found a solution to conciliate individual and group rights according to local needs with the support of anthropological knowledge. However, these needs must be evaluated on a constant, case-by-case basis. Wiessner's scholarship offers substantive guidance for such assessment:

> In order to respond holistically to human needs and aspirations, we need to endeavor to protect both individuals and the groups relevant to them. The vulnerability of individuals created the need for individual human rights; the vulnerability of groups—particularly of cultures—creates the need for their protection. The critical question of relevance to the human rights project is: what deprivations of values targeting individuals as members of groups have taken place in recent history, and in order to achieve a world public order of human dignity, how might these deprivations be remedied? To answer this question, we need to understand exactly what the claims are that arise in the essential interaction between individuals and the groups relevant to them.[96]

5   Conclusion

Anthropological expertise plays a critical role in adjudicating indigenous land rights. It may not decide lawsuits by itself, but legal practice shows that it is a milestone for decision-making and legal reasoning.[97] Beyond that, the guarantee of other key rights of indigenous peoples, such as self-determination, according to Article 3 of the United Nations Declaration on the Rights of Indigenous Peoples, relies on it. As stated by the eminent Brazilian attorney, Mrs. Deborah Duprat, who was for many years in charge of the national office for protecting indigenous peoples: anthropological mediation is a critical step in the process of indigenous peoples' self-determination.[98] Accordingly, anthropology elucidates indigenous peoples' own social organization and territorial patterns.

---

96   Wiessner, *supra* note 3, at 262.
97   Dalmo de Abreu Dallari, *Argumento Antropológico e Linguagem Jurídica, in* A perícia antropológica em processos judiciais 107, 114 (1994).
98   Deborah Duprat, *Entrevista com a Doutora Deborah Duprat (6 Câmara/MPF-PGR) por Fábio Mura e Alexandra Barbosa da Silva (Mar/Abr 2015), in* Laudos antropológicos em perspectiva 17 (2015).

Whereas expert witnessing and evidence are commonly debated among anthropologists, they were neglected in the legal scholarship on the IAHRS. This chapter has filled this gap and articulated the sophisticated evidentiary process in the IAHRS with a critical perspective embedded in anthropology-based scholarship. Concisely, it has offered a didactic legal framework of expert evidence and explored anthropological elements therein, thus producing an interdisciplinary reading on procedural issues in human rights complaints. This analysis has delved into the international landmark decision in the *Awas Tingni* case due to its legal significance in establishing anthropological evidence as a critical feature in the IAHRS.

The dialogue between law and anthropology is a critical asset for advancing the rule of law and human rights. It is relevant not only for procedural issues, such as expert evidence and the setting of reparations due to socioenvironmental damage, but also for dealing with challenges regarding conflicts of fundamental rights. Cultural defense, animal sacrifice, and *jusdiversity* are topical issues in this regard. This chapter demonstrates that this interdisciplinary dialogue entails substantial ideas for understanding and shaping legal notions, including property and possession, according to the unique needs of individuals and groups.

Law can interact with the knowledge created by other disciplines in its natural endeavor of promoting human dignity through diversity-paved means. Borrowing the term from Lévi-Strauss, this task can be designated legal *bricolage*. In collecting theoretical bits and unrelated academic pieces from abroad, law finds itself in front of a mirror—looking at the silhouette of its assumptions and reflecting upon the weight of its doctrines. This interdisciplinary communication is challenging but, above all, enriching and compelling, as it constitutes a vital path toward the holistic development of personal capabilities and collective human flourishing.

Acknowledgments

The author thanks the Inter-American Court's library staff for providing court documents, without which this chapter would not have been possible.

PART 6

Cultural Heritage Law

∵

CHAPTER 25

The UNESCO World Heritage List – Revisited

*Michael Kilian**

1   Introduction[1] and Fundamentals[2]

In 2022, UNESCO's World Heritage Convention (hereinafter WHC)[3] has been in existence for fifty years. International cultural heritage law has always

---

*   Dr. iur. habil. (Tübingen), Full Professor of Public Law, Public International Law, European Law, Law of Finance and Environment at Martin Luther University in Halle-Wittenberg (1992–2014); previously Professor of Public Law at the University of Heidelberg. Judge, Saxony-Anhalt Constitutional Court (1993–2000). Of Counsel, PHP Law, Leipzig and Dresden, since 2015.

1   In 2003, the author already submitted an interim assessment of the World Heritage List: Michael Kilian, *Die Weltkulturerbeliste der UNESCO aus völkerrechtlicher und aus nationalstaatlicher Sicht. Zugleich ein Beitrag zu den Reflexwirkungen des sogenannten soft law im Völkerrecht, in* Constanze Fischer-Czermak, Andreas Kletecka, Martin Schauer & Wolfgang Zankl, Festschrift Rudolf Welser 457–475 (2004). With respect to this publication, the author would like to express his deep appreciation to Professor Dr. Eva-Maria Seng of the University of Paderborn, for her sharing valuable materials in the field of the history of art and culture, as listed in the next note.

2   Eva Seng, *Denkmalpflege und kulturelles Erbe,* MUT No. 497, January 2009, at 68–85; Eva Seng, Lecture, xxxth German Conference of Historians of March 3, 2009 in Marburg, Section of "Canon Formation between the Experience of the Public and the History of Reception," entitled *Die Welterbeliste: zwischen Kanonbildung und Kanonverschiebung* (unpublished manuscript, 15 pp.); Eva Seng, *Kulturlandschaften. Die Rückgewinnung des immateriellen Kulturerbes in die Landschaft, in* Demokratie – Kultur – Moderne Perspectiven der Politischen Theorie 201–220 (Lino Klevesath & Holger Zapf eds., 2011); Eva Seng, *UNESCO-Weltkulturerbe und der Gedanke der Nachhaltigkeit,* Deutsche UNESCO-Kommission e.V., UNESCO heute, 2011, Nr. 2, at 77–80; Eva Seng, *Kulturerbe zwischen Globalisierung und Lokalisierung, in Europäisches Kulturerbe – Bilder, Traditionen, Konfigurationen, in* 23 Arbeitshefte des Landesamts für Denkmalpflege Hessen 69–82 (Winfried Speitkamp ed., Internationale Tagung Universität Kassel 8.-9. October 2010 (Wiesbaden 2013)); Eva Seng, *World Cultural Heritage: Cultural Identity and the War on Works of Art. Introduction, Sketch of Problems and Objects, in* German National Museum Nürnberg, CHIA 2012 Nürnberg. The Challenge of the Object, 33rd Conference of the International Council of History of Art, Congress Proc. Part. 11, (2013), at 430–434; Eva Seng, *Materiell gleich Immateriell/immateriell gleich materiell. Die zwei Seiten einer Medaille, in* Arbeitskreis Theorie und Lehre der Denkmalpflege e.V., Denkmale – Werke – Bewertung, Denkmalpflege im Spannungsfeld von Fachinstitutionen und bürgerschaftlichem Engagement 49–55 (2013); Eva Seng, *Patrimoine-Global-Régional-Glocal: Patrimoine matériel et immatériel, une alternative?, in* Les Cahiers du CFPCI n. 3. Le patrimoine culturel

languished in the shadows of the remainder of international law.[4] Still, UNESCO's World Cultural and Natural Heritage List, created by the Convention[5] of 1972,[6] counts among the very rare statements of international law – besides the UN Charter and the human rights instruments – which has won the general awareness of the global community, and has even achieved a degree of popularity.[7] It has become an routine part of travel ads and a concern of every tourism association,[8] and it has triggered the creation of further, similar lists, in particular, the list of intangible cultural heritage.[9] It has also spawned, on the national level, a panoply of pertinent lists with which numerous countries and regions adorn themselves. A further progeny of international cultural heritage law on the regional level is the European Union's "cultural capitals" list. At times, this list engenders contentious public debates, as recently occasioned by

---

immatériel. Regards croisés de France et d'Allemagne 20–34 (2015; Eva Seng, *The Situation of German Heritage – during the Past Forty Years*, in Patrimoine et architecture. Matériel / immatériel. 40 ans de patrimoine 1970–2010. Cahier nos. 21–22 (Avril 2015), Office de patrimoine et des sites. Département de l'enseignement du logement et de l'énergie, République et Canton de Genève, at 34–49; Eva Seng, *Authentizität und kulturelles Erbe – Genese und Aufnahme des Authentizitätsaspektes in die Welterbekonvention* (unpublished manuscript 2018, 18 pp.); Eva Seng, *Kulturerbe – global – regional – glokal. Materielles und Immaterielles Kulturerbe – eine Alternative?*, in Museum – Ausstellung – kulturelles Erbe, Vol. 4, Reflexe der Immateriellen und Materiellen Kultur (Eva Seng & Frank Göttmann eds., 2019), at 121–145.

3   UNESCO-Convention for the Protection of the World Cultural and Natural Heritage 16 November 1972, Bundesgesetzblatt [BGBl.] 1977 II 213, 216, in force since 1975. As to the foundation and history of UNESCO, see Kilian, *Die Weltkulturerbeliste, supra* note 1, at 457–466.

4   Michael Kilian, *Neue Medien ohne Grenzen? – Das Völkerrecht und der Schutz nationaler kultureller Identität zwischen Bewahrung und Weltkultur*, in Der Rundfunkbegriff im Wandel der Medien (Armin Dittmann, Frank Fechner & Gerald G. Sander eds., Berlin, 1997), at 69–112; as to the state of cultural heritage law in the EU, see Frank Fechner, *Auf dem Weg zu einem europäischen Kulturrecht*, in „In einem Vereinten Europa dem Frieden der Welt zu dienen … ," Festschrift Thomas Oppermann (Claus-Dieter Classen, Armin Dittmann, Frank Fechner, Ulrich Gassner & Michael Kilian eds., 2001), at 687–703.

5   Art. 11 Nr. 2 and Arts. 1 and 2 of the Convention.

6   The same year that Stockholm hosted the first UN conference on the environment.

7   *See* further details below.

8   For example, the German state of Saxony-Anhalt, home to a great number of world heritage sites, proudly advertises its World Heritage Card "Welterbe-Card: Anhalt-Dessau-Wittenberg"; the Autobahn features the billboard "Sachsen-Anhalt – Weltkulturerbe erleben" [Saxony-Anhalt: enjoy its world cultural heritage!] . The city of Dessau-Roßlau even features two cultural heritage sites, which is quite a rarity: the Bauhaus and the Wörlitzer Gartenreich.

9   Lyndel V. Prott, *An International Legal Instrument for the Protection of the Intangible Cultural Heritage?*, in Festschrift Oppermann, *supra* note 4, at 657 *et seq.*

the construction of the Waldschlösschenbrücke, a bridge over the River Elbe in Dresden.[10] In particular, it also strengthens national and regional identity.

In his interim assessment, the author concluded in 2003/2004 that the List, together with its associated lists (e.g. the "Red List" of World Heritage in Danger) and its Operational Guidelines constitutes an example of "soft" international law. Nevertheless, it engenders tangible, even legal effects as it radiates into the domestic law of states parties, particularly in their law regarding the conservation of monuments. It thus constitutes a success story of international law.[11]

Closely related to the concept of global protection of the environment and its banner cries of "One Earth" or "One World," developed in the 1960s,[12] the idea emerged of seeing world culture and particularly significant natural heritage sites as intrinsically connected and thus as a good to be protected by the world community. Environment and nature are, in any event, intersecting circles, and they ultimately form a unit.[13]

The idea of global protection of culture through international law was impelled by the immense losses of cultural heritage in World War II which produced the 1954 Hague Convention for the Protection of Cultural Property in the Event of Armed Conflict.[14] As early as the end of the 18th century, the Bishop of Blois (France) had already articulated the idea of protecting cultural heritage not only in wartime, but also in peace, against loss and neglect. This concept of the international protection of cultural and natural heritage gained traction the proposal of the Maltese Foreign Minister Arvid Pardo in the UN General Assembly to consider the entire ocean floor and the oceans themselves as the "common heritage of mankind" (a form of legal commons) and to place them under global legal protection as part of the international law of the sea.[15] This concept and the resulting regime, combined with the protection of the marine environment, entered the Law of the Sea Convention of 1982,

---

10   *Cf.* Michael Kilian, *Die Brücke über der Elbe: völkerrechtliche Wirkungen des Welterbe-Übereinkommens der UNESCO*, LKV 2008, at 248–254; *see also* Seng, *Welterbe zwischen Globalisierung und Lokalisierung, supra* note 2, at 70.

11   Michael Kilian, *Die Weltkulturerbeliste, supra* note 1, at 457–475; Die Presse, Wien, Beilage "Welterbe Wien", 20 February 2021, 46 *et seq.*

12   Michael Kilian, Umweltschutz durch internationale Organisationen 26, 51 *et seq.,* 416 *et seq.* (1986).

13   *Cf. id.* at 29–31.

14   *See further* Michael Kilian, *Kriegsvölkerrecht und Kulturgut,* Neue Zeitschrift für Wehrrecht 1983, at 41–57.

15   Pardo (1914–1999), of Italian ancestry, gave that speech in 1967.

albeit with significant modifications.[16] Thus at least one form of natural heritage common to all was subjected to a special legal regime and the concept of a common heritage took legal form. In parallel, UNESCO was transforming this idea into law in 1972, with the Convention concerning the Protection of the World Cultural and Natural Heritage, followed by the 2003 Convention for the Safeguarding of the Intangible Cultural Heritage.

The World Heritage List developed further. There are transnational heritage sites both of the natural and the cultural kind,[17] as well as cultural heritage sites at different places.[18] There are individual sites as well as "ensembles,"[19] integral entities,[20] and entire cultural landscapes.[21] Besides cultural and natural sites, there are also mixed world heritage sites.[22] The 2003 List of Intangible Cultural Heritage of 2003 completed the triad of world heritage, consisting of cultural, natural, and intangible heritage (such as rituals, customs, skills, and documents).

The novel section on "cultural landscapes" technically falls within the concept of cultural, not natural heritage. It is a mix between cultural and natural heritage and thus fills a gap.[23] Beyond that, further specialized UNESCO Lists were established for places whose protection was seen as urgent as that of cultural and natural heritage, e.g., biosphere reserves, so-called global geoparks, and underwater cultural heritage as special forms of natural heritage. They fill further gaps. More recently, the concept of the "world's documentary heritage" has been added, i.e. written and musical documents of various forms.

Our time is a time of lists, of measurements and rankings. Why shouldn't there be a world cultural heritage list? At the beginning of the 1970s, it followed a general trend within the incipient wave of digitalization, and it soon resonated in the general public.

The List started in 1975, featuring only 12 world heritage sites. It soon provoked political and scientific controversy among art historians, cultural

---

16   According to Art. 136 UNCLOS, only the area consisting of resources to be explored and exploited features as common heritage of mankind; for details, see Kilian, Umweltschutz, *supra* note 12, at 296 *et seq.*

17   E.g., the German-Polish Landscape Park in Muskau.

18   E.g., the Luther Memorial Sites in Wittenberg and Eisleben.

19   E.g., Berliner Museum Island, the castle of Schönbrunn.

20   E.g., Venice, or Vatican City.

21   Seng, *Kulturlandschaften. Die Rückgewinnung des immateriellen Kulturerbes in die Landschaft, supra* note 2, at 201–220. The concept first appeared in 1992.

22   E.g., Gartenreich Wörlitz, which comprises both parks and monuments.

23   E.g., regarding the classical sites in Weimar and the Luther memorial sites. Unfortunately, the City of Naumburg and its Cathedral together with the adjacent Unstrut valley and its castles was not included in the list.

scientists and within UNESCO itself.[24] There were questions about the inclusion and removal of sites from the list,[25] the scope and content of protection, the limitation and weighting of the list, losses, "uglifications,"[26] and destructions,[27] as well as urgent threats caused by the excessive designations of world heritage sites, especially via excessive tourism.[28] The war in Ukraine has provoked additional fears about the preservation and protection of cultural heritage.[29]

The most recent dislocations in world politics and the crisis of globalization and the democratic West has sowed doubts about the very idea of the "common heritage of mankind," the world heritage conventions and the lists, all of which are a chimera which conceals rather than overcomes the clash of civilizations identified by Samuel Huntington.[30]

A variety of novel issues and trends have emerged in the last couple of years regarding the List. They include:

– A paradigm shift with expanded criteria of inclusion in the Operational Guidelines and the introduction of so-called "tentative lists" by states parties.
– The problem of Eurocentrism and the issue of canon formation and canon shift (*Eva Seng*), combined with the rapid ascent of China.
– The issue of a setting a maximum number of sites in order to prevent a certain wearing-down effect.
– The relationship between natural and cultural heritage, and now intangible heritage, the various delimitations and intersections, and thus the blurring and merging of hard and soft (tangible and intangible) items of cultural heritage and skills.[31]

---

24   *Cf.* Seng, *Kulturerbe zwischen Globalisierung und Lokalisierung, supra* note 2, at 69–82.

25   E.g., Dresden, Vienna.

26   *Cf.* Wolfgang Freitag, *Das Ungeheuer von Loch Heumarkt – und kein Ende?* (Wien Mitte), Die Presse, Wien, 16 March 2022, at 14.

27   E.g., the destruction of the Buddha statues of Bamiyan, Afghanistan, of the museums in Bagdad, the Bridge of Mostar in Bosnia, the Old City of Aleppo, the Mausoleum of Timbuktu, or the earthquake destroying the City of Bam in Iran.

28   E.g., Fujiyama, Venice, the Grand Canyon, Machu Picchu, and various Alpine regions such as the Dolomites.

29   Regarding the continued existence of monasteries and churches, the protection of the City of Odessa, etc. *Cf.* Claudia Thurner, *Angst um das kulturelle Erbe*, Kronenzeitung Wien, 22 March 2022, at 6–7.

30   Samuel P. Huntington, *The Clash of Civilizations?*, 72(3) Foreign Aff. 22–49 (1993).

31   According to Eva Seng, the distinction between tangible and intangible cultural heritage is today "obsolete," as these concept merge into each other. She adduces the examples of

- The place of the lists in the determination of the identity of a state, a nation, a region, a city or a landscape;[32] the associated issues of postcolonialism, the safeguarding of identity, and protection against "cultural appropriation"; and the debate over robbery and booty of art with attendant issues of restitution.[33]
- The issue of the authenticity of a world heritage site.[34]
- As mentioned above, the issue of excessive tourism[35] and sustainability, related to the problem of creeping "McDonaldization," i.e. uniformization of cultures[36] or their hybridization (also called their "creolization").[37]
- The changes and novel developments in museum pedagogy and the relationship between the protection of cultural heritage and the preservation of historical monuments, including the issue of the reconstruction of lost monuments and old towns.[38]
- The discovery of the regional and the local within the framework of globalism and its interactions with the blurring frontiers of concepts and definitions of global – regional – local (so-called glocalization).[39]
- The relationship between world heritage protection and sustainability as part of the struggle against climate change.

---

the Cathedral of Reims and the phenomenon of dance. *Cf.* Seng, *Materiell gleich Immateriell/immateriell gleich materiell, supra* note 2, at 49–55.

32   *Cf.* Michael Kilian, Staatsästhetik. Ausgewählte Schriften (2022); Michael Kilian, *Ohne Leitbild. Von deutscher Republik im Zeitalter der Zuwanderung. Versuch einer Bestandsaufnahme, in* Republik, Rechtsverhältnis, Rechtskultur (Katharine Gräfin Schlieffen 2018), at 431–484, as well as from the perspective of art history, Seng, *World Cultural Heritage: Cultural Identity and the War on Works of Art. Introduction, Sketch of Problems and Objects, supra* note 2, at 430–434.

33   E.g., the return, by Germany, of the so-called Benin sculptures in 2022 to Nigeria.

34   *Cf.* Michael Kilian, *Die Rekonstruktion von verlorenen Baudenkmalen – Wiederherstellung und Bewahrung einer ästhetischen Umwelt? – Ein Plädoyer zur Ausformung eines erweiterten Denkmalschutzbegriffs*, Festschrift Werner Rengeling (Jörn Ipsen & Bernhard Stüer eds., 2008), at 105–126.

35   *See, e.g.,* Carsten Heinke, *Rügens Bild von einer Küste* (*Naturpark Jasmund*), Die Presse Wien, 2 April 2022, at R 3.

36   Seng, *Kulturerbe zwischen Globalisierung und Lokalisierung, supra* note 2, at 69, referring to George Ritzer, Die McDonaldisierung der Gesellschaft (1995).

37   Seng, *Kulturerbe zwischen Globalisierung und Lokalisierung, supra* note 2, at 69 *et seq.*

38   *Cf.* Seng, *Denkmalpflege und kulturelles Erbe, supra* note 2, at. 68–85.

39   This is understood to be an intermixture (hybridization) of the global and the local. *Cf.* Seng, *Patrimoine-Global-Régional-Glocal: Patrimoine materiel et immatériel, une alternative? supra* note 2, at 20–34; Seng, *Kulturerbe zwischen Globalisierung und Lokalisierung, supra* note 2, at 70 *et seq.*

Only some of these issues can be dealt with in Part III of this contribution, particularly those that have a closer relationship to cultural heritage law. Prior to that, I will briefly address the structure and content of the List.

2 The List of 2003 as Compared with the Current List

2.1 *The World Cultural and Natural Heritage List*
2.1.1 Classifications and Special Features of the List
UNESCO's List was first subdivided into four "regions": Africa, America, Asia and Europe. These regions, however, deviate from the exact geographic allocation. "Africa" does not include North Arabia and the Arab countries; "Asia" also includes Australia and Oceania, while "Europe" also covers Israel, Turkey and the countries of the Caucasus. It also includes the entirety of Russia up to the Pacific Ocean, even though Europe, according to general understanding, ends at the Urals. "America," on the other hand, only covers South and Central America (Latin America) and the Caribbean, while the U.S. and Canada are allocated to Europe.[40] Thus one wanted to create a sort of "Kulturkreise" (*Leo Frobenius*),[41] cultural areas which belong together on the basis of common ideas. In the meantime, Australia, New Zealand, and Oceania are listed separately.

2.1.2 The List in 2003
In 2003, close to thirty years after its inception in 1975, the World Heritage List consisted of the following entries:

At the time of the 27th session of the General Conference of UNESCO in October 2003, the List encompassed 129 States with 754 cultural and natural heritage sites overall, including 582 cultural sites, 149 natural sites, and 23 mixed cultural-natural heritage sites.[42]

The distribution was as follows:

Asia:	173 sites
Europe:	331 sites
Africa:	89 sites

---

40   As to the issues of allocation, with further details, see Kilian, *Die Weltkulturerbeliste, supra* note 1, at 467 *et seq.*

41   Leo Frobenius, Vom Kulturreich des Festlandes (1923). *See also* Kurt von Boeckmann, Vom Kulturreich des Meeres (1924).

42   Sources: Wikipedia, and the home page of the German UNESCO Commission, at https://www.unesco.de/. My own count then resulted in 752 sites, of which 617 were cultural heritage sites and 162 natural heritage sites. *See* Kilian, *Weltkulturerbeliste, supra* note 1, at 466.

America: 136 sites
Australia and Oceania: 23 sites.

The various sites and objects (the number of each can differ) were distributed in the following way:

Asia:[43]   142 cultural heritage and 33 natural heritage sites
Europe:[44]   298 cultural heritage and 35 natural heritage
                             sites
Africa: 62 cultural heritage and 33 natural heritage sites
America: 99 cultural heritage and 50 natural heritage sites
Australia and Oceania: 16 cultural heritage and 11 natural heritage sites

At that time, Europe's share of all world heritage sites amounted to 44%; as to cultural heritage sites, this share was 48.3%, while it was only 22% of the natural heritage sites.

2.1.3   The List in 2021
In July 2021, the World Heritage List featured a total of 1154 sites in 157 of the present states parties:[45]

897 are cultural heritage sites;
218 are natural heritage sites;
39 are mixed cultural-natural heritage sites;
40 are cross-border or transnational heritage sites.[46]

The distribution among the current five UNESCO areas is as follows:

Africa and Arabia: 127
Americas: 163
Asia: 304
Australia/Oceania: 34
Europe: 383
without allocation: 7

---

43   Including the Arabian Peninsula.
44   Including Russia up to the Pacific Ocean.
45   *World Heritage Site*, https://en.wikipedia.org/wiki/World_Heritage_Site; https://www
      .unesco.de/.
46   E.g., historic seaside towns in Europe.

Distribution according to: cultural heritage natural heritage mixed heritage:

	cultural heritage	natural heritage	mixed heritage
Africa:	49	47	6
Arabic States:	80	5 + 1	3
Americas:			
North America:	20	22	2
Central and South America	107	39	7
Australia and the Pacific:	8	16	6
Israel:	7		
Caucasus:	9	2	
Turkey:	17	2	
Asia:	192	56	6
Europe (without Israel, Caucasus,Turkey):	453	67	10

The List of Europe includes various multiple counts (e.g., European seaside towns).[47]

2.1.4 Changes

Within twenty years, Europe's share of the total number of world heritage sites has decreased from 44% to only 26.4%. Adding, however, North America, the Caucusus, Turkey, and Israel to the List again, the share is significantly higher (approximately 45%).

The number of national cultural and world heritage sites within the various states parties of the World Heritage Convention have the following ranking in August 2021:

Italy:	58[48]
China:	56
Germany:	51
Spain:	49

---

47   For example, the transnational world heritage site "Great Spa Towns of Europe" includes one Belgian, three German (an additional three had been nominated), a French, an Italian, an Austrian (an additional one had been nominated), three Czech (another one had been nominated), and a British spa town, in total eleven spa towns. https://www.unesco.de/kultur-und-natur/welterbe/welterbe-deutschland/die-bedeutenden-kurstaedte-europas. Still, important spa towns such as Bad Homburg v.d.H., Wiesbaden and Bad Ischl did not make it to the List.

48   Approximately 50% of occidental art is considered to be located in Italy.

France:	49
India:	40
Mexico:	35
Great Britain:	34
Russia:	30
United States:	24

Thus, besides the United States, four non-European states have ascended to the top group. Still, with Italy, Germany, Spain, France, Great Britain and Russia, six of ten states in that group are European. China, in 2002 not yet present on that list, has pushed itself within twenty years to the second place; India ascended to the sixth, and Mexico to the seventh rank.

2.1.5 Special Lists

The "Red List" of endangered cultural and natural heritage sites included 23 sites in 1999.[49] In 2021, 52 sites are listed as especially threatened, double the number of 1999.[50]

Only three sites have been deleted from that list, including one located in Germany (Elbe View in Dresden).

A tentative list of sites which the individual states parties have suggested for nomination as world heritage sites constitute a representative list worthy of preservation as cultural and natural heritage sites of the future. It now includes 463 cultural and 124 natural heritage candidate sites, in total 629 institutions (often located in several places) within 139 countries.[51] Purely national lists exist in 186 states, including currently 1,720 sites in 179 countries. The remaining conceivable seven states' lists are presently unfilled.[52]

2.2 *The List of Intangible Sites as an Expansion and Completion of the World Heritage List*

It made sense to follow up on the list of tangible cultural sites with a list of intangible world heritage sites. The filling of this gap had been asked for, particularly, by non-European countries and was achieved in 2003.[53]

---

49   Kilian, *Die Weltkulturerbeliste, supra* note 1, at 468.

50   UNESCO World Heritage Centre – List of World Heritage in Danger, https://whc.unesco .org/en/danger/.

51   The German list includes eight sites, plus one site already nominated. Tentativliste, https://de.wikipedia.org/wiki/Tentativliste.

52   Sources:wikipedia, https://www.unesco.de/.

53   Seng, *The Situation of German Heritage – during the Past Forty Years, supra* note 2, at 49–56; Seng, *Kulturerbe zwischen Globalisierung und Lokalisierung, supra* note 2, at 79 *et seq.*

The present UNESCO List of Intangible Cultural Heritage unifies two lists and a register: the Representative List of the Intangible Cultural Heritage of Humanity, the List of Intangible Cultural Heritage in Need of Urgent Safeguarding, and the Register of Good Safeguarding Practices. They have been established since 2008 within the framework of the Convention for the Safeguarding of the Intangible Cultural Heritage. These lists trace their origin to a list of "masterpieces of the tangible and intangible heritage of mankind," put together between 2001 and 2005 in supplementation of the existing World Heritage List.[54] Until 2005, it listed 90 items of intangible heritage which were integrated into the new Representative List in November 2018.

Intangible forms of cultural expression are, primarily, dance, theater, music, and oral traditions, in addition to customs, festivals, and artisanship. By 2019, many states had already joined the Convention, almost as many as the states parties of the World Heritage Convention.

There are presently 180 states parties to the Convention for the Safeguarding of the Intangible Cultural Heritage. The List of Intangible Cultural Heritage was augmented by 47 new entries in 2021, and, in 2019, included 463 forms of cultural expression in 124 countries.[55] The Tentative List includes 131 entries, of which there are 117 forms of culture and 14 so-called model programs.[56]

On this list, the non-European world, especially the Asian countries of China, Japan, Vietnam, and Indonesia, is represented much more strongly than on the tangible Cultural Heritage List, Numerous skills are registered simultaneously in many countries.

The United States does not have an entry on this list at this moment. Due to its late accession to the Convention in 2013, Germany now is only represented with four entries, two of them shared with several other countries.

Supplementing the tangible and intangible world culture and natural heritage lists there are other lists, including the World Documentary Heritage List with 427 entries in 2021, the Underwater Heritage List, 177 Geoparks, and 727 Biosphere reserves.[57]

---

54   As early as 1997, the UNESCO introduced a "masterpiece program," followed by three proclamations in 2001, 2003, and 2005. The masterpieces hailed from all regions of the world and so laid the foundation for today's Representative List of the Intangible Cultural Heritage of Humanity.

55   Sources: wikipedia; Deutsche UNESCO-Kommission homepage 2022, https://www.unesco.de.

56   From Germany, there are 22 entries and 3 applications.

57   Sources: wikipedia; https://www.unesco.de/.

3   The Development of the Operational Guidelines

The Operational Guidelines issued between 1978 and 1997 refined the Convention's criteria for inclusion in the List with six additional criteria. As of 2003, the Guidelines displayed three groups of cultural and natural heritage, for which in total six or four criteria, respectively, were established; these criteria could also be used cumulatively. The most recent Guidelines of 2021[58] were expanded further and now encompass, in Article 1, three cultural heritage and three natural heritage groups, one mixed group, and cultural landscapes with three typologies. The criteria for the existence of the "outstanding universal value" of a site were circumscribed using ten criteria (II. D). These criteria are subject to the yardsticks of "integrity" and/or "authenticity" (II. E. 79.-86., 87.-95.). Overall, the List has to be representative, balanced, and credible (II. B.).

The tentative lists serve as a "planning and evaluation tool" and are to be found in II. C.; the List of World Heritage in Danger (the Red List) in IV. B. Every year, 35 nominations are allowed now (Nr. 61.c), moveable items are excluded (Art. 1).

The Guidelines further regulate in great detail and comprehensively the safeguarding of the world heritage site (e.g., via the setting of precise boundaries and buffer zones) and their management (II. F.), the procedure of inclusion (III.) and monitoring (IV.) with the Red List as the key instrument and the procedure of deletion from the List (IV. C.). Detailed regulation is also provided with assistance to financially weak states parties (VII.) and the emblem of the List as well as its use (VIII.).[59]

The Guidelines also demonstrate the vast apparatus hiding behind the List: besides the states parties, represented by the national UNESCO world heritage commissions, there are the General Assembly of the States Parties to the Convention, the UNESCO World Heritage Committee, the Committee's Secretariat (i.e. the World Heritage Center) and several advisory bodies, i.e. ICCROM, ICOMOS, and IUCN. In addition, there is the cooperation with other international governmental and non-governmental organizations as well as national, regional, and local partners (I. C.-I.). Guideline I. J. also lists a plethora of conventions and programs which envelop the World Heritage Convention with a thick structure of regulations and other legal measures.

---

58   UNESCO-WHC.21/01 31 July 2021.

59   In 1854 already, a special blue-white emblem of protection was established for the safeguarding of cultural heritage in armed conflicts: this emblem has to be displayed prominently.

There is a remarkable delimitation of the regions in V. B. No. 203, which distinguishes between the Arabian States, Africa, Asia and the Pacific (including also Australia, New Zealand, Oceania, although they compose the "Fifth Continent," geographically speaking), Latin America, and the Caribbean as well as Europe and North America. The tentative lists are organized accordingly. As detailed above, the regions feature additional allocations that differ from their usual understanding and from geography.

Starting with the masterpieces of humankind, originally appearing to be quite simple, complemented by a few Guidelines, a doctrinal structure has developed which is nothing short of the UN Convention on the Law of the Sea. The UNESCO World Heritage Guidelines of July 31, 2021 now cover 83 pages with 290 numbered paragraphs, which comprise a total of 188 pages in 15 annexes. Thus the scope of the Guidelines has quadrupled since their first issuance in 1977.[60] Overall, one may speak of a virtually closed international regime of cultural heritage law, akin to the Law of the Sea Convention.

4   The Traditional Critique of the World Heritage List and New Trends in the Debates on the Safeguarding of the World Heritage

4.1   *The Traditional Critique*

The distribution especially of the cultural heritage sites has earned early criticism, primarily because of its concentration in Europe. The narrow conception of a monument, based on European ideas, necessitated supplementations which have led to an expanded definition. The question also was raised whether a "natural" limitation ("capping") of the List was not necessary in order to preserve its function of concentrating global attention.

The desired popularizing effect of the List vastly extended beyond its original intention, which was primarily to ensure safeguarding the world heritage sites against neglect and destruction. Thus the radiating effect of the List led to ever more numerous applications for inclusion and a virtual competition between states as to who can boast of the most heritage sites. Here as well debate ensued as to whether it was necessary to limit the number of applications per state.

The List's success appeared to turn to its detriment: Aspects of the prestige of states, the waning of the effect of drawing attention via too many nominations to the List combined with overly generous criteria for inclusion as well

---

60   *See also* Seng, *Authentizität, supra* note 2, at 5.

as the endangerment of many sites caused by rapidly growing cultural tourism (excessive tourism) led to the concern that the previously undisputed rank of the lists in both of their departments was diminishing, leading to the danger of devaluing the individual world heritage sites, leaving them only with nominal, no more intrinsic value.

The critique of 2001 focused on the imbalances of the List, especially its Eurocentrism, the preponderance of the cultural sites over the natural sites as well as the lack of categories which could lead to the filling of the gap of protection. Thus, for example, the characterization as a historical monument of the architecture of the 20th century and of industrial sites was scarcely if at all taken into consideration. There was a considerable need to catch up. The same was true for cultural areas belonging together (i.e. culturally connected to each other, such as the Luther towns of Eisleben and Wittenberg) beyond the individual cultural object. Also, the intrinsic value of the movements of historicism and eclecticism of the 19th century had only slowly been recognized and considered worthy of protection.

The legal content of the List also faced quite a number of reservations. For example, the concept of "common heritage" was considered too vague, even though it was decisive with respect to the popularization of the entire UNESCO enterprise. Nothing made it more popular than this easily understandable slogan, which ended up becoming the motto of the whole movement: the preservation not only of the environment, but, specifically, of the world's culture and its individual, especially valuable components. The "common heritage of mankind" thus developed into a concept which became mainstream in the public and the media and familiar in all languages.

There were obviously a number of questions: which object is particularly worthy of protection, which one has virtual "world class rank"? The often controversial answers necessitated the issuing of clarifying administrative regulations. The legally binding effect of the Convention, its List and the Guidelines as one legal "package" raised the question as to whether the List itself could be internationally legally binding. After all, one had developed additional techniques: the "Red List" on the world heritage in danger and the threat to delete once included world heritage sites from the List. This action was taken in a few cases and deletions from the List were effectuated.

Taking into account the international law concepts of hard law, soft law and mere reflections of the law, one can conclude that there is a legal institutionalization via autonomous UN specialized organization (UNESCO), the Convention, and UNESCO organs (UNESCO WGC, national committees, expert councils) as well as Lists and Guidelines. Thus the List is more than a mere posting for advertising purposes.

The idea of *soft law* has first been developed in international environmental law and found its widespread expression in international economic law, such as the (legally non-binding) "Charter on Economic Rights and Duties of States" of 1974, part of the debate over a "New International Economic Order." In this context, international economic law developed numerous recommendatory codes of conduct, guidelines, and declarations of principles.[61] Soft law, though not legally binding, "may gain substantial normative relevance as a mechanism of guiding behavior."[62] Its "law-shaping effect" (*Karsten Nowrot*) can be evidenced in many ways today.[63] Besides its contribution to the formation of customary international law, the effect of soft law can also be seen in the behavior of many states, the interpretation of international treaties and even in the jurisprudence of international and supranational bodies. In the case of the UNESCO World Heritage List, one can recognize this effect even in the decisions of domestic courts and administrative bodies.[64] Soft law thus has the effect of "supporting end supplementing the law."[65]

The List as a component of the UNESCO World Heritage Convention, which, itself, constitutes a multilateral international treaty, sums up the entire world heritage and defines and delimits it at the same time. The Convention, including its List, contains a mandate for optimizing the protection and safeguarding of the world's heritage. It includes legal commitments, albeit not enforceable, in the form of obligations to protect and preserve as well as duties of information-gathering of all kinds. The UNESCO World Heritage Committee and its subordinate bodies have comprehensive tasks of monitoring. UNESCO may also render advice regarding world heritage sites to states seeking assistance and provide financial support as well as expert knowledge.

Admittedly, though, these are "soft legal commitments" without enforcement sanctions (apart from the Red List warnings and the deletions from the List), but may nonetheless sanction in the case of a country's ignoring or neglecting its tasks and duties. There, the content of the sanction is of a rather more symbolic character, but it may draw the attention of the world community via processes of "blaming and shaming" and intangible diminutions of prestige of a state (though it had no appreciable effect in the case of the Dresden bridge). Mere debates and announcements, however, may lead to

---

61   Karsten Nowrot, §§ 2, 102 *et seq.*, Rd. 77 *et seq.*, *in* Internationales Wirtschaftsrecht (Christian Tietje ed., 2009); *see also* August Reinisch, *id.*, at. §§ 8, 351 *et seq.*, Rd. 20 *et seq.*

62   Nowrot, *id.*, Rd. 80.

63   *Id.*

64   *Cf.* the examples of German and Austrian law, which simply illustrate this phenomenon.

65   Nowrot, *supra* note 61, Rd. 83.

national and local consequences, e.g., in the area of city planning, as shown in the case of the first district of Vienna.[66]

In sum, one may speak in the case of the Convention and the List of a *"lex imperfecta"* which may have effects of guiding behavior which may ultimately protect world heritage sites "softly" via the creation of worldwide publicity. Culture, ultimately, also lives via psychology and the attention paid to it. The List thus embodies pragmatism, radiating effects, and the compulsion to react. The integration of conferences on the protection of culture and monuments and resulting texts, mostly due to private initiatives (such as the Charter of Athens, the Charter of Venice, and the Document of Nara/Japan) generates a focus for international debate which may serve to shape legal reactions in international law. Thus there are reflections in the domestic and international "ideology of monuments," which radiate into national and international law of safeguarding culture. The popularizing effect of the List is further enhanced by the Internet and the public presence and dissemination of information on the various world heritage sites.[67] This advertising effect contributes, in no small measure, to the indirect effect of the List on politics.

The author, in 2003, indicated a number of interior and exterior functions of the List, with "interior" functions meaning functions within the state, and "exterior" functions those outside of the state. Interior functions include:

1. the function of enhancing prestige and identification;
2. the function of globally communalizing all heritage sites ("one world");
3. the function of informing the public; and
4. the function of indirectly protecting and preserving the site.

Exterior functions are:

1. the function of drawing attention to the site;
2. the function of documentation;
3. the functions of warning and support;
4. the functions of blocking and pressure to publicly justify changes; and
5. the economic function.

4.2 *Canon Building and Canon Shift, in Particular, Eurocentrism*

The "latent" discussion about canons (*Eva Seng*) is a longstanding phenomenon in the history of ideas,[68] dating back to the classical period in the 18th

---

66   *Cf.* Die Presse, Wien, Beilage „Welterbe Wien," *supra* note at 11 *et seq.*, 18 *et seq.*
67   *Id.* at 20 *et seq.*
68   Harold Bloom, The Western Canon: The Books and School of the Ages (1994).

century.[69] It is not limited to the UNESCO World Heritage List. According to Seng, five issues play a role in this debate:[70]
- the issue of the representativeness of the List;
- the issue of the participants in the debate;
- the issue of societal acceptance and reception; as well as
- the issue of the influence of the general public on these processes.

The *content* of the List has been redefined several times: only since 1990 the art of women is also perceived or recognized; the same is true for extra-European or extra-North American art in the globally multi-ethnic world.[71] The safeguarding of intangible cultural heritage had been discussed as early as 1948 after the destructions of World War II; a pertinent financial fund, however, was not agreed upon.

Only in 1959 the endangerment of the Temple of Abu Simbel by the building of the Aswan Dam over the Nile alarmed the world and led, upon the request of Egypt and Sudan, to the first assumption of a common global responsibility by non-affected states for cultural heritage sites. In 1972, then, the UNESCO World Heritage Convention was adopted, which entered into force in 1976 upon ratification by 20 states. Up to the present day, it generated a veritable "cult" (*Eva Seng*) around historical heritage. In 2009, 186 states had become parties to the Convention; the Federal Republic of Germany had already joined it in 1976, the German Democratic Republic shortly before its end, in 1988.

After a somewhat muted beginning, the Convention experienced explosive development since the 1900s. Only in 2000, 61 world heritage sites were added, before countermeasures against this flood-like development could be taken, lest the exclusivity of the List be threatened. New nominations were limited to 30 a year. And states already heavily represented were only allowed one nomination per year. This limitation, however, was alleviated later. What was desired was a balance between the world's regions. At that time, the List consisted of 878 monuments in 145 countries (679 cultural heritage sites and 174 natural heritage sites, with 25 mixed sites) according to the definitions of Articles 1 and 2 of the Convention, which included ten criteria. This result made the Convention one of the most successful instruments with public appeal.

The issue of the representativeness of the List, in particular, the preeminence of Europe, was heading the debate, as the goal was the "equal rank of

---

69   Seng, *Die Welterbeliste zwischen Kanonbildung und Kanonverschiebung, supra* note 2, at 2.

70   *Id.* at 1 *et seq.*

71   *Id.* at 2.

all cultures."[72] Nevertheless, the heritage site in question has to be of "out-standing universal value," which necessitated a balance of the List as to its content. From the beginning, there was the issue of the balance between cultural and natural sites. In 1987 and 1989, respectively, demands for an independent global reference list, i.e. no notices by member states, which also should include non-member states. In 1994, an expert group was established in order to draft a global strategy. The IUCN indicated 219 natural heritage sites, distributed among eight bio-geographic regions, and further sites with cultural significance were added. For a long time, this list was used as reference list for the inclusion of new natural heritage sites. Since the identification of cultural heritage sites had to take into account too many "soft factors," no reference list managed to be established for them.

For this reason, ICOMOS in 1993, conducted a global study, which concluded the following: Europe was represented too heavily via its historical townships and Christian churches; in addition, there was the "architecture of the elite" (castles, fortresses, and palaces). Scarcely represented were monuments of the 20th century, testimonies to cultures still living, regional cultural traditions, and archeological sites. The preponderance of historical aesthetic typologies did not do justice to the global diversity of cultures.

Eurocentrism, according to Seng, had its causes in the criteria of inclusion, which all originated in the occidental tradition of protection of art and monuments, and which failed to take into account anthropological aspects. Four problems resulted: too much monumentalism, aestheticism, geographical distribution and authenticism, i.e. the claim of authenticity. The classical architectural heritage predominated; pilgrims' and trade routes were left out; there were very few early extra-European sites, such as the Taj Mahal, Angkor Wat, and Borobudur.[73] More than 50% of all sites were thus located in Europe and North America.

The Eurocentrism of the List was long attributed to the prevailing European/North American theory of art and monuments. The latter, however, has undergone quite some change, resulting in many openings. The Eurocentrism critique, also, does not apply to sites of natural heritage, as Europe, highly cultivated through centuries, and rather small, area-wise, does not include many outstanding natural heritage sites, in contrast to other world regions, e.g.,

---

72   Seng, *Kulturerbe zwischen Globalisierung und Lokalisierung, supra* note 2, at 75 *et seq.* For
      a comprehensive analysis, see Nikola Braun, Globales Erbe und regionales Ungleichge-
      wicht: Die Repräsentationsprobleme der UNESCO-Welterbeliste (2007).

73   These sites, however, had long been appraised as highly important in Europe, the world
      region leading in art history.

Africa. Traditionally, Europe is divided into small parts and populated densely. It boasts of a very long history of (in German) *"Hochkultur"* [= advanced civilization] distributed among more than forty independent states (including the UK, France, Germany, Spain, Italy, and Greece) and an extraordinary density of cultural heritage sites (Germany, Austria, Italy, the Netherlands, and Belgium). Besides the island states, Europe is the continent of the small and mini-states. In Europe, there are no vast territorial states, often devoid of humans, in which there are indeed very few world heritage sites. Its division into small parts and its cultural density ultimately turned out to be its disadvantage.

In addition to the existing List there were tentative lists (lists of suggestions and applications) for future world heritage sites requested to be included by member states, and evaluated by ICOMOS in each case. Here, as well, Europe had a head start over other world regions due to the great number of states located there.

Overall, there was a *shift* from the traditional *iconic sites/best of the best* to *the representation of the best/best of the representative*, from *outstanding universal value* to a number of sites considered typical, i.e. from the elitist to the mundane, from far back in time to what happened recently, from the tangible to the intangible. The general direction was veering toward a substantially broader representation of world heritage overall.

The *procedure* for the inclusion of new sites reflects a "separation of powers": the sole initiative rests with the member state of the Convention; the monopoly of inclusion *vel non* lies with the UNESCO World Heritage Committee.

Especially in Germany, a federal state, the application process is further differentiated and includes, due to their sovereignty over cultural issues, the federal states and the local communities as well, while the representation abroad rests with the federal government. The same is true for the German Tentative List.[74] Thus there are several levels of discussion: (1) the international/supranational level; (2), the national level; and (3) the regional/particlar level, with the German federal states observing the principle of proportionality. Generally, the application procedure has been shifted from the expert bodies to the political actors and the media.[75]

Social acceptance of the UNESCO Lists is high; its reception in then public, local politics and tourism is "overwhelming" (*Eva Seng*). The Red List is discussed passionately, as evidenced by the vigorous debate over the view of the Dome of Cologne, the First District of Vienna, and the Dresden

---

74 Seng, *Die Welterbeliste zwischen Kanonbildung und Kanonverschiebung. supra* note 2, at 10.
75 *Cf.,* in the case of Vienna, Die Presse, Wien, Beilage "Welterbe Wien", *supra* note 11, at 20 *et seq.*, 26, 42 *et seq.*, 64 *et seq.* and passim.

Waldschlösschen Bridge. Rejections, as seen in the case of Heidelberg, engender debates of disappointment, not only in the city at issue, which is perceived to have been denied a seal of approval to which it felt to be entitled.

The *influence of the public* increases ever more. Reactions by the UNESCO commission are feared by politicians, although not always observed.[76] It is very rare that international legal instruments are discussed by the general public with such intensity and passion. Admittedly, this is a great success for UNESCO, an insitution that has not evaded controversy.[77]

Overall, pursuant to the debates over elitism there have been a number of "shifts" (*Eva Seng*): monuments were replaced by cultural heritage, high culture by ordinary culture; the idea of sustainability was introduced as well as the concept of cultural landscapes and the protection of ensembles; a broad discourse with unimagined participation of the general public has developed, and in European-North American art history many openings toward new directions occurred.

4.3   *In Particular: The Issue of Authenticity*

The issue of authenticity was particularly important for the European view of the protection of monuments.[78] It was only the Charter of Venice of 1964 (a private, non-governmental text) that referenced the necessity to also take into account the surroundings of a monument (protection of the ensemble). It had been overlooked that many sites with monuments of second or third rank were part of a greater context and only from that context derive their full cultural meaning (e.g., Paris). To be added is the useful function of a monument, which necessitated changes in use and supplementations. Mere restorations had only been allowed in exceptional situations (e.g., St. Mark's Tower in Venice). The re-establishment of an ideal state was frowned upon. Necessary complementary parts had to be visibly detached, time layers had to be demonstrated, and harmonious insertions had to be aspired to.[79] The 1994 Document of Niara (also a private, non-governmental text) took this global policy into account.

The demand for authenticity could no longer, by itself, force the determination of a protectable monument. Instead, other sources of information, such as documents, plans, customs, traditions, techniques, skills, etc.) had to be drawn

---

76   Seng, *Die Welterbeliste zwischen Kanonbildung und Kanonverschiebung supra* note 2, at 12. The UNESCO List also exerts great influence on the respective national lists, cf. Seng, *Kulturerbe zwischen Globalisierung und Lokalisierung,* ssupra note 2, at 78 *et seq.*

77   *See* Kilian, *Die Weltkulturerbeliste, supra* note 1, 464 *et seq.*

78   *Cf.* Seng, *Authentizität, supra* note 2 (unpublished manuscript, 2019).

79   "Architecture of adaptation," *cf.* comprehensively, Dieter Bartetzko, Verbaute Geschichte: Stadterneuerung vor der Katastrophe (1986).

on to gain information about the credibility of the aspiring world heritage site. Only this way the different attitudes and traditions of extra-European regions and their "understandings of authenticity" could be taken into account on a level of equality. This was true, in particular, for Asia and there, in particular, Japan.

In 1994, a UNESCO working group developed an Additional Catalog for World Heritage Sites, including now also places where fossils were found, the history of technology,[80] industrial landscapes, natural landscapes, and cultural landscapes (e.g., terraced rice plantings). To this end, regional conferences were held in order to identify such sites and fill the gaps. In 1992, the concept of "cultural landscape" was introduced to include the interaction between humans and nature. It was to protect three expressions of culture: (1) parks: gardens and humans; (2) landscapes dealing with humans and nature (living/ fossil landscapes); and (3) religious, spiritual, artistic, historical associations, intermixed with elements of nature. One thinks , in particular, about the safe-guarding of indigenous cultures (i.e. Uhern Kata Tjuta in Australia, Sukur in Nigeria, Tongariro in New Zealand) and cultural routes as meeting-points of cultures or trade.[81]

The notion of "authenticity" became the key concept for the re-orientation of the List after 2002 and was already referred to in the discussion of the debate over canons. It experienced its breakthrough to the general public, the media, and art history research.[82] This way, via the World Heritage List and the Guidelines, it entered international law.

Authenticity means genuineness, originality, and the "aura" of it (*Walter Benjamin*).[83] At the same time, it embodies credibility, truthfulness, reliability, and sincerity. Relevant, at first, only with respect to the tangible heritage in the World Heritage Convention of 1972, its further development was nudged forward by the Document of Nara. The Convention for the Safeguarding of the Intangible Cultural Heritage of 2003, however, does not use this concept and it is not not discussed up to today in this context. Points of contact are, hew-ever, in the area of artisanal techniques and in the transitions from tangible to intangible heritage.[84]

---

80 For exampler, the Geislinger Steige, built around 1850, is the steepest regular railway track in Europe.

81 Seng, *Kulturerbe zwischen Globalisierung und Lokalisierung, supra* note 2, at 77–78.

82 Seng, *Authentizität, supra* note 2, at 1.

83 *See Das Kunstwerk im Zeitalter seiner technischen Reproduzierbarkeit* (vier Fassungen 1935–39), Zeitschrift für Sozialforschung 1936, 7 *et seq.*, 16 (new ed. Suhrkamp 2007).

84 Seng, *Kulturerbe zwischen Globalisierung und Lokalisierung, supra* note 2, at 70, 79 *et seq.*

The original ten criteria for the inclusion of a site into the List did not include this concept. This changed, however, with the Guidelines of July 1977, which required a "test of authenticity" regarding its design, materials, execution, and surroundings of the site. Original structures and forms could be modernized and supplemented later, to the extent that those additions embodied artistic or historical value of their own. The historical development and the layers of time in the respective environment was to be documented. This requirement was first implemented in the case of the reconstructed Historic Center of Warsaw (which initially was not supposed to be included).

Originally, the Charter of Venice had strictly refused to allow reconstructions and accepted only so-called *anastylons* (the putting together of existing component parts). Only preservation measures were supposed to be allowed, which raises the question of what to do with in their own way unique replicas.[85] Restorations were to be included only in exceptional cases.[86] The Guidelines mandated that reconstructions were only admissible on the basis of vast, detailed documentations or social-psychological studies. In this respect, UNESCO was advised by the International Council on Monuments and Sites (ICOMOS), established in 1965. As a result of this debate, the World Heritage List was now understood to be not solely a static document, but a dynamic one subject to constant change, further emphasizing the requirement of the uniqueness of a site.

Overall, the debate over theory also proved to be tilted toward Europe, as emphasized by the United States, Canada, and, in particular, Asia, and where the Charter of Athens had not been recognized. In Europe, especially, the debate focused on the restoration of central monuments destroyed in the First[87] and, particularly, the Second World War.[88] At the same time, one feared unreflected reconstructions in the nature of "Disneyland."[89]

The central focus of the international debate over authenticity was the *relationship of stone monuments to wooden monuments,* common to Asia, primarily. Dominating here is Japan, where sacred wooden buildings are often rebuilt after twenty years and moved to other locations; a similar practice exists in

---

85   E.g., the one-to-one replica of the door to Paradise of the Cathedral of Florence by Ghiberti, which is now located at WMF in Geislingen/Steige, and has now been better maintained than its original.

86   E.g., St. Mark's Tower in Venice (the Campanile) which crumbled in 1902 and was reconstructed one-to-one.

87   E.g., the Cathedral of Reims, the Ypres Cloth Hall, the Library of Leuven, Belfries in Flanders.

88   E.g., the Dresden Neumarkt and the Frauenkirche.

89   As they are known, e.g., in China, where Heidelberg Castle was rebuilt in its original state.

China. In the Buddhist context, the time frame of such change is about 300–400 years. To this end, a special ICOMOS commission, the so-called Vernacular Commission, was established in 1985. In addition to the Asian states, Norway also moved for taking into account more wooden buidlings, because it has the centuries-old tradition of wooden churches.

Overall, what is relevant is the authenticity of the underlying spirit, not the physical essence of the site. After all, stone sites – as shown by the cathedral workshops – have to be renewed constantly as well. In order to assess authenticity, education and training, communication and dialogue are needed. In the case of reconstructions, it has been agreed upon that they must be "readable" – for them not to be able to fake something that never existed that way.[90]

Of decisive significance was the Document of Nara (Japan) mentioned above, which led to a revision of the criterion of authenticity after UNESCO had established a World Heritage Center of its own as the permanent secretariat of the World Heritage Committee. Due to its wood architecture, Norway insisted, as to authenticity, on five aspects which had not been taken into account sufficiently up to then:

Design/form, material/substance, technology/traditional goals/function as well as context/spirit of a cultural site. Authenticity thus should no longer solely orient itself by reference to the value of a site's monument as such, but would draw upon all available sources of information. Thus buildings made of wood, straw, bamboo, clay or limestone could also be authentic.[91] The result would be a balanced, representative World Heritage List in contrast to Eurocentrism. Subsequently, upon pressure by the Asian member states, the test of authenticity was first weakened, in a reconception of the conditions of inclusion in the List, and it was totally abolished in 2005. Instead, the Guidelines of 2021 include a separate chapter on "authenticity" as mentioned above.

The criticism regarding the *imbalance between the Cultural and the Natural Heritage List* and the global reference list of cultural heritage sites led to the drafting of a "global strategy toward a balanced and credible World Heritage List."[92] Especially Christianity should recede in favor of other religions; monuments of the 20th century should be included, as well as testimonies of still living (indigenous) cultures, regional cultural traditions, and archeological sites.

---

90 Seng, *Authentizität, supra* note 2, at 9 *et seq.*, referring, as examples, to St. Michael's Church in Hildesheim, the Speyer Cathedral, the Residence of Würzburg and other sites rebuilt after wars or natural catastrophes. *See also* Bartetzko, *supra* note 79.

91 For examples, see Seng, *Authentizität, supra* note 2, at 12–13.

92 As stated above, there were perceived to be too many cities of the European Middle Ages, too many Christian sites of the Gothic, too many castles, etc.

The List thus would reflect global cultural diversity and not primarily historical and aesthetically oriented typologies, i.e. anthropological aspects rather than European conceptualizations of art and monuments.

Especially Asian, African, and Latin American members asked for a further convention, the Convention on the Safeguarding of the Intangible Cultural Heritage, adopted in 2003. This request was consistent: substance and materiality should play a lesser role than tradition, repetition and transmission of cultural practices from generation to generation. The criteria of authenticity were thus replaced by the "principle of dynamic tradition."[93] "Cold societies" should be afforded better protection than "hot societies."[94]

The List was intended to change from a documentation of European substantiatedness to the reflection of essence. In order to achieve that, a paradigm shift was necessary: as to the material, from stone to, e.g., wood; as to execution and practice, to smaller, more ordinary forms, the addition of numerous sources of information, such as artisanal techniques, the inclusion of indigenous sites and anthropological concepts of hot/cold societies with hybrid phenomena of preservation and progress, craft as link between tangible and intangible cultural heritage, etc.

Overall, there has been, in theory and practice, a marked shift of the World Heritage List "away from Europe." The loss of influence of the cultural region of Europe is evident. Ultimately, it is a battle between cultures expressing different ways of lives in the age of globalization.

4.4   *The Principle of Sustainability*

In the context of world cultural heritage, *sustainability* means protecting the culture of remembrance for today's and future generations.[95] The concept, coined in environmental law, has been known from forestry since 1713. The term "cultural heritage" was, as mentioned above, introduced by the Bishop of Blois in the face of widespread destruction of cultural sites, in particular churches and monasteries, during the French Revolution. Emer de Vattel saw the protection of cultural heritage in wartime as a necessary component of international law. In the 19th century, cultural heritage was celebrated in the movement to safeguard historical monuments, which, itself, had its roots in

---

93   Seng, *Authentizität, supra* note 2, at 14.

94   Seng, *Authentizität, supra* note 2, at 15 and two examples at 15 *et seq.* (the Narrensprung in Rottweil, and the New Museum in Berlin).

95   *Cf.* Seng, *UNESCO-Weltkulturerbe und der Gedanke der Nachhaltigkeit, supra* note 2, at 77–80.

Romanticism.[96] Immanuel Kant's distinction between civilization and culture as the intellectual-artistic creation in contrast to technology and business further sharpened the understanding of cultural heritage. An expanded conception of culture (as advanced by *Edward Taylor*) also included customs, usages, skills of humans in society, etc.

Concepts of cultural protection were developed by the League of Nations and the United Nations, especially in the form of UNESCO. Culture was supposed to promote peace and solidarity, as exemplified by the rescue of Abu Simbel. In 2005, the idea of an expanded concept of culture begot the "Convention on the Prevention and Promotion of Diversity of Cultural Expressions."[97] The Convention on the Safeguarding of the Intangible Cultural Heritage of 2003 included in its List, analogous to the World Heritage List, customs, rituals, festivals, and knowledge of practices (even if only transmitted orally), etc. This treaty is also based on an expanded concept of culture. As early as 1992, UNESCO established a program called "Memory of the World," which was designed to help archives, libraries, documentation centers, memorial sites, and museums address the impending loss of the memory of humankind via digitalization, Up to now, more than 120 documentations have been digitized, a further aspect of the principle of sustainability.

Sustainability finally includes the goal of cultural education,[98] as the world heritage lists expanded the interest in culture from the sophisticated experts to the general public. The preservation of the sites became a mandate for education and a general trend, evidencing the cooperative and mediating mission of culture. *Eva Seng* thus asks for a long-term strategy for the world heritage sites in the face of climate change, tourism and societal change toward sustainable reservation and transmission of the world's cultural heritage.[99]

---

96   Violet le Duc, Schinkel and others.

97   Convention on the Protection and Promotion of Diversity of Cultural Expressions, adopted at the 33rd Session of the UNESCO General Conference of October 3–21, 2005, preceded by the General Declaration on Cultural Diversity, adopted at the 31st Session of the UNESCO General Conference of November 2001. As to its assessment and the gatering of information, see the analysis of the brochure on "*Good Practices from around the Globe*" by the German UNESCO Commission, featuring 40 projects of all levels. *See also* Seng, *Kulturerbe zwischen Globalisierung und Lokalisierung, supra* note 2, at 69–70.

98   In Germany, the visitorship of world heritage sites doubled by 2009. Seng, *Kulturerbe zwischen Globalisierung und Lokalisierung, supra* note 2, at 79.

99   *Cf.* the UN General Assembly Resolution of December 2010. In 2006, UNDP's International Development Fund was expanded with the promotion of "culture and development," funding 18 programs in developing countries. The EU also has funded a cultural experts pool since 2010–12. Seng, *Kulturerbe zwischen Globalisierung und Lokalisierung, supra* note 2, at 80.

4.5   *Consequences for the Legal Assessment of the List*

The debates as described led to a worldwide departure from the European conception of art and monuments, particularly reflected in the law on historical monuments, and the global acceptance of a an ideology of art and monuments with significantly expanded legal concepts of protection. Those concepts reflected back to the European law on the protection of culture and monuments, triggering novel interpretations and legal supplementations. The extent of this influence on the jurisprudence of historical monuments would need separate analysis.

As far as international law is concerned, the discussions led to a hardening of soft law with multiple effects on national projects that would interfere with a listed world heritage site (Dresden, the Upper Middle Rhine Valley, Cologne, Vienna). One could classify this situation as an intermediate form of "hard" soft law which could not simply be ignored by domestic zoning, environmental or cultural protection law. This assessment is reinforced by the fact that the media and the general public, e.g., via citizens' initiatives, assume the protective function of the law and are empowered to exert pressure on politicians and the administration.[100]

5   The Beginning of a World Cultural Order?

While the 1954 Hague Convention for the Protection of Cultural Property in the Event of Armed Conflict was a first, rather isolated attempt to protect the world's cultural heritage in an extreme situation, i.e. that of war, the World Heritage Convention of 1972–1975 opened up wide the gates to a global, peaceful preservation of culture. This treaty was followed, consistently, by the 2003 Convention on the Safeguarding of the Intangible Cultural Heritage, and, ultimately, also consistently, the 2005 Convention on the Protection and Promotion of the Diversity of Cultural Expressions[101] on the basis of a General Declaration by UNESCO of November 2001.

By adding the WTO's regulations protecting intellectual property (TRIPS), which also include cultural creations in the fields of music, art, literature, architecture, and sculpture, as well as the rules on the *cultural*

---

100   *See* the examples cited by Kilian, *Die Weltkulturerbeliste, supra* note 1, at 457/458. They
       include projects averted in the Upper Middle Rhine Valley, in Stralsund, in Potsdam, and
       in the proximity of Wartburg Castle.
101   UNESCO Convention of October 20, 2005, in force since March 18, 2007.

exception/exemption[102] of world trade law (based on the GATT and, since 1995, the WTO)[103] as well as parts of the international information order, one can discern, from what appears to be, at first blush, a rather random mosaic of legal rules and objects of protection the beginning of a global cultural order.

What is to be desired is a convention which safeguards the preservation of the global cultural infrastructure, of cultural institutions such as museums, exhibitions, opera houses, theaters, etc., a protection of the infrastructure of culture, whose scope and funding, even in cultured states like Germany, is ever more reduced. There is thus a significant gap in the global preservation of the most important musems, theaters, opera houses, etc. which are threatened by closures and deep cuts in support.

Are we witnessing now the emergence of new "sectoral world order" (*Wolfgang Graf Vitzthum*),[104] in analogy, say, to the protection of the marine environment or the world trade regime: a "world order of culture"? Without doubt, this would be a desirable outcome, in light of the most noble mission of culture: to serve the goals of peace and understanding.

6 Final Remarks

One hallmark of international law is the establishment of sectoral world orders. Those are more or less closed partial regimes of segments of international law recognized as important:[105] the law of the sea, the law of the environment and climate change, world trade law, humanitarian international law, international criminal law, etc. Together, they form a comprehensive framework of order. Part upon part, they can ultimately build a closed composite order of global international law.

---

102   *Cf.* Kilian, *Neue Medien ohne Grenzen?, supra* note 4, at 99 *et seq.*

103   The Transatlantic Trade and Investment Partnership (T-TIP) Agreement discussed the concept of "cultural exception."

104   *Cf.* Kilian, *Weltkulturerbeliste, supra* note 1, at 475; further details at Wolfgang Graf Vitzthum, *The Search for Sectoral World Orde*rs, *in* Aspekte der Seerechtsentwicklung (1980), at 273 *et seq.*, the emergent international environmental order, Kilian, Umweltschutz, *supra* note 12, at 396 *et seq.*, 400 *et seq.* Such sectoral world orders include, e.g., the Bern radiofrequency order as precursor and early beginning, followed by the order of the Law of the Sea, the New International Information Order, and the attempt at creating a New International Economic Order.

105   With respect to the law of the conference and the resulting convention, Wolfgang Graf Vitzthum once spoke of the world home of international law, in which every room is freshly painted, one by one.

UNESCO's World Heritage List provided the impetus to establish, step by step, in the subsequent decades, a world order of culture: the protection of cultural heritage, natural heritage, intangible cultural heritage, documents, the biosphere, and much more.

There is, however, the danger of a breakdown of the "one-world idea" of "world culture"[106] (inspired by Johann Wolfgang von Goethe's notion of "world literature") via most recent dislocations within the phenomenon of globalization. The emerging world cultural order is thus already threatened by fissures and disintegration; it meets with resistance and opposition. One hears already talk of a Global South, splitting off from the Global West, and pursuing its own goals. These developments are manifested in the formation of the BRICS group of states and the effects of the conflict in the Ukraine on the non-Western world.

In parallel to the legal tendencies of the formation of a sectoral cultural and monuments world order, even a world order of education and tourism, one can see the rise of Asia in the areas of economic and cultural policy. This is true, in particular, for China (the "Empire of the Middle"), which aspires to an order of its own. The enhanced power and unbroken self-confidence of Asia (the "Global South") is demonstrated by the growing share of China and other Asian countries in the total inventory of the world's cultural heritage. The debates over the revision of the List since 2002, particularly regarding the issues of regional distribution, identity and authenticity, as well as the diversification of the forms of world cultural heritage, ultimately evidence, in parallel, a significantly dwindling influence of the ideas of Europe and the West on international cultural policy and, concomitantly, on world affairs.

---

106   *See* Seng, *Kulturerbe zwischen Globalisierung und Lokalisierung, supra* note 2, at 69.

CHAPTER 26

Reflections on Cultural Identity and Diversity as Common Heritage of Humanity

Fausto Pocar*

1   Introduction

Qualifying cultural diversity as common heritage of humanity may appear to be a paradox, since cultural diversity is almost by definition characterized by distinct approaches and values, which may not have common features but rather reflect different views and lifestyles of the plurality of human communities that compose humankind. It must be borne in mind, however, that, as a matter of international law, diversity has been regarded as a value in itself, to the point that it has been assumed as a basic ground for the protection of fundamental rights in the first international legal instrument ever adopted to describe international human rights and in most subsequent documents.[1] In this context, these brief reflections on the role of cultural identity and diversity as a common heritage of humankind – dedicated to Siegfried Wiessner, an eminent jurist who has extensively contributed to general international law and has shown a special interest in human rights and the protection of indigenous communities, and who honoured me with his friendship for decades – are aimed at contributing to clarify the role of cultural identity and diversity in the light of the framework of the international guarantees for the observance of human rights.

---

*   Professor Emeritus of International Law, University of Milan.

1   *Cf.* Article 2(1), Universal Declaration of Human Rights, UNGA Res. 217 A (III), 10 December 1948 (hereafter "UDHR" or "Universal Declaration"), which stresses that human rights must be enjoyed without distinction of any kind, without however mentioning expressly culture in the non-exhaustive list of prohibited grounds for distinction that it retains. *See also*, with respect to States' general obligation to protect human rights, Article 2 of the two International Covenants of 16 December 1966, respectively on Economic, Social and Cultural Rights (hereafter "ICESCR") and on Civil and Political Rights (hereafter "ICCPR").

2   Culture and Cultural Diversity in the UNESCO Declaration

For the purposes of discussing the place of cultural diversity in international
law and its belonging to the common heritage of humanity, it is hardly necessary to engage in a thorough definition of the terms "culture" and "cultural
diversity." Admittedly, a full and detailed analysis of these terms might help in
identifying exactly the scope of the notion and the holders of rights in the cultural domain. However, such an analysis could not be limited to legal considerations but would also require a sociological and anthropological discussion of
the values, expressions and symbols that characterize a culture, and it would
lead us far beyond the purposes of the present essay. In this context, reference
will therefore be made to the well-known definition that was agreed upon, in
line with the conclusions of several previous conferences, when the Universal
Declaration on Cultural Diversity was adopted in 2001.[2]

The 2001 Declaration is based on a comprehensive notion of "culture," which
is defined in the preamble as the "set of distinctive spiritual, material, intellectual and emotional features of society or a social group, and that it encompasses, in addition to art and literature, lifestyles, ways of living together, value
systems, traditions and beliefs."[3] As such, it comprises a list of features and
values, not necessarily exhaustive, which characterize a society or a social
group. It is worth noting that the accent is put on culture as a collective value
referring to a group of persons.[4]

As to "cultural diversity," it is regarded in the 2001 Declaration as a factual
necessity. Article 1 states that culture "takes diverse forms across time and
space. This diversity is embodied in the uniqueness and plurality of the *identities of the groups and societies* making up humankind. As a source of exchange,
innovation and creativity, cultural diversity is as *necessary* for humankind as
biodiversity is for nature."[5] The consideration that cultural diversity is a factual necessity implies, according to the Declaration, its value as the common

---

2   The Declaration was adopted by the General Conference of UNESCO, 31st session, 2 November
     2001 (hereafter "2001 Declaration"). The Declaration itself mentions, in a footnote, that the
     definition adopted is based on the conclusions of the World Conference on Cultural Policies
     (Mondialcult, Mexico City, 1982), of the World Commission on Culture and Development
     (Our Creative Diversity, 1995), and the Intergovernmental Conference on Cultural Policies for
     Development (Stockholm, 1998).
3   *Cf.* 5th paragraph of the preamble, 2001 Declaration.
4   *See* the 6th paragraph of the preamble, which notes that "culture is at the heart of contem-
     porary debates about identity, social cohesion, and the development of a knowledge-based
     economy."
5   Italics added.

heritage of humanity. Article 1 indeed concludes that: "in this sense [that is in the sense that cultural diversity is as necessary as biodiversity], it is the *common heritage of humanity* and should be recognized and affirmed for the benefit of present and future generations."[6]

The role of cultural diversity as connoting the multiplicity of the identities of the groups and societies existing in the world is reaffirmed and further clarified in subsequent provisions of the 2001 Declaration, especially in Article 2 on cultural pluralism, according to which "[i]n our increasingly diverse societies it is essential to ensure harmonious interaction among people and groups with varied and dynamic *cultural identities* as well as their willingness to live together."[7] Thus, while cultural diversity is a factual notion, cultural pluralism captures the inner political dynamic of that diversity in a democratic society and, through the participation and inclusion of all citizens, ensures social cohesion and vitality. As such, it "gives policy expression to the reality of cultural diversity" and "is conducive to cultural exchange and to the flourishing of creative capacities that sustain public life." This is a feature which is further stressed in the provisions on creativity, which "draws on the roots of cultural tradition, but flourishes in contact with other cultures," with the consequence that "cultural heritage in all its forms must be preserved, enhanced and handed on to future generations as a record of human experience and aspirations, so as to foster creativity in all its diversity and to inspire genuine dialogue among cultures."[8]

3 Cultural Diversity and Human Rights

Although the 2001 Declaration as such does not have any binding force on the States that voted for its adoption, reference has been made so far to it rather than to the subsequent Convention for the Protection and Promotion of the Diversity of Cultural Expressions,[9] which was meant to translate the principles affirmed in the Declaration into positive law. The 2001 Declaration represents indeed, as will be shown, a significantly new perspective with respect to the relationship between cultural diversity and human rights, especially cultural rights, likely to indicate different ways and means for their protection, that are not entirely taken on by the subsequent convention.

---

6 Italics added.
7 Italics added.
8 *Cf.* Article 7, 2001 Declaration.
9 The Convention was adopted by the General Conference of UNESCO, 33rd session, 20 October 2005 (hereafter "2005 Convention").

A discussion of this relationship requires to look back to how culture has played a role in the definition of human rights in the half century that preceded the 2001 Declaration and to how this issue is intertwined with the question of the recognition of rights to minorities and their members.[10] It has already been noted[11] that the Universal Declaration of Human Rights does not mention culture among the prohibited distinctions for the entitlement to human rights, even if it does not exclude that it may be comprised in a list that is clearly non-exhaustive and open to additions.[12]

The recognition in the Universal Declaration of a cultural right that "everyone has the right freely to participate in the cultural life of the community,"[13] may support joining culture to the list. A mention of the cultural life of the community employs, however, an expression that only in part defines the right so recognized, especially because it does not clarify the meaning of the community to which reference should be made. It certainly implies the existence

---

10   This paper will refer particularly to minorities, bearing in mind that the reference also includes indigenous populations in so far as they may be, and most frequently are, qualified also as minorities vis-à-vis the remainder of a country population. The protection of the rights of indigenous populations may however require special and different measures as compared with minorities, including in many cases, when indigenous populations can also be qualified as peoples, the recognition of their right to self-determination, a question that has been highly debated especially in connection with the distinction made sometime in legal doctrine and case-law between internal and external self-determination: see, e.g., Siegfried Wiessner, *Rights and Status of Indigenous Peoples: A Global Comparative and International Legal Perspective*, 12 Harv. Hum. Rts. J. 57, 116–120 (1999); Milena Sterio, Secession in International Law. A New Perspective 10, 27 (2018); Supreme Court of Canada, *In re Secession of Quebec* (1998) 2 S.C.R. 217. On the other hand, the monitoring functions of international bodies on the implementation of minorities' rights and indigenous peoples' rights are also distinct: *see, in general,* Elsa Stamatopoulou-Robbins, *Cultural Rights in International Law: Article 27 of the Universal Declaration and Beyond* 163 ff. (2007). More in particular, as concerns the ICCPR, whose Article 1 sets forth the right of all peoples to self-determination, the Human Rights Committee has accepted its competence to monitor this article's implementation under the States' reporting procedure, but has declined to hear individual cases brought on behalf of indigenous populations claiming a violation of their right to self-determination, and limited its consideration of such cases to alleged violations of minorities' rights under Article 27 of the Covenant: see Communication No 167/1984, *Ominayak and Lubicon Lake Band* v *Canada*, views 26 March 1990, UN Doc. CCPR/C/38/D/167/1984 (1990). For these reasons, references will not be made here to indigenous populations as such and to the relevant literature on the subject.

11   *Supra* note 1.

12   Like the UDHR, the 1966 Covenants prohibit distinction "of any kind, such as..."; furthermore, the enumeration of the prohibited distinctions in the list ends by referring in general to "other status", which may also comprise culture.

13   Article 27 UDHR.

of a group or society with common ways of living and values, but it does not specify whether any group or society is coming into play, other than the state-community to which a person belongs. Bearing in mind that the Universal Declaration is not directly aimed at establishing States' obligations,[14] and that another article mentioning a community does not refer to a state-community,[15] one may argue that the provision also intended to comprise any group or society irrespective of their qualification. However, the circumstance that the Universal Declaration was adopted within the framework of the United Nations Charter and the Member States' obligations to protect human rights therein described, as well as that the word "community" is employed in the provision concerning duties to the community which clearly refers to States,[16] may lead to a different conclusion.

This different conclusion may also be supported by the fact that the Universal Declaration ignores altogether any mention of rights of persons belonging to social groups as minorities or indigenous populations, probably also out of the concern not to encourage minority groups to act as entities representing the interests of a particular community vis-à-vis the State representing the interests of the entire population,[17] as well as to foster the development of movements aiming at independence from colonial domination.[18]

---

14 Although the UDHR, as a resolution of the UNGA, does not have binding force by itself, its legislative role may find support in the constant reference to it in State practice for defining the scope of international obligations in the human rights field.

15 Cf. Article 18 on the freedom to manifest religion or belief "alone or in community with others", where, however, the community is a qualified one.

16 Cf. Article 29(1) UDHR.

17 The question of including in the UDHR a provision on national minorities was discussed, but eventually a Soviet Union's proposal in that sense was rejected because of the complexity of the issue. The real reason for excluding minorities from the UDHR was rather the negative position of the States which were carrying out a policy of assimilation of the numerous immigrants and of the indigenous populations on their territory. Whether similar reasons contributed also to excluding cultural groups from the draft convention on genocide has been pointed out by Johannes Morsink, *Cultural Genocide, the Universal Declaration, and Minority Rights*, 21 Hum. Rts. Q. 1009–1060 (1999). The UNGA adopted therefore a separate resolution entitled "Fate of Minorities," in which it stated the UN "cannot remain indifferent to the fate of minorities," and requested the Council to ask the Commission on Human Rights and the Sub-Commission on the Prevention of Discrimination and the Protection of Minorities to make a thorough study of the problem of minorities, in order that the UN may be able to take effective measures for the protection of "racial, national, religious or linguistic minorities": UNGA Res. 217 C (III), 10 December 1948.

18 The UDHR was meant to promote the proclaimed rights and freedoms "among the peoples of Member States themselves and among the peoples of territories under their jurisdiction": *see* the chapeau of the dispositive part of the Declaration.

A similar and even more prudent approach to cultural rights appears to characterize much later the International Covenants aimed at imposing legal obligations on States reflecting the principles proclaimed in the Universal Declaration. It is noteworthy – and somewhat disturbing – that the ICESCR restricts cultural rights to a detailed description of the obligation of States Parties to ensure the right to education at all levels, which is no doubt extremely important and instrumental for the protection of all human rights (not just cultural rights), and, when it comes to other cultural rights, it simply reproduces the principle proclaimed in the UDHR without adding any required qualification, as earlier mentioned, but rather increasing ambiguity and even suggesting a restrictive interpretation. Article 15(1)(a) imposes on States parties the obligation to recognize the right of everyone "to take part in cultural life," dropping the mentioning of a community and thus deleting any reference to the collective dimension of cultural life. This text seems to limit the States Parties' obligations to ensuring the individual right to participate in cultural life as permitted and regulated by the State rather than as collectively developed in non-state communities.[19]

The question of the recognition of a right to culture of minorities, neglected in the UDHR and in the ICESCR, was, however, addressed in the other Covenant adopted at the same time, as a matter of civil and political rights. According to Article 27 of the ICCPR "in those States in which ethnic, religious or linguistic minorities exist, persons belonging to such minorities shall not be denied the right, in community with the other members of their group, to enjoy their own culture, to profess and practice their own religion, or to use their own language." This provision – the only binding provision in international treaty law – represents an important step forward in expressly recognizing the culture of a group or a community having cultural characteristics different from those of the other remainder of the population.

However, although it emphasizes that the right of persons belonging to minorities to enjoy their own culture may be exercised in community with the other members of the group, by setting aside the option of recognizing a collective right of the community as such, the text fails to expressly set out an obligation of the States Parties to ensure an adequate protection of that culture in its collective dimension. Second, the scope of application of the provision is limited to States in which minorities exist, thus allowing States parties

---

19   This possible reading has been regarded later as unwarranted in subsequent interpretations: *see,* however, *infra* at note 31. *See also* for a progressive but prudent interpretation of this provision Roger O' Keefe, *The 'Right to Take Part in Cultural Life' under Article 15 of the ICESCR,* 47 Int'l & Comp. L.Q. 904–923 (1998).

to challenge the existence of minorities on their territory.[20] Furthermore, it restricts the concerned minorities to those qualified as ethnic, religious and linguistic, thus excluding other minorities, especially cultural groups that may not meet these qualifications.[21] Lastly, by saying that persons belonging to minorities "shall not be denied the right ... to enjoy their culture", it does not provide an express positive obligation of the States parties to fully ensure the individual right to enjoy a minority culture.[22]

---

20   This was especially the case of France, which, on acceding to the Covenant, made a declaration stating that "in the light of article 2 of the Constitution of the French Republic [according to which, inter alia, the language of the Republic is French], the French Government declares that article 27 is not applicable so far as the Republic is concerned." The interpretation of this declaration is uncertain. On one hand, the Human Rights Committee has rightly pointed out that the rights protected under Article 27 should be kept distinct from the rights that States are bound to ensure to all individuals under the Covenant without discrimination, and thus that "States parties who claim that they do not discriminate on grounds of ethnicity, language or religion wrongly contend, on that basis alone, that they have no minorities" (see HRC, General Comment No 23, Article 27, 8 April 1994, CCPR/C/21/Rev.1/Add.5, para 4). On the other hand, the Committee has decided in several individual cases under the Optional Protocol that "France's 'declaration' made in respect of this provision [art. 27] is tantamount to a reservation and therefore precludes the Committee from considering complaints against France alleging violations of Article 27 of the Covenant": see Communication No. 347/1988, *S.G.* v *France*, Inadmissibility decision 1 November 1991, *Selected Decisions of the Human Rights Committee under the Optional Protocol*, vol. 4, CCPR/C/OP/4, para 5.3), with a dissenting Individual Opinion of Rosalyn Higgins; see also No. 549/1993, *T. Hopu and T. Bessert* v *France*, Views 29 July 1997, *ibidem*, vol. 6, CCPR/C/OP/6, para 4.3.

21   The question whether culture should also be mentioned as qualifying by itself as a protected group was discussed in the Sub-Commission during the elaboration of a definition of minorities but eventually answered negatively, on the assumption that a reference to ethnicity, rather than to race as initially proposed, alongside religion and language, would be sufficient to cover the cultural characteristics of the protected groups (*cf.* UN Doc. E/CN.4/Sub.2/SR.48). *See also*, in the sense that culture is essentially linked to ethnicity, Ruwadzano P. Makumbe, *An alternative conceptualization of indigenous rights in Africa under the international human rights law framework*, Deusto J. Hum. Rts. 143, 146 (2018). It is interesting that a similar approach was also followed, together with other arguments (*see supra* note 17), in rejecting the proposal to include cultural groups from the protected groups under the 1948 Convention on the Prevention and Punishment of the Crime of Genocide, although the question may be still open under customary international law: see Fausto Pocar, *Genocide (prevention)*, Dictionnaire encyclopédique de la justice pénale internationale 480 (Olivier Beauvallet ed., 2017).

22   The existence of a positive obligation to ensure the protection of the existence and the exercise of the right recognized in Article 27 against denial or violation has, however, been maintained by the Human Rights Committee: see General Comment No 23, *supra* note 20, para 6.1.

4   The UN Declaration on the Human Rights of Members of
      Minorities

The problems that the interpretation of Article 27 ICCPR could raise prompted
the preparation of a study on the implementation of the principles therein
set out,[23] and later the establishment of an open-ended working group of the
Commission on Human Rights tasked with drafting a declaration on the rights
of members of minorities within the principles set forth in the said provision.[24]
The work, however, was dragging on for some years, until the outbreak of
the war in the Balkans at the beginning of the nineties of last century accelerated the drafting of a document on minorities' rights; the Declaration on
the Human Rights of Persons Belonging to National or Ethnic, Religious and
Linguistic Minorities was eventually adopted in 1992.[25]

This instrument – the only UN instrument specifically devoted to minorities' human rights – was a breakthrough as regards the protection of the
collective identity of the minorities, although it keeps the focus on the individual rights of persons belonging to minorities that characterizes Article 27
of the ICCPR.

As compared with the ICCPR provision, the 1992 Declaration contains a
more detailed description of the implications of the right to enjoy their own
culture, to profess and practice their own religion and to use their own language,[26] and, more importantly, departs from the statement that States should
simply not deny these rights. It provides the positive obligation of States to
take measures to ensure that persons belonging to minorities may exercise
fully and effectively all their human rights and fundamental freedoms without
any discrimination and in full equality before the law, as well as to take measures to create favourable conditions to enable persons belonging to minorities

---

23   *See* Francesco Capotorti, *Study on the Rights of Persons belonging to Ethnic, Religious and
      Linguistic Minorities*, E/CN.4/Sub.2/384 and Add. 1–7 (1977). The study was conducted as
      of 1971 within the framework of the Sub-Commission on Prevention of Discrimination
      and Protection of Minorities by the author as Special Rapporteur and was concluded in
      1977.
24   The recommendation that the Commission on Human Rights consider drafting a declara-
      tion on the rights of members of minorities was made by the Sub-Commission following
      a suggestion the Special Rapporteur, who observed that, particularly as regards ethnic and
      linguistic minorities, "the implications of such minorities to preserve their own culture
      and use their own language are not clearly defined" and that it would have been useful to
      draw up certain principles for guidance. *See* Capotorti, *supra* note 23, para 617.
25   The Declaration was adopted without a vote by a UNGA resolution: A/Res/47/135, 18
      December 1992 (hereafter "1992 Declaration").
26   *Cf.* Article 2, 1992 Declaration.

to express their characteristics and to develop their culture, language, religion, traditions and customs, except when specific practices are in violation of national law and contrary to international standards.[27]

Even more importantly, these provisions are preceded by and represent the development of a general obligation of States to recognize the collective dimension of the minorities. According to Article 1 of the 1992 Declaration, "States shall protect the existence of the national or ethnic, cultural, religious and linguistic *identity* of minorities within their respective territories and shall encourage conditions for the *promotion of that identity*. States shall adopt appropriate legislative and other measures to achieve those ends."[28] On one hand, this provision sets forth an obligation for States to recognize and protect the existence of the minorities' identity and to act in favor of promoting such identity; on the other hand, it imposes on States an obligation to adopt positive measures to ensure that the goals of protection and promotion of that identity are achieved. Here is the breakthrough, since no earlier UN instrument had expressly provided for the protection of the collective dimension of minorities or other groups. Although merely cultural groups are not protected as such, this development is particularly significant with respect to the cultural identity of the protected groups, since culture is a common necessary qualification of any group of persons, irrespective of other grounds for defining that group.

With respect to the relationship between culture and human rights, the 1992 Declaration shows also an important development. Setting the protection and promotion of the cultural identity of social groups like the minorities as the primary obligation of States, as well as setting that obligation before all the provisions concerning the individual human rights of the members of the minorities,[29] the Declaration affirms that such protection and promotion are

---

27   *Cf.* Article 4(1) and (2), 1992 Declaration.

28   Article 1(1) and (2), 1992 Declaration. Italics added. The importance of this provision in the 1992 Declaration is also stressed by Joseph Yacoub, *Cultural diversity and international law. In the field of human rights and identities*, Sens Public. Revue internationale. International Webjournal 1–12 (2010), *available at* http://www.sens-public.org/IMG/pdf/SensPublic _JYacoub_Cultural_diversity_Multilinguism_and_Ethnic_minorities_in_Sweden.pdf.

29   It may be interesting to recall that until the last meeting of the session of the drafting working-group which discussed and finalized the text of the Declaration, the provision concerning the obligation of States to protect and promote the identity of minorities appeared in the preliminary documents as article 4, after the other state-obligations concerning the specific rights of persons belonging to minorities now enshrined in articles 2–4, and that the order was expressly changed at the last reading to emphasize the priority and the role that the recognition of the existence and the protection and promotion of the collective identity of the group plays for the enjoyment of the individual human rights of its members.

a requirement or a prerequisite for the enjoyment of the human rights of their members, particularly cultural rights. In other terms, the recognition of the collective identity of the group is a condition for the protection of the individual rights of its members, and not the other way round, as it could be drawn by a mere reference to the protection of individual rights of the members of the group.

5   The Impact of the UN Declaration on Minorities

This new perspective has clearly influenced the subsequent interpretation of the existing provisions concerning cultural rights as laid down in the Covenants. With respect to the ICCPR, a couple of years later the Human Rights Committee stated that "although the rights protected under Article 27 are individual rights, they depend in turn on the ability of the minority group to maintain its culture, language or religion," and that "positive measures by States may also be necessary to protect the identity of a minority."[30] As to Article 15 of the ICESCR on the right to take part in cultural life, the guidelines for the submission of State reports solicited information on the promotion of cultural identity as a factor of mutual appreciation among individuals, groups, nations and regions, and the commentary of the then president of the relevant monitoring Committee ("CESCR") underlined the constantly growing awareness of the importance of cultural identity, especially for groups such as minorities, indigenous peoples, immigrants, and others whose cultural roots and traditions differ from those of the majority.[31]

---

30   *See* General Comment No 23, *supra* note 20, para 6.2.

31   *See* Philip Alston, *Commentary* (on Article 15 ICESCR), UN Manual on Human Rights Reporting 154 (1997). This perspective has been later developed in a more recent General Comment issued by the CESCR on Article 15 of the Covenant, where the Committee however maintains that the right of persons belonging to minorities to take part in the cultural life of society and also to conserve, promote and develop their own culture, "entails the obligation of State parties to recognize, respect and protect minority cultures as an essential component of the identity of the States themselves." This proposition appears indeed to downplay the role and the importance of the specific cultural identity of the minority and to conflate it with the identity of the State, in contrast with the view expressed in the 1992 Declaration and later in the 2001 Declaration which refer to the culture of a minority and respectively of a group as distinct from the culture of the society as a whole: *cf.* CESCR, General Comment No 21, Right of everyone to take part in cultural life (art. 15, para. 1a) (2009), UN Doc. E/C.12/GC/21, at 32. *See*, however, on the progress that this General Comment represents in the clarification of the States' obligations under Article 15 ICESCR, Athanasios Yupsanis, *The Meaning of 'Culture' in Article 15(1)(a)*

In this context, it is not surprising that the new perspective could influence the 2001 Declaration in stating, a few years later, that the cultural identity of social groups is a necessary component for affirming that cultural diversity is a common heritage of humankind. Furthermore, dealing with cultural diversity and human rights, especially cultural rights, in their individual dimension,[32] the Declaration insisted, as mentioned earlier, on cultural identity as a qualification of groups and societies, and stated that the diversity of cultural identities implies a commitment to human rights and fundamental freedoms, in particular the rights of persons belonging to minorities and those of indigenous populations.[33] By insisting on the cultural identity of social groups, it departed from the mere reference to the individual dimension of human rights that characterized previous human rights instruments and emphasized the need for the safeguard and the promotion of the collective identity for the full enjoyment of human rights.

Although it may be true that an indirect reference to a need for the protection of the cultural identity of the group may be drawn implicitly from a provision focused on the enjoyment of the individual right to take part in the cultural life of the community, it is not without significance, however, that the importance of the protection of the cultural identity as such has been recognized in the 2001 Declaration, especially in the light of the consideration that such a recognition was missing in all previous international instruments.

The question remains open, however, and even the 2001 Declaration does not resolve it expressly, whether the so affirmed obligation to protect the existence and to promote the cultural identity of a social group is also accompanied by the obligation to do it with respect to any cultural group irrespective of other qualifications of that group. The precedent instruments appear to express themselves in the negative. Article 27 of the UDHR refers to an individual right to participate in the cultural life of the community, without qualifying the latter, but avoiding any reference to minorities or other groups.

As to the only binding instruments, Article 15 of the ICESCR repeats the wording of the UDHR but with the deletion of the word "community," and Article 27 of the ICCPR provides for the right of members of minorities to enjoy their own culture, but explicitly restricts this right to members of ethnic,

---

of the ICESCR – *Positive Aspects of CESCR's General Comment No. 21 for the Safeguarding of Minority Cultures*, 55 German Y.B. Int'l L. 346–383 (2012); Laura Pineschi, *Cultural Diversity as a Human Right? General Comment No. 21 of the Committee on Economic, Social and Cultural Rights*, Cultural Heritage, Cultural Rights, Cultural Diversity 29–53 (Silvia Borelli & Federico Lenzerini eds.,2012).

32   *See, particularly,* Article 5, 2001 Declaration.

33   Article 4, 2001 Declaration.

religious and linguistic groups, on the assumption that culture is comprised in these qualifications, especially in the qualification of a group as ethnic.[34] Other groups, including cultural minorities, do not enjoy the same protection. The same applies to the 1992 Declaration, which was "inspired" by the provisions of article 27 of the ICCPR and did not discuss its scope as to the definition of minorities.[35]

The only document, which does not contain a limitation as to the qualifications of the concerned groups, but only uses the expression "groups and societies making up humankind," is therefore the 2001 Declaration, which mentions that cultural diversity implies a commitment to human rights and refers, in particular, to rights of persons belonging to minorities without any qualification. It is true that it also specifies that the reference is made to human rights "as guaranteed by international law," but only for the purpose of prohibiting to invoke cultural diversity to infringe upon human rights or to limit their scope. Thus, an interpretation of the Declaration that extends the protection and includes cultural groups among those eligible for protection as such may be permitted.

6   The Convention on the Diversity of Cultural Expressions

The task of transposing the 2001 Declaration into positive law has been taken on, as it has already been mentioned, by the Convention on the Protection and Promotion of the Diversity of Cultural Expressions, concluded in Paris in 2005.[36] The Convention, however, appears to take a step back from the 2001 Declaration, and to return to a former perspective, omitting – except for a preambular recital – a reference to the obligation to protect the collective identity of cultural groups and limiting itself to providing for the protection of the individual right of the members of the community to take part in their own cultural life. Unlike the 2001 Declaration, even when it refers to a dialogue among cultures, it intends the protection and promotion of such a dialogue as based on "the diversity of cultural expressions,"[37] which is a formulation that does not underline the identity of different cultural groups as such, but rather the

---

34   *See supra* note 21.

35   Except for adding the qualification "national" to the minorities comprised within the protected groups, in order to distinguish groups that may be characterized by a nationality though belonging to the same ethnicity (an issue that does not need to be discussed here).

36   *See supra* note 9.

37   Art. 1(a), 2005 Convention.

different ways of manifestation of culture by the members of a group and thus the individual rights of each of them.

In this perspective, the 2005 Convention underscores that "cultural diversity can be protected and promoted only if human rights and fundamental freedoms, such as freedom of expression, information and communication, as well as the ability of individuals to choose cultural expressions, are guaranteed."[38] Under this provision, the protection and promotion of cultural diversity depends therefore on the safeguards provided for individual human rights, especially the right to freedom of expression, and requires such guarantee as a condition. This approach is manifestly different from the approach of the 2001 Declaration in so far as the latter predicated that the defense of cultural diversity implies a commitment to human rights and fundamental freedoms, especially cultural rights of the persons belonging to minorities and those of indigenous peoples, and among them the right to quality education and training that fully respect their cultural identity and the right to participate in the cultural life of their choice.[39]

In this context, it seems appropriate to note that the protection and promotion of the freedom of cultural expressions, which is no doubt a significant feature of the protection of the protection of the freedom to participate in cultural life, does not exhaust the scope of the required protection, as it is the case for other human rights, where the scope of the freedom to publicly exercise a right does not cover entirely the protection of the right itself. The rights to freedom of thought and to hold opinions are relevant examples. While these rights enjoy an absolute protection, without the possibility of any restriction, the freedom to manifest one's thought or to express opinions is subjected to restrictions prescribed by law which may be necessary for the respect of the rights of others or for the protection of national security, public order, public health or morals.[40] In the light of these examples, it may not be a daring conclusion to state that also the cultural identity of a social group should enjoy protection irrespective of the protection afforded to the members of the group in expressing that identity.[41] Hence cultural diversity, resulting from

---

38   Art. 2(1), 2005 Convention.

39   *Cf.* Articles 4 and 5, 2001 Declaration.

40   *Cf.*, in particular, Article 19, ICCPR. *See also*, in the same sense, Article 18 of the same treaty regarding the freedom of thought, conscience and religion.

41   Incidentally, freedom of expression must be safeguarded in full equality, even vis-à-vis persons all belonging to a social group characterized by the same cultural identity, whereas, under international law, as it has been seen at the beginning of these notes, cultural diversity is a matter concerning the plurality of the identities of the groups and societies making up humankind.

the existence of different cultural identities, should be protected as such without an intermediary role of the diversity of cultural expressions, as the 2005 Convention seems to posit.

This conclusion is all the more justified as the cultural identity of a group, like the freedom to hold opinions, is not subjected to restrictions of any kind, unlike the freedom of expression of opinions which, as it has just been clarified, may face inherent limitations and, in case of public emergency, formal derogations under the law.[42] Defining the scope of the protection of cultural diversity through the protection of cultural expressions implies therefore a restriction of the recognition of cultural diversity to the ways different cultures are manifested by its members, with the risk of subjecting the protection of cultural diversity to the limitations that it may encounter under national law, as it implicitly derives from the text of the 2005 Convention. It cannot go unnoticed in this respect, and cannot be unintentional, that the Convention mentions among its objectives "to reaffirm the sovereign rights of States to maintain, adopt and implement policies and measures that they deem appropriate for the protection and promotion of the diversity of cultural expressions on their territory,"[43] and reiterates this objective among the guiding principles of the Convention[44] and the obligations of the States parties.[45]

Thus, the Convention does not provide for precise obligations of States parties to promote and protect the identity of cultural groups and societies as such, but only to protect aspects of their identity as far as they are an expression thereof, with the limitations that freedom of expression may suffer under international human rights law. Consequently, the collective identity enshrined in the culture of groups and societies is protected only indirectly, insofar as it is reflected in its cultural expression by members of such groups or societies. The same applies, as a result, to the protection of cultural diversity as a common heritage of humanity.

---

42   *Cf.* Article 4, ICCPR. For the distinction between limitations or restrictions to, and derogations from human rights, see especially Rosalyn Higgins, *Derogations under Human Rights Treaties*, 48 Brit. Y.B. Int'l L. 81–319 (1976); and, more recently, Ilaria Viarengo, *Deroghe e restrizioni alla tutela dei diritti umani nei sistemi internazionali di garanzia*, 88 Rivista di diritto internazionale 955–997 (2005).

43   Article 1 (h), 2005 Convention.

44   Article 2(2), 2005 Convention.

45   Article 5(1), 2005 Convention.

7   Conclusion

The conclusion of these brief notes is that, notwithstanding the efforts made by the international community and its organizations, positive specific obligations of States to promote and protect the cultural identity of groups and societies, and thus consequently their cultural diversity, are still missing in international treaty law, although a progressive interpretation of existing binding as well as non-binding instruments may reduce the significance of that gap. Whether an analysis of international practice may lead to conclude that customary international law is moving towards a greater recognition of the cultural identity of groups and societies is an issue that would require a thorough and detailed consideration of situations having distinct historical, social, economic and legal features that it may be difficult to compare and from which it may be difficult to draw uniform conclusions, other than the existence of an aspiration of the international community to protect cultural diversity as a common heritage of humanity. All the more because the practice shows that States have frequently manifested a clear reluctance to recognize the collective identity of social groups other than that of the majority population, probably out of the fear that the recognition of such identities might eventually result in a threat to the preservation of the territorial integrity of the State and eventually undermine their sovereignty.

CHAPTER 27

Cultural Heritage in International Indigenous Rights Declarations: Beyond Recognition

Lucas Lixinski*

1 Introduction

The landscape on the rights of Indigenous peoples has shifted considerably in the early 21st century. Two major international instruments – the United Nations Declaration on the Rights of Indigenous Peoples of 2007 (UNDRIP)[1] and the American Declaration on the Rights of Indigenous Peoples of 2016 (ADRIP)[2] – have been adopted, leading to much celebration and further galvanizing among Indigenous rights activists and academics alike.[3] Further, domestic and international jurisprudence has increasingly recognized the rights of Indigenous peoples in a range of contexts from land rights to consultation to the impacts of land evictions on the integrity of a people to a broader embrace of economic, social, and cultural rights.[4] While these developments have represented undeniable advances in the area of Indigenous rights, there is still much additional work to be done.

---

* Professor, Faculty of Law & Justice, UNSW Sydney; Associate, Australian Human Rights Institute. Some of this chapter builds on previous and forthcoming work. *See* Lucas Lixinski, *Indigenous (Intangible) Cultural Heritage and the Unfulfilled Promises of Rights Declarations, in* Indigenous Rights: Changes and Challenges for the 21st Century 41–58 (Sarah Sargent & Jo Samanta eds., 2019); and Lucas Lixinski, *Article 11, in* United Nations Declaration on the Rights of Indigenous Peoples: Article-by-Article Commentary (Jessica Eichler et al. eds., *forthcoming*). It also builds on the work of the International Law Association's Committee on Participation in Global Cultural Heritage Governance, which ended its mandate in June 2022 and of which I had the honor to serve as Rapporteur.

1 United Nations Declaration on the Rights of Indigenous Peoples (UNDRIP), A/61/295 (Adopted 13 December 2007).

2 American Declaration on the Rights of Indigenous Peoples (ADRIP), AG/RES. 2888 (XLVI-O/16) (Adopted at the third plenary session, held on June 15, 2016).

3 In relation to the UNDRIP, see, for instance, Siegfried Wiessner, *The Cultural Rights of Indigenous Peoples: Achievements and Continuing Challenges*, 22 Eur. J. Int'l L. 121–140 (2011).

4 For a critical overview in particular of international jurisprudence, see Beatriz Garcia & Lucas Lixinski, *Beyond Culture: Reimagining the Adjudication of Indigenous Peoples' Rights in International Law*, 15 Intercultural Hum. Rts. L. Rev. 127 (2020).

One of the particular areas in which more work needs to be done is the area of Indigenous rights in relation to their cultural heritage. There are many long and painful accounts of historical and ongoing appropriation of Indigenous knowledge, artefacts, and even bodies in the name of colonialism, science, and the shared heritage of humanity.[5] In all these moves, Indigenous voice has remained largely absent or elusive, under protestations of cultural heritage as being a vehicle for national identity which either flew in the face of Indigenous resistance,[6] or appropriated it to generate a claim for distinctiveness for elites of non-Indigenous ancestry.[7] While both declarations contain provisions on cultural heritage, these provisions for the most part are only declaratory acknowledgements of Indigenous peoples having a right to access their own heritage. While declaratory recognition and access are very important, particularly considering that Indigenous rights are fundamentally grounded on culture,[8] they tend to fall short of giving Indigenous peoples full control over their heritage, let alone provide for remedies. In other words, we pay lip service to a fundamental facet, if not normative foundation, of Indigenous rights, but do not do enough to shore up effectiveness of these rights. As a result, the foundation of Indigenous rights remains on shifty grounds.

I argue in this chapter that, if we are serious about the emancipatory potential of these two instruments, we need to do more to move beyond declaratory recognition, and need to increasingly lend teeth to cultural heritage rights. While the declarations were in many respects what was possible to achieve at the time, and a positive step forward, we must not allow for complacency. I further argue that the best way to ensure the effectiveness of these instruments is to go in a different direction from what they propose: while these declarations announce substantive rights, in many ways I suggest the best responses to these claims lie in institutional design instead. Better institutional design means an *a priori* engagement with Indigenous needs and voice, which sets

---

5 For a collection of essays, see The Sound of Silence: Indigenous Perspectives on the Historical Archaeology of Colonialism (Tiina Äikäs & Anna-Kaisa Salmi eds., 2019).

6 Denis Byrne, *The Ethos of Return: Erasure and Reinstatement of Aboriginal Visibility in the Australian Historical Landscape*, 37 Historical Archaeology 73 (2003).

7 The Americas are a very typical example. *See* Lucas Lixinski, *Central and South America, in* The Oxford Handbook of International Cultural Heritage Law 878 (Francesco Francioni & Ana Filipa Vrdoljak eds., 2020).

8 Karen Engle, The Elusive Promise of Indigenous Development: Rights, Culture, Strategy (2010).

much firmer ground for Indigenous peoples' participation, allowing them to set the fundamental parameters within which their claims are discussed.[9]

In order to pursue these claims, the next part of this chapter focuses on the ways in which Indigenous cultural heritage rights appear in the two declarations. The section after that makes the claim that the language in these instruments does not go far enough, and that remedies and institutional design are necessary to enable the full potential of Indigenous aspirations.

A word on positionality is warranted: I am not myself Indigenous, nor do I claim to have the answers to what Indigenous peoples wish and aspire to at the specific level. What I can do instead from my relatively privileged position of a white male cisgender and able-bodied Latin American migrant now an academic in a Global North institution, is simply to drive home the message that better spaces for Indigenous voice and direction are needed, and can be carved out, through building on the achievements of rights declarations. To do so, however, first requires scrutinizing the content and reach of these declarations, particularly in the area of cultural heritage.

2   Cultural Heritage in International Indigenous Rights Declarations

Both the UNDRIP and the ADRIP contain a number of specific provisions on Indigenous heritage safeguarding. Considering the centrality of culture for Indigenous rights, the existence of these provisions is not surprising. They focus on the markers of culture found in heritage, both tangible and intangible, and introduce avenues for the recognition and safeguarding of Indigenous heritage. The most significant problem with the idea of protecting culture as heritage is the very commodification that necessarily ensues, in a way that "cultural heritage becomes revered over, and disembodied from, the very peoples associated with it."[10] For the purposes of the survival of a culture, culture as heritage is still seen as an effective (or at least appropriate) advocacy tool, despite the grave risk of commodification and folklorization. The objective of cultural survival seems to fit well within the limits of self-determination in the

---

9   International Law Association, Participation in Global Cultural Heritage Governance – Final Report (2022) ("ILA Committee on Participation Final Report") (on file with the author).

10   Engle, Elusive Promise, *supra* note 8, at 142.

UNDRIP and ADRIP.[11] The UNDRIP and ADRIP both protect Indigenous heritage, containing several provisions on these themes.

There are many provisions on Indigenous culture in these declarations. Dorough and Wiessner call attention to multiple provisions in the UNDRIP in particular.[12] The main provisions on Indigenous heritage in the UNDRIP (Articles 11 and 31)[13] speak primarily of the right to practice and revitalize traditions, with some reference to remedies (Article 11.2) and control (Article 31.1). For the purposes of this chapter, I will focus primarily on the practice under Article 11 UNDRIP, which encapsulates Indigenous heritage more broadly, without being captured by the debates on intellectual property rights prompted by Article 31.

Article 11 is often read as meaning, fundamentally, a diffuse right to culture which contains within itself the right to cultural heritage. The right to culture has been interpreted in line with broader trends, connecting cultural heritage and human rights, which focus on "access," "contribution," "participation," and

---

11   The full provision is as follows: "Article 3. Indigenous peoples have the right of self-determination. By virtue of that right they freely determine their political status and freely pursue their economic, social and cultural development." For a broader discussion of heritage listing as self-determination, coupling the Wayúu example with Ladakh Buddhist Chanting in India, see Lucas Lixinski, *Heritage Listing as Self-determination*, *in* Heritage, Culture, and Rights: Challenging Legal Discourses 227 (Andrea Durbach & Lucas Lixinski eds., 2017).

12   Dalee Sambo Dorough & Siegfried Wiessner, *Indigenous Peoples and Cultural Heritage*, *in* The Oxford Handbook of International Cultural Heritage Law 407, 412–413 (Francesco Francioni & Ana Filipa Vrdoljak eds., 2020) (including also articles 7, 10, 12, 13, 14, 16, 18, 19, and 25).

13   The full provisions are as follows: "Article 11. 1. Indigenous peoples have the right to practice and revitalize their cultural traditions and customs. This includes the right to maintain, protect and develop the past, present and future manifestations of their cultures, such as archaeological and historical sites, artefacts, designs, *ceremonies*, technologies and visual and performing arts and literature. 2. States shall provide redress through effective mechanisms, which may include restitution, developed in conjunction with indigenous peoples, with respect to their cultural, intellectual, religious and spiritual property taken without their free, prior and informed consent or in violation of their laws, traditions and customs." (emphasis added) and "Article 31. 1. Indigenous peoples have the right to maintain, control, protect and develop their cultural heritage, traditional knowledge and traditional cultural expressions, as well as the manifestations of their sciences, technologies and cultures, including human and genetic resources, seeds, medicines, knowledge of the properties of fauna and flora, oral traditions, literatures, designs, sports and traditional games and visual and performing arts. They also have the right to maintain, control, protect and develop their intellectual property over such cultural heritage, traditional knowledge, and traditional cultural expressions. 2. In conjunction with indigenous peoples, States shall take effective measures to recognize and protect the exercise of these rights."

"enjoyment."[14] The right to culture rarely means control over one's culture. It is noteworthy that there is no direct reference to the right to control said culture, or to own it, rather the rights spelled out are rights of use and enjoyment, which might imply a comparatively weaker form of human rights protection. By making culture central to rights and identity, but control over the same culture and its meanings and uses unattainable, Indigenous rights end up being weakened. In other words, the recognition of Indigenous cultural rights, by not being stronger on control, can have disempowering effects. Article 11 refers to a series of specific manifestations of culture, which map onto different domains of heritage, even if the term is not stipulated in the provision; in fact, "heritage" only appears once in the entire UNDRIP, in Article 31 (which does use the word "control").

Among the possible meanings of culture in relation to Indigenous rights, culture as heritage is arguably one of the weakest manifestations, because (international) heritage law speaks of stewardship over the culture in the name of society as a whole, while state-centrism prevails as a proxy for the group.[15] However, there is much promise to heritage, because it can be about control over its uses and meanings. There is growing practice suggesting increasing control by communities, including Indigenous communities, over their heritage. Control over culture shaped as heritage holds the promise to deliver more than actually facilitating access and participation; it can also catalyze more tangible forms of power. Therefore, reading heritage out of Article 11 is not only inconsistent with its meaning just beneath the surface of terminological choices, it also undermines what can be its strongest tool to deliver change in favour of Indigenous peoples.

The two parts of Article 11, taken together, suggest a focus on the right to cultural heritage that is more specific than a broad right to culture. While the language of rights is present, Article 11 focuses on specific "manifestations" of culture, and calls for remedies in relation to Indigenous "cultural, intellectual, religious and spiritual property."

Article 11 distinguishes itself from the other provisions for its focus on the practice and revitalization of culture and cultural heritage through its maintenance, protection, and development. It is also the only provision in the

---

14   Yvonne Donders, *Cultural Heritage and Human Rights, in* The Oxford Handbook of International Cultural Heritage Law 379, 400–401 (Francesco Francioni & Ana Filipa Vrdoljak eds., 2020).

15   *See generally* Engle, The Elusive Promise, *supra* note 8 (looking at culture as heritage, culture as land, and culture as development).

UNDRIP that focuses explicitly, while not exclusively,[16] on Indigenous tangible cultural heritage, comprising "archaeological and historical sites" and "artefacts," combined with a focus on intangible cultural heritage (ICH), which includes "ceremonies, technologies and visual and performing arts and literature." These examples of manifestations of culture ("ceremonies, technologies and visual and performing arts and literature") are replicated in Article 31, but not the emphasis on practice and revitalization.

Article 11 traverses several specific themes. It outlines the different domains of Indigenous culture and cultural heritage, and grants Indigenous peoples the rights to practice, revitalize, maintain, protect, and develop their cultural heritage across multiple generations ("past, present and future manifestations of their cultures").

Article 11(2) focuses on remedies to the taking of Indigenous cultural property, suggesting restitution ("may include restitution," which was particularly controversial language in the drafting of the UNDRIP, explaining the use of the conditional "may"),[17] and highlighting that the taking of cultural heritage should be deemed illicit when carried out "without their free, prior and informed consent [FPIC] or in violation of their laws, traditions and customs." It therefore imposes a burden on the taker of proving FPIC, a central principle of international human rights law,[18] which is inadequately applied in contexts outside of international human rights where emphasis is placed on cultural heritage rights of Indigenous peoples, particularly as far as international investment law is concerned.[19] Alternatively, if requiring proof of FPIC is impossible, there is a burden on Indigenous peoples themselves to prove the violation of their laws, traditions and customs.

The drafting history of what is now Article 11 suggests early and continuous support by Indigenous peoples for the idea of protection of the different domains of Indigenous cultural heritage since the 1987 UNWGIP preparatory

---

16   Alexandra Xanthaki, *Culture: Articles 11(1), 12, 13(1), 15, and 34, in* The UN Declaration on the Rights of Indigenous Peoples: A Commentary 273, 274 (Jessie Hohmann & Marc Weller eds., 2018).

17   Federico Lenzerini, *Reparations, Restitution, and Redress: Articles 8(2), 11(2), 20(2), and 28, in* The UN Declaration on the Rights of Indigenous Peoples: A Commentary 573, 587 (Jessie Hohmann & Marc Weller eds., 2018).

18   Stephen Young, Indigenous Peoples, Consent and Rights: Troubling Subjects (2019); and Cathal M. Doyle, Indigenous Peoples, Title to Territory, Rights and Resources: The Transformative Role of Free Prior and Informed Consent (2014).

19   Valentina Vadi, *The Protection of Indigenous Cultural Heritage in International Investment Law and Arbitration, in* The Inherent Rights of Indigenous Peoples in International Law 203, 233–235 (Antonietta di Blasé & Valentina Vadi eds., 2020).

meeting. What is now Article 11(1) was overall one of the least controversial provisions in the debates leading to the UNDRIP's adoption.[20] Underlying the protection of Indigenous culture is the idea of safeguarding what Erica-Irene Daes saw as the overarching principle that "Indigenous peoples possess distinctive cultural characteristics which distinguish them from the prevailing society in which they live,"[21] requiring, in turn, extensive protective safeguards for Indigenous culture and heritage in the future instrument.[22] However, states were concerned early on about the positive obligations required by this type of language, notably obligations allowing for cultural accommodation in the way of funding cultural preservation measures and cultural programs, for instance, standing in contrast with the negative obligations in Article 27 ICCPR.[23]

It is noteworthy that the Declaration of Principles adopted at the 1987 UNWGIP meeting was much stronger in some respects than the adopted text of Article 11. For one, it emphasized that Indigenous peoples "continue to own and control their material culture,"[24] instead of it just being a right to "practise and revitalize" said culture. Further, it is worth pointing out, the reference is to "material culture," which does not include the wealth of intangible culture that in many respects is the backbone of Indigenous heritage (much of which left to be addressed in Article 31). The provision also included a reference to human remains, now within the purview of Article 12, and, importantly, a declaration that "no technical, scientific or social investigations, including archaeological excavations, shall take place in relation to indigenous nations or peoples, or their lands, without their prior authorization, and their continuing ownership and control."[25] It is worth noting that the latter has disappeared from the adopted UNDRIP.

All of these debates insisted on the need for appropriate remedies, but what is now Article 11(2) has gone largely unchanged, except for the separation

---

20   Xanthaki, *supra* note 16, at 287–288.

21   Commission on Human Rights, *Standard-Setting Activities: Evolution of Standards Concerning the Rights of Indigenous People – New Developments and General Discussion of Future Action – Note by the Chairperson-Rapporteur of the Working Group on Indigenous populations, Ms. Erica-Irene Daes, on criteria which might be applied when considering the concept of indigenous peoples*, UN Doc. E/CN.4/Sub.2/AC.4/1995/3 (21 June 1995), para. 14.

22   Note also that Dalee Sambo Dorough and Siegfried Wiessner argue that protecting Indigenous cultural heritage was arguably the key driver for the UNDRIP. *See* Dorough & Wiessner, *supra* note 12, at 408.

23   Xanthaki, *supra* note 16, at 280.

24   Commission on Human Rights, *Declaration of Principles Adopted by the Indigenous Peoples – Prep Mtg of UNWGIP July, 1987*, UN Doc. E/CN.4/Sub.2/1987/22, Annex V, para. 11.

25   *Id.*, para. 13.

between the two paragraphs (initial suggestions and commentary thereto conflated the two ideas in a single provision). It is worth noting that there was
relatively little debate around the concepts in what is now Article 11, with more
extensive debates happening in relation to other heritage provisions in the
UNDRIP, particularly Article 31.

Existing practice around the themes of Article 11, both before, during the
drafting, or after the adoption of the UNDRIP suggest that the recognition
of the importance of Indigenous cultural heritage across both tangible and
intangible heritage (Article 11(1)) is a settled matter of customary international
law. In its resolution on the rights of Indigenous peoples, the International
Law Association (ILA) would, however, identify a more general right, that is,
respective obligations to protect cultural identity, or cultural heritage, also as a
conduit for land rights.[26] What is less settled, even if there is growing support
behind it, is the customary status of remedies and restitution in relation to
Indigenous cultural property (Article 11(2)), despite the ILA's general recognition of remedies as customary.[27]

There is in other words is a mismatch between the declaratory recognition
of Indigenous rights over their culture and actual enforcement and remedies.
There is a growing body of practice on such recognition, particularly in the
realm of participation in heritage management, and on declaring the importance of Indigenous cultural heritage for cultural identity and other human
rights. The connection to other human rights instrumentalizes cultural heritage concerns by making culture just an element to prove a violation of a
different right, such as property or integrity, which makes it harder for international practice to focus specifically on remedying cultural harm using the
language and mechanisms of cultural heritage.

While using heritage as vehicles for other claims is not a problem, it is perfectly possible and reasonable that Indigenous peoples have claims to their

---

26   Dorough & Wiessner, *supra* note 12, at 424–425. In a broader sense, the ILA recognized, in
      para. 6 of its Resolution No. 5/2012 on the Rights of Indigenous Peoples:
          States are bound to recognise, respect, protect and fulfil indigenous peoples' cultural
      identity (in all its elements, including cultural heritage) and to cooperate with them in
      good faith – through all possible means – in order to ensure its preservation and trans-
      mission to future generations. Cultural rights are the core of indigenous cosmology, ways
      of life and identity, and must therefore be safeguarded in a way that is consistent with the
      perspectives, needs and expectations of the specific indigenous peoples.
          Int'l Law Ass'n Res. No. 5/2012, Rights of Indigenous Peoples (2012), http://www.ilahq
      .org/index.php/committee 6.
27   Dorough & Wiessner, *supra* note 12, at 426.

heritage, which are not often captured by existing international rights frameworks that focus on "culture" more broadly. Cultural heritage gives definition to culture and allows for stronger claims for control, while the softer language of cultural rights focuses on access and participation. The right to heritage in Article 11 UNDRIP can and should be an integral part of the conversation, rather than being left to the side in favour of a primary focus on culture more broadly. Further, in other legal contexts discussed below, heritage belongs to the state, not to (Indigenous) peoples. The lack of heritage-specific practice also translates into fewer measures in terms of remedies and restitution; the adoption of which needs to be guided by Indigenous voices and self-determination, and by a commitment to treating Indigenous culture as Indigenous peoples', and to a right meritorious of protection beyond a broad commitment to culture or as a pathway to land rights. We need to move past declaratory engagement and put more emphasis on remedies, so that we can really deliver on the promise of Indigenous control over their heritage.

The practice under Article 11 supports this argument about an excessive focus on declaratory recognition with little in the way of remedies, too. There are two United Nations specialized agencies whose work speaks directly to the content and rights in Article 11 UNDRIP: the United Nations Educational, Scientific, and Cultural Organization (UNESCO), and the World Intellectual Property Organization (WIPO). The work of the latter in particular engages more closely with Article 31, and sheds light on the matter of remedies.

UNESCO tends to place emphasis on the recognition of the existence and importance of Indigenous heritage. UNESCO cultural heritage instruments in general do not contain rights language, focusing instead on states' prerogatives in relation to heritage in their territories.[28] They therefore suggest a co-management arrangement between states and Indigenous peoples[29] that, in fact, arguably goes against the UNDRIP and the focus on Indigenous control over their own heritage.[30] That said, Article 15 of the Convention for the Safeguarding of the Intangible Cultural Heritage (ICHC) can help in inverting the logic, by requiring the participation of communities in the identification and management of ICH; FPIC is required for inscription of intangible heritage on international lists for the purposes of visibility, awareness-raising, and

---

28   For this discussion, see generally Lucas Lixinski, International Heritage Law for Communities: Exclusion and Re-Imagination 50–51 (2019).

29   Gro B. Ween, *World Heritage and Indigenous rights: Norwegian examples,* 18(3) Int'l J. Heritage Stud. 257 (2012).

30   Sam Grey & Rauna Kuokkanen, *Indigenous governance of cultural heritage: searching for alternatives to co-management,* 26(10) Int'l J. Heritage Stud. 919 (2020).

attraction of safeguarding resources, which must be conducted in accordance with the terms of the ICHC and its Operational Directives (albeit, as I have documented elsewhere, the implementation of FPIC in this context is not without its problems).[31] The ICHC only refers to Indigenous peoples once, in its preamble ("communities, in particular indigenous communities"). The exclusion of Indigenous peoples from the operative text of the treaty was intentional, because drafters wanted to broaden the instrument's scope; in fact, the ICHC is also criticized for not mentioning Indigenous peoples as "peoples".[32] Likewise, the Operational Directives to the ICHC only use the word "Indigenous" three times, always in the context of vulnerable groups, including migrants, refugees, persons with disabilities, and in light of safeguarding the practices of these vulnerable groups and including them in listing processes.[33]

Nevertheless, Article 11 UNDRIP recognizes that intangible heritage is a core part of Indigenous cultural heritage. The ICHC is therefore worth considering when it defines ICH as "the practices, representations, expressions, knowledge, skills – as well as the instruments, objects, artefacts and cultural spaces associated therewith – that communities, groups and, in some cases, individuals recognize as part of their cultural heritage", which includes "(a) oral traditions and expressions, including language as a vehicle of the intangible cultural heritage; (b) performing arts; (c) social practices, rituals and festive events; (d) knowledge and practices concerning nature and the universe; (e) traditional craftsmanship."[34]

At least 26 elements of intangible cultural heritage that pertain to indigenous peoples are inscribed on the three lists created by the ICHC,[35] across 23 countries in all continents.[36] These represent about 5% of all the elements on the international lists created by the ICHC, and over 12% of the States parties, hence underscoring the importance of the recognition of Indigenous cultural

---

31   For a critique, see Lucas Lixinski, Intangible Cultural Heritage in International Law (2013).

32   Janet Blake, *The Preamble, in* The 2003 UNESCO Intangible Heritage Convention: A Commentary 19, 30 (Janet Blake & Lucas Lixinski eds., 2020).

33   *Operational Directives for the Implementation of the Convention for the Safeguarding of the Intangible Cultural Heritage* (2018), paras. 174, 194, and 197.

34   Convention for Safeguarding of the Intangible Cultural Heritage 2003 (adopted 17 October 2003, entered into force 20 April 2006) 2368 UNTS 3 (ICHC), Article 2.

35   The three lists are: the List of Intangible Cultural Heritage in Need of Urgent Safeguarding; the Representative List of the Intangible Cultural Heritage of Humanity; and the Register of Programmes, projects and activities for the safeguarding of the intangible cultural heritage.

36   UNESCO, *Browse the Lists of Intangible Cultural Heritage and the Register of good safeguarding practices* (2020), at https://ich.unesco.org/en/lists?text=indigenous& multinational=3&display1=inscriptionID#tabs.

heritage. Despite the ICHC not stipulating many rights for Indigenous peoples, it may still be useful to raise visibility and awareness of Indigenous heritage, as well as committing states to safeguarding said heritage whenever the territorial State chooses to recognize it.

The 1972 World Heritage Convention,[37] on the other hand, has taken much stronger action in relation to Indigenous peoples and Indigenous sites on the World Heritage List, even though there are still fundamental limitations.[38] In direct response to the adoption of the UNDRIP, the World Heritage Committee has reformed the "Operational Guidelines for the implementation of the World Heritage Convention" to include to the requirement to obtain Indigenous peoples' free, prior, and informed consent in the process of listing and managing their heritage as well as recognizing Indigenous peoples as rights-holders in relation to their own heritage.[39] The *UNESCO Policy on Engaging with Indigenous Peoples* (2018) pays particular attention to the rights of Indigenous peoples in relation to their heritage, that can also be considered World Heritage.[40]

Lastly, in relation to remedies specifically, there are two treaties on cultural objects that must be considered. The first is the 1970 UNESCO Convention on the Means of Prohibiting and Preventing the Illicit Import, Export and Transfer of Ownership of Cultural Property, which requires that cultural objects taken illicitly from one territorial State to another be returned.[41] However, this treaty is not retroactively applicable, which means it is of limited use for Indigenous artefacts taken away from Indigenous territories during colonization even if the Indigenous rights movement has helped shape the implementation of the treaty in significant ways.[42] Despite the temporal limitations of the treaty, the 1970 Convention is the UNESCO treaty that focuses most clearly on remedies, even if the beneficiaries of the return of cultural objects are territorial states, and not Indigenous peoples themselves, as tends to be the case in international

---

37   Convention concerning the Protection of the World Cultural and Natural Heritage 1972 (adopted 23 November 1972, entered into force 15 December 1975) 1037 UNTS 151 (WHC).

38   Ana Filipa Vrdoljak, *Indigenous Peoples, World Heritage, and Human Rights*, 25 Int'l J. Cultural Prop. 245 (2018).

39   UNESCO, *World Heritage and Indigenous Peoples*, at https://whc.unesco.org/en/activities /496/.

40   UNESCO, *UNESCO policy on engaging with indigenous peoples* (2018), at https://en.unesco .org/indigenous-peoples/policy.

41   Convention on the Means of Prohibiting and Preventing the Illicit Import, Export and Transfer of Ownership of Cultural Property 1970 (adopted 14 November 1970, entered into force 24 April 1972) 823 UNTS 231 (1970 Convention).

42   As discussed in detail by Ana Filipa Vrdoljak, International Law, Museums and the Return of Cultural Objects (2006).

cultural heritage law more broadly. One recent example is the Quimbaya Cultural Treasure dispute, where the Colombian government is seeking the return from Spain of a collection of Indigenous cultural artefacts, but little to no consultation of the affected Indigenous peoples, let alone a promise that their return, if it eventuates, would benefit the concerned Indigenous peoples.[43]

The other relevant treaty is the 1995 International Institute for the Unification of Private Law Convention (UNIDROIT) where all references to human rights in the instrument are in fact references to the rights of Indigenous peoples.[44] This treaty, outside of UNESCO, is fundamental in its recognition of direct rights of heritage holders because it harmonizes domestic private law in the area of cultural objects. Its multiple references to the rights of Indigenous peoples to obtain remedies constitutes an essential component of good practice that could be relevant as far as Article 11(2) is concerned.

Still on remedies, but looking at a different specialized agency, the WIPO's work on traditional knowledge (TK) and traditional cultural expressions (TCES), which has been ongoing for over 20 years at the time of writing, has relied extensively on Indigenous peoples in the drafting process. The 2019 versions of the TK and TCEs draft articles suggest that the instruments should be interpreted in a way that only improves upon, and never detracts, from the content of the UNDRIP.[45] The TK articles are useful in that one of the draft options clearly defines the conduct from which a remedy can be sought by Indigenous peoples, defining misappropriation as "Any access or use of traditional knowledge of the [beneficiaries] indigenous [peoples] or local communities, without their free, prior and informed consent and mutually agreed terms, in violation of customary law and established practices governing the access or use of such traditional knowledge."[46] The brackets demonstrate how contentious the language still is, but that they are still a possibility at all speaks to important developments that should be at the forefront of UNDRIP implementation. Much of this language is fairly similar to Article 11(2) of the UNDRIP, using the label of "misappropriation" instead can be helpful in giving more leverage to domestic law mechanisms.

---

43 For a discussion, see Diego Mejía-Lemos, *The "Quimbaya Treasure," Judgment SU-649/17*, 113 Am. J. Int'l L. 122 (2019).

44 UNIDROIT Convention on Stolen or Illegally Exported Cultural Objects (Rome, 24 June 1995). See also The 1995 UNIDROIT Convention Academic Project, *Human Rights*, at https://1995unidroitcap.org/human-rights/.

45 The Protection of Traditional Cultural Expressions: Draft Articles (Facilitators' Rev. June 19, 2019) (TCEs Articles), Article 12; and The Protection of Traditional Knowledge: Draft Articles (Facilitators' Rev. June 19, 2019) (TK articles), Article 13.

46 TK articles, alternative 4 in Article 1.

Further, both the TCEs and TK draft articles draw an important distinction between right to a heritage that is sacred or secret, and heritage that is still a part of cultural identity but over which control is not as restricted.[47] This nuance is important in assessing remedies for violations of rights established in Article 11 UNDRIP, as it helps set the tone for balancing the enforcement of the right(s), since the closer the practice to the core of a people's identity, the more the balance shifts in favour of indigenous peoples.[48] In other words, if the cultural practice is considered essential to an Indigenous people's culture, the right of Indigenous peoples to maintain and control their culture is more likely to take precedence over the rights of third parties whose activities directly or indirectly interfere with developing or maintaining that cultural practice or site. That said, the goal should still be control by Indigenous peoples, the assumption of need to balance with third parties can be problematic because it works from a baseline that favours non-Indigenous potential rights holders, instead of the actual rights holders in a declaration on the rights of Indigenous peoples.

With respect to remedies, the TCEs draft establishes important elements to give full effect to Article 11(2) UNDRIP, and deserves being quoted in full:

> [10.1 Member States shall, [in conjunction with indigenous [peoples],] put in place accessible, appropriate, effective, [dissuasive,] and proportionate legal and/or administrative measures to address violations of the rights contained in this instrument. Indigenous [peoples] should have the right to initiate enforcement on their own behalf and shall not be required to demonstrate proof of economic harm.
>
> 10.2 If a violation of the rights protected by this instrument is determined pursuant to paragraph 10.1, the sanctions shall include civil and criminal enforcement measures as appropriate. Remedies may include restorative justice measures, [such as repatriation,] according to the nature and effect of the infringement.][49]

---

47   TK articles, alternatives 2 and 3 in Article 5; TCEs articles, alternatives 2 and 3 draft Article 5.

48   For a discussion of the balancing test in relation to cultural identity, see Lucas Lixinski, *Balancing Test: Inter-American Court of Human Rights (IACtHR)*, *in* Max Planck Encyclopedia of International Procedural Law (Hélène Ruiz Fabri ed., 2019).

49   TCEs articles, alternative 2 in Article 10.

Relatedly, the TK articles also contain important proposed language to guide the implementation of Article 11(2) UNDRIP: "6.4 [Where appropriate, sanctions and remedies should reflect the sanctions and remedies that indigenous people and local communities would use.]"[50] Therefore, the activities of this UN specialized agency can be particularly useful in strengthening the remedies framework for Indigenous peoples in Article 11(2) UNDRIP, notably, by opening more pathways for practice of culture that is controlled by Indigenous peoples, and creating more enforceable remedies.

In other words, the better practice in relation to remedies happens outside of the UNDRIP, via other instruments, and the UNDRIP is used to anchor declaratory recognition instead. My use of the word "anchor" here is calculated: while the UNDRIP language can be used simply as the initial step in a process of remedying harm, it can also slow down that process, if all that one considers to be appropriate consideration of Indigenous rights and perspectives is a reference to the relatively weak language of the UNDRIP.

This declaratory trend is emulated by regional human rights courts. For the most part, the jurisprudence of regional human rights bodies on Indigenous culture and heritage has highlighted the importance of cultural heritage when demonstrating ancestral ties to lands, in relation to the right to participate in cultural life, and in underscoring the collective dimensions of Indigenous human rights.[51] There have also been cases where the destruction of Indigenous heritage constituted a violation of Indigenous peoples' rights. In *Moiwana Community vs. Suriname*, for example, the Court found a violation of the right to humane treatment because burial sites were destroyed and the remains of community members who had been killed by the national army were not returned.[52] Despite jurisprudence from the African, European, and Inter-American human rights bodies on Indigenous rights, and growing references to the UNDRIP, the IACtHR *Case of Kichwa Indigenous People of Sarayaku*

---

50 TK articles, alternative 2 in Article 6:
51 Expert Mechanism on the Rights of Indigenous Peoples, Promotion and protection of the rights of indigenous peoples with respect to their cultural heritage, UN Doc. A/HRC/30/53 (19 August 2015), paras. 32–33 (citing IACtHR, *Mayagna (Sumo) Awas Tingni Community v. Nicaragua*. Judgment of 31 August 2001. Series C, No. 79, para. 153; IACtHR, *Yakye Axa Indigenous Community v. Paraguay*. Judgment of 17 June 2005. Series C, No. 125, para. 131; and ACHPR, *Centre for Minority Rights Development and Minority Rights Group International on behalf of Endorois Welfare Council v. Kenya*, 276/2003 (2010), para. 241). *See also* Michele D'Addetta, *The Practice of the Regional Human Rights Bodies on the Protection of Indigenous Peoples' Right to Culture*, XXXIX(5) Rivista Giuridica Dell'Ambiente 587 (2014).
52 IACtHR, *Case of the Moiwana Community v. Suriname. Preliminary Objections, Merits, Reparations and Costs.* Judgment of June 15, 2005. Series C No. 124, paras. 98–100.

v. Ecuador is the only one that directly invokes Article 11 UNDRIP, but does so to affirm the Court's "recognition of the right to cultural identity of indigenous peoples" under international law.[53]

Article 11 is a central provision in the UNDRIP to promote control over culture and cultural heritage. However, practice to date has focused mostly on access and participation, both of which require merely declaratory value, but miss any sufficient embedment in remedy frameworks which are central to giving hard effect and enforcement to the provision. We may be past the point of getting the ideas in Article 11(1) UNDRIP endorsed by states, and attention should now move towards enforcement of remedies for Indigenous peoples contained in Article 11(2) as a tool to promote the very control that is promised in Article 11(1).

Article 11, however, should be employed not to simply reinforce ways in which the rights to culture and cultural identity have been implemented via other treaties; rather, the provision should be used to challenge the significant leeway that states enjoy in implementing the right. Article 11 should be applied with the objective of diminishing state prerogative in relation to other (enforceable) rights of relevance to Indigenous culture and heritage. International law in this area assumes a baseline in favor of states, which Article 11 can help shift towards Indigenous peoples. It is not for Indigenous peoples to accommodate others seeking to exploit their culture, but rather the other way around. In this sense, Article 11 UNDRIP has the potential to render cultural heritage, as an expression of culture, more central to articulating Indigenous claims.

In addition to the UNDRIP, the ADRIP benefits from close to ten years of use of the UNDRIP (not to mention it did not have the African bloc's last-minute push against self-determination),[54] and therefore has somewhat more sophisticated provisions on cultural heritage, even if the key provisions on heritage[55]

---

53   IACtHR, *Case of Kichwa Indigenous People of Sarayaku v. Ecuador. Merits and Reparations.* Judgment of June 27, 2012. Series C No. 245, para. 215–217.

54   For this history, see Karen Engle, *On Fragile Architecture: The UN Declaration on the Rights of Indigenous Peoples in the Context of Human Rights*, 22(1) Eur. J. Int'l L. 141 (2011).

55   The full provisions are as follows: "SECTION THREE: Cultural identity. Article XIII. Right to cultural identity and integrity. (1) Indigenous peoples have the right to their own cultural identity and integrity and to their cultural heritage, both tangible and intangible, including historic and ancestral heritage; and to the protection, preservation, maintenance, and development of that cultural heritage for their collective continuity and that of their members and so as to transmit that heritage to future generations. (2) States shall provide redress through effective mechanisms, which may include restitution, developed in conjunction with indigenous peoples, with respect to their cultural, intellectual, religious and spiritual property taken without their free, prior and informed consent or in violation of their laws, traditions and customs. (3) Indigenous people have the right to the recognition

are somewhat similar in tone to those in the UNDRIP. A notable difference between the UNDRIP and the ADRIP is that the language in the latter, precisely benefitting from activity under the former, is more assertive in some respects. The ADRIP places stronger emphasis on control over heritage, as well as reparations and restitution, which are more tentatively addressed in the UNDRIP. Regional practice in the Americas on the relevant provisions of the UNDRIP and the ADRIP shows this preference towards stronger language.

The text of Article XIII(1) ADRIP suggests the recognition of much broader rights to cultural identity and integrity, and to heritage. Unlike UNDRIP Article 11(1), which focuses on the right to practice and revitalize cultural traditions and customs, this article addresses the right of Indigenous peoples to their "own cultural identity and integrity." In other words, culture is something that belongs to and is owned by the concerned Indigenous peoples and over which they have a right to exercise control, rather than something which they merely have a right to practice and revitalize. Furthermore, Article XIII(1) is broader in scope, as it explicitly includes all heritage "whether tangible or intangible."

The focus of instruments like ADRIP on cultural identity and integrity can help alter the equation in favour of indigenous peoples when Courts and states are balancing the rights of Indigenous peoples with the interests of other actors. By making heritage the central claim, rather than a platform for another claim, and by focusing on control over "practice and revitalization" which suggest a focus on procedural matters like access and participation, these provisions can be interpreted to be pivotal in allowing Indigenous peoples to control their

---

and respect for all their ways of life, world views, spirituality, uses and customs, norms and traditions, forms of social, economic and political organization, forms of transmission of knowledge, institutions, practices, beliefs, values, dress and languages, recognizing their inter-relationship as elaborated in this Declaration." And "Article XXVIII. Protection of Cultural Heritage and Intellectual Property (1) Indigenous peoples have the right to the full recognition and respect for their property, ownership, possession, control, development, and protection of their tangible and intangible cultural heritage and intellectual property, including its collective nature, transmitted through millennia, from generation to generation. (2) The collective intellectual property of indigenous peoples includes, inter alia, traditional knowledge and traditional cultural expressions including traditional knowledge associated with genetic resources, ancestral designs and procedures, cultural, artistic, spiritual, technological, and scientific, expressions, tangible and intangible cultural heritage, as well as the knowledge and developments of their own related to biodiversity and the utility and qualities of seeds and medicinal plants, flora and fauna. (3) States, with the full and effective participation of indigenous peoples, shall adopt measures necessary to ensure that national and international agreements and regimes provide recognition and adequate protection for the cultural heritage of indigenous peoples and intellectual property associated with that heritage. In adopting these measures, consultations shall be effective intended to obtain the free, prior, and informed consent of indigenous peoples."

own culture on their own terms and to have access to adequate remedies in relation thereto.

Bearing in mind the declaratory work that the two declarations do, and the potential for remedies in the other international instruments discussed above, the next section focuses on the shift from recognition to remedies. In discussing remedies, in particular, the chapter queries whether remedies in substantive law are the gold standard, or rather whether institutional design might instead offer some more promising avenues to make room for Indigenous voice and rights implementation.

3   From Recognition to Remedies to Institutional Design

The declaratory recognition work that these instruments do is important. After all, recognition of cultural heritage, as a marker of culture, can be an important galvanizing factor, a banner of sorts around which an Indigenous people or peoples can rally and organize politically. In other words, to be able to name one's heritage as one's own, even if said naming does not immediately translate into anything else, can still have some effects. Because cultural heritage carries important symbolic value, it is important that the law guarantees this type of recognition.

Acknowledgment that certain heritage is Indigenous without assigning clear control to Indigenous peoples themselves, however, can also leave this heritage exposed to co-option by a nationalistic project, for instance, which can lead to it being manipulated for the benefit of nation-making, or, worse still, so as to modify its meaning and uses in ways that alienate Indigenous peoples from their own heritage. International cultural heritage law, by and large, can have exclusionary effects with respect to communities, particularly Indigenous communities, in that heritage law outside of the Indigenous context is often framed within state-centric regimes, as indicated above.[56] Therefore, without a clear assignation of control, let alone substantive remedies through which Indigenous communities can make claims about violation of their interests over their own heritage, recognition does not get us very far in terms of allowing the political and identity-based organization of Indigenous peoples to turn into concrete legal, political, economic, or otherwise structural change.

The move to control and remedies, thus, allows us to more fully explore the possibilities of using heritage not just as a symbolic marker of identity, but as

---

56   For a further discussion of this critique, see Lixinski, International Heritage Law for Communities, *supra* note 28.

a lever to promote the change that Indigenous peoples wish to seek in relation to their status vis-à-vis the settler colonial state within which they exist, up to articulating claims for self-determination. There is potential for heritage to stand as a marker of a call for greater self-determination, as indicated above, but often this potential is over-promised and remains unfulfilled. The reasons for this failure are not just that self-determination itself has been legally weakened to mean largely only internal self-determination; rather, the primary reason is that remedies available to allow communities to seize control over their heritage in their own terms, rather than in the terms of heritage being subject to the design of a nation-state (which is also where self-determination leaves us).

Further, for certain types of heritage, as the ADRIP and UNDRIP themselves acknowledge, remedies are required as the only pathway to redress harm that impinges upon the core of Indigenous identity (such as removal of cultural objects, and particularly human remains). Remedies offer a clear language through which Indigenous peoples can present themselves as claimants, exercise agency before the legal process, and claim for the return of their cultural heritage to them, placing this heritage within their control.

But the focus only on tangible heritage (and particularly cultural objects) in these instruments obscures the fact that harm to heritage, particularly intangible heritage, can be much more pervasive. The destruction of Indigenous intangible cultural heritage would not qualify, on a textual reading of the relevant provisions of ADRIP and UNDRIP, as "property taken." Therefore, the available remedies under these instruments focus only on specific or specifiable discrete instances, and misses structural and more pervasive harm to Indigenous identity through other forms of heritage.

Further, the focus on remedies, much as the focus on declaratory recognition of Indigenous rights over their heritage, is based on substantive law that accepts a legal process framework and assumes its neutrality. In practice, however, the rules for the exercise of Indigenous agency are tightly controlled by gatekeeping measures such as standing and rules of participation, checked by institutions that operate from a settler-colonial baseline. One instance is what happens with the return of Indigenous human remains under United States law. Despite legislation that is progressive in terms of recognition, and even remedies, the institutions implementing this legislation create obstacles for Indigenous peoples to even qualify as claimants, let alone be able to recover those remains and other objects taken from Indigenous graves in the name of colonial science.[57]

---

57   For a broader discussion, see Susan Benton, *A Paradox of Cultural Property: NAGPRA and (dis)possession, in* The Routledge Companion to Cultural Property 108 (Jane Anderson &

In other words, the incorporation of substantive responses, via declaratory recognition and / or remedies, does important work, but can also be limited in how much it does to promote real structural reform. Instead, I suggest that one must take a step back, and focus also on institutional design. That is one of the conclusions of the ILA Committee on Participation in Global Cultural Heritage Governance, which assessed participation rules across over 40 international and regional institutions, as well as over 30 domestic jurisdictions. Specifically, the final report of the Committee recommended that:

> Decision-makers (like states), gatekeepers (such as experts), and other affected stakeholders shall be included in governance decisions with respect to heritage and shall all be considered in equal terms in heritage governance matters, except when the interest of minorities warrants more privileged status to these groups.

> The incorporation of actors beyond the state and experts in governance processes after these processes have already been decided necessarily renders their input less valuable and actionable, making therefore a case also for co-design of regimes to ensure that participation is equal across all levels.[58]

To use a sports metaphor: by changing these background structural norms, one is able to change the game itself, rather than just allowing new players to come to the pitch and having to learn how other people have played the game for centuries and engage in a game that has historically been stacked against them. This critique echoes a basic critique of Third World Approaches to International Law, which suggests it is unfair to expect the "third world" to engage in the rules of international law which were designed not only in their absence as subjects, but specifically considering these states and peoples as objects. The same can be said of Indigenous peoples, as a "fourth world": international and domestic background legal norms, in relation to cultural heritage but also more broadly, have been designed not only in the absence of Indigenous voices, but also with the implicit or explicit aim of using Indigenous peoples to promote settler-colonial goals (therefore, treating Indigenous peoples as objects of the law). Even law protective of Indigenous interests has more often

---

Haidy Geismar eds., 2017); and D Rae Gould, *NAGPRA, CUI and Institutional Will, in* The Routledge Companion to Cultural Property 134 (Jane Anderson & Haidy Geismar eds., 2017).

58   ILA Committee on Participation Final Report, *supra* note 9, para. 140(3).

than not been designed in the absence of Indigenous voices themselves, which explains historical and ongoing paternalistic effects underlying these norms.[59]

There is a strong case to be made, therefore, to move towards institutional design as a response to Indigenous claims for emancipation, in relation to but not limited to control over Indigenous heritage. International legal institutions, especially international human rights courts, are not averse to designing institutions with a rights-centric framework front and center, and in fact in many instances have been very adept at it, albeit indirectly.[60]

The direct design of institutions would allow Indigenous peoples to have direct input in norms (and their implementation) affecting them, as well as to control heritage, its uses and meanings, in ways that promote Indigenous identity and other goals, rather than a narrative that necessitates reconciling with a nationalistic project. Freed from the necessity being framed by the colonial encounter, Indigenous peoples can reconsider the narratives around their heritage, how they organize politically and economically around it, and the choices they make about the identity embodied in said heritage.

The downside of this move towards institutional design is the potential it has to unsettle existing norms and institutions. But doing so acknowledges and attempts to correct historical imbalances. As the ILA Committee on Participation also recommended:

> Heritage actors should be recognized in their diversity, with legal instruments and processes designed to facilitate participation in cooperative ways that also account for and incorporate this diversity.
>
> Different levels of participation may be accorded when doing so will assist in correcting historical disadvantage, and / or ongoing power asymmetries. Special consideration, and greater participatory powers, should probably go to historically oppressed and marginalized minorities, including Indigenous groups. Doctrines like abuse of rights can play a central role in mediating the potential for abuse of these powers, and constructive disagreements can be exploited by different actors, always with a view to levelling power imbalances. In the event of unresolvable conflicts among the equivalent preferences of different actors, a status quo protective of heritage should prevail.[61]

---

59   *See for instance* Gillian Cowlishaw, *Erasing Culture and Race: Practising 'Self-Determination'*, 68 Oceania 145 (1998).

60   *See generally* David Kosař & Lucas Lixinski, *Domestic Judicial Design by Regional Human Rights Courts*, 109 Am. J. Int'l L. 713 (2015).

61   ILA Committee on Participation Final Report, *supra* note 9, para. 140(1).

The correction of power imbalances means that greater power goes, in several instances, to Indigenous peoples themselves to decide the fate of their heritage. To the extent international law, particularly in the area of Indigenous rights, is devoted to the idea of promoting human flourishing, and imagining a society that reckons with past harm and is seriously committed to not repeating it, then the risk of upending the status quo to achieve the promise of justice to Indigenous peoples seems a high but fair price to pay.

4   Concluding Remarks

International instruments on Indigenous rights have come a long way to cement the declaratory recognition of Indigenous claims. They have, however, fallen short on providing clear access to remedies and control over heritage and its potentials by Indigenous peoples. The stakes of this gap are particularly high in the context of cultural heritage, which is often captured by nationalistic myth-making at the expense of Indigenous peoples' distinctiveness identities and self-determination. If we are serious about the potentials of these instruments to emancipate Indigenous peoples and enable their flourishing, we need to do better. Better access to remedies and control is one crucial step, but there is still largely untapped potential in going further, and addressing the core of institutional design, so that international and domestic norms and institutions can more aptly reflect the work they should do with Indigenous peoples as opposed to forcing Indigenous peoples to fit into pre-existing colonial moulds. Better institutional design engages Indigenous voice and rights more openly and directly, and lives up to the promise of international law in relation to self-determination and the foundation of a more just global society.

Acknowledgments

The views expressed in this chapter are entirely mine, but I am incredibly grateful to the members of the ILA Committee for the enlightening discussions that shaped my thinking in this area.

PART 7

Space Law

∵

CHAPTER 28

The Beginning of the End of International Space Law

Ram S. Jakhu* and Nishith Mishra**

1   Introduction

Human beings are a curious species. Throughout history, we find great pleasure in accepting and meeting challenges, and in making efforts in overcoming
what we refer to as "hurdles"[1] or obstacles. We then compete, through collective
involvement and participation, to overcome those hurdles: the greater number of challenges fulfilled, or hurdles overcome, the more powerful a group
of human beings claims to be. For a prolonged period of our shared human
history, a small and powerful group of people have used laws and regulations to
control, govern and enhance the welfare of organized communities in various
domains throughout the world. From monarchs to emperors, from authoritarian dictators to modern forms of democratic governance setups and structures
across the world, leaders have, understandably and presumably with honest
intentions and reasoned approaches, aimed to prevent "lawlessness," "rule of
the jungle," or situations where "survival of the fittest" prevails.

The domain of outer space is not an exception in this regard. The adoption
of laws, both national and international, is one such effort to overcome hurdles that we have placed on our collective path of achieving welfare for all of
humankind in the space domain.

---

*   Full Professor, Institute of Air and Space Law, Faculty of Law, McGill University, Montreal,
    Canada.

** Research Assistant, Institute of Air and Space Law, Faculty of Law, McGill University,
    Montreal, Canada.

1   The authors refer to laws and regulations as "hurdles" for there is something very intrinsic
    and basic in every human being to long for boundless expansion. If we achieve something,
    our immediate natural reaction is to look for what is next for us to be able to conquer and
    achieve. This, fortunately or unfortunately, has been the most basic drive in all of humanity's
    history and our existence. This drive has also given us all the modern comforts that we are so
    used to in today's world. Thus, in a way, any limitation placed on our attempt(s) to seamlessly
    or effortlessly expand, whether we admit them in as many words or not, naturally becomes a
    hurdle or an obstacle.

In the context of this Chapter, international law refers to those legal instruments or principles which have gained international acceptance and have been classified as universally accepted sources of international law in accordance with Article 38(1) of the Statute of International Court of Justice.[2] After centuries of relentless exploitation and colonization and two devastating world wars, the international community came together to create institutions and enact laws and regulations at the international level that were universally recognized and adhered to. However, with the passage of time, the preference of the international community has seemingly changed and continues to change. All the while, newer forms of international regulations are being explored and devised to match the rapid pace in advancements in technological sectors, and extra-legal factors are having a marked influence on the adoption and application of international law.

As law-making, at least at the international level, is a complex and time-consuming process, humanity or a group of its representatives have sought to overcome the "hurdles," time and again, by trying to find ways, mechanisms and mannerisms to act and achieve their goals indirectly what they have otherwise prohibited themselves to do directly. In this regard, John Locke's version or idea of the "end of law" resonates through the passage of time and is contained in the basic notion that "the end of law is not to abolish or restrain, but to preserve and enlarge freedom. ..."[3] His version of "law" and implications of the "end of law" were thus securely built around ideas of liberty and expansion, and freedom from oppression or violence to be enjoyed by all or a majority of human beings. This appears to have been centered around the needs of the

---

2   Statute of the International Court of Justice, Jun. 26, 1945, 33 U.N.T.S. 993, art. 38(1):

    The Court, whose function is to decide in accordance with international law such disputes as are submitted to it, shall apply: (a) international conventions, whether general or particular, establishing rules expressly recognized by the contesting States; (b) international custom, as evidence of a general practice accepted as law; (c) the general principles of law recognized by civilized nations; (d) subject to the provisions of Article 59, judicial decisions and the teachings of the most highly qualified publicists of the various nations, as subsidiary means for the determination of rules of law.

3   John Locke, *Second Treatise of Government*, 1690, *in* The Project Gutenberg eBook of Second Treatise of Government (Re-released: Apr. 22, 2003), https://www.gutenberg.org/files/7370/7370-h/7370-h.htm#CHAPTER_II, at ch. 6 § 57 (last visited Oct. 20, 2022):

    So that, however it may be mistaken, the end of law is not to abolish or restrain, but to preserve and enlarge freedom: for in all the States of created beings capable of laws, where there is no law, there is no freedom: for liberty is, to be free from restraint and violence from others; which cannot be, where there is no law: but freedom is not, as we are told, a liberty for every man to do what he lists: (for who could be free, when every other man's humour might domineer over him?) but a liberty to dispose, and order as he lists, his person, actions, possessions, and his whole property, within the allowance of those laws under which he is, and therein not to be subject to the arbitrary will of another, but freely follow his own.

time and has been enjoyed by the international community, albeit by a small group of nations, till as late as the 20th century.

Fast forward to the developments of the first two decades of this century: human beings are now increasingly capable of expressing and conveying ideas and notions of a valued human life. They are able to do so promptly and impactfully in an increasingly global and inter-connected world made possible, in part, through space-based technologies, aided and assisted also through technologies such as the Internet of Things ("IoT"), social media, Artificial Intelligence ("AI") and cyber technologies. Through the proliferation of and increased access to new technologies, traditionally and historically imparted laws and regulations, particularly international law and international relations along with its validity and social acceptance, have been and are being torn apart bit by bit. It is often said that there is strength in numbers, yet the actual manifestation of such strength, increasingly and largely through the actions and conduct of a few States and their non-state actors, is creating (has created, and will continue to create) a scenario that is shaking the very foundations of existing international relations and international law, including in the space domain.

Human activities in the space sector have had their own role to play in providing numerous societal and economic benefits[4] as well as humanitarian assistance to humankind.[5] Almost all spheres of modern-day outreach and allied activities are facilitated through and impacted by, at least in part, space-based or space-related technologies. Indeed, a direct consequence of developments in the space sector, including in the growth of satellites and space-based

---

4   *See, generally,* Satellite Industry Association, *Executive Summary of the 2022 State of the Satellite Industry Report,* (Jun., 2022), https://sia.org/news-resources/state-of-the-satellite-industry-report (last visited Oct. 12, 2022).

5   *See, e.g.,* United Nations Department of Economic and Social Affairs – Sustainable Development, United Nations Office for Outer Space Affairs, https://sdgs.un.org/un-system-sdg-implementation/united-nations-office-outer-space-affairs-unoosa-24523, highlighting:

    2.4 The benefits of space technology are wide-reaching and have the potential to support all of the SDGs; it is part of UNOOSA's mission to ensure that everyone has equal opportunities to contribute to and access these benefits …

    3.3 As part of its mission to ensure that all countries and international and regional organizations have access to space-based information to support disaster and risk management, UNOOSA's UN-SPIDER program is engaged in a number of advisory support initiatives to support Member States.

    3.5 Harnessing science, technology and innovation for the SDGs: Science, technology, and innovation are essential drivers of space exploration, and are at the heart of nearly every project undertaken by UNOOSA. Initiatives that directly involve the use of space science and technology include UN-SPIDER, Space4Water, and Space4SDGs.

communications, is intensified globalization and the proliferation of new technologies and applications.

Through discussions of a variety of events and changes that are impacting today's globalized world, in this Chapter, the authors explore and enunciate whether we are witnessing the beginning of the end of international space law, or whether in reality, humanity is going through a transitional phase. In other words, the question we intend to address is whether international law, and international space law in particular, is drastically changing or withering away. As the conduct of States through international relations, and now more than ever through the conduct of a State's private or non-governmental entities, have a direct impact on the making and implementation of international space law, the authors intend to demonstrate the impact that a variety of global events and policies of major powers have on the success or failure, strength or weakness of international space law.

The end of law results in law of the jungle, i.e. a state of affairs in which some gain absolute freedom while the freedom of others is significantly restrained, if not totally lost. In today's world, the complete end of law may not be conceivable. However, limiting the scope of law, its routine disregard, ineffective implementation, intentional weakening or clear violations of international law, including international space law, with impunity, is cause for alarm and also hints at the beginning of the end of the rule of law. It is in this sense that the authors have used the term "the end of law" in this Chapter.

The authors feel privileged to be invited to contribute a Chapter to this collection of essays honoring Professor Dr. Siegfried Wiessner who is a world-leading expert in international law, international human rights, and international indigenous law. His scholarship and contribution to space law is unmatched. After almost 40 years, Professor Wiessner's seminal paper "*The Public Order of the Geostationary Orbit: Blueprints for the Future*" still remains a classic masterpiece of academic brilliance that encapsulates highly complex issues related to space law, telecommunications law, international relations and space technologies from the perspective of global public order. This Chapter is intended to support Professor Wiessner's assertion that "congruence of interest and the experience of mutual benefits would be the foundation for the public order of a resource [the geostationary orbit in outer space] now universally recognized as indispensable."[6]

---

6   Siegfried Wiessner, *The Public Order of the Geostationary Orbit: Blueprints for the Future*, 9 Yale J. World Pub. Order 217 (1983 [1985]), http://digitalcommons.law.yale.edu/yjil/vol9/iss2/2/.

2 Tracing the Beginning of the End of International Space Law

Before adverting to a discussion on some of the important changes affecting the global space landscape (*see* sections 2.2 and 3 below), it is appropriate to first present the background, the origins and the core and foundational principles of the contemporary international legal framework governing space activities and conduct.

2.1 *Origins, Recent Trends and Core Principles of International Space Law*

At the dawn of the Space Age, the international community rallied behind the two Cold War superpowers and reached consensus on binding legal commitments in the form of five United Nations ("UN") space law treaties.[7] These instruments capture the essence of international space law and contain the core and foundational legal principles governing space activities and conduct.

From the inception of the international regulation of outer space, the international community recognized the UN system as the international forum for the regulation of outer space affairs. Under its first resolution on outer space, in 1958, the UN General Assembly took a historic step in establishing an international institution specifically for the consideration of space affairs. The then *ad hoc* Committee on the Peaceful Uses of Outer Space (predecessor of what would later be formally recognized as United Nations Committee on the Peaceful Uses of Outer Space, or UNCOPUOS)[8] was composed of States from all regions of the world representing not only spacefaring powers, but also non-spacefaring powers from both the developed and developing countries.

---

7   They are: Treaty on Principles Governing the Activities of States in the Exploration and Use of Outer Space, including the Moon and Other Celestial Bodies, Jan. 27, 1967, 610 U.N.T.S. 205 (entered into force Oct. 10, 1967) [*Outer Space Treaty* or *OST*], preceded by, G.A. Res. 1962 (XVIII), U.N. GAOR, 18th Sess., Supp. No. 15, U.N. Doc. A/5515 (1963), Declaration of Legal Principles Governing the Activities of States in the Exploration and Use of Outer Space, at 15 [*1963 Declaration of Legal Principles*]. *See also* Agreement on the Rescue of Astronauts, the Return of Astronauts and the Return of Objects Launched into Outer Space, Apr. 22, 1968, 672 U.N.T.S. 119 (entered into force Dec. 3, 1968) [*Rescue Agreement*]; Convention on International Liability for Damage Caused by Space Objects, Mar. 29, 1972, 961 U.N.T.S. 187 (entered into force Sep. 1, 1972) [*Liability Convention*]; Convention on Registration of Objects Launched into Outer Space, Jun. 6, 1975, 1023 U.N.T.S. 15 (entered into force Sep. 15, 1976) [*Registration Convention*]; and Agreement Governing the Activities of States on the Moon and Other Celestial Bodies, Dec. 5, 1979, 1363 U.N.T.S. 3 (entered into force Jul. 11, 1984) [*Moon Agreement*].

8   G.A. Res. 1348 (XIII), Question of the peaceful use of outer space (Dec. 13, 1958).

The 1958 decision of the UN General Assembly further underlined the need "to avoid the extension of present national rivalries into" outer space, and the desire to promote "energetically the fullest exploration and exploitation of outer space for the benefit of mankind."[9]

From the outset, the exploration and use of outer space was envisioned, specifically and categorically, as the "province of all mankind,"[10] which was prompted by the recognition that this unique domain is part of the global commons. In other words, the precepts of international space law were based on the unprecedented recognition that the space domain is not a *domaine réservé* as space activities of one State may potentially have implications for the activities of other States.

With the exception of the Moon Agreement,[11] the other four UN space law treaties instantly garnered widespread acceptance of the international community, considering the historically small number of States that had space capabilities. Newly independent developing countries and some emerging or newer space powers at that time, often seeking economic or technological assistance to advance their own space programs and having their interests recognized, sided with either one or both of the two major spacefaring superpowers, i.e. the United States ("U.S.") and the Union of Soviet Socialist Republics ("USSR" or "Soviet Union"). As a result, progress in the field of law-making for the space domain at the international level was relatively easy and quicker in comparison with other terrestrial domains.

Moreover, the principles contained in the five UN space law treaties, especially in the Outer Space Treaty, can be marked and categorized as safeguarding the inclusive interests of all States. The Outer Space Treaty expanded to outer space the scope of enlightenment approach to international relations and law that was initiated in the Charter of the United Nations. This Treaty encapsulated a set of legal principles, morals and values which were held in the highest regard by the international community to ensure that the exploration and use of outer space remain the province of all mankind. Echoing the 1958 UN General Assembly resolution, the Outer Space Treaty reiterated and codified that the exploration and use of outer space, which includes the Moon and other celestial bodies, must be carried out for the benefit and in the interests of all countries, irrespective of their degree of economic or scientific

---

9   *Id.* at Preamble.
10   Outer Space Treaty, *supra* note 7, at art I.
11   Moon Agreement, *supra* note 7.

development.[12] All States are free to explore and use outer space without discrimination of any kind, on a basis of equality, and in accordance with international law.[13] Additionally, the Outer Space Treaty guarantees free access to all areas of celestial bodies and freedom for scientific exploration,[14] while also declaring that outer space is not subject to national appropriation by any means.[15]

This Treaty also prohibits the placing of nuclear weapons or weapons of mass destruction in orbits around the Earth, and obliges States to use the Moon and other celestial bodies exclusively for peaceful purposes.[16] These principles naturally aligned with the general disarmament objectives of the international community at that time, which was still recovering from the long-term impacts of World War II and feeling the immediate effects of the Cold War. In addition, the recognition of astronauts as "envoys of mankind" captured the common understanding and need to infuse a humanitarian perspective and context to the exploration and use of outer space.[17]

In many ways, the Outer Space Treaty, as is the regulation of outer space and space activities in general, was very innovative in its global governance approach. Disagreements between the then USSR and its Western counterparts (predominantly the U.S.) regarding participation of the private sector or non-governmental entities in space activities were amicably resolved and led to some unique law-making.[18] Unlike general international law, under

---

12   Outer Space Treaty, *supra* note 7, at art. I ¶ 1.

13   *Id.* at art. I ¶ 2.

14   *Id.* at art. I ¶ 3.

15   *Id.* at art. II.

16   *Id.* at art. IV.

17   *Id.* at art. V.

18   The provision of Article VI of the Outer Space Treaty, having its origin in the *1963 Declaration of Legal Principles*, *supra* note 7, at ¶ 5, was a compromise reached between the views initially forwarded by the United States appealing for non-state actors participation in space activities, and the Soviet Union that advocated only for State participation in space activities. This compromise was conveyed to the United Nations General Assembly in its meeting of the Eighteenth Session. This was also noted as a core compromise by the Soviet delegation during deliberations regarding Article VI of the Soviet Draft Treaty (which later formed the basis for Article VI of the Outer Space Treaty) later on in 1966. *See, generally,* Comm. on the Peaceful Uses of Outer Space, Rep. of the Legal SubComm. on its Fifth Session, Summary Record of the Sixty Seventh Meeting, Jul. 25, 1966, U.N. Doc. A/AC.105/C.2/SR.67 (1966), at 3: Statement of Mr. Morozov, USSR, noting that:

     In the plenary committee's discussion on the matter, the Soviet delegation had proposed, in document A/AC.105/L.2, that article 7 should state that all activities of any kind pertaining to the exploration and use of outer space should be carried out solely and

international space law, the States bear responsibility for national activities, including those of its non-governmental/private entities and without any requirement for attribution to the appropriate State.[19] The State that launches or procures the launch of a space object and each State from whose territory or facility an object is launched must bear international liability for damage caused by space objects, even if such a launch were conducted by private companies within the State.[20] Furthermore, the Outer Space Treaty requires the national and international registration of all space objects, both civil and military, launched into outer space, and recognizes the State of registration's enduring national jurisdiction over space objects launched into Earth orbits or further.[21] Most importantly, the States have undertaken to assure that their national space activities, conducted both by its governmental agencies as well as private corporations, are carried out in conformity with the provisions set forth in the Outer Space Treaty.[22]

Encapsulating the unique nature of outer space and legally entrenching space as a shared global commons, there are provisions on safeguarding against harmful contamination, co-operation, mutual assistance and due regard to the corresponding interests of all States.[23] Further, there is a provision regarding prior consultation,[24] which is an expression of the views and aspirations of spacefaring as well as non-spacefaring nations, including those of the developing countries to safeguard the inclusive interests of all countries.[25] More importantly, these fundamental provisions establish a fair balance of interests of all States and the international community as a whole.[26]

---

exclusively by States. Many delegations, however, had insisted that in the view of the conditions prevailing in certain countries activities in space could not be confined to the State.

19   Outer Space Treaty, *supra* note 7, at art. VI.

20   *Id.* at art. VII.

21   *Id.* at art. VIII.

22   *Id.* at art. VI.

23   *Id.* at art. IX.

24   *Id.*

25   *See, generally,* Ram S. Jakhu, *Developing Countries and the Fundamental Principles of International Space Law, in* New Directions in International Law 351–373 (R.G. Girardot et al. eds., 1982).

26   *See* United Nations General Assembly, First Committee, on its Twenty-first Session, Official Records of the 1492nd Meeting, Dec. 17, 1966, U.N. Doc. A/C.1/SR.1492 (1966) at 427, wherein the U.S. expressed that the Outer Space Treaty "established a fair balance between the interests and obligations of all concerned, including the countries which had as yet undertaken no space activities." *See also* Comm. on the Peaceful Uses of Outer Space, Legal SubComm. on its Fifth Session, Summary Record of the Fifty Seventh Meeting, Jul. 12, 1966, U.N. Doc. A/AC.105/C.2/SR.57 (1966), at 12, wherein the Soviet Union emphasized

Further, the Outer Space Treaty affirms the applicability of general international law, including the UN Charter, to outer space.[27] This affirmation is so forward-looking that it can also be applied in the regulation of newer technologies such as cybertechnology and AI technologies in the conduct of space activities. Moreover, the other four UN space law treaties contain provisions that expand on some of the legal provisions contained in the Outer Space Treaty and regulate specific aspects of the exploration and use of outer space, including the Moon and other celestial bodies. In all, these comprise the core and foundational principles of international space law.

In areas where the international community could not accept binding treaty provisions, the core framework of international space law has been supplemented by a few United Nations principles and declarations,[28] which mostly cover and address sectoral applications of space technologies. In other aspects of regulation of space activities, the international community has been adopting annual UN General Assembly resolutions. Notable instruments in this regard are resolutions on the prevention of an arms race in outer space (PAROS)[29] and resolutions on international co-operation in the peaceful uses of outer space.[30]

In sum, through a combination of binding treaty provisions and UN General Assembly resolutions, it is easy to see the preference of the international community towards valuing, providing for and protecting inclusive interests and freedom of all States without any discrimination, and with the desire to assert and enhance the space domain as a global commons.

---

that this treaty was designed "to guarantee that the interests, not only of individual States, but of all countries and of the international community as a whole, would be protected."

27   Outer Space Treaty, *supra* note 7, at art. III. *See also, generally,* Ram S. Jakhu, Steven Freeland & Kuan-Wei Chen, *The Sources of International Space Law: Revisited,* 67 Zeitschrift für Luft- und Weltraumrecht 606 (2018).

28   G.A. Res. 37/92, Principles Governing the Use by States of Artificial Earth Satellites for International Direct Television Broadcasting (Feb. 4, 1983); G.A. Res. 41/65, Principles relating to Remote Sensing of the Earth from Outer Space (Jan. 22, 1987); G.A. Res. 47/68, Principles Relevant to the Use of Nuclear Power Sources in Outer Space (Feb. 23, 1993); G.A. Res. 51/122, Declaration on International Cooperation in the Exploration and Use of Outer Space for the Benefit and in the Interest of All States, Taking into Particular Account the Needs of Developing Countries (Feb. 4, 1997) [*Benefits Declaration*].

29   *See, e.g.,* G.A. Res. 36/97, Prevention of an arms race in outer space (Jan. 15, 1982); G.A. Res. 76/22, UNGA Res. 36/97, UN GAOR, 36th Sess, Supp No 51, UN Doc. A/RES/36/97[C] (1981); G.A. Res. 76/22, Prevention of an arms race in outer space (Dec. 6, 2021). *See also* G.A. Res. 76/23, No first placement of weapons in outer space (Dec. 6, 2021).

30   *See, e.g.,* G.A. Res. 76/76, International Cooperation in the Peaceful Uses of Outer Space (Dec. 9, 2021); G.A. Res. 74/82, International Co-operation in the Peaceful Uses of Outer Space (Dec. 13, 2019); G.A. Res. 73/91, International Co-operation in the Peaceful Uses of Outer Space (Dec. 7, 2018); and so on.

2.2   *An Emerging Trend toward Exclusive Interests of Some States*

Although a number of the above-mentioned legal principles have been adopted to safeguard and enhance inclusive interests of all countries, recently, the actual conduct of some major spacefaring nations has started a contradictory trend. Within a few years after the negotiation of the Moon Agreement in 1979, developments in the space sector indicated a move towards exclusive interests of some leading spacefaring nations. Space activity and conduct quickly became a hallmark of geopolitical hegemony, a means for asserting economic and strategic superiority and dominance,[31] and hinted at the beginning of unilateralism. Currently, the increasing participation, presence and ever-expanding assertiveness of non-governmental or private entities have further made exploration and use of the space domain more complex and difficult. The presence and increased reliance on conduct of private space actors is impacting the conduct of their States in matters related to space technologies and in formulation and application of international space law.

In terms of terminologies and parlance used in legal consciousness research and methodologies, as appropriately summarized and captured by Chua and Engel,[32] State actions and conduct in the space domain is broadly reflective of the "identity" held by spacefaring nations (Identity School of Thought)[33] as well as their "hegemonial" conduct (Hegemony School of Thought).[34]

---

31 *See, e.g.,* since 1958, the space policies and laws of the United States have often reiterated that the U.S. must maintain global leadership or dominance in the space sector. One of the main objectives of the National Aeronautics and Space Act of 1958, Pub. L. No. 85-568, 72 Stat. 426–438 (Jul. 29, 1958) (as amended), at § 102(d)(5) is the "preservation of the role of the United States as a leader in aeronautical and space science and technology. ..." Since then, this approach consistently continued and the latest space policy issued by the Biden Administration, *United States Space Priorities Framework* (Dec. 2021), https://www .whitehouse.gov/wp-content/uploads/2021/12/United-States-Space-Priorities-Frame work-_-December-1-2021.pdf, at 4, (last visited Oct. 10, 2022) states, "The United States is the world leader in space. ... Worldwide interest in space offers the United States opportunities to expand this network while opening new avenues for U.S. leadership and collaboration with allies and partners."

32 Lynette J. Chua & David M. Engel, *Legal Consciousness Reconsidered*, 15 Ann. Rev. L. & Soc. Sci. 335, 337 (2019).

33 The Identity School of thought in legal consciousness relies on the foundation that the place of law in people's lives is intimately connected to their sense of who they are, which is itself a product and producer of their worldview. Scholars further argue, for example, that for the marginalized, "law may seem a double-edged sword"; as they assert legal rights based on an identity protected by the law to win acceptance and inclusion, yet they find themselves constructing an identity that may actually be stigmatized and oppositional.

34 The Hegemony School of legal consciousness has typically seen law as a pervasive and powerful instrument of State control. Citing previous works in the field, Chua & Engel

The identity held by major spacefaring nations and their respective attempt(s) to achieve global leadership and dominance has resulted in the following acts, trends or phenomena:

a. There has been a rise in unilateralism both in law-making as well as conduct in outer space, even at the cost of sidelining UN law-making processes and foundational principles of international space law. For example, in recent years there has been a trend whereby a few States have through their national space legislation authorized private companies to appropriate and exploit natural resources of the Moon and other celestial bodies.[35] Such unilateralism displayed by a handful of States is a noteworthy instance of hegemonial conduct, and also emblematic of the inability of the international community to respond to and to remedy such departures or deviations from decades-long trusted principles of law (*see also* section 4.4 below).

b. There has been a failure to continue to evolve the framework of international space law, or more broadly, a failure to holistically expand and engage the global space governance system to ensure it is better suited for modern times.[36] Since 1979, no space law treaty has been adopted by the UNCOPUOS which goes to show that its role as the main international forum for the progressive development of international space law is gradually being undermined. Outside the UN framework, no progress has been made either. As a consequence, the expansion of international space law is virtually at a standstill.

---

summarized the views held by scholars in this field as: (i) law was "all over," a "shadowy presence" of "power and of compulsion," (ii) law as "majestic," or (iii) law as a "game." with some attempting to go against it. Moreover, to the radical environmentalists, law is a hegemonic power to be challenged *in toto* for protecting an illegitimate social order.

35   *See, e.g.*, United States, Space Resource Commercial Exploration and Utilization Act, 2015, 51 U.S.C. 513; Luxembourg, Law of July 20th 2017 on the exploration and use of space resources; United Arab Emirates, Federal Law No. (12) of 2019 on the Regulation of the Space Sector; and Japan, Space Resources Act, 2021. *See also* The Artemis Accords: Principles for Cooperation in the Civil Exploration and Use of the Moon, Mars, Comets, and Asteroids, https://www.nasa.gov/specials/artemis-accords/img/Artemis-Accords-signed -13Oct2020.pdf [*Artemis Accords*]. The original signatories were representatives from Australia, Canada, Italy, Japan, Luxembourg, the United Arab Emirates, the United Kingdom, and the United States. As of October, 2022, there are 21 Signatories to the Artemis Accords, which is a non-binding international instrument.

36   Ram S. Jakhu & Kuan-Wei Chen, *The Need for Expanding Current Global Space Governance*, *in* Liber Amicorum Sergio Marchisio: Il diritto della comunità internazionale tra caratteristiche strutturali e tendenze innovative 1091, Vol. II, Part III (Editoriale Scientifica, Italy, 2022).

c.   Certain States are refusing to accept their legal status under international space law as a "launching State,"[37] which is contrary to a principle that "once a launching State always a launching State." Such refusal effectively shakes the foundations of international space law which holds the launching State liable for any damage caused by space objects belonging to its public agencies and private entities.[38]

d.   Several launching States have not been fulfilling their obligation to register with the UN Secretary-General their space objects,[39] including those that are being used in military space activities, that have been launched into Earth orbit or beyond.[40]

---

37   Outer Space Treaty, *supra* note 7, at art. VII; Liability Convention, *supra* note 7, at arts. II, III.

38   For example, on July 29, 2003, the Permanent Mission of the Kingdom of the Netherlands to the United Nations (Vienna) informed the United Nations that Netherlands is "not the 'launching State', 'State of registry', or 'launching authority' for the purposes of (a) the Convention on International Liability for Damages Caused by Space Objects (General Assembly resolution 2777 (XXVI), annex), (b) the Convention on Registration of Objects Launched into Outer Space (resolution 3235 (XXIX), annex), or (c) the Agreement on the Rescue of Astronauts, the Return of Astronauts and Return of Objects Launched into Outer Space (resolution 2345 (XXII), annex), respectively." *See* Comm. on the Peaceful Uses of Outer Space, *Note verbale dated 29 July 2003 from the Permanent Mission of the Netherlands to the United Nations (Vienna) addressed to the Secretary-General*, U.N. Doc. A/AC.105/806 (Aug. 22, 2003). Similarly, when INMARSAT was transformed from an intergovernmental organization to a private company (Inmarsat Ltd.), the United Kingdom notified the United Nations on 9 September 2002, that "the United Kingdom is not the "launching State", "State of registry" or "launching authority" for the purposes of" (a) the Liability Convention, (b) the Registration Convention, or (c) the Rescue and Return Convention, respectively. *See,* Comm. on the Peaceful Uses of Outer Space, *Note verbale dated 9 September 2002 from the Permanent Mission of the United Kingdom of Great Britain and Northern Ireland to the United Nations (Vienna) addressed to the Secretary-General,* U.N. Doc. ST/SG/SER.E/417/Rev.1 (Dec. 3, 2002). When notifying to the United Nations the information about of its space objects to be registered in the UN Register of Objects, in accordance with article IV of the Registration Convention, the US often adds that it might not be "a launching State" for some of its registered space objects. For example, on 23 September 2022, the US sent information about several of its space objects to be registered with the UN and indicated that "consistent with its long-standing registration practice, the United States is not necessarily a launching State for each of the space objects it registers." *See,* United Nations Secretariat, *Note verbale dated 23 September 2022 from the Permanent Mission of the United States of America to the United Nations (Vienna) addressed to the Secretary-General,* U.N. Doc. ST/SG/SER.E/1076 (Oct. 5, 2022). *See also,* Comm. on the Peaceful Uses of Outer Space, *Note verbale dated 5 February 2015 from the Permanent Mission of the United States of America to the United Nations (Vienna) addressed to the Secretary-General,* U.N. Doc. ST/SG/SER.E/739 (Jul. 23, 2015).

39   Registration Convention, *supra* note 7, at art. IV.

40   According to the United Nations Office for Outer Space Affairs which maintains the UN Register of Objects Launched into Outer Space, as of Nov. 24, 2022, about 85 percent of

e. There has been neglect on the part of major spacefaring nations to respect the principles contained in Article IX of the Outer Space Treaty. This provision provides the basis to ensure that the space and terrestrial environment is protected from harmful contamination, and obliges States to have due regard to the corresponding interests of other State Parties when conducting space activities.[41] In addition, as missions to the Moon and the Mars are about to take place, primarily for exploitation of natural space resources, the possibility of contamination may be expected on other celestial bodies.[42]

f. There has been a recent unilateral move to formally and expressly negate the long-standing consensus that outer space is a global commons,[43] which in turn hints at the dismantling of the foundations on which international space law has been envisioned and promulgated.

g. Most importantly, recent years have witnessed an exponential increase in the privatization and commercialization of space activities as well as in space militarization and weaponization. Such trends have resulted in greater congestion and competition in outer space. They have also been responsible for the creation of an enormous amount of pollution in the

---

all such space objects have been registered. See, United Nations Office for Outer Space Affairs, United Nations Register of Objects Launched into Outer Space, https://www .unoosa.org/oosa/en/spaceobject register/index.html (last visited Nov. 25, 2022).

41 *See* Committee on Space Research, COSPAR *Policy on Planetary Protection*, approved on Jun. 3, 2021, https://cosparhq.cnes.fr/cospar-policy-on-planetary-protection/ (last visited Dec. 12, 2022). Through this and pursuant to Article IX of the Outer Space Treaty, the COSPAR has adopted its non-binding Planetary Protection Policy, which is the basis for Planetary Protection Policy of States involved in mission to celestial bodies, including to other planets in our solar system. It remains to be seen if the international community will come up with appropriate planetary protection international regulations, procedures and standards that would sufficiently protect space-earth environment and the humans that are expected to travel to and stay on celestial bodies and planets, especially the Moon and the Mars.

42 Fiona Macdonald, *Humans Have Already Left More Than 400,000 Pounds of Junk on The Moon*, Science Alert (Feb. 1, 2018), https://www.sciencealert.com/we-ve-hardly-visited -but-humans-have-already-left-more-than-400-000-pounds-of-waste-on-the-moon (last visited Dec. 12, 2022); Adam Mann, *The Moon could soon have a space junk problem: Impending lunar impact heralds future pollution on our natural satellite*, Science (Feb. 22, 2022), https://www.science.org/content/article/moon-could-soon-have-space-junk -problem (last visited Nov. 22, 2022); Cagri Kilic, *Mars is littered with 15,694 pounds of human trash from 50 years of robotic exploration*, Sep. 28, 2022, https://www.space.com /mars-littered-with-human-trash (last visited Nov. 22, 2022).

43 *See, e.g.*, United States, *Encouraging International Support for the Recovery and Use of Space Resources*, E.O. 13914 (Apr. 6, 2020), https://www.federalregister.gov/documents /2020/04/10/2020-07800/encouraging-international-support-for-the-recovery-and-use-of -space-resources (last visited Oct. 17, 2022).

form of, and in particular, space debris.[44] These are significant developments in the space domain, and the integrity and sustainability of the
global space governance system demands that the rule of law over these
matters is maintained and expanded. So far, the international community remains unable to effectively regulate such developments and activities. (for further details, see Section 4 below);

h.   Finally, there is a lack of effective and formal mechanisms to register
      disagreement and disputes. In general, the major spacefaring nations
      have shown an aversion towards setting up of and creating a functional
      international organization to regularly deal with issues related to inter-
      national space law and regulations (*see* section 5 below).

All of the above trends seem to be contrary, and pose a threat, to some of the
most fundamental principles of international space law that are contained
in the five UN space law treaties. These trends indicate, at least in part, the
gradual and ongoing move by some major spacefaring States as well as their
private companies and actors towards undermining the role and importance
of international space law for protecting inclusive global interest in favor of
enhancing and protecting their individual exclusive interests. There are several extra-judicial and general factors that have also influenced the conduct of
States and their private corporations alike in attempting to circumvent existing
binding international legal obligations. Some of these factors are discussed in
the next section below.

3   Politics of International Law Affecting International Space Law

3.1   *From "Leave No One Behind" to "Each Their Own"*

Perhaps the most immediate, pertinent and prevalent factor towards the current state of affairs in international relations is marked by increasing mistrust
among States, rise in aggressive nationalism, and decline in international
co-operation and multilateralism. In addition, there is an utter failure on the
part of world governments to envisage and deliver, for present and future
generations of humanity, a world that lives and thrives within the carrying

---

44   *See, generally*, Ram S. Jakhu, Joseph N. Pelton & Nishith Mishra, *Satellite Constellations
      and Orbital Pollution: Need for New Policies and Regulations, in* Outer Space Future for
      Mankind – Issues of Law and Policy 267, 273 (Marietta Benkö & Kai-Uwe Schrogl eds.,
      2021).

capacity of our planet Earth. As a result, the world is divided into "haves" and "have-nots."

As an example, in September 2015, Heads of State and Government and High Representatives adopted the United Nations General Assembly Resolution *"Transforming our world: the 2030 Agenda for Sustainable Development."*[45] This resolution contains 17 Sustainable Development Goals and 169 Targets to stimulate action over a period of 15 years till the year 2030;[46] with a declaration and pledge that no one will be left behind;[47] and emphasizing the need to take into account different national realities, capacities and levels of development.[48] Amongst several other shared visions, goals, agendas and action plans, a resolution was adopted with a view to "envisage a world free of poverty, hunger, disease and want, where all life can thrive."[49]

Every year since the adoption of the UN 2015–2030 Agenda goals, the UN has annually released Sustainable Development Goals Reports.[50] The 2022 version of the report,[51] however, paints a rather worrying picture by observing that "[a]s the world faces cascading and interlinked global crises and conflicts, the aspirations set out in the 2030 Agenda for Sustainable Development are

---

45 G.A. Res. 70/1, Transforming our world: he 2030 Agenda for Sustainable Development (Sep. 25, 2015).

46 *Id.*; *see also* United Nations Department of Economic and Social Affairs, *The 17 Goals*, https://sdgs.un.org/goals (last visited Oct. 15, 2022).

47 *Id.* at ¶ 4. Moreover, it is appropriate to note here that although fashioned with the agenda of "leaving no one behind," the availability and delivery of vaccines (or rather, its unavailability for the marginalized and underdeveloped sections of our society) to protect against the Covid-19 pandemic is a case at hand as to how human beings still inhabit a grossly unfair and untrustworthy environment, primarily due to vaccine nationalism.

48 *Id.* at ¶ 5.

49 *Id.* at ¶ 7:
    We envisage a world free of poverty, hunger, disease and want, where all life can thrive. We envisage a world free of fear and violence. A world with universal literacy. A world with equitable and universal access to quality education at all levels, to health care and social protection, where physical, mental and social well-being are assured. A world where we reaffirm our commitments regarding the human right to safe drinking water and sanitation and where there is improved hygiene; and where food is sufficient, safe, affordable and nutritious. A world where human habitats are safe, resilient and sustainable and where there is universal access to affordable, reliable and sustainable energy.

50 *See* United Nations Department of Economic and Social Affairs, *Implementation Progress*, https://sdgs.un.org/goals (last visited Oct. 15, 2022).

51 United Nations, *The Sustainable Development Goals Report 2022*, https://unstats.un.org /sdgs/report/2022/The-Sustainable-Development-Goals-Report-2022.pdf (last visited Oct. 15, 2022).

in jeopardy."[52] The vision of the 2030 Agenda seems to have fallen apart, and along with this, it appears as though somewhere down the line humanity has lost the plot. Needless to say, most human beings realize that there is no Plan B as there is no Planet B.

A few years marked by a pandemic, climate change events, a global recession resulted in the growth of aggressive nationalism that has influenced the approach and action of States. Consequently, States are moving away from an all-inclusive approach (i.e. leaving no one behind) to preserving and protecting their own national interests. Instead of our collective long-term survival goals, dealing with comparatively short-term crises appears to be the priority of the day. Understandably, the world of today is dealing with crises of unprecedented proportions. However, should this mean that we abandon our collective efforts to save humanity from challenges that threaten our very survival?

Today, the space sector also has the potential to contribute to almost all the 17 Sustainable Development Goals of humanity. For this purpose, the UN General Assembly adopted the *"Space 2030 Agenda: space as a driver of sustainable development"* resolution.[53] Among other things, the benefits of space technology and activities to humanity have been classified and categorized as follows: (a) agriculture, (b) global health, (c) environment, (d) sustainable development, (e) disasters and assistance in their management, (f) education, (g) human settlement, (h) transportation, (i) communication, (j) humanitarian assistance and research and development, and (k) international peace and security.[54] Space technologies also provide us with modern comforts and facilities and impact almost all sphere of human activities in many direct as well as indirect ways.

Unfortunately, current approaches being adopted by States on matters that pertain to the very survival of humanity and its ability to live within the

---

52   *Id.* at ¶ 2, noting:

>   As the world faces cascading and interlinked global crises and conflicts, the aspirations set out in the 2030 Agenda for Sustainable Development are in jeopardy. With the COVID-19 pandemic in its third year, the war in Ukraine is exacerbating food, energy, humanitarian and refugee crises – all against the background of a full-fledged climate emergency. Using current data, the Sustainable Development Goals Report 2022 provides evidence of the destructive impacts of these crises on the achievement of the Sustainable Development Goals (SDGs).

53   G.A. Res. 76/3, The "Space2030" Agenda: space as a driver of sustainable development (Oct. 25, 2021) [*Space 2030 Agenda*].

54   United Nations Office for Outer Space Affairs, *Benefits of Space for Humankind*, https://www.unoosa.org/oosa/en/benefits-of-space/benefits.html (last visited Oct. 16, 2022).

carrying capacity of Earth hints at a rather pessimistic future that humanity may encounter in the near future.[55] All of our collective conduct in the form of international law making and international relations subtly points towards this trend. The rise in nationalism, the increasing number and scale of international conflicts as well as widespread protests calling for radical changes in national governmental regimes also appear to be a natural consequence of the self-serving course of action adopted by some States. In addition, as most of the world's population increasingly lives in undemocratic countries, the need and respect for the rule of law, both at the national and international levels, is dangerously receding. In the context of space activities and conduct, this raises a vital point, i.e. if States are unwilling to alter their approach and course of action in matters that relate to our very survival, would their conduct be any different in the space domain?

3.2   *Reasons for the Gradual Decline in International Co-Operation*
Acknowledging the overwhelming view that no individual legal consciousness (even in State sovereignty-based legal systems) arises in a social vacuum,[56] the temporary downfall and subsequent revival of legal consciousness literature has been predicated on its ability to come up with and propound the rather newly crafted "relational legal consciousness continuum."[57] Although, historically, ideas and notions of legal consciousness research and methodologies have been applied by scholars and academicians at the national level only,

---

55   *See* Stacy Liberatore, *Humans are using 73% more natural resources than the Earth produces in a year – with wealthy nations living out of their means fueling the problem*, The Daily Mail (Apr. 27, 2021), https://www.dailymail.co.uk/sciencetech/article-9518051/Humans-using-73-natural-resources-Earth-produces-year-study-reveals.html (last visited Nov. 15, 2022); Jerusalem Post Staff, *World natural resources may run out by 2040 – study*, Jerusalem Post (Jul. 25, 2021), https://www.jpost.com/health-science/world-natural-resources-may-run-out-by-2040-study-674844 (last visited Nov. 15, 2022).

56   Chua & Engel, *supra* note 32, at 342.

57   *Id.* For, in the relational legal consciousness continuum, there is space to examine (a) conduct of specific spacefaring nations (at an individual level) as the collective morals or conscience or values shared by people in a specific geographic territory or socio-cultural and economic context i.e. a specific nation (in a State-sovereignty based international system) then takes the form of international positions (legal as well as political) taken by a nation State at the global level; (b) conduct of a conglomeration of States organized and acting collectively through formal or informal groups, often with collective economic, military or other objectives; and (c) conduct of the entire international community and the effect that geo-political developments or other factors have on international law in general, and in turn, how the conduct of nations in international law or international relations affects their attitude and behaviour in the conduct of space activities and international space law.

recent efforts point towards a growing interest in the examination of these aspects at an international level as well.

Placed in the international context, say, for example, in the context of the UN, the tasks of maintaining international peace and security and promoting international cooperation have typically been retained by the Security Council, which is composed of 15 Member States, but dominated by five Member States who are permanent members. The increase in the general mistrust of other States in view of the privilege being exercised selfishly by the permanent Member States of the Security Council, often in the form of their veto power(s) being repeatedly exercised only in their self-interest, has had a tremendous effect on international law in general.[58] While there has always been a tacit recognition of this power disparity in international relations, several trends and developments have turned the tide of international concerns and relations towards a more individualistic, nationalist and unilateral approach to addressing what are issues of global concern. In recent years, we have witnessed the rise of more States with noteworthy economic and military might and with potential to influence international relations on a global scale. Further, in addition to a "revert back to the basic instinct of survival" course of action being adopted by States due to increasing instances of the threat or use of force and conflicts, we are also seeing aggressive armament, decline in rules-based multilateral trade, continuing environmental degradation and associated climate change events, destruction of ecosystems and loss of biodiversity and natural resources, overpopulation and an increase in refugee and other humanitarian crises, pandemics and medicine nationalism, global food insecurity, growing energy crises on a global scale and the continuous destruction of unique cultures of indigenous peoples. Naturally, all of these trends in international relations and the current state of the world have also penetrated to the domain of international space law, space activities and conduct.

---

58   *See, generally, Security Council – Veto List*, https://www.un.org/Depts/dhl/resguide/ scact _veto_table_en.htm. *See also* Michael Ramsden, *Uniting for Peace: the Emergency Special Session on Ukraine*, https://harvardilj.org/ 2022/04/uniting-for-peace-the-emergency-spe cial-session-on-ukraine (last visited Oct. 20, 2022), highlighting how the international community, specifically the United Nations General Assembly, engaged a reinvigorated 72-year old legal instrument, the Uniting for Peace Resolution (G.A. Res. 377 (V), Uniting for Peace (Nov. 3, 1950)) to determine that "Russia has committed aggression in Ukraine and this provides the first such internationally authoritative determination that this conduct occurred". Moreover, the use of the Uniting for Peace mechanism is a symptom of the UN's institutional failure, with the many (i.e. the 193 members of the Assembly) attempting to do through a process of collective legal interpretation what the few have failed to do through Chapter VII decisions (i.e. the 15 members of the Security Council, especially when a permanent member exercises its veto power).

While historically the two major spacefaring nations, the United States and the Russian Federation (former USSR) have been dominant in the space domain, in the past three decades a few States have started making noteworthy progress in that area. Today, more than 70 space agencies exist in the world. More than 15 States and their private companies possess the ability to launch space objects, and seven States have the capability to send a probe to extra-terrestrial locations such as the Moon, Mars, or deep space.[59] Moreover, in the NewSpace 4.0 era, activities of private enterprises or non-governmental entities often exceed the activities of most States.[60] Since these developments are essentially and exclusively directed at profit-making, space activities are shifting away from international cooperation and from protection of the core principles of international space law focused on inclusive benefits and interests of all States.

There have been some other factors contributing to the gradual decline in international co-operation in space activities. UNCOPUOS has been unable to make States commit to binding legal agreements, even in matters of urgent and pressing concern to the international community. Such matters include the issue of ever-increasing space debris and the unilaterally declared intentions of a select few spacefaring States to extract and exploit space natural resources for exclusive national benefits. The long-term sustainability of outer space has further been threatened by States conducting anti-satellite tests that result in the destruction of their own satellites in orbit,[61] and other experiments and maneuvers that heighten international mistrust and tensions.[62]

---

59   World Population Review, *Countries with Space Programs*, https://worldpopulationre view.com/country-rankings/countries-with-space-programs (last visited Oct. 22, 2022).

60   Svetla Ben-Itzhak, *Companies are commercializing outer space. Do government programs still matter?*, Washington Post (Jan. 11, 2022), https://www.washingtonpost.com /politics/2022/01/11/companies-are-commercializing-outer-space-do-government-pro grams-still-matter (last visited Oct. 24, 2022), noting:

        Over the last 15 years, commercial activity in space more than tripled, growing from $110 billion in 2005 to nearly $357 billion in 2020. Commercial activity in 2020 accounted for about 80 percent of the estimated $447 billion global space economy that year. Morgan Stanley projects that the sector will rocket to more than $1 trillion by 2040, with growth concentrated in the commercial space sector.

61   Secure World Foundation, *Anti-Satellite Weapons: Threatening the Sustainability of Space Activities*, https://swfound.org/media/207392/swf-asat-testing-infographic-may2022.pdf (last visited Oct. 12, 2022).

62   *See, e.g.*, Matthew Mowthorpe, *The Russian space threat and a defense against it with guardian satellites*, The Space Review (Jun. 13, 2022), https://www.thespacereview.com /article/4401/1 (last visited Oct. 12, 2022).

All these observations are not *per se* a critique of existing international space law. It is the failure of the international community to review and update this legal regime that has led to a situation that such an important and for-ward-looking treaty as the Outer Space Treaty is facing challenges to its foun-dational principles. Added to the general despair with regard to the strength and nature of the law governing outer space and outer space activities, the possibility of major space power(s) withdrawing from this principal treaty is not unthinkable.[63] Coupled with a period of unilateral onslaught on signifi-cant international treaties and States' reluctance to negotiate or strengthen international agreements on matters of utmost importance to humanity, like the climate change issue, the global space governance regime is at a crucial inflexion point.

The deteriorating state of general international relations is a key contrib-utor to the current state of affairs. In the context of international space law, international relations have had an impact since the time States negotiated and adopted the Moon Agreement but then proceeded not to become party to the treaty that was designed to clarify the law as it applies to activities in the exploration, exploitation and use of natural resources of the Moon and celestial bodies.[64]

---

63   Ram S. Jakhu & Steven Freeland, *A Vital Artery or a Stent Needing Replacement? A Global Space Governance System Without The Outer Space Treaty?, in* Proceedings of the Interna-tional Institute of Space Law 505 (IISL, 2018).

64   *For example,* the United States actively participated in the negotiation of the Moon Agree-ment and supported the inclusion of the Common Heritage Principle in its Article 11. However, it never signed or ratified the treaty, showing its indifference to this fifth UN space law treaty for forty years and finally rejected it in 2020. The 2020 U.S. President Executive Order 13914, *supra* note 43, asserts that

the United States does not consider the Moon Agreement to be an effective or nec-essary instrument to guide nation states regarding the promotion of commercial partic-ipation in the long-term exploration, scientific discovery, and use of the Moon, Mars, or other celestial bodies. Accordingly, the Secretary of State shall object to any attempt by any other State or international organization to treat the Moon Agreement as reflecting or otherwise expressing customary international law.

Similarly, other major space powers and the permanent members of the UN Security Council (i.e. China, France, Russia and the United Kingdom) have not ratified the Moon Agreement either. Moreover, another member State, Saudi Arabia, has sent on 05 January 2023 its intimation to withdraw from the Moon Agreement (*see supra* note 7) which will come into effect on and from 05 January 2024. *See* United Nations, *Saudi Arabia – With-drawal,* Depositary Notification and Reference: C.N.4.2023.TREATIES-XXIV.2 (Jan. 5, 2023), https://treaties.un.org/doc/Publication/CN/2023/ CN.4.2023-Eng.pdf (last visited Jan. 19, 2023). This is a unique and unprecedented development as this is the first time ever a State has withdrawn from any of the UN space treaties. This may initiate a trend for abandoning not only this Agreement, but also other instruments of international space law.

In a way, all these changes and shifts propelled the course of action that the international community has adopted since the early years of this century. The lack of flexibility shown by Russia and China on one side, and the United States and some of the European powers on the other, has made it impossible for the negotiation, let alone adoption, of a subsequent international treaty on the regulation of outer space. Persistent geopolitical differences between Russia and the U.S., and more recently with People's Republic of China, are major barriers to cooperation in controlling placement of weapons in outer space.[65] For instance, geopolitical, economic, legal and other related factors and disagreements led to the rejection of the Sino-Russian draft Treaty on the Prevention of the Placement of Weapons in Outer Space and of the Threat or Use of Force Against Outer Space Objects (PPWT)[66] by the United States and other allied States. In the meantime, the intentional destruction of a State's own satellites in space has emerged as a means of showcasing military space power and capabilities. All of these trends jeopardize the long-term sustainability of outer space activities and the freedom of exploration and use of outer space by all States.

---

65 *See, e.g.*, G.A. Res. 76/23, No First Placement of Weapons in Outer Space (Dec. 8, 2021), initiated by the Russian Federation whereby States make a political commitment not to be the first to place weapons in outer space. The United Nations General Assembly adopted it with a vote of 130 in favor to 35 against and with 20 abstentions. The United States is one of the States that opposed this Resolution. Similarly, in 2022, the United States initiated and called for unilateral declarations not to conduct destructive direct-ascent anti-satellite missile testing. The UN General Assembly First Committee endorsed this United States initiative with a vote of 154 in favor to 8 against and with 10 abstentions. Russia and China opposed this Resolution. Both these very good initiatives can be expected to make important contributions to control a space arms race and should be adopted by all States, but geopolitical differences inhibit international cooperation in this regard.

66 Conference on Disarmament, Letter dated 12 February 2008 from the Permanent Representative of the Russian Federation and the Permanent Representative of China to the Conference on Disarmament addressed to the Secretary General of the Conference transmitting the Russian and Chinese texts of the draft "Treaty on Prevention of the Placement of Weapons in Outer Space and of the Threat or Use of Force against Outer Space Objects (PPWT)" introduced by the Russian Federation and China, (Feb. 29, 2008), U.N. Doc. CD/1839; Conference on Disarmament, Letter dated 10 June 2014 from the Permanent Representative of the Russian Federation and the Permanent Representative of China to the Conference on Disarmament addressed to the Acting Secretary-General of the Conference transmitting the updated Russian and Chinese texts of the draft "Treaty on Prevention of the Placement of Weapons in Outer Space and of the Threat or Use of Force Against Outer Space Objects (PPWT)" introduced by the Russian Federation and China, (Jun. 12, 2014), U.N. Doc. CD/1985.

3.3   *New Technologies Outpace Treaty-Making*

The deterioration in international relations is not the sole cause of the current state of affairs of our globalized world. The pace of technological developments coupled with the fact that the treaty-making process at the international level is very slow and tedious are equally potent factors. As a result, the desire for binding legal commitments through international treaties and agreements on a multilateral basis is no longer the preferred means of conducting international relations. Such a trend is particularly evident when looking at the way the international community approaches the legal regulation of technologies that have developed after the onset of space activities, such as cybertechnology, use of Autonomous Weapons Systems, and most recently, AI systems.[67]

As they stand today, the preferred means of regulating these newer technologies have been soft law (non-binding) instruments such as guidelines, UN General Assembly resolutions, and the establishment of a UN Group of Governmental Experts,[68] which deliberate and make suggestions to the international community as to the relevant legal principles that 'may' be applied and adhered to by States on the basis of voluntary political commitments. Moreover, the general reluctance of States to undertake international responsibility for actions of private actors (which, in the context of these newer technologies, may be an individual "person," natural or legal) has largely prevented meaningful international agreements in these areas. As a result, technological progress is by far outpacing its regulation. For example, the only universally agreed-upon document addressing the use of AI systems comes in the form of the United Nations Educational, Cultural and Scientific Organization's Recommendations on the Ethics of Artificial Intelligence.[69] Significantly, it

---

67   For these newer technologies, the effects that they have had on the international community and the well-being of human beings largely overshadow the impacts that space technologies have had in their initial years and decades of development. Moreover, as opposed to space activities and conduct, where governments and their actions were largely able to prevent meaningful participation of non-governmental entities or private enterprises for almost half a century, there is private participation in development and handling of the newer technologies from the very beginning.

68   The basis of cybersecurity at the United Nations was laid by the work of the United Nations Group of Governmental Experts (UN GGE) between 2004 and 2021, which continues to date. *See, e.g.,* UN OEWG and GGE, https://dig.watch/processes/un-gge (last visited Oct. 25, 2022). Similarly, in areas of UN processes for regulation of lethal autonomous weapons systems, *see,* United Nations Office for Disarmament Affairs, *Background on Laws in the CCW,* https://www.un.org/disarmament/the-convention-on-certain-conventional -weapons/back ground-on-laws-in-the-ccw/ (last visited Oct. 25, 2022).

69   United Nations Educational, Scientific and Cultural Organization, *Recommendations on the Ethics of Artificial Intelligence,* (Nov. 23, 2021), U.N. Doc. SHS/BIO/REC-AIETHICS/2021,

does not deal specifically and effectively with any important aspect of its legal regulation.

All of this has had a significant impact in creating a general aversion of States toward entering into binding legal commitments for the regulation of space activities as well. The complexities and challenges presented by private sector participation, such as issues related to insurance and re-insurance, consumer protection, antitrust and competition, commercial transactions and agreements on a bilateral basis, etc. are increasingly in the domain of private international law; and this also has resulted in the general decline of acceptability of instruments of public international space law as well as in multilateralism.

The next section of this Chapter discusses a few notable developments in space activities and the negative impact they have had on the expansion of international co-operation and respect for international space law.

4   Noteworthy Actions of States Significantly Affecting International Space Law

As put forth in the introductory part of this Chapter, it is in the inherent nature of human beings to identify obstacles and then devise mechanisms and mannerisms through which such obstacles are overcome. This fundamental human nature, fortunately or unfortunately, plays all the way up to the very regulation of international actions and conduct of international relations, including in the space domain. The following discussion captures the most critical developments and issues, the continuation or resolution of which will determine the success or failure of international space law.

4.1   *Unbridled Privatization and Commercialization of Space Activities*
Owing to the economies of scale and entrepreneurship, States and their agencies have historically been unable to match the pace and growth that private sector participation is able to deliver. While accepting the undeniable role that governments play in legal and other forms of regulation of space activities, the growth of the private space sector has dwarfed the technological capabilities and relevance that governmental agencies have provided in the past. The rapid and unprecedented onset of private sector participation in space activities has been possible due to tremendous technological advancements, such as reusable rocket launchers, increase in the number of satellites that can be

deployed per launch activity, and the ability to induct newer forms of technology quickly to manage on-orbit operations of satellites and their constellations. As an example, the onset of commercialization and privatization of the aviation sector took many State players out of the equation entirely and in turn had reduced the role of States to providing air defense. A similar trend may be currently observed in the space sector as well.[70]

In relation to activities in the space domain, the hegemonial conduct of certain States has sometimes seeped deep into the attitude of their private corporations. For instance, one large private space corporation has unilaterally and quite explicitly expressed its views that international law is not applicable to a specific space activity or on a celestial body.[71] While such expressions might have typically not mattered in other areas of international regulation, it is a matter of concern when that particular entity owns and operates nearly half of all active satellites in Earth orbits.[72] The global presence and transboundary outreach of a few private enterprises raises a very important issue of "if and/ or when" these enterprises be treated as subjects of international law. There is also a growing concern about the increasing influence of major private space companies and their multibillionaire executives in national regulatory frameworks and in international relations.

The launch and operation, by private companies, of mega-constellations comprising thousands of satellites are expected to result in the creation of considerable space debris and the occupation of a fairly large number of radio frequency bands, which are a limited international natural resource. Lack of effective control of space debris would make it expensive, and often prohibitive, for newer States to launch and manage their space objects and assets. Further, control over radio frequencies is being increasingly seen as attempts at establishing a monopoly in outer space to the exclusion of new entrants into the space domain.[73] Such private space corporations have been able to carry

---

70   Barring the States that do not yet allow for direct private participation in space activities, this trend is being observed in most States that do allow for such participation.

71   *See, e.g.,* Anthony Cuthbertson, *Elon Musk's SpaceX will 'make its own laws on Mars,* The Independent (Oct. 28, 2020), https://www.independent.co.uk/space/elon-musk-spacex -mars-laws-starlink-b1396023.html (last visited Oct. 12, 2022).

72   Primoz Rome, Every Satellite Orbiting Earth and Who Owns Them, Jan. 18, 2022, https:// dewesoft.com/blog/every-satellite-orbiting-earth-and-who-owns-them (last visited Oct. 12, 2022).

73   Peter B. De Selding, *French Space Command: Europe must react to U.S., Chinese constellations' land grab in low Earth orbit, Space Intel Report* (Jun. 21, 2021), https://www .spaceintelreport.com/french-space-command-europe-must-react-to-u-s-chinese -constellations-land-grab-in-low-earth-orbit/ (last visited Oct. 25, 2022).

on their operations with no or little regard for the appropriate protection of dark and quiet skies[74] as well, and the emerging environmental impact their activities may have on various stakeholders.

Additionally, as a result of privatization of space activities, there has been a blurring of the distinction between public (governmental) and private sector involvement in foreign wars and conflicts.[75] The governmental agencies of major space powers are increasingly relying on the commercial launchers, satellite and services of the private sector for military purposes.[76] The dual-use nature of numerous commercial satellites has contributed towards growing mistrust among States. It is evident there is a failure to effectively regulate such private companies or non-governmental entities. Article VI of the Outer Space Treaty obliges States to authorize and continuously supervise the activities of private space operators, and States must ensure that all activities of private enterprises are carried out in compliance with the provisions of the Outer Space Treaty. In addition, the considerably dominant position of private space corporations may be contrary to the principles contained in Article I of the Outer Space Treaty pertaining to the exploration of outer space for the benefit and in the interests of all mankind, the freedom of exploration and use of outer space without discrimination of any kind and on a basis of equality.[77]

---

74   *See, e.g.*, United States National Science Foundation & NOIRLab, SATCON2 Policy Working Group Report (2022), https://noirlab.edu/public/media/archives/techdocs/pdf /techdoc037.pdf (last visited Sep. 27, 2022). It should also be noted that challenges posed by mega satellite constellations on dark and quiet skies have negative implications for cultural rights of indigenous peoples who have close affinity to astronomy. *See, e.g.*, Ciara Finnegan, *Indigenous Interests in Outer Space: Addressing the Conflict of Increasing Satellite Numbers with Indigenous Astronomy Practices*, Laws (Mar. 22, 2022), https://www. mdpi.com/2075-471X/11/2/26 (last visited Oct. 15, 2022).

75   Gillian Tett, *Ukraine's Starlink problems show the dangers of digital dependency*, Financial Times (Oct. 13, 2022), https://www.ft.com/content/692a222b-7823-4308-80a1-afa05111351c (last visited Oct. 25, 2022).

76   In doing so, these States are set on re-enacting the course of action which was earlier seen in the aviation sector. However, to reiterate, a critical difference between these two sectors is that the exploration and use of space domain have been marked and considered as the province of all mankind. Thus, naturally, any advancements in military technologies, capabilities and actions are viewed by the international community with apprehension. In turn, this reduces trust and multilateralism in the enacting of new treaties, laws and regulations.

77   The only attempt in this regard was made in the negotiation and adoption by the United Nations General Assembly of the non-binding 1997 Benefits Declaration whose provisions are without any teeth. *See generally,* Benefits Declaration, *supra* note 28.

Humanity must keep in mind that private companies, owing to their profit-seeking motivations and exploitative tendencies, will carry on their activities in outer space in a similar manner as they have done and continue to do on Earth. The barbarism shown by, for example, the British East India Company in the 16th and 17th centuries, and the environmental damage caused by British Petroleum[78] in the 21st century, can be expected to be repeated in some form in outer space by irresponsible and unregulated corporations. Again, the unwillingness and inability of some States to tackle this issue[79] contribute further towards the gradual and ongoing decline in respect for international space law. The profound impact that privatization of space activities has had on an increase in military space activities is also noteworthy.

4.2 Grave Danger Posed by Increasing Space Arms Race and Space Militarization

The sharp increase in military space activities (or "militarization of space") is typically associated or linked with the attitude to assert dominance and to expand both defensive and offensive capabilities. While the hegemonial nature and conduct of major spacefaring nations and ambitions for dominance have been quite apparent and discussed in earlier sections, factors supporting the increased onset of military activities and capabilities in space are also marked by the need to maintain the "relevance" of governmental agencies in the form of support that they can provide to protect the space assets and infrastructure of both governmental agencies and private enterprises.

A report by the Secure World Foundation highlights the global counterspace capabilities of Australia, China, France, India, Iran, Japan, North Korea, Russia, South Korea,the United Kingdom and the United States.[80] Moreover, major spacefaring nations have also been setting up their own space force divisions or other agencies as part of their military capabilities and structures. The rules of engagement for space wars are being considered and drafted, and space

---

78   Dominic Rushe, *BP set to pay largest environmental fine in US history for Gulf oil spill*, The Guardian (Jul. 2, 2015), https://www.theguardian.com/environment/2015/jul/02/bp-will -pay-largest-environmental-fine-in-us-history-for-gulf-oil-spill (last visited Nov. 22, 2022).

79   In this context, an issue of urgent concern is that: if one of the leading spacefaring nations, such as the United States, which has historically been vigilant in the promulgation of laws and regulations, is unable to keep up with the pace of development of the private sector and the complexities being presented by it, it remains dubious at best whether other States, including emerging spacefaring States, would be able to do so promptly and aptly.

80   Brian Weeden & Victoria Samson, Global Counter Space Capabilities – An Open Source Assessment, (5th ed. 2022), https://swfound.org/media/207346/swf_global_counterspace _capabilities_es_2022_en.pdf (last visited Oct. 25, 2022).

war games are being conducted. All of this implies that the space domain is becoming a war-fighting domain.[81] The phenomena of newer forms of weapons and systems in space, the dual-use nature of most space objects, and the rise of many emerging spacefaring nations who also wish to possess their own military space capabilities, etc. have all contributed towards the growth of global military space activities and capabilities. In addition, the rise of aggressive nationalism, conflicts, mistrust in the global arena mentioned before have also contributed significantly to the militarization and weaponization of outer space. The conduct of some spacefaring nations has inspired others to follow suit. The deliberate and intentional destruction of their own satellites by the United States, China, Russia, and India can be said to have expanded the weaponization of space, accelerated a space arms race and caused pollution in the space environment in the form of space debris. Other States may soon be motivated to conduct their own anti-satellite tests.

The use of satellites (even of private companies of non-combatant States) in actual war has given rise to serious controversies among nations with respect to these satellites being legitimate targets, and possible actions which are/may be needed to protect them. War or hostilities in space would have devastating consequences for humanity. The International Committee of the Red Cross has warned that "the weaponization of outer space would increase the likelihood of hostilities in outer space" and the "human cost of using weapons in outer space that could disrupt, damage, destroy or disable civilian or dual-use space objects is likely to be significant."[82] Thus, in specific situations and for the use of certain kind of military tactics and maneuvers in space, certain States can be considered to be in violation of their fundamental obligations under the Outer Space Treaty for carrying out all their space activities, including military space, "in the interest of maintaining international peace and security and promoting international co-operation and understanding."[83] All in all, the unwillingness of the major space powers to take steps to reduce or halt the

---

81   In 2019, NATO "recognised space as a new operational domain." *See, e.g.,* North Atlantic Treaty Organization, *NATO's approach to space*, Oct. 6, 2022, https://www.nato.int/cps/en /natohq/topics_175419.htm (last visited Oct. 26, 2022). *See also* Marcia Smith, *Top Air Force Officials: Space Now Is A Warfighting Domain*, May 17, 2017, https://spacepolicyonline .com/news/top-air-force-officials-space-now-is-a-warfighting-domain/ (last visited Oct. 26, 2022).

82   International Committee of the Red Cross, *The Potential Human Cost of the Use of Weapons in Outer Space and the Protection Afforded by International Humanitarian Law*, IRRC No. 915 (Apr. 8, 2021), https://www.icrc.org/en/document/potential-human-cost-outer -space-weaponization-ihl-protection (last visited Dec. 12, 2022).

83   Outer Space Treaty, *supra* note 7, at art. III.

growth of militarization and weaponization of outer space activities has been and continues to be a major factor towards the decline in development of and respect for international space law.[84]

4.3   Great Challenge of Space Pollution (Contamination) Caused by Space Debris

Admittedly, the space environment is vast and larger than one can imagine. However, if we consider the current technological capabilities of even the most advanced spacefaring nations, the portion of usable space environment in orbits around the Earth that can sustain commercial space operations is fast diminishing.[85] Considering the specificities of the space environment, this is due to the aggravated problems being posed by space debris elements in Low Earth Orbits. The orbital velocity of satellites and the possibility of a cascading effect in space where debris elements or an active satellite colliding with each other has the potential to affect the space operations of all of humankind, is making space operations in outer space even more unsafe and hazardous.[86] This problem is further complicated by the launch, or proposed launch, of tens of thousands of satellites in the form of large-scale (mega) satellite constellations in already crowded portions of low Earth orbits. In addition, while risks to missions in Earth orbits remain unchecked, spacefaring nations have also been creating space debris in the Moon's orbits.[87]

Despite these urgent and pressing issues, the international community has been unable to agree on binding legal commitments to halt the generation of or to significantly reduce the ever-increasing amount of space debris. This course of action hits at the very foundational principles of international space law, i.e. to explore and use space for the benefit and in the interests of all

---

84   For the control and regulation of space arms race the international community has made several efforts in the form of draft treaties, UN General Assembly resolutions, draft codes of conduct, unilateral declarations, etc. but none of them has succeeded yet or has been able to make any positive and effective change.

85   *See* Carmen Pardini & Luciano Anselmo, *Evaluating the impact of space activities in low earth orbit*, 184 Acta Astronautica 11–22 (2021), noting the key result of a preliminary analysis of the 2021 study that "we have already 'filled up' one-third to one-half of the 'capacity' of LEO able to sustain long-term space activities."

86   This has sometimes been also referred to as the "Kessler Syndrome": *See* Donald Kessler & Burton G. Cour-Palais, *Collision Frequency of Artificial Satellites: The Creation of a Debris Belt*, 83 J. Geophysical Research 2637 (1978).

87   Paolo Guardabasso & Stéphanie Lizy-Destrez, *Lunar orbital debris mitigation: characterisation of the environment and identification of disposal strategies*, 8th European Conference on Space Debris, Conference Proceedings of the European Space Agency – Space Debris Office, 2021, https://conference.sdo.esoc.esa.int/ proceedings/sdc8/paper/42 (last visited Dec. 12, 2022).

countries. The presence of space debris necessarily also acts as a natural obstacle to the entry of newer States wishing to conduct space activities as it makes it more challenging and expensive for these emerging spacefaring nations and their private corporations to launch, to conduct and to sustain operations in outer space. To safely navigate through the cloud of space debris requires technological advancement over and above the most basic technological prowess for the simple launch and operation of a space object. More importantly, it is estimated that the "distribution of rocket body launches and reentry leads to the causality expectation (that is, risk to human life) being disproportionately borne by populations in the Global South, with major launching states exporting risk to the rest of the world."[88] Due to the ongoing proliferation of space debris, it becomes increasingly important to not only launch and operate space objects but also to keep a constant track of space debris and other redundant elements through Space Situational Awareness ("SSA") and Space Traffic Management ("STM") capabilities. Even a large majority of spacefaring nations do not currently have these capabilities.

Soft law instruments in the form of Space Debris Mitigation Guidelines[89] have been incorporated into respective national legislations and other policy documents of some States.[90] However, in the absence of any formal legally binding instrument of international space law on the subject matter, and in

---

88   Michael Byers et al., *Unnecessary risks created by uncontrolled rocket reentries*, Nature Astronomy (Jul. 11, 2022), https://www.nature.com/articles/s41550-022-01718-8 (last visited Nov. 22, 2022).

89   United Nations Office for Outer Space Affairs, *Space Debris Mitigation Guidelines of the Committee on the Peaceful Uses of Outer Space* (endorsed by G.A. Res. 62/217, Dec. 22, 2007), https://www.unoosa.org/pdf/publications/st_space_49E.pdf (last visited Oct. 15, 2022); Inter-Agency Space Debris Coordination Committee, *IADC Space Debris Mitigation Guidelines*, Revision 3 of June, 2021, IADC-02-01 [collectively, *Space Debris Guidelines*].

90   *See* United Nations Office for Outer Space Affairs, *Compendium of space debris mitigation standards adopted by States and international organizations*, Part 1: National mechanisms, http://www.unoosa.org/oosa/en/ourwork/topics/space-debris/compendium.html (last visited Oct. 20, 2022). For a few examples in the international context: *see*, International Organization for Standardization, *Standard 24113 'Space systems – Space debris mitigation requirements,'* ISO Reference Number 24113:2019(E), (3rd ed. July, 2019); *European Code of Conduct for Space Debris Mitigation*, Jun. 28, 2004, Issue 1.0. For national legislations: *see, e.g.*, China, *Space Industry Standard – Orbital Debris Mitigation Requirements*, QJ3221-2005 (came into effect in 2006, and revised in 2015); Russia, *Space Technology Items. General Requirements for Mitigation of Near-Earth Space Debris Mitigation*, GOST R 52925-2018, adopted by Order of the Federal Agency for Technical Regulation and Metrology Order No. 632-st of Sep. 21, 2018 (effective as of Jan. 1, 2019); France, *Decree on Technical Regulation issued pursuant to Act n°2008-518 of 3rd June 2008*, Mar. 31, 2011, at arts. 21, 40; Canada, *Remote Sensing Space Systems Act*, Nov. 5, 2005, S.C. 2005, at ch. 45 § 9; United States Government, *Orbital Debris Mitigation Standard Practices*, Nov. 2019 update, at objective 4: Postmission disposal of space

the absence of an appropriate mechanism to initiate and engage processes towards the making of such a formal legal instrument, it remains uncertain whether the recommendations of some of these Guidelines have passed onto the domain of customary international space law. The effectiveness, if any, of these Guidelines remains extremely limited as the number of space debris continues to increase, as can be clearly seen in Figure 28.1 below:

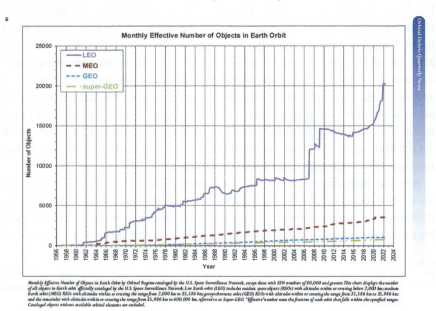

FIGURE 28.1   Source U.S. NASA, *Orbital Debris Quarterly News*, Volume 26, Issue 2, June 2022

In September 2011, the U.S. National Research Council warned that space debris has reached a "'tipping point', with enough currently in orbit to continually collide and create even more debris, raising the risk of spacecraft failures. ..."[91] A decade later, in 2021, while admitting that "[O]ne of the biggest global challenges facing the space sector is orbital congestion and space debris", the G7 Leaders "pledged to take action to tackle the growing hazard of space debris as our planet's orbit becomes increasingly crowded."[92] It remains to be seen if,

structures, https://orbitaldebris.jsc.nasa.gov/library/usg_orbital_debris_mitigation_stan dard_practices_november_2019.pdf (last visited Oct. 20, 2022), and so on.

91   Eyder Peralta, *Space Debris Has Reached A 'Tipping Point'*, Sep. 1, 2011, https://www.npr .org/sections/thetwo-way/2011/09/01/140114894/study-space-debris-has-reached-a-tip ping-point (last visited Nov. 12, 2022).

92   United Kingdom Space Agency Press release, *G7 nations commit to the safe and sustainable use of space*, Jun. 13, 2021, https://www.gov.uk/government/news/g7-nations-commit-to -the-safe-and-sustainable-use-of-space (last visited Dec. 12, 2022). *See also* Staff Writers,

and when, this pledge will be fulfilled. Without more proactive space debris remedial or removal measures, there is very limited, if any, hope for a meaningful solution in the near or medium term to the space debris problem that is caused by a few spacefaring nations, and which is expected to pose constraints on the freedom of use of outer space by all States. If no Active Debris Removal ("ADR") efforts are undertaken, it is believed that even if no new space objects are launched and given the number of objects already in orbit, the space environment (at least in the most used Earth orbits) might not be sustainable. There are numerous legal, organizational and strategic challenges to effective ADR operations, but none of them are being seriously addressed at the international level.

4.4 Exploitation of Natural Resources of the Moon and Other Celestial Bodies

As terrestrial natural resources are expected to be depleted soon, the impetus to explore and exploit space natural resources has increased significantly over the past ten years or so. Although, commercial exploitation and appropriation of natural resources of the Moon and other celestial bodies may appear to be in the realm of science fiction, various States and their private companies are actively planning their missions for this purpose.

Recent unilateral attempts to support such activities highlight the nature of exploitation of natural resources in the space environment. Some States have taken national legislative initiatives to authorize their private companies to exploit and appropriate space natural resources.[93] Other States may follow this lead. These steps may be necessary to create domestic administrative processes for implementing their international obligation regarding authorization and continuous supervision that is required under Article VI of the Outer Space Treaty. However, this trend presents concerns at the international level. Such unilateral regulatory efforts related to the exploitation and appropriation of space natural resources are believed to circumvent the UN law-making process and bypass the role of UNCOPUOS on matters that are clearly the concern of all of humanity. Similarly, they also seem to be contrary to the provisions of Article II of the Outer Space Treaty that prohibit national appropriation by any means, and Article 11 of the Moon Agreement, which designates natural

---

NASA funds projects to study orbital debris, space sustainability, Space Daily (Sep. 15, 2022), https://www.spacedaily.com/reports/NASA_funds_projects_to_study_orbital_debris _ space_ sustainability_999.html (last visited Nov. 14, 2022), noting:

   Orbital debris is one of the great challenges of our era, said Bhavya Lal, associate administrator for the Office of Technology, Policy, and Strategy (OTPS) at NASA Headquarters in Washington.

93   See supra note 35.

resources of the Moon and celestial bodies as the common heritage of mankind. The Moon Agreement further calls for the establishment of an international framework to facilitate the orderly and safe development, rational management, and equitable sharing of such natural resources.

Compounding the issue with regard to the exploitation of space natural resources, the legal status of outer space as a global commons has unilaterally been rejected.[94] A number of, mainly Western, States have signed the U.S.-led Artemis Accords. Though these Accords mainly reiterate some of the provisions of the Outer Space Treaty, they also "affirm that the extraction of space resources does not inherently constitute national appropriation under Article II of the Outer Space Treaty."[95] Even though by signing the Artemis Accords the signatories have made only political commitments, one author believes that these Accords are "reflecting an increasing acceptance of an interpretation of [the Outer Space Treaty] Article II – the non-appropriation principle – that would permit the recovery and exploitation of space resources."[96] This opinion is not shared by others. While the Artemis Program and Artemis Accords are Western initiatives, Russia and China have planned their own program called the "International Lunar Research Station" for the exploration of resources of the Moon[97] and have invited other nations to join them.[98]

It appears that conflicts with respect to the exploitation and appropriation of natural resources of the Moon and other celestial bodies are already emerging.[99] The national legislations of some States and the Artemis Accords

---

94   *See* E.O. 13914, *supra* note 43, noting: "Outer space is a legally and physically unique domain of human activity, and the United States does not view it as a global commons." *See also* United States, American Space Commerce Free Enterprise Act of 2019, H.R.3610, at § 80309, "Global commons – Notwithstanding any other provision of law, outer space shall not be considered a global commons."

95   Artemis Accords, *supra* note 35, at § 10 (2).

96   John Goehring, *The Russian ASAT Test Caps a Bad Year for the Due Regard Principle in Space*, Jan. 12, 2022, https://www.justsecurity.org/79820/the-russian-asat-test-caps-a-bad-year-for-the-due-regard-principle-in-space/ (last visited Nov. 16, 2022).

97   Stuart Clark, *Russia and China team up to build a moon base*, The Guardian (Jun. 25, 2021), https://www.theguardian.com/science/2021/jun/25/russia-china-team-up-build-moon-base (last visited Nov. 22, 2022).

98   Andrew Jones, *China, Russia open moon base project to international partners, early details emerge*, Space News (Apr. 26, 2021), https://spacenews.com/china-russia-open-moon-base-project-to-international-partners-early-details-emerge/ (last visited Nov. 22, 2022).

99   Andrew Jones, *NASA and China are eyeing the same landing sites near the lunar south pole*, Space News (Aug. 31, 2022), https://spacenews.com/nasa-and-china-are-eyeing-the-same-landing-sites-near-the-lunar-south-pole/ (last visited Nov. 22, 2022). It may be recalled that one of the main objectives for the adoption of the Moon Agreement was "to

raise many questions on humanity's commitment to the collective objectives and motives of the sustainable use of outer space, and a trend towards taking specific measures for preventing the disruption of the existing balance of the environment of the Moon. Some believe that the conclusion of the Artemis Accords is contrary to the multilateral approach to space resources exploitation.[100] Though the UNCOPUOS has established a Working Group on Legal Aspects of Space Resource Activities,[101] given the treaty-negotiating history of the UN and desires of major spacefaring States to have exclusive access to and control over space natural resources that are said to carry high economic value, the conclusion of any international agreement to regulate such resources cannot be expected soon.

5   A Suggestion for Stopping the Ending of International Space Law

All of our observations show the tremendous impact that many factors have had on the development, invocation, application and respect of international space law. Attempts to regulate newer technologies together with the rapidly changing scope of international relations demonstrate that the general preference of major powers is changing and that they are nowadays unwilling to commit themselves to binding international obligations. A number of contributory factors, as discussed in preceding sections, are directly or indirectly responsible for such a state of affairs. Moreover, it may take some time for the international community to rally and gather support towards a reconsideration of what constitutes essential components or mechanisms of international legal regulation. If humankind is at an inflexion point and undergoing a transitional phase that will make or break the international system pertaining to the regulation of space domain and outer space activities, in the short term to medium term, the authors suggest the strengthening, clarification and expansion of the

---

prevent the moon [and other celestial bodies] from becoming an area of international conflict." *See* Moon Agreement, *supra* note 7, at Preamble. Moreover, the Outer Space Treaty has been designed to avoid the repetition of the efforts (even wars) to acquire overseas territories during the colonization period in human history.

100   Athar ud din, *The Artemis Accords: The End of Multilateralism in the Management of Outer Space?*, (2022) 20:2–3 Astropolitics 135 – 150.

101   United Nations Office for Outer Space Affairs, Working Group on the Legal Aspects of Space Resource Activities, https://www.unoosa.org/oosa/en/ourwork/copuos/lsc /space-resources/index.html (last visited Nov. 22, 2022).

core principles of international space law that are promulgated in the five UN space law treaties.

While specific instances of deviations or departures from the rule of law, including international law, are not infrequent, problems arise when such departures and deviations become the accepted behavior or norm, and manifest themselves as visible and noteworthy trends. Efforts to combat the effect of such influences demand flexibility, adaptability and dynamism in approach. In the space domain, it is not that law-making has completely come to a halt but has significantly slowed to a level that would not be able to keep up with the pace of technological advancements and progress. In addition, the process of law-making in the form of binding commitments (including treaties) has shifted to the adoption of non-binding guidelines and reports of groups of governmental experts, which are seen as the preferred mode of norm-making. Recently, there are also attempts at circumventing the United Nations process of law-making and an alarming trend of unilateral actions of some advanced spacefaring nations, often to the detriment of multilateralism, and away from international measures and safeguards which ensure the protection and enhancement of the collective and inclusive interests of humankind.

As calls are being made to expand the framework of the global space governance system,[102] it is important to reemphasize that these newer and upcoming developmental or expansionist legal regimes must build on the foundations of existing core principles of international space law, and must view the core legal principles as stepping stones towards the next "big thing." In an attempt to expand the "freedoms of some," which creates geopolitical frictions and undermines laws that have been put in place to serve the needs of all, we are observing an increase in "deviant" actions and conduct by some States and their private enterprises. Any attempt to address and overcome existing frictions must be made by trying to strengthen and revise the consensus-based global legal order with the greatest possible participation of all stakeholders.

Activities related to the exploration and use of outer space, including the Moon and other celestial bodies, are complex from a scientific, technical, economic, societal, geopolitical, and strategic perspective. They are expected to become even more complex and extensive as the number and nature of space activities and stakeholders increase in the near future. The significant impact that space activities have on life globally makes the space domain a critical infrastructure both at national and international levels. In a world that

---

102   See Jakhu & Chen, *supra* note 36.

is rapidly moving away from bi-polarization and towards a multi-polar global order, law needs to be viewed as an evolving process and not something that is fixed or frozen in time. It is, therefore, crucial for the international community, acting collectively and preferably through the UN, to place high value and emphasis on the need to expand and update international space law, to enhance space law capacity-building, and to underline and place emphasis on the communal benefits of space for all.

The current attitude of States, especially of the major space powers, towards international space law and law-making process will certainly not be conducive to the development and sustainability of space activities, both of space-faring and for non-space faring States. In fact, the current *ad hoc*, piecemeal, un-coordinated, fragmented approach to a global space governance framework is detrimental to long-term sustainability of space activities. The needs and priorities of space actors, both old and new, will give rise to unforeseen challenges that would need to be met. This is the reason for the need for a more holistic approach to the coordination, adoption and application of international treaties as well as national laws and regulations pertaining to space domain and space activities. Considering all the above-mentioned perspectives, it is therefore imperative that the global governance regime for outer space must be devised and developed on a multilateral, comprehensive, coordinated and regular basis. This can only be achieved, as previously suggested by the authors,[103] through an intergovernmental organization dedicated to space affairs.

Through strength in numbers and multilateralism, the ability to rally States and other relevant stakeholders to secure a common objective is what is needed to ensure the long-term safety, security and sustainability of the space domain. In the view of the authors, the inclusive interests encapsulated in the five UN space law treaties included the implied responsibility that there should have been/ be an international organization to ensure the effective application and continual update of international space law. As such, an international organization as a specialized agency of the UN and charged with the main task of expanding and strengthening the global space governance framework should actively facilitate the progressive development of international space law, in cooperation with other international organizations and the private sector, and oversee its effective implementation. Only such an international body could effectively and routinely address regulatory requirements of the day as well as the needs of the future to ensure the widespread and international

---

103   *See, e.g.*, Jakhu, Pelton & Mishra, *supra* note 44, at 273.

acceptability and implementation of laws that enhance and further the collective interests of all countries and all humanity.

In addition to the issues of space militarization and weaponization, congestion and concerns about space debris, there are and will be numerous issues that will need to be addressed. Such issues include matters related to planetary protection, planetary defense, cybersecurity, space weather, space transportation systems, standardization of space ports, space traffic management, space travel and tourism, threats to dark and quiet skies,[104] technical assistance to developing countries, the equitable sharing of space benefits, and the need to protect various cultures, especially indigenous cultures and those that are on the verge of extinction.[105] It is logical that they all should be addressed by a single intergovernmental body, in cooperation with other appropriate international, regional and local institutions and the private sector.

Jean Monnet, the postwar architect of European unity, once said that *"Nothing is possible without men [people], but nothing is lasting without institutions."*[106] Monnet's wisdom must be followed for the creation of intergovernmental

---

104   Some mega-constellations of satellites (including the ones that are proposed to be launched) are threatening and will continue to threaten the work of astronomers and astronomical societies. This is due to "reflectivity of sunlight" from panels installed in the satellite(s), thus raising issues of "light pollution" originating from Low Earth Orbits. In turn, this is becoming a major problem or hindrance at our collective attempts of preserving and protecting dark and quiet skies, which is considered to be a global commons and of cultural significance to various peoples, especially indigenous peoples. *See* Aparna Venkatesan, et al., *The impact of satellite constellations on space as an ancestral global commons*, Nov. 6, 2020, (2020) 4 Nature Astronomy 1043–1048.

105   The United Nations estimates that there are about 5,000 different cultures of more than 500 million indigenous peoples who live in about 90 countries and are susceptible to extinction. *See, e.g.,* United Nations, *We need indigenous communities for a better world*, https://www.un.org/en/observances/indigenous-day/background (last visited Nov. 16, 2022); United Nations, Department of Economic and Social Affairs, *Indigenous Peoples – Culture*, https://www.un.org/development/desa/indigenouspeoples/mandated-areas1/culture .html (last visited Nov. 16, 2022). *See, also,* in the context of cultural genocide: Christopher White, *Pope Francis says Catholic Church committed cultural 'genocide' of Canada's Indigenous peoples*, National Catholic Reporter (Jul. 30, 2022) https://www .ncronline.org/news/vatican/pope-francis-says-catholic-church-committed-cultural -genocide-canadas-indigenous (last visited Nov. 16, 2022).

106   *See,* also, Monticello, *Quotations on the Jefferson Memorial*, https://www.monticello.or g/research-education/thomas-jefferson-encyclopedia/quotations-jefferson-memorial/ (last visited Nov. 22, 2022), wherein one may note the words carved on the walls of the Jefferson Memorial that state,

   I am not an advocate for frequent changes in laws and constitutions, but laws and institutions must go hand in hand with the progress of the human mind. As that becomes more developed, more enlightened, as new discoveries are made, new truths discovered and manners and opinions change, with the change of circumstances, institutions must advance also to keep pace with the times.

organization with a mandate to continuously address, through multilateral process, global space affairs and consequently to stop the ending of international space law.

6   Final Remarks and Conclusion

The current state of affairs of the world is grave. As early as the year 2004, the then UN Secretary-General cautioned the international community that "the rule of law is at risk around the world. ... Again and again, we see laws shamelessly disregarded. ... [N]o one is above the law, and no one should be denied its protection. ... [A]ll countries need a framework of fair rules and the confidence that others will obey them."[107] Fast forward almost two decades, in 2022, humanity must again contend with the harsh reality that the Doomsday Clock stood at 100 seconds to midnight,[108] and the fact that "[o]ur world is in peril – and paralyzed" as international law is undermined by geopolitical divisions.[109]

As has been outlined above, there is overall consensus in the international community that space is a "global commons," the exploration, use and long-term sustainability of which is a common ground to unite the many differing views of States and bring them into a single and pointed action plan and agenda. There is a critical difference between space as a global commons, and an emerging view that space is no one's domain or that space is a war-fighting domain. Each and every State participating in space activities has the individual and shared responsibility to protect the whole of the space domain. If the view that space is no different than other domains to facilitate war-fighting and exclusive interests of a select few nations gains traction, it could potentially result in an attempt by a few States to shirk the most basic responsibilities as regards their approach and conduct in this domain.

To facilitate the end-goal of benefit-sharing and navigate the differentiated power and capability dynamics between spacefaring and non-spacefaring nations, the implementation of initiatives such as the Space 2030 Agenda[110]

---

107   *See, e.g.*, United Nations News, *Addressing UN Assembly, Annan urges nations to restore respect for rule of law*, Sep. 21, 2004, https://news.un.org/en/story/2004/09/115712 (last visited Nov. 22, 2022).

108   John Mecklin, *At doom's doorstep: It is 100 seconds to midnight – 2022 Doomsday Clock Statement*, Jan. 20, 2022, https://thebulletin.org/doomsday-clock/current-time/ (last visited Nov. 22, 2022).

109   United Nations Secretary General, *Secretary-General's address to the General Assembly*, Sep. 20, 2022, https://www.un.org/sg/en/content/sg/speeches/2022-09-20/secretary-generals-address-the-general-assembly (last visited Nov. 22, 2022).

110   *See* Space 2030 Agenda, *supra* note 53.

appear to be a good basis to build on. Following the commonly agreed objective of securing space as a driver for the achievement of sustainable development goals could potentially lead to a reversal of trend and an increase in trust among States and cause a "butterfly effect" in the legal regulation of all spheres of human activities. Further, it is hoped that this will in turn increase participation and trust in multilateralism, and thereby lead to a corresponding increase in the effectiveness and value of international law and international space law.

Every aspect of each space activity or space-related issue need not be regulated by binding international treaties; but it is equally true that every such activity or issue cannot and must not be governed only by soft law (non-binding) instruments such as guidelines, United Nations General Assembly resolutions, etc. In certain situations, it may not be helpful and appropriate to wait for non-binding political commitments to develop into customary international law. The mode of development of rule of law for each space activity or issue must be determined, on a case-by-case basis, taking into consideration the nature of the activity or issue and the consequences of non-regulation within an appropriate time period.

While it remains to be seen if international law in general is in a transitory phase or has undergone a drastic change for the good, considering all the ways in which space activities as well as newer technologies need to be coordinated and regulated, it is crucial to reiterate that international law remains a "means to an end." If the objectives of humanity remain steadfast and firm, concretized by an increase in the numbers of States supporting and advancing inclusive interests agendas in space activities, there should be flexibility in the way that humankind is seeking to "end the law" (in its current form) with objectives of, as John Locke puts it, the preservation and expansion of freedom of all.

It is difficult to highlight or present a single event or even a chain of events that started a trend towards States disregarding international space law. Likewise, it is equally difficult to mark the exact time period that indicates the beginning of the end of international space law. Nonetheless, it is believed that the beginning of the end has already occurred and continues unabated. In using the phrase "beginning of the end," the authors do not in any way imply that an end is not stoppable . Rather, it is an urgent call to the international community to take appropriate actions and timely recourses.

A domain, the exploration and use of which is the province of all humankind, must remain so for all present and future generations. International as well as intergenerational equity is of prime importance for the management, use and preservation of a shared global commons. While international law, international relations and conduct are a product of the times we live in, the collective human consciousness pertaining to our space ambitions and goals, expressed and mediated in the form of legal principles and aspirations contained in the five UN space treaties, must be expanded and strengthened enough to survive the current onslaught of unilateralism and worrying trends that are threatening to accelerate the ending of international space law.

If the rule of law is allowed to end or be significantly weakened in the space domain, the freedom of exploration and use of outer space by all, without discrimination of any kind and on a basis of equality, will significantly diminish, and threaten our common future, and humanity's survival in the long term. The time to act is "now" for the future of young people as well as that of their children or grandchildren, on the Earth but also in outer space and on the Moon and other planets.

Acknowledgments

The authors acknowledge with sincere gratitude the help provided by Professor Steven Freeland, Mr. Kuan-Wei Chen and Mr. Bayar Goswami in reviewing and providing valuable comments on the earlier draft of this Chapter that improved its quality. Notwithstanding this invaluable help, the authors remain exclusively responsible for any errors contained in this Chapter.

CHAPTER 29

Space, Satellites and Siegfried Wiessner's Universe of Human Aspirations: Preventing and Punishing Mass Murder Crimes through Aerial Satellite Evidence

Qerim Qerimi*

Abstract

This chapter seeks to build on Professor Siegfried Wiessner's pioneering work about Earth-space interaction from a legal perspective. It explores his far-sighted vision of the distinct place of space and its use in pursuit of his paramount intellectual goal of an ever-larger universe of core human values. These values, however, remain elusive in unfortunate real-world events involving mass atrocities. Against this specific context and drawing on Wiessner's insights and premises, the chapter seeks to uncover the many roles and challenges of space-based technology to arrest mass murder crimes, as conceived under international law.

1 Introduction

"The use of space has grown exponentially. It is impossible today to conceive of international communications, weather forecasting, or the screening of the riches of the earth without the help of space-based devices."[1] This articulate language marks the opening statement of Professor Siegfried Wiessner's

---

*   Qerim Qerimi is a professor of international law, international law of human rights, and international organizations at the University of Prishtina. He is also a visiting professor and member of the Law and Development Research Group at the University of Antwerp Faculty of Law. Additionally, he is a current member of Council of Europe's European Commission for Democracy through Law (Venice Commission) and chair of its sub-commission on the protection of national minorities, and serves as Rapporteur for Oxford International Organizations (OXIO). He holds a J.S.D. (Ph.D. in Law) from St. Thomas University School of Law, Miami, FLORIDA, and has subsequently pursued postdoctoral research at Harvard Law School on a Fulbright scholarship.

1   Siegfried Wiessner, *The Public Order of the Geostationary Orbit: Blueprints for the Future*, 9 Yale J. World Pub. Ord. 217, 217 (1983).

inspiring article, entitled "The Public Order of the Geostationary Orbit: Blueprints for the Future."[2] Published in 1983, with the *Yale Journal of World Public Order*, the predecessor to the current *Yale Journal of International Law*, the work's exemplary character emanates from not only it forming part of the pioneering legal contributions on the Earth-space arena, but also, and perhaps most importantly, the vision it emboldens and the values it embraces. An almost sixty-page article, inclusive of over 300 footnotes, is no exception to the author's method of work, an otherwise thorough and disciplined quest for truth in pursuit of a clearly specified guiding light, which is a world public order of human dignity, empirically expressed through a set of eight core human values encompassing the totality of human aspirations.

The author imagines an array of functions space-based technology can perform and defines his ultimate quest as one that seeks to invent a model that would promote "the aspirations of all participants in the global arena."[3] In consonance with the system of human values that he has so characteristically and compellingly promoted throughout his academic career, his concerns—as exhibited throughout this work—have been around such preeminent goals as "equitable access," "distribution of benefits," or "widespread direct access to the geostationary orbit."[4] He appeals for an "inclusive regime."[5] He has an eye to the future, envisioning the imperative of adjusting the balance of equity between the "initial consensus" and "new developments of technology, demand, and composition of the world community."[6]

A précis of this work appeared in 1985 in the *ITU Telecommunication Journal*, with the title "Communications in the Earth-Space Arena: Translating Equity into Hertz and Degrees from the Greenwich Meridian."[7] Based on the format and the forum, one can deduce that its intentions were to aid the world of practice, primarily the International Telecommunication Union, the oldest UN specialized agency, with responsibility on matters related to information and communication technologies. In this article, Professor Wiessner observes, "the communication and information industry has become one of the most vital in the world"[8] and that "[t]he fastest expanding part of it is space

---

2 *Id.*

3 *Id.* at 273.

4 *See, e.g., id.* at 271.

5 *Id.* at 239 & 272.

6 *Id.* at 271.

7 Siegfried Wiessner, *Communications in the Earth-Space Arena: Translating Equity into Hertz and Degrees from the Greenwich Meridian*, 52 ITU Telecommunication J. 304 (1985).

8 *Id.* at 304.

communications."[9] Exhibiting the same goals and values as in the main work, namely *The Public Order of the Geostationary Orbit: Blueprints for the Future*, he concludes, "Technology and human ingenuity have made the band of space around the planet a natural resource of advanced global civilization."[10] The same advanced degree was, however, lacking as far as its regulation was concerned.[11] The same remains true even with the most contemporary public order for many aspects of technology regulation.

Beyond formal regulatory frameworks, however—as envisaged by Professor Wiessner—the uses of space-based or space-enabled technology have grown exponentially, and he himself has referred to their modern-day applications as problem-solving devices. One such instance is when applying the insights of Policy-Oriented Jurisprudence to the problem of human rights abuses in internal conflict in a 1999 *American Journal of International Law* article (Symposium on Method). More specifically, when referring, among others, to "the increased realization of individual accountability for human rights abuses"[12] because of the "virtual omnipresence of information on these events, generated by satellite and other sophisticated communication technology."[13]

Building on these insights and drawing inspiration upon them, this chapter seeks to uncover the many roles and challenges of space-based or space-enabled technology to prevent and punish mass murder crimes, as conceived under international law, namely genocide, crimes against humanity, and war crimes. More specifically, the objective of this chapter is threefold: (1) to define and describe the scope of application of modern space-related technology to contexts involving human rights abuses; (2) to ascertain the role and probative value of aerially derived evidence; and (3) to identify the criteria that would form part of the method of proof, making the use of satellite-based evidence both procedurally permissible and practically plausible. In terms of method, it will mostly look into the existing praxis of international courts and tribunals. Most international criminal tribunals, including here the International Criminal Tribunal for the former Yugoslavia (ICTY) and the International Criminal Court (ICC), have relied on aerially obtained evidence. The fundamental questions to be explored in this chapter include the identification of the criteria used to administer and admit this evidence and the associated challenges.

---

9   *Id.*
10   *Id.* at 310.
11   *Id.*
12   *See* Siegfried Wiessner & Andrew R. Willard, *Policy-Oriented Jurisprudence and Human Rights Abuses in Internal Conflict: Toward a World Public Order of Human Dignity*, 93 Am. J. Int'l L. 316, 332 (1999).
13   *Id.*

2   Application of Modern Space-Related Technology to Contexts
         Involving Human Rights Abuses

In his 1983 article, Professor Wiessner speaks of a broad range of spheres in
which space and satellite systems interact and find application for the benefit
of humanity. Until the time of his writing, he notes that the "main use of the
geostationary orbit ... has been for communications, both domestic and international."[14] Another dimension that is as valid today as it was back then is that
"it would be naive, finally, to overlook the fact" that the geostationary orbit is
also used in many different ways for reasons of national security. Ultimately,
Professor Wiessner projects—and does so accurately—that the "future of the
geostationary orbit is bright."[15] Its validity is rooted in the constant expansion
of space technology and its uniquely diverse applications. The present inquiry
however concerns only a particular segment, as it relates to the nature and
scope of the specific application of aerial imagery in international legal and
judicial processes involving mass atrocities. It examines the existing body of
jurisprudence of international courts and tribunals.

The inquiry becomes of an ever-growing imperative as comprehensive satellite imagery is being utilized more frequently by humanitarian organizations,
private companies, and open source platforms to complement and support
investigations of an international criminal law, human rights law and humanitarian law nature. References could be made to the Satellite Sentinel Project,
a partnership between the Enough Project and DigitalGlobe, to collect and
analyze satellite imagery of atrocities in both Sudan and South Sudan; the U.S.
Holocaust Memorial Museum's "Crisis in Darfur" Project in partnership with
Google Earth; or the Amnesty International's "Decode Darfur" Project. Indeed,
Amnesty International has decided to make extensive use of modern technology devices in pursuit of various human rights causes, from use of machine
learning in human rights investigations to the potential for discrimination
within the use of machine learning, in particular with regard to policing, criminal justice, and access to essential economic and social services.[16]

In the case of Russia's invasion of Ukraine and its ensuing actions, one case in
point is robust evidence emerging from Maxar Technologies' satellite imagery.[17]
Countless videos and photographs could likewise serve important evidentiary

---

14   Wiessner, *supra* note 1, at 220.
15   *Id.* at 224.
16   *See* Mathias Risse, *Human Rights and Artificial Intelligence: An Urgently Needed Agenda*, 41
      Hum. Rts. Q. 1 (2019).
17   *See* Maxar Technologies' website at https://www.maxar.com/news-bureau.

purposes.[18] One can well imagine an important place for aerially-obtained evidence in the ongoing proceedings instituted by Ukraine against the Russian Federation in the case of *Allegations of Genocide under the Convention on the Prevention and Punishment of the Crime of Genocide*.[19] As the body of such evidence increases, so is the need to also verify its authenticity and reliability, which in modern days is often challenged by fake, manipulative technological processes.[20]

To provide supplementary context to the developing trends in the use of alternative digital applications, the UN investigation team in Iraq has released a technology tool to collect evidence against ISIS.[21] The platform allows ISIS victims to upload photographs and other proof of abuse to help investigate, prosecute and put perpetrators behind bars. In other words, it gives victims a voice and justice. It empowers "members of impacted communities to come forward with their accounts."[22] The initial results of the initiative have "underlined the significant scale of evidentiary material that will ultimately be collected, stored and made available in criminal proceedings."[23] This is not the first time that UN investigators are resorting to technology for help, as they have done it before to build cases against ISIS militiamen. For instance, "4K

18   *See*, among others, the following reports from Washington Post: Meg Kelly, Elyse Samuels & Karly Domb Sadof, *Russian attacks hit at least 9 Ukrainian medical facilities, visual evidence shows*, Wash. Post, March 12, 2022, https://www.washingtonpost.com/world/2022/03/12/ukraine-hospital-attacks-video/; Annabelle Timsit, *Pregnant mother whose photo showed tragedy of maternity hospital bombing in Ukraine dies with her baby*, Wash. Post, March 14, 2022, https://www.washingtonpost.com/world/2022/03/14/pregnant-woman-baby-death-mariupol-maternity-hospital.

19   International Court of Justice, *Allegations of Genocide under the Convention on the Prevention and Punishment of the Crime of Genocide* (Ukraine v. Russian Federation), https://www.icj-cij.org/en/case/182 (10 Mar. 2022).

20   *See, e.g.*, the following reports from BBC News, CNN and Associated Press: *Marianna Spring, How to spot false posts from Ukraine*, March 13, 2022, https://www.bbc.com/news/blogs-trending-60654288; Daniele Dale, *Fact check: Pro-Russia social media accounts spread false claims that old videos show Ukrainian 'crisis actors'*, CNN, March 10, 2022, https://edition.cnn.com/2022/03/10/politics/fact-check-ukraine-not-actually-crisis-actor-fakes/index.html; Amanda Seitz & David Klepper, *Propaganda, fake videos of Ukraine bombard users*, AP News, February 25, 2022, https://apnews.com/article/russia-ukraine-technology-europe-media-social-media-80f729025396abf9ad9e4e9d0b4f5ece.

21   *See* Statement by the Special Advisor and Head of the United Nations Investigative Team to Promote Accountability from Crimes Committed by Da'esh/Islamic State in Iraq and the Levant, Karim Asad Ahmad Khan, S/2020/1193, 21 December 2020, https://www.securitycouncilreport.org/atf/cf/%7B65BFCF9B-6D27-4E9C-8CD3-CF6E4FF96FF9%7D/s_2020_1193.pdf.

22   *Id.* at 2.

23   *Id.* at 3.

drones" had been used to capture high-quality footage of mass graves and the sites of ISIS atrocities. Additionally, "3D laser scanners" on the ground can be powerful tools to help build credible cases.

In parallel with the practice of these actors, courts have begun testing *new waters*—perhaps only a natural outcome given the technology-bound time we live in—by continuing to create and develop practices and procedures around evidence that transcends *viva voce* witness testimony. This evidence, diverse and challenging (in terms of authentication, security, and verification), yet inescapable and instrumental to prevent and punish crime, can be based on such sources as photographs, aerial and satellite images, audio and video recordings, phone records, forensic evidence of the kind of DNA, ballistic and blood tests, as well as a multitude of digital information generated from devices as phones, computers, tablets, iPads, and other digital devices.

It should additionally be noted here that the newer types of technologically derived evidence are often linked to, or transmitted through, open sources, in particular the widely accessible platforms such as Facebook, Twitter or YouTube. For instance, evidence from Facebook has been referenced as a key source of evidence in *The Gambia v. Myanmar case* before the International Court of Justice in a case related to the application of the Genocide Convention.[24] All in all, the hitherto unforeseen magnitude of smart phones and other imaging applications and platforms—including a significant number of high-resolution imaging satellites—offer fertile grounds for an abundance of surveillance. There is a high degree of probability that, once something happens, it stands a good chance of being recorded in one or another way, either by a camera on earth or a satellite in orbit. The next section will offer an overview of pioneering cases from the practice of international courts and tribunals dealing with the acceptability of evidence obtained from these sources.

3   The Role and Probative Value of Aerially Derived Evidence

Back in 1999, as part of a symposium on method, Professor Wiessner co-authored an article, published with the American Journal on International Law, entitled *Policy-Oriented Jurisprudence and Human Rights Abuses in Internal Conflict: Toward a World Public Order of Human Dignity*.[25] Applying

---

24   *See* International Court of Justice, *Application of the Convention on the Prevention and Punishment of the Crime of Genocide* (The Gambia v. Myanmar) (Nov. 11, 2019), https://www.icj-cij.org/public/files/case-related/178/178-20191111-APP-01-00-EN.pdf.

25   Wiessner & Willard, *supra* note 12.

the tenets of Policy-Oriented Jurisprudence, Wiessner explored and advanced solutions to the recurring problem of human rights abuses in internal conflicts, both from a preventive and a punitive perspective. He aptly recognized the variety of factual contexts and decision variables involved in the matter at hand, which in turn engages "a range of goals for the international community, including restoring minimum order where it has been breached, reducing the expectation of violence, reestablishing practices of a productive civil society, eliminating or mitigating the factors that could, in varying combination, reignite particular conflicts, and deterring the occurrence of comparable offending behavior in the society at issue and in others that are watching."[26] Most relevant to the immediate context under scrutiny, however, remains the observation about the role of modern technology in this mix of methods to prevent and punish abuse in internal conflict:

> Important conditioning factors for the increased realization of individual accountability for human rights abuses include the virtual omnipresence of information on these events, generated by satellite and other sophisticated communication technology. Vivid images of the mass slaughters in Rwanda and the blood spilled in Sarajevo's Sniper Alley fill the living rooms around the world and cannot fail to leave an impact.[27]

Indeed, the impact exerted from data generated by satellites and other modern technology has left its footprints in the decision processes surrounding those cases. An institutional body of prime importance for holding -to account those responsible for some of the worst atrocities committed since the Second World War, the International Criminal Tribunal for the former Yugoslavia (ICTY) has resorted to aerial satellite evidence in order to establish the guilt of the perpetrators.

3.1   *The Practice of the ICTY*

The ICTY, through its trial and appeals chamber judgments, has developed an extensive and exemplary body of jurisprudence on the crimes forming the subject of its jurisdiction, namely genocide, war crimes, and crimes against humanity; in particular, on the elements of these crimes, modes of individual and command responsibility, issues of evidence and proof, and other aspects

---

26   *Id.* at 317.
27   *Id.* at 332.

of international criminal law.[28] The ICTY, complemented by its sister ad hoc tribunal, the International Criminal Tribunal for Rwanda (ICTR)—both established by the UN Security Council under its Chapter VII powers of the UN Charter—is the first contemporary international criminal tribunal to generate an extremely comprehensive wealth of law.[29]

With regard to evidence coming from non-traditional sources, including aerial satellite evidence, the ICTY has had occasion to deal with it. It has in fact dealt with the matter of such evidence in several cases, notably in the *Krstić, Blagojević, Popović et al.,* and *Tolimir* cases, in which the Trial Chambers admitted aerial images offered by the prosecution; images that were used to show areas of earth that, the prosecution alleged, were disturbed in the digging of mass burial sites in the vicinity of Srebrenica.[30]

Aerial images were also admitted by the ICTY that showed buildings, vehicles, large groups of prisoners, and bodies.[31] These aerial images have been provided by the U.S. Government and disclosed to the Prosecution pursuant to Rule 70 of the ICTY's Rules of Procedure and Evidence.[32] This Rule allowed the Prosecutor to receive confidential information on a limited basis and under certain conditions, thus allowing for a tolerable, yet necessary, degree of flexibility to be applied in international criminal proceedings. In this case, the Trial Chamber noted the fact that the U.S. Government made it clear that the Prosecution "is not authorized to discuss in courtroom proceedings any information relating to the technical or analytical sources, methods, or capabilities of the systems, organizations, or personnel used to collect, analyze, or produce these imagery-derived products."[33]

The accused challenged the reliability of these images, on the grounds that no evidence was presented on their origin, the method of their creation, the

---

28   *See, e.g.,* Jennifer Trahan, Genocide, War Crimes and Crimes Against Humanity: A Topical Digest of the Case law of the International Criminal Tribunal for the former Yugoslavia (2006).

29   *See, e.g.,* The Legacy of Ad Hoc Tribunals in International Criminal Law: Assessing the ICTY's and ICTR's Most Significant Legal Accomplishments (Milena Sterio & Michael P. Scharf eds., 2019).

30   *Prosecutor v. Zdravko Tolimir,* Case No IT-05-88/2-T, Trial Judgment, ¶¶ 65, 67–68, 70, 435, 454, 457, 459, 478, 561, 564 (Dec. 12, 2012) [*Tolimir* Trial Judgment]; *Prosecutor v. Radislav Krstić,* Case No IT-98-33-T, Trial Judgment, ¶¶ 114, 223, 229, 230, 238, 250, 253, 258 (Aug. 2, 2001); *Prosecutor v. Vidoje Blagojević and Dragan Jokić,* Case No IT-02-60-T, Trial Judgment (Jan. 17, 2005); and *Prosecutor v. Vujadin Popović et al,* Case No IT-05-88-T, Public Redacted Judgment, Volume I, ¶¶ 73–75 (Jun. 10, 2010).

31   *Tolimir* Trial Judgment, *id.* ¶ 67.

32   *Id.* ¶ 68.

33   *Id.*

manner of their editing, how to interpret them, or whether they were delivered to the Prosecution in their original form or previously modified.[34] Although the Chamber agreed with the accused that evidence lacked "on the method of creation of these images,"[35] it pointed out that "this does not impair the credibility of aerial images in general."[36] In this connection, the Chamber noted that former investigators from the Office of the Prosecutor have extensively testified about the use of aerial images and that such images have often complemented forensic archaeological or anthropological reports.[37] For example, the fact that gravesites were first identified and then located "by aerial images points to their authenticity and utility as evidence."[38] Additionally, the Chamber noted that the authenticity or interpretation of an aerial image has often been corroborated by the testimony of witnesses.[39] What is ultimately critical is the ICTY's finding that aerial images can be "reliable and of probative value."[40]

In its jurisprudence, the ICTY has likewise admitted a large number of intercepted communications, communications that could potentially also be recorded by satellites or other aerial technology.[41] The Tribunal suggested that the reliability of intercepted communications would depend on the methods used to conduct interceptions and recording.[42] Independent corroboration of the intercepts may also be demanded in certain cases. In the *Tolimir* case, the Chamber corroborated the intercepts with other documents, such as notes taken by UN officials, telephone books obtained, and aerial images.[43] In one specific instance referred to by the Tribunal, the intercept of a conversation "was corroborated by both a Croatian intercept and a UNPROFOR report of the same conversation."[44]

The Trial Chamber has also discussed a specific scenario, for which there is at least a theoretical possibility, which is the possibility that the intercepted material be in some way tampered with before it came into possession.[45] However, in the case at hand, taking all relevant circumstantial factors into consideration,

---

34   *Id.* ¶ 69.
35   *Id.*
36   *Id.* ¶ 70.
37   *Id.*
38   *Id.*
39   *Id.*
40   *Id.*
41   *Id.* ¶ 63.
42   *Id.* ¶ 64.
43   *Id.* ¶ 65.
44   *Id.*
45   *Id.* ¶ 66.

the Chamber came to the conclusion that "the overwhelming weight of the evidence is in favor of the reliability and authenticity of the intercepts," and that it was "satisfied that, as a whole, the intercepts have a high degree of validity in relation to the conversations they purport to record."[46]

A number of elements can be identified and established from the practice of the ICTY as far as the admission and probative value of aerially obtained evidence is concerned. *First*, this international tribunal has admitted aerial images as valid evidence and that such evidence can be admitted authoritatively in international trials or proceedings. *Secondly*, this evidence can serve multiple purposes, which in the concrete cases before the Tribunal were linked to the confirmation of the presence and locations of gravesites, reburial activities, buildings and vehicles, groups of prisoners, and bodies. *Thirdly*, while the Tribunal noted the evidence's lack on the method of creation of these images—certainly preferable so as to remove any contestation—this fact in itself does not invalidate the credibility of aerial images as evidence in general. *Fourth*, the Tribunal clearly confirms the utility of evidence generated by aerial images. *Fifth*—though not always or on an exclusive basis—the authenticity or interpretation of an aerial image often requires corroboration by witnesses' testimony. *Sixth* and ultimately, aerially-generated evidence can be both credible and of probative value.

The work of the ICTY as an ad hoc tribunal with limited territorial scope—now on a global scale—has been in many ways carried out by the International Criminal Court (ICC). This court has been also confronted with evidence generated by modern technology.

3.2   *The Practice of the ICC*

In August 2017, the ICC, the permanent criminal court established by the Treaty of Rome in 1998, issued an indictment for the arrest of a Libyan warlord, Mahmoud Mustafa Busayf Al-Werfalli ("Al-Werfalli"), based on satellite images and videos taken of the executions ordered or conducted by him.

Those satellite imagery and videos were posted on social media by his followers. Geographical features seen in the videos—buildings, roads, trees and hills—were located via time-stamped high-resolution satellite images.[47] In this way, video, photos, satellite images, and other data are triangulated to verify events at a specific time and place. In the case of the Libyan warlord, much

---

46   *Id.*

47   Bellingcat Investigation Team, "How a Werfalli Execution Site Was Geolocated," Bellingcat (Oct. 3, 2017), https://www.bellingcat.com/news/mena/2017/10/03/how-an-execution-site -was-geolocated/.

of the analysis was done by humans engaged in many hours of painstaking review of satellite imagery. The original source, however, lies in space.

The arrest warrant issued on 15 August 2017 against Al-Werfalli, an alleged commander of the Al-Saiqa Brigade of the Libyan National Army (LNA), is the first ever arrest warrant based solely on social media evidence (generated by satellite imagery), albeit corroborated and confirmed by other authoritative sources. Mr. Al-Werfalli is accused of mass executions in or near Benghazi, Libya. He is accused in the context of seven incidents against 33 persons in the non-international armed conflict in Libya, from on or before 3 June 2016 until on or about 17 July 2017 and in the context of an eighth incident which took place on 24 January 2018, when Mr. Al-Werfalli allegedly shot dead 10 persons in front of the Bi'at al-Radwan Mosque in Benghazi.[48] A second arrest warrant was issued by the Pre-Trial Chamber I of the ICC on 4 July 2018.[49] The Chamber finds reasonable grounds to believe that Mr Al-Werfalli bears criminal responsibility both for (*i*) his direct participation to the commission of the crime (article 25(3)(a) of the ICC Statute); and (*ii*) as a superior, for the commission of crimes by his subordinates under his ordering (article 25(3)(b) of the Statute).

Both warrant arrests were issued publicly and could be communicated to any State or international organization for the purpose of its execution. Mr. Al-Werfalli is still not in ICC custody.

The wider pertinent context is defined by an investigation launched over the situation in Libya by the United Nations Security Council. On 26 February 2011, the UN Security Council decided unanimously to refer the situation in Libya since 15 February 2011 to the ICC Prosecutor, stressing the need to hold accountable those responsible for attacks, including by forces under the control of those responsible, on civilians. After conducting a preliminary examination of the situation, the ICC Prosecutor concluded, on 3 March 2011, that there is a reasonable basis to believe that crimes under the ICC's jurisdiction have been committed in Libya, since 15 February 2011, and decided to open an investigation in this situation.

---

48   International Criminal Court, Pre-Trial Chamber I, *In the Case of the Prosecutor v. Mahmoud Mustafa Busayf Al-Werfalli* (Aug. 15, 2017), https://www.icc-cpi.int/sites/default/files/CourtRecords/CR2017_05031.PDF.

49   International Criminal Court, Pre-Trial Chamber I, *In the Case of the Prosecutor v. Mahmoud Mustafa Busayf Al-Werfalli* (Jul. 4, 2018), https://www.icc-cpi.int/sites/default/files/CourtRecords/CR2018_03552.PDF.

In its Second Warrant of Arrest in the *Al-Werfalli* case, the ICC scrutinized the source and validity of the evidence before it. This analysis is most prominently captured in paragraph 18 of the Second Warrant of Arrest. It reads:

> The Chamber is satisfied that the ... mentioned video has sufficient indicia of authenticity in order to be relied upon at this stage of the proceedings. The Chamber notes, in particular, that the Prosecutor has submitted an expert report on the authentication of the video, prepared by a renowned, independent institute. Having analysed the video and its key frames, the report concluded that there were no traces of forgery or manipulation in relation to locations, weapons or persons shown in the video. The location has also been confirmed by a witness, who stated that the video was shot "[i]n front of the mosque at Al-Salmani" where "[a] day before [...] there was a bombing".[50]

The Chamber relied on further evidence before it, which it considered to have provided reasonable grounds to believe that Mr. Al-Werfalli is directly responsible for the killing of the 10 persons on 24 January 2018. In particular, the Chamber took note of a public statement made by the spokesperson of the Libyan National Army (LNA) on or around 7 February 2018, in which Al-Werfalli had admitted to the killings.[51] A letter allegedly sent by the LNA's commanding General, Khalifa Haftar, to the Prosecutor of the Court confirmed that Al-Werfalli "killed some detained terrorists [...] as a reaction to the bombings" of 23 January 2018, this being additionally supported by a United Nations report submitted to the Chamber.[52]

Given the gravity of the crime, it is obvious that an abundance of credible evidence is at least desirable. Yet, the prime source of information here remains video footage based on satellite imagery, a revolutionary act of using smart spatial machines to detect and potentially deter future crime. Yet, the advancements in technology have created many faces of it: beyond its ability to record and hence collect decisive evidence, it is likewise capable of modifying its results through what is known as the "deep fakes," an Artificial Intelligence application that makes it look like a person said or did something he or she did not.[53] "Deep fakes" is otherwise defined as "manufactured imagery that is

---

50   *Id.* ¶ 18.
51   *Id.* ¶ 19.
52   *Id.*
53   Jon Christian, *Experts Fear Face Swapping Tech Could Start an International Showdown*, The Outline (Feb. 1, 2018).

developed via generative adversarial networks, a process that pits two neural networks against each other."[54]

In the case at hand, the ICC has essentially acknowledged the risks and indicated this through the institution of methods that it used in order to assign credence to the presented evidence, as it noted, at this stage of the proceedings. It means that when dealing with the merits, it could potentially supplement or modify this stance. This notwithstanding, the Court made it clear that such open source and/or aerially-collected evidence has been subjected to expertise for authentication.

Two elements could be discerned here for the confirmation of the validity of any such type of evidence: *one*, that authenticity ought to be confirmed; and, *two*, that this confirmation should come from independent expertise; in this case, "a renowned, independent institute." Certainly, a specialized independent institution as a collective body of experts adds compelling value to the confirmatory process. However, should it be individual expertise, the finality of its credence might demand that it is provided by at least two experts and that—to analogously borrow from the jurisprudence of the ICJ in a related context of newspaper, radio and television reports—such expertise should be "wholly consistent and concordant as to the main facts and circumstances"[55] of the evidence.

Indeed, the ICC itself has had occasion to shed light on the methods designed to verify and confirm the authenticity of the open source evidence, which would certainly encompass evidence that might have been collected by satellite imagery and other means enabled by modern technology. In the case of *Prosecutor v. Katanga and Chui*, the ICC made specific observations with regard to its reliance on documentary evidence with particular characteristics, more specifically videos, films, photographs and audio recordings.[56]

Before video or audio material could be admitted, the Court postulated that it would require evidence of originality and integrity.[57] The Court has additionally developed criteria for determining reliability, acknowledging that "there is no final list of possible criteria."[58] However, the key factors that furnish the reliability criteria include the source of the information, nature and

---

54   Alexa Koenig, *"Half the Truth is Often a Great Lie": Deep Fakes, Open Source Information, and International Criminal Law*, 113 AJIL Unbound 250, 252 (2019).

55   *US Hostages*, Merits, Judgment of 24 May 1980, ICJ Rep. 1980, pp. 9–10, ¶ 13.

56   *Prosecutor v. Germain Katanga and Mathieu Ngudjolo Chui*, ICC-01/04-01/07, Decision on the Prosecutor's Bar Table Motions, ¶ 24 (Dec. 17, 2010).

57   *Id.* ¶ 24d.

58   *Id.* ¶ 27.

characteristics of the item of evidence, contemporaneousness, purpose, and adequate means of evaluation.[59]

Beyond aspects of evidence and its admission, one other critical step characterizing the wider process of documenting crime and establishing guilt is the method of proof.

4   Questions of Proof for Finding the Truth in Mass Atrocity Cases

Among many professional functions performed during his academic career, Professor Siegfried Wiessner served as a member of the Executive Council of the American Society of International Law. In that capacity, he was asked to comment on the ICJ's judgment in the *Case of Bosnia and Herzegovina v. Serbia and Montenegro* related to the Application of the Convention on the Prevention and Punishment of the Crime of Genocide, the first contentious genocide case in the history of the World Court. The comment then appeared in the Newsletter of the American Society of International Law of Spring 2007.[60] Professor Wiessner qualified this ICJ decision as "a triumph of diplomatic caution over the Court's duty to gather sufficient facts to establish the truth."[61] He commended the Court's interpretation of the Convention that states can commit genocide themselves or be accomplices to it as breaking new grounds for state accountability.[62] He also noted the Court's "bold if somewhat questionable extension of the res judicata doctrine," which opened the door for the merits stage.[63] His comment becomes critical when moving to a more slippery part of the decision and at the same time crucial for the end result of a case with historic proportions. Its substance is best captured by the following succinct statement:

> These commendable interpretations of the Convention are ... undermined by the Court's pursuit of the facts. One may not quarrel with the Court for raising the standard of proof from a preponderance of the evidence to the Court's "full conviction" that the crime has been "clearly established" for crimes of "exceptional gravity." In fact, the Court relies

---

59   *Id.*
60   See *Council Comment: The International Court of Justice's Decision in the Bosnia and Herzegovina v. Serbia and Montenegro*, Newsletter of the Am. Soc'y Int'l L. 2007.
61   *Id.* at 9.
62   *Id.*
63   *Id.*

almost exclusively on decisions of the ICTY made "beyond a reasonable doubt." In areas of disputed facts, where final ICTY findings are not available, particularly regarding the Respondent's control over the Bosnian Serb army, it should have acceded to the Applicant's request for unedited copies of the relevant minutes of the Respondent's Supreme Defense Council meetings and asked for them under Article 49 of its Statute. When the quasi-civil standard of proof becomes elevated to a quasi-criminal standard, then the duty of the Court to find the truth has to be similarly augmented. Lamentably, the Court, on the basis of incomplete facts, failed to fully grasp and legally sanction a centerpiece of the horrendous atrocities committed in Europe at the end of the 20th century.[64]

This commentary speaks not only of the distinct significance of questions of proof to the case at hand—involving a most supreme crime—but also of the perpetual validity of the proper method of proof as an indispensable instrument for finding the truth in any case. Questions of proof have obviously followed the Court in other cases and have potential to be determinative of outcome in many opening cases, including the related ongoing proceedings in *The Gambia v. Myanmar case* before the ICJ, which is now at the merits stage.[65] While there has been no specific case relating to evidence enabled by modern technology in front of the ICJ so far—perhaps also because of its broader scope of jurisdiction and the nature of cases brought before it—evidence from Facebook has nonetheless been referenced as a key source in *The Gambia v. Myanmar Case*. It is in this connection that this new genocide case will be discussed in more detail, along with the principles of method as developed by the ICJ over the years or indeed decades.

4.1   *The Gambia vs. Myanmar Case concerning the Application of the Genocide Convention*

Beginning in October 2016 and then again in August 2017, Myanmar's security forces engaged in so-called "clearance operations" against the Rohingya population, in Rakhine State, Myanmar (also known as Burma). The operations were characterized by brutal violence and serious human rights violations on

---

64   *Id.*

65   *The Gambia v. Myanmar, supra* note 24. *See* Judgment on Preliminary Objections of 22 July 2022, https://www.icj-cij.org/public/files/case-related/178/178-20220722-JUD-01-00-EN.pdf, *infra* note 85.

a mass scale. As a result, an estimated 745,000 people were forced to flee to Bangladesh.[66]

The UN Human Rights Council mandated an Independent International Fact-Finding Mission on Myanmar (FFM). According to FFM, the treatment of the Rohingya population during the "clearance operations" amounts to genocide, crimes against humanity, and war crimes. In its final report, published in September 2019, the FFM concluded that "the State of Myanmar breached its obligation not to commit genocide under the Genocide Convention under the rules of State responsibility,"[67] and found that Myanmar continues to harbor "the genocidal intent to destroy the Rohingya in whole or in part as a people."[68] The report "documented extensive roles that Facebook and other social media platforms played" in these events.[69]

With regard to the specific usage of Facebook, the 2018 Report of the Independent International Fact-Finding Mission—the mission's first report—sets out the stage. It reads in its perhaps most relevant paragraph implicating the role of the military leadership via Facebook:

> The nature, scale and organization of the operations suggest a level of preplanning and design by the Tatmadaw leadership that was consistent with the vision of the Commander-in-Chief, Senior General Min Aung Hlaing, *who stated in a Facebook post on 2 September 2018*, at the height of the operations, that "the Bengali problem was a longstanding one which has become an unfinished job despite the efforts of the previous governments to solve it. The government in office is taking great care in solving the problem."[70]

The report further notes that "[s]atellite imagery and first-hand accounts corroborate widespread, systematic, deliberate and targeted destruction, mainly

---

66 *See* Qerim Qerimi, *'All You Can Do is Pray': Implications for Human Rights Advocacy of the Lack of Recognition of Ethnic Cleansing as an International Crime on its Own*, 10 J. Hum. Rts. Practice 508 (2018).

67 Detailed findings of the Independent International Fact-Finding Mission on Myanmar, A/HRC/42/CRP.5, para. 220 (Sep. 16, 2019). Also *available at* https://www.ohchr.org /Documents/HRBodies/HRCouncil/FFM-Myanmar/20190916/A_HRC_42_CRP.5.pdf. [FFM, 2019].

68 *Id.*

69 *Id.* ¶ 466.

70 Report of the independent international fact-finding mission on Myanmar, A/HRC/39/64, para. 35 (Sep. 12, 2018) (emphasis added). Also *available at* https://www.ohchr.org/Documents /HRBodies/HRCouncil/FFM-Myanmar/A_HRC_39_ 64. pdf. [FFM, 2018].

by fire, of Rohingya-populated areas ...,"[71] also adding that, "[t]he role of social media is significant. Facebook has been a useful instrument for those seeking to spread hate, in a context where, for most users, Facebook is the Internet."[72]

On 11 November 2019, the Republic of The Gambia instituted proceedings against Myanmar in the ICJ for violating the Genocide Convention.[73] In its application instituting proceedings and requesting provisional measures of protection, The Gambia relied heavily on the findings of the UN FFM. Indeed, those findings represent the key segments of evidence submitted to the Court.[74]

During the first round of oral observations before the ICJ on its request for the indication of provisional measures, The Gambia made extensive use of the reports and findings of the UN fact-finding mission, specifically related to the use of social media.[75] A relevant part of these observations is expressed in the following terms: "The Rohingya are a distinct ethnic and religious group in Myanmar's Rakhine State, where they have had historical presence for centuries ... As set out in the Application, the genocidal acts against them have been a long time in the making. They incubated in toxic hate speech – on Facebook and Twitter – by which Myanmar demonized an entire group as 'illegal Bengali immigrants', 'terrorists' and 'jihadists'; 'maggots' and 'dogs' ... The UN Mission has pointed to the 'systematic oppression and persecution of the Rohingya. ... from birth to death'; and their 'extreme vulnerability [as] a consequence of State policies and practices implemented over decades.'"[76] As a result of these circumstances, both Facebook and Twitter have subsequently suspended the account of the commander-in-chief of Myanmar's armed forces.[77]

Also during the second round of oral observations, The Gambia continued its argument based on evidence from Facebook.[78] For its part, Myanmar reacted only during the second round of oral observations, stating that "the

---

71   *Id.* ¶ 42.

72   *Id.* ¶ 74.

73   *See* International Court of Justice, *Application of the Convention on the Prevention and Punishment of the Crime of Genocide* (The Gambia v. Myanmar) (Nov. 11, 2019), https://www.icj-cij.org/files/case-related/178/178-20191111-APP-01-00-EN.pdf.

74   *Id. See* in particular ¶¶ 38, 44 & 45.

75   *See* The Gambia's first round of oral observations, *available at* https://www.icj-cij.org/files/case-related/178/178-20191210-ORA-01-00-BI.pdf.

76   *Id.* ¶ 9.

77   *Id.*

78   Second round of oral observations of The Gambia on its request for the indication of provisional measures, *available at* https://www.icj-cij.org/files/case-related/178/178-20191212-ORA-01-00-BI.pdf. *See* in particular ¶¶ 7, 10 & 42.

statement on the Facebook post [by the commander-in-chief of Myanmar's army] is one to which many different meanings can be attached."[79]

The ICJ issued its Order, adopting provisional measures, on 23 January 2020.[80] All indicated measures of protection were adopted unanimously by Court members. However, what is more relevant to the present discussion is the Court's reliance on the reports of the UN fact-finding missions, inclusive of evidence collected from Facebook and other social media. For instance, the Court noted that the reports of the Fact-Finding Mission have indicated that the Rohingya in Myanmar have been subjected to acts which are capable of affecting their right of existence as a protected group under the Genocide Convention, such as mass killings, widespread rape and other forms of sexual violence, as well as beatings, the destruction of villages and homes, denial of access to food, shelter and other essentials of life.[81]

On the basis of the detailed findings in the reports of the UN fact-finding mission, the Court was "of the opinion that the Rohingya in Myanmar remain extremely vulnerable."[82] The Court further took note of the detailed findings of the Fact-Finding Mission on Myanmar submitted to the Human Rights Council in September 2019, which refer to the risk of violations of the Genocide Convention, and in which it is "conclude[d] on reasonable grounds that the Rohingya people remain at serious risk of genocide under the terms of the Genocide Convention."[83]

In light of those considerations, the Court found that there is a real and imminent risk of irreparable prejudice to the rights invoked by The Gambia.[84] What is significant in this case is the decisive value the Court accorded to the findings of the UN fact-finding missions in making its conclusion and issuing the order. A note must be added here that the Court may, however, look at the evidentiary basis and its value under a different test at the merits stage.

In a further decision of 22 July 2022, the Court rejected all preliminary objections raised by Myanmar and found that it has jurisdiction, on the basis

---

79   The second round of oral observations of Myanmar on the Request for the indication of provisional measures by The Gambia, *available at* https://www.icj-cij.org/files/case-related /178/178-20191212-ORA-02-00-BI.pdf. *See* in particular ¶¶ 8 & 9.

80   See International Court of Justice, *Application of the Convention on the Prevention and Punishment of the Crime of Genocide* (The Gambia v. Myanmar), Request for the Indication of Provisional Measures, Order (Jan. 23, 2020), https://www.icj-cij.org/files/case-related /178/178-20200123-ORD-01-00-EN.pdf.

81   *Id.* ¶ 71.

82   *Id.*

83   *Id.*

84   *Id.* ¶ 75.

of Article IX of the Genocide Convention, to entertain the application filed by The Gambia.[85] It therefore declares the application admissible,[86] opening the door to the decision on the merits.

Given the decisive value it accords in its decision on provisional measures, the next sub-section will address the question of the method utilized in the two reports of the UN Human Rights Council's Fact-Finding Mission on Myanmar and the criteria already developed by the ICJ to assess the legal value of such reports.

4.2   *The Methodology of Fact-Finding Reports and the ICJ Jurisprudence*

The 2018 FFM Report on Myanmar has addressed specifically the question of method. The report based its factual findings on the "reasonable standard" of proof.[87] This standard was considered to have been met "when a sufficient and reliable body of primary information, consistent with other information, would allow an ordinarily prudent person to conclude that an incident or pattern of conduct occurred."[88]

In terms of primary information, the FFM conducted 875 in-depth interviews with victims and eyewitnesses, which had been both randomly selected and targeted. The FFM has also obtained satellite imagery and authenticated a series of documents, photographs and videos. According to the FFM, it relied "only on verified and corroborated information."[89]

In its 2019 report, the FFM confirmed that it continued to base its factual findings on the "reasonable grounds" standard of proof, and that the mission continued to employ the same method as in its 2018 report.[90] For this second report, in the period between February and June 2019, the FFM conducted 419 interviews with victims and witnesses. Again, it obtained and analyzed satellite imagery, photographs and videos, and a variety of documents. It then "cross-checked the information against secondary information assessed as credible and reliable, including organizations' raw data or notes, expert interviews, submissions and open source material."[91]

---

85   *See* International Court of Justice, *Application of the Convention on the Prevention and Punishment of the Crime of Genocide* (The Gambia v. Myanmar), Preliminary Objections, Judgment (Jul. 22, 2022), https://www.icj-cij.org/public/files/case-related/178/178-20220722-JUD-01-00-EN.pdf.

86   *Id.* ¶ 115.

87   FFM, 2018, *supra* note 70, ¶ 6.

88   *Id.*

89   *Id.* ¶ 7.

90   FFM, 2019, *supra* note 67, ¶ 31.

91   *Id.* ¶ 32.

In its past judicial practice, the ICJ has dealt with the probative value of UN or other organizations' reports, advancing important elements in order to establish the validity of such reports. In its 2005 judgment in the *Case Concerning Armed Activities on the Territory of the Congo (Democratic Republic of the Congo v. Uganda)*, the Court decided not to take into account elements of United Nations reports which rely only on second-hand sources.[92] Indeed, the Court has not relied on various other reports offered as evidence for reasons of finding them "uncorroborated, based on second-hand reports, or not in fact saying what they are alleged to say ..., or even in some cases partisan."[93] In its 2022 judgment concerning reparations in this case, the Court clarified that it would consider UN reports as reliable evidence "only to the extent that they are of probative value and are corroborated, if necessary, by other credible sources."[94] As regards a study prepared by a team of University experts, the Court stated that it needs to be treated with caution,[95] reaffirming its statement from the 2005 judgment that "it will treat with caution evidentiary materials specially prepared for this case and also materials emanating from a single source."[96]

The Court has additionally noted that it prefers contemporaneous evidence from persons with direct knowledge, and that it also gives weight to evidence that has not been challenged by impartial persons for the correctness of what it contains.[97] Moreover, the Court has noted that evidence obtained by examination of persons directly involved, and who were subsequently cross-examined by judges skilled in examination and experienced in assessing large amounts of factual information, merits special attention.[98]

Having regard to the aforementioned pronouncements from the practice of the ICJ, the two FFM reports would appear to comply with a number of requisite criteria, such as its reliance on primary sources and corroborated by other credible sources. Moreover, the reports are not prepared for the specific ICJ case on the matter, and obviously, the mission's materials do not emanate

---

92   International Court of Justice, *Case Concerning Armed Activities on the Territory of the Congo (Democratic Republic of the Congo v. Uganda)*, Judgment of 19 December 2005, I.C.J. Reports 2005, ¶ 159 [DRC v. Uganda, 2005].

93   *Id.*

94   International Court of Justice, *Armed Activities on the Territory of the Congo (Democratic Republic of the Congo v. Uganda) Reparations*, Judgment of 9 February 2022, I.C.J. Reports 2022, ¶ 215 [DRC v. Uganda, 2022].

95   *Id.* ¶ 358.

96   DRC v. Uganda, 2005, *supra* note 92, ¶ 61.

97   *Id.* ¶ 61.

98   *Id.*

from a single source. The evidence is contemporaneous and does not appear to have been challenged by impartial persons. However, the evidence obtained has not been cross-examined by judges or factual findings made by a court of law such as, for instance, the ICTY in the *Bosnia Genocide case*. This can alternatively be mitigated by the Court itself, as it has the power prescribed in the Statute to consider expert opinions and also question the experts.[99] However, even assuming that the Court accepts the credibility of the reports and the validity of the findings, it is another question as to what significance it gives to them. More importantly, although the Court might rely on findings of fact, it is fully autonomous, however, to make its own legal analysis and come to its legal conclusions, which can diverge from those of the fact-finding mission.

5   Conclusion

The discussion in this chapter has revealed the many facets of modern technology and its indubitable utility in the pursuit of justice in situations involving mass atrocity crimes. Drawing on Professor Siegfried Wiessner's writings, beginning as far back as 1983, this chapter has portrayed a distinct place for space-based or space-enabled technology in pursuit of a world public order of human dignity. In return, it has testified to his foresighted claim of the bright future of the geostationary satellite orbit.

In correlation with Professor Wiessner's writings, three specific dimensions have been closely examined, namely the scope of application of modern space-related technology to contexts involving mass atrocity crimes, the role and probative value of aerially derived evidence, and questions pertaining to the method of proof.

As further revealed by the exposed trends in this chapter, specialized international courts and tribunals have already embraced evidence generated by space-based or other means of modern technology. Given the scale and speed of advances in technology, it is to be naturally anticipated that international courts and tribunals will more frequently conduct judicial proceedings on the basis of evidence generated by space-based and other modern means of technology. Their value becomes ever more important and inescapable especially in hardly accessible political and security zones. In such contexts or arenas, aerially-generated evidence may not only play a decisive role, but indeed may

---

99   Statute of the International Court of Justice, Arts. 50 & 51.

well be the only available effective instrument capable of generating reliable evidence in the pursuit of truth and justice. At least in this sense, *space* or smart technologies in space are an indispensable ally of materializing hope to prevent crime and preserve life, as well as, in other contexts, discover truth and provide justice.

CHAPTER 30

The Consciousness of Astronautical Ethics

*Roy Balleste**

It is a unique opportunity to be one of the authors in this special *Festschrift* in honor of Siegfried Wiessner. I know that any attempt to honor my mentor and friend—Siegfried Wiessner—would require much more than the few words I will share in this essay. There is so much to be said about this great scholar and humanitarian. I hope he finds the following words as my most profound sign of admiration, affection, and respect. I still remember the first day I met Professor Wiessner. On that day, he opened for me a door to the most crucial legal field of our lifetime: international law. Today this field continues to defy time and space as it takes humanity into a new frontier that challenges all perceptions of reality. Outer space law is now the frontier of exploration and future human discovery. In this essay, within the pages of its three sections, I share with my mentor Siegfried Wiessner and all other readers the strange new worlds that he once inspired in me.

1   On Counterspace

> The test of a man isn't what you think he'll do. It's what he actually does.
> FRANK HERBERT, *Dune*[1]

I would like to believe that in one thousand years, humanity will be better. I choose to believe that human civilization will expand through the galaxy in that time. It is a vision of a civilization launching into the cosmos. Our

---

*   Dr. Roy Balleste is Professor of Law and Law Library Director at Stetson University. He has focused his scholarship on the evolving regulatory challenges of cybersecurity law, cybersecurity in outer space, cyber operations, and cyber conflict, and is a core expert and editorial board member of the Manual on International Law Applicable to Military Uses of Outer Space (MILAMOS). Balleste holds a J.S.D. in Intercultural Human Rights (St. Thomas University); LL.M. in Air and Space Law (McGill University); LL.M. in Intercultural Human Rights (St. Thomas University); M.S. in Cybersecurity (Norwich University); and a J.D. degree (St. Thomas University).

1   Frank Herbert, Dune 575–576 (1965; 2005).

planetary society has progressed substantially since the days of Admiral Piri Reis,[2] explorer Ferdinand Magellan,[3] and Antarctic explorer Sir Ernest Shackleton.[4] Those ageless mariners remind us of human ingenuity and the blueprints of what later evolved into the Space Age. Looking back in time also reminds us of great cruelty observed amongst human beings suffering in conflicts worldwide. Although history is a helpful guide to navigating the present human rights standards, humanity continues to allow ancient cruelties to persist in our midst. The crimes against humanity on the battlefield are one of a series of calamities that plague our existence. Whether this cruelty responds to political forces or not, human beings have a long journey ahead to achieve enlightenment which is the object of my hopes for the future. But it may take longer than a thousand years.

A new age for humanity approaches from above the heavens and the human mind is tied to its divine consciousness. It is a consciousness linked to the life of those that surround us. "The conscious mind is thus a multiplex of aptitudes, attitudes, and feelings including intuiting, imagining, and creating new ideas and innovative solutions to problems."[5] I suppose that imagination starts new endeavors that leave a lasting legacy for future generations. I imagine that if we could move forward in time, we would see wondrous worlds populated by our distant inheritors.

Let me illustrate this point. Frank Herbert begins the first book of his masterpiece sci-fi novel *Dune* with a mystery. The story's beginning takes us first to the far future and to a distant planet known as Caladan, where Duke Leto and his noble family are the rulers.[6] This family is at the center of the story and traces its roots to our present human civilization.[7] The head of the family, Duke Leto of the House Atreides, also belongs to the greater noble class of a

---

2   *See* José Juan Montejo, Los Enigmas de Piri Reis y Otros Navegantes 45 (2016). [Spanish Edition]. [The Enigmas of Piri Reis and Other Navigators].

3   *See* Laurence Bergreen, Over the Edge of the World (2003).

4   *See* Alfred Lansing, Endurance: Shackleton's Incredible Voyage (1959).

5   Joseph P. Hester, *Reflections on Humanity's Moral Consciousness: Uncovering the Foundation of Values-based Leadership*, 13(2) Journal of Values-Based Leadership 115 (2020).

6   *See* Kim Becker, *'Dune' Reveals the Elements Essential to Every Science Fiction Story*, StudyBreaks (May 18, 2022), https://studybreaks.com/culture/reads/science-fiction-elements/. *See also* Sean T. Collins, *'Dune' for Dummies: Everything You Need to Know Going Into the Sci-Fi Blockbuster* (October 12, 2021), https://www.rollingstone.com/movies/movie-features/dune-for-dummies -1228259/.

7   Adam Rosenberg, *What is 'Dune'? Everything you should know about Frank Herbert's sci-fi epic*, Mashable (September 15, 2020), https://mashable.com/article/what-is-dune-book-universe -explainer.

vast society that expands the universe.[8] The main character at the center of
the story is Duke Leto's son, Paul Atreides.[9] The emperor has ordered Duke
Leto to move and govern *Arrakis—Dune—Desert Planet.*[10] Naturally, the story
begins with young Paul Atreides, who is about to face a test.[11] From the beginning of the story, Paul and those around him are surrounded by unexpected
events lurking on the horizon. A conspiracy takes form, and a conscious moral
approach eventually defines the Atreides.[12] "It is consciousness that makes
available our moral capacity, an indispensable aptitude definitive of human
life."[13] When we think of human activity in a complex interplanetary society,
as described in *Dune*, it would probably engender this type of moral reflection.
Dune's Book I has an important lesson: the human condition is directly tied to
society's ethical standards in outer space.

Paul's inner story is surrounded by an impending conflict between his family and the House Harkonnen, a rival family.[14] Our present days seem equally
troubled by similar human elements. Terrestrial conflicts threaten to extend
themselves toward outer space. Astronomy professor Chris Impey noted
China's actions in destroying "one of its weather satellites with a missile" and
the outcome materialized as "tens of thousands of pieces of shrapnel, all large
enough and traveling fast enough to destroy another satellite or pose a threat
to the International Space Station."[15] India and, most recently, Russia conducted anti-satellite missile tests.[16] These activities could signal the start of
what is dubbed as counterspace. "Counterspace is a mission, like counterair,
that integrates offensive and defensive operations to attain and maintain the
desired control and protection in and through space."[17] Outer space is now

---

8   Collins, *supra* note 6.
9   Rosenberg, *supra* note 7; *see also* Manohla Dargis, *'Dune' Review: A Hero in the Making,
      on Shifting Sands*, N.Y. Times (October 29, 2021), https://www.nytimes.com/2021/10/20
      /movies/dune-review.html.
10   Jon Michaud, *Dune Endures*, The New Yorker (July 12, 2013), https://www.newyorker.com
      /books/page-turner/dune-endures.
11   Herbert, *supra* note 1, at 3–6 (1965; 2005).
12   Collins, *supra* note 6.
13   Hester, *supra* note 5.
14   Collins, *supra* note 6.
15   Chris Impey, *Is conflict in space inevitable?* The Hill (October 8, 2021), https://thehill.com
      /opinion/international/575903-is-conflict-in-space-inevitable/
16   *Id.*
17   United States Air Force, *Counterspace Operations*, Air Force Doctrine Publication 3–14
      – Counterspace Operations, LeMay Center for Doctrine Development and Education
      (January 25, 2021), https://www.doctrine.af.mil/Portals/61/documents/AFDP_3-14/3-14
      -D05-SPACE-Counterspace-Ops.pdf.

more than a frontier. It is a new strategic arena where superiority and control may mean the difference between security and vulnerability.[18] It is now known that "[t]he United States activated two command centers for the Space Force, the branch of the military designed to conduct its operations in outer space."[19] Professor Impey asked, "[i]s this crescendo of activity a harbinger of international space warfare?"[20] At present, the concept of counterspace operations seems inescapable.

Perhaps the most worrisome threat of our times is nuclear conflict. While many individuals may have left behind the accompanying fears of the late 1980s, the threat of nuclear conflict has resurfaced recently. This turn of events casts a sense of doom for our future. "A final characteristic of nuclear war is its environmental effect, including the spread of dangerous radiation and changes to the global climate. The effects of a nuclear conflict would not be limited to the geographical area that was attacked, but instead would spread to affect the globe."[21] The potential dust, smoke, and debris paint an ominous horizon.[22] A conflict in outer space will most likely affect the other warfighting domains: land, sea, air, and cyber.[23] A solution must be found so that space remains free for use and exploration. This freedom of exploration is the true spirit of astronautical ethics:

> Outer space, including the Moon and other celestial bodies, shall be free for exploration and use by all States, without discrimination of any kind, on a basis of equality and in accordance with international law, and there shall be free access to all areas of celestial bodies.[24]

When we think about the development of space law, we must consider how various national militaries are integrating counterspace doctrine and

---

18   *Id.*

19   Chris Impey, *supra* note 15.

20   *Id.*

21   Wendy N. Whitman Cobb, *Making a Moral Case for Nonconflict in Space: Expanding Strategic Norm to Taboo*, Wild Blue Yonder (March 16, 2020), https://www.airuniversity.af.edu /Wild-Blue-Yonder/Articles/Article-Display/Article/2106715/making-a-moral-case-for -nonconflict-in-space-expanding-strategic-norm-to-taboo/.

22   *Id.*

23   Kestutis Paulauskas, *Space: NATO's latest frontier*, NATO Rev. (March 13, 2020), https:// www.nato.int/docu/review/articles/2020/03/13/space-natos-latest-frontier/ index.html.

24   *Treaty on Principles Governing the Activities of States in the Exploration and Use of Outer Space, including the Moon and Other Celestial Bodies*, 27 January 1967, 610 U.N.T.S. 205, art I (2) (entered into force 10 October 1967) [Outer Space Treaty].

technologies for future wars.[25] "According to the 2020 U.S. Defense Space Strategy, China and Russia have weaponized space as a means to reduce U.S. and allied partners' freedom of operation in space."[26] Have the nations of the world abandoned the true spirit of space exploration as enshrined in the Outer Space Treaty? Professor Myres McDougal would remind us that "the minimum we might mean by a Regime of Outer Space is that all important decisions with respect to space activities are taken by legal process."[27] McDougal would also remind us that the basis for a public order in outer space depends on the existence of a free society.[28] This proposition is exacerbated by the future uncertainties of Roscosmos' operations due to the Russian government's aggression in Ukraine. Russia's invasion of Ukraine has fractured the moral fabric of the international world order. "Outraged by Western sanctions imposed over its invasion of Ukraine, Russia may end its collaboration onboard the International Space Station in favor of China."[29] This fact on its own seems harmless and exclusively political. Yet, "China and Russia are developing and testing multiple counterspace technologies that potentially threaten U.S. and allied partners' space assets."[30] These counterspace technologies may include, for example, direct ascent weapons to destroy a satellite, lasers, high-powered microwave weapons, nuclear weapons, the jamming of radio frequency signals, or attacks on the data sent via cyberspace.[31] These array of threats, and others, offer a chilling presage of future events. In contrast to these threats, the famous Prussian general Carl von Clausewitz would compare this changing landscape of warfare in our times to a chameleon seeking to fit within the societal values that influence the eventual character of war.[32] The future claims of States regarding their use of outer space may be less driven by the cooperation that existed at the genesis of space exploration and more about offensive and defensive measures. Perhaps it will be "far more difficult to identify the characteristics of conflict in space given that actual, kinetic combat has not

---

25   Stephen M. McCall, *Space as a Warfighting Domain: Issues for Congress*, Congressional Research Service (August 10, 2021), https://sgp.fas.org/crs/ natsec/IF11895.pdf.

26   *Id.*

27   Myres S. McDougal, *The Prospect for a Regime in Outer Space, in* Law and Politics in Space 105 (Maxwell Cohen ed., 1964).

28   *Id.* at 105.

29   Antony Ashkenaz, *Russia threatens to abandon NASA on ISS and join China's space mission*, Express (April 29, 2022), https://www.express.co.uk/news/science/1602809/ russia-news -space-threatens-abandon-nasa-iss-china-space-mission-moon-base.

30   McCall, *supra* note 25.

31   *Id.*

32   Brandon T. Euhus, *A Clausewitzian Response to "Hyperwarfare*, 48(3) US Army War College Quarterly: Parameters 66 (2018).

occurred."[33] Space exploration, I suppose, will further be threatened by how space conflict shapes in its various forms.[34]

Continuous lessons of the past color the threat of conflict beyond our planet's boundaries. Cruelty may probably arise out of human activity in outer space. I suppose that new technologies will impact human space activity. Judge Manfred Lachs noted that "[i]n assessing the present, one must not forget that it grew out of the past and that events should be evaluated in their proper perspective."[35] Indeed, Lachs explains that our communities and societies serve as a catalyst for science, technology, and law.[36] As Lachs noted, we must remember that nature must be harnessed to satisfy humanity's needs.[37] In *Dune*, Paul Atreides's mother is relieved to know that his son has passed the test; that his son is human.[38] This test was meant to unleash him. But unleash him from what? "Once men turned their thinking over to machines in the hope that this would set them free. But that only permitted other men with machines to enslave them."[39] These words uttered by the Revered Mother Gaius Helen Mohiam carried a profound meaning. Then Paul quoted: "Thou shalt not make a machine to counterfeit a *human* mind."[40] Politics—the continuity of human affairs—required separating the human mind from the artificial mind.[41] The human mind that promises to take humanity into outer space will succeed only if technology is properly managed. I submit to you that the famous author, Sir Arthur C. Clarke, pondered the idea of astrophysics and the existence of many other universes. As Clarke put it, "insofar as I understand anything that [astrophysicists] are talking about," our universe is peculiar.[42] In Clarke's view, the specific variables necessary for life—"which as far as one could see, God could have given any value He liked"—were precisely calibrated to allow for our existence.[43] Clarke would agree that humanity exists where it is supposed to be

---

33   Wendy N. Whitman Cobb, *Making a Moral Case for Nonconflict in Space: Expanding Strategic Norm to Taboo*, Wild Blue Yonder (March 16, 2020), https://www.airuniversity.af.edu /Wild-Blue-Yonder/Articles/Article-Display/Article/2106715/making-a-moral-case-for -nonconflict-in-space-expanding-strategic-norm-to-taboo/.

34   *Id.*

35   Manfred Lachs, *Thoughts on Science, Technology and World Law*, 86(4) Am. J. Int'l L. 673, 675 (1992).

36   *Id.* at 677.

37   *Id.*

38   Herbert, *supra* note 1, at 13.

39   *Id.* at 14.

40   *Id.*

41   *Id.*

42   Arthur C. Clarke, Tales from Planet Earth 100 (1990).

43   *Id.*

and not in any other place.[44] The desire to live, exist, and evolve transcends any notion of artificiality. It is an innate trait of human beings to discover and seek answers. If this natural trait represents our conscious reality, why do so many acts of States seem inclined to sabotage the future? It is not to be wondered then that "the most important objective in regard to space sought by the principal participants obviously continues to be the enhancement of their power and security."[45] The uneasy truce amongst States, as noted by Professor McDougal, Lasswell, and Vlasic in the 1960s, and one defined by power and security continues to this day.[46]

Turning to near-future space conflicts, if these occur, the assumption is that we will observe a code of behavior based on the rules of war. I think negotiations at the States' level will not be enough. While plenty of analysis has been associated with the theory of just war, in reality, this concept seems irrelevant when related to wars of aggression. I note my service in the U.S. Army during the final months of the Kosovo war. While not directly participating in-country on ground operations, I participated in a succeeding supporting role. It was frustrating and mindboggling to see from afar how a group of human beings caused so much pain and suffering to another group. The war of aggression by Serbia in Kosovo was a reminder that the United Nations Security Council processes were imperfect and would probably fail again.[47] In a reflection of those memories, the struggles of Paul Atreides ironically resonate in recent conflicts. For example, the Middle East has been compared to Arrakis, a place exploited and ignored by the major powers.[48] The political machinations have been influenced by the Middle East oil, and in *Dune*, by its spice.[49] Now natural gas is at the center of the conflict in Ukraine.[50] But oil or natural gas is not the supreme commodity of our times. It is information and, in particular, online data. In *Dune*, "it is the quest to control the 'spice' that drives the economic,

---

44   *Id.*

45   Myres S. McDougal, Harold D. Lasswell & Ivan A. Vlasic, Law and Public Order in Space 17 (New Haven and London: Yale University Press, 1963).

46   *Id.*

47   https://warontherocks.com/2019/03/the-kosovo-war-in-retrospect/.

48   William A. Senior, *Frank Herbert's Prescience: 'Dune' and the Modern World*, 17(4) Journal of the Fantastic in the Arts 317 (2007).

49   Senior, *supra* note 48.

50   *See, e.g.*, Associated Press, *Ukraine halts Russian gas exports to Europe at eastern transit point*, Euronews (May 11, 2022), https://www.euronews.com/2022/05/11/ ukraine-halts -russian-gas-exports-to-europe-at-eastern-transit-point.

political, and military action of the empire."[51] Spice, an energy source for inter-stellar travel, becomes the strategic commodity of control and power.[52]

The events in *Dune* represent Frank Herbert's vision of a linear and progressive historical outcome that may not always be "predictable, [yet, events] are nonetheless logical and understandable."[53] *Dune* serves as an allegory for our times and one that anticipated "many of the issues that face us most insistently today: production and price of oil, environmental threats, the escalating instability of the Middle East, Muslim fundamentalism, the erosion of monolithic world powers, the failure – or abandonment – of diplomacy, and the staggering cost in lives, money, and matériel."[54] The point to be made is about technology and its use. Judge Lachs notes that his desire to acknowledge how "science and technology have become essential parts of history and the present ... [and] that the future will to an even greater degree be dependent on the various methods and tools used to make products of human genius [to] serve the needs and interest of ... the international community."[55] When we turn to the challenges associated with space exploration, we discover our limitations of technological knowledge. There is still much to be understood about our place in the solar system and our membership in the galaxy.

2   Strange New Worlds

A new life awaits you in the Off-world colonies!
A chance to begin again in a golden land of opportunity and adventure![56]

Not all events are about the crisis that may surround our future civilization. Our planet offers ecstatic beauty in many places, known and remote. Our works

---

51   Paul R. Camacho, *American Warfare in the Twenty-First Century*, 19(1) New England J. Pub. Pol'y, 201, 202 (2003).

52   Gwyneth Jones, *Metempsychosis of the Machine: Science Fiction in the Halls of Karma*, 24(1) Science Fiction Studies 1, 3 (1997). *See also* Fatemeh Mirjalili, *The Proper Reading Order For Dune*, Slashfilm (May 23, 2022), https://www.slashfilm.com/871699/the-proper-reading. -order-for-dune/.

53   Lorenzo DiTommaso, *History and Historical Effect in Frank Herbert's 'Dune,'* 19(3) Science Fiction Studies 311 (1992).

54   Senior, *supra* note 48.

55   Lachs, *supra* note 35, at 699.

56   Fictional advertisement from *Blade Runner* (1982), considered one of the greatest sci-fi films of all time. The movie was based on Philip K. Dick's original 1968 novel, *Do Androids Dream of Electric Sheep?* (Del Rey, 2017). *See also Blade Runner*, Imdb, online: http://www .imdb.com/title/tt0083658/.

of art, music, global landscapes, architecture, and traditions are magnificent representations of that beauty. I truly believe that we will surmount the present and future conflicts simply because human nature enshrines love, beauty, happiness, and fraternity. We can only wonder about those strange new worlds that humanity will visit someday. Imagine worlds not like our own, but equally fascinating, majestic, and scenic. What if one of these strange new worlds is habitable? These thoughts are the inspiration that Philip K. Dick shares with us in his novel, *Do Androids Dream of Electric Sheep?*[57] Most popularly known as the novel behind the motion picture *Blade Runner*, this visionary work is considered one of our time's most fascinating noir sci-fi stories.[58] Both, the book and the motion picture are concerned with "the ethics of artificial intelligence and what it means to be human."[59] Once again, we encounter notions of a technology that may threaten or improve humanity's ability to develop a new age of discovery in outer space. In *Blade Runner*, Earth's environment has turned hostile, yet Philip K. Dick reminds us of the meaning of being alive.

Our planet is in a galaxy like no other. From a distance, it may look like many others. The closest world with intelligent life—if any—is not known to us. In between, there are millions of planets, and thousands of potential exoplanets spreading across the galaxy. But life may be rare, for planets harboring life may be unique and hard to find in the universe.[60] Yet, our existence's noble purpose is to explore new worlds. To think about our purpose in life could be perceived as an exercise of self-indulgence. Still, it is appropriate—once in a while—to take that proverbial short look into the past, if just to see the road already traveled, and immediately imagine the road ahead. My friend Siegfried Wiessner should be proud of that road because we see it as his legacy. Some may perceive this legacy as tied to Wiessner's fortune in life. But what is that exactly, that fortune. The best way to describe it would be to identify specific moments in time.

---

57   Douglas E. Williams, *Ideology as Dystopia: An Interpretation of 'Blade Runner,'* 9(4) Int'l Pol. Science Rev. / Revue Internationale de Science Politique (1988): 381, 384 (1988). ["Ridley Scott's Blade Runner became first a 'cult' film, and then a national institution: it is one of only fifty films to be deposited in the Library of Congress, Washington DC, on the basis of its contribution to film culture'"]. *See also* Nigel Wheale, *Recognizing a 'Human-Thing': Cyborgs, Robots and Replicants in Philip K. Dick's 'Do Androids Dream of Electric Sheep?' And Ridley Scott's 'Blade Runner,'* 3(3) Critical Survey 297–304. (1991).

58   Ben Sherlock, *Blade Runner: 10 Tropes Of Film Noir (& How It Puts A Sci-Fi Twist On Them)*, Screenrant (August 22, 2020), https://screenrant.com/blade-runner-film-noir-tropes-sci-fi-twist/.

59   *Id.*

60   Carl Sagan, *in* The Meaning of Life: Reflections in Words and Pictures on Why We Are Here 73 (David Friend and the Editors of LIFE eds., 1991).

Siegfried Wiessner has always reminded us that "human rights are inviolable." My memories take me back to his many lessons during the Juris Doctor program. It was also an honor to be part of the second class of his prestigious and highly respected graduate program in intercultural human rights. One central theme of the program has been the use of law as a tool for achieving a global order of human dignity and the many aspects that this endeavor entails.[61] For example, Wiessner noted that "to achieve a global order of human dignity responding to human needs and aspirations, the quest should be redirected from the cataloguing of states' grants of power or tolerance of indigenous peoples' authorities toward looking instead for the proper starting point: the authentic claims and aspirations of indigenous peoples."[62] Yet, Wiessner understands—as I do—that our technological world complicates the efforts to attain that global order of human dignity. While human beings are more connected than ever, individuals are also exposed to new forms of threats that endeavor to interfere with their dignity. This state of affairs requires the foundation for astronautical ethics. If we move from the surface of our planet and beyond our atmosphere, in the immeasurable vastness of the cosmos, human activities will be surrounded by unexpected threats originating from technology and other natural sources. Similarly, McDougal and Feliciano note:

> The "rapid multiplication and diffusion of weapons capable of shattering the globe, ... the continued, if decelerated, hostile polarization of power in the world arena, ... the ever more precarious equilibrium between the polar opponents [−] ... all these and many other aspects of the contemporary world arena magnify with chilling insistence, even for the willful blind, the urgent need for rational inquiry into the potentialities and limitations of our inherited principles and procedures for controlling violence between peoples and for the invention and establishment of more effective alternatives in principles and procedures."[63]

Blade Runner is about that future life on colony planets and those still on Earth.[64] It is a life supported by androids that serve their human masters. Yet,

---

61 Siegfried Wiessner, *Indigenous Sovereignty: A Reassessment in Light of the UN Declaration on the Rights of Indigenous Peoples*, 41 Vand. J. Transnat'l L. 1141, 1170 (2008).

62 *Id.*

63 Myres S. McDougal & Florentino P. Feliciano, *International Coercion and World Public Order: The General Principles of the Law of War*, 67(5) Yale L.J. 771 (1958).

64 Dylan Schuck, *If You Can't Rewatch 'Blade Runner' Before '2049,' Read This*, The Hollywood Reporter (October 6, 2017), https://www.hollywoodreporter.com/movies/movie-news/blade-runner-original-movie-plot-synopsis-you-need-before-2049-1046355/.

these androids have become self-aware, and a group of them—at the center of the story—have escaped their owners and traveled back to Earth.[65] *Blade Runner* shows us a society that has given androids, by design, a forbidding lifespan of just four years.[66] The story highlights four androids—Nexus 6 replicants—who successfully escaped and searched for their creator, Eldon Tyrell, hoping he would extend their lives.[67] Their short lifespan adds a degree of cruelty to the replicants' bondage.

In a future society of outer space and off-world commerce, technology reigns at its center with these "extraordinarily sophisticated robots or androids ... [that] do the hazardous and most demanding work" as slaves.[68] It is not difficult to see that slavery in any form, even for replicants, would be wrong. On Earth, the Los Angeles Police Department employs bounty hunters with a mandate to "retire" these artificial lifeforms.[69] This state of affairs is significant because that human creation—artificial intelligence technology—blurs the distinction between humans and synthetic lifeforms.[70] "Indeed, the super-sophisticated androids or replicants ... have so drastically narrowed the gap itself as to cast serious doubt on the tenability of the distinction at its very core."[71] Rick Deckard, the story's main character, is the blade runner who must hunt and retire the replicants.[72]

Blade Runner shows us a future much more complicated than our own. Yet, the elements surrounding the story are not necessarily alien to our potential future. The story infers that these replicants may behave better than human beings. But what is a real human? The 17th-century French philosopher, René Descartes, pondered this dilemma.[73] "If there were machines bearing images of our bodies, and capable of imitating our actions as far as it is morally possible, there would still remain two most certain tests whereby to know that they were not therefore really men."[74] In *Blade Runner*, the Voight-Kampff test is

---

65   *Id.*

66   *Id.*

67   Williams, *supra* note 57, at 385.

68   *Id.* at 384.

69   David Barnett, *Are we living in a Blade Runner world?* BBC (November 11, 2019), https://www.bbc.com/culture/article/20191111-are-we-living-in-a-blade-runner-world.

70   Williams, *supra* note 57, at 384.

71   *Id.*

72   *Id.* at 385.

73   *See* Lorraine Boissoneault, *Are Blade Runner's Replicants "Human"? Descartes and Locke Have Some Thoughts*, Smithsonian Magazine (October 3, 2017), https://www.smithsonianmag.com/arts-culture/are-blade-runners-replicants-human-descartes-and-locke-have-some-thoughts-180965097/. *See also* René Descartes, Discourse on the Method (2008).

74   *Id.*

used to address Descartes' question as it is administered by blade runners to identify replicants.[75] Replicants have developed feelings and a desire to defend life.[76] This trait represents a "security threat to those [humans] they were intended to serve, an eventuality that has been compensated for by coding them genetically."[77] These androids simply represent a tool to be used to propel the human agenda in space. One of the most dramatic moments in the story is the "bone-chilling climactic battle" between Deckard and the replicant group's leader, Roy Batty.[78] Batty had previously operated as a combat unit.[79] Another point to highlight is using technology in space for military purposes. If technology is to serve humanity for the better, its military applications must be considered in conjunction with any new development in the rules of war. Practice, not theory, will define humanity's activities in outer space. Siegfried Wiessner highlights Professor Michael Reisman's work in his reminder about this very consideration.[80] "In the practice of law, beyond the area of explicit legislation or regulation, the application of such prescriptions often takes place in a highly institutionalized environment which mandates adherence to certain pressures of role and structure of argument."[81] If our present history is to serve as witness and judge, then our international political mechanisms are far from applying good practice. The beginning of our new life in outer space requires something more. Both Professor Reisman and Wiessner have dedicated their efforts and scholarship to the goals of a world order of human dignity. As noted by these outstanding scholars, these goals have been guided by policy-oriented jurisprudence.[82] Wiessner explains that "policy-oriented jurisprudence postulates explicitly the overriding goal toward which all activity and interaction should be directed. The overriding goal is to foster a commonwealth of human dignity and all trends, projections, and alternatives can be appraised in terms of their compatibility with this goal."[83] No doubt our human civilization has a long way to go to fulfill that goal, yet Wiessner's wisdom points us in the best

---

75   *Id.*

76   Myres S. McDougal & Florentino P. Feliciano, *supra* note 63, at 771.

77   Williams, *supra* note 57, at 385.

78   David Sims, *The Real and Unreal in Blade Runner 2049*, The Atlantic (October 12, 2017), https://www.theatlantic.com/entertainment/archive/2017/10/the-real-and-unreal-in -blade-runner-2049/542574/.

79   *Id.*

80   Siegfried Wiessner, *Law as a Means to a Public Order of Human Dignity: The Jurisprudence of Michael Reisman*, 34 Yale J. Int'l L. 525, 529 (2009).

81   *Id.*

82   Siegfried Wiessner & Andrew R. Willard, *Policy-Oriented Jurisprudence*, 44 German Y.B. Int'l L. 96 (2001).

83   *Id.* at 103.

direction. As noted earlier, there are moments in time that remain vivid in our minds. Siegfried Wiessner has left many of these moments in my life, and no doubt, in the lives of the many people he has touched with his wisdom. The moments in time represented as "tears in rain."[84] Every single time I heard my friend speaking, it became one special moment in time. Moment by moment, revealing to us the mysteries of life through the tool that we know as law.

On Earth, the requirement for new energy sources will be a significant incentive to enter into a new age of exploration. And there are more incentives out there in the great expanse. What will be our role to play as species in the cosmos? We are all fascinated with outer space's mysteries and the opportunities it may offer to improve our existence. "The point is not to declare that space is only for warfighting, that war in space is inevitable, or that space-power is exclusive to the military. Such a declaration, instead, functions to clarify and delineate relationships."[85] This is how I envision the role of astronautical ethics. I see it from a unique lens or philosophy for a better life. It is a search for meaning as we endeavor to use international law as a vehicle to develop these ethics and shine a light on those who need it. In fact, Judge Lachs may have perceived it in a similar manner. Lachs noted that "[t]he main tool is obviously law, made-made international law: humanity's response to the discovery of the laws of nature, and man-made devices its key to controlling their human application with wisdom and patience."[86] It is this wisdom and patience that offers a degree of policy-oriented jurisprudence.

The most unforgettable scene in *Blade Runner* is near its end. Batty traps Rick Deckard on a high roof, and Deckard is about to fall from that high roof.[87] This scene is accentuated by Roy Batty's "death scene, as he saves Deckard's life and crouches over him, imparting his strange, alien memories to his would-be assassin before expiring."[88] Roy's final words may represent the echoes of a human consciousness returning into the universe:

> I've seen things you people wouldn't believe: attack ships on fire off the shoulder of Orion. I've watched C-beams glitter in the dark near the

---

84   Batty, *infra* note 89.
85   Everett C. Dolman, *Space Is a Warfighting Domain*, 1(1) ÆTHER: A Journal of Strategic Airpower & Spacepower 82, 84 (2022).
86   Lachs, *supra* note 35, at 699.
87   Blade Runner, Imdb, *supra* note 56.
88   Sims, *supra* note 78.

Tannhauser Gate. All those ... moments ... will be lost... in time, like ... tears ... in rain ... Time to die.[89]

The nature of the cosmos, what we perceive with our consciousness, may compel an inquiry away from *just in bello* and *jus ad bellum* and more precisely, as U.S. Navy Lieutenant Euhus notes, toward the *casus belli*.[90] Indeed, we have an obligation to protect our future by understanding the meaning of traveling to planets and from there to other galaxies. Warfare in outer space must be avoided if we are to fulfill our place in the cosmos. "If an entity uses robots to conduct a massive offensive and destroys the opponent's entire robot army, does the war end? Or did a naïve population just realize they would have to fight the war themselves?"[91] Regardless of our military strategies, I believe there is an aspect that is less explored yet equally relevant. The mysteries of the human condition will be clarified if those future brave explorers— astronauts—survive the harsh realities of our present global conflicts. Our terrestrial troubles threaten to reach beyond our celestial borders. Yet, there are those who believe that the spirit of outer space law will serve as a shining beacon in the years to come. Siegfried Wiessner is one of those believers.

3   And All My Hopes

All men dream, but not equally. Those who dream by night in the dusty recesses of their minds, wake in the day to find that it was vanity: but the dreamers of the day are dangerous men, for they may act on their dreams with open eyes, to make them possible.

T. E. LAWRENCE, *Seven Pillars of Wisdom*[92]

This *Festschrift* is an opportunity to remember that humanity, for the most part, has a noble nature. Siegfried Wiessner also appreciates this nature. It is a nature for good that will never be lost like tears in the rain. It is a nature for good that overflows the many lessons that Professor Wiessner has shared with his students all these past fruitful years. These lessons now inspire me to dream.

---

89   Roy Batty is a fictional character from *Blade Runner* and the original 1968 novel, titled *Do Androids Dream of Electric Sheep? See Biography for Roy Batty*, Imdb, online: http://www .imdb.com/character/ch0002845/bio. *See also supra* note 56.

90   Euhus, *supra* note 32, at 13.

91   *Id.*

92   T. E. Lawrence, Seven Pillars of Wisdom 12 (1926; 2017).

In my view, as humanity continues to learn new methods of travel, outer space will emerge as the new frontier. And the lessons of *Dune* echo into the successful continuity of human affairs in space. These affairs depend on the human mind separated from the artificial mind.[93] It is the human mind that must conquer technology for the betterment of humanity. Similarly, Blade Runner reminds us of the very core of our human existence, our purpose in life, and our legacy as stewards of the planet.

The new age of exploration will also rely on what we perceive as the meaning of our existence. Carl Sagan's appreciation for our unique opportunities as technological beings incorporated a conscious effort to highlight the immensity of this life's purpose:

> The hard truth seems to be this: We live in a vast and awesome universe in which, daily, suns are made and worlds destroyed, where humanity clings to an obscure clod of rock. The significance of our lives and our fragile realm derives from our own wisdom and courage.
>
> *We* are the custodians of life's meaning.[94]

New outer space wonders are found every week. Our probes send back magnificent images of a frontier many never thought they would see. Now we are aware of thousands of exoplanets and many capable of sustaining life. When I hear individuals speak against space exploration and question its necessity, I imagine those individuals centuries ago who probably wrestled with the challenges associated with the entry of Spanish and Portuguese explorers into the world's great oceans. Every time I have stood up in front of El Escorial, the palace and monastery of King Philip II of Spain, I am reminded that this is not just a monument to a king or an empire. It is a monument to those men that began a journey of discovery in the fifteenth century. We have learned so much more since those times. Novelist William Burroughs once noted the following:

> I believe mankind's biological destiny is in space, and dreams are our lifeline to that destiny ... Why are we here? This is the Space Age, and we are here to go.[95]

---

93   Herbert, *supra* note 1, at 14.

94   Carl Sagan, *supra* note 60.

95   William Burroughs, *in* The Meaning of Life: Reflections in Words and Pictures on Why We Are Here 124 (David Friend and the Editors of LIFE eds., 1991).

Humanity has learned how exploration carries responsibilities. These responsibilities are owed, for example, to the indigenous populations and to the natural environment of those places yet to be discovered. But if humanity must enter a new age of discovery, it must learn to incorporate the entire solar system into its legal domain. My friend Siegfried would remind us that "[a] more *substantive*, or "thick," concept of the rule of law would aspire to filling the idea of the law with notions of substantive justice."[96] Justice must shine on the actions of those who now enter the new age of exploration. McDougal and Burke observed that "[t]urning from historic achievement to the contemporary world arena, an observer cannot fail to note the increasing demands, unparallel in scope and complexity, for extension of the exclusive authority of states over the oceans of the world."[97] By extension, the same observation would apply to the cosmic ocean and its astronautical ethics. In particular, the ethics associated with commercial and military activities with a defining role in the future.

To me, our understanding of our status in the cosmos is incomplete. True, it might be a case of mirages and false hopes if humans remain at odds with each other. Clausewitz noted, "[t]he invention of gunpowder and the constant improvement of firearms are enough in themselves to show that the advance of civilization has done nothing practical to alter or deflect the impulse to destroy the enemy, which is central to the very idea of war."[98] So, how would I describe our purpose in the cosmos? I would say that the answer would be rooted in a deep understanding of what is the *rule of law*. "If now, you ask me what guarantee I can offer that this my own faith about the Good in this institution of our law is better than another's—what does Reason show me to warrant this particular faith of mine against mistake—I have no answer."[99] Life reflects human activities. Beyond our atmosphere, human activities will be beyond expectations in the immeasurable vastness of the cosmos. And all my hopes rely on the goodness of humanity and the space law that will catalyze a new age of exploration.

If we could trace the evolution of international space law, what could we find? Siegfried Wiessner helps us see some of that answer in his brilliant article titled *The Public Order of the Geostationary Orbit: Blueprints for the Future.*

---

96 Siegfried Wiessner, *The Rule of Law: Prolegomena*, Zeitschrift für deutsches und amerikanisches Recht, 82, 83 (2018).

97 Myres S. McDougal and William T. Burke, *Crisis in the Law of the Sea: Community Perspectives versus National Egoism*, 67(4) Yale L.J. 539, 540 (1958).

98 Peter Paret, Clausewitz and the State, The Man, His Theories, and His Times 384 (2018).

99 K. N. Llewellyn, *On the Good, the True, the Beautiful, in Law*, 9(2) U. Chicago L. Rev. 224, 230 (1942).

I have had the privilege to read this article many times, and every time it delivered something new and helpful to my understanding of space law. Wiessner begins his analysis as follows:

> The use of space has grown exponentially. It is impossible today to conceive of international communications, weather forecasting, or the screening of the riches of the earth without the help of space-based devices. Full-scale industrialization of outer space is under way, and space has become a critical arena for military strategists in the global duel.[100]

The very first footnote of this article is also impressive, as Wiessner acknowledges the valuable comments of several individuals, including luminaries such as Professors Myres S. McDougal, W. Michael Reisman, and Carl Q. Christol.[101] The article intended to address a problem that continues to challenge space law practitioners to this day: the "saturation of the geostationary orbit."[102] Wiessner took a unique and pragmatic approach as he searched for a solution. He proposed "a flexible framework of inclusive control over the area, based on the view of the orbit as a *res publica internationalis*."[103] Recognizing that the GEO or "geostationary orbit is a complicated astrophysical phenomenon," Wiessner tackled the science, law, and politics behind the allocation of satellite spaces in this limited and valuable orbit. As I noted once before, "Wiessner would probably say that the geostationary orbit is directly related to the claims for access to that resource, where States are mainly interested in their own security, which is also susceptible to external demands from the other States, the private sector, and international organizations."[104]

The formulation of a solution requires the clarification of the reason for the technology that serves our goals and sentient beings. In this case, "the GEO is not just congested but is accessible only to those who can reach it."[105] Wiessner's applicability and reimagination of law in the context of the management of the geostationary orbit, and throughout his vast scholarship, shares with us his vision. A portion of that vision also observes—superbly—the following:

---

100   Siegfried Wiessner, *The Public Order of the Geostationary Orbit: Blueprints for the Future*, 9
         Yale J. Int'l L. 217 (1983).
101   *Id.*
102   *Id.*
103   *Id.* at 218.
104   Roy Balleste, *Space Horizons: An Era of Hope in the Geostationary Orbit*, 35 J. Envtl. L. &
         Litig. 165, 188 (2020).
105   *Id.* at 181.

First, law is essentially a matter of choice. Prescriptions do not flow, like the laws of natural science, from immutable experience and observation. Kepler's laws are but factual limits, objective ramifications of the bulk of highly flexible rules designed to guide human behavior. Often, these rules are inherited; sometimes, they are fairly novel, like the general public order of outer space. Always, they are subject to change.

Second, resource control and exploitation are subject to various regimes, or public orders, which have developed over time in the process of continuous interaction as outlined above. The regimes differ according to the nature of the resource, the conditions necessary for its optimum use, including its conservation, and the prevailing socio-economic context.[106]

Professor Wiessner has taken the law in his hands and has delivered in return legal scholarship as works of art as well as science. To ponder his legal scholarship is to perceive his mind and his love for his fellow human beings. "So it comes about that right craftsmen of the law can discover that they have 'been talking prose all their lives'—which means, in this instance, that they have been doing legal poetry. They have been artists, they are artists, art is of the essence of their daily work."[107] This is the legacy that Professor Siegfried Wiessner leaves with us. It is a message representing a chain of knowledge passed on to him by his mentors, and compounded by his wisdom, now becomes a shining light for those who have had the privilege to learn from him. So many thoughts, memories, and images come to mind as I reflect on all the conversations with my friend Siegfried.

Life is a true mystery. It could be defined as the cumulative efforts of many hours, days, months, and years. It is its own universe. "Many and strange are the universes that drift like bubbles in the foam upon the River of Time."[108] When we look back in time, what do we see? My friend Siegfried Wiessner can look back with pride. He has touched many lives, and many have been his acts of kindness. And it is now our opportunity to repay a small measure of that kindness. Looking back in time, I see the wisdom of my dear mentor, from whom I have learned not just about international law but about the source of astronautical ethics. My friend Siegfried Wiessner is one of those men that dreams by day because he has acted on his dreams with open eyes and made them possible.

---

106   Wiessner, *supra* note 100, at 236.
107   Llewellyn, *supra* note 99.
108   Arthur C. Clarke, Tales from Planet Earth 219 (1990).

PART 8

International Investment Law and Arbitration

∴

The Search for Truth v. The Preservation of the Integrity of International Investment Arbitration Proceedings: The Issue of Admissibility of Illegally Obtained Evidence under the Revised ICSID Arbitration Rules

*Stephan Wilske**

The truth will set you free.

JOHN 8:32, NCB

•••

Pilate responded, "What is truth?"

JOHN 18:38, NCB

∴

1 Introduction

It is well known that our honoree Professor Dr. Siegfried Wiessner has a vivid interest in different perspectives of international law, including a theoretical perspective,[1] a contemporary (and even practical) perspective[2] as well

---

* Stephan Wilske, Dr. iur., Maître en Droit (Aix-Marseille III), LL.M. (The University of Chicago, Casper Platt Award); admitted in Germany and in the State of New York and to various U.S. federal courts, including the U.S. Supreme Court; FCIArb; Partner at Gleiss Lutz, Stuttgart; Lecturer at the Universities of Heidelberg and Jena, Member of the American Law Institute (ALI) and Vice President of the CAAI Court of Arbitration.

1 General Theory of International Law (Siegfried Wiessner ed., 2017); Siegfried Wiessner & Andrew R. Willard, *Policy-Oriented Jurisprudence and Human Rights Abuses in Internal Conflict: Toward a World Public Order of Human Dignity*, 93 Am. J. Int'l L. 31 (1999).
2 *See* W. Michael Reisman, Mahnoush H. Arsanjani, Siegfried Wiessner & Gayl S. Westerman, International Law in Contemporary Perspective (2004).

as a humanitarian perspective.[3] This author is still very grateful for Siegfried Wiessner contributing his article on *The Rule of Law: Prolegomena* to the Farewell Issue of *Zeitschrift für Deutsches und Amerikanisches Recht* (ZDAR) in 2018.[4] Quite obviously, Siegfried Wiessner must have an interest in truth and is certainly an academic truth seeker. However, in practice, the question is often not only whether a piece of evidence reflects truth (however truth may be defined[5]) but also whether there are limits in the methods for seeking the truth. In the international dispute arena, the question may boil down to the question of admissibility of illegally obtained evidence. A lot could be written about the "fruit of the poisonous tree" in various fields of law, but as the authors to this *liber amicorum* were reminded to limit their contribution, this author will mainly address the issue of admissibility of illegally obtained evidence under the revised ICSID Arbitration Rules.[6] Thus, the focus is not on fraudulent evidence,[7] but on truthful evidence that was obtained by dubious means.

2   The Revised ICSID Arbitration Rules and the IBA Rules on the Taking of Evidence in International Arbitration

In 2018, the International Centre for Settlement of Investment Disputes ("ICSID") started the process of modernizing its 2006 Arbitration Rules. The overall goal was to update and simplify its rules while taking into account general trends towards more efficiency and transparency in international arbitration.[8]

---

3   Siegfried Wiessner, Die Funktion der Staatsangehörigkeit [The Function of Nationality] (1989); Siegfried Wiessner, *Asylverweigerung ohne Anerkennungsverfahren* [Denial of Asylum without Process of Recognition], 7 Europäische Grundrechte-Zeitschrift 473 (1980); Siegfried Wiessner, *Rights and Status of Indigenous Peoples: A Global Comparative and International Legal Perspective*, 12 Harv. Hum. Rts. J. 57 (1999), to mention but a few.

4   Siegfried Wiessner, *The Rule of Law: Prolegomena*, Zeitschrift für Deutsches und Amerikanisches Recht (ZDAR) 85 (2018) (The relaunch of this journal with the title *Transatlantic Legal Journal* is scheduled for summer 2023 and this author hopes for valuable contributions from our honoree in the future issues).

5   *See, e.g.*, Philip Roth, The Great American Novel 19 (1973): "Well, what may seem like the truth to you," said the seventeen-year-old bus driver and part-time philosopher, "may not, of course, seem like the truth to the other fella, you know." "THEN THE OTHER FELLOW IS WRONG, IDIOT!"

6   Richard Happ & Stephan Wilske, *The new ICSID Arbitration Rules – are they really new? What's the Catch?* 13 Korean Arb. Rev. 77 (2022).

7   *See* on this topic the very illustrative study by W. Michael Reisman & Christina Parajon Skinner, Fraudulent Evidence before Public International Tribunals: The Dirty Stories of International Law (2014).

8   Happ & Wilske, *supra* note 6.

After four years, and five working papers, the 2022 ICSID Arbitration Rules came into effect on 1 July 2022.

2.1 The Arbitral Tribunal's Role in the Taking of Evidence[9]

Pursuant to Rule 36(1) of the 2022 ICSID Arbitration Rules, the "Tribunal shall determine the admissibility and probative value of the evidence adduced" by the parties. The wording of the current rule thus describes the role of the tribunal more proactively in the process of taking the evidence as compared to 2006 ICSID Arbitration Rule 34(1), which stated that "the Tribunal shall be the judge of the admissibility of any evidence adduced and of its probative value." Indeed, the taking of the evidence is one of the primary tasks of the tribunal. Whereas Rule 36(1) addresses only the arbitral tribunal's power in determining the admissibility and probative value of the evidence, Rules 36(3), 39(1), and 40(1) provide the tribunal with the authority to seek evidence actively. However, ICSID arbitration remains an adversarial process. Adducing and producing evidence is primarily up to the parties. When evidence is produced by the parties, it is then the tribunal's task to determine whether that evidence is admissible and to what extent the probative value of the evidence suffices to satisfy the producing party's burden of proof.

It is a long-established practice that tribunals exercise jurisdiction over the process of the taking of evidence. This applies especially to the admissibility and probative value of the evidence adduced, as can also be drawn from Rule 36(1), and to the weighing of the evidence. As for establishing the facts and determining whether the parties satisfied their respective burden of proof, it is for the tribunal to decide. Thus, tribunals control the process of the taking of evidence.

2.2 Admissibility of Evidence

When determining the admissibility and probative value of the evidence adduced, the tribunal generally has broad discretion.[10] The tribunal's discretion is, however, not unfettered, but restricted through general principles of

---

9 The following analysis of Article 36 of the 2022 ICSID Arbitration Rules draws upon the commentary of Stephan Wilske & Björn P. Ebert on Chapter V (Evidence) of ICSID Rules and Regulations 2022: Article-by-Article Commentary (Richard Happ & Stephan Wilske eds., 2022).

10 Luke Sobota & Gaëtan Verhoosel, *Chapter 24: Written and Oral Procedures, in* The ICSID Convention, Regulations and Rules: A Practical Commentary para. 24.2, (Julien Fouret, Rémy Gerbay & Gloria M. Alvarez eds., 2019); Richard Happ, *Rule 34 ICSID Rules, in* Institutional Arbitration Article-by-Article Commentary 965 (Rolf A. Schütze ed., 2013).

law and international law.[11] Hence, when exercising its discretion, the tribunal engages in a balancing of applicable legal principles and the relevant interests of the parties.[12] Depending on the specific circumstances, the tribunal thereby may consider aspects of fair process, the right to be heard and the right to present one's case, good faith, abuse of process, etc.

The tribunal may further be guided by the 2020 IBA Rules on the Taking of Evidence in International Arbitration ("IBA Rules"). Although tribunals are entitled to order the application of the IBA Rules,[13] it is more common for the IBA Rules to serve as persuasive authority in the process of determining the admissibility of evidence adduced.[14] Parties are free to agree on the application of the IBA Rules or to agree that the tribunal may be guided by the IBA Rules when considering the admissibility of evidence and other evidentiary issues.[15] Indeed, in the absence of an agreement by the parties, the direct application of the IBA Rules was considered controversial by some tribunals in past arbitral awards. For instance, the tribunal in *Noble Ventures v. Romania* argued that the IBA Rules were primarily created to be utilized in the field of commercial arbitration.[16] Nonetheless, taking guidance from the IBA Rules is common practice in investor-state arbitration.[17] Since the IBA Rules foster efficient and fair taking of evidence, they have led to a harmonization and predictability of the process.[18] The IBA Rules are thus often seen as best practice

---

11   Richard Happ, *Rule 34 ICSID Rules, in* Institutional Arbitration Article-by-Article Commentary 965 (Rolf A. Schütze ed., 2013).

12   Saar Pauker, *Substance and procedure in international arbitration,* 36 Arbitration International 3 (2020); Christoph H. Schreuer, Loretta Malintoppi, August Reinisch & Anthony Sinclair, The ICSID Convention. A Commentary 644 (2009).

13   Jörg Risse & Heiko Haller, *So kommen die IBA-Rules zur Anwendung, in* Beweis im Schiedsverfahren 123 (Walter Eberl ed., 2015); S.I. Strong & James J. Dries, *Witness Statements under the IBA Rules of Evidence: What to Do about Hearsay?* 21 Arbitration International 301 (2005).

14   Christoph H. Schreuer, Loretta Malintoppi, August Reinisch & Anthony Sinclair, The ICSID Convention. A Commentary 642 (2009).

15   Richard Happ, *Rule 34 ICSID Rules, in* Institutional Arbitration. Article-by-Article Commentary 965 (Rolf A. Schütze ed., 2013).

16   *Noble Ventures, Inc. v. Romania* (ICSID Case No. ARB/01/11), Arbitral Award, 12 October 2005, para. 20, citing para. 2 of Procedural Order No. 1 of the tribunal.

17   *See* paragraph 1 of the Preamble of the IBA Rules, which describes that the IBA Rules are broadly meant to be used in "international arbitrations," and Tobias Zuberbühler, Dieter Hofmann, Christian Oetiker & Thomas Rohner, IBA Rules of Evidence 1 (2012), who point to the fact that the word "commercial" was deleted from the initial title of the IBA Rules to acknowledge that they are meant to be used both in commercial and in investment arbitration.

18   Zuberbühler et al., IBA Rules of Evidence, *supra* note 17, Preamble, paras. 4, 6, 7 (2012).

in international arbitration.[19] Accordingly, even the tribunal in *Noble Ventures v. Romania* concluded that the IBA Rules can provide guidance.[20] Indeed, the notorious Procedural Order No. 1[21] in ICSID arbitral proceedings often provides that the tribunal *"will be guided"* by the IBA Rules.

2.3   The Tribunal's Broad Discretion

Admission of evidence in an ICSID arbitration is a procedural matter not governed by national law, but only by international law. As noted above, although tribunals enjoy broad discretion with respect to evidence, several legal principles recognized in international law may restrict tribunals' discretion to decide on the admissibility of evidence under Rule 36(1) 2022 ICSID Arbitration Rules. Limits to tribunals' discretion under Rule 36(1) may also derive from an agreement by the parties or the IBA Rules. While parties seldom agree on the direct application of the IBA Rules, the IBA Rules are commonly considered as persuasive authority that provides guidance for the admissibility of the evidence.

In international law, it is a long-established practice that an international tribunal is the judge of the admissibility of the evidence with very few limitations.[22] In practice, however, tribunals are reluctant to exclude evidence as inadmissible.[23] On the one hand, this may be due to the fact that the unjustified exclusion of evidence as inadmissible affects a party's right to present its

---

19   *See, e.g.*, Gary B. Born, 2 International Commercial Arbitration 2377 (3d ed. 2021), (referring, *inter alia*, to a 2012 study of Queen Mary, University of London that had found that the IBA Rules were used in 60% of the international arbitrations that were surveyed).

20   *Noble Ventures, Inc. v. Romania* (ICSID Case No. ARB/01/11), Arbitral Award 12 October 2005, para. 20.

21   *See* Stephan Wilske & Chloë Edworthy, *The Predictable Arbitrator: A Blessing Or A Curse?*, Austrian Y.B. Int'l Arbitration 77, 85–86 (2017) (referring to anecdotes in the arbitration community about arbitrators' "standard form" Procedural Order No. 1 which is circulated by the "auto-pilot" arbitrator in advance of the preliminary meeting between arbitral tribunal and the parties and without any attention paid to the particularities of the case in hand; see also IBA Arb40 Subcommittee, Compendium of arbitration practice (2017), Chapter 2 (Procedural Order No 1)(https://www.ibanet.org/document?id=Compendium-of-arbitration-practice).

22   *See Middle East Cement Shipping and Handling Corporation S.A. v. Arab Republic of Egypt*, Award of 12 April 2002, ICSID Case No. ARB/99/6, para. 75; Luke Sobota & Gaëtan Verhoosel, *Chapter 24: Written and Oral Procedures, in* The ICSID Convention, Regulations and Rules: A Practical Commentary para. 24.28, (Julien Fouret, Rémy Gerbay & Gloria M. Alvarez eds., 2019).

23   *See EDF (Services) Ltd. v. Romania*, Procedural Order No. 3 of 29 August 2008, ICSID Case No. ARB/05/13, para. 47; Cherie Blair & Ema Vidak Gojković, *WikiLeaks and Beyond: Discerning an International Standard for the Admissibility of Illegally Obtained Evidence* 33(1) ICSID Review – Foreign Investment L.J. 235, 238 (2018).

case.[24] On the other hand, in order to avoid a tough decision, arbitral tribunals sometimes decide not to reject evidence as inadmissible but to assign little or no evidentiary value to the individual pieces of evidence in the course of weighing the evidence. This might not seem convincing from a dogmatic point of view but might serve to some extent as a counter-weight to restraint in the exclusion of evidence (at least for conflict-averse arbitrators).

Generally speaking, the decision on the admissibility of evidence depends on the individual circumstances and merits of the given case. Within the realm of public international law, tribunals must balance several principles when deciding on the admissibility of evidence. Notably, that includes the parties' right to be heard. The right to be heard suggests the admissibility of the evidence, as this right requires, as a general rule, that the parties are authorized to present all of their evidence.[25] However, tribunals must also consider the principles of good faith and due process in their decision-making.[26] These principles as well the parties' procedural right to fair process and the principle of equality of arms[27] may rather imply a dismissal of the evidence, despite the importance of the parties' right to be heard. Therefore, the decision of the tribunal on the admissibility of evidence requires a balancing of different rights and principles.

2.4   *Grounds for Inadmissibility of Evidence*

The tribunal's discretion to determine the admissibility of the evidence adduced is subject to limitations deriving from general principles of law. While the 2022 ICSID Arbitration Rules, in particular Rule 36(1), do not provide for explicit limitations to the tribunal's discretion, general principles of public international law as well as general principles of law and any agreement of the parties may provide for limitations.

In this regard, the principles of good faith and procedural fairness are frequently referred to by tribunals, and a violation of these principles may result in the inadmissibility of the respective evidence. Within the realm of public international law, the principle of good faith requires parties "to deal honestly and fairly with each other, to represent their motive and purposes truthfully, and to refrain from taking unfair advantage."[28] Hence, the tribunal may refuse

---

24   Zuberbühler et al., IBA Rules of Evidence, *supra* note 17, Article 9, para. 6.

25   Blair & Vidak Gojković, *supra* note 23, at 235; Zuberbühler et al., IBA Rules of Evidence, *supra* note 17, at 182; Nitya Jain, *Can an Arbitral Tribunal Admit Evidence obtained through Cyber-Attack?* Kluwer Arbitration Blog (27 January 2019).

26   *EDF (Services) Ltd. v. Romania*, Procedural Order No. 3, *supra* note 23, para. 47.

27   Jain, *supra* note 25.

28   *Phoenix Action Ltd. v. Czech Republic*, Award of 15 April 2019, ICSID Case No. ARB/06/5, para. 107.

to admit evidence to the record if there are good and sufficient reasons to believe that either the principle of good faith or that of procedural fairness has been violated or that the integrity of the proceedings might be impaired. The violation of either principle has to be evaluated depending on the individual circumstances of the given case.[29] When determining whether the principle of good faith or the principle of procedural fairness is violated, tribunals consider not only the facts alleged to indicate such a violation, but also the burden of proof and probative value of the evidence concerned. Additionally, tribunals may consider whether the privacy of the other party would be compromised or violated. For instance, in *Methanex v. United States of America*, the tribunal found that the disputing parties owe each other a general legal duty to conduct themselves in good faith during the arbitral proceedings and to respect the equality of arms between them.[30] On that basis, the tribunal refused to admit evidence that the claimant had improperly obtained from searching through the respondent's internal trashcans, which included personal notes, private correspondence and material expressly subject to legal privilege.[31]

The approach according to which a violation of general principles of law may result in the evidence's inadmissibility is also confirmed by the IBA Rules. Pursuant to Article 9(2)(g) of the IBA Rules, evidence might be excluded if there are "considerations of procedural economy, proportionality, fairness or equality of the Parties that the Arbitral Tribunal determines to be compelling." Indeed, the IBA Rules provide for more detailed grounds for inadmissibility of evidence produced or evidence sought by one of the parties to the dispute. In this regard, Article 9(2) of the IBA Rules authorizes the arbitral tribunal, at the request of a party or on its own initiative, to exclude from evidence or production of evidence any document, statement, oral testimony or consideration of the evidence under any of the following circumstances: lack of relevance or materiality (Article 9(2)(a)); for reasons due to legal impediment or privilege (Article 9(2)(b)); evidence which is unreasonably burdensome to produce (Article 9(2)(c)); loss or destruction of the document (Article 9(2)(d)); commercial and technical confidentiality, such as trade secrets (Article 9(2)(e)); and evidence with political or institutional sensitivity, also known as "national security privileges" (Article 9(2)(f)).[32] The list of these examples should not, however, be considered

---

29 *EDF (Services) Ltd. v. Romania*, Procedural Order No. 3, *supra* note 23, para. 47.

30 *Methanex Corporation v. United States of America*, UNCITRAL Award on Jurisdiction and Merits of 3 August 2005, Part II Chapter I, para. 54.

31 *Id.*, Part II Chapter I, para. 54; Brigitta John, *Admissibility of Improperly Obtained Data as Evidence in International Arbitration Proceedings,* Kluwer Arbitration Blog (28 September 2016).

32 Zuberbühler et al., IBA Rules of Evidence, *supra* note 17, Article 9, paras. 36–49.

as conclusive, but rather as open to several other procedural situations or circumstances that call for the exclusion or inadmissibility of the evidence.[33]

One of the most cited reasons for the inadmissibility of evidence, which is also mentioned in the IBA Rules (see Article 9(b) and (f) of the IBA Rules), is confidentiality, legal privilege, and sensitivity of the evidence. Yet, the concept of confidentiality and legal privilege differs under national law. Whereas legal privilege is a well-known concept in common law jurisdictions, such as the legal system of the United States or the United Kingdom, civil law jurisdictions follow a different approach. Invoking legal privilege in international arbitration therefore comes with its challenges. In this regard, the tribunal may be guided by the IBA Rules. Article 9(4) of the IBA Rules includes the following pieces of evidence under legal privilege: communications between the parties and their attorneys; communications between the parties with the purpose of settlement negotiations; the expectations of the parties and their advisors at the time the legal impediment or privilege is said to have arisen; any possible waiver of any applicable legal impediment or privilege; and the need to maintain fairness and equality between the parties. A further factor that may lead the tribunal to conclude that certain evidence is inadmissible or should be excluded from consideration of the evidence is of particular importance in international arbitration, namely the fact that there are often parties, counsel, and arbitrators from different jurisdictions and diverse legal backgrounds involved and, thus, compromises for procedural fairness are required. For instance, if tribunals were to strictly apply the national law applicable to each party (including its counsel), this could result in one party being able to invoke a broader legal privilege, while the other party may be required to disclose more potential evidence due to limited or narrower legal privilege. This applies even more to ICSID arbitration, where the investor, by virtue of the requirement of Article 25 of the ICSID Convention, often has a different legal background than the respondent state. In light of the differences of the concept of confidentiality and legal privilege, it is often necessary for the tribunal to determine the rules applicable in relation to confidentiality and legal privilege under the specific circumstances of the arbitration concerned.

In practice, especially the national security privileges play a crucial role in ICSID arbitration. Politically sensitive documents include for instance technical data on weapons, algorithms used for encryption programs and similarly confidential information of international organizations such as the United Nations, the World Bank or the International Monetary Fund, but may also

---

33   *Id.,* Article 9, para. 18.

include documents of the respondent state.[34] These documents are usually classified as secret or top secret. Under Rule 36(1), as well as according to Article 9(2) and (3) of the IBA Rules, it is within the tribunal's discretion to reject such evidence as inadmissible.

Legal privilege, confidentiality, and sensitivity of the evidence play a crucial role when it comes to document production. Often parties cite confidentiality, legal privilege or sensitivity when refusing to produce requested documents.

When the tribunal excludes evidence due to the inadmissibility of the evidence, it is within the tribunal's discretion to impose the costs connected with a challenge or request to exclude evidence on a party if it breached the general principles of good faith and procedural fairness. This is also provided for in Article 9(7) of the IBA Rules.

2.5   *Evidence Obtained by Irregular Means*

As in other legal proceedings, the tribunal in an investor-state dispute might be confronted with evidence obtained by irregular means. Examples of illegally obtained evidence, with which ICSID tribunals were confronted, are evidence obtained from computer hacking,[35] interception of electronic (privileged) communication[36] and audio recordings without the knowledge of the person being recorded.[37] A famous case of (potentially) illegally obtained information/data is WikiLeaks.[38] In the meantime, with WikiLeaks now being part of the public domain, it will be extremely difficult for a party to convince a tribunal to ignore potentially outcome-determinative documents because of a potential breach of national laws many years ago; in particular, many releases relate to issues of genuine public interest, and international as well as national courts and tribunals have allowed documents that have been leaked through WikiLeaks to be admitted as evidence.[39] Further, the assessment of the admissibility as evidence of leaked documents also has to consider the public debate of these documents, which results in loss of their potential confidential nature.

---

34   Zuberbühler et al., *supra* note 17, Article 9, para. 46 (2012).

35   *Caratube International Oil Company LLP v. Republic of Kazakhstan*, ICSID Case No. ARB/08/12, Arbitral Award, 5 June 2012.

36   *Libananco Holdings Co. Limited v. Republic of Turkey*, ICSID Case No. ARB/06/8, Arbitral Award, 2 September 2011.

37   *EDF (Services) Ltd v. Romania*, ICSID Case No. ARB/05/13, Arbitral Award, 8 October 2009.

38   Blair & Vidak Gojković, *supra* note 23, at 236, stating that U.S. laws were violated.

39   Blair & Vidak Gojković, *supra* note 23, at 242–250 (2018); Moritz Keller & Lukas Tepke, *Beweisaufnahme in der internationalen Schiedsgerichtsbarkeit* [Taking of Evidence in International Arbitration], *in* Liber Amicorum Günther Horvath (Axel Reidlinger, Eliane Fischer & Bertram Burtschler eds., forthcoming in 2022).

The leading case in international law on the admissibility of evidence obtained by irregular means is the *Corfu Channel Case* between the United Kingdom and Albania.[40] In its judgment, the ICJ did not exclude the evidence obtained by the United Kingdom as inadmissible even though the Court had characterized the act through which the United Kingdom obtained the evidence as a violation of international law.[41] This may be due to the fact that Albania had not complained about the inadmissibility of the evidence, but had also relied, at least in part, on the actions of the United Kingdom to support its own claim of violation of territorial sovereignty.[42] Hence, it follows from the ICJ's judgment that illegally obtained evidence is not automatically inadmissible in the realm of public international law.[43]

In investor-state arbitration, evidence obtained by irregular means is similarly not *per se* inadmissible.[44] ICSID tribunals have not resorted to the Anglo-American doctrine of the "fruit of the poisonous tree," which may not be transferred to ICSID arbitration.[45] Rather, every case has to be evaluated separately depending on its own merits and circumstances and the tribunal has to conduct a balancing of interests.[46] In this regard, tribunals consider various general principles as well as the interests of the parties.[47] On the one hand, the rule of law and access to justice in international legal proceedings call for the consideration of all relevant evidence by the tribunal.[48] On the other hand, however, there are limits to the discretion of the tribunal, due to which illegally obtained evidence may not be considered as admissible.

In the first place, tribunals evaluate whether the party relying on the illegally obtained evidence was itself involved in the illegal activity.[49] In this respect, the *clean hands doctrine* plays a crucial role.[50] Generally speaking, unlawfully obtained evidence is more likely to be admissible if the party relying on the evidence has clean hands with respect to how it obtained the

---

40   *Corfu Channel Case (UK v. Albania)*, Merits, April 9, 1949, 1949 ICJ Reports 4.

41   *Id.* at 13 *et seq.*, 34 *et seq.* The act in question was a minesweeping operation by warships of the United Kingdom in Albanian waters in violation of Albanian sovereignty.

42   *Id.* at 26, 32 *et seq.*; *see also EDF (Services) Ltd. v. Romania*, Procedural Order No. 3, *supra* note 23, para. 36.

43   Blair & Vidak Gojković, *supra* note 23, at 241.

44   *Id.* at 256 (2018); Richard Happ, *Rule 34 ICSID Rules, in* Institutional Arbitration Article-by-Article Commentary 188 (Rolf A. Schütze ed., 2013).

45   Happ, *Rule 34 ICSID Rules, supra* note 44, at 186.

46   *EDF (Services) Ltd v. Romania*, Procedural Order No.3, *supra* note 23, paras. 36, 47.

47   Saar Pauker, *supra* note 12; Christoph H. Schreuer, Loretta Malintoppi, August Reinisch & Anthony Sinclair, The ICSID Convention. A Commentary 651 (2009).

48   Blair & Vidak Gojković, *supra* note 23, at 236.

49   Jain, *supra* note 25; Blair & Vidak Gojković, *supra* note 23, at 256.

50   Blair & Vidak Gojković, *supra* note 23, at 256 (2018).

evidence, and more likely to be inadmissible if that party does not have clean hands.[51] Whenever a party tries to benefit from its own unlawful behavior, the provided evidence tends to be inadmissible (this general guideline, however, is subject to significant exceptions[52]). Allowing a party to rely on such evidence would clash with the principle of *ex turpi causa non oritur actio* (a right cannot stem from a wrong).[53] As an example, in *Libananco v. Turkey*, the respondent relied on evidence obtained through interception of the claimant's electronic communications, and included communications between the claimant and its legal counsel. The claimant emphasized the respondent's unclean hands with respect to such evidence and the tribunal consequently excluded the respective evidence from the arbitration proceeding.[54]

Besides consideration of the *clean hands doctrine*, it is important to assess whether the public interest favors rejecting evidence as inadmissible. Public policy considerations could favor inadmissibility of the evidence because either the act of obtaining the evidence or the usage of the evidence would contravene public policy. These public policy considerations include, for instance, professional privilege, diplomatic immunity and diplomatic inviolability.[55] In this context, Article 9(2)(f) of the IBA Rules, according to which the tribunal may "exclude any document from evidence on the grounds of special political or institutional sensitivity," plays an important role.

Apart from the *clean hands doctrine* and considerations of public interest, there are many other aspects that might influence the tribunal's decision. Often, tribunals assess whether the interest of justice favors the admission of the evidence.[56] Thereby, the importance of the provided evidence as well as the risks associated with the inclusion of the illegally obtained evidence is considered.[57] Tribunals also consider interests of procedural integrity and equality of arms.[58] Evidence obtained through torture, etc. would most likely be considered to be inadmissible

---

51   As for WikiLeaks, this approach would result in the admissibility of documents obtained from WikiLeaks.

52   *See* Stephan Wilske & Teresa Schiller, *Jurisdiction Over Persons Abducted in Violation of International Law in the Aftermath of United States v Alvarez-Machain* 5(1) The University of Chicago Roundtable, 205–242 (1998); and Stephan Wilske, *Abduction, Transboundary*, *in* Max Planck Encyclopedia of International Law (Rüdiger Wolfrum ed., 28 July 2022), para. 8 (describing the conflicting principles of *ex iniuria ius non oritur* and *male captus, bene detentus*).

53   Blair & Vidak Gojković, *supra* note 23, at 256.

54   *Libananco Holdings Co. Limited v. Republic of Turkey*, ICSID Case No. ARB/06/8, Decision on preliminary issues, 23 June 2008, paras. 48, 82 (1.16, 1.17).

55   Blair & Vidak Gojković, *supra* note 23, at 257.

56   *Id.* at 258.

57   Jain, *supra* note 25.

58   Blair & Vidak Gojković, *supra* note 23, at 258.

in order not to impair the integrity of the proceedings. After a balancing of all interests, the tribunal might allow the illegally obtained evidence if there is no other – especially lawfully obtained – evidence available to prove an important aspect of the case. Lastly, the tribunal might also decide to allow illegally obtained evidence to be submitted in the arbitration in order to avoid issuing an award which would be factually wrong in light of the true facts of the case.[59]

3   Conclusion and Outlook

Obviously, the search for truth is not always as easy and uncontroversial as it may appear at first glance. Rather, the search for truth must be balanced against other international legal values such as the preservation of the integrity of arbitral proceedings. There might well be situations where the wisdom of the *Glimmer Twins* applies:

> The moon is up
> The sun goes down
> And you can't have it both ways round.[60]

However, we can be assured that our honoree Siegfried Wiessner is best suited to balance seemingly contradicting values in the best achievable manner. In the spirit of the recently concluded *SIXTY* concert tour of the Rolling Stones, let us unite to wish our honoree not only the endurance, creativity, and enthusiasm of this iconic band, but also their blessing: *May the good Lord shine a light on you, warm like the evening sun.*[61]

Acknowledgments

Many thanks for a critical review of the manuscript go to my colleague and friend Todd J. Fox, Attorney-at-Law (New York, New Jersey, Pennsylvania) who was kind enough to revive his old-time law review editor skillset for this contribution.

---

59   Jain, *supra* note 25.

60   The song *Moon Is Up* is written by the *Glimmer Twins* Mick Jagger and Keith Richards and was released on the Rolling Stones' album *Voodoo Lounge*, Virgin Records (1994).

61   This quote is taken from the song *Shine a Light*, written by Mick Jagger and Keith Richards and first released on the Rolling Stones' album *Exile on Main Street*, Rolling Stones Records (1972).

PART 9

Constitutional Law and Jurisprudence

∴

A "Public Order of Human Dignity" and Justice as an "Open Concept": The Missing Lessons of Legal Education

*Jay Silver**

Lawyers are the stewards of a system of justice. Their professional duty, their livelihood, and their sense of personal satisfaction are organically bound up in the provision of justice. While legal education seeks to provide aspiring lawyers with the rules of law, the tools of advocacy, and the analytical skills to fulfill their chosen roles in the system, two vital elements of a comprehensive legal education are missing. The first is how we can recognize justice within the context of law? We must ask whether justice entails a set of necessary and sufficient conditions? Just because one might intuitively recognize that a just result has been produced in a legal matter does not mean one can identify the principles upon which it is based any more than one who recognizes the taste of a particular cake automatically knows how to bake it. The second missing lesson is equally basic. It addresses the potential and the path of law in shaping a world in which the dignity of all people is respected and their aspirations are facilitated.

With respect to the first lesson – the constituent elements of justice – we might ask if the dictionary enlightens us?

The answer is no. It informs us only that justice is "the quality of being just."[1] It falls to philosophy to provide us with the meaning of justice. Unfortunately, jurisprudence has not been up to the task. Bentham's quantitative utilitarian theory of justice collides head on with individual rights theory. The adage that it is better that, according to Voltaire,[2] five guilty persons go free – Blackstone said ten,[3] Benjamin Franklin a hundred,[4] and John Adams referenced an

---

* Professor of Law and Director of the Criminal Law Certificate Program at St. Thomas University College of Law.

1 Merriam Webster Dictionary, at https://www.merriamwebster.com/dictionary/justice (last visited January 26, 2022).
2 Voltaire, Zadig et autres contes (1747).
3 William Blackstone, Commentaries on the Laws of England xx (J.B. Lippincott Co., Philadelphia, 1893).
4 Benjamin Franklin, *Letter from Benjamin Franklin to Benjamin Vaughn* (Mar. 14, 1785), *in* The Works of Benjamin Franklin 11 (John Bigelow ed., 1904).

unspecified number[5] – than that one innocent person be convicted stands in opposition to Bentham's "hedonic calculus" whereby "[i]t is the greatest happiness of the greatest number that is the measure of right and wrong."[6]

Neither orientation alone fits our intuitions of justice. However, many guilty parties that Blackstone *et al.* would release will wreak havoc on the community. On the other hand, the net savings of life achieved by seizing a fellow sleeping on a park bench to keep five others alive with his organs strikes us as repugnant.[7] Over time, Bentham's formulation has come under fire on a number of fronts, including its consequentialist and hedonic nature.[8] To better understand the requirements of justice in the context of the legal system, we must set out to identify whether there is a particular set of lofty principles that must be observed before the necessary and sufficient conditions of justice are met. The authoritative *Stanford Encyclopedia of Philosophy* echoes this sentiment, urging us to "try to make sense of such a wide-ranging concept by identifying elements that are present whenever justice is invoked."[9]

Law students contemplate many of these principles every day in their studies. The cases they ponder often turn on the need for equal treatment under law, the doctrine of precedence, and the proportionality between prohibited conduct and punishment, and many more principles, not to mention the need for impartiality and sound reason. Perhaps they can divine whether there is a list of the necessary and sufficient conditions of justice. To this end, a modest

---

5   Rob Warden & Daniel Lennard, *Death in America under Color of Law: Our Long, Inglorious Experience with Capital Punishment*, 13 Nw. J. L. & Soc. Pol'y 194, 206 (2018). The adage had a much earlier birth, going back at least to Maimonides in the 12th Century. Maimonides, Sefer Hamitzvot [Book of the Commandments], commentary on *Negative Commandment 290*, at https://www.chabad.org/library/article_cdo/aid/961920/jewish/Negative-Commandment -290.htm. *But cf.* Dick Cheney, Meet the Press (NBC), 14 December 2014, *quoted in* Anthony Zurcher, *Cheney: 'No problem' with detaining innocents*, BBC News 21 December 2021 ("I'm more concerned with bad guys who got out and released than I am with a few that, in fact, were innocent.").

6   Jeremy Bentham, A Fragment on Government: Being an Examination of What Is Delivered, on the Subject of Government in General, in the Introduction to Sir William Blackstone's Commentaries (1776).

7   This scenario is close cousin of the classic "case of Sam" in the critique of utilitarianism. *See, e.g.*, Donald Palmer, Does the Center Hold? An Introduction to Western Philosophy 278–79 (6th ed. 2014).

8   John Stuart Mill was a critic, as well, espousing a qualitative form of utilitarianism in which some pleasures are of a higher order than others. *The History of Utilitarianism* 2.2, Stanford Encyclopedia of Philosophy, at https://plato.stanford.edu/entries/utilitarianism-history/.

9   David Miller, *Justice*, Stanford Encyclopedia of Philosophy (2017), at https://plato.stanford. edu/entries/justice/.

exercise involving forty-six upper class law students elicited from each a list of such conditions, to the extent each felt such a list existed.

The exercise revealed two findings regarding soon-to-be-lawyers' view of justice. The first is the assumption among all the respondents that there is such a list, and the second involves the various principles that make up their lists. Although the lists varied greatly, one half of the students believed that equal treatment and the consistency and notice provided by *stare decisis* were universal principles of justice, while one quarter added impartiality to the list as well.[10]

The job of the lawyer is like that of the philosopher when faced with an assumption about a foundational issue. It must be critically analyzed. And so we embark on an examination of whether there is a set of high principles whose application constitutes the necessary and sufficient conditions of justice and, if so, which they are.

Impartiality certainly sounds like a universal requirement of justice and a good place to start. It's even written into the Bill of Rights as a requirement of jurors in criminal trials. The last thing we want is a judge or a juror to be predisposed toward one party or the other before a hearing has even begun.

The concept, however, is not quite as simple as it may sound. How, for example, does one suppress implicit biases of which one is, by definition, unaware? Moreover, impartiality requires more than just the absence of preconceived notions about the parties that skews a decision maker's judgment. It includes the neutral and disinterested processing of the information presented in a legal matter upon which the outcome may turn. Our processing, however, is highly idiosyncratic. We are not blank slates. Our particular experiences, our culture, and our values, and beliefs shape what we perceive and the inferences we draw from it. Our conclusions may feel objective and unbiased to us, but the widely differing judgments of others will feel just as objective to them. One of the most dramatic examples was the deep racial divide over the 1995 acquittal of O.J. Simpson on murder charges, whereby a CNN/Time Magazine poll found that, after months of watching trial on television, whites were four times more likely to disagree with the verdict than blacks.[11] True impartiality, it turns out, is a mirage. The best we can hope for from a decision maker is the absence of virulent bias, of self-interest in the outcome, and of material preconceptions.

---

10 Documentation of the exercise is available from the author.

11 *Races disagree on impact of Simpson trial,* CNN/Time Magazine Poll (October 6, 1995) (Sixty-two percent of whites polled believed Simpson was guilty, while only fourteen percent of blacks did).

Surely, we want law, procedure, the contemplation of issues, and the ultimate dispositions in legal matters to be based on sound reasoning. As we conceive of it, sound reasoning factors in all relevant information, including emotional repercussions, although proper critical analysis is not itself warped by emotion. But our capacity for unskewed reasoning turns out to be more limited than we think. Take, for instance, the "trolley-problem," an age-old thought experiment. In the most well-known version of it, the respondent is asked to imagine that a trolley car is bearing down on a group of five individuals who will be fatally run over. The subject is told that he or she is standing at a lever next to the trolley tracks and can redirect the trolley onto another track where only one person will die. The respondent is then asked which of the two available options – pushing the lever to save four lives or not pushing it at the expense of four lives – is the right thing to do? The experiment has been repeated innumerable times on thousands of subjects from different cultures across the continents, and the vast majority – over 90 percent – answer that they would divert the trolley by pushing the lever to reduce the loss of life.[12]

But a variation on the first trolley scenario suggests an odd inconsistency – and thus unsoundness – in our capacity for rational calculus of the greatest happiness for the greatest number. In it, instead of standing at a lever that can redirect the trolley, the respondent imagines that he or she is standing on a bridge under which the trolley, still bearing down on five workers on the track. In this version of the problem, though, the five individuals can be saved only if the respondent pushes a large person standing next to him or her off the bridge onto the tracks. The person pushed will perish as a result, but the lives of the five imperiled workers will be preserved. With this version, at least half the respondents indicated that pushing the large person off the bridge is *not* the proper thing to do, even though it means four more lives than necessary will die.[13] For decades, commentators have searched for a moral distinction reconciling the two seemingly conflicting responses, but with no agreement on the rationale.

Neuroscience may now be suggesting the answer. Functional magnetic resonance imaging has recently shed light on the involvement of the emotional centers of the brain in some, but not all, human decision-making. Apparently, certain issues take a detour through a repository of emotional content that helps shape our ultimate conclusion. As Professor Anthony Damasio, author of *Descartes' Error: Emotion, Reason and the Human Brain*, explains:

---

12   John Cloud, *Would You Kill One Person to Save Five? New Research on a Classic Debate*, Time (Dec. 8, 2011) at https://healthland.time.com/2011/12/05/would-you-kill-one-person-to-save-five-new-research-on-a-classic-debate/.

13   *Id.*

[T]he brain has at least two systems for assessing ... options for action and of representations of future outcomes. [In one,] we use logical reasoning and knowledge to decide that we will do X instead of Y. Another system, probably evolutionarily far older, acts even before the first one. It activates biases related to our previous emotional experience in comparable situations. These non-conscious biases affect the options and reasoning strategies that we present to our conscious selves.

We do ourselves a disservice when we think of human beings as exclusively logic- or knowledge-driven, and fail to pay attention to the role of the emotions. The two systems are enmeshed because that is the way our brain and the rest of our body have been put together by evolution.[14]

Professor Joshua Greene has woven imaging and the trolley problem together, comparing the regions of the brain involved in respondents' answers to whether or not they'd push the lever to divert the trolley, and whether or not they'd push the large person off the bridge. Sure enough, the processing of responses to the former question took the route directly through the center for rational thought while the latter detoured through an emotional center.[15] As such, the consistent, logic-based critical analysis that advances justice may well, in a variety of circumstances, be beyond our reach.

An element that seems at least as vital to justice as any other is equal treatment under law. From *Brown v. Board of Education*[16] to *Loving*[17] to *Obergefell*,[18] the High Court's most celebrated decisions have advanced the principle in the fight against discrimination.

However, when we recall French novelist Anatole France's remark that "[t]he law, in its majestic equality, forbids the rich as well as the poor to sleep under bridges, to beg in the streets, and to steal bread,"[19] we realize that the principle of equal treatment can sometimes ring hollow. Moreover, subjecting young children or incompetent persons to the same criminal sanctions as normal adults would, as one of a thousand examples, represent a gross *injustice*.

---

14   Antonio R. Damasi, *The Science of Emotion*, at https://www.loc.gov/loc/brain/emotion /Damasio.html. *See generally* Daniel Kahneman, Thinking Fast and Slow (Farrar, Straus, and Giroux 2011).

15   Joshua Greene, *Moral Cognition*, at https://www.joshua-greene.net/research/moral -cognition.

16   347 U.S. 483 (1954).

17   388 U.S. 1 (1967).

18   576 U.S. 644 (2015).

19   Anatole France, Le Lys Rouge, [The Red Lily] chap. 7 (1894) at https://fr.wikisource.org /wiki/Le_Lys_rouge/VII.

As Aristotle, Thomas Jefferson, and others are said to have remarked, "There is nothing so unequal as the equal treatment of unequals."[20] Accordingly, equal treatment under law, while often a basic component of justice, is not always a necessary condition of it.

Perhaps consistency in the outcomes of similar cases – a principle that provides fairness and notice as to what the law requires – is a necessary element. Our strong allegiance to the principle of *stare decisis* suggests that it is. As the Supreme Court has put it, *stare decisis* "promotes the evenhanded, predictable, and consistent development of legal principles, fosters reliance on judicial decisions, and contributes to the actual and perceived integrity of the judicial process."[21] But now think back to the consistent outcomes that *stare decisis* provided in the days of Jim Crow laws and *Plessy v. Ferguson*,[22] and we see that, in a number of cases, consistency can be the very bane of justice.

How about mercy? In a famous line from *The Merchant of Venice*, Portia advises that mercy "is an attribute to God himself; and earthly power doth then show likest God's when mercy seasons justice."[23] Indeed, both the Old and New Testaments repeatedly assure us that God is merciful in his or her judgments of us,[24] so surely mercy is a necessary attribute of justice.

But then we recall the sentiments of Agatha Christie's Hercule Poirot: "Too much mercy ... often resulted in further crimes which were fatal to innocent victims who need not have been victims if justice had been put first and mercy second."[25] And of the Prince's warning in *Romeo and Juliet* that "[m]ercy but murders."[26] God herself tells us that mercy is not always a feature of justice, with Romans warning: "never avenge yourselves, but leave it to the wrath of God, for it is written, 'Vengeance is mine, I will repay, says the Lord,'"[27]

---

20   *See, e.g.,* Peggy Bittick, *Equality and Excellence: Equal Opportunity for Gifted and Talented Children*, 36 S. Tex. L. Rev. 119, 144 n. 142 (1995); and Leading with Trust, *Are You Playing Fair? You better be, because your people are keeping score*, at https://leadingwithtrust .com/2011/07/31/are-you-playingfair/#:~:text=A%20quote%20from%20Aristotle%20 speaks, recognized%20and%20valued%2C%20not%20diminished. While the quotes are widely attributed to both historical figures, it appears that it appears that it has not been found in their writings.

21   *Payne v. Tennessee*, 501 U.S. 808, 827 (1991).

22   163 U.S. 537 (1896).

23   William Shakespeare, The Merchant of Venice, Act 4, scene 1, line 182.

24   At least 17 times. *See, e.g.,* Deuteronomy 4:31 ("For the Lord your God is a merciful God."); Psalm 103:8 ("The Lord is merciful.").

25   Agatha Christie, Hallowe'en Party 131 (1969).

26   William Shakespeare, Romeo and Juliet, Act. 3, Scene 1, line 197 (1597).

27   Romans 12:19.

a sentiment that Lot's wife and the first-born males of ancient Egypt were testaments to. So, like the first two principles we considered, we can say that mercy is often an important feature of justice, it's just not a universal one.

Ahhh. Fairness. That must be an attribute of justice. But while "unfair justice" would be an oxymoron, fairness is more a synonym for justice than a component part.[28]

Proportionality between an offense and the resultant sanction feels like a necessary quality of justice. No one would say that the punishment needn't fit the crime, and the Eighth Amendment bans inordinately harsh punishment. The catch here is that proportional sanctions occur in limited areas of the system, such as the adjudication of criminal and civil offenses, and a legal system is called on to do justice in a vast array of matters where punishment is not an issue.

Truth is surely the foundation of justice. Indeed, the *Ten Commandments* make it a sin to lie. Without accurate knowledge with respect to a legal matter, there is nothing for justice to sink its teeth into. The question thus becomes, is the discovery of material truths in a matter a necessary feature of justice. While justice rests on some quantum of truth, many material truths are hidden, in the name of justice, from the fact finder. Possession of illicit drugs that have been unlawfully seized by police, a penitent's confession to a priest, and matters of national security are a few of the plethora of examples of truths we suppress.

Let's think for a moment beyond our own system in which we proudly tout the right to a jury trial in criminal prosecutions. Surely this fundamental procedural safeguard is a universal requirement of justice. Even John Adams and Thomas Jefferson could agree on that. Said Jefferson, "The wisdom of our sages and the blood of our heroes has been devoted to the attainment of trial by jury. It should be the creed of our political faith."[29] Adams echoed his rival: "Representative government and trial by jury are the heart and lungs of liberty. Without them we have no other fortification against being ridden like horses, fleeced like sheep, worked like cattle and fed and clothed like swine

---

28   Collins English Dictionary, at https://www.collinsdictionary.com/dictionary/english /justice. (January 26, 2022).

29   *See, e.g.,* Garvin Isaacs, *Juror Appreciation Project to Emphasize Importance of Trial by Jury,* 87 Okla. B.J. 1924, 1924 (2016).

and hounds."[30] Trial by one's peers in the community was a bold and enlightened check on government persecution or undue pressure on the judge.[31]

Again, though, not even the vaunted right to a trial by one's peers is a requisite feature of justice in all legal regimes. Let's take the case of a country with a very different demography, culture, economy, and topology than ours. For example, Mongolia, which lies uneasily between Russia and China, was for many years a Soviet satellite that had, by necessity, adopted the Soviet-style system of justice in which confessions – often coerced – and show trials were the norm.[32] Following détente, the Mongolian government asked the highly-esteemed international law and human rights expert and honoree of this Festschrift, Professor Siegfried Wiessner, to tour the country, meet with government leaders and heads of NGOs, observe legal proceedings, and tour penal facilities to help draft a revised code of criminal procedure that afforded genuine due process to suspects and defendants.[33]

---

30   David Kolbe 14, *The American Criminal Jury Trial – Justice and Democracy in Action* 14, 16 Law and World (2020); *A Forgotten History: Trial by Jury and the American Revolution*, West Virginia Association for Justice *at* https://www.wvaj.org/?pg=TrialbyJuryAmerican Revolution#:~:text=In%201774%20founding%20father%20John,clothed%20like%20 swine%20and%20hounds.%22.

31   Duncan v. Louisiana, 391 U.S. 145, 153 (1968) ("The guarantees of jury trial in the Federal and State Constitutions reflect a profound judgment about the way in which law should be enforced and justice administered. A right to jury trial is granted to criminal defendants in order to prevent oppression by the Government. Those who wrote our constitutions knew from history and experience that it was necessary to protect against unfounded criminal charges brought to eliminate enemies and against judges too responsive to the voice of higher authority. The framers of the constitutions strove to create an independent judiciary but insisted upon further protection against arbitrary action. Providing an accused with the right to be tried by a jury of his peers gave him an inestimable safeguard against the corrupt or overzealous prosecutor and against the compliant, biased, or eccentric judge. ... [T]he jury trial provisions ... reflect a fundamental decision about the exercise of official power—a reluctance to entrust plenary powers over the life and liberty of the citizen to one judge or to a group of judges. Fear of unchecked power ... found expression in the criminal law in this insistence upon community participation in the determination of guilt or innocence.").

32   *See, e.g., Stalled Reform* in Confessions at Any Cost, Police Torture in Russia, Human Rights Watch (1999) at https://www.hrw.org/legacy/reports/1999/russia/Russ99o-11.htm

33   Documents on file with author. Professor Wiessner was a logical and common choice for an endeavor of this type and magnitude. Indeed, at any particular moment over more than three decades, he has been just as likely to be delivering a presentation half-way around the world on human rights for indigenous and disenfranchised peoples as he been to be meeting with students in the dynamic Intercultural Human Rights program that he and Professor Roza Pati built or brilliantly speaking truth to power in his writing. His devotion to the oppressed and marginalized and his long and admirable list of accomplishments have made him an awesome force for human rights around the world. *See also*

On the trip to Mongolia, Professor Wiessner brought along the author of this Essay, who has written on defendants' rights, to assist him. That the revisions we were to suggest must include trial by jury was, in my view, an imperative of justice from the very start. Professor Wiessner wanted to learn more before drawing that conclusion. As it turns out, much of the country consists of small, nomadic communities in which families live in circular, wood-framed, portable tents known as *gers* and move every few months to grassier "steppes" (or grasslands) for their goats, sheep, cows, and horses to graze.[34] It soon became evident that, while the jury system is a vital feature of justice from our country's large metropolis' to towns with a single stoplight, it would do more to tear the social fabric apart in much of our host's country than it would to further justice.

The prospect of members of highly interdependent nomadic families condemning their neighbors would more wreak havoc on the community than any drought could. Professor Wiessner was wise to wait, and the author gained a deeper understanding of the organic relationship of culture and justice.

Compliance with each of the principles considered so far is often a necessity of a just outcome in a legal matter, but, as seen, none are universal requisites. There may be at least one such principle, though. Access to competent, affordable legal resources and legal redress is yet another key principle of justice. Those involved in the legal system in any manner or who seek its involvement need lawyers to translate arcane law to them and assert their rights and defend themselves. A system of justice from which poor citizens are excluded is a contradiction in terms. Access to lawyers and the courts will not alone yield justice, but here we finally seem to have at least one universal condition of it.

With respect to these cherished principles, our concept of justice seems to lack an enumerable set of necessary and sufficient conditions. Philosopher Ludwig Wittgenstein said the same of the games people invent, in which there is no set of features in common with all of our games. Wittgenstein called our notion of games an "open concept."[35] Upon reflection, justice would appear to be an open concept as well.

Which doesn't make it unidentifiable or irreducible, merely indefinable. Justice may be analogous to what Justice Potter Stewart said about the definition of obscenity fifty years ago in *Jacobellis v. Ohio*: "[P]erhaps I could never

---

CNBC, *St. Thomas University Professor Appointed To Vatican's Pontifical Council Of Justice And Peace* at https://www.cnbc.com/ id/100128169.

34 Michael Turtle, *Mongolian Nomadic Life*, The Travel Turtle at https://www.timetravelturtle .com/nomadic-life-in-mongolia/.

35 Ludwig Wittgenstein, Philosophical Investigations: The German Text with an English Translation 36e (P.M.S. Hacker & Joachim, eds., G.E.M. *et al* trans., Blackwell Publ'g Ltd. 4th ed. 2009).

succeed in intelligibly [defining it]. But I know it when I see it."[36] Perhaps, in the end, the best that can be said is that, in any particular case, the open concept of justice draws what it requires from among the constellation of grand principles.

This conclusion, coupled with law students' common but mistaken assumption that a set of necessary and sufficient conditions does exist, underscores a basic, unfulfilled task of legal education. But the missing lessons in the study of law don't end here. Law graduates generally come away from their studies never having deepened a shallow and misleading understanding of other foundational principles. As a result, they may never have contemplated a broader view of justice than the study of our case law and statutes generally affords, or the higher possibilities of law, or the full role of lawyers in society.

A simplistic understanding of the rule of law is a good example. Whether by politicians, network pundits, or law professors, the notion of the "rule of law" is easily bandied about these days. The Republican National Committee that, for example, endorsed the sacrosanct concept of the rule of law no less than thirteen times in its 2020 political platform,[37] is the same group that later issued a resolution characterizing the January sixth insurrection as "legitimate political discourse."[38]

The rule of law is, in and of itself, spoken of as a basic and requisite feature of justice.[39] While it is true that a strong rule of law can often be a laudable feature of a particular system of justice, it is just as true – though generally unnoticed – that it can also be a feature of an infinitely repressive system. The harsh, inflexible, and stultifying commands of North Korean law, for example, reflect a more absolute rule of law than in democratic regimes, yet subvert justice itself. Accordingly, scholars have been distinguishing between the "thick" rule of law – thick with due process – and the thin, North-Korean variety.[40]

Another missing lesson involves the analytical research papers typically required of law students in a seminar or a class. Uncovering or further investigating existing problems in our law and legal system is normally the focus

36   *Jacobellis v. Ohio*, 378 U.S. 184, 197 (1964, Justice Stewart concurring).

37   Republican National Committee, *The Republican Party Platform, 2020* (2020) at https:// ballotpedia.org/The_Republican_Party_Platform,_2020 . .

38   Josh Dawsey & Felicia Sonmez, *'Legitimate political discourse': Three words about Jan. 6 spark rift among Republicans*, The Washington Post at https://www.washingtonpost.com /politics/2022/02/08/gop-legitimate-political-discourse/.

39   American Bar Association, The Rule of Law at https://www.americanbar.org/groups/public _education/ resources/rule-of-law/.

40   Siegfried Wiessner, *The Rule of Law: Prolegomena,* German-American Law Review (2018) at SSRN: https://ssrn.com/abstract=3293042 or http://dx.doi.org/10.2139/ssrn.3293042.

of a student research paper. It would serve students well – not to mention the common interest – if they were guided to the problem-solving approach of the New Haven School of Jurisprudence, of which the late Professors Myres McDougal and Harold Lasswell and now Professor Michael Reisman and Professor Wiessner have been its driving forces. Under that approach, much as a doctor wouldn't simply diagnose a patient's illness and close the case, those who take on law-related problems do not simply restrict themselves to the articulation of problems in doctrine, practice, and society and then conclude they've fully addressed the topic. The next step must be to formulate workable corrective measures consonant with the values and hopes of those who are subject to the law in order to overcome or ameliorate the problem. As Professor Wiessner explains:

> The essential difference to traditional approaches to law is that the New Haven School of Jurisprudence addresses problems in society and ... allow[s] us to find, in rational, inter-disciplinary analysis, (1) the parameters of the social ill or problem the law has to address; (2) to review the conflicting interests or claims; (3) to analyse the past legal responses in light of the factors that produced them; (4) to predict future such decisions; and (5) to assess the past legal responses, invent alternatives and recommend solutions better in line with a good order, a preferred order we term a "public order of human dignity."[41]

Ultimately, this dignity-centered approach serves as an adjustment to the traditional tethering of law to stale concepts, special interests, and the view of law as a bounty to be fought over by warring legislative factions. The New Haven view focuses instead on the identification of individual and community needs and aspirations and the adoption of doctrine that best facilitates them. After all, as Professor Wiessner wrote,

> We do not see the law from the perspective of a person looking up to it in abject rêverie. Instead, we see law as one instrument that serves human beings, not the other way around. We ought to consider ourselves the masters of the law; we should make it serve our needs and our aspirations – particularly our aspirations. Here is where the positive – and, to an extent, normative – feature of the New Haven approach comes in.

---

41   Siegfried Wiessner, *The New Haven School of Jurisprudence: A Universal Toolkit for Understanding and Shaping Law*, 81 Asia Pacific L. Rev. 45, 48 (2010), at SSRN: https://ssrn.com/abstract=2011130.

> Maybe there is a grain of American optimism in it. What it is calling forth is a good law, and this is a touchstone that often is not offered, allowed or even defined by traditional jurisprudence.[42]

In this sense, the New Haven approach can be said to liberate conventional legal reasoning from its restraints that fail – at least, in part, by design – to serve the common interest, , and to attempt to peacefully change the law, via persuasion in a democratic society, when it does not. There is no better time to acquaint tomorrow's shapers of law with this "policy-oriented jurisprudence" than in their own efforts to tackle a significant problem in their research papers, arriving at a solution that would maximize access by all to the processes of shaping and sharing all things humans value, the classical definition of a public order of human dignity.

Similarly, perhaps the most important missing element in the three years that our future lawyers study the legal system is the general failure to question or stray from the orthodox view of the development and purpose of law. In a world in which the wealthy and influential further engorge themselves at the cost of all others and nationalist movements ignoring any form of the rule of law grow stronger in most every nation, the New Haven approach stands in direct contrast and ought to be introduced to those who will become the next stewards of the legal system. Rather than espousing a particular set of rules, the approach represents an alternative theory for the development of law in which the fundamental operating principle is the dignity of every member of the community. Professor Reisman put it eloquently:

> Unless one is willing to perpetuate the imbalance in accessibility to the material amenities of life, which distinguishes the lives of the highest social strata in North America, Western Europe and Japan from life elsewhere on the globe, the process of development will require changes in conceptions of development everywhere. The alternative is a global order of "zero-sum" and "winner take all", an order sustained by violence in which only some live lives of dignity while the lives of others are nasty, brutish and short. One of the urgent challenges of development theory and praxis is to avert such a dystopic future and to contribute to the achievement of a world public order of human dignity.[43]

---

42   *Id.* at 51.

43   W. Michael Reisman, *A Policy-Oriented Approach to Development*, 3 J. Int'l & Comp. L. 141, 148 (2016). *See also* Mahnoush H. Arsaniani, Jacob Cogan, Robert Sloane & Siegfried

The New Haven School isn't starry-eyed. It recognizes that the transformation from our current troubled and imbalanced system to a dignity-centric system must occur in stages. Traditionally, law and legal proceedings are presented to future lawyers as a series of rights and remedies governing citizens' commercial activities and social relations. If law were to effectively provide for security, equality, fair proceedings, and just deserts, it would generally be seen as having fulfilled our ambitions for a just system. The New Haven approach envisions that this ostensible endpoint in the maturation of law need only represent a "minimum public order" in the longer quest for a higher "public order of human dignity." With respect to this "optimum public order,"[44] Professor Wiessner notes that "[t]he touchstone would be whether the law ... responds to those needs and aspirations of human beings and, more specifically, would afford maximum access by all to all things humans value."[45]

To accomplish this, legal analysis and legal education must reach far beyond entrenched doctrine and conventional interpretive standards. An understanding of law must probe deep beneath the text. The forces beyond law that shape and maintain doctrine, those who benefit from a law and those who are subjugated by it, and the underlying politics and ideology must become the focus of legal analysis and legal education. Law students must come to see that the vast disciplines outside of law can become the tools of lawyers and lawmakers in solving society's problems. Indeed, a century ago, Professor Wesley Newcomb Hohfeld called for the "critique of our principles and rules of law according to considerations *extrinsic* or *external* to the principles and rules as such, that is, according to the psychological, ethical, political, social, and economic bases of the various doctrines and the respective purposes or ends sought to be achieved thereby."[46]

Wiessner, Looking to the Future: Essays on International Law in Honor of W. Michael Reisman (2011) at https://brill.com/view/title/15834.

44 Human dignity would appear to be another "open concept." To begin with, it has at least three main senses. It can refer to an innate, inalienable quality shared by all human beings, a feature of the way one views or treats him or herself, or the treatment accorded to a person by others or by circumstance. The New Haven School clearly employs the third sense of the term and thus faces the challenge of enumerating the foundational features of an order of human dignity. By requiring equality, personal security, fair procedure, and just desserts in a "minimum public order" and the above "touchstones" of an "optimum public order," the New Haven School provides a meaningful description of what, left alone, would represent a mere slogan.

45 *Supra* note 41, at 51.

46 Wesley Newcomb Hohfeld, *A Vital School of Jurisprudence and Law*, Fundamental Legal Conceptions 332, 351 (Cook ed. 1923).

Introducing students to the New Haven approach carries benefits beyond acquainting them with an alternative blueprint for the development of law. It can spark enlightening classroom discussion, for example, on the notion of human dignity in a world as culturally, philosophically, and politically as diverse and as stratified as ours. Even matters that seem to appear crystal clear at first glance may generate discussion. Take, for example, the assumption of an absolute ban on torture in a system grounded in personal dignity and then imagine that a terrorist who has been taken into custody is known to have planted a nuclear explosive in a large city and that torture is likely – and the only way – to get him to disclose the location of the device in time to disarm it and save millions of lives. By preventing torture in this scenario, could it be asserted that the law had violated the personal dignity of not just one person, but of millions?[47]

The missing lessons are clear. The future stewards of the system of justice should understand that justice itself has no automatic checklist of constituent rights and principles, and instead that, much like an artist painting from a pallet of colors, justice is the art of making just the right choices from the pallet of lofty principles. And, to the extent that the current formulation of law serves special interests, the failure of legal education to expose students to an alternative system that recognizes the primacy of individual human dignity, rather than sidestepping the issue, is itself inconsistent with justice.

Acknowledgments

The Essay is dedicated to Professor Siegfried Wiessner who has, over the decades, been an inspiration to me, a mentor, a font of wisdom, and a good friend. I remain in awe of the unique and vital human rights program he built, his global contributions to the well-being of indigenous and disenfranchised peoples, and that brilliant mind of his that works overtime in the common interest. Many thanks to Professors Roza Pati and Michael Reisman for their hard work in organizing and editing this Festschrift and, moreover, their own devotion to the protection of the most vulnerable groups on the planet and to Dr. Beth Krancberg for her wise insights on an earlier draft.

---

47   *See, e.g., Justice with Michael Sandel* – BBC: *Torture and human dignity*, Harvard U. at
       https://www.youtube.com/watch?v=7FR-FuhN2HM.

CHAPTER 33

The Public Authority Defense, January 6, 2021, and the Following Orders Defense: A Juxtaposition

*Alfredo Garcia**

The assault on the United States Capitol on January 6, 2021 tested the fabric of American democracy. Disrupting the formal transfer of presidential power, a violent mob descended on the capitol, instigated by then-President Trump's false claim that the election he lost was fraudulent and that he was the legitimate winner. The assault was costly: five people lost their lives and numerous others suffered serious injuries. In the process, the attackers searched for Vice President Pence, whose role was ceremonial, because they considered him derelict for refusing to alter the election's outcome. While Pence and members of Congress feared for their safety in the face of the attack, President Trump failed to quell the assault for over three hours, refusing to minimize the damage by persuading his followers to desist.

Were these followers merely duped by the President, who exhorted them to "take back their country," or were they cognizant of the illegal nature of their violent enterprise? As Commander-in-Chief of the Armed Forces, was Trump ordering his adherents to take military action to "preserve" American democracy? Although many of those in the crowd may have been in the military, none of them were actively serving in the armed forces. As such, the assaulters were not engaged in military action and following the orders of their commander. Similarly, was Trump, as their "commander," obligated to prevent them from carrying out an illegal order? From a military standpoint, were the assaulters "following orders," and did Trump correlatively have the "command responsibility" to preclude or mitigate what he knew to be an illegal order?

Of course, the defense of following orders and its obverse, command responsibility, is only applicable to military operations and not to actions by civilians. Nevertheless, the civilian counterpart to the defense in American jurisprudence is the defense of public authority. Under that concept, criminal defendants may contend that their otherwise illegal acts were rendered permissible by the directives or assurances of public authorities. In this essay, I propose to

* Dean Emeritus and Professor, St. Thomas University College of Law.

compare, contrast, and juxtapose the military following orders defense with its civilian public authority counterpart. I plan to do so in the context of the January 6th assault on the United States Capitol. The aim behind this analysis is to illuminate whether the public authority defense is normatively viable for the January 6th attack; and whether the following orders defense adumbrates that enquiry. Indeed, the essay will highlight a case in which the defendant, a former military officer, has asserted the public authority defense to defend against a criminal indictment for his actions on the day of the assault. In addition, the failed invocation of the defense by President Trump's advisor, Stephen K. Bannon, in response to criminal contempt charges, based on a defiance of a subpoena by the January 6th Committee, will illustrate the limits of the defense.[1]

Let us begin by briefly outlining the obeying orders defense and applying it, hypothetically, to the individuals who violently assaulted the Capitol on that fateful and tragic day. As a general proposition, the military cannot exist without a command and hierarchical structure premised on soldiers obeying the orders of a superior. As one scholar has succinctly put it: "No military force can function effectively without routine obedience, and it is the routine that is stressed. ... But there is some ultimate humanity that cannot be broken down, the disappearance of which we will not accept. ... Trained to obey 'without hesitation,' they nevertheless remain capable of hesitating."[2] In essence, the quote captures the two sides of the following orders coin: while routine obeyance is indispensable to military efficiency and success, it is also tempered by the constraints embedded in fundamental human rights.

The obeying orders defense has an ancient lineage, although it is commonly associated with the Nuremberg military tribunals that determined the guilt of the Nazi individuals for war crimes and crimes against humanity. Under the London Charter of the International Military Tribunal, Principle IV, following orders of a superior does not relieve a defendant "from responsibility under international law, provided a moral choice was in fact possible to him."[3] The

---

1   *See* Alan Feuer & Michael S. Schmidt, *The Jan. 6 Panel After 8 Hearings: Where will the Evidence Lead*, N.Y. Times, July 22, 2022, for a summary of the January 6th riot as set forth by the Congressional Committee Hearings on the January 6th assault. The case involving the military officer who invoked the public authority defense is *United States v. Gabriel Garcia*, CRIMINAL NO. 21-CR-129 (U.S.D.C. District of Columbia). Stephen K. Bannon was convicted of two counts of contempt of Congress for defying a subpoena from the January 6th Committee on July 22, 2022. *United States v. Stephen K. Bannon* CRIMINAL NO. 21-CR-670 (U.S.D.C. District of Columbia).

2   Michael Walzer, Just and Unjust Wars 311 (3rd ed. 2000).

3   London Charter of the International Military Tribunal, Principle IV.

defense, if applicable, did not absolve the defendant, but served as a mitigating factor in sentencing.

Similarly, modern international law norms hew to that model. The Rome Statute, which established the basis for the International Criminal Court, provides under Article 33 of the statute as follows: "The fact that a crime within the jurisdiction of the Court has been committed by a person pursuant to an order of a Government or of a superior, whether military or civilian, shall not relieve that person of criminal responsibility unless ... the person was under the legal obligation to obey the orders ...; the person did not know that the order was unlawful and the order was not manifestly unlawful." The Article then clarifies that orders to commit genocide or crimes against humanity are unlawful.[4] In addition, the defense does not negate criminal liability but mitigates the punishment.

The United States Supreme Court, in a civil case arising from the Mexican American War in the 1840s, remarkably adhered to the same precept. *Mitchell v. Harmony*[5] dealt with a civil suit by a plaintiff to recover the value of property seized by a military officer during the war. Chief Justice Taney, writing for the majority, summarily rejected the officer's argument that he was following the orders of his military superior. Because, according to the Court, an "urgent necessity" did not exist, Mitchell had no legal authority to seize the property. Therefore, the order to seize the property amounted to an "illegal act." Indeed, Justice Taney underscored that "it can never be maintained that a military officer can justify himself for doing an unlawful act, by producing the order of a superior."[6]

Taney, however, did not end his analysis by discarding the superior orders defense. Rather, he felt compelled to emphasize that, even if applicable, the defense merely mitigated the potential punishment and did not serve as a complete defense. He finished by stressing that "the order may *palliate* [emphasis added], but it cannot justify."[7] Accordingly, the highest court in the United States affirmed the legal principles underlying the superior orders defense as early as the mid-nineteenth century: it is not a defense to a criminal charge to allege one was obeying illegal military orders; and even if the defense is viable, it only serves to "palliate" the punishment and not to negate guilt.

---

4   Rome Statute of the International Criminal Court (1998), Part 3: General Principles of Criminal Law, Article 33: Superior orders and prescription of law.

5   54 U.S. 115 (1852).

6   *Id.* at 137.

7   *Id.*

In the following century, a defendant relied on the defense in one of the most egregious and notorious cases in American military history. The massacre of defenseless men, women and children occurred on March 16, 1968, during the Vietnam War. Lieutenant William L. Calley, Jr. was charged with "systematically" shooting and killing, with other soldiers, a "large number of defenseless old men, women, and children."[8] He was found guilty, upon being court-martialed, of the premeditated murder "of not fewer than 22 Vietnamese civilians of undetermined age and sex, and of assault with intent to murder one Vietnamese child."[9] As Judge Ainsworth aptly noted, the massacre at My Lai village was "one of the most tragic chapters in the history of this nation's armed forces."[10] Calley appealed his conviction in both the military and civilian appellate courts, but lost his appeals.[11]

Calley's principal defense at his court-martial trial was that he was not legally responsible for the killings because he had been ordered to kill the civilians in the village by his immediate superior, Captain Medina.[12] Medina disputed Calley's testimony, contending that his instructions, presumably over radio the day before the massacre, was to use "common sense" and not to shoot and kill defenseless women and children.[13] The appellate court approved the court-martial trial judge's instruction to the jury "that an order to kill unresisting Vietnamese would be an illegal order, and that if Calley knew the order was illegal or should have known it was illegal, obedience to an order was not a valid defense."[14] In conclusion, the court ratified the jury's finding that either Captain Medina did not issue the order, or if he did, the order was illegal and was not a defense.[15] To summarize, the superior orders defense, both in international and Anglo-American law, looks askance at the defense and permits it only to reduce punishment and not to disprove guilt. Further, international law sets forth the parameters of the defense by requiring that the defendant had an obligation to obey the orders, did not know the order was unlawful and the order was not manifestly unlawful. Under the American iteration, the defense is comparable to the international one: the obligation to obey is presumed but the order is not valid if the defendant knew or should have known that the order was illegal.

---

8   *Calley v. Callaway*, 519 F.2d 184, 190 (1975).

9   *Id.*

10   *Id.*

11   *Id.* at 190–91.

12   *Id.* at 193.

13   *Id.*

14   *Id.*

15   *Id.* at 194.

Though in the guise of asserting the public authority defense, which we will explore in the second half of this essay, Gabriel Augustin Garcia, a defendant indicted on six criminal counts related to the January 6th assault, contends that, as a military officer, he was following the orders of his Commander-in-Chief, when he unlawfully entered the Capitol building that fateful day.[16] In his motion, Garcia adverts to the speech President Trump gave preceding the assault on the Capitol in which he exhorted his followers to "take back their country," and that they would not take back their country "with weakness." Garcia's motion emphasizes that he is a "retired military officer still subject to the Uniform Code of Military Justice [who] was following the orders of his Commander-in-Chief ... and reasonably relied on then [sic] President's assurances to lawfully walk over the Capitol and peacefully exercise his First Amendment right to express his political grievances at the Capitol."[17]

Conflating the public authority and superior orders defenses, Garcia's motion furnishes a vehicle to examine the defenses both discretely and comparably. Let us first focus on the obeying orders defense in the context of the January 6 incursion of the Capitol building. Does Garcia have a colorable defense given his status and the President's actions? First, Garcia was a civilian, not a military officer, at the time of the assault. It is questionable whether he was still subject to the Uniform Code of Military Justice. Indeed, he is not facing, as Calley did, a court-martial proceeding based on acts performed under active military duty. Instead, Garcia has been indicted by a civilian tribunal for allegedly violating federal statutes.

Nevertheless, let us assume that Garcia was on active duty at the time of the events in question. The indictment against Garcia charges him with six criminal counts: civil disorder, obstruction of an official proceeding, entering and remaining in a restricted building or grounds, disorderly and disruptive conduct in a restrictive building or grounds, disorderly conduct in a Capitol building and parading, demonstrating, or picketing in a Capitol building.[18] The following orders defense requires Garcia to establish that he was following the Commander-in-Chief's order and that he did not know or reasonably should have known that the order was illegal. This raises several issues: did President Trump issue an order; did he know his order was illegal; did Garcia know, or should he have known that the President's order was illegal?

---

16   *See infra* note 1, United States v. Gabriel Augustin Garcia, CRIMINAL NO. 21-CR-129 (U.S.D.C. District of Columbia), Notice of Entrapment by Estoppel Defense, filed January 28, 2022.

17   *Id.*

18   *Id.*

Did President Trump issue an order to his followers when he spoke to them at the Ellipse? Garcia alleges in his motion to rely on the public authority defense that Trump ordered him, and presumably his other followers who were military veterans, to "take back their country," and not to do so with "weakness." But there is one part of the President's speech that also could be construed as a call to action. President Trump told the crowd, "And we fight like hell. And if you don't fight like hell, you're not going to have a country anymore."[19] Of course, one could argue that President Trump was speaking metaphorically. Combined with the other parts of the speech highlighted in Garcia's motion, however, and President Trump's peroration, "so let's walk down Pennsylvania Avenue," it is plausible to consider the speech as an order.

If the President issued an order, did he know it was illegal? The Select Congressional Committee on January 6th conclusively demonstrated that President Trump knew his claims of a stolen election were without foundation.[20] He not only lost over sixty cases challenging the results, but also was told by many advisors, including his own Attorney General, that there was no basis for the claim that fraud marred the election and affected the outcome.[21]

The third question is the critical one for the obeying orders defense: did Garcia know, or should he have known that the Commander-in-Chief's order was illegal? Trump's speech at the Ellipse was riddled with numerous allegations of electoral fraud. For example, he argued that there were 205,000 more ballots than eligible voters in Pennsylvania. President Trump also stated that election officials in Georgia were "crooked," and the election results there were "fraudulent." He referred to election irregularities in Wayne County, Michigan. More telling was the President's assertion to the crowd that, unless the electoral result was reversed, Americans would "have an illegitimate President."[22]

While it is evident that Trump knew that he lost the election, a follower listening to his speech on January 6th might have been persuaded otherwise. Given how defiantly Trump had challenged the results before the speech, and his claims of fraud during his speech, a supporter might be inclined to believe his claims. Indeed, the prevalence of conspiracy theories in American history has been documented by historian Richard Hofstadter in his essay, later expanded into a book, entitled *The Paranoid Style in American Politics*.[23] On the

---

19   *See, for example*, a text of the speech as excerpted in NPR, at npr.org/2021/02/10/966396848 / read-trump-jan-6-speech-a-key-part-of-impeachment-trial.

20   *See* Feuer & Schmidt, *supra* note 1.

21   *Id.*

22   *See supra* note 19.

23   The original article was published in the November, 1964 issue of *Harper's Magazine*, at 77–86. The latest edition of the book is, Richard Hofstadter, The Paranoid Style in American Politics and Other Essays (2008).

other hand, a rational actor would not be blinded or duped into believing such a series of fantastical and audacious theories, none of which are supported by facts. A jury in a court-martial trial would have a difficult time accepting the notion that Garcia acted from a genuine belief in the illegitimacy of the election.

Garcia, however, has professed that his protest was about "democracy, not destruction.[24]" In a news conference he held on the anniversary of the riot, Garcia attempted to deflect the charges against him by claiming that "[a]t the end of the day, I didn't go there to destroy property, burn, loot, or do any of that stuff.[25]" A friend who organized the news conference confirmed the view that the protest was not about Trump, but rather about voter fraud. She stressed, "Everybody seems to think this is a Trump thing. It wasn't a Trump thing. It was an American thing, and it's about preserving our freedoms. It's about voter fraud."[26] These statements, though seemingly genuine, are delusional in view of the incontrovertible evidence refuting the claim of voter fraud. Garcia's weak defense reaffirms Hofstadter's historical analysis documenting the "paranoid" penchant in American politics.

It would also be difficult, moreover, for Garcia to establish the defense under the international law version. To successfully invoke the defense, Garcia would have to convince the fact finder that he was under a legal obligation to obey the order, that he did not know the order was unlawful, and that the order was not manifestly unlawful. It is apparent that the order to disrupt the congressional certification of a legitimate election, as confirmed by the judiciary branch, was manifestly unlawful. From that premise, it follows that Garcia was not under a legal obligation to follow Trump's orders. Whether Garcia did not know that the order was unlawful is irrelevant, because he would fail to satisfy the first and third prongs of the defense.

Even if Garcia succeeded and convinced the fact finder to accept the defense, the best outcome he would achieve is a reduction in his sentence and not an outright acquittal. As we have seen, the superior orders defense is limited; it merely mitigates the potential punishment. Extrapolating from that tenet, one would have to question the extent to which a judge would be willing to significantly reduce the sentence under the circumstances. After all, Trump lost the election by a comfortable margin, the judiciary found no evidence of fraud in

---

24 Jamie Guirola, *'A lot of Misrepresentation': Miami Proud Boys Member Charged in Riot Defends Entering Capitol*, NBC Miami, January 6,2022 at https://www.nbcmiami.com /news/local/a-lot-of-misrepresentation-proud-boy-charged-in-riot-defends-entering -capitol-/2655494/.

25 *Id.*

26 *Id.*

the election, and the orderly transition of presidential power is a hallmark of American democracy.

Let us now turn to the public authority defense, which differs from the superior orders defense because it affords a full defense to criminal charges. Furthermore, as we have previously noted, it has been invoked by Gabriel Garcia as a defense to federal criminal charges. Stephen K. Bannon also unsuccessfully raised the defense to counter the contempt of Congress charges for which he was ultimately convicted.

As the title implies, the public authority defense is predicated on the defendant relying on the authority of a public official in the belief that his criminal acts are sanctioned by the government. In effect, the defense serves to nullify the defendant's guilt. It is rooted in the principle that, although a mistake of law is not a defense to a criminal offense, an exception exists if the defendant reasonably relies on either the authority of a government official or an official interpretation of the law.[27] A brief excursion into the relevant federal case law and rule of procedure will guide our analysis.

In a prominent and high-profile case illustrating the scope of the defense, several defendants were indicted and convicted of burglarizing the office of Daniel Ellsberg's psychiatrist, and thereby conspiring to violate Dr. Fielding's civil rights.[28] On appeal, the defendants argued that their convictions should be overturned because the trial court prevented them from offering evidence and rejected a jury instruction based on their good faith reliance on the apparent authority of a governmental official (Assistant to the President for Domestic Affairs) to break into the office without warrant.[29] The defendants had been recruited for the job by former CIA agent E. Howard Hunt, who would later play a role in the Watergate break-in that led to President Nixon's resignation.

Of course, the principle that ignorance of the law is not an excuse is deeply embedded in Anglo-American jurisprudence.[30] Nonetheless, there are exceptions to the mistake of law defense. Among those exceptions is the claim of good faith reliance on a government official's authority. As the court observed in *Barker*, the defendants, who previously worked with the CIA and Hunt, had a viable explanation for their "good faith reliance on Hunt's apparent authority

---

27   *See, for example, United States v. Anderson*, 872 F.2d 1508(11th Cir. 1989), *cert. denied, 493 U.S. 1004 (1989); United States v. Barker*, 546 F.2d 940 (D. C. Cir. 1976); *United States v. Tallmadge*, 829 F.2d 767 (9th Cir. 1987).

28   *United States v. Barker*, 546 F.2d at 941–44.

29   A second basis for the appeal was that the civil rights statute required the government to establish the defendants had the specific intent to violate the law.

30   *See, for example, Lambert v. California*, 355 U.S. 225 (1957).

and their consequent failure to inquire about the activities they were to undertake on his behalf."[31] The court reversed the defendants' conviction, the *Barker* court concluded that there was "abundant evidence" from which the jury could have found that Barker and his co-defendant, Martinez, believed they were engaged in a national security operation lawfully authorized by the CIA.[32]

Since the *Barker* opinion, courts have been loath to recognize the apparent authority version of the defense.[33] Derisively labeling it the "CIA" defense, the Eleventh Circuit Court of Appeals rejected the "apparent authority" defense in a couple of cases in which the defendants maintained that their criminal acts were committed in concert with or with the implied or express approval of the CIA.[34] In *United States v. Rosenthal*, the defendants were under the impression that someone they thought was a CIA agent implied that their drug smuggling acts were undertaken to advance national security interests. The *Rosenthal* court rejected the defense, citing a Second Circuit court opinion for the proposition that a "defendant may only be exonerated on the basis of his reliance on real and not merely apparent authority."[35]

Collectively, these opinions supersede the broad scope of the defense the *Barker* court enunciated. Rather, the mistake of law defense now rests on the real, not the apparent, authority of the governmental agent or agency. For our purposes, this distinction is consequential. If the official who expressly or impliedly authorizes the criminal acts has no legal authority to do so, then the defendant cannot invoke the defense. The three cases rejecting the apparent authority form of the defense constrain its borders to actors who can sanction the otherwise criminal offenses. As delineated in the opinions, "because the CIA had no real authority to authorize such violations of the law, the defendant's theory 'that they were acting on apparent authority of a CIA agent is not a viable defense.'"[36]

Intertwined with the public authority defense is the variant invoked by both Stephen Bannon and Gabriel Garcia in their respective cases: entrapment by estoppel.[37] Procedurally, the public authority defense must be affirmatively invoked, with appropriate notice to the government. Federal Rule of Criminal

---

31   *United States v. Barker*, 546 F.2d at 966 (Leventhal, J., dissenting).

32   *Id.* at 949.

33   *See, for example, United States v. Rosenthal*, 793 F.2d 1214 (11th Cir. 1986), *cert. denied*, 480 U.S. 919 (1987); *United States v. Anderson, supra* note 27.

34   *See Rosenthal and Anderson, supra* note 33 and *United States v. Duggan*, 743 F.2d 59 (2d Cir. 1984).

35   *United States v. Anderson*, 872 F.2d at 1515 (citing *United States v. Duggan*).

36   *Id.*, citing *Duggan, supra* note 34.

37   *See* United States v. Gabriel Garcia and United States v. Stephen K. Bannon, *supra* note 1.

Procedure 12.3 requires a defendant who intends to rely on the defense to "serve upon the attorney for the government a written notice of such intention ... [and] shall identify the law enforcement or Federal intelligence agency on behalf of which ... the defendant claims the actual or believed exercise of authority occurred."[38] In addition, the government must admit or deny that the public authority existed. The aim of the rule is to provide the government with sufficient advance notice before trial to prepare and to counter the defense.[39]

As an affirmative defense, what must the defendant establish in order to satisfy the elements of entrapment by estoppel? The Fifth and Ninth Circuit Courts of Appeals have set forth the contours of entrapment by estoppel in a series of opinions. These opinions will be the lens through which we assess the normative foundation for the defense in the context of the January 6th assault on the Capitol.

The crux of entrapment by estoppel is that a government official misled the defendant to believe his actions were legal and that the defendant reasonably relied on the representation when he committed the offense. For example, in *United States v. Tallmadge*,[40] the defendant was charged with the statute that prohibits convicted felons from receiving firearms.[41] When he received the firearms from the federally licensed dealer, Tallmadge was assured by the dealer that he could purchase the firearm because his previous felony conviction had been legally reduced to a misdemeanor. Tallmadge informed the dealer about the expungement of the felony. The court reasoned that because the government had, in effect, made the licensed dealer a federal agent "in connection with the gathering and dispensing of information on the purchase of firearms." Consequently, the buyer of firearms "has the right to rely on the representations of a licensed firearms dealer ... that a person may receive and possess a weapon if the felony conviction has been reduced to a misdemeanor."[42]

Similarly, in *United States v. Clegg*,[43] the defendant was charged with exporting firearms in violation of federal law.[44] Clegg supplied weapons to Afghan rebels during the Soviet occupation, allegedly with the solicitation, encouragement, and assistance of United States officials affiliated with various agencies of the government.[45] Relying on *Tallmadge*, the court concluded that, a fortiori,

---

38   Fed.R.Crim.P. 12.3.

39   *See United States v. Abcasis*, 785 F. Supp. 113, 117 (E.D.N.Y. 1992).

40   829 F. 757 (9th Cir. 1987).

41   18 U.S.C. § 922 (h) (1) 1982.

42   *United States v. Tallmadge*, 829 F.2d at 774.

43   846 F.2d 1221 (1988).

44   18 U.S.C. § 922 (a) (1) (1982) and 22 U.S.C. § 2778 (b) (2), (c) (1982).

45   *United States v. Clegg*, 846 F.2d at 1222.

Clegg was entitled to invoke the defense. The court noted that "if Tallmadge was entitled to rely on the representations of the gun dealer as a complete defense, we can hardly deny the same defense to Clegg."[46] The court's holding underscores the distinction between the superior orders and public authority defenses: the latter is a complete defense while the former is only a partial one.

Gabriel Garcia relies on *United States v. Trevino-Martinez*,[47] in support of his motion to rely on the entrapment by estoppel defense.[48] In that case, the defendant was charged with illegally entering the country after having been deported. Trevino-Martinez alleged that he reasonably relied on the issuance of a nonimmigrant visa by the United States consulate in Monterrey, Mexico when he re-entered the United States. Therefore, he maintained that the trial court erred in denying a jury instruction on the entrapment by estoppel defense.[49] Upholding the trial court's ruling, the appellate court rejected the defense because Trevino-Martinez did not disclose his previous deportation to the consulate when he applied for the visa. In effect, the court concluded, "he was not actively misled by the government since the consulate did not assure Trevino that his actions were proper."[50] Therefore, Trevino-Martinez failed to support the elements of the defense: "[that] a government official or agent actively assures a defendant that certain conduct is legal and the defendant reasonably relies on that advice and continues or initiates that conduct."[51]

The threshold inquiry under the defense is whether a government official misled the defendant. Stephen Bannon's reliance on the entrapment by estoppel defense to his contempt of Congress charges, therefore, was fatally flawed. Bannon's failure to comply with a Congressional subpoena did not result from the advice of a government official or agency. President Trump was no longer a federal official, thereby precluding Bannon's claim that he was not complying because Trump had asserted executive privilege. Further, no governmental agency (for example, the Justice Department) had "sanctioned his default."[52]

Let us return to Gabriel Garcia's motion to rely on the entrapment by estoppel defense. Garcia argues that President Trump's speech at the Ellipse on January 6, 2021 amounted to a military order to disrupt the proceeding destined to certify Biden's electoral victory. Garcia amply meets the first prong of

---

46   *Id.* at 1224.

47   86 F.3d 65 (5th Cir. 1996).

48   *See United States v. Gabriel Augustin Garcia, supra* note 16.

49   *Id.* at 69.

50   *Id.* at 70.

51   Id. at 69.

52   *See United States v. Stephen K. Bannon, supra* note 1, United States Response to Defendant's Notice Under Federal Rule of Procedure 12.3.

the defense: President Trump was a government official; indeed, he was the highest civilian and military official of the United States, the President and Commander-in-Chief.

The second prong of the defense is more problematic. Did President Trump assure Garcia, and by implication all supporters listening to his speech, that their acts in disrupting the Congressional certification of the electoral results were legal? Garcia refers to a specific part of the speech in which President Trump states: "We are going to walk down, and I'll be there with you. ... We are going to the Capitol... We're ... going to try and give them [Republicans] the kind of pride and boldness that they need to take back our country."[53] Of course, the recent hearings conducted by the Select Committee on January 6 have corroborated that President Trump intended to go with his supporters to the Capitol but was prevented from going by his Secret Service agents.[54]

President Trump, as the evidence has confirmed, knew that his claim of electoral fraud was spurious. Did he therefore mislead Garcia into believing that storming the Capitol building was legal? Garcia emphasizes in his motion that his actions were a peaceful exercise of "his First Amendment right to express his political grievances at the Capitol."[55] As he has put it, his actions were meant to redress his grievances against voter fraud and to preserve democracy – lofty ideals indeed.[56] However misguided Garcia may have been, the argument that he was misled by his Commander-in-Chief to disrupt the electoral process is colorable, if not viable. What more reasonable reliance on governmental authority does one need other than an assurance given by the highest civilian and military official in the land? A loyal soldier, Garcia initiated the conduct endorsed by his commander.

In contrast to the following orders defense, therefore, Garcia has a more compelling argument by relying on the entrapment by estoppel defense. However illegal Trump's orders may have been, and whether Garcia should have known they were unlawful, are not germane to the defense that he was misled and acted in reasonable reliance of an assurance by the highest official in the country that his acts were legal.

The government is placed in a Hobson's choice by contesting Garcia's motion. As a thoughtful commentator has observed, how does the Justice Department "thread the needle" of "potentially holding the former president and others responsible for conduct that allegedly led to the insurrection,"

---

53   *Id.*

54   *See* Feuer & Schmidt *supra* note 1.

55   *United States v. Gabriel Garcia, supra* note 16.

56   *See supra* note 26.

while opposing Garcia's motion that he reasonably relied upon the advice of a government official?[57]

Conclusion

Most Americans would like to eradicate the unfortunate assault on the Capitol on January 6, 2021 from their consciousness. Democracy stood at the precipice when a sitting American president sought to upend his defeat and remain in power through unlawful means. Aristotle remarked that "democracies are often corrupted by the insolence of demagogues." The statement captures the essence of what occurred on January 6th. Neither the superior orders nor the entrapment by estoppel defenses justify the assault on the Capitol. Perhaps both defenses could mitigate the punishment of the individuals who violated the law, but they cannot negate the collective guilt of the offenders.

---

57   Andrea L. Moseley, *Permission to Violate the Law? Public Authority Defenses in the Limelight*, https://grandjurytarget.com/2022/02/08/permission-to-violate-the-law-public-authority -defenses-in-the-limelight/.

CHAPTER 34

Childhood Gender Transitioning and Human Flourishing

*June Mary Zekan Makdisi**

Professor Siegfried Wiessner has inspired countless students and academics throughout the world. He shines his lamp for the benefit of advancing knowledge, participating in community, and providing active caring for others. I treasure his advice and friendship as do so many others. Under his guidance, students from the Intercultural Human Rights Program have gone on to become world-class leaders. We remember these students collectively: a flag from each nation of origin flies in the St. Thomas law school atrium. Each flag also stands as tribute to the far-reaching influence of Professor Wiessner, as each student fosters his mission to advance human flourishing as the end of law.

This essay explores human flourishing in the context of childhood transgender identity and body alteration to mimic another sex. To honor Professor Wiessner, this essay will trace important elements of the New Haven method.[1]

1 Delimitation of the Problem: Upsurge in Transgender Identity and Transitioning in Children

There have always been children who sensed an incongruence between their biological sex and their gender. Previously, their existence has been in extremely small numbers, and most were biological boys. In the past decade, there has been an increase of almost 2000% in clinic referrals of both boys and girls. This rapid escalation of children with gender identity issues accompanies

---

* Professor of Law Emeritus, St. Thomas University School of Law; B.A., University of Pennsylvania; M.S., University of Pennsylvania; J.D., University of Tulsa College of Law.
1 *See* Siegfried Wiessner, *Doctors of the Social Order: Introduction to New Haven Methodology*, Handbook on Human Trafficking, Public Health and the Law: A Spring School from the New Haven Perspective 8 (Wilhelm Kirch, Siegfried Wiessner & Roza Pati eds., 2014) (explaining the methodology and stating that the purpose of law is to bring about human flourishing).

a simultaneous and dramatic shift to girls, who now outnumber boys with perceived gender incongruence three to one.[2]

1.1   *Internal and External Influences*

All children suffer confusion and anxiety as they begin to mature sexually. "Puberty brings profound bodily and psychological changes that threaten any adolescent with feelings of loss of control."[3] The gender-dysphoric child must have something beyond the normal anxieties – either some type of functional impairment or "clinically significant distress." In addition, he or she must message a "marked incongruence" between the biological sex and the professed gender for at least six months, manifested by two or more of the symptoms specified by the American Psychiatric Association's fifth edition of its *Diagnostic and Statistical Manual of Mental Disorders*. The list specifies a strong desire: to eliminate or prevent the development of primary (external and internal sex organs that are present at birth) or secondary (e.g., breast or facial hair) sex characteristics; to have the opposite sex's characteristics; to be the other (or alternative) gender; to be treated as the other (or alternative) gender; and to have a strong conviction that one's feelings or reactions are typical of the other (or alternative) gender.[4]

Unlike the traditional preschool manifestation of gender dysphoria, the majority of today's dysphoric children are not only female, but also commence gender dysphoria during adolescence. Ob-gyn, public health researcher Lisa Littman labels this atypical expression "rapid-onset gender dysphoria."[5] No medical theory has explained the cause of gender dysphoria.[6] However, Dr. Littman has found that a majority of the girls with rapid-onset gender dysphoria had immersed themselves in social media for a prolonged period of time. She also found a high correlation (seventy times the expected rate) of rapid-onset dysphoric girls having friends who identified as trans. Her explanation, at least for rapid-onset dysphoria? "Peer contagion."[7]

---

2 Abigail Favale, The Genesis of Gender 167 (2022).

3 Marcus Evans, *'If Only I Were a Boy …': Psychotherapeutic Explorations of Transgender in Children and Adolescents*, 38 British J. Psychotherapy 269, 275 (2022), *available at* https://doi.org/10.1111/bjp.12733.

4 Am. Psychiatric Assoc., *Gender Dysphoria Diagnosis*, https://www.psychiatry.org/ psychiatrists/cultural-competency/education/transgender-and-gender-nonconforming-patients/gender-dysphoria-diagnosis (last visited July 6, 2022).

5 Abigail Shrier, Irreversible Damage 13 (2020).

6 Mark A. Yarhouse, Understanding Gender Dysphoria 61, 67–73 (2015) (analyzing several hypotheses, but concluding that no one knows the medical cause of gender dysphoria).

7 Shrier, *supra* note 5, at 25–27.

A number of explanations have arisen to explain the attractiveness of identifying as the opposite gender. Some children create an "illusory ideal self" to escape from the pubescent transition to adulthood.[8] Some girls who might earlier have considered themselves tomboys believe that their preference for male activities or apparel must mean that they are trans. Other girls who are sexually attracted to girls receive more cachet as "trans" than as lesbian, especially if they come from a family with conscious or unconscious anti-homosexual attitudes.[9] For still other girls, casting themselves as the opposite gender is a reaction to unwanted sexual attention from boys.[10] Others were bullied and sought medical transitioning with a belief that the intervention would solve their problems.[11] For boys, like girls, being considered transgender may have greater social status than being gay. Some believe that they will get into less trouble as girls.[12]

The gender dysphoric child may express a great deal of certainty in his or her judgment of gender incongruence, and in the desire to create a transgender avatar for relief.[13] It is not unusual for children to be adamant about things they badly want.[14] A scientific explanation for a child's, including adolescent's, strong emotional expression of their heartfelt desire is that the part of the brain that controls consequential thinking, judgment, decision-making, and emotions – the prefrontal cortex – is undeveloped. The prefrontal cortex does not achieve full development until early adulthood.[15]

---

8   Evans, *supra* note 3, at 269–70, 274.

9   *Id.* at 269, 282; Shrier, *supra* note 5, at 13.

10   Favale, *supra* note 2, at 176.

11   Anna Churcher Clarke & Anastassis Spiliadis, *'Taking the Lid Off the Box': The Value of Extended Clinical Assessment for Adolescents Presenting With Gender Identity Difficulties*, 24 Clinical Child Psychol. 338, 340 (2019), *available at* https://www.researchgate .net/publication/330911243_'Taking_the_lid_off_the_box'_The_value_of_extended _clinical_assessment_for_adolescents_presenting_with_gender_identity_difficulties.

12   Richard P. Fitzgibbons, *Transsexual Attractions and Sexual Reassignment Surgery: Risks and Potential Risks*, 82 Linacre Q. 337, 341 (Nov. 2015), *available at https://www.ncbi.nlm .nih.gov/pmc/articles/PMC4771004/*.

13   Evans, *supra* note 3, at 270, 272.

14   Debra Soh, The End of Gender 143 (2021).

15   Barbara Annis & Keith Merron, Gender Intelligence 25 (2014); Adele Diamond, *Normal Development of Prefrontal Cortex from Birth to Young Adulthood: Cognitive Functions, Anatomy, and Biochemistry, in* Principles of Frontal Lobe Function 466, 487 (D. Stuss & R. Knight eds. 2002), *available at* chrome-extension://efaidnbmnnnibpcajpcglclefindmkaj /http://devcogneuro.com/Publications/ChapterinStuss&Knight.pdf; Sharon M. Kolk & Pasko Rakic, *Development of Prefrontal Cortex*, 47 Neuropsychopharmacology 41, 41 (2022), *available at* https://doi.org/10.1038/s41386-021-01137-9.

1.2   *Clinical Focus*

Prior to the fifth edition of the *Diagnostic and Statistical Manual of Mental Disorders* (DSM-V), there was no entry for gender dysphoria. Previously, the *Manual* had an entry for gender identity disorder (GID), with criteria less stringent than the current model under the new term. The GID diagnosis pathologized gender nonconformity and justified treatment.[16] Treatment for GID was psychotherapy, with the psychologist exercising "watchful waiting" while coming to understand the source of gender discomfort.[17] Studies showed that most children resolved their gender incongruence, paralleling their gender identity with their biological sex.[18]

Declassifying GID had the effect of normalizing gender nonconformity because it was no longer considered a mental disorder by the American Psychiatric Association, the publishers of the DSM-V.[19] The DSM-V's inclusion of a more stringent gender dysphoria diagnostic classification in place of the GID paved the way for a medicalized treatment of a diagnosed child. Although the prevalence of other psychiatric symptoms in the gender dysphoric child were specifically acknowledged, clinicians could make gender dysphoric symptoms themselves be the primary focus, with a goal of treating them with hormones and even surgery.[20]

Several influential organizations have made recommendations on providing care to children qualifying for chemical intervention to suppress puberty. The American College of Obstetrics and Gynecology suggests that oral contraceptives, intrauterine devices or an implant containing progesterone could be given to suppress menses in biological females. The purpose is to prevent the child's distress if she begins to menstruate.[21] The American Academy of Pediatrics and the Endocrine Society guidelines call for administering gonadotrophin-releasing hormone (GnRH) analogues at the outset of puberty to

---

16   Amber Ault & Stephanie Brzuzy, *Removing Gender Identity Disorder from the Diagnostic and Statistical Manual of Mental Disorders*, 54 Soc. Work 187, 187 (2009), *available at* https://www.jstor.org/stable/23719302.

17   *Abigail Shrier, Top Doctors Blow the Whistle on 'Sloppy' Care*, Common Sense 3 (Oct. 4, 2021), https://www.commonsense.news/p/top-trans-doctors-blow-the-whistle?s=r.

18   Soh, *supra* note 14, at 141 (eleven long-term studies); Devita Singh et al., *A Follow-Up Study of Boys with Gender Identity Disorder*, Frontiers in Psychiatry, Mar. 29, 2021, *available at* https://www.frontiersin.org/articles/10.3389/fpsyt.2021.632784/full.

19   See Ault & Brzuzy, *supra* note 16, at 187.

20   Am. Psychiatric Assoc., *supra* note 4.

21   Jason Richard Rafferty et al., *Ensuring Comprehensive Care and Support for Transgender and Gender-Diverse Children and Adolescents*, 142 Pediatrics e1, e7 (Oct. 4, 2018), *available at* http://publications.aap.org/ pediatrics/article-pdf/142/4/e20182162/1066566/peds 20182162.pdf (Policy Statement, Am. Acad. Pediatrics).

allow time for an adolescent to consider whether to make a permanent gender transition.[22] The goal is to block puberty by preventing the development of secondary sex characteristics (such as the development of female curvature or an Adam's apple in males) that would make it more difficult to pass oneself off as a member of the opposite biological sex.[23] The puberty blockers work by shutting off the pituitary to prevent the child's body from releasing sex hormones.[24] The GnRH analogues are optimally administered in the early stages of puberty, which typically begins somewhere between the ages of eight and thirteen for girls and between nine and fourteen for boys.[25] Although the Endocrine Society recommends initiating treatment at about sixteen years of age, physicians will start them as early as age thirteen or fourteen.[26]

The two most common puberty blockers are leuprolide, delivered by periodic injection, and histrelin, administered over twelve months as a subcutaneous implant. The former drug has been approved by the FDA for treating central precocious puberty in pediatric patients. The latter drug has been FDA approved for treatment of prostate cancer. Neither these nor any other drugs have been approved by the FDA for treatment of gender dysphoria.[27] The annual cost of this treatment, without insurance, can range between $4000 and $25,000.[28]

Puberty blockers pause sexual development; to phenotypically transition to the opposite sex, cross-sex hormones must be taken. Beginning at about age sixteen,[29] the regime continues throughout life. Natal females take testosterone and natal males take estrogen plus an androgen inhibitor. Once this hormonal regime has begun, many physical changes are irreversible. These include

---

22   Heather Boerner, *What the Science on Gender-Affirming Care for Transgender Kids Really Shows*, Sci. Am. (May 12, 2022), *available at* https://www.scientificamerican.com/article /what-the-science-on-gender-affirming-care-for-transgender-kids-really-shows/#.

23   Shrier, *supra* note 5, at 82.

24   *Id.* at 165; Boerner, *supra* note 22.

25   Cleveland Clinic, *What Are Puberty Blockers?* Jan. 10, 2022, *available at* https://health .clevelandclinic.org/what-are-puberty-blockers/.

26   Daphne Sashin, *What is Transitioning?* WebMD (Dec. 13,2020), https://www.webmd.com /parenting/what-is-transitioning.

27   Johanna Olson-Kennedy et al., *Histrelin Implants for Suppression of Puberty in Youth with Gender Dysphoria: A Comparison of 50mcg/Day (Vantas) and 65mcg/Day (SupprelinLA)*, 6 Transgender Health 36, 37 (2021), *available at* https://www.ncbi.nlm.nih.gov/pmc/articles /PMC7906230/.

28   Jack L. Turban, *Pubertal Suppression for Transgender Youth and Risk of Suicidal Ideation*, 145 Pediatrics, Feb. 1, 2020, at 1, 6, *available at* https://publications.aap.org/pediatrics/article /145/2/e20191725/68259/Pubertal-Suppression-for-Transgender-Youth-and.

29   Clarke & Spiliadis, *supra* note 11, at 341.

Adam's apple protrusion, voice changes, and breast development. The effect on fertility is unknown.[30] It is likely that these irreversible changes are hormonally induced in many children at a very young age because the Endocrine Society advises against taking puberty blockers for longer than two years, and some children begin taking puberty blockers before becoming teens.[31]

The final stage for transitioners is irreversible sex reassignment surgery, also called gender-affirming surgery. Eighteen is the minimal age recommended by the Endocrine Society, but because more children are undergoing chemical transitioning earlier, more undergo the surgery at an earlier age.[32] Theoretically, the only surgery available to minors is a double mastectomy to remove healthy, but unwanted, breasts.[33]

1.3 *Gender Affirming Social Transitioning*

While receiving chemical intervention to prevent passing through puberty, and even before, the child is expected to receive gender-affirming care, ideally including the child's family.[34] This social affirmation is recommended by the American Academy of Pediatrics (AAP) for any child who expresses "*partially* or completely in their asserted gender by adapting hairstyle, clothing, pronouns, name, etc."[35] Self-identification, then, is the sole criterion; neither the requisite distress associated with gender dysphoria nor adult authorization is necessary since the AAP removed the mental disorder classification for those who claim that their gender does not match their biology. Absent diagnostic criteria, the behavior and assertion of a child that he or she is transgender (or other nonbinary identity) warrants affirmation.

Some children prefer to keep their transgender identity private; others make their trans identity public. Public social transitioning informs those with whom the child associates that expressed gender rather than biological sex connotes who they are. The communication to others is expressed by taking on a new name and attire, and professing a desire to participate in activities typical of the expressed gender. The child's social transitioning also includes charging others to identify the child by the incongruent gender rather than by birth sex.

To facilitate a child's desire to create this new identity at school, a variety of organizations have devised programs specifically geared to training teachers

---

30   Rafferty et al., *supra* note 21, at e6, Table 2.
31   See Boerner, *supra* note 22.
32   Sashin, *supra* note 26.
33   Boerner, *supra* note 22.
34   Rafferty et al., *supra* note 21, at e5.
35   *Id.* at e6 (Policy Statement, Am. Acad. Pediatrics) (author's emphasis).

on how to support children coming out as trans. In addition, curricular guides instruct teachers and administrators on how to implement trans instruction within the curriculum as early as kindergarten.[36] Teachers are encouraged to affirm the child's gender identity by using the child's chosen name and pronouns. In a position of authority in the classroom, affirming teachers model behavior and viewpoint.[37] This authority can extend beyond the classroom. For example, if a parent does not affirm his or her own child's gender identity, a resource guide that is supported by the National Teacher's Association considers the child's teacher to be a "neutral professional" who is in the best position to "assess and identify the child's needs and recommend a course of action."[38] In 2019, the 800-delegate membership of the California Teachers Association State Council approved a course of action that enabled students as young as twelve years old to leave campus during school hours in order to receive gender hormone treatments without parental permission.[39]

1.4   *Puberty Blockers*

All pharmaceutical products have side effects, including those that youth take to chemically halt puberty. Using puberty blockers can result in myriad medical problems. Side effects include weight gain, rashes, irritability, headaches, mood swings, hot flashes, reduced height, a decrease in bone density, and insufficient genital skin for male-to-female surgery.[40]

Some say that any physical harm is outweighed by the benefits to the child's psyche. For example, denying puberty blockers will result in a less optimal post-puberal transition result because once some secondary characteristics such as an Adam's apple develop, the process cannot be reversed.[41] In addition, some studies claim that if gender-dysphoric children do not chemically

---

36   *See, e.g.,* The Transgender Training Institute, *Want to Better Understand & Be More Affirming of Trans & Non-Binary People?* https://www.transgendertraininginstitute.com /training-services/; https://www.eventbrite.com/cc/k-12-educators-47179 (online training session) (last visited July 4, 2022); Asaf Orr et al., *Schools In Transition: A Guide for Supporting Transgender Students in K-12 Schools,* https://www.hrc.org/resources/schools-in -transition-a-guide-for-supporting-transgender-students-in-k-12-s (produced by the HRC Foundation and supported by the National Education Association); GLSEN, *Developing LGT-BQ-Inclusive Classroom Resources,* https://www.glsen.org/activity/inclusive-curriculum -guide (last visited July 9, 2022).

37   Orr et al., *supra* note 36.

38   *Id.* (produced by the HRC Foundation and supported by the National Education Association).

39   Shrier, *supra* note 5, at 59, 247 n.1.

40   Cleveland Clinic, *supra* note 25.

41   Evans, *supra* note 3, at 281.

suppress puberty, their depression, self-harm, and suicidal ideation increases. This rate is significantly higher than that of same-aged cisgender children. With treatment, however, the studies reported that most of the children had less severe depression and fewer thoughts of suicide or self-harm during the year after beginning treatment.[42] Not highlighted in these reports is that a large proportion of children with gender dysphoria have one or more mental health co-morbidities. Children with co-morbid psychological issues have suicide ideation statistics similar to that of gender-dysphoric children.[43] This finding casts doubt on assertions that gender dysphoria is the sole root of the suicidal thoughts.

The AAP recognizes that children who identify as transgender, regardless of whether they experience gender dysphoria, have high rates of co-morbidities such as depression, anxiety, eating disorders, autism, self-harm, and suicide. However, the Academy blames the co-morbid mental health illnesses primarily on stigma, discrimination, and other like matters.[44] Since it disregards the comorbidities as significant in dealing with gender dysphoria, the Academy also disregards the former standard of neutral, "watchful waiting," considering that therapeutic treatment "outdated," and favoring instead gender-affirming care.[45]

Research on the physical efficacy of puberty blockers is undisputed. However, the narrative studies that assert psychological benefit cannot claim scientific proof because of the methodological flaws that challenge the conclusions drawn. Some of the researchers themselves have recognized the limitations in their research protocols. These included small sample sizes, improper survey questions, and lack of control groups by which to compare results.[46] Additional defects encompassed survey recruitment methods that resulted in skewed samples.[47] Other studies included trans youth of only one sex; had insufficient short- and long-term follow-ups; and infused research bias because

---

42 Boerner, *supra* note 22; Diana M. Tordof et al., *Mental Health Outcomes in Transgender and Nonbinary Youths Receiving Gender-Affirming Care*, JAMA Network Open, at e4, e8, e10, Feb. 25, 2022, https://jamanetwork.com/journals/jamanetworkopen/ fullarticle/2789423; Turban, *supra* note 28, at e1, e2–6.

43 Bianca Machado Borba Soll et al., *Descriptive Study of Transgender Youth Receiving Health Care in the Gender Identity Program in Southern Brazil*, 12 Frontiers in Psychiatry 1, Mar. 4, 2021, *available at* https://www.frontiersin.org/articles/ 10.3389/fpsyt.2021.627661/full.

44 Rafferty, *supra* note 22, at e3–4.

45 *Id.* at e3–5.

46 Turban, *supra* note 28, e2–7.

47 Roberto Angelo et al., *One Size Does Not Fit All: In Support of Psychotherapy for Gender Dysphoria*, 50 Archives Sexual Behav. 7, 8 (2021), *available at* https://link.springer.com /article/10.1007/s10508-020-01844-2.

all the trans youth in the studies came from supportive families. Protocols also did not track the other psychotropic medications given to the youth in the studies, so there was no way of knowing whether puberty blockers had any causative effect on improvement.[48] This failure to track other psychotherapeutic medications is significant given the large proportion of gender-dysphoric children who have one or more mental health problems.[49]

Another consideration with respect to gender identity studies is that a more scientific evaluation of treatment approaches is prevented by a growing trend to overstate positive and minimize negative findings.[50] Contrary results and contrary professional voices are too often suppressed.[51] The renowned vaginoplasty specialist who performed thousands of bottom surgeries, including on Jazz, has said that she is not a fan of puberty blockers. She explained that puberty stimulates sex organ development and also the erotic potential that makes orgasm possible. Erotic potential is not cured with surgery. She said that the problem is often overlooked, and the party line on affirmation provides no room for dissent.[52]

In addition to the problems discussed above, there is concern that the long-term consequences of using puberty blockers are unknown.[53] Short-term effectiveness studies may help users to obtain insurance coverage for treatment, but it does not answer the question of true benefit. Further data is needed to determine long-term efficacy, safety, and side effects.[54] Among the unknown consequences of using puberty blockers is its effect on prefrontal cortex development. The interference caused by puberty blockers may affect cognitive functions such as decision-making and emotion.[55] Since the brain,

---

48   Tordof et al., *supra* note 42, at e4, e8, e10; Turban, *supra* note 28, at e2–7.

49   Soll et al., *supra* note 43.

50   Alison Clayton, *Commentary: The Signal and the Noise – Questioning the Benefits of Puberty Blockers for Youth with Gender Dysphoria – a Commentary on Rew et al.*, Child & Adolescent Mental Health (2021) at e1, *available at* https://acamh.onlinelibrary.wiley.com/doi/full/10.1111/camh.12533.

51   *See, e.g.,* Angelo et al., *supra* note 47, at 11 (letters commenting on the inaccuracy of a JAMA Psychiatry article rejected by the publishers); Soc'y for Evidence Based Gender Med., *The AAP Silences the Debate on How to Best Care for Gender-Diverse Kids* (Aug. 9, 2021) (denied an exhibitor table at the annual AAP conference), https://segm.org/AAP_silences_debate_on_gender_diverse_youth_treatments; Shrier, *supra* note 5, at 27–30; 123–29 (researchers fired from jobs, book award reversed, false ethics accusations, following pressure from activists to discredit proponents of non-affirmative psychotherapy).

52   *Shrier, supra* note 17, at e1–4.

53   Clayton, *supra* note 50 (England suspended using puberty blockers on children under sixteen because of the unknown risks).

54   Olson-Kennedy et al., *supra* note 27, at 41–42; Shrier, *supra* note 5, at 13.

55   Diamond, *supra* note 15, at 494.

musculoskeletal structure and sexual development all occur within a social context, we do not know how the body will respond when the timing of naturally occurring puberty does not coincide with these other developmental milestones.[56] Moreover, the very hormones that the body is denied when puberty is blocked are the very ones that could help resolve the child's dysphoria, if they had been allowed to be released.[57]

Evidence that deprivation of pubescent hormones prevents a trans-identifying child from naturally overcoming gender incongruence may be seen in the high percentage of children who desist when puberty blockers are not administered. All of the eleven studies done between 1972 and 2013 demonstrated that most children who had identified with a gender opposite of their sex desisted.[58] One long-term study showed that almost all of the boys who persisted in their dysphoria were really homosexual or bisexual.[59] This means that if the clinician in that study had initiated current chemical protocol instead of neutrally waiting, those children would have undergone unnecessary medical intervention with life-long maintenance and reproductive consequences when the persisters' real condition more approximated homosexuality. A lower acceptance rate of homosexuality in their home environment was theorized as a possible explanation for their presenting as trans.[60]

Desistance studies have been refuted and said to be irrelevant by some because they were done before gender dysphoria became a medical diagnosis.[61] Before the DSM-5 established the criteria of *distress* for gender incongruence as a treatable disorder, a child's feeling of gender incongruence *itself* was considered the disorder.[62] The verity of bodily form was unquestioned. The mind's reluctance to recognize that reality was not automatically affirmed, as doing so would add to the child's confusion over self. Instead, clinicians treated the child holistically, searching for the source of the disorder and attempting to understand the child's reasons in escaping from the truth of their material selves. Therefore, the desistance studies remain valuable because they

---

56   Soh, *supra* note 14, at 156 (interview with endocrinologist William Malone).

57   *Id.* at 158.

58   *Id.* at 141 (studies published between 1972 and 2013 showed desistence of between 60% and 90%).

59   Singh et al., *supra* note 18.

60   *Id.*

61   Thomas D. Steensma & Peggy T. Cohen-Kettenis, *A Critical Commentary on "A Critical Commentary on Follow-Up Studies and "Desistence" Theories About Transgender and Gender Non-Conforming Children"*, 19 Int'l J. Transgenderism 225, 225–26 (2018), *available at* https://www.tandfonline.com/doi/full/10.1080/ 15532739.2018.1468292.

62   Shrier, *supra* note 5, at 150.

successfully refute the need to mindlessly affirm and begin puberty blocker interventions.

This is especially true since a diagnosis of gender dysphoria is based on a very loose standard having no discernible medical measurement, and is mostly generated by self-reports of distress that could be coached to satisfy a child's desire for trans medication. Some clinicians have been misled into believing that gender affirmation with its consequential progression to puberty blockers and beyond is the best, and only, treatment for children presenting with gender dysphoria. Published studies and professional organizations such as the AAP have encouraged it. At times, clinicians have pushed unwilling parents into consenting to therapy by presenting them with misleading suicide statistics and suggesting that withholding therapy increases their child's risk of suicide.[63]

When a diagnosis of gender dysphoria is based on symptoms and studies of low certainty, it warrants caution not only with respect to the diagnosis but also with respect to how other psychological conditions may have impacted the expressed gender incongruence. Although clinicians have a lot of room to interpret whether symptoms accord with a diagnosis of gender dysphoria or if they arise from other causes,[64] AAP guidelines remark that clinicians may focus on reports of dysphoria as if distinct from other co-morbidities.

When clinicians apply gender-affirmative care and medical transitioning, insufficient consideration may be given to a child's inability to understand his or her deep emotions or to think consequentially. How can there be true consent when the child's immature prefrontal cortex prevents him or her from thoughtful deliberation about the long-term effects of medical interventions used to treat gender *distress*?[65] Moreover, prescription medicine for mental conditions such as depression or anxiety disorders address the *un*healthy parts of the body whose dysfunction is considered the source of the problem. By contrast, medicine prescribed to treat the emotional distress associated with gender dysphoria renders dysfunctional *healthy* body parts.

Therefore, automatically affirming social transformation is not in a child's best interest because it puts the child on a pathway to puberty blocking, which

---

63   *Id.* at 138.

64   Yarhouse, *supra* note 6, at 90.

65   Joleen M. Schanzenbach, *Navigating Treatment of Gender Dysphoric Teens*, Ethics & Medics 1 (June 2022).

itself is a gateway to receiving cross-sex hormones and undergoing sex reassignment surgery.[66]

1.5   *Cross-Sex Hormones and Gender-Affirming Surgery*

There is very little information on the use of cross-sex (gender-affirming) hormones on youth. In the first prospective U.S. study, only data from fifty-nine of the initial one hundred youths, aged twelve to twenty-three, could be collected for the two-year study. Twenty-two percent of these candidates began cross-sex hormonal treatment at younger than sixteen, which is below the Academy-recommended age. The researchers recognized study limitations including data insufficiency and inconsistent adherence to medication among the candidates. They concluded that the therapeutic goals had been reached and that, despite noted side effects, it was safe for youth to use gender-affirming cross-sex hormones for about two years.[67]

Cross-sex hormones are effective in inducing the desired secondary sex characteristics, but also cause side effects. These include cardio-vascular problems, diabetes, painful orgasm, and cancer.[68] Complications also include weight gain, stroke, limited sexual function, and infertility. The risk of permanent infertility increases with prolonged use, even after stopping hormone therapy.[69]

On account of age, few children have received surgical treatment. Sex reassignment surgery mutilates a healthy reproductive system, brings about permanent infertility, and is irreversible.[70] Distress, however, is said to be relieved by these alterations: Short-term studies conclude that gender-affirming care, including cross-sex hormones and gender-affirming surgery decreases depression, anxiety, and suicidal thoughts.[71] But the claims may be overstated. Many patients fall off the grid; the follow-up rate is only about ten percent.[72]

---

66   The World Prof'l Ass'n for Transgender Health Standards of Care for the Health of Transsexual, Transgender, and Gender-Nonconforming People 11 (7th ed. 2012), *available at* https://www.wpath.org/publications/soc; Angelo et al., *supra* note 47, at 12.

67   Johanna Olson-Kennedy et al., *Physiologic Response to Gender-Affirming Hormones Among Transgender Youth*, 62 J. Adolescent Health 397 (2018), *available at* https://www.ncbi.nlm.nih.gov/pmc/articles/PMC7050572/.

68   Soh, *supra* note 14, at 159.

69   Mayo Clinic, *Feminizing Hormone Therapy*, https://www.mayoclinic.org/tests-procedures/feminizing-hormone-therapy/about/pac-20385096 (last visited June 17, 2022).

70   Fitzgibbons, *supra* note 12.

71   *E.g.*, Tordof et al., *supra* note 42 (methodological biases similar to the studies on puberty blockers).

72   Walt Heyer, Gender, Lies and Suicide 85 (2013).

Forty-one percent of transgender persons have attempted suicide compared with fewer than two percent of the general U.S. population. Worse yet, the attempted suicide rate for those who underwent gender affirmation surgery was reportedly higher than for those who did not.[73] A long-term study capturing data from almost the entire population of Sweden who had undergone sex reassignment surgery over the course of thirty years confirms this position. That study concluded that high rates of depression, suicide, and psychiatric hospitalizations for comorbid mental illness continued after surgery.[74] Therefore, surgical interventions may not bring about the professed psychological benefits.

A growing number of detransitioners also makes one wonder about the prudence of gender-affirming care.[75] Many detransitioners relate that they never would have undergone the life-changing transition if a professional had helped them explore their underlying problems, and their own doubts about transitioning.[76] This suggests that at the onset of gender dysphoric symptoms, children should not be automatically affirmed in their incongruency. Instead, they should be treated with compassionate, but neutral therapy that explores all their mental states and illnesses and treats them in conjunction with their gender dysphoria. This would prevent their taking a potentially unnecessary path that destroys their bodily integrity.

1.6   *Social Transition and Affirmation*

Professional societies, clinicians, and other advocates assert that gender affirmation that involves nothing more than changing hairstyle, clothing, name, and so forth promotes well-being.[77] They say that transgender expressiveness is not a mental disorder, and that whoever tries to change a child's gender expression acts inappropriately.[78] Gender itself, they say, is a social construct.[79] Thus, it can be fluid because defining one's own self-identity is at the heart

---

73   *Id.* at 68 (citing *Injustice at Every Turn: A Report of the National Transgender Discrimination Survey*).

74   Cecilia Dhejne, *Long-Term Follow-Up of Transsexual Persons Undergoing Sex Reassignment Surgery: Cohort Study in Sweden*, PLoS One (Feb. 22, 2011), at e5–7, https://www.ncbi .nlm.nih.gov/pmc/articles/PMC3043071/.

75   Soc'y for Evidence Based Gend. Med., *Detransition: A Real and Growing Phenomenon*, SEGM, May 30, 2021, https://segm.org/first_large_study_of_detransitioners.

76   Evans, *supra* note 3, at 280.

77   *See, e.g.*, Rafferty et al., *supra* note 21, at e6.

78   *Id.* at e4 (Oct. 4, 2018).

79   *See* Jan Bentz, *Paradise Contested: A Plagiarized Genesis Is the Source for a Secular Utopia*, Touchstone, Jan.-Feb., 2022, at 32, 35.

of liberty.[80] Gender transitioning thereby reflects a "deep need to be one's authentic self."[81]

In support of the benefits of gender affirmation, this group points to studies that have found that children who received gender affirmation had better mental health outcomes than those who did not. Those studies found that those who did not receive gender affirmation had increased self-harm, depression, and suicidal thoughts.[82] Proponents also point out that since no harm is done to the body, social transition is reversible.[83] Therefore, gender affirmation in the form of social transitioning is said to be both beneficial and neutral.

Social transitioning is physically reversible, yet 90% of the children who socially transition move on to medically transition. The social gender transition variable appears to be a uniquely vital predictor of gender dysphoric persistence.[84] Some might believe that the high persistence rate must mean that gender transitioning was right for those children. Others might reflect on the child's humiliation in re-gendering to their birth sex after previously telling the world that the two didn't match.[85] One might think that the child was courageous in making the announcement initially, especially if the child subsequently suffered mistreatment from others.[86] Imagine how much worse it might seem, in the psyche of a child, to suffer the further indignation of retraction of such a monumental disclosure.

Since almost all socially transitioning children go on to change their bodies, it cannot be a neutral choice to affirm them. It is, therefore, important to consider not just the psychological benefit of any affirmation, but also affirmation in its substantive context.

Substantively, what does it mean to affirm gender over biological sex? Affirmation communicates to the child that mind and body are not intrinsically a unified one. The child need not accept limitations presented by a physical being (at least where gender is concerned), and can create his or her own unity – choosing and creating a body to fit the mind's identity desire. Yet there is no scientific "evidence that it is possible for a mind to be in the wrong body."[87]

---

80   See George McKenna, *The Odd Couple: Freedom and Liberty*, The Hum. Life Rev., Fall 2021, at 5, 13 (Pew survey showed that teens espoused this view).

81   Orr et al., *supra* note 36, at e14.

82   Boerner, *supra* note 22.

83   Rafferty et al., *supra* note 21, at e6.

84   See Singh et al., *supra* note 18; Boerner, *supra* note 22.

85   Debra Soh, *supra* note 14, at 148.

86   See Rafferty et al., *supra* note 21, at e7 (openly transgender children may be victimized).

87   Edward J. Furton, *Philosophical Puzzles about Transgenderism*, Nat'l Cath. Bioethics Ctr. (July 16, 2021), https://www.ncbcenter.org/messages-from-presidents/puzzles.

One does not affirm a person with body dysmorphic disorder, let alone provide a medical treatment to excise an otherwise healthy limb. Likewise, one neither affirms one who suffers from anorexia nor suggests liposuction to treat the mind-body incongruence.[88] Both conditions are treated as psychological problems. By contrast, one who believes that his or her sex is incongruent with its parallel gender is affirmed in the belief and also ushered on to alter the body to conform to the mental image.

Approving transgendered self-identity embraces a post-modernist view that truth is mere perception and not objective. Those who affirm a transgender identity collude in a falsehood, and moral harm results. Moral harm is not insignificant; it matters.[89] As adults, we should not be perpetrating lies and, with them, attempting to secure freedom from reality.[90] Professing one's gender to be something other than one's biological form is a rebellion against nature's constraints, which "touches on every aspect of what it means to be human."[91] Instead, we should recognize that development, including sexual development, arises from its original form.[92] That is not to say that a child who undergoes a gender identity crisis does not suffer. Some say that if they work with their biological body as gift despite its discordance with their self-gendered perception, their earthly challenge will be met with eternal reward from God.[93]

Affirming an individual child's transgender identity does not just have an effect on that child; the affirmation affects the whole community in which that child interacts. For other children, it can create confusion. They are told that they must accept another child as being of the opposite gender, despite the obvious conflict with what their eyes are telling them.[94] They must accept a new and false understanding of physical reality because they are told to do so by teachers and other adults who stand in positions of trust.

If told that another child whose physical reality is so clear is really another gender, a child might begin to wonder about himself. Is he or she really someone else, too? If the other opposite-gendered child garners positive attention for that opposite-gendered identity, maybe it would be a good thing to do the same, a child might reason. This train of thought sounds rational to a child

---

88   *Id.*
89   McKenna, *supra* note 80, at 10.
90   *See* Reno, *infra* note 101, at 66.
91   *Id.* at 65.
92   Margaret E. Mohrmann, *On Being True to Form, in* Health and Human Flourishing 89, 93 (Carol R. Taylor & Roberto Dell'oro eds., 2006).
93   Yarhouse, *supra* note 6, at 67–73.
94   Fitzgibbons, *supra* note 12, at 337–348.

because a child's prefrontal cortex, because of its immaturity, lacks the capacity to understand complexities or to weigh the consequences of their decisions.

In a way, affirming social transitioning triggers an accommodation by everyone in that child's environment to conform to that child's desire. Many may celebrate the child's transgender identity as being true to self. Others will feel coerced into proclaiming a lie when they are made to identify the child by a pronoun that corresponds to the opposite sex. Although not dealt with in this essay, that sounds like forced speech, which strikes me as unconstitutional – at least when it occurs in the context of public schools.

Creation of in-school affirmative environments for transgendered children educates children to accept perception over reality. Insistence on classroom conformity to the school's gender policy also teaches children something else. When school instruction contradicts parental and religious teachings, it teaches children to doubt the wisdom of authority. If conflict exists with an understanding of something so profoundly basic as the unity of engendered sex, other authoritative pronouncements also may be disregarded. In effect, requiring children to concede to perception over reality invalidates contrary parental instruction and the values that go along with them. This interferes with parents' inherent right to bring up their children in accord with their own religion and values.[95]

Additional accommodation problems exist with respect to sharing multiple occupancy private places such as restrooms and dressing rooms. Children are taught from an early age to be modest – that's why we wear clothing and do not undress in public. But when they are forced to share private spaces with a different-sex child because that child wants to be that sex, it *un*teaches that basic rule on modesty.

Accommodating transgender identities also impacts sports participation, at least where natal females are concerned. Male bodies are known to have competitive athletic advantage over female bodies in many sports because of natural endowments associated with their karyotype. Policies that require natal males who identify as females to be allowed to participate on competitive female athletic teams deconstructs the level playing field that Title IX was said to institutionalize. Thus, prioritizing gender identity over biology appears to be a backward step in the context of female sports.

Affirming social transition tends to result in body alteration. Therefore, it is not neutral with respect to the child. It is also not neutral with respect to the community. Affirmation causes moral harm by approving subjective

---

95   *See* Stephen L. Carter, The Culture of Disbelief 179 (1994).

perception as if it were objective truth. It directly or indirectly teaches what value to place on sex and gender in relation to each another.[96] If that value differs from the parents' whose children must adhere to the school-determined policies, then gender affirmation accommodations usurp parental rights, including values teaching. Finally, gender affirmation impacts privacy and interferes with equitable competition in girls' competitive sports.

2   Clarifying My Observational Standpoint: The Key Value of Rectitude

The New Haven School of Jurisprudence counsels clarifying one's observational standpoint regarding the problem under review. The New Haven method specifies that an order of human dignity, which is the goal of law and measuring-stick of existing law, would allow for maximum access by all to the shaping and sharing of values set forth in those laws. Here, where alteration of a core aspect of humanity is at issue, it is vital to include the value of rectitude as a key aspect in assessing law. People of faith look to God for guidance in shaping their own views and evaluating what constitutes morally correct behavior. My observational standpoint is that of a person of faith.

With respect to the problem at hand, the value of rectitude and thus moral considerations is in rendering healthy body parts unhealthy. It is not the person's desire to alter his or her body that is immoral, but rather acting upon it to violate the integrity of the healthy body through medical alteration.[97] A physician's first rule is to do no harm. Maintaining bodily integrity despite the emotional pain of feeling incongruent to the gender it represents is to submit to God's will, recognizing His dominion over us.[98] The body is a gift from God, and gender is "grounded in the physical reality of the body."[99] Therefore, gender cannot be a mere psychological or social construct.[100]

Altering the body to coincide with a personal notion of sexual self is a visible rebellion against nature and against God as Creator. Therefore, "transgenderism has tremendous metaphysical significance as a symbol of successful

---

96   *See id.* at 204.

97   Yarhouse, *supra* note 6, at 48. See also June Mary Z. Makdisi, *Application of the Principle of Totality and Integrity in American Case Law,* The Nat'l Cath. Bioethics Q. 43, 43, 52 (Spring 2012).

98   Yarhouse, *supra* note 6, at 59.

99   Nicholas Tonti-Filippini, *Sex Reassignment and Catholic Schools,* The Nat'l Cath. Bioethics Q. 85, 94 (Spring 2012).

100   *Id.*

rebellion."[101] Deliberately marring the body denies the integrity of maleness and femaleness and its sacred image.[102] It also challenges the complementarity between male and female, thereby attacking the concept of family.[103]

These moral considerations apply to all forms of gender-affirming care. Social affirmation implicitly fosters an untruth about the body and challenges God as Creator.

3   Legal Trends and Conditioning Factors: Legal Battles Over Child Transgender Issues

In recent months, a number of states have passed legislation to curb childhood gender transitioning. More than one hundred fifty state bills have been introduced in 2022 related to LGBTQ issues. Most deal with limiting child gender transitioning and limiting child athletic competition to biological sex.[104] These state legislative responses to the explosion of transgender-identifying children and the simultaneous demand for accommodation suggests that those states do not consider child gender affirmation and treatment to be in the common good.

3.1   *Conditioning Factors*
The legislative provisions push back against the incursion of modernist cultural views. State policies expressed in legislation include protecting children and safeguarding parental rights to bring up children with parental moral and religious values.[105] Adherents of traditional religions believe that moral standards are established by their Creator, and that objective truth stems from God. Postmodernist culture, by contrast, removes God from the equation in determining what is true or good. They hold that our autonomous selves construct

---

101   R. R. Reno, *Transgenderism: Escaping Limits*, First Things, June-July 2022, at 65, 66.

102   Yarhouse, *supra* note 6, at 46–49.

103   Fitzgibbons, *supra* note 12, at 348–50 (referencing Popes Benedict XVI and Francis).

104   *Florida Isn't the Only State Pushing Legislation that could be Harmful to LGBTQ Students* (CNN March 29, 2022), *available at* https://www.cnn.com/2022/03/10/us/states-anti-lgbtq-legislation-florida/index.html.

105   Matt Lavietes & Elliott Ramos, *Nearly 240 Anti-LGBTQ Bills Filed in 2022 So Far, Most of Them Targeting Trans People*, NBC News (March 20, 2022, 6:00 AM), https://www.nbcnews.com/nbc-out/out-politics-and-policy/nearly-240-anti-lgbtq-bills-filed-2022-far-targeting-trans-people-rcna20418.

our truths. Under this view, we are both sources and masters of truth.[106] Moral judgments, then, are said to be "essentially human and socially conditioned."[107]

These contrasting starting points and methodological reasonings set the basis for conflicting views on whether to embrace transgender identity. A majority of religious adherents tend to view gender as determined by biological sex.[108] Others do not feel the need; only self and culture, and not traditional religious views, are deemed relevant.[109]

Cultural attitude about sex and progeny also drives the cultural acceptance of transgender identity. Increasingly, sex has become disassociated from its natural consequence of reproduction. Instead, sex has become more about love and intimate relationship.[110] Reducing sexual meaning in that way gives rise to a perspective that natal sex is not truly relevant. Sex can be seen as a social construct that need not be adopted. Sex can, instead, be whatever gender one desires.[111]

Adolescents are particularly vulnerable to cultural trends because they are falling away from traditional moral reasoning. In its place, they are adopting a pseudo-religious view with a generalized belief in God who wants us to be good, but who is not much involved in day-to-day life.[112] Life's purpose appears to mostly concern about oneself rather than community, with life's central goal devoted to being happy and feeling good about oneself.[113] Against this backdrop, donning a transgender identity can be embraced as a means of solving problems and feeling better.

Media likely plays a meaningful part in orienting teens to a transgender solution. Media has glamorized famous people who transitioned. For example, Olympic medalist (and Kardashian relative) Bruce Jenner underwent

---

106   William Desmond, *Pluralism, Truthfulness, and the Patience of Being, in* Health and Human Flourishing 53, 54–55, 62 (Carol R. Taylor & Roberto Dell'oro eds., 2006).

107   Jaggi Vasudev, Inner Engineering: A Yogi's Guide to Joy 46 (2016).

108   Michael Lipka & Patricia Tevington, *Attitudes About Transgender Issues Vary Widely Among Christians, Religious 'Nones' in U.S.*, Pew Research Ctr. E2, e3 (July 7, 2022), https://www.pewresearch.org/fact-tank/2022/07/07/attitudes-about-transgender-issues-vary-widely-among-christians-religious-nones-in-u-s/.

109   *See* Liane Jackson, *Aiming at Educators*, ABA J., June-July 2022, 24, 25 (traditional gender values are outdated).

110   Christine E. Gudorf, *Gender and Human Relationality, in* Health and Human Flourishing 185, 196–99 (Carol R. Taylor & Roberto Dell'oro eds., 2006).

111   Yarhouse, *supra* note 6, at 50; Fitzgibbons, *supra* note 12, at 337–350.

112   McKenna, *supra* note 80, at 12.

113   *Id.*

sex-reassignment surgery and became Caitlyn.[114] One teen in particular was made famous for gender transition. Jazz became a prominent transgender child at six years old when interviewed by Barbara Walters in 2007.[115] Jazz continues to be in the public eye in the *I Am Jazz* programs,[116] and has been identified as one of twenty-five most influential teens in America.[117] The internet, too, puts teens in touch with transgender ideas, support, and encouragement for youth transitioning.[118]

A panoply of clinical professional organizations has also embraced the movement, approving childhood gender transitioning under a rubric of "affirmation."[119] The American Academy of Pediatrics (AAP), which produces guidelines for clinicians, has discarded the previously included "gender iden- tity disorder," and replaced it with "gender dysphoria." Significantly, the AAP has decided that it is no longer the *incongruence* that matters, but only the *distress* generated by the discordance. This diagnostic reformation was not accidental.[120] Research on the benefits of gender-affirming care was insufficiently conclusive for there to have been a medically scientific basis for the statement.[121] In fact, based on the inconclusive scientific evidence, and contrary to AAP recommen- dations, "almost all clinics in the world use what's called the watchful waiting approach to helping gender-diverse children."[122] Thus, the reason for the diag- nostic shift was to influence public policy.[123]

---

114   *See, e.g.*, OSSA, *Caitlyn Jenner's Transition: The Most Controversial Moments*, YouTube (Aug. 31, 2018), https://www.youtube.com/watch?v=rjkP4jKyIoo.

115   Alexander Kacala, *'Proud to Be Me': Jazz Jennings Reflects on New Season Detailing 100- Pound Weight Gain*, Today (Nov. 30, 2021), https://www.today.com/health/diet-fitness /-jazz-star-jazz-jennings-talks-100-pound-weight-gain-rcna7017.

116   *I Am Jazz* (TLC network), https://go.tlc.com/show/i-am-jazz-tlc.

117   Shrier, *supra* note 17.

118   *See, e.g.*, It Gets Better Project, https://itgetsbetter.org/blog/resources-for-trans-gnc-and- intersex-youth/ (last visited July 16, 2022) (listing national and state organizations serving trans youth); tyef, http://www.transyouthequality.org/for-youth (last visited July 16, 2022) (stating "trans is cool!" and providing resources for children and teens).

119   Boerner, *supra* note 22.

120   *See* M. Gregg Bloche, *Medicalizing the Constitution?* The New Eng. J. Med. e3 (May 25, 2022), https://www.nejm.org/doi/full/10.1056/NEJMp2201440?query=TOC&cid=NEJM +eToc%2C+May+26%2C+2022+DM1081728_NEJM_Non_Subscriber&bid=994189298.

121   *See supra*, Part 1.

122   Tad Pacholczyk, *Challenging the Establishment on Childhood Gender Transitions*, Nat'l Cath. Bioethics Ctr. e2 (May, 2021) (*Making Sense of Bioethics*), www.ncbcenter.org (quoting James Cantor, Director of the Toronto Sexuality Center).

123   *See* Bloche, *supra* note 120, at e3. Similar attempts by professional organizations to influ- ence public policy can be seen elsewhere. *See, e.g.*, June Mary Zekan Makdisi, *Genetically Correct: The Political Use of Reproductive Terminology*, 32 Pepp. L. Rev. 1 (2004) (changing

In discarding gender incongruence as disordered and adopting a medical-ized definition for its distress, sex and gender became sanctioned as fluid, and distress garnered a treatment consecrated as "medically necessary." Deeming treatment "medically necessary" triggers compliance by practicing clinicians, with a predictable consequence of parents surrendering to professional "med-ical" advice.[124] Many parents succumbed because they were told that without gender-affirming treatment, their child would be likely to commit suicide, even though suicide ideations may have had at least as much to do with the child's other mental health conditions.[125]

By adopting a standard of care deemed "medically necessary," the AAP also empowered others to take advantage of the professional charge. The label opened up the availability of insurance coverage for treatment. It also pro-vided justification for educators to impose a gender-affirming atmosphere in schools. The AAP itself advocated for it by alleging a need for "safe" schools in reference to gender care.[126]

As expected, many schools have adopted policies that accommodate the wishes of children expressing transgender identities. Schools have ready-made curricular guides and training programs gleaned from the internet to develop and maintain a gender-affirming environment.[127] Gender coaches who affirm and advocate for gender transitions are also available, even for elementary school children.[128] Planned Parenthood has also stepped up to provide school programs and teachers, and to provide in-school Wellbeing Centers for high school students. The Centers' purpose is "to create a safe space" in schools to "address the social, emotional, and sexual health needs of young people."[129]

---

terminology to promote doing research on human embryos). *See also* Erin Morrow Hawley, Op-Ed., *Planned Parenthood's Politicized Diagnosis*, Wall St. J., Aug. 2, 2022, at A13. Planned Parenthood has changed some of its abortion narrative on ectopic pregnancy. Also, the American College of Obstetrics and Gynecology (ACOG), in its newly-released *Guide to Language and Abortion*, recommends not using such terms as "unborn child" and "baby," and recommends referring to the milestone fetal heartbeat as "fetal cardiac activ-ity." Such terminology is designed to support abortion by avoiding humanizing unborn children. *Id.*

124   Pacholczyk, *supra* note 122.

125   Soh, *supra* note 14, at 160–61, 165; Shrier, *supra* note 5, at 103.

126   Rafferty et al., *supra* note 21, at e8 e10.

127   *See, e.g.,* The Transgender Training Institute, *Want to Better Understand & Be More Affirming of Trans & Non-Binary People?* https://www.transgendertraininginstitute.com /training-services/; https://www.eventbrite.com/cc/k-12-educators-47179 (online training session) (last visited July 4, 2022); Orr et al., *supra* note 36; GLSEN, *supra* note 36.

128   Fitzgibbons, *supra* note 12 (teaching that gender is a spectrum).

129   Press Release, Planned Parenthood, *Planned Parenthood Los Angeles Announces Land-mark Program Partnership of High School-Based Wellbeing Centers Across L.A. County*

Planned Parenthood already offers puberty blockers and sex-change hormones for sixteen-year-olds at some non-school clinics.[130]

When children exhibit transgender behavior at school, parents don't always know. Parental lawsuits against schools have been reported, claiming that schools are making gender-identity decisions for their children and keeping them in the dark. Vernadette Broyles, a lawyer in a Massachusetts case, explains how it typically happens. First, an adolescent experiencing depression, anxiety, or low self-esteem goes onto the internet and, based on YouTube videos, decides that the root of his or her problem is in identifying with the wrong gender. The child then confides in a trusted teacher or guidance counselor, who affirms the child's self-identified solution. Counseling sessions with the student commence without the parents' knowledge. After that, and again without notice or discussion with parents, teachers and staff are instructed to refer to the child by a new name and associated pronouns.[131] Schools have even begun to install "transition closets" on their premises. Their purpose is to enable students to leave home wearing parent-approved clothing, and then to change before beginning classes.[132] This induced separation of children from parental supervision perpetrates a fraud on parents. It also indirectly teaches children that is acceptable to lie to and distrust parents.

(Dec. 11, 2019), https://www.plannedparenthood.org/about-us/newsroom/ press-releases /planned-parenthood-los-angeles-announces-landmark-program-and-partnership-of -high-school-based-wellbeing-centers-across-l-a-county.

130   See, e.g., Planned Parenthood MarMonte, *Gender Affirming Hormone Therapy*, https://www .plannedparenthood.org/planned-parenthood-mar-monte/patient-resources/gender -affirming-care (last visited July 12, 2022).

131   Matt McDonald, *Parents Say Public Schools Make 'Gender Identity' Decisions for Them*, Nat'l Cath. Reg., June 5, 2022, at 3 (child was eleven years old). Additional lawsuits against middle schools have been reported for gender transition conduct in schools without parental notice. The reported suits were in California ("predatory brainwashing" of girl evidenced by audio recording of general teacher strategy); Florida (secret meetings grooming child for new gender); New Hampshire (using name and pronouns of opposite sex); and Wisconsin (changing girls' names to boys'). Alice Giordano, *Advocates Say Girls Are Main Target of Transgender Movement*, The Epoch Times, April 20–26, 2022, at A1, A3.

132   Steve Warren, CA *Public School Bypasses Parents with 'Transition Closet' for Teens Who Want to Cross-Dress in Class*, CBNNEWS (Feb. 25, 2022), https://www1.cbn.com/cbnnews /us/2022/february/ca-public-school-bypasses-parents-with-transition-closet-for-teens -who-want-to-cross-dress-in-class (California high school); Alice Giordano, *Secret Gender Transition Closets Discovered in Public Schools*, The Epoch Times, April 27-May 3, 2022, at A1, A5 (Colorado middle school).

3.2   *State Legislative Action*

Several states have enacted legislation to safeguard the protection of children, to prevent schools from usurping parental rights, and to defend against school interference with religious freedom. These state interests have congealed into three focused forms of statutory policies: parental rights to bring up their children in matters relating to gender; state interests in protecting children against bodily harm; and maintaining Title IX fairness in interscholastic female sports.

3.3   *Florida*

On March 28, 2022, Florida's governor signed the Parental Rights in Education Bill which reinforced the fundamental parental right to make decisions over child upbringing. The provisions require notifying parents of changes in services or monitoring of the student's health or well-being, unless disclosure would result in abuse, abandonment or neglect.[133] Sexual orientation or gender identity instruction is prohibited for children in *kindergarten through third grade*, otherwise, it must be age and developmentally appropriate.[134] Significantly, the statute has teeth insofar as it gives parents a right of action against schools.[135]

The legislative provisions appear modest. Schools must notify parents if their children exhibit gender-change behaviors, but have an exception for anticipating extreme parental reactions of abuse, abandonment, or neglect. Gender identity instruction is not prohibited. It is precluded only for very young children. One has to wonder why anyone would find these provisions objectionable or why it would be important for school teachers to broach subjects related to sexuality with children who have not yet reached a double-digit age. Young children are unable to functionally process the sex instruction. Their immature prefrontal cortexes disable them from consequential thinking, and their age and dependence on adults makes them naturally susceptible to influences from the quasi-parental authority of school teachers.

Nevertheless, the law was widely criticized, identified as the "Don't Say Gay" bill. Perhaps criticism was primarily directed toward two provisions of the Parental Rights in Education Act that impede unrestricted promotion of progressive views on gender and other nontraditional ideas about sexuality. The Act provides that before administering any health screenings or well-being questionnaires to children in grades kindergarten through third grade, the school district must both provide parents with the questionnaire or screening

---

133   Fla. Stat. § 1001.42(8)(c)1 & 2 (2022).

134   *Id.* § 1001.42(8)(c)3 (emphasis by author).

135   *Id.* § 1001.42(8)(c)7.

form and obtain parental permission to proceed with either.[136] In addition, at the beginning of the school year, school districts must notify parents of health care services offered at their children's schools, and parents may decline specific services.[137]

The former provision prevents the planting of ideas into children's heads guised as seemingly neutral questionnaires and health screenings. It is likely that gender questions would be part of the screenings because of AAP guidance. The AAP encourages gender screening as part of health maintenance, urging primary care physicians to "*routinely* inquire about gender development in children and adolescents."[138] Questionnaires also have an opportunity to introduce subject matter about gender that parents may consider too adult for their children. Parents might also find that the concepts presented contradict their religious beliefs and interfere with their parental rights in child upbringing. Without this legislative protection, questionnaires (surveys) and health screenings (interviews) would likely be exempt from parental oversight.[139] Therefore, the law appropriately safeguards parental rights, and its enactment removes the opportunity for invisible gender indoctrination of children in kindergarten through third grade.

The Act gives parents an opportunity to opt out of whatever health care services they find objectionable. It also safeguards parental rights to determine the wellbeing of their children. It is not the AIDS and pregnancy testing that is forbidden, nor the provision of birth control. The statute does not require that parents be informed when their children make use of such services. It only ensures that parents either consent or withhold consent for particular services at the beginning of each year, and that they have access to the services actually provided to their children – if they want that information.[140]

The uproar about the legislation might be because promotors would like to separate children from parental oversight when it comes to gender and sexual behavior. Some consider traditional values that are taught at home to be "indoctrination" and "outdated."[141] Educators certainly have the right to consider parental instruction on morals "outdated." It does not, however, give them the right to usurp parental prerogatives and substitute their own moral values for those of the parents. Without the statutory protections, children

---

136   *Id.* § 1001.42(8)(c)6.

137   *Id.* § 1001.42(8)(c)5.

138   Rafferty et al., *supra* note 21, at e5 (emphasis by author).

139   *See* 45 C.F.R. § 46.101(b)(2) (2009).

140   *See* Fla. Stat. § 1001.42(8)(c)1 (2022) (parental right of access to health records maintained by the school).

141   Jackson, *supra* note 109, at 25.

could be counseled on gender transitioning and groomed for hormonal treatment without any input from parents. The statute does not appear to prevent such counseling; it only requires that parents first grant permission.

3.4   *Other States*

Tennessee and Alabama have recently enacted gender education laws. Tennessee grants parents an opportunity to examine the gender identity curriculum and opt out. Similar to Florida's law, the gender identity curriculum includes materials, instruction, and questionnaires.[142] Alabama only requires that any instruction concerning gender identity be appropriate for age and development in kindergarten through fifth grade. Tacked to the law is a bathroom provision: "[M]ultiple occupancy restrooms or changing areas" must be used only in accord with natal sex.[143]

The Texas Family Code protects children from abuse in the form of physical injury and mental or emotional injury that results in material impairment in the child's development or psychological functioning.[144] In February, 2022, the Texas Attorney General issued an opinion letter in response to the Chair of the House Committee on General Investigating. The Chair wanted to know whether it constituted statutory child abuse when gender reassignment surgeries were performed, or when puberty blockers or cross-sex hormones were administered to children who did not have medically verifiable sex disorders. The reason for the request was to determine whether an investigation should be initiated when such conduct occurred.[145]

The Texas A.G. opined that participating in these procedures constituted statutory abuse. He noted that permanent infertility resulted from some of the procedures, which violates a child's fundamental right to procreate.[146] Other procedures can cause serious physical and mental health harms. The opinion acknowledged a lack of scientific consensus on benefits, and that medical evidence also does not demonstrate benefits from the procedures. In addition, the opinion noted that there is no evidence of improved long-term mental

---

142   Tenn. Code Ann. § 49-6-1308 (2021).

143   H.B. 322, Reg. Sess. (Ala. 2022) (enrolled) (signed by governor Apr. 7, 2022). https://openstates
       .org/ al/bills/2022rs/HB322/.

144   Tex. Fam. Code Ann. § 261.001(1) (2021).

145   Whether certain medical procedures performed on children constitute child abuse, Op.
       Att'y Gen. KP-0401 (2022), *available at* https://www.texasattorneygeneral.gov/opinions
       /ken-paxton/kp-0401 [hereinafter A.G. Opinion].

146   *Id.* at 3, 5–6.

health benefits from the hormonal or surgical procedures.[147] With medical or scientific uncertainty, states have wide discretion to legislate.[148]

A recognition that states have broad legislative powers when there is scientific uncertainty may explain why positive transgender outcomes are overstated and why negative transgender outcomes are suppressed.[149] Only with medical and scientific certainty can transgender proponents successfully argue for the illegality of state legislation concerning the health and wellbeing of state citizens.

In support of state statutory power to enact the legislation, the Texas A.G. made reference to *Bellotti v. Baird*.[150] Quoting from the opinion, he noted that "due to 'the peculiar vulnerability of children,'" the state's power is "at its zenith when it comes to protecting children" because, unlike adults, children cannot weigh the long-term consequences "to make critical decisions in an informed, mature manner."[151] The state has a *parens patriae* interest in safeguarding the welfare of children independent from that of their parents.[152]

Alabama also enacted legislation against medical and surgical sex-change interventions performed on children without specified sex disorders, making violation a felony.[153] In addition, the Alabama statute prohibits nurses, teachers, counselors, and other administrative personnel in any school from withholding a child's perceived gender incongruency from his or her parents or guardians, and prohibits them from encouraging or coercing a minor to do so.[154] Similar to Texas, Alabama's statutory policy is meant to protect children from harm. Similar to Florida, Alabama's statutory policy safeguards parental rights.

Legislative reasoning for the Alabama statute resembles that of Florida. It recognized that some children self-report a feeling of discordance between their sex and identity. It further explained that although its cause is unknown, it usually resolves by late adolescence. Nevertheless, some medical professionals push for medical alterations beginning with chemical treatments that are not FDA approved for the condition. The interventions prevent the child from experiencing the process of sexual development and produce side effects that are known to be harmful. Unknown is the effect on cognitive development.

---

147   *Id.* at 3–4.
148   *Id.* at 4, citing *Gonzales v. Carhart*, 550 U.S. 124, 163 (2007).
149   *See* Clayton, *supra* note 50, at e1.
150   Bellotti v. Baird, 443 U.S. 622 (1979).
151   A.G. Opinion, *supra* note 145 (quoting *Bellotti*, 443 U.S. at 634 (1979)).
152   *Id.*
153   2022 Ala. Acts 2022–289 § 4, *available at* https://arc-sos.state.al.us/cgi/actdetail.mbr /detail?year=2022&act =%20289&page=bill (formerly Ala. S.B. 184).
154   *Id.* § 5.

Expected risk of taking cross-sex hormones is permanent sterility; unknown is the long-term risks of taking puberty blockers. Several studies have shown that medical interventions do not resolve the underlying psychological problems. Minors, and often their parents, are unable to fully understand and appreciate the risks and life-long difficulties resultant from the intervention. Therefore, medical and surgical interventions should not be presented to, or determined for, minors to address their sex and identity discordance. The result of a wait-and-see approach is that a large majority of children with signs of gender non-conformity will resolve to gender conformity by late adolescence.[155]

Arkansas, like Alabama, has statutory provisions prohibiting medical and surgical gender transition procedures, absent verifiable sex disorder, and provides for a private right of action for violation, as well as an A.G. enforcement action. It specifies that the statute applies to medical intervention as well as referrals for minors under the age of eighteen, adding that provision or referral would subject the violator to disciplinary action for unprofessional conduct.[156] An additional statutory distinction is that no public funds, even indirectly, may be "used, granted, paid, or distributed to any entity, organization, or individual that provides gender transition procedures to an individual under eighteen (18) years of age."[157]

On March 2, 2022, Iowa's governor signed legislation that banned students who were defined as males at birth, or shortly thereafter, from participating in female sports.[158] It applies to all accredited educational institutions, including universities who are members of national athletic associations. It says nothing about natal males, but ensures a level playing field for natal females. Only natal females may participate in interscholastic female sports.[159] Like the teeth in Florida's law, a private right of action is granted for violations. It adds a private right of action for retaliation, but also provides a number of protections for educational institutions.[160]

The Utah legislature also successfully enacted sports legislation, overriding the governor's veto.[161] Incorporating Title ix's promotion of fairness for female athletes, the statute provided that persons who are genetically and

---

155 *Id.* § 2.

156 Ar. Code Ann. §§ 20-9-1501(6), 20-9-1502, 20-9-1504 (2021).

157 *Id.* § 20-9-1503.

158 HF2416_GovLetter.pdf (providing governor's letter and approved Bill). The new statute, appended to the governor's letter, is codified as Ala. Code § 261I.1 and § 261I.2 (2022). *Id.*

159 Ala. Code § 261I.2(1) (2022).

160 *Id.* § 261I.2(2–5).

161 Press Release, Utah Senate, Legislature Overrides Veto on H.B. 11 (Mar. 25, 2022), *available at* https://senate.utah.gov/legislature-overrides-veto-on-h-b-11/.

anatomically male at birth may not compete in interscholastic female sports.[162] In the event that a final court ruling invalidated the provisions, Utah also enacted an alternate measure.[163] The alternate statutory measures provided for gender-designated participation. If a student fell within an evidence-based, baseline range of physical characteristics established by a commission, whose members included medical professionals, that child would be approved to compete in accord with their gender identity.[164] Competitive gender-identified sports eligibility did not necessarily extend to use of gender-preferred facilities such as bathrooms and showers. Schools and athletic associations could adopt reasonable rules and policies for the safety and privacy of students as long as reasonable accommodations were also granted to transgender-identifying students.[165]

Three states overrode governors' vetoes in enacting female sports legislation. Kentucky passed legislation providing that sixth through twelfth grade boys could not participate in girls' sports and specified that sex was determined at birth.[166] North Dakota's ban on natal male membership on female sports teams included all public elementary and secondary schools.[167] Indiana's statute is similar to Utah's, but restricts natal males from participation on female teams, and not just in competitions. Like Iowa's sports statute, it offers a private right of action, retaliation protection, and educational institution protections. However, Utah adds a grievance procedure and limits damages.[168]

A number of Bills in these and other states are percolating in legislatures.[169] Several states have provisions relating to gender identity issues at schools. Some bill proposals would prohibit gender identity instruction.[170] Some would

---

162   Utah Code Ann. §§ 53G-6-901(3) & 53G-6-902(1)(b) (2022).

163   Id. § 53G-6-1002.

164   Id. §§ 53G-6-1003 & 1004.

165   Id. § 53G-6-1005.

166   Ky. Rev. Stat. Ann. § 156.070(2)(g) (2022), available at https://apps.legislature.ky.gov /record/22rs/hb23.html. The statute was vetoed by the governor on April 6, 2022 and overridden in both chambers on April 13, 2022. Id.

167   N.D. Cent. Code §14-02.4 (2022) (enacted, overriding governor veto). https://www.ndlegis .gov/assembly/67-2021/bill-actions/ba1298.html.

168   Ind. Code § 20-33-13 (2022).

169   ERLC, Explainer: States Propose Bills Related to Parental Rights, Gender Identity, and Sexuality (May 13, 2022), https://erlc.com/resource-library/articles/explainer-states-propose -bills-related-to-parental-rights-gender-identity-and-sexuality/.

170   E.g., H.B. 616, 134th Gen. Assemb., Reg. Sess. (Ohio 2022) (in Comm.) (not in grades K-3; O.K. if age-appropriate in grades 4 – 12); H.B. 7539, Jan. Sess., Gen. Assemb., Reg. Sess. (R.I. 2022) (in Comm.) (no gender identity instruction in sex ed); H.B. 4605, 124th Gen. Assemb., 2021–22 Sess. (S.C. 2021) (none under age eighteen) (dead).

grant parents a right to inspect documents such as questionnaires and opt out.[171] Some proposed legislation would not permit mandatory gender diversity training.[172] Other proposed legislation refers to name and pronoun use.[173] A number of bill proposals restrict medical gender transitioning on children.[174] A number of states already ban male participation in female sports, and several states have proposed such legislation.[175]

3.5   *Federal Action*

The President signed an Executive Order on June 15, 2022, which specifically asserts that the Order is meant to target "harmful and discriminatory" state legislation. The Order gives directives to the Secretaries of Health and Human Services and the Department of Education on how to deal with states and to encourage state adoption of the policies generated by the Departments, pursuant to the Order.[176]

The HHS Secretary was charged with developing and sending sample policies to states on expanding access to "medically necessary" gender identity care, and to working with the states in implementing the expansion of gender-affirming care.[177] To ensure that services would not utilize a wait-and-see methodology, the HHS Secretary was to establish an initiative that would discourage professional use of "so-called conversion therapy" on youth. To facilitate, the Secretary was to "consider whether to issue guidance clarifying for HHS programs and services agencies that so-called conversion therapy

---

171   *E.g.*, H.B. 2011, 55th Leg., 2nd Reg. Sess. (Ariz. 2022) (no action); S.B. 1654, 58th Leg., 2nd Reg. Sess. (Okla. 2022) (dead); Assemb. B. 963, 2021–22 Leg. (Wis. 2022) (vetoed by governor on Apr. 15, 2022), https://docs.legis.wisconsin.gov/ 2021/proposals/ab963.

172   *E.g.*, H.B. 4343, 124th Gen. Assemb. (S.C. 2022) (dead).

173   *E.g.*, H.B. 7539, Reg. Sess. (R.I. 2022) (in Comm.) (parental right to determine names and pronouns); H.B. 4605, 124th Gen. Assemb., (S.C. 2021) (dead) (no coerced use of pronouns); A.B. 963, (Wis. 2021) (gov. veto) (parental right to determine names and pronouns).

174   *E.g.*, S.B. 514, 2021–22 Sess. (N.C. 2021) (no gender medical treatments below age twenty-one; parent notification of social transitioning); S.B. 442, 101st Gen. Assemb., Reg. Sess. (Mo. 2021) (died in committee) (no gender reassignment treatment below age eighteen); H.B. 427, 67th Leg., Reg. Sess. (Mont. 2021) (failed) (no gender medical treatment for minors).

175   Katie Barnes, *Alabama to Wyoming: State Policies on Transgender Athlete Participation*, ESPN, June 7, 2022, https://www.espn.com/espn/story/_/id/ 32117426/state-policies-transgender-athlete-participation (for all 50 States, identifies gender-identity sports participation and whether rules found in statute, bill proposal, or school/athletic association).

176   Exec. Order No. 14,075, 87 Fed. Reg. 37,189 (June 21, 2022).

177   *Id.* at §§ 2(a) & 7(b).

does not meet criteria for use in federally funded health and human services programs."[178]

The Order seeks to have all states implement the AAP recommendation of ensuring medical therapy when children say they want to physically transition, and, until then, promoting gender-affirming therapy for transgender-identifying children in schools. By utilizing the "medically necessary" language set forth in the AAP, the Order removes the need to consider whether the therapies it proposes are actually medically necessary. Given that medical necessity is still being debated,[179] use of the term must be less about healthcare and more about politics. It is likely that the HHS will try to put pressure on states to adopt its sample policies, perhaps by means of regulation and financial incentives that would encourage states to devise pro-care statutes and structure a Medicaid platform for Order-suggested care.

The Order's reference to conversion therapy can be seen as an attempt to intimidate or otherwise discourage professional therapists from utilizing a neutral wait-and-see therapy for children who exhibit signs of gender nonconformity. First, the Order identifies actual conversion therapy as "discredited."[180] But the regulations that HHS is to "consider" devising are not limited to preventing actual conversion therapy. Instead, the HHS is to consider finding that "so-called" conversion therapy would not meet the criteria for federally funded programs.

The addition of the qualifying term "so-called" is significant. A therapeutic approach that does not immediately affirm a child's self-described transgender identity frequently has been conflated with conversion therapy, which many have thought to be coercive in its use in the homosexual context. The implication is that neutral, non-affirming gender therapy for children works the same way as non-neutral conversion therapy. By attempting the comparison, the executive order's choice of terms also guides readers to think that a transgender identity is inborn, the way that many consider homosexual orientation to be. The irony is that the whole concept behind transgender identity

---

178   *Id.* at §3(a)(i).

179   *See* James McTavish & Tadeusz Pacholczyk, *Clarifying Key Issues around Conversion Therapy*, 21 The Nat'l Catholic Bioethics Q. 571, 575 (2021). The American College of Pediatricians determined that "[c]urrently, there is no conclusive medical evidence that children who experience gender incongruence receive long-term benefits from medical and surgical interventions associated with 'gender transition.'" *Id.* (quoting the American College of Pediatricians). See also *supra* Part 1.

180   Exec. Order No. 14,075, 87 Fed. Reg. 37,189 at §1. This is a clear effort to remind everyone that conversion therapy had previously been used by therapists to change a patient's homosexual orientation. *See* Soh, *supra* note 14, at 154.

and sex/gender fluidity is that it is *not* inborn. A further irony is that by unquestioningly affirming, affirmative care therapy itself may be considered a type of conversion therapy insofar as it endorses and thereby encourages a child to change his or her inborn nature.[181]

If there were no threat to a professional's independent judgement, many therapists would apply a standard therapeutic approach, treating the patient holistically and exploring not only the symptoms presented, but also underlying issues.[182] But, by using the "so-called" qualifier, the Order makes clear that holistic psychotherapy would not garner Medicaid reimbursement, or federal funding under any other health services program. This is sad since there are "increasing numbers of detransitioners ... who regret not having received exploratory psychotherapy to help them understand their distress ... before they underwent irreversible medical and surgical treatments. Equally concerning, a number report that when doubts about their own transgender status arose, their therapists continued to affirm them as transgender."[183] A double standard seems to exist. A neutral, questioning, wait-and-see approach that explores reasons for gender incongruence is disqualified as so-called conversion therapy. At the same time, a gender-affirming approach is approved even though the consequences of its application generally cement a child's conversion to another gender.[184]

In the same executive order, the Secretary of Education was charged with establishing a Working Group "to support LGBTQI+ at schools" and, through it, to develop and send sample policies to states. The expressed content of the policies was "to promote safe and inclusive learning environments in which all LGBTQI+ students thrive."[185] In addition, school-based health services, including mental health services, were to be supportive of transgender-identifying students.[186]

The sample policies directly address state legislation that places the power of pronoun identifiers and name choice in the hands of parents. The effect of the Department of Education regulations generated by the Order would be to remove that choice from the parents and put it squarely in the hands of a child, who can in turn make name and pronoun demands on others. The Order also facilitates organizations like Planned Parenthood, which offers off-campus

---

181   *See* Soh, *supra* note 14, at 155. *See also* Angelo, *supra* note 47, at 12, and McTavish & Pacholczyk, *supra* note 179, at 577.

182   Schanzenbach, *supra* note 65.

183   Angelo et al., *supra* note 47, at 13. *See also* Heyer, *supra* note 72, at 45, 107–27.

184   McTavish & Pacholczyk, *supra* note 179, at 577.

185   Exec. Order No. 14,075, 87 Fed. Reg. 37,189 at § 8(a).

186   *Id.* at §§ 2(b) & 8(b).

medical transition care, to have a presence on school campuses. These school-based, gender-affirming health services could easily incorporate the very questionnaires and interviews that some states seek to disallow because of their gender-orienting inquiries.

States will also feel constraints from federal agency actions generated by the two executive orders that the President issued in 2021 with respect to trans adults and trans-identifying children. The January, 2021 Order expressed a policy that it was sex discrimination to prevent transgender-identifying children from using their gender-preferred private spaces, such as restrooms, and to prevent them from participating in sports consistent with their self-identified gender. The Order's policy asserted that the stated principles found support in the Equal Protection Clause and in *Bostock v. Clayton*, which found gender identity to be included within Title VII's purview of "sex" in the context of employment discrimination. All agency heads were directed to implement the January, 2021 policy and to assure that all existing federal regulations and other documents did not conflict with the Order.[187] The March, 2021 Order expressed a policy that Title IX's prohibition against sex discrimination in educational programs and activities, and charges of sexual harassment, were to apply to transgender-identifying children. The Order directed the Secretary of Education to review all regulations and documents and to adjust them to be consistent with the Order. The Secretary was to issue new guidance, specifically with respect to Title IX, and to incorporate sexual harassment as a sex discrimination enforcement mechanism.[188]

Both 2021 executive orders have the same purpose: to ensure that gender-identification is treated as if it were the same as biological sex. Enforcement is achieved through sex discrimination charges, thereby effectively penalizing contradictors who may be subject to federal regulation. While the January order was directed to all agencies, who were to certify that sports participation and use of shared private space such as restrooms would accord with self-identified gender, the March order had an additional purpose. It gave the Education Department the power to weaponize Title IX as a means of normalizing the "gender equals sex" value. It did so by directing that sexual harassment complaints fell within the purview of Title IX, and that complaints about not being treated according to self-identified gender constituted sex discrimination. The Order's long-term effect, if successful, would be to have youth

---

187 Exec. Order No. 13,988, 86 Fed. Reg. 7,023 (Jan.20, 2021) (citing Bostock v. Clayton, 140 S. Ct. 1731, 590 U.S. __ (2020)).

188 Exec. Order No. 14,021, 86 Fed. Reg. 13,803 (Mar. 8, 2021).

believe that gender is the same as sex, and then to pass this new-found value on to the next generation.

The 2021 Orders' directives instigated swift agency action. In June, 2021, the Department of Education issued a Notice of Interpretation. In it, the Notice incorporated the January order's policy to utilize *Bostock* to conclude that discrimination on the basis of sex would encompass gender identity under Title IX. It also listed several federal cases to support its position that children should be treated in accordance with their self-identified gender.[189]

Then, in January, 2022, the Department of Education issued a proposed rule interpreting Title IX to include complaints by transgender-identifying students within its anti sex-based discrimination and sexual harassment protections. The Department also promised a separate rule proposal to further address Title IX's application to athletics.[190]

Legal commentators have concluded that the Department's interpretive rule proposal does not accord with Title IX's enacted purpose. Moreover, the proposed rule's redefinition of "sex" to include "gender identity" would require every educational institution that receives federal money to allow biological men to enter into women's locker rooms and other female-only spaces, seemingly contrary to the original legislative intent.[191] The agency itself, in interpreting the statute, had specified that institutions could offer separate restrooms, locker rooms, and other such facilities: "A recipient [of federal funds] may provide separate toilet, locker room, and shower facilities on the basis of sex, but such facilities provided for students of one sex shall be comparable to such facilities provided for students of the other sex."[192] This rule would make no sense unless it were recognized that there is a need to treat sexes, with different biological features, differently. The commentators also observe that Title IX never mentions sexual harassment, and that the proposed

---

189   Exec. Order No. 14,021, 86 Fed. Reg. 13,803 (Mar. 8, 2021). U.S. Department of Education *Confirms Title IX Protects Students from Discrimination Based on Sexual Orientation and Gender Identity* (June 16, 2021), *available at* https://www.ed.gov/news/press-releases/us -department-education-confirms-title-ix-protects-students-discrimination-based-sexual -orientation-and-gender-identity. See, *e.g.*, Grimm v. Gloucester Cnty, Sch. Bd., 972 F.3d 586 (4th Cir. 2020)(first case on the list).

190   *See* Press Release, U.S. Dep't Educ., *The U.S. Department of Education Releases Proposed Changes to Title IX Regulations, Invites Public Comment (June 23, 2022), available at* https:// www.ed.gov/news/press-releases/us-department-education-releases-proposed-changes -title-ix-regulations-invites-public-comment.

191   *See, e.g.*, Jennifer C. Braceras & Inez Feltscher Stepman, Op-Ed,. *Biden's Title IX Rewrite Is an Assault on Women's Rights*, Wall St. J., June 2, 2022, at A17.

192   34 C.F.R. § 106.33 (2022).

rule expanding sexual harassment to include speech would compel students, teachers, and others to use only child-directed names and pronouns.[193]

The HHS also proposed a rule in January, 2022. It interpreted the Patient Protection and Affordable Care Act (ACA) to require coverage of medical transitioning. Since the HHS classified gender transition as medically necessary, denying the service would be considered presumptively discriminatory.[194] During the notice and comment period, a number of Christian organizations issued a joint letter to HHS, objecting to the proposed rule. They asserted that the rule did not make any allowance for a health care professional's judgment as to whether the intervention was medically necessary for an individual patient. In support of its individualized care position, they cited a number of large-scale studies that challenged the HHS perspective that medical transition was medically necessary. The letter also pointed out that the proposed rule suffered from the same litigated religious liberty infirmity that courts found present in the original Act.[195]

In accord with HHS's proposed rule, the Department of Justice issued a warning letter to all State Attorneys General in March, 2022. It gave notice that a failure to provide "medically necessary" gender-affirming treatment to minors would subject states to penalties for violating the ACA, Title IX, and other laws.[196]

Simultaneous with executive action, Congress drafted the Equality Act to include gender identity within the rubric of sex in previously enacted statutes.[197] The legislation implies that it would be discriminatory to deny medical gender

---

193 Braceras & Stepman, *supra* note 191. A Wisconsin school district has already launched a Title IX investigation against three middle school boys for "mispronouncing" because they referred to a classmate who wants to be identified as "them" as "her." The school district concluded that it was a punishable sexual harassment offense even when the reference is not directed to the student. Rick Esenberg, Op-Ed., *The Pronoun Police Come for Middle Schoolers*, Wall St. J., May 24, 2022, at A17.

194 HHS Notice of Benefits and Payment Parameters for 2023, 87 Fed. Reg. 584 (proposed Jan. 5, 2022) (to be codified at 45 C.F.R. pts. 144, 147, 153, 155, 156 & 158).

195 Letter from Thomas Brejcha, Thomas More Soc'y; David Nammo, Christian Legal Soc'y; Anthony R. Picarello, Jr., Michael F. Moses, & Daniel E. Balserak, U.S. Conf. Cath. Bishops; Ellen Gianoli, Nat'l Assoc. Cath. Nurses; Galen Carey, Nat'l Assoc. Evangelicals; & Joseph Meaney, Nat'l Cath. Bioethics Ctr., to Ctrs. for Medicare & Medicaid Serv., Dept. Health & Human Serv. (Jan. 26, 2022), *available at* chrome-extension://efaidnbmnn-nibpcajpcglclefindmkaj/https://www.usccb.org/about/general-counsel/rulemaking/upload/1.26.2022.proposed.rule_.hhs_.health.plans_.pdf.

196 Letter from Kristen Clarke, Assistant Att'y Gen., Civ. Rts. Div., U.S. Dep't Just. (Mar. 31, 2022), *available at* https://www.justice.gov/opa/pr/justice-department-reinforces-federal-nondiscrimination-obligations-letter-state-officials.

197 Equality Act, H.R. 5, 117th Cong. (1st Sess. 2021).

transition to those who sought it.[198] It also implies that professionals could not effectively protect children from unneeded medical transitions because, similar to executive statements, the Act labels conversion therapy as discrimination.[199] Its policies would have broad application because it would apply to individuals as well as to health care institutions. In addition, it specifically excludes faith-based exceptions.[200] The Equality Act would also ensconce its gender-equals-sex values within public education: It seeks to enable eligibility for participation in single-sex sports and other activities to hinge solely on gender identity, and it would require single-sex restrooms, dressing rooms, and other multiple occupancy facilities to be available to those who self-identified as that gender, regardless of their physical sex.[201]

The state and federal actions discussed in this section are in obvious and direct conflict with each another. The next section will explore how some of the conflicts may resolve.

4   Projecting Future Trends in Decision

State legislation is grouped around a few main issues. Some state policies safeguard children from bodily harm caused by medical transitioning interventions. Others focus on preventing the usurpation of parental rights in child upbringing. Still others seek to safeguard competitive opportunities for female athletes, as originally envisioned in Title IX.

Federal actions focus on these same issues, but employ a discrimination narrative to thwart state efforts. Under the federal approach, requiring children to wait until their prefrontal cortexes mature before making potentially irreversible changes to their anatomy and physiology would be unlawful discrimination. Requiring children to compete in accord with their sex on single-sex teams, or to use shared bathrooms in accord with their anatomical sex would be unlawful discrimination, when a child proclaims to be of a different gender. Using parent-designated names and sex-corresponding pronouns would be unlawful discrimination, if contrary to the child's preference. On-campus health services would be allowed to perform mental health

---

198   *Id.* § 2(a). *See also* Wesley J. Smith, Op-Ed., *Biden Administration Policies Push Puberty Blocking, Transition Surgeries for Transgender Children,* The Epoch Times, Apr. 13–19, 2022, at A17.

199   H.R. 5 § 2(a)(7).

200   *Id.* §§ 3(a)(4), 3(b), & 9(b).

201   *Id.* §§ 2 (a)(10), 5 & 9(b)(2).

services, but permitting clinicians to make individualized choices on whether to apply gender-affirming therapy would be unlawful discrimination. Not discriminatory would be to maintain gender-affirming care on school campuses to facilitate transition while also keeping parental influence at arm's length.

The federal gender-identity discrimination policies seem off kilter and not in accord with historical application. Previously, unlawful discrimination laws championed equal opportunities for Blacks and biological females. Those laws protected persons from being disqualified purely on the basis of immutable traits having nothing to do with the substance of the foregone opportunities. Unlike race and sex characteristics, however, gender identity is not immutable. Therefore, in order to take strategic advantage of discrimination laws that would disable states from formulating their own health and wellbeing gender policies, gender had to fall within the rubric of sex. Subsuming gender identity within the definition of sex blurs the immutability distinction and allows the anti-discrimination framework to slide into place. Whether the federal strategy succeeds may depend upon how *West Virginia v. Environmental Protection Agency*[202] affects treatment of agency interpretations.

In the past, *Chevron* deference gave agencies a wide berth to interpret federal statutes.[203] If deference continues, then federal policies will have a good chance of thwarting contrary state policies to the extent that the states receive federal funds in those contexts. Continued deference, however has been called to doubt by the recent Supreme Court decision in *West Virginia v. Environmental Protection Agency*. In that case, the Supreme Court held that the agency had overstepped its authority to devise regulations that fundamentally revised the statute.[204]

With respect to Title IX, sex discrimination in "any education program or activity" receiving federal funding is unlawful.[205] To clarify, Title IX provides exceptions to demonstrate what sorts of discrimination would not be unlawful. It specifically allows institutions to "maintain separate living facilities for the different sexes."[206] It also specifically recognizes that maintaining single-sex sororities, youth organizations and conferences is not unlawful discrimination.[207] The statute itself recognizes that sex differences matter. Agency interpretation codified the material distinction when its regulation

---

202   West Va. v. Environmental Prot. Agency, No. 20-1530 (U.S. June 30, 2022).

203   *See* Chevron v. Natural Res. Def. Council, 467 U.S. 837 (1984).

204   *West Va. v. Environmental Prot. Agency*, No. 20-1530 at e5.

205   20 U.S.C. § 1681(a) (2019).

206   § 1686.

207   §§ 1681(a)(6) & (7).

allowed federally supported institutions to have separate toilets, locker rooms, and shower facilities for males and females.[208] Therefore, current agency rule-making attempts to encompass gender identity within the framework of Title IX sex-discrimination at educational institutes appears to be a seismic shift that cannot be explained on the basis of Congressional intent. Since proposed interpretive rules appear to fundamentally revise the statute, it would seem that the reasoning in *West Virginia v. Environmental Protection Agency* could successfully challenge the agency actions.

West Virginia v. Environmental Protection Agency also might be applied to limit agency proposals that require all clinicians to treat transgender-identifying children with the one-size-fits-all gender-affirming care. The agencies look like they are using what scientists say rather than what scientists prove to support their policy. Moreover, they are treating a moral question about gender transitioning as if it were nothing more than a medical issue.[209] The U.S. case also might be used to successfully challenge agency interpretation rules that would force states to cover medical transitioning for children. It seems beyond agency authority to require state programs to cover medical treatments pursuant to the ACA that the FDA has not approved for child transitioning.

The proposed Equality Act, which mirrors executive branch policies, may not become law. If it does, it suffers from several infirmities and may not survive a challenge, at least as applied to children. It is difficult to imagine that there would be no faith-based exception for a clinician who would consider it immoral to potentially sterilize a child with non-FDA approved treatments – especially when that child has not been given a chance to undergo the non-invasive traditional therapy that could render more drastic medical measures unnecessary. It is also difficult to imagine that a federal Act could disable parents from supervising the moral education of their children with respect to transgender and other sexual issues. Parents already have sex ed opt out rights in many states, including California.[210]

If federal action fails, states would be free to legislate for the health and well-being of their respective state populations.[211] Some states would enact

---

208   34 C.F.R. § 106.33 (1980).

209   *See* Bloche, *supra* note 120.

210   *See* Michelle Ball, *Sex Education and Parents Right to Opt Out*, Law Office Michelle Ball (Apr. 14, 2021), https://edlaw4students.com/sex-ed-opt-out/ (California education attorney).

211   *See* Dobbs v. Jackson Women's Health Org., 597 U.S. __, 6, 142 S.Ct. 2228 (2022) (moral issue of abortion returned to the states). *See also* June Mary Zekan Makdisi, *The Affordable Care Act: Does It Improve Health and Does It Live Up to Human Rights Standards*, 10 Intercultural Hum. Rts. L. Rev. 117, 121 (2015).

policies consistent with those discussed in this essay while other states would not. California and other states are currently pursuing legislative action to enable out-of-state children to have medicalized gender care in their states while also avoiding arrest and extradition orders from the children's home states.[212]

5   Appraisal

When a child is distressed over perceived incongruity between sex and gender, that child should be treated with compassion and affirmed in his or her human dignity. Administered care should be holistic, in recognition that the psychological disturbance may not be stemming uniquely from the child's sense of gender incongruity, and also in recognition that gender incongruities usually resolve on their own. Therapists should model neutral listening, not mindless affirmation of a child's self-diagnosis, especially since affirming social change almost always leads to body alteration. Even though there is a small percentage of children who will remain gender dysphoric when gender-affirming care is not applied, there is no way to predict which child will persist into adulthood.[213] Therefore, it seems inconsistent with community flourishing to have all children set on a path toward gender transitioning just because some children will persist in their gender incongruency.

Children do not have the reflective capacities of adults. Therefore, we have many laws that restrict their rights. Children may not become licensed drivers until they are sixteen. Children are not granted a right to vote. Children are under the authority of their parents, guardians, teachers, and the state. Children may not drink or gamble, or see certain movies because the content is deemed not in their best interests to see. In general, children may not consent to non-emergency medical care.

We have all sorts of protections for children because we know that they are unable to properly evaluate and to self-protect in many circumstances. Among these is the area of sexual behavior. Sex with a "consenting" child below a certain age is criminalized as rape because the child does not have the capacity to

---

212   S.B. 107, 2021–22 Leg., Reg. Sess. (Ca. 2022) (in Comm.); Press Release, Scott Wiener, Cal. Sen, Dist. 11, *LGBTQ Lawmakers in 19 States Have or Will Introduce Laws to Protect Trans Kids from Civil and Criminal Penalties When Seeking Gender-Affirming Care* (May 3, 2022), *available at* https://sd11.senate.ca.gov/news/20220503-lgbtq-lawmakers-19-states-have-or-will-introduce-laws-protect-trans-kids-civil-and.

213   Soh, *supra* note 14, at 147.

consent. We also are wary of child predators because they have the ability to groom children who are naturally vulnerable, and even more so when the child also suffers from social anxieties.

It seems cruel to permit children, who we find incapable and too inexperienced to make a great variety of decisions, to be placed in control making profound, life-altering decisions. As children, they are at an age of greatest vulnerability and least capacity. A delay should be made. But it should not be to delay puberty, during which time the body releases hormones that may resolve the child's perception of gender incongruity. Instead, the delay should be in the life-altering decisions themselves. In today's world, until a child sorts out the important matter concerning gender identity, a child is free to wear androgenous clothing and hairstyles in public schools. And, because of cultural acceptance of equality, children have an opportunity to participate in gender-atypical as well as gender-typical activities. We can and should affirm children's interests, but not affirm their desire to be other than who they are. We need to coach them to bring out the best of who they already are, not coach them into believing they are somebody else.

Human flourishing embraces a search for truth. Altering physical reality to mimic perception is not searching for truth, but escaping from it. Laws that enforce perception over truth do not advance human flourishing. Laws that promote secrecy that interferes with family trust do not advance, but undermine human flourishing. And laws that promote unquestioning affirmation that will lead to harmful medical interventions on a child's healthy body do not further, but detract from human flourishing.

Even though gender-care treatments can alter the body visually, the material nature of the person's embodied self remains unchanged. A person's XX or XY karyotype, present in each and every somatic cell, remains consistent throughout life. The karyotype continues its task of generating sex-related products, unless inhibited. For that reason, "[i]f the hormonal treatments are stopped, the karyotype will reassert its dominance in the biology of the individual."[214]

Laws that compel citizens to affirm a child's gender perception that will most likely lead to that child's lifelong commitment to suppression of natural physiology appear inconsistent with community as well as individual flourishing. Laws that protect child vulnerability and prevent them from being used as unwitting soldiers in an adult revolt against nature can best ensure human flourishing.

---

214   Tonti-Filippini, *supra* note 100, at 94.

CHAPTER 35

To Procreate or Not to Procreate

*Lauren Gilbert**

1 Introduction

My life has been filled with happenings that have led me to contemplate the meaning of motherhood, particularly with regard to unwed mothers and their children. I write this piece in honor of Professor Siegfried Wiessner, Professor of Law and Director of the LL.M./J.S.D. Program in Intercultural Human Rights, St. Thomas University College of Law, on his seventieth birthday. It is a privilege to participate in this *Festschrift* honoring his career. I am particularly grateful for all that he has taught me over the last twenty years about the importance of viewing rights through the lens of human dignity. I found that principle – that the purpose of law should be to allow all persons to achieve their fullest potential – particularly illuminating as I researched and wrote this very personal piece.

I was (and have always been) an unwed mother. It is an essential part of my identity. My mother was an unwed expectant mother at the age of 17 until my maternal grandmother, Sally, pressured her to marry my father, a marriage that lasted about a year-and-a-half and ended in a burst of violence. Carrie Buck from the infamous case *Buck v. Bell*[1] was an unwed mother who, at the age of 16, was impregnated by the nephew of her foster parents, the Dobbs,[2] and quickly shipped off after her baby's birth to the Lynchburg Colony for the Epileptics and Feeble-Minded in Virginia where she was made the test case for eugenic sterilization.[3] Anna Buck (no relation) was a librarian in Manchester, Vermont and

---

* Professor of Law, St. Thomas University College of Law; J.D., University of Michigan Law School; B.A., Harvard University.
1 Buck v. Bell, 274 U.S. 200 (1927).
2 I found it ironic that Carrie Buck's foster parents had the same name as the decision overturning a woman's right to reproductive freedom, Dobbs v. Jackson Women's Health Organization, 142 S.Ct. 2228 (2022) (hereinafter, *Dobbs*). I began this article after the draft was leaked, S. Ct., No. 19-1392 (Feb. 10, 2022) (hereinafter *Dobbs* draft), and made final revisions after the full decision came out. Little changed from the draft to the final decision, with the exception of the addition of concurring and dissenting opinions and the majority's response.
3 *See* Stephen Jay Gould, *Carrie Buck's Daughter*, 2 Const. Comment. 331, 334–336 (1985); Paul A. Lombardo, Three Generations, No Imbeciles: Eugenics, The Supreme Court and Buck v. Bell (Updated Edition 2022).

the birth mother of Marilyn.[4] Anna gave up Marilyn for adoption shortly after her birth in 1933.[5] Eighty-eight years later, Marilyn confirmed through genetic testing that her biological father was Eric Allen,[6] the pastor from 1931 to 1939 of the First Congregational Church of Manchester.[7] He was married at the time to my great grandmother, Nina, and had five other children, including my grandmother, Sally. Anna stayed during her pregnancy at a home for unwed mothers before giving up her baby for adoption.[8] She returned shortly thereafter to Manchester, no one else the wiser, and resumed her position as town librarian.[9]

If law's role, as this collection posits, should be "to allow humans to achieve their full potential – to thrive, to achieve happiness and satisfaction, full mental and physical health," then women need to be able to control their own reproductive destinies.[10] Real stories of unwed pregnant women, past, present and future, shed a light on how the laws in this country have evolved to ensure greater recognition for a woman's fundamental right to reproductive and family autonomy. Today, these rights are in jeopardy now that the U.S. Supreme Court in *Dobbs v. Jackson Women's Health Center*[11] has overturned the constitutional right to abortion. While other countries have moved forward in protecting a woman's right to terminate her pregnancy,[12] approximately half the States already have either limited or banned abortion.[13]

---

4   Letter from Marilyn W. to Polly and Kim (Feb. 1, 2022) (hereinafter "Marilyn W. Letter") (on file with the author).

5   *Id.* at *1.

6   *Id.* at *2.

7   The First Congregational Church Manchester, Vermont: 1784–1984 (1894), p. 101 [hereinafter, "First Congregational Church of Manchester"].

8   Marilyn W. Letter, *supra* note 4, at *1.

9   First Congregational Church of Manchester, *supra* note 7, at 101; Silver Fork at the Old Library, Gallery and History, at https://thesilverforkvt.com/gallery-history/ (with a pictures of Anna Buck, including a 1964 celebration in her honor for her over 50 years of service as Mark Skinner Library Head Librarian).

10   Although I often refer to a woman's right to abortion, I recognize that persons who do not identify as women, including non-binary persons and transgender men, also can become pregnant and are similarly entitled to the right to an abortion.

11   *Dobbs, supra* note 2.

12   *Id.* at 2340-2341 (Breyer, Sotomayor & Kagan, J., dissenting). *See also* Julie Turkewitz, *Colombia Decriminalizes Abortion, Bolstering Trend Across Region*, N.Y. Times, Feb. 22, 2022; Natalie Kitroeff & Oscar Lopez, *Mexico's Supreme Court Votes to Decriminalize Abortion*, N.Y. Times, Sept. 7, 2021; Daniel Politi & Ernesto Londono, *Argentina Legalizes Abortion, a Milestone in a Conservative Region*, N.Y. Times, Dec. 30, 2020; Thirty-sixth Amendment of the Constitution Act 2018 (Ireland's constitutional amendment repealing abortion ban and allowing for termination of pregnancy, to be regulated by statute).

13   Quoctrum Bui, Claire Cain Miller, & Margot Sanger-Katz, *How Abortion Bans Will Ripple Across America*, N.Y. Times, June 24, 2022.

The abortion issue is framed by the *Dobbs* decision and pro-life advocates as being about the states' interest in the protection of human life; yet the rights of women and other pregnant persons are almost invisible in the final opinion, which takes a hyper-formalistic approach in applying the equal protection and due process clauses. Implicit in the opinion is a stunted view of parenthood and the family. Indeed, at the 2022 Convention of the National Rifle Association (NRA) in Houston, Texas, in response to the school shooting in Uvalde, Texas three days earlier that killed 19 elementary school children and two of their teachers, Senator Ted Cruz and former President Donald Trump insisted that the cause of gun violence was not the lack of gun control, but rather, the breakdown of the American family, fatherless children, untreated mental illness, and the existence of "evil."[14]

Such assertions raise serious concerns. Whose rights to life, liberty and the pursuit of happiness do we really care about? In both Alito's leaked opinion and in the final *Dobbs* decision, Justice Alito emphasizes that in deciding whether a right is fundamental, the Court looks at whether the right is essential to our Nation's "scheme of ordered liberty," and that this depends on whether the right is "deeply rooted in [our] history and tradition."[15] Women, however, did not have voting rights until 1920 with passage of the 19th Amendment[16] and it took until the 1970s for the Court to extend the guaranties of equal protection to sex-based discrimination.[17] Are women's rights to bodily integrity and control over their reproductive lives "deeply rooted in [our] history and tradition"? *Dobbs* concludes that abortion is not. It is not part of the "ordered liberty" protected by the 14th Amendment due process clause because, according to the decision, it is neither enumerated in the Constitution nor was it rooted

---

14 Isaac Arnsdorf, *Trump, Cruz join NRA leaders in defiant response to Uvalde shooting*, Wash. Post., May 27, 2022; Eric Radner & Jeff Zeleny, *Trump, other Republicans reject gun reforms at NRA convention that showcases nation's split*, CNN Politics, May 28, 2022 at https://www .cnn.com/2022/05/27/politics/uvalde-donald-trump-nra-convention/index.html; *Trump and Cruz speak at NRA convention days after school shooting*, https://www.youtube.com /watch?v=nPHaU55uD1I&t=5795s at 1:39:25–1:48:50 ("broken families, absent fathers").

15 *Dobbs Draft, supra* note 2, at *5; *Dobbs, supra* note 2, at 2242.

16 United States Constitution, Amendment XIX, passed by Congress June 4, 1919, ratified Aug. 18, 1920.

17 *See, e.g.,* Reed v. Reed 404 U.S. 71 (1971) (invalidating a gender classification as not rationally related to a legitimate government interest); Frontiero v. Richardson, 411 U.S. 677 (1973) (classifications based on sex, like those based on race, are inherently suspect and must be subjected to strict judicial scrutiny); Craig v. Boren, 429 U.S. 190 (1976) (settling on intermediate scrutiny, Court found that "classifications by gender must serve important governmental objectives and must be substantially related to achievement of those objectives.").

in history and tradition at the time the 14th Amendment was ratified in 1868.[18] Nor, according to *Dobbs*, are abortion regulations sex-based classifications subject to heightened scrutiny under equal protection analysis.[19]

What then *is* "ordered liberty"? In 1923, in *Meyer v. Nebraska*[20] the Court identified some of the unenumerated liberty interests it said were protected by the due process clause:

> Without doubt, [liberty] denotes not merely freedom from bodily restraint but also the right of the individual to contract, to engage in any of the common occupations of life, to acquire useful knowledge, to marry, establish a home and bring up children, to worship God according to the dictates of his own conscience, and generally to enjoy those privileges long recognized at common law *as essential to the orderly pursuit of happiness by free men.*[21]

Unsurprisingly, this broad, often contested concept of liberty[22] was, even then, not enjoyed by women on the same terms as men. On the contrary, throughout history, men's pursuit of happiness often depended on women's subordination within the domestic sphere. Indeed, in 1872, in *Bradwell v. the State of Illinois*,[23] in voting to uphold an Illinois statute that prohibited women from being licensed to practice law, Justice Bradley wrote in a concurring opinion that

> The paramount destiny and mission of woman are to fulfil the noble and benign offices of wife and mother. This is the law of the Creator. And the rules of civil society must be adapted to the general constitution of things, and cannot be based on exceptional cases.[24]

---

18   *Dobbs, supra* note 2, at 2252-2253. *See also* McDonald v. City of Chicago, 561 U.S. 742 (2010) (where Alito, J. found that the right to possess a handgun in the home was part of the fundamental right to keep and bear arms enshrined in the Second Amendment and enforceable against the states through the Fourteenth Amendment due process clause).

19   *Dobbs, supra* note 2, at 2245.

20   262 U.S. 390 (1923).

21   *Id.* at 399. [Emphasis added.]

22   The Court has been inconsistent over the years in embracing this definition of liberty, frequently citing *Meyer v. Nebraska* as a source of unenumerated rights, but at other times, repudiating its definition of liberty, claiming that it was only dicta and/or that it was decided during the free-wheeling *Lochner* era. *See, e.g.,* Kerry v. Din, 576 U.S. 86, 94 (2015) (negative treatment); Conn v. Gabbert, 526 U.S. 286 (1999)(negative); Albright v. Oliver, 510 U.S. 266, 294 (1994)(J. Stevens, dissenting).

23   83 U.S (16 Wall.) 130 (1872).

24   *Id.*

In *Muller v. Oregon*,[25] in 1908, in upholding a maximum hours law for women after striking down similar laws for men, the Court stated that "as healthy mothers are essential to vigorous offspring, the physical well-being of woman becomes an object of public interest and care in order to preserve the strength and vigor of the race."[26] Later, with the end of the *Lochner* era and new limits on freedom of contract, the Court upheld a state minimum wage law on the basis that protecting women against unscrupulous employers was a legitimate end for the exercise of state power.[27] Soon thereafter, applying the more deferential rational basis test, the Court also upheld a paternalistic law denying a woman equal access to the job of bartender in the name of protecting her.[28] Not until the 1970s did the Court apply heightened scrutiny to laws discriminating on the basis of sex.[29]

By the 1970s, gender equality found itself in tension with the doctrine of marital privacy that was the basis for the Court's decision in *Griswold v. Connecticut*.[30] In *Griswold*, the Court, in striking down Connecticut's ban on the use of contraceptives by married couples, described the right of marital privacy as "a right of privacy older than the Bill of Rights."[31] As the Court in the 1970s began to strike down laws discriminating on the basis of sex under equal protection analysis, the right to privacy in *Griswold* evolved into a much broader right to privacy under fundamental rights analysis. Striking down a Massachusetts statute regulating the sale and use of contraceptives as violating the equal protection clause, the Court found that

> the marital couple is not an independent entity with a mind and heart of its own, but an association of two individuals each with a separate intellectual and emotional makeup. If the right of privacy means anything, *it is the right of the individual married or single*, to be free from unwarranted governmental intrusion into matters so fundamentally affecting a person as the decision whether to bear or beget a child.[32]

---

25 208 U.S. 412 (1908).

26 *Id.* at 421.

27 West Coast Hotel Co. v. Parrish, 300 U.S. 379, 398 (1937) (upholding minimum wage law for women).

28 *See, e.g.,* Goesart v. Cleary, 335 U.S. 464 (1948) (preventing the licensing of a woman as a bartender unless she was the wife or daughter of a male who owned the bar).

29 *See supra* at note 17.

30 381 U.S. 479 (1965).

31 *Id.* at 486.

32 Eisenstadt v. Baird, 405 U.S. 438, 453 (1972). [Emphasis added.]

This was no doubt an expansion of the right to privacy recognized in *Griswold,* and implicated both the due process and equal protection clauses. *Eisenstadt v. Baird* laid the groundwork for the Court's recognition of other unenumerated rights, including the right to abortion a year later in *Roe v. Wade*,[33] the right to sexual intimacy in consensual, private, relationships,[34] and eventually, the right to same-sex marriage.[35] If the conservatives on the Court could turn the clock back, it would probably be to *Eisenstadt v. Baird.*

Over the last eighty years, the U.S. Supreme Court has recognized both a fundamental right to procreate[36] as well as a fundamental right to not procreate.[37] With the Court's decision in *Dobbs* overturning the nearly 50-year-old right to abortion, scholars and advocates for reproductive and sexual rights have raised serious concerns about what might be next.[38] The same "history and tradition" test that Justice Alito applies in *McDonald v. City of Chicago*[39] in analyzing whether there is a Second Amendment right to possess handguns, he applies to abortion. While in *McDonald* he upholds the right to possess handguns in defense of hearth and home as constitutionally protected,[40] in the *Dobbs* decision he concludes that the abortion right is not an essential component of "ordered liberty" because it is neither enumerated in the Constitution nor rooted in history and tradition.[41] As the dissent noted, this analysis from the *Dobbs* decision could easily be extended to other unenumerated rights, including the right to interracial marriage, to contraceptives, to private, consensual sexual intimacy outside of marriage, including in same-sex relationships, and to same-sex marriage.[42] It could also be extended to other unenumerated rights, such as the right of parents to custody and to control

---

33   Roe v. Wade, 410 U.S. 113 (1973); Planned Parenthood v. Casey, 505 U.S. 833 (1992).

34   Lawrence v. Texas, 539 U.S. 558 (2003).

35   Obergefell v. Hodges, 576 U.S. 644 (2015).

36   Skinner v. Oklahoma, 316 U.S. 535, 541 (1942) ("marriage and procreation are fundamental to the very existence and survival of the race").

37   *Eisenstadt, supra* note 32, at 453.

38   *See, e.g.,* Leah Litman & Steve Vladeck, *The Biggest Lie Conservative Defenders of Alito's Leaked Opinion Are Telling,* Slate, May 5, 2022, *available at* https://slate.com/news-and-politics /2022/05/conservatives-lying-impact-samuel-alito-leaked-draft-opinion-roe.html; Melissa Murray, *How the Right to Birth Control Could Be Undone,* N.Y. Times, May 2, 2022, *available at* https://www.nytimes.com/ 2022/05/23/opinion/birth-control-abortion-roe-v -wade.html.

39   561 U.S. 742 (2010).

40   *Id.* at 767.

41   *Dobbs, supra* note 2, at 2242-2243, 2249.

42   *Dobbs, supra* note 2 (Breyer, Sotomayor & Kagan, JJ., dissenting at 2338).

the upbringing of their children, particularly if done beyond the confines of Justice Scalia's "unitary family."[43]

This paper focuses on the rights of unwed women, both then and now, including both their reproductive rights and rights to family autonomy. There is a history and tradition in this country of preventing unwanted pregnancy which has included the abortion decision, but it has taken different form at different points in history. Under the common law and early American history, abortion in most states was not a crime prior to quickening.[44] Chastity, like modern day abstinence, became a social value in large part because of the consequences of unwanted pregnancy.[45] Unwed motherhood was treated at multiple periods in history as a threat to the social order and to be avoided,[46] the stigma attaching itself to so-called "bastard children."[47] Thinking back to Nathanial Hawthorne's *Scarlet Letter*, such families were often met with derision from the broader society.[48] By the 19th century, many states had passed Bastardy Acts that went so far as to require the incarceration of unwed mothers until they either paid a bond or named the putative father.[49]

In the 1920s and 1930s, when the stories of Carrie Buck and Anna Buck unfolded, when these Bastardy Acts were still in place, white women with unplanned pregnancies had little choice but to either marry before giving birth or to give the baby up for adoption. Poor white women like Carrie Buck were labeled as "feeble-minded" for having sex outside of marriage and exiled from the community. Many, like Carrie Buck and her mother, had their children taken away from them.[50] Anna Buck's middle-class status in Manchester,

---

43   Michael H. v. Gerald D., 491 U.S. 110, 123 (1989) (narrowing rights of biological fathers to those that develop within the context of the unitary family).

44   *Roe, supra* note 33, at 132–133.

45   *See* Lea Vandervelde, *The Legal Ways of Seduction*, 48 Stan. L. Rev. 818, 885 (1996).

46   Jonathan L. Hafetz, *"A Man's Home is His Castle?": Reflections on the Home, the Family and Privacy During the Late Nineteenth and Early Twentieth Centuries*, 8 Wm. & Mary J. Women & L. 175, 178 (2002); Carla Spivack, *To "Bring Down the Flowers": The Cultural Context of Abortion Law in Early Modern England*, 14 Wm. & Mary J. Women & L. 107, 118–119 (2007).

47   1 William Blackstone, Commentaries *434 (Project Gutenberg ed. 2009).

48   Nathaniel Hawthorne, The Scarlet Letter (1850). The Scarlet Letter tells the story of Hester Prynne, who gave birth to a daughter, Pearl, after having a sexual liaison with the Reverend Dimmesdale, who she refused to identify as the father. She was forced to stand in the public pillory and to wear the scarlet letter A as punishment for the crime of adultery. Both she and her daughter were shunned by the community.

49   *See* Daniel Hatcher, *Don't Forget Dad: Addressing Women's Poverty by Rethinking Forced and Outdated Child Support Policies*, 20 Am. U. J. Gender Soc. Pol'y & L. 775, 778 (2012).

50   Adam Cohen, Imbeciles: The Supreme Court, American Eugenics, and the Sterilization of Carrie Buck (2016) at 20.

Vermont, as town librarian was jeopardized by the looming scandal of her unplanned pregnancy with a married pastor.

By the 1970s, even as women as a class gained new rights, including reproductive rights, this was met with a backlash.[51] Congress overwhelmingly passed the Equal Rights Amendment in 1972, but it did not get the necessary 38 state ratifications by the June 30, 1982 deadline. Throughout the 1970s and early 1980s, the ERA was fought bitterly by conservative women and men who saw it as a threat to the family and conservative values.[52]

I argue that, notwithstanding *Dobbs*, existing jurisprudence clearly establishes that the decision to procreate or not procreate is a fundamental right that belongs to the individual, and that it is essential to each person's self-determination. In Part I, I briefly review the common law history and treatment of unwed motherhood, according to Blackstone and other legal scholars, along with constitutional doctrine involving unwed mothers and natural fathers. In Part II, I recount some less well-known but illuminating details of Carrie Buck's case and her family history. In Part III, I discuss the case of Anna Buck, who, to preserve her place in her community, hid her pregnancy and gave her baby up for adoption. I place Anna Buck's story within the context of Vermont's Bastardy Act, as applied by the Vermont Supreme Court. In Part IV, I tell my own story of single motherhood and the choices I made. In Part V, I discuss the *Dobbs* decision, and how its formalistic due process and equal protection analyses are compartmentalized so as to read out of existence any potential violations of a pregnant woman's rights. I discuss the implications of the *Dobbs* decision for women and girls and other pregnant persons of different classes, races, and levels of education and for the children many will be forced to bear. I conclude that the *Dobbs* decision is fundamentally flawed because, by focusing on 1868, a time when women were excluded from the political process, it disregards developments in women's rights in the 20th century, defines the fundamental rights at stake too narrowly and, in finding no equal protection violation, ignores the evidence of hostility towards women who seek to control their reproductive destinies.

---

51   *See, e.g.,* Geoffrey R. Stone, Sex and the Constitution (2017) at 401–403 (discussing the rise
      of the Christian Right after Roe v. Wade was decided).
52   *See, e.g.,* Donald T. Critchlow, Conservativism: A Women's Crusade 4, 222 (2005).

2   The Common Law, Unwed Women and Bastard Children

At common law, according to Blackstone, children were of two sorts: legitimate or bastards.[53] A legitimate child was one born in lawful wedlock. The marriage had to precede the birth.[54] A bastard child was one born outside of lawful matrimony. Blackstone explains that

> For, if a child be begotten while the parents are single, and they will endeavour to make an early reparation for the offence, by marrying within a few months after, our law is so indulgent as not to bastardize the child, if it be born, though not begotten, in lawful wedlock …[55]

Thus, women's only recourse to avoid the social stigma of bastardy was to marry the father before the child was born, if that was even an option. Blackstone distinguished the common law rule from civil law and canon law, which allowed for removal of the stigma of bastardy if the parents married after the child's birth. He said that the purpose of marriage was to "fix upon some certain person, to whom the care, the protection, the maintenance, and the education of the children should belong" which was better served by legitimating only those children born into wedlock, in light of the problems of proof that might otherwise arise.[56]

Children born out of wedlock were considered "filius nullius," the children of no one. They could not be heir to anyone nor have any heir, except of their own body, because they were kin to nobody.[57] Although Blackstone stated that they were entitled to maintenance from the father, based upon oath of the mother,[58] other scholars have emphasized that, initially, neither biological parent had a duty to the child, although eventually this responsibility was placed on the shoulders of their unmarried mothers.[59] By the 19th century, many U.S. states, including the State of Vermont, passed laws known as Bastardy Acts, which allowed the unwed mother to bring a claim against the biological father for maintenance. These laws were the early equivalent of modern child support laws, and were later repealed and/or reframed as such, although the same

---

53   1 William Blackstone, Commentaries *434 (Project Gutenberg ed. 2009).

54   *Id.*

55   *Id.* at 442–443.

56   *Id.* at 443.

57   *Id.* at 447.

58   *Id.* at 446.

59   Melissa Murray, *What's So New About the New Illegitimacy?*, 20 Am. U. J. Gender Soc. Pol'y & L. 387, 390 (2012).

basic idea never changed: prevent the child from becoming a burden on the State.[60]

Melissa Murray underscores in her article, *What's So New About the New Illegitimacy,* that by the late 1960s, even as the Supreme Court moved away from common law notions of illegitimacy, the law strongly favored the traditional family.[61] In 1968, in *Levy v. Louisiana*[62] and *in Glona v. American Guarantee & Liability Insurance Co.,*[63] the Supreme Court struck down Art. 2315 of the Louisiana Civil Code as applied, in *Levy,* to orphaned children bringing a wrongful death action after the death of their unwed mother, and in *Glona,* to a mother bringing a wrongful death action after the death of her nonmarital son. In both cases, the lower courts dismissed their suits because they did not fall within the definition of "survivor," based solely on the fact of illegitimacy. The Supreme Court found that the statutory scheme involved invidious discrimination: while States were free to legislate with regard to nonmarital sexual conduct, the means chosen here were not rationally related to the State's interest in promoting morals.[64]

Even so, Professor Murray points out that neither decision challenged the "view that the marital family was –and should be – favored and encouraged as a matter of public policy."[65] She argues that the Court found in the plaintiffs' favor in both cases because they did not conform to traditional conceptions of unwed mothers and bastard children, under which "illegitimacy posits a never-ending cycle in which children become heirs to their parents' immorality and lax values."[66] Ms. Levy regularly took her children to church on Sundays. She supported them through work as a domestic, without relying on public benefits. Ms. Glona had given birth, out-of-wedlock, to her son in her youth but later married a man who informally recognized him.[67]

A comparable theme runs through the canonical unmarried father cases.[68] These cases begin in 1972 with *Stanley v. Illinois,*[69] where Mr. Stanley, the unwed father of children he had lived with and raised, challenged a statute that automatically made his children wards of the State upon their mother's

---

60   Hatcher, *supra* note 49, at 779.
61   Murray, *supra* note 59, at 393–394.
62   391 U.S. 68 (1968) (cited in Murray, *id.,* at 391–393).
63   391 U.S. 73 (1968) (cited in Murray, *id.*).
64   *Levy,* 391 U.S. at 71; *Glona,* 391 U.S. at 74–75.
65   Murray, *supra* note 59, at 393.
66   *Id.* at 394.
67   *Id.* at 395–396.
68   *Id.* at 399.
69   405 U.S. 645 (1972).

death. The Court struck down the statute, citing previous decisions (including *Meyer v. Nebraska*) that the right to conceive and to raise one's children was one of the "basic civil rights of man" that has found protection in the due process and equal protection clauses of the 14th Amendment as well as the Ninth Amendment.[70] The Court found that it violated Mr. Stanley's due process rights to deny him the opportunity to prove he was a fit parent[71] and that it denied him equal protection where the State of Illinois took custody of his children without a hearing while only taking custody of children of unmarried mothers after a hearing and proof of neglect.[72]

After *Stanley*, a series of cases followed that attempted to define the rights of unwed biological fathers.[73] They culminated in 1983 in *Lehr v. Robertson*,[74] where the Court reviewed each of the preceding cases, including *Stanley*, finding that a biological connection was not enough to create parental rights. Rather, it depended on whether the unwed father had "demonstrate[d] a full commitment to the responsibilities of parenthood by 'com[ing] forward to participate in the rearing of his child'."[75]

Then, in 1989, in *Michael H. v. Gerald D.*,[76] the Court found that an adulterous unwed biological father, Michael H., whose biological child, Victoria, had been born into an existing marriage, did not have a fundamental right to parent his child, despite his active involvement in her life.[77] Justice Scalia relied heavily on the common law marital presumption, citing to an 1836 treatise on Adulterine Bastardy.[78] In declining to overturn a California statute which denied a natural father the right to rebut the presumption that a child born into an existing marriage was the child of that marriage, Justice Scalia looked at both the purpose behind the marital presumption[79] and at whether there was a history and tradition of States awarding substantive parental rights to the

---

70   *Id.* at 651.

71   *Id.* at 657–658.

72   *Id.* at 658.

73   *See* Quilloin v. Walcott, 434 U.S. 246 (1978); Caban v. Mohammed 441 U.S. 380 (1979).

74   Lehr v. Robertson, 463 U.S. 248 (1983).

75   *Id.* at 261 (quoting *Caban, supra* note 73, at 389).

76   Michael H. v. Gerald D., 491 U.S. 110 (1989).

77   *Id.* at 127.

78   H. Nicholas, Adulturine Bastardy 1 (1836) (cited with approval in *Michael H., supra* note 76, at 124).

79   Justice Scalia noted that the primary rationale under the common law for the marital presumption was an aversion to having children declared illegitimate, thus depriving them of rights of inheritance and succession and making them wards of the State. *Michael H., supra* note 76, at 125 (citing with approval to Schouler, M. Grossberg, Governing the Health 201 (1985); and 2 J. Ken, Commentaries on American Law *175).

natural father of a child conceived within, and born into, an existing marital union that wished to embrace the child. He found none.[80] Therefore, Michael H. had no fundamental right to be Victoria's father because their relationship had not been treated as a protected family unit under the historic practices of society.[81] Scalia distinguished the other unwed father cases as resting less upon biological fatherhood plus an established parental relationship, and more "upon the historic respect ... traditionally accorded to the relationships that develop within the unitary family."[82] Although Scalia did not limit the "unitary family" to marital children, including *Stanley* in distinguishing *Michael H.* from the other unwed father cases, he clearly ranked the father-mother dyad as superior to other forms of the family.

3   The Tragedy of Carrie Buck and her Daughter Vivian

Most law students are familiar with *Buck v. Bell*,[83] the Supreme Court opinion which concludes with Justice Holmes' disturbing rationale for upholding Virginia's statute providing for the sterilization of "mental defectives."[84] The less-well-known story behind the Carrie Buck case, however, is deeply unsettling for what it says both about judicial review as well as society's treatment of poor, unwed mothers in the early 20th century. The two-page ruling in the Supreme Court Reporter begins with a brief recitation of the "facts":

> Carrie Buck is a feeble-minded white woman who was committed to the State Colony above mentioned in due form. She is the daughter of a feeble-minded mother in the same institution, and the mother of an illegitimate feeble-minded child.[85]

Carrie Buck, as we now know, was not "feeble-minded," but rather a woman of normal intelligence who was one of almost 20,000 forced eugenic sterilizations performed in the United States by 1935.[86] Harry Laughlin, who prepared a "family history" of the Bucks for the case, was superintendent of the

---

80   *Michael H., supra* note 76, at 127.
81   *Id.*
82   *Id.* at 123.
83   Buck v. Bell, 274 U.S. 200 (1927).
84   *Id.* at 207.
85   *Id.* at 205.
86   *See, e.g.,* Chemerinsky, Constitutional Law 951 (6th Ed. 2020), citing Stephen Jay Gould, *Carrie Buck's Daughter*, 2 Const. Comment., *supra* note 3, at 336.

Eugenics Record Office and a leader of the eugenics movement. His goal was to eliminate from the gene pool what he described as the "most worthless one-tenth of our present population" through eugenic sterilization of those with "degenerate hereditary traits."[87] Carrie Buck became the test case. In his family history of the Bucks Laughlin writes that "[t]hese people belong to the shiftless, ignorant and worthless class of anti-social whites of the South."[88] He concludes, never having met Carrie, that "the evidence points strongly towards the feeble-mindedness and moral delinquency of Carrie Buck being due, primarily, to inheritance and not environment."[89]

Over the years, there have been several excellent works on the *Buck* case.[90] This is what we know. Carrie Buck was from Charlottesville, Virginia, literally from the other side of the tracks.[91] She was born in 1906 to a poor white woman, Emma Buck, whose husband had disappeared.[92] She was taken from her mother when she was three or four years old and sent to live with the Dobbs, a foster family, for whom she performed chores around the house.[93] Emma Buck, who had other children out of wedlock, was deemed to be feeble-minded and later sent, when Carrie was fourteen and still living with the Dobbs, to the Lynchburg Colony for Epileptics and the Feeble-Minded.[94] Carrie would join her there a few years later.

When Carrie was sixteen years old, while Mrs. Dobbs was out of town, Mrs. Dobbs' nephew, Clarence Garland, had sex with Carrie.[95] The circumstances are not entirely clear, but Carrie said repeatedly over the years that he forced himself upon her and then promised he would marry her.[96] Several scholars have concluded that she was raped.[97] At a minimum, Garland seduced her, which was also a crime at the time.[98] Upon discovering the pregnancy,

---

87 Gould, *id.,* at 332–333.

88 *Id.* at 336–337.

89 *Id.* at 335.

90 *See, e.g.,* Gould, *supra* note 3; Lombardo, *supra* note 3; Cohen, *supra* note 50; Khiara M. Bridges, *White Privilege and White Disadvantage,* 105 Va. L. Rev. 449 (2019).

91 Lombardo, *supra* note 3, at 116.

92 Cohen, *supra* note 50, at 19.

93 *Id.* at 20–21.

94 *Id.* at 22.

95 Lombardo, *supra* note 3, at 140.

96 *Id. See also* Cohen, *supra* note 50, at 24.

97 *Id. See also* Gould, *supra* note 3, at 336; Bridges, *supra* note 91, at 455.

98 Lombardo writes that under Virginia law, a "man who 'under the promise of marriage' had an 'illicit connection with any unmarried female' could be sentence to up to ten years in prison, as long as the woman was of 'previous chaste character.'" Lombardo, *supra* note 3, at 141.

Mrs. Dobbs and her husband, J.T., set out to have her committed and sent away to the Lynchburg Colony, claiming that she had been feeble-minded since the age of ten or eleven, showing signs of sexual promiscuity from a very young age.[99] The Dobbs were in a pickle. Pregnancy out-of-wedlock carried a social stigma and their reputation in the community as foster parents would be seriously damaged. Furthermore, if Carrie went forward with her story that their nephew had raped her, he could be criminally charged.[100] If she were to claim seduction on promise of marriage, his best defense would be that she was not of previous chaste character. It was thus in the Dobbs' interest to blame it on heredity, accuse her of promiscuity and have her sent away.

The superintendent of the Lynchburg Colony, Dr. Albert Priddy, who sought to expand the sterilization of "feeble-minded" women at the Colony, was in close contact with members of the eugenics community.[101] They were looking for a test case that they could take to the U.S. Supreme Court. They were ecstatic. Carrie was the ideal subject. Her mother had already been institutionalized. They would prove that she was the feeble-minded daughter of a feeble-minded woman and had given birth to a feeble-minded child.[102]

Carrie's baby was born on March 28, 1924 and taken away from her. Two months later, Carrie was sent to the Lynchburg Colony, where she remained until she was sterilized in October 1927, not long after the Court's decision in *Buck v. Bell*. Her daughter, Vivian, was placed with the Dobbs, who eventually adopted her, but tragically died at age eight of a complication from measles.[103] Although Carrie, upon her release, was anxious to return to the Dobbs' home, Mrs. Dobbs rejected her request.[104] In *Carrie Buck's Daughter*, Steven Jay Gould, a Harvard biologist and historian of science, poignantly ends his article, published a year after Carrie died in 1983, telling how, by a quirk of fate, Carrie was buried just a short walk from her daughter's grave.[105]

Paul Lombardo has exhaustively documented in his work that not only was Carrie Buck not feeble-minded but that the entire case was built on a series of lies manufactured by a group of eugenicists who saw her case as the perfect test case.[106] Her appointed lawyer, Irving Whitehead, was an ardent eugenicist

---

99   Lombardo, *supra* note 3, at 114–115.
100   *Id.* at 141. Cohen, *supra* note 50, at 24.
101   Lombardo, *supra* note 3, at 60.
102   *Id.* at 108.
103   *Id.* at 190.
104   Lombardo, *supra* note 3, at 188.
105   Gould, *supra* note 3, at 339.
106   Lombardo, *supra* note 3, at xiii. *See also* Gould, *supra*, note 3, at 336; Bridges, *supra* note 91, at 453–456.

who was hand-picked to represent her and to create a paper trail that was unassailable, going through the motions without serving her interests.[107] Indeed, Lombardo emphasizes that procedures were scrupulously followed in building the case for sterilization.[108]

This going through the motions is what makes Justice Holmes' findings all the more devastating. After stating the "facts," he goes on to state that

> There can be no doubt that so far as procedure is concerned the rights of the patient are most carefully considered, and as every step in this case was taken in scrupulous compliance with the statute and after months of observation, there is no doubt that in that respect *the plaintiff in error has had due process at law*.[109]

The Court concludes that

> It is better for all the world, if instead of waiting to execute degenerate offspring for crime, or to let them starve for their imbecility, society can prevent those who are manifestly unfit from continuing their kind ... Three generations of imbeciles are enough.[110]

Harvard Professor Steven Jay Gould, an evolutionary biologist, was the first to conclude that Carrie's case was "never about mental deficiency; it was always a matter of sexual morality and social deviance."[111] Feeble-mindedness was nothing but a euphemism for women who failed to conform to the sexual mores of society. Carrie was taken advantage of by the Dobbs' nephew, raped or seduced, then blamed by the Dobbs for becoming pregnant. She was institutionalized "to hide her shame" and no doubt the father's identity,[112] and to protect the Dobbs' reputation in the community.[113]

Upon her institutionalization, Dr. Priddy, the superintendent of the Lynchburg Colony, examined Carrie and classified her as "feeble-minded of the lowest grade Moron class" and as "a moral delinquent."[114] At trial, he

---

107   Lombardo, *supra* note 3, at 148.
108   *Id* at 106 – 107.
109   *Buck v. Bell, supra* note 1, at 207 [emphasis added].
110   *Id.*
111   Gould, *supra* note 3, at 336.
112   *Id.*
113   Cohen, *supra* note 50, at 24–25.
114   Lombardo, *supra* note 3, at 107.

described her as congenitally and incurably defective."[115] There was no reliable evidence at the time of trial, however, that either she or her daughter were "feeble-minded." The "evidence" came from the family study prepared by Harry Laughlin of the Eugenics Record Office. Although Laughlin never met her, relying on information gathered by Dr. Priddy, he concluded that she had a chronological age of 18 years but a mental age of 9 years, and was thus an imbecile. He found that she had led a life thus far of "immorality, prostitution, and untruthfulness," came from "a shiftless, ignorant and worthless class of people," that her feeble-mindedness was hereditary, and she was the "potential parent of socially inadequate or defective offspring."[116] Regarding her daughter Vivian, despite vague testimony by a social worker that there was something "not quite normal" about the seven-month-old baby, years later, Steven Jay Gould, with the help of Lombardo, tracked down Vivian's report cards from the years before her death and found that she "was a perfectly normal, average student, neither particularly outstanding nor much troubled."[117]

Carrie Buck's trial and appeal were a sham coordinated by the very people entrusted to protect her. No one at the time fought for her parental rights or her bodily integrity. Her sterilization was built on a cover-up and on the ambitions of a team of eugenicists.[118] Her younger sister, Doris, who had been placed with another family after her mother's institutionalization, was sent to the Lynchburg Colony in 1926 at the age of 13, while Carrie's case was still in the courts, having been accused of "running wild" and "meeting men."[119] The Colony Board issued an order for Doris's sterilization soon after Carrie was released from the Colony.[120] At the time she was told she was having an appendectomy, but did not learn she had been sterilized until 1980, when she was in her sixties.[121] They lived long enough to see their histories rediscovered and an ACLU lawsuit brought against the Lynchburg Colony on their and others'

115   *Id.*
116   Carrie Buck Trial Transcript, pp. 32–34, Digital Documents, *available at* https://buckvbell .com/downloads.html.
117   Lombardo, *supra* note 3, at 338.
118   *Id.* at xii.
119   *Id.* at 186.
120   *Id.* at 187.
121   *Id.* at 251.

behalf, but the suit was dismissed in 1981, based in large part on Justice Holmes' ruling in *Buck v. Bell*.[122] Doris died in 1982 and Carrie died the following year.[123]

4   The Story of Anna Buck and her Daughter Marilyn

Anna Buck was a librarian in Manchester, Vermont and church clerk at the First Congregational Church of Manchester when in 1932, she became pregnant by the Reverend Eric Allen,[124] the pastor of Manchester's First Congregational Church.[125] Reverend Allen was married at the time to my great-grandmother, Nina, and had five other children by Nina, including my grandmother, Sally. To hide her pregnancy, Anna left Manchester for several months to be treated for a supposed "kidney problem."[126] She stayed at the Elizabeth Lund Home for unwed mothers in Burlington, Vermont, giving birth to a baby girl in spring 1933.[127] The child, whose birth name was Ruth,[128] was adopted by a childless couple when she was three months old who changed her name to Marilyn.[129] Anna, who was in her early forties when Marilyn was born,[130] returned to Manchester, no one else the wiser, and resumed her positions as town librarian and church clerk.[131] It appears that she never married or had other children.[132]

When Marilyn was in her early teens, some people in her town asked her if she had been adopted. When she questioned her adoptive parents, they tearfully acknowledged that it was true. They shared with her a typed document, several pages in length, which Anna had prepared. Marilyn supposed that most women who gave up their children wished to keep their identity secret,

---

122   Poe v. Lynchburg Training School and Hospital, 518 F. Supp. 789, 792 (W.D. Va. 1981) ("the fact remains that the general practice and procedure under the old Virginia statute were upheld by the highest court in the land in *Buck v. Bell*").

123   Lombardo, *supra* note 3, at 254–256.

124   Marilyn W. Letter, *supra* note 4, at *2.

125   First Congregational Church Manchester, *supra* note 7, at 101.

126   Marilyn W. Letter, *supra* note 4, at *1.

127   *Id.*

128   Ancestry Messaging from Marilyn W. at ancestry.com/messaging (last checked 6/17/22) (on file with author).

129   *Id.*

130   Cemetery Records, Anna B. Buck, at https://www.findagrave.com/memorial/12353391/.

131   First Congregational Church of Manchester, *supra* note 7, at 101; Silver Fork at the Old Library, Gallery and History, at https://thesilverforkvt.com/gallery-history/(with various pictures of Anna Buck, including a 1964 celebration in her honor for her over 50 years of service as Mark Skinner Library Head Librarian).

132   *See* Cemetery Records, Anna B. Buck, *supra* note 130.

but Anna wrote in great detail about her parents and siblings, that she was a librarian in Manchester, and about Marilyn's father, Eric R. Allen, his birth date, education, and that he was a Congregational minister.[133]

In the early 1950s, when Marilyn was in her late teens, she went with her fiancé Bill, who she later married, to the library where Anna Buck worked, with the intention of introducing herself. She spotted her mother, who looked a lot like her, but "when the face-to-face moment was there," she writes, "I could not go through with it. I knew that my adoptive parents, especially my mother would be heartbroken."[134] She made no further attempts to contact Anna Buck or to learn more about her biological family until years later.[135]

Marilyn contacted the First Congregational Church in Manchester in 2021.[136] They sent her a copy of the church history, including a chapter focused on Reverend Allen's pastorate from 1931 until 1939.[137] She found his obituary and learned the names of her half-siblings.[138] She also learned from the church history that he and Anna had started at the Church at almost the same time in 1931,[139] but that he had left the church in 1939 while she continued as church clerk.[140]

In 2021, when Marilyn was 88 years old, she confirmed through Ancestry.com her relationship to the Allen Family Tree, with several DNA matches, including to me, my half-brother, and my cousin.[141] She reached out to my mother who shared the news with Eric Allen's descendants. We were enthralled. We knew that my great-grandfather had been forced out of the First Congregational Church for reasons that remained unclear. We also knew that he had then left his wife and five children and moved to California and later to Mexico where he took up farming.[142] My great-grandmother had to leave the manse and find lodging elsewhere with her youngest children. His deserting his family and

---

133   Marilyn W. Letter, *supra* note 4, at *1.
134   *Id.*
135   *Id.*
136   *Id.* at 1–2.
137   First Congregational Church of Manchester, *supra* note 7, at 101,104.
138   Marilyn W. Letter, *supra* note 4, at *2.
139   First Congregational Church of Manchester, *supra* note 7, at 101, 103 (As Church Clerk, Anna Buck recorded after one of the first annual meetings of the Allen years that "The feeling of good fellowship and brotherhood of all those connected with the church has been raised a very market degree in the last year by the leadership of our earnest, faithful, and loyal leader, Mr. Allen.")
140   First Congregational Church of Manchester, *supra* note 7, at 101, 104.
141   Marilyn W. Letter, *supra* note 4, at *2. *See also* Ancestry Messaging from Marilyn W. at ancestry.com/messaging (last checked 6/17/22).
142   Email from J. Allen (grandson), March 15, 2022 (on file with author).

leaving them in near poverty was part of the family lore, each of us seeing it through our own lens,[143] but his relationship with Anna Buck had been a secret until Marilyn, at the age of 88, shared it with us. By that time, her half-siblings had died, and no one living knew whether this had been a skeleton in all their closets.[144]

As a professor of family law, I am interested in how this story fits within the legal culture at that time and how Vermont's legal system regulated parents of children born out of wedlock. I hope in future research to compare Vermont's legal system with that in other parts of the country, in terms of how they characterized and regulated unwed motherhood. By the early 1800s, Vermont had in place a Bastardy Act which allowed an unwed mother to sue the biological father for maintenance.[145] The Vermont Supreme Court interpreted the Act as applying to both unmarried and married men. In *Beattie v. Traynor*,[146] the Vermont Supreme Court upheld an oral agreement entered into by an unwed

---

143 Email from P. Allen-S. (granddaughter), Feb. 28, 2022 ("For our beloved Gran Nina, what an incredibly sad time this must have been for her... And how quickly the door into this tragic occurrence must have been closed. If anything, the mystical adventurer Eric Allen who slept with rattlesnakes, battled cougers and ended up with a Mexican beauty named Rosa has been somewhat diminished by an un-acknowledged daughter named Marilyn."); Email from J. Allen (grandson), March 3, 2022 ("Don't mean to sound a sour, cautionary note, but it seems to me that speculation about the state of our common Allen grandparents' marriage, Grandfather Eric's and Anna's relationship apart from the sexual liaison, and other aspects of this fascinating story, beg further investigation and additional information before we draw any conclusions or pass judgment on anyone") (On file with author).

144 *See, e.g.,* Email from E. Allen (grandson), March 15, 2022 ("My take on the Allen stoicism is that it was less calculated than you suggest. More like a congenital predisposition to keeping skeletons firmly locked in their closets."); Email from J. Allen, March 15, 2022 ("Stoicism and a stiff upper lip are Allen family traits, as is denial. Together, those probably inherent characteristics may explain what I've gone out on a limb to accuse our elders of: a cover-up and a deliberate concealment of the existence of their half-sister from us.") (On file with author).

145 *See* Haven v. Hobbs, 1 Vt. 238, 243 (1828) ("when any single woman shall be delivered of any bastard child, or shall declare herself to be with child, and that such child is likely to be born a bastard, and shall charge any person in writing, and on oath before any justice of the peace, with being the father of the same, the justice may issue his warrant for the apprehending of the person so charged, may bind him over to the next term of the County Court; and if the County Court shall adjudge such person to be the father, to charge him "with the payment of money for the assistance of the mother, for her expenses already accrued in the premises, and for the future support of the child.")

146 114 Vt. 238 (1945).

mother and married father where he agreed to support the child in exchange for the mother not bringing a bastardy suit.[147]

Ms. Beattie, the mother, brought the case against Traynor, the administrator of the estate of the father, Clarence Smith, after Smith's death. The Vermont Supreme Court had many opportunities to dismiss the case. It could have found that the oral agreement was outside the Statute of Frauds;[148] that the Bastardy Act did not apply to suits against married men;[149] that the agreement was meretricious, because it was based on an adulterous relationship;[150] that there was not adequate consideration;[151] or on the basis of her delay in enforcing their agreement.

Yet the Vermont Supreme Court took a surprisingly enlightened approach. Overturning the lower court, it found that the Vermont Legislature intended to make single *and* married men liable for supporting their illegitimate children.[152] It dismissed the defendant's argument that the agreement should not be enforced because it was based on an adulterous relationship.[153] It found that the agreement was salutary and not illegal in providing for the support and education of an innocent child.[154] After the case was remanded and made its way back to the Court, it wrote:

> It is a matter of fine speculation whether a married man with business experience and of substantial means would be less likely to have illicit sexual intercourse or to make such a contract than a single man. We have been referred to no statistical studies upon the subject. ... By reputation in any community the greater number of, and the most promiscuous, seducers of women are often married men, and able business men and men of wealth are no exception.[155]

As an unwed mother, Anna Buck's story intrigues me. There are so many questions that remain unanswered. Did she ever consider keeping her child? Why did she stay on at the Church working with my great-grandfather? Why was he eventually forced out in 1939? Did my great-grandmother learn the truth? One

---

147   *Id.* at 239.
148   Beattie v. Traynor, 114 Vt. 495, 497–498 (1946).
149   Beattie v. Traynor, 114 Vt. at 240 (1945).
150   *Id.* at 242.
151   *Id.* at 241.
152   *Id.* at 240.
153   *Id.* at 242.
154   *Id.*
155   Beattie v. Traynor, 114 Vt. 495, 503 (1946).

can speculate that she did and that his departure must have been connected to his relationship with Anna, since he not only left the church but left his family as well. But then why wasn't Anna ostracized? To me, Anna Buck showed great resilience in navigating through difficult terrain and in not allowing an unplanned pregnancy to derail her life.

5 My Story

In my last semester of law school, in the midst of final exams, I realized that I was pregnant. The day of my last exam, I dropped off a urine sample before going to take my exam. A couple of days later, the test came back positive. The father was a fellow law student. We had dated the previous semester, broken up, and then had one last fling in April after celebrating with a group of classmates. My whole life was ahead of me. I had accepted an offer from Arnold & Porter in Washington, D.C., as an associate. I knew that there was no future between this person and myself. But I wanted to have a baby and I was 27-years-old.

My child's father was a devout Catholic. When we had sex the first time and I told him that I felt awkward, his response was that he believed in a forgiving God. Yet later, when I told him that I intended to have the baby and assumed that he was against abortion, he told me that I should have talked that over with him first. He pressured me to give her up for adoption, saying that she would be better off with a mother and father. I refused. My devastated grandmother, when confronted with yet another unplanned pregnancy, insisted on writing to his father to propose that we marry. To appease her, I acquiesced. She sent the letter, but after my child's father learned of the letter, he informed me that he had told his father that the matter was between the two of us. I don't think we ever spoke again, although he wrote me several hand-written letters over the years with regard to our daughter.

Work at a fast-paced law firm was extremely demanding, both before and after I gave birth. The firm, however, had an excellent maternity policy which they extended to me even though I joined them well into my pregnancy. Selfishly, I took the maximum: three months of paid and three months of unpaid leave, returning to work when Megan was six months old, just as we were beginning to bond. Those first few months back were overwhelming for both of us. I felt a failure as a mother and inadequate as a lawyer. Even though I worked part-time (80%), this meant that when everyone else was there until 2:00 a.m., I was able to go home at 8:00 p.m.

At first I shared a house and a baby-sitter with another single mother, Nancy, but it didn't work out. I forgot my umbrella one day and came home to find my daughter crawling across the floor crying uncontrollably while the sitter made toast and coffee in the kitchen. I moved out, got my own place, and found an excellent care-giver, Marta, an Ecuadorian. Megan was much happier, but I was miserable, especially when Megan started calling Marta "Mami." So I applied for a Fulbright to teach international trade law in Costa Rica. I had studied international trade in law school and worked on several high profile international trade cases at Arnold & Porter. I put together a strong application and was awarded the Fulbright.

In early 1991, when Megan was just two, I traveled with her to Costa Rica on my Fulbright, where I was able to achieve, for the first time since her birth, work-family balance, teaching international trade law one evening a week at the National University's School of International Relations and doing research and writing the rest of the week. I published my first OpEd. I stayed in Costa Rica when my Fulbright ended, working with the Inter-American Institute of Human Rights on matters related to the Salvadoran Peace Process. My life was on track.

In 1992, while still in Costa Rica, I became pregnant. Megan was three. My boyfriend in Costa Rica was a Salvadoran refugee. I liked him, and upon learning I was pregnant, considered having the child, but when I told him I was pregnant, he told me, somewhat embarrassedly, that he had another girlfriend, a Costa Rican, and that she was also pregnant with his child. He didn't pressure me, one way or the other. I was using birth control at the time, a diaphragm, but contraception had failed. I went to a gynecologist to confirm the pregnancy and remember how shocked I was by the doctor's clear message that, of course, I had to have the child; abortion was illegal in Costa Rica.

I did try to terminate my pregnancy in Costa Rica. I went to the pharmacist, but he only could suggest that I go to an herbalist in the Central Market in San Jose. I consulted with a friend whose ex-husband was a doctor. She told me that it was hard to get a safe abortion in Costa Rica and that I should fly to Miami. She said there was one Costa Rican doctor who had some contraption that he put around your neck for inducing abortions by vibrations. I contacted a clinic in Miami but was told that they could not perform the abortion until I was at least six weeks pregnant. I went to the Central Market and cooked up the herbal remedy, but to no avail.

So at six weeks, I traveled to Miami for the abortion. It was a miserable experience, as I lay awake the whole time, but the nurse held my hand throughout. I briefly cried when it was over. What I remember most vividly was the recovery room where I chatted with other women who were there. Many of the women were either Haitian or Latina (mostly Mexican or Central American). It was a surprisingly empowering experience, to share our different reasons for terminating our pregnancies. One Haitian girl with whom we were talking was very young, about fifteen. A nurse interrupted us to tell her that she had to repeat the procedure because they had not removed the entire fetus. A Mexican woman talked about how she and her partner had several other children and could not afford another. I felt sad but knew I had made the right choice.

My Salvadoran boyfriend wanted to continue our relationship. I broke it off, because I believed that his Costa Rican girlfriend needed his support more than I did. Also, I enjoyed the autonomy of being able, as a single woman, to make my own choices about my future. The silver lining to Megan's father's lack of interest in her or me was that I did not have to get his permission, even when I left the United States.

Later that year, I was selected by the United Nations to be an attorney-investigator on the Truth Commission for El Salvador, traveling there with Megan in September and hiring a full-time baby-sitter to care for her during the endless hours that we worked. It was only for seven months and the only time in my life, aside from those first months back at work, where I felt like I was neglecting her, but it was still hard on both of us, mostly on her. Megan and I eventually returned to the United States near the end of that stint and then back to the Washington, D.C. area where, after a long job search, I began my career in academia in 1994.

Megan's father dutifully paid child support, but it would be years before he would ask to meet her, and only after her admission to Yale University. She graduated first in her class from Phillips Exeter Academy. She graduated *magna cum laude* from Yale, where his parents attended her graduation. She successfully defended her dissertation in East Asian Studies at Princeton University in August 2022 and has a postdoctoral fellowship at the University of Texas-Austin where she is teaching Premodern East Asian History.

Over the years, I have met many single mothers, including my students. Although we come from different backgrounds, ethnicities, and experiences, we often bond because we share the same resilience and commitment to being good parents and seeing our children succeed. Having lived through both my parents' various dysfunctional marriages, I find the idea that a child is always better off in a traditional family with a mother and a father almost laughable.

One last story: When I was 11 months old, my father, unhappy with my mother's cooking, took a plate of food and threw it across the room into the wall. My mother, who was only 18 at the time, showed the courage to pick me up and move back in with her parents rather than waiting for the further incidents of violence that would have followed. (He would go on to physically abuse his second and third wives.) My grandmother had been so concerned about my being born a bastard that she pressured my mother to marry a man she did not love and who my grandmother never even liked. I was conceived in 1960 in Connecticut in the backseat of a 1957 Chevy at a time when contraception was not legal. My mother was not much older than Carrie Buck at the time, and probably would have been considered "feeble-minded" if she had lived in the same era. I am glad that I and my daughter exist, and that we have been able to flourish in our own ways, but I also believe that my mother would have found greater personal fulfillment if she had had control over her reproductive life back in 1960.

6   Ordered Liberty, Sex and the Single Mother

What are the implications of *Dobbs* for the modern Carrie Bucks and Anna Bucks of this country as well as for poor women of color who were not even of concern to policymakers and eugenicists back then?[156] With the Court's ruling in *Dobbs* that there is no constitutional right to abortion and that the matter should be left to the States to decide, the right to choose will depend largely on where a person lives and what resources they have. Middle and upper class women seeking an abortion likely will be able to obtain medication abortions or travel to states where abortion is legal while poor women and girls and other pregnant persons will face considerable hardship if they choose to terminate their pregnancies. The latter are more likely to resort to black markets or backroom abortions.[157] The decision also raises concerns regarding reproductive rights in general, including the rights to procreate and not procreate, and to raise ones children outside of the traditional family without undue interference from the State. *Dobbs* and the State laws being enacted across the country are a serious threat to pregnant individuals' right to self-determination.

---

156   Bridges, *supra* note 91, at 466 ("Thus, it is not an overstatement to say that, *on the whole, eugenicists working in the early twentieth century were uninterested in people of color*") (emphasis in original).

157   *See, e.g.,* Stephania Taldrid, *A Texas Teen-Agers Abortion Odyssey*, The New Yorker, June 20, 2022; Vanessa Williamson & John Hudak, *The War on Abortion Drugs will be just as racist and classist,* Brookings Inst. (May 9, 2022) available at https://www.brookings.edu/blog /fixgov/2022/05/09/the-war-on-abortion-drugs-will-be-just-as-racist-and-classist); Susan A. Cohen, *Abortion and Wom, at en of Color: The Bigger Picture,* 11 Guttmacher Institute 3 (Aug. 6 2008); Sandhya Dirks, *Abortion is also about racial justice, experts and advocates say,* NPR (May 14, 2022) (available at https://www.npr.org/2022/05/14/1098306203/abortion -is-also-about-racial-justice-experts-and-advocates-say).

The specific issue before the Court in *Dobbs* was a narrow one: whether "all pre-viability prohibitions on elective abortion are unconstitutional".[158] Rather than deciding the case on these narrow grounds, the majority seized the opportunity to overturn *Roe* and *Casey*.[159] Rejecting *stare decisis*, it concludes that *Roe* was "egregiously wrong" from the start and that the reasoning in *Roe* and *Casey* was "exceptionally weak".[160] Although it acknowledges the existence of unenumerated rights, it concludes that abortion is not one of them. It distinguished abortion from other unenumerated rights such as marriage, the right to procreate, contraception, intimate sexual relations, and same-sex marriage on the basis that abortion destroys fetal life.[161]

Twenty-six states in the *Dobbs* litigation had asked the Court to overrule *Roe* and *Casey* and give States the authority to regulate abortions.[162] At least half the states are likely to pass restrictive abortion laws.[163] Thirteen states already have passed trigger laws banning most abortions, including in cases of rape, incest, and fetal abnormalities, many of which already have gone into effect.[164] In April 2022, Florida and Arizona passed laws like Mississippi's banning abortions after fifteen weeks of pregnancy, and, a year later, Florida passed a six-week ban.[165] As the dissent in *Dobbs* points out, this is just the beginning. Some States will try to block women from traveling out of State to obtain an abortion or from receiving abortion medications through the mail. Some may criminalize the provision of information or funding to women seeking abortion services in other States. Nothing in the decision precludes Congress from prohibiting abortions nationwide.[166] And even if these laws include an exception to save a woman's life, doctors are unclear at when that exception will kick in. In short, as the dissent states, the majority

---

158   *Dobbs, supra* note 2, at 2244.

159   *Id.* at 2242.

160   *Id* at 2243.

161   *Id.*

162   *Id.* at 2242.

163   *How State Abortion Laws Could Change if Roe Is Overturned*, N.Y. Times, updated June 17, 2022.

164   *Id.* (lists 10 states with existing or trigger laws banning most abortions with no exception for rape or incest).

165   *See* Alison Durkee, *Arizona Enacts 15-Week Abortion Ban – Same as Mississippi Law Supreme Court Now Weighing*, Forbes, April 14, 2022; Wynne Davis, *Florida Gov. Ron DeSantis signs a bill banning abortions after 15 weeks*, NPR, April 14, 2022; Arek Sarkissian, *DeSantis Signs Florida's 6-Week Abortion Ban into Law*, Politico, April 13, 2023.

166   *Dobbs, supra* note 2, at 2318 (Breyer, Sotomayor, and Kagan, JJ., dissenting).

would allow States to ban abortion from conception onward because it does not think forced childbirth at all implicates a woman's rights to equality and freedom. *Today's Court, that is, does not think there is anything of constitutional significance attached to a woman's control of her body and the path of her life.*[167]

Before applying the due process clause, Justice Alito disposed of the equal protection claims. He concluded that abortion regulations cannot be challenged under the equal protection clause because they are not a "sex-based classification subject to heightened scrutiny".[168] The regulation of a medical procedure that only one sex can undergo, he said, relying on *Geduldig v. Aiello,* a controversial 1974 decision,[169] does not trigger heightened scrutiny unless done with a discriminatory purpose.[170] *Dobbs* concludes that the Court already had found that "the goal of preventing abortion does not constitute invidiously discriminatory animus against women."[171] It fails to recognize the interrelationship between a pregnant woman's liberty interests in bodily integrity and self-determination and the equal protection concerns raised when the State dictates her reproductive role.[172]

---

167   *Id.* at 2323. [Emphasis added.]

168   *Id.* at 2245.

169   Geduldig v. Aiello, 417 U.S. 484 (1974); General Electric Co. v. Gilbert, 429 U.S. 125, 145 (1976) (extending *Geduldig's* reasoning to Title VII), superceded by Pregnancy Discrimination Act of 1978. *See also* Newport News Shipbuilding and Dry Dock Co. v. E.E.O.C., 462 U.S. 669 (1983) ("When Congress amended Title VII in 1978, it unambiguously expressed its disapproval of both the holding and the reasoning of the Court in the *Gilbert* decision. ... The first clause of the Act states, quite simply: "The terms 'because of sex' or 'on the basis of sex' include, but are not limited to, because of or on the basis of pregnancy, childbirth, or related medical conditions.")

170   *Dobbs, supra* note 2, at 2245 - 2246. *Dobbs* references the Brief of Equal Protection Constitutional Law Scholars as Amici Curiae. *Id.* It does not address their argument that subsequent decisions of the Court, like *United States v. Virginia* and *Nev. Dep't of Hum. Res. v. Hibbs,* clarified that "equal protection principles apply with equal force to pregnancy-based classifications." Brief of Equal Protection Constitutional Law Scholars Serena Mayeri, Melissa Murray, and Reva Siegel as Amici Curiae in Support of Respondents, Dobbs v. Jackson Women's Health Organization, No. 19-1392, 2021 WL 4340072 (Sept. 20, 2021) at *3 [hereinafter Amicus Brief of Equal Protection Scholars].

171   *Dobbs, supra* note 2, at 2246.

172   Brief of Amici Curiae National Women's Law Center and 72 Additional Organizations Committed to Gender Equality in Support of Respondents, Dobbs v. Jackson Women's Health Organization, No. 19-1392, 2021 WL 4441329 (Sept. 20, 2021) at 8–10 [hereinafter NWLC Amicus Brief].

The Court in *Dobbs* then turns to *Casey's* "bold assertion"[173] that the abortion right is part of the liberty protected by Fourteenth Amendment's due process clause. It warns that "we must guard against the natural human tendency to confuse what that Amendment protects with our own ardent views about the liberty that Americans should enjoy."[174] It claims that "history and tradition ... map the essential components of our Nation's concept of ordered liberty."[175] The majority concludes that there is "an unbroken tradition of prohibiting abortion on pain of criminal punishment [that] persisted from the earliest days of the common law until 1973."[176] It relies most heavily on the observation that when the Fourteenth Amendment was adopted in 1868, "three quarters of the States had made abortion a crime at any stage of pregnancy."[177] It discounts the findings from *Roe* that neither English common law nor most States had criminalized abortion prior to "quickening", concluding that the reason for drawing a line at quickening was because, at the time, fetal movement was the first well-defined *evidence* of life.[178] It emphasizes that no common law case or authority treated abortion as a positive right prior to 1973.[179]

The Court, however, (to paraphrase *Brown v. Board of Education*[180]) cannot turn the clock back to 1868, when women were excluded from the political process. It should have taken account of the 19th Amendment, ratified in 1921, which gave women the right to vote, and the jurisprudence of the 1970s, which recognized women's right to full and equal participation in society, including the right to control their reproductive destiny. As the dissent in *Dobbs* points out:

> The majority's core legal postulate, then, is that we in the 21st century must read the Fourteenth Amendment just as its ratifiers did. ... If the ratifiers did not understand something as central to freedom, then neither can we. ... If those people did not understand reproductive rights as

---

173   *Dobbs, supra* note 2, at 2246.

174   *Id.* at 2247.

175   *Id.* at 2235.

176   *Id.* at 2253-2254.

177   *Id.* at 2236. *See also* Kavanaugh, J. concurring at n. 1 ("As I see it, the dispositive point in analyzing American history and tradition for purposes of the Fourteenth Amendment inquiry is that abortion was largely prohibited in most American States as of 1868 when the Fourteenth Amendment was ratified, and that abortion remained largely prohibited in most American States until *Roe* was decided in 1973").

178   *Id.* at 2251-2252.

179   *Id.* at 2251.

180   Brown v. Board of Education, 347 U.S. 483, 492–493 (1954).

part of the guarantee of liberty conferred in the Fourteenth Amendment, then those rights do not exist.

But, of course, "people" did not ratify the Fourteenth Amendment. Men did. ... Those responsible for the original Constitution, including the Fourteenth Amendment, did not perceive women as equals, and did not recognize women's rights. When the majority says that we must read our foundational charter as viewed at the time of ratification ... it consigns women to second-class citizenship.[181]

The *Dobbs* majority justifies its analysis by relying heavily on the majority opinion in *Washington v. Glucksberg*,[182] where the Court unanimously found that there was no fundamental right to physician-assisted suicide. Five justices in *Glucksberg* would have defined the right in question with the greatest degree of specificity. They would have asked whether the liberty protected by the Due Process clause "includes a right to commit suicide which itself includes a right to assistance in doing so."[183]

The four concurring justices differed in their analyses. Three focused on the concept of human dignity. Justice O'Connor said that, under a different set of facts, the Court might "address the question whether suffering patients have a constitutionally cognizable interest in obtaining relief from the suffering that they may experience in the last days of their lives."[184] Justice Stevens argued that a dying patient has the right to die with dignity.[185] Justice Breyer defined the right to die with dignity as involving "at its core ... personal control over the manner of death, professional medical assistance and the avoidance of unnecessary and severe physical suffering-combined."[186]

---

181   *Id.* at 2325
182   521 U.S. 702 (1997).
183   *Id.* at 723.
184   *Id.* at 737 (O'Connor, J., concurring).
185   *Id.* at 788 (Stevens, J., concurring).
186   *Id.* at 790 (Breyer, J., concurring). The majority's approach in *Glucksberg* of defining the fundamental right with the greatest degree of specificity has often been met with criticism by both concurring and dissenting justices. See, e.g., *Bowers v. Hardwick*, 478 U.S. 186, 199 (1986) (Blackmun, J., dissenting) ("This case is no more about 'a fundamental right to engage in homosexual sodomy,' as the Court purports to declare than *Stanley v. Georgia* was about a fundamental right to watch obscene movies ... Rather, this case is about 'the most comprehensive of rights and the right most valued by civilized men,' namely, 'the right to be let alone.'"); *Michael H. v. Gerald D.*, 491 U.S. 110, 132 (1989), (O'Connor, J., concurring) (I concur in all but footnote 6 of Justice SCALIA's opinion. This footnote sketches a mode of historical analysis to be used when identifying liberty interests protected by the Due Process Clause of the Fourteenth Amendment that may be somewhat

Justice Souter, in contrast, focused on ordered liberty. He would have asked "whether the statute sets up one of those 'arbitrary impositions' or 'purposeless restraints' at odds with the Due Process Clause of the 14th Amendment."[187] Answering that question in the negative, he defined ordered liberty as requiring a balancing of the individual's liberty interests against the demands of organized society, quoting Justice Harlan's dissent in *Poe v. Ullman*:[188]

> Due Process has not been reduced to any formula; its content cannot be determined by reference to any code. The best that can be said is that through the course of this Court's decisions it has represented the balance which our Nation, built upon postulates of respect for the liberty of the individual, has struck between that liberty and the demands of organized society. ... The balance of which I speak is the balance struck by this country, having regard to what history teaches are the traditions from which it developed as well as the traditions from which it broke. That tradition is a living thing.[189]

The Court repeatedly has recognized that the liberties protected by the due process clause include certain personal choices central to human dignity and self-determination.[190] This broader concept of ordered liberty, which recognizes that while history and tradition are a starting point they do not set its outer boundaries, is part of our jurisprudence.[191] As the Court said in *Obergefell*, "the past alone [cannot] rule the present."[192]

---

inconsistent with our past decisions in this area. [Citations omitted]. On occasion the Court has characterized relevant traditions protecting asserted rights at levels of generality that might not be 'the most specific level' available"). This particular approach was specifically rejected by Justice Kennedy in *Lawrence v. Texas*, 539 U.S. 558 (2003) in overturning *Bowers v. Hardwick* as incorrectly decided. Id. at 567 ("[The decision in *Bowers*] discloses the Court's own failure to appreciate the extent of the liberty at stake. To say that the issue in *Bowers* was simply the right to engage in certain sexual conduct demeans the claim the individual put forward, just as it would demean a married couple were it to be said marriage is simply about the right to have sexual intercourse.").

187   *Glucksberg, supra* note 182, at 752 (Souter, J., concurring).
188   Poe v. Ullman, 367 U.S. 497, 542 (1961) (Harlan, J., dissenting).
189   *Id.* at 542 (quoted with approval in Washington v. Glucksberg, 521 U.S. at 765 (Souter, J., concurring).
190   *See, e.g.,* Loving v. Virginia, 388 U.S. 1 (1967) ("the freedom to marry or not marry, a person of another race resides with the individual and cannot be infringed by the state"); *Eisenstadt, supra* note 32, at 453; *Lawrence v. Texas*, 539 U.S. 558, 572 (2003); *Obergefell v. Hodges*, 576 U.S. 644, 663-664 (2015).
191   *Id.*
192   *Obergefell, supra* note 190, at 664.

In sharp contrast, Justice Alito and the Court in *Dobbs* rely on a static concept of tradition, frozen in time, that would force many women back into the domestic sphere and a maternal role. It could, potentially wipe out the last fifty years of jurisprudence on women's rights. *Dobbs* speaks repeatedly of "ordered liberty" but engages in empty formalism. It compartmentalizes its analyses without considering the relationship between the liberty interests at stake and the impact of abortion bans on women's equal status in society. By relying on the state of the law in 1868, *Dobbs* also gives short shrift to historical evidence that, under the common law and early American history, by not criminalizing pre-quickening abortion, there appears to have been a protected liberty interest up until a certain point in pregnancy, regardless of whether it was treated as the woman's right.[193] The Court's rationale in *Roe* and *Casey* for drawing a bright line at viability was not "egregiously wrong" but built on an evolving history and tradition of weighing the interests of the pregnant person against the State's interest in potential life.[194]

The Court's analysis of the due process and equal protection issues in *Dobbs* is not only fragmented but disingenuous. Laws based on sexual stereotypes about the way men and women are exist, at least in part, because of an underlying animus[195] towards those who do not conform to traditional models of womanhood or the family. Let us return to the stories of Carrie Buck and Anna Buck who were very different people but whose stories are connected in time. Carrie Buck was a poor white girl in Virginia whose foster parents, the Dobbs, labeled her as feeble-minded when she became pregnant by their nephew at aged sixteen; they took away her child, quickly shipped her off to

---

193   *As* Lea Vandervelde illustrates in her article *The Legal Ways of Seduction, supra* note 45, at 821, the common law extended rights to the fathers of unwed women, rather than the women themselves, allowing fathers, for example "to sue for sexual interference with their daughters' services while their daughters were working outside the household's confines." As a result, since the law, prior to the mid-19th century did not allow women to bring their own claims, single women lacked the legal autonomy and actual autonomy needed to be independent. *Id.* at 821–822.

194   *Roe v. Wade, supra* note 33, at 133–134.

195   The Merriam-Webster dictionary describes animus as "a usually prejudiced and often spiteful or malevolent ill will"; or, alternatively, as "an inner masculine part of the female personality in the analytical psychology of Carl Gustav Jung." (available at https://www .merriam-webster.com/dictionary/animus). According to Wiktionary, animus originated from Latin, where it was used to describe ideas such as the rational soul, life, mind, mental powers, courage or desire. In the early nineteenth century, animus was used to mean "temper" and was typically used in a hostile sense. In 1923, it began being used as a term in Jungian psychology to describe the masculine side of women (available at https://en .wiktionary.org/wiki/animus#English).

the Lynchburg Colony to hide the scandal, and called for her sterilization and permanent institutionalization.[196] Anna Buck was a respectable middle-aged unmarried woman from Manchester, Vermont, working as church clerk and town librarian. When she became pregnant by the town's married pastor, she had to make difficult choices to preserve her reputation and place in the community. Ill-will towards this pregnant teenager drove the Dobbs' decision to label her as promiscuous and send her to the Lynchburg Colony. If Anna Buck had chosen to keep her child, she likely would have been met with animus by the church elders, the broader community and certainly, the Reverend Allen's family. She would have worn a scarlet letter.[197]

There is a nearly 50-year history and tradition of women being able to control their own reproductive destinies that connects to a much longer history of laws designed to protect unwed women from unwanted pregnancies. Over the last 230 years, the means have changed as the views of the role of women within and outside of marriage have evolved. Contraceptives have become more widely available. The shame and social stigma of unwed motherhood has largely, but not entirely, dissipated.[198] The Court in *Roe* and *Casey* recognized that women's ability to flourish and to fully participate in society on the basis of equality with men depended on their ability to control their reproductive lives and to make those crucial decisions without undue interference by the State.[199] Under *Dobbs*, fifty different States will now get to decide what rights a pregnant person has over her own body.

I have sought to interweave these stories of single motherhood with the *Dobbs* decision. Anna Buck's story is linked with my story, the story of Carrie Buck, and all the single women who were confronted with an unplanned pregnancy and had to decide whether to have a child, give the child up for adoption, marry, or raise the child on their own. To limit their choices, as the *Dobbs* decision does, denies many women the opportunity to control their own destinies. Women's control over their bodily integrity and their reproductive lives, to self-determination, is vital to their human flourishing. We must return it to its place as an essential component of our uniquely American concept of ordered liberty.

---

196   Lombardo, *supra* note 3, at 3.
197   Nathaniel Hawthorne, The Scarlet Letter (1850). *See also* Rickie Solinger, Wake Up Little Susie (Routledge 2000) (documents how race shaped the experiences of single mothers in the 1950s and 1960s, how both Black and white unwed mothers faced shame and stigma, and how the cultural meaning of pregnancy and the institutional response varied on the basis of race).
198   *Dobbs, supra* note 2, at 2258-2259.
199   *Casey, supra* note 33, at 856.

CHAPTER 36

Children's Picture Books and the Rule of Law: The Jurisprudence of "The Poky Little Puppy"

Lenora Ledwon[*]

> Five little puppies dug a hole under the fence and went for a walk in the wide, wide world.
> JANETTE SEBRING LOWREY, The Poky Little Puppy[1]

∴

Can a children's picture book be a law book? My university bookstore does not think so. The first time I assigned The Poky Little Puppy for a law school seminar, I received a call from the bookstore asking if I made a mistake filling out the ISBN. After all, The Poky Little Puppy does not look like the typical law school casebook. It is not hundreds of pages long; it is not bound in dark, somber colors; it is not prohibitively expensive; it is not intimidating. But this short, colorful, inexpensive picture book for children is indeed a law book.

Law and Literature scholars, with some notable exceptions, have rarely turned their attention to children's literature.[2] As for the genre of children's picture

---

[*] Professor of Law, St. Thomas University College of Law. Ph.D., University of Notre Dame; J.D., University of Michigan.

[1] Janette Sebring Lowrey, *illustrated by* Gustaf Tenggren, The Poky Little Puppy n.p. (Golden Books (1970)(1942). (Note: The Poky Little Puppy, like many children's picture books, does not have page numbers. It is 24 pages long, including the title page.)

[2] For a sampling of some of the relatively rare (but truly excellent) scholarship addressing law and children's literature, see the following: Sarah Hamilton, *Over the Rainbow and Down the Rabbit Hole: Law and Order in Children's Literature*, 81 N.D. L. Rev. 75 (2005)(analysis of legal ideology in Alice in Wonderland and The Wonderful Wizard of Oz, including how the stories might affect children's legal and social development); Thomas C. Klein, *Imperfect Order: Reflections of the Law in Two Classic Children's Novels*, 12 Tex. Wesleyan L. Rev. 303 (2005) (examines the portrayal of law in The Wind in the Willows and Shiloh); Mary Liston, *The Rule of Law Through the Looking Glass*, 21 Law & Literature 42 (2009) (examines legal authority in such children's classics as Alice in Wonderland, The Phantom Tollbooth, and Harry Potter and the Order of the Phoenix); William P. MacNeil, *"Kidlit" As "Law-And-Lit": Harry Potter and*

books (i.e., books where illustrations accompany every page of the story), such works have received even less attention from legal scholars.[3] While analyses of law in literary works by canonical authors such as Shakespeare and Dickens abound, analyses of law in children's literature are far fewer, perhaps because children's literature is considered insignificant when compared to works in the traditional Western canon. Yet, children need the opportunity to imagine how to live in a world under a rule of law. Picture books such as The Poky Little Puppy provide that opportunity. As James Boyd White reminds us, law is a constitutive activity: interpreting, understanding, and imagining changes in the law are ways we constitute our society and ourselves.[4] A picture book may be one of the very first jurisprudential stories with which a young child imaginatively engages.[5] The Poky Little Puppy, an illustrated story about a rule-breaking, curious little puppy, suggests lessons in jurisprudence for readers both young and old.

Where does law come from? Is it always present as a set of universal moral imperatives? Or does law have little to do with morality and everything to do

---

the Scales of Justice, 14 Law & Literature 545 (2002)(discusses Harry Potter and the Goblet of Fire in terms of the jurisprudence of magic); Katherine J. Roberts, Note, Once Upon the Bench: Rule Under the Fairy Tale, 13 Yale J.L. & Human. 497 (2001)(analyzes fairy tales for insights into how the literary genre can shape ideas of law); The Law and Harry Potter (Jeffrey E. Thomas and Franklin G. Snyder eds., 2010) (collection of articles analyzing aspects of law and legal culture in the world of the Harry Potter books).

3 Scholarly works analyzing law and children's picture books include the following: Alyssa A. Dirusso & Letitia Van Campen, Law and Literature Junior: Lawyers in Books for Young Children, 11 Whittier J. Child & Fam. Advoc. 39 (2011)(examines portrayals of lawyers in books for preschoolers and early elementary school students); Desmond Manderson, From Hunger to Love: Myths of the Source, Interpretation, and Constitution of Law in Children's Literature, 15 Law & Literature 87 (2003) (masterful explication of the picture book, Where the Wild Things Are, as a source of law); Symposium: Exploring Civil Society Through the Writings of Dr. Seuss 58 N.Y.L. Sch. L. Rev. 495 (2013/2014) (fascinating collection of articles analyzing children's picture books by Dr. Seuss in the context of various issues concerning the nature of civil society in the twenty-first century, such as gay rights, children's rights, and global citizenship, among other topics); Jonathan Todres & Sarah Higinbotham, A Person's A Person: Children's Rights in Children's Literature, 45 Colum. Hum. Rts. L. Rev. 1 (2013) (well-written analysis using Dr. Seuss's Horton Hears a Who! and Yertle the Turtle to explore the role of children's literature in children's rights discourses, suggesting a new field of study in children's rights and children's literature); Ian Ward, Law and Literature: Possibilities and Perspectives (1995) (in Chapter Five, Ward undertakes a jurisprudential analysis of Beatrix Potter's illustrated children's book, The Tale of Peter Rabbit).

4 James Boyd White, The Judicial Opinion and the Poem: Ways of Reading, Ways of Life, in Heracles' Bow: Essays on the Rhetoric and Poetics of the Law 107(1985).

5 Ian Ward, discussing Beatrix Potter's classic picture book, The Tale of Peter Rabbit, comments that this picture book "is probably the first jurisprudential text that a young child will ever encounter." Ward, Law and Literature, supra note 3, at 100.

with the threat of state-sanctioned violence? Who is a legal subject? When is law (and justice) visible? These jurisprudential questions are all present in The Poky Little Puppy. An entire law school curriculum could be structured around topics raised by this picture book. The story encompasses issues of justice, statutory interpretation, punishment (retribution versus restitution), and even a very Foucauldian notion of self-discipline (the naughty puppies decide on their own to fill in the hole they dug under the fence). In fact, the text could be used as an overview of many topics taught in law school (law school in a nutshell via a children's picture book).[6]

While the book outwardly inclines toward a legal philosophy of positivism, it also has a strong countervailing undercurrent of natural law. Additionally, the social contract it envisions for its future law-abiding citizens is strangely undercut by its admiration for the rule-breaking poky little puppy. Despite its outward endorsement of the rule of law, the story exhibits an implicit, lingering admiration for independence and rebellion.

In exploring the jurisprudence of The Poky Little Puppy, this article will first provide some brief background on children's picture books and the publication history of The Poky Little Puppy (including its long-running best-seller status, its place within the Little Golden Books publishing imprint, and a summary of the plot and illustrations). Second, this article will interrogate the jurisprudence of the text, including analysis of the text's construction of responsible citizens and its sometimes puzzling message about the nature of rights and duties under the rule of law. Finally, we will conclude by exploring the relationship between law and love in the text. The dialogic possibilities inherent in the way in which picture books are consumed (typically, an adult reads the picture book to a young child, in an act of loving engagement) means that stories about rules have the potential to be part of an ongoing conversation about law and justice between adult and child.

---

6 For example, **Property** issues can be explored beginning with the physical object itself (the actual book). A children's picture book such as "The Poky Little Puppy" usually is purchased by an adult as a gift for a child, raising issues of gift. (Young children rarely have the ability to make such a purchase by themselves, and typically receive picture books as a gift.) On the inside front cover of "The Poky Little Puppy," as is common for every Little Golden Book, is the legend, "This Little Golden Book belongs to ..." followed by a place for the child to print their name. Thus, concepts of the ownership of chattel (tangible personal property) can be explored via the book. **Tort** issues abound, including trespass and the destruction of property (the puppies dig a hole under the fence in the story). **Copyright** issues include issues of work for hire (see this Article's section on the publication history of Little Golden Books). **Punishment** (the puppies don't get dessert when they break the rules) and **Restitution** (the puppies fill in the hole they made under the fence) are some of the other legal issues that arise in the book.

1   Children's Literature: Didacticism and Entertainment

Historically, children's literature as a distinct literary genre developed from two different streams of literature: entertainment and didacticism.[7] The entertainment stream received a boost in the fifteenth century when William Caxton (the first English printer) began publishing tales from the oral tradition.[8] Such folk and fairy tales subsequently were collected in popular editions in the seventeenth and eighteenth century by Charles Perrault and by Jakob and Wilhelm Grimm, and continue in popularity today.[9] The didactic stream is rooted in books of religious instruction for children, with the advent of Puritanism in the seventeenth century.[10] Lessons about morality and correct behavior in such books of religious instruction were aimed at saving the soul of the child.[11] But, of course, instruction works best if blended with artistry.[12] Readers will be more willing to consume a text if there is something pleasurable in it.[13]

Perhaps the first illustrated book written for children was John Amos Comenius's *Orbis Pictus* (1658), which was something like a dictionary for children with accompanying woodcut illustrations.[14] (Thus, knowledge was imparted with the added interest provided by the woodcut images.) Improvements in the printing press and growing literacy during the Industrial Revolution widened the market for children's literature, and illustrators found

---

7   Judith Saltman, The Riverside Anthology of Children's Literature 2 (6th ed. 1985).

8   *Id.*

9   *Id.*

10   *Id.*

11   *Id.*

12   "The history of children's literature is marked not only by didacticism and the impulse to instruct but also by literary innovation and artistry." Carrie Hintz & Eric l. Tribunella, Reading Children's Literature: A Critical Introduction 37 (2nd ed. 2019).

13   This is something Sir Philip Sidney clearly understood in the 16th century in his great critical essay, *An Apology for Poetry*, where he writes that poetry should "teach and delight." (He explains the necessity for mixing in delight alongside of instruction: "[W]ithout which delight they [readers] would fly as from a stranger..."). Sir Philip Sidney, *An Apologie For Poetrie, in* A Defence of Poesie and Poems n.p. (1891), https://www.gutenberg.org /files/1962/1962-h/1962-h.htm (last visited July 23, 2022). We see the same idea in the lyrics from a well-known Disney song: "A spoonful of sugar makes the medicine go down." Robert B. Sherman & Richard M. Sherman, *A Spoonful of Sugar, in* Mary Poppins (Walt Disney Productions, 1964).

14   Denise L. Matulka, A Picture Book Primer: Understanding and Using Picture Books 10–11 (2008).

audiences eager for books that included illustrations (such audience interest has continued to this day).[15]

Even today, children's picture books often have a didactic or instructional quality, and these books may teach young children the rules and norms for entry into the surrounding culture.[16] As such, these books for young children might be understood as constructing model citizens under the rule of law.[17] Obedience to the law thus would seem to be the presumptive "happy ending," the passport for entry into civil society. As texts reinforcing hegemonic norms of polite behavior through lessons about obedience and submission to the rules, such stories appear overtly authoritarian. However, as Alison Lurie notes, "Most of the great works of juvenile literature are subversive in one way or another."[18] Unpacking the workings of the rule of law in The Poky Little Puppy

---

15   *Id.* at 11. In the nineteenth century, English illustrator Randolph Caldecott ("father of the picture book") used illustrations to complement text in books for children. *Id.* at 1. As Salisbury and Styles note, "The picturebook as it is today is a relatively new form. We may debate its true origins but it is only 130 years or so since Randolph Caldecott began to elevate the role of the image in the narrative." Martin Salisbury with Morag Styles, Children's Picturebooks: The Art of Visual Storytelling 7 (2012).

16   Desmond Manderson states, "Children's fables are without a doubt pedagogical and normative; we would not set such store by them were it not so. [cite om] And they are profoundly influential in the child's constitution." Manderson, *From Hunger to Love, supra* note 3, at 91. Manderson goes on to explain the crucial significance of children's literature: "[C]hildhood is the scene of the mythic emergence of sociability in each and every life, repeated and constantly renewed. Children's literature, then is not *like* myth. It is myth. Children's literature is not a source of information *about* social structure of subjectivity in our society. It is the very site of their emergence. Children's literature is not a series of texts *about* the law. It is a source of law." *Id.* at 92.

17   As Manderson notes, "Because law is synonymous with the symbolic order, it is produced in the dialogue and discourse all about us: in all the things that we read and say, in the music we listen to, and the art we grow up with. [cite om] ... [T]here *are* nevertheless texts that provide an important discourse through which we develop assumptions as to the meaning, function, and interpretation of law; assumptions that are tested and implemented in those daily events throughout our lives. The texts that play this important role are not the *Magna Carta* or *Marbury v. Madison*. They are our children's books." Manderson, *From Hunger to Love, supra* note 3, at 92.

18   Alison Lurie, Don't Tell the Grown-Ups: Why Kids Love the Books They Do 4 (1990). Lurie points out that children reading Beatrix Potter's *Peter Rabbit* love that rebellious little bunny: "But when I asked a class of students which character in the book they would have preferred to be, they voted unanimously for Peter, recognizing the concealed moral of the story: that disobedience and exploration are more fun than good behavior, and not really all that dangerous, whatever Mother may say.... Consciously or not, children know that the author's sympathy and interest are with Peter, and with Tom Kitten and the Two Bad Mice; with impertinent, reckless Squirrel Nutkin, and not with the other timid, good squirrels or with obedient, dull little Flopsy, Mopsy, and Cottontail." *Id.* at 95.

reveals some surprising tensions in what might seem to be a simple picture book for children.

2   Publishing Background: Little Golden Books and The Poky Little Puppy

The Poky Little Puppy, which has continuously been in print since 1942, lays good claim to being the number one best-selling children's picture book of all time.[19] The book is part of the original Little Golden Books imprint of Simon and Shuster, now published by Random House.[20] Little Golden Books are still recognizable today by the eye-catching strip of gold foil along the spine. (Gold as a color signifies value, although the books themselves are inexpensive.) The series was launched in 1940 as an affordable purchase (sold for 25 cents) at a time when hardcover picture books for children were much more expensive.[21] Golden Books are lightweight and easy for small hands to hold. The books have a distinctively recognizable look, and, contrary to established publishing practice, the names of author and illustrator do not appear on the cover (putting the focus on the series rather than on creators).[22] Although Little Golden Books have sold well over the years, they have received little critical attention from reviewers.[23] Popularity did not translate to critical acclaim.

---

19   Publisher's Weekly reports that, as of 2001, "The Poky Little Puppy" was the number one best-selling hardcover children's book in the U.S., having sold nearly 15 million copies. Diane Roback, ed., *All-Time Bestselling Children's Books*, publishers weekly (December 17, 2001) https://www.publishersweekly.com/pw/by-topic/childrens/childrens-industry-news /article/28595-all-time-bestselling-children-s-books.html.

20   Lowrey, Poky Little Puppy, *supra* note 1, at copyright page.

21   Leonard S. Marcus, Golden Legacy: How Golden Books Won Children's Hearts, Changed Publishing Forever, and Became an American Icon Along the Way 32, 49 (2007). The first printing of 600,000 sold so quickly that within five months of launch, 1.5 million copies had been sold. *Id.* at 49. (In the late 1930s the average price of a children's picture book was close to $2.00, making the Little Golden Books quite a bargain. *See* Marcus at 32.) The current edition of The Poky Little Puppy is still quite affordable for a children's hardcover picture book, listing at $4.99 on Amazon. https://www.amazon.com/gp/product /0307021343?tag=randohouseinc7913-20 (last visited July 30, 2022).

22   Marcus, Golden Legacy, *supra* note 21, at 59. "The focus remained on the book itself as part of a larger entity. It was as though each volume in the line was a piece of a puzzle that children moved closer to completing every time they went shopping with their parents." *Id.*

23   *Id.* at 56. The Little Golden Books "were designed as impulse-buy items that parents would purchase not because an authority had praised them but because the books were affordable, visually appealing, and ready at hand. The librarian-critics, who prided themselves

The Poky Little Puppy was one of the original twelve Golden Books and the only book based on an original story (rather than on folktales and other materials in the public domain).[24] The relatively unknown author of the story (Janette Sebring Lowrey) received the flat fee of seventy-five dollars for her work on the story.[25] The illustrator, Gustaf Tenggren, on the other hand, was a star in the early group of Golden Book artists and, as a marquee talent, Tenggren could opt for a better payment structure.[26] The charming illustrations and deceptively simple story of the poky little puppy combine to create an imaginative space for readers to consider ways to be in the world.

3   Book Summary: The Dynamics of Words and Pictures

"Five little puppies dug a hole under the fence and went for a walk in the wide, wide world."[27] So begins the simple plot of the book. A poky puppy and his siblings break the law three times by repeatedly digging a hole under a fence in order to explore the outside world. Along the way, they encounter the rule of law in the form of a prohibition against digging under the fence. The plot movement is one of oscillation between leaving home for the larger world and returning back home. The familiar tension between two competing desires (security versus exploration) encapsulates the process of growing up in many

---

on being cultural gatekeepers and moral guardians of the nation's youth, suddenly realized, much to their dismay, that in the case of Little Golden Books, they had been factored out of the equation." *Id.* at 58.

24   *Id.* at 60.

25   *Id.* at 63.

26   *Id.* As Leonard Marcus notes, "The Artists and Writers Guild had two standard contracts for nonstaff authors and illustrators. One contract provided for the outright purchase of all rights to the freelancer's contribution to a book, and the other granted a modest royalty payment based on sales. The latter contract was held in reserve for marquee figures, such as Gustaf Tenggren and Margaret Wise Brown, whose association with the Golden list brought prestige as well as profit to the line. Those lucky enough to belong to that group could choose to draw funds against future earnings, an arrangement that helped tide over some authors but in other cases had the adverse effect of putting the author ever deeper in the company's debt. Perhaps with that prospect in mind, those invited to choose between contracts sometimes preferred to accept one-time payment of a sum that exceeded the amount of the royalty-arrangement advance by just enough to make it a tempting option." *Id.* at 125–126.

27   Lowrey, Poky Little Puppy, *supra* note 1, n.p.

children's books.[28] We all desire the familiar safety and comforts of home, but we also desire to leave home and explore the world.

Why puppies as main characters? Children's picture books often feature animals, not only because animals can be cute and appealing, but also because readers will anthropomorphize animals; the puppies become the equivalent of human children.[29]

How do words and pictures interact in a picture book such as this? The dynamics of words and pictures can be complex, as sometimes the two work in tandem, sometimes one mode will be dominant, and sometimes there may even be tension between the two. Words can create a "cognitive map" to help the reader determine the significance of a particular picture.[30] Additionally, the words themselves can have a visual component (we will see this with a hand-lettered sign that will be key to the plot). It is significant that, while the mother is never pictured, illustrations of the puppies and their surroundings take up the majority of space on the pages. Generally, as Molly Bang notes, "The larger an object is in a picture, the stronger it feels."[31] With the focus on the puppies, the reader will feel an affinity with them and an interest in what is the focalization point of many of the illustrations.

---

28   "The idea and experience of home and leaving home are tied to the very definition of what it means to be a child, so domestic and adventure fiction have emerged as two central genres of children's literature." Hintz & Tribunella, Reading Children's Literature, *supra* note 12, at 233. As Hintz and Tribunella note, "The experience of childhood is marked by negotiations between one's desires and the restrictions placed on those desires by other people, available resources, and the conditions of the environment." *Id.* at 239.

29   Perry Nodelman comments that casting an animal protagonist may highlight the tension between animal desires versus obedience to societal codes: "The story of Peter Rabbit sums up a central dilemma of childhood – whether one should act naturally in accordance with one's basic animal instincts or whether one should do as one's parents wish and learn to act in obedience to their more civilized codes of behavior. The importance of that dilemma may explain why picture books about creatures who look and sometimes act like animals but who talk and sometimes act like humans continue to be so prominent: these curiously ambiguous creatures actually represent our understanding of childhood better than any less ambiguous creature might." Perry Nodelman, Words About Pictures: The Narrative Art of Children's Picture Books 116 (1988).

30   *Id.* at 213.

31   Molly Bang, Picture This: How Pictures Work 90 (rev. ed. 2016). As Bang explains, "We generally feel more secure physically when we are big than when we are little, because we're more capable of physically overpowering an enemy. One of the easiest ways to make a protagonist – or a threat – appear strong is to make it *very* large." *Id.*

4   Beginnings

The cover of the book displays the title ("The Poky Little Puppy") in bright yellow handwritten lettering, against a light blue sky. While the word "The" is written in cursive, the remaining words create the impression of having been hand painted (the words are in chunky, all capital letters, foreshadowing the handwriting on the signs that will appear later in the book). The handmade aspect of the letters and the bright yellow color creates a cheerful, friendly tone. "A Little Golden Book" appears in the extreme upper left, in tiny cursive letters. The traditional gold foil wraps around the binding of the book. The largest image on the cover is a drawing of a chubby puppy. The puppy looks out at the reader, as if interrupted in the midst of exploring the many interesting bugs and flowers that surround it on the hillside. The puppy's body is angled down as it stands on the green hillside, with its head close to the ground. It is ready to get back to examining the world closely. The cover illustration suggests to the reader the answer for why the titular puppy is poky: it is poky (always late) because it is curious and takes the time to closely explore. The puppy desires to understand the world.

5   Rule-Breaking and Freedom

Upon opening the book (after the title/copyright page), the reader sees a double page illustration with typeface story text running across the bottom. The reader's eyes will be drawn first to the illustration filling the upper two-thirds of this double page spread. Four charming little puppies are exploring at the top of a hill, each looking in different directions. (One puppy is nearly upside down, with only its backside visible to the reader.) The bright tempera colors of green grass and the blue sky make a pleasing contrast to the brown, white and gray of the puppies. But while the words at the bottom third of the page begin with an act of rule-breaking ("Five little puppies dug a hole under the fence...."), the picture does not show the action of digging.[32] Instead, the picture shows the puppies exploring the hillside and wondering where the fifth puppy could be. So the book begins with an absence: where is the main character? The puppies' search for their poky brother is also the reader's visual search: where can this poky puppy be? The words, which will be repeated several times during the story, serve the function of teaching a young child about basic spatial

---

32   Lowrey, Poky Little Puppy, *supra* note 1, n.p.

directions such as up and down ("Through the meadow they went, down the road, over the bridge, across the green grass, and up the hill, one right after the other.")[33] The words also help instruct a child in counting (the puppies count themselves, and realize the fifth puppy is missing). Another significant absence is the absence of an illustration of the key event of rule-breaking: the pictures do not show the puppies digging the hole. What is the effect of not showing the act of transgression (i.e., digging the hole)? Perhaps it lessens or diminishes the "badness" of the puppies, when the first visual the reader sees is of the four puppies romping on the hill, rather than of them wantonly destroying property. While the story verbally begins with a description of an act of rule-breaking, the illustrations begin with freedom.

6   Pleasures of the Text

By this early stage, the reader will be enjoying the endearing illustrations and engaging story. In the next two pages, the simple words and pictures alternate placement between top and bottom of the page. (The words and illustrations change places from top to bottom, just as the story describes going up or down a hill.) The words tell us that the poky puppy is not going down the hill (the only thing going down is a fuzzy caterpillar) and not coming up the hill (the only thing coming up is "a quick green lizard").[34] Note also the emphatic rhythm in the word choice, tailor-made for reading aloud – "quick green lizard." The pictures are close-up, detailed tempera illustrations of a caterpillar heading down toward the bottom of the page, and a lizard heading up to the top of the page, surrounded by grass and flowers. No puppies are visible, but the intense, close-up focus and attention to details in the colorful illustrations put the reader in the position of a puppy looking very closely at something in nature. The close perspective and experiential immediacy of the pictures recasts readers themselves into poky puppies. One must slow down and become poky to examine the illustration closely and to speak out loud the alliterative words. (Additionally, the practice of an adult reading this picture book out loud to a child often involves the fun of slowing down and encouraging the child to participate in counting out loud the number of puppies, or in repeating a quirky phrase such as "roly-poly, pell-mell, tumble-bumble.")

On turning the page, the reader sees another double-page spread, and, for the first time, sees the poky puppy. The puppy is sniffing the ground near

---

33   *Id.*
34   *Id.*

the bottom of the hill, while his siblings watch from the top of the hill. In the following pages, his siblings scamper down the hill accompanied by another catchy and alliterative passage that will be repeated several times throughout the story ("And down they went to see, roly-poly, pell-mell, tumble, bumble, till they came to the green grass").[35] The poky puppy smells the enticing aroma of rice pudding, and when his siblings smell the dessert, they scamper home. Here, the text repeats the directions as the siblings run home (over, under, up, through, etc.). The child reader will be learning directions, as well as learning about the variety of sensory perceptions, such as smell.

7   Unjust Desserts

The next page begins with a strangely disquieting spectacle of procedural unfairness. The mother says, "So you're the little puppies who dig holes under fences! .... No rice pudding tonight!"[36] The words suggest a direct juridical cause and effect: break the rules and you are punished. But the picture shows the poky puppy joyfully eating an entire dish of rice pudding. How are we to understand this picture, juxtaposed as it is with words recounting punishment for rule breaking? The picture does not show the mother (she remains an unseen voice of the law throughout the story), nor does it show the other four puppies, who have been sent straight to bed; instead, the illustration shows the poky puppy enjoying an entire dish of rice pudding. How does this come to be? All five of the puppies took part in digging the forbidden hole, but only four were punished. Why is the poky puppy rewarded with a delicious dessert? The text explains that the poky puppy returns home late, after everyone is asleep. He eats up all the pudding and goes to bed, "happy as a lark."[37] It is his pokiness (his curiosity in exploring the world) that makes him perennially late ("poky"), but it seems unfair that he gets rice pudding while the others do not. The emotional satisfaction of the visual spectacle of seeing an adorable puppy heartily enjoying a tasty treat must be balanced against the written words that tell us that four puppies were sent to bed without dessert. (Food, of course, is a subject of abiding interest to young children, and the relative gentleness of the punishment still will be keenly felt by young readers.) There is something unsettling here, and it resonates with Rawls' notion of justice as

---

35   *Id.*
36   *Id.*
37   *Id.*

procedural fairness.[38] Equal treatment requires that all five puppies should be punished equally, since all five helped dig the hole. We will see this pattern (rule-breaking followed by punishment for some but not for all) repeated twice more in the story.

8   Making Law Visible

The first time the puppies break the law, the law itself is only visible in the form of the physical fence. The fence is a boundary whose existence presupposes the presence of law. The fence demarcates different spheres. There is inside the fence and outside the fence. Breaching the boundary (by digging a hole) violates the law. The mother makes the interpretation of the law explicit when she scolds the puppies the first night ("So you're the little puppies who dig holes under fences! ... No rice pudding tonight!")[39]

The next morning, the law becomes more visible and more explicit. (The fence was, perhaps, too vague a symbol of law.) Now, someone has put up a sign that reads, "DON'T EVER DIG HOLES UNDER THIS FENCE!"[40] (We may presume the mother made the sign, but the story never identifies the maker.) The sign looks like very much like a statute. If the fence was, perhaps, more representative of a norm or customary law, the sign looks like a written declaration of law. The sign is hand-lettered in all capital letters with an extra-large exclamation point. (In contrast, the text of the story is in a consistently sized and mechanically produced serif typeface.) The sign's handwritten letters are in all capitals and the oversize exclamation point at the end gives emphasis to the rule. The text of the law here is simultaneously words and illustration. The handwritten lettering of the law displays a disjunction between appearance of the letters and the meaning of the words. On the one hand, the meaning of the words is strict and threatening. The fact that the letters of the sign are in all capitals, followed by an exclamation point, suggest a severity to the law. But on the other hand, the handwritten sign gives it a homey, personal touch.

---

38   Rawls proposes the concept of "justice as fairness," meaning that there are two basic principles that rational people would accept in advance of knowing their position in society: "the first requires equality in the assignment of basic rights and duties, while the second holds that social and economic inequalities ... are just only if they result in compensating benefits for everyone, and in particular for the least advantaged members of society." John Rawls, A Theory of Justice 14–15 (1971).

39   Lowrey, Poky Little Puppy, *supra* note 1, n.p.

40   *Id.*

The accompanying illustration adds a humorous gloss to this explicit law. Centered in the page is the sign itself, but directly beneath the sign the reader sees the chubby backside of the poky puppy; he is vigorously digging a hole beneath the sign (flouting the law in the very face of the law). Dirt is flying as the puppy busily works to squeeze himself under the fence.

The text now repeats the opening lines of the story with a slight addition: "The five little puppies dug a hole under the fence, just the same, and went for a walk in the wide, wide world."[41] The addition of "just the same" is the equivalent of "nonetheless" or "despite the prohibition." This suggests that the puppies intend to flout the law. Despite the written statutory language, the puppies deliberately choose to dig the hole.

The story then repeats the pattern we saw in the beginning: the four puppies go through, down, over, across, and up, and the reader sees a charming drawing of a frog on the hill, from a very close-up perspective (as if a child or a puppy were crouching as near as possible to observe the frog at close range). When the puppies finally find their poky brother, he is sitting with his ears perked up, listening intently to the delicious sound of custard being spooned into bowls. The four puppies run home (with the text repeating the catchy descriptions). Once again, their mother is displeased that the puppies dug the hole under the fence. Once again, she sends the four puppies to bed without dessert. Once again, the poky puppy returns home late and eats up all the dessert by himself.

9   The Pattern Changes

The following morning, the sign now reads: "DON'T EVER EVER DIG HOLES UNDER THIS FENCE!"[42] (The addition of the second "ever" is written in extra-large text, for emphasis). The puppies again dig a hole and repeat the journey. They look for their poky brother but only see (illustrated in loving, nose-to-the-ground detail) natural objects and creatures (a grass snake, a grasshopper, flowers on the hill). When they finally find their poky brother, he is closely examining a wild strawberry. They deduce strawberry shortcake is on the menu. The four puppies race home. Once again, their mother sends them to bed without dessert.

But something different happens this time. The four puppies wait until they think their mother is asleep and proceed to fill up the hole. (The illustration shows four wide-eye puppies tucked in bed, peeking to see if the coast is

---

41   *Id.*
42   *Id.*

clear for them to secretly fill in the hole.) Significantly, the four puppies seek to make things right without their mother's prompting of threats or rewards. Their mother sees them filling in the hole, tells them they are good puppies, and gives them strawberry shortcake.

This time, when the poky puppy finally gets home, the dessert has been eaten up by the other puppies. His mother says, "What a pity you're so poky! Now the strawberry shortcake is all gone!"[43] (What are we to make of this comment? Is the mother perhaps subtly suggesting that the poky puppy not only has missed out on dessert but missed out on the opportunity to make things right?) The poky puppy goes to bed without shortcake and "he felt very sorry for himself."[44] The illustration shows the poky puppy tucked in bed, looking perturbed.

10 Endings and Beyond

The very last page of the book is where we might expect a moral or some takeaway for the child reader. The ending does and does not suggest a moral. The words state that the next morning, someone put up a new sign: "NO DESSERTS EVER UNLESS PUPPIES NEVER DIG HOLES UNDER THIS FENCE AGAIN!"[45] The statutory language seems clear enough (in this version, the law not only spells out the prohibition but explicitly states the punishment). But the illustration accompanying the words conceivably undercuts the force of law. The sign is once again in bold handwritten lettering, and the poky puppy is looking up at the sign, with his back to the reader. But the imposing sign and the red fence are strangely angled away from the reader (toward the right of the page). The puppy is squarely situated beneath the sign, apparently reading it. The puppy is on the same angle or plane of vision as the reader (i.e., squarely seated). We see the puppy and look up and over his shoulder to read the sign. The child reader again will feel an affinity with the puppy. Not only will the child put themself in the place of the puppy because of anthropomorphism, but the child will be on the same literal plane of sight as the puppy. The puppy is looking up at the written law. What is the puppy thinking? Is he going to obey the law? The incongruous angle of the sign and fence creates a gently humorous tone. The law does not seem to be squarely planted. The puppy, despite being lower than (beneath) the law, has a solidity and stability. Has he learned

---

43   *Id.*
44   *Id.*
45   *Id.*

his lesson? What exactly is the lesson the child reader might take from the book?

11   Law's Story

In desiring to explore the world, the poky puppy and his siblings break the law three times. The first time, the law is simply represented by the fence. The second and third times, the law appears in the form of a hand-lettered sign in all capitals ("DON'T EVER DIG HOLES UNDER THIS FENCE!") and then another even more emphatic iteration ("DON'T EVER EVER DIG HOLES UNDER THIS FENCE!").[46] After the four puppies have filled in the hole, the final version of the law/sign reads, "NO DESSERTS EVER UNLESS PUPPIES NEVER DIG HOLES UNDER THIS FENCE AGAIN!"[47]

The nature of the law, where it comes from and what it means, is part of the interpretive puzzle of the story; this book requires the child not only to interpret the words and interpret the pictures, but also to interpret the interrelationship between words and pictures. How do the words and pictures interact to tell a juridical story? What precisely is that story?

Significantly, while the first words in the story describe breaking the law ("Five little puppies dug a hole under the fence..."), the first picture does not show the actual rule-breaking; instead, the reader only sees the glorious results of freedom from containment. The first (double-page) illustration shows four puppies in a charming natural setting, exploring the world. Thus, the relationship between picture and words creates an implicit tension. The initial effect of breaking the law looks delightful. Even when the inevitable punishment ensues (no dessert), it seems very strange that the poky puppy is not punished two out of the three times. Why, in point of fact, does the poky puppy get two desserts and only one punishment? Is the text divided against itself, in that it champions the rule of law on the surface, but implicitly encourages the reader to root for the poky little puppy? Can the text have it both ways?

The law acts as a barrier to desire. The puppies desire to explore the greater world, but the law (in the form of the fence and sign) blocks the way. Just as in Shakespearean comedies, the law in this children's picture book is a blocking force, an obstacle to the anticipated happy ending.[48] The law must be

---

46   *Id.*

47   *Id.*

48   The law (usually in the form of a parental figure) frequently blocks the way to happiness in both children's literature and Shakespeare's comedies. In The Poky Little Puppy,

accommodated before there can be a happy ending. All five of the puppies break the law three times by digging a hole under the fence to go out in the world. But the poky puppy (unlike his siblings) is only punished once. Is that procedurally fair? Will the poky puppy finally learn how to live under a rule of law? What exactly is the jurisprudence of the story? While the text seems to be imbued with legal positivism (the idea that law is simply rules from the state/ sovereign, with no necessary connection to morality), the fact that the four puppies take the initiative to make a moral decision to fix a wrong makes the text resonate with natural law principles.[49] All in all, this is a much stranger text than one might initially think.

12   What is Law? Where is Law?

What messages about lawfulness and illegality might the reader take from this picture book? When we unpack the story, the application of rules seems procedurally unjust, in a Rawlsian sense, in the first two cases: the four siblings get punished, but the poky puppy gets dessert. This is procedurally unfair despite the reason behind the poky puppy's lack of punishment. (He avoids punishment,

---

the mother withholds dessert as punishment when the puppies dig under the fence and break the rules. Shylock's contract for a pound of flesh must be dealt with before Portia and Bassanio can be happy. William Shakespeare, The Merchant of Venice. As literary scholar Northrop Frye notes, "We notice how often the action of a Shakespearean comedy begins with some absurd, cruel, or irrational law: the law of killing Syracusans in the *Comedy of Errors*, the law of compulsory marriage in *A Midsummer Night's Dream*, the law that confirms Shylock's bond, the attempts of Angelo to legislate people into righteousness, and the like, which the action of the comedy then evades or breaks." Northrop Frye, Anatomy of Criticism: Four Essays 166 (2000) (1957).

49   "Legal positivism," often discussed in light of the writings of H.L.A. Hart, can be defined as "The theory that legal rules are valid only because they are enacted by an existing political authority or accepted as binding in a given society, not because they are grounded in morality or in natural law." Black's Law Dictionary1033 (10th ed. 2014). "Natural law," on the other hand, can perhaps be best understood as, "A philosophical system of legal and moral principles purportedly deriving from a universalized conception of human nature or divine justice rather than from legislative or judicial action; moral law embodied in principles of right and wrong." Black's Law Dictionary 1189 (10th ed. 2014). Natural law generally concerns "the intersection between law and morals." Raymond Wacks, Philosophy of Law: A Very Short Introduction 1–2 (2d ed. 2014). Thus, a primary distinction between legal positivism and natural law concerns the issue of the relation between law and morality: "The highest common factor among legal positivists is that the law as laid down should be kept separate – for the purpose of study and analysis – from the law as it ought morally to be.") *Id.* at 26.

not because he is willfully hiding, but because he is so curious about the world that he is always late.) What does the text expect of children? What does the text expect of adults? The text never explicitly justifies the prohibition against digging so we are left to speculate. (If obedience to the rule of law is predicated on whether legal subjects recognize law's legitimacy or perceive it as being just, that is a difficult task, as the puppies must figure out the law's justification for themselves.) Is the rule meant to protect the puppies from the dangers of the outside world? Is the rule meant perhaps to protect the property interest of the homeowner? Perhaps the text implicitly endorses a different type of law, more akin to natural law, exemplified by the decision of the four puppies to fill in the hole. This action seems to have a moral component; it is good to repair what you have broken. We can contrast this implicit natural law with the more positivist rules we see earlier in the text, represented by the fence and the sign.

The Fence. The first law the puppies encounter is the physical structure that is the fence. The structure itself stands for law. Who built it, why it was built, or how long it has been there are never explained: it just is. The fence is a barrier, a demarcation of a boundary and a signifier of ownership and control. The fences simply exists as a rule, with no clear connection to morality. It seems positivist in its existence. It separates and marks off the inside and the outside. There is everything inside the fence (the puppies, their home, their mother) and everything outside the fence (the wide world). The meaning seems clear – do not transgress. But perhaps it is not so clear to the puppies. They desire to explore the world and the fence blocks their way.[50] Nothing in the text suggests they feel guilt over digging the first hole. It takes the voice of the (unseen) mother to interpret their action as transgression and mete out punishment: "So you're the little puppies who dig holes under fences! ... No rice pudding tonight!"[51] This pattern happens three times, and each time rule-breaking is followed by punishment (at least for four of the five puppies). But why? Is the law of the fence natural law, in the sense that this is a law intrinsically linked

---

50   Discussing picture books, including The Poky Little Puppy, Ellen Handler Spitz notes, "Children's disobedience seems invariably to involve crossing a boundary that has been set by adults ... But, we must ask, what do such boundaries feel like to young children? Not as fixed and permanent. Rather, more like fences ... that – whether physical, emotional, intellectual, or social – *can* perhaps be bypassed. This is in part because growing and changing, each child keeps testing his or her developing strength against the resistance. ... To explore classic picture books is thus to discover how children expand their worlds through misbehavior – and how mischief can be a surprisingly constructive, and even creative, means by which children adapt to, and seek to revise, societal and familial boundaries." Ellen Handler Spitz, Inside Picture Books 161–162 (1999).

51   Lowrey, Poky Little Puppy, *supra* note 1, n.p.

with morality? If so, the rule must have something to do with not disturbing established boundaries (but established by whom?) or perhaps it relates to the idea that it is not right (not moral) to take/break things that are not yours.

If the law of the fence aligns with legal positivism, then the law of the fence is simply the law of the state. Rules are rules, with no relationship to notions of morality, and rule-breaking must be met with punishment. Child developmental psychologists might describe this pattern as demonstrating "immanent justice": the concept that breaking a rule, regardless of the circumstances, must result in punishment.[52]

13 The Seen and Unseen World of Law

What do we not see in this picture book? From the context, as well as verbal and visual cues, the story seems to be set in the dream-world of 1940's middle-class American suburbia, complete with a picket fence (albeit red, rather than white), a stay-at-home mother who bakes delicious meals and an absent father. (Given the 1942 publication date, it is possible to imagine a father serving in WWII, although the father is never mentioned.) The voice of the law is the voice of the unseen mother. The mother is the enforcer of rules. She is the one who administers punishments and rewards. The reader never sees the mother, but the mother interacts verbally with the puppies, admonishing them when they do wrong. Presumably, it is the mother who erects the sign and who subsequently alters the sign to make the rule even more explicit. But the story only tells us that "someone" put up the sign. This makes the origins of the law deeply mysterious to its subjects. Why not simply say that the mother (or someone else) makes the sign? When the maker of law is concealed or hidden, the justification or morality of the law also is unclear. The command is simply a command, the voice is the voice of authority, and, by implication, the legal subject has no business interrogating the morality of the law.

---

52 "Immanent justice," as postulated by noted developmental psychologist Jean Piaget, is "the belief that rules are fixed and immutable and that punishment automatically follows misdeeds regardless of extenuating circumstances. Children up to the age of 8 equate the morality of an act only with its consequences; not until later do they develop the capacity to judge motive and subjective considerations." American Psychological Association, APA Dictionary of Psychology, definition of *"immanent justice,"* https://dictionary.apa.org /immanent-justice (last visited July 23, 2022). Piaget describes "immanent justice" as the child's belief in "automatic punishments which emanate from things themselves." Jean Piaget, The Moral Judgment of the Child 251 (1965)(1932).

Because she is not presented visually in the story, the mother paradoxically seems to be everywhere. She somehow sees the four puppies when they fill in the hole, even though they do not see her and they think she is asleep. (The law never sleeps.) This invisible parental presence acts as a juridical authority (and probable source of law). As such, the mother is very much the sovereign/ the state, in terms of legal positivism. She punishes when the puppies break the rules, but she does not make any explicit connection between morality and the rules. She never tells the puppies why the rule exists, or whether it might even be a rule that is beneficial (perhaps it is meant to protect the puppies from any dangers that may lurk in the outside world). Interestingly, the law twice changes (by becoming more explicit) in response to the puppies' actions. This suggests that the law may be organic (in line with the jurisprudence of Cardozo, among others) and not immutable.[53] At first, there is just the fence. Then, a printed sign appears prohibiting digging. Next, the sign is modified to have an increased intensity/seriousness. Lastly, the sign clearly states the punishment and clarifies that the law applies to puppies ("No desserts ever unless puppies never dig holes under this fence again!").[54] At first, the law is the unspoken boundary represented by the fence (common law). Next, the law is spoken by the sovereign, who administers punishment (interpretation by the judge). Then, the law becomes written (statutory). Next, the law is clarified (re-written, with emphasis and a slight revision). Finally, after the four puppies fill in the hole, the law is revised one final time to clarify both the rule and the punishment. So the law seems to change over time, based on the actions of the puppies.

The law is not the only thing with the potential to change. Surely, puppies (and children) also have the potential to change. When the four puppies unselfishly go out into the night to fill in the hole, they do not do so with the hope of reward. Instead, they seem to intuit that this is the right thing to do. It is an act of kindness and restoration. Have they changed? Their mother pronounces them "good" and lifts the punishment after they fill in the hole. They have changed in that they have taken action to repair what they have broken.

Has the poky puppy changed? This is less clear, and it is the poky puppy, after all, who is the focalization of the story. (He is the title character, the protagonist, the character with whom the reader most identifies.) The emphasis of the text, both visually and in words, is on the poky puppy. He is adventurous and curious. He gets desserts twice (when his siblings do not), in what seems like an unfair application of the law. But the third time, his pokiness not only means he misses out on dessert, but he also misses out on taking part in

---

53   Cardozo famously stated, "A Constitution has an organic life." Browne v. City of New York, 241 N.S. 96, 111 (1925).

54   Lowrey, Poky Little Puppy, *supra* note 1, n.p.

the restitutionary act of his siblings. What will the poky puppy do next? Has he learned his lesson? The text notes that he felt very sorry for himself after he did not get the final dessert, but is self-pity the path to moral decision-making? Does the story reinforce the idea of obedience to the law? Will the poky puppy continue to explore, but find a different way around or through the boundary without digging a forbidden hole? Will he continue to be poky?

14   Imagining Law/Imagining Our Future Selves

The entire design of this children's picture book creates imaginative space; the words, pictures, and the interactions between words and pictures all work together to clear the way for a child's imagination to engage with questions of law and justice. On the one hand, the story clearly has a didactic thrust. After absorbing the story, a young child will understand that actions create consequences: rule-breaking (digging the hole) results in punishment (four puppies are twice sent to bed without dessert) and good little puppies must follow the rules. Is this all there is to the story, a simple lesson in not breaking rules? If this is all, then the story is a "safe" text, one that reinforces the status quo of power dynamics between children and adults, i.e., between those who are subject to the law and those who make the law.

But there is an additional takeaway from the story. A child also will learn that it is a moral good to fix things you break (the four puppies fill in the hole without prompting from their mother and then she rewards them with dessert and tells them that they are good). The puppies make things right not with any expectation of being rewarded, but simply because they have come to understand that you should fix what you break. (This is a moral lesson, "sweetened" by the subsequent dessert.) How do they learn this? This seems to be a lesson they have learned through their own imaginative understanding of what these rules could possibly mean.

Despite the all-too-apparent didactic elements in the story, the interesting implicit tension between words and illustrations operates to open up the text to other possibilities. In particular, the book opens space for a conversation or dialogue between child and adult about rules, justice, and ways to be in the world.

15   Law and Love

Consider the kinetic activity of reading a picture book. Books such as The Poky Little Puppy are written for young children who cannot yet read or may be just learning to read (hence, such stories often rely heavily on illustrations).[55] Because a young child is not yet proficient in reading, the activity of reading a picture book must be a shared one. Typically, an adult will read the book to the child, often at bedtime.[56] In fact, by the mid-twentieth century, the soothing ritual of shared bedtime reading "became a metonym for proper parenting and an idealized middle-class childhood."[57]

Does the cozy scene of a parent reading a bedtime story to a child actually reify a top-down power dynamic? When an adult reads a picture book to a child, is this activity nothing more than a thinly veiled process of socialization into the rule of law foisted on a child subject? Who benefits from instructions in how to behave? The adult benefits by having a well-behaved child, and presumably the child benefits by being socialized into the rules of behavior mandated in a particular culture (and thus avoiding negative consequences for unacceptable behavior).[58] But if the child is subject to law, shouldn't the

---

55   Brian A. Klems, *Defining Picture Books, Middle Grade, and Young Adult*, Writer's Digest (December 15, 2009), https://www.writersdigest.com/writing-for-kids/defining-picture -books-middle-grade-and-young-adult#:~:text=Picture%20books%20are%20 published%20for,center ed%20around%20one%20main%20character.

      Klems notes that publishers generally follow several subcategories for children's books, based on the age group, including toddler books, picture books, easy readers, middle grade, and young adult. "Picture books are published for children ages 4 to 8 years old and rely heavily on pictures and illustrations to tell the story. This is a big-tent category, where the definition can vary greatly from publisher to publisher, but picture books are typically about 1,000 words long and centered around one main character. Examples include *Where the Wild Things Are* by Maurice Sendak, *The Carrot Seed* by Ruth Krauss, and *The Polar Express* by Chris Van Allsburg." *Id.*

56   Ellen Handler Spitz notes that picture books, unlike electronic media, "[R]equire the participation of warm, breathing adult human partners who have available laps, keen eyes and ears, arms adept at holding while turning pages, and perhaps a flair for the dramatic." Spitz, Inside Picture Books, *supra* note 50, at 2. Spitz also notes that the story The Poky Little Puppy, "[T]o all young children's immense delight, rewards the slowest, most curious puppy. ... until, at the end of the story, proper adult values reassert themselves, and this poky little puppy is duly sent off to bed 'without a single bite of shortcake.'" *Id.* at 160.

57   Robin Bernstein, *"You Do It!": Going-to-Bed Books and the Scripts of Children's Literature*, 135.5 PMLA 877, 878 (cite om)(2020). Bernstein notes that the practice of an adult reading to a child at bedtime began largely in the latter part of the nineteenth century, and was a result of a number of factors, including: "not only the growth of the picture book industry but also the spread of isolated sleeping in which children occupied individual bedrooms, the expansion of electricity and heating systems that shifted evening reading beyond the hearth to other domestic spaces, and a bevy of newly crowned psychological experts who persuaded parents that children need 'a calm, happy atmosphere at bedtime...'" (cite om) *Id.*

58   As Desmond Manderson states, "The bed-time story is the contemporary instrument of this subtle, loving, but relentless socialization by which the child becomes fit and fitted

child also at least have some modicum of agency?[59] Children, as well as adults, should have the right to flourish and the right to human dignity. The implications of the power dynamics of children's books have been debated by literary scholars for decades, with no clear consensus.[60] Perhaps the child's agency and engagement with the rule of law in the text can exist in the kinetic experience of enjoying the story. If we think of how we, as adults, read to children, or recall how we were read to as a child, we may see the possibility for a conversation. This includes not just loving interaction between child and adult (pointing to a picture, counting objects, repeating funny words or phrases, etc.) but also an opportunity for the child to imaginatively participate in meaning making.

Is there space for playfulness and pleasure in a picture book that teaches a lesson about rules? Even in picture books with overtly didactic lessons about good versus bad behavior, there may be room for playfulness. Texts are rarely completely hegemonic or completely subversive.[61] Scholars have suggested various ways the child can be an active participant in unpacking the meaning in picture books including working with the dynamics of kinship systems

---

out for adult life and law. This is the necessary corollary of contemporary legal pluralism. Since law exists in the everyday, it must be learned in the everyday, too..." Manderson, *From Hunger to Love, supra* note 3, at 95.

59 Todres and Higinbotham point out, "Even today, although the most widely accepted international human rights treaty is a treaty on children's rights, children's rights are still marginalized in mainstream academic legal circles." (referring to The Convention on the Rights of the Child, G.A. Res. 44/25, 44th Sess., U.N. Doc. A/RES/44/25 (Nov. 20, 1989)). Todres & Higinbotham, *A Person's A Person, supra* note 3, at 4.

60 Bernstein notes, "For almost four decades, scholars have debated the implications of one characteristic of children's literature: it is the only major category of literature that is generally written by one group (adults) for another group (children)." Bernstein, *"You Do It!" supra* note 57, at 879. While some scholars find that "children's literature appears to address a readership that it in fact constructs, at times forcibly...", other scholars maintain that "children exert agency in their practices of reading." Bernstein, at 879. Jacqueline Rose famously argues, "Children's fiction is impossible, not in the sense that it cannot be written (that would be nonsense), but in that it hangs on an impossibility, one which it rarely ventures to speak. This is the impossible relation between adult and child. ... Children's fiction sets up a world in which the adult comes first (author, maker, giver) and the child comes after (reader, product, receiver), but where neither of them enter the space in between." Jacqueline Rose, The Case of Peter Pan or the Impossibility of Children's Fiction 1–2 (1984).

61 Hintz & Tribunella, Reading Children's Literature, *supra* note 12, at 36. "Texts rarely just do one or the other [exist as subversive or hegemonic texts], and reading children's literature critically can involve considering how a text reinforces or resists hegemonic values." *Id.* Additionally, as Bernstein points out, "Adults, like children, often resist scripts. Adults, like children, often choose naughtiness over obedience." Bernstein, *"You Do It!" supra* note 57, at 886.

and considering the kinetic experience of reading aloud as an opportunity for a conversation between adult and child.[62] The conversation should be a dialogue, not a power struggle.

Imagine some of the topics that might arise in such a conversation. What makes the puppy poky? Is it fair that the poky puppy got the first two desserts? Why did the four puppies fill in the hole? Why did the mother give dessert to the four puppies after they filled in the hole? What do you think the poky puppy will do next? Is he going to find a different way to explore the wide world? What is the puppy thinking in the last picture as he is looking up at the sign?

16   After the Ending

The Poky Little Puppy outwardly inclines toward a jurisprudence of legal positivism, but has a strong undercurrent of natural law, based on the actions of the four puppies. Significantly, despite the book's overt endorsement of the rule of law, the social contract it envisions for its future citizens is undercut by its admiration for the independent poky puppy. Being poky means being curious about the world, taking the time to look closely, to listen intently, and to interpret. The poky puppy is good at interpreting. He sniffs (and understands that his mother is making rice pudding). He listens (and hears pudding being spooned into bowls). But interpreting law/rules is a difficult skill. Perhaps his siblings were quicker to interpret the idea of making things right because they suffered the punishment twice. What will he do next, after the book is closed? After the book is ended, readers have a potential opportunity to participate in reflection and meaning-making and imagine possibilities for

---

62   Marah Gubar, for example, suggests that children can have agency in reading practices if we consider a kinship model that "maintain[s] that children and adults are fundamentally akin to one another, even if certain deficiencies routinely attend certain parts of the aging process." Marah Gubar, *The Hermeneutics of Recuperation: What a Kinship-Model Approach to Children's Agency Could Do for Children's Literature and Childhood Studies*, 8.2 Jeunesse: Young People, Texts, Cultures 291, 299(2016) as quoted in Bernstein, *"You Do It!"*, *supra* note 57, at 879. Desmond Manderson notes that the practice of an adult reading to a young child "offer[s] even to the youngest listener ways of *participating* in giving meaning to the text, and offer therefore a path to responsibility." Manderson, *From Hunger to Love*, *supra* note 3, at 129. He adds that there are linguistic, aural and pictorial opportunities for interpretation: "Like Talmudic *Mishnash*, the verses of a book like *Where the Wild Things Are* form the framework for a conversation: about the story, about Max's experience of the story, about the child's own and parallel experiences. In all these ways, the story provides a dialogic space for the acknowledgment and for the mediation of children's own emotions." *Id.* at 130.

living and thriving in a rule-based society. The reader may well suspect that the puppy will continue to be poky, and that perhaps he will contrive other ways to explore. The poky puppy has his own deeply lived experiences of the wide world precisely because he is poky and takes time to savor the smell of a wild strawberry.

Acknowledgements

The author wishes to thank Professor Siegfried Wiessner for years of kindness, erudition, and deeply thoughtful scholarship. Professor Wiessner is an exemplar of the humane legal scholar and teacher dedicated to the pursuit of human dignity for all.

CHAPTER 37

Policy-Oriented Jurisprudence and Constitutive Process in Mexico: Toward a Public Order of Human Dignity in Turbulent Times

*Jaime Olaiz-González**

A central part of policy-oriented jurisprudence is its very distinctive notion of the law. For the New Haven School, "law is conceived [as] *decision,* composed of both perspectives and operations; as *authoritative decision,* combining elements of authority and control; and not as occasional choices, but as a *continuous process* of authoritative decision, both maintaining the constitutive features by which it is established and projecting a flow of public order decisions for the shaping and sharing of community values."[1]

This distinctive concept of law as a continuous process of authoritative decision reveals a unique perspective when put vis-à-vis the theory and practice of constitutional change.

The traditional doctrine on constitutional change frames it as episodic, i.e. a phenomenon that occurs rarely and under extraordinary or exceptional conditions of the social process. This is the fundamental argument of Bruce Ackerman's constitutional moments theory.[2] Let us call it *the conventional approach.*

In contrast, if we see the theory and practice of constitutional change through the focal lenses of the New Haven School, we will discover a very different perspective.

Whereas constitutional moments are predicated as a new grammar of political legitimation, constitutional change, rather than being episodic, can also be conceived equally as a continuous and authoritative process of decision characterized by an unceasing effort of refinement and innovation that may include, on occasion, some regressions and distortions to be corrected at the due time. Let us call this *the unconventional model.*

---

* Professor of Constitutional Theory and International Law at Universidad Panamericana Law School, Mexico City.

1   W. Michael Reisman, Siegfried Wiessner & Andrew Willard, *The New Haven School: A Brief Introduction,* 32 Yale J. Int'l L. 575, 579–580 (2007).

2   Bruce Ackerman, We the People, I: Foundations 3–33 (1991).

© JAIME OLAIZ-GONZALEZ, 2023 | DOI:10.1163/9789004524835_038

Altogether, this continuous process of constitutional recalibration towards a public order of human dignity approximates more efficiently the operational code of contemporary constitutional transformations, in contrast to the conventional theory based on the episodic nature of constitutional change.

The unconventional model of constitutional change may reveal itself as especially insightful within polities immersed in the daunting processes of political and social redefinition such as has been the case of Mexico over the last two decades, in which it has struggled to conduct a process of political liberalization within a context of increasing violence and ideological radicalization.

This chapter will embark on mapping and comparing the processes of authoritative decision in Mexico during the process of political liberalization between 1990 and 2018, and the ones that resulted from a radical shift in power after the presidential election of 2018. This study aims to define the content of pending constitutional changes aimed at approximating in more effective ways a public order of human dignity.

This work is a tribute to the scholarship and intellectual legacy of our dear Professor Siegfried Wiessner, a champion of policy-oriented jurisprudence, continuing and developing the legacy of Professors Myres McDougal and Harold Lasswell, and, more saliently, the jurisprudential work of our dear mentor, Professor Michael Reisman.

1   The Framework

In a nutshell, development is the series of decision processes and decision outcomes that approximate a given society towards a public order of human dignity.[3] These processes are articulated in continuous political transformations and predicated through constitutional change portraying a new grammar of legitimation based upon the shaping and sharing of the goal values of a world order of human dignity. This understanding equates development to human flourishing and condenses the goals that any contemporary liberal democracy should set to achieve. But not all political transformations and constitutional changes are considered development. Those transformations "incompatible with human dignity can be characterized as retrogressions or as 'disdevelopmental.'"[4]

---

3   W. Michael Reisman, *Development and Nation Building: A Framework for a Policy-Oriented Inquiry,* 60 Maine L. Rev. 309, 310 (2008).

4   *Id.*

This approach towards development was the order of the day of Mexico's constitutive process of authoritative decision between 1988 and 2018. Our scope of inquiry is the transformative period of political liberalization in Mexico between 1988 and 2000, and its consolidation until 2018. This thirty-year span set the foundations of Mexico as a modern liberal democracy after the long tenure of the PRI's single-party rule. This transition to democracy entailed momentous constitutional and statutory reforms that deconcentrated political power from a mighty Presidency to new-fledged independent agencies, state governments, and an increasingly influential civil society claiming a more active role in the constitutive process.

I contend that over the three decades before 2018, Mexico's major policies and structural reforms were articulated around the chief goal of creating a constitutional and normative framework that promoted, shaped, and shared the most cherished values of a liberal democracy to foster and maximize development. At the center of such undertaking was an underlying premise of human dignity and human rights protection. But all this changed with the momentous presidential election of 2018 that brought into power a governing coalition with a remarkably different set of values. When put in practice through policy, the result of this change has been catastrophic, including clear retrogressions from all that was achieved nearly three decades ago. Despite the government's "transformative" rhetoric, what Mexico has experienced since 2019 is in fact what I have defined as *regression through transformation.*[5]

In this chapter, I will explore the past and present dynamics of Mexico's constitutive process. The first part of our analysis will be focused on the process of democratic liberalization of the 1990s. This process was maintained until 2018, when a new governing coalition rose to power with the chief goal of dismantling the legacy of the liberal democratic regime of the last three decades. The second part of the chapter will explore the set of retrogressive changes that this political transformation has entailed and its ramifications against the consolidation of a public order of human dignity. The last part will appraise the defective constitutional design that resulted from the liberalization process and will also formulate two strategies for the transformation of the constitutive process to put Mexico back on the developmental track more consistent with the expectations of a public order of human dignity.

---

5   Jaime Olaiz-González, *Regresión por Transformación: Cambio Constitucional en México en tiempos de la denominada 'cuarta transformación'*, Cuestiones Constitucionales Revista Mexicana de Derecho Constitucional, Num. 45, July-December 2021, at 238–278.

2   In the Quest for Development: The Constitutive Process in the
Period of Political Liberalization (1988–2018)[6]

In this section, we will explore the relevant participants and the dynamics that characterized the constitutive process over the three-decade period of political liberalization. A special feature of this analysis refers to the expected goals and intended outcomes that all relevant participants involved in the constitutive process of authoritative decision in Mexico should seek to secure. As Michael Reisman explains,

> A person engaged in performing any decision function that involves choosing should examine the demands of particular actors in terms of their congruence with the common interest, expressed as preferred patterns of production and distribution of every value within a system of stable minimum order.[7]

Hence, the activity of postulating and clarifying a set of public order goals ought to be characterized not only by the array and sometimes conflicting expectations and perspectives of the relevant actors, but also by what a given society in a particular time and place demands.

In the case of Mexico and its current predicaments, we should start by making a distinction between securing a minimum public order[8] by lowering the dominant expectations of violence, and the establishment of a desirable optimum public order of human dignity, in which all value categories are comprehensively fostered and achieved.

To do this, we start from the identification of the eight familiar values postulated by policy-oriented jurisprudence: power, wealth, enlightenment, skill, well-being, affection, respect and rectitude. From our perspective, a contextual focus is preferable to the conventional approach, based upon the predominance of one value over the rest. In our view:

---

6   Part II of this chapter is an adaptation from my J.S.D. dissertation at the Yale Law School, which explores the constitutive process of authoritative decision in Mexico and its possibilities of transformation from a historical and contemporary perspective. *See* Jaime Olaiz-González, *At the Turn of the Tide: A Framework for a Policy-Oriented Inquiry into Strategies for the Transformation of the Constitutive Process of Authoritative Decision in Mexico* (2015), https:// openyls.law.yale.edu/handle/20.500.13051/17634 (accessed 16 October 2022).

7   Michael Reisman, *A Jurisprudence from the Perspective of the "Political Superior,"* 23 N. Ky. L. Rev. 605, 619 (1996).

8   Harold D. Lasswell & Myres S. McDougal, Jurisprudence for a Free Society: Studies in Law, Science and Policy 34–35, 197–198 (1992).

A contextual focus emphasizes the multiple interrelationships between value production and distribution in all value categories. What can be achieved with respect to any one value is dependent on what can be achieved with all other values; positive developments in one value category may entail retrogressions or disdevelopments in others.[9]

This clarification, emphasizing the appropriateness of using a contextual focus in contradistinction with the "one-value predominance" approach, is particularly relevant in a scenario such as the case of Mexico.

2.1   *Participants*
2.1.1   Governmental Institutions

Governmental institutions bore the greatest influence on the constitutive process in Mexico. Putting it succinctly, they were the awarders, as well as the awarded. They controlled all initiatives in varying degrees and at all stages – from cradle to grave.

2.1.1.1   *The Presidency*

History has witnessed the President playing a decisive role in Mexico's political decision-making. The constant of our political ethos, the "concentration of power,"[10] has afforded the Presidency almost insurmountable power. A direct consequence of this constant has been the total absence of the creativity and imagination that a political system requires in order to serve all strata of society effectively.

For the last three quarters of the past century, the President was the embodiment of the political system as whole.[11] The Legislature and the Judiciary were

---

9   Reisman, *Development and Nation Building, supra* note 3, at 311.
10   Jo Tuckman, Mexico. Democracy Interrupted 84 (2012). Tuckman describes the concentration of power in the Mexican presidency: "[A] kind of political solar system [where] the president – the sun – provided the guiding force for almost everybody, from the governors to intellectuals, the unions to the Church, and the media to the opposition political parties. They moved around the system with different degrees of subordination to the center, [but] their movements were always controlled to some degree. [In the era of political plurality] the waning of the sun's gravitational pull released the planets to roam more freely, but the absence of more concerted efforts to deepen democratization meant that they did so with their own orbits largely intact. Some floated off towards irrelevance and began to lose their satellites, but others began drawing in more floating bodies, gaining greater weight and importance in the definition of how the whole system works." *Id.*
11   Daniel Cosío Villegas, El sistema político mexicano. Las probabilidades de cambio (1976). Daniel Cosío has provided in the eyes of many specialists, the best analysis of the political system in Mexico and the presidentialism that resulted after the Mexican Revolution.

little more than his minions, acting on his absolute authoritative will. The 1980s witnessed a gradual shift in the equation of power. The electoral triumph of the main opposition party brought about an erosion of presidentialism. The vacuum created by the demise of the earlier hyper-presidentialism generated frenetic power grabbing among the rest of the participants. Since then, and until 2018, the President's powers were shackled considerably and brought under the permanent scrutiny of the other actors. However, public memory, though generally considered short, retains the imprint of earlier times: It is often argued that the President has been held hostage to the partisan interests of myopic participants, thus depriving him from working on an agenda of his own, which many consider a boon for the greater good of the nation.

2.1.1.2   *Congress*

The legislative arm of government experienced a newfound independence until 2018. Previously, it had functioned more or less as an appendage to the President's will. However, since 1997, there was an increase in the number of opposition parties represented in Congress, thereby altering the balance of power. The President's party no longer enjoyed absolute control of Congress. This new political reality compelled Congress to conduct an inner deliberation within the different political lobbies in order to develop the constitutive process. They have made Congress the arena where they spar with one another in an attempt to express their interests over those of others in the most meaningful manner.

Since Congress is the primary arena of political decision-making, lawmakers, however, make a concerted effort to keep the institution insulated from public participation and scrutiny. As a result, there is heightened unaccountability. Hence, lawmaking is considered as distanced from the actual identifications, expectations and demands of the constituents.

2.1.1.3   *The Judiciary*

The Judicial Branch also experienced a regenerative independence. In 1995, the Judiciary was restructured and became more transparent and accountable to the public. Until 2018, appointments of Supreme Court Justices were based more on merit rather than political affiliation. Even though the selection process was still controlled by the political parties, Congress, and the Presidency,

---

Cosío's concept of the so-called "concentric circles" depicting how the whole political system spun around the President and how all decisions were ultimately taken by him during his term in power – "a sexennial monarchy" as Cosío refers to it - is a key notion for understanding the political ethos in Mexico after the Revolution.

the independence of the Judiciary as an institution remained unblemished. However, for this very reason, the Judicial Branch experienced problems of counter-majoritarianism, particularly while justifying judicial review.[12] By introducing televised deliberations and providing informative access to court material, the Supreme Court attempted to gain greater legitimacy[13] after decades of silent subordination to the President. Over the following years, it endeavored in asserting the "right degree of independence."[14] Notwithstanding these laudable efforts, the excessive length of judicial deliberations and the time taken to arrive at decisions coupled with a lack of professionalism at the lower strata of the Judiciary greatly mars its public reputation.

Until recent years, the Supreme Court focused predominantly on private law adjudication, following the so-called "dispute resolution model" which views adjudication solely as a process to resolve private disputes. The other, often ignored model, is "structural litigation." This refers to that form of adjudication that emerged in the United States during the Civil Rights era. It is characterized by two main features: the awareness that the basic threats to civil liberties are posed not by individuals, but by the state apparatus; and that unless that apparatus is restructured, the threats to constitutional rights will not be eliminated.[15] Structural litigation remains a panacea for our Judiciary. As Professor Bruce Ackerman eloquently describes, the Judiciary, in enforcing constitutional rights, can take up either of two attitudes: One is to allow the natural separation of political and legal times to persevere until society witnesses the evolution of social mores, or second, to embrace judicial activism in the attempt to meld political and legal processes while adjudicating constitutional rights. Consequently, this process would create a strong precedent

---

12   I am referring to Alexander Bickel's "counter-majoritarian" difficulty. *See* Alexander M. Bickel, The Least Dangerous Branch. The Supreme Court at the Bar of Politics 16–23 (1986).

13   *See* Robert A. Burt, The Constitution in Conflict 374 (1992). Professor Burt refers to the legitimacy of the Judiciary in these terms: "The Supreme Court must never conclude that its authority to act or to withhold action is unquestionably legitimate. For the same reason, the Court must never conclude that other institutions or individuals have unquestionably authority to coerce anyone."

14   On the independence of the Judiciary, *see* Owen M. Fiss, *The Right Degree of Independence, in* Transitions to Democracy in Latin America: The Role of the Judiciary 55 (Irwin P. Stotzky ed., 1993); *see also* Robert A. Burt, *Judicial Independence and Constitutional Democracy: Lessons from the U.S. Experience, in id.* at 287.

15   Owen M. Fiss, The Law as It Could Be 48–58 (2003). Professor Fiss explains the two predominant models of adjudication in the United States and, in contrasting them, defends the social value of structural litigation to protect civil rights.

for the protection of these rights for posterity. It is this kind of activism that is expected from the Mexican judiciary in these trying times.

2.1.1.4   *The Bureaucracy*

Traditionally, members of the official party composed the state apparatus. The bureaucracy was considered to be simply an extension of the ruling party. The appointment of public officials was contingent on their political affiliation and ability to win the favor of the party elites, a practice that continued for several decades. It created a general perception that the only formula for bureaucratic success was to work for the government and muster political favor. Such practices – still prevalent in the state apparatus – undermined the quality of public service. The lack of accountability of public officials stemming from being under the protection of political superiors was gradually eroded but has failed in undoing the damage caused by decades of dysfunction. However, the technocrats were a pleasant exception to this state of malfunction. This category consisted of upper-level public officials educated in the best institutions in Mexico and abroad and endowed with exceptional professional skills. Their efficiency saved the day for the Mexican bureaucracy, the silver lining in the cloud, and the bright side of a bad situation. On many occasions, their work even improved the performance of the state organizations in which they worked.

2.1.1.5   *Political Parties*

The Mexican political system is based on a multiparty structure, which serves as the link between the citizens and the State. At the dawn of the Mexican Revolution, the political factions clustered together as the Partido de la Revolución Mexicana (PRM), which was later transformed into the Partido Nacional Revolucionario (PNR). Later, in 1929, it attained its present form as Partido Revolucionario Institucional (PRI – Institutionalized Revolution Party). The peculiar feature of the PRI was that it concentrated the power of ordinary citizens – chiefly, workers and peasants. It also centralized the full range of political ideologies, from the most liberal to the most libertarian. The President was not only the head of state, but also the head of the party. He had the unique privilege of appointing his successor to the Presidency. He also approved all nominees for each local and federal election. The party's allegiance to the President was unquestionable. However, in the 1970s, Mexico bowed to international pressure and allowed opposition parties to have greater representation in Congress with the goal of enhancing democratic plurality. A series of constitutional reforms were undertaken as a result. These reforms gave opposition parties sufficient representation to dislodge the PRI monopoly on the decision-making process in Congress.

Political parties have a life of their own, unaffected by social movements or public criticism. They have shown that they possess the final word in the decision-making process, which they have molded according to their interests. Frequent political bargaining, undertaken secretly, coupled with mere lip service to transparency, goes a long way in distancing the People from the political process.

A regressive constitutional reform allowed only political parties to enter into contracts to buy airtime on television broadcasts in order to promote their electoral programs. This privilege undermined the access of other participants to one of the most common forms of information dissemination. The Judiciary reviewed this reform and surprisingly upheld its constitutionality. As a consequence, political parties have the sole right to the use of the mass media to reach out to the People, thus delivering a deathblow to free debate between all constituents.[16]

Campaign finance for political parties is another characteristic feature. Each year, political parties are assigned almost 1.1% of the annual budget for the financing of their campaigns.[17] The threshold of accountability for this budgetary allocation is almost non-existent, and corruption is rampant in the management of these budgets.

Opinion polls demonstrate that political parties are losing public confidence, and that the average citizen does not feel adequately represented by any of them.[18]

2.1.1.6 Labor Unions

One of the greatest achievements of the Mexican Revolution was the establishment of freedom of association and the protection of the working class

---

16 In October 2, 2008, the Supreme Court granted a writ of certiorari to a group of citizens and private associations that filed a collective pleading challenging the constitutionality of the legislative procedure that was followed for the electoral reforms made in 2007 preventing citizens and organizations different from political parties to access the mass media – radio and television, in particular – to convey their ideas. The case was remanded to the lower court and it granted jurisdiction in January 16, 2009.

17 See Presupuesto de Egresos de la Federación para el Ejercicio Fiscal 2022, https://www .diputados.gob.mx/Leyes Biblio/pdf/PEF_2022.pdf (accessed 26 November 2022).

18 The same study, conducted in 2017, shows that the least well regarded/least respected institutions in Mexico are the political parties, rating 4.4/10 of public approval. See Rolando Ramos, Se mantiene la baja confianza en las instituciones, El Economista, 1 February 2018, https://www.eleconomista.com.mx/politica/Se-mantiene-la-baja-confianza-en-las -instituciones-20180201-0145.html (accessed 26 November 2022).

expressed explicitly in various constitutional provisions. This resulted in the labor unions attaining significant influence in the state apparatus, becoming an extension of the official party. The original purpose of the unions – that of protecting the interests and rights of their members – was quickly forgotten, as they zealously embraced the dominant political ideology and became tools of political mobilization and expression of support.

After the decay of the hegemonic party, unions remained active participants in the process of decision-making, either by encouraging initiatives that would increase their privileges, or by opposing initiatives that would subject them to transparency and accountability. The degree of opacity prevailing in the management of unions has eroded their public image and they are now widely seen an obstacle to development.[19]

2.1.1.7   *The Military*

The triumphant generals of the revolution, after consolidating the constitutional regime, established a professional military. The subsequent years of the revolution saw the military presiding over the government. In the mid 1940s, power shifted from military to civilian control.[20] Since then, the military has played such an important institutional role that it has become one of the most revered public institutions in Mexico.[21] Due to an unwritten code, the military did not take an active part in the political process. However, in matters of national security, it used to play a discreet, but key role in decision-making that changed dramatically in 2019.

2.1.2   Non-Governmental Organizations

Even though non-governmental organizations enjoy diminished influence as compared to governmental organizations, the current process of political transformation in Mexico has endowed the former with enough power and authority to influence and, in some cases, even control, the processes of decision-making. I will now briefly enumerate their roles in the constitutive process.

---

19   Polls taken in 2017 show that public support for unions and its leaders is of 4.6/10. *See* Ramos, *supra* note 18.

20   On the matter of civil-military relations, earlier works of Samuel Huntington are particularly instructive. *See* Samuel Huntington, The Soldier and the State. The Theory and Politics of Civil-Military Relations (1957).

21   As a poll taken in 2017 demonstrates, the public holds the military in higher regard than other institutions studied, rating 7.0/10 in public acceptance, and ranking just below the universities and the Church. *See* Ramos, *supra* note 18.

2.1.2.1   Private Sector (Businessmen)

When I refer to the private sector, I mean a very small group of groups, associations and individual businessmen representing a large portion of the private wealth in Mexico. These business elites are formidable actors in the constitutive process, particularly in economic affairs. As the government embraced privatization, reduced its size and assigned several contracts to the private sector, it gained the enduring allegiance of the business elite. However, this allegiance was not always unconditional. By the end of the 1970s, the chambers of commerce and most business associations began to demand greater accountability in public functions and a fairer taxation policy. Notwithstanding these ripples of dissent, the private sector has generally played a central role in pushing initiatives, chiefly tax policies, favorable to their interests.

2.1.2.2   The Media

The media are perhaps the most influential participants in the process today. Due to their unparalleled public reach and lenient regulation, the media— particularly television networks—have acquired an increasing influence on public affairs. Doing little more than serving as the unofficial press service of the prevailing government, the media have progressively experienced a greater degree of independence.

However, in managing and conveying information, the media are not subject to any regulation either, in addition to their lack of a shared code of ethics. This absolute lack of a control mechanism results in the media being used as an instrument of intimidation against proponents of reform and regulation, effectively alienating proponents of change from the constitutive process.

As the law stands today, the only political participants allowed to communicate their ideas through television networks are political parties. This incestuous relationship between political parties and "independent" television networks is one of the most concerning threats to democracy. It is the most obvious assault on the freedom of citizens to take part in public affairs.

2.1.2.3   Non-Governmental Organizations (stricto sensu)

The so-called "third sector"[22] has acquired greater importance over the last two decades. Since the origin of non-governmental organizations was outside the state apparatus, their survival and perdurability has depended on their commitment to their goals and the support of particular sections of society

---

22   The expression "third sector" is commonly used in Mexico to denote the Non-Governmental Organizations in order to distinguish them from traditional public (governmental structure) and private (business organizations) institutions.

that they serve (for example, women, children, elders, environment, human rights). Their participation in the constitutive process is gradually increasing. They address a mosaic of subject matters and offer a more objective analysis of a range of issues. In many ways, they have been pioneers in the attempt to open the constitutive process to non-traditional participants.

2.1.1.4   Intellectuals

Intellectuals have traditionally been the critics of the status quo. For over a century, they have criticized the way in which the government relates to the citizens. From the very beginning of the authoritarian regime, intellectuals denounced the lack of political plurality and political freedom in Mexico. They embodied public reason. However, due to the authoritarian practices of the ruling party, intellectuals were frequently silenced by intimidation or coercion, with many fleeing the country as a result. Those who stayed were often suppressed or made to express a sympathetic view of the regime.

However, it was the intellectuals who provided the narrative of the constitutive process that followed the Mexican Revolution, as well as of the distribution of power amongst the elites over the next decades. They also brought to light the failures of the political system as well as the challenges that lay in the path to democratization. They provided the agenda of change for the democratic regime that followed.

2.1.2.5   The Church and Religious Associations

The Roman Catholic Church has played a decisive role in Mexico ever since the Spanish colonial regime. Due to ideological dualism, the tension between the Church and the State has been a constant. After the end of the Mexican Revolution, the State undertook a radical campaign against the Catholic Church that escalated into a war, generally known as "*Guerra Cristera.*"[23] The outcome of this war was a shaky truce between both groups. The Church limited its role to spiritual ministry. In the 1990s, after a series of constitutional reforms that granted legal standing to religious associations, including the Roman Catholic Church, the institutional relations between these institutions and the state attained an unprecedented degree of tolerance and communication. Historically, Mexico has been almost 90% Catholic, and the religious fervor of its population is evident in a diversity of cultural and social institutions. However, in the last decades, the growing number of sects and religious faiths

---

23   The most prolific historical work pertaining to the "*Guerra Cristera*" is by Jean Meyer. *See* Jean Meyer, La Cristiada (1975).

has weakened the dominance of the Catholic Church in Mexico. This notwith-standing, Catholicism remains the preferred religion of the political elite.

2.1.3   Other Participants
2.1.3.1   *Local Leaders*
Local leaders exhibit some of the clearest expressions of influence in the micro-constitutive process. They conduct unilateral decision-making in regions. Due to the historical trend of concentration of power, these leaders enjoy substantial independence in local decision-making. At one time, local leadership served as one of the main assets of the ruling party in its attempt to maintain control over the nation. By bestowing political favors and economic rewards, the party relied on local leaders to assure and/or manipulate the local electoral results in order to retain power in the region.

Due to the high degree of poverty in large parts of Mexico, local leaders still control most decisions. This is primarily because they are the only ones sufficiently capable of obtaining the necessary means of subsistence for their communities. Unscrupulous participants often take advantage of the situation to obtain the acquiescence of the local leader to conduct their illegal activities without hindrance. In exchange, they reward the leader with financial support that is significantly greater than the contributions that they receive from the government.

2.1.3.2   *Illicit Participants*[24]
Over the last twenty years, organized crime has spread its tentacles through-out Mexico, leading to a rise of instances of violence and intimidation. The emergence of this anti-social force has led to a breakdown of the constitutive process. Drug organizations, local gangs, warlords, and thugs have systemat-ically bribed key public officials and now conduct their business with impu-nity. Furthermore, they have attained such a high degree of power that they have managed to undermine the functioning of key governmental institutions. But their threat to society goes further than this: Their continuous efforts to increase their influence has resulted in a brutal and bloody struggle that has spilled onto the roads, putting innocent lives at risk. Due to this reality, the

---

24   Professor Reisman explains that criminals are rarely brought into refined legal discussion
        and regrets this tendency, due to the fact that thugs are instructive as a power phenom-
        enon. Therefore, by following the teachings of his mentor Harold Lasswell, Professor
        Reisman proposes to include thugs and organized crime as participants in any consti-
        tutive process of authoritative decision analysis. *See* W. Michael Reisman, *International
        Lawmaking: A Process of Communication,* 75 Am. Soc'y Int'l L. Proc. 110 (1981).

incidence of violence in Mexico is extremely high. Illicit participants are today the most dangerous threat to our peaceful existence.

2.1.3.3   *Indigenous Peoples*[25]

There are approximately 62 indigenous communities in Mexico, numbering around 10 million people; most of these have their own language and customs. Since the Spanish colonial regime, the majority of indigenous communities have been able to preserve their traditions. They live in relative isolation from the rest of the population. Their livelihood comes primarily from agriculture and craftwork. Due to them often being unable to speak Spanish, their participation in the constitutive process is minimal. However, as a political concession and due to international pressure, the state has created public offices and programs to assist the advancement of indigenous people.[26] However, these programs have been unsuccessful in bringing about social integration and they remain marginalized from the process of decision-making. For this reason, their expectations are the lowest among all the social groups in Mexico.

2.1.3.4   *Foreign Governments*

As interdependent as we are in today's metamorphosed world, the influence of foreign governments on the constitutive process cannot be underestimated as an important variable influencing decision-making in Mexico. Due to significant foreign investment in Mexico, the demands of foreign nationals for safety and security have always been an important consideration for the government. Foreign governments often engage in dialogue with their Mexican

---

25   An authoritative voice pertaining to the study of the rights of indigenous peoples is Professor Siegfried Wiessner. As Chair of the International Law Association's Committee on the Rights of Indigenous Peoples, he played a leading role in the development and adoption of ILA Resolution No. 5/2012 on the Rights of Indigenous Peoples, *see* https://ila .vettoreweb.com/Storage/Download.aspx?DbStorageId=1243& StorageFileGuid=401ee841 -8ad2-4e35-8aaf-beebd9b3aa4e (finding customary international law rights to indigenous peoples' traditional lands and resources, as well as their heritage and wide-ranging autonomy, all culturally determined). *Cf.* Siegfried Wiessner, *El Estado y los pueblos indígenas: la importancia histórica de la resolución No. 5/2012 de la ILA (Asociación de Derecho Internacional)*, 51 Ars Iuris 209 (2016). For an initial vanguard study, *see* Siegfried Wiessner, *Rights and Status of Indigenous Peoples: A Global Comparative and International Legal Perspective*, 12 Harv. Hum. Rts. J. 57, 127 (1999).

26   As Professor Reisman underscores, the responsibility of states to the indigenous peoples within their borders has acquired international currency and is now the subject of a number of initiatives to forge a common policy expressed in multilateral conventions and declarations. He also explains that when these claims have been made by the elites of the smaller groups, they have been framed in terms of "group rights." *See* Michael Reisman, *Autonomy, Interdependence, and Responsibility,* 103 Yale L.J. 411 (1993).

counterparts to advocate for the interests of their nationals. Furthermore, in terms of strategic geopolitics, foreign governments pay close attention to the outcomes of the macro- and micro-constitutive processes in Mexico. The classic example of this communicative process of mutual cooperation is best exhibited in the relations with the United States. The United States, because of its own political, economic and national security interests, is a permanent participant in ordinary decision-making in Mexico.

Having provided a brief description of the participants in the constitutive process, I will now proceed to describe the perspectives, situations, bases of power and outcomes that characterize decision-making in Mexico.

2.2   *Perspectives*

2.2.1   Identifications

As a result of cohabitation and intermarriage between native communities and Spanish colonizers in the 16th century, there is rich social diversity in Mexico. However, this heterogeneity has not prompted a historical consensus on national identity. On the contrary, vast social and economic stratification has influenced the presence of a constant feeling of struggle and resentment between the haves and the have-nots. The former consists primarily of descendants of European immigrants in the 16th and 17th centuries, and the latter of the indigenous people. Considering that development has not been inclusive enough to lead to an equal distribution of wealth in society, there has historically existed an insurmountable gap between the privileged classes and the vast majority of the rest of the population. Thus, socio-economic status is a key variable of social differentiation in Mexico.

These asymmetries have a great impact on the distinction between urban and rural settings. On the one hand, between urban groups of major cities and those of smaller, relatively backward cities, and on the other hand, between rural townships close to industrialized regions, which tend to be more prosperous, and those further away. Among each one of these social settings—urban and rural, centralized, and distant—there exist great differences in social stratification. These differentiations perpetuate inequalities that undermine the very essence of democracy by inhibiting a significant section of the society from taking an active part in the constitutive process.

Hence, it has been very difficult to define a common identity among the Mexican people. For various socio-economic, cultural, religious, political, and ideological reasons, Mexican society is greatly fragmented. In fact, ideological dualism has played a crucial role in dividing Mexican society since the 19th century. The struggle between conservative and liberal views of reality has kept the country at odds ever since. This lack of basic common identifications constitutes an essential element for the elaboration of further strategies that would enhance identity as Mexicans; an in depth-analysis of the strife within Mexican society is beyond the scope of this work, however.

2.2.2   Expectations

The absence of a strong national identity had a visible impact on the expectations of groups and individuals in Mexico. The more advantaged socio-economic groups are characterized by very high expectations. They share a self-imposed burden to help alleviate Mexico's many problems. For them, the main question in the constitutive process is whether they would be able to retain their privileges and way of life in case of any potential reform. As long as this is answered in the affirmative, these groups pledge themselves to reform. Gradualism and steady progress are the distinctive expectations for these groups. On the other side of the spectrum, among the less privileged groups, living a life of poverty and extreme deprivation, the expectations are very low. They are satisfied with two square meals a day, enough seed to sow, and the hope for a fruitful harvest. They aspire to a peaceful existence with little or no participation in the constitutive process – this reduces their expectations substantially.

Between these two extremes, there lies a middle class that constitutes the critical mass of the process of decision-making in Mexico. It spurs reform of the constitutive process by arguing for greater inclusiveness, democratization, and human dignity. Unlike the advantaged groups that are concerned only with retaining and enlarging their privileges, this middle class strives for a better distribution of all the values that were mentioned at the inception of this work. Inclusiveness is the key element of this task. Unlike the less-privileged groups at the bedrock of the social structure,[27] the middle class has at the center of its concerns the quest for transformation in order to alleviate the condition of the dismally oppressed masses.

In terms of expectations, however, one variable has a particularly strong influence on the constitutive process: the violence that has prevailed in Mexico in the last decades. Whether from actual or implicit intimidation, violence has shaped the way in which the constitutive process is conducted in Mexico, as well as its outcomes. The incidence of violence is significant due to the struggle between the State and organized crime groups, gangs, and drug cartels in focalized parts of the country. Extensive poverty in the peripheries of major cities also increases the crime rate. Notwithstanding the numerous expressions of

---

27   Numbering about 60 million people.

dissatisfaction and demands for more security from urban citizens, the government has been overwhelmed in its efforts to lower the expectations of violence that characterize the constitutive process.

2.2.3   Demands

A lack of widespread common national identity in Mexico and a great variety of expectations lead to manifold demands. The current participants in the decision-making process both in its macro- and micro-dimensions are unwilling to let other participants diminish their influence. Conversely, those at the margins of the process struggle to gain entry. There is a distinct connection between identifications and expectations with demands. As has been explained above, the level of expectations corresponds to the degree of demands that each group brings to the attention of the incumbent authorities. For instance, the demands of privileged participants (such as political parties and labor unions) are significantly more numerous and pressing than the demands of the less privileged. Paradoxically, of course, it ought to be the other way around. However, as organized as political parties, unions, business associations are, it is easier for them not only to express their demands but also to pressure the decision makers to favor them. The voice of the downtrodden is made to resound in the ears of the decision maker only when there is a significant mobilization. The misery of the unprivileged finds voice mainly through the efforts of the middle class, who shape and form common interests.

Consistent with the goal of minimum order, the most relevant appeals to common interests include those directly related to the maintenance of this order: a decrease in intimidation and violence as instruments of change.[28] In the present case, the relevance of this demand and its fulfillment cannot be overstated.

2.3   *Situations*

Governmental participants predominantly conduct the process of authoritative decision in Mexico in a centralized manner. Since Mexico City is the seat of federal power, all major decisions are made by the political elites located there. As has been explained previously, the process is neither transparent nor significantly deliberative. Decisions are made at the "center" without a fair sense of their broader implications for the rest of the country. Consequently, conflicts

---

28   Myres McDougal, Harold D. Lasswell & W. Michael Reisman, *The World Constitutive Process of Authoritative Decision, in* Myres S. McDougal & W. Michael Reisman, International Law Essays. A Supplement to International Law in Contemporary Perspective 191 (1981). The original version of this article was published in 19 J. Legal Ed. 253, 403 (1967).

arise between federal, state and local levels of government.[29] However, decentralization remains a goal of modern federalism. That being said, the most concerning practice pertaining to "situations" or "arenas" of decision-making in Mexico is the restriction of decision-making to a handful of elites, elites who may not possess legitimate authority. They tend to discuss national affairs privately, and their deliberations are completely inaccessible to ordinary citizens. The great concern pertaining to situations of authoritative decision-making in Mexico –- as occurs in most Latin American countries[30] – is that there are no transparent procedures for the administration of the constitutive process. This fosters political gerrymandering and corruption. Moreover, *ex post* public scrutiny of decisions is often fruitless.

2.4   Bases of Power

Power has been the defining feature of decision-making in Mexico. This is in part due to the legacy of authoritarianism imposed by the official party for over seven decades, during which the President and his appointees exercised power with full discretion over a lenient citizenry. Power was managed as a means of control and intimidation, rather than as a capacity and willingness to make a preferential expression effective.[31] The difference is small, yet fundamental: when power is used to make a preferential expression effective by intimidation or violence, it is inconsistent with the value of human dignity. Conversely, if exercised with an aim to minimize expectations of intimidation and violence, it is consonant with human dignity and will be regarded as exercise of legitimate power.

Authority, as the basis of power in the constitutive process, has been overshadowed by raw power in Mexico. The use of violence and intimidation

---

29   In this respect the opinion of Cuauhtémoc Cárdenas, a prominent Mexican politician, former Governor of the State of Michoacán and Presidential candidate in 1988, 1994 and 2000, is particularly useful to emphasize the importance of downscaling the areas for decision-making in order to enhance the participation of local and state governments. Interview with Cuauhtémoc Cárdenas, Mayor of Mexico City 1997–1999; Governor of Michoacán 1980–1986; in Mexico City (Apr. 10, 2012).

30   A comprehensive study pertaining to the functioning of the bureaucracies and decision-making processes in Latin American has been made by Professor Susan Rose-Ackerman, underscoring the wide differences of institutional operation in the region. Her insights into the Mexican case are extremely relevant here. *See* Susan Rose-Ackerman, *Public Administration and Institutions in Latin America,* article prepared for the "Copenhagen Consensus," Consulta de San José de Costa Rica, September 11, 2007.

31   Reisman, *supra* note 24, at 110–111.

against those who seek to take lawful part in the process is the clearest example of how authoritarianism overshadows authority.[32]

2.5 *Outcomes*

In describing the outcomes of decision-making in Mexico, I have categorized them in terms of the eight preferred values: power, wealth, enlightenment, well-being, skill, affection, respect and rectitude.[33] The perspectives mentioned above serve to shed some light on the condition of each of these values.

2.5.1 Power

Considered as the capacity and willingness to make preferential expressions effective, power is currently exercised only by the most advantaged participants in the constitutive process. It is their choice and theirs alone to share their power with others. Since authority is still not the basis for prescriptions in Mexico, the disruptive effects of violence often undermine effective decision-making. Consequently, if power remains concentrated in the hands of a few, the possibilities of transformation are minimal.

2.5.2 Wealth

About 70% of Mexico's national wealth is concentrated among a thousand families. At the other end of the spectrum lie around 40 million people who live in abject poverty. The distribution of wealth is highly imbalanced. Under the current situation, the rich get richer and the poor poorer. The only way to change this dynamic is to devise mechanisms of social and political inclusiveness for the less privileged.

2.5.3 Enlightenment

Basic literacy has not sufficed in making Mexican society inclusive. Notwithstanding the fact that illiteracy in Mexico is relatively low, the quality of basic education is mediocre. One of the greatest obstacles to development in education is the lack of professionalism in the teaching ranks. Due to the overriding influence of their labor union and the power of union leaders, teachers enjoy great benefits that are not on par with their performance.

---

32   Hannah Arendt, On Revolution 27–28 (2006). Here, Arendt's reflections on violence and its connections with authority are particularly relevant. In explaining the connections between violence and revolution, Hannah Arendt gives the example of the Roman republic as a model of a polity where authority, and not violence, ruled the conduct of the citizens.

33   Reisman et al., *supra* note 1, at 580.

Since they are not subject to performance evaluations and are often involved in political activities, the students receive deficient education, which is in turn reflected in a lack of expectations and diminished accomplishments.

2.5.4   Well-Being
Although there has been an increase in life expectancy in Mexico, public health services are strained to their maximum capacity and are now at their breaking point. This is primarily due to the growing number of elderly people needing continuous medical attention. Disease in remote areas of the country is rampant, increasing mortality and lowering life expectancy.

2.5.5   Skills
There was a considerable advancement in the development of skills after the conclusion of the Revolution. A large educational enterprise created a vast framework of institutions where knowledge was transmitted and shared in order to foster socio-economic development. However, a demand of broader dissemination of skills still exists.

2.5.6   Affection
Mexico is a traditional and conservative nation, where the institution of the family is at the epicenter of an individual's life. The degree of social affection is intimately related to the sentiments that people develop towards their families and friends. However, as stratified as our society is, exclusiveness has increased. This has undermined the values of loyalty among inclusive groups.

2.5.7   Respect
Respect is determined by one's socio-economic position. The higher the position, the higher the degree of respect. There is a tendency to appreciate both individual and exclusive behavior. Merit-based social recognition is becoming increasingly important and accepted. However, the lack of a common identity prevents group members from perceiving themselves as full participants in the social process.

2.5.8   Rectitude
Anomie[34] is the worst enemy of rectitude in Mexico. The internalization of personal codes is dependent on how firmly human values have been implanted.

---

34   Carlos Nino, Un país al margen de la ley (2005).

Bribery and corruption are widespread practices that tend to undermine the rectitude of individuals.

For these reasons, individuals are often less interested in taking part in a process that systematically marginalizes them. Moreover, the lack of historical memory makes it easy for the citizenry to overlook the misdeeds and abuses of its representatives, which further impedes accountability and the development of a notion of a responsible mandate in Mexico.

3   Regression through Transformation: The Constitutive Process in Times of the So-Called Fourth Transformation

As a continuum, political transformations and constitutional change sometimes entail progress and evolution. Others entail regressions and deterioration. Both scenarios have important implications for the constitutive process.

The continuous nature of political transformations and constitutional change evinces the interplay between progress and regress, between reform and preservation, and the way in which each vision articulates a distinctive series of values to assert its political authority.

As described in the previous section, Mexico's political transformations over the past three decades and until 2018, were characterized by an institutional and societal effort to approach the values of liberal democracy: rule of law, human rights protection, effective separation of powers, the promotion of economic development through international cooperation, and environmental sustainability.

These goals reflected the values promoted by policy-oriented jurisprudence, and they very well represented the dominant mindset of the past three generations in Mexico, whose perspectives were deeply infused into a culture of merit, respect, integrity, dialogue, tolerance, equal opportunity, and a continuous search for progress.[35]

But this process was dramatically interrupted and reversed by the national election of 2018, in which a new governing coalition championing the opposite values of those that guided Mexico's transition to democracy since the 1980s, took power based upon a retributive populist platform with the chief goal of

---

35   Somewhere else, I have explored in detail the features that characterized the constitutive process in Mexico between 1988 and 2015, during the period of political liberalization. *See* Olaiz-González, *supra* note 5, at 183–340.

dismantling the legacy of institutions and procedures of the most transformative and modernizing period in Mexico's contemporary history.[36]

In this section, I will embark on elaborating the features that characterize the present phase of Mexico's constitutive process and the daunting implications that they entail.

The current constitutive process is defined by an official narrative that deepens the tensions between the haves and the have-nots, the educated and the non-educated, the professional middle class and the grantees of the government's social programs, and we can continue with more binary classifications in which the governing coalition presents itself as the champion of the less favored groups.

As will be seen, the contrast with the former constitutive process is astonishing, and these new dynamics have interrupted Mexico's quest for a more consolidated public order of human dignity. So, let us explore the manifold changes that this new government has produced in the constitutive process of authoritative decision-making in Mexico.

3.1 Participants

3.1.1 Governmental Institutions

Over the past three years, there has been a radical shift of the relevant actors in the constitutive process and of their perspectives. In many respects, these participants, their mindsets and behavior resemble the actors, institutions, and practices that dominated in the 1970s, before the transformative period of political liberalization. In many ways, the operational code of the single-party rule of the 1970s is the blueprint of the present administration.

3.1.1.1 The Presidency

After a steady process of adjusting the Mexican presidency to liberal-democratic standards over the past three decades, since 2019, this government has reinstated its former supra-constitutional and influential role as the epicenter of state policy. This administration has been characterized by an overwhelming inclination to act outside constitutional limits, to ignore legal rules, for the sake of its own idea of justice, and by overtly interfering in the spheres of the other branches of government.[37]

---

36   *Id.* at 183–238.

37   María Amparo Casar, *La ilegalidad y el presidente*, Nexos (March 2020) at https://www
      .nexos.com.mx/?p=47085.

Claiming its unprecedented popular support, the President daily sets a confrontational tone, by exacerbating a Manichean narrative of *with us or against us,* instead of conceiving the Presidency as a critical unifying institution.

Practical subordination of most political actors has intensified this institutional regression to the point that there is not any difference between the Mexican presidency today and that of the single-party rule that dominated Mexican politics between 1928 and 2000. In consequence, the actions of the President directly affect the behavior of the rest of the relevant participants in the constitutive process as we will see below.

3.1.1.2 *Congress*

Since 2018, the new governing coalition controls the Legislative Branch with an ample majority. The Lower House – Chamber of Deputies – best represents the subordination of the official party deputies (Congressmen) to the dictates of the President, by approving his proposed legislation without any type of deliberation. The Senate, however, remains as a more professional legislative body, in which – notwithstanding the majority that the official party also enjoys – a better study of proposed legislation and parliamentarian deliberation still prevails in the law-making process.

Over the first half of the administration (2018–2021), the governing coalition enjoyed a qualified majority of two thirds to amend the constitution and with it, it passed 56 constitutional amendments,[38] chiefly pertaining to the militarization of public safety; to incorporate, at a constitutional level, mandatory imprisonment for new crimes such as corruption and tax evasion; to protect governmental social programs; to reverse the former constitutional reform on education, implemented in the previous administration, which promoted evaluation of teachers through merit and competition; to reduce the size of government by introducing a state policy of extreme austerity, undermining professional public service; among others. Most of these amendments were constitutionally challenged by the political opposition and some independent agencies before the Supreme Court, to no significant avail.

There was, however, an important shift in the mid-term elections of 2021, in which the governing coalition lost its qualified majority to amend the Constitution,[39] entailing the corresponding institutional paralysis and making the government explore further legislative changes at a statutory instead of a

---

38 *See* https://www.diputados.gob.mx/LeyesBiblio/sumario.htm (accessed 26 December 2022).

39 Anatoly Kurmanaev & Oscar Lopez, *Mexico's President Grip on Congress Slips, Showing Limits to His Mandate,* N.Y. Times, 7 June 2021, at https://www.nytimes.com/2021/06/07

constitutional level, with the corresponding political tensions and legal challenges that such scenarios bring along.

This limited, but decisive new distribution of power in Congress has prevented the governing coalition of passing two extremely regressive constitutional amendments: on the one hand, an amendment aiming at reshaping the energy sector to favor state-owned companies,[40] and on the other hand, a political reform purposely designed to dismantle the Electoral Branch,[41] as an independent, non-partisan, professional agency in charge of the organizing, policing, and validating elections in Mexico. Again, the government's goal is to bring back the electoral system to the pre-democratic era in which elections were controlled by the government, and the official party was at the same time, the granter, and the grantee of power.

3.1.1.3   *The Judiciary*

One of the most revolutionary institutional transformations of the past three decades was that of the Mexican Supreme Court of Justice in becoming a full-fledged constitutional court, enjoying autonomy and independence to fulfill its instrumental constitutional role. This transformation resulted in an unprecedented progeny of judicial precedents that represented an evolutionary leap of the Court's interpretative and adjudicatory processes.[42]

But this trend was interrupted with the election of 2018. Since then, the Court and the Federal Judiciary have endured constant pressure and criticism from the President himself, who claims that the Court and the federal judges have subordinated themselves to the interests of the haves to the detriment of the demands of the have-nots, the people. Furthermore, in a clear transgression of the principle of the separation of powers, he has publicly pressured the members of the Court to rule in favor of all his passed legislation that was challenged before the Court. In his view, the Court should abide first to justice,

---

/world/americas/mexico-election-results-lopez-obrador.html (accessed 26 December 2022).

40   Kirk Semple & Oscar Lopez, *Mexico Set to Reshape Power Sector to Favor the State*, N.Y. Times, 7 March 2021, at https://www.nytimes.com/2021/03/07/world/ americas/mexico-energy-sector-privatization.html?action=click& module=RelatedLinks&pgtype=Article.

41   *An 'electoral reform' in Mexico will make elections less safe*, The Economist, 20 December 2022, at https://www.economist.com/the-americas/2022/12/20/an-electoral-reform-in-mexico -will-make-elections-less-safe (accessed 26 December 2022).

42   I have explored this in other works. *See* Jaime Olaiz-González, *Mexican Supreme Court under Pressure: Between Affirmation or Accommodation*, 14(4) ICL J. – Vienna J. Int'l Const'l L. (January 2021). *See also* Jaime Olaiz-González, *Mexican Supreme Court: Legislative Omission – Analysis on Congress' Failure to Enact Legislation Regulating Official Advertising in Mexico*, 12(3) ICL J. – Vienna J. Int'l Const'l L. (November 2018).

rather than to the Constitution and the law. To attain this goal, the President has embarked on gradually packing the Court with loyalists, notwithstanding, in some cases, their lack of qualifications.[43]

From the vantage point of the Court, it has fluctuated over the last three years between affirming its independence, compromising when necessary, or ultimately, subordinating some of its momentous decisions to the President's dictates.[44]

To implement his plans, López Obrador and his coalition passed an overarching series of statutory reforms that were eventually challenged at the Supreme Court. The Court's President deliberately put on hold the deliberation of most of these lawsuits to prevent further antagonism with the government, at the same time as he was ushering in a momentous constitutional amendment to restructure the Judicial Branch. In some other cases, the Court validated some of López Obrador's reforms, such as in the case of the popular referendum of 2021.[45]

Thus, there is consensus among legal circles and academia that a minority of the Court and its former President have undermined its independence by abdicating their responsibility to unequivocally affirm the Court's role as the custodian of the Constitution.[46] Perhaps the best illustration of this was the Court's reluctance to declare the unconstitutionality of statutory amendments passed in 2019 and 2020, incorporating mandatory imprisonment for some specific crimes such as corruption and tax evasion, in violation of the principles of presumption of innocence and due process, and breaching the rules of the Inter-American System of Human Rights that ban unjustified mandatory imprisonment.[47]

This case presented a golden opportunity for the Court not only to affirm the incorporation of international human rights law standards at a constitutional level, but, even more importantly, to start defining the boundaries of a

---

43   After being appointed to the Court in 2018 and 2019 respectively, Associate Justices Juan Luis González-Alcántara Carrancá and Margarita Ríos-Farjat have demonstrated their independence in an important set of decisions taken by the Court over the last couple of years.

44   Olaiz-González, *Mexican Supreme Court under Pressure, supra* note 42.

45   *Id.*

46   Mariana Velasco-Rivera, *When Judges Threaten Constitutional Governance: Evidence from Mexico,* I-CONnect, Blog of the International Journal of Constitutional Law, 16 June 2022, at http://www.iconnectblog.com/2022/06/when-judges-threaten-constitutional-governance -evidence-from-mexico/ (accessed 26 December 2022).

47   Jaime Olaiz, Daniel Torres, Sebastián Incháustegui, *Whispers of Change. On Mexico's Supreme Court Ongoing Debate on the Unconstitutionality of Constitutional Amendments,* Verfassungsblog on Matters Constitutional, 22 September 2022, at https://verfassungsblog .de/whispers-of-change/ (accessed 26 December 2022).

needed Basic Structure Doctrine amid the ongoing political and institutional assault.[48] Instead, and based upon outdated formalistic arguments, the majority of the Court refrained from invalidating mandatory imprisonment as is, except for the case of tax evasion.[49]

All in all, the Supreme Court is passing through a period of momentous self-definition: to choose between persevering in becoming a full-fledged constitutional court or succumbing to the pressure to play a more modest role in the constitutive process as in the times of the single-party rule.

3.1.1.4   The Bureaucracy

Starting from members of the Cabinet to the rest of the government, professional and specialized public service is no longer valued or rewarded. In fact, the leitmotif of the incumbent administration is "90% honesty, 10% skill," in clear and deliberate contrast with the technocratic identity of previous administrations.[50]

This trend is closely related to the continuous effort of President López Obrador to dismantle not only public professional service within the government itself, but also the number of distinctive independent agencies that resulted from the institutional decentralization that characterized the democratization process that started in the 1990s and continued until the structural reforms of 2014.

The present conditions of Mexican bureaucracy are far from good. They can be summarized in three words: chaos, incompetence, and inefficiency. With the new administration, thousands of seasoned public servants at all levels of the federal government were sacked or forced to resign due to substantial

---

48   As we will see below, the Basic Structure Doctrine was first enunciated by the Supreme Court of India in 1973, when it established specific limits to the amendDent powers of constitutional amendments, setting forth an inviolable domain within the constitution that cannot be changed under any circumstances.

49   Acción de Inconstitucionalidad 130/2019 [Challenge to the Constitutionality of Laws], 15 November 2019, filed by the National Commission of Human Rights.

50   Roderic Ai Camp, Mexico's Mandarins. Crafting a Power Elite for the Twenty-First Century 183, 252 (2002). Ai Camp argues that the Mexican technocrats, the "técnicos" as he refers to them, have left a distinctive imprint on their Latin American peers, "The técnicos, as a group, are worth examining because *they perhaps more than any other power elite group in Mexico influenced the major trends in public policy, trends which confronted and reformed the country's economic and political structures*" (emphasis added). Quoting Harvard professor Raymond Vernon, he describes them as having "a common ideology which, harnessed to the government apparatus, constituted a strong force in shaping the behavior of the public sector in Mexico... Accordingly, the strength of the technicians lies not so much in their powers to shape policy directly as in their capacity to choose the technical alternatives which are presented to their political masters," *id.* at 176–177.

changes to their contracts. The underlying premise of this gradual deterioration is the frontal antagonism of the President and his supporters against the so-called neoliberal period of the last three decades.

However, the ramifications of this go beyond politics. Critical areas of public policy such as health services, education, public safety, among others, have been affected due to the lack of experience or competence of the new public officials. Sensitive processes ranging from public contracting to the participation in numerous international fora have been left in the hands of amateurs, to put it mildly, who ultimately discredit the government and Mexico's reputation around the globe.

3.1.1.5   *Political Parties*
In this respect, there has also been a radical change with the new distribution of power: the political pluralism that defined the last twenty-five years, has given way to a renewed de facto single-party rule that has embarked on a systemic effort to undermine or even eliminate any significant political opposition, to no avail so far. The mid-term elections of 2021 evinced that political parties in Mexico are divided in two blocks: the official party (Morena) and its allies (the Green Party and the Labor Party) presenting themselves as the legitimate speakers of the people and willing to circumvent the Constitution and legality to achieve their goals, on the one hand; and on the other, the traditional parties – PRI, PAN, and PRD – clustered in a factual coalition to protect the constitutional order against the abuses of the government.

In many ways, the present situation of political parties resembles the days of the single-party rule of the PRI for most of the second half of the past century.

3.1.1.6   *Labor Unions*
Unions have pledged their fidelity to the incumbent governing coalition. The most important labor unions have aligned themselves to the project of López Obrador with some corresponding effects such as a considerable rise of the minimum wage and passing legislation banning outsourcing. As in the past, these labor unions have been somehow absorbed by the official party.

3.1.1.7   *The Military*
Perhaps the most relevant participant along with the President in Mexico's constitutive process, the Military is passing through momentous transformations. The new administration has assigned to the armed forces an array of duties that range from public safety, airports administration, construction of key infrastructure projects, such as a new domestic airport neighboring Mexico City, a regional train in the Yucatán Peninsula, or an oil refinery in the

southeastern state of Tabasco; to the vaccination campaign during the COVID-19 pandemic, administering national ports or fighting gasoline-theft from the pipelines of the state-owned oil company – PEMEX –, or customs and border patrol to detain illegal immigrants.

The arbitrariness in which these functions have been assigned, has produced several claims before the Supreme Court, challenging their constitutionality. One of the major concerns is the normalization of the military overseeing and conducting operations related to public safety across the country in the form of the so-called National Guard. In this regard, the Constitution explicitly prescribes that this body will be structured under civilian command.[51] However, in implementing it, the administration left the National Guard and its regulation and operations under the authority of the Military. In a recent decision, a majority of the Court validated the package of statutory reforms that enabled the present militarization of public safety.[52]

3.1.1.8   State Governors

During the period of political liberalization, state governors enjoyed unprecedented independence and unchallenged political power in their respective states. During this time, the President refrained from interfering in state politics by appointing or deposing state governors, as was customary in the past.

Since 2019, this also has changed: Due to the increasing concentration of power in the Presidency, the power of state governors has gradually decreased, by subordinating them again to the dictates of the President, who has overwhelming control over them either for the appropriations assigned by the Ministry of Economy, or for pending investigations of corruption and other charges in the Attorney General's Office, or simply for expectations of future political rewards within the governing coalition.

3.1.1.9   Independent Agencies

One of the hallmarks of the political liberalization of the 1990s and 2000s, was the flourishing of independent agencies – protected at a constitutional level – that in many ways represented the spirit of the transition to democracy, based upon structural policies of deconcentration of political power and maximizing technical specialization of some sensitive areas subject to increasing public scrutiny and transparency. All of this was very much in tune with Bruce

---

51   Mexico Constitution, Article 21, at https://www.diputados.gob.mx/LeyesBiblio/pdf/CPEUM.pdf (accessed 26 December 2022).

52   Controversia Constitucional 90/2020 [Constitutional Controversy], 23 June 2020, filed by the Chamber of Deputies.

Ackerman's influential ideas of a new model of separation of powers,[53] when the landmark institution that resulted from those transformative years was an independent electoral authority – the Electoral Branch – in charge of organizing and validating elections in Mexico. Alongside, there were other equally relevant agencies overseeing issues such as central banking, antitrust, human rights protection, telecommunications, transparency and access to public information, energy, evaluation of the quality of education, the census bureau, and since 2014, law enforcement.

Nonetheless, with the new government, most of these independent agencies have been under constant siege. The governing coalition has used the existing legal framework to gradually undermine the functioning of these agencies,[54] ultimately leading them to practical obsolescence or irrelevance. From the government's standpoint, these agencies are superfluous, hence unnecessary, and in fact, represent an interference in governance and unjustified public spending. Playing the card of austerity, the government has unleashed a systematic attempt to obliterate most of these agencies – more saliently, the National Electoral Institute – by passing a series of statutory amendments that in short aim at totally crippling the efficiency and independence of these institutions that have overseen critical areas of the social, economic, and political process in Mexico over the past twenty-five years.

3.1.2   Non-Governmental Actors

3.1.2.1   *The Private Sector*

In contrast with their former role, business elites are not enjoying the same degree of influence in the constitutive process. This is due to manifold reasons, but two are predominant: On the one hand, this government's distrust and animosity against anything that is not dependent on the overarching system of public spending and social programs. From the government's vantage point, private enterprise is seen as a distortion of good governance and of public affairs. In their view, at best, private business should run in the same direction as the government and moderate its earnings to favor a more balanced distribution of wealth. On the other hand, the President harbors a strong prejudice against the most important business associations such as the *Consejo Coordinador Empresarial* (CCE) and the *Consejo Mexicano de Negocios,* or COPARMEX, that represent a substantial portion of the private wealth in

---

53   Bruce Ackerman, *The New Separation of Powers,* 113 Harv. L. Rev. 647 (2000).

54   David Landau, *Abusive Constitutionalism,* 47 U. Calif. Davis L. Rev. 189, 191–215 (2013). According to Landau, abusive constitutionalism is "[the] use of mechanisms of constitutional change in order to make a state significantly less democratic than it was before."

Mexico. In his view, these associations have served as custodians and grantees of the so-called neoliberal period – that implemented the structural economic reforms that allowed Mexico to enter the global free trade and investment system – and were neglectful in bridging the historical gap between the haves and the have-nots.

With these two dominant biases, the government has focused on undermining Mexico's private sector by aggressive policies such as increasing taxes or implementing radical cuts to tax benefits, blocking the creation of new companies, denying economic relief to small and medium businesses during the pandemic, arbitrarily canceling important infrastructure projects such as the new international airport in Mexico City[55] or an international brewery plant in the northern state of Baja California.[56]

This has created a hostile environment for national and foreign private enterprise and investment, with an increasingly unclear perspective. From 2019 to 2021, 1.6 million businesses closed in Mexico, from a total of 4.9 million in 2018, before the pandemic.[57]

3.1.2.2   *The Media*
Independent media and major information networks are also passing through challenging times for free press and journalism. According to reports from *Reporters without Borders,* Mexico is one of the most dangerous countries in which to practice journalism.[58] Just in 2022, Mexico ranked first in the number of journalists killed, with eleven such fatalities.[59] The underlying problem is the government's continuous hostility against press, media, journalists, and commentators that inform the public about its inefficiency, failures, and abuses. Again, as with other relevant participants, the governing coalition questions the integrity of most journalists, press, and media since from its view, they do

---

55   Anthony Harrup, *Mexico to Cancel $13.3 Billion Mexico City Airport Project,* Wall Street J., 29 October 2018, at https://www.wsj.com/articles/mexicans-vote-to-cancel-13-3-billion -mexico-city-airport-project-1540789177 (accessed 26 December 2022).

56   Santiago Pérez, *Mexican City's Residents Reject Constellation Brewery in Referendum,* Wall Street J., 23 March 2020, at https://www.wsj.com/articles/mexican-citys-residents -reject-constellation-brewery-in-referendum-11584974431 (accessed 26 December 2022).

57   INEGI, Estudio sobre Demografía de los Negocios, 2021, at https://www.inegi. org.mx /contenidos/saladeprensa/ boletines/2021/EDN/EDN_2021.pdf (accessed 26 December 2022).

58   Reporters without Borders, *This is already the deadliest year ever for Mexico's media,* 16 December 2022, at https://rsf.org/en/already-deadliest-year-ever-mexico-s-media (accessed 26 December 2022).

59   *Id.*

not serve the people, but private and de facto interests that are against the government's "transformative" agenda.

3.1.2.3   Non-Governmental Organizations (stricto sensu)

As with private enterprise, NGOs are considered a problem by the governing coalition. Since the beginning of the administration, all social programs that had been subsidized by the government to channel welfare assistance and social benefits through the work of civil organizations (NGOs) were terminated. Due to this government's inherent distrust of anything that is not state-controlled, NGOs represent an area of independent association and spontaneous collaboration of individuals who operate beyond the direct control of the government, and therefore, are less likely to fit the subordinate role that this administration expects from the governed. As with other participants, it is very challenging nowadays to function as an NGO in Mexico, considering the continuous animosity of the governing coalition. In numerous times, the President himself has not only questioned the work of philanthropy and social assistance that NGOs do but has officially requested the U.S. Department of State to stop funding some of these organizations,[60] such as *Mexicanos contra la Corrupción y la Impunidad* (MCCI), an NGO that conducts and publishes investigations on the state of the rule of law and corruption in Mexico.[61] In the President's view, such funding constitutes an interference in Mexico's domestic affairs and violates the principle of non-interference. However, his request has not been granted.

3.1.2.4   Intellectuals

In tune with the growing global criticism against science, merit, evidence, and objectivity, the governing coalition and more saliently President López Obrador have unleashed a large-scale campaign against Mexico's scientific, academic, and intellectual community. They accuse them of perpetuating the enduring inequality in Mexico in as much as they were the ones that planted the seeds in the members of the governing elites – when they were students – in the period of political liberalization.

---

60   Associated Press, *Mexican President Pressures U.S. to Stop Aid for NGO,* 19 May 2021, at https://apnews.com/article/latin-america-kamala-harris-mexico-city-united-states -mexico-44e5b30424afcd5990e97ca072d75fe4.

61   *See* https://contralacorrupcion.mx/ (accessed 26 December 2022).

López Obrador labels the most prominent intellectuals in Mexico as corrupt and complicit in what he defines as "the abuses of the neo-liberal past."[62] He rejects merit and qualification, praising instead ideology, retribution, and blind support to his policies. Whoever thinks differently is accused of being corrupt and harassed in the President's daily press conferences.

But this hostility has gone far beyond the presidential rhetoric: Since the beginning of the administration, the governing coalition has conducted a systematic attack against the different agencies that oversee public policy on culture, education, science, and technology. A good illustration of this is the gradual dismantling of the National Council of Science and Technology (CONACYT) that, among other mandates, implements the National System of Researchers (SNI) based on an objective appraisal of scientific production of academics across the country. This agency has become increasingly ideologized and has undermined the merit-based system of acknowledging, promoting, and rewarding scientific work and its contributions. Another example is the dismemberment of one of the most prestigious institutions of public education in Mexico, the *Centro de Investigación y Docencia Económicas* (CIDE), due to its influence on public policy over the last twenty years and to its reluctance to become a single-thought institution.

An elemental motivation of all this is the President's belief that academic preparation and the resulting degrees create in fact a power elite detached from the needs of the people (mostly have-nots) and, instead of working in their favor, academics and intellectuals promote the endurance of privileges and inequality in Mexico, hence, their influence in the constitutive process should be eradicated.

3.1.2.5   *The Church and Religious Associations*

In ten years, the number of Catholics in Mexico has decreased from 85% to 78% of the population.[63] This is mainly due to an increase in the number of protestants or non-religious individuals: From 2010 to 2020, the number of non-Catholics grew from 10 to 16 million people,[64] and the non-religious doubled from 4.6 to 9 million people.[65] These figures have had an impact on the constitutive process: the Catholic Church is no longer as influential within

---

62   Christine Murray, *Mexican president's war on 'neoliberalism' moves on to campus,* Financial Times, 4 November 2021, at https://www.ft.com/content/2e8fdbce-9fa3-4d1c-b9b3
-f53dbf4dcb42 (accessed 26 December 2022).

63   INEGI, Censos y Conteos de Población y Vivienda 2020, Religión, at https://www.inegi
.org.mx/temas/religion/ (accessed 26 December 2022).

64   *Id.*

65   *Id.*

political elite circles as it was in the past. Moreover, most of the prominent members of the governing coalition are non-Catholics or agnostic. In addition to this, the Catholic Church has assumed a position of moderate criticism of the government's policy to fight the drug cartels and the increasing violence across the country, after the killings of two Jesuit priests by a drug kingpin in the northern state of Chihuahua.[66] Since these killings and many others of Catholic priests, the relations between the government and the Church have deteriorated.

3.1.2.6   *Foreign Governments and Investors*

Globalization and interdependence are realities that the new governing coalition finds difficult to appreciate. Starting from López Obrador's belief that the best foreign policy is domestic, Mexico has isolated itself from the most relevant international fora over the past four years. In addition, it has lost its credibility with foreign governments and investors due to a deep and outdated nationalistic approach when addressing foreign investment protection in strategic areas of Mexico's economy.[67] From the government's vantage point, foreign investment and international cooperation are used as political tools to preserve and maximize the privileges not only of foreign investors, but also of the Mexican oligarchy that they traditionally partner with. In clear retribution for this, the government has focused its efforts on canceling major infrastructure projects – as in the cases of the new airport in Mexico City or a brewery plant in Mexicali – with the corresponding payment of substantial compensation to foreign investors to settle their legitimate claims.[68] It has also reversed licenses for electricity and energy generation and distribution to major foreign companies such as Iberdrola, and passed legislation that favors state-owned oil and electricity companies – *Petróleos Mexicanos* (PEMEX) and the *Comisión Federal de Electricidad* (CFE), respectively – to the detriment of contracts with foreign investors to participate on equal conditions in the market. This

---

66   Associated Press in Mexico City, *Two Jesuit Priests and Man Seeking Sanctuary Killed in Mexican Church,* The Guardian, 21 June 2022, at https://www.theguardian.com /world/2022/jun/21/two-jesuits-priests-killed-mexico-church (accessed 26 December 2022).

67   Mary Anastasia O'Grady, *Mexico Criminalizes Investment,* Wall Street J., 1 May 2020, at https:// www.wsj.com/articles/mexico-criminalizes-investment-energy-market-opening -amlo-lopez-obrador-biden-morena-supreme-court-11651432097 (accessed 26 December 2022).

68   Mary Anastasia O'Grady, *Mexico's Democracy Test,* Wall Street J., 25 November 2018, at https://www.wsj.com/articles/mexicos-democracy-test-1543176225 (accessed 26 December 2022).

policy has put Mexico in default of numerous Bilateral Investment Treaties (BITs) and free trade agreements – chiefly the USMCA. Therefore, these issues have created increasing tensions with the U.S. government through its Trade Representative, triggering dispute settlement talks within the framework of the USMCA.[69]

In addition to this hostile political environment against foreign investors, the growing and uncontrolled violence across the country has produced an equally rising concern about investing in Mexico due to the increasing influence of the drug cartels in local and state governments.

As a result of all of this, foreign investment sank to a historic low of less than 15 billion dollars in 2021 compared to 24 billion dollars in 2014,[70] and Mexico is no longer in the top twenty-five more attractive countries for foreign investment.[71]

3.1.2.7   *Organized Crime*

Since 2019, drug cartels and criminal organizations are running amok across Mexico. In contrast to its predecessors, the López Obrador administration has chosen appeasement – to put it mildly – as the chief policy to deal with the increase of the expectations of violence produced by the drug cartels. According to General Glen Van Herck, head of the U.S. Northern Command (NORAD), "[organized] crime controls between 30 and 35% of the territory in Mexico, and that is one of the reasons for the increase in the number of migrants arriving each day at the southern border of the United States."[72] This aggressive and uncontested expansion has given organized crime de facto control over the array of micro-constitutive processes in at least one-third of the country, and with particular influence in local, state, and national elections. In the mid-term national election of 2021, organized crime and drug cartels killed

---

69   Kanishka Singh, *Mexico, U.S. Trade Officials Discuss Energy, Corn Exports, Environment,* Reuters, 2 December 2022, at https://www.reuters.com/world/americas/mexico-us-trade-officials-discuss-energy-corn-exports-environment-2022-12-02/ (accessed 26 December 2022).

70   *Cf.*https://tradingeconomics.com/mexico/foreign-direct-investment(accessed26December 2022).

71   *Cf.* https://www.kearney.com/foreign-direct-investment-confidence-index (accessed 26 December 2022).

72   José López Zamorano, *México 'ingobernable': narco controla hasta 35% del país, dice EU,* El Financiero Bloomberg, 18 March 2021, at https://www.elfinanciero. com.mx/nacional /controla-el-narco-hasta-35-del-territorio-en-mexico-alerta-eu/ (accessed 26 December 2022).

89 candidates during the campaign.[73] No doubt such growth has required some collaboration from public officials bribed by the drug cartels at all levels of local, state, and federal government. The impression is that the fight against drug violence has already been lost by this administration.[74]

The so-called political tsunami of 2018,[75] that brought López Obrador and his social movement to power, has entailed not only a radical change of Mexico's political landscape and power dynamics, but has also fundamentally transformed the constitutive process that prevailed over the past three decades. Let us explore the implications of such transformations.

3.2   *Perspectives*
3.2.1   Identifications
Two major polarizations divided Mexico in the past two centuries and resulted in terrible civil wars: First, the Reform War in the mid-19th century between liberals and conservatives; and the second, the Revolution in 1910, between the supporters of President Porfirio Díaz (*porfiristas*) and those of the leader of the revolutionary movement (*revolutionaries*), Francisco I. Madero - a northern businessman and writer.

These two events defined the course of Mexican history and its constitutional and political arrangements. López Obrador has devoted his administration and presidential rhetoric to replicating these historic scenarios by constantly fueling division and polarization in Mexican society, that in his particular mindset is simply divided in two camps: Those that support his project – that he describes as the Fourth Transformation, as a continuation of the legacy of the Independence, the Reform, and the Revolution – and represent the liberal wing, and those that are against it, whom López Obrador refers to as the conservative faction.

This simplistic characterization of political opposition distorts a much more complex political reality: what the President describes as conservative factionalism is rooted in fact in a growing concern over the constant arbitrariness and legal marginality that this administration has normalized. In his view of

---

73   Mary Beth Sheridan, *Mexico's deadly elections: Crime groups target candidates in a fight for turf,* The Washington Post, 2 June 2021, at https://www.washingtonpost.com/world/interactive /2021/mexico-midterm-election-candidates-killed/ (accessed 26 December 2022).

74   The Editors, *Mexico is Losing the Fight Against Drug Violence,* Wash. Post, 27 September 2022, at https://www.washingtonpost.com/business/mexico-is-losing-the-fight-against-drug -violence/2022/09/27/68dff846-3e64-11ed-8c6e-9386bd7cd826_ story.html (accessed 26 December 2022).

75   Jorge Buendía & Javier Márquez, *2018: ¿Por qué el tsunami?*, Nexos, num. 499, 36–42 (July 2019).

reality, López Obrador has succeeded in dividing the country into two sides as no other President has done after the Revolution. Hence, inclusive identifications are at the lowest possible level.

3.2.2 Expectations

In most national and international rankings, Mexico has lost ground compared to past administrations. Considering the growing violence, the low performance of the economy, and the overarching polarization, Mexicans are less optimistic than in previous years. This can be illustrated by the growing number of migrants to the United States,[76] or the historic figures of capital flight to safer jurisdictions.[77]

Furthermore, this administration has launched a campaign against qualified and competitive education based on merit, contending – just as in the case of the private sector, or the intellectuals – that this model contributed to the enduring social and economic inequalities that persist in Mexico. Hence, the former expectation that a good education and individual effort would serve as a basis for progress is no longer shared or promoted. In these deteriorating dynamics, the middle class is the most injured since it is not part, on the one hand, of the favored groups (mainly low-income households, that represent more than half of the population) by the extensive network of social programs of this regime, or, on the other hand, of the wealthiest families in the country that have already allocated their main assets abroad or ultimately, have fled Mexico. No, the middle class, coping with the hostility and regressive policies of this administration, waits for an unlikely change in power in the presidential election of 2024.

3.2.3 Demands

To understand the prevailing contrast of demand that defines the constitutive process in Mexico nowadays, it is necessary to describe the government's interpretation of its constitutional mandate: From the landslide victory in 2018, López Obrador has focused his core policies on developing and implementing a huge network of social programs based upon unprecedented public spending to benefit low-income households – that represent the vast

---

76   *Cf.* https://www.pewresearch.org/fact-tank/2021/07/09/before-covid-19-more-mexicans-came-to-the-u-s-than-left-for-mexico-for-the-first-time-in-years/ (accessed 26 December 2022).

77   Michael O'Boyle, *Rich Mexicans are fleeing to Miami and funneling money overseas,* Financial Post, Bloomberg News, 17 July 2020, at https://financialpost.com/news/rich-mexicans-are-fleeing-to-miami-and-funneling-money-overseas (accessed 26 December 2022).

majority of the country – aiming at consolidating a strong electoral base. He has also focused on enacting regressive legislation designed to dismantle the legacy of the period of political liberalization, even as, in most cases, such changes were in clear contravention of the Constitution. To justify it, the government claims that it is endowed with a majoritarian popular support from the election of 2018, and that such democratic legitimacy trumps any constitutional or legal limits. This administration and its policies can be characterized as an *anything-goes* attitude towards the Constitution, the rule of law, the principle of separation of powers, the protection of minority rights; in sum, as a complete disdain for the pillars that sustain any liberal democracy.

Consequently, present demands are conditioned by ongoing polarization: Those that support the President – mainly low-income, non-educated people – demand more benefits from the government through its vast framework of social spending programs implemented since 2019 in the form of non-merit-based scholarships, cash payments and rewards, and subsidies. On the opposite side are those that do not benefit from these programs and witness the gradual destruction of the legacy of the transition to democracy in the 1990s – chiefly, the professional middle class – and demand a law-abiding government that respects the rules of democracy, human rights, separation of powers, free speech, due process, equality before the law, in sum, that respects and protects the Constitution.

3.3   *Situations*

Centralized decision-making continues as the dominant trend in Mexico's constitutive process. However, this administration has exacerbated it by concentrating more power in the Presidency. The undermining of independent agencies and of constituted powers such as Congress and the Supreme Court, has resulted in a de facto allocation of more power in the Executive Branch, in clear retrogression from the achievements of the past three decades. Furthermore, the Cabinet does not enjoy minimal independence to articulate its policies. On the contrary, everything is decided by the President himself, as it used to be during the PRI single-party rule. The result is the reversal of the gradual transfer of power for decision-making at all levels of the national government – that was replicated at state and local levels – that dominated between the 1990s and 2018.

Additionally, the informal power that some economic elites enjoyed in the past to shape decision has also been weakened due to the overwhelming expansion of the government's interference in all areas of the social process.

3.4   *Bases of Power*

Legality has been replaced by raw political power as the chief basis of power in Mexico. The instrumentalization of majoritarian popular support as the key element of political legitimation – and ultimately, of decision-making – has erased almost three decades of a continuous struggle to consolidate a culture of legality in the authoritative decision-making process. As posited before, now anything goes in Mexico as long as it serves the interests of the governing coalition. The boundaries between legality and arbitrariness have been deliberately blurred by playing the card that whatever the President does as the legitimate speaker of the people, should be considered legal. If we add to this that violence and intimidation still play a critical role in the constitutive process and reinforce expectations of violence, the quest towards a minimum public order of human dignity seems today even more remote.

3.5   *Outcomes*

The description of preferred outcomes is based upon the eight values of the New Haven School:

3.5.1   Power

Contrary to presidential rhetoric, this new government has not entailed the transfer or creation of new enfranchised participants in the constitutive process. Their victory in 2018 only entailed an elite replacement. The system, its institutions, and procedures, remains practically unchanged. In multiple deceptive attempts, the government has implemented illegal referendums on matters regarding infrastructure and involving foreign investment,[78] to apparently "leave the final word to the people." However, these referendums were conducted in violation of the Constitution and the law, serving just as an effective political marketing strategy to justify arbitrary governmental decisions and to antagonize the business sector and foreign investors.

3.5.2   Wealth

By the end of 2022, there were more people in poverty than in 2018. According to the last census, the number of people in poverty grew from almost 52 million

---

78   James M. Roberts & Giovanna Milano, *Mexico Needs Rule of Law, Not Self-Serving Referendums from Lopez Obrador,* The Heritage Foundation, 10 August 2021, at https://www .heritage.org/americas/commentary/mexico-needs-rule-law-not-self-serving-referendums-lopez-obrador (accessed 26 December 2022).

in 2018 to almost 56 million in 2020.[79] Some recent estimates predict that, for 2022,[80] the number of people in poverty will reach 58 million: this is an average increase of 1.5 million poor people per year since 2018. If this trend continues, this government and its policies will have generated 8 more million people in poverty, notwithstanding the unprecedented aggressive social spending with electoral purposes of the last four years.

3.5.3   Enlightenment

The number of students in basic and middle education has consistently decreased in the last four years.[81] These are the figures: as to basic education, only 75% of students attend school, out of the total population between 3 and 11 years old. In 2018, it was 86%.[82] As to education – students between 12 and 14 years old – as of 2018, only 84% attend school.[83] Higher education is an option for only 22% of the population between 18 and 24 years old.[84] However, the greatest problem is not attendance, but the quality of education. Based upon its distrust of independent agencies, this administration dismantled the National Institute for the Evaluation of Education (INEE), which oversaw and appraised the quality of education in Mexico; thus there is no longer an independent and professional body to assess such an important issue. Furthermore, in 2019, the governing coalition abrogated the momentous constitutional amendment on education passed in 2014 during the Peña administration. It introduced mandatory constant evaluation for teachers.[85] Considering that this amendment promoted a system of privileges and differentiation based on merit, –, López Obrador, with electoral goals in mind, introduced a new constitutional amendment that basically brought things back to the status-quoante, the

---

79   INEGI, *Población en situación de pobreza*, 2018–2020, at https://www.inegi.org.mx/app/tabulados/interactivos/?pxq=Hogares_Hogares_15_9954f9c6-9512-40c5-9cbf-1b2ce96283e4&idrt=54&opc=t (accessed 26 December 2022).

80   Diego Ore, *Ranks of Mexican poor swell to reach nearly half the population,* Reuters, 5 August 2021, at https://www.reuters.com/world/americas/ranks-mexican-poor-swell-reach-nearly-half-population-2021-08-05/ (accessed 26 December 2022).

81   INEGI, *Características educativas de la población*, 2020–2021, at https://www.inegi.org.mx/temas/educacion/ (accessed 26 December 2022).

82   *Id.*

83   *Id.*

84   *Id.*

85   Oxford Business Group, *Major reforms in Mexico to improve standards in educational system,* at https://oxfordbusinessgroup.com/overview/back-school-major-reforms-are-set-improve-standards-across-system (accessed 26 December 2022).

2014 reform,[86] treating the policy on education more as a political and electoral issue, rather than as a long-term State policy that requires a professional, non-partisan approach.

3.5.4   Well-Being

This administration has crippled the National Health System in Mexico. It abrogated universal health care – known as *Seguro Popular* – and centralized the purchase of medications to supply the vast network of public hospitals in the country. This has significantly impaired universal access to health services and has caused a disturbing shortage in the supply of medications nationwide. If we add to this scenario the tragic way in which the government tackled the COVID-19 pandemic, this will explain why the life expectancy in Mexico has dramatically decreased from 74 years in 2019 to 70 in 2020.[87]

3.5.5   Skills

Due to the present policies against maximizing the quality of education , the deficit of skills needed to make Mexico more competitive is a trademark of this administration. The President himself criticizes the culture of competitiveness, specialization, and technological improvement as causes of inequality, praising instead, the most rudimentary – almost primitive – modes of production such as the so-called *trapiche,* a wooden mill to produce juice from raw sugar. This misappreciation of skills, combined with the pervasive public spending for his social programs, has generated a passive, unskilled, and unprepared generation with no means to be productive . This is well explained by Adriana García, head of Economic Analysis at the think-tank *México ¿Cómo vamos?,*

> [The] main problem is that the social spending strategy of this administration is designed to attract the population to the government in the short term, but it doesn't support the creation of skills that will help people in the medium and long term. It's direct short-term transfers. People are not acquiring knowledge or labor skills.[88]

---

86   Anthony Harrup, *Mexican President Seeks to Revoke Education System Overhaul,* The Wall Street Journal, 12 December 2018, at https://www.wsj.com/articles/mexican-president-seeks-to-revoke-education-system-overhaul-11544648739 (accessed 26 December 2022).

87   World Bank, Life expectancy at birth, total (years) – Mexico, 2020, at https://data.worldbank.org/indicator/SP.DYN.LE00.IN (accessed 26 December 2022).

88   Nathaniel Parish Flannery, *Why is Mexico's President López Obrador so Popular?,* Forbes, 16 November 2022, at https://www.forbes.com/sites/nathaniel parishflannery/2022/11/16

3.5.6 Affection

Notwithstanding its tradition as a very family-centered society, Mexican families have also been affected by the ongoing political and ideological polarization. It has become commonplace to see families divided due to present political preferences. Overall, Mexicans are less happy than in the previous decade: according to survey data of 2022, 65% of Mexicans considered themselves happy, in contrast to 75% that felt that way in 2011.[89]

3.5.7 Respect

Sources of moral authority are becoming increasingly problematic under the present regime. Until recent years, respect resulted from personal and professional integrity, coherence, honesty, loyalty, cultivation, empathy, and merit. These attributes are no longer appreciated, since the dominant narrative – infused by the government's rhetoric or the actions from organized crime – is that power – mainly political – or that based upon violence and intimidation, produces respect. From this view, power is enough to be respected regardless of other personal qualities.

3.5.8 Rectitude

Corruption continues as one of the major structural concerns of Mexico's constitutive process, regardless of the presidential rhetoric insisting that corruption has been eradicated from the top levels of the government. The lack of transparency and scrutiny over most parts of the government's policies and more specifically on its unprecedented public spending, has generated a growing sentiment of impunity among the ruling elite for whom anything goes.

4 Conclusion: Appraisal and Strategies for Transformation toward a Public Order of Human Dignity in Mexico through Constitutional Change

A political earthquake shocked Mexican politics in the summer of 2018: a non-traditional political coalition led by Andrés Manuel López Obrador won the general election by a landslide claiming to usher in the so-called "Fourth

---

/mexicos-presidents-social-programs-are-effective-at-boosting-his-popularity/?sh=6b
f9512a3688 (accessed 26 December 2022).

89   IPSOS, *Encuesta sobre felicidad global*, 26 April 2022, at https://www.ipsos.com/es-mx
/felicidad-global-lo-que-hace-feliz-la-gente-en-la-era-del-covid-19-salud-familia-y-obje
tivos (accessed 26 December 2022).

Transformation" in Mexico, only preceded by the Independence (1810), the Reform (1857), and the Revolution (1910). This coalition and its leader set as a goal a 180-degree change of public life in Mexico in which the have-nots would finally claim their demands for influence and justice in a country increasingly unequal. Since then, a radical platform has been implemented to dismantle a great number of institutions that had resulted from the prior process of political liberalization that we have described in this chapter. A retributionist impetus has characterized the work of the government and has produced greater numbers of people in poverty, a dislocation of important institutions and procedures undermining the rule of law, a growing sense of foreign investors' distrust in Mexico, a perplexing alienation of Congress and the Judiciary to the dictates of the President, and a worrying irrelevance of the Constitution.

In sum, this recent political transformation anticipated a radical change in the features that have historically characterized Mexico's constitutive process. However, the mid-term election of 2021 signaled a reduction of the popular support of the governing coalition, depriving it – among other things – of its congressional majority to amend the constitution. This outcome watered down the ambitions of the administration and put a check on their apparently unlimited power.

This account shows the pernicious effects overt majoritarianism has had in the constitutive process and its disturbing implications for the quest for a public order of human dignity. But it would be misleading to assign the current situation solely to the regressive policies of the governing coalition. In retrospect, the ongoing deterioration of the institutions and procedures that resulted from the political liberalization process of the 1990s was abetted by a defective constitutional design that failed to insulate the constitutional order against the majoritarian populist siege.

I will offer in this section two modest proposals for the transformation of the constitutive process, aiming, in the short term, at preventing further constitutional regressions, and in the mid and long terms at maximizing a public order of human dignity in Mexico. Both proposals may require some adjustments in the present constitutional design and a substantial shift in the Supreme Court's operational code to scrutinize constitutional amendments.

But before entering into the details of these proposals, a caveat: their feasibility depends upon two conditions. First, it requires a new distribution of power in Congress, to enable the constitutional block to overcome the present control of the governing populist side over the legislative process. Second, it requires a majority of the Court interpreting and adjudicating on non-formalistic or conventional grounds, but rather with substantive and functional approaches.

4.1   *Incremental Constitutional Change (ICM)*

As of today, anything can be added, deleted, or changed in the Mexican Constitution, as long as the formal procedure of Article 135 of the Constitution is observed, requiring two-thirds of members of Congress and a simple majority of the state legislatures to pass a constitutional amendment. This mechanism has served to pass more than 750 amendments to the Constitution since 1921.

However, this flexibility has made the Mexican Constitution one of the most disharmonic and incoherent constitutions in the world and has trivialized the Constitution itself . The staggering number of amendments has not improved the lives of the governed.

Therefore, I contend that it is necessary to introduce what in diverse studies of comparative constitutionalism is described as the *constitutional escalator*,[90] i.e. a classification of constitutional prescriptions, principles, rights, values, and procedures that, depending on their relevance within the polity, deserve a differentiated degree of constitutional protection to prevent the abuse by incumbent majorities. For instance, in the hypothetical case that a majoritarian coalition may pretend to change the republican form of government, in addition to the existing procedure (Article 135), a mechanism of *incremental constitutional change* (ICM) or *constitutional escalator,* may require a previous analysis by the Supreme Court on the constitutionality of the proposed amendment, and – if approved by Congress and the state legislatures – to submit it via referendum to the considered judgement of the people, requiring a minimum of 65% of voters saying Yes to validate such a radical amendment.

This ICM or constitutional escalator, can be articulated in a federal statute regulating the procedure for constitutional amendment enshrined in Article 135 of the Constitution.

4.2   *The Need of a Basic Structure Doctrine (BSD) in Mexico*

Historically, the Supreme Court has adopted a self-restraint doctrine preventing it from scrutinizing the validity of constitutional amendments in Mexico. Its view is based upon a formalistic understanding of the Constitution, of the separation of powers principle, and the role of the Court in a democracy. Accordingly, he Court has failed to act in the context of abusive and threatening majoritarianism.[91]

---

90   Yaniv Roznai, Unconstitutional Constitutional Amendments. The Limits of Amendment Powers 164–167 (2017).

91   David Landau, *Abusive Constitutionalism,* 47 U. Calif. Davis L. Rev. 189, 191–215 (2013).

In such daunting scenarios, comparative constitutionalism proves enlightening: to prevent the constitutional assault of political majorities, either constituent assemblies or constitutional courts have articulated the so-called *Basic Structure Doctrine* (BSD), that Yaniv Roznai explains,

> [According] to this doctrine, the amendment power is not unlimited; rather, it does not include the power to abrogate or change the identity of the constitution or its basic features.[92]

The BSD was introduced by the Supreme Court of India in the *Kesavananda Bharati Sripadagalvaru v. Kerala* case,[93] and Richard Albert describes the elements that comprise the basic structure of the Indian Constitution and that offer a good illustration of the features that may constitute the BSD of any modern liberal democracy:

> [The] concept of the basic structure was said to include the supremacy of the constitution, the republican and democratic forms of government, the secular character of the state, the separation of powers, and federalism.[94]

The present challenging scenario requires an activist Court willing to set the boundaries of a basic structure doctrine in Mexico, defining the most fundamental values, principles, and institutions that may not be transgressed under any circumstances. The most legitimate body to conduct such a definition is a constituent assembly, but the present political fragmentation in Mexico makes it highly unlikely in the foreseeable future.

This BSD will allow the Supreme Court to exercise its constitutional mandate with enough legitimation to check the potential abuses of incumbent political majorities assaulting the constitutional order and may also serve as a deterrent for future governing majorities.

It remains to be seen if the next general election in 2024 will bring Mexico back on the track of the liberal democracy that it aspired to be on before 2018, or, to the contrary, will lock it in a retrogressive spiral away from a public order

---

92   Yaniv Roznai, Unconstitutional Constitutional Amendments. The Limits of Amendment Powers 42–43 (2017).

93   *Kesavananda Bharati Sripadagalvaru v. Kerala,* 1973 SCC (4) 225.

94   Richard Albert, Constitutional Amendments. Making, Breaking, and Changing Constitutions 151–152 (2019).

of human dignity. In the meantime, these two strategies for transformation may serve to pave the way for a more effective constitutive process that would be more resistant to the abuses of majoritarianism and would, at the same time, promote actual human flourishing in Mexico's quest for a public order of human dignity.

PART 10

Law and the Environment

∵

Upholding the Philosophy of International Environmental Law through the Domestication of Environmental Conventions: An Imperative for Nigeria

Jude O. Ezeanokwasa*

Abstract

Nigeria has actively participated in the development of international environmental law (IEL) right from the Stockholm Conference (1972) on human environment and has ratified many environmental conventions. Accordingly, it has created at the municipal level legal and institutional regimes for environmental protection at both the federal and state levels. Despite these, a significant gap is created between Nigeria's environmental credentials at the international and municipal levels by the non-domestication of many environmental conventions. This chapter examines the domestication law in Nigeria and points out the effects of non-domestication of environmental conventions in the country and the barriers inhibiting the domestication of environmental conventions.

1 Introduction

International environmental law (IEL) grew out of the concerns in the global community for the protection of the human environment from harmful effects of human activities. It grew out of the understanding that the human environment is one and cannot be parceled out amongst the States despite their political independence and sovereignty. For this reason, environmental issues like climate change, ozone depletion, acid rain, etc. are not threats to particular

* Ph.D. (Law), J.C.D. (Canon Law), LL.M, J.C.L., B.L., B.Th., B.Phil. Senior Lecturer, Department of International Law & Jurisprudence, Nnamdi Azikiwe University, Awka, Nigeria; Formerly Acting Dean, Faculty of Law, Nnamdi Azikiwe University; Adjunct Professor of Law, St. Thomas University, Miami Gardens, Florida; Judge, Metropolitan Tribunal of Archdiocese of Miami, Florida, USA and Diocesan Tribunal of Catholic Diocese of Awka. He is a priest of the Catholic Diocese of Awka, Nigeria. Email: jo.ezeanokwasa@unizik.edu.ng.

countries but rather threats to the entire global community, and thus global efforts are needed to address them. Nigeria has appreciated these truths and thus has keenly partnered with other members of the international community in the development of IEL from the Stockholm Conference in 1972 on the human environment through the Rio Conference in 1992 on Environment and Development and the Johannesburg World Summit on Sustainable Development in 2002. It has followed these active international initiatives with the ratification of many environmental conventions, indicating the intention to give legal effect to these instruments in its municipal sphere. Nigeria has brought home the gospel of the global environmental movement with the creation of legal and institutional regimes at the national, state and even local government levels to further the goals of this movement.

While all this is laudable and commendable, there is the undeniable fact of a dissonance between Nigeria's environmental credentials at the international level and its environmental initiatives at the municipal level. Many environmental conventions ratified by the country are not domesticated, despite the constitutional provisions for their domestication and the international law principle of *pacta sunt servanda*. Record shows that between 1972 and 2020 Nigeria ratified about 77 environmental treaties,[1] and, as of 2021, only about 6 have been domesticated by the National Assembly.[2] This poor domestication record is general as it pertains also to non-environmental treaties. As of 2013, Nigeria was a party to about 400 treaties, but only 10 were duly domesticated by the National Assembly.[3] Headlines such as the following corroborate this fact: "Nigeria yet

---

1   *International Environmental Agreements (IEA) Database Project: MEAs to which Nigeria has taken membership actions, available at* https://iea.uoregon.edu/country-members/Nigeria.

2   The domesticated treaties are: International Convention for the Safety of Life at Sea (Ratification and Enforcement) Act 2004, Treaty to Establish Rotterdam Convention on the Prior Informed Consent Procedure for Certain Hazardous Chemicals and Pesticides in International Trade (Ratification and Enforcement) Act 2005, and United Nations Convention on Carriage of Goods by Sea (Ratification and Enforcement) Act 2005. Others are: International Convention on Civil Liability for Oil Pollution Damage (Ratification and Enforcement) Act 2006, International Convention on the Establishment of an International Fund for Compensation for oil Pollution Damage 1971 as Amended (Ratification and Enforcement) Act, 2006, and International Convention for the Prevention of Pollution from Ships, 1973 and 1978 Protocol (Ratification and Enforcement) Act 2007. *Treaties Ratified by National Assembly of Nigeria, available at* https://laws.lawnigeria.com/2021/03/05/treaties-ratified-by-national-assembly-of-nigeria/.

3   C. E. Okeke & M. I. Anushiem, *Implementation of Treaties in Nigeria: Issues, Challenges and the Way Forward*, 9(2) Nnamdi Azikiwe U. J. Int'l L. & Jurisprudence 225–226 (2018). Ibrahim Yusuf, *Nigeria Loses Billions due to Non-compliance with Bilateral Agreements, available at* https://thenationonlineng.net/nigeria-loses-billions-due-non-compliance-bilateral-agreements/.

to domesticate over 95% of treaties, protocols—Reps",[4] "FG yet to domesticate 400 treaties, agreements, protocols – Rep",[5] and "Could the Non-domestication of Nigerian Treaties Affect International Energy Investment Attraction into the Country?"[6] The many environmental conventions not domesticated by Nigeria create a disharmony between Nigeria's international participation and roles in environmental protection, on the one hand, and its local efforts towards the same goal, on the other. A better and more effective synergy and coherence with the international environmental law community will be forged when Nigeria domesticates all the environmental conventions it ratifies. This will also create sincerity in its relations within the international community. In urging Nigeria to do the needful in this regard this chapter examines the domestication law in Nigeria and points out the effects of the non-domestication of environmental conventions in the country as well as the barriers inhibiting the domestication of environmental treaties in the country. The chapter concludes with a call on Nigeria to domesticate ratified environmental conventions as a way of being coherent with its active participation in the development of IEL and living up to the demands of its leadership role in the African region. The chapter is divided into eight parts. Part I is the introduction, and Part II clarifies the key concepts regarding the topic, while Part III retraces the historical development of modern international environmental law. Part IV examines the place of the principle of *pacta sunt servanda* in the implementation of environmental conventions in Nigeria. Part V examines the effects of the non-domestication of environmental conventions in Nigeria, while Part VI reviews the legal regime for the implementation of environmental conventions in the country. Part VII looks at the barriers to the domestication of environmental conventions in Nigeria, and Part VIII includes the conclusion and recommendations.

I deeply thank Professor Roza Pati for involving me in this project for honoring our friend, a great and humane scholar, Professor Siegfried Wiessner, who has spent years in the academia promoting human dignity through legal publications and teaching.

---

4 Tordue Salem, *Nigeria Yet to Domesticate Over 95% of Treaties, Protocols—Reps*, *available at* https://www.vanguardngr.com/2021/03/nigeria-yet-to-domesticate-over-95-of-treaties-proto cols-reps/.

5 Ade Adesomoju, FG *Yet to Domesticate 400 Treaties, Agreements, Protocols – Rep*, Punch Newspaper, Online, Jan. 8, 2020, *available at* https://punchng.com/fg-yet-to-domesticate -400-treaties-agreements-protocols-rep/.

6 Chinenyendo Nriezedi-Anejionu, *Could the Non-Domestication of Nigerian Treaties Affect International Energy Investment Attraction into the Country?*, 28 Afric. J. Int'l & Comp. L. 122–144 (2020). *Available* at https://www.euppublishing.com/doi/full/10.3366/ajicl.2020 .0305#abstract.

2   Clarification of Key Concepts

2.1   *International Environmental Law*

International Environmental Law (IEL) is that branch of public international law that concerns itself with the legal protection of the world environment either through bilateral, multilateral, sub-regional, regional or worldwide environmental agreements.[7] Its sources broadly coincide with the sources of the public international law, namely, international conventions, international customary law, general principles of law, as well as evidence of international law as found in judicial decisions and juristic writings.[8] Judicial decisions and juristic writings that would act as evidence of international environmental law must be those that relate to the protection of the environmental media. The purpose of IEL is to secure through agreements the carrying capacity of the world environment without undermining the developmental and economic activities of States.[9] From this perspective, IEL strives to ensure sustainable development through sustainable exploitation of the world's resources while protecting the broad environmental media of air, land and water from harmful degradation and pollution.[10] It emerged from the understanding that the world environment and human existence are rendered vulnerable by unregulated or ill-regulated developmental activities of human beings.[11] It also demonstrates the understanding that despite the political independence and sovereignty of

---

7   *International Environmental Law, available at* https://www.encyclopedia.com/environ
ment/energy-government-and-defense-magazines/international-environmental-law.

8   *See* Art. 38(1), Statute of the International Court of Justice, 3 Bevans 1179, 59 Stat. 1055, T.S.
No. 993. Judicial decisions and judicial decisions and the teachings of the most highly
qualified publicists of the various nations, according to article 38(1)(d), qualify as "subsidiary means for the determination of rules of law," i.e., as evidence.

9   *See Why Do We Need International Environmental Law, available at* https://www
.briangwilliams.us/sustainable-development/why-do-we-need-international
-environmental-law.html .

10   *See* Arosh Martin, *The Role of International Environmental Law in Achieving Sustainable
Development Goals, available at* https://www.researchgate.net/publication/357639784
_The_role_of_international_environmental_law_in_achieving_Sustainable_development
_Goals; *International Environmental Law, available at* https://www.encyclopedia.com
/environment/energy-government-and-defense-magazines/international
-environmental-law.

11   *UN Secretary-General's message on World Environment Day | 5 June 2022, available at*
https://iraq.un.org/en/184790-un-secretary-generals-message-world-environment-day
-5-june-2022. Florencia Ortuzar Greene, *International Environmental Law: History and
Milestones, available at* https://aida-americas.org/en/blog/international-environmental
-law-history-and-milestones. Philippe Sands & Jacqueline Peel, Principles of International Environmental Law 3–5 (2012).

countries, the world environment is not parceled out, but is a continuum, such that what happens in one area of it has effects in other areas. Being an aspect of public international law, it regulates the activities of the members of the international communities, typically States.

2.2   *Domestication*

Domestication is another key concept in this chapter. It is a term used in the context of the relationship between international law and domestic law. It is a concept connected essentially with the dualist theory of the relationship between international law and municipal law. The dualist theory, with Heinrich Triepel as the leading proponent, treats international law and domestic legislation as belonging to two separate and independent systems of law such that the validity and enforceability of an international norm in a domestic system is dependent on the rule of domestic law authorizing the application of that international norm.[12] In other words, a rule of international law has no binding force in a country until it is formally enacted as law inside that country. This is the phenomenon of domestication. The rule of international law is said to be domesticated when it has been enacted into law inside a country. The international and domestic systems are separate and independent because while international law is the manifestation of the common will of sovereign states, domestic laws represent the common will of the citizens of each given State.[13] The two separate and independent legal systems have two separate and independent legislative organs. It follows therefore that laws made in one system are foreign to the other system and thus cannot bind that other system without that other system formally incorporating the laws into its own system. Usually, the ratification of treaties and conventions is done by the heads of government, that is, the executive arm of government, which, under the doctrine of separation of powers, does not ordinarily have the competence to make laws for the State. The ordinary power to make laws for the State under the doctrine of separation of powers belongs to the legislature. Domestication therefore avails the legislature the opportunity to exercise its legislative competence over agreements signed by the executive in the international community. In effect, norms of international law are foreign and unenforceable in a domestic

---

12   Madelaine Chiam, *Monism and Dualism in International Law, available at* https://www .oxfordbibliographies.com/view/document/obo-9780199796953/obo-9780199796953 -0168.xml.

13   Vishwas Chitwar, *International and Municipal Law: An Ultimate Guide, available at https://* *blog.ipleaders.in/international-and-municipal-law-an-ultimate-guide/;* Carolyn A. Dubay, *General Principles of International Law: Monism and Dualism, available at* http://www .judicialmonitor.org/ archive_winter2014/generalprinciples.html.

legal system until those norms are incorporated into the extant law of a country in the manner provided by the constitution of the country. Thus, Eke sees domestication as "the process of incorporating the provisions of a treaty or convention into the extant law of a country in order to give it force of law in that country."[14] Domestication is, therefore, the gateway for international conventions to have legal binding force inside a country. Nigeria is a dualist country pursuant to the constitutional provision demanding that any treaty entered into by the country must be passed by the National Assembly before it can have the force of law in the country.[15] Other dualist countries include, *inter alia*, Australia[16] and Ghana.[17]

The opposite of the dualist theory is the monist theory. Its foremost proponent was Hans Kelsen who held that international law and domestic law form part of a single universal legal system and inside this system there is a hierarchical relationship between international law and domestic law.[18] International law is superior to domestic law and so prevails in any conflict between the two laws.[19] For countries that subscribe to the monist jurisprudence, once an international treaty or convention is made, it automatically has binding effect in their domestic law and would be enforced by the domestic courts. These countries include France,[20] Switzerland,[21] the Netherlands[22] and Kenya.[23] In France, for instance, ratified treaties upon publication prevail over its domestic laws.[24]

---

14   Sandra Eke, *Non-Domestication of Treaties in Nigeria as a Breach of International Obligations*, *available at* https://www.mondaq.com/nigeria/international-trade-investment/1013006 /non-domestication-of-treaties-in-nigeria-as-a-breach-of-international-obligations -sandra-eke#:~:text=Nigeria%20is%20a%20signatory%20to,been%20domesticated%20 in%20our%20laws.&text=In%20Nigeria%2C%20ratifying%20or%20signing,before%20- it%20can%20be%20enforceable.

15   Section 12, 1999 Constitution of the Federal Republic of Nigeria (hereinafter CFRN).

16   Cheryl Saunders, Adrienne Stone & Joshua Quinn-Watson, *A Constitution Shaped by Distance*, *available at https://pursuit.unimelb.edu.au/articles/a-constitution-shaped-by -distance*.

17   Justice Srem-Sai, *Committing Ghana to International Agreements: A Review of the Roles of Parliament and the President*, 29(2) Afric. J. Int'l & Comp. L. 204–22 (2021).

18   Chiam, *Monism and Dualism, supra* note 12. Torben Spaak, *Kelsen on Monism and Dualism*, *available at* https://papers.ssrn.com/sol3/papers.cfm?abstract_id=2231530.

19   Chiam, *Monism and Dualism, supra* note 12.

20   David Sloss, *Domestic Application of Treaties* (2011), *available at* https://papers.ssrn.com /sol3/papers.cfm?abstract_id=1826102 .

21   *Id.*

22   *Id.*

23   Art. 2(5) and (6), Kenya Constitution 2010.

24   *See* Art. 55, 1958 French Constitution.

However, the monist/dualist dichotomy is not absolute. Some countries like the USA and South Africa operate mixed monist-dualist systems. In the USA, international law applies directly in courts in some instances, but not others.[25] In South Africa, customary international law applies directly in courts,[26] but international treaties and other such agreements have to be domesticated before they have binding force.[27] Nigeria also operates a mixed monist-dualist system because labor-related treaties can be enforced by the National Industrial Court without needing to be domesticated.[28] By this token, a labor-related convention that also concerns the environment can be enforced in the country once it is ratified. But the attention of this chapter is on environmental conventions that are unconnected with labor which cannot be judicially enforced in the country without domestication.

In Nigeria, pursuant to the ruling of the Supreme Court *per* Ogundare, JSC [Justice of the Supreme Court], in *Abacha v. Fawehinmi*,[29] a domesticated treaty enjoys a status higher than that of any other statute besides the Constitution. The ruling was given on the question of the relationship between the domesticated African Charter on Human and Peoples' Rights and other domestic statutes. According to Ogundare, JSC, "the Charter possesses a greater vigor and strength than any other domestic statute."[30] This judgment has been serially criticized for giving a domesticated treaty a status higher than other statutes. The position of the critics is that the domesticated treaty is enforceable because it has been made a domestic statute and by that fact it is ordinarily at par with every other domestic statute and not higher.[31] Be that as it may, the ruling remains the law until set aside by the same apex court or by legislation.

2.3 *Environmental Conventions*

The next key concept in this chapter is the notion of an "environmental convention." Convention is a noun used in different contexts like legislative law[32]

---

25 Stephen P. Mulligan, *International Law and Agreements: Their Effect upon U.S. Law*, Cong. Research Service, Sept. 19, 2018, *available at* https://sgp.fas.org/crs/misc/RL32528. pdf. Only treaties qualifying as "self-executing" apply directly in U.S. courts. *Cf.* Foster v. Neilson, 27 U.S. (2 Pet.) 253, 254 (1829) and Medellín v. Texas, 552 U.S. 491 (2008).

26 Art. 232, South African Constitution 1996.

27 Art. 231(2), South African Constitution 1996.

28 S. 254(C)(2), 1999 CFRN (As Amended).

29 (2000) FWLR (Pt.4) 553 at 586.

30 *Id.*

31 *See* Okeke, *Implementation of Treaties in Nigeria, supra* note 3.

32 In this context, a convention assembly refers to a deliberative assembly consisting of delegates elected for the purpose of policy-making and purposes other than normal

and constitutional law,[33] but in this chapter it generally "refers to all kinds of agreements, compacts or treaties entered into by the nations, such as Geneva Convention."[34] Conventions are treaties or agreements between countries.[35] They may be of a general or specific nature and may be entered into between two or multiple states.[36] Conventions between two states are called bilateral treaties, whereas conventions between a small number of states (but more than two) are called plurilateral treaties; and conventions between a large number of states are called multilateral treaties.[37]

An environmental convention is an international treaty or agreement that deals with the protection of the global environment from pollution, degradation and excessive exploitation, and it is geared towards ensuring sustainable development. The fact that an environmental convention deals with the protection of the global environment does not mean that the subject matter of the convention must immediately and directly affect the world environment. The particular subject of a convention could immediately affect particular areas of the world. For instance, a convention on desertification does not mean that all parts of the world are immediately impacted by desertification. The world environment is one, and a degradation of it in one part is a degradation of the one human environment. The International Environmental Agreements (IEA) Database Project presents an environmental convention as "an intergovernmental document intended as legally binding with a primary stated purpose of preventing or managing human impacts on natural resources."[38] Particular environmental issues that have been taken up by environmental conventions include: climate change,[39] ozone layer protection,[40] biodiversity protection,[41]

---

legislation. *Convention Law and Legal Definition, available at* https://definitions.uslegal
.com/c/convention/.

33   In this context, it is mostly used to refer to a deliberative assembly, which amends, revises or helps in framing a constitution of a state. *See Convention Law and Legal Definition, available at* https://definitions.uslegal.com/ c/convention/.

34   *Id.*

35   *International conventions, available at* https://www.law.cornell.edu/wex/international
_conventions.

36   *Id.*

37   *Id.*

38   *International Environmental Agreements (IEA) Database Project, available at* https://iea
.uoregon.edu/international-environmental-agreements-ieas-defined.

39   *E.g.,* UN Framework Convention on Climate Change, which entered into force on March 21, 1994.

40   *E.g.,* Vienna Convention for the Protection of the Ozone Layer, which entered into force on September 22, 1988.

41   *E.g.,* Biodiversity Convention, which entered into force on December 29, 1993.

desertification,[42] and the movement of harmful and hazardous substances.[43] Environmental conventions are tools for promoting cooperation amongst the members of the international community either at the bilateral, plurilateral or multilateral dimensions for the protection and enhancement of the world environment under the principle of shared responsibility in tackling global environmental issues.[44] They are also tools for promoting cooperation for the development of international environmental law and international environmental actions. Environmental conventions play a significant role in shaping actions for addressing domestic environmental problems and promoting sustainable development.[45] All these purposes of environmental conventions are understood and appreciated by Nigeria, hence it charges its flagship environmental protection agency, the National Environmental Standards and Regulations Enforcement Agency (NESREA) with the duty and responsibility of, *inter alia*, enforcing environmental conventions.[46]

2.4   *Nigeria*

Nigeria is a country in West Africa. It borders Cameroon in the east, the Republic of Benin in the west, the Atlantic Ocean in the south, the Niger Republic in the north, and Chad in the northeast. It is a federal republic comprising 36 States and the Federal Capital Territory, Abuja. It covers an area of 923,769 square kilometers (356,669 sq. mi.) with a population of about 215,763,437 million,[47] making it the most populous country in Africa.[48]

---

42   *E.g.*, UN Convention to Combat Desertification, which entered into on December 26, 1996.

43   *E.g.*, Basel Convention on the Control of Transboundary Movements of Hazardous Wastes and Their Disposal, which entered into force on May 5, 1992. Bamako Convention on the Ban of the Import into Africa and the Control of Transboundary Movement and Management of Hazardous Wastes within Africa. It entered into force on April 22, 1988.

44   United Nations, *World Leaders Stress Shared Responsibility, Immediate Action, as High-Level Segment of Johannesburg Summit Continues, available at* https://www.un.org/press /en/ 2002/envdev690.doc.htm; M. Cordier, T. Poitelon & W. Hecq, *The Shared Environmental Responsibility Principle: New Developments Applied to the Case of Marine Ecosystems, available at* https://www.tandfonline.com/doi/full/10.1080/09535314.2018.1520691.

45   Edith Brown Weiss, *The Evolution of International Environmental Law*, 54 Japanese Y.B. Intl.L.1, 27(2011).

46   S. 7(c) NESREA Act.

47   Worldometer, *Nigeria Population (Live), available at* https://www.worldometers.info /world-population/nigeria-population/.

48   Worldometer, *African Countries by population (2022), available at* https://www.worldome ters .info/population/countries-in-africa-by-population/.

3   The Development of Modern Environmental Law

The development of the modern international environmental law is anchored on the binding effect of environmental conventions in municipal legal systems. And a channel for the binding effect of environmental conventions in municipal legal systems is domestication. The development of modern international environmental law gained greater momentum with the 1972 United Nations (UN) Conference on the Human Environment held in Stockholm, Sweden. Unlike the concept of international environmental law of preceding centuries, the modern concept sees the world environment as a subject of protection and regulation given that its carrying capacity is being hampered by harmful anthropogenic activities. International environmental agreements in the pre-Stockholm era focused on particular issues that were of interest to the parties to the agreement. The environment was hardly seen as a single subject for protection; for instance, pre-1900 international environmental agreements, though numerically few, focused mainly on boundary waters, navigation, and fishing rights.[49] With the prevailing international law rule of national sovereignty over natural resources in a country at the time, these agreements were made because of direct common ownership of these bodies of water. With few exceptions, these agreements did not address pollution issues.[50] The twentieth century (1900–1972) witnessed international agreements shifting to the protection of environmental issues of particular interests; for instance, early in the century about four agreements were made for the protection of species of commercial value like migratory birds, birds useful to agriculture, fur seals, and wild animals, birds and fish in Africa.[51] The 1930s and 1940s witnessed the making of agreements that aimed at the protection of fauna and flora in specific regions, such as the Western hemisphere and Africa.[52] The period between 1950 and 1970 saw countries focusing on two environmental problems, *viz.* marine pollution from oil and damage from civilian use of nuclear energy, and they negotiated several agreements with respect to them.[53] The African Convention on the Conservation of Nature and Natural Resources was concluded in 1968 and the Ramsar Convention on Wetlands was concluded in 1971. A major setback to these earlier developments of international environmental law in the twentieth century is that there was little development of international

---

49   Weiss, *The Evolution of International Environmental Law, supra* note 45, at 2.
50   *Id.*
51   *Id.*
52   *Id.*
53   *Id.*

environmental rules or principles.[54] This is not surprising because the agreements were more or less *ad hoc* in nature and so could not produce principles that could be further developed and applied to other situations.

The Stockholm conference ushered in a new era of international environmental law, an era that saw the world environment as a single unit that belonged to the global community and, thus, needs to be protected by the same global community. For this reason, the protection of the global environment falls squarely on the shoulders of the UN as the highest international organization. Particular situations that created this understanding include the following.

a. The awareness that the sustainability of human life in the world is a matter dependent substantially on the environment and its sustainability. This awareness came from the many harmful effects on life from environmental damage emanating from the World Wars.[55] It also derived from harmful effects on life resulting from unregulated or ill-regulated developmental activities.

b. The world environment with the oceans, polar regions, and celestial bodies, such as the moon, sun and other planets, constitute a common human heritage that is not parceled out to states, but rather demands worldwide protection and conservation.

c. The planet is confronted with serious environmental challenges that can only be addressed through international co-operation.[56] Acid rain, ozone depletion, climate change, loss of biodiversity, toxic and hazardous products and wastes, pollution of rivers and depletion of freshwater resources are parts of the issues that international environmental law is being called upon to address.[57]

d. The recognition that ecological problems previously seen as matters of domestic concern have international implications –at the bilateral, subregional, regional or global levels – that can be addressed by international law and regulation.[58]

---

54 *Id.*

55 *See* The Long Shadows: A Global Environmental History of the Second World War (Simo Laakkonen, Richard Tucker & Timo Vuorisalo eds., 2017). Thomas B. Robertson, *The Nature of World War II*, *available at* https://origins.osu.edu/connecting-history /nature-world-war-ii-operation-husky-environmentalism-defense-industry?language _content_entity=en. Drew Heiderscheidt, *The Impact of World War One on the Forests and Soils of Europe*, 7(3) Ursidae: Undergrad. Res. J. U.N.Col. 1, 1–11 (2018).

56 Sands, Principles of International Environmental Law, *supra* note 11, at 3.

57 *Id.*

58 *Id.*

e.   The realization that certain ecological hazards like climate change, ozone depletion and desertification do not respect national boundaries, meaning therefore that international co-operation, whether bilateral, plurilateral, subregional, regional or global, is needed to address them.

f.   The recognition of the obligations of the UN as the international organization responsible for maintaining world peace and security since environmental problems that are transboundary could be objects of international discord.[59]

g.   The recognition that the need for world development requires a healthy attention to the environment in order to realize sustainable development.

The conference was well attended with 114 of the then 131 UN members present.[60] It resulted in the creation of the UN Environment Program (UNEP), the first international organization concerned exclusively with the protection and conservation of the environment.[61] It is headquartered in Nairobi, Kenya. The conference produced the Stockholm Declaration, a 26- principle document that focuses on the rights and obligations of citizens and governments with regard to the preservation and improvement of the environment. These principles have been incorporated in many post-Stockholm environmental agreements. For instance, principle 21, which talks of the right of a State to exploit its resources in accordance with its environmental policies and which affirms the obligation of a State not to cause transboundary injury has been incorporated into many treaties like the Biodiversity Convention, the Vienna Ozone Convention, the Convention on Long-Range Transboundary Air Pollution (LRTAP) and the UN Convention on the Law of the Sea (UNCLOS).[62] Other multilateral environmental agreements inspired by or associated with the Stockholm Conference include the 1972 Convention for the Prevention of Marine Pollution by Dumping of Wastes and other Matters, the 1972 Convention for the Protection of World Cultural and Natural Heritage, and the 1973 Convention on International Trade in Endangered Species of Wild Fauna and Flora (CITES).[63]

The euphoria for the Stockholm Conference in the developed countries did not reverberate across the board of the global community, as developing

---

59   *See* Art. 1(3) & (4) UN Charter.
60   Lakshman Guruswamy, International Environmental Law in a Nutshell 38 (2012).
61   *Id.*
62   *Id.* at 39.
63   Weiss, *The Evolution of International Environmental Law, supra* note 45, at 6.

countries approached the Stockholm environmentalism with suspicion and fear.[64] They considered it to be at the expense of their economic development since the new ideas, processes and technologies being spurned by it entailed more costs and possibly market restrictions for their products. Attempts to address their fears which began before the Stockholm Conference with the Founex Committee continued after the Conference with the World Commission for Environment and Development (WCED) 1983 (otherwise known as the Brundtland Commission)[65]; its main objective was "to re-examine the critical issues of environment and development and to formulate new and concrete action proposals to deal with them."[66] The Commission in its report, titled *Our Common Future,* developed the principle of sustainable development (SD), which it defined as a "development that meets the needs of the present without compromising the ability of future generations to meet their own needs."[67] The principle not only accommodated the interests of both the developed and developing countries, but also broadened the concept of international environmental law to now embrace also the regulation of activities for economic development.[68] It held that environmental protection and economic development were not mutually exclusive, but could go together. In other words, economic growth was both desirable and possible in the same breath with environmental protection. To cement the successes recorded and draw up a worldwide plan for SD, the Commission called for an international conference that would act as a successor of the Stockholm Conference and advance its legacy. This was the 1992 UN Conference on Environment and Development held in Rio de Janeiro, Brazil, otherwise known as the Earth Summit or Rio Conference.

---

64   Michael Manulak, *Developing World Environmental Cooperation: The Founex Seminar and the Stockholm Conference, in* International Organizations and Environmental Protection, 103, 105–107 (2016). *Available at* https://www.researchgate.net/publication/326392380 _Developing_World_Environmental_Cooperation_The_Founex_Seminar_and_the _Stockholm_Conference.

65   The commission was created by a resolution adopted at the 38th session of the UN General Assembly in December 1983, *available at* https://idl-bnc-idrc.dspacedirect.org/bitstream / handle/10625/8942/WCED_79365.pdf?sequence =1&isAllowed=y.

66   *Id.*

67   *Sustainable Development, available at* https://www.ic.gc.ca/eic/site/693.nsf/eng/h_00019 .html.

68   Sumudu Atapattu, *From "Our Common Future" to Sustainable Development Goals: Evolution of Sustainable Development under International Law, available at* https://wilj.law .wisc.edu/wp-content/uploads/sites/1270/2020/01/36.2_215-246_Atapattu.pdf.

The Earth Summit, with over 178 countries and 117 heads of state in attendance, was welcomed as the greatest summit level conference in history.[69] Such a high-level attendance indicated a broad global acceptance of the agenda of the Summit and particularly the acceptance of the new paradigm of sustainable development fashioned by the Brundtland Commission. Key contributions of the Earth Summit to the development of IEL are the Rio Declaration, the Agenda 21 – an action plan for the planet, the Global Consensus on Sustainable Development of Forests (Forestry Declaration),[70] the ceremonial signing of the UN Framework Convention on Climate Change (UNFCCC) and the Biodiversity Convention.[71]

Some scholars are critical of the Conference in terms of the development of IEL. For Guruswamy, "[t]he Earth Summit palliated from the strict environmental focus and momentum already generated by the Stockholm Conference." He further maintained that "the Earth Summit arguably weakened international efforts to secure environmental protection."[72] It is submitted that this perception is incorrect; it manifests a misunderstanding of the Stockholm Conference. The environmentalism of the Stockholm conference was not an environmentalism that was opposed to economic development. This would have been counterproductive. It was only an environmentalism that grew from the background of the damning side effects of the economic advancement of the developed world and so called for restraint and balance with concerns for environment protection and conservation. Hence, it did not call for the halt of every economic activity in the developed countries. This is precisely what the Rio conference did by formally and explicitly integrating environmental protection with economic development and by so doing actualized the intention of the Stockholm conference. Affirming this reasoning, Weiss considers the Rio Conference as being, together with the Stockholm conference, of foundational relevance in the development of IEL. According to her, the period from 1972 to 1992 (from Stockholm through the Rio Conference) is the basic framework in the development of IEL.[73]

Another major step in the development of IEL came with the 2002 UN World Summit on Sustainable Development (WSSD) in Johannesburg, South Africa.

---

69   *United Nations Conference on Environment and Development, available at* https://www .britannica.com /event/United-Nations-Conference-on-Environment-and-Development.

70   A non-legally binding Authoritative Statement of Principles for a Global Consensus on the Management, Conservation and Sustainable Development of All Types of Forests (1992), U.N. Doc. A/CONF. 151/26, v. 3.

71   Guruswamy, International Environmental Law, *supra* note 60, at 44.

72   *Id.* at 45.

73   Weiss, *The Evolution of International Environmental Law, supra* note 45, at 4.

The Summit was scheduled primarily to motivate the implementation of Agenda 21. However, its attention was directed more to problems created by poverty as different from environmental degradation.[74] The Conference produced two documents, *viz.* a political Declaration, otherwise called the Johannesburg Declaration on Sustainable Development, and an Implementation Plan. The Implementation Plan drawn for Agenda 21 embraced different new goals to be pursued in the following 20 years. These include poverty eradication,[75] changing unsustainable patterns of consumption and production,[76] and protecting and managing the natural resource base of economic and social development.[77] With the Declaration, the world rededicated itself to sustainable development, this time not only with the two pillars of environmental protection and economic development, but with a third pillar added, that is, social development. Article 5 of the Declaration states: "we assume a collective responsibility to advance and strengthen the interdependent and mutually reinforcing pillars of sustainable development – economic development, social development and environmental protection – at the local, national, regional and global levels."[78] Social development, which was subsumed in economic development, with the wssd became a distinct but interdependent pillar of sd. This must have been from the realization that poverty and other inhuman social conditions also result in environmental degradation and pollution.

In summary, from Stockholm to Johannesburg, the concept of iel evolved from the mono pillar of environmental protection to the threefold pillars of environmental protection, economic development and social development, all under the umbrella framework of sd. iel therefore becomes more or less an all embracing course that caters not for just the "abstract" environment, but rather one that sees adequate and effective environmental protection and conservation as something that is to be done along with the social and economic development of persons and peoples. This extensive and broad understanding of iel generated corresponding and extensive interests in international environmental conventions as a way of securing holistic human well-being and development. The effect is the proliferation of environmental conventions resulting in the so-called "treaty congestions" in international environmental

---

74   Guruswamy, International Environmental Law, *supra* note 60, at 51.

75   Ch. ii, wssd Implementation Plan.

76   Ch. iii, *id.*

77   Ch. iv, *id.*

78   Art. 5, wssd Declaration.

law.[79] This is a sign that international environmental law had matured and come to stay within the framework of sustainable development.

The many environmental conventions have been grouped under the following five clusters: Biodiversity Conventions, Atmosphere Conventions, Land Conventions, Chemicals and Hazardous Wastes Conventions, and Regional Seas Conventions and Related Agreements.[80]

As a responsible member of the international community and a leading country in the African region, Nigeria has participated in the development of modern IEL through participation in the IEL conferences such as

---

79   Bethany Hicks, *Treaty Congestion in International Environmental Law: The Need for Greater International Coordination*, 32 U. Rich. L. Rev. 1643 (1999). *Available at https://scholarship .richmond.edu/cgi/viewcontent.cgi?httpsredir=1&article=2324&context=lawreview*. Donald Anton, *Treaty Congestion' in International Environmental Law*, *in* Routledge Handbook of International Environmental Law, (Shawkat Alam, Jahid Hossain Bhuiyan, Tareq M.R. Chowdhury & Erika J. Techera eds., 2012). *Available at* https://papers.ssrn.com/sol3 /papers.cfm?abstract_id=1988579.

80   *Biodiversity conventions*: deal with the protection of individual species, the protection of ecosystems and also promote sustainable use of resources. Examples: Convention of Biological Diversity (CBD), Convention on International Trade on Endangered Species 19 (CITES), and Convention of Migratory Species (CMS). *Atmosphere conventions*: deal with the protection of the environment by eliminating or stabilizing anthropogenic emissions of substances that threaten to interfere with the atmosphere. Examples: Vienna Convention on the Protection of the Ozone Layer and its Montreal Protocol, and United Nations Framework Convention on Climate Change and Kyoto Protocol. *Land conventions*: deal with combating desertification and mitigating the effects of drought in countries experiencing serious drought and/or desertification, especially in Africa. Example: UNCCD. *Chemicals and hazardous wastes conventions*: deal with protecting human health and the environment from pollution by specific chemicals and hazardous substances by aiming to control trade. The mechanisms used in trade control include: prior informed consent, phase outs, restriction and reduction in production and use of certain chemicals, and reduction of production of hazardous wastes and their transboundary movements. Examples: Stockholm Convention, Basel Convention, Rotterdam Convention, and Bamako Convention. *Regional seas conventions and related agreements*: deal with the protection and sustainable use of marine and coastal resources. Example: The Global Programme of Action for the Protection of the Marine Environment from Land-based Activities. Wangare Kirumba, *Domestication of Multilateral Environment Agreements (MEAs) in Kenya: Case study of United Nations Framework Convention on Climate Change (UNFCCC) in Muranga County*, *available at* http://erepository.uonbi.ac.ke/bitstream/handle/11295 /75394/Kirumba_Domestication%20of%20multilateral%20environment%20agreements %20(MEAs)%20in%20Kenya%20Case%20study%20of%20United%20Nations%20 Framework%20Convention%20on%20Climate%20Change%20(UNFCCC)%20in%20 Muranga%20County.pdf?isAllowed=y&sequence=1.

the Stockholm Conference,[81] the Rio Conference,[82] the Johannesburg World Summit on Sustainable Development,[83] and, more importantly, by adopting/ ratifying many of the IEL instruments which have since entered into force. Such instruments include the Stockholm Declaration, the Rio Declaration, and the Convention on Persistent Organic Pollutants.[84] Ratification is a formal confirmation by a State that it is bound by a treaty.[85] Ratification comes with the inherent obligation under the principle of *pacta sunt servanda* of actualizing within the country the aims and objectives of the conventions. The question then is, how far has Nigeria gone in having these conventions acquire binding force within its territorial confines under the spirit of ratification? Ratifying an environmental convention without going further to domesticate it is inchoate and ineffectual. Before examining this, it is important we first examine the nature of the obligation incurred by Nigeria under the international law principle of *pacta sunt servanda,* which is also a rule of the Vienna Convention on the Law of Treaties (VCLT).

4   *Pacta Sunt Servanda* **and the Implementation of Environmental Conventions in Nigeria**

Pacta sunt servanda is a principle of customary international law which has also acquired treaty force by being enshrined in the 1969 Vienna Convention on the Law of Treaties 1969 (VCLT). Article 26 of VCLT with the heading *pacta sunt servanda* states: "Every treaty in force is binding upon the parties to it and

---

81   *United Nations Conference on the Human Environment – List of Participants, available at* https://documents-ddsny.un.org/doc/UNDOC/GEN/NL3/217/10/PDF/NL321710.pdf? Open Element.

82   *See* the statement of Dr. Lawrence C. Anukam, leader of the Nigerian delegation at the first meeting of the preparatory committee for the United Nations Conference on Sustainable Development, New York, May 17, 2010, where he said: "Nigeria participated actively in all the major processes leading to the Earth Summit in Rio in 1992, at the Summit itself, and all the follow-up activities. Following the Earth Summit, we developed our National Agenda 21 to operationalise and implement the outcomes of the Summit." *Available at* https://sustainabledevelopment. un.org/content/documents/17626Nigeria.pdf.

83   WSSD *Statements: Nigeria, Zimbabwe, available at* https://www.scoop.co.nz/stories /WO0209/ S00024/ wssd-statements-nigeria-zimbabwe.htm.

84   Entered into force on May 24, 2004. See *Stockholm Convention on Persistent Organic Pollutants, in* United Nations Treaty Collection, *available at https://treaties.un.org/pages/View Details.aspx?src=IND&mtdsg_no=XXVII-15&chapter=27&clang=_en.*

85   Ratification refers to the international act whereby a state establishes its consent to be bound by a treaty. Art 2(b) Vienna Convention on the Law of Treaties.

must be performed by them in good faith." This makes *pacta sunt servanda* as a treaty principle pre-eminent to *pacta sunt servanda* as a principle of customary international law, at least in the discussion of the import of the ratification of environmental conventions. This is particularly so because modern environmental conventions, the subjects of our discussion, came into force after 1969.

Pacta sunt servanda thus makes treaty making a serious business, which demands every party like Nigeria to be resolved to discharge the consequential responsibilities within its municipal territory. Article 26 of VCLT gives two preconditions for the binding force of a treaty, namely: (a) that the treaty must be in force, and (b) that the obligations must be discharged in good faith. A treaty that is in force is a treaty that has gone through the formative processes and is promulgated to bind parties from a stated date. It must not be a treaty that is suspended[86] or terminated.[87] The demand for a treaty obligation to be discharged in good faith indicates that a treaty cannot be discharged in any manner. It must be discharged in ways that uphold its aim and not ways that undermine it. Any manner of discharging a treaty that defeats its aim can be considered as being in bad faith. Thus, Dörr and Schmalenbach opined that the duty of good faith "requires that a party to a treaty shall refrain from any acts calculated to prevent the due execution of the treaty or otherwise frustrate its objects."[88] Article 29 confines the duty on a State to performing the treaty duties only within its own territory. This serves to prevent a State from meddling in the affairs of another State in breach of the sovereignty principle of general international law. Yet Article 26 does not stipulate the extent of the obligation it places on the shoulders of parties. Is it an obligation to take particular steps towards performing the treaty obligations or simply a broad and general obligation of seeing to it that the intent of the treaty is realized using any means of its choice in so far as the means is used in good faith? The position in international law jurisprudence is that it does not demand from a State any specific form of action in giving life to the provisions of a treaty. This is based on the basic principle of international law that States are at liberty on how to discharge their international obligations.[89] Thus, Mendez

---

86   Art. 72(a) VCLT.

87   Art. 70(a) VCLT.

88   Vienna Convention on the Law of Treaties 445–46 (Oliver Dörr & Kirsten Schmalenbach eds., 2011); Timothy Meyer, *Good Faith, Withdrawal, and the Judicialization of International Politics, available at* http://www.qil-qdi.org/good-faith-withdrawal-and-the-judicialization -of-international-politics/#:~:text=nature%20of%20treaty.,,or%20otherwise%20frustrate%20its%20objects.

89   Mario Mendez, *The Legal Effects of Treaties in Domestic Legal Orders and the Role of Domestic Courts, available at* https://www.researchgate.net/publication/300180665_The _Legal _Effects_of_Treaties_in_Domestic_Legal_Orders_and_the_Role_of_Domestic_Courts.

wrote: "whilst treaties are to be performed in good faith, it remains the case that they are in principle no exception to the basic precept of international law that States are free to determine how they meet their international obligations."[90] Going further, he stated: "treaties do not as a general rule impose specific requirements as to how the substantive obligations that they lay out should be realized in the domestic legal orders of the Contracting Parties."[91] Several interconnected factors are advanced to support this position. They include the following. (i) The core factor of the sovereignty of a State.[92] (ii) Already, states have developed different means of complying with treaty obligations and so it would make no sense for treaties to busy themselves with this. In short, international law leaves this to the domestic legal order to determine. Usually this is provided for in municipal constitutions.[93] (iii) A recent detailed assessment concluded that there is no general obligation under general international treaty law, customary international law, or general principles of international law requiring States to open their courts for invocation of treaty norms by individuals.[94] (iv) All the same, whatever the effect given domestically to treaty obligations, a State cannot invoke its internal law as justification for a failure to perform.[95] In other words, a State cannot be heard to say that it has failed to discharge its treaty obligations because the domestic legal order has impeded its discharge of the obligations. VCLT makes this point clearly in article 27, which provides that: "A party may not invoke the provisions of its internal law as justification for its failure to perform a treaty. This rule is without prejudice to article 46."[96] Article 46(1) provides that a State may not invoke the fact that its consent to be bound by a treaty has been expressed in violation of a provision of its internal law regarding competence to conclude treaties as invalidating its consent unless that violation was manifest and concerned a rule of its internal law of fundamental importance. According to article 46(2), a violation is manifest if it would be objectively

---

90   *Id.*

91   *Id.*

92   *Id.*

93   Anthony Aust, Modern Treaty Law and Practice 182 (2007).

94   Mendez, *The Legal Effects, supra* note 89.

95   *Id.*

96   The substance of this article was already relied on in the advisory opinion of the Permanent Court of International Justice in *Treatment of Polish Nationals and Other Persons of Polish Origin or Speech in the Danzig Territory*, (1932) PCIJ SER. A/B, No. 44 (Polish Nationals in Danzig)) where the Permanent Court of International Justice strongly held that: "[*i*] *t should, however, be observed that ... a State cannot adduce as against another State its own constitution with a view to evading obligations incumbent upon it under international law or treaties in force.*"

evident to any State conducting itself in the matter in accordance with normal practice and in good faith.

There are, however, exceptions where the principle of *pacta sunt servanda* means that a State has the obligation to follow a specific line of action in order to discharge its treaty obligations. This is where the specified line of action was part of the terms of the agreement such that by ratifying the treaties parties consented also to following the specified line of action or doing certain things in order to discharge the treaty obligations.[97]

What the immediate foregoing means is that the domestication of a treaty, as a means of implementing treaty obligations, is not a direct duty under *pacta sunt servanda* as a rule of VCLT. Nor is it a rule of customary international law, nor that of a general principle of law under article 38(1)(c) of the ICJ Statute. All that *pacta sunt servanda,* particularly as a rule of VCLT, demands is that the aims and objectives of a treaty be achieved inside a State. All the same, general international law devolved the determination of the specific means of implementation of treaties to constitutional mechanisms of countries. It is in awareness of this that Nigeria in its constitutional history has always provided for the domestication of conventions.[98] The extant 1999 Constitution states in section 12(1) that "[n]o treaty between the Federation and any other country shall have the force of law except to the extent to which any such treaty has been enacted into law by the National Assembly."[99] This makes it relevant to examine the legal regime for domestication in Nigeria. Before we do this, it is necessary that we look at the effects of the poor domestication records of environmental conventions.

5   Effects of the Non-Domestication of Environmental Conventions in Nigeria

The non-domestication of many environmental conventions ratified by Nigeria takes a lot of steam from Nigeria's commitment to modern-day environmentalism and has many negative effects in the country.

97   Mendez, *The Legal Effects, supra* note 89.
98   Section 69, 1960 CFRN; section 74, 1963 CFRN; section12, 1979 CFRN; section 13, 1989 CFRN.
99   Section 12(1) CFRN.

5.1   It Inhibits the Growth of Environmental law in Nigeria

Modern environmental law as seen above developed from international conferences and conventions, thereby making these conventions crucial in the development and growth of international law in the individual countries. For Okeke and Anushiem, "domesticated treaties do not only fill the gaps in the Nigerian legal system, but also expand its frontiers."[100] In appreciation of this fact, Ethiopia, which like Nigeria is fundamentally dualist in the implementation of international treaties, is constitutionally monistic in the implementation of environmental conventions. It treats environmental issues as human rights issues and thus guarantees constitutionally the right to clean and healthy environment. In addition, appreciating the importance of international instruments for the domestic development and guarantee of human rights, it provides constitutionally for the interpretation of the provisions of its human rights and freedom to be in consonance with international covenants and instruments ratified by it.[101] This boils down to interpreting its constitutional environmental rights provisions to be in consonance with any environmental convention ratified by it. This keeps environmental law in Ethiopia very dynamic as it readily adjusts to the international standard once a treaty is ratified. The importance of treaties in the development of the domestic legal order has received judicial confirmation from the Nigerian Supreme Court *per* Achike, JSC, who stated, "it is crystal clear today that treaties may create rights and obligations not only between member states themselves, but also between citizens and the member states, and between the ordinary citizens themselves."[102] These rights and obligations with respect to environmental conventions are strong instruments for the development of environmental law in Nigeria. So, for Nigeria to become lethargic in the deployment of this beneficial constitutional mechanism of domestication in respect of environmental conventions is to inhibit the growth of environmental law in the country.[103]

5.2   It Weakens Environmental Protection in the Country

Aware of the indispensable place of environmental conventions for environmental protection in Nigeria, the National Environmental Standard and

---

100   Okeke, *Implementation of Treaties in Nigeria, supra* note 3, at 221.

101   Art. 13(2), 1996 Ethiopian Constitution.

102   *Abacha & Ors v Fawehinmi,* (2000) LPELR-14(SC).

103   *See* Jude Ezeanokwasa, *Legal Regulations on Air Pollution Control and Industrialisation in Nigeria,* 1(1) Unizik J. Bus. 103, 115.

Regulations Enforcement Agency (NESREA) Act, (as amended), which established the principal environmental protection agency for the country, the NESREA, assigned to NESREA, *inter alia*, the function of enforcing environmental conventions. Section 7(c) NESREA Act states:

> [T]he Agency shall enforce compliance with the provisions of international agreements, protocols, conventions and treaties on the environment, including climate change, biodiversity, conservation, desertification, forestry, chemicals, hazardous wastes, ozone depletion, marine and wild life, pollution, sanitation and such other environmental agreements as may from time to time come into force.

Given that by the force of section 12(1) of the 1999 Constitution no convention can be enforced without first being domesticated, it entails that the plethora of undomesticated environmental conventions cannot be enforced by the NESREA. To this extent the NESREA is incapacitated in achieving its statutory mission of protecting, developing and conserving Nigeria's environment.

5.3   *It Undermines Sustainable Development in the Country*
This is a direct corollary to the immediate foregoing point. Environmental conventions are key purveyors of sustainable development as they ensure that economic development is carried out in a manner that is sensitive to the health of the environment and sensitive to the social well-being of individuals involved. Environmental conventions achieve this developmental balance through their regulatory mechanisms. When they are not domesticated, it means that these rules cannot be legally enforced and sustainable development suffers. The Niger Delta area of Nigeria, which is the cash cow of Nigeria in terms of oil money, is in a sorry state from the perspective of sustainable development[104] because of the non-domestication of many environmental conventions that would have aided the fight against environmental pollution there.[105]

---

104   Paul Peters Ugboma, *Environmental Degradation in Oil Producing Areas of Niger Delta Region, Nigeria: the Need for Sustainable Development*, 4 Int'l J. Sc. & Tech. 75–85(2015). Amnesty International, *No clean up, no justice: Shell's oil pollution in the Niger Delta, available at* https://www.amnesty.org/en/latest/news/2020/06/no-clean-up-no-justice-shell-oil-pollution-in-the-niger-delta/. Ighodalo Akhakpe, *Oil-Environmental Degradation and Human Security in the Niger-Delta region of Nigeria: Challenges and Possibilities*, 8(26) Eur. Scientific J. 77–92, *available at https://www.eujournal.org/index.php/esj/article/view/570/0.*
105   These conventions include the Bamako Convention.

5.4   *It Forecloses the Right of Federating Units to Benefit from Environmental Conventions*

The Nigeria Constitution has arranged the legislative competences of the federal and state governments in such a manner that only the National Assembly can legislate on foreign affairs,[106] and by that token only it can domesticate treaties. This runs along the line of the exclusive competence of the federal executive, like the praxis in many federations, in representing the country in international diplomatic relations and in the consequent activities of treaty negotiations and ratifications. Under this arrangement, it is the federal executive that negotiates and ratifies every treaty regardless of whether the subject-matter is constitutionally within the competence of the federal government or state government. In other words, in the realm of diplomatic relations and treaty negotiations and ratification, Nigeria is one entity represented by the President. A similar exclusive competence is enjoyed by the National Assembly with respect to the domestication of treaties pursuant to section 12 of the Constitution. The only difference is that on matters within the legislative competence of State Assemblies, the bill for the domestication of a treaty, after it has been passed, shall not be sent to the President for his assent, but rather has to be ratified by a majority of all the Houses of Assembly in the Federation.[107] In the context of environmental conventions, this means that unless the National Assembly considers it necessary to pass into law a bill for the domestication of an environmental convention whose subject is within the legislative jurisdiction of State Assemblies, the States in Nigeria cannot take advantage of such conventions in protecting and developing their environment. The Supreme Court *per* Ogundare, JSC, in *Abacha v. Fawehinmi*,[108] echoed this statutory implication when it held that "it is therefore manifest that no matter how beneficial to the country or the citizenry an international treaty to which Nigeria has become a signatory may be, it remains unenforceable, if it is not enacted into law of the country by the National Assembly."[109] The non-domestication of environmental conventions by the National Assembly forecloses the right and power of the States to protect and develop their environment and it becomes very telling for the environmental protection of the country.

---

106   Item 26 Exclusive Legislative List 1999 CFRN.
107   S. 12(3), 1999 CFRN.
108   *Abacha & Ors v Fawehinmi,* [2000] 6 NWLR (Part 660) 228.
109   *Id.* at 356–57.

5.5 It Betrays the Cooperation That Should Exist between Parties to a Convention

As seen earlier on, environmental conventions are tools for promoting cooperation amongst the members of the international community for the protection and enhancement of the world environment under the principle of shared responsibility in tackling global environmental issues. There is full and meaningful cooperation when every party to a convention sees that the legal provisions of the agreement are enforceable in its territory. It is when this is done that the mechanism for achieving the objectives of the convention is legally in place in the territories of the country parties. Without the domestication of these conventions in Nigeria therefore, the cooperative bond that should exist between Nigeria and other States parties in the pursuit of the environmental goals of the conventions is betrayed and sabotaged.

5.6 It Inhibits Foreign Direct Investment (FDI) in Nigeria

What has become a recurrent slogan on the lips of the leadership of Nigeria and leading politicians both at the federal and state levels is the need for foreign direct investments to boost the economy.[110] One feature of conventions as treaties is that they create enforceable rights and obligations that establish legally binding expectations between citizens of one country and citizens of other countries, and between citizens of one country and other sovereign States. It is on the basis of these rights and obligations that citizens of one country can enter into business and investment relationships with citizens of other countries or even other countries. Now that many environmental conventions are not domesticated by Nigeria, it means that these rights and obligations cannot be judicially enforced in Nigeria. The effect is that countries and citizens of countries that have these conventions domesticated would not like to engage in investment relations where these environmental rights and obligations are involved because they cannot be enforced in Nigerian courts. After assessing the effects of the non-domestication of treaties by Nigeria in international energy investments, Nriezedi-Anejionu found that it will, *inter alia,* "affect the admissibility of treaty provisions in Nigerian courts and lead to difficulty in the application of exhaustion of local remedies (ELR) and fork-in-the-road[111] and

---

110   Nriezedi-Anejionu, *Could the Non-Domestication of Nigerian Treaties, supra* note 6.

111   This is a clause in investment agreements which provides that "the investor must choose between the litigation of its claims in the host State's domestic courts or through international arbitration and that the choice, once made, is final." Rudolf Dolzer & Christoph Schreuer, Principles of International Investment Law 267 (2nd ed. 2012).

exclusive forum[112] clauses in investment treaties."[113] Going further, she wrote: "Putting together all the issues associated with the non-domestication of relevant energy investment treaties, Nigeria risks being perceived as an unattractive investment destination by potential investors."[114] Again, she stated:

> It could also affect the smooth resolution of disputes concerning denial of justice and expropriation, as well as result in Nigeria having a non-compliant status and denying the investor the opportunity to use a less costly dispute settlement mechanism. It could also constitute an obstacle to Nigeria achieving its investment interests. In addition, it could erode investors' confidence to invest in the country and result in other far-reaching effects that could affect FDI inflow.[115]

An ELR requires a foreign investor, in case of dispute, to first exhaust local remedies before resorting to diplomatic remedies.[116] If the environmental treaty relied upon by the foreign investor is not domesticated by Nigeria, the ELR principle cannot guarantee this right in Nigeria for *nemo dat quod non habet* (no one gives what he does not have). In effect, companies and businesses enjoying the benefits of environmental treaties in other countries would not like to invest in or do business with Nigeria where such benefits and safeguards are not guaranteed.[117] Thus, Nriezedi-Anejionu would consider the non-domestication of environmental treaties as a major challenge to the application of beneficial international investment rules and principles to environment-related investments in Nigeria.[118]

5.7 *It Obscures the Awareness of the Existence of the Conventions in Nigeria*

Nigeria's dualist jurisprudence implies that environmental conventions as part of international law pertain to a legal sphere distinct and independent of the domestic legal realm. For this reason, they are ordinarily unknown to

---

112   An exclusive forum clause is a clause in a contract that stipulates the court and location where the parties would like to have their legal dispute decided. *Cf. Forum Selection Clause, available at* https://www.law.cornell.edu/wex/forum_selection_clause.

113   Nriezedi-Anejionu, *Could the Non-Domestication of Nigerian Treaties, supra* note 6.

114   *Id.*

115   *Id.*

116   Berk Demirkol, *Exhaustion of Local Remedies, available at https://jusmundi.com/en/document/publication/en-exhaustion-of-local-remedies.*

117   Nriezedi-Anejionu, *Could the Non-domestication of Nigerian Treaties, supra* note 6.

118   *Id.*

the domestic legal system. The only way to bring them to the knowledge of the domestic system is through domestication, and the Constitution has provided for it. Their non-domestication therefore obscures the awareness of their existence in the domestic society. It is only when a convention is brought to the knowledge of the people that they can apply it in concrete situations. This fact was underscored in 2013 in the public lamentation of Dayo Bush-Alebiosu, a member of the House of Representatives and chairman of the House Committee on Treaties and Protocols in the National Assembly, to the effect that he could not state with accuracy the number of treaties that had been signed by Nigeria.[119] Unfortunately, this ugly situation has not improved today.[120] Law, as an instrument of social engineering and re-engineering, begins its work with the people being aware of its existence.

With all these negative effects of the non-domestication of environmental conventions in Nigeria, it becomes apposite to inquire into the legal regime for domestication in the country.

6   The Legal Regime for the Implementation of Environmental Conventions in Nigeria

The Treaties (Making Procedure, Etc) Act,[121] the Constitution of the Federal Republic of Nigeria 1999 (as amended), and the Constitution of the Federal Republic of Nigeria (Third Alteration) Act, 2010 constitute the legal corpus regulating the implementation of treaties in Nigeria and by that token, they regulate the implementation of environmental convention in the country. They deserve individual examination.

6.1   *The Treaties (Making Procedure, Etc) Act*[122]
The Treaties (Making Procedure, Etc) Act was originally promulgated in 1993 as a Decree by the Military, and after the return of democracy in 1999, it was redesignated as an Act in 2004. Amongst the reasons for redesignation would have been to align the decree with the 1999 Constitution, or else there is no way the decree could have, in section 1(1), referred to the Exclusive Legislative

---

119   Channels Television, *Non-domestication of Treaties Deprives Nigerians of Expected Benefits—BushAlebiosu*, *Available at* https://www.channelstv.com/2013/11/25/non-domestication -of-treaties-deprives-nigerians-of-expected-benefits-bush-alebiosu/.

120   Salem, *Nigeria Yet to Domesticate, supra* note 4; Adesomoju, FG *Yet to Domesticate, supra* note 5.

121   Cap T20 LFN 2004.

122   *Id.*

List in the 1999 Constitution. This is a short piece of legislation consisting of only 7 sections. Its long title reads: "An act to provide, amongst other things, for treaty-making procedure and the designation of the Federal Ministry of Justice as the depository of all treaties entered into between the Federation and any other country." The scope of the Act is limited to the making of any treaty between the Federation and any other country on any matter on the Exclusive Legislative List of the 1999 Constitution.[123] In other words, its provisions do not apply to the making of any treaty on any matter in the concurrent and residual lists of the Constitution. It provides in section 2 that all treaties to be made between the Government of the Federation and any other country shall be classified as specified by the Act. Section 3(1) of the Act classifies the treaties into three, namely: (a) law-making treaties, being agreements constituting rules which govern inter-state relationships and co-operation in any area of endeavor and which have the effect of altering or modifying existing legislation or which affects the legislative powers of the National Assembly; (b) agreements which impose financial, political and social obligations on Nigeria or which are of scientific or technological import; and (c) agreements which deal with mutual exchange of cultural and educational facilities. The Act goes further in section 3(2) to specify the process for getting each of these categories of treaty enforceable in Nigeria. According to section 3(2)(a), treaties in section 3(1)(a) need to be enacted into law before they can acquire binding force. This class of treaties embraces environmental conventions that constitute rules which govern inter-state relationships and cooperation in any area of endeavor, and which have the effect of altering or modifying existing legislation or which affects the legislative powers of the National Assembly.

An instance of such a rule-making environmental convention is the United Nations Convention on Conditions for Registration of Ships 1986 which in article 17(1) enjoins contracting parties to take any legislative or other measures necessary to implement this Convention. Section 3(2)(b) of the Act provides that the treaties or agreements specified in paragraph (b) of section 3(1) need to be ratified before they can be implemented in the country. In other words, such agreements do not have to be enacted into law by the National Assembly as provided by section 12(1) of the CFRN. All that is required for them to be implemented is ratification. And section 3(2)(c) provides that the treaties or agreements specified in paragraph (c) of section 3(1) may not need to be ratified before they can also be implemented in the country. Such agreements can be implemented in the country even without being ratified. An instance

---

123   S.1(1), Treaties Act.

of such an agreement would be article 2(a) of the Vienna Convention for the Protection of the Ozone Layer which obliges parties to co-operate by means of systematic observations, research, and information exchange in order to better understand and assess the effects of human activities on the ozone layer and the effects on human health and the environment from modification of the ozone layer.

What the foregoing implies is that domestication, strictly speaking, does not apply to the classes of treaties mentioned in section 3(1)(b) and (c) of the Act, but is required only for the class of treaties mentioned in section 3(1)(a) where the agreement must go through the legislative process at the National Assembly before it can have the force of law. Agreements that impose financial, political, and social obligations on Nigeria or which are of scientific or technological import can be implemented by Nigeria without them needing to be domesticated. The same is true of agreements which deal with mutual exchange of cultural and educational facilities. They can be implemented without needing to be domesticated. Section 3(3) of the Act defines treaties or agreements to mean instruments whereby an obligation under international law is undertaken between the Federation and any other country and they include "conventions", "Act", "general acts" "protocols", "agreements" and *"modi vivendi,"* whether they are bilateral or multi-lateral in nature.

A lacuna in the Treaties Act is that while it designates the Federal Ministry of Justice as the depository of all treaties entered into between the Federation and any other country,[124] it fails to specify the agency that should initiate domestication at the National Assembly for agreements that require it. The power of the Ministry of Justice to receive and keep treaties as the depository does not automatically include the power to initiate domestication bills at the National Assembly. It should also be the duty of the Ministry of Justice to inform the National Assembly of ratified treaties in its repository. This lacuna is responsible for the gap between the Ministry of Justice and the National Assembly on account of which the latter is lamenting lack of information on the treaties ratified by the Executive.[125]

---

124   S. 4 Treaties Act.
125   Salem, *Nigeria Yet to Domesticate, supra* note 4; Adesomoju, FG *Yet to Domesticate, supra* note 5.

6.2   *The Constitution of the Federal Republic of Nigeria 1999 (As Amended)*

The domestication of treaties has been an integral part of Nigerian constitutional history[126] since independence.[127] The 1999 Constitution in section 12 states:

1. No treaty between the Federation and any other country shall have the force of law except to the extent to which any such treaty has been enacted into law by the National Assembly.

2. The National Assembly may make laws for the Federation or any part thereof with respect to matters not included in the Exclusive Legislative list for the purpose of implementing a treaty.

3. A bill for an Act of the National Assembly passed pursuant to the provisions of subsection (2) of this section shall not be presented to the President for assent, and shall not be enacted unless it is ratified by a majority of all the Houses of Assembly in the Federation.

This is the constitutional basis of the doctrine of domestication in Nigerian law. Subsection 1 makes the National Assembly the exclusive gateway for any treaty between the Federation and any other country to have the force of law in the country. The fact that the domesticated treated will have the force of law only to the extent that it is enacted into law implies that the National Assembly can excise portions of it or qualify some provisions of it before passing it into law. The Supreme Court affirmed the indispensability of the National Assembly in the domestication process when it held that "an international treaty entered into by the Government of Nigeria does not become binding until enacted into law by the National Assembly."[128]

The exclusive power of the National Assembly in the domestication of treaties has particular implications on the legislative competence of the State Assemblies under Nigerian federalism. Legislative competences in Nigerian federalism, like in many federations, are shared between the federal government or central government and the federating units or states.[129] Under the 1999 Constitution, the National Assembly enjoys exclusive legislative competence on matters in the Exclusive Legislative list.[130] Both the National Assembly and the Houses of Assembly of the various States enjoy concurrent

---

126   *See supra* note 98.

127   Nigeria gained independence from England on October 1, 1960.

128   *Abacha & Ors v Fawehinmi*, (2000) LPELR-14(SC) 11–12.

129   J.O. Arowosegbe, *Techniques for Division of Legislative Powers under Federal Constitutions*, 29 J. L., Pol'y & Globalization 127–134 (2014).

130   S. 4(3) CFRN states: "The power of the National Assembly to make laws for the peace, order and good government of the Federation with respect to any matter included in the

legislative competence on matters in the Concurrent Legislative list, whereas matters in the Residual Legislative list belong exclusively to the legislative competence of the State Assemblies. By the wide power given to the National Assembly by section 12(1), the Houses of Assembly of the various State have no say even on matters that ordinarily belong to their legislative competence. This is a mirror of the praxis in many federations where the federal executive enjoys exclusive competence in diplomatic relations and the making of treaties as the official representative of the sovereign State.[131] The pre-eminent powers of the National Assembly on treaty making over the federating States is confirmed by section 12(2) of the Constitution, which states: "The National Assembly may make laws for the Federation or any part thereof with respect to matters not included in the Exclusive Legislative list for the purpose of implementing a treaty." In other words, insofar as it concerns the implementation of a treaty, the legislative competence of the National Assembly is all-encompassing; it can make laws on matters in Exclusive, Concurrent and Residual legislative lists. In effect, the implementation of a treaty reduces all the constitutional legislative lists to just one and it is entrusted to the National Assembly. However, concerning matters ordinarily outside the Exclusive Legislative List, the domesticating powers of the National Assembly is qualified; it is not full and exclusive. To be domesticated, such treaties, pursuant to section 12(3), shall not be ratified by the assent of the President which is the protocol reserved for the ratification of treaties on matters in the Exclusive Legislative List. Instead, they shall be ratified by a majority of all the Houses of Assembly in the Federation.

Given the absolute provision of section 12(1) of the Constitution as to the indispensability of the intervention of the National Assembly for a treaty to have the force of law in Nigeria, section 3(2) of the Treaties Act appears to derogate from section 12(1) of the Constitution to the extent that it provides for certain treaties that can have the force of law without needing to be enacted into law by the National Assembly. It is submitted that, essentially, it is no

---

Exclusive Legislative List shall, save as otherwise provided in this Constitution, be to the exclusion of the Houses of Assembly of States."

131   Hugo Cyr, *Treaty Powers of Federated States and International Law*, available at http:// juspoliticum.com/article/Treaty-Powers-of-Federated-States-and-International-Law-1117 .html. Karol Karski & Tomasz Kamiński, *Treaty-Making Capacity of Components of Federal States from the Perspective of the Works of the UN International Law Commission*, available at https://www.researchgate.net/publication/323346732_TreatyMaking_Capacity _of_Components_of_Federal_States_from_the_Perspective_of_the_Works_of_the_UN _International_Law_Commission.

derogation from section 12(1). What it does is to isolate law-making agree-ments[132] from non-law-making agreements[133] and to provide for the necessity of enacting into law the law-making agreements before they can assume their status as pieces of legislation within the Nigerian domestic legal system. Non-law-making agreements, that is, agreements which impose financial, political and social obligations on Nigeria, or which are of scientific or technological import, and also agreements which deal with mutual exchange of cultural and educational facilities can be enforced in the country as such without needing to be made legislative rules. The power of the National Assembly under section 12(1) of the Constitution is a power to create for the country acts of legislation out of law-making international agreements and not the power to create legis-lation out of international agreements that are of concessionary or political or contractual character.[134]

6.3   *The Constitution of the Federal Republic of Nigeria (Third Alteration) Act, 2010*

This is an Act to alter the 1999 Constitution of the Federal Republic of Nigeria for the establishment of the National Industrial Court (NIC).[135] In section 6, the Act assigns jurisdictions to the NIC, and amongst them is the competence to apply any labor-related international convention or treaty ratified by Nigeria without the treaty needing to be enacted into law by the National Assembly pursuant to section 12(1) CFRN. It states specifically:

> Notwithstanding anything to the contrary in this Constitution, the National Industrial Court shall have the jurisdiction and power to deal with any matter connected with or pertaining to the application of any international convention, treaty or protocol of which Nigeria has ratified relating to labour, employment, workplace, industrial relations or matters connected therewith.[136]

---

132   A law-making agreement establishes a legal regime "towards all the world rather than towards particular parties." Catherine Brolmann, *Law-Making Treaties: Form and Function in International Law,* 74 Nordic J. Intl L. 383, 384 (2005).

133   These are "reciprocal" or "concessionary" obligations of a contract treaty, which provide for "a mutual interchange of benefits between the parties, with rights and obligations for each involving specific treatment at the hands of and towards each of the others individ-ually." *Id.*

134   *Id.* at 384. *See also* Gerald Fitzmaurice, *Third Report on the Law of Treaties,* U.N. Doc. A /CN.4/115, YILC 1958, Vol. II, at 27, article 18 para. 2.

135   Long title: Constitution of the Federal Republic of Nigeria (Third Alteration) Act, 2010.

136   S. 6, Third Alteration Act, S.254(C)(2) 1999 CFRN (As Amended).

This provision introduces a monist dimension to the implementation of international treaties under Nigerian law. An environmental convention that is labor-related would therefore be enforced judicially without needing to be enacted into law in the manner prescribed by section 12(1) CFRN.

The examination of the legal regime for the implementation of environmental conventions in Nigeria reveals that Nigeria is not lacking in a legal regime for the implementation of environmental conventions. It has a sufficient legal regime for the implementation of environmental conventions. Its legal regime embraces both the dualist (the Treaties Act and section 12 CFRN) and monist (section 254(C)(2) CFRN) avenues for the implementation of environmental conventions. Being that the possibility of a direct implementation of environmental conventions via the NIC is limited to labor-related issues, the domestication channel remains the broad-based avenue for the implementation of environmental conventions in the country. Unfortunately, this avenue has been put to little use even though many environmental conventions have been ratified by Nigeria. This makes it germane to explore the barriers that hinder the non-domestication of many environmental conventions in the country.

7 Barriers to the Domestication of Environmental Conventions in Nigeria

The non-domestication of environmental conventions in Nigeria is a product of many factors that are not very independent of one another. They overlap in some circumstances, principal amongst which are the following.

7.1 *The Duty of Initiating Domestication Is Unassigned*

Neither the Constitution nor the Treaties Act assigned the duty of introducing the bill for the domestication of a treaty to any agency. Section 12 CFRN only states the necessary and precedent requirement of domestication for a treaty to have a binding force in Nigeria and the extent of the domestication powers of the National Assembly, but it has no provision on who should introduce the bill for the domestication of a treaty in the National Assembly. It cannot be presumed that since the National Assembly is the national legislature, it falls to it alone to initiate the domestication process for treaties. It is also within the powers of the President to introduce Executive bills which can include bills for the domestication of treaties.[137] The lack of this clear-cut provision on

---

137   Lawpadi, *How Laws Are Made in Nigeria, available at* https://lawpadi.com/11-steps-to
-how-a-law-is-made-in-nigeria/.

who should initiate bills for the domestication of treaties is responsible for the blame game that goes on between the Federal Ministry of Justice (the depository of ratified treaties) and the National Assembly on the non-domestication of treaties including environmental conventions.[138] The National Assembly claims that it does not domesticate treaties because it has no information on the treaties ratified by the country.[139] Since the Treaties Act has made the Federal Ministry of Justice, a sector in the executive arm of government, the depository of ratified treaties, it is administratively better that the presidency bears the responsibility of introducing the bills for the domestication of these treaties. Moreover, it is the presidency that negotiated and ratified them.

7.2 Lack of Political Will

Political will refers to the impetus in following up with the appropriate and effective policy, law, or decision in public or political administration on the part of individuals who have the power to enforce a particular law, policy or decision. It is needed at all levels of governance and administration, national, state, local, etc. However efficient a legislation, policy or decision may be, without the will of the relevant authority for its enforcement, little positive result can be recorded. In this chapter, attention is paid to the lack of political will at the national level where the issue of domestication pertains. Many factors contribute to the lack of political will.

First is the age-long fear amongst developing countries that environmental protection is at the expense of their economic development. A corollary to this fear is the belief that greater economic development resulting in material prosperity far outweighs any damage that might be caused by resource exploitation, use and pollution.[140] This belief has not changed much over the years, and Nigeria is no exception to this mindset. Evidence is the lukewarm attitude of successive governments in Nigeria towards environmentalism. A glaring case is the continued flaring of gas in the country despite there being a legislation since 1979 prohibiting it from January 1st, 1984. Section 3(1) of the Associated Gas Re-injection Act states:

> Subject to subsection (2) of this section, no company engaged in the production of oil or gas shall after 1 January, 1984 flare gas produced in association with oil without the permission in writing of the Minister.

---

138 Salem, *Nigeria Yet to Domesticate, supra* note 4; Adesomoju, FG *Yet to Domesticate, supra* note 5.

139 *Id.*

140 Guruswamy, International Environmental Law, *supra* note 60, at 36.

Subsection 2 provides:

> Where the Minister is satisfied after 1 January, 1984 that utilization or
> re-injection of the produced gas is not appropriate or feasible in a partic-
> ular field or fields, he may issue a certificate in that respect to a company
> engaged in the production of oil or gas
> a.   specifying such terms and conditions, as he may at his discretion
>   choose to impose, for the continued flaring of gas in the particular
>   field or fields; or
> b.   permitting the company to continue to flare gas in the particular
>   field or fields if the company pays such sum as the Minister may
>   from time to time prescribe for every 28.317 Standard cubic metre
>   (SCM) of gas flared:
>
> Provided that, any payment due under this paragraph shall be made in
> the same manner and be subject to the same procedure as for the pay-
> ment of royalties to the Federal Government by companies engaged in
> the production of oil.

Gas flaring has continued unabated in the country despite its being prohibited by this statute.[141] The provision of subsection 2(b) to the effect that gas
flaring can continue on payment of money says it all on the subordination of
environmental protection to economic gains. Another example of the luke-
warmness of government towards environmental protection is the case of the
exclusion of the oil and gas sector from the regulatory powers of the national
environmental agency, the National Environmental Standards and Regulation
Enforcement Agency (NESREA). The agency was established with the objective
of having

> the responsibility for the protection and development of the environ-
> ment, biodiversity conservation and sustainable development of Nigeria's
> natural resources in general and environmental technology, including
> coordination and liaison with relevant stakeholders within and outside

---

141   Kingsley Mrabure & Benedicta Ohimor, *Unabated gas flaring menace in Nigeria. The need
       for proper gas utilization and strict enforcement of applicable laws*, 46 Commonwealth L.
       Bull. 753–779 (2020). Institute for Security Studies, *Are Nigeria's promises to end gas flar-
       ing merely hot air, available at* https://issafrica.org/iss-today/are-nigerias-promises-to-end
       -gas-flaring-merely-hot-air.

Nigeria on matters of enforcement of environmental standards, regulations, rules, laws, policies and guidelines.[142]

But the above power to protect the Nigerian environment is shielded from the
oil and gas sector, the very sector where gas flaring, oil spillage and other forms
of oil-related environmental pollution go on daily. The agency is barred from
enforcing environmental protection standards, regulations, rules, laws, policies and guidelines in the oil and gas sector. For instance, stating the functions
of the agency, section 7(g) of the NESREA Act provides: "They shall enforce
compliance with regulations on the importation, exportation, production, distribution, storage, sale, use, handling and disposal of hazardous chemicals and
waste *other than in the oil and gas sector* (emphasis added)." A similar exception is imposed with respect to the enforcement of regulations and standards
on noise, air, land, seas, oceans and other water bodies.[143] The exception is also
granted to the oil and gas sector in the enforcement of environmental control
measures through registration, licensing and permitting systems.[144] The oil
and gas sector is also exempted from the regulatory functions of the agency as
they relate to conducting environmental audits and establishing a data bank
on regulatory and enforcement mechanisms of environmental standards.[145]
Nigeria's non-ratification of the Bamako Convention on the Ban of the Import
into Africa and the Control of Transboundary Movement and Management
of Hazardous Wastes within Africa further evidences its subscription to the
unwholesome philosophy of "developmentism" that believes that economic
development outweighs whatever environmental degradation that is left in its
trail. Nigeria is a signatory to this Convention, which entered into force in 1998,
yet it has neither ratified it nor implemented it.[146] The Convention came as a
reaction of African countries to the Basel Convention on the Transboundary
Movement of Hazardous Wastes. Displeased that rather than ban outright
the transboundary movement of hazardous wastes into mostly developing
countries, the Basel Convention protected this movement. African countries

---

142   S. 2, NESREA Act 2018.

143   S. 7(h), NESREA Act 2007 (as amended).

144   S. 7(j), *id.*

145   S. 7(k), *id.*

146   *List of Countries which have signed, ratified/acceded to the Bamako Convention on the
       Ban of the Import into Africa and the Control of Transboundary Movement and Manage-
       ment of Hazardous Wastes within Africa. Available at* https://au.int/sites/default/files
       /treaties/7774-sl-bamako_convention_on_the_ban_of_the_import_into_africa_and_the
       _control_of_transboundary_movement_and_management_of_hazardous_wastes
       _within_africa.pdf .

negotiated and adopted the Bamako Convention to, *inter alia*, ban the import of hazardous wastes into Africa.[147]

Another cause of lack of political will is tribalism/ethnicism, which is recognized as a fault line of Nigeria.[148] This is the socio-political malaise whereby tribal/ethnic considerations come uppermost in making government policies, decisions, and legislations as well as in enforcing them. The effect is that many public authorities see their offices as being mainly for the good of the members of their ethnic nationalities or tribes or for the punishment or subjugation of their rivals. Regarding the domestication of environmental conventions, this unpatriotic mindset would result in relevant public authorities not being disposed to see an environmental convention that does not directly and immediately benefit their ethnic group enacted into law. The callous attitude of the federal government to responding adequately to the endemic oil-sector-related pollution can be attributed to the fact that the Niger Delta region (where oil is produced) is not composed of any of the dominant ethnic nationalities in the affairs of the country.[149]

7.3   *Ignorance of the Vulnerability of the Human Environment*

Despite the over fifty years of modern international environmental law, there is still widespread ignorance about the vulnerability of the human environment in Nigeria. People are usually aware of environmental issues that directly affect their immediate surroundings, but, beyond this point, they know little of how their actions can ill affect their immediate environment and the global environment on a long term. This connotes ignorance of the relevance of environmental conventions. Babalola, Babalola and Okhale studied the awareness and accessibility of environmental information in Nigeria using Delta State as a case study. Their finding is that the residents of Warri Central Local Government Area of Delta state, Nigeria, are very much aware of the environmental implication of soil erosion, bush burning, pipeline vandalization, and oil spillage, but most of them do not regard the burning of fuel wood for household cooking

---

147   Guruswamy, International Environmental Law, *supra* note 60, at 359–360.

148   Babatunde Adeshina, *Ethnicity as potent contributor of political conflicts in Nigeria, available at* https://www.grin.com/document/372182; Collins Adeyanju, *Politics of Ethnicity in Nigeria: The Way Forward. Available at* https://www.foresightfordevelopment.org/featured /ethnicity-tribalism.

149   Amnesty International, *Niger Delta Negligence, available at* https://www.amnesty.org / en/latest/news/2018/03/niger-delta-oil-spills-decoders/. Cyril Obi, *Nigeria's Niger Delta: Understanding the Complex Drivers of Violent Oil-related Conflict*, XXXIV(2) Africa Development 103–128 (2009).

as a source of environmental pollution.[150] They are aware of the environmental implication of soil erosion, bush burning, pipeline vandalization, and oil spillage because they experience directly and firsthand the environmental hazards of these occurrences in their area. But they do not understand that the use of fuel wood leads to deforestation. Ibrahim and Babayemi administered questionnaires to 1000 undergraduates of the University of Ibadan on environmentalism and they found a low level of awareness and knowledge of what it is all about.[151] Countering this ignorance is an area environmental NGOs distinguish themselves in developed countries,[152] but Nigeria is yet to have very active environmental NGOs. When much of the citizenry is ignorant about the environment and its polluters, they cannot muster the pressure to demand that government domesticates environmental conventions.

7.4   Poor Handling and Documentation of Treaties by the Federal Ministry of Justice

The Treaties (Making Procedure, Etc) Act[153] established the Federal Ministry of Justice as the depository for signed and/or ratified treaties. This evidently serves the need for records for ratified treaties for ease of domestication. However, there are indications that these records do not exist. It made headline news in 2017 that there was no record of treaties signed by Nigeria.[154] According to Adesomoju, "The Federal Government says it does not have an accessible, comprehensive and updated register of treaties and conventions to which Nigeria is a signatory."[155] Going further, Adesomoju reported: "The government stated that the nation lacked a list of both multilateral and bilateral treaties, not to talk of a published compendium."[156] The effect of this, according to

---

150   Yemisi Babalola, Akinola Babalola & Faith Okhale, *Awareness and Accessibility of Environmental Information in Nigeria: Evidence from Delta State*, available at https://www.researchgate.net/publication/268415529_Awareness_and_Accessibility_of_Environmental_Information_in_Nigeria_Evidence_from_Delta_State.

151   F. Ibrahim & O. Babayemi, *Knowledge and Attitude of a Group of Nigerian Undergraduates Towards Enviromentalism*, available at https://citeseerx.ist.psu.edu/viewdoc/download?doi=10.1.1.414.915&rep=rep1&type=pdf.

152   Aswin Azis, *The Role of Non-Governmental Organizations (NGO's) in Shaping Environmental Policies*, available at https://www.atlantis-press.com/proceedings/ulicoss-21/125968232; Eghosa Ekhator, *The Role of Non-Governmental Organisations in the Environmental Justice Paradigm* 8(2) Nnamdi Azikiwe U. J. Int'l L. & Jurisprudence 28–37 (2017).

153   Cap T20 LFN 2004.

154   Ade Adesomoju, *No record of treaties signed by Nigeria, says FG*, available at https://punchng.com/no-record-of-treaties-signed-by-nigeria-says-fg/.

155   *Id.*

156   *Id.*

him, among other things, is that many of the international agreements, such as human rights treaties and conventions are unimplemented.[157] When there is no proper handling and documentation of ratified treaties, including environmental conventions, domestication would be hampered. The National Assembly cannot domesticate an environmental convention that is lost.

8   Conclusion and Recommendations

As the leading African country that has participated very actively in the development of modern IEL, it is very unbecoming that Nigeria should be found wanting in the domestication of the many environmental conventions it has already ratified. Continuing on this lane is a disappointment to many less privileged African countries that look up to it for regional leadership in the area of environmental protection and development. It is also a disappointment to numerous Nigerian men and women who, whether as scholars or as players in the private sector, champion concerns for a healthy and clean environment. Nigeria cannot afford to present itself still as unconvinced of the propriety and necessity of the philosophy of sustainable development, which stands on the tripod of environmental protection, economic development and social development. Unfortunately, this is the unenviable position Nigeria gives itself with the non-domestication of many environmental conventions. Nigeria certainly can do better, and it should go ahead and do better.

To successfully do better, the Treaties Act should be amended to make it the duty of the presidency to introduce bills in the National Assembly for the domestication of treaties. This would forestall the blame game between the National Assembly and the executive. Nigeria needs to develop an environment culture that hinges on widespread and deep enlightenment on the environment, and the causes and effects of its pollution and degradation. This would help individuals to appreciate its vulnerability and consequences on human life. This would, in turn, make individuals able to resist every temptation to play down environmental protection whether as private individuals, public servants, politicians or policy makers. The fact that Nigeria has not domesticated many ratified environmental conventions means that there are individuals in government who, whether as politicians, legislators, public servants, or policymakers, do not sufficiently appreciate the importance of environmental protection. With a proper environment culture, the political will to domesticate ratified environmental conventions would increase.

---

157   *Id.*

CHAPTER 39

International Obligations and Duties Leading to Protecting Vulnerable States from the Climate Crisis

*Cosmin I. Corendea**

1   Introduction

It is a great privilege to contribute to this Festschrift in honor of Professor Siegfried Wiessner and his wonderful academic career and lifetime contribution to international law, whom I had the honor to learn from, both as a student and academic fellow. Soon after I had the opportunity to become Professor Wiessner's LL.M. student, I learned his fundamental theory on Policy-Oriented Jurisprudence, which, assisted by the progressive interpretation of law, helped me develop the International Hybrid Law Concept, a legal norm extensively used these days in climate change and human mobility research and litigation. This demonstrates the fantastic influence Professor Wiessner exercises in the international law arena, and his immense impact on the expansion of law, in general.

Today, I am honored to work with Professor Wiessner as an academic fellow, being one of the few who returned to his wonderful graduate program to teach as a visiting professor.

2   The International Law Regime

2.1   *General Obligations of the State*

States, in the international law context, acquire international obligations and responsibilities by expressing consent and becoming signatories to international treaties and conventions. Treaties create obligations based on the customary

*   Professor of Climate Law and Policy, Refugee and Migration Law and International Comparative Law; founding Vice Dean for Jindal School of Environment and Sustainability and member of the founding faculty for the LL.M. Programme in Environmental Law, Energy and Climate Change with WWF, in Delhi, India. Dr. Corendea is credited for initiating and developing "international hybrid law," an international legal concept which synergizes human rights, environmental and refugee/migration law in international climate law, revealed in his seminal book on this subject: Legal Protection of the Sinking Islands Refugees.

international law principle of *pacta sunt servanda* which posits that "agreements are binding."[1] This principle is considered as one of the oldest and a fundamental international law principle. It lays down that all the subjects of international law ought to fulfill their rights, duties, and obligations in good faith.[2] In the legal context, this principle establishes the "character of international law as law" and brings forth the binding nature of the law.[3] Further, consent remains crucial as it is only through consent States can establish rules which are legally binding in nature.[4]

Thereby, treaties usually do not impose obligations on States that have not signed or ratified them, due to the lack of "consent," unless the treaties codify or reflect customary international law. If a treaty reflects customary international law, then non-parties compulsorily become bound by it,[5] unless they have been persistent objectors to that customary international law rule.

Obligations under international law don't merely include duties, but also rights of the State. These duties and rights ought to be exercised in *good faith* and in conformity with the purposes and principles of the law, without causing any bias or harm to the interests and rights of other subjects of the law. Further, the content, as well as the method of establishing and exercising international obligations, must be in accordance with the principles and rules of international law.[6] The principle of good faith mandates that both the implementation of the rules which impose obligations as well as the very fulfilment of the obligation must be done while refraining from those actions which could defeat the object and purpose of the rule.

Under international law, every State is obliged to fulfil its obligations in good faith, arising particularly out of:[7]

a.   the UN Charter; treaties; or customary international law and general principles of law recognized by civilized nations.

The binding (or non-binding) nature and the scope of State obligations under international law in the area under review have been primarily defined and

---

1   Vienna Convention on the Law of Treaties, art.26, May 23, 1969, U.N.T.S. Vol. 1155, at 331 (entered into force January 27, 1980).

2   *Id.* at Preamble.

3   *Id.* at art. 26.

4   *Id.*

5   Michael Akehurst, *Custom as a Source of International Law,* 47 Brit. Y.B. Int'l L. 1, 29 (1976).

6   U.N.General Assembly, *Declaration on Principles of International Law concerning Friendly Relations and Cooperation among States in accordance with the Charter of the United Nations,* U.N. Doc. A/RES/2625(XXV) (Oct. 24, 1970).

7   I.I.Lukashuk, *The Principle Pacta Sunt Servanda and the Nature of Obligation Under International Law,* 83 Am. J. Int'l L. 513–518 (1989).

shaped through the UN Covenant on Economic, Social and Cultural Rights (ICESCR) and, particularly, the Limburg Principles on the Implementation of the ICESCR, if this treaty has been accepted by the State at issue or the principle at issue reflects customary international law.

2.2   *Obligations of the State under International Environmental Law*

Under traditional international law, the responsibility of the State would be limited to the damage caused by it, when it can be clearly and reasonably proved that the State's unlawful activity caused the said damage. However, with respect to environmental issues, this traditional international law framework has proven to be inadequate as it suffers from various shortcomings such as difficulty in proving liability, and determining the nature of responsibility of non-State offenders.[8] Therefore there has been a steady shift towards a regime of international co-operation under international environmental law.

The nature and extent of State responsibility and obligations have been defined and laid down through various treaties, conventions and resolutions by international bodies. The United Nations General Assembly adopted a wide range of resolutions, and, after the Stockholm Conference of 1972, the United Nation Environment Programme (UNEP) was set up.[9] This organization played a crucial role in the development and evolution of conventions concerning the protection of the environment.

The obligations of the State can be better understood through the rights provided under international law, one such being the international human right to a clean environment.[10] Further, there exists a wide range of human rights provisions which intersect with environmental responsibility, such as the right to life, the right to an adequate standard of living, the right to health, and the right to food. The Stockholm Declaration (1972) laid down in its preamble that the environment was "essential to ... the enjoyment of basic human rights – even the right to life itself."[11] Further Principle 1 of the Declaration

---

8   Krista Singleton-Cambage, *International Legal Sources and Global Environmental Crises: The Inadequacy of Principles, Treaties, and Custom,* 2 ILSA J. Int'l & Comp. L. 171, 174–179 (1995).

9   U.N.General Assembly, *2997 (XXVII). Institutional and financial arrangements for international environmental cooperation,* U.N. Doc.A/RES/27/2997 (Dec.15, 1972).

10 United Nations Human Rights Council, *The human right to a clean, healthy and sustainable environment,* U.N.Doc.A/HRC/RES/48/13 (Oct.18, 2021).

11 Declaration of the United Nations Conference on the Human Environment, in *Report of the United Nations Conference on the Human Environment,* chap.1, U.N. Doc.A/CONF.48/14 (1972) [hereinafter Stockholm Declaration].

states, "Man has the fundamental right to freedom, equality and adequate conditions of life, in an environment of a quality that permits a life of dignity and well-being."[12]

Additionally, the African Charter on Human and People's Rights of 1981 provides that "all people shall have the right to a general satisfactory environment favorable to their development."[13] It is also stated in Article 11 of the Additional Protocol to the American Convention on Human Rights of 1988 that "everyone shall have the right to live in a healthy environment" and that "the states parties shall promote the protection, preservation and improvement of the environment."[14]

2.3 *State Responsibility and the Environment*

State responsibility towards the environment arises from those principles that have acquired the nature of customary international law, as well as from treaties that the States have become party to. To understand these responsibilities, certain general principles of environmental law that have been established through treaties, customary practices and soft law engagement must be discussed.

2.3.1 The Principle of Territorial Sovereignty

The principle of territorial sovereignty, through Principle 21 of the Stockholm Declaration, has been deemed to be part of customary international law by the ICJ in its 1996 Advisory Opinion on *The Legality of the Threat or Use of Nuclear Weapons*.[15] However, its initial conceptions can be traced back to many UN General Assembly resolutions.[16]

According to this principle, every State has the sovereign right to (i) make its own policies relating to natural resources present within its territorial boundaries; (ii) exploit its own natural resources – all in accordance with the UN Charter and international law principles. This right, however, is accompanied

---

12   *Id.* at Principle 1.
13   Organization of African Unity (OAU), *African Charter on Human and Peoples' Rights* (*"Banjul Charter"*), June 27, 1981, CAB/LEG/67/3 rev. 5, 21 I.L.M. 58 (1982).
14   Organization of American States (OAS), *Additional Protocol to the American Convention on Human Rights in the Area of Economic, Social and Cultural Rights* (*"Protocol of San Salvador"*), Nov.17, 1988, A-52 (entered into force Nov.16, 1999).
15   Legality of the Threat or Use of Nuclear Weapons, Advisory Opinion, I.C.J. Reports 1996, p.226 (July 1996).
16   Phillipe Sands, Jacqueline Peel, Adriana Fabra & Ruth MacKenzie, Principles of International Environmental Law 191 (3d ed. 2012); *see, e.g.,* U.N.G.A. Res. 523 (VI) (1950); Res. 626 (VII) (1952); Res. 837 (IX) (1954); Res. 1314 (XIII) (1958); Res. 1515 (XV) (1960).

by the responsibility to respect other States' sovereignty and not to take measures that may cause damage to other States' environment.[17]

This principle not only provided for the making of policy and exploitation of resources but also for the safeguarding of a State's environment – the Preamble of the Basel Convention, for example, granted the right to ban import of hazardous wastes.[18] Further, the Preamble to the 1992 Biodiversity Convention explicitly stated that States have sovereign rights over their natural resources.

However, the limitations of a blanket application of the principle of territorial sovereignty were observed onward of 1970.[19] For instance, regarding matters where jurisdiction was unclear, as on the high seas and in the atmosphere, States could not exercise their sovereign rights of exploitation. While Principle 12 of the Rio Declaration did not permit unilateral action (it only provided for said action to be avoided), it was interpreted that there was no prohibition of it. Yet, the *Iron Rhine* case[20] holds that certain considerations of environmental protection will apply if extra-territorial power is exercised by States. This statement was based on the decision by the Permanent Court of International Justice (PCIJ) in the *Lotus* case[21] where it was opined that power may not be exercised extra-territorially except in cases of a permissive rule that may be derivative of customary or treaty law. Part of this treaty law though not customary law is the practice of seeking Prior Informed Consent.

2.3.2   Prior Informed Consent

Prior Informed Consent (PIC) emphasizes the need for prior (before action is taken) and informed consent of the party which may be affected by the action. PIC has been utilized in two manners in international law. The first manner is signified by Article 8(j) of the 1992 Biodiversity Convention which mandates the need for the prior and informed consent of indigenous peoples before the utilization of their traditional knowledge. The second manner is that regarding the transfer of waste from one State to another. In this manner, the transferor State must seek and gain the Prior and Informed Consent of the transferee

---

17   Stockholm Declaration, *supra* note 11, at Principle 21.

18   Convention on the Control of Transboundary Movements of Hazardous Wastes and Their Disposal, Mar.22, 1989, 1673 U.N.T.S. 126 (entered into force May 5, 1992) [hereinafter Basel Convention].

19   Phillipe Sands, Jacqueline Peel, Adriana Fabra & Ruth MacKenzie, *supra* note 16, at 192.

20   Iron Rhine Arbitration (Belgium v Netherlands), Award, ICGJ 373 (PCA 2005), (May 24, 2005), ¶223.

21   S.S. "Lotus" (France v. Turkey), Judgment No 9, P.C.I.J. Series A No. 10, ICGJ 248 (PCIJ 1927) Sept.7, 1927).

State for any waste that it wants to export, so as to ascertain that the trans-feree State has the capacity to manage the waste. This need for PIC has been enshrined under Principle 14 of the Rio Declaration.

This Transfer has been manifested in two ways: (i) substance-by-substance method; and (ii) shipment-by-shipment method. The substance-by-substance method is depicted in the 1998 Rotterdam Convention[22] which mandates information exchange, while the shipment-by-shipment method is illustrated by Article 6 of the 1989 Basel Convention.

The concept of PIC, however, cannot be deemed to be a principle of custom-ary international law.[23]

2.3.3   The Principle of Preventive Action

The Principle of Prevention/Preventive Action is envisioned under Principle 21 of the Stockholm Declaration of 1972. However, it digresses from Principle 21 in the purpose of its formulation and application. Principle 21 aims to uphold the principle of sovereignty in order to protect other States from suffering damage, while the Principle of Preventive Action focuses its attention on minimizing environmental damage.[24] Further is the State to not only prevent transbound-ary harm, but also domestic (intra-jurisdictional) harm.[25]

Before being recognised as a principle of customary international law, pre-ventive action appeared in other instruments[26] like the Article 193 of the UN Convention on the Law of the Sea (UNCLOS)[27] which recognised a "duty to pro-tect and preserve the marine environment," the Preamble of the United Nations Framework Convention on Climate Change (UNFCCC),[28] and Principle 2 of the Rio Declaration.[29]

---

22   Rotterdam Convention on the Prior Informed Consent Procedure for Certain Hazardous Chemicals and Pesticides in International Trade, Sept.10, 1998, U.N.T.S. Vol. 2244, at 337 (entered into force Feb.24, 2004) [hereinafter Rotterdam Convention].

23   Pierre-Marie Dupuy & Jorge E. Viñuales, International Environmental Law 77 (2d ed. 2018).

24   Phillipe Sands, Jacqueline Peel, Adriana Fabra & Ruth MacKenzie, *supra* note 16, at 201.

25   *Id.*

26   Pierre-Marie Dupuy & Jorge E. Viñuales, *supra* note 23, at 59.

27   Convention on the Law of the Sea, Dec. 10, 1982, 1833 U.N.T.S. 397. Article 193 states that, "*States have the sovereign right to exploit their natural resources pursuant to their environmental policies and in accordance with their duty to protect and preserve the marine environment.*"

28   United Nations Framework Convention on Climate Change, May 9, 1992, U.N.T.S. vol. 1771, p. 107 (entered into force March 21, 1994).

29   U.N.General Assembly, *Annex I: Rio Declaration on Environment and Development, adopted* June 14, 1992, U.N.Doc.A/CONF.151/26 (Vol. I) (Aug.12, 1992) [hereinafter Rio Declaration].

However, citing Principles 21 and 2 of the Stockholm Declaration and the Rio Declaration, the ICJ opined in its *Advisory Opinion on the Legality of Nuclear Weapons*[30] that the Principle of Prevention is a principle of general international law.[31] Further, the ICJ in the *Pulp Mills* case[32] stated that the customary principle of preventive action has its roots in "due diligence."

At present, the Principle of Preventive Action is considered a principle of general international law encompassing within its ambit treaties that aim to prevent, *inter alia*,[33] air pollution,[34] adverse effects of climate change,[35] and "degradation of the natural environment."[36]

2.3.4 The Principle of Co-Operation

The Principles of Co-operation and Good Neighbourliness are to be interpreted *en ensemble*, according to Article 74 of the UN Charter.[37] Co-operation was established as a duty under GA Resolution 2625 (XXV).[38] This principle is a representation of the maxim *sic utere tuo et alienum non laedas*[39] and is referred to in Principle 24 of the Stockholm Declaration and Principle 27 of the Rio Declaration which give importance to co-operation in good faith in matters that concern the environment.

Principle 2 states that, '... *the responsibility to ensure that activities within their jurisdiction or control do not cause damage to the environment of other States or of areas beyond the limits of national jurisdiction.*'

30 Legality of the Threat or Use of Nuclear Weapons, *supra* note 15.

31 Pierre-Marie Dupuy & Jorge E. Viñuales, *supra* note 23, at 59.

32 Pulp Mills on the River Uruguay (Argentina v Uruguay), Judgment, I.C.J. Reports 2010, at 14, ¶101.

33 Phillipe Sands, Jacqueline Peel, Adriana Fabra & Ruth MacKenzie, *supra* note 16, at 202.

34 Convention on long-range transboundary air pollution, Nov.13, 1979, U.N.T.S. Vol. 1302, at 217 (entered into force March 16, 1983), art. 2.

35 United Nations Framework Convention on Climate Change, *supra* note 28, at art.2.

36 Agreement on the Conservation of Nature and Natural Resources, *adopted on* July 9, 1985, art. 11. (Agreement still not in force; *see 1985 Agreement on the Conservation of Nature and Natural Resources*, Centre for International Law, National University of Singapore, https:// cil.nus.edu.sg/databasecil/1985-agreement-on-the-conservation-of-nature-and-natural -resources/.

37 United Nations, *Charter of the United Nations*, June 26, 1945, 1 U.N.T.S. XVI (Oct.24, 1945), art. 74. It states that, "*Members of the United Nations also agree that their policy ... must be based on the general principle of good-neighborliness, due account being taken of the interests and well-being of the rest of the world, in social, economic, and commercial matters.*'

38 U.N. General Assembly, *supra* note 6.

39 Phillipe Sands, Jacqueline Peel, Adriana Fabra & Ruth MacKenzie, *supra* note 16, at 203.

The obligation to co-operate has been recognized in two manners[40]: general co-operation with regard to the treaty's objectives; and co-operation for specific commitments like the sharing of information, environmental impact assessment, application of the principle of prior informed consent,[41] and the prevention of transboundary harm.[42]

In the matter of the *MOX Plant*,[43] the ITLOS held that the duty to co-operate is a fundamental principle. It is a principle that represents the duty to share information, specifically that regarding emergency and to evaluate the environmental impacts of activities.

2.3.5   The Principle of Sustainable Development

The Principle of Sustainable Development was first featured in the Preamble of the 1992 EEA Agreement,[44] though the term was coined in the Brundtland Report of 1987 which defined it as "development that meets the needs of the present without compromising the ability of future generations to meet their own needs." It has since become a principle of international law, as per the 2002 Delhi Declaration of Principles of International Law Relating to Sustainable Development.[45]

Four interlinked principles fall within Sustainable Development's ambit: (i) the principle of intergenerational equity which addresses the preservation of natural resources; (ii) the principle of sustainable use which emphasizes the "sustainable" or "wise" exploitation of natural resources; (iii) the principle of equitable use which promotes inter-state consideration of "need"; and (iv) the principle of integration which states that environmental sustainable development must be integrated with economic and other development plans (purporting necessary intersectionality). These elements were brought together under Article 33 of the Lomé Convention of 1989. Further, Principle 4 of the

---

40   *Id.* at 204.

41   Rotterdam Convention, *supra* note 22.

42   Draft articles on Prevention of Transboundary Harm from Hazardous Activities, *adopted on* Aug.10, 2001, U.N. Doc. A/RES/56/82 (2001), U.N. Doc. A/56/10, art.4.

43   MOX Plant (Ireland v. United Kingdom), Provisional Measures, Order of 3 December 2001, ITLOS Reports 2001, at 95.

44   Agreement on the European Economic Area (Oporto), May 2, 1992, O.J.E.C. No. L1 (entered into force January 1, 1994).

45   International Law Association, *New Delhi Declaration of Principles of International Law Relating to Sustainable Development*, 49 Netherlands Int'l L. Rev. 299 (2002).

Rio Declaration[46] and Principle 13 of the Stockholm Declaration also emphasize the principle of integration.

Though it is considered a "principle" of international law, the ICJ in the *Gabčíkovo-Nagymaros Project* case[47] referred to it as a "concept" and reaffirmed it in the *Pulp Mills* case.[48] However, upon referring to it as a "principle" under the ICJ, the Permanent Court of Arbitration clarified that as a principle, sustainable development meant the application of all other environmental law principles.[49]

2.3.6   The Precautionary Principle

The Precautionary Principle began appearing in instruments of international law around the 1980s.[50] It is formulated in Principle 15 of the Rio Declaration as a principle that promotes action being taken without the absence of scientific certainty being a hindrance. Principle 15, however, includes the criterion of cost-effectiveness which is absent from earlier conceptions of the principle.[51]

This principle's primary objective is to allow pre-emptive measures to be taken "precautionarily" where there is a lack of scientific evidence for the damage being caused to the environment. It has widely been used for the protection of the marine environment, though its general applicability linked to sustainable development was highlighted in the Bergen Ministerial Declaration of 1990. This general applicability, however, did require that such environmental threat must be "serious" or "irreversible" for the principle to apply – this can also be seen in Article 3(3) of the 1992 Climate Change Convention.

Though the scope of the principle is unclear, its objective can be determined to be the regulation of activities that may cause harm to the environment

---

46   Rio Declaration, *supra* note 29, Principle 4. It states that, "[i]*n order to achieve sustainable development, environmental protection shall constitute an integral part of the development process and cannot be considered in isolation from it.*"

47   Gabčíkovo-Nagymaros Project (Hungary/Slovakia), Judgment, ICJ Reports 1997, at 7.

48   Pulp Mills on the River Uruguay (Argentina/Uruguay), Judgment, ICJ Reports 2010, p. 14.

49   Pierre-Marie Dupuy & Jorge E. Viñuales, *supra* note 23, at 93.

50   Phillipe Sands, Jacqueline Peel, Adriana Fabra & Ruth MacKenzie, *supra* note 16, at 217.

51   *See generally,* International Convention Relating to Intervention on the High Seas in Cases of Oil Pollution Casualties, 1969, U.N.T.S.vol.970, p.211 (May 25, 1975), Arts. I and V(3) (a); Vienna Convention for the Protection of the Ozone Layer, March 22, 1985, U.N.T.S. vol. 1513, p. 293 (entered into force Sept. 22, 1988), Preamble; Montreal Protocol on Substances that Deplete the Ozone Layer, Sept. 16, 1987, U.N.T.S. Vol. 1522, at 3 (entered into force Jan. 1, 1989), Preamble; and U.N. General Assembly, *Bergen Ministerial Declaration on Sustainable Development in the ECE Region* in *Report of the Economic Commission for Europe on the Bergen Conference,* U.N. Doc. A/CONF.151/PC/10 (Aug. 6, 1990), at 18–28.

notwithstanding the lack of conclusive evidence regarding the potential damage to the environment.[52] This, however, raises the question of burden of proof which traditionally lies on the party seeking regulation/prohibition. The principle, however, supports an alternative approach wherein the party wishing to carry out the activity must prove that it does not harm the environment.[53] This alternative approach, however, is not accepted by the ICJ.[54]

The status quo of the law can be determined by the ICJ's opinions on the principle's applicability. In the *Nuclear Tests (New Zealand v. France)* case,[55] the ICJ refrained from commenting on the principle of precaution, but opined that the principle was gaining support in terms of becoming a part of international law given its evolution to meet the evidentiary difficulty that often surfaces.[56] Further on, in the *Gabčíkovo-Nagymaros* case[57] the ICJ avoided talking about the principle, but did order and emphasize the need for precautionary measures.[58] Finally, in the *Pulp Mills* case, the ICJ rejected the reversal of the burden of proof but in doing so recognised the precautionary principle as part of international law.[59]

2.3.7   The Polluter Pays Principle

This Polluter Pays Principle posits that the cost of environmental degradation must be borne by the person causing the pollution – that is the producer, and eventually the consumer. Though this principle has not garnered as much support as the aforementioned principles, Principle 16 of the Rio Declaration enshrines it and speaks for the promotion of "internalisation of environmental costs... that the polluter should, in principle, bear the costs of pollution. ..."

With this principle, however, come several problems such as the determination of the larger cost, the probability of the damage being caused in order to pre-emptively implement the cost, and the determination of the individual's cost.

---

52   Phillipe Sands, Jacqueline Peel, Adriana Fabra & Ruth MacKenzie, *supra* note 16, at 222.
53   *Id.*
54   Pulp Mills on the River Uruguay, *supra* note 32, where the ICJ rejected the reversal of the burden of proof.
55   Nuclear Tests (New Zealand v. France), Judgment, ICJ Reports 1974, at 457.
56   Phillipe Sands, Jacqueline Peel, Adriana Fabra & Ruth MacKenzie, *supra* note 16, at 223.
57   Gabčíkovo-Nagymaros Project, *supra* note 47.
58   *Id.*
59   Pulp Mills on the River Uruguay, *supra* note 48.

2.3.8   The Principle of Common But Differentiated Responsibility
            (CBDR)

This principle talks about a common responsibility that must be differentiated among States on the basis of capabilities and historical accounts of responsibility (or lack thereof).[60] By considering the capabilities, this principle recognises the need for development of certain States as compared to others – this can be seen in Principle 7 of the Rio Declaration which says that "States have common but differentiated responsibilities. The developed countries acknowledge the responsibility that they bear in the international pursuit for sustainable development. ..."

The determination of what is a common responsibility rests primarily on the proprietorship of the resource in question – if it is not owned by a single State, it often becomes of common concern.[61] This is reflected in the Preamble of the 1992 Climate Change Convention wherein climate change is deemed to be a "common concern of humankind," as well as in the Preamble of the 1992 Biodiversity Convention.[62] While this principle has been used in areas such as Antarctica, the deep seabed, the ozone regime and, and international trade, it is applicable to the three major areas of the ozone layer, climate change, and biodiversity.[63]

When considering differentiated responsibility, certain criteria such as special needs, future economic development of developing countries, and historic contributions to causing an environmental problem are considered. For instance, the United Nations Convention on the Law of the Sea of 1982 considered the future economic needs of nations, while the nation's means of disposal and capabilities were considered in the 1985 Vienna Convention.[64] By considering these criteria, convention compliance deadlines are often relaxed for developing countries and other such graces are provided.[65]

---

60   Pierre-Marie Dupuy & Jorge E. Viñuales, *supra* note 23, at 83.
61   Phillipe Sands, Jacqueline Peel, Adriana Fabra & Ruth MacKenzie, *supra* note 16, at 234.
62   Convention on Biological Diversity, 1760 UNTS 79, 31 ILM 818, 1992 at Preamble.
63   Pierre-Marie Dupuy & Jorge E. Viñuales, *supra* note 23, at 83.
64   Convention for the Protection of the Ozone Layer, 1513 UNTS 293, 26 ILM 1529, 1988, at Article 2.
65   Phillipe Sands, Jacqueline Peel, Adriana Fabra & Ruth MacKenzie, *supra* note 16, at 235.

2.4 *International Law Cases Upholding Principles of International (Environmental) Law*

2.4.1 The ICJ's Advisory Opinion on the Legality of Threat or Use of Nuclear Weapons of 8 July 1996[66]

The ICJ, by a vote of thirteen to one, decided to comply with the request for an advisory opinion by the UN General Assembly. It was unanimously decided that there is neither customary, nor conventional, international law that gives any specific authorization to the threat or use of nuclear weapons.

In doing so, the ICJ referred to the PCIJ's opinion in the *Lotus* case[67] where it was held that restrictions upon the sovereignty and independence of States cannot be presumed.[68]

Having established the stance of the Court on the general threat or use of nuclear weapons, certain questions regarding the prohibition on the basis of international principles must be considered.

The Court considered the argument made before it, regarding the protection of environment under Protocol I of 1977 to the Geneva Conventions of 1949.[69] It was argued that by not prohibiting the use of nuclear weapons, the environment is put at great risk of damage.

However, the Court opined that this obligation, though applicable during both wartime and peacetime, would not infringe upon the right to self-defence of a State. The Court did, however, say that necessity and proportionality must be observed, keeping in mind this obligation and environmental considerations. The Court additionally noted Principle 24 of the Rio Declaration and emphasized the duty of the States to provide environmental protection in times of war.

The Court opined, while considering the General Assembly resolution 47/37 of 25 November 1992 on "Protection of the Environment in Times of Armed Conflict," that, though existing international law does not prohibit the use of nuclear weapons, it does place a general obligation to give proper heed to environmental considerations while implementing principles and rules in armed conflict.[70]

The Court later considered principles of international humanitarian law in order to determine the legality of threat or use of nuclear weapons. In doing

---

66   Legality of the Threat or Use of Nuclear Weapons, *supra* note 15.
67   S.S. "Lotus," *supra* note 21.
68   *Id*
69   *Id.*
70   *Id.*

so, the Court acknowledged the Hague Conventions (1899 and 1907) and the Geneva Conventions (1864, 1906, 1929 and 1949) and noted the prohibitions they place on chemical and bacteriological weapons. Further, the Court noted the "cardinal principles"[71] which include the principle of civilian protection and the principle of avoiding unnecessary suffering of combatants (which limits the weapons States may use) and held that these principles are to be abided by by States regardless of their ratification of the conventions, given their customary nature.

The Court opined that by becoming part of *jus cogens* under Article 53 of the Vienna Convention on the Law of Treaties of 1969, humanitarian law cannot be violated.

The Court addressed concerns regarding whether humanitarian law that existed prior to the invention of nuclear weapons would apply to nuclear weapons, and opined that it would, no matter the qualitative and quantitative difference between nuclear weapons and conventional arms.

The Court went on to examine the principle of neutrality, which protected neutral territory from belligerent incursion, and opined that it was part of customary international law, thus making it applicable to the threat or use of nuclear weapons.[72]

The key finding of the Court allows for the threat or use of nuclear weapons in an "extreme circumstance of self-defence, in which the very survival of a State would be at stake":

By seven votes to seven, by the President's casting vote,

> It follows from the above-mentioned requirements that the threat or use of nuclear weapons would generally be contrary to the rules of international law applicable in armed conflict, and in particular the principles and rules of humanitarian law;
>
> However, in view of the current state of international law, and of the elements of fact at its disposal, the Court cannot conclude definitively whether the threat or use of nuclear weapons would be lawful or unlawful in an extreme circumstance of self-defence, in which the very survival of a State would be at stake.[73]

---

71   Legality of the Threat or Use of Nuclear Weapons, *supra* note 15, ¶78, at 257.

72   *Id.* ¶89, at 261.

73   *Id.*, ¶105, at 44.

2.4.2   The ICJ's Judgment on Pulp Mills on the River Uruguay (Argentina
           v. Uruguay) of 20 April 2010[74]

This case arose before the ICJ on application by the Argentine Republic
("Argentina") against the Eastern Republic of Uruguay ("Uruguay") for constructing mills on the left bank of the river Uruguay in breach of a treaty signed
between both States.

After extensively discussing its jurisdictional authority, the Court moved
onto discussing the procedural obligations between the States. With the sharing of information being in dispute, the Court noted that the obligation to
inform the Administrative Commission of the River Uruguay ("CARU") as well
as the other State in order to negotiate was present under the 1975 Statute of
the River Uruguay ("1975 Statute") that both States had signed. It pointed to
the principle of prevention as a customary international rule and opined that
informing CARU was a necessary step to fulfil the obligation of prevention. The
Court held, for reasons based on the facts, that since Uruguay did not transmit
the correct information in a procedurally sound manner to CARU, it breached
its obligation under Article 7 of the 1975 Statute.

Further, in deciding Uruguay's breach in notifying Argentina, the Court
referred to the principles of sovereignty (the obligation to not cause transboundary harm) and co-operation.

The Court also noted that the 1975 Statute was "perfectly in keeping with
the requirements of international law … since the mechanism for co-operation
between States is governed by the principle of good faith," citing Article 26 of
the Vienna Convention of 1969 – thus confirming the applicability of the principles in bi/multilateral treaties that bound States.[75]

The Court, though averse to the reversal of the burden of proof under the
precautionary principle, recognized the legal authority of the principle of
precaution.[76]

Considering the principle of equitable and reasonable use, the Court held
that all pre-existing legitimate uses of the river must be taken into account and
said that "if the interests of the other riparian State in the shared resource and
the environmental protection of the latter were not taken into account," then
the principle cannot be said to have been complied with.[77]

While considering the measures to be taken to avoid change in the ecological
balance, the Court noted that to prevent transboundary harm, co-ordination

---

74   Pulp Mills on the River Uruguay, *supra* note 32.
75   *Id.* ¶145, at 67.
76   *Id.* ¶164, at 71.
77   *Id.* ¶177, at 75.

must be engaged in by both parties. The duty to implement the principle of prevention and co-ordination imposed an obligation on both States to "take positive steps to avoid changes in the ecological balance."[78] Whereas, considering the question of whether or not Uruguay conducted an Environmental Impact Assessment ("EIA"), the Court opined that it was agreed upon by the States to conduct an EIA and so it bound them (under the principle of co-ordination), and that such EIA must be conducted prior to the implementation of the project. Regarding the content of the EIA, the Court held that the UNEP Goals and Principles are not binding on the parties but are mere guidelines to be considered, and that the scope and detail of the report depended on the environmental significance of the effect the project may have.

The Court, on the matter of protection of biodiversity, held that both States had the obligation to preserve the aquatic environment including its flora and fauna.

3   The Climate Change Regime

The existing climate change legal framework can be explored through two main instruments: the National Adaptation Plan(s) ("NAP(s)") and the Nationally Determined Contributions ("NDCs").

3.1   *National Adaptation Plans*
The 7th Conference of Parties ("COP") in 2001, under Article 4.9 of the United Nations Framework Convention on Climate Change ("UNFCCC"), established the least developed countries ("LDC") work program entitled "National Adaptation Programmes of Action" ("NAPA").[79] This was developed to support the LDCs in their journey to address and mitigate climate change. The COP further established the "Least Developed Countries Fund" ("LDCF") to fund the LDCs in preparing and implementing their NAPAs[80] and also to fund the LDC Expert Group ("LEG"), which would provide technical support and act as an advisor to the LDCs.[81]

---

78   *Id.* ¶185, at 76.
79   *National Adaptation Programmes of Action,* United Nations Climate Change (July 13, 2022), https://unfccc.int/topics/resilience/workstreams/national-adaptation-programmes -of-action/introduction.
80   *Id.*
81   *Id.*

The NAPA was later incorporated into a larger framework titled "National Adaptation Plan" ("NAP"). The latter was introduced through the 16th COP (2010) in Cancun and applied to all countries regardless of their development stage. It intends to identify medium and long-term adaptation needs, which enables parities to develop and enforce mitigation and adaptation plans. The NAP is envisioned to be "comprehensive and provide a system in which countries can iteratively create and update adaptation plans."[82] The Paris Agreement is the key source of law which establishes a duty on the state party to formulate and release a National Adaptation Plan.

3.2   *Nationally Determined Contributions (NDCs)*

The NDCs were introduced through the Paris Agreement.[83] Under Article 4, Paragraph 2[84] of the Paris Agreement, a request for each country to create and communicate their plan of action with respect to climate change, which is termed as their "Nationally Determined Contributions," is established. The Paris Agreement, however, does not provide for any specific standard or limit, keeping in mind that the control of emissions and NDCs would be different for developing countries.

The NDCs are submitted every five years to the UNFCCC Secretariat. The last submitted NDC was in 2020, and 2025 would be the upcoming deadline for the revised NDC. The Paris Agreement provides that each successive NDC should represent a progression compared to the previous NDCs submitted by the State.

3.3   *NDCs and NAPs: Instruments of International Obligation*

The requirement of NDCs creates an international procedural obligation on the State, through the usage of the words "prepare, communicate, and maintain successive [NDCs] that it intends to achieve" in the Paris Agreement, creates a procedural obligation on each State.[85] Further, the usage of the term

---

82   LDC Expert Group, *The National Adaptation Plan Process: A Brief Overview*, United Nations Framework Convention on Climate Change (Dec. 2012), https://unfccc.int/files/adaptation /application/pdf/nap_overview.pdf.

83   Paris Agreement to the United Nations Framework Convention on Climate Change, Dec. 12, 2015, T.I.A.S. No. 16-1104.

84   *Id.* at art.4(2). It states, "*Each Party shall prepare, communicate, and maintain successive nationally determined contributions that it intends to achieve. Parties shall pursue domestic mitigation measures, with the aim of achieving the objectives of such contributions.*"

85   Benoit Mayer, *International Law Obligations Arising in relation to Nationally Determined Contributions*, 7(2) Transnat'l Env'tal L. 251 (July 2018); Christina Voigt, *The Compliance*

"shall" in Article 4.2, instead of "should," indicates the legally obligatory nature of this requirement.[86]

Moreover, Article 4.2 creates an obligation on individual parties, as the parties collectively cannot constitute a legal personality, and thereby cannot collectively undertake legal obligations.[87] An alternative interpretation, which would lead to a collective obligation, would be inconsistent with the usage of the word "shall," which aims to create a legal obligation. Therefore, the obligation in the said provision applies to each party individually.[88] This further establishes that the Paris Agreement clearly lays down a legal duty upon each party including obligations of procedural nature.

Further, the second sentence of Article 4.2 indicates it to be an obligation based on conduct wherein the parties to the agreement ought to "pursue measures" which they reasonably believe will achieve the objective.[89] Therefore, there is an obligation to pursue the measures and obligations, determined by the parties, in good faith.[90] This can be contrasted with the obligation based on results, wherein the party would breach its obligation on the ground that the mitigation objectives of its NDC have not been realized.[91] Thereby, the objectives of the NDCs constitute a benchmark for the stringency of the measures; they ought to be pursued by the State;[92] and a party to the Paris Agreement could breach its obligations of conduct by failing to take relevant measures

---

and *Implementation Mechanism of the Paris Agreement*, 25(2) Rev. Eur., Comp. & Int'l Env'tal L. 161 (2016).

86   *Cf.* Peter Lawrence & Daryl Wong, *Soft Law in the Paris Climate Agreement: Strength or Weakness? 26 Rev. Eur., Comp. & Int'l Env'tal L.* 276 (2017).

87   Benoit Mayer, *supra* note 85.

88   Harald Winkler, *Mitigation, in* The Paris Agreement on Climate Change: Analysis and Commentary 141, 147 (Daniel Klein et al. eds., 2017).

89   Daniel Bodansky, *The Paris Climate Change Agreement: A New Hope?*, 110 Am. J. Int'l L. 288 (2016); Vienna Convention on the Law of Treaties, *supra* note 1; Daniel Bodansky, *The Legal Character of the Paris Agreement*, 25 Rev. Eur., Comp. & Int'l Env'tal L. 142, 146 (July 2016); Daniel Bodansky, Art and Craft of International Environmental Law 103 (2010).

90   Unlike the affirmation of a goal in Art. 4.2(b) UNFCCC, the second sentence of Art. 4.2 Paris Agreement contains a clear obligation of conduct for the parties to pursue this aim. *Cf.* Bodansky, n. 7 above, p. 146; Daniel Bodansky, *The Paris Climate Change Agreement: A New Hope?, supra* note 80, at 304; Sebastian Oberthür & Ralph Bodle, *Legal Form and Nature of the Paris Outcome*, 6 Climate L. 40 (2016); Annalisa Savaresi, *The Paris Agreement: A New Beginning?*, 34(1) J. Energy & Natural Resources L. 16, ¶ 6.

91   Benoit Mayer, *supra* note 85.

92   *Cf. Christina Voigt, The Paris Agreement: What Is the Standard of Conduct for Parties?, 26 Questions Int'l L.* 17, ¶20 (March 2016), http://www.qil-qdi.org/paris-agreement-standard-conduct-parties (interpreting Art. 4.2 as requiring measures which are "meaningful and, indeed, effective to function as a means to this end").

even if its mitigation commitment had nevertheless been realized.[93] The procedural obligation can be established through an "obligation of result" which is judicial or quasi-judicial proceeding.[94]

The International Court of Justice in the *Nuclear Tests Case*[95] laid down certain conditions under which unilateral acts may create legal obligations on States. This includes "when it is the 'intention' of the State making the declaration that it 'should become bound' according to its terms"[96]; "that intention confers on the declaration the character of a legal undertaking, the State being thenceforth legally required to follow a course of conduct consistent with the declaration."[97] In the context of NDCs, the States parties' intention is to be completely bound by their respective NDCs' terms.[98]

3.4   *Climate Change Cases Upholding the NAPs and NDCs*[99]

3.4.1   Urgenda Foundation v. The State of Netherlands (2019)[100]

The Netherlands, as part of Annex I countries and thus under the IPCC scenario in AR4 of 2007, has formulated a target and suggested to reduce greenhouse gas emissions by 25% to 40% in 2020 and by 80% to 95% in 2050, both compared to 1990 emissions. In this case, the Supreme Court of The Netherlands recognized that the reduction agreements made by the countries, in various climate conferences and under the UNFCC, are not legally binding in themselves. However, at the same time, the Court observed that in the Dutch Constitutional system, the agreements made (in this case to reduce greenhouse gas emissions) fall within the competence of the government, which is subject to parliamentary oversight.

The Court laid down grounds under which the international commitments will have a binding effect on the state. These grounds can be briefly

---

93   *See, e.g.,* Certain Activities Carried Out by Nicaragua in the Border Area (Costa Rica v. Nicaragua) and Construction of a Road in Costa Rica along the San Juan River (Nicaragua v. Costa Rica), Judgment, I.C.J. Reports 2015, at 665, ¶156.

94   Christina Voigt, *supra* note 92, at 18.

95   *Nuclear Tests (Australia v France)*, Judgment, I.C.J. Reports 1974, p.253.

96   *Id.* at ¶43.

97   *Id.*

98   Annalisa Savaresi, *The Paris Agreement: A Rejoinder*, EJIL: Talk! (Feb. 16, 2016), http://www.ejiltalk.org/the-paris-agreement-a-rejoinder/.

99   Stacy-Ann Robinson & D'Arcy Carlson, *A just alternative to litigation: applying restorative justice to climate-related loss and damage*, 42 Third World Q. 1384 (2021).

100   The State of Netherlands v. Stichting Urgenda, Supreme Court of Netherlands, 19/00135 (Dec. 20, 2019), http://climatecasechart.com/climate-change-litigation/wp-content/uploads/sites/16/non-us-case-documents/2020/20200113_2015-HAZA-C090045 6689_judgment.pdf.

summarizedas, a) Is there support of the international community with respect to the commitment in question? b) Does this target apply to the Netherlands as an individual country?

3.4.2 Juliana v. United States[101]

The case of *Juliana* was filed in the U.S. state of Oregon by twenty-one members of the youth under the claim of violation of their constitutional right to life, liberty, property and threat to essential public trust resources. This case was instituted against the President, the United States, and federal agencies. The plaintiffs argued that the government continued to "permit, authorize, and subsidize fossil fuels" despite the knowledge of its harmful consequences, particularly in its role in fueling climate change, which is causing injury to the plaintiffs.

The injuries alleged ranged from psychological harm, impairment to recreational interests, medical conditions and damage to property. Claims were made of violations of a) substantive rights under the Due Process clause of the Fifth Amendment; b) rights under the Fifth and Fourteenth Amendments to equal protection of the law; c) rights under the Ninth Amendment; and d) violations of the public trust doctrine. Through this suit, the young plaintiffs sought declaratory relief, and sought for the court to issue an injunction ordering the government to implement a plan to "phase out fossil fuel emissions and draw down excess atmospheric carbon dioxide."

This case, unlike *Urgenda*, was filed on grounds of civil rights rather than international obligations. However, it is interesting to note that the plaintiffs attempted to hold the U.S. government responsible under its NDC commitments. This suit was not successful in the lower court, but the case is still pending in the appellate court.[102]

4   The Human Mobility Regime[103]

There is a numerous and diverse range of factors which drives human mobility, such as conflict, political instability, environmental degradation, climate change, poverty, marginalisation and poor governance.[104] Mobility is linked to

---

101   947 F.3d 1159 (9th Cir. 2020).

102   *Id.* at ¶101.

103   Advisory Group on Climate Change And Human Mobility, 2015.

104   Dr. Gary Milante, *Mobility and migration*, Stockholm International Peace Research Institute. https://www.sipri.org/research/peace-and-development/peacebuilding-and-resilience /mobility-and-migration.

larger underpinnings of social, economic, and political elements. It includes various factors ranging from international patterns "of demand for and supply of labor; the relative cheapness of international transport; the advent of electronic communication; and the emergence of transnational family networks."[105] A key factor in mobility is "social, economic and demographic inequalities whether experienced in terms of employment opportunities, resources, education or human rights."[106]

One of the early discussions on the relationship between environment, climate change and migration was in the First Assessment Report of the IPCC in 1990.[107] The report stated that climate change could lead to human migration.[108] However, more contemporary research has shown that behaviors of migration due to climate change expand over a larger range of variation in reasons. Aside from mass forced displacement, anticipatedmigration comes out of "adaptation." According to patterns, albeit without empirical data, it is observed that most of the short-distance migration is caused by environmental considerations. These short-distance migrations often occur within borders, rather than across borders, and may leave people "trapped" at the location where they may face the harsh effects of climate change. Further, it is also believed that sequential migration may end up forcing people to move more toward new destinations facing the adversity of climate change.[109]

4.1 Contribution of Climate Change to Human Mobility

Climate Change and the resulting negative effects impact settlements and economic areas, thereby influencing and contributing to the migration movement.[110] These weather occurrences are predicted to be more frequent and intense in the future, thereby creating an impact on disaster displacement, migration, and planned relocation.[111]

---

105   *Migration and human mobility: Thematic Think Piece*, IOM, UNDESA (2012), https://www
       .un.org/millenniumgoals/pdf/Think%20Pieces/13_migration.pdf.
106   *Id.*
107   IPCC, *Climate Change: The IPCC Scientific Assessment*, Intergovernmental Panel on
       Climate Change (J.T. Houghton, G.J. Jenkins & J.J. Ephraums eds., 1990).
108   IPCC, *Climate Change: The IPCC 1990 and 1992 Assessments*, Intergovernmental Panel on
       Climate Change 103 (1992).
109   *Migration and human mobility: Thematic Think Piece, supra* note 105.
110   Dr. Dorothea Rischewski, *Human mobility in the context of climate change*, German Federal Ministry for Economic Cooperation and Development (BMZ), (2017), https://www
       .giz.de/en/worldwide/67177.html.
111   *Id.*

The impact of climate change on human mobility can already be seen and studied through the case of island States as well as coastal regions of the Pacific, the Caribbean and the Philippines.[112] These regions have experienced intense storms, flooding, and rising sea levels.[113] Further, the regions of East and West Africa have been severely impacted by climate change, through phenomena such as dry spells and flash floods.[114]

The UNFCCC recognized the importance and relationship between human mobility and climate change, through the adoption of the 2010 Cancun Adaptation Framework.[115] The 2015 Paris Agreement, adopted during COP21, led to the recognition of climate migrants, for the first time in an international policy arena.[116]

Migrating as a precautionary action has been observed in *environmentally motivated migrants*. These migrants leave a region that may potentially be adversely affected by climate change, because they "pre-empt the worst" and by doing so, suffer harm to their livelihoods.[117] This harm can be avoided by implementation of appropriate policies.[118] It has been observed that such migration emerges out of primarily economic reasons, and may or may not be permanent in nature.

Another form of migration is seen among *environmentally forced migrants* who, instead of "pre-empting the worst" are simply "avoiding the worst" by escaping the imminent loss of livelihood.[119] This kind of migration has been observed to be mostly permanent in nature, arising out of calamities such as a loss of topsoil (leading to unsuitable agricultural conditions) and/or a rise in the sea level.[120] The IOM has elaborated on a rather all-inclusive definition for migrants who get displaced due to climate change, to succinctly encapsulate the soon-to-be endemic of environmental migration.[121]

---

112   *Id.*

113   *Id.*

114   *Id.*

115   IOM, *Human Mobility in the UNFCCC*, Environment Migration Portal, https://environmentalmigration.iom.int/human-mobility-unfccc.

116   *Id.*

117   International Organization for Migration, Expert Seminar: Migration and the Environment (2008), https://environmentalmigration.iom.int/sites/g/files/tmzbdl1411/files/idm_10_en .pdf.

118   *Id.*

119   *Id.*

120   *Id.*

121   The IOM had proposed the following definition for environmental migrants. *"Environmental migrants are persons or groups of persons who, for compelling reasons of sudden or progressive changes in the environment that adversely affect their lives or living conditions,*

4.2 *Human Mobility Cases Upholding Climate Change*
4.2.1 Teitiota v. New Zealand, (2014) NZCA 173

The case of *Teitiota v. New Zealand*[122] is one of the eminent landmark cases of climate migrants. There, Teitiota, a Kiribati citizen sought asylum in New Zealand on grounds of "changes to his environment" due to adverse impacts of climate change such as rise in sea level.[123] However, the petition was rejected by the national courts of New Zealand on grounds of lack of a "serious violation of human rights" and that the applicants did not fulfil the criteria to be a refugee in international human rights law under the 1951 Refugee Convention.[124] The court also expressed its concern about "expanding the scope of the Refugee Convention and opening the door to millions of people who face hardship due to climate change."[125] Despite the dismissal of the complaint to the UN Human Rights Committee,[126] the judgment is significant, as it acknowledged the relationship between climate change, migration and human rights. It went on to hold that "climate change induced migration can occur through sea level rise, salinization, land-degradation, or through intense storms and flooding" and highlighted the need for countries to take actions towards prevention and mitigation of climate change.[127]

The crucial takeaway from the UN Human Rights Committee views was how it opined that "the government should not return migrants to countries where [their] lives would be threatened by climate change," thereby reaffirming the non-refoulement obligations on the part of a sending State, as enshrined under

---

are obliged to leave their habitual homes, or choose to do so, either temporarily or permanently, and who move either within their country or abroad." IOM, *Discussion Note: Migration and the Environment*, MC/INF/288 (Nov.1, 2007), https://www.iom.int/sites/g/files/tmzbdl486/files/jahia/webdav/shared/shared/mainsite/about_iom/en/council/94/MC_INF_288.pdf.

122   Also referred to as *Teitota v. Chief Executive Ministry of Business, Innovation and Employment,* as it was titled during its trial in regional New Zealand Courts.

123   Teitiota v. Chief Executive of the Ministry of Business, Innovation and Employment (2014) NZCA 173, https://forms.justice.govt.nz/search/Documents/pdf/jdo/b8/alfresco/service/api/node/content/workspace/SpacesStore/70056dfa-a205-4baf-9d8d-e97ed5244899/70056dfa-a205-4baf-9d8d-e97ed5244899.pdf.

124   *Id.*

125   *Id.*

126   The complaint was based on the grounds of violation of the right to life under the International Covenant on Civil and Political Rights (ICCPR), particularly due to rise in sea level which left Kiribati uninhabitable for all its residents.

See Press Release, *Historic UN Human Rights case opens door to climate change asylum claims,* UN News (2020), https://www.ohchr.org/en/press-releases/2020/01/historic-un-human-rights-case-opens-door-climate-change-asylum-claims.

127   *Id.*

Article 6 of ICCPR.[128] The case of *Teitiota v. New Zealand,* along with the views in *Portillo Cáceres v. Paraguay,* has "crystallise[d] a deeper and wider body of jurisprudence and practice on the existence of an 'undeniable relationship' between environmental protection and the right to life in dignity."[129]

4.2.2 AC (Tuvalu) [NZIPT 800517–520][130]

The Tribunal in this case noted that there was an increasingly recognized obligation that was placed on States to protect the rights of people in the context of natural disasters. For this, the Tribunal cited the Committee on Economic, Social and Cultural Rights and the Committee on the Rights of the Child.

The Tribunal noted the contribution of Professor Walter Kälin in his article titled *"The Human Rights Dimension of Natural or Human Made Disasters"*[131] in saying that a positive duty is imposed by human rights provisions to protect and enable the enjoyment of rights against infringements of such rights or other eminent "dangerous situations"[132] and emphasizing that, under Articles 6 and 7 of the ICCPR, such positive obligations are becoming more significant. The Tribunal further referred to *AF* (*Kiribati*), and noted that the right not to be arbitrarily deprived of life in the context of "natural disasters" fell under the ambit of section 131 of the Immigration Act 2009. Further, it reaffirmed that such a positive obligation was applicable in cases of man-made as well as natural disasters.

5 Inclusion of Climate Change and Human Mobility under the International Law Regime

Human mobility in the light of climate change was flagged as a global concern by the UNFCCC in 1992. During the 16th Conference of Parties (COP-16), human mobility was integrated into the UNFCCC.

---

128   Kate Lyons, *Climate refugees can't be returned home, says landmark UN human rights ruling* The Guardian (2020), https://www.theguardian.com/world/2020/jan/20/climate-refugees -cant-be-returned-home-says-landmark-un-human-rights-ruling. This case marks a legal tipping point" and "opens the door way" to future claims by people whose lives have been affected and threatened by climate change and global warming.

129   Ginevra Le Moli, *The Human Rights Committee, Environmental Protection and the Right to Life,* 69Int'l & Comp. L. Q. 735, 750 (2020).

130   AC (Tuvalu), [2014] NZIPT 800517-520, https://forms.justice.govt.nz/search/Documents /IPTV2/ RefugeeProtection/ref_20140604_800517.pdf.

131   Walter Kälin, *The Human Rights Dimension of Natural or HumanMade Disasters,* 55 German Y.B. Int'l L. 119 (2012).

132   *Id.* at 127.

According to the Sixth Assessment Report of the IPCC, "climate and weather extremes are increasingly driving displacement in all regions, with small island states disproportionately affected."[133] Climate change has generated vulnerability, through displacement and involuntary migration resulting from extreme weather and climate events.[134] The report further states that "mid- to long-term displacement will increase with intensification of heavy precipitation and associated flooding, tropical cyclones, drought and sea level rise."[135]

Thereby, as identified by the IPCC report, an increase in adaptive capacities minimizes the negative impacts of climate-related displacement and involuntary migration. Further, "it improves the choice under which migration decisions are made, ensuring safe and orderly movements of people within and between countries."[136]

The role of NAPs/ NDCs becomes crucial in the context of human mobility and climate change, as it enables parties to the UNFCC, to create strategies and policies which address adaptation needs.[137]

Additionally, it is noted that the negative forms of mobility can be significantly reduced if disaster risk reduction strategies and NAPs and NDCs include integration migration. By addressing displacement and/or (planned) relocation in the documents mentioned above, resilience toward climate change would be built among communities, which is deemed to be essential for sustainable development.[138] The common trend observed among the countries which decided to mention displacement and/or migration in their NDCs is that most of these countries are small-island countries, who are disproportionately affected by climate change. Because there is an immediate sense of urgency in most of these countries, displacement and migration have made their way into the NDCs. Alternatively, there are countries which have no mention of displacement or migration. These countries, which are vastly larger in number, have not undertaken any obligations or measures in the arena of human mobility.

---

133   IPCC, *Climate Change 2022: Impacts, Adaptation, and Vulnerability. Contribution of Working Group II to the Sixth Assessment Report of the Intergovernmental Panel on Climate Change* (H.-O. Pörtner, D.C. Roberts, M. Tignor, E.S. Poloczanska, K. Mintenbeck, A. Alegría, M. Craig, S. Langsdorf, S. Löschke, V. Möller, A. Okem, B. Rama eds., 2022), https://www.ipcc.ch/report/ar6/wg2/downloads/report/IPCC_AR6_WGII_Summary ForPolicymakers.pdf.

134   *Id.*

135   *Id.*

136   *Id.*

137   Lilian Yamamoto, Diogo Andreola Serraglio & Fernanda de Salles Cavedon-Capdeville, *Human mobility in the context of climate change and disasters: a South American approach*, 10 Int'l J. Climate Change Strategies& Management 65 (2018).

138   *Migration and human mobility: Thematic Think Piece, supra* note 95.

The major takeaway from the study of the NDCs of all the countries is that, only countries significantly affected by climate change, most often sea level rise, have strived to undertake measures with respect to human mobility. However, the larger portion of parties to the Paris Agreement, have not undertaken any such obligations, measures, or plan of action.

6   Conclusion

There is an urgency in regard to improving the contemporary state of human mobility arising out of environmental considerations. More, the general protection of rights in the context of climate change could also be improved, by taking into consideration an assessment of vulnerabilities, such as the socio-economic factors (gender and related wage-gaps), the economic classification and its relation with occupations that are directly contingent upon the environment, and other cultural factors. This would form the basis of further policy changes and creations.

Furthermore, though it is understood that climate change and its effects cannot be predicted with great precision, a study of the pattern of migration along with environmental factors being affected by human-intervention would allow for the development of preemptive policies. Inclusion of the vulnerable and the most-affected communities in policy designing would allow for a more holistic development of policies. This recommendation is interlinked with the introduction of an intersectional lens, since it allows for the consideration of a wider range of factors pertinent to the (potentially) most affected. Also, non-State actors and corporations should be involved for the purposes of facilitating migration and pushing forward the cause of inclusive policies.

The legal equation is quite simple: States do have an international obligation to protect against the pernicious effects of climate change under international law, including the obligations taken under the Paris Agreement, through the NAPs and the NDCs.

States should urgently consider enhancing domestic policies and measures in order to prevent displacement, to facilitate the inevitable intra-State and/or inter-State increasing migration and preventively create relevant and efficient policies to maintain planned relocation, as the last resort. All these pre-emptive measures would address significant segments of the current and future climate mobility scenarios.[139]

---

139   *See* Cosmin Corendea, *Hybrid Legal Approaches Towards Climate Change: Concepts, Mechanisms and Implementation*, 21(1) Annual Survey Int'l & Comp. L. 29 (2016).